ISAIAH BERLIN

AFFIRMING

LETTERS 1975–1997

Edited by Henry Hardy and Mark Pottle

with the assistance of Nicholas Hall

Additional research · Brigid Allen, Victoria Benner, James Chappel,
Georgina Edwards, Hugh Eveleigh, Jason Ferrell, Steffen Groß, Nicholas Hall,
Serena Moore, Eleonora Paganini, Kim Reynolds, Teisha Ruggiero,
Patrick Wise-Walsh

Archival Research · Michael Hughes

Consultant Russianists · Tatiana Pozdnyakova, Josephine von Zitzewitz

Consultant Hebraist · Norman Solomon

Transcription · Betty Colquhoun, Esther Johnson

These days, where there is so much strife, so much war and so much
destruction, to do something which is civilised in intent, and I hope in
result, at the top end of what is possible in a civilisation: what a privilege,
eh? What a privilege!

Peter Maxwell Davies[1]

[T]here is no doubt that [Isaiah Berlin] showed in more than one direction the unexpectedly large possibilities open to us at the top end of the
range of human potential.[2]

1 Interview broadcast on the Six O'Clock News, BBC Radio 4, 31 January 2014, about his 10th
  Symphony, written in the teeth of leukaemia. For Peter Maxwell Davies see 212/8.
2 'Sir Isaiah Berlin', obituary, *Independent*, 7 November 1997, 18.

Also by Isaiah Berlin

*

KARL MARX

THE HEDGEHOG AND THE FOX

THE AGE OF ENLIGHTENMENT

RUSSIAN THINKERS

CONCEPTS AND CATEGORIES

AGAINST THE CURRENT

PERSONAL IMPRESSIONS

THE CROOKED TIMBER OF HUMANITY

THE SENSE OF REALITY

THE PROPER STUDY OF MANKIND

THE ROOTS OF ROMANTICISM

THE POWER OF IDEAS

THREE CRITICS OF THE ENLIGHTENMENT

FREEDOM AND ITS BETRAYAL

LIBERTY

THE SOVIET MIND

POLITICAL IDEAS IN THE ROMANTIC AGE

With Beata Polanowska-Sygulska
UNFINISHED DIALOGUE

Uniform with this volume
FLOURISHING: LETTERS 1928–1946
ENLIGHTENING: LETTERS 1946–1960
BUILDING: LETTERS 1960–1975

*

For more information on Isaiah Berlin visit
⟨*http://berlin.wolf.ox.ac.uk/*⟩

AFFIRMING
LETTERS 1975–1997

———

ISAIAH BERLIN

Edited by Henry Hardy and Mark Pottle
with the assistance of Nicholas Hall

Chatto & Windus

London

1 3 5 7 9 10 8 6 4 2

Chatto & Windus, an imprint of Vintage
20 Vauxhall Bridge Road
LONDON SW1V 2SA

Chatto & Windus is part of the Penguin Random House group of companies
whose addresses can be found at global.penguinrandomhouse.com

Penguin
Random House
UK

First published by Chatto & Windus in 2015

www.vintage-books.co.uk

A CIP catalogue record for this book is available from the British Library

ISBN 9781784740085

Designed in the Dept of Typography & Graphic Communication,
University of Reading

Typeset by Deltatype Ltd, Birkenhead, Merseyside
Printed and bound by Clays Ltd, St Ives plc

Penguin Random House is committed to a sustainable future for our business, our readers
and our planet. This book is made from Forest Stewardship Council® certified paper.

In memory of Stuart Hampshire

1914–2004

The answer is 'Yes.'

Isaiah Berlin pp Pat Utechin[1]

IB was one of the great affirmers of our time.

John Banville[2]

---

1 To Edna Ullmann-Margalit, 5 November 1997, the day of his death. The question was whether he was willing that the Margalits should publish the statement on Israel and the Palestinians that he had sent them (568), but the answer stands here more broadly for IB's life-affirming tempera-ment, celebrated in the title of the present vol. For Pat *Utechin, IB's secretary, see 633.
2 'Learning a Lot about Isaiah Berlin', review of L3, NYRB, 19 December 2013, 44–7 at 47. (William) John Banville (b. 1945), novelist, long-standing enthusiast for and reviewer of IB.

CONTENTS

[...] a rapid torrent of descriptive sentences, fresh, lucid, direct, interspersed with vivid and never irrelevant digressions, variations on the same theme in many keys, [...] quotations real and imaginary, verbal inventions, [...] mordant personal observations and cascades of vivid images [...], which, so far from either tiring or distracting the reader by their virtuosity, add to the force and swiftness of the narrative. The effect is one of spontaneous improvisation: exhilarating conversation by an intellectually gay and exceptionally clever and honest man endowed with singular powers of observation and expression.

IB, 'Herzen and His Memoirs', AC2 245

No doubt the twenty-fifth century will recognise my eminence.

To Charles Blattberg, 19 March 1996

ILLUSTRATIONS

The subject is IB where not otherwise stated

SECOND PLATE SECTION

CREDITS

Credits name as many as are known to the editors of the following: photographer / agent / copyright owner / owner of original.

Illustrations in the text (listed by page)

Plates

All photos are from albums kept by Aline Berlin and members of her family, photographers unknown, unless stated otherwise

  1 ITV

  2 unknown photographer / Raymond Carr private collection / scan courtesy of María Jesús González

  5 BBC

  7 Bernard Lee ('Bern') Schwartz / © National Portrait Gallery, London

11 Sandra Burman

13 Dominique Nabokov

14 David V. Hankey / Nicholas Utechin

18 Dominique Nabokov

21 Gemma Levine

26 Billett Potter

29, 30 Pat Utechin

31 Gillman & Soame (B. J. Harris)

32 ⟨www.johnbattenphotography.co.uk⟩

33 © Norman McBeath 1992

34 Steve Frost

36 BBC

38 Nigel Francis / © The Lucian Freud Archive / Bridgeman Images / courtesy Berlin Charitable Trust

PREFACE

[U]nder pressure from people like you I may change or modify or sharpen this view.

To Claude Galipeau, 5 January 1991

Is this satisfactory? I do hope so. If not, do go on pressing me. I don't mind a bit: it is only Pat upon whose shoulders the dreadful burden of my answers lies.

To HH, 17 April 1991

I

IN THIS fourth and final volume of his selected letters, Isaiah Berlin – having retired at the end of the previous volume as President of Wolfson College, Oxford – completes his four-year Presidency of the British Academy in London and returns to his spiritual home in Oxford, All Souls College, as a Distinguished Fellow.[1] Throughout the last two decades of his life he is as profuse a correspondent – mostly by dictation – as ever, though the publication in this period of several collections of his essays, and one short monograph, leads gradually to a change in tone and emphasis, as his readers write to ask for clarification of this or that point in his work. He replies punctiliously, and often at considerable length – to the despair of his secretary, Pat Utechin, who, though she admired his conscientiousness, felt that he could have been more selective and economical in his responses.[2]

But Berlin firmly believed that it was the responsibility of a thinker who published his ideas to reply to all serious requests for elucidation from whatever quarter. The result is a body of correspondence that should be seen as an integral part of his *oeuvre*, comprising as it does a sort of running commentary on his more formal work that sometimes throws supplementary light on his central ideas, clearing away some of the misunderstandings that occasionally arose from the more condensed and allusive statements in his published essays. Among many other subjects, he returned repeatedly to pluralism of values and of cultures, political liberalism, national consciousness and other forms of belonging, and the essential ingredients of human nature, as opposed to human characteristics that vary between persons, groups, cultures or epochs; and he chewed over and refined what he had said and written and thought about these subjects before.

Pluralism is a particular leitmotif of the letters from these years; and

---

1 25/2.
2 She once told HH that, if she had to type another explanation of pluralism, she would explode. She did have to do this, more than once, but remained entire.

pluralism is the doctrine above all that he might reasonably have claimed
as his own creation, at any rate in the fully explicit form in which he stated
it.[1] He first set it out clearly, indeed canonically, in 1958 in 'The One and
the Many', the final (eighth) section of *Two Concepts of Liberty* (reprinted
in *Four Essays on Liberty* in 1969), but it was some thirty years before the
sustained investigation by others of this radically disturbing view began to
gather momentum – largely, perhaps, as a result of the publication, from 1978
onwards, of further collections of his previously scattered essays, in some of
which he had more to say about the doctrine in question. As Charles Taylor
has written:

> Isaiah's plurality thesis was not only a blow to various totalitarian theories of
> positive liberty, it was also deeply unsettling to the moral theories dominant
> in his own milieu. It is one of the paradoxes of our intellectual world, which
> will be increasingly discussed in the future, why this latter point was not
> realised. The bomb was planted in the academy, but somehow failed to go
> off.[2]

However that may be, the bomb well and truly went off in the last two
decades of the twentieth century, when pluralism's relevance to the contemporary world became even greater than it was at the end of the 1950s.
Indeed, the continuing timeliness of Berlin's crucial idea is one of the main
reasons for the vigour of the discussion that has centred upon it. All the
issues that gather round the question of the proper limits to tolerance of
difference – multiculturalism, nationalism, fundamentalist extremism and
terrorism, cultural imperialism – turn on whether pluralism is true, and, if
so, what its implications are for our conduct in particular circumstances. As
Berlin himself wrote about this 'important topic' in 1993: 'I have for many
years thought the problem of the incommensurability, and still more the
incompatibility, of some values to be central to all ethical, social, political
and aesthetic issues, and could never find any treatment of this topic in what
is commonly called "the literature".'[3]

Other notable general themes that recur include the continuously worry-
ing conflict between Israel and the Palestinians, on which he makes a rare
public statement at the end of his life (included here), and many of his observations on which are, sadly, just as applicable today as when he made them;
the related question of Jewish identity, both in general and as it affected
himself; and the fall of Communism and its impact on Eastern Europe. More

---

1 For some material relevant to the question of the degree of his originality see ⟨http://berlin
   .wolf.ox.ac.uk/lists/pluralism/index.html⟩.
2 'Plurality of Goods', in *The Legacy of Isaiah Berlin*, ed. Ronald Dworkin, Mark Lilla and Robert B.
   Silvers (NY, 2001), 113–19 at 117.
3 To Ruth Chang, 4 January 1993. This brief statement was provided at RC's request for her edited
   vol. *Incommensurability, Incomparability and Practical Reason* (Cambridge, 1997), inspired by his
   work and dedicated to his memory, but was not incorporated there.

specifically, he continues to respond as acutely and entertainingly as ever to a wide range of public events, and to letters from his close friends – though death contracts their number as the years pass.[1] He reports on his travels to Australia and the Pacific, to Japan and Iran, and to the USSR, which he revisits in 1988 for the first and only time since he had taken his new wife there in 1956. We hear his views on current political issues in America and Britain (Reagan and Thatcher), in Israel (Shamir and Begin), and in the Soviet Union (Gorbachev, Yeltsin, Solzhenitsyn and Sakharov). These are the years of continuing IRA terrorism, the Camp David accords, the Islamic revolution in Iran, the Soviet invasion of Afghanistan and the ensuing US-led boycott of the Moscow Olympics; the unmasking of Anthony Blunt as the 'fourth man', the formation of Solidarity in Poland, Israel's invasion of Lebanon and the Falklands War; the Chernobyl disaster, the fall of the Berlin Wall, Khomeini's fatwa against Salman Rushdie, the Gulf War and the collapse of the Soviet Union. We hear from Berlin on all these subjects in his letters, and about a large supporting cast of thinkers, composers, musicians, and other prominent and unprominent persons.

As for his personal life, Berlin is offered but declines a life peerage, is awarded the Agnelli Prize for his contribution to ethical thought, and celebrates his seventieth and (especially) eightieth birthdays; he remains until 1987 on the board of Covent Garden and has much to say about opera; he talks to Michael Ignatieff, mostly on tape, over ten years and appoints him his biographer; and he continues his working partnership with Henry Hardy, which results in eight published volumes in his lifetime, and prepares the ground for seven more after his death, as well as for the four-volume edition of his letters which the present volume completes. He has a long and (eventually) distressingly bitter correspondence with Stalin's daughter, Svetlana; he enters into a controversy with Noam Chomsky about a contribution by the latter to *Index on Censorship*; he reflects on the mental depredations of old age (remarkably slight in his own case, viewed from outside); he lends his name, directly or indirectly, to causes in which he believes, and affords assistance to correspondents who make an appeal to him.[2]

His rate of publication scarcely slackens. His book *Vico and Herder: Two Studies in the History of Ideas* – heavily revised versions of work published earlier, with a substantial new introduction – appears in 1976. He writes essays on romanticism, operatic performances and (separately) surtitles,

---

1 'The older I get the fewer friends I have; some of them are falling like leaves from a tree. I spend my time going to memorial services [...]. So do come. Let us meet before we expire – once, or many times.' To Carl Schorske, 2 January 1995.

2 For example, he writes to David Raphael 25 September 1990, asking for his help with one such: 'I have been in correspondence with an Iranian girl for a year or two now – she asks for books, she asks questions about political theory, she explains her position, etc. – her English is not very good but there is something touching about a lonely Iranian student of philosophy, particularly political philosophy, who begs for help from the West.'

and a number of further aspects of Vico; on Hume and Hamann, utopian ideas, nationalism, and Einstein and Israel; on his meetings with Akhmatova and Pasternak, relativism, the 'three strands' in his life and the dispatches he drafted in Washington for the Foreign Office during the Second World War; on Mozart at Glyndebourne, the unexpected survival of the Russian intelligentsia, Jewish Oxford, the London Library and the nature and development of his own ideas. Alongside this new work, seven volumes of collected essays (the first four originally appearing under the unifying title *Selected Writings*) and one new freestanding book (on J. G. Hamann) are published and attract a great deal of critical attention – most but not all of it positive – and, as noted above, much correspondence from curious readers. Some of these volumes include work from earlier years that had not previously been published, including pieces – especially a long essay on Joseph de Maistre and the origins of Fascism, and his study of Hamann – which he revises extensively. Indeed one volume, *The Sense of Reality*, consists almost entirely of previously unpublished material. He also translates Turgenev's play *A Month in the Country* for a new production by Peter Gill at the National Theatre.

His presidential addresses to the British Academy appear in its *Proceedings*. He contributes forewords, reviews books, writes letters to the press, replies in print to published criticisms of his work, and gives some seventy interviews, mostly for publication or broadcast.[1] Notable among the interviews are those with Michael Berkeley, Frans Boenders, John Drummond, Nathan Gardels, Michael Ignatieff, Ramin Jahanbegloo (which became a book, *Conversations with Isaiah Berlin*), Peter Jay, Enrique Krauze, Lars Roar Langslet, Bernard Levin, Sue Lawley, Steven Lukes, Bryan Magee, Beata Polanowska-Sygulska, Igor Shaitanov and Vsevolod Shishkovsky (the last two in Russian).

He writes pen-portraits of those he has met and often known well: Thomas Armstrong, David Ben-Gurion, David Cecil, Martin Cooper, Patricia Douglas, Nahum Goldmann, Harry d'Avigdor Goldsmid, Alexander and Salome Halpern, Herbert Hart, Auberon Herbert, Maynard and Lydia Keynes, Teddy Kollek, Yehudi Menuhin, John Plamenatz, Dorothy de Rothschild, Yitzhak Sadeh, Stephen Spender, Jacob Talmon, Charles Taylor, John Wheeler-Bennett, Virginia Woolf and others. And all the time the letters pour forth in all directions. He was one of the last great letter-writers of an age brought to an end by the Internet.

---

1 'I have always refused to be interviewed': to Robert Silvers, n.d. [27? March 1979]. 'I *loathe* interviews': to Kyril FitzLyon, 20 March 1978.

II

Letter after letter!

To HH, 4 December 1978

The proportion of available letters included in this volume is similar to that in its predecessor: a very slightly larger percentage (just under a fifth) of a somewhat smaller pool of transcribed material. Cutting has once more been painful, and the material on the cutting-room floor includes many excellent letters. In particular, there was room for only a sample of his letters about his conception of human nature and human values, all of which should be read by any interpreters of his ideas who wish to see the full, sometimes puzzlingly unclear and/or contradictory, picture. In order to make more of these letters available to scholars in a timely fashion, a further selection has been posted online.[1] For excluded letters on other topics readers will for the time being need to consult Berlin's papers in the Bodleian Library in Oxford, at any rate until the project of adding many of them to the online Isaiah Berlin Virtual Library (IBVL) has been completed.

All the other provisos stated in the preface to the previous volume apply here too. One additional point that may be worth spelling out concerns punctuation. As before, we have felt ourselves free to tidy the presentation and punctuation of typed letters (without, of course, changing the wording except where there was an obvious misdictation or mistranscription). Much of this aspect of his letters stems from his secretary: his inclusion of punctuation in his dictation was somewhat sporadic and unreliable. Moreover, both when one is composing prose viva voce, and when one is transcribing shorthand or recorded dictation, it is often difficult to choose the best punctuation while in transit, as it were: the logical structure of a long sentence is sometimes unclear until it is complete, if then. Berlin's sentences are notorious for their length and complexity, though they do mostly, in the end, wind safe to sea. As typed by Pat Utechin, they tend to exhibit a structurally ambiguous and taxingly extended series of dashes, and we have broken them up liberally by inserting or substituting full stops, colons, semi-colons, commas and parentheses – and occasionally even dashes where, exceptionally, there were none – hoping and believing that the result is easier to follow. Manuscript items, however (again as in previous volumes), are transcribed faithfully, except where obsessive fidelity would entail serious difficulty in comprehension. In these autograph communications readers may observe Berlin's

---

1 At ⟨http://berlin.wolf.ox.ac.uk/published_works/a/more-explaining.pdf⟩. Other published letters, a number of them in the appendices to revised editions of IB's collections of essays, are listed at ⟨http://berlin.wolf.ox.ac.uk/lists/bibliography/index.html⟩, and more letters to Beata Polanowska-Sygulska appear in UD.

characteristic use of colons and dashes as rhetorical signposts – breathing
marks – more than as conventional literary punctuation.[1]

We should also record that we have made some minimal cuts to avoid
distracting, boring or irritating the reader with repetitive and insubstantial
matter of the kind that often opens and closes letters: 'Thank you for your
letter of 1 January, which I have only just seen on my return from a week in
London' etc. When letters are read in bulk, these formalities can become
tiresome. We have also suppressed certain formulaic riffs to which Berlin was
given, for instance apologies for not writing by hand, of which there are hundreds of instances, often similarly worded. In all such cases, of course, cuts
are marked with ellipses. It has to be admitted, too, that Berlin's increasingly
frequent letters of condolence naturally tended to draw on the same stock of
thoughts and images, and this explains why there are not more of them here.

What we say at the start of the second section of the preface to *Building*
applies to the present volume as well, and we shall not repeat it in full here.
Our principles of selection remain the same, so that we continue not to
censor interesting material that reveals Berlin's feet of (albeit top quality)
clay, and occasionally omit passages that do, or might, offend the living.[2] In
this latter connection we have sometimes followed Berlin's own advice to his
friend Irving Singer: 'The best idea [...] is to send the offensive passage to the
subject and ask if he (she) minds.'[3] Berlin could be catty in his letters – 'I am
an intemperate writer and probably made a number of unjustifiable remarks
about all kinds of good people'[4] – and had a bee in his bonnet about certain
bêtes noires; but against this must be set the fact that he was an enormously
kind man who, in general, could not bear to do anyone else down. He once
asked a colleague why a particular election to a fellowship had been made,
since the successful candidate was no good. The colleague reasonably replied
that in his reference Berlin had said that that he was one of the most distinguished graduate students in political theory in the university. 'You should
never have taken any notice of that,' Berlin replied in dismay. Indeed, it was
often said in the university that his references should be discounted, since he
would always praise his students indiscriminately.

During the years covered by this volume an extensive correspondence
occurred between Berlin and Henry Hardy, much of it about Berlin's core
ideas.[5] Because of the possible conflict of interest that this fact may be
thought to create, we should like to make explicit that the choice of which
(parts) of these letters to include was made solely by Mark Pottle (who also

---

1 The letter of 20 May 1987 to Kay Graham is a particularly striking example.
2 '[P]ut in anything you like, save the bits I have listed [...], which might cause unnecessary pain (as
   opposed to permissible pain).' To Morton White, 14 August 1995.
3 Letter of 2 January 1991.
4 To Kyril FitzLyon, 11 December 1980.
5 'Let me be brief (a quality characteristic of neither of us).' IB to HH, 2 November 1979.

wrote the entry on HH in the biographical glossary and the connective tissue on pp. 11–12). Some of those that have been excluded are in the online file referred to above.[1]

As before, we have set a limit to the explanations we provide, assuming in general that words included in the *Concise Oxford English Dictionary* do not (all) require glosses. But we have translated most words and phrases in foreign languages, including French, since it is no longer safe to assume that familiarity with this or any other foreign language is part of everyone's basic intellectual furniture. We have also supplied, as footnotes or linking passages, information that we hope will enable the widest range of readers to understand the letters. Many will need no such introduction to the topics at hand, but we have aimed for consistency and comprehensiveness, and have designed our apparatus to make Berlin's letters accessible to future generations, and to cultures different from our own. The same approach informs our biographical footnotes: we provide basic information, wherever possible, for everyone mentioned in the text, even for such universal figures as Shakespeare. This will irritate some readers, maybe, but seems to us preferable to a more selective policy that, in its arbitrariness and partiality, would inevitably reflect the cultural assumptions, predilections and interests of the editors and the civilisation to which they belong, to the potential disadvantage of readers in the future, and indeed of those alive today who are not schooled in the Western liberal culture in which IB was himself steeped. It also seems useful to us to provide the years of birth and death of even the best-known figures.

We should like to express our special gratitude to the two colleagues who have worked most closely with us in the preparation of this final volume. Our research associate Nicholas Hall has managed to find precise answers to innumerable queries, and has proved as deft at handling Internet databases and search engines as he has been resolute in tracking down elusive quarries in the Bodleian Libraries and elsewhere. All of the burdens we have laid upon him he has shouldered uncomplainingly and efficiently, enabling us to concentrate on other aspects of the editorial task. Without him this book would never have appeared anything like as soon as it has. In parallel with his work for us he has been editing the diaries and letters of the remarkable Welsh journalist Gareth Jones (1905–35), one of the first to bring the Ukrainian famine of 1932–3 to the attention of the world. Our archivist Georgina Edwards has patiently prepared our holdings for transfer to other homes at the end of Wolfson's 'Berlin Papers Project', which began in 1990 and reaches its conclusion with the present volume. She has also managed

---

1 Some, too, are quoted in HH, 'Dear Isaiah', ⟨http://berlin.wolf.ox.ac.uk/writings_on_ib/hhonib/barcelona.pdf⟩.

the project office with quiet tact and effectiveness, as well as working for Brasenose Archives when she has not been working for us.

The other Trustees of the Isaiah Berlin Literary Trust, and Berlin's family, have once again helped us with the preparation of the text, reading drafts and making suggestions from which we have profited. We have also been assisted in various ways by Nick Allen, Shlomo Avineri, Simon Bailey, Liz Baird, Thomas Binder, Etan Bloom, Vernon Bogdanor, Peter Boswell, Elena Bonham Carter, Alfred Brendel, Irene Brendel, Terrell Carver, Charles, Prince of Wales, Meir Chazan, Elena Chukovskaya, Joshua Cherniss, Nick Clarke, Aimee Collis, Angela Courtney, Alan Crookham, George Crowder, Judith Curthoys, Robin Darwall-Smith, Timothy Day, Dimitris Dimitrakos, Arie Dubnov, Lazar Fleishman, Adam Garfinkle, Erin George, Susie Gilbert, Martin Goodman, John Goodwin, Simon Green, Samuel Guttenplan, Sue Hales, Becky Hardie, Mary Hardy, Thérèse Herbert, Robin Hessman, Anthony Hippisley, Hirata Masako, Kei Hiruta, Leofranc Holford-Strevens, Jennifer Holmes, David Hutson, Michael Inwood, Baruch Knei-Paz, Lars Roar Langslet, Wolfram Latsch, John Levy, Alistair Lexden, Martin Liddy, Yigal Liverant, John Livingstone, Paul Luna, Grant McIntyre, Bryan Magee, Paolo Mancosu, Yehuda Meltzer, David Miller, Serena Moore, Gaye Morgan, Claus Moser, Kanami Nakatake, Penelope Newsome, Nicky Nevin, Georges Nivat, Kate O'Donnell, Bertell Ollman, Peter Oppenheimer, Lionel Orchard, Lewis Owens, Christopher Phipps, Michael Quinn, Jane Rawson, Henry Richardson, Bridget Riley, Sylva Rubashova, Arthur Ruppin, Dean Ryan, Philip Schofield, Sandy Scholey, Colin Shindler, John Simpson, Adam Sisman, Rowena Skelton-Wallace, Alexander Sokolov Grant, Matthew Spender, Keith Thomas, Jennifer Thorp, John Tooley, Eyal Tsur, David Vital, Wang Qian, Brandon Ward, Edmund Weiner, Caro Westmore, Leon Wieseltier, Mirko Wischke, Susan Wood, Fred Worms, Bondo Wyszpolski, Philip Ziegler, and the staff of the ODNB; and by many others, especially archivists, librarians and other institutional officers, too numerous to list here exhaustively, who have often gone well beyond the call of duty in answering our enquiries. Nor should the professional team listed on the half-title page be left unmentioned: we have relied on them in countless ways.

Our title is intended to reflect both Berlin's (re-)affirmation in his letters of his important views on central human questions; and also his ebullient and life-affirming personality, so vividly on display in his correspondence, and so neatly and serendipitously encapsulated in the last and briefest item in the book: 'The answer is "Yes." '

We record in sorrow that, while this volume was in preparation, the death of Berlin's widow Aline, an original Trustee of The Isaiah Berlin Literary Trust,[1] deprived this project of a most generous and constant supporter and

1 Created 26 November 1996.

friend, whose enthusiasm, practical aid and unmatched personal knowledge has sustained us over the years. We have also lost another faithful Trustee[1] and friend in Jon Stallworthy, professor of English and fellow of Wolfson, poet, publisher, editor, biographer and expert on war poetry: in more than one of these guises he was an immense help to us, and his position as elder statesman of College was especially valuable to the work of the Trust. We are sad that Lady Berlin and Professor Stallworthy did not live to see the publication of the final volume, but they did see a draft text.

To Lady Berlin and all our benefactors over twenty-five years, large and small, financial and moral, who not only enabled us to complete this edition of letters, but also made possible the preparation of all the volumes by Berlin that have appeared since 1990, we say a final heartfelt thank you. They have not been systematically identified in previous volumes, so let us now name them all, in alphabetical order: Aline Berlin, Peter Halban and the Berlin Charitable Trust; Gilbert de Botton; Gerald Chan and the Morningside Foundation; Katharine Graham; the Trustees of the Isaiah Berlin Literary Trust; the Jacob Rothschild GAM Charitable Trust; Lewis Owens and EdmissionUK; Antony Percy; Jacob Rothschild and the Rothschild Foundation; Geoffrey Wilkinson and the Wilkinson Charitable Foundation; Ken Wilson and the Ford Foundation; the successive Presidents and fellows of Wolfson; and Leonard Wolfson and the Wolfson Foundation. The thorough research needed for a full scholarly edition of letters by such a wide-ranging and allusive correspondent as Berlin takes time and does not come cheap, and our debt to these wonderful examples of charitable giving is immeasurable. Nor must we pass over those whose non-pecuniary support proved indispensable: in particular Alan Bullock, who with great gusto raised the initial funding for the project, and continued in this role until Berlin died; and successive Bursars of Wolfson, whose tolerance and generosity have made a significant contribution to our *esprit de corps*. To these too we record our unforgettable debt.

We now bid farewell to Berlin's letters, their recipients and readers, after a journey that began in earnest for one of us a quarter of a century ago.[2] The younger of us is the same age as Berlin was when he became President of Wolfson, the elder (now an old-age pensioner) the same age as when he retired from that position. As we reflect on what Berlin had been and done by our ages, and on the letters he wrote after his retirement – so much more numerous than those printed here – we marvel increasingly at the intellectual energy and creativity of this warm, fizzing, fluent, generous epicentre of enthusiastic engagement with people and their ideas, this extraordinary man and his capacious, penetrating, lucid, unpretentious, articulate mind,

---

1 Since 2008.
2 Forty years ago, if one includes the period of work on IB's collections of essays that directly or indirectly generated many of the letters written after his retirement.

with its relish for life in all its manifestations: a mind whose contents he shared so liberally with his correspondents, and one with which we have been fortunate to keep company for so long.

Towards the end of his (and Berlin's) life, his friend the satirist John Wells described him persuasively to one of us as 'the best human being I have known'. Berlin's own words to Chaim Weizmann also come to mind: 'My association with you has been in all my life the thing in which I felt more pride and moral satisfaction than anything else whatever – not to speak of the personal pleasure and the sense of justification for one's existence which it provided and provides.'[1]

HENRY HARDY
MARK POTTLE[2]

---

1 Letter of 16 September 1948.
2 Mark Christopher Pottle (b. 1959), historian, teacher and editor; fellow, Wolfson, 1992–9 and since 2011; principal editor of the diaries and letters of Violet Bonham Carter; co-editor of a number of original WW1 documents; research associate, *Oxford Dictionary of National Biography*, 2000–2; co-editor of L3 and L4. For HH see 624.

CONVENTIONS AND ABBREVIATIONS

The format of the names, addresses and dates in the letter-headings has been standardised, and the most common addresses abbreviated as follows:

All Souls	All Souls College, Oxford
Headington House	Headington House, Old High Street, Headington, Oxford
Paraggi	500 Scalini, Paraggi, Santa Margherita Ligure, Italy

All Oxford colleges except New College, Exeter College and Christ Church (which is not known as 'Christ Church College') are referred to in the notes without the word 'College'. 'Corpus' or 'CCC' is Corpus Christi College and 'Univ.' is University College. All Colleges mentioned are in Oxford unless otherwise stated, and Universities are in general referred to without including the word 'University' (so 'Cambridge', 'Columbia', 'Exeter', 'London' etc.), unless the context does not make clear that a university is in question.

Knighthoods are in general indicated by the date and rank of the earliest entitlement to be addressed as 'Sir' (e.g. 'KCMG 1949'), and any subsequent upgrades (e.g. 'KCB 1953, GCMG 1955, GCB 1960') are omitted. Plain 'Kt' means Knight Bachelor, the bottom rung of the ladder of knighthood. Life peers are referred to as such rather than by their longer specific titles (e.g. 'life peer 1976' not 'Baron Bullock of Leafield 1976').

Page references are not introduced with 'p.' or 'pp.' when the context makes it obvious that that is what they are. Cross references of the form '(256/6)' mean 'see page 256, note 6'.

Originals are typed unless said to be in manuscript. The location of these originals is provided as part of the index of correspondents. Where we have used carbon copies (retained by Berlin's secretaries), this is stated:[1] Berlin often amended top copies, and we should be grateful to see top copies of any letters, whether or not included here, but especially if we have used a carbon for a letter selected for inclusion. Signatures have been added (in square brackets) to letters of which we have seen only carbons. The date of dictated letters (i.e. most letters) may be the date of dictation, of typing, or of the expected addition of IB's signature.

Though in general 'house style' has been held constant through the volumes, consistency has not been rigidly imposed. During the quarter-century of the preparation of this edition, subeditorial fashions have changed, and some of these changes are reflected in the editorial matter in successive volumes, for example in an increased preference for lower-case initial letters in job titles (within limits: 'prof. of philosophy', but 'Wayneflete Prof. of Metaphysical Philosophy'), gender-neutral

---

1 In this period carbon copies gradually give way to photocopies, often made before IB signed (and frequently amended) the top copy. The term 'carbon' appearing after the date signifies both carbon copies proper and pre-signature photocopies. (Neither IB nor his secretaries used email.)

appellations ('chair') and religion-neutral dates ('BCE', 'CE'); the style of Berlin's own text, however, has not been too anachronistically updated. Additional abbreviations have been introduced to save space. Finally, the vast development of the Internet while the edition has been in progress has made it ever more possible to track down detailed information in a manageable time, and this sometimes shows.

People and other subjects requiring a gloss are in general footnoted when they are first referred to, but not otherwise. The index will quickly locate this introductory note (its page reference being given in italics) if it is needed to elucidate a later reference. Recipients of letters are referred to by their initials in notes to letters received by them.

Listed below are people referred to more than once without a surname (given in the text in square brackets for single surnameless references). The incomplete versions of their names in the left-hand column are not annotated unless they are used for the earliest reference to their bearers; rather, these names can be assumed to refer to the individuals in the right-hand column unless we state otherwise, or the context makes clear that someone else is meant. Many but not all of these individuals, together with other important or frequently mentioned people, are subjects of the entries in the biographical glossary that precedes the indexes, and are glossed only briefly on their first occurrence, when an asterisk before the surname indicates that an entry is to be found in the glossary, thus: 'Isaiah *Berlin'.

AA	Anna Akhmatova	Jacob	Jacob Rothschild
Adam	Adam von Trott	Jean	Jean Floud
Aline	Aline Berlin	Joe	Joseph Alsop
AJPT / Alan	A. J. P. Taylor	Kay	Katharine Graham
Alexandra	Alexandra Schlesinger	Lionel	Lionel Trilling
Alfred	Alfred Brendel	Lucia	Lucia White
Bob	Robert Silvers	Marietta	Marietta Tree
Chuck	Charles Taylor	Mary	Mary Bennett
Diana	Diana Cooper /	Maurice	Maurice Bowra
	Hopkinson / Trilling	Nicolas	Nicolas Nabokov
Dominique	Dominique Nabokov	Noel	Noel Annan
Douglas	Douglas Jay	Pod	Norman Podhoretz
Edmund / EW	Edmund Wilson	Renée	Renée Ayer, later
Freddie	A. J. Ayer		Hampshire
Goronwy	Goronwy Rees	Stephen	Stephen Spender
Henry	Henry Paget (Lord	Stuart	Stuart Hampshire
	Anglesey)	Teddy	Teddy Kollek
Herbert	H. L. A. Hart	Wystan	W. H. Auden
Iris	Iris Murdoch		

A list of other abbreviations follows. For publication details of books listed see ⟨http://berlin.wolf.ox.ac.uk/lists/books/index.html⟩.

⟨?⟩	enclose (*a*) substantial manuscript additions to typed items made by IB (or by secretaries in carbons), but not most small MS corrections; (*b*) URLs, last accessed on 30 November 2013, but subject to change[1]
[?]	uncertain transcription of preceding word; if preceded by space, illegible word
[ ]	gap in carbon typescript where typist could not interpret IB's dictation
...	authorial ellipsis
[...]	text omitted by editors
AC; AC2	IB, *Against the Current*; 2nd ed.
AD [numeral]	Anno Domini ('in the year of the Lord', i.e. the stated number of years after the conventional year of birth of Jesus of Nazareth); numerically equivalent to CE
AGM	annual general meeting
ANU	Australian National University (Canberra)
AP	Associated Press
b.	born
BA	British Academy
[numeral] BCE	the stated number of years before the Common Era; numerically equivalent to BC (before Christ)
the Berlins	Aline and Isaiah Berlin
BI	*The Book of Isaiah: Personal Impressions of Isaiah Berlin*, ed. HH)
BIS	British Information Services
BLitt	*baccalaureus litterarum* (bachelor of letters)
Bt	Baronet
CAABU	Council for the Advancement of Arab–British Understanding
CBE	Companion of the British Empire
CC	IB, *Concepts and Categories*
CCC, Corpus	Corpus Christi College
[numeral] CE	the stated number of years after the beginning of the Common Era; numerically equivalent to AD
CH	Companion of Honour
CIA	Central Intelligence Agency
CIB	Ramin Jahanbegloo, *Conversations with Isaiah Berlin*
Co.	company
Commons	House of Commons (UK Parliament)
CND	Campaign for Nuclear Disarmament

1 The editors will be grateful to be notified of any changes to these URLs, and of other updatings and corrections, all of which will be posted at ⟨http://berlin.wolf.ox.ac.uk/published_works/a/corrections .html⟩ before being incorporated in future impressions. Please write to henry.hardy @wolfson.ox.ac.uk.

CP	Communist Party
CPGB	Communist Party of Great Britain
CPSU	Communist Party of the Soviet Union
CTH; CTH2	IB, *The Crooked Timber of Humanity*; 2nd ed.
CUNY	City University of New York
CW	Karl Marx, Frederick Engels, *Collected Works* (London, 1975–2005) [referred to by volume and page, thus: CW iii 172]
d.	died
DBE	Dame Commander of the Order of the British Empire
DCL	Doctor of Civil Law
dept	department
DPhil	*doctor philosophiae* (doctor of philosophy)
ed.	edition / edited by (one editor)
eds	editions / edited by (more than one editor)
EEC	European Economic Community ('Common Market')
ENO	English National Opera
FBA	Fellow of the British Academy
FIB; FIB2	IB, *Freedom and Its Betrayal*; 2nd ed.
FDR	Franklin Delano Roosevelt
FO	Foreign Office (London)
FRG	Federal Republic of Germany
FRS	Fellow of the Royal Society
FRSE	Fellow of the Royal Society of Edinburgh
GDR	German Democratic Republic (East Germany)
HF; HF2	IB, *The Hedgehog and the Fox*; 2nd. ed.
HH	Henry Hardy
HM	Her / His Majesty['s]
hon.	honorary
HUJ	The Hebrew University of Jerusalem
IAS	Institute for Advanced Study, Princeton
IB	Isaiah Berlin
IBAC	*Isaiah Berlin: A Celebration* (418)
IBLT	Isaiah Berlin Literary Trust
IBVL	Isaiah Berlin Virtual Library, ⟨http://berlin.wolf.ox.ac.uk/⟩
IDF	Israeli Defense Forces
IRA	Irish Republican Army
IUJF	Inter-University Jewish Federation
JC	*Jewish Chronicle*
Jr	Junior
KM; KM5	IB, *Karl Marx*; 5th ed.
Kt	Knight
L	IB, *Liberty*
L1	The first volume (1928–46) of this edition of IB's letters
L2	The second volume (1946–60) of the same

L3	The third volume (1960–75) of the same
LLD	*legum doctor* (doctor of laws)
LMH	Lady Margaret Hall (Oxford college)
Lords	House of Lords (UK Parliament)
LPO	London Philharmonic Orchestra
LRB	*London Review of Books*
LSE	London School of Economics (and Political Science)
Mass.	Massachusetts
m.	married
MC	Military Cross
MCC	Marylebone Cricket Club
Met	New York Metropolitan Opera
MI	Michael Ignatieff, *Isaiah Berlin: A Life* (London/New York, 1998)
MIT	Massachusetts Institute of Technology
MI Tape	recording of interview by Michael Ignatieff (interviews conducted 1988–97), followed by tape no. and date of interview
MK	Member of Knesset (Israeli parliament)
MLitt	*magister litterarum* (master of letters)
MP	Member of Parliament
MSB	Oxford, Bodleian Library, MS. Berlin, followed by specific shelfmark and folio(s), e.g. MSB 232/1–3 = MS. Berlin 232, fos 1–3
NATO	North Atlantic Treaty Organization
n.d.	no date
NGO	non-governmental organisation
NKVD	People's Commissariat for Internal Affairs (USSR)
NRP	National Religious Party (Israel)
NY	New York
NYRB	*New York Review of Books*
NYT	*New York Times*
NYU	New York University
ODNB	*Oxford Dictionary of National Biography*
ODQ	*Oxford Dictionary of Quotations*
OM	Order of Merit
OUP	Oxford University Press
PhD	*philosophiae doctor* (doctor of philosophy)
PI; PI2; PI3	IB, *Personal Impressions*; 2nd ed.; 3rd ed.
PLO	Palestine Liberation Organization
POI	IB, *The Power of Ideas*
pp	*per pro[curationem]*, through the agency of (after name of correspondent, and before name of person signing on his/her behalf: e.g. IB pp PU)
PPE	Philosophy, Politics and Economics (Oxford undergraduate course)
PPS	Parliamentray Private Secretary; second postscript

PRO	Public Record Office
prof.	professor
PS	postscript / Private Secretary
PSM	IB, *The Proper Study of Mankind*
PU	Pat Utechin
repr.	reprinted
RIBA	Royal Institute of British Architects
ROH	Royal Opera House, Covent Garden, London
RR	IB, *The Roots of Romanticism*
RT; RT2	IB, *Russian Thinkers*; 2nd ed.
SM	IB, *The Soviet Mind*
SOAS	School of Oriental and African Studies
SPD	Sozialdemokratische Partei Deutschlands (German Social Democratic Party)
Sr	Senior
SR	IB, *The Sense of Reality*
SS	Stephen Spender / Schutzstaffel (the 'Defence Corps' of the Nazi Party)
TCE; TCE2	IB, *Three Critics of the Enlightenment*; 2nd ed.
THES	*The Times Higher Education Supplement*
Times	*The Times* (London)
TLS	*The Times Literary Supplement*
trans.	translated by
UCL	University College London
UCLA	University of California, Los Angeles
UD	IB and Beata Polanowska-Sygulska, *Unfinished Dialogue*
UGC	University Grants Commission
UN	United Nations
UNESCO	United Nations Educational, Scientific and Cultural Organization
UNHCR	United Nations High Commissioner for Refugees
Univ.	University College
UNRRA	United Nations Relief and Rehabilitation Administration
US	United States (of America)
USSR	Union of Soviet Socialist Republics
VH	IB, *Vico and Herder*
vol. / vols	volume(s)
Wasp	White Anglo-Saxon Protestant
WSC	Winston [Spencer-]Churchill
WW1	First World War
WW2	Second World War

STILL PRESIDING

The British Academy *suite et fin*

1975–1978

The assassination of Lord Moyne,[1] the British resident minister in Cairo, on 6
November 1944 by two members of the Jewish underground terrorist organiza-
tion Lehi[2] had been greeted with outrage, not only in Britain but among moder-
ate Zionists in Palestine. The killers were hanged in Cairo on 23 March 1945;
thirty years later their bodies were handed over by the Egyptian authorities to
the Israeli government, and on 26 June 1975 the Prime Minister, Yitzhak Rabin,[3]
led thousands of mourners in what had the appearance of a state funeral.
Terrorist outrages, whether in Britain or the Middle East, had by then become a
depressingly frequent feature of modern life, prompting The Times *to observe,*
of the adulation of Lord Moyne's assassins:

Of course these people have to be brave, whether they are Jews or Arabs or
Irishmen or of any other nationality. Of course by their own lights they are
patriots. But the great men who led the Israeli nation [in 1944] did not accept the
support of murder, and it is a reflection on the men who lead Israel now that
they accept other and lower standards. As do almost all Arab leaders.[4]

This judgement presaged a troubled era in the Middle East, and if IB grew criti-
cal of British press reporting on Israel in these years, he also grew increasingly
critical of the Israeli leadership, and the fate of of Israel consumed him until his
dying day.

TO STEPHEN SPENDER[5]

1 July 1975

Headington House

Dear Stephen,

[...] I entirely agree with you about Lord Moyne etc. It is both immoral
and colossally stupid – a gift to the PLO, the biggest they have ever received.
And according to our Peter,[6] who is in Jerusalem now, they have no sense at
all of anything being odd or wrong. I feel both angry and depressed about
this, and feel a kind of unworthy relief that I am on record about the Moyne
assassination: in a published lecture in Jerusalem I did say that it did the
Zionist movement fatal damage,[7] and it seems to be pursuing it still.

1 Walter Edward Guinness (1880–1944), DSO 1917 and bar 1918, 1st Baron Moyne 1932, Conservative
   and Unionist politician; secretary of state for the Colonies 1941–2; leader, Lords, 1941–2; deputy
   minister of state, Cairo, 1942–4, resident minister 1944.
2 Lohamei Herut Israel, or Lehi (Fighters for the Freedom of Israel), founded by Avraham Stern
   1940 after a split in the Irgun (233/7), and known as the 'Stern Gang'.
3 Yitzhak Rabin (1922–95), Jerusalem-born Israeli general and statesman, became leader, Labour
   Party, April 1974 in succession to Golda Meir; prime minister 1974–7, 1992–5; his work for regional
   peace was acknowledged by the 1994 Nobel Peace Prize (awarded jointly to Rabin, Shimon Peres
   and Yasser Arafat); assassinated by an Israeli extremist 1995 while still in office (468).
4 'The Terrorists Receive a Welcome in Israel', Times 26 June 1975, 17a–c at 17c.
5 Stephen Harold *Spender (1909–95), poet, critic, playwright.
6 Peter Francis *Halban (b. 1946), son of Aline Berlin and Hans Halban; publisher.
7 *Zionist Politics in Wartime Washington* (Jerusalem, 1972), repr. in L1; see L1 687–8, 690–1.

Mrs Gandhi does not surprise me – she is an awful woman and capable of anything.[1] Next time I see Iris[2] I shall certainly very gently ask for her views.
Yours ever,
     Isaiah

TO JEAN FLOUD[3]

   31 July 1975 [*manuscript*]

                                                                    Paraggi

Dear Jean,

   [...] I've just read about Akhmatova's[4] life, a memoir,[5] a very sensitive & distinguished woman's reminiscences of her: it is solemn, terribly sad, tragic & full of deaths & – round the nearest corner – torture and executions – & moving as Solzhenitsyn[6] – who is *terrifying* – is not: because extremely personal and interwoven with old fashioned, noble rules of conduct: of what one does & doesn't do: what good literary manners are: what one can & what one cannot say (going back to Emily Dickinson or Chekhov or Jane Austen):[7] all this in the midst of unimaginable brutalities, hunger, squalor, blood – in which these ladies – the writer, Lydia Chukovsky,[8] & her heroine, Akhmatova, & all their friends, remain uncontaminated, unbroken, sensitive, articulate, dignified, morally impeccable, not priggish even, and a wonderful, I hope irremoveable reproach to history & E. H. Carr,[9] and all the contemptible 'impassive' recorders of the majestic march of the forces of progress.[10]

1 An editorial in that day's *Times*, 'The Indian Dictator' (15a–c), described the events leading to the declaration of a state of emergency in India, 24 June 1975, at the behest of Indira Priyadarshini Gandhi (1917–84) née Nehru, prime minister 1966–77, 1980–4. The state of emergency was ostensibly a response to civil unrest in the wake of her conviction on charges of electoral corruption, 12 June, but facilitated the arrest of hundreds of her political opponents.
2 (Jean) Iris Murdoch (1919–99), DBE 1987, novelist and philosopher; m. 1956 John Bayley (262/4); fellow, St Anne's, 1948–62; lecturer in philosophy, Royal College of Art, 1963–7; friendly with Indira Gandhi at Badminton School, Bristol, where they were boarders, and at Somerville, where they were contemporaries.
3 Jean Esther *Floud (1915–2013), sociologist and college head.
4 Anna Andreevna *Akhmatova (1889–1966) née Gorenko, Russian poet visited by IB 1945–6.
5 Lidiya Chukovskaya, *Zapiski ob Anne Akhmatovoi* [*Notes about Anna Akhmatova*] i, 1938–1941 (Paris, 1976), reviewed by IB in 'In absentia: Some Books of the Year', TLS, 23 November 1979, 4. Extracts were included in the collection *Pamyati Anny Akhmatovoi: stikhi, pis'ma* [*In Memory of Anna Akhmatova: Poems, Letters*] (Paris, 1974), 43–198, and the 1976 book was translated as *The Akhmatova Journals* (London/NY, 1994). The 2nd vol., covering 1952–62, was first published in French as Lidia Tchoukovskaïa, *Entretiens avec Anne Akhmatova*, trans. Lucile Nivat and Geneviève Leibrich (Paris, 1980), and in the original Russian later the same year. The 3rd and last vol., covering 1963–6, was published in Russian in Moscow 1997. Neither of the last 2 vols has yet appeared in English.
6 Aleksandr Isaievich *Solzhenitsyn (1918–2008), Russian writer and dissident.
7 Emily Elizabeth Dickinson (1830–86), US poet ranked with Walt Whitman (266/3) in the US canon; Anton Pavlovich Chekhov (1860–1904), one of the foremost Russian dramatists and short-story writers; Jane Austen (1775–1817), pre-eminent and much loved English novelist.
8 Lidiya Korneevna *Chukovskaya (1907–96), Russian writer and poet.
9 Edward Hallett *Carr (1892–1982), historian; friend and ideological opponent of IB.
10 For IB's criticisms of Carr's historical method see 515–16 and L3 76, 84–5, 401.

I don't know who first protested against this appalling vulgarity: Schiller[1]
I *think*: Herder[2] thought it all avoidable: Schiller, not. But there, I must not
go on: I've just discovered a dreadful mistake in "Vico" – my account of him,
I mean.[3] How could I *not* have known that Nicholas of Cusa (1401–1464)[4]
anticipated Vico's account of what Ryle[5] always calls 'maths'? Can I insert
a footnote noting, but not overrating this fact?[6] Why has *no one else* I've read,
noticed it? I am *no* scholar, but sometimes muddled amateurs like me (I don't
underrate myself: but I *am* that:) stumble on tiny facts like this, of interest
to *nobody* save a few Vicomaniacs who will (because they haven't discovered
this themselves) certainly ignore it. Perhaps Mat[t]hews[7] is right: perhaps
scholarship – learning – does not matter that much: & Lockwood's[8] name
is much more important than Prof. Kristeller's[9] (who managed to *prove* that
Minucius Felix[10] wrote X or Y *two* months *after* it had been thought earlier:
"but Prof Kristeller' Morgenbesser[11] asked "what difference does this make?'
'*What difference?*' K. answered '*What difference*?!? Two months!"

Here in Paraggi it is peaceful. My health is slowly being restored by old
fashioned tonics & a new diet (I do *love* that: *any* doctor can twist me round
his little finger: I know I am being twisted, but having a servile nature, *like*
it). I am informed that I am *toxic*: not infected: but need detoxication: so
I munch boiled vegetables, keep off meat. Bob Silvers[12] has, I hear, become
a vegetarian by conviction: converted by an article by Singer[13] in his own

1 (Johann Christoph) Friedrich von Schiller (1759–1805), philosopher, dramatist, poet, one of the
   central figures of German Romanticism.
2 Johann Gottfried Herder (1744–1803), philosopher, poet, critic; an important influence in German
   Romanticism, especially on the young Goethe.
3 Giambattista Vico (1668–1744), Italian philosopher and jurist, regarded by IB as 'one of the boldest
   innovators in the history of human thought' (POI 53). VH was in its final stages of preparation.
4 Nicholas of Cusa, German cardinal and philosopher, wrote extensively on mathematics and
   astronomy, asserting before Copernicus that the earth rotated.
5 Gilbert Ryle (1900–76), Waynflete Prof. of Metaphysical Philosophy, Oxford, and fellow,
   Magdalen, 1945–68; editor of *Mind* 1947–71; a leading figure in Oxford linguistic philosophy.
6 Done: see VH 21/1 (at 142), TCE 40/3. IB had claimed that Vico was the first to propound his theory
   that mathematical knowledge was certain (only) because we ourselves created mathematics.
7 Robert Charles Oliver ('Robin') Matthews (1927–2010), economist and historian; fellow, St John's,
   Cambridge, 1951–65; Drummond Prof. of Political Economy, Oxford, and fellow, All Souls, 1965–
   75; Master, Clare, Cambridge, 1975–93 (and prof. of political economy 1980–91); David Lockwood
   (next note) was a beneficiary of Matthews's successful campaign on behalf of the Social Sciences
   section of the BA.
8 David Lockwood (1929–2014), prof. of sociology, Essex, 1968–95.
9 Paul Oskar Kristeller (1905–99), Berlin-born philosopher specialising in Renaissance humanism;
   Woodbridge Prof., Columbia, 1968–73.
10 Marcus Minucius Felix (*fl.* 200–40), Christian apologist.
11 Sidney Morgenbesser (1921–2004; plate 13), John Dewey Prof. of Philosophy, Columbia, 1975–99,
    famous for his wit, and much loved by IB.
12 Robert Benjamin *Silvers (b. 1929), co-founder and co-editor, NYRB.
13 Peter Albert David Singer (b. 1946), Australian moral philosopher, known for his work on animal
    rights and bioethics; professor of philosophy, Monash, 1977–99; later (since 1999) Ira W. DeCamp
    Professor of Bioethics, University Center for Human Values, Princeton; author, *Animal Liberation:
    A New Ethics for Our Treatment of Animals* (London, [1975]).

journal: he eats fish because they suffer less (how do we know?) – does he
wear leather shoes?[1] He is coming for 2 days with his Countess[2] [...].
Love
    Isaiah

TO JEAN FLOUD
    12 August 1975 [*manuscript*]

                          As from, & indeed from, Paraggi

Dear Jean,
    [...] I am bored: not profoundly: I seldom am, owing to my shallow &
rapidly adaptive nature, and lack of creative neuroses or important traumas
or a deep, dark German inner life, and a genuine absence of self absorption
& self importance – not tragic but sublime, unbearable but formidable and
spiritually important deep self-lacerating storms – but to the extent that my
extravert nature permits, I *am* bored with myself: this has come on as a result
of forcing myself to plunge into a huge ragbag of notes on romanticism etc.[3]
which shows me to myself in a chaotic & trivial light: my notes are copious,
unreadable (to me), unsystematic, not stupid (for the most part) but dust &
ashes compared to real thinkers (of whom I am relieved to tell you, I know
none in our country). Ryle thinks he is one: he is, I think, mistaken: Leavis[4]
does: but he is not *that*: there are no real ideas – only techniques & anath-
emas & a view of the subject – to feed off – Eliot[5] *was* one, I think: deeply
unsympathetic: so were Arnold[6] and Wittgenstein:[7] Oakeshott[8] thinks he is

1 Peter Singer, 'Animal Liberation', review of Stanley and Rosalind Godlovitch and John Harris,
  Animals, Men and Morals: An Enquiry into the Maltreatment of Non-Humans (London, 1971), appeared
  in the NYRB 5 April 1973, 17–21. Since then Robert Silvers has been more or less vegetarian.
2 Grace Maria Dudley (b. 1923) née Kolin, Countess of Dudley 1961, former wife of, 1st (1946–59),
  Prince Stanisław Albrecht Radziwiłł, 2nd (from 1961 until his death in 1969), William Humble Eric
  Ward, 3rd Earl of Dudley; since 1975 she has been Silvers's partner.
3 In the years after the delivery of his Mellon Lectures on romanticism in 1965, especially after his
  retirement from Wolfson, IB continued to read widely with a book on romanticism in mind.
  In the last decade of his life he started afresh on the task of pulling his notes together, but the
  new synthesis continued to elude him, and not so much as a sentence of the intended work was
  written. Cf. RR2 xix–xx.
4 Frank Raymond Leavis (1895–1978), literary critic; editor of the quarterly review *Scrutiny* 1932–53;
  fellow, Downing, Cambridge, 1936–62; reader in English, Cambridge, 1959–62.
5 Thomas Stearns Eliot (1888–1965), OM 1948, US-born British poet, critic and publisher.
6 Matthew Arnold (1822–88), poet, writer and inspector of schools; his later essays and his view of
  the literary critic's proper social role made him an important influence on figures as diverse as
  Max Weber, T. S. Eliot, F. R. Leavis and Lionel Trilling.
7 Ludwig Josef Johann Wittgenstein (1889–1951), Vienna-born philosopher, initially Bertrand
  Russell's protégé at Cambridge, prof. of philosophy there 1939–48; naturalised British citizen
  1939; inspired the Cambridge school of analysis between the wars and influenced the analytic
  philosophy of post-war Oxford.
8 Michael Joseph Oakeshott (1901–90), fellow, Nuffield, 1949–50; prof. of political science, LSE,
  1951–69.

one, but believe me (for I have no proof) he is a *feeble* heir of Montaigne[1] &
Burke,[2] with not one idea, or even formulation, to call his own: & his influence, which is certainly a fact, is a means of letting people off the disagreeable task of serious self examination. Even Bagehot[3] was a giant compared
to him – a real original, an English phenomenon, smaller than, but analogous to, Dr Johnson & Cobbett[4] & the probably underrated Morley.[5] What
on *earth* am I doing writing this cross & probably envious denunciation of
everybody? [...]
Yours
    Isaiah

*While he was President of Wolfson, July 1966 to March 1975, IB's foreign travel
had mostly been limited to trips to the East Coast of the US, principally Boston,
New York and Washington. Though these visits were frequent and enjoyable,
he looked forward to the time when he would retire from Wolfson 'and be, as
Khrushchev[6] said about himself, "a free Cossack" (not an entirely convincing
image so far as I am concerned)'.[7] In anticipation of that freedom he accepted
the position of visiting lecturer at the History of Ideas Unit of the Australian
National University at Canberra, from September to November 1975. Aline[8]
accompanied him throughout. Their outward journey took in Tahiti (plate 3) –
'little boys & girls, in tidy uniforms, looking like Gauguin paintings, dutifully
intone "nos ancêtres, les Gaulois ..."[9] – it is all too beautiful, sun drenched,
remote – very agreeable and not to be seriously tolerated for more than a week (4
days for us)';[10] and then Fiji – 'Aline points out the aesthetic & cultural superiority of French colonies – rigorous direct rule – to British ex-colonies, free, & not
miserably poor, & full of Indians & glum to a degree. Silent unhappy New*

1 Michel Eyquem de Montaigne (1533–92), influential French moralist, originator of the modern
essay genre.
2 Edmund Burke (1729/30–97), Dublin-born politician, political theorist and philosopher, author of
Reflections on the Revolution in France (London, 1790).
3 Walter Bagehot (1826–77), political commentator and economist; editor of *The Economist* 1860–77;
author of *The English Constitution* (London, 1867); one of the leading journalists of the Victorian
era.
4 Samuel Johnson (1709–84), known as Dr Johnson (LLD, Dublin, 1765), essayist, biographer, critic
and lexicographer, author of the magisterial *A Dictionary of the English Language* (London, 1755).
William Cobbett (1763–1835), political writer and farmer who combined social conservatism with
a radical democratic political agenda; his *Political Register* appeared weekly 1802–35.
5 John Morley (1838–1923), 1st Viscount Morley 1908, politician and writer; editor, *Fortnightly
Review*, 1867–82; Liberal MP 1883–1908, cabinet minister under Gladstone and Asquith, and highly
rated by the latter.
6 Nikita Sergeevich Khrushchev (1894–1971), Ukraine-born Soviet leader, 1st secretary, CPSU,
1953–64, prime minister 1958–64.
7 To Kay Graham, 4 November 1974.
8 Aline Elisabeth Yvonne *Berlin (1915–2014), IB's wife and from 1997 widow.
9 'Our ancestors, the Gauls ...'.
10 To Patricia and Bernard Williams, 10 September 1975.

Zealand couples and unconvincing dances by bored native children'.[1] *Australia, where they arrived in mid September, was a revelation, confounding the apprehensions that IB had experienced in the comfort of his home in Headington.*

TO HUGH TREVOR-ROPER[2]

30 August 1975 [*manuscript*]

Headington House

Dear Hugh,

I am writing this on the very eve of leaving these shores for Australia – God knows why; senile curiosity – I wish I weren't going: I have no wish to lecture or hold classes or travel: even the prospect of Tahiti or Bali does not allure me: full of juke boxes & malaria, I imagine, and tax haven seekers. But I promised to go in a moment of irrational Wanderlust, long ago, & now my words have come home to roost. So we go. Alas, this means that I cannot dine with the Brethren till Hilary:[3] sad: I'll lift a glass of Australian Burgundy in a silent toast: but do not intend to drink the contents. [...]

My heart sinks. A synthetic image composed of Wheare, Crombie, Hancock and the late Warden of Rhodes House[4] swims before my eyes: miserere.[5]

Yours,
    Isaiah.

TO JEAN FLOUD

6 October 1975 [*manuscript*]

Australian National University, Canberra

Dear Jean,

Canberra is an unattractive city. Scattered like Los Angeles – without even Los A's queer, sinister, eccentric quality, it has no centre, no flavour, no real life. The academics are perfectly nice & friendly, but it is a relief to go to

---

1 To Iris and William Hayter, 16 September 1975.
2 Hugh Redwald *Trevor-Roper (1914–2003), historian.
3 Hilary Term. The members of 'the Club' (plate 2), a private all-male Oxford dining society, called one another 'Brother'. 'My election stultified the original idea: it was originally meant for conservative, snobbish, well-born fellows of colleges – that's how it was in the nineteenth century, and roughly until I was elected. The idea that persons with left-wing or even mildly liberal views, Jews etc. could be members was, I am sure, never entertained.' To HH, 28 September 1992.
4 All Australians at Oxford: Kenneth Clinton Wheare (1907–79), Kt 1966, constitutional expert, Rector, Exeter, 1956–72; Alistair Cameron Crombie (1915–96), lecturer in history of science, Oxford, 1953–83, and fellow, Trinity, 1969–83; (William) Keith Hancock (1898–1988), historian, 1st Australian fellow of All Souls 1924–30, Chichele Prof. of Economic History, Oxford, and fellow, All Souls, 1944–9; Carleton Kemp Allen (1887–1966), Kt 1952, jurist, Warden, Rhodes House, 1931–52.
5 'Pity [me].'

Sydney or Melbourne or anywhere, even if it means talking about Hamann.[1] Kamenka,[2] my boss, is a disarming, affable, know-all, with a rather pedantic ambitious Chinese wife[3] who lacks the higher attributes very conspicuously: she works hard & is not sympathetic: Herbert[4] thinks highly of her. Sydney is a very attractive, brash town: the harbour is *marvellous*, even I noticed that: the Opera striking & too small for what it is: given that one wishes to do something violently unforgettable it shd dominate more [...]: John P.[5] much appreciated here: his death widely mourned by D. McCallum[6] & the U. of Sydney – I got a lot of credit for claiming to be a friend of his. Melbourne is *very* different: rich, British to a degree, snobbish, with a 'hotel in which we were put up which outdoes England in Edwardian conveniences & curlicews[7] (including calling Room Service – 'Pantry'.) My host, a Chilean called Veliz[8] who was at L.S.E. in the early 50ies: very gay & affable, all his colleagues (including himself) seemed to have listened to my notorious Comte Lecture[9] & thought it *execrable*; they all claimed that life, vicissitudes, old age brought them round to my side: I felt like some aged reactionary after the failure of a revolution. I am lecturing too much & working quite hard to earn my visit: the kangaroos, emus, koala bears, parrots *are* worth inspecting: so is the Melbourne art gallery. Tasmania, Adelaide, N. Zealand, are still to come. They are *not* like America: yet they are too, you know (as Americans say) like the Middle West 30 or so years ago. The upper crust speak English with only the *faintest* digger accent: some speak a horrible artificial neither honest

1 Johann Georg Hamann (1730–88), German theologian and philosopher, and leading anti-rationalist thinker; one of the subjects of TCE; in October 1965 IB delivered the Woodbridge Lectures at Columbia on 'Two Enemies of the Enlightenment', Hamann and Joseph de Maistre: 'I am now reading and scribbling notes about Hamann – the terrible, obscure and religious bigot of the eighteenth century where romanticism sprang from as much as anywhere. He did have certain bold ideas, but seems to have no real predecessors – just my thing.' To Stuart Hampshire, 4 January 1962.
2 Eugene Kamenka (1928–94), German-born Australian philosopher and Marxian scholar of Russian Jewish descent; emigrated to Australia 1937; founding head, History of Ideas Unit, Institute of Advanced Studies, ANU, 1968–93, prof. of the history of ideas 1974–93; collaborated on many academic publications with his 2nd wife Alice Tay (next note).
3 Alice Erh-Soon Tay (1934–2004), Singapore-born academic, human rights activist and lawyer; Challis Prof. of Jurisprudence, Sydney, 1975–2001; director of the Centre for Asian and Pacific Law 1993–8; m. 1964 Eugene Kamenka.
4 Herbert Lionel Adolphus *Hart (1907–92), philosopher of law.
5 John Petrov Plamenatz (1912–75), Montenegrin-born social and political theorist; fellow, All Souls, 1936–51; lecturer in social and political theory, Oxford, 1950–67; fellow, Nuffield, 1951–67; Chichele Prof. of Social and Political Theory (IB's successor), Oxford, and fellow, All Souls, 1967–75; subject of a memoir in PI.
6 Douglas McCallum (1922–98) prof. and head, School of Political Science, New South Wales, 1964–87.
7 sc. 'curlicues'.
8 Claudio Veliz (b. 1930), Chilean historian and sociologist, LSE PhD 1959, prof. of sociology, La Trobe, Melbourne, 1972–89, of history, Boston, 1990–2002.
9 (Isidore Marie) Auguste François Xavier Comte (1798–1857), French positivist philosopher and pioneer of sociology. IB's inaugural Auguste Comte Memorial Trust Lecture, 'History as an Alibi', was delivered at the LSE 12 May 1953: for Veliz's view on this see 114/3.

Australian nor B.B.C: Geelong Grammar School (C. of E.) is a *marvellous* piece of fair haired, blue eyed England, real public school stuff, up to date, clean fun, not too many dagoes or cockneys, with a *splendid* headmaster (Sir H. Fisher's[1] brother)[2] & headmaster's wife:[3] I adored our visit there: for a sociologist with a sharp eye & adequate irony & malice, Australia is a wonderful hunting ground: what about Vaizey?[4] I believe they were madly relieved to *liberate* themselves: some because they knew him & didn't like the idea: some out of straight local chauvinism. The vitality *is* infectious: but to live here cd be difficult: too wholesome, too provincial, nobody to talk to. Norman Chester[5] is I am astonished to say, *detested*: thought nasty, stupid (intellectually) & lacking in all virtues. So at least all the politics dept chaps. I love them all: I really do: they aren't in the least like either Wheare or Crombie: they *look* like Chester, & turn out to be salt of the earth & vastly friendly despite my queer accent etc: & Aline goes for bush walks with their ladies [...].

    love

    Isaiah

TO PAT UTECHIN

    25 October 1975 [*manuscript*]

                                            Canberra

Dear Pat

    New Zealand over; nice, tame country: *very* remote from everywhere: *very* pleased with itself, social justice, classlessness (lower middle class throughout:) & very nice, friendly, decent, anglophile, jealous of Australia & disapproving of its antics; Canterbury University is like a Scots university in 1890; peace, harmony & remarkably dull. Marxists should study it. Australia is like Paris by comparison. My Canberra lectures are done (thank God) now only Tasmania & Adelaide (latter spoken of with class conscious scorn as genteel & snobbish in advanced Canberra circles) + 2 radio programmes (unavoidable if offence to be avoided) + short address to Australian Academy (I shall

---

1 Henry Arthur Pears ('Harry') Fisher (1918–2005), Kt 1968, fellow, All Souls, 1946–73, barrister, banker, judge, and IB's successor as President, Wolfson, 1975–85.

2 Charles Douglas Fisher (1921–78), headmaster of the Church of England grammar school, Brisbane, 1970–3, Geelong Church of England grammar school, Victoria, 1974–8; oversaw the difficult task of transforming Geelong into a truly co-educational establishment.

3 Anne Gilmour (b. 1930) née Hammond; studied music at the Guildhall School of Music and Drama, London, 1948; m. 1952 Charles Fisher (6 children) and actively supported his teaching career.

4 John Ernest Vaizey (1929–84), life peer 1976, prof. of economics, Brunel, 1966–82, head, School of Social Sciences, 1973–81; 'in 1975 he suddenly accepted the vice chancellorship of Monash University, Melbourne. He came, he saw, he withdrew, to the consternation of his friends, though they knew that he was volatile and impulsive' (Robert Blake, ODNB).

5 (Daniel) Norman Chester (1907–86), Kt 1974, lecturer in public administration, Manchester, 1936–45; fellow, Nuffield, 1945–54, Warden 1954–78.

talk about lack of funding in Britain: dully professional address: cannot be bothered to seek to shine upon them: *they* wish to shine, not to be shone upon, as Noel Coward[1] once said about *himself* at the Asquiths[2] – when he found *they* shone on *him*)[3] & then heigh ho! To Bali [...].
I.B.

When he retired from the Presidency of Wolfson in 1975 IB's reputation was assured, but not his legacy. He had published few books, and no original monograph, and he would fail to emulate his predecessors in the Mellon Lectureship, Kenneth Clark[4] and Ernst Gombrich,[5] who had each turned their series into an important book, since his own planned work on romanticism did not materialise.[6] In the eyes of critics he was a talker, not a writer,[7] a mistaken impression that he self-deprecatingly reinforced in his own correspondence, where there are repeated confessions about his indolence. In reality he was industrious, and had published well over 150 pieces by the mid 1970s,[8] a fact established by an enthusiastic, somewhat obsessive, young editor, Henry Hardy,[9] who first met Berlin when he applied to do a BPhil in philosophy at Wolfson in 1972. HH was excited by the challenge of publishing more of IB's work, and with IB's initially somewhat grudging consent proceeded, in his spare time, to produce four volumes of his uncollected essays 1978–80; a fifth appeared in 1990, shortly before HH left his post at OUP to begin full-time work on IB's papers.[10] There was undeniably a tension between their respective views of the project, HH wanting to publish more books, more frequently, than IB was really happy with: 'Why

1 Noël Pierce Coward (1899–1973), English actor, playwright, novelist and composer of light music.
2 The family of Herbert Henry Asquith (1852–1928), 1st Earl of Oxford and Asquith 1925, Liberal prime minister 1908–16, and his wife Margaret Emma Alice ('Margot') (1864–1945) née Tennant.
3 Not traced as a remark by Coward. The formula has also been attributed to Edgar Vincent, Lord d'Abernon – see Nicholas Haslam, *Redeeming Features: A Memoir* (London, 2010), 256 – but it has a longer pedigree: e.g. in *History of the United States, or, Republic of America* (Philadelphia, 1843), 76, Emma Willard writes 'it was the part of [Roger] Williams to shine, and theirs to be shone upon' .
4 Kenneth Mackenzie Clark (1903–83), life peer 1969, OM 1976, art historian; Slade Prof. of Fine Art, Oxford, 1946–50, 1961–2; became internationally known through his TV series *Civilisation*, first broadcast by the BBC 1969; Mellon Lecturer 1953.
5 Ernst Hans Josef Gombrich (1909–2001), Kt 1972, Austrian-born art historian; prof. of the history of the classical tradition, London, and director, Warburg Institute, 1959–76; Mellon Lecturer 1956.
6 L3 214.
7 Maurice Bowra wrote to Noel Annan in 1971, when IB was appointed to the OM: 'Though like Our Lord and Socrates he does not publish much, he thinks and says a great deal and has had an enormous influence on our times.' Noel Annan, 'A Man I Loved', in Hugh Lloyd-Jones (ed.), *Maurice Bowra: A Celebration* (London, 1974), 53.
8 By 2014 the constantly updated online bibliography of IB's published work at ⟨http://berlin.wolf .ox.ac.uk/lists/bibliography/index.html⟩ listed 470 items.
9 Henry Robert Dugdale *Hardy (b. 1949), editor and publisher.
10 This move followed HH's appointment by IB as one of his literary executors in 1988, as a result of which HH inspected IB's voluminous papers (he never threw much away); discovered, to his astonishment, a wealth of relatively finished unpublished material; and persuaded IB, slowly and with some difficulty, that the task of dealing with the papers should begin while the author was still alive, and could explain and interpret.

this tearing hurry?' he wrote to him in May 1979.[1] *But as the years went by IB came to acknowledge what he owed to his 'devoted friend': 'such reputation as I now have is almost certainly due to his collections of my scattered pieces into little books, which have suddenly converted me from someone who has hardly written anything into an almost indecently prolific author'.*[2]

TO HENRY HARDY

13 November 1975

Australia

Dear Henry,

I have just sent you a jolly postcard, and this is the grave letter that follows. I am glad that you love your job and that you like London[3] like Dr Johnson. As for books having to be of the same size – I agonised bitterly over squeezing drops of blood out of my, of course, very long written text of *Karl Marx*.[4] The chief editor, the late H. A. L. Fisher,[5] assured me (after I had pleaded tearfully to let me publish two books) that the restrictions on space would be the making of the book. This could be true, though I did not feel it at the time. It is like censorship in Russia in the nineteenth century: if it is not too efficient, the response to the challenge can act as a tremendous stimulus. On the other hand, there is, I believe, a letter from Hegel[6] to his publisher, Cotta,[7] explaining that if Cotta really wants the book to be longer, he, Hegel, would be perfectly willing to expand it to any required length.[8] Rhetorical writers, like Hegel and me, can do this; and it is very shaming (it actually happened with *The Hedgehog and the Fox*).[9]

1 IB to HH, 14 May 1979.
2 To Genia Lampert, 13 June 1994.
3 HH was then working for the small educational publishing firm Open Books in Soho.
4 IB's biography of the revolutionary and thinker Karl Heinrich Marx (1818–83), co-founder (with Friedrich Engels) of modern Communism, was first published 1939 and has never been out of print; it is now in its 5th edition, ed. HH (Princeton, 2013). IB wrote over 100,000 words, which he cut to the published length of 75,000 words.
5 Herbert Albert Laurens Fisher (1865–1940), OM 1937, historian and politician; author of the 1918 Education Act; Warden, New College, 1925–40; much admired by IB.
6 Georg Wilhelm Friedrich Hegel (1770–1831), German philosopher, succeeded Fichte as prof. of philosophy, Berlin, 1818–31; a profound influence on European thought, notably on Marx and Engels. One of the 6 main subjects of FIB.
7 Johann Friedrich, Freiherr Cotta von Cottendorf (1764–1832), German publisher.
8 This may refer to Hegel's letter to Cotta of 22 January 1831, in which he writes, 'We have agreed on twenty-two florins per sheet for an edition of a thousand copies. My deletions and additions – I have entirely reworked most of it – will more or less balance out. There will be a few sheets more than in the first edition.' If so, IB improves the story, as so often. *Hegel: The Letters*, trans. Clark Butler and Christiane Seiler (Bloomington, [1984]), 670.
9 IB, *The Hedgehog and the Fox: An Essay on Tolstoy's View of History* (London, 1953). The original, shorter, version of HF, based on a lecture delivered in Oxford, was published 1951 under the somewhat less memorable title 'Lev Tolstoy's Historical Scepticism' in *Oxford Slavonic Papers* 2 (1951), 17–54; 2 years later, at the inspired suggestion of George Weidenfeld (341/7), joint founder 1948 of the publishing house Weidenfeld and Nicolson, it was reprinted in a revised and expanded

[...] As to my bits and pieces – I am not at all surprised that my footnotes are inaccurate. I am wildly unscholarly and I am sure the book on Vico will be exposed mercilessly by some pundit.[1] Yet I long for accuracy, even pedantry. It would be nice to think that my confusions are the vice of some mysterious virtue, but I fear this is not so. I am really most grateful to you for all that you can do in this and every way. I have heard nothing about David Shapiro.[2] I wonder what kind of introduction he will write? Aileen Kelly[3] has discovered the same horrible inaccuracy on my part when she read my piece on *Fathers and Children*.[4] I need help at every stage, I see, and am very lucky to have both her and you. [...]

We adored Australia. It does not make England seem in the least remote, as it certainly looks from New York or San Francisco. Australians are all too aware of England and English, even when they are slightly touchy about it, like e.g. my friend Professor Passmore,[5] who complains that the BBC constantly makes snide references to Australians, which I believe to be quite groundless. I loved all the Australians I met, particularly philosophers. The Anderson legend is exceedingly intriguing,[6] and George Paul is a great Australian hero like Austin in America.[7] If I were exiled from England and

form under its present famous title, afforced principally by 2 additional sections on Tolstoy and Maistre, written at Weidenfeld's request to bulk out the text.

1 There are indeed several reviews that took issue with IB's account of Vico. The one that most impugned his scholarship was Hans Aarsleff, 'Vico and Berlin', *London Review of Books*, 5–18 November 1981, 6–7; IB replied at 7–8. An exchange of letters followed, in the last of which (3–16 June 1982, 5) IB referred to 'Whitehead's pertinent observation about scholars "who know so much and understand so little". Professor Aarsleff's two philippics seem to me to be excellent illustrations of this sad truth.' We have not been able to trace the remark attributed to Whitehead.

2 David Michael Shapiro (b. 1934) met IB when, as an undergraduate at New College, he was one of 4 freshmen allowed to attend a seminar given by IB and E. H. Carr on precursors of the Russian Revolution; thereafter he was an academic Russianist; reader in government, Brunel, 1972–88; director, Nuffield Council on Bioethics, 1991–7. Shapiro was originally to be the editor of RT (contract dated 1968), a role subsequently taken over by HH and Aileen Kelly.

3 Aileen Mary Kelly (b. 1942), assistant lecturer in Slavonic studies, Cambridge, 1975–8, lecturer 1978–2001, later (2001–9) reader in intellectual history and Russian culture; fellow, King's, since 1975. She writes that IB 'inspired my interest in Russian thinkers' and that his 'moral vision has been the constant standard by which I have measured their failings and their strengths'. *Toward Another Shore: Russian Thinkers between Necessity and Chance* (New Haven and London, [1998]), ix.

4 *Fathers and Children: Turgenev and the Liberal Predicament*, the 1970 Romanes Lecture (Oxford, 1972); repr. in RT. A critical review by Richard Freeborn in the TLS (L3 519/2) led IB to ask Aileen Kelly to check his text, and numerous corrections were made in a 1973 reprint.

5 John Passmore (1914–2004), prof. of philosophy, Research School of Social Sciences, ANU, 1958–79, University Fellow in History of Ideas 1980–2, visiting fellow 1983–94; visiting fellow, All Souls, 1978.

6 John Anderson (1893–1962), Challis Prof. of Philosophy, Sydney, 1927–58, a left-wing but anti-Communist thinker whose anti-conservatism made him a philosophical hero to Australian intellectuals resisting the stifling conformity of the 1950s and 1960s. His lionisation by the 'Sydney Push', a rougher version of Bloomsbury (including, e.g., Germaine Greer and Clive James) made him in that respect a local analogue of G. E. Moore.

7 George Andrew Paul (1912–62), fellow and philosophy praelector (i.e. tutor), Univ., 1945–62; died of exposure after capsizing a dinghy on Coniston Water, Lake District. John Langshaw Austin (1911–60), fellow, All Souls, 1933–5; fellow and philosophy tutor, Magdalen, 1935–52; White's Prof.

transported to Australia, I should not complain. It is a large, rich, wide world with an open and fascinating future, unexhausted and not corrupt or guilt-ridden like much of America. In fact, I have become an Australophile. We must certainly discuss determinism and responsibility. The people who say they are not fond of blaming seem to me to indulge in a form of writers' vanity.

Yours ever,

Isaiah   [...]

TO LIDIYA CHUKOVSKAYA

20 November 1975 [*translation of Russian manuscript*][1]

As from All Souls

[Dear Lidiya Korneevna,

I have behaved *despicably* towards you: I received your *splendid* letter in 1973,[2] in which you told me very very interesting things about Chekhov and AA's and B[oris] L[eonidovich Pasternak]'s[3] attitudes towards him (which clarified many things for me), and then a year later you sent me your remarkable (I don't know why you belittle yourself – I have never in my life read anything less banal) book about Herzen.[4] And I repaid you with base ingratitude – I did not even send you confirmation of my having received the book – [...] I am simply a good-for-nothing, do not deserve even a drop of respect, and do not even dare to ask for a pardon. Where am I writing to you from now? From the Far East – where all of a sudden I have a couple of hours of 'leisure' – I am on my way home to Oxford from Australia. The truth of the matter is:

1) I'm not used to writing in Russian and I don't have any real language at my disposal – it's what the Italians call 'mancanza di parole'[5] – because I stopped writing and thinking in Russian as long ago as 1919, when I was 10, but there is nothing that is, if not more excruciating, then at least more insuperable, than to be full of English words and thoughts, but not to have the chance to pour all of them through the excessively narrow 'neck' of the bottle, especially for a person in whose head there is a constant jumble or jungle (as here on the island of Java where I currently am) – thickets of unnecessary words. Oh, how I envy those who think in well-ordered,

of Moral Philosophy, Oxford, and fellow, CCC, 1952–60. IB liked and admired them both.
1 The translation is by Katharine Judelson and Sylva Rubashova (see 637/1).
2 Dated 12 September 1973.
3 Boris Leonidovich *Pasternak (1890–1960), poet, novelist and translator.
4 Lidiya Chukovskaya, '*Byloe i dumy' Gertsena* (Moscow, 1966). Aleksandr Ivanovich Gertsen (Herzen) (1812–70), Russian revolutionary thinker and writer; one of IB's heroes because of his rejection of any attempt to justify violent means in pursuit of utopian ends; his major works were his political essays, collected as *S togo berega* (*From the Other Shore*, 1847–50), and his memoirs, *Byloe i dumy* (*My Past and Thoughts*, 1852–68); IB's essays on Herzen have done much to form the contemporary view of his personality and ideas.
5 'Shortage of words'.

logically coherent and clear thoughts (you yourself can certify that I write chaotically with grammatical and all sorts of other mistakes), and that's why I kept postponing and putting off my reply despite the fact that your letter and book touched me very much and still go on doing so today.

2) I have also read some things you wrote about AA:[1] and this made a big impression on me and reminded me of so many things I had 'lived through and thought through'[2] that I did not know (and still don't) how to say something to you which is not totally inadequate.

All that taken together paralysed me. This letter is not a letter but just an inappropriate substitute for one: and just a plea for compassion (how horrible my Russian is!). On the subject of Chekhov I do understand: the whole of that generation – both the Symbolists and the Acmeists[3] – the whole of that 'silver' age could not delight in Chekhov: the distance between Baudelaire–Verhaeren–Nietzsche,[4] and Graeco-Roman classical literature and Dante[5] and so on and Chekhov is too great.

As soon (I almost wrote soone[6] – I'm mixing up everything) as I return to England, I shall try to find those articles by Marshak[7] which you mentioned. We probably have all Marshak's writings. But I don't know anything about Samoilov, Kornilov or Mezhirov:[8] how and where can I find them? The more famous ones are not to my liking. And KI's[9] collected works we do have – I plan to sit down and read *everything*: I have only just shed my bureaucratic office and professorship – thank God – and now I have the chance to go back to Russian books! Apart from their literary value this is refreshing nostalgia

---

1 Presumably the extracts from LC's memoirs of AA in *Pamyati Anny Akhmatovoi* (4/5).

2 'Perezhitogo i peredumannogo': in quotation marks, presumably, as a familiar Russian phrase.

3 Symbolism and Acmeism were literary movements belonging to the so-called silver age of Russian poetry (c.1890s–1917). The Russian Symbolists, like the broader European movement of that name (c.1880–95), reacted against realism in literature, favouring the use of symbols to convey an otherwise inaccessible meaning. The Acmeist school, which emerged c.1911, rejecting symbolist mysticism for lucid, logical depictions of everyday reality, was led by Nikolay Gumilev and Sergey Gorodetsky; Anna Akhmatova and Osip Mandel'shtam were members.

4 The Russian Symbolists were influenced by all 3 writers: the French poet and critic Charles Baudelaire (1821–1867); the Belgian francophone poet Émile Verhaeren (1855–1916); and the German philosopher Friedrich Wilhelm Nietzsche (1844–1900).

5 Dante Alighieri (1265–1321), Italian poet and philosopher; author of the epic poem *La divina commedia* (c.1307–20).

6 In the Russian his near-mistake was 'toliko' for 'tol'ko'.

7 Samuil Yakovlevich Marshak (1887–1964), Jewish Russian poet, children's author and translator, from 1925 head of the children's literature section of the state publishing house (later the children's state publishing house), Leningrad. LC worked with him there for 9 years, until both left the organisation 1937. She refers to 3 of Marshak's poems in her letter to IB: 'Pozhar' ('The Fire'), 1923; 'Myach' ('The Ball'), 1926; 'Pochta' ('The Post Office'), 1927; see Marshak, *Sobranie sochinenii* (Moscow, 1968–72) i 83–7, 21–2, 88–93.

8 C20th Russian poets: David Samoilov, pseudonym of David Samuilovich Kaufman (1920–90); Vladimir Nikolaevich Kornilov (1928–2002); Aleksandr Petrovich Mezhirov (1923–2009).

9 Korney Ivanovich Chukovsky (pseudonym of Nikolay Vasil'evich Korneichukov) (1882–1969), author, literary critic, translator, publisher; famous for his children's writing, in prose and verse. Oxford's Taylor Slavonic Library holds his collected works: *Sobranie sochinenii* (Moscow, 1965–9).

– B. L. Pasternak in his day *scolded* me for regarding everything truly Russian through enamoured eyes. That's true: in my old age recidivism is setting in – I *can* even read Levitov[1] and Co. (whom your father despised). And Herzen! He is the greatest love of my whole life and for that reason I was thrilled to read your 'étude': Lenin[2] quotes 'and all', as the English would say. You too (if you will permit me to say so) have a 'heart-driven mind':[3] no one in the West has written about the *unique nature* of *My Past and Thoughts*: recently I met one of Herzen's French great-grandsons: he remarked sadly that all that Western intellectuals, even French Communists, who don't read Russian know about Herzen is the Russophobic filth which E. H. Carr wrote about him before the war in his *Romantic Exiles*:[4] the sharp and even talented libel on Russian nineteenth-century émigrés. About Herwegh[5] one can and should forget: in spite of his friendship with Wagner[6] and Marx he was not a poet of talent – a man justly forgotten. Tolstoy,[7] on the other hand, who did not *really* like H[erzen] personally, was right: even Dostoevsky[8] called H[erzen] a poet: and Belinsky[9] (as always in relation to his friends) was right on the mark, at the very core of Herzen's talent. What is your attitude to Belinsky? Old Russian ex-Formalists – as, for example, Roman Jakobson[10] and his disciples – 'dethroned' him, but I feel *warm* towards him. Despite all his raging, mistakes and misunderstandings, he, precisely he, created that new current of literary criticism which is called 'commitment', 'engagement',

1　Aleksandr Ivanovich Levitov (1835–77), Russian writer.
2　Vladimir Il′ich Lenin (1870–1924) né Ul′yanov, Russian revolutionary Communist, founder and leader of the Bolshevik Party; head of the Council of People's Commissars 1917–24.
3　Belinsky's (note 9 below) characterisation of Herzen in a letter to him of 6 April 1846: 'um [...] oserdechennyi'. V. G. Belinsky, *Polnoe sobranie sochinenii* (Moscow, 1953–9) xii 271.
4　*The Romantic Exiles* (London, 1933).
5　Georg Friedrich Rudolph Theodor Herwegh (1817–1875), German political poet. On his relations with Herzen, see Herzen's *My Past and Thoughts*, part 5, 'Story of a Family Drama'. He had an affair with Herzen's wife Natalie.
6　(Wilhelm) Richard Wagner (1813–83), German composer, librettist, theorist, conductor and director; established his own opera house, the Bayreuther Festspielhaus in Bavaria, to stage his master-work *Der Ring des Nibelungen*, the 1st complete performance of which occurred there 1876. IB did not respond well to Wagner, despite strenuous efforts to educate himself: 'we have recently seen the TV version of the Bayreuth *Ring*, by which I was almost converted to Wagner' (to Miriam Sambursky, 27 January 1983); 'I can live very well without Wagner but I cannot deny that *Tristan* is a major work of genius which has altered the history certainly of music and perhaps of many other things as well' (to Victor Weisskopf, 20 February 1990).
7　Lev Nikolaevich Tolstoy (1828–1910), Russian writer, most famous for his novels *War and Peace* and *Anna Karenina*. IB found Tolstoy endlessly fascinating, and it was the view of history advanced in *War and Peace* that inspired the celebrated essay best known as *The Hedgehog and the Fox*.
8　Fedor Mikhailovich Dostoevsky (1821–81), Russian novelist.
9　Vissarion Grigor′evich Belinsky (1811–48), influential Russian radical journalist and literary critic; a 'Westerniser' like Herzen, he believed that the ideals and institutions of the countries that were heirs to the Enlightenment held out the best promise of political liberty and scientific progress in Russian society.
10　Roman Osipovich Jakobson (1896–1982), Russian-born US linguist and literary theorist, a central figure in the European movement in structural linguistics known as the Prague School; Cross Prof. of Slavic Languages and Literatures and General Linguistics, Harvard, 1949–65; visiting Institute Prof., MIT, 1957–70.

which has developed so widely and interestingly in the West over the last thirty to forty years: the attitude to art which does not break down the individual into pieces – into roles – does not separate the citizen from the writer, politics from ethics, the public from the private. All this came from Russia, from her great writers – but the father of all this is, I think, despite the antipathy shown him by Dostoevsky after 1849 and by Tolstoy, after all, Belinsky; it 'raked over' literature throughout the world; and everything which you say so astutely, vividly and with such profound, sincere and cogent emotion, without pathos, about Herzen's integrity – about the imprint of his personality on everything he wrote – is part of the same phenomenon. The world is divided between those who love this integrity and those to whom it is profoundly repellent: Proust,[1] Eliot, Stravinsky[2] and so on: 'we' and 'the others'. The pleasure your book gave me defies description. There you have it.

Someone told me that you are intending to write a critique of Nadezhda Mandel'shtam's second book.[3] I hope you will do it, although it is clear how much bitterness must seethe within that breast.[4] But even so, re-establishing the truth and justice is worthwhile: about me as well she wrote nonsense – although not bitter, and the mistakes are more or less to be understood – but even so it's complete nonsense, not a word of truth.[5] But those are all trifles. This letter I shall send off to you in Singapore or Siam – I hope it will reach you. I am not capable of waiting till Oxford – 'it is aflame and burning'[6] – my

1 (Valentin Louis Georges Eugène) Marcel Proust (1871–1922), French novelist, author of À la recherche du temps perdu (In Search of Lost Time, 1913–27), ranked 1st by IB in his top 10 'Books of the Century' (557).
2 Igor Fedorovich Stravinsky (1882–1971), Russian-born composer, conductor, pianist and writer; IB supplied the original inspiration, and in due course the biblical libretto, for his cantata for baritone solo and chamber ensemble Abraham and Isaac (1962–3), whose premiere occurred at the Israel Festival in August 1964.
3 Nadezhda Yakovlevna Mandel'shtam (1899–1980), Russian writer, widow of the Acmeist poet Osip Emil'evich Mandel'shtam (1891–1938), who died en route to a Siberian labour camp; the 1st 2 vols of Nadezhda's memoirs, Vospominaniya (NY, 1970) and Vtoraya kniga (Paris, 1972), trans. Max Hayward as Hope Against Hope and Hope Abandoned (London, 1971, 1974), depicted, respectively, her husband's persecution and death, and her experience of widowhood, all set against a backdrop of Stalinist repression and cultural degradation. Her statements on various people, including Lidiya Chukovskaya, were often hotly contested. During the 1970s LC wrote much of a book correcting Nadezhda's account; the unfinished text was published as Dom poeta [The House of the Poet] in LC's Sochineniya v dvukh tomakh (Moscow, 2001) ii 7–238.
4 Nadezhda Mandel'shtam saw herself as a (great) writer in her own right, on the same level as her husband and Akhmatova, not simply 'the wife of a writer' (a job description in Russia) who preserved his legacy – which is how Chukovskaya and others saw her (a main source of the bitterness) – and wished to settle accounts with her detractors. The quality of the prose in her memoirs might be thought to justify her self-estimation. Cf. the letter of 31 May 1977 to Stanley Mitchell (54).
5 Nadezhda Mandel'shtam had reported in her Vtoraya kniga (Paris, 1972), 403, that a group of Oxford students who visited Leningrad in 1954 was said to have been sent by IB. In fact none of them was from Oxford, and IB, who knew nothing of the visit, did not send them. These errors are corrected in a footnote in the English translation by Max Hayward, Hope Abandoned (London/NY, 1974), 357/†.
6 The title of one of the chapters of LC's book on Herzen (14/3), 140. The phrase is taken from a letter from Turgenev to Mikhail Evgrafovich Saltykov-Shchedrin, 19 January 1876.

sense of guilt. Once again I bow my head and ask for forgiveness. *Everything which you sent me, KI's article and your book and especially the letters, is very precious to me. If you will have mercy on me (and close your eyes to my spelling), please send me an answer, otherwise I shall never forgive myself.*
    Yours sincerely
        Isaiah Berlin]

In spring 1975 Joe Alsop[1] made one of his many visits to Israel, which he had supported unswervingly over the years. He was shocked by the 'drastically altered attitude'[2] that he found there towards the US secretary of state, Henry Kissinger,[3] who only a short time before had been feted for his diplomacy during the Yom Kippur War. Alsop feared that this hostility heralded a breakdown in US–Israeli relations, which would be disastrous to both countries; and he discerned in it a fatal inability on the part of Israel's political class to show that unity in peacetime that it habitually found in time of war: 'I'm afraid the time has come for you Israelis to tackle the hardest problem that has ever faced you – the problem of genuine Middle Eastern peacemaking, with Israel participating in a positive way. You cannot, after all, contemplate a state of permanent bellig-erency between you and your Arab neighbors.' Implicit in Alsop's approach was his belief in Kissinger's diplomacy, which reflected changes in US policy, notably a greater degree of engagement with Egypt under Anwar Sadat.[4] In a long open letter 'to an Israeli friend' in the New York Times *in December 1975, Alsop urged Israel to come to its senses, recalling what President Ford[5] had said to him 'long ago, and I think with unchallengeable good sense: "Most Americans are willing to take great risks to preserve the state of Israel, but they are not willing to take great risks to preserve Israel's conquests." Therein lies the basic Israeli dilemma, and I needn't underline it any further for you.'*

1 Joseph Wright ('Joe') *Alsop (1910–89), journalist.
2 This quotation and those that follow are from Alsop's 'Open Letter to an Israeli Friend', *New York Times Magazine*, 14 December 1975, SM5, 16–17, 52, 54, 58, 60, 63–4, 66–8, at 17, 64, 67.
3 Henry (né Heinz) Alfred Kissinger (b. 1923), German-born US diplomat; instructor, dept of gov-ernment, Harvard, 1954–9, associate prof. 1959–62, prof. 1962–9; national security adviser 1969–75, secretary of state 1973–77; Nobel Peace Prize 1973 with the North Vietnamese politician and mili-tary leader Le Duc Tho (who declined the award) for negotiating the January 1973 Paris Peace Agreement that brought a ceasefire in the Vietnam War; after the Yom Kippur War of October 1973 he embarked on intense shuttle diplomacy designed to bring peace to the Middle East.
4 Anwar Mohammed al-Sadat (1918–81), Egyptian statesman, President 1970–81 in succession to Nasser; reversed Nasser's policy of military and economic links with the USSR, expelling Soviet military advisers 1972, and severing ties by 1976; after Egypt's costly involvement in the Yom Kippur War of 1973 he effected a rapprochement with the US, and sought peace with Israel, signing the Camp David Accords with Menachem Begin 1978, for which they shared the 1978 Nobel Peace Prize; Egypt was subsequently expelled from the Arab League, and Sadat assas-sinated by Islamic fundamentalists; he was succeeded by Hosni Mubarak.
5 Gerald Rudolph Ford (1913–2006) né Leslie Lynch King, Jr, US President 1974–7; Republican rep-resentative, Michigan, 1949–73; House minority leader 1965–73; became Nixon's Vice President October 1973 after the resignation of Spiro Agnew; became President 9 August 1974 after the resignation of Nixon, who faced impeachment over his role in the Watergate affair (27/5).

TO JOSEPH ALSOP

23 December 1975

Headington House

Dear Joe,

[...] A kind friend has sent us your Letter to an Israeli Friend. I am ready to accept your main theses as valid, including the unfortunate fact that local Israeli politics are the cause of irrational behaviour on the Israel government's part; and do not even wish to question your belief that Dr K[issinger] cannot err. What left Aline and me – to use your own expression – thunder-struck (you were thunderstruck, I think, three times – once was enough for us) was the tone and style and turn of phrase in your piece. Even Arthur Schlesinger,[1] who wrote furiously to me about Rabin's allegedly open oppo-sition to McGovern during the last election,[2] did not vent his spleen in public. Edwin Montagu[3] once, when Secretary for India, spoke of Lord Curzon's[4] 'bullying, hectoring tone':[5] I think there is more than a touch of Curzon in your thunderbolts. I remember that you spoke in somewhat similar fashion here once, and blew the British ambassador to Israel – Ledwidge[6] – out of the water: that was positively enjoyable, if rather cruel; and I remember that you spoke to me in somewhat similar terms when the blacks were rioting at Watts[7] – about what would happen to them if they persisted in harry-ing the whites. But your fierce admonitions to 'you Israelis' [...] can only, it seems to me, be counterproductive.[8] It might cause resentful stiffening on the part even of Israeli doves, who go far beyond Mr K[issinger]'s and your policies in concessions to the Arabs; add grist to the mill of those who, like

1 Arthur Meier *Schlesinger, Jr (1917–2007), writer, academic and commentator.
2 George Stanley McGovern (1922–2012), Democrat senator, South Dakota, 1963–81; strongly liberal, he was his party's presidential candidate 1972, when he lost heavily to his Republican opponent Richard Nixon. Rabin regarded McGovern as less likely to support Israel than Nixon, and gave a clear public indication of this preference in a radio interview in Israel, June 1972. Yuval Elizur, 'Israeli Preference for Nixon Hinted', *Washington Post*, 11 June 1972, A1, A23.
3 Edwin Samuel Montagu (1879–1924), Liberal politician, secretary of state for India 1917–22, in which capacity he introduced important reforms; obliged to resign 1922 at the instigation, as he saw it, of the foreign secretary, Lord Curzon (next note).
4 George Nathaniel Curzon (1859–1925), Kt 1916, Baron Curzon of Kedleston (Irish peerage) 1898, Marquess Curzon of Kedleston 1921; Unionist MP 1886–98, Viceroy of India 1898–1905; in Lloyd George's war cabinet 1916–19, foreign secretary 1919–24.
5 In a speech in Cambridge, 11 March 1922, Montagu spoke of 'one of those plaintive, hectoring, bullying, complaining letters which were so familiar to Lord Curzon's colleagues and friends': 'Premier "Dictator", Declares Montagu', *Washington Post*, 12 March 1922, 2.
6 (William) Bernard John Ledwidge (1915–98), KCMG 1974, diplomat; UK ambassador to Finland 1969–72, to Israel 1972–5.
7 In August 1965 the largely African American Watts district of Los Angeles saw nearly a week of serious rioting, during which there was widespread damage to property and more than 30 were killed; at the root of the troubles were racial tensions, exacerbated by poor relations between the police and the local community.
8 Alsop had written: 'The cruel fact remains that you Israelis now find yourselves in a peacetime situation that can well be more dangerous than any of Israel's four wars.' op. cit. (18/2), 67.

Mrs Meir[1] (Dr K[issinger], whom I saw two Saturdays ago in London, spoke pretty savagely of her), believe that *all* Gentiles must ultimately betray the Jews, that Israel's only hope is in its own prowess and the help of Jews, that it is better to die gloriously than in squalor like Czechoslovakia or S. Vietnam; and, finally, increase hostility to Israel in the United States on the part of those who think that the interests of the US and Israel are incompatible, and that Israel is a pure embarrassment to be sloughed off. This, surely, is not what you intend? But so far as your piece is likely to have an effect, I cannot see how it can fail to have precisely this one. Dr K[issinger] was quite clear that his difficulties e.g. in Angola[2] and with Syria[3] are due to the belief that the US will not indefinitely resist Russian pressure in the Middle East, because of the US public reaction to Vietnam – rampant neo-isolationism etc. Israel's tiresomeness is merely episodic in all this – he realises that Rabin's stubbornness is due to political weakness, and *can* be overcome in the end; but not by open menaces. As for Syria – do you really think that the USSR will permit a settlement in which it plays no real part? But, issues apart, it is your *fury* with Israel's errors and unbelievable blundering diplomacy that we find so flabbergasting. Why now? Why when they are down? In a despairing mood?

We plainly must have a conversation *à deux* – or *à trois* if Aline wishes to be present – about all this some time. To think that you and Izzy Stone[4] should find yourselves on the *same* platform! Forgive me for this last quip, but it is irresistible: and sadly accurate. [...]

Where are we to discuss your piece? Preferably in Headington House – come and stay for as long as you like – our love for you is undiminished, despite this *huge* peccadillo. [...]

love

Isaiah

---

1 Golda Meir (1898–1978) née Goldie Mabovich, Ukrainian-born US-educated Israeli politician, leading figure in the Mapai Party; foreign minister 1956–66, prime minister 1969–74.
2 After its war of independence from Portugal (1961–74), Angola was consumed by an even longer civil war (1975–2002), in which the 2 sides were supported by the US and USSR; in autumn 1975 Henry Kissinger warned Cuba and the USSR about the build-up of their forces in Angola in support of the Communist MPLA, which soon emerged as the dominant force in the Angolan struggle.
3 In his attempt to pacify the Middle East, Henry Kissinger forged an understanding between Egypt and Israel that led to the signing of the Sinai Interim Agreement in September 1975; Syria, however (regarded as a Soviet protégé), objected, seeing Kissinger's diplomacy as a US plan to undermine Arab unity for Israel's benefit; in this light, there was unlikely to be agreement over the Golan Heights, which Israel had taken from Syria during the Six Day War 1967, and retained during the Yom Kippur war 1973.
4 Isidor Feinstein ('Izzy') Stone (1907–89), journalist made famous by his self-published newsletter *I. F. Stone's Weekly*, reputed for its independent investigative journalism, though reflecting Stone's distinctly individual left-wing perspective; Stone was notably critical of Israel – poles apart from Joe Alsop.

⟨Stuart[1] is astonished by your switch. Unable to explain it – he thinks it is just plain anti-Israel.

MERRY XMAS: HAPPY NEW YEAR AND TURN OUR THOUGHTS TO LOVE AND FRIENDSHIP.⟩

TO JOSEPH ALSOP

15 January 1976

Headington House

Dearest Joe,

Your letter[2] arrived an hour ago, and was read avidly by Aline and me. Let me begin by assuring you that my feelings are no more changed than yours – my love for you and devotion to you are not and cannot be affected by differences of opinion or even disapproval and, confidence for confidence, let me assure you in the most hideous secrecy that of course the kind friend who sent your article to me was none other than Arthur,[3] who must have felt pleasure in the thought that the contrast in my mind between his distinct coolness towards Israel – deriving from Adlai[4] – with your firm support, which I did not fail to rub in, might at last be shaken. I do not blame him for this natural, irresistible impulse to make a little trouble between us. But for God's sake don't speak to him, or anyone, about it – bad blood cannot do anyone any good.

Your letter is, of course, a magnificent analysis of the position, which I fully accept. I did not in my letter quarrel with a single detail of your exposition of the facts: it was masterly, convincing, profoundly depressing for anyone who desires the good of either Israel or America. I did not and do not doubt its realism or complete good faith. Nor am I surprised by the fact that a good many American Jews – you correctly call them Jewish Americans – have been shaken by your analysis and agonised by the problem that it created for them personally. You must not be surprised that if a friend imparts home truths in public – however salutary these may be – particularly that one who, in complete sincerity, says that he finds it painful to say such things but that he can no other – [he] may be suspected of imperfect friendship. As my hero Herzen said long ago, when one is in trouble one turns to one's friends for love,

1 Stuart Newton *Hampshire (1914–2004), philosopher.
2 A 9-page defence of his 'Open Letter to an Israeli Friend' dated 8 January 1976.
3 IB had written to Schlesinger the previous day, 14 January: 'I have reproved Joe and received a powerful, not altogether relevant, letter, bursting with love for the secretary of state [Henry Kissinger]. The substance of what Joe says is very likely true, even in its minutest details, but the tone! Such candour puts a distinct strain on the warmest professions of a friendship.'
4 Adlai Ewing Stevenson (1900–65), US Democrat politician; governor, Illinois, 1949–53, presidential candidate 1952, 1956; beaten to the Democratic nomination by JFK 1960, and his ambassador to UN 1961–5; Schlesinger took sabbaticals from Harvard to work on Stevenson's 1st 2 campaigns, transferring his allegiance to JFK 1960.

not justice; help, not truth.[1] This is the difference between being a friend and being a judge. If you say, 'Others are deceiving you, I alone tell you the truth', you take the risk of being misunderstood. It is a risk that must be taken if the alternative is destruction through illusion.

The question in this case is whether this was the hour and this the manner of telling the truth. That it is largely true, I repeat, I do not myself doubt. You know far more about the movement of American opinion and American politics than I ever shall, so I accept what you say without the slightest hesitation. I am prepared to believe it absolutely. But then, in my letter to you, I did not question *that* [...]. Nor am I – like most of the Foreign Offices of Western Europe (including certainly the British one), or many Israelis – critical of the main lines of Kissinger's diplomacy: some of it has failed, but much of it succeeded brilliantly, and the detaching of Sadat from the Soviet Union is a major achievement which has, of course, radically altered the situation in the Middle East. It is mere short-sightedness and obstinacy on the part of the Israelis to behave not only as if Sadat were a bitter enemy in the long run (which he is) but also in the short run (which he is not). Long runs are made of short runs – to ignore the latter is very foolish (I am told that 'worse than a crime – a mistake' was said not by Talleyrand,[2] as commonly assumed, but by Boulay de la Meurthe in connection with the murder of the duc d'Enghien[3] – you might investigate). None of this do I question. We are of one mind about all that. I am to meet Mrs Meir[4] at lunch tomorrow – a huge lunch – questions may be asked, but I shall probably not be brave enough to make your points to her in public (as perhaps I should).

What I questioned and still question is [...] the minatory tone of your piece. I have no doubt that you did agonise over how to put it all in so delicate a situation, and in speaking, after all, to friends – but I think that your irritation with them did out, in places, *very* fiercely.[5] [...] there are such things as self-fulfilling prophecies: if you say 'Beware, you are digging your own grave'

1 'Friendship and love must avoid cold, legal justice. Love is in its very essence biased and partial; that's love's character.' Diary entry for 31 May 1843. A. I. Gertsen [Herzen], *Sobranie sochinenii v tridtsati tomakh* (Moscow, 1954–66) ii 283–4.

2 Charles Maurice de Talleyrand-Périgord, Prince de Bénévent (1754–1838), French politician and diplomat.

3 'C'est pire qu'un crime, c'est une faute' (often translated as 'It is worse than a crime, it is a blunder') was indeed first said by Antoine Jacques Claude Joseph Boulay de la Meurthe (1761–1840) on hearing of the execution of Louis Antoine de Bourbon, duc d'Enghien (1772–1804), according to C.-A. Sainte-Beuve, *Nouveaux lundis* (1863–70) xii 52. Alsop quoted this: op. cit. (18/2), 60.

4 Golda Meir arrived in London from Washington 12 January 1976 as guest of a number of Jewish organisations in Britain.

5 Alsop wrote that he had worked 'non-stop on this single article for close to two months, precisely because I did *not* want to seem to turn against Israel', but also that 'it seemed to me close to a duty to throw a good big rock into the pond, so to say, in order to start waves of realistic discussion' (8 January 1976).

– if you say this *orbi et urbi*[1] – you surely make that grave more probable; that, indeed, is often the purpose of all such strictures. The chances of its causing repentance in time can only exist if the warning is accompanied by threats of real pressure, as with the denunciations of Soviet treatment of the Jews, which work because all kinds of sanctions *are* actually involved.

So it all comes to the question, not of whether what you say is true, or important, or well-meant – none of which I question – but whether it should have been said in that form, that place, to the whole wide world. About that I am prepared to argue when we meet: I believe that the immediate effect is to strengthen anti-Israel feeling. The question is whether so desperate a move is needed. [...]

Yours ever,

Isaiah

26 February 1976: publication of IB's Vico and Herder: Two Studies in the History of Ideas.

TO QUENTIN SKINNER[2]

15 March 1976

Headington House

Dear Skinner,

Thank you for your letter about my book.[3] I am glad I sent it to you for many reasons which you can easily think of, but in particular, of course, because you are one of the few people in England, it seems to me, who are deeply interested in these problems and have contributed very fruitfully to their discussion. Whom can I talk to about these matters? Who in Oxford is really interested? Alan Ryan[4] somewhat, Stuart Hampshire to a degree, not Tony Quinton,[5] for all his omnivorous intellectual curiosity. And who in England? That is one of the reasons for which I enjoy going to America, where I can find people to talk about these things. [...]

1 Usually 'urbi et orbi', 'to the city [originally Rome] and to the world', a papal address and blessing at Easter and Christmas.
2 Quentin Robert Duthie Skinner (b. 1940), historian of ideas; prof. of political science, Cambridge, 1978–96, Regius Prof. of Modern History 1996–2008.
3 VH.
4 Alan James Ryan (b. 1940; plate 11); fellow, New College, 1969–87, Warden 1996–2009; lecturer in politics, Oxford, 1969–78, reader 1978–87; prof. of politics, Princeton, 1988–96, Oxford 1997–2010; author of introduction to KM4 (repr. as foreword to KM5); later trustee, IBLT (from 2002), and visiting scholar, Princeton (from 2009).
5 Anthony Meredith ('Tony') Quinton (1925–2010; plate 28), life peer 1982; philosopher and college head; fellow, All Souls, 1949–55, New College 1955–78; President, Trinity, 1978–87; '[H]is no-nonsense Dr Johnson tendency, coupled with the Humean sensibility of an 18th-century man of letters, gave him a conception of philosophy that was more wide-ranging and pluralistic than that of his socialite, socialist friend and fellow empiricist, A. J. (Freddie) Ayer' (Jane O'Grady, *Guardian*, 22 June 2010, 37).

I cannot deny that what interests me most, both about Vico and Herder, are the ideas which still seem to me to be living, hares that are still running, issues that are of permanent concern, at least of lasting concern, to other societies. But I am sufficiently conscious of (at least, I think and hope I am) the situations and issues that gave birth and strength and content to these ideas: the anti-medieval and anti-clerical drive of the Renaissance, the acute political, or politico-theological, controversies of the sixteenth century, which made some of these things into issues for which men fought and died, and with which they were concerned if only for mere survival. I do not trust myself, as an amateur historian, sufficiently – indeed, I do not trust myself at all in this respect – to relate these ideas to their contexts in a way in which you, for example, quite rightly wish and seek to do. I am delighted to think that I should have been of the slightest assistance to you in this respect. I am very far from thinking that ideas give birth to ideas in some timeless medium: I do believe that the book makes this clear, not merely by precept, but in the way in which it is actually written. Anything that you write about the genesis of historicism in pre-Vico times would of course be of the greatest interest to me. I could never acquiesce in the idea that Vico came out of the study of the classics, or reading Bacon,[1] still less out of Neapolitan empirical science, which the worthy and learned and personally very nice, but faithfully Marxist, Badaloni[2] tries, in my opinion so hopelessly, to demonstrate. No faithful member of the Party could possibly trace ideas approved of by Marx to nationalist or theological disputes, unless these things can be 'unmasked' in turn to demonstrate deep social conflict. [...] But I need not preach all this to you. [...]

Yours sincerely,

    Isaiah Berlin

PS [...] The thing to me about Vico and Herder is that they opened windows on to new prospects. Nothing is ever more marvellous, and men who do it are rightly excited, and indeed overwhelmed. [...]

---

1 Francis Bacon (1561–1626), 1st Viscount St Alban 1621, statesman and philosopher; Lord Chancellor 1618–21, impeached for corruption and briefly imprisoned in the Tower 1621; regarded by later generations as the inventor of scientific method, as presented in his *Novum Organum* (London, 1620).

2 Nicola Badaloni (1924–2005), proponent of Marxist historiography and author of *Introduzione a G. B. Vico* (Milan, 1961); taught pedagogy and then history of philosophy in modern languages dept, Pisa, 1953–66, dept of letters and philosophy 1967–98; also taught at the Scuola Normale Superiore di Pisa 1969–82.

TO ROWLAND BURDON-MULLER[1]
17 March 1976

Headington House

Chérissime Rowland,

First, let me thank you for your present [...] – the handkerchiefs are exquisite and I am in much need of them (according to Aline), particularly as she thinks that the layers of dust on the lenses of my spectacles, besides obstructing vision, are an exaggeration of my academic untidiness. Liberated from Wolfson, I am now installed in a large panelled room in All Souls College, as a kind of life fellow of All Souls under a statute which is an old, eighteenth-century abuse by which I profit.[2] Long may it last. I keep warning my colleagues of the fearful dangers that they face from the envious glances directed at their ancient institution, not merely by other colleges in Oxford (this was always the case), but also by government and Parliament and the Labour Party and many another narrow-eyed group and sect, to whom All Souls is the quintessence of *ancien régime*. Nor are the views and personality of my dear friend John Sparrow,[3] in whose society I find such pleasure, an antidote to such suspicions.

We are at the moment in the throes of trying to elect his successor, as he will be seventy next year and obliged to retire. By huge efforts we managed to scale down the list of twenty-three possible candidates, all members of the College, to twenty; and last Saturday, by even more agonised efforts, got these down to seven – all excellent men, as everyone is not tired of explaining, any one of whom would do the job splendidly. I do not think this at all, nor does anyone else. The real battles will begin in May. I am (rightly) suspected of belonging to the progressive camp: that is to say, an adherent of someone reasonably young, with sharp and critical capacities, stern academic standards and a reasonably strong social conscience – as against some cosy old conservative who will let things be, and be totally incapable of keeping the College afloat in the rough weather which it is bound to encounter, both financially and politically. The mood is still reasonably friendly, but it is idle to expect that candidates who burn with ambition should behave altogether naturally towards people whom they suspect of being unlikely to vote for them. It is like an extended political convention, or a Papal conclave,

---

1 Rowland Burdon-Muller (1891–1980), Eton- and Oxford-educated cosmopolitan, connoisseur of the arts and interior designer who lived for most of his life in the US; IB greatly enjoyed his trenchantly expressed and radical views on politics and current affairs, which he mostly did not share.

2 The title of the class of fellow to which he was elected is 'Distinguished Fellow'. 'Distinguished Fellowships are held by former fellows who have attained distinction in the service of the Crown, law, literature, science, art, education or public service': ⟨http://www.all-souls.ox.ac.uk/content/The_Categories_of_Fellowship⟩. 'I am now ensconced in All Souls, with a room and a telephone, an ancient, retired person': to Bertell Ollman, 25 May 1977.

3 John Hanbury Angus *Sparrow (1906–92), Warden, All Souls.

just kept from boiling over by a useful hypocritical pretence that nothing is happening, that everyone loves everyone equally, that everyone is modest and self-effacing and thinks that others are far better qualified to have the job than they are. Still, it is quite entertaining: after [an] absence of some ten years, I attended my first College meeting the other morning, and it was as if the ten years had never been: everyone was exactly like themselves. The great political figures and ambassadors – Lord Hailsham[1] and Lord Sherfield[2] and Sir Keith Joseph[3] and Douglas Jay[4] and Lord Wilberforce[5] – all delivered splendid speeches, as if on the benches of the House of Lords; while the junior fellows were oppositional, a trifle arrogant, agreeably subversive, and had obviously ganged up against the establishment. All very enjoyable. I cannot believe that Oxford will remain quite so unchanged in the years to come, but in the meanwhile it is all rather comforting. They kept me as a fellow, but would not do so for Rowse,[6] because he had become too megalomaniac, remorselessly boring and offensive to guests, varying his conversation with long, self-laudatory speeches, harangues against the masses of his critics or other enemies, punctuated by occasionally unctuous flattery of those he thought important for his purposes.

The country in general seems to be in a state of complacent depression: everyone knows that we are slowly going downhill, that unemployment is increasing, that the pound is declining. (The news on the wireless now always begins with words like 'The pound has had another uncomfortable day – it ended in a lower state than it started. Our economics correspondent

---

1 Quintin McGarel Hogg (1907–2001), 2nd Viscount Hailsham 1950, peerage disclaimed 1963, life peer 1970; KG 1988; fellow, All Souls, 1931–8, 1961–2001; barrister and Conservative politician; Lord Chancellor under Edward Heath 1970–4, under Margaret Thatcher 1979–87.

2 Roger Mellor Makins (1904–96), KCMG 1949, 1st Baron Sherfield 1964, diplomat and civil servant; fellow, All Souls, 1925–39, 1957–96; UK ambassador to the US 1953–6, joint permanent secretary, treasury, 1956–9; chair, UK Atomic Energy Authority, 1960–4.

3 Keith Sinjohn Joseph (1918–94), Bt 1944, CH 1986, life peer 1987; fellow, All Souls, 1946–60, Distinguished Fellow 1971–94; Conservative MP 1956–87, cabinet minister under Harold Macmillan, Edward Heath and Margaret Thatcher; one of the small group of Tory radicals driving Thatcherism.

4 Douglas Patrick Thomas Jay (1907–96), life peer 1987, journalist, economist and politician; fellow, All Souls, 1930–7, Distinguished Fellow 1968–96; Labour MP 1946–83, President, Board of Trade, 1964–7.

5 Richard Orme Wilberforce (1907–2003), Kt 1961, life peer 1964, barrister and judge; fellow, All Souls, 1932–2003, elected examination ('prize') fellow in the same year as IB; judge, chancery division, high court of justice, 1961–4; lord of appeal in ordinary 1964–1982; chancellor, Hull, 1978–94; music (especially opera) enthusiast (see letter of 15 May 1992, 441).

6 (Alfred) Leslie Rowse (1903–97), Cornish-born historian and poet; fellow, All Souls, 1925–74; Rowse felt rejected when he failed to be elected Warden of All Souls 1952, and became convinced that his colleagues there, and in the University at large, were determined to underrate his achievements, which for him included identifying the 'Dark Lady' of Shakespeare's later sonnets, a claim that 'became emblematic of the failings exhibited in the later stages of his career as a whole – a high-handed way with the evidence, disdain for the work of other scholars, vituperative responses to criticism, unshakeable belief in his own genius' (Stefan Collini, 'Look Back in Pique', TLS, 23 May 2003, 3).

predicts that worse is to come.') Nobody knows, or pretends to know, what will happen next. The parties go through the routine of attacking each other, but it is all a little like the last days of some old regime, though in the case of England, where everything ultimately happens very slowly and decorously, this may take a long time.

Your fellow resident[1] Solzhenitsyn made a powerful appearance on television,[2] in which he said that the West was in open decay, that the Soviet Union could seize it with bare hands (a Russian idiom) whenever it chose, that the collapse of morale was everywhere noticeable, and that, in short, our sins had found us out. This is rather like the sort of speeches that Pétain[3] used to make during the Vichy regime, and George Kennan[4] in America is somewhat liable to. Dr Kissinger, oddly enough, says much the same thing, but from the other end. Now that the United States [has] refused to take action in Angola, he is clear that China, which only needed the United States as a shield against Russia, is sheering away (the invitation to Nixon[5] was intended to under-line who they thought their true friends were, as against broken reeds like Ford and Kissinger); [that] the Russians, who only need the United States as a shield against China, are equally disillusioned by the total collapse of the Executive in the face of Congress;[6] that Syria, which at one time looked like beginning to nibble out of America's hand, unlike Egypt, which is positively eating out of it, is now much tougher, because they rightly assume that the United States would not intervene whatever anyone did in the Middle East; that the Israelis, now that they knew that America would not in fact come

1 Burdon-Muller had moved in 1971 from Boston to Lausanne in Switzerland, the country where Solzhenitsyn spent the first 2 years of his exile, from February 1974, in Zurich.

2 In February 1976 Solzhenitsyn made his 1st visit to Britain. In an interview broadcast 1 March on the BBC's prestigious current affairs programme *Panorama* he criticised the decadence of the West, which had made too many 'concessions' to the USSR: 'How can one lose one's spiritual strength, one's willpower, and possessing freedom not value it, not be willing to make sacrifices for it?' The political and spiritual weaknesses of the West, he argued, were strengthening the Soviet authorities, and weakening internal opposition to the regime. *Warning to the Western World* (London, 1976), 11, 11–12.

3 (Henri) Philippe Benoni Omer Joseph Pétain (1856–1951), French general who became a national hero as the defender of Verdun 1916–17, but fell from grace as the collaborationist last prime minister of the Third Republic from 16 June 1940, a capacity in which he concluded an armistice with the invading Germans that left his government in control of two-fifths of French territory, governed from the spa town of Vichy; tried for treason July–August 1945 and sentenced to death, commuted to life imprisonment.

4 George Frost Kennan (1904–2005), US diplomat, historian and influential exponent of the policy of containment of the USSR, on which he was an acknowledged expert; US ambassador to Yugoslavia 1961–3; prof., school of historical studies, IAS, Princeton, 1956–74.

5 Richard Milhous Nixon (1913–94), Republican US President 1969–74; Eisenhower's Vice President 1953–61; defeated by Kennedy for the presidency 1960, but elected 1968, and re-elected 1972; resigned office – the first President ever to do so – after Congress began impeachment proceedings over his involvement in the June 1972 break-in to the Democratic National Committee headquarters at the Watergate offices in Washington, DC. In July 1971 Nixon accepted an invitation to visit China: his much-publicised and highly successful visit in February 1972 was viewed unfavourably by Moscow.

6 i.e. Nixon's resignation (previous note).

to their physical defence, even though it might lecture those who attacked them, were now preparing for their last desperate stand; and that as a result of all these self-inflicted injuries, the West was probably done for sooner than anyone supposed. Moreover, every senator and representative had now increased his staff to about a hundred persons (I believe this to be true), consisting of research assistants, public relations men, secretaries, letter-answerers etc., none of whom had been checked by the security agencies and [who] are consequently penetrated by the Russians – in short, that the last hours of the great American Republic were not far off. Obviously things are not quite as black as this, but I must admit that the old anti-Vietnam coalition seems as depressed as the defeated hawks. Nobody is very keen on anybody as presidential candidate (why am I piling Pelion on Ossa of gloom for your benefit? I really ought to stop). The number of persons who feel positively favourable to either Reagan[1] or Ford is minute; the old liberals, the Kennedy mafia, are in favour of the worthy Udall,[2] who does not appear to have much chance; Senator Jackson[3] is popular only with labour, Jews and cold warriors; Humphrey[4] may be chosen in an exhausted way because nobody can think of anyone else; and various Southern governors are regarded with natural suspicion and contempt by the entire Northern establishment.

In England nobody really loves either Mr Wilson[5] or Mrs Thatcher[6] either. Whom are we to look to? Mao[7] is now literally unintelligible – makes peculiar noises which three secretaries try and translate into intelligent utterances. Nobody knows what he is really saying – his dynamic wife[8] pretends

1 Ronald Wilson Reagan (1911–2004), Hollywood actor turned politician; Republican governor of California 1967–75, US President 1981–9; running as the more conservative candidate 1976, he was beaten to the Republican presidential nomination by the incumbent, Gerald Ford (18/5).

2 Morris King ('Mo') Udall (1922–98), professional basketball player turned politician; Democrat member, Arizona, house of representatives, 1961–91; unsuccessfully sought the Democratic Party nomination 1976: 'Mo's too funny to be President' was the columnist James J. Kilpatrick's epitaph on Udall's campaign (1st use untraced).

3 Henry Martin ('Scoop') Jackson (1912–83), Democrat senator, Washington State, 1953–83; unsuccessful candidate for the Democratic presidential nomination 1972, 1976; advocate of social justice at home, and of the positive influence of US power abroad; an important influence on neoconservatives during the Reagan and George W. Bush administrations.

4 Hubert Horatio Humphrey (1911–78), Democrat politician; senator, Minnesota, 1949–64, 1971–8; Vice President under Lyndon Johnson 1965–9; Democrat presidential nominee 1968, losing to Richard Nixon; briefly considered running again 1976 despite having cancer.

5 (James) Harold Wilson (1916–95), KG 1976, life peer 1983; Labour MP 1945–83, elected party leader February 1963; prime minister 1964–70, 1974–6; leader, Opposition, 1963–4, 1970–4.

6 Margaret Hilda Thatcher (1925–2013), OM 1990, life peer 1992; elected Conservative Party leader 1975; prime minister 1979–90 – the longest-serving in the C20th, and the 1st woman to hold that office.

7 Mao Zedong (1893–1976), founder of the CP of the Chinese People's Republic 1949, chair 1949–76, head of state 1949–59. His health deteriorated markedly during 1976 and he died in Beijing 9 September.

8 Jiang Qing (1914–91), Chinese actress and politician, m. Mao Zedong 1939 as his 3rd wife; her political influence increased dramatically during the Cultural Revolution, but after Mao's death she was arrested and sentenced to death (subsequently commuted to life imprisonment) in a show trial 1980–1; her death in prison 1991 was reported as suicide.

she knows what he wants, but the three secretaries sometimes interpret him differently. So that is rather odd, too. Mrs Gandhi has gone wrong.[1] Tito locks up his opponents rather more vigorously than before.[2] Where are we to look for liberty, progress, the pursuit of happiness? I realise that this is exactly how people talked in, for example, 1810 – those who thought that the real Europe was before 1789 decided in 1810 that Europe was dying, if not dead; but it was in fact entering upon one of the most vigorous periods of its existence. And so it may be now. All I am saying is merely the function of age and habits of thought formed too long ago. So we must gird ourselves for the new world and will it to be grist to some new mill, with which we must identify ourselves. I do not really know what this means in practice, but I am sure it is the right attitude, rather than jeremiads over what cannot be restored. What do you feel? All these things cannot seem quite so acute in Lausanne, but perhaps they do?

Joe Alsop, having observed the collapse of all his aspirations and hopes, and the end of the old Wasp ascendancy, and the retreat from the principles of Theodore Roosevelt and the American Century,[3] is now entirely preoccupied with his huge history of collecting (of works of art) and of taste, in which he is encouraged by various German professors. As he is very industrious and very resolute and very intelligent, he may yet produce an interesting volume on all this.[4]

Although I am entirely devoid of all visual sense, as you know, I have agreed to become a Trustee of the National Gallery[5] in the belief that I can act as a mouthpiece for various young historians of art and aesthetes like Francis Haskell[6] and Stuart Hampshire, who otherwise cannot get their view heard. I am willing to repeat their opinions parrot-wise, and defend their suggestions as if they were my own, and in this way I might be of some tiny use. Why was I appointed? Because I am thought quite harmless and no nuisance to the establishment. Covent Garden has just had a splendid visit

1 4/1.
2 Josip Broz Tito (1892–1980) né Josip Broz, Croatian-born Yugoslav marshal and Communist statesman; prime minister 1945–53, President 1953–80; under his dictatorship Yugoslavia was expelled from the Soviet bloc 1948 and remained non-aligned; restrictions on academic freedom in the country elicited a protest, December 1974, from a group of international scholars and scientists, including A. J. Ayer, Noam Chomsky and Jürgen Habermas; in summer 1975 there was a spate of politically motivated arrests there, the targets being principally pro-Soviet dissidents.
3 Theodore Roosevelt (1858–1919), Republican US President 1901–9, believed that US military leadership was essential to world peace, and was awarded the Nobel Peace Prize 1906 for negotiating the end of the Russo-Japanese War (1904–5).
4 He did: The Rare Art Traditions: The History of Art Collecting and Its Linked Phenomena Wherever These Have Appeared (NY/London, 1982) was favourably if not uncritically reviewed in the TLS (Martin Kemp, 'Prizes and Their Price', 25 March 1983, 294).
5 'Latest Appointments', Times, 25 June 1975, 16d.
6 Francis James Herbert Haskell (1928–2000), art historian; prof. of the history of art, Oxford, and fellow, Trinity, 1967–95.

from La Scala – the young conductor Abbado[1] is magnificent, the orchestra is far better than ours, so is the chorus; the singers are very adequate, and their visit was one enormous triumph (so, curiously enough, was the visit of the Covent Garden company to Milan). They performed *Simon Boccanegra*, *La Cenerentola* and the Verdi[2] *Requiem* here, to entirely packed houses which went into justified transports of enthusiasm; while our company did *Peter Grimes*, *Benvenuto Cellini* and *La clemenza di Tito* in Milan, apparently also wildly acclaimed. Mr Healey,[3] the Chancellor of the Exchequer, who attended the performance of *Boccanegra* the night after the Queen,[4] made a speech in perfectly good Italian – he had served on the Italian front during the war, kept up his Italian, and made several excellent jokes. The Italians were tremendously impressed and said that no Italian Minister of Finance had ever attended a performance at the Scala, still less Covent Garden, and would not have been able to make a speech in literary English. The director of the Scala, Grassi,[5] said it was a wonderful thing that England and Italy, said to be hurtling to their financial doom amid the storms of inflation, were both able to put on splendid performances of this kind, and how wonderful it was to be the two most bankrupt nations in Europe. [...]

Yours ever ⟨with much love
    Isaiah

Wilson resigned this morning. No real reason given.[6] I expect this refutes much of what I say: I am not much of an observer of the public scene.⟩

TO MARTIN GILBERT[7]

6 April 1976

Headington House

Dear Martin,
    My handwriting is unreadable and my secretary has been in hospital.

1 Claudio Abbado (1933–2014), Milan-born conductor; principal conductor, La Scala, Milan, 1968–72, music director 1972–6, artistic director 1976–86; Covent Garden debut 1968; principal conductor, London Symphony Orchestra, 1979–88; music director, Vienna State Opera, 1986–91; principal conductor, Berlin Philharmonic Orchestra, 1989–2002.
2 Giuseppe Fortunino Francesco Verdi (1813–1901), Italian composer, the pre-eminent figure in C19th Italian opera.
3 Denis Winston Healey (b. 1917), life peer 1992; Labour MP 1952–92, secretary of state for defence 1964–70, chancellor of the exchequer 1974–9; served with distinction in North Africa and Italy with the Royal Engineers 1940–5.
4 Elizabeth Alexandra Mary (b. 1926), Queen Elizabeth II; succeeded her father, George VI, 1952.
5 Paolo Grassi (1919–81), Milan-born theatrical impresario, founder 1947 and director 1947–72 of the Piccolo Teatro di Milano; superintendent, La Scala, Milan, 1972–7.
6 Wilson was the 1st prime minister to retire voluntarily since Stanley Baldwin (1937); he was undoubtedly exhausted after many years in office, and his health was deteriorating; indeed, he may already have started to notice the onset of Alzheimer's disease, which later seriously afflicted him. But he must also have judged it an opportune moment, politically, with the endorsement in the June 1975 referendum of his policy of continued membership of the EEC.
7 Martin John Gilbert (1936–2015), Kt 1995, historian; fellow, Merton, 1962–94; appointed Churchill's

This explains the delay in my answer reaching you – please forgive me. I felt ashamed afterwards of not breaking my silence, and relieved at the fact that no one asked me to. Your quotation from Ruppin's[1] instructions to his children moved me genuinely.[2] I do put this guilt-inducing question to myself, perhaps not every day, but frequently enough to cause discomfort. Should I, for example, have spoken sternly to Syme[3] (that is the man, I assume, to whom you were referring – the man who disapproved of the creation of Israel)? But on that occasion I thought that anyone prepared to go and receive an Honorary Degree at Tel Aviv was sufficiently reconciled to the facts not to need either a sermon or the excommunication which Talmon[4] was contemplating.

To come to the substance of your letter. It was, I admit, a depressing occasion.[5] To ignore attacks is, I agree, weak and generally mistaken; but on the other hand, to deny allegations is never entirely convincing – people will always think there is something in a charge, and assume that the answer is a routine reaction to be discounted, particularly if it comes from obviously interested parties such as Zionists or bearers of Jewish names; at best, if there is a controversy, in, say, *The Times*, the effect on the uncommitted reader is probably to assume that there is something in what both parties say, that this is a predictable dogfight to be ignored by those not directly involved. But of course it does not follow that there is nothing to be done and that one must simply sit still with folded hands and suffer lies and calumnies patiently and peacefully, or, perhaps, with feigned indifference. What, then – as Chernyshevsky called his novel, and Lenin repeated – is to be done?[6] [...] I firmly believe that the best thing that can be done is to send people to Israel. What they experience there, even if they are critical, refutes more lies and allegations, and leaves a deeper impression, than anything else that can be done. Do you think this not valid?

official biographer 1968; his many works include a number on the Holocaust; a Jew and champion of Israel.

1 Arthur Ruppin (1876–1943), born in Rawicz (Poland); Zionist, demographer and sociologist; helped shape the pattern of Jewish settlement in Palestine; joined HUJ 1926, founding its sociology dept.

2 The 'instructions' are probably those implicit in the question Ruppin used regularly to ask his children: 'What did you do today for the Jewish people?' (Ruppin's grandson Arthur to Arie Dubnov, 25 April 2014). Cf. 'Ruppin-like principles' later in this letter.

3 Ronald Syme (1903–89), Kt 1959, OM 1976, Roman historian; Camden Prof. of Ancient History, Oxford, 1949–70, fellow, Wolfson, 1970–89; hon. DLitt, Tel Aviv, 1975.

4 Jacob Leib Talmon (1916–80), Polish-born Israeli historian; lecturer, HUJ, 1949–60, prof. of modern history 1960–80.

5 An unidentified meeting held at the Oxford Centre for Hebrew and Jewish Studies, Yarnton Manor, 4 miles NW of Oxford.

6 The 1863 novel *What Is To Be Done?* by Nikolay Chernyshevsky (1828–89) argued for radical collectivism, and prescribed the duty of the intellectual as leading the masses to socialism. IB described it as having 'a literally epoch-making effect on Russian opinion' (RT 228), and Lenin, admiring the work, adopted its title for a 1902 study (subtitled *Burning Questions of Our Movement*), in which he proposed the creation of a 'vanguard' party to lead the working class to Marxism.

Secondly, I think that students, particularly the representatives I met at the IUJF, are more energetic, more convinced and convincing, closer to the truth, and more sympathetic as human beings, and so likely to create more good will, than the average academic. A young man I met in London recently seemed to me much better aware of both the difficulties and the possibilities than the group at Yarnton who depressed you (and me) so terribly. The attacks on Israel – at least, the most formidable – come from the misguided young, who are often idealistic, passionate and often plumb wrong. The Third World and its rhetoric has become the escape world in which all those who are discontented with the institutions in the West can invest their confused idealism. I doubt if Israel need have got itself into the wrong camp in which they are now situated if they had not been so complacent and so blind – it was not so even over Suez in 1956, still less in 1967.[1] What, you may ask, has altered a situation in which even the Italian Communist Party could split over pro- and anti-Israel sentiment during the Six Day War? But all that is spilt milk. Anyway, it seems to me that students, not dons, are those who need convincing, and only other students – with the exception of a handful of teachers whom they trust and admire – can perform this most uphill task. If there is any financing to be done, it should go towards them. In short, you and I must speak to them, and forget about the dons for the moment.

The third point is that we literally need what the Soviets used to call 'the propagandist's handbook', on the assumption that propaganda is not necessarily false, dishonest, unscrupulous, but only an effective way of exposing falsehood and saying what one truly believes. Somebody – you? I? a handful of us in Oxford? if not we, then who? it cannot be left to others – must compile a list of the commonest charges against Israel, the commonest slogans, the commonest libels; and then get experts to provide us with answers, and then translate these answers into language which people can understand rather than the stale homilies of professional Zionists. Maybe some of these charges are genuine: if so, they should be admitted. If we believe in this cause at all, there is no need to suppress the truth or suggest falsehood. It sounds uncritical, and full of simple faith, but I have believed this all my life and see no reason for retreating from this now.

Consequently, be of good cheer. Don't be got down by that rather dreary occasion; let the committee go its own way and do what it can, for it certainly cannot do any harm. But in the meanwhile, despite your overwhelming preoccupations, which I understand, set aside, on Ruppin-like principles, a Sunday afternoon during which you and I and Shukman[2] and one Israeli dove (who will be familiar with all the objections, and will not want to

---

1 Israel secretly colluded with Britain and France to invade Egypt during the Suez Crisis of October–November 1956; during the Six Day War of June 1967 it launched a pre-emptive strike against hostile neighbouring Arab states.
2 Harold ('Harry') Shukman (1931–2012), historian, Russian scholar and translator, born in London

condone and exonerate) get together – four persons is perfectly enough – to
see what are the questions and what the answers are [...].

Yours ever,

Isaiah

TO WILLIAM EMPSON[1]

20 May 1976

Headington House

Dear William,

I have a personal favour to ask of you. If the British Academy were to
invite you to become a fellow, I suspect that your first impulse would be to
decline. This institution may well mean very little or nothing to you, but
I think that if we met I could convince you that its activities have not been
useless – that it does give grants to people and finance enterprises some of
which you would positively approve of and none of which you would utterly
condemn. The fact that its fellowship should have been offered to you years
and years ago, and that it came as a shock to me and others to discover that it
had not (nor was it, I suspect, to Eliot)[2] – disgraceful as this fact is – will not,
I hope, deter you from accepting. I need not enlarge to you on the less estimable characteristics of literary specialists in England, and probably elsewhere;
enough of them in the relevant section of the Academy now feel repentant
to have shamed the rest, and they should not be penalised for seeing the light,
however late. If you refuse, this fact will remain a standing reproach to the
Academy, which I, who have a short while ago become its President, will find
personally as well as functionally painful. So please do not reject us. [...]

Perhaps I am quite wrong in thinking that your instinctive reaction would
be to ignore the proffered hand, but I somehow do not think I am. If I may
say so, you shine so brightly by your own light that you confer distinction on
institutions rather than derive it from them; moreover, journeys to London
may be irksome to you. So let me once again entreat you not to spurn us; if
only as a pure, private act of kindness to myself.

No need to answer this if you do not feel like it.

Yours ever,

Isaiah (Berlin)

⟨Of course this letter is madly indiscreet and wholly improper: We have never

to a Russian Jewish emigré family; fellow, St Antony's, 1961–98 (director, Russian Centre, 1981–91);
lecturer in modern Russian history, Oxford, 1969–98.

1 William Empson (1906–84), Kt 1979, poet and literary critic, author of the influential *Seven Types
of Ambiguity* (London, 1930); prof. of English literature, Sheffield, 1953–71. Empson was elected
FBA 1 July.

2 FBA was not among the many honours collected by T. S. Eliot.

written so to anyone else, or ever expect to again: but I find the prospect of quite understandable disdain from you too awful.⟩

TO BERNARD WILLIAMS[1]

31 May 1976

Headington House

Dear Bernard,

Thank you ever so much for your most welcome letter about my posthumous Selected Writings. It was very good of you to look at them all again. Whatever you may say, it must have been something of a nuisance and a bore – no, no, don't reassure me, it must, it must. However, I am quite sure that you are right: 'Verification' has some historical justification, and I am glad you liked the piece on hypothetical propositions etc. I remember how stern Stuart was with me for ignoring the formal and material modes, and how Strawson[2] quite correctly pointed out various obvious objections which phenomenalists could make, which I still think not worth bothering about, since all that matters is the central issue. All I write is by nature dishevelled – the well-combed and neatly fitting wigs of Warnock[3] and other Wykehamists are not for me. If this sounds like making a romantic virtue out of irremediable mental disorder ('The chaos of the papers on your table doubtless represents equal chaos in your mind', said the eminent Irish scholar Myles Dillon[4] to me once), it is just that. Anyway, thank you very much indeed – I shall act according to your advice and report to Henry Hardy, who will be much relieved. My contempt for my own works cannot really be assuaged; nevertheless, I am of course delighted to hear from someone as critical and as truthful as you undoubtedly are that they may not be quite as worthless as in some sense I shall continue to think them to be.

Mack Smith and Mathias look rather gloomy,[5] but Mack Smith will recover and resume his usual stony glare; Mathias will take a little longer. I have persuaded Michael Dummett[6] not to tell Tony [Quinton] that his name is no

1 Bernard Arthur Owen *Williams (1929–2003), philosopher.
2 Peter Frederick Strawson (1919–2006), Kt 1977, fellow and philosophy praelector (i.e. tutor), Univ., 1948–68; Waynflete Prof. of Metaphysical Philosophy, Oxford, and fellow, Magdalen, 1968–87.
3 Geoffrey James Warnock (1923–95), Kt 1986; educated at Winchester and New College, both founded (1382, 1379) by William of Wykeham, Bishop of Winchester 1366–1404; fellow and philosophy tutor, Magdalen, 1952–71; Principal, Hertford, 1971–88.
4 Myles Dillon (1900–72), philologist and Gaelic scholar; director, School of Celtic Studies, Dublin Institute for Advanced Studies, 1960–8.
5 Denis Mack Smith (b. 1920), historian of Italy; fellow, Peterhouse, Cambridge, 1947–62; senior research fellow, All Souls, 1962–87; Extraordinary fellow, Wolfson, 1987–2000. Peter Mathias (b. 1928), economic historian; Chichele Prof. of Economic History, Oxford, and fellow, All Souls, 1969–87; Master, Downing, Cambridge, 1987–95. Both were unsuccessful candidates to succeed John Sparrow as the Warden of All Souls (25).
6 Michael Anthony Eardley Dummett (1925–2011), philosopher; fellow, All Souls, 1950–79; Wykeham Prof. of Logic, Oxford, and fellow, New College, 1979–92.

longer being considered, since (a) he knows it, and (b) not all truth liberates. Michael Howard[1] wanders disdainfully up and down the College, with
a slightly Rowse-like expression on his face ('The fools!' etc.). Pat Neill[2] came
to the opera with us on Friday, just to show that there were no hard feelings.[3]
Wallace-Hadrill[4] cannot bring himself to come to the SGM[5] because he is
in such a state – I am rather sympathetic, but a thin skin is neither a necessary nor a sufficient condition for this particular post, though touching in
itself. [...]

Yours ever,
Isaiah

TO DIANA TRILLING[6]
7 October 1976
Headington House

Dearest Diana,

I should have answered your letter of 2 August weeks, and indeed months,
ago. It took a very long time to arrive, my handwriting is illegible – to inflict
it upon [you] would be an act of gratuitous cruelty, something which during
the prayers on the Jewish Day of Atonement one promises not to perpetrate
(I think it is called 'causeless hatred' – apparently well-grounded hatred is
OK). So I write now. [...]

I do not know Martha's Vineyard, of which you speak, but I do know
whom you mean by the lady dictator[7] – my views are, I am sure, identical

---

1 Michael Eliot Howard (b. 1922), MC 1943, Kt 1986, later (2005) OM; fellow, All Souls, 1968–80,
Chichele Prof. of the History of War 1977–80; Regius Prof. of Modern History, Oxford, and
fellow, Oriel, 1980–9; Robert A. Lovett Prof. of Military and Naval History, Yale, 1989–93.

2 (Francis) Patrick Neill (b. 1926), Kt 1983, life peer 1997, lawyer and public servant; fellow, All Souls,
1950–77, Warden 1977–95; vice chancellor, Oxford, 1985–9.

3 Neill was the succeesful candidate in the Wardenship election, in which IB had backed Bernard
Williams; after the result was known he wrote to BW, 15 May: 'I am very very depressed, & feel
flat: I shall never cease to regard you as a king over the water – does Patricia feel secretly relieved
or not?' For Patricia Williams see 634.

4 (John) Michael Wallace-Hadrill (1916–85), medieval historian; senior research fellow, Merton,
1961–74; fellow, All Souls, 1974–85, Chichele Prof. of Modern History, Oxford, 1974–83.

5 Stated General Meeting: one of the at least biannual regular meetings of the fellows of All Souls.

6 Diana Trilling (1905–96) née Rubin, m. 1929 the critic Lionel Trilling (36/7); an author and critic
in her own right, she contributed to publications such as the New Yorker, the Nation and Partisan
Review, a journal with which her husband was also closely associated. 'Her special targets were
always cant or empty rhetoric in any form, providing her critical work with its distinguishing
characteristic, its insistence that all ideas needed to be rooted in rationality and morality' ('Diana
Trilling', obituary, Times, 26 October 1996, 23d–g at 23f).

7 Lillian Florence ('Lilly') Hellman (1905–84), dramatist and screenwriter, considered one of
America's finest playwrights in the 1930s and 1940s; blacklisted during the McCarthy era (260/3),
when she denied belonging to the CP, though in fact a member 1937–49. For her self-dramatising
inventions in her memoirs she was denounced as an inveterate liar by Mary McCarthy on TV, 25
January 1980, whereupon she embarked on an ill-advised legal action ended only by her death.
She owned a beach house on Martha's Vineyard.

with yours. This is, I know, an opinion not shared by a number of our friends, at least mine – yours may have better judgement. My old and dear friend George Backer,[1] whom I do not suppose you ever knew, [who] was a nice man and tried to be an intellectual, touchingly, and did many acts of kindness to myself and others, seems to have had an intimate relationship with her many years ago; he died last year. Edmund Wilson,[2] whom I loved and respected, seemed to tolerate her and indeed even like her; Joe Alsop, of all people, had her to stay quite recently because she said that he had behaved honourably during the McCarthy period; she came to tea here, at her request, when her *Candide*[3] was being played at the local theatre, and I was uncomfortable and she later said that she, too, had felt extremely constricted and uneasy. I first met her, I think, at lunch with the Hayters,[4] or at least, with William Hayter, in Washington: it had something to do with his service in Moscow, some topic of conversation during the war which she wished to have with him, and I thought her very unattractive then. I am sure she is gifted and knows many things, that her writings are characteristic of a phase of American opinion, and so on, but there is something about her personality which I find that I cannot abide. It may be a purely chemical reaction – it is not her opinions. I can talk perfectly comfortably to a Communist like Hobsbawm;[5] I quite enjoy my personal relations with my opinionated and not wholly scrupulous enemy E. H. Carr, whom I positively like even while I am stirred to considerable indignation by his way with historical facts; I do not mind the wicked A. J. P. Taylor,[6] the wicked, or ex-wicked, I. F. Stone – in this respect I am sure I am far less principled than you are – but the dictatrix you speak of, and indeed Lionel's[7] old friend Lord Snow,[8] are more than I can take. Can it be

1 George Backer (1903–74), Democrat US politician, Jewish activist, theatrical sponsor and writer; publisher and editor, *New York Post*, 1939–42.

2 Edmund Wilson (1895–1972), US critic and essayist; associate editor, *New Republic*, 1926–31, book reviewer, *New Yorker*, 1944–8; 'a man, as you must know, of passionate loves and hates, likings and dislikes, admiration and contempt' (to Jeffrey Meyers, 14 June 1993).

3 Operetta by Leonard Bernstein, first performed on Broadway 1956, with a libretto by Lillian Hellman; it had a short run at the New Theatre in Oxford 1959 before transferring to the West End; the text used in the 1974 revival and subsequent productions is by Hugh Wheeler.

4 William Goodenough Hayter (1906–95), KCMG 1953, diplomat, college head; UK ambassador to the USSR 1953–7; Warden, New College, 1958–76; m. 1938 Iris Marie Hoare (1911–2004) née Grey.

5 Eric John Ernest Hobsbawm (1917–2012), Marxist historian, long-standing member, CPGB; prof. of economic and social history, Birkbeck, London, 1970–82, of politics and society, New School for Social Research, NY, 1984–97. He and IB spoke on democracy at a weekend school conference in the Beatrice Webb House, Holmbury St Mary, Surrey, 1959. IB confronted Hobsbawm on the recent suppression by the Chinese of a rebellion in Tibet. IB: 'How can you condone that?' Hobsbawm: 'It is the imposition of civilisation on barbarism.' Dimitris Dimitriakos to Nicholas Hall, 16 January 2015.

6 Alan John Percivale *Taylor (1906–90), historian.

7 Lionel Trilling (1905–75), US critic and essayist, taught English at his alma mater, Columbia, from 1932, prof. 1948–74; in 1977 IB was one of the first invited speakers at an annual seminar instituted there in his honour; his *The Liberal Imagination* (NY, 1950) became a bestseller, establishing him as an exemplary Cold War US intellectual.

8 Charles Percy Snow (1905–80), Kt 1957, life peer 1964, writer and scientific administrator; IB

to do with their appearances? I do not wish to think this. Still, the face is the only mirror of the soul that we possess, and extreme coarseness of expression is not wholly irrelevant, therefore. [...]

Now, as to the seminar for Lionel, [...] for the title, do you think that 'Nationalism: Its Origins and Unforeseen Career',[1] or something of that kind, will do? What I should like to talk about, if that is permitted, is the origins of nationalism at the end of the eighteenth and beginning of the nineteenth century; and the fact that none of the prophets of the nineteenth century, though they predicted practically everything, had an inkling of the fact that it would be, with racism, the dominant influence of our own time – and how come? You must tell me if this seems adequate to you, for it is all I can possibly do: my ideas are fewer and fewer; I cling to anything that comes to my head with pathetic avidity, for fear of total pauperisation. I have no shelf full of books of appalling and undisputed authority to lean on, none of the pride in their indisputable authority of the stern Central European masters who know, and have always known, that they have the truth and that those who question it are either fools or rogues. This hardly ever happens in English-speaking countries: I suppose that Dr Leavis and Trevor-Roper are exceptions in England – who are the American equivalents? [...]

Our friend David Pryce-Jones,[2] son of Alan,[3] has written a biography of Unity Mitford,[4] Hitler's[5] friend. I doubt if such a biography was really worth writing, but since her sister is the Duchess of Devonshire,[6] a tremendous

viscerally disliked Snow, 'whose writings no serious person could possibly admire' (to Hugo Brunner, 7 July 1980).

1 This was a topic IB returned to more than once (see IBVL). His first published treatment was 'A Note on Nationalism', *Forethought* (Windsor, [1964]), 9–14, repr. in POI2.

2 David Eugene Henry Pryce-Jones (b. 1936), author and literary editor; his mother, Thérèse ('Poppy') (1908–53) née Fould-Springer, was a close friend of Aline Berlin, whose family he knew from childhood; special correspondent, *Daily Telegraph*, 1966–82; later (since 1999) senior editor, *National Review*; his biography *Unity Mitford: A Quest* (London, 1976) brought him face to face with her brother-in-law and defender, Oswald Mosley, on the television programme *Tonight*, hosted by Melvyn Bragg, in November 1976; of this encounter the critic Clive James observed: 'Devoid of any capacity for self-criticism, Sir Oswald is never nonplussed when caught out: he simply rattles on with undiminished brio. [...] If it had done nothing else but encourage Sir Oswald to expose himself, Pryce-Jones's book [...] would have performed a service.' 'Sir Oswald's Whoppers', *Observer*, 21 November 1976, 28.

3 Alan Payan Pryce-Jones (1908–2000), writer and critic; editor, TLS, 1948–59.

4 Unity Valkyrie Freeman-Mitford (1914–48), 4th of the 6 daughters of 2nd Baron Redesdale; joined her future brother-in-law Oswald Mosley's British Union of Fascists 1933; contrived to meet Hitler 1935 and frequently accompanied him and other Nazi leaders thereafter; her personal anti-Semitic manifesto, 'Brief einer Engländerin' ['Letter of an Englishwoman'] appeared in *Der Stürmer: Nürnberger Wochenblatt zum Kampf um die Wahrheit*, 30 July 1935 (a PS reads 'If you happen to find space for this letter in your newspaper, please publish my full name. I do not want to sign "UM", but want everyone to know that I am a "Jew-hater" '); she attempted suicide in Munich 3 September 1939 on the outbreak of war between Britain and Nazi Germany.

5 Adolf Hitler (1889–1945), Austrian-born German Fascist leader, became head of the (then) small National Socialist German Worker's (Nazi) party 1921; chancellor, Germany, January 1933, dictator 1933–45; committed suicide 30 April 1945 as the Red Army advanced through Berlin.

6 Deborah Vivien ('Debo') Cavendish (1920–2014) née Freeman-Mitford, Duchess of Devonshire,

upper-class cabal has been formed to do everything possible to prevent publication (which they cannot do); to persuade all the persons who have given
information to deny that he has reproduced them correctly, and sign affida-
vits to that effect; to get journals either to ignore it or review it unfavourably.
As an example of such influence as portions of our aristocracy still possess,
it is an extraordinary spectacle. The book may or may not be any good, but
a conspiracy against it is very unattractive, headed as it is, ultimately, by her
brother-in-law Sir Oswald[1] himself, who I daresay is not over-anxious to have
his past revealed in colours very different from those of his own autobiography.[2] This is re-advertised with blurbs in its favour by Lord Boothby,[3]
Michael Foot,[4] Crossman,[5] A. J. P. Taylor and Harold Macmillan,[6] all of
whom acclaim the author as a wonderful fellow. Perhaps it was like this in
the Renaissance and the Roman Empire? Sincerity and integrity: when and
where?

    Yours ever, ⟨with fondest love⟩
    Isaiah   [...]

youngest of the 6 Mitford sisters; m. 1941 Lord Andrew Robert Buxton Cavendish (1920–2004),
from 1950 11th Duke of Devonshire; together they devoted themselves to the preservation and
development of the vast ducal palace at Chatsworth in Derbyshire.
1 Oswald Ernald Mosley (1896–1980), 6th baronet, British Fascist leader; successively a Conservative,
  Independent and Labour MP 1918–24, Labour 1926–31; founded the New Party 1931 and, after its
  collapse, the British Union of Fascists, October 1932; imprisoned 1940–3 as a security risk (under
  Defence Regulation 18B).
2 'His fine autobiography, My Life, published in [London in] 1968, was a defence of his political
  career and an account of his policies for the future' (Robert Skidelsky, biographer of Mosley,
  ODNB).
3 Robert John Graham ('Bob') Boothby (1900–86), KBE 1953, life peer 1958; Conservative MP 1924–
  58; PPS to Winston Churchill 1926–9; parliamentary secretary, Ministry of Food, 1940–1 (resigned
  over a financial impropriety).
4 Michael Mackintosh Foot (1913–2010), journalist, author, Labour politician; leader, Commons,
  1976–9, Opposition 1980–3.
5 Richard Howard Stafford Crossman (1907–74), Labour politician and diarist; an Oxford contemporary, if never a close friend, of IB, to whom he gave his first job in 1932, as a lecturer in
  philosophy at New College; fellow and philosophy tutor, New College, 1930–7; MP 1945–74 and
  government minister under Harold Wilson 1964–70.
6 (Maurice) Harold Macmillan (1894–1986), 1st Earl of Stockton 1984, publisher and Conservative
  statesman; prime minister 1957–63, chair, Macmillan (publishers), 1963–74, president 1974–86;
  chancellor, Oxford, 1960–86. The paperback of Mosley's My Life, 'A book to read in time of crisis,
  always foretold by the author', was advertised in these terms in the TLS (12 November 1976,
  1432) along with positive comments from Foot, Macmillan and Taylor (who, with Crossman and
  Boothby, were also cited on the book itself); according to Taylor, Mosley was 'an orator of the
  highest rank. [...] He was never unpatriotic' ('The Leader Who Got Lost', Observer, 20 October
  1968, 29), while Macmillan acknowledged 'great talents and great strength of character': Winds
  of Change (London, 1966), 263.

TO NICOLAS NABOKOV[1]

21 December 1976

Headington House

Chérissime Nicolas,

[...] I remember your saying that you were contemplating a new book on 'Les riches heures du CIA'.[2] If you were serious about this, let me earnestly advise you not to do this. One's memory is not infallible; the subject is, to say the least, sensitive; you and I, flown by the sheer joy of the variety of life, are apt to colour events and persons – dates, faces, events go round kaleidoscopically in one's mind, and this particular topic is likely to cause furious rejoinders, denials, explosions, from old enemies, old friends, new enemies, new friends, neutrals of all sizes and types who will, rightly or wrongly, regard themselves as misrepresented, maligned, compromised, libelled, and from reviewers who will enter the fray. I doubt if you can want to be for the rest of your life the centre of unending rows: even the most innocent gossip leads to that, as well you know. So let me strongly advise you to leave that minefield alone, and, like me, confine yourself to the spoken word, which causes trouble enough, but less than printed ones.

I am constantly pressed to write my own memoirs: I have no intention of doing so, partly because I am too little interested in myself and regard everything I have done as being even more worthless than perhaps some of it is; but mainly because to write about other people (even in the charming, if candid, fashion in which you write about e.g. Auden,[3] or myself)[4] is always a kind of invasion of privacy; and I believe that the people in Bloomsbury who believed that personal relations came before anything were not mistaken – 'private faces in public places are wiser and nicer than public faces in private places'.[5] People should be left to live in peace. You won't quite agree, but you will agree sufficiently to avoid causing inevitable pain and distress, even to some not entirely sympathetic persons.

That is my sermon to you this Christmas: the snow lies heavily upon the ground here, and reminds me of my visit to Akhmatova in 1945. I did describe it to Miss Amanda Haight, who has written a biography of AA;[6] although her account of me is scrupulous, accurate, based on what I myself

1 Nicolas *Nabokov (1903–78), composer and cultural administrator.

2 Presumably a humorous play on the title of the *Très riches heures du Duc de Berry*, a famous illuminated C15th book of prayers.

3 Wystan Hugh Auden (1907–73), poet and writer, went down from Christ Church 1928, the year IB went up to CCC: for their 1st meeting see 511.

4 See Nabokov's *Bagázh: Memoirs of a Russian Cosmopolitan* (London, 1975), 209–11 (IB), 216–17 (Auden).

5 'Private faces in public places / Are wiser and nicer / Than public faces in private places.' Auden, *The Orators: An English Study* (1932), epigraph dedicatory (to Stephen Spender).

6 Amanda Chase Haight (1939–89), author of *Anna Akhmatova: A Poetic Pilgrimage* (Oxford, 1976); on learning of her untimely death IB wrote to Richard McKane, 24 November 1989: 'I think her

told her – yet, yet, I am appallingly embarrassed by the information now afforded to the public of my personal relationship with the poetess, even though it is related briefly and decently, in neutral, impersonal terms. I do not think this is unique sensitiveness: I perfectly understand what Wystan meant when he wanted all his private letters destroyed, and thought that writers had the right not to disclose their private lives, and that others, who did so, were interlopers and vulgar gossip-writers. If one writes imaginative prose or verse, where the facts of one's private life have a certain relevance (as, goodness me, they certainly did in the life of Anna Andreevna), critics have a certain horrible right to draw the curtain; but even this right they ought to use sparingly and not beyond absolute necessity. T. S. Eliot, who, in his will, asked that no biography of him should be written, seems to me to have behaved more sympathetically than Edmund Wilson, our old friend, who I think wanted Edel[1] to write one. Or perhaps he only wanted Edel to edit his letters. But at least fifty or a hundred years ought to pass, unless one is completely 'historical'.

I don't know why I suddenly decided to preach this long sermon to you, as if for publication! Be kind, and destroy this letter after you have read it: I should be distressed to think that anyone other than you is likely to read it, by whatever accident, even though it contains no secrets.

Now to really important things: I am not at all clear about Renée [Hampshire]'s cat – is it alive? is it dead? I fear I may be unable to go to a Christmas lunch with the Hampshires,[2] at which no fewer than two black couples are being entertained, as well as a complement of the halt, the blind, the lame which Renée has accumulated. Bob and his Countess can give you an account of their tea in Wadham: the best moment was when Renée asked about details of the lunch they had with us, and the Countess claims that she described the sweet in particular detail – the glaze on the soufflé, the little things which surrounded it, the exquisite taste, and explained that as we had no servants (which is true, our Spaniards are gone),[3] Aline certainly prepared this herself. Renée said 'I really do not think, perhaps, that Aline did it herself ... really not ... I do not think ...'. [...]

We shall be virtually alone for the next fortnight here, no social engagements, no visitors. I am, or pretend to be, too feeble to move until the New Year. Bliss. I hope you too are in this condition. Nobody believes that you or

book, though not absolutely first-rate, is indispensable. She was charming, sensitive, intuitive and a very honest person, and Akhmatova truly loved her.'

1 Joseph Leon Edel (1907–97), literary critic and biographer, taught at NYU from 1950, prof. 1955–66, Henry James Prof. of English 1966–72; Citizen's Prof. of English, Hawaii, 1972–8; 1963 Pulitzer Prize for vols 2–3 of his biography of Henry James; edited 4 vols of Edmund Wilson's diaries 1976–86.
2 For Renée Hampshire see 619.
3 We have not identified the Spanish couple in question. Their successors were the Portuguese couple Casimiro and Claudina Botelho, whom Aline had recently employed to look after her, IB and Headington House, which they did from 17 December 1976 to 27 July 2001.

I like this kind of life, but we do: you here in the summer, I here in the winter. Perhaps more difficult in New York.

See you in April, love to Dominique,

Yours,

Исай-ликуй[1]

TO LEONARD SCHAPIRO[2]

29 December 1976

Headington House

Dear Leonard,

Thank you very much for sending me the second edition of *The Origin of the Communist Autocracy*.[3] Well do I remember the circumstances of the first publication. All I can say is that historic justice has been done – your reputation has risen as that of Chatham House has fallen.[4] Who now thinks of it as an institution of central importance where foreign statesmen count it a privilege to speak? I read the second preface with pleasure: the good Lenin and bad Stalin[5] really is a pathetic fallacy, by which many disappointed ex-Communists still live. I wonder if some very, very early Christians felt this about Paul, as Renan plainly did.[6] And talking of preachers, I only have two qualifications. I do not believe in 'the banality of evil'.[7] I think this is

1 'Isai-likui', apparently a nickname based on 'Isaie, likui!', 'Isaiah, rejoice!', the opening of the 'Dance of Isaiah' wedding hymn at the end of the Orthodox Christian wedding service ('Isaiah, rejoice! A virgin is with child'), during which the priest leads the couple 3 times round a table.

2 Leonard Bertram Naman Schapiro (1908–83), a St Paul's contemporary and lifelong friend of IB (224); admitted to the bar, Gray's Inn, 1932, practised 1946–55; lecturer, dept of politics, LSE, 1955–75, prof. of political science (with special reference to Russian studies) 1963–75.

3 *The Origin of the Communist Autocracy: Political Opposition in the Soviet State, First Phase, 1917–1922* (London, [1955]; 2nd ed., London/Cambridge, Mass., 1977).

4 Schapiro's indictment of the Soviet regime began life as a research proposal supported by the Royal Institute of International Affairs at Chatham House. Its pursuit there was made difficult by E. H. Carr, who chaired the Institute's Soviet and East European studies subcommittee. Schapiro epitomised to Carr 'all that was going wrong with Soviet studies in the Cold War climate' and Carr used his dominance in the subcommittee to 'lash out' at him: Jonathan Haslam, *The Vices of Integrity: E. H. Carr, 1892–1982* (London, 1999), 157. On the subcommittee's recommendation Chatham House declined to publish Schapiro's work, to the angry incredulity of IB, who had consistently supported it. It was eventually published under the auspices of the LSE, with the backing of Karl Popper. IB's 'commitment to the success of Schapiro's enterprise soon became a touchstone for battles with Carr's "errant" intellect' (ibid. 159), and he resigned his membership of Chatham House over the affair.

5 Joseph Vissarionovich Stalin (1879–1953) né Djugashvili, general secretary, central committee, Communist Party 1922–53; after outmanoeuvring his rivals, notably Trotsky and Bukharin, he was effectively dictator of the USSR from 1929; adopted the name 'Stalin' ('man of steel') c.1911.

6 Joseph Ernest Renan (1823–92), French philosopher, historian and scholar of religion, author of the widely read and highly controversial *Vie de Jésus* (Paris, 1863), and a life of the early Christian leader St Paul 'the Apostle' (c.4 BC–c.AD 63) né Saul of Tarsus, *Saint Paul* (Paris, 1869).

7 A reference to Hannah Arendt's *Eichmann in Jerusalem: A Report on the Banality of Evil* (London/NY, 1963).

psychologically false, as, indeed, I think most of what the late Miss Arendt[1] said, though she was no doubt perfectly sincere – but too German for me. I believe that those who function in totalitarian systems either do so with conviction, i.e. believing that they are doing good, or despite mild qualms, 'That is the way we live now', 'There has been a great mutation', 'This is the turn that history has taken' – but that implies a certain awareness of deviation from the old moral code, which one may disregard in practice but which one has not forgotten in theory, and which occasionally pricks one. What I do not believe is that any of the minor officials simply mechanically perform their duty, totally unaware of why this might be thought upsetting by some of their own kith and kin. In Italy, for example, the bulk of the population regarded Fascism with cynicism but not with indifference; in Russia, part cynicism, part conviction. And so on. But I may well be mistaken. I often am.

My second qualification is about the great African saint.[2] There was a bit of Lenin in him too. After all, he was the first person, so far as I know, who openly justified the torture of heretics, and the application of violence to them. No doubt it was done before, both by Christians and Jews, but the justification – in his case, against the enormities of the Donatists – had not been enunciated before in explicit terms. [...] Anyway, I regard all the great Christian persecutors, and finally the secular ones as well, as direct descendants, ideologically, of St Augustine. That he was a genius is clear; his sainthood appears to me more than dubious. I have always wondered why the Orthodox Church went beyond beatification, though even that seems to me to pay homage to the blackest, fiercest, most intolerant tradition in Christianity: from Calvin through Dzherzhinsky is no great distance.[3]

But I still believe that this book is the greatest single original contribution

1 Johanna ('Hannah') Arendt (1906–75), German-born Jewish philosopher and political theorist; left Germany for France 1933, France for the US 1941, settling in NY. IB first met her 1942, and developed an extreme aversion to her and her works, but she is widely regarded as one of the most influential political philosophers of her era.

2 St Augustine of Hippo (354–430), Christian theologian and philosopher, bishop of Hippo Regius 395–430. His justification of coercion by the Church arose from his thinking on the Donatist heresy in North Africa, a schismatic movement named after its leader, the Carthaginian prelate Donatus (d. c.355). St Augustine initially repudiated coercion, but came to see fear as a necessary weapon in the battle to win back souls to the Church: '[T]here is an unjust persecution which the wicked inflict on the Church of Christ, and there is a just persecution which the Church of Christ inflicts on the wicked. She, indeed, is happy because she suffers persecution for justice's sake, but they are unhappy because they suffer persecution for injustice's sake. Therefore she persecutes out of love, they out of hatred.' Augustine to Boniface, Letters 4, trans. Sister Wilfrid Parsons (NY, 1955), 152 (letter 185, written in 417, chapter 11).

3 Jean Calvin (1509–64), French-born theologian and Protestant reformer, settled in Geneva 1541, establishing theocratic rule there; Calvinism emphasised particular election (some are chosen by God for salvation), predestination and justification by faith alone, and in England gave rise to the religious extremism of Puritanism. The Bolshevik Feliks Edmundovich Dzerzhinsky (Polish Feliks Dzierżyński) (1877–1926), son of a Polish nobleman, participated in the October 1917 Revolution (November in the Western calendar); that December he became head of the first Soviet secret police, the Cheka, and, like that body, was for ever identified with the mass political terror that consolidated the Lenin and Stalin regimes.

to the history of Bolshevism made by anyone in our time. I hope it will be reviewed afresh and as it deserves.

Yours,

Isaiah

TO CLARISSA AVON[1]

14 January 1977 [*manuscript*]

Headington House

Dearest Clarissa,

You must have imagined often and often what it would be like:[2] you knew in advance – past crises when it nearly happened, or looked as if it would, had, you thought perhaps, prepared you for it, yet when it does happen, it is very different: and rather worse; and nothing can ever be the same. Everyone will tell you – and they will say no more than the truth – that the love and devotion and wisdom and what the Bible calls lovingkindness with which you preserved Anthony & made him happy and prolonged his days, were beyond praise & beyond description – noble, moving and magnificent beyond words. Marriage to you was surely the best and to him the most deeply satisfying thing even in his brave and dedicated life, filled with achievements: you sustained him and made him happy at an agonizing time in his career – nor do I believe that ever before had he been with anyone who gave him so much help, confidence, loyalty, and love as surely you did. But the cost to you must have been, at times, very great: not appalling because you loved him; still, if, as Pasternak says in *Dr Zhivago*, all life is a sacrifice,[3] no one has lived more truly than you: (forgive me for this solemn address! but I truly mean every word I say: I cannot say it to your face: but I can write it, and I am glad and anxious to say it at last) – no one has lived a better or nobler life, and I (and surely all who know you) feel boundless admiration for you and for what you have been and are. To have had a life so free from the smallest, the least hint of meanness, of moral squalor (as Bloomsbury used to call it), of any concession, of compromise, not to have evaded, not to have falsified one's own feelings or perception of reality – to have stayed clear and fearless about it all – surely this is a matter of the highest pride? And all this with humour, gaiety, amusement, love of life & people, and not the beginning of complaint, where

1 (Anne) Clarissa Eden (b. 1920) née Spencer-Churchill, niece of Winston Churchill, m. 1952 (Robert) Anthony Eden (296/1); Lady Eden from 1954, Countess of Avon from 1961; as an unmatriculated philosophy pupil of IB's at Oxford during the war she became a close friend.

2 Anthony Eden died at his home, Alvediston Manor, Wiltshire, 14 January 1977; he had suffered bouts of recurring ill health after a botched operation to remove gall stones 1953, and had resigned as prime minister 1957 on medical advice; his wife cared for him devotedly throughout.

3 Pasternak writes of 'the two concepts which are the main part of the make-up of modern man – without them he is inconceivable – the ideas of free personality and of life regarded as sacrifice'. *Doctor Zhivago*, trans. Max Hayward and Manya Harari (London, 1958), 19.

others would have felt that they were owed so much for acting so – I cannot tell you how marvellous this seems to me, how vastly superior to the run of the mill people you are often surrounded by I think you to be: all this besides and over and above the deep love I bear you. [...] And I'll never forget with what courtesy & friendliness Anthony behaved towards me: I am not exactly "his type" – Aline much more so; hence, gratitude. She, of course, wants to send every possible loving message to you also. I'll wait for your signal. And if you summon me, & when you do, I'll go on babbling as always, until you stop me. In the meanwhile if there is anything we can do, you know you have but to convey it [...]. You will have a superhumanly large correspondence to cope with: *don't*, I beg you earnestly, *don't* acknowledge this in any possible way. I know this [is] all inadequate, inevitably: but perhaps too inadequate. Sorry.

My warmest warmest love
Isaiah

TO BONDO WYSZPOLSKI[1]

25 January 1977

Headington House

Dear Mr Wyszpolski,

[...] About the filming of historical biographies: I wish I could be of help to you, but I fear I cannot. No doubt we do judge of the past in terms of our own experience, view it through spectacles coloured by contemporary conditions – the very thing that Vico warned us against so strongly. How is one to avoid anachronism?[2] Vico and many subsequent writers tell us that there are certain laws of development of society whereby we can determine what the prevailing concepts, the prevailing outlook and language and view of life must have been in this or that age; but we must not attribute to those who lived in it thoughts or feelings or motives which could only have occurred at a later stage. Whether such laws exist, and if so what they are, has ever since been a matter of dispute. Others maintained that one must simply steep oneself in the life of the past by a species of sympathetic insight, which enables one to put oneself in the shoes of people who belong to times and places, other cultures, not too remote in either time or space; but how

1 Bondo Wyszpolski (b. 1950), Pasadena-born writer and interviewer on the arts, and exhibition curator; arts and entertainment editor, *Easy Reader* (South Bay, California), since 1994.
2 BW was writing a script for a film on Lorenzo de' Medici, and asked (10 January 1977): 'Is there a usual fault with filmed historical biographies that I should be wary of? Do you believe it possible to convey, visually, not only a realistic picture of the times, but a portrait of such an individual that can emerge without too much distortion? Or will the average, modern viewer automatically judge the main action from today's standards? Indeed, is he even *capable* of doing otherwise?' He went on to refer to 'the need to see [a] culture as the culture saw itself', and to explain why he was asking IB for his views: 'I have neither colleagues nor the necessary well-read friends.'

can one ever tell whether one's 'insight' into a past age, or groups, or individuals, is correct? There are some historical tests, of course, of coherence with known facts; some psychological laws, perhaps, or even sociological ones, which – while they may not be precise – are better than nothing; still there is a pervasive doubt about all such reconstructions. This troubles, or should trouble, historians and biographers, and film scriptwriters, perhaps, more than it does. [...] When I read about the history of events in the 1930s, through which I lived, written by young men who have not, I sometimes do not believe that it is the world I remember that they are writing about. There is a [...] book by Professor Hay, of Edinburgh, on the Renaissance, which I find useful.[1] If I were you, I should do what you yourself have thought of – read Machiavelli,[2] read Guicciardini,[3] read *The Lives of the Painters*, particularly the famous one of Michelangelo[4] – something will seep through. For instance, when Machiavelli writes to someone that his writing may be rather illegible because he has been tortured recently,[5] the fact that he refers to such torture as a pretty normal occurrence, and complains of its effects rather as we might of arthritis or a headache (perhaps it is different behind the Iron Curtain, or in Argentina or Chile, or Iraq), does convey to me the distance between us and them – there is something about this in a not very good book by Lytton Strachey – *Elizabeth and Essex* – where he stresses how unlike us the Elizabethans were.[6] I once saw a performance of an Elizabethan play, *The Witch of Edmonton*,[7] which conveyed to me the different world of witchcraft, superstition and brutality. This emerges from second- and third-rate works

1 Denys Hay (1915–94), who taught at Edinburgh 1945–80 (prof. of medieval history 1954), wrote widely on the Renaissance; IB is probably referring to his *The Italian Renaissance in Its Historical Background* (Cambridge, 1961; 2nd ed. 1977).

2 Niccolò di Bernado dei Machiavelli (1469–1527), Florentine political theorist, dramatist and historian, best known for his disconcerting discourse on contemporary statecraft *Il Principe* (*The Prince*), written 1513, published in Florence 1532.

3 Francesco Guicciardini (1483–1540), Florentine diplomat and historian; ambassador to Aragon 1512–14; in the service of the papacy 1515–34; author of *L'historia d'Italia*, the most important contemporary record of Italy 1494–1534; incomplete at his death, it was published posthumously in Florence 1561.

4 Giorgio Vasari, 'Michelangelo Bonarroti Fiorentino: pittore scvltore et architetto', in *Le vite de piv eccellenti architetti, pittori, et scvltori italiani, da Cimabve insino a' tempi nostri* [*The Lives of the Most Excellent Italian Architects, Painters and Sculptors, from Cimabue to Our Times*] (Florence, 1550), [part 3,] 947–91; revised in the 2nd. ed., *Le vite de' piu eccellenti pittori, scultori, e architettori* (Florence, 1568), as 'Vita di Michelagnolo Buonarruoti Fiorentino pittore, scultore, & architetto', [part 3 (ii),] 715–96. For Michelangelo see 436/3.

5 Letter untraced.

6 (Giles) Lytton Strachey (1880–1932), biographer and literary critic. 'More valuable than descriptions, but what perhaps is unattainable, would be some means by which the modern mind might reach to an imaginative comprehension of those beings of three centuries ago [...]. But the path seems closed to us. [...] With very few exceptions – possibly with the single exception of Shakespeare – the creatures meet us without intimacy; they are exterior visions, which we know, but do not truly understand': *Elizabeth and Essex: A Tragic History* (London/NY, 1928), 8.

7 A Jacobean play by Thomas Dekker, John Ford, William Rowley and perhaps (an)other(s), written 1621 and first published as *The Witch of Edmonton: A Known True Story, Composed into a Tragi-Comedy* (London, 1658).

much more vividly than from first-rate ones, which have universal themes – more from minor Elizabethan writers than from Shakespeare,[1] or from minor Renaissance storytellers than from printed poets. [...]

Yours sincerely,
Isaiah Berlin

On 20 February 1977 an opinion poll in Israel predicted that the ruling Alignment (Labor) list would lose heavily in the 17 May Knesset elections, resulting in a right-wing government for the first time in Israel's history. The prediction proved correct, and there was a sea change in Israeli politics, with Menachem Begin's[2] Likud[3] winning one-third of the votes. IB had viewed such a possibility with dismay, and he viewed its consequences with increasing concern.

TO DAVID VITAL[4]

16 March 1977

Headington House

Dear David,

Your melancholy letters plunge me into melancholy too, but I am sure that you do not, alas, exaggerate, and that the situation is as gloomy as you paint it. The rumours are that Yadin[5] will accumulate about thirty seats. If he gets anywhere near this, what will he do with his army? In which direction will he march them? One must obviously prefer him to the NRP,[6] even though I constantly remember Weizmann[7] found the company of Itche-Mayer Levin[8] more congenial than that of his officially closer allies. That

1 William Shakespeare (1564–1616), English poet and playwright, equally adept at comedies, histories and tragedies; considered one of the greatest dramatists ever to have lived; cf. 190.
2 Menachem Begin (1913–92), Israeli politician; leader of the right-wing Likud bloc 1973, prime minister 1977–83 (took office 20 June).
3 'Union', right-wing alliance, established in Israel 1973, which won the Knesset elections of 1977 under Begin's leadership, ending the era of Mapai–Labor dominance.
4 David Vital (b. 1927) né David Vital Grossman, son of the Zionist leader and journalist Meir Grossman; Israeli political scientist and historian of post-Emancipation Jewry; in government service 1954–66 (Foreign Ministry and Intelligence Service) before returning to academia; Nahum Goldmann Prof. of Diplomacy, Tel Aviv, 1977–95. An undergraduate pupil of IB's at New College, Vital undertook his 3-vol. history of the Zionist movement (Oxford, 1975–87) at IB's pressing.
5 Yigael Yadin (1917–84) né Sukenik, Israeli army officer, archaeologist and politician; founding member and leader throughout of the short-lived (1976–8) centrist Democratic Movement for Change, which won 15 seats in the elections to the Knesset in May 1977, and subsequently joined the government of Menachem Begin, though not needed for a majority; it soon began to disintegrate into a number of small parliamentary groups.
6 National Religious Party; established 1956, it participated in most governments of Israel for the next 5 decades; until the 1967 Six Day War it was considered moderate, but thereafter its nationalistic elements strengthened, especially in response to the formation of the Gush Emunim movement 1974 (286/2).
7 Chaim *Weizmann (1874–1952), 1st President, Israel.
8 Yiddish familiar form of the name of Yitzhak-Meir Levin (1893–1971), Polish-born Orthodox rabbi

was founded on a certain mutual cynicism, which is not the right recipe for the present, whatever situations it is thought to be suitable for; will he not be a bit too tough? You may say 'It is all very well for you, sitting there on the lawn at All Souls, to indulge in doveish sentiments and recommend liberal concessions from us, when for us it is a matter of life or death.' Yet I think it is possible to go too far in defying the Americans. I have a recurrent nightmare of Carter,[1] if faced by too much obstinacy on the part of unyielding Israeli hawks, losing his temper and blowing up like Bevin.[2] If America retreats from the scene – and the arguments that it simply cannot do so, in its own interest, are not convincing – then I think the future of Israel really is dark. So long as it does not do this, there is not merely hope but a great deal of it; I do not think it matters a rap what either the UK or Europe does about all this. But I must not go on philosophising in the void.

Do you know a man called Iverach McDonald,[3] who used to be foreign editor of *The Times*, and then deputy editor, I think, and now retired, who is going to Israel for the twin purpose of visiting Biblical sites – he is a solid Scotsman, brought up on the Old Testament and knows it backwards – and to gather material for the last volume of the history of *The Times* which he is writing [...]?[4] [...] he told us that when he was last in Palestine, in 1956, he asked the taxi-driver about the hill down which they had come, 'What is it?' 'A hill,' said the driver. Iverach then said 'Ye mountains of Gilboa, let there be no dew, neither let there be rain upon you, nor fields of offerings; while the shield of the mighty is vilely cast away, the shield of Saul, as though he had not been anointed with oil.'[5] The driver said, 'I don't know what you mean; it has rained here for three days since Monday, what is all this about dew?' [...]

Yours ever,
   Isaiah

and longstanding MK 1949–71, where he was associated with the ultra-orthodox Haredi-Hassidic party Agudat Yisrael.

1 James Earl ('Jimmy') Carter (b. 1924), Democrat governor of Georgia 1971–5, US President 1977–81.

2 Ernest Bevin (1881–1951), trade unionist and Labour politician; as secretary of state for foreign affairs, 1945–51, Bevin had to balance Zionist aspirations in Palestine with those of the Arab population. He reacted angrily to Truman's unilateral endorsement 1946 of substantial Jewish immigration at a time when he was trying to limit this, and was outraged by the terrorist operations against British targets of the Irgun and the Stern Gang (3/2).

3 Iverach McDonald (1908–2006), Scottish Highlander; subeditor, *Times*, 1935, foreign editor 1952, managing editor 1965–73; translator of Pushkin and Proust.

4 McDonald wrote (only) vol. 5 of *The History of The Times* (London, 1935–), *Struggles in War and Peace, 1939–1966* (1984), which was not of course the last volume of the history.

5 From David's song for Saul and Jonathan, 2 Samuel 1: 21. The King James Bible reads 'for there' in place of 'while'.

TO MORTON WHITE[1]

16 March 1977

[Headington House]

Dear Morton,

Your handwriting gives me great pleasure. This is a really sure sign of affection – one's immediate reaction to handwriting on envelopes or letters seems to me a more direct symptom of one's feelings than almost anything save the sight of a face or a figure. There used to be a screen in the All Souls buttery, where lunch is eaten; one never knew who was coming in, one heard steps, but then one suddenly saw a face as it appeared from behind the screen; spirits immediately rose or fell, perhaps not dramatically, or even stayed still (not very often) – one then knew at least whose company one liked, and who lowered one's spirits. So with handwriting.

Yes, I remember Aline's condition on the way to the airport. She is really a kind of centaur, half woman, half car – David Pears[2] is also like that. When in a car they become spiritually and physically fused with it, its behaviour is theirs, its sensations are those of limbs, intimately connected with thought and feeling and will (is there such a thing as will? perhaps not, but I do not like to think it or even have it said).

We are to go to Japan during the first week in April; before that, New York for about five days for me (Aline may come a day or two before). What am I doing there? You may well ask. I have been asked to deliver one of the three Trilling seminars. I liked Lionel Trilling, but not extravagantly; I liked him more towards the end of his life than when I first met him; unlike most of his friends in Oxford – Hampshire, for example, or Hart, who liked him less as time went on and thought him pompous, pretentious, while I thought him touching, not very clever, sensitive, responsive, silvery, without cutting edge, neither a great scholar nor a great critic, but disarming and in need of sympathy and encouragement, famous and admired as he was: and in every respect a very decent, reputable man, even though he was taken in by a certain sort of European glossiness and false style (Barzun).[3] Anyway, be that as it may, Diana, his wife, is a savage and impossible termagant of whom I am genuinely fond despite her furious onslaughts, faintly reminiscent of her old radical past (she used to begin sentences 'When Li and I were members of the Communist Party', when in fact they never were, converts

---

1 Morton Gabriel *White (b. 1917), philosopher and historian of ideas.

2 David Francis Pears (1921–2009), philosopher; lecturer, Oxford, 1950–72, reader 1972–85, prof. of philosophy 1985–8; fellow and philosophy tutor, CCC, 1950–60; student (i.e. fellow), Christ Church, 1960–88.

3 Jacques Martin Barzun (1907–2012), French-born historian of ideas and of culture; prof., dept of history, Columbia, 1945–60, Seth Low Prof. of History 1960–7, University Prof. 1967–75; ran the famous 'Great Books' graduate seminar with Lionel Trilling 1946–72.

of Sidney Hook[1] though in some sense they must have been). When she asked me to 'deliver' one of these seminars, I found it difficult to refuse, and now it is like a halter round my neck, a perpetual unlifting weight. I have worked up a piece I once wrote for *Foreign Affairs*, called 'The Bent Twig',[2] on nationalism, into something which may do, but may not. My 'discussants' are to be Gertrude Himmelfarb[3] and Michael Walzer[4] – neatly disposed to the right and the left of me, I suppose. My only real point in the entire piece, which I have spun out and spun out to make it look like an offering, is that nobody in the nineteenth century predicted the fantastic rise of nationalism in our own time; nobody, save perhaps Moses Hess,[5] and he merely said that a fusion of Communism and nationalism was desirable, not certain to occur.

Anyway, it is not an intellectually exciting subject, and I shall be glad to be rid of it, and shall certainly not publish it.[6] This happens in the first week in April. Then I propose to unload this on to the poor Japanese, together with something about Utopias and what stopped people producing them, on the whole, after the eighteenth century – there were some, but they haven't the confidence of the old worked-out visions.[7] Will the Japanese like that? I wonder. I am rather nervous of going there – I have no idea what to expect. I do know two or three Japanese scholars who were at Oxford and who did seem to me intelligent, but Freddie Ayer[8] gave me a harrowing description of what it is like to be the guest of the Japan Foundation – how one is given dinner by twenty-five Japanese professors of whom only three understand English; a great deal of affable smiling, good will one could cut with a knife, but not much communication. They then sit down in a U-shaped manner around one, and one of them says, 'Won't you say a few words?', and this means that they want a lecture of an hour and a half. 'Without four prepared lectures, you cannot go to Japan', said Freddie to me severely, before reading a chapter of his autobiography, in which I am much mentioned, sometimes with favour, sometimes more ambivalently.[9] It will be a very honest, rather

1 Sidney Hook (1902–89), prof. of philosophy, NY, 1939–72; research fellow, Hoover Institution on War, Revolution and Peace, Stanford, 1973–89; gravitated from Marxism to anti-Communist democratic socialism, and helped found the Congress for Cultural Freedom 1950, an anti-Communist advocacy group that (it was revealed 1966) was secretly funded by the CIA.

2 'The Bent Twig: A Note on Nationalism', *Foreign Affairs* 51 (1972), 11–30; repr. in CTH.

3 Gertrude Himmelfarb (b. 1922), prof. of history, CUNY, 1965–88; combative historian of C19th ideas who has urged the return of 'Victorian' moral standards in public policy.

4 Michael Walzer (b. 1935), prof., Harvard, 1966–80; prof., School of Social Science, IAS, Princeton, 1980–6, UPS [United Parcel Service] Foundation Prof. 1986–2007; co-editor, *Dissent*, since 1976; contributing editor, *New Republic*, 1977–2014.

5 Moses né Moritz Hess (1812–75), German Jewish writer, socialist and early Zionist, subject of IB's Lucien Wolf Memorial Lecture 11 December 1957, published as *The Life and Opinions of Moses Hess* (Cambridge, 1959; repr. in AC).

6 It was in fact published, first in a Spanish translation, then in English as 'Nationalism: Past Neglect and Present Power', *Partisan Review* 46 (1979), 337–58; repr. in AC and PSM.

7 *Decline of Utopian Ideas in the West* ([Tokyo], 1978: Japan Foundation); repr. in CTH.

8 Alfred Jules ('Freddie') *Ayer (1910–89), philosopher.

9 A. J. Ayer, *Part of My Life* (London, 1977), in which Ayer writes of IB: 'He once described me to

uninteresting book, I suspect, which will tell the story of his life, omitting its
'affective' aspects, the only thing that has a genuine vitality. He will do this
out of decent feeling – why should all those ladies be for ever compromised?
But it will make the book a rather mechanical jog-trot, I fear. It is Russell's[1]
book, I think, which inspires him with the idea of doing it: he identifies
himself with Russell to a very profound degree.

I am glad that the new head of the Institute[2] pleases you. Here too, there
are some changes: we have elected a new Warden of All Souls – a very nice,
sweet, good, honourable, utterly blameless, kind, amiable lawyer[3] […]. The
rival candidate was Bernard Williams, whose supporters assured him that it
was in the bag. I turned out to be the only person who warned him that it
might well not be so, and was sorry to be so true a prophet. I think I really am
getting rather old. I feel the strain of having to squeeze ideas out of myself;
when called upon to give a lecture or write an article, it is more painful than
it used to be, and I think that what I say is less worth saying, in spite of my
tendency to reckless generalisation. The generalisations are just as reckless
as they were, but paler. If you can imagine such a thing as reckless truisms,
these are what I seem to myself to be generating. […]

Yours ever,
    [unsigned]

*On 10 April 1977 IB and Aline flew from New York to Toyko for a three-week
stay in Japan as the guests of the Japan Foundation, which promoted cultural
exchanges, and IB revelled in the opportunity to experience a way of life unlike
any he had known. As he wrote to Joe Alsop: 'If only I had listened to you more
gratefully about China, I might have been able to understand this culture better.
I am rather overwhelmed by its gravity, aestheticism, unbroken roots in a past
remote from the West – or anything but itself.'[4]*

TO DIANA TRILLING

23 April 1977 [*manuscript postcard*]

                                                                Kyoto, Japan
Strange country. The courtesy is exquisite and unending: did Lionel ever

a common friend as having a mind like a diamond, and I think it is true that within its narrower
range my intellect is the more incisive. On the other hand, he has always had the readier wit, the
more fertile imagination and the greater breadth of learning' (99).
1 Bertrand Arthur William Russell (1872–1970), OM 1949, 3rd Earl Russell 1931; mathematician,
  philosopher, author and anti-nuclear campaigner; fellow, Trinity, Cambridge, 1895–1901, 1944–70;
  Nobel Prize in Literature 1950; the 1st vol. of his *Autobiography of Bertrand Russell* (3 vols, London,
  1967–9) in particular is regarded as a masterpiece.
2 Harry Woolf (1923–2003), Willis K. Shepard Prof. of the History of Science, Johns Hopkins,
  1961–76; director, IAS, Princeton, 1976–87.
3 Patrick Neill (35/2).
4 To Joe Alsop, 21 April 1977.

come here? He wd have loved the low toned tact and infinite trouble which people take in avoiding the slightest conceivable source of embarrassment from any act to anyone: there is a terrific intensity of feeling, repressed, disciplined by ritual, turned to an elaborate game, but charming, civilised, and at times greatly comical: It is like living in a state of continuous formal play, in which all the moves are predictable, but nevertheless give constant pleasure, because so beautifully made: *most* odd & unlike what we call human relations. I go lecturing away to polite expressionless heads who seem to have no English. Nice, all the same. L's name *very* well known here. [...]

TO GLEB STRUVE[1]

5 May 1977

Headington House

Dear Gleb Petrovich,

[...] I met AA twice in the Soviet Union, on both occasions in her room in Leningrad.[2] The first time was in the autumn of 1945 – late October or November – the date is probably noted in the poem 'Cinque', which speaks of two voices, which will be familiar to you.[3] This was the far longer, and more 'fundamental' meeting. I then returned to Moscow. I left the Soviet Union via Leningrad in early January 1946. I called on AA in the afternoon of 5 January (not in the evening, for my train left for Helsinki, I seem to recollect, before midnight). According to AA, it was on the day after this that microphones were openly inserted into the ceiling of her room, and she began to be harassed after that (although I do not wish to be cited as reporting all this: if you wish to use this information, it had better be referred to as 'communicated by AA to friends during one of her visits to the West', or something like that). As for the verses in 'Stalin cycle',[4] she did ask me whether I understood the motive for them. I said that everyone who knew the circumstances did so, that no decent human being held them against her – she seemed satisfied. Much the most eccentric thing in Amanda Haight's book is the proposition, which she obviously took quite literally and believed, that AA and I 'started the cold war'.[5] AA did say this to me, but apt as she was to romanticise her

1 Gleb Petrovich Struve (1898–1985), Russian-born Balliol-educated literary historian, translator, poet and critic; prof. of Slavic languages and literatures, Berkeley, 1947–67; a specialist in Soviet literature, he produced editions of the works of writers suppressed by the Soviet authorities, including Akhmatova.

2 As St Petersburg was called 1924–91.

3 The poems of *Cinque* give dates of composition, not the date of the meeting, which was 15–16 November 1945.

4 'In Praise of Peace', a cycle of poems published by Akhmatova 1950 in the weekly *Ogonek*, nos 14, 36, 42; ostensibly supportive of the Stalinist state, they were written in an attempt to improve the plight of her son, Lev Nikolaevich Gumilev (617), who had been re-arrested.

5 'He will not be a beloved husband to me / But what we accomplish, he and I, / Will disturb the Twentieth Century.' From the 'Third and Last' dedication to Akhmatova's *Poem without a Hero*,

own life and that of others, I do not myself think that she believed this in any ordinary sense of the word, although it entered into her vision of her own and her country's past, conceived as a tragic drama.

You speak of the review in the *New Yorker* of Amanda Haight's book[1] – I have not seen it, but it seems to me that the quality of the reviews in that journal lapsed a long time ago; I do not know who the literary editor may be, but I am quite clear that he does not know his business. I should be grateful if you did not repeat this to George Steiner,[2] who takes immense pride in being, as he thinks of it, Edmund Wilson's successor, when in fact he is not worthy of tying his bootstraps. Nor, for that matter, am I. But I do not write reviews for the *New Yorker*; and in view of the somewhat ironical treatment of my works – which they, I believe, think to be friendly – I never shall.

Yours ever,
    Isaiah Berlin

TO MASAO MARUYAMA[3]

23 May 1977

Headington House

Dear Professor Maruyama,

I felt, and so did my wife, throughout our three weeks in Japan, that we were moving in a noble and coherent dream of great beauty and some strangeness. It was a transcending experience, in some ways the strongest cultural impact I have ever suffered in my life; but (and perhaps this is an indication of a certain shallowness of nature on my part), however disturbing, it was always enjoyable. It was sometimes tantalising – not exactly inscrutable, but composed of an infinity of perspectives, so that each door opens into a prospect that leads one to the next, to an apparently infinite *enfilade*,[4] each of which is completely satisfying in itself and yet creates a yearning for that which lies behind it. I am not expressing myself very clearly, and all this romantic patter is merely an attempt to convey how strange and marvellous I found it all. You never warned me, during our meetings in Oxford, how firmly, despite all the modernisation and Westernisation of the Japanese cities and economic life, the independent Japanese culture had in fact been

in *The Complete Poems of Anna Akhmatova*, trans. Judith Hemschemeyer, ed. Roberta Reeder, 2nd ed. (Boston, Mass./Edinburgh, 1994), 547.

1 *Anna Akhmatova: A Poetic Pilgrimage* (39/6), reviewed by Naomi Bliven, *New Yorker*, 11 April 1977, 137–9.

2 (Francis) George Steiner (b. 1929), Paris-born US writer and academic; fellow, Churchill, Cambridge, since 1961, Extraordinary Fellow since 1969; prof. of English and comparative literature, Geneva, 1974–94; 'he is not a man whose views I can conceivably take seriously on any subject' (to Joe Alsop, 3 March 1981).

3 Masao Maruyama (1914–96), Japanese political theorist; prof. of the history of East Asian (especially Japanese) political thought, dept of law, Tokyo, 1950–71.

4 'Vista'.

preserved. Beside it, England, and particularly America, must surely seem crude, chaotic, shoddy, horribly uncontrolled. All this on the basis of three weeks in Japan! What right have I to generalise, or say anything at all about a life and a civilisation of which I have only seen the tip of the topmost part of the surface. [...]

I suspect that even China is more intelligible to Westerners than Japan, if only because the contact of the Chinese with foreigners is longer, more continuous, and so the adaptation is greater. But I think this insulation a marvellous thing – the desire to knock down walls and cause familiarity between everyone and everyone can go too far. A fastidious withdrawal is a precondition of certain forms of artistic creation and spiritual self-protection, without which all values tend to assimilation, identity – that is, evaporate altogether. But again, I am beginning to indulge in fine writing.

What I really wish to say is that I know well that it is [...] really to you that we owe it all. For fear of further fine writing, let me say that it has been the most marvellous visit of our life; and that nothing, even a second visit to Japan, could ever equal it; and that for this I shall always remain profoundly grateful to you. I am not really used to VIP treatment, but even that was done with such exquisite tact and courtesy that it was never oppressive, never excessive. I must not go on. You will, I am sure, know that I cannot put into words my real feeling; but I wish you to know that it is unique and delightful, and that you are its primary begetter. [...]

Yours sincerely,
Isaiah Berlin

TO STANLEY MITCHELL[1]

31 May 1977

Headington House

Dear Mitchell,

[...] Did I really send you two newspaper cuttings from the NYT? Why should I have wished to draw your attention to juvenile sex delinquency? Of course, I am capable of anything, but this does seem rather 'undermotivated', as they say nowadays. As for China and Beethoven[2] and Schubert,[3] that I might well have sent you. Did we talk about China in any connection? I recollect nothing. [...] I have, since I sent the cutting, been to Australia, where I heard the Shanghai Symphony Orchestra. They played extremely well, but

1 Stanley Mitchell (1932–2011), born in London's East End to a family of Russian Jewish extraction, became a translator and Russian scholar; inaugural lecturer in Russian literature, Essex, 1965–75; thereafter pursued a peripatetic academic career; his translation of Pushkin's *Eugene Onegin* (London, 2008), begun 1966, has been widely praised.
2 Ludwig van Beethoven (1770–1827), phenomenally gifted and influential German composer and pianist whose career bridged the classical and Romantic eras.
3 Franz Peter Schubert (1797–1828), prolific Austrian composer, much loved by IB (57).

their looks – [...] fantastically *gleich*[*ge*]*schaltet*[1] – did rather frighten me: as [they] did, indeed, some of the pro-Chinese Australian Labour Party stalwarts who were sitting next to me. They marched in, in their identical suits; smiled, all of them for exactly the same number of seconds; ceased smiling at precisely the same split second; first played traditional Chinese music on the old instruments, rather marvellously, I thought; then the 'revolutionary' music, which was a very feeble dilution of Soviet music of the 1920s, i.e. Glazunov[2] with water, weak, conventional, Western salon music, remote from any possible individual content, sugary and characterless; then *Waltzing Matilda*, dazzlingly done, a compliment to Australia which caused pleasure and amusement in the audience. [...]

I wish I knew how to assess the situation in a country as genuinely remote from us as China. I have just been to Japan, and that is truly a strange civilisation. Under the veneer of skyscrapers and Sony and colossal efficiency and student revolt there is an ancient civilisation, rigid, strange, complicated, much more remote from us than any part of Europe or Russia or India than the books about it seem to convey – at least, I thought so. Since I don't speak Japanese, this could only be judged from general behaviour: non-verbal communication has its limits. I should love to go to China, but I am terribly conscious of the fact that if one does not speak the language, and does not stay for, say, two or three months in one place, so that one can get the hang of how things are done and what thoughts are thought, one is at the mercy of governments, propagandists, counter-propagandists and one's own outlook and biases. All that people in the West read about Russia in the 1920s – not the history but the reportage – and still more in the 1930s, or at any rate vast quantities of it, seem[s] absurdly distorted now, both ways. At least in this case I know the language and I have been there, and have my own impressions, such as they are, to rely on; but the only books to do with anything in the Soviet Union which seem to me authentic, and not to be preaching a sermon of some kind, are the angry – but humanly angry – books of Madame Mandel′shtam. Full of resentments against this or that person, but these are ordinary, human reactions, sometimes moving, sometimes expressions of the kind of bitchy jealousies which occur in any literary and artistic community – but all natural, spontaneous and intelligible. I get a sense of absolute authenticity about these books which I do not get about others. You may well disagree.

Do let us talk about Benjamin.[3] I do not claim to understand much of what

---

1 'Regimented'.
2 Aleksandr Konstantinovich Glazunov (1865–1936), Russian composer in the Romantic tradition of Tchaikovsky; pupil of Rimsky-Korsakov; director, St Petersburg Conservatory, 1905–30; occupied a respected position in the Soviet repertory despite leaving USSR 1928 and settling in Paris.
3 Walter Bendix Schönflies Benjamin (1892–1940), Berlin-born literary critic and essayist of Ashkenazi descent; met and befriended Bertolt Brecht 1929; went into exile in Paris 1933;

he wrote, but he was clearly an extremely sensitive, gifted and tormented man, who, if he had remained in any Communist country, would have ended badly; not as badly as he did end, perhaps – he might just have survived – but would more likely have returned to Switzerland, where he was during the First World War, and been unhappy and indignant there too. Anyhow, he is a far more sympathetic critic and human being than (to me) Brecht,[1] who is far more gifted, and whose poetry I think wonderful, far better than the plays, in whom there is a core of disdainful contempt for human stupidity and weakness and muddle, and an ultimate inhumanity disguised as humanism which leads to those, to me horrifying, cynical jokes, which nevertheless are extremely intelligent and often, of course, very good: i.e. the difference between people who, if ordered to shoot their friends, have no compunction about pressing the trigger, and those who at least feel qualms, whether they do it or not. Would you deny that Brecht belongs to the first category? Nevertheless, he is, without a doubt, a major figure. As for Pushkin,[2] the mere name lifts the spirit of all Russians, whether they read him or not. He is a unique phenomenon. [...]

Yours,

Isaiah Berlin

TO DAVID VITAL

23 June 1977

Headington House

Dear David,

[...] You can imagine what my views of the prospective government are, and you are not mistaken. And I, in my turn, as you rightly say, can imagine yours. Everyone seems agreed that the old government had to go. As for the quarrel with America, I do not think there is an analogy with Beneš/Hácha:[3]

committed suicide September 1940 when held at the Spanish border attempting to flee to the US after the German invasion of France.

1 Bertolt (né Eugen Berthold Friedrich) Brecht (1898–1956), German dramatist, producer and poet; emigrated to the US during the Fascist era, but settled in East Berlin 1949.

2 Alexander Sergeevich Pushkin (1799–1837), Russia's greatest poet.

3 Edvard Beneš (1884–1948), President, Czechoslovakia, 1935–8, 1945–8; though prepared to make concessions over the Sudetenland in order to secure peace with Nazi Germany, he resigned in October 1938 after the signing of the 4-power Munich Agreement (30 September) between Britain, France, Germany and Italy, the terms of which were dictated to Czechoslovakia and led to its dismemberment. In March 1939 Beneš's successor Emil Hácha (1872–1945) was reduced to the status of a puppet President after Hitler invaded what remained of the Czech lands. IB appears here to reject an analogy between the Sudetenland and the occupied West Bank, in the sense that he did not believe that withdrawal from the latter would put an Israeli prime minister in the humiliating position that Beneš and Hácha had found themselves in over the Sudetenland, where they were effectively powerless to stop the destruction of the Czech state; IB came to see 'no other solution than the giving up of the West Bank and fortifying the frontiers of the reduced Israel' (to Josef Cofel, 18 February 1992).

if Carter finds Arafat,[1] Assad,[2] Saudi Arabians etc. sensible, reasonable etc., as he well may (whether they are or not, particularly if they are not), and Israel obstructive in what looks like an obstinate way, and then loses his temper, like Bevin, the consequences to Israel may well be grave – graver, I think, than if there are concessions of what I should regard as a reasonable and you a dangerous and intolerable kind. But I do not expect you to agree with me about that.

I suffer from an incurable distaste – that is too weak a word – for all that Begin stands for.[3] I should not think a Dayan[4] government bad at all, since he is aware of what both Russia and America can be and do, which I feel sure that Begin is not. The notion that Israel can stand alone, supported only by South Africa, or *sub rosa* by Iran, without Europe or America, and defy public opinion, however erroneous such opinion may be, seems to me wildly impracticable and dangerous. That is why I think that [...] when Israel is attacked for, say, judicial torture, it is far better that it should invite the International Jurists, or some body not obviously corrupt or biased, like the United Nations, and at least retain a certain amount of general good will in the United States, Scandinavian countries, etc., than that it should stand proudly aloof, cross its arms on its breast and make itself ready for a final stand. But perhaps all this exaggerates the extremes between which it is placed – perhaps Likud will not go too far, perhaps the resistance of the unions will modify its stand, perhaps my nightmare is groundless. I hope so. I have a feeling that the consensus between Israel and the Diaspora that existed for more than sixty years has been all but snapped – that there is no common ground, no natural affinity or possibility of informal contact as there was between the old discredited government and the Jews outside the country, between Likud and the Jews of America and Europe. This is a major rift which bodes no good. However, I must stop being a Cassandra and hope that you are right. [...]

    Yours ever,

    Isaiah

1 Mohammed Abdel-Raouf Arafat As Qudwa al-Hussaeini (1929–2004), known as Yasser Arafat, Palestinian leader; co-founder, Fatah (a political and military party comprising the largest faction of the PLO) 1958, leader 1958–2004; chair, PLO executive committee, 1969–2004; President, Palestinian National Authority, 1996–2004; Nobel Peace Prize 1994 with Shimon Peres and Yitzhak Rabin.

2 Hafez al-Assad (1928–2000), Syrian Baath politician, President 1971–2000; a former air force officer from the Alawi sect, he came to power in a series of coups; succeeded by his son Bashar al-Assad (b. 1965).

3 IB held Begin, formerly commander of Irgun (233/7), responsible for acts of terror, including the bombing of the King David Hotel in Jerusalem 22 July 1946; his hostility was untempered by the (joint) award of the Nobel Peace Prize to Begin.

4 Moshe Dayan (1915–81), Israeli general and politician, rose to prominence during the 1948 War of Independence; chief of staff, IDF, 1955–8, minister of defence 1967–74, foreign minister 1977–9, a post in which he played an important part in the negotiations with Egypt that led to the Camp David accords.

TO YEHUDI MENUHIN[1]

TO YEHUDI MENUHIN[1]

18 July 1977

Headington House

Dearest Cousin,

I stand before you in sackcloth and ashes, for I have not acknowledged your book:[2] this was an appalling solecism on my part, the only reason for which was the disorder of my life, which anyone visiting the room in which I am writing could deduce from the permanent chaos that prevails in it – and also the fact that I have put off the pleasure of reading it until I go to Italy (today), where everything is delightful, and this would be a *bonne bouche* to look forward to. I have read nothing for two, three, four, five months – not even the biography of my friend Freddie Ayer, which, since references to me evidently appear *passim*, and since everyone minds about what is said about them, whether they admit this or not, might have driven all other reading from my desk and mind. But it hasn't. That, too, I shall read in Italy with, I suspect, mixed feelings. All this only to explain my misconduct.

Now, about Schubert.[3] Of course I also love him to distraction, particularly the late works, but really everything, even the works that others find mechanical or dull or over-extended, for if one loves a composer or a writer truly, one loves the padding, the canvas, as well as the images upon it – anything that is characteristic of the composer. This, indeed, is what love entails: to love only what is best or most beautiful is quite, quite different. That is what I feel about Brahms, about Debussy, but not about Bach or Mozart or Beethoven or Schubert or Rembrandt or Piero della Francesca or Pushkin, or, oddly enough, Berlioz.[4] But I cannot write about any of these things: writing about music is in any case something that a very few critics have

1 Yehudi Menuhin (1916–96), 4th cousin to IB, US-born British violinist of Russian Jewish descent and world renown: 'he belongs to the category of those who combine a certain sweet idealism and otherworldliness and worship of moral and aesthetic ideals with a certain sense of self-importance, a feeling that he has a role to play in affairs, and that when crises appear it is up to people like him to sound off' (to Teddy Kollek, 30 August 1988).

2 Menuhin's recently published autobiography, *Unfinished Journey* (London, 1977): 'The reviewers were very enthusiastic in print; privately, two or three spoke of it as cloying, sugary, acutely embarrassing. But Menuhin's public position in England is such that nobody is allowed to say a word against him. Indeed, he is a very nice man, my seventh cousin [but see previous note], and I love him.' To Rowland Burdon-Muller, 12 May 1977.

3 YM had invited IB (letter of 12 July 1977) to contribute a chapter, on any aspect of Schubert's music, to a book he had been asked to edit.

4 Johannes Brahms (1833–97), German composer and pianist; (Achille) Claude Debussy (1862–1918), French composer and critic; Johann Sebastian Bach (1685–1750), German composer and organist of sacred and secular works, active during the Baroque era, one of the outstanding figures in Western music; Wolfgang Amadeus (né Johannes Chrysostomus Wolfgangus Theophilus) Mozart (1756–91), Austrian composer, keyboard player, violinist, violist and conductor whose prodigious talents were exhibited in every musical genre of the day; Rembrandt Harmenszoon van Rijn (1606–69), Dutch artist; Piero della Francesca (c.1415–1492), Renaissance Italian painter and art theorist; (Louis) Hector Berlioz (1803–69), French composer.

ever succeeded in doing at all adequately. Has any musical critic ever really opened your eyes or ears to anything? Do you remember all those sentimental pages by Aldous Huxley, or Rolland, or E. M. Forster?[1] No good, embarrassing, useless.

Romanticism is a terrible subject, on which I do intend to write one day, but only on the intellectual origins, or perhaps the social milieu in which it was born, is it possible to write sense: on the ideology and on the history, but not on the actual embodiments, the works of art – at least, I have never read anything in the least satisfactory, and much that is insincere and pretentious. No, I could not do it, I wish I could. What do words like 'profound' when applied to music mean? In virtue of what do we say that the posthumous quartets are 'deeper' than the works of Sullivan[2] or Menotti?[3] The metaphor is one from a well: how much further can we press the simile? Why a well? Because the water is dark and no bottom is visible? What is meant by calling music 'dark' or expressive of some unattainable ideal or height? And so on and so on. But I will not waste your hours with all this frustration. Nor should I inflict it on the innocent reader. But thank you ever so much for thinking of me. Perhaps when I am in my late nineties, like Sir Robert Mayer,[4] and have written my pages on the intellectual origins of romanticism, I may have more to say. But I suspect not even then. Wittgenstein was right: music is a field *wovon man nicht sprechen kann.*[5] He thought there were only four great composers: Haydn,[6] Mozart, Beethoven, Schubert; possibly Labor,[7] a Czech

1 Aldous Leonard Huxley (1894–1963), English novelist and essayist, contributed a weekly column on music to the *Westminster Gazette* 1922–3. The French writer Romain Rolland (1866–1944), Nobel Prize in Literature 1915, published studies of *Beethoven* (Paris, [1903]) and *Haendel* (Paris, 1910), and also *Musiciens d'autrefois* and *Musiciens d'aujourd'hui* (both Paris, 1908). The most celebrated music criticism of E. M. Forster (1879–1970), OM 1969, English novelist and critic, occurs in chapter 5 of *Howard's End* (London, 1910), 29–42: 'Beethoven took hold of the goblins and made them do what he wanted. [...] He gave them a little push, and they began to walk in a major key instead of in a minor, and then – he blew with his mouth and they were scattered! Gusts of splendour, gods and demigods contending with vast swords, colour and fragrance broadcast on the field of battle, magnificent victory, magnificent death!' (31).
2 Arthur Seymour Sullivan (1842–1900), Kt 1883, composer, best known for his partnership with the librettist William Schwenck Gilbert (1836–1911), which produced 14 'Gilbert and Sullivan' comic operas 1871–96.
3 Gian Carlo Menotti (1911–2007), Italian composer, librettist and conductor, mainly domiciled in US from 1928; achieved considerable popularity with his modern opera buffa works, realising his aim of bringing opera closer to Broadway audiences, if at the expense of some originality, in the opinion of critics.
4 Robert Mayer (1879–1985), Kt 1939, German-born philanthropist; after making his fortune in metals he became a patron of music in Britain, co-founding the LPO with Thomas Beecham 1932.
5 Ludwig Wittgenstein, *Tractatus Logico-Philosophicus* (London, 1922), proposition 7 (the last sentence of the book), 'Wovon man nicht sprechen kann, darüber muss man schweigen' ('Whereof one cannot speak, thereof one must be silent'). One cannot, for him, explain music in words.
6 (Franz) Joseph Haydn (1732–1809), influential Austrian-born composer of German descent.
7 Josef Labor (1842–1924), Czech pianist, organist and composer, blind from childhood; settled in Vienna, and became a friend of the pianist Paul Wittgenstein (who lost his right arm in WWI), the philosopher's elder brother; in Ludwig's frequently stated opinion Labor was one of the six truly great composers, the one missing from IB's list being Brahms.

who taught him and his brothers – not, I fear, an immortal – and if anyone professed a love of Wagner, he never spoke to such a person again.[1] A little extreme, I think, but on the right lines.

Yours ever, with much love,
    Isaiah

In October 1977 IB went to Iran, accompanied by Aline, as the President of the British Academy, to open a new building for the British Institute of Persian Studies in the Embassy compound in Teheran. The Institute had been founded in 1961 as one of the overseas research bodies sponsored by the Academy, and that occasion had been marked by a visit and lecture by Maurice Bowra,[2] then the President of the Academy. Sixteen years later IB followed in his friend's footsteps, delivering a lecture entitled 'The Rise of Cultural Pluralism' at the official opening of the new building. The guest of honour was Her Imperial Majesty the Shahbanu of Iran,[3] who had contributed generously to the cost of the building, and who brought with her a retinue of courtiers who wondered how long the lecture – which they would be obliged to sit through – would last. According to Peter Brown,[4] the Secretary of the British Academy, who was present:

Isaiah, already unsure of his reception, had arranged with the Institute's director, Dr David Stronach,[5] that he [Stronach] would give a signal from the back of the hall when the time came to conclude. He was soon in his stride, in full rhapsodical flow, but a section of the audience became increasingly restless. Stronach became alarmed and after what I remember (perhaps falsely?) as only a few minutes gave the agreed sign, bringing Isaiah good-humouredly to a juddering halt, more or less mid paragraph.[6]

---

1 We have been unable to confirm this perhaps exaggerated claim, probably associated with Wagner's allegedly damaging effect on the classical tradition in music rather than with his anti-Semitism.

2 (Cecil) Maurice *Bowra (1898–1971), Kt 1951, classicist, academic administrator and wit.

3 Farah Pahlavi (b. 1938) née Diba, the French-educated daughter of an officer in the Imperial Iranian Armed Forces who had graduated at the elite French military academy of Saint-Cyr; m. 1959 Muhammad Reza Pahlavi (64/1) as his 3rd wife; styled Shahbanu ('the Lady Shah'), and from 1967 Empress of Iran.

4 Peter Wilfred Henry Brown (b. 1941), academic administrator; assistant secretary, SOAS, 1968–75; deputy secretary, BA, 1975–83, secretary 1983–2006.

5 David Brian Stronach (b. 1931), archaeologist; 1st director, British Institute of Persian Studies, Tehran, 1961–80; prof. of Near Eastern archaeology, Berkeley, 1981–2004.

6 Peter Brown to Nicholas Hall, 17 November 2013. Tariq Ali (97/3) wrote about this visit in his review of David Caute's *Isaac and Isaiah: The Covert Punishment of a Cold War Heretic* (New Haven and London, 2013), *Guardian*, 20 June 2013: '[IB] was at his happiest when close to power, an instinctive courtier, unless insulted or ignored. During the 1970s he was invited to Iran, then under the Shah, when dissidents were being hanged naked or toasted on racks by the hated secret police. He accepted. His fee was never disclosed, but the subject of his talk [...] irritated the empress Farah Pahlavi. He was barely halfway through when the empress signalled a factotum to bring her torture to an end and stop the lecture. Berlin later confided to a friend that it was as if he had been "stung by several wasps". But why had he gone in the first place?' The above editorial headnote provides the literal answer to Ali's rhetorical question: IB went on official business, and

The official reception afterwards proved more successful, and the Berlins, with Peter Brown and Max Mallowan,[1] then toured the major sites in Iran (plate 8), hosted by the Institute. Brown recalls IB 'making no concessions to the heat, in dark suit, and, in the car with the windows firmly closed, talking as only he did, mainly Oxford gossip'.[2] On his return to England in early November IB fell ill with atrial fibrillations, and then a form of hepatitis, which sent him to hospital for a fortnight.

TO HENRY HARDY

21 November 1977

Headington House

Dear Henry,

[...] You ask me whether I really rate my essays as low as I sometimes affect to do – believe me, it is no affectation. I do not believe in any great mine of potential talent in myself still unexploited. I do, indeed, believe that Aileen and Roger[3] and yourself overestimate my work: I think this must be because of the fervour with which I talk at times about things in which I am interested, rather more than the intrinsic value of the ideas themselves. I should like to think that I am wrong about this – nothing is nicer than praise by honest men – but I remain unshakeably convinced that I have all my life been overestimated.

So say what you will. I feel terrible about this: rather like the man who at some testimonial dinner was praised to the skies by the man who proposed his health. He gracefully acknowledged, with pleasure, all the handsome things that had been said about him, but said that there was perhaps one attribute of his which had not been mentioned by anyone and of which he felt proudest of all – his conspicuous modesty. I remember, too, although I was not present, that there was a famous Balliol dinner, at which praise was showered on the Master, Lord Lindsay,[4] who, in reply, among other things, after thanking everybody for everything, said that there was one thing that he had missed – nobody had spoken of a nice, honest chap called Sandy

so far from accepting a fee he later wrote to the BA to point out that, in his opinion, he had been undercharged for his personal expenses. He sent a cheque for the shortfall.
1 Max Edgar Lucien Mallowan (1904–78), Kt 1968, archaeologist; fellow, All Souls 1962–71; prof. of Western Asiatic archaeology, London, 1947–62; director, British School of Archaeology, Baghdad, 1947–61; president, British Institute of Persian Studies, Tehran, 1971–8.
2 loc. cit. (59/6).
3 Roger Neil Hausheer (b. 1945), Germanist and historian of ideas; St Catherine's modern languages 1965–9; Wolfson graduate student 1969–80, Charter Fellow 1991–2; taught at Oxford, Giessen, Bradford (lecturer in German 1980–2002) and elsewhere; later (since 2007) visiting prof., Montenegro at Podgorica; a friend, admirer and interpreter of IB, on whom he has written several pieces, including introductions to AC and PSM (the latter of which he co-edited with HH).
4 Alexander Dunlop Lindsay (1879–1952), 1st Baron Lindsay 1945, philosopher and Christian socialist; Master, Balliol, 1924–49; Principal, University College of North Staffordshire (Keele University 1962), 1949–52.

Lindsay. I don't want to be like that! Is that vanity? Perhaps. All I really want
said is that although even I recognise that some of my pieces are less good
than others, I do not think any of them begin to reach the level of some of
the writers I truly admire, e.g. Herzen, or Brandes[1] or Edmund Wilson, to
name only three men who had something new and important to say and
knew how to say it. So there.

Yours,

Isaiah

TO KYRIL FITZLYON[2]

6 December 1977

Headington House

Dear Kyril,

[…] You are right that the point you take up is of fundamental importance, because the problem is a contemporary one in a number of countries
and with regard to a number of governments.[3] You are perfectly right: when
I say that 'morally sensitive men' shied away from any kind of co-operation
with the Tsarist government, I do indeed mean the former of your two
alternatives – not objections to specific undertakings, but reluctance to be
involved, or even to support, governmental activities in any large and positive sense (of course I do not mean in the field of public health, let us say, or
the *zemstva*,[4] or teaching in schools or universities). What I mean is accepting
posts from the government or in politically important areas. Roughly what
Spanish liberals must have felt under the Franco regime[5] – liberals, and not
merely Communists or other extremists, or even socialists. When someone
like Madariaga,[6] who was certainly no leftist, emigrated from Spain after

1 Georg Morris Cohen Brandes (1842–1927), Danish literary theorist and critic; IB drew on his
  works in the preparation of his 1965 Mellon Lectures on 'Sources of Romantic Thought', published 1999 as RR.
2 Kyril *FitzLyon (b. 1910), diplomat and translator.
3 KF had written to IB, 29 November, about a point 'of fundamental importance' arising from IB's
  'Old Russia', *Guardian*, 24 November 1977, 14, a review of 2 books of photographs published in
  London 1977, Marvin Lyons, *Russia in Original Photographs, 1860–1920*, ed. Andrew Wheatcroft,
  and KF and Tatiana Browning (eds), *Before the Revolution: A View of Russia under the Last Tsar*:
  namely, whether 'morally sensitive men' (IB's phrase) were 'wrong to co-operate on the general
  level' with a government that they opposed, 'while withdrawing co-operation on particular
  issues'. The question related not only, historically, to the opponents of the Tsar in pre-1917 Russia,
  but also, Fitzlyon argued, to modern dissidents 'such as Sakharov in the Soviet Union or Shahak
  in Israel […], who] do co-operate with their governments on the general level, even if they refuse
  to co-operate with them in, or bitterly attack them for, acts of which they disapprove'.
4 The *zemstvo* (plural *zemstva*) is an elected local government council in Russia: the *zemstvo* system
  was established by Tsar Alexander II 1864.
5 The nationalist government of Generalissimo Francisco Franco y Bahamonde (1892–1975), dictator of Spain from 1939 until his death.
6 Salvador de Madariaga (1886–1978), Spanish diplomat and historian; King Alfonso XIII Prof. of
  Spanish, Oxford, and fellow, Exeter, 1928–31; Spanish ambassador to the US 1931, to France 1932–4;

occupying all those eminent positions, he did so because he could not collaborate in helping the Franco regime; this was surely true of a large number of enlightened persons in Imperial Russia [...].

You say that 'regime' means something new and transitory.[1] Surely not: when Tocqueville[2] speaks of the *Ancien Régime*[3] what this refers to is the centuries of the French monarchy. The word is much less used now, perhaps: it is mainly used not for new, but for old, established, traditional governments – the tsarist regime, the French monarchy. If people do not talk about the 'royal regime' in England, it is because the word 'regime' does connote something authoritarian, something repressive – there is an undoubtedly pejorative flavour to the word – which the citizens of this country or Scandinavia do not in fact feel about their governments, for the most part. I suspect that Persians of a certain kind might well use it for the political order in Iran, whether the present one or the old; and I admit that when people do talk about 'the Soviet regime' they wish, consciously or unconsciously, to transfer to the Soviet Union the kind of unfriendly, negative feeling which those who applied it to tsarism in fact, whether consciously or unconsciously, felt and wished to convey. It seems to me to connote something old, heavy, traditional, frozen.

Let me go on. You say that 'most men, whether morally sensitive or not, co-operate with the established order – tsarist or any other – however much they may criticise it, simply because they take it for granted and merge (or, perhaps, confuse) the two concepts of *government* and *country*'. To acquiesce is not to co-operate: 'inner emigration' – opting out – is *a* method of non-collaboration, condemned by 'resisters', but very different, surely, from co-operation? Then you mention Sakharov[4] and Shahak.[5] I should be inclined to deny this. The essence is not co-operation: Sakharov does more than criticise, he condemns Soviet practices. Shahak is close to thinking Israel a criminal state – he would certainly not accept a post in it (the main difference being, I suppose, that Sakharov was put out of his post whereas Shahak continues to be a professor at the Hebrew University – so far as one can see, unmolested by the authorities). Shahak would be outraged if you suggested

Spanish permanent delegate, League of Nations, 1931–6; after the outbreak of the Spanish Civil War 1936 he went into self-imposed exile, returning to Oxford, where he remained a staunch opponent of Francoism.

1 KF had written that he would find it easier to agree with IB's belief in the impossibility of 'morally sensitive men' co-operating with Tsarism if that 'had been a "regime" rather than an established social order. For to most minds the term "regime" conveys something new and transitory.'

2 Alexis Charles Henri Clérel de Tocqueville (1805–59), French historian, politician and political thinker; author of *De la démocratie en Amérique* (Paris, 1835–40) and *L'Ancien Régime et la Révolution* (Paris, 1856), a study of the society and politics of pre-revolutionary France.

3 'Old political system'.

4 Andrey Dmitrievich *Sakharov (1921–89), theoretical physicist and dissident.

5 Israel Shahak (1933–2001) né Himmelstaub, Polish-born Israeli chemist, political commentator and activist; lecturer, then prof. of chemistry, HUJ, 1963–90; a fierce critic of Israel's Palestinian policy and of Orthodox Judaism, and a leading figure in the Israel League for Human and Civil Rights (chair 1970–90).

to him that he was co-operating with the government: he certainly does *not* identify government and country. Nor, surely, does Sakharov. The Russians I speak of were patriotic enough – Sakharov is, and perhaps Shahak also (at least he believes in what he calls the 'tradition of Judaism' as a spiritual tradition – I suspect he has no use for either state or nation). These people think they do more good by staying in a country whose government, and indeed whose whole political structure, they abhor and regard as immoral, because (I think they would so justify this) they think they do more good by resisting from within than harm by making use of its public services or being members of at least some of its non-political institutions. I think that if you could prove to them that the state derives more benefit from their presence than their absence, they would be morally forced to say that emigration was preferable. [...]

Yours,

Isaiah

TO KYRIL FITZLYON

4 January 1978

Headington House

Dear Kyril,

[...] As for co-operation with the state, I really do disagree with you: acquiescence is not co-operation. Sakharov worked as a scientist in the Soviet Union because he is a patriot and it was a natural thing to do. When he convinced himself that it was an immoral government, he spoke out in a manner which, no one could doubt, would lead to some sort of repression. I do not think there is any valid sense of the word in which he could be said to co-operate with the regime. I think the same is true of Shahak – he will not emigrate because he probably thinks that it is his duty to denounce an evil government, as did the prophets of old. Some of the dissidents in Russia probably feel the same. Avvakum[1] did not seek to emigrate either, and no one could say that he collaborated, towards the end of his life, with the government of Tsar Alexis. The vast bulk of any population, whatever they may feel, set about their own business, which may in some cases be the government's business, and hope for the best. The historical role of the intelligentsia in Russia is precisely not to do that. Again, I do not in my turn wish to apportion praise or blame: I only wish to say that to live in a country and to some degree not disobey its laws is not to co-operate with it – unless one

---

1 Avvakum Petrov (*c.*1620–1682), Russian archpriest who led the 'Old Believers' in opposition to the reforms of the Russian Orthodox Church instituted by the Patriarch Nikon during the reign of Aleksey Mikhailovich Romanov, Tsar Alexis (1629–76; ruled 1645–76). Avvakum was imprisoned for 14 years, after which he was burned at the stake; his autobiography appeared in English as *The Life of the Archpriest Avvakum* (London, 1924).

thinks that all subversion from within is immoral as such, no matter what the government or the situation. Would you not have to say that Solzhenitsyn, before he was expelled, was collaborating with the regime? That all the dissidents, expelled or unexpelled, are? By just living there and willy-nilly obeying the laws of the land? That can surely not be right, otherwise the notion of co-operation loses meaning. [...]

Yours ever,

[unsigned: IB in hospital with possible hepatitis]   [...]

5 January 1978: publication of IB's Russian Thinkers, edited by HH and Aileen Kelly, with an introduction by Aileen Kelly.

TO BERNARD WILLIAMS

10 February 1978

Headington House

Dear Bernard

I ought to have written before, but, as you know, was physically incapacitated – and still am, but to a much lesser degree. I am now convinced that the virus was implanted in me in Persia (David Pears, naturally, has a parallel case of a pop painter, summoned to paint the Shah[1] and his family, who has suffered a similar fate) and is a perfectly appropriate punishment for meeting the Empress: had I actually met the Shah I might not have escaped with my life (I do see how comfortable metaphysical superstitions can be when science fails to produce a clear answer, as in my case).

But that is not the purpose of this letter. In the first place, let me tell you that I think your introduction to my philosophical works is a *heroic* act of friendship[2] – almost approximating to the sort of heroic martyrdom much discussed by Dummett and his friends – and really is further from my deserts than almost anything that has ever happened to me. [...]

Secondly, let me tell you that I am reading *Descartes*[3] with immense enjoyment. I thought I was not interested in him, but your book seems wonderful to me – I love learning about thinkers and their thoughts, and carry your book from room to room in Headington House, which is the only exercise I am permitted at the moment. [...]

1 Muhammad Reza Pahlavi (1919–80), Shah of Iran 1941–79, the last reigning monarch of the Iranian Pahlavi dynasty, brutally repressed political opponents, and was overthrown and exiled in the 1979 revolution that brought to power the theocracy of the Shiite Muslim leader Ayatollah Khomeini (109/6).

2 In his preface to CC, IB refers to 'this act of what I can only describe as heroic friendship' without specifying which friend he is referring to. This letter resolves any possible ambiguity.

3 Bernard Williams, *Descartes: The Project of Pure Enquiry* (Harmondsworth, 1978). René Descartes (1596–1650), French philosopher, mathematician and scientist, regarded by many as the father of modern philosophy.

Last night I listened to a scientist on Radio 4 who said how terrible I was and how marvellous Magee,[1] if only he were allowed to deliver a lecture himself: 'Every time Magee spoke, it all burst into flames', said Professor Laithwaite,[2] until I plunged the whole thing again into ghastly unintelligible patter. Very good for me (presumably).

Yours ever, with deep gratitude

Isaiah

TO SAMUEL AND MIRIAM SAMBURSKY[3]

3 March 1978

Headington House

Dear Shmuel, dear Miriam,

Thank you ever so much for your letters. It is delightful to receive such letters at any time, but particularly when one is in a slightly depressed state, from which, however, I am now proud to inform you that I have fully emerged. The nature of my ailment remains obscure: the doctors talk learnedly about this or that virus, but they are like physicians in Molière[4] or Shaw[5] (*The Doctor's Dilemma* still has some life in it – did you know that the hero was Marx's son-in-law?).[6] They will not confess that they simply do not know, and use Latin terms in a vain attempt to conceal their perfectly natural and excusable ignorance. However, they have behaved very decently to me – not given me pills or disagreeable treatment against unknown causes, but let nature do her work. I have a certain sympathy for my mother,[7] who was terrified of doctors and medicines all her life (not surgeons, oddly enough), and regarded

1 Bryan Edgar Magee (b. 1930), writer, philosopher and broadcaster; MP 1974–83 (Labour 1974–82, SDP 1982–3); a familiar figure on British television and radio from the 1970s (sometimes fronting his own series), he has published widely, including works on Schopenhauer and Wagner and volumes of autobiography. IB refers here to 'An Introduction to Philosophy', his interview with Magee on the 1st of the latter's *Men of Ideas* series, recorded 23 May 1976 (plate 5), and first aired on BBC2 TV 19 January 1978.

2 Eric Roberts Laithwaite (1921–97), prof. of heavy electrical engineering, Imperial College London, 1964–86; a well-known broadcaster on science, he reviewed Magee's interview of IB on BBC Radio 4's arts review programme, *Kaleidoscope*, 8 February.

3 Samuel (Hebrew 'Shmuel') Sambursky (1900–90), German-born Israeli scientist and historian; m. 1938 Miriam Grunstein/Greenstein (a 2nd marriage for both) (1911–89); physicist, HUJ, 1928–59; 1st director, Research Council of Israel, 1949–56; dean of the science faculty, HUJ, 1957–9; founded Institute for the History and Philosophy of Science 1959, prof. 1959–70.

4 Pseudonym of Jean Baptiste Poquelin (1622–73), French comic playwright, actor and director; *L'Amour médecin* (1665) portrays a handful of doctors, all charlatans, who invariably disagree over a given diagnosis.

5 George Bernard Shaw (1856–1950), Dublin-born playwright, essayist, critic and socialist; Nobel Prize in Literature 1925; among his plays was a satire on the medical profession, *The Doctor's Dilemma: A Tragedy* (1906).

6 Shaw used Edward Bibbins Aveling (1849–98), partner of Marx's daughter Eleanor 1884–98, as a model for a character in the play, the clever but financially and sexually unscrupulous Louis Dubedat.

7 (Mussa) Marie *Berlin (c.1880–1974), IB's mother.

taking an aspirin as a major risk, to be embarked on only in desperate situations, when the headache became too unbearable – and lived until the age
of 94, and died very peacefully. If I were not so colossally indolent, I should
mind my inactivity far more than I do. As it is, I secretly enjoy it – not having
to go to committees, deliver lectures, give appointments to notorious operators and bores is pure gain.

I was very sorry not to present his prize to Dodds.¹ I shall send you Freddie
Ayer's autobiography – the comparison with Dodds is to the advantage of ...
but I shall not anticipate your verdict. I had no idea that all his life Ayer was
constantly measuring himself against me – on the whole to his advantage,
I daresay rightly. He played no such part in my life – I don't think anyone has.
But it is a queer sensation to realise that one had, all unknowingly, played
a curious role throughout someone else's existence – not a wholly negative
one, by any means, but still, embarrassing because so totally unintended and
so unlike one's image of oneself. [...]

In the meanwhile, here we sit, hoping for reasonable behaviour by the
present leaders of Israel. There is an extraordinary contrast between the attitude of the British 'quality' media – The Times, the Guardian, the BBC, which
are on the whole critical and hostile, and deplore Israel's fatal obstinacy in
the face of Sadat's admirable initiatives – and the American press, the New
York Times, the European Times-Herald² etc., which remain sympathetic to
Israel and optimistic. I don't know if you saw a letter by Siegmund Warburg³
in The Times at the beginning of last week. The sentiments were such as we
all might agree with; nevertheless, my immediate, unreflected reaction was
that there was something terribly pompous and monomaniacal in lecturing
the state of Israel in the pages of The Times: whom was he addressing, whose
conduct did he intend to improve? He wrote as a spokesman of all the moderate Jews in the Diaspora, chiding the Israeli government for its chauvinism
and blindness – and this was naturally followed by a letter of strong support
by Anthony Nutting.⁴ If he had written to the Jerusalem Post, it might at least

1 IB's illness had prevented him from presenting the Duff Cooper prize for non-fiction to the
  eminent classicist Eric Robertson Dodds (1893–1979), Regius Prof. of Greek, Oxford, and student
  (i.e. fellow), Christ Church, 1936–60, for his autobiography Missing Persons (Oxford, 1977), which
  IB compares with A. J. Ayer's Part of My Life (49/9).
2 Presumably the International Herald Tribune.
3 Siegmund George Warburg (1902–82), Kt 1966, German-born British merchant banker of Jewish
  descent, played a crucial role in revolutionising post-war banking in the City of London; director, S. G. Warburg, 1946–69, president 1970–8, chair, advisory council, 1978–82. His letter, 'Israel's
  Stance in the Peace Talks', appeared 18 February 1978, 15d–e: 'there exists a great number of Jews
  both in Israel and abroad who acclaim President Sadat's initiative and advocate a positive and
  imaginative response to it by Israel' (15e).
4 (Harold) Anthony Nutting (1920–99), 3rd Bt 1972, Conservative politician and author, MP 1945–56,
  minister of state for foreign affairs 1954–6, resigned over Suez. His letter, 'Israeli Settlements',
  appeared 23 February 1978, 17f: 'No fair-minded person can fail to applaud the courage and
  wisdom of Sir Siegmund Warburg's letter [...]. President Sadat has offered co-existence: it is not
  too late for Mr Begin to steer Israel away from the holocaust.'

have stirred some debate. As it is, it was ultimately an apologetic letter: 'Do not believe that we are all blind nationalists; G. Schocken,[1] other Israelis, people like me, who are legion, are decent, liberal moderates; do not identify us with these terrible nationalists, set on a fatal course' etc. He intended, I think, to say the same to Sadat when they met in Paris, and was only held back by the fact that the others with him declined to accompany him if he proposed to embark on that kind of oration. All this, I need hardly tell you, is confidential, and I would not be sending it through the post if I was not in so feeble a condition at the moment, and consequently over-reckless. I wonder if you agree, or if you think I am being too conventionally reasonable about all this: I simply do not believe in preaching to sovereign states from abroad unless they perpetrate outrages – and then it does little good, but at least it is right to cry out. [...]

Much love from us both,
Isaiah

TO BERNARD WILLIAMS
21 March 1978

Headington House

Dear Bernard,

Let me tell you that your performance on the Magee show was far and away the best to date.[2] He told me that you had to do it twice – that is probably a fact about him rather than yourself or the 'performance' itself. I hope the original talk has not perished – the ur-dialogue is indispensable to future doctoral work. Comparison of sentences could make the fortune of more than one professor of the subject. You were the only performer to date who did not appear to be prearranged, pre-packed – everyone else seemed to be that, without exception. The lowest point was certainly Mr Barrett.[3] Freddie is not altogether wrong when he said that all he reported Heidegger[4] as saying was that (a) all men are mortal, and some are worried about it,

1 Gershom Gustav Schocken (1912–90), German-born Israeli journalist, writer and politician; editor of the liberal and independent daily newspaper Ha'aretz 1939–90; Progressive Party MK 1955–9.

2 Bernard Williams's talk with Bryan Magee in the Men of Ideas series, 'The Spell of Linguistic Philosophy', was broadcast on BBC2 TV 2 March. Magee interviewed fifteen leading philosophers for the series (all identified in this letter except Anthony Quinton and IB himself), which was published as Men of Ideas: Some Creators of Contemporary Philosophy (London, 1978), subsequently retitled Talking Philosophy: Dialogues with Fifteen Leading Philosophers (Oxford, 2001).

3 William Christopher Barrett (1913–92), prof. of philosophy, NYU, 1950–79; his episode of Men of Ideas, 'Heidegger and Modern Existentialism', went out 9 February.

4 Martin Heidegger (1889–1976), prof. of philosophy, Freiburg, 1928 (his students included Hannah Arendt and Herbert Marcuse); joined Nazi Party 1933; forbidden from teaching 1945, a proscription lifted 1951, though Heidegger continued to work alone; his major work, Sein und Zeit (Halle, 1927), was translated as Existence and Being ([London], 1949) and subsequently as Being and Time (Oxford, 1962).

(b) we did not choose our parents. I did not share the general impression of Marcuse's[1] overwhelming charm, and thought Hare[2] a caricature of an Oxford philosopher of a certain date, the leading Beckmesser[3] in his field. Loyalty prevents me from continuing with the list. I enjoyed Quine,[4] and since I do not crave for novelty, listened with pleasure both to Chuck[5] and to Freddie. I am all poised for Searle,[6] Chomsky[7] and Putnam[8] – all of whom I believe have something to say. I shall be sorry to miss Dworkin[9] and Iris – if I am well enough, we may go to Italy for ten days or so in April. We shall be glued to our radios, with news of the by then almost certain civil war, and be back just in time for the joy of listening to Gellner.[10] [...]

Yours ever,

Isaiah

1 Herbert Marcuse (1898–1979), German-born US philosopher and social theorist, prominent member of the influential Frankfurt School: 'a most intelligent and delightful man who correctly maintains that E. H. Carr has neither understanding of nor interest in ideas of any kind and should be prevented from writing about them. How could I dislike anyone who thought that?' (to Bertell Ollman, 18 December 1962, L3 136).

2 Richard Mervyn Hare (1919–2002), fellow and philosophy tutor, Balliol, 1947–66; White's Prof. of Moral Philosophy, Oxford, and fellow, CCC, 1966–83.

3 In Wagner's opera Die Meistersinger von Nürnberg (1868) Sixtus Beckmesser, the town clerk and a Meistersinger, is a comic creation epitomising pedantry and a narrow reliance on rules.

4 Willard van Orman Quine (1908–2000), leading US philosopher and logician; associate prof. of philosophy, Harvard, 1941–8, prof. 1948–56, Edgar Pierce Prof. of Philosophy 1956–78.

5 Charles Margrave ('Chuck') Taylor (b. 1931; plate 11), Canadian philosopher; prof. of philosophy, McGill, 1973–6; Chichele Prof. of Social and Political Theory, Oxford (IB's successor but one), and fellow, All Souls, 1976–81; prof. of political science and philosophy, McGill, 1982–98.

6 John Rogers Searle (b. 1932), US philosopher of mind and language; a Rhodes Scholar, he studied and taught at Oxford 1952–9; assistant prof., Berkeley, 1959–64, associate prof. 1964–7, prof. from 1967.

7 (Avram) Noam Chomsky (b. 1928), US linguist, public intellectual and political moralist, joined MIT 1955, Institute Prof. in the dept of modern languages and linguistics (subsequently linguistics and philosophy) 1976–2002; known more widely for his political activism than for his formative work in linguistics; his opposition to the Vietnam War made his name internationally.

8 Hilary Whitehall Putnam (b. 1926), US philosopher of science, mathematics, language and mind; prof. of philosophy, Harvard, 1965–2000; active in the 1960s US anti-war movement, and member of the Maoist Progressive Labor Party 1968–72; his interview, broadcast 6 April, was on the philosophy of science.

9 Ronald Myles ('Ronnie') Dworkin (1931–2013), US-born legal and political philosopher and public intellectual; prof. of jurisprudence, Oxford, and fellow, Univ., 1969–98.

10 Ernest André Gellner (1925–95), social philosopher and anthropologist; prof. of philosophy, LSE, 1962–84; William Wyse Prof. of Social Anthropology, Cambridge, 1984–93; author of Words and Things (London, 1959), a devastating critique of linguistic philosophy; not much admired by IB, who regarded him as 'an anthropologist with an unnecessary interest in philosophy' (to Ruth Chang, 1 January 1996).

IB's four-year term as President of the British Academy came to an end at the annual meeting of 29 June 1978, though in practice he held the reins for a little longer. One of his last tasks was to canvass opinion among members of the governing council, and four ex-Presidents, as to who should be his successor. By March 1978 three candidates had emerged, Helen Gardner,[1] Robert Blake[2] and Kenneth Dover,[3] and of these the latter had the most support. IB therefore planned to recommend him for the presidency at the annual meeting on 29 June: in theory an alternative candidate could be proposed, but in practice this never happened. Dover's nomination, and therefore certain election, were not welcomed by Hugh Trevor-Roper, who wrote to IB in protest: IB replied by pointing out that the President was effectively a figurehead who had much less influence than was supposed, and this was certainly his experience of the post; but it did not prove so for Dover, who in the first year of his presidency was embroiled in a controversy over whether Anthony Blunt[4] should remain a fellow of the Academy after being exposed as a Soviet spy. IB was relieved to have avoided this controversy, writing to Myron Gilmore[5] in July: 'thank God my British Academy job is almost over and I can relapse into a reasonable degree of indolence, which has always been my ideal since, I think, I was in the womb'.[6]

TO HUGH TREVOR-ROPER

24 March 1978

Headington House

Dear Hugh,

Thank you very much for your letter. You may well be right – I do not know Sir K. Dover at all well, indeed scarcely at all. I have not spoken to him on more than three, or at most four, occasions, and then for not more than ten minutes or so. [...] But having started the democratic process, there is, so far as I can see, no way of stopping it. Kenneth Dover got more votes than anyone else by about three heads. I have written to all the members of the BA Council to say that, unless I hear to the contrary, I shall assume that the Council wishes me to approach Dover, Helen [Gardner], Robert

1 Helen Louise Gardner (1908–86), DBE 1967, FBA 1958, fellow and English literature tutor, St Hilda's, 1942–66, reader in Renaissance English literature, Oxford, 1954–66; Merton Prof. of English Literature, Oxford, and fellow, LMH, 1966–75.
2 Robert Norman William Blake (1916–2003), life peer 1971, FBA 1967, historian, biographer of Disraeli; student (i.e. fellow) and politics tutor, Christ Church, 1947–68; Provost, Queen's, 1968–87; joint editor, *Dictionary of National Biography*, 1980–90.
3 Kenneth James Dover (1920–2010), Kt 1977, classicist; FBA 1966; fellow and classics tutor, Balliol, 1948–55; prof. of Greek, St Andrews, 1955–76; President, CCC, 1976–86; President, BA, 1978–81.
4 Anthony Frederick Blunt (1907–83), KCVO 1956–79; art historian and spy; surveyor, King's pictures 1945–52, Queen's pictures 1952–72; adviser, Queen's pictures and drawings, 1972–8; director, Courtauld Institute of Art, 1947–74.
5 Myron Piper Gilmore (1910–78), Renaissance scholar, prof. of history, Harvard, 1954–74, director, Harvard University Center for Italian Renaissance Studies, Villa I Tatti, Florence, 1964–73.
6 To Myron Gilmore, 12 July 1978.

[Blake] in this order, which corresponds to their relative popularity. I could, I suppose, have a 'run-off' in the French manner, but I suspect that if I did the result would be exactly the same. The opposition to both Helen and Robert is so great on the part of some people that, as often happens in such cases, a harmless person who has the smallest number of opponents gets in – that, I suspect, is how *I* came to be appointed.

You did, when we saw each other, suggest Herbert Hart, and even lightly mentioned the name of the Cornish poet,[1] but while the second is not to be seriously considered by rational men anxious to avoid public ridicule, the former would, of course, be very good indeed – and indeed, would, I think, be elected by acclamation, were it not that he is too old. [...] But do not repine! The influence of the President is smaller than you might suppose: apart from presiding over the Council and some committees, he has very few things in his gift – the annual speaker at the dinner and, at most, one appointment or two inside the Academy.

I promise to do my best to reinforce the new Council with stout-hearted and rational beings, of powerful personality, who will resist any aberrant figure. And, indeed, if your gloomy anticipations prove correct, this will pave the way to pre-eminent merit next time. As I told you when we met, since I shall be consulted by the new President, if I am alive, in 1982, I shall raise my voice most emphatically in favour of yourself. Remember that troughs create a demand for crests – this zigzag or see-saw will surely operate! [...]

Yours ever,

Isaiah

⟨Better burn this letter! I apprehend the fate of your filing cabinets – what will posterity make of the stimulus to this letter, and the indiscretions of which we shall be thought guilty – why *shd* posterity be titillated in this way? Even assuming that such trifles are thought rewarding, what right have they? What, as someone said in a similar context, have they done for *us*?⟩[2]

TO JACOB TALMON

28 April 1978

Headington House

Dear Yaacov,

[...] Of course I did not mean to say that one is not allowed to criticise

---

1 A. L. Rowse (26/6).

2 This joke is found in various forms, the earliest of which is given by Joseph Addison, who records 'an old Fellow of a Colledge' saying *'We are always doing something for posterity, but I would fain see posterity do something for us'*: *Spectator* 8 no. 583 (20 August 1714), [2]. The wit in question is Thomas Stafford (1641/2–1723), fellow, Magdalen, 1667–1723: *Remarks and Collections of Thomas Hearne* (Oxford, 1885–1921) viii, ed. under the superintendence of the committee of the Oxford Historical Society, entry for 27 February 1722/3, 50 (*'What good will Posterity do for us?'*).

a sovereign state,[1] however harshly, if one feels like it, even unjustifiably. I have no such Bismarckian feelings,[2] and the Hegelian state is anathema to me. I meant something else: critics of the central policies of a country, if they live abroad, whether they are citizens or otherwise connected, usually only do this if they are deeply provoked; that is, if they think that the policies are shameful, or betray the central values of a nation which mean something to the critics; that is, unless the critics are indifferent to the country and simply do it because they feel like it or because they are in fact hostile to the country in question. Americans did it in the case of the Vietnam war, and one could understand them; even they only did it inside America; those who did it from abroad were not listened to, carried little weight. In the case, however, of Israel, Jews sometimes feel – particularly if they feel self-important – that it is a veritable enterprise to which they are contributors, and that this alone gives them a right to give advice and complain publicly, in the newspapers of the countries in which they live, if their advice is not followed; and this irritates me.

This is all I meant by saying that Israel was a sovereign state – it is not simply the headquarters of a world Zionist organisation. I do not accept Ben-Gurion's[3] view of *Auslandsjuden*[4] as having specific obligations to Israel. If they choose to live in the Diaspora, they are perfectly entitled to their choice: they may be criticised by Israelis or Zionists for choosing a mode of life which is attacked as morally or socially or politically inferior, of bartering full national existence for comfort, security or money – this is sometimes just and sometimes unjust, but all men are liable to criticism from all other men, and this is as it should be. But to denounce the policies of Israel's present government, which, like you, I also think mistaken and dangerous, and in the long run suicidal, and that in the pages of a journal – the London *Times* – which is anti-Israel as part of a set policy, seems to me unhelpful and merely likely to strengthen the hand of the enemies of the state: it did not surprise me when virtually the only supporter of Sir Siegmund turned out to be Antony Nutting, a friend of the PLO.

I was afraid that Zionists might write letters and accuse Sir Siegmund of 'disloyalty', and that too, would have been bad – he owes no loyalty to Israel:

---

1 In the letter (4 April 1978) to which IB is replying, JT had written: 'You say that you do not feel self-righteous enough […] to join busybodies in giving advice to a sovereign state. […] The situation is crying out for wise, tactful, but firm intervention by experienced, personally disinterested and influential people. One thing is to recoil from stepping in where angels fear to tread, another to invoke the sacredness and inviolability of the Hegelian state.'

2 Otto Eduard Leopold von Bismarck (1815–98), Duke of Lauenburg, Prussian statesman, chancellor of the German Empire 1871–90 (the 'Iron Chancellor'), architect of German unity; he was a fierce champion of the German state against its critics, and IB was highly critical of Hegel's similarly authoritarian view of the state in FIB, referring to 'the celebration of the authority and the power and the greatness of the state as against the whims or individual inclinations of this or that citizen or subject' (102).

3 David *Ben-Gurion (1886–1973), 1st prime minister, Israel.

4 'Jews living abroad'.

at best, devotion to it, which in fact, although he said that he had always been a friend of that country, was very much not the case in 1949 when I crossed the ocean on the same boat and he denounced Israel's war of independence as wickedly anti-British, in a bitter argument with a fellow banker called Kramarsky.[1] Since then he has greatly changed his views, and is a follower of Nahum Goldmann.[2] But I have a feeling that when Israel [behaves] badly he is indignant, and even, perhaps, feels ashamed, but is not upset as one is when one is anxious for the state of someone or something one loves and is emotionally identified with. I do not begin to deny his right to speak out if he chooses, but I cannot help feeling that there is an element here of the second son in the Haggadah – ' "What is this activity that you are engaged upon?" – you and not we'[3] – and my own attitude is correspondingly affected.

It is another matter if Raymond Aron,[4] who is a professional commentator, and expected to pronounce on all the central questions of the day, speaks out; and I need hardly tell you that the protest of the 30,000 in Tel Aviv delighted me;[5] so did the manifesto of the New York intellectuals,[6] who by no stretch of the imagination could be regarded as dedicated to abstract liberal principles without emotional ties to Israel; and if a similar manifesto were to be drafted in England (I have not seen the American one) in the name of genuinely pro-Israel academics and intellectuals, I should be ready to support it; but I suspect that in England there is no 'intelligentsia' as there is in New York or Chicago, nor a blindly loyal instrument of any Israeli government, such as appears – or until today appeared – to exist in the United States. [...]

So, as far as I can see, there is no real disagreement between us, not even

1 Siegfried Kramarsky (1893–1961), German-born NY banker, philanthropist, art collector and Zionist; chair 1955–61 of the advisory committee of Hadassah, the national women's Zionist organisation, of which his wife, Lola, was president 1960–4.
2 Nahum Goldmann (1895–1982), Lithuanian-born German-educated Zionist and Jewish leader, a leading figure in the establishment of the World Jewish Congress 1936, acting presdeint 1949–51, president 1951–77; president, World Zionist Organization, 1956–68: subject of a memoir in PI3. 'A man of strong independent views he clashed many times with the Israeli governments, whom he often accused of not adopting more flexible and imaginative policies towards the Palestinian Arabs and the Arab states generally': 'Dr Nahum Goldmann', obituary, Times, 31 August 1982, 10f–h at 10f.
3 In the Haggadah, the Hebrew text of the Passover Seder, this question about the Passover night's activities is asked by the wicked son: by saying 'you' and not 'we' he deliberately distances himself from the community.
4 Raymond Aron (1905–83), French sociologist, political philosopher, journalist and author; columnist, Figaro, 1947–83; prof. of sociology, Sorbonne, 1956–68.
5 c.40,000 Israelis took to the streets of Tel Aviv 1 April 1978 to urge their government to hasten the achievement of peace: the demonstration was organised by Peace Now, which had staged a much smaller demonstration in Jerusalem 2 days earlier.
6 A group of 36 US Jews, including 'rabbis, scholars, writers and community leaders', among them the Nobel laureate Saul Bellow, sent a message of support 20 April 1978 to the organisers of the Peace Now (137/5) protest in Tel Aviv earlier that month (previous note). They declared themselves 'lifelong friends of Israel': 'It is because of our commitment that we are disturbed by the Begin Government's response to President Sadat's peace initiative.' Linda Charlton, '36 Jews in US Applaud Israelis Who Urged Flexibility on Peace', NYT, 21 April 1978, A1, A6 at A1.

an apparent one. I think you genuinely misunderstood my use of 'sovereign state' as being an expression of awe before this super-individual, organic expression of the World Spirit. I need not tell you that those are not my sentiments. [...]

Yours ever,
Isaiah

TO ARTHUR SCHLESINGER

2 May 1978

Headington House

Dear Arthur

Thank you ever so much for your letter of 20 March, which I enjoyed very much indeed, particularly the news of Prich.[1] I am distressed about his blindness, it gives me fearful guilt, I ought to go and see him or write to him or something – and yet I do not know what to say, our last meeting was so awkward, and he constantly suspects me of doing things out of compassion and not affection. I will try and think of a method of approach.

We are in a peculiar political position: all the polls indicate that the Conservatives will win, for no better reason than the general systolic system of ups and downs, action and reaction (what is the Marxist dialectic doing?). Yet it is plain that the Conservative team is dim to a degree: the voters have never heard of half of them – Heath[2] and Mrs Thatcher mean something to the voters, but the shadow cabinet in general, virtually nothing at all, and rightly so. I wish David Harlech[3] and Roy Jenkins[4] were not quite such shadowy figures themselves by now: the former, at least, retired from genuinely active politics by his own wish; but Roy, I think, made a genuine mistake – I think if he had hung on, even if he had harried the present government somewhat from the back benches, he would have had a better chance of

1 Ed(ward) Fretwell Prichard, Jr ('Prich') (1915–84), Kentuckian New Deal lawyer with whom IB briefly shared a house in Washington 1943; convicted 1949 of ballot-stuffing in a senatorial election in his home state, Prichard resurrected his reputation as a champion of higher education, and towards the end of his life bravely bore the afflictions of kidney failure and blindness.
2 Edward Richard George ('Ted') Heath (1916–2005), KG 1992, Conservative MP 1950–2001; leader, Opposition, 1965–70; prime minister 1970–4, taking Britain into the EEC 1973; again leader, Opposition, 1974–5; ousted as party leader by Margaret Thatcher, February 1975, thereafter holding no government office.
3 (William) David Ormsby-Gore (1918–85), 5th Baron Harlech 1964, Conservative MP 1950–61; UK ambassador to Washington 1961–5, where he enjoyed a particularly close relationship with JFK; deputy leader, Conservative Party, Lords, 1966–7, but soon resigned, having lost any appetite for front-line politics; founder chair of Harlech Television (HTV) from 1967.
4 Roy Harris Jenkins (1920–2003), life peer 1989, OM 1993, politician and author; MP (Labour) 1948–76, (SDP) 1982–7, Home Secretary 1974–6; soundly beaten in the 1976 Labour leadership contest, he resigned from government to become President, European Commission, 1977–81; prime mover behind the formation of the centrist SDP 1981, and its 1st leader 1982–3; chancellor, Oxford, 1987–2003.

returning to real political activity than he now seems to me to have. But somewhere there is a lack of that minimum will to power which any successful politician must surely have, some surrender to social life and comfort, the gentlemanly existence and a sane and moderate view of the political and economic scene, without the risks and the heat and the in-fighting which are, perhaps, required for genuine effectiveness. The doughnut is of the highest order of consistency and suitability to the palate of the most demanding, but there is just not enough jam at the centre. I think this was always so. There is no lack of ambition, only of willpower to satisfy it. [...]

Let us turn to a more serious and sadder subject. Is it really true that Nicolas died of medical errors? I think that perhaps Dominique, who stayed here and talked about all this, it seemed to me, very sanely and calmly, is right when she said that Nicolas had lost all desire to live; perhaps as a result of the CIA/*Encounter* row,[1] he found himself offside, as it were, bombinating in a void,[2] without a specific function, with only vague negotiations about this or that musical festival. The Congress of Cultural Freedom kept him going, and after it collapsed he only had his personal friends, and this was not quite enough – and therefore he could not in any case have lasted long. This is melancholy, and may be true – what do you think? I had a heart-warming and rather rending letter from Avis[3] which conveyed the impression that doctors had doomed him. Perhaps it does not matter now. I wrote a little piece about him in the London *Times* because I was sure that nobody else would, and to my astonishment they printed it almost at once.[4] He leaves a deep gap in my life; I really was very attached to him. He was exhausting company, of course, but his warmth, imagination, profound inner independence and what I can only call the sad nobility of a man in permanent exile – he was not cosmopolitan, and certainly [not] gallicised or americanised or in any way wishing to throw roots in any foreign land – but, like his more gifted, far less sympathetic cousin Vladimir,[5] an aristocrat in exile with bags permanently packed to return to his native land, which he knew he would never reach, and therefore clinging to every genuine fragment of it, which to some extent I represented, and, oddly enough, Russian Jews in Israel, where he once told

1 L3 432/1.
2 The phrase is from Rabelais, *Gargantua and Pantagruel* 2. 7, where the title of one of 'the fine books in the library of St Victor' is given as *A Most Subtle Question, Whether a Chimera Bombinating in the Void [in vacuo bombinans] Can Dine on Second Intentions.* 'Bombinans' is a Rabelaisian coinage, apparently based on Latin *bombilare*, to buzz.
3 Avis Howard Bohlen (1912–81) née Thayer, widow of IB's close friend US diplomat Charles 'Chip' Bohlen (156/3).
4 It is not clear whether IB realised that his name had by now for a long time been seen as one to conjure with.
5 Vladimir Vladimirovich Nabokov (1899–1977), novelist, born to a wealthy family in St Petersburg, 1st cousin of Nicolas Nabokov, left Russia with his family 1919; lived in Europe before moving to the US 1940; naturalised 1945; prof. of Russian literature, Cornell, 1948–59; best known for his novel *Lolita* (Paris, 1955).

me he alone felt comfortable, because he could talk to these people who talked in a language totally familiar to him, even when they were comical bourgeois, without any [misunderstanding?], and made him feel at home.[1]

Last week I went to lunch with R. Grierson[2] to meet the Harrimans.[3] He is fantastically preserved, and not even very deaf. As is the American custom, he was asked to address the table on the present state of affairs, and did so, very nicely, in the presence of E. Heath and small fry like Aline and me and some lady from Harvard and I cannot now remember who else. He defended Carter, but complained that he took nobody's advice, and having been elected on an anti-Washington ticket he found it difficult to come to terms with the bogey. He said that the Soviet Union had no intention of making war because it did not want atom bombs to fall on its surface, and that Brzezinski[4] was utterly wrong about all that; that what the Soviet Union was doing in the horn of Africa was highly undesirable,[5] but that the United States was not prepared to do anything about that because they left that to the British, who must take the initiative in this matter, which is clearly not going to happen, if only because of lack of means. When told that, Averell shrugged his shoulders. I heard Macmillan about a week before suddenly burst forth at a dinner in Oxford about what a nightmare it was to have to live through the same ghastly history once again: appeasement in the 1930s, when he occasionally asked himself if he was mad, or if Baldwin and Chamberlain were – or perhaps they were right.[6] Sam Hoare,[7] after all, was an intelligent

1 For once IB's sentence fails to construe.
2 Ronald Hugh Grierson (1921–2014) né Rolf Hans Griessmann, Kt 1990, German Jewish émigré banker and public servant; director, S. G. Warburg & Co., 1958–68, 1980–6; vice chair, General Electric Co., 1968–91.
3 (William) Averell Harriman (1891–1986), US politician, businessman and diplomat, heir to a rail-road fortune, held numerous appointments under Democrat administrations from Roosevelt to Johnson; US ambassador to the USSR 1943–6, to Great Britain April–October 1946; ambassador at large 1961, 1965–9; m. 1971 his 3rd wife (as her 3rd husband) Pamela Beryl (1920–97) née Digby, who became a Democratic Party fundraiser and activist, and President Clinton's ambassador to France 1993–7.
4 Zbigniew Kazimierz Brzezinski (b. 1928), Warsaw-born national security adviser to President Carter 1977–81; regarded Soviet policy in the Horn of Africa (next note) as a direct threat to US interests, and to balance this advocated completion of the diplomatic rapprochement with China begun under Nixon.
5 During the Ethio-Somali War of July 1977 to March 1978 (also known as the Ogaden War) the USSR supplied substantial military aid to Ethiopia, which proved decisive in repelling the Somali invasion of the disputed Ogaden region in the east of that country. In response to the build-up of Soviet arms and Cuban troops in Ethiopia, the US gave military aid to Somalia, a country that had previously been in the Soviet orbit: a notable example of the Cold War being fought by proxy.
6 Stanley Baldwin (1867–1947), 1st Earl Baldwin of Bewdley 1937, prime minister 1923–4, 1924–9, 1935–7, was succeeded by (Arthur) Neville Chamberlain (1869–1940), prime minister 1937–40; they were 2 of the 15 politicians identified by Michael Foot, Peter Howard and Frank Owen (under the collective pseudonym 'Cato') in Guilty Men (London, 1940) as the principal architects of appeasement.
7 Sir Samuel John Gurney Hoare (1880–1959), 1st Viscount Templewood 1944, Conservative polit-ician; another of the Guilty Men (previous note), he resigned as foreign secretary December 1935

man and he believed that an arrangement with the Germans was possible – perhaps he, Macmillan, and his friends were having nightmares, not seeing reality straight, but they turned out to be right. Once again, appeasement was in full swing, this time of the Russians, and the Russians could and should be stopped in Africa, but [...] the other side could only come through South Africa, which was taboo, a moral leper; therefore this was precluded, so the Russians were bound to win, against no resistance. Averell does not believe this at all, nor in the end (I add pompously) do I.

What on earth is George Kennan at?*[1] Why does he think that these tired old men in the Kremlin only want a reasonable degree of security, and why does he think that in that case Angola or Ethiopia are so important to them? Reluctantly, I find that I vote with Pipes,[2] without enthusiasm. Of course, you can say that Soviet policy has always been defensive, but that defence in their eyes consists in occupying positions before the enemy does so, and that the frontiers of the Soviet Union are not secure, so long as combinations of strength against it are in principle possible. This form of defensiveness does not stop until all possible sources of danger have been liquidated – not in the name of ideology or the happiness of mankind, purely pre-emptively.

Mistaken and dangerous though I think Mr Begin's policies to be (I own to a personal loathing of him ever since 1946–7 – my hatred of terrorism has become absolute – and yet, when I used to read about the Russian terrorists in the 1880s and 1890s[3] I used to think that ...), I understand this rather better. It is not true to say that in these days of atomic weapons, no frontiers are all that important, that security is unobtainable when nuclear war is a threat, etc. I do not believe that, in the case of small countries, nuclear war is a threat. I do not believe that, despite all the Cassandras, there will be a major conflict in this century; not, at least, until the Chinese are ready. But that wars can occur with conventional weapons which do not threaten the world order, and that small countries are in danger of that, I do believe. The danger to

when the terms of the Hoare–Laval Pact with the French prime minister Pierre Laval, designed to appease Mussolini, were made public.

1 Kennan's *The Cloud of Danger: Current Realities of American Foreign Policy* (Boston, 1977; London, 1978) had recently appeared: 'Kennan's sad new book perfectly portrays a fashionable post-Vietnam mood about foreign affairs. Exhausted, disillusioned, and nearly without hope, Kennan says "Goodbye to All That". [...] In dealing with the Soviet Union, Kennan would have us apply diplomatic persuasion and the power of a good example rather than deterrent military strength. The goal of our efforts, he urges, should be to coax that country away from paranoid fears of encirclement.' Eugene V. Rostow, 'Searching for Kennan's Grand Design', *Yale Law Journal* 87 (1978), 1527–48 at 1529.

2 Richard Edgar Pipes (b. 1923), Polish-born US historian and Russian specialist; Frank B. Baird, Jr, Prof. of History, Harvard, 1958–96 (director, Russian Research Center, 1968–73); Reagan's appointee as adviser on East European and Soviet affairs, National Security Council, 1981–2. A hard-line anti-Communist, he regarded détente as 'a foreign policy based on ignorance of one's antagonist and therefore inherently inept': *US–Soviet Relations in the Era of Détente* (Boulder, CO, 1981), xv.

3 Narodnaya volya (The People's Will), a Russian revolutionary terrorist organisation responsible for the assassination of Tsar Alexander II 1881.

the Israelis comes obviously from the Arabs, supported by various Soviet-supplied Cubans, not from starting a world war on the field of Armageddon, where the Kings of Israel kept their horses. Israeli policy is plainly suicidal, simply because they cannot govern a million and a half Arabs, under whatever arrangements, without being duly blown up, as the Czechs were by the Sudets.[1] So they must retreat, in sheer self-interest, not to please the UN or the great powers; but so long as Begin is there, they won't: he resembles de Valera[2] more than anyone else that I can think of, and there is nobody in the world less likely, it seems to me, to begin to engage Mr Carter's sympathies, or, indeed, anyone's but the Poles', whose more old-fashioned generals (of Pilsudski's day)[3] he seems to me to model himself on. If one has to choose between fanatics and political operators, I should unhesitatingly choose the latter, and that is the only choice in Israel at present, it seems to me. Sad but true. Perhaps it is true of most countries. Having reached this sublime thought, I must stop. But not before telling you how ashamed I feel that you should have been asked to produce a blurb for my Russian book[4] – you should not have done it. [...]

Yours ever & ever

Isaiah

⟨*Secretly I have *never* thought his ideas on Russia bore on reality: it was, in all its shyings to & fro, half a private fantasy. But *don't*, on pain of I don't know what, *reveal* to anyone this heretical thought!⟩

---

1 sc. Sudeten Germans.
2 Éamon (né Edward George) de Valera (1882–1975), Irish statesman, one of the foremost figures in the struggle for independence from Britain; Taoiseach (prime minister) 1937–48, 1951–4, 1957–9, President 1959–73; the comparison with Begin indicates IB's view of de Valera as a fanatical and narrow nationalist, a political monist of the sort he could not abide; see L2 691.
3 Jósef Klemens Piłsudski (1867–1935), Polish general and statesman; effectively dictator of Poland 1926–35.
4 RT (64); AS's endorsement read 'The most brilliant and engaging intellect of our time'.

EXPLAINING

'Retirement'

1978–1997

I do not at all wish to die: I am full of curiosity.

To Arthur Schlesinger, 12 July 1978

TO ARTHUR SCHLESINGER

12 July 1978

Headington House

Dear Arthur,

Indeed I received your letter about Nicolas's death – I had some inkling that this was what must have happened, although Dominique loyally more than half concealed it.[1] I think that she thought that he would not live long anyway: he had lost the desire to live – was visibly declining – and she did not want to make too much fuss about something which she in any case regarded as inevitable, although I may not be doing her justice. But it is a shocking story all the same. Iatrogenic death is something which occasionally terrifies me too. I do not really mind dying very much – do you? Pain I am afraid of, but death not much. On the other hand, I do not at all wish to die: I am full of curiosity. I have no wish to act; I am a natural observer – unkind persons might say voyeur – of history; but I simply long to know what happens next. What will happen to the Soviet Union, what to China, what to Israel? How will it all end? Who will do what? I want to know about the twenty-second and twenty-third centuries, and far beyond that – not all time and all existence, but very large portions of it, both the *grandes lignes* and individuals' lives. That is why I find Tolstoy so sympathetic as a novelist, and, indeed, as involved in a desperate attempt to explain what it is that he is trying to do when he knows that it is, according to his own theory, irrational and in any case impossible.

Your piece on Nicolas[2] is excellent. Even more so is your piece on Solzhenitsyn.[3] He is all that you say. But not very remote from George Kennan, as far as I can see. The mixture of despair of materialism, desire to retract oneself into one's own special calling – these in a minor measure are George's too, are they not? In any case, you have got Solzhenitsyn absolutely right. His gifts, his courage, his immense effect are undeniable, and an asset to the human race: he seems to be the only individual who has ever succeeded in inflicting genuine damage on the Soviet regime – nobody else has done it, even in a small measure. Because he wrote what he wrote, all kinds of unknown folk – peasants in Italy, workers in France, probably downtrodden peons in Latin America, Arabs, Indians etc. – are all dimly aware that terrible things go on inside the Soviet Union, and that is why Communist parties have to put on Euro-Communist guises, or perhaps genuinely deviate somewhat; why even orthodox Communist parties have to explain that while their ideals are still impeccably Marxist, yet they wish to have nothing to do

1 AS had written to IB (21 May) that Nabokov had succumbed to a fever soon after undergoing routine prostate surgery. According to Nabokov's widow, Dominique, his elderly doctor had forgotten to prescribe post-operative antibiotics: 'I have no doubt', AS wrote, 'that Nicholas was killed by his physician's carelessness.'

2 An obituary of Nicolas Nabokov published in the *Century Yearbook: 1979* (NY, 1979), 271–3.

3 'The Solzhenitsyn We Refuse to See', *Washington Post*, 25 June 1978, D1, D4.

with concentration camps, repression etc.; why M. Elleinstein[1] has to associate himself with denunciations of the latest Soviet trials, and so on. It is an extraordinary achievement: it could only have been done by someone who was not a member of the intelligentsia but was obviously of proletarian origin and had been to a camp himself, and was not a Jew, not an intellectual, not a Westerniser, etc. Of course, Sakharov is my man, as he is, I am sure, yours: that is the authentic noble liberal voice, very like Herzen's – everything he says seems to me true, unanswerable and more simply and better put, braver and more moving, than any other voice in the world today.

As for Solzhenitsyn, he is, so far as I can see, much more like the seventeenth-century schismatics, to whom Peter the Great[2] was an evil ruler, tsar of a kingdom organised by Satan, which had to be, if not destroyed, at any rate resisted at all costs, and destroyed if possible. All those early eighteenth-century followers of the Archpriest Avvakum, who regularly burnt themselves rather than submit to Peter's proscription or his tax-gatherers, were made of the same stuff as Solzhenitsyn is now. There is something spiritually grand and terrifying about that. But he is to me a sort of early Soviet man turned inside out – the mirror image of a fanatical Communist of earlier days, who knows the answer, who will stop at nothing to convert people to it, who thinks that every means is justified if the sacred end is to be brought about, save that his end is at least capable of being respected by theocrats (of whom you and I do not think well), while in the Soviet Union today there are no ends except self-perpetuation and survival, so far as I can see. There may be faithful Communists in Romania, Yugoslavia, Peru, and for all I know East Germany, certainly Japan, maybe even in America and England – none in the Soviet Union in the sense that none of them believe that after the seas of blood some glorious consummation can in principle be reached. Not even fanatics – what more terrifying condemnation can the rulers of a nation be guilty of?

[…] Do telephone immediately you touch the soil of Italy – as Diana Cooper[3] used to say 'First the loo, then telephone me.' She is marvellous still – I have never seen anything like it – most beautiful, exquisitely preserved; aged eighty-six, I should say; perhaps a little too white, too frail in some of her movements, but a monument to a culture which, whatever else may be said against it, had plenty of spirit and appetite for life. She goes to every party she is asked to and trembles nervously before it – like me before delivering a lecture. As Raymond

1 Jean Elleinstein (1921–2002), French historian; lecturer, Poitiers, 1969–89; a long-standing member of the French CP, he fell from favour in the 1970s after criticising the rigidity of its leadership.
2 Petr Alekseevich Romanov (1672–1725), Peter I ('the Great'), Tsar of Russia 1682–1725 (jointly with his half-brother Ivan until 1689), regarded as the creator of modern Russia; in modernising society he subordinated the Church and continued the persecution of the schismatics (319/2) begun in the reign of Tsar Alexis (63/1).
3 Diana Olivia Winifred Maud Cooper (1893–1986) née (Lady Diana) Manners, famous in Edwardian society for her beauty, was a highly successful actress, society hostess and autobiographer. When her husband was created Lord Norwich 1952 she retained the style 'Lady Diana Cooper'.

Asquith[1] once said about her, 'She has no heart, but her brain is in the right place.'[2] That is perhaps a little too harsh – I think there is a heart there, myself – but you see what I mean. Anyway, she is particularly super-admirable. [...]
⟨Fondest love to Alexandra⟩
Yours ever,
   Isaiah

7 September 1978: publication of IB's Concepts and Categories: Philosophical Essays, *edited by HH, with an introduction by Bernard Williams.*

TO ANTHONY STORR[3]

29 September 1978

Headington House

Dear Storr, ⟨– am I allowed to call you Anthony?⟩

Thank you ever so much for sending me your lecture on Newton.[4] I read it with the greatest pleasure and agreement. Of course Manuel[5] goes too far – he is over-exuberant, enslaved by Erikson,[6] and goes overboard. How could any serious person, even the most fanatical Freudian or Eriksonian, believe that deprivation and lack of love would by itself produce rejection of the notion of action at a distance and the invocation of ether? The idea that causality or gravitation is a kind of pushing or pulling, and that this entails contact between bodies, is a common-sense notion, and the contrary of this – however valid in fact – seems counter-intuitive. Nobody, so far as I know, questioned Newton's conclusions about this, whether or not they were deprived of parental love at an early age (am I talking like a philistine?). As for self-depreciation, I wonder: I received a full measure of parental love at all times – my father[7] died when I was forty-four, my mother twenty years later; yet every line I have ever written and every lecture I have ever delivered seems to me of very little or no value.

1 Raymond Asquith (1878–1916), eldest child of H. H. Asquith; scholar, lawyer, prospective Liberal candidate and wit; died of wounds at the Somme, 15 September 1916.
2 Attributed to Patrick Houston Shaw-Stewart (1888–1917) at L3 12.
3 (Charles) Anthony Storr (1920–2001), psychiatrist, author, broadcaster; clinical lecturer in psychiatry, Oxford, 1974–84; fellow, Green, 1979–84.
4 Untraced, but evidently concerned with the psychological roots of scientific genius, in particular that of the natural philosopher and mathematician Isaac Newton (1642–1727), Kt 1705. AS develops this subject in *The School of Genius* (London, 1988).
5 Frank Edward Manuel (1910–2003), intellectual historian noted for his work on utopian thought; Alfred and Viola Hart University Prof., Brandeis, 1977–86; author of (inter alia) *A Portrait of Isaac Newton* (Cambridge, Mass., 1968), which argues that we can discern psychoanalytically relevant features of Newton's life in many of his scientific ideas. For instance, Manuel maintains that, deprived of love – an emotion that might be said to act at a distance – and distrusting it, Newton also distrusted the action at a distance that seemed to be part of his theory of gravity, and was led to consider the idea that a medium such as ether might be invoked to transmit gravitational force.
6 Erik Homburger Erikson (1902–94), German-born US developmental psychologist and psychoanalyst; prof. of human development and lecturer in psychiatry, Harvard, 1960–70; IB thought well of his *Young Man Luther: A Study in Psychoanalysis and History* (London, 1958) (L3 579).
7 Mendel Borisovich *Berlin (1884–1953), timber trader, IB's father.

After every lecture I feel a sense of shame, which seems equal on all occasions; and as some of my lectures must be worse than others, while the degree of shame seems constant, this is no doubt a neurotic symptom.

So withdrawal of parental love cannot be a necessary cause of this condition. Remoteness, a relative absence of intimate personal relationships, is, as I think you show, a genuine ingredient of certain types of genius. It is certainly true of Einstein,[1] who was himself aware of his absence of contact with human beings; although in his case it certainly did not take the form of a desire for power or glory. Still, I am sure that Popper[2] is wrong to dismiss psychopathology in this regard: I am sure you are right about that. The withdrawn quality, a certain inhumanity, uncosiness, of the scientists of genius I have met – Bohr (for all his humane sentiments), Einstein, von Neumann, Dirac; even such people as Jack Haldane, for all his ebullience, or R. Oppenheimer – is very marked.[3] This applies far more to abstract, conceptual thinkers than to experimentalists, I suspect: it applies, indeed, to Keynes[4] himself and to the philosophers you list – Russell pre-eminently. I suspect that mathematicians and physicists and certain types of philosophers, especially logicians, have this far more than biologists or physiologists: abstract thinkers rather than those intent on curing the ills of the body or mind – Florey,[5] or Lister,[6] or Abraham[7] (cephalosporin) or Pasteur[8] or Alan Hodgkin.[9]

1 Albert Einstein (1879–1955), German theoretical physicist famous for the development of relativity theory; Nobel Prize in Physics 1921.

2 Karl Raimund Popper (1902–94), Kt 1965, Austrian-born philosopher of science; senior lecturer in philosophy, Canterbury University College, Christchurch, New Zealand, 1937–45; reader in logic and scientific method, LSE, 1945–9, prof. 1949–69.

3 Niels Henrik David Bohr (1885–1962), Danish physicist, Nobel Prize in Physics 1922 for his work on the structure of atoms; John (né János Lajos) von Neumann (1903–57), Hungarian-born US mathematician, pioneer of game theory and computing; Paul Adrien Maurice Dirac (1902–84), British theoretical physicist, Nobel Prize in Physics 1933 with Erwin Schrödinger for their discovery of new productive forms of atomic theory; John Burdon Sanderson ('JBS' / 'Jack') Haldane (1892–1964), geneticist, biometrician, philosopher and populariser of science; (Julius) Robert Oppenheimer (1904–67), US theoretical physicist, director 1943–5 of the Los Alamos laboratory in New Mexico, where he led the 'Manhattan Project', which developed the atomic bomb.

4 John Maynard Keynes (1883–1946), 1st Baron Keynes 1942, arguably the most influential economist of the C20th; his The General Theory of Employment, Interest and Money (London, 1936) laid the foundations of modern macroeconomics.

5 Howard Walter Florey (1898–1968), Kt 1944, life peer 1965, OM 1965, Australian-born experimental pathologist and bacteriologist; prof. of pathology, Oxford, and fellow, Lincoln, 1935–62; Provost, Queen's, 1962–8; 1945 Nobel Prize for Physiology or Medicine with Alexander Fleming and Ernst Chain for their work on penicillin.

6 Joseph Lister (1827–1912), baronet 1883, 1st Baron Lister 1897, OM 1902, pioneer of antiseptic surgery; prof. of surgery, Glasgow, 1860–9; prof. of clinical surgery, Edinburgh 1869–77, King's London 1877–93.

7 Edward Penley ('Ted') Abraham (1913–99), Kt 1980; fellow, Lincoln, 1948–80, and prof. of chemical pathology, Oxford, 1964–80; played a crucial role in the development of penicillin, and subsequently of the antibiotic cephalosporin.

8 Louis Pasteur (1822–95), French chemist and microbiologist, considered one of the most important medical scientists of the C19th; developed the 'pasteurisation' technique, as well as vaccines against anthrax and rabies; founding director, Institut Pasteur, Paris, 1887–95.

9 Alan Lloyd Hodgkin (1914–98), KBE 1972, OM 1973; physiologist, Nobel Prize in Physiology or

It may well be that the capacity for intentness for long periods upon highly general ideas, as opposed to constant contact with empirical facts, is due to or at least 'helped' by some trauma, some form of withdrawal from individual or social integration with persons and things. So that in the utopia in which everyone was integrated, adjusted, happy, fully realised, less progress would be made in the abstract branches of knowledge. Is the desire for a unified world picture – everything in place, everything fitting in, no loose ends, every entity in its unique, proper place (a passion I do not suffer from, if suffer is the word) – a sign of wanting to compensate for some broken relationship? It is one of the oldest and most central human tendencies – all desire for perfection in metaphysical, political, social, aesthetic, psychological terms – which is the largest part of Western thought, and Eastern too, I expect – seems to spring from this. I think it unrealistic, and indeed, dangerous, and liable to lead to fanaticism and ruthless repression of unaccountable differences – tyranny in the world of practice – but I seem to myself to be in a small minority, in any society in any period known to us. I'd love to know what you think about that. [...] Do let us meet soon.

Yours sincerely,

Isaiah B

IB's collected pen-portraits of his contemporaries, Personal Impressions, *was to include (at HH's suggestion) a personal impression of the author himself, in the form of an introductory essay written by his friend Noel Annan.[1] IB however was mortified when he saw an early draft, and wrote to Bob Silvers: 'Despite all his excellent qualities, and my affection – and indeed, respect – for him, and the friendship that has bound us for years, I should not have dreamt of choosing him to write this introduction.'[2] He found*

a good many passages in it wholly inappropriate. I shall have to have a private talk with Lord Annan about all this, as I fear (though I beg you not to pass this on to anyone) I could not dream of letting the volume appear with the introduction in its present form – it seems to me both inaccurate in its report of my opinions and in places acutely embarrassing. I am so sorry to feel so strongly, but I fear that the data justifies it. I have consulted one or two others, who feel rather more strongly than I do. I do not look forward to my long talk with Lord Annan on this topic – I can imagine what my feelings would be if the position were reversed.[3]

Medicine 1963; fellow, Trinity, Cambridge, 1936–78, Master 1978–85; John Humphrey Plummer Prof. of Biophysics, Cambridge, 1970–81.

1 Noel Gilroy *Annan (1916–2000), historian and academic administrator.
2 To Robert Silvers, n.d. [27? March 1979].
3 To John Charlton, his editor at the Hogarth Press, 28 September 1978.

TO NOEL ANNAN

2 October 1978

Headington House

Dear Noel,

You can imagine with what acute embarrassment I am writing this. That I am infinitely grateful to you for writing about me at all, you can imagine – all the nice things, particularly when they are more than my due, I enjoy like so many delicious lollipops which one rolls upon one's tongue with increasing delight. I am prepared to go on repeating this to you until you experience a sense of satiation. There are, of course, also bits which seem to me in need of condensation or alteration.[1] This is inevitable, and I feel awful about having to discuss them – how can one possibly claim the slightest objectivity in a matter which concerns oneself so intimately? [...]

'Studies in praise'[2] – so they are. Perhaps you could say something about the fact that I enjoy being able to praise – I always have. I daresay I am guilty of a (sometimes frustrated) tendency to hero-worship: I am greatly excited by occasions for meeting men or women of genius – Freud,[3] Einstein, Virginia Woolf,[4] Russell, Pasternak, Picasso,[5] Stravinsky – and massive though my defects no doubt are, the desire to do down is not one of them; the 'feet of clay'[6] of which you speak in your piece [are] something I am happy to discuss, without, I believe, much personal feeling, much as one might do so with characters in fiction. And, funnily enough, I think the highly critical Keynes – if you look at his essays in biography – also enjoyed offering encomia. To be able to do it, besides being a great pleasure (which Austin, of all people, once told me was one of *his* greatest pleasures in the case of those who deserved them), enhances one's world and one's life.

[...] I think you really do exaggerate my scepticism. It is true that I am highly sceptical of final solutions of any kind. Of panaceas, in fact. But what have I against monetarism, deficit budgeting, syndicalism?[7] I do not think I have views on these. I am not totally against participatory populism, even,

1 IB goes on to raise a series of points about Annan's draft introduction to PI, sometimes quoted in the notes. PI references are given for Annan's final text.

2 PI xiv.

3 Sigmund (né Sigismund Schlomo) Freud (1856–1939), Austrian neurologist, founder of psychoanalysis; escaped from Vienna to London in June 1938; for IB's visit to see him at his London home, when he was in the final stage of cancer of the jaw, see IB to Peter Gay, n.d. [1985?], 275, and MI 91–2.

4 (Adeline) Virginia Woolf (1882–1941) née Stephen, novelist, publisher, critic; for IB's 1933 meeting with her see L1 68–71, 79 ('I continue to adulate').

5 Pablo Diego José Francisco de Paula Juan Nepomuceno María de los Remedios Cipriano/ Crispiniano de la Santísima Trinidad Ruíz Picasso (1881–1973), Spanish painter, sculptor, printmaker, draughtsman, ceramicist and designer, generally regarded as the most influential and versatile artist of the C20th; the co-founder, with Georges Braque, of the cubist movement.

6 PI xxix.

7 'Monetarism, deficit budgeting, participatory populism, syndicalism and inevitably Communism

since I regard equality as one of the ultimate goals of men, and its rejection as such is deeply unsympathetic to me; against even such moderate conservatives as David Cecil,[1] Rees-Mogg,[2] Tony Quinton or Raymond Carr[3] I should be inclined to defend equality as a sacred value – obliged, no doubt, to yield to other equally ultimate values when there is a collision, but certainly to be practised wherever it cannot be shown to be doing positive damage. The notion that all culture is founded on inequality, and that culture is the one value we must defend with our lives, are neither of them propositions I am prepared to defend.

[...] I am not at all against believing that life *can* be ordered for the better, following a rule of conduct or a critique of culture or a method, even a scientific law – often one can, and if one can, one should (I say didactically).[4] [...]

I do not say that 'In fact you cannot pursue one good end without setting another on one side':[5] I say that one cannot *always* do this – equality and freedom may sometimes be reconciled and sometimes not. This sounds very boring, but it is surely true: there are forms of inequality which diminish freedom, forms of oppression which destroy equality, etc. The agonising choice arises when they do conflict, and to deny that they ever can is what I preach against – not that one is caught at every moment of life and choice between these terrible alternatives. Life is not one long effort to impale oneself on one horn of a dilemma in order to avoid the other. Peaceful 'trade-offs' *are* possible: and not agonising (always).

[...] 'Positive' freedom is not 'diminishing the freedom of the few in order to increase the freedom of the many',[6] but the alleged freedom of the 'real' self, or 'the self at its best', at the expense of what we ordinarily judge a man's personality to be – with its attributes, wishes, needs. So that the experts who divine the 'true' needs of the 'true' self are thus justified in setting aside what people actually say they love or hate or need or aspire to, as the pronouncements of the insufficiently enlightened, developed, 'empirical', 'lower', 'self'. We do this in the case of children or very benighted undeveloped human

---

are for him all delusions; and if men back them they will lose their freedom as well as their shirt.' Cf. PI xvi.

1 (Edward Christian) David Gascoyne Cecil (1902–86), son of the 4th Marquess of Salisbury, and grandson of the 3rd Marquess, the great Victorian prime minister; fellow, New College, 1939–69, Goldsmiths' Prof. of English Literature, Oxford, 1948–69; one of IB's lifelong friends.

2 William Rees-Mogg (1928–2012), life peer 1988, city editor, *Sunday Times*, 1960–1, political and economic editor 1961–3, deputy editor 1964–7; editor, *Times*, 1967–81.

3 (Albert) Raymond Maillard Carr (1919–2015), Kt 1987, historian of Spain and Latin America; fellow, All Souls, 1946–53, New College 1953–64; fellow, St Antony's, 1964–6, Sub-Warden 1966–8, Warden 1968–87.

4 Omitted in PI.

5 Cf. PI xv.

6 'People [...] listen respectfully to political thinkers who declare that they have discovered a far better kind of freedom, positive freedom, which enables you to argue that although you have to diminish the freedom of the few, you increase the freedom of the majority.' Cf. PI xvii.

beings (so Mill maintained),[1] but, whether or not it is permissible there, the question is whether this can be extended to all men, as in theory Hegel, Green,[2] Bosanquet[3] etc. maintained – whether or not you identify the 'real' authoritative self with the state, the Church, the people, the class, the party etc. So when you say 'can be reconciled', this should be 'can always, in the end, be reconciled'; and for 'but they cannot' I wish to read 'but they some-times cannot'; and for 'ideology' I should substitute 'the one true, infallible ideology'.[4] Otherwise I should find myself marching with Oakeshott and all kinds of irrationalists and obscurantists. Whereas I wish to align myself with the non-Utilitarian Mill, with Erasmus, Diderot, Turgenev, Herzen, Schumpeter[5] and, indeed, E. M. Forster & Co. – a very different company. To be anti-absolutist, to believe in constant corrigibility, is not to reject ideas, theories, rational constructions as such. I look on Russell as politically sympathetic; Quintin Hogg and Burke as the opposite.

[...] Austin: he did indeed reject the idea of a logically perfect language, but Wittgenstein – the later Wittgenstein – rejected this before him, as against his own former self and against Russell.[6] So that is not the central reason for my admiration of Austin, though of course it is part of it. [...] What I truly admired about him was that he was prepared to take every problem as it came, and tried to solve it in its own terms, as it were, and not force it into a Procrustean bed of a single, all-embracing system, and so transform its formulation that it ceased to be the problem that in fact it was, or else [was] rejected as a pseudo-problem, because it did not fit, as some logical positivists (e.g. Freddie) tended to do. When you say that Austin reinforced my 'unbounded' suspicion of all ideologies,[7] at most what he did was to reinforce my suspicion of all total ideologies which profess to solve everything

---

1 John Stuart Mill (1806–73), liberal philosopher and economist. 'It is, perhaps, hardly necessary to say that this doctrine [that the individual is sovereign over himself] is meant to apply only to human beings in the maturity of their faculties. We are not speaking of children, or of young persons below the age which the law may fix as that of manhood or womanhood.' Mill, *On Liberty* (1859), chapter 1: *Collected Works of John Stuart Mill*, ed. J. M. Robson and others (Toronto/London, 1963–91), xviii 224.
2 Thomas Hill Green (1836–82), liberal Idealist philosopher, White's Prof. of Moral Philosophy, Oxford, and fellow, Balliol, 1878–82.
3 Bernard Bosanquet (1848–1923), philosopher and social theorist; fellow, Univ., 1870–81, lecturer 1871–81; prof. of moral philosophy, St Andrews, 1903–8; Gifford Lecturer, Edinburgh, 1911–12; strongly influenced as a Balliol undergraduate by T. H. Green.
4 See PI xvii–xviii: 'surely the different aspects of truth and goodness can always be reconciled. But Berlin declares that sometimes they cannot. Ideology answers the questions "How should I behave?" and "How should I live?" People want to believe that there is one irrefutable answer to these questions. But there is not.'
5 Desiderius Erasmus (c.1466–1536), Dutch humanist and theologian; Denis Diderot (1713–84), French *philosophe* and encyclopedist, a leading figure in the Enlightenment; Ivan Sergeevich Turgenev (1818–83), Russian novelist and dramatist; Joseph Alois Schumpeter (1883–1950), Austrian-born economist.
6 Cf. PI xviii.
7 Omitted in PI.

by the one true system; which is somewhat different. He did look on ordinary language as a pointer to true meaning; but he believed in teamwork and systems. I don't (much).

[…] Why is man a free agent because he thinks?[1] Is there something totally incompatible between determinism and thinking? I do not think so – but this is a vast philosophical issue – perhaps you should not prejudge it with one firm sentence. […]

I do not think that I intend to throw doubts on religious morality as such,[2] only on one that excludes all non-religious values. On Utilitarianism, yes, but the case of Kant[3] is much more complicated: I am deeply pro-Kantian on certain issues, e.g. his obscure but epoch-making doctrine of the freedom of the will, his concept of the moral autonomy of the individual, his doctrine of human beings as ends in themselves, and of moral values as constituted by human commitment to them (I won't go into the niceties of what this means, how far Kant held it, etc.), which seem to me of the first importance, and to which I am wholly sympathetic. So I am not to be taken as an opponent of Kantian morality *tout court* – I should leave this last sentence out altogether. Since Stuart has always maintained that I was an unregenerate Humean, and Hume[4] is a Utilitarian, the whole issue is distinctly complex. I think that if I am described as wanting to throw doubt on any moral or political system which is founded on, or includes, an unalterable hierarchy of values binding on all men at all times in all places, capable of providing an objective and unalterable solution to every moral and political (and aesthetic) problem, this would be true. But not much more than this.

[…] I cannot deny my love of gossip,[5] though whether – and this raises a point of principle – it is appropriate to produce a portrait of me in this introduction rather than reflections on the pieces contained in the volume is something we might have a word about. I really do feel that I am being obituarised, and emerge corpse-like in consequence. However true, kind or revealing the picture may be, I cannot deny that I sweat with embarrassment. Is this 'hypersensitive' (something that none other than Lord Drogheda[6]

1 Omitted in PI (on the issue see 310/4).
2 Omitted in PI.
3 Immanuel Kant (1724–1804), German philosopher, regarded as the central figure in modern philosophy; prof. of logic and metaphysics, Königsberg, 1770–96; his theory of morality resists simple summary, but central to it is the identification of morality with human freedom and the idea that freedom consists in our being both authors of, and obedient to, the moral law, a universal law arrived at by reason alone.
4 David Hume (1711–76), philosopher, as well as historian and man of letters, best known in philosophy for his naturalism, empiricism and scepticism in theory of knowledge, metaphysics and morality. He had a major influence on Kant, as well as on such diverse figures as Rousseau, Bentham and Darwin.
5 The draft, but not the published text, speaks of 'what he greatly enjoys, gossip with close friends in which his inexhaustible interest in people is given full rein'.
6 (Charles) Garrett Ponsonby Moore (1910–89), 11th Earl of Drogheda 1957; bought *Financial Times* 1945 (merging it with the *Financial News*), managing director 1945–70, chair 1971–5; secretary to

called me)? Oh dear. But I do feel this strongly, so if you could take some of this out! Do! It is intolerable, awful of me, but I do feel it, so I do *beg* you to hold your hand.

[…] Namier:[1] he insisted not so much that the history of ideas was a non-existent subject,[2] as that Marx's ideas in particular were not worth bothering about. Nor did he, in spite of his ironies, ever actually tell me that my approach was worthless – only that I was wasting my time on Marx, and that the philosophy of history seemed a morass to him. […]

I certainly do find in the rise of the state of Israel an argument against deterministic history of an impersonal kind; but the English resistance in 1940 seems to me just as much an argument against it; so does Hitler's attack on Russia, which need not have occurred but which has altered our world.[3] The fate of the whole of central and Eastern Europe – that turned on the decision of an individual, too. So the modern history of the Jews is not the sole, or even the greatest, piece of evidence against determinism in my mind. But it *is* one, and I do say it.

[…] I do not think that history is the history of great men at all:[4] I think there are turning points at which great men can give a decisive impulsion in one direction or another, but that there *is* an analysable texture of impersonal events. I think this is a genuine misinterpretation of what I believe.

[…] Do I say 'Do not ask these sorts of questions about great men'?[5] I do not think I forbid people to ask them when writing about their appearance on 'the stage of history'.[6] I do think that some personal qualities may not be relevant. But your text rather makes it appear that I think great men are beyond moral scrutiny, rather as Hegel maintained that they were. And this I should absolutely deny.[7] […]

That's all. Will you forgive me? Have I rewarded generosity with meanness? Behaved abominably? Will you forgive me? Please?

yrs

Isaiah   […]

the board, ROH, 1951–8, chair 1958–74; IB greatly admired Drogheda's rule at Covent Garden, despite his sometimes imperious style.

1 Lewis Bernstein Namier (1888–1960) né Ludwik Niemirowski, Kt 1952, prof. of modern history, Manchester, 1931–53, first met IB in summer 1937 and once wrote to him: 'how intelligent you must be to understand all you write' (letter of 10 February 1955: see L2 530–1).

2 Cf. PI xxiii.

3 Cf. PI xxvii.

4 Omitted in PI.

5 'You do not ask, writes Berlin, when you consider the career of the great, questions which would be perfectly appropriate if you were considering the life of one of your friends – you do not ask whether he was kind, upright, sensitive or whether he was naturally good company.' Cf. PI xxvii.

6 IB compares Churchill to 'a great actor – perhaps the last of his kind – upon the stage of history'. PI 22.

7 'Great men are seldom good men.' To Fumiko Sasaki, 6 April 1994.

TO ISAAC STERN[1]

[7 October 1978][2] Tabernacles, First Day [*carbon*]

[Headington House]

Dear Isaac,

I, for my part, have just emerged after six hours of *Götterdämmerung* and am myself in a distinctly twilit condition. But Colin Davis[3] conducted it extremely well. It is, I fear, undeniable that Wagner is probably the most powerful cultural influence of the entire nineteenth century, who made a difference far beyond music – in all the arts, in politics, in literature. It was a 'Prom' evening – only £2 for sitting on the floor of the auditorium, and the passionate, not to say violent, enthusiasm of all those rough youths and far-out girls was tremendous – not a very good or hopeful sign, I thought. It is the violence that excites them. Wagner as an idol of radical youth in England is something new. It is not merely all that verbiage about his revolutionary activities in 1849, the careful omission not only of the anti-Semitism but of the violent Prussian nationalism in 1870, and hideous delight at the crushing of the French and the worship of Bismarck (all carefully left out), but the story and the music themselves of *The Ring* – the combination of sex, violence and apocalyptic mystique – that gets them, I think. Your old friend Bernstein[4] is not very far from it all, but never mind (I am being too bitchy).

[…] The German ambassador[5] was next to me at supper during the work, and when I cautiously observed to him that I thought there was a lot of Wagner in Hitler,[6] he said 'Why do you not also say that there is a very great deal of Hitler in Wagner?' Better for him to say it than for me, I thought. But I rather warmed to him after that, especially after he told me that he thought that Wagner ought to be shortened by huge, judicious cuts. I told him that Bing[7] felt the same way about it, and that Diamand[8] once told him that the entire *Ring* was being done somewhere in one evening – 'just the highlights,

1 Isaac Stern (1920–2001; plate 7), Ukrainian-born US violinist of Russian Jewish descent.
2 The 1st day of Tabernacles in 1978 was 16 October, but the performance IB refers to occurred 7 October. IB evidently had a brainstorm about the dates.
3 Colin Rex Davis (1927–2013), Kt 1980, conductor; musical director, ROH, 1971–86; chief conductor, Bavarian Radio Symphony Orchestra, 1983–92; principal conductor, London Symphony Orchestra, 1995–2007; conducted 3 *Ring* cycles in Covent Garden September–October 1978 to great acclaim, the last of which was a 'Prom cycle': IB refers here to the 7 October performance of the last opera, *Götterdämmerung*.
4 Leonard (né Louis) Bernstein (1918–90), US composer, conductor and pianist; composer of *West Side Story* (Broadway 1957, film 1961) and the film score for *On the Waterfront* (1954).
5 Hans Hellmuth Ruete (1914–87), West German ambassador to the UK 1977–80.
6 In the passage omitted above IB called Wagner 'the old proto-Nazi'.
7 Rudolf Franz Joseph Bing (1902–97), KBE 1971, Vienna-born naturalised British opera manager, helped found the Edinburgh Festival 1947; general manager, Met, 1950–72.
8 Peter Diamand (1913–98), Berlin-born arts administrator; left Germany 1933, becoming Dutch national; PS to Artur Schnabel (331/4); director, Edinburgh Festival, 1965–78.

just the thing for you, Rudi' – and Rudi answered 'Highlights? I didn't know there were any.' [...]
Yours,
[Isaiah]

TO PATRICK NEILL
27 November 1978

Headington House

Dear Mr Warden,

Fifteen or more years ago a motion to make women eligible for fellowships at the College was proposed at an SGM: I voted against it.[1] I have regretted this ever since. I have changed my mind because I cannot think of a single rational objection to this proposal. May I state my position in the form of comments on Bryan Wilson's[2] very well written and persuasive list of objections to your paper? [...]

As for the argument [...] that this move would create 'inevitable bitter divisions within the College', even the most overdue reforms can do this: the abolition of the marriage ban, more than a century ago,[3] led to bitter feeling on the part of the unbending Tories [...], but nobody now, so far as I know, sheds tears over this departure from tradition. There was, after all, some bitterness when we went back on our decision to admit graduates:[4] I am glad to say that these wounds seem to have healed completely. I am the last person to minimise the importance of harmony and good feeling, but to resort to its claims as decisive would render all serious change, however intrinsically desirable, impossible. I cannot persuade myself that the consequences of this change would be anything like as divisive as Wilson and others dread. This seems to be unduly pessimistic. [...]

Keeping in line with others. Wilson's point is, I take it, that we are already so different from other colleges that any unpopularity which may result

1 The 1962 motion, which had no realistic chance of passing, was regarded by IB as 'a demonstration of exasperated hostility by the *jeunesse*' towards the reactionary Wardenship of his close friend John Sparrow. Though swayed by the example of his 'master' John Stuart Mill, a noted advocate of women's rights, IB nevertheless voted against. IB to Charles Taylor, 23 February 1962, L3 80–1.

2 Bryan Ronald Wilson (1926–2004), reader in sociology, Oxford, 1962–93, fellow, All Souls, 1963–93. He had introduced the visiting fellowship programme at All Souls, and was thus not against reform in principle. 'He did not, however, welcome the arrival of women, fearing that they might disrupt the scholarly ambience by discussing domestic trivialities' (Eileen Barker, ODNB).

3 This was a college, not a University, matter. Celibacy was originally a condition of holding a college fellowship. Holders of certain posts in the University, e.g. professors, could marry unless they also held a college fellowship, as indeed could heads of colleges. By the late 1860s a few colleges, including New College, had altered their statutes to allow fellows to marry, but it was not until 1882, after the University of Oxford Commission of 1877, that all such college statutes were changed, sometimes with residual restrictions.

4 See L3 236–7.

from staying as we are should not greatly matter. I agree. But the point, surely, is that our other differences from other colleges have a rational basis: there is a strong case for a college dedicated exclusively to research, even though its members, both professors and research fellows, are involved in teaching duties – this is defensible on purely academic grounds, as a unique benefit to learning. No such argument can be produced for the exclusion of women. I cannot find a rational basis for this argument, which appears to me to be founded, ultimately, on uncritical adherence to tradition, or even prejudice. [...]

I have no quarrel with Wilson's desire to see that 'the value and richness of particular and distinctive traditions and arrangements' and 'all unique and individual differences' should, so far as possible, be preserved, if only for the sake of variety of life. But I part company with him if, in my view, these differences are based on, or lead to, obvious breaches of natural justice, which can only be defended either on grounds of unyielding conservatism, or (what I cannot help regarding as) prejudice.

The case for admitting women is both that of simple justice, and, on the assumption that the central purpose of the College is the promotion of learning (which, so far as I know, nobody has yet questioned), that the opening of the doors to women of high intellectual and personal qualifications could only contribute to this end. All Souls has the best research facilities, in a very wide field, of any institution in England. To deny suitably qualified women their use for the sole reason that they are women seems to me indefensible. To stand out against the rest of the University either in the name of a principle, or even of a form of life, which seems to us to be so important that we should be morally justified in fighting for this to the last, if need be alone (or in the company of Oriel),[1] seems to me perfectly right. My argument is not that we must march with the times and join the great majority of colleges, without considering the implications for us. But I fail to detect any such principle, or a seriously threatened way of academic life that must be defended at all costs. For these reasons I should like to associate myself with the position you have taken. I have no doubt that both sides in this dispute are wholly sincere and concerned solely with the welfare of the College; but your letter, and Bryan Wilson's, have made it clear to me on which side I stand.[2]

Yours sincerely,
Isaiah Berlin

1 By 1978 Oriel was the only men's college not to have decided to admit women as undergraduates; it remained single-sex until 1986.
2 Women became eligible for fellowship in All Souls in 1979, and the 1st female fellow, Susan Hurley (150/2), was elected in 1981.

TO HENRY HARDY

4 December 1978

Headington House

Dear Henry,

Letter after letter! Noel Annan's piece is far better than it was, but there are still one or two 'bad' bits – not very important ones, but one in particular which would embarrass too many people without cause. I will write to him again. Sincere and laudatory as his introduction is, and now shorn of its direct errors of fact, especially about philosophy (for which we have to thank Stuart Hampshire), and warm-hearted as it plainly is, I shall, I am afraid, have gooseflesh whenever I think of it, for the rest of my life. Hubert Henderson[1] once told me, about Sir Roy Harrod's[2] life of Keynes, that everything in it was two or three degrees out, just wrong by a thin margin, and that this produced a continuous feeling of irritation, when things were nearly but never quite right about a man whom he knew – or thought he knew – far better than Harrod knew him, which caused him to refuse to review it. About pieces on oneself, one must speak with greater humility and caution: a man hears his own voice quite differently from the way others hear it; nevertheless, I shall never be quite reconciled to it. You will think that I am making far too much of all this. I expect I am. I shall not say a word about this to you again. All I ask is that people should not write or say to me anything about how well captured my views and personality [are], how exact, and yet generous, the vignette is. But they will. No more on that. [...]

I am still looking for the carnivorous sheep.[3] As in the case of the quotation from E. M. Forster,[4] I am convinced that it is in de Maistre[5] – but I cannot lay everything else aside to look for it in the collected works, so perhaps it would be as well if we resorted to one of our well-known subterfuges, and

---

1 Hubert Douglas Henderson (1890–1952), Kt 1942, economist; fellow, All Souls, 1934–52; Drummond Prof. of Political Economy, Oxford, 1945–51.

2 (Henry) Roy Forbes Harrod (1900–78), Kt 1959, economist; student (i.e. fellow) in modern history and economics, Christ Church, 1924–67; Nuffield Reader in International Economics, Oxford, 1952–67; author of the official biography *The Life of John Maynard Keynes* (London, 1951).

3 IB had attributed to Maistre a witticism that was in fact (as HH later discovered) due to the critic Émile Faguet (who was, nevertheless, paraphrasing Maistre): 'To say that sheep are born carnivorous, but everywhere eat grass, would be just as reasonable [as saying, with Rousseau, "Man is born free, but is everywhere in chains"].' Émile Faguet, 'Joseph de Maistre', *Politiques et moralistes du dix-neuvième siècle*, 1st series (Paris, 1899), 41. Maistre himself had written: 'What does he [Rousseau] mean? [...] This mad pronouncement, *Man is born free*, is the opposite of the truth.' *Oeuvres complètes de J. de Maistre* (Lyon, 1884–7) ii 338.

4 Probably 'Everything must be like something, so what is this like?' (L1 212/1); less probably, 'Only connect' (L2 269/1), 'telegrams and anger' (L2 594/3) or 'if I had to choose between betraying my country and betraying my friend, I hope I should have the guts to betray my country' (L2 394/2).

5 Joseph Marie, comte de Maistre (1753–1821), ultramontane French writer who regarded the horrors of the French Revolution as divine judgement on the secularism of the Enlightenment. The last of the 6 main subjects of FIB.

said, 'de Maistre somewhere says' – or something of that sort. What do you think?

Yours ever,
Isaiah   [...]

TO NOEL ANNAN
7 December 1978

Headington House

Dearest Noel,

My gratitude can no longer be conveyed by mere epistolary prose: it is a great deficiency not to be either a creative, or at least an interpretative, artist, so that one can convey emotion by means of direct expression – dance, song, poetry, beating a tom-tom in a special rhythm. I really am most grateful to you for all your patience in making these, to me, relief-bringing changes. At this point, I ought simply to say all this again and sign. But – forgive me even more generously than you have before – I cannot quite do that: there are a few trivial points which I should like to make, and one or two (not more, I swear) untrivial ones. [...]

I do not really want to be too nasty about MCC Jews:[1] there are some who assimilate so successfully that one really cannot mind what they are or do; if there are any members of 'say' the Jessel[2] family who preferred the MCC to Jerusalem, I could not mind. I do not mind those who have really forgotten Zion. I am not against assimilation if it can be done, only against ghastly and conscious efforts to do so, which actually prevent it. [...] I do not wish to be thought what I am not – a fanatical anti-assimilationist, as most Zionists, of course, are, but I (deeply) am *not*. I admit to taking some pleasure in detecting what Namier called 'trembling Israelites';[3] with their children and grandchildren, who have ceased to tremble and ceased to be Israelites in all but form or religion, I really have no quarrel: I had none with the late Lord Melchett,[4] I have none with the present Lord Reading,[5] not

1 The points in this letter arise from a revised draft of Annan's piece. For the MCC Jews see PI xxiv.
2 George Jessel (1824–83), Kt 1873, jurist, Master of the Rolls 1873–83, son of a Jewish coral merchant; his elder son, Charles James Jessel (1860–1928), was made a baronet 1883 in a posthumous tribute to his father, while the younger son, Herbert Merton Jessel (1866–1950), a Liberal Unionist MP, was created 1st Baron Jessel 1924; both sons married daughters of the lawyer and Liberal MP Sir Julian Goldsmid, Bt, and they and their descendants were thoroughly assimilated into the British establishment.
3 PI xxiv.
4 Julian Edward Alfred Mond (1925–73), 3rd Baron Melchett, banker and industrialist; chair of the newly nationalised British Steel Corporation 1967–73.
5 Michael Alfred Rufus Isaacs (1916–1980), 3rd Marquess of Reading, 1st cousin of Julian Melchett (previous note), and grandson of the Liberal politician Rufus Daniel Isaacs, 1st Marquess, whose ministerial career began in Asquith's pre-war cabinet.

even Sybil Cholmondeley[1] or Antoinette's[2] French relations – quite different from my contemporary at Oxford, Roy Beddington,[3] to whom one only had to mention Jews to throw him into cold and hot fits, if you see what I mean. It is the open or secret wincing that is awful.

[...] Only two things, and then I cease, I swear it. But these *are* genuine issues.

[...] About my 'dual loyalty being stretched and strained':[4] though I say, I think, that my position was not a wholly comfortable one, my loyalty to England was not in fact stretched or strained. My position was perfectly clear to me: quite apart from loyalty, or a sense of gratitude for my too unobstructed career, I was clear that I was a servant of the British government and had chosen to be so quite freely; I was not a conscript; as long as the war lasted I had no right to work for any other master, or, if I was asked to do something too outrageous, then I had no doubt that I had to decline and opt out – resign, or be shot, so to speak; but not to disobey. Since I was a civilian and under no constraints (I had not even signed the Official Secrets Act, for some reason), my obligation in this respect appeared to me to be all the stronger. And I found no difficulty in relations with my colleagues, most of whom were anti-Zionists in some degree, sometimes to an acute degree; they knew my views (those who were interested), and this may have made for some discomfort when the topic came up; but *not* for 'stretching and straining loyalties'.

My second point is that, as persons of foreign origin, but more particularly Jews, have often been suspected of double allegiance – to their country *and* their race (or community, or the state of Israel, etc. etc.) – which seemed to the somewhat anti-Semitic Harold Nicolson[5] a good reason why Jews should not be employed by the Foreign Office; and since this is a still pretty generally

---

1 Sybil Rachel Bettie Cecile Cholmondeley (1894–1989) née Sassoon, Marchioness of Cholmondeley, daughter of a Sassoon and a Rothschild, scandalised her family 1913 by marrying a gentile, George Horatio Charles Cholmondeley, 5th Marquess of Cholmondeley 1923; she converted to Christianity after WW2.

2 Antoinette Nicole Eugénie de Gunzbourg (1910–86) née Kahn, 2nd wife from 1924 of Aline Berlin's brother Philippe Georges de Gunzbourg.

3 Julian Roy Beddington (1910–95), artist, writer and fisherman, hailed from a family of well-established English Jews named Moses who, in the late C19th, Anglicised their name by adopting that of a Surrey village; this did not protect Beddington, who 'suffered an anti-Semitism at school that he never forgot. At Rugby he spent his time in the artroom' (James Fergusson, 'Roy Beddington', obituary, *Independent*, 6 June 1995, 12); cf. 546.

4 Annan had written: 'It is possible in England – difficult at times, but in no way absurd or inconsistent – to be loyal to one's country and also to Zionism. For a few years during the war Berlin worked on the staff of the British Embassy in Washington and he describes with candour here exactly how this dual loyalty was stretched and strained.' This remark was no doubt stimulated by IB's 1972 lecture *Zionist Politics in Wartime Washington* (3/7), originally to have been included in PI, but later dropped. Cf. PI xxv–xxvi, 219–20 below, L3 510/2, MI 117–18.

5 Harold George Nicolson (1886–1968), KCVO 1953, diplomat, politician and writer; National Labour MP 1935–45, parliamentary secretary, Ministry of Information, 1940–1, governor, BBC, 1941–6.

accepted view; anything which implies that to be a Jew is to be under such strains (this used to be alleged against Catholics, but no longer is, I think) seems to me to provide tinder for xenophobia in general and anti-Semitism in particular. Dual allegiance *is* an issue: it is not true that it is not one at all. Weizmann was often asked what he would do if his British loyalties – which, as you know, were considerable – came into collision with his Zionist ones. This did happen in the end, and he wrote a moving letter to the Foreign Secretary – Bevin (!) – which was suppressed at the time by an official in the Foreign Office, Bernard Burrows,[1] who thought it was wrong to forward any letter from such an awful man to the Foreign Secretary: but that is another story.[2] My point is that since I did not suffer from this strain – though no doubt some Zionists thought that I should have done, and that I was a British stooge – my situation should *not* be given as an illustration of such tension. I reached my decision without conscious reflection; I took the supremacy of total loyalty to England for granted. [...]

Have I abused your devotion, patience and generosity? Have I behaved intolerably? Have I gone too far? At any rate, I am ashamed of going on so. The only really serious point is the one about dual allegiance and the straining of loyalties, not so much because of biographical accuracy as because of the generalised implications for others, the use that could be made of it by evil-minded persons (imagine Ali[3] or *Private Eye*[4] on this – imagine a cartoon of me, stretched and strained, with a hideous-looking Begin on the left and a frightful-looking Churchill on the right, each beckoning). Anyway, you have behaved with great sweetness and nobility and beauty of character, and I have been tiresome, niggling and a strainer and stretcher of your great but not unlimited patience.

I fall on my knees before you and cover my face.

Yours,

    Isaiah

TO CHIMEN ABRAMSKY[5]

    II December 1978

Headington House

Dear Chimen,

    Thank you ever so much for your letter of I December. Heaven knows

1 Bernard Alexander Brocas Burrows (1910–2002), KCMG 1955, diplomat; UK Embassy, Cairo, 1938–45; Foreign Office 1945–50; permanent British representative to North Atlantic Council 1966–70.
2 Told in IB's interview with Allegra Mostyn-Owen and Hugo Dixon, *Isis*, 17 May 1985, 8–9 at 8; cf. MI 94–5.
3 Tariq Ali (b. 1943), writer, editor, broadcaster and left-wing political activist; editor, *Black Dwarf* 1968–70, *Red Mole* 1970–3; editorial board, *New Left Review*, since 1982.
4 British satirical current affairs magazine founded 1961.
5 Chimen Abramsky (1916–2010), Minsk-born historian, bibliographer, book collector and

why I was awarded the Jerusalem Book Prize.[1] When I was asked to say a few words impromptu on Jerusalem Radio I 'screwed it up', to use Nixon's unforgettable phrase, though the result may not be as fatal as Watergate's.[2] I am no good at spontaneous interviews: no thoughts come into my head. I was asked in what way the three traditions in which I grew up – Russian, Jewish and British – fit into my character. How does one answer that? I can think of an answer to it now – but not on the spot.[3] Similarly, when I was asked what I regarded as the leading principle of my life – have I one? – I denied it, and emerged as a feeble opportunist and pragmatist (I expect). Thirdly, who would I award such a prize to now, as a champion of liberty, etc.? Popper, said I firmly – he does not like being described as a Jew, does not care for Israel, and his last works are not at all to my taste. Having given absurd answers to all these questions, I am covered with shame. But I am genuinely happy to receive this prize, because any form of recognition from that quarter naturally delights me. [...]

Yours,

Isaiah

TO NOEL ANNAN

3 January 1979

Headington House

Dearest Noel,

[...] No one has ever harried a potential benefactor so much since Maurice harried Roy Harrod about the *Times* obituary that Roy had undertaken to compose – and in the end it was a palimpsest of Harrod and the boys at Wadham.[4] I am grateful to you for saving me from the fury of the decent assimilated Jews – some of Aline's cousins, for example. [...]

My relationships with people: I can certainly have affable relations with people I think awful and embarrassing, but in certain cases the awfulness

long-standing friend of IB, who, with James Joll, helped establish his academic career; lecturer in modern Jewish history, UCL, 1966–9, reader 1969–74, Goldsmid Prof. of Hebrew and Jewish Studies 1974–83.

1   IB was the recipient 1979 of the Jerusalem Prize for the Freedom of the Individual in Society, a biennial literary award.

2   Interviewed by David Frost for television in March 1977 (broadcast that May), Nixon said of Watergate: 'I screwed up terribly in what was a little thing and it became a big thing.' The 'little thing' was seeking to protect from the consequences of their illegal actions his senior aides H. R. ('Bob') Haldeman and John Ehrlichman. Less self-serving was his confession to his chief of staff Alexander Haig and press secretary Ron Ziegler, at the White House 6 August 1974, three days before his resignation: 'Well, I screwed it up good, real good, didn't I?' *The Memoirs of Richard Nixon* (London: 1978), 1068.

3   See 'The Three Strands in My Life', *Jewish Quarterly* 27 nos 2–3 (Summer/Autumn 1979), 5–7, and, as 'Upon Receiving the Jerusalem Prize', *Conservative Judaism* 33 no. 2 (Winter 1980), 14–17; repr. in PI2.

4   Bowra's colleagues at Wadham.

does create sympathy and affection – rather like bores, whom I was accused by Nabokov of liking too much. But the case of the sinister and evil is different, believe me. Lord Snow I regard as merely awful, tremendously unattractive, but not sinister or evil. [...] Really evil people, or those who seem so to me, I cannot manage at all – if Sir Oswald or Lady Mosley[1] were in the room, I should, I think, walk out without hesitation. I was acutely uncomfortable in the presence of Lords Beaverbrook,[2] Cherwell,[3] Radcliffe[4] and – what peerage did Tom Driberg take?[5] Them I thought genuinely evil, and Beaverbrook and Driberg sinister too. I felt horror in their presence and tended to leave rooms. I do not think Lord Eccles[6] or Lord Home[7] or any member of the Mitford[8] and Foot[9] families are in the least evil, but would rather not have met them. If

1 Oswald Mosley m. 1936 (they were each other's 2nd spouses) Diana (1910–2003) née Freeman-Mitford, 4th child and 3rd of 6 daughters (there was one brother) of David Freeman-Mitford, 2nd Baron Redesdale; the wedding, in Joseph Goebbels's drawing room, was attended by Hitler, whose gift was a signed photograph in a silver frame; husband and wife were both interned in Britain on security grounds during WW2.

2 (William) Max(well) Aitken (1879–64), 1st Baron Beaverbrook, Canadian-born businessman, Conservative politician and newspaper magnate, owner, *Daily Express* and *Evening Standard*, used his newspapers to promote his personal and political agenda; IB found him 'revolting in every way' (to Mary McCarthy, 7 August 1964, L3 196).

3 Frederick Alexander Lindemann (1886–1957), 1st (and last) Viscount Cherwell 1956, physicist and government scientific adviser relied on by Winston Churchill; Dr Lee's Prof. of Experimental Philosophy (i.e. physics), Oxford, and fellow, Wadham, 1919–56; he elicited 'extreme sentiments' from those who met him and, while kind-hearted, could be shockingly cynical: ' "One shouldn't kick a man when he's down", said a guest in the Christ Church common room. Lindemann replied, "Why not? It's the best time to do it because then he can't kick you back" ' (Robert Blake, ODNB).

4 Cyril John Radcliffe (1899–1977), KBE 1944, life peer 1949, 1st Viscount Radcliffe 1962, lawyer and public servant; fellow, All Souls, 1922–37; lord of appeal in ordinary 1949–64.

5 Thomas Edward Neil Driberg (1905–76), journalist and left-wing Labour politician, joined the CPGB at the age of 15 but was expelled 1941; on editorial staff, *Daily Express*, 1928–43; life peer 1975 (Baron Bradwell of Bradwell juxta Mare). His reckless appetite for risky homosexual encounters did not diminish with age, and he became 'A sort of stout Dracula': Gore Vidal, *Palimpsest: A Memoir* (London, 1995), 199.

6 David McAdam Eccles (1904–99), KCVO 1953, 1st Viscount Eccles 1964, businessman and Conservative politician, minister in the governments of Churchill, Eden, Macmillan and Heath; 'his undoubted elegance and good looks won him the nickname "Smarty Boots", which to his rivals also reflected his smugness and excessive confidence in his own abilities' (Martin Pugh, ODNB).

7 Alexander Frederick ('Alec') Douglas-Home (1903–95), Conservative politician, prime minister 1963–4, succeeded as 14th Earl of Home, but disclaimed his peerages for life 1963; Kt 1962, life peer 1974; as PPS to Neville Chamberlain he accompanied the prime minister to the final meeting with Hitler in September 1938, and defended the Munich agreement for the rest of his life.

8 David Bertram Ogilvy Freeman-Mitford (1878–1958), 2nd Baron Redesdale, soldier and landowner, his wife Sydney (1880–1963) née Bowles, and their 6 daughters, Nancy (1904–73), Pamela (1907–94), Diana (1910–2003), Unity (1914–48), Jessica (1917–96) and Deborah (1920–2014), popularly known as 'Diana the Fascist, Jessica the Communist, Unity the Hitler-lover; Nancy the Novelist; Deborah the Duchess and Pamela the unobtrusive poultry connoisseur' ('Those Utterly Maddening Mitford Girls', Ben Macintyre, *Times*, 12 October 2007, 23a–d at 23c), whose only brother, (Major) Thomas David (1909–45), died of his wounds 30 March 1945 while serving with the King's Royal Rifle Corps in Burma.

9 The West-Country Foot family was deeply imbued with the ideals of the radical Liberal tradition. Isaac Foot (1880–1960), Liberal politician and orator, and his wife Eva (1878–1946) née

I can conveniently ignore their presence or go to the other end of the room,
I do so systematically. I am not very discriminating, but in the presence of
what I feel to be genuinely evil I shrivel. Unlike Maurice, I cannot say 'I like
shits.' On the other hand, I do like some awful people too, and still do. Next
time we meet, we might go over our respective lists. You have 'the two most
corrupt couples in London' on yours; I have some as good. Do not, I beg
you, overestimate my frontiers of tolerance. I draw the line at the Italian and
Spanish aristocracy, but I like Philip Johnson,[1] Mrs Longworth.[2] I shivered in
the presence of Chips Channon.[3] And so on. I cannot be as uncensorious as
all that. I could go on for ever, of course – everyone is delighted to be allowed
to talk about themselves from time to time. But I know from the example of
certain common friends what a fearful bore this can be – I must stop at once.
  With endless gratitude,
  Yours,
    Isaiah

TO JACOB TALMON
  29 January 1979

                                                      Headington House

Dear Yaacov,
  [...] Physical health is everything: we both have something to complain
of – you, perhaps, more than I. But I, too, during my brief visit to America in
November (Yale, Washington etc.), was once more subjected to my irregular pulse and extreme discomfort. No sooner did I come back to England
than on the whole it abated: it is a pure result of tension, and in America

Mackintosh had 7 children, and 4 of their 5 sons had careers in public life: Dingle Mackintosh
Foot (1905–78), Kt 1964, politician and lawyer, solicitor general in Harold Wilson's Labour government 1964–7; Hugh Mackintosh Foot (1907–90), life peer 1964, colonial administrator and diplomat, last British governor of Cyprus 1957–60; John Mackintosh Foot (1909–99), life peer 1967,
solicitor and Liberal politician, chair, UK Immigrants Advisory Service, 1970–8, one of whose
children was Paul Mackintosh Foot (1937–2004), journalist and Trotskyite; Michael Mackintosh
Foot (1913–2010), journalist, author and politician, deputy leader, Labour Party, 1976–80, leader,
Opposition, 1980–3.
1 Philip Cortelyou Johnson (1906–2005), US architect whose NY designs included the plan of the
  Lincoln Center (1964). During the 1930s his Fascist sympathies took him to Hitler's Potsdam rally
  1933: 'his later ostentatious work on behalf of causes associated with Judaism were seen by many
  as gestures of atonement' ('Philip Johnson', obituary, *Times*, 28 January 2005, 69a–70a at 69e).
2 Alice Lee Roosevelt Longworth (1884–1980), eldest daughter and 1st child of Theodore Roosevelt
  and his 1st wife Alice, who died 2 days after childbirth; m. 1906 the Republican Congressman
  Nicholas Longworth (1869–1931), and conducted a long but discreet affair with Senator William
  Borah (260/2), who was, by her own admission, the father of her only child, Paulina; IB enjoyed
  her deliberately provocative, liberal-baiting views (259).
3 Henry ('Chips') Channon (1897–1958), Kt 1957; Conservative MP 1935–58; right-wing and pro-
  appeasement, he is principally remembered for his posthumously published diaries, in which he
  wrote in 1935: 'I am riveted by lust, furniture, glamour and society and jewels.' *'Chips': The Diaries
  of Sir Henry Channon*, ed. Robert Rhodes James (London, 1967), 38.

I never feel relaxed. Even dinner parties induce it. At any rate, I came back to England a patient, swallowed some sort of new pills given me by a clever Jewish doctor (what an anti-Semitic phrase!), which seem to have done me good.

So now I gird my loins to go to the deeply troubled land of Israel. It all began with an invitation from the Princeton Institute to deliver a lecture on Einstein's impact on general thought as part of the centenary[1] celebrations which they are holding there. I replied as politely as I could to Dr Woolf, of the Institute, that, while his impact on the conception of the physical universe was obviously transforming, and his impact on the philosophy of science, according to some, significant (it was genuine, but smaller than people suppose), his impact on the world of general thought was, to say the least, problematic. There is no doubt about Newton's impact on the entire Enlightenment, or Darwin's[2] [...] or Freud's on our world – but Einstein's? I should say virtually none. Of course relativity was interpreted as relativism – everything is relative, etc. – but he happened to believe the precise opposite, that there was an objective material world, independent of human thought, and that although our concepts were not, as he had once believed, themselves derived from experience (which Mach[3] had taught), but were arbitrary creations of the ever-creative human imagination and intellect, nevertheless the many possible ways of describing this world were only valid if they corresponded to some kind of external reality, of which men were a part but which, *pace* Marx, they did not – so far as natural science was concerned – affect in any way. I did not say all this to Dr Woolf, but I did say that I did not think that the subject he proposed for me existed. He wrote back very politely and said that what he had meant was the world in which Einstein had lived; I replied once again that the German world was known to others better than to myself, the Princeton world also, and that I was totally unqualified to deal with this topic. I then received a similar invitation from Washington, which I declined in similar terms. I then received one from Jerusalem: Aline said that I could not refuse everything and that, whatever my pulse and its rhythms, I must do something. So I agreed to say a few words by way of introduction to Isaac Stern and his orchestra – and this I have composed and wonder whether it begins to be adequate. I suffer from despising everything I write: what others write is objective, valid, important, true, original, at least sometimes; what I write is invented by me, so what value can it possibly have? [...]

1 Of Einstein's birth on 14 March 1879.
2 Charles Robert Darwin (1809–82), naturalist, geologist and originator of the theory of natural selection set out in his *On the Origin of Species by Means of Natural Selection, or the Preservation of Favoured Races in the Struggle for Life* (London, 1859).
3 Ernst Waldfried Josef Wenzel Mach (1838–1916), Austrian physicist and philosopher of science, whose strongly empiricist work was a precursor of logical positivism; Einstein too acknowledged his influence.

Your letters to me are the only totally convincing account of Israeli politics that I receive: I occasionally go to meetings of a little group in London which is addressed by the Israel ambassador,[1] who has just been sacked unceremoniously and gratuitously by Dayan, simply because he did not like him. He is a perfectly good ambassador, dignified, socially highly acceptable, and intelligent – there was no real reason for dismissing him with the kind of brutal suddenness which shocked and distressed everyone who liked him here. He was not marvellous, but he was much more than adequate; this seems to me fairly symptomatic of the way in which Israeli policy is conducted now, with total disregard for other lands and reactions in the most influential circles, both in great matters and in minute ones like this. [...]

In the meanwhile, all that you say about the policies of the Israel government is painfully true: when I was in Washington in mid November the mood was sharply anti-Israel, on the part of friend and foe alike (this is true of official circles in England too – but it was always truer of establishment opinion in England so far as officials were concerned than even in America – with the sole exception of the State Department and the Foreign Office, which were always at one on this issue). Nor is the idea of sending Harold Wilson to the United States to collect money for the Technion[2] a very marvellous one, it seems to me – although rich American Jews are as naive as rich British Jews, and the savour of even an ex-Prime-Minister with Wilson's particular characteristics may give them naive pleasure and a false sense of important allies in important places.

To go back to Washington: when I was there Henry Kissinger said more or less what you said to me – that partition was the only sensible and practicable solution. He maintained that by talking about home rule on the West Bank the Begin government had given away all its cards, that home rule was clearly unrealisable – and must lead to war or to an Arab state; that the frontiers of such a state are preselected by offering the entire West Bank for home rule, and that this leaves Israel with no diplomatic or military cards to play – which seemed to him unaccountably stupid. 'Unaccountably' is the only inappropriate word, it seems to me, but he is surely right – large concessions but not complete cession of territory on the West Bank seems the only feasible alternative. And I have a terrible feeling that Israel is behaving rather as the European powers did vis-à-vis German claims in the early 1930s – what was not given to the Democrats was given to Bruning; what was not given to

1 At this time 'Israel' was the official adjectival form of the word in Israel, 'Israeli' being reserved for citizens of the country. IB's usage varies. Avraham Kidron (1919–82), Israeli intelligence officer and diplomat, director, ministry of foreign affairs, 1973–6, Israeli ambassador to the UK 1977–9, to Australia 1979–82; he was said to have been recalled from London because Menachem Begin was dissatisfied with him (Moshe Dayan was then the foreign minister).

2 The Israel Institute of Technology, founded 1912; its main campus is on Mount Carmel, in Haifa. Harold Wilson had emphasised the importance of science and technology during his premiership.

Bruning was offered to Schleicher or Groener; what was not offered to them was offered to Papen, and so to Hitler.[1] In other words, a somewhat precarious but not hopeless peace could have been purchased years ago by concessions far smaller than those which now seem, even to the allies of Israel, ridiculously small; there was a moment when enough Arabs would have accepted them and it would have been difficult for the others to fight a war to reject them. Still, all this is speculative and would-have-been history which E. H. Carr and other realists reject as unworthy of serious men. How wrong, how deeply wrong, such people are: nothing in history can be understood save in terms of possible alternatives – it is only disbelief in the existence of alternatives, i.e. [...] a rigid determinism (I am back on my hobby-horse), that makes history so dreadfully boring. Carr's history of the Soviet Union,[2] although very full of material, carefully and excellently written, is one of the most tedious and dreary books in existence: if ever the archives, or even a part of them, are opened, it will have to be rewritten very radically.

Morton White, of the Princeton Institute, keeps tempting me with offers to collaborate with him in writing a piece on historical method, philosophically considered, and perhaps I shall do it. History is certainly much too important to be left to historians – with certain exceptions. [...]

With much love,

Yours ever,

Isaiah

TO DAVID ABERBACH[3]

12 April 1979

Headington House

Dear Aberbach,

[...] You ask me about Nietzsche. Remember that the blond beast[4] is made to serve, if not nationalist, at least racist purposes; that the contempt for Christianity and liberalism is quite enough to go on with for a Fascist regime

---

1 The European powers made a series of concessions to Germany in the early 1930s which came too late to prevent the rise of extremism there. IB mentions the last 3 chancellors of the Weimar Republic before Hitler assumed that office in January 1933: Heinrich Brüning (1885–1970), 1930–2 (459/6); Franz Joseph Hermann Michael Maria von Papen (zu Köningen) (1879–1969), June–November 1932; Kurt Ferdinand Friedrich Hermann von Schleicher (1882–1934), 1932–3. Before Brüning, Hermann Müller (1876–1931) of the Social Democratic Party was chancellor 1928–30. Karl Eduard Wilhelm Groener (1867–1939), former chief, German general staff (1919), was minister of defence 1928–32.

2 A History of Soviet Russia (London, 1950–78): 14 vols.

3 David Aberbach (b. 1953), then a doctoral student at Linacre (MLitt 1977, DPhil 1980); prof. of Hebrew and comparative studies, Dept of Jewish Studies, McGill, since 1987.

4 A metaphor used by Nietzsche whose meaning is disputed, but which can be interpreted as having racial overtones: 'One must not underestimate the predator deep in all these noble races, the glorious blond beast [blonde Bestie], lusting after prey and victory.' Zur Genealogie der Moral: Eine Streitschrift (Leipzig, 1887) 1. 11.

– the ideas of Nietzsche, in a vulgarised form, were widespread among people who never read a line of him, as the ideas of Marx and Freud are today. He certainly had an influence on Italian Fascism, and on German militarism and imperialism. You are right that he deprecated German nationalism and praised the Jews – at least in contrast with the despised Christians. You must remember, however, that his sister[1] was married to a ferocious nationalist who became a Nazi – Förster[2] – and was a violent nationalist and anti-Semite herself: and she forged a certain number of his writings, which later editors have had to cope with [...]. Nietzsche was not a nationalist, but he added – or rather, the vulgarisation of his ideas added – the notions of self-assertive elitism, craving for violence, and contempt for liberalism, internationalism, pacifism etc., which in the end produced the critical mass which issued into Fascism of the pagan variety, i.e. Italian and German, with imitations in south and north-eastern Europe, as opposed to the Iberian peninsula, where it was intimately linked with the Church. [...]

Yours ever,
Isaiah Berlin

TO NOEL ANNAN

12 May 1979

Headington House

Dearest Noel,

Your letter arrived half an hour ago, and I wish to answer it immediately, without reflection, and record my deep gratitude to you for responding as you have to my genuine *cri de coeur* [...].

Now, about the facts themselves. In spite of All Souls, New York, Jerusalem, the British Academy, I am not a public figure in the sense in which, let us say, A. J. P. Taylor, or Graham Greene,[3] or Arthur Schlesinger, or Arnold Toynbee,[4] or Kenneth Clark are. Truly, I am not; and because I am not, I was terribly hesitant about accepting either a knighthood or the OM, because I thought it would give undue prominence to basically unpublic

1 Elisabeth Förster-Nietzsche (1846–1935) née Nietzsche, younger sister of Friedrich Nietzsche, became his guardian and literary executor after his breakdown 1889, and after his death published corrupted editions of his works, designed to make him appear the prophet of her own extreme nationalist and anti-Semitic outlook. She became an ardent Nazi, and Hitler and other Nazi leaders attended her funeral; m. 1885 Bernhard Förster (next note).

2 Bernhard Förster (1843–89), anti-Semitic German propagandist and far-right politician, emigrated to Paraguay 1886 with Elisabeth Förster-Nietzsche, and established there the Aryan colony of Nueva Germania 1887; committed suicide after this collapsed, leaving his wife to confront a financial scandal; she returned to Germany 1893.

3 (Henry) Graham Greene (1904–91), OM 1986, novelist.

4 Arnold Joseph Toynbee (1889–1975), historian; director of studies, Royal Institute of International Affairs, and research prof. of international history, LSE, 1925–55; made famous in Britain and America by the success of the 2-vol. abridgement (with D. C. Somervell: Oxford, 1946–7) of vols 1–10 of his 12-vol. *Study of History* (London, 1934–61).

activities and a life which, so far as I could make it so without betraying loyalties or convictions, was purely marginal to the central issues and activities of any region of national life (let alone the central current). [...] you will not persuade me that I am a natural object of public interest – I need to be built up by artificial means, by masters of the media, in order even to seem to be so. I wish I were like Moore,[1] but I admit I am not, philosophical genius apart; neither am I like C. S. Lewis[2] or Leavis or even awful Lord Snow (whose public praise naturally embarrasses me); or a man who stands for certain views, a kind of ideologue, identified with a movement, like Laski[3] or Tawney[4] or Cole,[5] or even Oakeshott – more like Butterfield[6] (at most), not quite as bad as what Crossman and a good many others thought and think me to be – a well-disposed, amiable rattle. Do not, I beg you, think this is simply an attempt, stimulated by some kind of genuinely felt false modesty (if you see what I mean), to opt out of an exposed position in which I am liable to receive both kicks and ha'pence. [...]

Yours ever, with much love [...].

Isaiah

TO ARTHUR SCHLESINGER

28 May 1979

Headington House

Dear Arthur,

[...] We came back from Jerusalem a short while ago, where I was more or less forced to undergo a TV interview, and the prime minister of that country,[7] on the next day, informed me that he had watched this interview

---

1 George Edward Moore (1873–1958), OM 1951, prof. of philosophy, Cambridge, and fellow, Trinity, 1925–39; he was regarded as one of the great teachers of philosophy, and his influence was felt far beyond his chosen discipline. IB recalled giving a paper at a symposium in the 1930s at which Moore presided: 'he said "When Mr Berlin says [whatever it was], I consider that he is absolutely right. Nobody can deny his statement that [whatever it was]" – at this point I felt very proud – "but in saying that, what is Mr Berlin saying? He is saying nothing." And then the demolition.' To Dr Thomas, 14 January 1991.

2 Clive Staples Lewis (1898–1963), writer, scholar and Christian apologist; fellow and English tutor, Magdalen, 1925–54; prof. of medieval and Renaissance English, Cambridge, 1954–66; best known for the 7 vols of his allegorical Christian fairy-tales for children, *The Chronicles of Narnia* (London, 1950–6).

3 Harold Joseph Laski (1893–1950), Marxist-influenced political theorist; Graham Wallas Prof. of Political Science, LSE, 1926–50; executive committee, Labour Party, 1936–49, chair 1945–6.

4 Richard Henry Tawney (1880–1962), economic historian and social reformer; prof. of economic history, LSE, 1931–49.

5 (George) Douglas Howard Cole (1889–1959), Fabian socialist and political theorist; Chichele Prof. of Social and Political Theory, Oxford (IB's predecessor), and fellow, All Souls, 1944–57; research fellow, Nuffield, 1957–9.

6 Herbert Butterfield (1900–79), Kt 1968; prof. of modern history, Cambridge, 1944–63, Regius Prof. 1963–8, Master, Peterhouse, 1955–68.

7 Menachem Begin.

and that the announcer had said about me that I was well known to be opposed to the Herut[1] party, and in particular to himself, although I would not say so in public. 'I was rather intrigued by that,' he said: 'Professor Berlin, what have you against me?' Disarming but embarrassing. I failed to satisfy him. He is a very unattractive and politically deplorable man, and I hate all terrorists anyway (I would not rule out the justifiability of terrorism in some situations). But, despite your beliefs to the contrary, I am bound to say that it is not a hotbed of nationalism – far from it – and is both liberal and democratic beyond most countries in the world, if by 'liberal' is meant total freedom of expression. Arabs can say terrible things about Jews, the poor can be openly rude to the rich, without being made to suffer for it by any overt public action; and rights are protected, though there is some inequality of status as between Arabs and Jews, due to gnawing doubts about survival, either nationally or individually, on the part of the Jews; by 'democratic' all I think that I mean is that the government, or those in power, have systematically to curry favour with the citizens for fear of being thrown out. I know of no other effective definition of democracy – neither majority rule nor equality of rights nor representative government, etc., etc. But lest this degenerate into a piece of Zionist propaganda abhorred by Izzy Stone, I shall come to a rapid end. Do let us discuss this in the summer when we meet. [...]

    Yours,

      Isaiah

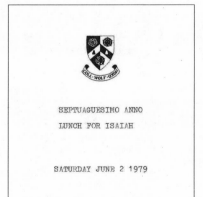

A Festschrift to mark IB's seventieth birthday was presented to him at a lunch in Wolfson on 2 June 1979. Pat Utechin's copy of the menu is shown here. 'Septuagesimo [*sic*] anno [expleto]' ('Now that seventy years have passed') is an allusion to Pope Pius XI's 1931 encyclical *Quadragesimo anno*.

---

1 'Freedom', the main right-wing party in Israel from its 1948 foundation, led by Menachem Begin, until its merger with Likud 1988.

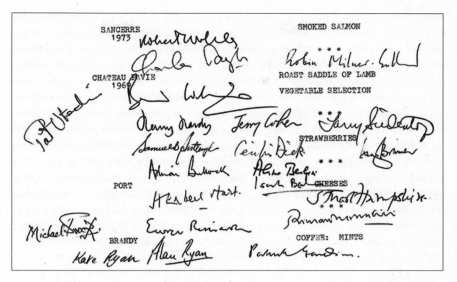

The menu is signed by the contributors who attended, and by other guests, here identified in parentheses: Robert Wokler, Charles Taylor, Robin Milner-Gulland, Pat Utechin, Bernard Williams, HH, Jerry [G. A.] Cohen, Larry Siedentop, Samuel Guttenplan (373/4), Cecilia Dick (Domestic Bursar, Wolfson), Hugo Brunner (228/2), Adrian Bullock (Production Manager, General Division, OUP), Aline Berlin, IB, Herbert Hart, Stuart Hampshire, Michael Brock (Warden, Nuffield; formerly Vice President and Bursar, Wolfson), George Richardson (Secretary to the Delegates and Chief Executive, OUP), Richard Wollheim, Kate Ryan (on a maternity break between publishing jobs; wife of Alan Ryan), Alan Ryan, Patrick Gardiner.

7 June 1979: publication of IB's Against the Current: Essays in the History of Ideas, *edited by HH, with an introduction by Roger Hausheer.*

TO QUENTIN SKINNER

19 June 1979

Headington House

Dear Quentin (if I may: I really cannot do anything else after your review of vol. 3 of my posthumous works),[1]

[…] All that you say seems to me entirely true – particularly my irresistible attraction to those moments in the history of ideas when some effective deviation, or better still overturn, occurs, some radical turning point after which nothing is ever quite the same. I think this happened after Aristotle,

1 QS's largely laudatory review of AC, 'Inside Story', *New Statesman*, 8 June 1979, 830–1.

with the Stoics and Epicureans;[1] it happened when the Jews and Greeks collided; then Machiavelli,[2] then the German historicists and Romantics,[3] but then, despite Marx and Freud, never again to the same degree. I am prone to exaggeration and this may be going too far: but it is the isolated original swimmers against the stream, even those who stand stock still and do not let the stream carry them away – the exceptions, not the upholders and disciples of a continuous tradition – the swerve, not a regular curve, almost plottable, a species of historical analytic geometry, moving inexorably in some direction or other. I suspect that all this is ultimately temperamental, that Fichte[4] was right – that as a man's temperament, so his philosophy. This has no bearing on the validity of doctrines, but a strong one on why some people think the thoughts they do. At any rate, you have penetrated my not very effective disguises, as also has Kołakowski in the *Guardian*:[5] it is a source of genuine pride to me, and, of course, gratitude too, that you should have written as you have. [...]

Yours very sincerely,
Isaiah

TO ROWLAND BURDON-MULLER
16 July 1979

Headington House

Dearest Rowland,

[...] I have just been rung up by a man and asked to write personal letters to the Home Secretary and the Foreign Secretary – or at least to sign a letter with five or six other signatories – demanding that we receive 15,000

1 Aristotle (384–322 BCE), one of the greatest figures in Western philosophy, studied under Plato and tutored the young Alexander the Great; the Stoics, followers of the philosophical school founded c.300 BCE by Zeno of Citium; the Epicureans, followers of the philosopher Epicurus (342–270 BCE). IB's view of this 'overturn', for him a key moment in the emergence of the idea of individual 'negative' liberty, is elaborated in 'The Birth of Greek Individualism: A Turning Point in the History of Political Thought' in L, one of his 3 1962 Storrs Lectures at Yale on 'Three Turning Points in Political Thought' ('The Greeks'; 'Machiavelli'; 'Romanticism'); links to texts of the last 2 are in the IBVL at ⟨http://berlin.wolf.ox.ac.uk/lists/nachlass/index.html⟩.
2 See IB's 'The Originality of Machiavelli' in AC and PSM.
3 See RR.
4 Johann Gottlieb Fichte (1762–1814), Idealist philosopher and German nationalist. One of the 6 main subjects of FIB. In his first introduction (1797) to his *Foundations of the Science of Knowledge* of 1794–5 he wrote, 'What sort of philosophy one chooses depends [...] on what sort of man one is; for a philosophical system is not a dead piece of furniture that we can reject or accept as we wish; it is rather a thing animated by the soul of the person who holds it.' *Johann Gottlieb Fichte's sämmtliche Werke*, ed. I. H. Fichte (Berlin, 1845–6), i 434; quoted from *Fichte: Science of Knowledge (Wissenschaftslehre) with the First and Second introductions*, ed. and trans. Peter Heath and John Lachs (New York, [1970]), 16.
5 Leszek Kołakowski (1929–2007), Polish-born philosopher and historian of ideas, left his homeland for the West, 1968, after facing official censure for his advocacy of democratisation and reform; senior research fellow, All Souls, 1970–95; 'Gallery of Subversives', *Guardian*, 14 June 1979, 10, is his review of AC.

Vietnamese refugees in England.[1] Of course we must be as generous as we can to these unfortunate people: the British record with regard to refugees in the 1930s is quite decent – that is, the Home Office behaved quite well and the Foreign Office abominably. But if I know anything about governments, particularly Conservative governments, the idea that Lord Carrington[2] or Mr William Whitelaw[3] will be stirred by a letter written by six worthy and well-meaning persons saying that we ought to be kind to the Vietnamese has little sense of reality. So I encouraged the man to produce a letter for a newspaper, which I was prepared to sign, not this kind of useless private pressure.

There is a great deal of selective indignation going on: those who were against the Vietnam War are not particularly stirred about the Vietnamese refugees, and prefer not to think about Cambodia at all;[4] those who were for it are not particularly stirred about Chilean or Argentinian victims.[5] The Persian situation draws reactions from everyone: the right don't like the defeat of the Shah and the discomfiture of the West, but approve Khomeini's[6] anti-Communism – the left is totally silent. I wish I were a Catholic or a Communist with a moral and political director who would tell me exactly what to think. As it is, I am, as I have always been, an understander of too many sides in too many cases, and therefore quite useless. [...]

Yours ever,
   Isaiah

1 From September 1978 there was a dramatic increase in the numbers of Vietnamese fleeing Communist rule: the majority, the so-called 'boat people', left by sea; by October an estimated 115,000 of the 250,000 who were thought to have fled Vietnam and Cambodia since 1975 had still to find a home; that month 346 Vietnamese, rescued by a British ship in the South China Sea, arrived in London (David Nicholson-Lord, 'Vietnamese Refugees Taste British Way of Life', *Times*, 18 October 1978, 2d–g).

2 Peter Alexander Rupert Carrington (b. 1919), 6th Baron Carrington 1938, MC 1945, Conservative statesman; secretary of state for defence 1970–4, for energy 1974; foreign secretary 1979–82; secretary general, NATO, 1984–88.

3 William Stephen Ian ('Willie') Whitelaw (1918–99), 1st Viscount Whitelaw 1983, Kt 1990; Conservative politician; defeated for the Conservative leadership by Margaret Thatcher 1975; deputy leader, Opposition, and spokesman on home affairs 1975–9; Home Secretary 1979–83; Lord President of the Council and leader, Lords, 1983–8.

4 IB suggests that responses to the Cambodian genocide were conditioned by the legacy of the war in Vietnam, opponents of that war being unwilling to entertain the possibility that large-scale atrocities were being perpetrated by an indigenous leftist regime, not least because the atrocities were widely reported in the Western media, which was held to be biased and mendacious.

5 The victims of the brutal military dictatorships of Augusto Pinochet in Chile, 1973–90, and of Jorge Rafael Videla in Argentina, 1976–81; an estimated 30,000 Argentinians are thought to have been tortured and killed by the junta during its *guerra sucia* (dirty war) against political opponents, c.1976–83, and 3,000 in Chile after the CIA-backed coup that deposed the democratic government of Salvador Allende 11 September 1973; including prisoners tortured in Chile, more than 40,000 were affected.

6 Ruhollah Khomeini (1900–89), Iranian Shiite Muslim leader (ayatollah), who returned to Iran from exile in France in February 1979 to lead the revolution that had overthrown the Shah; he inaugurated the theocratic Islamic Republic of Iran.

TO IRVING SINGER[1]

19 July 1979

Headington House

Dear Irving,

[...] The Harvard ceremony was extraordinary.[2] I was genuinely flattered by being offered this degree, for I have warm feelings towards Harvard, which so far as I am concerned has always been very kind to me, as you know – but the whole spectacle! The passing of the generations, the class of 1904, the oldest living Harvard man, the bath-chairs, the shepherds who were appointed to guide the honorand sheep – in my case, John Clive[3] in the morning, which was all right since he is an old friend and I am attached to him; in the afternoon, John Updike,[4] who had written a particularly hostile review of my book on Vico and Herder in the *New Yorker*;[5] neither he nor I alluded to this in any fashion, though I did mention Vico once or twice in an absent sort of way, just to see if there was the faintest reaction; there was; but I affected not to see that. Do you read his novels? I read one, I cannot remember its name, but it seemed to me mainly pornographic, although skilfully written: he is obviously pleased with himself; he spent a year in Oxford at the Ruskin School, talked wistfully about that, was perfectly friendly, and so, in a slightly insincere way, was I.

However, there were embarrassments: at the dinner on the night before, some cad had revealed the fact that it was in fact my birthday (6 June), so the President felt obliged to announce this to the assembled company, a cake was produced, at very short notice evidently, with three little candles – I suppose this was felt to be better than two, and two better than one – which I duly blew out, and a short speech of welcome was made. Obviously I was expected to answer in some witty, irresistible fashion, but I did not. I simply could not do it. One thing is that I am incapable of spontaneous reactions in public, though I have a lot of *pensées d'escalier*[6] afterwards and feel shame at

1 Irving Singer (1925–2015), Harvard-educated philosopher; associate prof. of philosophy, MIT, 1959–69, prof. 1969–2013.
2 IB received an hon. LLD from Harvard on his 70th birthday, 6 June 1979.
3 John Leonard Clive (1924–90) né Hans Leo Kleff, Berlin-born Jewish American historian; assistant prof. of history and general education, Harvard, 1952–60; assistant/associate prof. of history, Chicago, 1960–4; prof. of history and literature, Harvard, 1965–75, William R. Kenan, Jr, Prof. of History 1978–89.
4 John Hoyer Updike (1932–2009), Harvard-educated Pulitzer-Prize-winning American novelist, poet and short-story writer.
5 'Texts and Men', a review of Barthes's *Sade/Fourier/Loyola* and VH, *New Yorker*, 4 October 1976, 148–56: 'here, in a set of warmed-over lectures that breathe a stale air of recapitulation, glitters a brilliant exercise of knowledge, a plausible collation of obscure texts that enables us to enter into the intellectual adventures and horizons of the Renaissance as no instancing less concrete could do'.
6 'Afterthoughts' (literally 'staircase thoughts').

having cut a *bruta figura*;[1] so all I did was to bow and say 'Thank you' under my breath. Some sensitive persons applauded, in approval of no speech, others looked slightly cross. I should have felt even more embarrassed had the German Chancellor[2] been present, but fortunately he did not arrive until the next day.

Then, at dinner with the Mason Hammonds,[3] where we stayed, John Clive read a comical poem in my honour, which was very prettily and ingeniously composed, and again, I lowered my head and muttered that I was very grateful. I did not leap to my feet and say 'Unused as I am to public speaking, I cannot let this occasion pass without ...'. I did not do too well – however, I do not suppose anyone will remember this too strongly against me.

I am a natural recipient of hon. degrees because I am harmless and, when two much more controversial figures are suggested to those who take an interest in such things, the two parties clash over the rival merits of incompatible candidates, and I am chosen as a compromise solution. I have a feeling that I owe my entire career to this kind of thing; I do not complain; to be overestimated is not the most painful of states; I am about to be given an hon. degree at Sussex University, where a riot by the undergraduates is expected, not so much against me personally as against the University and reactionaries in general, with whom I am identified. Still, I am seventy, as you know – it is not my world, I say to myself, I cannot cope with it, let the young (men of sixty) deal with it as best they can. [...]

Yours,

Isaiah

TO MAX FISCH[4]

19 September 1979 [*carbon*]

Headington House

Dear Professor Fisch,

[...] Let me answer your enquiry: the inaccurate account of my conversation with Sheffer[5] was in Sir Alfred Ayer's autobiography,[6] now, I think, in paperback, in which he says that my chief reason for abandoning philosophy for the history of ideas and the like was Sheffer's insistence that one needed

1 'Unfeeling impression', i.e. having given the impression of insensitivity.
2 Helmut Heinrich Waldemar Schmidt (b. 1918), German statesman, author and publisher; SPD Bundestag member, FRG, 1953–61, 1965–87, chancellor 1974–82; publisher, *Die Zeit*, 1983–9; commencement day speaker, Harvard, 1979.
3 Mason Hammond (1903–2002), Pope Prof. of the Latin Language and Literature, Harvard, 1950–73, m. 1935 Florence Hobson (1909–99) née Pierson.
4 Max Harold Fisch (1900–95), US historian of philosophy and science; prof. of philosophy, Illinois, 1946–69; senior editor, Peirce Edition Project, Indiana at Indianapolis, 1976–91.
5 Henry Maurice Sheffer (1882–1964), Ukraine-born US logician and philosopher; prof. of philosophy, Harvard, 1938–52.
6 op. cit.(49/9), 98.

mathematical logic to do philosophy nowadays, and that I was not prepared
to embark on that course. In fact, of course, Sheffer believed in something
directly opposite. He was a logician of very great talent himself and he
thought that the relation of logic to philosophy was somewhat marginal.
He hated logical positivism passionately; he said that if he had known what
Carnap[1] and 'his miserable crew' were going to convert philosophy into, he
would rather not have written himself, for he regarded himself as partially
responsible for this development. His attitude to Russell, by the time I met
him, was ambivalent: he admired his genius and of course was a disciple
as a logician. His main burden was that whereas in logic and psychology
progress was possible, as it was in the natural sciences, so that what was
superseded became obsolete, this was not the case in epistemology, ethics
and general philosophy: 'How can you speak of a scholar in ethics? A man
learned in the theory of knowledge?' He thought it was a marvellous subject
in itself, ruined by positivists, but no more capable of progress than, say,
criticism or the arts. [...]
    Yours sincerely,
      [Isaiah Berlin]   [...]

TO RORY CHILDERS[2]
  21 September 1979 [*carbon*]

                                       Headington House
Dear Professor Childers,
    [...] I do indeed, as my secretary told you, contemplate writing some-
thing about my meetings with Russian writers in the autumn of 1945[3] – the
most interesting by far were, of course, Pasternak and Akhmatova. Whether
what I say about them will prove of any interest, now that so much has been
written about both, is another matter, but I do intend to record something,
even though my memory about events of more than thirty years ago is apt
to be both inaccurate and selective. I kept no notes at the time and have only
kept my memory fresh by talking about it to friends from time to time. This
is no doubt what storytellers in primitive societies tend to do – it does not,
I am afraid, do anything to guarantee accuracy or truth.
    Now, as to your specific enquiries. You are perfectly right that the *Poem
without a Hero* does carry references to my visit; and so do other poems by

1 Rudolf Carnap (1891–1970), German logical positivist philosopher, leading member, Vienna
  Circle; prof. of philosophy, Chicago, 1936–52, UCLA 1954–62.
2 Roderick Winthrop ('Rory') Childers (1931–2014), cardiologist; assistant prof. of medicine,
  Chicago 1964–9, associate prof. 1969–76, prof. from 1976; grandson of the novelist and Irish
  nationalist Robert Erskine Childers, Rory Childers was an authority on modern Irish culture, but
  also learned Russian in order to read the works of Anna Akhmatova and Osip Mandel'shtam, on
  both of whom he published.
3 This he did the next year: 'Meetings with Russian Writers in 1945 and 1956' is included in PI.

Akhmatova, in particular *Cinque* (I have a volume of her poems inscribed by her with the first poem of *Cinque*),[1] and a good deal in *Shipovnik*, *Polnochnye stikhi* and elsewhere. All this was confirmed to me by Amanda Haight, who, as you know, was close to Akhmatova in her last years. [...] I do not propose in my memoir to speculate on the subject of why it is that I am indeed 'the guest from the future', nor why my visit brought her 'doom'[2] – I expect that my visit, the first by any foreigner since 1917, did complicate her position somewhat, and although I am assured by various Soviet scholars that Zhdanov[3] would have condemned her in any case, she herself was convinced that Stalin himself was personally furious about the fact that she allowed me to call on her – I was an official of the British Embassy and therefore necessarily a spy. She confirmed this to me when she received her honorary degree in Oxford. She solemnly and repeatedly told me that she and I began the cold war and wrought fateful changes in the fate of the world – I think she really believed this in some sense. I do not know if you have read the touching and fascinating memoir of her by Lydia Chukovskaya – she there speaks of the fact that once an idea implanted itself in AA's mind she drew rigorously logical consequences from it and believed them all and was immovable.

I shall, of course, be glad to send you my memoir once it is published; you may then, of course, use it as you please, but I would beg you to wait until you receive it. On the other hand, I must explain that I do not intend to interpret Akhmatova's characteristically self-revealing poems so far as they have any relationship to myself; this could only be speculative, as well as an unheard-of vulgarity and unbearable exploitation of what was purely personal in my brief meetings with her, and must remain so. I propose in my memoir to confine myself to our conversations about literature and literary personalities appropriate for public discussion. I am sure you will understand and appreciate my reluctance to go further. There was nothing secret or mysterious about our meetings; she was a great poet and I was her respectful visitor; nevertheless, to speculate about mood and feeling is something that I cannot and will not bring myself to do, now or ever. I have answered in that sense to the many enquiries which, as you rightly suppose, have been addressed to me.

1 The 2nd poem in the published cycle, and the 2nd to be written.
2 In the 'Third and Last' dedication to *Poem without a Hero*, Akhmatova writes that her visitor, named in the body of the poem as 'the guest from the future', will bring her 'pogibel'', 'doom'. Cf. L1 651, where the word is translated as 'death'.
3 Andrey Aleksandrovich Zhdanov (1896–1948), Soviet government and CP official, close associate of Stalin; as a cultural inquisitor 1944–8 he oversaw the brutal campaign against Western influence in Soviet society that led to a purge of artists, writers and composers; Akhmatova, called by Zhdanov 'half nun, half harlot' 1946, was singled out for special treatment, being expelled from the Union of Soviet Writers; Zhdanov died suddenly in August 1948, and Stalin later accused a group of Jewish doctors of his murder. Zhdanov's anathema, 'Doklad t[ovarishcha] Zhdanova o zhurnalakh "Zvezda" i "Leningrad" ', was published in *Zvezda* 1946 no. 7–8, 3–6, and elsewhere.

I ought to add that although I am the person to whom the third dedication[1] was made – and this is widely known both in the West and in the Soviet Union – this cannot be stated or even hinted at in any Soviet publication. Zhirmunsky[2] felt very embarrassed by this. I told him that I understood perfectly and that he did not need to offer the apologies that he did. Nevertheless, he continued to say how unfortunate this was, and begged me not to think ill of him for succumbing to authority. He was an exceptionally brave, honest and altogether decent man, and behaved exceptionally well to Akhmatova herself when she was in disgrace. I assured him of my full understanding of his problem, but he remained inconsolable. […]

Yours sincerely,
    Isaiah Berlin

TO CLAUDIO VÉLIZ
    27 September 1979

                                                    Headington House

Dear Claudio,

Thank you ever so much for your heart-warming letter of 15 September, and in particular for the *Clare Market Review*.[3] I understand very well the impression that my unfortunate lecture – unfortunate because I read one line out of every four, as I told you, and got confused and muddled in the course of reading it – must have made on the enthusiastic *lumières*[4] in the then still dominant LSE tradition (for all that Laski had been replaced by Oakeshott, who introduced me with such ironical disparagement[5] – even though he treats me with positive affection now, particularly when in his cups, we are not, and never can be, friends, or even opponents bound by a mutual feeling of respect). I expect all this is personal in the end, and feel humiliated by this

1 The 1st dedication is to the memory of the soldier-poet Vsevolod Gavrilovich Knyazev (1891–1913); the 2nd to the dancer (inter alia) Olga Afanas'evna Glebova-Sudeikina (1885–1945), the object of Knyazev's unrequited love, the apparent cause of his suicide; the 'Third and Last' to IB, who, however, is not explicitly named.
2 Viktor Maksimovich Zhirmunsky (1891–1971), Russian literary scholar and philologist; awarded an hon. DLitt at Oxford 1966, when he called on IB; they discussed inter alia Anna Akhmatova, whose poems Zhirmunsky was editing – *Stikhotvoreniya i poemy* (Leningrad, 1976) – and Zhirmunsky told IB, on Akhmatova's authority and at her request, which of her poems were wholly or partly inspired by their meetings. These poems are listed in 'The Guest from the Future', an appendix to 'Meetings with Russian Writers in 1945 and 1956' in PI.
3 Véliz had written to Berlin, 15 September, enclosing a copy of an 'absurdly impertinent' review that he had written 1955, when editor, *Clare Market Review*, the journal of the LSE Students' Union, of IB's inaugural Auguste Comte Memorial Trust Lecture (9/9); Véliz had dwelt on the 'glaring shortcomings' of IB's case against determinism and historical inevitability (Lent 1955, 2–4 at 3).
4 Proponents of the Enlightenment.
5 'Listening to him you may be tempted to think that you are in the presence of one of the great intellectual *virtuosos* of our time, a Paganini of ideas' (LSE Archives, Oakeshott 1/3). Cf. L2 364.

thought. Blatant *amour propre* in this respect is something I would rather be without.

And here are Michael Foot on one hand and Lord Lambton[1] on the other – both equidistant from me politically, neither the objects of my admiration or regard (yet I have never met either) until this moment. But now that they have both written exceedingly friendly notices of the book I sent you ...[2] Why should a little, or even much, undeserved praise go such a long way with me? Is it so with you? I admire Dr Leavis, on whom flattery had no effect whatever – if anything, it was counterproductive: George Steiner once wrote an admiring article about him in *Encounter*,[3] which increased Leavis's already violent hostility to him and his writings. I do not wish to go so far. But I wish I had a little of that particular kind of Stoic *ataraxia*[4] – imperviousness to praise or blame. Virginia Woolf once told me that she never read reviews of her books; I wondered whether she really could be so strong and independent and contemptuous; her diaries reveal she read them all and suffered agonies from the unfriendly ones;[5] I feel comforted – nothing is more comforting than the weaknesses of persons obviously superior to oneself in almost every other way, do you not find? [...]

Yours,

Isaiah

TO NOEL ANNAN

20 October 1979

Headington House

Dear Noel,

I am consumed with guilt at not having replied to your marvellous (and I mean that) letter about Belinsky and Leavis.[6] Of course you are right.

1 Antony Claud Frederick Lambton (1922–2006), son of 5th Earl of Durham (1884–1970), disclaimed peerage for life 1970; permitted to sit in Parliament using courtesy title Viscount Lambton; Conservative MP 1951–73.
2 IB has confused 2 books. Foot had reviewed AC in *Tribune* ('A Gallery of Socialist Outsiders', 27 July 1979, 6) and Lambton Herzen's *From the Other Shore*, trans. Moura Budberg [and IB], and *The Russian People and Socialism*, trans. Richard Wollheim (London, 1956), in the *Spectator* ('Hope amidst Despair', 25 August 1979, 21), complimenting IB on his introduction to the latter volume.
3 George Steiner, 'F. R. Leavis', *Encounter* 18 no. 5 (May 1962), 37–44.
4 'Indifference'; literally 'not being disturbed'.
5 See e.g her reaction to reviews of *The Years* in April 1937: 'E.M. [Forster] says *The Years* is dead and disappointing. [...] All the lights sank; my reed bent to the ground. Dead and disappointing – so I'm found out and that odious rice pudding of a book is what I thought – a dank failure. No life in it. [...] Now this pain woke me at 4 a.m. and I suffered acutely. All day [...] I was under the cloud. But about 7 it lifted; there was a good review, of 4 lines, in the *Empire Review*.' *A Writer's Diary*, ed. Leonard Woolf (London, 1953), 280.
6 In 'Art for Liberation's Sake', an interview with Miriam Gross (*Observer*, 5 August 1979, 35), IB described the English literary critic F. R. Leavis as a direct descendant of Belinsky. The day after publication Noel Annan wrote to IB to explain why he could not accept this proposition. While he agreed that both Belinsky and Leavis stood 'against art for art's sake', and believed in 'a direct

Belinsky, for all his occasional fanaticism and wrong-headedness, was infinitely responsive to human relationships – sometimes too much so. His letters, never translated, are the most moving records of an agonised and warm-hearted human being, to whom his relations with his friends meant almost everything, whose views on literature and morality and politics are always sympathetic (at least to me, and I am sure to you) even when perverse; there is never the hectoring, bullying tone of the infallible Savonarola,[1] dispensing praise and blame as an instrument of divine justice, inflexible, implacable. Leavis could not have been adored by Turgenev (whom he thought little of – on the only occasion when I met him he said as much), or Herzen, who would have looked on him as an inquisitor and an enemy of all that he himself believed in – the variety of life and character and the play of the imagination wherever it chose to dart, a source of exhilarating vitality and not of a faith from which any deviation was frivolity or sin. In short, you are right. My only defence is an addiction[2] to what in the end is a moral approach, in Belinsky's case held in check by an astonishing literary sensibility not often to be observed in Western criticism – but you are right about the crude exaggerations practised by poor old Leavis.

Suddenly one afternoon I was rung up by a lady who said that she was Greek, and a great-granddaughter[3] of Belinsky, and could I meet her? I felt excited, and asked her to lunch in an Oxford restaurant. There appeared before me an exquisite Athenian beauty, with beautiful manners like those of the kind of Greek diplomats you would meet in fairly grand circles in Paris, absolutely charming, highly cultivated, with a beautifully brought up daughter who offered me a bag of Greek pistachio nuts, which I accepted. Belinsky's wife[4] – a dreary schoolmistress – and her daughter[5] went to Corfu, it seems, for a holiday, where the daughter met a fairly grand Greek,[6] married him, and died in Athens. The great-granddaughter spoke not a word of Russian, and we did not have much in common, but I was amused and pleased by the whole thing. I liked her much more than I think Belinsky would have done.

Yours ever,
Isaiah

connection between what a writer is and the value of what he writes', Belinsky was interested in the writer as a complete human being, and sought 'to illustrate the man by his works and vice versa. Leavis means no such thing. He despises biography. For him "the man" is a *persona* which emerges from the printed page of his writings.'

1 Girolamo Ṣavonarola (1452–98), ascetic Dominican monk, fought worldly corruption, and briefly controlled Florence 1494–5; excommunicated by Pope Alexander VI 1497; publicly hanged 1498 as a heretic in the city's Piazza della Signoria.
2 On the part of Belinsky and Leavis.
3 Theodora Rembos (b. 1955), in fact Belinksy's great-great-granddaugher.
4 Mariya Vasil'evna Orlova (1812–90).
5 Olga Vissarionovna Benzi (1845–1904) née Belinskaya.
6 Athenian lawyer George Benzi.

In a written Commons answer issued on 15 November, Mrs Thatcher revealed
that in April 1964 Anthony Blunt, then Surveyor of the Queen's Pictures, had
admitted to the security authorities, in return for immunity from prosecution,
that 'he had been recruited by and had acted as a talent-spotter for Russian intel-
ligence before the war, when he was a don at Cambridge, and had passed infor-
mation regularly to the Russians while he was a member of the Security Service
between 1940 and 1945'.[1] The announcement followed revelations in Andrew
Boyle's[2] The Climate of Treason: Five Who Spied for Russia (London,
1979), published on 6 November. It transpired that Blunt had first come under
suspicion in 1951, after enquiries into the defection to the USSR that year of the
spies Guy Burgess[3] and Donald Maclean;[4] Blunt had assisted in the arrangements
for their flight, and was subsequently interviewed eleven times by the author-
ities without confessing. His exposure as the 'fourth man' in the Cambridge spy
ring with Maclean, Burgess and Philby[5] was front-page news in Britain on 16
November 1979; a month later IB wrote to Arthur Schlesinger: 'As for Blunt, it is
subject no. 1 among virtually everyone you know. So far I have attended no dinner
party at which violent altercations broke out, as there is a reasonable degree of
unanimity about his conduct. I talked to Mr Boyle myself, which I now slightly
regret, as everything came out in no degree libellously, but inaccurately.'[6]

TO ANDREW BOYLE

13 November 1979 [*carbon*]

Headington House

Dear Mr Boyle,

Like the majority of your reviewers, I am reading your book, *Climate*
of Treason, with great interest. To my surprise, I find myself quoted in it,
although I clearly recollect that when we talked at the Athenaeum, I did so
on the understanding that you would not do this, a condition to which you
agreed. But since there is nothing to be done about that, let that be.

The main purpose of my writing – apart from congratulating you on the
deserved success of your book – is to point out certain inaccuracies, at any
rate so far as facts about myself are concerned.[7] [...]

1 *Parliamentary Debates* (Commons) 973, 15 November 1979, cols 679W–680W.
2 Andrew Philip More Boyle (1919–91), author, journalist, broadcaster; joined BBC 1947, founding editor, *The World At One, The World This Weekend, PM* etc. 1965–75.
3 The spy Guy Francis de Moncy Burgess (1911–63) joined the CPGB at Cambridge (where his drinking and homosexuality were already in evidence), the British secret service 1938.
4 Donald Duart Maclean (1913–83), diplomat and spy; after disappearing from the UK he and Burgess resurfaced in Moscow, where they afterwards lived and died.
5 Harold Adrian Russell ('Kim') Philby (1912–88), British intelligence officer and Soviet spy; the so-called 'third man' alongside Burgess and Maclean (492/2).
6 To Arthur Schlesinger, 12 December 1979.
7 As Noel Annan made clear in the TLS, the book could be criticised on many grounds, not least its inaccuracy, but not ignored: 'All Honourable Men', TLS, 7 December 1979, 83.

p. 196, para. 3. You say that I 'immediately smelled a rat'. This overestimates my acuteness. I had no idea, of course, that Burgess[1] had put up a scheme to Harold Nicolson,[2] vetted by Lord Perth[3] etc., about enlightening the Russians about the truth in the West. I was not told this at all – only that nobody in the British Embassy in Moscow knew much Russian, that there was no press attaché, that one was needed (all of which I believe was more or less false), and that I had the required qualifications. What seemed to me odd was that there was any work for a press attaché to do in Moscow – the idea of persuading the Soviet press to insert items favourable to Britain seemed an impossible task, even if this had not been the time of the Russo-German Pact.[4] Nevertheless, Harold Nicolson and Burgess between them said that, what with my knowledge of Russian, and the need to know what was going on in the Soviet press, there was a job I could do; and as nobody else offered me anything at the time, I accepted. I had not 'offered to help the country in any way I could'[5] – that would have been rather self-important. All I did was to fill in a form from the Ministry of Labour which was circulated to practically all Oxford dons. Nothing followed, and I was indeed told by a friend of mine, an Oxford poet called Phillips,[6] who worked in the Ministry of Labour, that I was unlikely to be offered a job because, as you say, I was born an alien. I knew this to be the rule, and although I was disappointed, it is quite incorrect to say that 'the slight had rankled'. Rightly or wrongly, I had not felt it to be a slight, only a piece of mechanical bureaucracy.

I am not clear whether you think that this imaginary 'slight' had anything to do with my acceptance of what I took to be the post of press attaché in Moscow, which I duly discussed with officials both in the Ministry of Information and the Foreign Office (not, however, the Northern Department

1 For IB's trip to the US with Burgess see L1 309–35. IB denied suspecting him of Communism.
2 Though married (to Vita Sackville-West, 490/4) with children, Nicolson also took male lovers, and his close interest in Burgess may at least in part have been sexual: 'Burgess could not have taken anyone in, yet did: after all, Harold Nicolson got him every job he ever had, so far as I know, and was in happy correspondence with him until the end' (to Alistair Cooke, 10 May 1989).
3 John David Drummond (1907–2002), 17th Earl of Perth 1951; lieutenant, Intelligence Corps, 1940, War Cabinet Offices 1942–3, Ministry of Production 1944–5; partner, Schroder's, 1945–56; minister of state for colonial affairs 1957–62 (resigned); first crown estate commissioner 1962–77.
4 The German–Soviet Treaty of Non-Aggression, 23 August 1939, negotiated by the Soviet foreign minister Vyacheslav Molotov and his German counterpart Joachim von Ribbentrop, joined previously implacable enemies in a marriage of convenience that provided mutual security and enabled them to destroy and partition Poland.
5 'Moreover, when war had broken out the year before, Whitehall had refused Berlin's offer to help the country in any way he could' (196). On this see MI 93. For IB's desire to help his country, cf. 'I [...] thought that I could perhaps be of service to the country, to however small [a] degree, if I could go to Moscow in some semi-official or official capacity [...]. There are a good many useful things which it seems to me that I could do.' To Lord Halifax, 21 June 1940; L1 303.
6 Possibly Thomas Williams Phillips (1883–1966), KBE 1934, one of the civil servants credited with creating the welfare state; Ministry of Labour 1919–44, deputy secretary 1924–34, permanent secretary 1935–44; Gaisford Greek Prose Prize, Oxford, 1905.

of the latter, e.g. Fitzroy Maclean,[1] who told me afterwards that it was he who informed Sir Stafford Cripps[2] and recorded his objection;[3] but it is perfectly true that I consulted a number of persons, including the celebrated *éminence grise* Lionel Curtis,[4] my colleague at All Souls, and only accepted after they all seemed to think that the idea was sound).

p. 197. I am said to have gone on a VIP flight to the United States.[5] This was not so: Burgess and I went by Cunarder, the *Antonia*, about 15,000 tons, which narrowly missed being hit by a torpedo a day or two out of Liverpool. We went not 'before the end of September', but in July, from Liverpool to Quebec and on to Montreal, New York, Washington. A few lines below this, you say that 'an urgent message arrived for them', i.e. Burgess and myself. An urgent message arrived for Burgess, recalling him, but none for me. In due course I asked that an enquiry be addressed to the Foreign Office as to whether I was to proceed alone to Moscow. The answer was that, as it was not intended to employ me in Moscow, I was free to do whatever I wished. I was offered a post in Washington by Stephen Childs[6] in his section of the embassy (he said he was short-handed and had authority to employ additional staff). I wrote to Harold Nicolson, my would-be employer, and said that it seemed to me best to return to Oxford, and asked his advice, which I felt I was bound to do. He replied that if any job was offered to one in wartime one had a duty to accept, and that I was in his opinion obliged to accept Childs's offer. Nevertheless, after doing the job on AP[7] of which you speak, I went home. I felt that I had something to do in Oxford and possibly something in Moscow, but that I was in Washington by pure chance and I did not wish to be, or seem to be, *embusqué*;[8] the last thing I wanted to do was to be a refugee from England at that moment. This may seem copybook patriotism but it is what I felt. I did detect a considerable anti-British bias in the AP despatches – I gather that this led to a démarche, and the tone was improved. I returned to England in October – I do not remember whether

1 Fitzroy Hew Royle Maclean (1911–96), 1st baronet 1957, army officer and Conservative politician; British Embassy, Moscow, 1937–9; Northern dept, FO, London, 1939–41; special operations in the war; MP 1941–74.
2 (Richard) Stafford Cripps (1889–1952), Kt 1930, Labour politician and lawyer; MP, East Bristol, 1931–50; UK ambassador to the USSR 1940–2; minister of aircraft production 1942–5; chancellor of the exchequer 1947–50.
3 See L1 319, 325, 329 ('Mr. Berlin is trying to double cross us. We had better telegraph to Sir S Cripps'), 334.
4 Lionel George Curtis (1872–1955), public servant and historian; fellow, All Souls, 1921–55.
5 'He [Burgess] departed with his Oxford protégé on a VIP flight to the United States before the end of September [1940]'.
6 Stephen Lawford Childs (1896–1943), British diplomat, attached to the League of Nations and the International Labour Organization during the 1920s and 1930s; BIS 1940–2; killed in an air crash between Iraq and Iran January 1943.
7 Associated Press. In September 1940 IB carried out an analysis of AP dispatches for the British Library of Information in NY; discussions were then under way about a possible long-term role for him in the US.
8 'A shirker'.

it was late October or not – on the same Pan Am plane as the ambassador, Lord Lothian[1] – via Lisbon, and after some delay there did indeed return to Oxford.

Maclean:[2] I can assure you that I did not know that Maclean had recluse-like habits, nor did I consider anything he did 'abnormal and unhealthy'.[3] I did not tax him on the subject. It was he who said to me that he seemed to meet nobody but conventional and pompous officials, that he understood that I knew some New Dealers (which was true), and could he meet some of them? Thereupon I persuaded a friend of mine whose husband was in uniform in the Pacific (they were both ardent New Dealers and both became exceedingly famous later – the lady is one of the best-known public figures in the United States now) to invite Maclean to dinner.[4] All the other guests were her friends and I had never met them before.

p. 292. The evening was indeed a disaster. Some remark of mine about Mrs Longworth did indeed set Maclean off. He said that persons who called themselves liberal had no business knowing reactionaries of her type; he could not understand how I could even be tempted to do so. All life was a battle and one should know which side one was on and stay faithful to it. One must be clear which side of the barricades one was on: relations with the enemy were not permissible – at this point he became exceedingly abusive. I replied that the civilisation we were fighting for – civilisation, as well as our lives – entailed the freedom to know anyone one pleased, just because one liked them, although in a crisis – war or revolution – one might have to shoot them; but that I did not accept the proposition that life was perpetual war between two sides (whatever they might be). Perhaps I should have realised from Maclean's speech that he was some sort of political extremist, e.g. a Communist or very left-wing socialist, or something of that kind; but the thought never entered my head. Indeed, I never knew that Burgess was a Communist either. Such imperceptiveness is rare, and as I said above, I think you have overestimated my sagacity.

The rest of the company thereupon joined in the debate, and took Maclean's side and attacked me passionately and unanimously. At this point an element of farce enters your account. You say that Maclean reached down and grabbed me by the lapels of my jacket (as he was towering over me). This did not occur, still less the interposition of Douglas Fairbanks, Jr[5] – he

1 Philip Henry Kerr (1882–1940), 11th Marquess of Lothian; UK ambassador, Washington, from August 1939 until his untimely death, 12 December 1940; succeeded by Lord Halifax.
2 Donald Maclean was then a colleague of IB's at the British Embassy, Washington.
3 'The recluse-like habits of the newcomer [Maclean] suggested anti-social traits which Berlin considered abnormal and unhealthy in a young and presumably ambitious diplomat' (291).
4 Katharine ('Kay') *Graham (1917–2001), journalist, and her husband Phil(ip); the year was 1944 (MI Tape 7, 8 February 1994; L1 532/1; MI 128).
5 Douglas Elton Fairbanks, Jr (1909–2000), hon. KBE 1949, DSC 1944; US actor, writer, producer and company director; served with distinction in the US Navy Reserve 1941–54, attaining the rank of captain; his successful Hollywood screen career, from 1923, included starring roles in *The Dawn*

was not present, nor was there the remotest likelihood of his being there: I have no idea what he was doing, but he was known neither to my hostess nor myself nor anyone present, so far as I know, and could not, I suspect, be described either as a New Dealer or an anti-New-Dealer. What I think I said to you was that, as the company attacked me, I felt like Douglas Fairbanks (Sr),[1] standing on a table in one of the old films, fending off a dozen assailants – but, unlike Douglas Fairbanks, receiving many painful wounds.[2] I think it must have been Douglas Fairbanks's name in your notes in this context that led you to Douglas Fairbanks, Jr, whose appearance in the story seems, on the face of it, pure fantasy.

I did indeed receive a letter of apology, but Maclean did not call upon me; nor did he say (enigmatically or otherwise) 'Why don't you join *us*?'[3] What he did do was to invite me to lunch at his house (in order to make up); I there met his wife[4] and one or two of her sisters. The conversation at first was quite amicable, but somehow the name of the Vice President of the United States, Henry Wallace,[5] was mentioned, and I expressed the opinion that he had a screw loose somewhere. Whereupon, after the ladies had left the room, Maclean did indeed have another tantrum, and said that Wallace was a splendid man, much admired by his wife and her family, and that I was very wrong to say such things about him, and should not do so again. After that, our relationship came, as you rightly say, to an end. I never, so far as I remember, spoke to him again and he did not conceal his dislike of me.

This is all, but as I am sure that you are concerned with total accuracy I feel that you will not mind my pointing out these inaccuracies. I shall now return to reading your fascinating book.

Yours sincerely,
Isaiah Berlin

Patrol (1930), *Little Caesar* (1931) and *Sinbad the Sailor* (1947); son of Douglas Fairbanks, Sr (next note).

1 Douglas Elton Thomas Ulman Fairbanks, Sr (1883–1939), Hollywood actor famous for his swashbuckling roles in silent films such as *Robin Hood* (1922) and the part-talkie *The Iron Mask* (1929).
2 IB enjoyed this image, and used it repeatedly: see L3 187, 212.
3 'Within a few minutes [Maclean's] basic anti-American prejudice betrayed itself again in another tantrum. As if desperately trying to make amends, Maclean said enigmatically: "Why don't you join *us*?" and left the room' (292). Boyle gives the impression that Maclean was casting a recruiting fly over IB, who here denies that this happened.
4 Melinda Maclean (1916–2010) née Marling, daughter of a Chicago oil executive; m. 1940, in Paris, Donald Maclean; joined him in the USSR with their 3 children 1953, but returned to live in the US 1979; she was aware of, and to a degree complicit in, her husband's spying.
5 Henry Agard Wallace (1888–1965), US Republican, then Democrat, then Progressive Party politician; secretary of agriculture 1933–40; FDR's Vice President 1941–5; secretary of commerce 1945–6; forced to resign 1946 after criticising Truman's strong anti-Communist line.

TO SHIELA SOKOLOV GRANT[1]

23 November 1979

Headington House

Dear Shiela,

[...] I did not stay with Goronwy[2] for long – his appearance is so terribly changed that it was all I could do not to give any sign of my shock. Mel Lasky[3] was announced as waiting to see him, and this rather curtailed my visit. Goronwy was perfectly clear-headed – we talked about Machiavelli, he spoke touchingly about the volume of my essays which he had reviewed so generously in *Encounter*,[4] and we only touched very lightly on the Blunt[5] affair. But he said that he had lived under a cloud for many years – I took this to refer to the friction with his friends over those articles.[6] I do not know what other cloud there might have been; anyway, I did not ask. I was terribly upset by the visit and am so still. He said that he would not see me again, but I promised to go and see him next week and shall fulfil that promise – but whether he will be alive by then it is impossible to say. I warned Lasky not to give any sign of shock when he went in to see him after me. [...]

As for a letter about Goronwy as I remember him, I am quite incapable of that; nor do I remember warning you, however sagely, about him: did I really do that? How awful and priggish, however right I may have been. I *have* changed.

Yours ever, ⟨with much love⟩

Isaiah

---

1 Shiela *Sokolov Grant (1913–2004), moralist, author, journalist and political commentator.
2 (Morgan) Goronwy Rees (1909–79), journalist and author, close friend of IB's from their undergraduate days; fellow, All Souls, 1931–46, Estates Bursar 1951–4; Principal, University College of Wales, Aberystwyth, 1953–7. A friend from 1934 of Guy Burgess, who 'told him in 1937 that he was an agent for the Comintern; many were later to allege that Rees, very sympathetic to Communism in the 1930s, was an agent or even a double agent himself' (Kenneth O. Morgan, ODNB).
3 Melvin Jonah Lasky (1920–2004), US journalist, author and critic; a leading figure in mobilising the anti-Communist left during the Cold War; editor of *Encounter* 1958–90, privy to the CIA funding that caused a scandal 1967.
4 Rees reviewed AC in his regular 'R' column in *Encounter*: 53 no. 4 (October 1979), 23–5, ending: 'There are few books published in our time which more dazzlingly illuminate some of the most crucial problems of Western culture and civilisation.'
5 Anthony Blunt had been publicly unmasked as a Soviet agent on 15 November: his knighthood was annulled the next day.
6 'Burgess Stripped Bare', a series of 5 articles in the *People* newspaper, 18 March to 8 April 1956, exposing Burgess's seedy life, and his activities as a spy. Cf. L2 526–7, esp. 526/1. Rees resigned as Principal at Aberystwyth after being severely criticised there over the publication of the articles.

TO MARGARET THATCHER

10 December 1979 [*carbon*]

[Headington House]

[Dear Prime Minister,]

May I begin by expressing my deep gratitude for the great honour, certainly more than my due, for which you most generously wish to put forward my name. However, I look upon a life peerage as conferring not only a title and certain privileges but also certain responsibilities which I do not feel capable of undertaking.

Consequently I hope you will forgive me if I decline this dignity. I should like to say once again that I am deeply conscious of how signal an honour it is for which you wish to recommend me – an act of singular kindness which I shall remember so long as I live.

Yours sincerely,
[Isaiah Berlin]
Sir Isaiah Berlin

TO DANIEL REES[1]

13 December 1979 [*manuscript*]

All Souls

Dear Daniel,

Your father's death is a deep grief to me. I was told that he was to be moved to a nursing home not far from Oxford on Friday: & so I arranged to see him today: & this morning someone from Encounter telephoned to say it was no good. Of course you must have gone over many times in your mind about how it would be – you knew as I did that he could not live long – but no matter what one imagines one's state of mind would be, when it happens it is always much worse: and nothing is ever the same; & the thought that I would never see him again – he told me so when I went to see him ten or so days ago – is one I cannot get used to at all.

I first got to know him when we were both undergraduates – in 1931 I think – & we became great friends: [...] & remained so through thick & thin – the thick used to occur now & then – things always looked brighter, gayer, more delightful when he was there: I loved his company more than anyone's in the thirties – and the forties & fifties – & really all the time, even when differences divided us, as happened in the mid-fifties – & when I saw him again, ten years or so ago, all the old feeling returned & his marvellously life enhancing exhilarating qualities, his imagination, his affectionateness, his

1 Daniel Jenkin Rees (b. 1948), one of the twin sons (and 5 children) of Goronwy Rees and his wife (m. 1940) Margaret Ewing ('Margie') (1921–76) née Morris.

warmth & vitality & bright qualities made up for everything. I knew that he was going through a difficult time after your mother was no more: & I used to have lunch with him, & see him in Oxford, & it was always a source of unique delight to me; nobody ever made things sparkle more in my existence: his voice, his laugh, haunt me now: I ought to have taken more trouble: seen him oftener: he was a genuine lifelong friend; & he thought so too: I must not go on [...]. I am terribly distressed: I hope something worthy of him is done or written: I shall do my best to come to the funeral – or if there is a memorial service – I am quite incapable of saying or writing anything: too much painful feeling.

Yours ever,

Isaiah Berlin

TO BRIAN KNEI-PAZ[1]

5 February 1980

Princeton

Dear Brian,

[...] Afghanistan is all the news here, as you may imagine. George Kennan has written an article for the *New York Times*[2] in which he thinks all this is bellicose hysteria induced by the American government; that, though no doubt the Russians are wicked to have attacked Afghanistan, and have done it very 'clumsily', yet Afghanistan is after all their neighbour, it has a very unstable political regime, they have been involved in its affairs for many years, why should America with its feeble resources wave the big stick? Indeed, what he says in the one remark worth quoting in the entire article is that it is unwise to wave a very small stick and to thunder all over the place. He goes on to say that it is very unwise to rely on the Middle East for oil and one must simply do without it. I assume he means that everybody should go on bicycles, which he genuinely believes in, even though it entails unemployment of forty or fifty million. No doubt a thunderous answer by Professor Richard Pipes will follow. [...]

So long.

Yours ever,

Isaiah

1 Baruch ('Brian') Knei-Paz (b. 1937) né Bruno Baruch Knapheis, Polish-born Israeli political theorist educated in Canada, met IB 1961 on arriving in Oxford as a Rhodes Scholar; BPhil in politics, Queen's, 1963, DPhil, St Antony's, under IB's supervision, 1974; taught political theory (from 1978 as prof. of political science) at HUJ 1966–2005, Hebraising his name after settling in Israel; m. 1963–4 to Baillie née Klass, IB's personal secretary 1965–7; books include *The Social and Political Thought of Leon Trotsky* (Oxford, 1978), based on his doctoral thesis.
2 'George F. Kennan, on Washington's Reaction to the Afghan Crisis: "Was This Really Mature Statesmanship?"', NYT, 1 February 1980, A27. The Soviet invasion of Afghanistan had begun the previous December.

TO CLAUDIO VÉLIZ

13 March 1980

Headington House

Dear Claudio,

[...] I have now religiously been 'through' *The Ring* two and a half times and it has still not 'taken' as it should have. I remember that Bernard Berenson[1] once told me that he was converted to Catholicism in the 1890s 'but it did not take' – I feel the same. I am only too willing to be carried away by a Dionysiac frenzy and become a slave of the monstrous Wagner for a time and experience that spiritual and evidently almost physical transformation which the disciples claim to have attained. It is no go: I remain obstinately unaffected. I realise, of course, that I am listening to and seeing works of genius, I follow the leitmotifs, I think the orchestral sounds magnificent, I wait to be swept off my feet – and remain stone sober. How often must I try? Or is it a hopeless business? What can it be that is so wrong with me?

Yours ever,

Isaiah

Anthony Blunt's exposure as a spy in November 1979 led to the annulment of his knighthood, and placed in doubt his fellowship of the British Academy. Early in 1980 the Academy's governing council voted narrowly for his expulsion, and a motion was put to the annual general meeting on 3 July, when the fellows voted against expulsion; a compromise resolution put forward by Lionel Robbins,[2] which IB had drafted (and favoured), stating that the Academy deplored Blunt's conduct but wished to take no further action, was not considered. IB lamented this, because in the weeks that followed a caucus grew within the Academy calling for Blunt's resignation, prompting A. J. P. Taylor to resign his own fellowship in protest at what he described as a witch-hunt. Blunt was not indifferent to the travails of the Academy, and after an exchange with Kenneth Dover, he resigned on 17 August, bringing the affair to an end. By then IB was in Italy, 'far – mercifully far – from all those anti-Blunt campaigns'.[3]

1 Bernard Berenson (1865–1959) né Bernhard Valvrojenski; art historian, collector, and authority on the Italian Renaissance; converted to Christianity from Judaism, becoming an Episcopalian, and then a Catholic.
2 Lionel Charles Robbins (1898–1984), life peer 1959; prof. of economics, LSE, 1929–61; director, ROH, 1955–81; chair, *Financial Times*, 1961–70; President, BA, 1962–7.
3 To Hugh Trevor-Roper, 23 September 1980.

TO BERNARD WILLIAMS

14 March 1980

Headington House

Dear Bernard,

[…] The Blunt situation grinds on: you have presumably by now received his reply (predictable, I should have thought), that he does not wish to appear before Council and explain his conduct to them. So Council has to meet again and decide whether to 'proceed'. The machinery having once started, I daresay it cannot by now be stopped. Richard,[1] in my view, has not done the cause much good by (apparently, according to Eric Hobsbawm) writing to the President in strong terms, threatening to resign etc.[2] The reaction is that council must not act under threats – as you may imagine, this is precisely how Kenneth Dover would react. Hobsbawm himself says that he wrote a more judicious letter, and received a judicious answer. Dover is fundamentally in favour of deprivation, but supposes that the fellowship will probably vote against this course. I wonder. It now looks as if, whichever way the thing goes, there will be some effusion of blood, and I cannot help feeling that this could have been avoided. I found to my surprise that two heads of Cambridge Colleges (Lord Dacre,[3] if I can call him such, and Robin Matthews), while expressing themselves as against expulsion, do not propose to attend because of a general feeling of awkwardness about it all. Eric Hobsbawm wishes me to make a powerful speech, but I cannot do this for I do not base my opinion (which is the same as yours) on any general principle about which I can speak with clear passion, as required on such occasions – it just is a question of where one draws the line, which can be asserted but not deduced from statable general truths.

Now to more delightful matters: the opera on 3 April is OK – it is indeed the Box and therefore DJ (alas).[4] Aline says we ought to rebel and appear in slacks, but I lack an adequate degree of courage. I might have done it in Lord Drogheda's day as a kind of belated act of public-school revolt (not very

1 Richard Arthur Wollheim (1923–2003; plate 11), FBA 1972, lecturer in philosophy, UCL, 1951–60, reader 1960–3, Grote Prof. of Philosophy of Mind and Logic 1963–82; prof. of philosophy, Columbia 1982–5, Berkeley 1985–2002.

2 Wollheim wrote to Kenneth Dover 21 February 1980 that he would 'have to consider very seriously' his membership of the Academy if Blunt either were expelled or felt compelled to resign.

3 Hugh Trevor-Roper was made a life peer at the recommendation of Mrs Thatcher's government 1979, and took as his title Baron Dacre of Glanton.

4 For a performance of Stravinsky's 1951 opera The Rake's Progress, with a libretto by W. H. Auden and Chester Kallman. One of the perks of being a director of the ROH was that IB could book the Royal Box on nights when no royalty wanted it, although this did entail the formality of wearing a dinner jacket.

characteristic of me, but more so, I say proudly, than you might suppose), but
I do not wish to irritate Claus[1] or John Tooley[2] – very undespotic figures. [...]
   Yours,
      Isaiah

TO BERTELL OLLMAN[3]

   31 March 1980

                                                          Headington House
Dear Bertell,
   [...] Your image of me as a violently provocative generator of socialists
by stimulating sharp reactions to my (I suspect you think over-vehemently
stated) views fascinates me. I see myself as the mildest, most uncertain,
tentative, undogmatic, excessively self-critical thinker (the late Crossman
once said to me with a sneer, 'What are you? You call yourself a thinker,
I suppose?'), a cause – too often, perhaps – of scepticism in others, but
not a rouser of passionate opposition save among fanatical Catholics and
Marxists not pervious to the slightest criticism or disagreement. Still, it may
be that Karl Marx believed himself to be an amiable, gentle soul who never
spoke much but was a marvellous listener. All the same, everything you have
ever said to me and about me has warmed, and still warms, the cockles of
my heart. I enjoyed your last visit more than I can say, and long for another.
   Yours,
      Isaiah

TO JOSEPH BRODSKY[4]

   8 April 1980

                                                          Headington House
Dear Iosif (if you continue to call me Sir Isaiah, I shall fall into a state of
wounded melancholy – you can spell it in the Russian or the English manner,

  1 Claus Adolf Moser (b. 1922), KCB 1973, later (2001) life peer, Berlin-born British statistician, college
    head, public servant and company director; prof. of social statistics, LSE, 1961–70, visiting prof.
    1970–5; director, Central Statistical Office, and head of Government Statistical Service 1967–78;
    Warden, Wadham, 1984–93; chair, ROH, 1974–87.
  2 John Tooley (b. 1924; plate 17), Kt 1979, assistant general administrator, ROH, 1960–70, general
    administrator 1970–80, general director 1980–8.
  3 Bertell Ollman (b. 1935), Marxist political theorist supervised by IB at Oxford (MPhil 1963, DPhil
    1967) and thereafter a close friend; lecturer, dept of government, West Indies, 1963–6; assistant
    prof., dept of politics, NYU, 1967, associate prof. 1972, prof. from 1974; m. 1959 Paule Yvonne
    Gaudemard (b. 1939).
  4 Iosif/Joseph Aleksandrovich Brodsky (1940–96), poet; born in Leningrad into a Jewish family; rec-
    ognised by Anna Akhmatova as the most gifted lyric poet of his generation; sentenced to internal
    exile in the Archangelsk region for 'social parasitism' 1964–5; involuntary exile from the USSR
    1972, settling in America; poet in residence and visiting prof. at Michigan, Columbia, Cambridge
    and elsewhere; Five College Prof., Mount Holyoke, 1986–96; Nobel Prize in Literature 1987.

but if you use my title I shall be forced to resort to *mnogouvazhaemy*[1] and that kind of thing),

[...] Have you read Chukovskaya's huge book of *entretiens*[2] with AA? Only the beginning appeared in Russian, and the rest for some reason in French (Albin Michel). I am reading it now – it is, of course, absorbing to me, but I see that 'objectively' it is rather flat. The devotion, indeed, love, for Pasternak combined with stern judgements on him, the nightmare in which all the *dramatis personae* live and speak, Lydia's torments about whether or not she should have spoken out at a meeting of the Writers' Union which condemned Pasternak,[3] which she thinks might have killed her father, the hostile gossip about Ivinskaya,[4] the lifting of the entire level whenever AA herself speaks, the calm and tragic dignity of everything directly connected with her, the abominations which she is forced to face, the courage and decency of the small group of friends who alone make her existence tolerable, the daily expectations of persecution, violence, death, and the unyielding creative activity – the unbelievable resources, the adamantine morality on which this is based – how can anyone in the West, the ordinary reader of Bob's paper[5] or my collected volume of obituaries[6] (which is what it will in effect be) begin to understand this?

What can I say but thank you very, very much, and for God's sake be careful of your health – preserve yourself. [...]

Yours,

Исаия[7]

TO WALTER EYTAN[8]

11 April 1980

Headington House

Dear Walter,

Trevor-Roper: I was asked about this everywhere, in Princeton, New York, someone telephoned me from Canada, Aline etc.[9] Trevor-Roper is not anti-

---

1 'Much respected'.

2 'Conversations'. For the book see 4/5.

3 Pasternak was expelled from the Soviet Writers' Union at their 28 October 1958 meeting, after the award of the Nobel Prize.

4 Olga Vsevolodovna Ivinskaya (1912–95), Russian poet and writer, friend and lover of Boris Pasternak: see 628.

5 The NYRB.

6 PI, published the following October (142).

7 'Isaiah'.

8 Walter George Eytan (1910–2001) né Ettinghausen, diplomat; Munich-born contemporary of IB at St Paul's and Oxford; 1st director general of Israel's foreign ministry 1948–59; Israeli ambassador to France 1959–70; political adviser to Israeli foreign minister Abba Eban 1970–2; chair, Israeli broadcasting authority, 1972–8.

9 The controversy sparked by Trevor-Roper's 'When Reason Failed: Vienna', a review of Carl Schorske's *Fin-de-Siècle Vienna: Politics and Culture* (NY, 1979), *New York Times Book Review*, 27

Semitic – at least, no more so than most persons of his education and milieu: this still holds. There was a time, which you may recollect, when he was positively pro-Zionist, and I dare say may be so still – save that your present government has ensured that almost no gentile (it seems to me) anywhere, and few Jews (at least in this country), can any longer offer unqualified support to Israel under its present government. You do not need me to tell you this: the Israeli ambassador[1] – a perfectly nice man, as you know – addressed a mixed Jewish/gentile group in Cambridge recently, and four or five of the Zionists present walked out during his words about the settlements: not a very good thing.

But back to Trevor-Roper. He sees himself, I think, as a kind of Gibbon[2] or Voltaire,[3] a mocker of everything mystical, religious, irrational, emotional – irony, reason, Whig civilisation are his ideals. I have not read Schorske's[4] book yet, but I suspect that he treats Herzl[5] as a product of the irrational and decadent atmosphere of Vienna with which he is concerned, that the hysterical reception of Herzl (I do not know where – perhaps Bulgaria) as a prophet and a prince is cited – and that this was enough for Trevor-Roper, who liked to coin a phrase for its own sake, to produce the offending sentence, just to *épater*[6] liberal idealists and the like, and make them squirm, which he enjoys. In addition to this, there was an incident here, which you may have heard about, when the defeat of a motion in Congregation to give the late Bhutto (when he was prime minister) an Oxford doctorate[7] was

January 1980, 1, 30–1; the opening paragraph concluded with 'the offending sentence' to which IB refers below: 'The same Vienna that inspired Adolf Hitler, an immigrant from Linz, inspired Theodor Herzl, an immigrant from Budapest. Zionism and Nazism had a common source – and more common features than can comfortably be spelled out.'

1 Shlomo Argov (1929–2003), Israeli ambassador to Mexico 1971–4, to the Netherlands 1977–9, to London 1979–82; the attempt on his life by members of the Abu Nidal terrorist group, who shot him outside the Dorchester Hotel in London 3 June 1982, leaving him paralysed, was the pretext for Israel's invasion of the Lebanon 4 days later: 'He was openly critical of the approach to the Middle East of the European Community, directing his barbs specifically against the Community's Venice declaration, which called for a role in peace talks for the PLO.' 'Shlomo Argov', obituary, *Times*, 24 February 2003, 27f.

2 Edward Gibbon (1737–94), whose *The History of the Decline and Fall of the Roman Empire* (London, 1776–88) was famous for its mordant criticism of the early Christian Church.

3 Voltaire (1694–1778), pseudonym of François-Marie Arouet, French writer, philosopher and paragon of the Enlightenment; strongly anticlerical, he used satire to expose the iniquities and intolerance of his times.

4 Carl Emil Schorske (b. 1915), cultural historian and socialist; prof. of history, Berkeley 1960–9, Princeton 1969–80.

5 Theodor (né Binyamin Ze'ev) Herzl (1860–1904), Austro-Hungarian Vienna-based Jewish journalist whose experience of reporting on the Dreyfus affair in Paris persuaded him that Jewish emancipation only heightened tensions between Jews and their neighbours, and that political Zionism was the answer; founder, World Zionist Organization, elected its 1st president at the inaugural Zionist Congress, Basel, 1897.

6 'Shock'.

7 A proposal to confer an honorary DCL on Zulfikar Ali Bhutto (1928–79), prime minister of Pakistan 1973–7, was rejected by Congregation 1975 (L3 593).

attributed by his champion, Trevor-Roper, to 'leftists and Jews',[1] about which I had occasion to reproach him;[2] and this may be an echo of that wound to his vanity. However, I shall one of these days take it up with him, and if anything interesting transpires shall report to you.

Yours ever,

Isaiah

PS I have no doubt that the average reader may well assume that Trevor-Roper is anti-Semitic, or at least Anti-Zionist, but although I hold no particular brief for him I do not believe that this is in fact so. [...]

TO HUMPHREY CARPENTER[3]

18 April 1980

Headington House

Dear Mr Carpenter,

[...] What I remember is this. In 1941 the then head of the British Information Services in New York – one of whose principal tasks was to engage the sympathies of the Americans in the British war effort – the very well-known and eminent historian C. K. (later Sir Charles) Webster,[4] muttered to me (and perhaps to others, but of that I know nothing) that a bad impression might be made on sympathetic, or potentially sympathetic, Americans by the spectacle of young Englishmen (I ought to say Britons), not connected in any way with the war effort, knocking about at large, *embusqués*,[5] in America; and in this connection he did indeed mention Auden, not surprisingly, since the case of Auden and Isherwood was, I imagine, at this time being referred to in the British press.[6] I have no idea whether Webster took any action in this matter – certainly I know nothing about any 'duress' or direct pressure applied to Auden. When I saw him in New York in 1941 he said nothing to me about it. It may all have been confined to Webster's private grumbles on the subject.

1 According to Christopher Hitchens the phrase was 'the Left and the Jews': 'Mr Bhutto's Lost Cause', *New Statesman*, 28 February 1975, 272. Cf. L3 593–6.
2 L3 596–7.
3 Humphrey William Bouverie Carpenter (1946–2005), author, broadcaster and musician; his *W. H. Auden: A Biography* was published the next year (London/Boston).
4 Charles Kingsley Webster (1886–1961), KCMG 1946; Stevenson Prof. of International History, LSE, 1932–53; director, BIS, NY, 1941–2; President, BA, 1950–4.
5 'Shirkers'.
6 Christopher (William Bradshaw) Isherwood (1904–86), writer, had known Auden at preparatory school, but was reintroduced to him 1925, and became an intimate friend and occasional literary collaborator. As the threat of war in Europe loomed, the pair decided to emigrate to the United States, sailing for NY in January 1939, 'a controversial decision seen in some quarters as little short of "desertion"' (Peter Parker, ODNB); both men became US citizens 1946. There is no indication that *The Times*, at least, raised their case, although the paper did report on a single question asked in the Commons of the Home Secretary (26 February 1942, 8a).

It is also true that Mrs Francis Biddle[1] herself (as you know, a well-known poet) did say to me, when I met her in Washington towards the end of 1941, that the deaths of gifted poets in the First World War, particularly English ones, was a melancholy story and ought not to be allowed to happen again, and that she hoped that Auden would be saved from such a fate. Again, she said nothing about doing something in this connection. It is possible that, since she was the wife of the Attorney General of the United States, her influence may have had something to do with the speeding up of his American naturalisation (I have no idea when this was accomplished). On this rather flimsy information, it is possible to erect any hypothesis about steps being taken to 'rescue' Auden from impending conscription. [...]

Yours sincerely,
    Isaiah Berlin

TO RICHARD PIPES

18 April 1980

Headington House

Dear Dick,

Thank you ever so much for Struve, vol. 2.[2] I still feel deep pride in the original dedication and have no doubt whatever that this is a major contribution not only to Russian intellectual history but to the history of ideas which led to the cataclysm of our times. Mrs Thatcher and I seem to be the only persons in the UK to approve fully of the Olympic boycott[3] – all the rest, if they do it at all, are à contre-coeur.[4] On the other hand the blockade of Iran[5] seems to me (if it is genuinely effective) likely to lead to the disintegration of that country, with the Soviet Union, Pakistan and various Baluchis and Kurds snatching at this and that, and in the end a new dictatorship, possibly from Moscow. I do not believe that the obvious answer, 'Well, what would you do in Carter's place?', is devastating: in his place I should simply play for time

1 Katherine Garrison Biddle (1890–1977) née Chapin, US poet, patron of literature and the performing arts, staunch advocate of civil rights; m. 1918 Francis Beverley Biddle (1886–1968), US lawyer and judge, attorney general 1941–5 and the primary US judge at the Nuremberg trials.
2 *Struve: Liberal on the Right, 1905–1944*, vol. 2 of RP's 2-vol. study of Gleb Struve's life and thought (Cambridge, Mass., 1970, 1980); vol. 1, *Struve: Liberal on the Left, 1870–1905*, is dedicated to IB.
3 Several countries, including West Germany, Canada, Japan and China, supported a US boycott of that summer's Olympic Games in Moscow, in protest at the Soviet invasion of Afghanistan. Mrs Thatcher's government supported the boycott, but left the decision on whether to compete to individuals, and their sports' governing bodies; though the British team that went to Moscow was much reduced, it was still the largest West European squad.
4 'Reluctant'.
5 In November 1979 a large group of radical Islamist students, supporters of the Iranian Revolution, occupied the US Embassy in Tehran, taking many hostages; several hostages were later released, but 52 were held until January 1981 in trying conditions. Among the options considered by President Carter to secure their release was a blockade of the Persian Gulf, but America's allies did not support this, and ultimately the idea was rejected.

and hope for the best – I see no other solution that holds the least promise of safety for the hostages or the oil. And that I suppose is what Israel ought to be doing too, though I would much, much rather that someone else – Peres,[1] Weizmann – did it in the place of the inflexible and monomaniacal Begin, who is thinking of nothing but his own record and place in history, and to hell with peace and freedom and prosperity in the short run, i.e. in this world. [...]

Yours,

Isaiah

In the course of his visits to Princeton, IB made the acquaintance of Svetlana Allilueva (Mrs Lana Peters),[2] daughter of Joseph Stalin, who had defected to the US from Russia in 1967, becoming a naturalised US citizen. IB had met her on relatively few occasions before she expressed an interest in settling in England, where she wished her child to be educated. She had only modest means, and few friends who could help her, and in 1982 IB made enquiries on her behalf, to see if she could gain admission to Britain, with a view to earning a living there by writing. He was convinced of her literary gifts, and was prepared to recommend her to the immigration authorities; he and Aline were even willing to help with the costs of her child's schooling. But he was also aware that her predicament was difficult, and that she might 'exaggerate the peace and dignity of life in England',[3] as it indeed proved. When in 1983 her expectations failed to materialise, she began to accuse IB, quite baselessly, of failing her.

TO LANA PETERS

25 April 1980

[Headington House]

Dear Svetlana,

[...] You are quite right about Americans and psychiatrists. In the old days it was done by priests, but the conversation of the average American, of the

1 Shimon Peres (b. 1923) né Szymon Perski, later (2008) hon. GCMG; Polish-born Israeli statesman and author; MK 1959–2007, leader, Israeli Labour Party, 1977–92, 1995–7 (and 2003–5), prime minister 1984–6, 1995–6, later (2007–14) President; Nobel Peace Prize 1994, jointly with Yitzhak Rabin (3/3) and Yasser Arafat (56/1).

2 Lana Peters (1926–2011) née Svetlana Iosifovna Stalina, daughter of Joseph Stalin and Nadezhda Allilueva, known in childhood as Stalin's 'little sparrow'. Her life was dominated by her father's legacy: on his death (1953) she changed her name to Allilueva, and defected to the US 1967, where she denounced her father and the USSR; m. 1970, 3rdly, William Wesley Peters, adopting the name Lana Peters. They divorced 1973, and, unable to settle in America, she moved to England 1982, where her younger daughter attended the Friends' School, Saffron Walden. Hoping for a reunion with the son and daughter she had left behind 1967, she returned to Moscow 1984, where she was granted Soviet citizenship, but the experiment was not a success, and after 2 years she returned to the US.

3 To Francis Graham-Harrison, 12 May 1982.

kind that you speak of and who tell you their TV-derived ideas, is so tedious that I should not be prepared to listen to them even for $35 an hour – nor even, perhaps, for $350, unless to keep the wolf from the door, to support my starving family. Of course you cannot write a book 'about America' of the kind they expect – you should not even think of it. If you need to increase your income there must be other ways of doing so.

I understand perfectly that you think that England might be a more civil-ised place to live in, that there is room for private life here, that everything is not open and public, that people do not talk to strangers as they talk to intim-ate friends, that they do not think that all facts are interesting and equally interesting, as they are certainly thought to be in some circles in America; though I must own that intellectually I have had a very good time in America myself, and find that there is a certain spontaneity, imagination, appetite for life, a freshness of approach which is sometimes lacking in the old country which I inhabit. Still, that only applies to small, semi-professional circles in New York, the largely Jewish culture which obtains there and is frowned at by 'middle America'.

Your idea of coming to England is in principle a good one. I imagine there are men and women of breeding and distinction with whom you could live and who would not invade your privacy and would treat you with courtesy and tact. The problem is, I need not tell you, how to find them. I do not really know how to set about this, although I should like to. We live with Oxford University at one end and a few old friends in London at the other. The unworldliness of the academic friends is balanced by the pro-nounced worldliness of our London friends and acquaintances. In neither world would such persons exist as (if I understand what it is that you would like – and I feel sure that I do) you are thinking of. I promise you to search for them.

I think I ought to warn you that when George Kennan came here he was bitterly disappointed. He had some image of a civilised, wise, deeply trad-itional, sensitive, reticent people who did not talk much, but when they did had something to say, and said it with charm and depth, if not of feeling, at any rate of experience. He imagined, I am sure, evenings at Oxford with distinguished thinkers and visitors from London, from the great world, of great refinement and insight, cultured, quiet and impressive. His dream was rudely shattered. He found a pretty provincial assembly, steeped in their own local gossip, talking about nothing but parochial issues in academic life, from which naturally he was excluded – in which he did not wish to be included any more than you with your Merry Wives of Princeton. His anglophile sen-timents suffered a dreadful shock, and he is not nearly so friendly to England as he expected to be. Nobody noticed his entering and leaving rooms – no visitors are lionised here, and that, so far as it goes, is very good. But the trouble is that life is depressed: incomes have gone down, there is much dreariness, neglect, boredom; the *vieille Angleterre*,[1] the civilised aristocrats, the marvellous novelists and poets, the urbane, cultivated statesmen – that England, believe me, is no more. The noise, the dirt, the obscenities in the streets are sometimes worse – because drained of life – than the equivalent in America. Solzhenitsyn's unfriendly reaction[2] was due [to] a certain perception of a lack of vitality, of letting things go down without much struggle. All this leads to a certain degree of tolerance, but it can also be lowering to the spirit. So I should not hurry to come to this country, whatever the circumstances, too soon, if I were you. You should come on a visit first and you will see for yourself. Believe me, I understand what it is that you wish to find and what to avoid, to be free from. 'Your' England really is something now in the past. There is mediocrity everywhere.

I am not aware if that for which you seek can truly be found today – not in France, not in Italy, still less in Germany, and Scandinavia and Holland are too stuffy and dull. Still, I shall go on looking. Let us assume that the world you are looking for is not imaginary, not a Utopia. I do not wish to discourage you too deeply – it may be that England in some respects, and particularly Scotland, would suit you better than America. Everything depends on individual relationships, on the degree of natural sympathy between individuals – no country can guarantee that. I think your ideas are not absurd in the least, I think that fundamentally you are probably quite right. I shall write to you again in a month or two and tell you whether I have any concrete ideas or have been frustrated. [...]

Yours,

[Isaiah]

The Hurva ('ruin') Synagogue in the Jewish Quarter of the Old City of Jerusalem had been rebuilt in the 1860s after lying in ruins for more than a century. During the 1948 Arab–Israeli War it was destroyed by the Arab Legion, and when the Old City came under Israeli control after the Six Day War, plans were made to rebuild it; but a controversy arose as to whether the building should be traditional in design – 'where it was, as it was' (a phrase originally used of the San Marco bell-tower in Venice when it collapsed in 1902) – or reflect a more modern Western aesthetic. IB appealed to his old friend Teddy Kollek,[3] the celebrated mayor of Jerusalem, to reject Denys Lasdun,[4] the architect who had been favoured by Charles Clore.[5] The synagogue was eventually rebuilt in its original style, and officially opened in 2010.

1 'Old England'.
2 In February 1976 (27).
3 Theodor ("Teddy') *Kollek (1911–2007), mayor of Jerusalem.
4 Denys Louis Lasdun (1914–2001), Kt 1976, British architect; designer of (inter alia) the brutalist (Royal) National Theatre on London's South Bank; his plans for the rebuilding of the Hurva Synagogue, 1978–81, were eventually rejected by the prime minister, Menachem Begin.
5 Charles Clore (1904–79), Kt 1971, businessman of Russian Jewish descent; many Jewish and Zionist

TO TEDDY KOLLEK

29 April 1980

[Headington House]

Dear Teddy,

Forgive this *cri de coeur*, but the thought is preying on me. Whoever I have spoken to about Lasdun as the architect of Hurva Synagogue expresses legitimate horror. I realise that this may have been the dying wish of the late Sir Charles Clore, but even so, it could be an aesthetic and political disaster – to restore is one thing, to rebuild another. What would the restoration of the Hurva cost? I should be prepared to recommend to the Rothschild Foundation that they do something in that direction if it was to save the city from real disaster. I beg you not to think that these are hysterical words, dictated in the middle of the night under the influence of nightmarish broodings. The late Sir Charles was not notable for his aesthetic tastes: the flat in the Weizmann Institute has at least ruined nothing, but the Clore and Wolfson structures in Jerusalem do that city very little honour, and their founders even less. A gentle, sensitive, imaginative but deeply traditional (Lasdun says he is, but he is not) architect, especially one good at exquisite pastiche (do not let them tell you that this is 'dishonest', that we must be of our time, that architecture is a progressive art, etc.: the Italian reconstructions on Rhodes and other ex-Italian islands are far better than the ghastly buildings by famous architects which have destroyed Tokyo or Regent's Street in London) – believe me, this would be better than a second-rate brutalist. You should come to England and look at his buildings here to satisfy yourself about the truth of what I say. [...] I kneel before you and beg for mercy for the city.

Yours,

Isaiah

TO ANNE KINDERSLEY[1]

9 May 1980 [*carbon*]

Headington House

Dear Anne,

[...] You are right in thinking that I am very reluctant to re-read my own letters, and I would naturally prefer that others did not see them either. I have no idea what I put in them. When I accidentally come across something that I have written to other people I am overcome by shame and self-reproach at

causes were the beneficiaries of his charitable donations.

1 Anne Kindersley (b. 1928) née Karminski, author; m. 1959 Richard Kerr Kindersley (1922–2010), diplomat, Russian scholar and fellow, St Antony's, 1967–89; AK was then working on the letters between her great-aunt Katherine Lewis, daughter of Elizabeth Lewis (one of the leading hostesses of her day), and Bernard Berenson; her findings have not been published.

both the content and the style. I have therefore never asked anyone to send back letters that they may have received from me. After my death I do not mind what happens, but during my lifetime I wish this cup to pass from me.

My letters to BB[1] cannot possibly shed any light on him – his to me may possibly do so, although I suspect not much. Still, if you want to see that, I do not wish to withhold it from you, but I would rather look at it myself first […].

Forgive me for being so difficult, but I suffer from very mixed feelings towards Berenson. He was, of course, a very gifted and remarkable man and a very beguiling talker, but I never thought him either a nice man or an honourable one, and all this was, of course, confirmed by those who investigated his relations with dealers and patrons. As I think I told you, when I first met him – in a train – I thought him quite awful and had no wish to see him again. When I did see him again twenty years later, I found his company enjoyable and interesting, but I did not like him even then, and I am put off by the thought of being connected with him in any way. […] When Schapiro[2] wrote his famous attack on him, and I was about to rise up to defend him, the late Ben Nicolson,[3] who knew him very well, assured me that at least eighty per cent of what Schapiro had said was entirely true and that loyalty could go too far.[4] I felt warmer towards BB then than I do now that I have read some of his letters, some of which seem loathsome to me. The truth was not in him, and sincerity was not one of his attributes. And – this will shock you – I did not think Nicky Mariano[5] was very genuine or sympathetic. Hence my general reluctance to think about that world. All this sounds terribly priggish, and perhaps it is, but it is how I feel and cannot help feeling. […]

You speak of BB's 'aesthetic view of life'. I do not believe in this much – he loved nature and the art of the past deeply and genuinely, I think, but his view of life was dominated by social ambition and security, and haunted by his buried past; the aestheticism was a rationalisation, a curtain to hide the materialism and cynicism of which he may have been ashamed but which he could not help. But there – I only say this to you, you must never publish a word of this, and I am quite prepared to be told that I am mistaken. […]

Yours,

[Isaiah]

1 Bernard Berenson; for IB's changing feelings towards him see L3 25–7, 176–8.
2 Meyer Schapiro (1904–96), Lithuanian Jewish art historian, artist and polymath; taught at Columbia, where he was prof. 1952–65, University Prof. 1965–73. L1 715, L2 797, L3 639.
3 (Lionel) Ben(edict) Nicolson (1914–78), art historian, editor, *Burlington Magazine*, 1947–78; a close friend of IB's from 1930s Oxford.
4 For IB's reaction to Meyer Schapiro, 'Mr Berenson's Values', *Encounter* 16 no. 1 (January 1961), 57–65, see L3 25–7. 'As I liked Schapiro much, much more than I ever liked Berenson (fascinated though I was by him), I thought I'd let him off my rejoinder. Hence it remained written but unpublished, but I stand by what it contains' (to HH, 25 October 1993).
5 Elizabetta ('Nicky') Mariano (1887–1968), Berenson's librarian and secretary from 1918, who in 1919 became his mistress, and an integral part of his life at I Tatti, his villa outside Florence.

TO YEHUDI MENUHIN

14 June 1980

Headington House

Dear Cousin,

Thank you ever so much for your plan for Jerusalem.[1] Admirable as it is, it presupposes a degree of peaceful collaboration between Jews and Arabs in Jerusalem which at present is very far to seek: whenever Teddy Kollek ceases to be Mayor, it will be further still. It needs the good will of King Hussein,[2] the Saudis etc. At least it is a far better scheme than trusteeship by the UN, which (in its previous incarnation) worked so badly in the Saar, Danzig, Memel etc.,[3] and which foolish, though no doubt sincere, pro-Arabs like Lord Caradon[4] are pressing for. I do not doubt that, if the Israelis come out with some such proposal, it will be fanatically turned down by any Arab who fears the fate of a traitor to his people; nor is there the slightest hope of the present government – soon may it go – reading a sentence of your proposal, as surely you well know; it is only the most doveish fringe of the admirable 'Peace Now'[5] group that could be induced to take it seriously. Still, it is a noble effort [...].

Yours ever, ⟨with much love⟩

Isaiah

1 We have not been able to find the plan to which IB here refers, but Menuhin was a long-standing advocate of Arab–Israeli integration in the city, and once submitted a detailed plan for this to Teddy Kollek, as he relates in 'A Shared Jerusalem', *Palestine-Israel Journal of Politics, Economics and Culture* 2 (1995) no. 2, 19–22.
2 Hussein bin Talal (1935–99), king of the Hashemite Kingdom of Jordan 1953–99; educated at Sandhurst, and a direct descendant of the prophet Muhammad, he maintained relations with both Western and Arab states, and secretly met with Israeli representatives throughout the 1970s and 1980s, playing an important role in the peace negotiations of the mid 1990s; Jordan and Israel signed a formal peace treaty 1994.
3 German territories whose future was determined by the League of Nations under the 1919 Treaty of Versailles: Saar was administered by France until 1935, when its population voted to return to Germany; Danzig was constituted a free city, but elected a Nazi majority to its parliament 1933, and was integrated with the Third Reich 1939; Memel was placed under French control, but was seized by Lithuania 1923 and renamed Klaipėda.
4 When made a life peer 1964 Hugh Foot took the title Baron Caradon.
5 In March 1978, when the peace talks with Egypt that led to the Camp David accords appeared to be collapsing, 348 reserve officers and soldiers from IDF combat units published an open letter to the prime minister, Menachem Begin, urging him in effect to adopt a 2-state solution, giving up land for peace. Tens of thousands of Israelis subsequently registered their support for this letter, and the Peace Now movement was born. IB was one of a number of Oxford figures who supported it: others included Herbert Hart, Alan Montefiore, Ronald Dworkin and Steven Lukes.

TO STEPHEN ROTH[1]

20 June 1980

Headington House

Dear Dr Roth,

Thank you for sending me the discussion paper 'The Erosion of Liberal
Support for Jewry'. It seems to me very well done. I have no doubt that,
apart from the general improvement of the position of Jews in the free
world during the last quarter of a century, the most important single factor
in eroding liberal support is the attitude which Israel appears to take towards
the problem of the Palestinian refugees – nothing did more harm than Mrs
Meir's celebrated statement that there were no Palestinians, which even her
own immediately popular image abroad did not dispel.[2] The Third World's
automatic support for Palestinians, with all its shades of sincerity and insin-
cerity, and the support for Israel by the USA, which seem to align it (Israel)
with the 'ex-colonialists', occasionally offset by patently anti-Israel moves
(whether political, as in the case of the UNESCO scandal,[3] or physical, as
in the case of terrorist attacks), worked against Israel. The present policy
on the West Bank settlements has, I fear, wholly counteracted the sympathy
of liberals over the savage attacks upon it by terrorists and the swelling tide
of pro-Arab propaganda, stimulated by causes which are familiar enough.
Moreover, the 'My country right or wrong'[4] attitude of a great many Jewish
communities, understandable enough both in Europe and especially in
America, goes directly counter to liberal sentiment in such matters. [...]

Yours sincerely,

Isaiah Berlin

1 Stephen Roth (1915–95), Hungarian-born international lawyer and Jewish leader, worked with
the Zionist underground in Hungary during WW2 and afterwards became involved in the World
Jewish Congress; as London-based director of its research arm, the Institute of Jewish Affairs,
1966–88, he enabled it to have 'a major impact on the intellectual and academic life of Anglo-
Jewry' ('Stephen Roth', obituary, Times, 11 August 1995, 19a–e at 19d).

2 In an interview with the Sunday Times published 15 June 1969, Mrs Meir stated: 'It was not as
though there was a Palestinian people in Palestine considering itself as a Palestinian people and
we came and threw them out and took their country away from them. They did not exist' (Basel
Amin Aqi, 'The Palestine Liberation Movement', Times, 25 June 1969, 15e–h at 15h).

3 In November 1974 UNESCO resolved to exclude Israel from its European regional group (which
amounted to expulsion), on the grounds that its archaeological works were damaging the historic fabric of Jerusalem. The relevant vote was initiated by Arab and Warsaw Pact states, and
was regarded by many as politically motivated. In response, the US Congress voted to withhold
the US contribution to UNESCO, and the resolution was reversed 1976.

4 A slogan originated by US Navy Commodore Stephen Decatur as a toast at an 1816 dinner: 'Our
country – In her intercourse with foreign nations may she always be in the right, and always successful, right or wrong.' Niles' Weekly Register (Baltimore) 10 no. 8, 20 April 1816, supplement, 136.

TO RUTH CHESHIN[1]

25 September 1980 [*carbon*]

Headington House

Dear Ruth,

[...] You are perfectly right, the Hurva problem is an infinite number of times more important than the music centre, and the results liable to be genuinely tragic (the Music Centre only mildly disastrous).[2] But there really is no point in my coming to look at Lasdun's plans. Quite apart from the fact that I can never visualise a building from elevations and explanations, however lucid, I should not be against this or that aspect or part of the plan, but am in principle against the whole thing – even more on political than on aesthetic grounds. Many bad moments as there have been, this is literally the worst moment that could so far be imagined for a dramatic piece of modernism, however modified, in the Old City. Why should we choose this moment to reinforce – as indirectly this does – the present government's politically disastrous insistence on flouting what is now literally world opinion? Nor is the idea of the expenditure of this kind of money, wherever it comes from, likely to be well received by anyone (except fanatics) in Israel's present economic situation.

I realise that Teddy feels committed to Mrs Duffield,[3] having gone so far: but could not the whole thing be at least postponed, for whatever reason, until a more rational government is in power, and no final decision be made? Lasdun, of course, will be impatient, as he has the reputation of being the most intolerable prima donna of all European architects (I do not know him personally, and base myself on the very emphatic evidence of his clients, e.g. the Vice Chancellor of the University of East Anglia,[4] who, as I remember, was driven mad by him, and the people at the National Theatre) – but the future of Jerusalem is perhaps more important.

1 Ruth ('Ruthi') Cheshin (b. 1937) née Salomon, Jerusalem-born champion of her native city; opened the 1st tourism dept, Jerusalem municipality, 1965; helped Jerusalem mayor Teddy Kollek establish the Jerusalem Foundation 1967 to co-ordinate worldwide support and fundraising for the development of 'an open, equitable and modern' multicultural city (*The Jerusalem Foundation: Annual Report 2013*, 7), director 1967–80, (1st) president 1980–2011; head, Mishkenot Sha'ananim, from 1973 (when it was restored and renovated by the foundation), later (from 2009) chair.

2 IB had supported Isaac Stern and Teddy Kollek in establishing the Jerusalem Music Centre in Mishkenot Sha'ananim 1973.

3 Vivien Louise Duffield (b. 1946), later (2000) DBE, philanthropist and public servant, daughter of Charles Clore: chair, Charles Clore 1979 Israel Foundation 1979–2000, later (1998) renamed the Clore Israel Foundation; Vivien Duffield Foundation 1987–2000; later (from 2000) Clore Duffield Foundation. Charles Clore had wanted the Hurva Synagogue restored, but his daughter did not share his view.

4 Frank Thistlethwaite (1915–2003), historian of America and university administrator; fellow, St John's, Cambridge, 1945–61; founding vice chancellor, UEA, 1961–80, where he had a formative influence over the architecture of the campus; IB visited UEA in 1967 in his search for an architect for Wolfson.

As you know, my view is that the synagogue should be reconstructed in a more or less pastiche-like manner, to fit entirely with its surroundings, and not be a monument to modern taste. My views are affected, I must confess, by the fact that I find no architecture more depressing than the old-fashioned avant-garde, which, as anyone of taste will tell you, Lasdun is regarded as representing (Jacob[1] will confirm this). The kind of architect you need is not someone who wishes to express his own powerful ego at all costs – even his admirers do not deny that Lasdun does just that, and it matters less in London (where some of his ugliest buildings are, as well as the one tolerable one) than it would in Jerusalem, for reasons which I need not enlarge upon.

So what is the use of my coming to say: 'For God's sake, don't madden the Arabs, don't add to the triumphs (enough have been celebrated lately) of the worldwide anti-Zionist forces, don't (this is almost the weakest part of my plea, because in the end subjective) ruin Jerusalem aesthetically, don't give a powerful handle to every enemy of Zionism in the world. A better day may come, when decent people will recover their love and enthusiasm for Israel – it may not be far off. Why commit yourself to something both irreversible and, in the opinion of every single person here whom I have spoken to, disastrous?'?

You cannot want me to come to Jerusalem to say this to Lasdun and Mrs Duffield. I know that Nelson Glueck[2] saved Jerusalem from Khan's[3] beautiful but totally unsuitable design, but I am incapable of that kind of bitter confrontation. So I shall come in November, as planned, three days before Jacob, and if it is a fait accompli shall beg you not to speak of it to me – I have never felt so depressed about anything in Israel before in my life, except the results of the last election, into the hands of whose victors this plan will surely play.[4] *Dixi et salvavi amimam meam. Ich kann nicht anders.*[5]

Yours,
     [Isaiah]

PS On a jollier note, thank God there is nothing by your friend in Oxford;

1 (Nathaniel Charles) Jacob Rothschild (b. 1936), 4th Baron Rothschild 1990, later GBE (1998), OM (2002), banker and philanthropist, close friend of the Berlins.
2 Nelson Glueck (1900–71), US-born archaeologist; director, American School of Oriental Research, Jerusalem, 1932–3, 1936–40, 1942–7 (also their field director and an agent for the US Office of Strategic Services in the latter period); president, Hebrew Union College, Cincinnati (where he was ordained rabbi 1923), 1947–71.
3 Louis Isadore Kahn (1901–74), Estonian-born US modernist architect, designed the Jonas Salk Institute of Biological Studies, La Jolla (1959–65); none of the 3 plans he proposed 1968–73 for the reconstruction of Hurva on monumental modernist lines was chosen.
4 The Knesset elections of 17 May 1977 returned Likud to power under Menachem Begin.
5 'Dixi et salvavi animam meam' ('I have spoken and saved my soul') is the closing sentence of Karl Marx's *Critique of the Gotha Programme* (1875). 'Hier stehe ich, ich kann nicht anders' ('Here I stand: I can do no other') is (dubiously) attributed to Martin Luther as part of his statement before the Diet of Worms 1521.

we have enough ugly buildings of our own and do not need him inflicted on us [...].

TO CHARLES, PRINCE OF WALES[1]

7 October 1980 [*manuscript*]

Headington House

Sir,

I am naturally delighted that the first volume of my hero's memoirs[2] should have given Your Royal Highness real pleasure: I agree that they do tend to show that plus ça change: the present despotism and the suffocating regime Herzen describes did have a hideous family resemblance: the governing class has changed, the methods have become more mechanised and the country is screwed together in the iron grip: but otherwise ... What seems to me to make Herzen so agreeable to read is his lively, spontaneous eloquence and his acute sense of the ridiculous; and also his personal distinction and charm as a wonderful raconteur. The fact that the Paris Rothschild[3] managed to extract Herzen's property out of the clutches of the Russian government (he seems to have done it just to show he could) made Herzen financially independent, rare among refugees; he could, and did, live in a Victorian gentleman's style, & this shows in his writings: & annoyed the grim, hardnosed Russian revolutionaries of a later generation, though they acknowledged him as a grandfather (he hated them). I propose, if I may, to send your Royal Highness the entire translation – four large volumes,[4] I fear it overlaps with the paperback, but can be dipped into – particularly the chapters on London where he lived – with much enjoyment: the writing seems to me at once moving and full of a kind of irresponsible gaiety (in the other & better sense of that valuable word).

We are most grateful for the invitation to the opera: may we come to *Lucia* on the 21st October? It is wonderfully good of you, Sir, to ask us. We look forward to it immensely.

---

1 Charles Philip Arthur George Mountbatten-Windsor (b. 1948; plate 33), eldest son of, and heir apparent to, Queen Elizabeth II; created Prince of Wales 1958.

2 HH had recently published in OUP's new paperback World's Classics series J. D. Duff's 1923 translation of parts 1 and 2 of Alexander Herzen's *My Past and Thoughts* as *Childhood, Youth and Exile* (Oxford, 1980), with IB's 1956 essay on Herzen from 'A Remarkable Decade' (in RT) as an introduction, and IB had sent a copy to the Prince of Wales.

3 James Mayer de Rothschild (1792–1868), founder and head of the Paris branch of the family. For the financial help and advice he rendered to Herzen (and a somewhat less enthusiastic view of Herzen) see Derek Offord, 'Alexander Herzen and James de Rothschild', *Toronto Slavic Quarterly* no. 19 (Winter 2007), ⟨http://sites.utoronto.ca/tsq/19/offord19.shtml⟩.

4 Alexander Herzen, *My Past and Thoughts: The Memoirs of Alexander Herzen*, trans. Constance Garnett (London, 1924–7; NY, 1924–6), revised by Humphrey Higgens, with an introduction by IB (London/NY 1968).

I remain Your Royal Highness's obedient servant
   Isaiah Berlin

30 October 1980: publication of IB's Personal Impressions, *edited by HH, with an introduction by Noel Annan.*

TO MIRIAM GROSS[1]

3 November 1980

                          Headington House

Dear Miriam,

   [...] On p. 12 of yesterday's copy of the *Observer*, under 'Sayings of the Week', I am quoted as saying 'A work of art is no good if it doesn't provoke a furore.' I have, of course, never made this idiotic statement, which is patently absurd, and feel deeply embarrassed to have it attributed to me, as you may well understand. I do not know what the source of it may be,[2] but I should be genuinely grateful if you could ask the Editor to publish a *démenti*, which ought to take the form of 'For Isaiah Berlin, read Ken Russell'[3] – or whoever it is. I really do feel humiliated by this – it is one of the silliest statements I have ever seen; and yet I am sure that lots of people who know me are capable of believing that I did in fact say it (unfortunately, they all know that I don't drink). So do please rescue me! The saying by Mary Warnock,[4] which immediately precedes my alleged epigram, is from her review of my book in the *Listener*.[5] I wonder what light this throws on anything. ⟨But it is a major (v. funny) méchanceté[6] – like that game in which one attributes the *least* characteristic statement to people. Cd the correction be printed in next week's Sayings of the Week, please?[7] Oh dear! What a monstrosity!⟩

   Much love,
      Isaiah

1　Miriam Marianna Gross (b. 1938) née May, Lady Owen 1993, assistant literary editor, *Observer*, 1964–9, deputy literary editor 1969–81, women's editor 1981–4; arts editor, *Daily Telegraph*, 1986–91; literary editor, *Sunday Telegraph*, 1991–2005; m. 1st 1965 John Gross (divorced 1988), 2nd 1993 Geoffrey Owen, Kt 1989.

2　The *Observer* subsequently told IB that the source was Stan Davis in 'Londoner's Diary', *Evening Standard*, 31 October 1980, but there is no mention of this in the edition we have been able to check.

3　Henry Kenneth Alfred ('Ken') Russell (1927–2011), film, television and opera director known for his flamboyance.

4　(Helen) Mary Warnock (b. 1924), DBE 1984, life peer 1985; fellow and philosophy tutor, St Hugh's, 1949–66; headmistress, Oxford High School for Girls, 1966–72; Talbot Research Fellow, LMH, 1972–6; senior research fellow, St Hugh's, 1976–84; Mistress, Girton, Cambridge, 1985–91.

5　In her review of PI, Warnock had written: 'Oxford is, and always has been, full of cliques, full of factions, and of a particular non-social snobbishness.' 'Isaiah Berlin's Friends', *Listener*, 30 October 1980, 583–4 at 583.

6　'Piece of spitefulness'.

7　A correction was printed on the letters page (16) of the issue of 9 November under the heading 'Sir Isaiah Berlin'.

TO KYRIL FITZLYON

5 November 1980

Headington House

Dear Kyril,

Thank you for your letter about my piece in the TLS.[1] For once I don't think that we disagree. When I say 'The revolution had stimulated great waves of creative energy in Russia in all the arts; bold experimentalism ...' etc., and then mention Kandinsky, Chagall, Soutine, up to Z for Zadkine,[2] plus all those producers, and speak of masterpieces, I did not, of course, mean that the revolution literally generated these waves out of some kind of void. By 'stimulated' I meant only something like 'excited', or 'created an atmosphere in which some of these works of art were produced'. Of course I do not begin to think that the art produced by the early revolutionary years (let alone later) was superior to that of the early years of the century. Despite Pasternak and his contemporaries, I would be prepared to go to the block (sorry about the dreadful pun) for saying that the generation of Blok, Bely, Vyacheslav Ivanov,[3] and the generation of painters and sculptors born in the 1880s and 1890s, not to speak of the much older Kandinsky, and for that matter the Arts Theatre – that all these were greatly superior to anyone whose *Blüthezeit*[4] occurred at any point during the Soviet regime. Despotism is sometimes not incompatible with great art, but this one certainly was.

What I was trying to stress, perhaps not clearly enough, was the contrast between the undoubted excitement generated in the very early years of the Revolution among groups of artists, writers, producers etc., and the dark night which fell so soon and extinguished all but the bravest dissidents. Of course you are right in saying that most of the names I cited belong to people whose talents grew to maturity before the Revolution – the fact that the painters, e.g. Kandinsky, Chagall, Soutine, Zadkine, Arkhipenko, Lipchitz,[5] all left Russia before 1914 (and some of them became what they became abroad: e.g. K. & C. & S. & L.) – although some of them returned during the war and the Revolution – is not important – they *were* products, however oppositional, of the pre-Revolutionary culture (I know I am not allowed to say 'the old

1 'Conversations with Russian Poets', TLS, 31 October 1980, 1233–6, a shortened version of 'Meetings with Russian Writers in 1945 and 1956' (112/3).
2 Vasily Vasil'evich Kandinsky (1866–1944), Russian abstract expressionist painter and art theorist; Marc Zakharovich Chagall (1887–1985) né Moishe Shagal, Russian-born French painter and graphic artist; Chaim Soutine (1893–1943), Russian modernist painter; Osip Zadkine (1890–1967), Russian-French cubist sculptor.
3 Aleksandr Aleksandrovich Blok (1880–1921), poet and playwright; Andrey Bely (1880–1934) né Boris Nikolaevich Bugaev, novelist, poet and literary theorist; Vyacheslav Ivanovich Ivanov (1866–1949), poet and playwright: key figures in the Russian Symbolist movement.
4 'Heyday'.
5 Aleksandr Porfir'evich Arkhipenko (1887–1964), Ukrainian-born sculptor; Jacques (né Chaim Jacob) Lipchitz (1891–1973), Lithuanian-born sculptor: both cubists.

regime'); my only point is that some of them were genuinely excited by 1917 and the brave new technological, art-for-the-masses world. [...]

It seems to me the situation is rather similar to, say, the effect of the French Revolution on, for example, David,[1] who produced masterpieces before it but was ideologically and artistically deeply affected by it (as, say, Fragonard and Isabey[2] were not); or as Delacroix or Courbet[3] reacted to 1848, even though they were mature artists by then. They were not 'made' by these revolutions any more than the relevant Russians, but they were caught up, at least for a time (Courbet for life) by them.

Some of these writers and artists ⟨& critics – Babel', Tynyanov, Eikhenbaum, A. Tolstoy, Shklovsky, Zoshchenko⟩,[4] not to speak of the producers, in Russia were certainly fresher and more alive during those few years before the guillotine fell than were the rather tired older writers, whether they remained in Russia or not [...]. With the exception of Mandel'shtam, Pasternak (and Akhmatova, who remained outside all this) I have no taste for either the tired old émigrés, internal or external, or real Soviet art and literature, Mayakovsky[5] et al. But when Roman Jakobson, Artur Lourié (the composer), Prokofiev, Chagall, Eisenstein[6] talked to me about how exciting those few early years were, I was prepared to believe it – it was all summer lightning, brief and unreal perhaps, but it occurred.[7] My only point in that piece was to contrast the relative freedom of art in that brief period with the appalling aftermath, the nobility and courage of Pasternak and Mandel'shtam and Akhmatova and their friends – the sort of thing Lydia Chukovsky wrote about – during those ghastly decades. They ⟨Pasternak, K.

---

1 Jacques Louis David (1748–1825), French neoclassical painter.
2 Jean Honoré Fragonard (1732–1806), French rococo painter; Jean Baptiste Isabey (1767–1855), French portraitist and printmaker.
3 (Ferdinand Victor) Eugène Delacroix (1798–1863), French romantic painter; (Jean Désiré) Gustave Courbet (1819–77), French realist painter.
4 All Russian writers in the Soviet era: Isaak Emmanuilovich Babel' (1894–1940) né Isaac Manievich Bobel, short-story writer, executed 1940; Yury Nikolaevich Tynyanov (1894–1943), novelist, critic and theorist, a leading exponent of Russian formalism, as was the literary critic Boris Mikhailovich Eikhenbaum (1886–1959); Aleksey Nikolaevich Tolstoy (1883–1945), White Russian emigré novelist much honoured by the regime when he returned to the USSR 1923; Viktor Borisovich Shklovsky (1893–1984), literary theorist and critic; Mikhail Mikhailovich Zoshchenko (1895–1958), satirical writer famous for his comic short stories, refused to conform to socialist realism and fell out of favour with the authorities, by whom he was denounced (with Akhmatova) in 1946.
5 Vladimir Vladimirovich Mayakovsky (1893–1930), Russian poet and playwright; successfully put futurism at the service of the Bolshevik revolution, but subsequently fell from favour; committed suicide.
6 Arthur Vincent Lourié (1892–1967) né Naum Izrailevich Luria, later known as Artur Sergeevich Lur'e, Russian futurist composer appointed commissar of music in Petrograd 1918 but left USSR 1922; Sergey Sergeevich Prokofiev (1891–1953), Russian pianist, composer and conductor; Sergey Mikhailovich Eisenstein (1898–1948), Riga-born stage and film director and film theorist.
7 An allusion to Alexander Herzen's 'Art [...] and the summer lightning of individual happiness: these are the only real goods we have.' 'Kontsy i nachala', 1st letter, 10 June 1862, in Kolokol no. 138, 1 July 1862; op. cit. (22/1) xvi 135.

Chukovsky, Shostakovich[1] *all* talked of how 'realized' they felt in the brief corridor⟩ *did* look with some nostalgia on 1917–22, even though Blok died of hunger and disease then. [...]

Yours ever,

[Isaiah]

TO MORTON WHITE

8 December 1980

Headington House

Dear Morton,

Thank you for your letter of 24 November anent value judgements in history. Are such judgements permissible? E. H. Carr, as you know, caricatures my view by saying that in effect I advocate saying to King John[2] (I think that is his example, but I cannot remember), after describing his activities, 'You cad!', or to Stalin 'You wicked fellow!'[3] I did not mean to say that historians are not forbidden to moralise – they have the same rights as any other men – whether they do it as historians or as human beings does not, as you say, matter very much. My difficulty is with question 2: Are moral judgements indispensable components of the historical work itself? This seems to me to be part and parcel of what you call 'another question' – the value judgement behind the arras.[4] It seems to me that the mere use of descriptive words, with no evaluative intent, itself carries evaluations. Apart from the fact that the selection of the facts, the emphasis etc. presuppose or embody a view as to what matters, and therefore matters to someone – the historian himself, his party, his society, mankind at large (which need not be made explicit, but

1 Dmitry Dmitrievich Shostakovich (1906–75), Russian composer: he was considerably younger than Pasternak and Chukovsky, and it seems improbable that he shared the contemporary artistic response to 1917 that IB attributes to them all, even if he looked back on the period with nostalgia.

2 John Plantagenet, known as John Lackland (1167–1216), son of Henry II and brother of Richard I, against whom he intrigued, and whom he in due course succeeded; king of England 1199–1216; forced by his barons to sign the Magna Carta at Runnymede 1215.

3 IB here appears to conflate 2 passages in Carr's *What Is History?* (London and NY, 1961). In one passage Carr attacks what he dubs the 'Bad King John theory of history', according to which individuals are the key historical agents, and says that IB 'pokes fun at people who believe in "vast impersonal forces" rather than individuals as the decisive factor in history' (39). Later he uses the example of a normally amiable man named Smith who one day attacks the reader verbally. Carr argues that the reader would explain Smith's behaviour in terms of its context (e.g. ' "Poor Smith! He must have been having more trouble with his wife" '), and that by doing so 'you would, I fear, incur the wrath of Sir Isaiah Berlin, who would bitterly complain that, by providing a causal explanation of Smith's behaviour, you had swallowed Hegel's and Marx's deterministic assumption, and shirked your obligation to denounce Smith as a cad' (89).

4 IB's metaphor is drawn from *Hamlet* 3. 4, in which Polonius hides behind an arras (a hanging tapestry curtain), eavesdrops on an exchange between Hamlet and his mother, and is stabbed to death by Hamlet for his pains. IB's claim is that it is not possible to make value judgements in human studies from an uninvolved perspective, to hide behind an arras separating us from our humanity.

nevertheless can be written between the lines easily enough) – there is also
the question of the words themselves. To say that Stalin or Hitler murdered
vast numbers of persons is different from saying that he killed them, or that
his policies were a cause of the rise in mortality in certain populations, or
that the average age of Jews or Volga Germans or whoever was a good deal
lower in 1938 than it had been in 1928, or 1908. The evidence on which these
statements are founded is much the same. The causal connection can be indicated in a neutral manner, which [...] would be positively misleading, or at
least indicate a Stalin-exonerating or Stalin-defending bias. No doubt there
are types of history – say, historical demography, based mainly on statistical
tables, or historical geography and the like – where the language really can
be made almost as 'value free' as it is in chemistry. But can 'ordinary' political
or general, social or even art history be written like that? Carr tries to get out
of it by distinguishing progressive from reactionary tendencies, as if this did
not imply a clear, sometimes exceedingly crude, set of values. [...]

    Yours ever,

    Isaiah   [...]

TO DITA SHKLAR[1]

    31 December 1980

                                Headington House

Dear Dita,

    [...] Your kind words about my piece on the Russian poets moved me
particularly, since you know the circumstances – who better? We know these
things both by [experience?] and heredity – knowledge by acquaintance, as
Russell pointed out, is quite different from knowledge by description, and
it is that that I was trying to convey. The behaviour of both Pasternak and
Akhmatova, and others, in the face of what they lived through, does vividly
transform one's (at any rate my) notions about moral freedom and dignity
[...]. It was not the 'massive evil' in Russia that was news to me; although,
of course, if one sees it face to face, as it were (knowledge by acquaintance
again), it makes a difference. It was the quality of the survivors of the pre-1914
culture under conditions of persecution which brought out its full grandeur,
not, for obvious reasons, so patent in the émigrés. It is a platitude to say that
critical situations exhibit the moral texture of individuals. In this case, I was
affected for life by seeing a combination of genius with nobility of character
and courage, virtues which do not necessarily go with artistic gifts. These
people were not only martyrs – blind fanatics, innocent children, ordinary

---

1 Judith Nisse ('Dita') Shklar (1928–92) née Yudita Nisse, Latvian-born political theorist; instructor,
  dept of government, Harvard, 1955–71, John Cowles Prof. of Government 1971–92; author of 'The
  Liberalism of Fear', in Nancy L. Rosenblum (ed.), *Liberalism and the Moral Life* (Cambridge, Mass.,
  and London, 1989).

people with no special attributes can be that – but by luck, or something else, we cannot tell what, they had the opportunity of rising above the world in which they lived, and did so. The moral effect is literally indescribable. So much for that terrible world, which I do not wish to visit again. I shall never go to the Soviet Union[1] – the mere thought that talking to people may have compromised them, even if ever so little, is too oppressive and guilt-inducing. I shall continue to watch from outside. [...]

You ask if Pasternak and Akhmatova thought that they were 'world-historical individuals'. Goodness knows: this is not confined to them, or to Russians. Robert Lowell[2] was rather like that too. I do not mean that any of them actually thought that they were fateful figures called upon to change the course of things, though Akhmatova did believe that she and I started the Cold War;[3] but that they were prone to a mythological view of life, in which everybody played certain parts, and if one departed from one's assigned role (as I did in Akhmatova's great fantasy, when I married),[4] it caused annoyance. I do not think that the horrors of Soviet, or even Russian, life were directly responsible for this: self-romanticisation and self-dramatisation have probably existed at all times. Hegel certainly thought of himself in these terms, so did M. Kojève,[5] who wished to have an influence on Stalin – or at least, the kind of relation which he imagined Hegel had to Napoleon,[6] not so much personal as two actors in the same cosmic drama. I have a feeling that George Kennan is liable to fantasies of this kind, too – he once told me that Gandhi[7] and he were the only men of any stature in political life who had spiritual vision. If you come to see me in Princeton in February, I'll tell you what he is saying now.

Much love,

Isaiah

---

1 IB visited the USSR with Aline in March 1988 (336–8).
2 Robert Traill Spence ('Cal') Lowell (1917–77), US poet known for his liberalism and opposition to the Vietnam war, regarded by contemporaries as the greatest US poet of his generation, comparable to Yeats, though this estimate now seems dated; 'Lowell seems to me very like some Tolstoyan character, blindly stumbling through and among groups of people greatly inferior to himself, don't you think?' (to Morton White, 3 December 1965).
3 Cf. 51–2, 113.
4 It was inconsistent with Akhmatova's somewhat mystical, world-historical view of her relationship with IB that he should have married: 'the fact that I had gone and got married in the most ordinary, banal fashion, insulted her' (to Lidiya Chukovskaya, 16–17 June 1981).
5 Alexandre Kojève (1902–68) né Aleksandr Vladimirovich Kozhevnikov, Russian-born French philosopher and politician of a somewhat megalomaniac stripe who helped create the European Union and declared himself (with some irony) a Stalinist; noted interpreter of Hegel.
6 Napoleon I (1769–1821) né Napoleone di Buonaparte, Corsican-born Emperor of the French 1804–15, one of the greatest historical figures of modern times, and admired as such by Hegel.
7 Mohandas Karamchand ('Mahatma', 'venerable') Gandhi (1869–1948), Indian political leader, religious and social reformer, apostle of non-violence, led India to independence 1947.

*One of the nineteenth-century Russian authors IB felt most in sympathy with
was Ivan Turgenev, and he had a hand in two productions of his comedy of
manners,* A Month in the Country *(1855), first staged in Moscow in 1872.
It was at IB's suggestion that a ballet based on the play, choreographed by
Frederick Ashton,[1] was set to the music of Chopin: the premiere at Covent
Garden on 12 February 1976, with music arranged by John Lanchbery,[2] was
soon established in the Royal Ballet's repertoire. Five years later IB was commissioned to translate the play for the National Theatre: 'There is absolutely
no need for a new English translation', he wrote to Andrzej Walicki:[3] 'Mrs
Garnett's[4] old version is perfectly good enough, both for reading and for acting;
but there is a perpetual pressure for new translations simply because they are
new, and for some reason I was tempted to do it – it was a kind of challenge.
I have now finished it, and it is a marvellous play, far better than I ever thought
before.'[5] IB's text was the basis of the production by Peter Gill[6] that opened at
the Olivier Theatre on 19 February 1981,[7] and* The Times *found words of praise
for the script: 'The new translation by Isaiah Berlin transmits the elegance of
the hothouse and (from hasty comparison) often finds one precise word where
other versions use an approximate two. It also underlines the larger metaphor
of departure; so that with the Governess's closing line, "I'm going too", a vista
appears of other and larger despotisms that are due to be abandoned.'[8] IB was
in the US with Aline on the opening night, 19 February, but early in January he
met the cast to discuss his translation and their staging.*

TO PETER GILL

10 January 1981 [*carbon*]

Headington House

Dear Mr Gill, ·

   I am so sorry to have left so precipitately, and to have talked so fast and so

---

1 Frederick William Mallandaine Ashton (1904–88), Kt 1962, OM 1977; principal choreographer,
   Vic–Wells Ballet (renamed Royal Ballet 1956), 1933–70, director 1963–70.
2 John Arthur Lanchbery (1923–2003), conductor and music arranger specialising in ballet music;
   among his arrangements was Kenneth Macmillan's *Mayerling* (1978); conductor, Royal Ballet,
   1959–60, music director 1960–72; music director, Australian Ballet 1972–8, American Ballet Theatre
   1978–80.
3 Andrzej *Walicki (b. 1930), philosopher and historian of ideas.
4 Constance Clara Garnett (1861–1946) née Black, translator of many Russian classics; IB recognised her achievement in making Russian literature available to English readers, but was dismissive of her 'plodding prose', and her insensitivity to the naturalness of Turgenev's dialogue. 'On
   Translating Turgenev', review of I. S. Turgenev, *Smoke, On the Eve, Virgin Soil, Fathers and Children*
   and *A House of Gentle Folk*, trans. Constance Garnett, *Observer*, 11 November 1951, 7.
5 Letter of 3 December 1980.
6 Peter Gill (b. 1939), playwright, actor, theatre director; director, Royal Court Theatre 1976–80,
   Royal National Theatre Studio 1984–90; assistant director, Royal National Theatre, 1989–97.
7 For the NT's poster advertising the production see 585.
8 Irving Wardle, 'Turgenev with All the Discomforts', *Times*, 21 February 1981, 8e–h at 8h.

much: was it the slightest use? I never got to my funeral, of course; I was an hour late and might just as well have stayed, and was afterwards very sorry that I didn't – I do mismanage my life.

I don't think I replied to that charming actress's question about why the Russians talked about the ends of life so much in those country houses – certainly not adequately. What I really meant was: Why don't they in Jane Austen's novels, and why do they in Turgenev? – for socially there is a certain analogy. There is no final answer – personal and provincial class habits differ from each other in different countries as they do, and none of the explanations given by sociologists and psychologists ever seems really convincing. But all I could and should have said, perhaps, is that in England or France there really is a certain continuity of life: the way people behave, and what they think or talk about, in the nineteenth century – even when they are self-conscious, as they are in, say, George Eliot,[1] even in Emily Brontë[2] – is not all that different from what similar persons might have talked about in the eighteenth century in similar circumstances socially and topographically. There is a line from Jane Austen to Mrs Gaskell,[3] Mrs Humphry Ward,[4] Virginia Woolf; there is a line from Sterne and Lamb to Betjeman.[5] But in Russia – that's what I should have said – the break from the past, effectively imposed by Peter the Great, who forced Western culture upon some of his subjects, was really revolutionary.[6] Russia never quite came to after that – they were Russians, with a set of national and family characteristics, superimposed on which was all that German and French and even English culture.

They were at once conscious of their own backwardness, and at the same time of the worried attitude towards them of Western Europe: the fear of the sheer brute physical power of Russia, shown after its triumphant march across Europe to Paris in 1815, mingled with contempt towards these uncouth barbarians, these pathetic imitators of the West who had everything to learn. All this created self-questioning in the intelligentsia, and a degree of

1 Mary Ann Evans ('George Eliot') (1819–80), novelist, admired as an acute observer of Victorian society, and commercially successful both in her lifetime and posthumously; her reputation was cemented with her greatest work, *Middlemarch: A Study of Provincial Life* (Edinburgh/London, 1871–2).
2 Emily Jane Brontë (1818–48), novelist and poet, sister of Charlotte and Anne and author of *Wuthering Heights* (London, 1847).
3 Elizabeth Cleghorn Gaskell (1810–65) née Stevenson, novelist, short-story writer and active humanitarian; biographer of Charlotte Brontë.
4 Mary Augusta Ward (1851–1920) née Arnold, novelist (wrote under her married name), philanthropist and political lobbyist; best known for her novel *Robert Elsmere* (London, 1888), which dealt with the religious and social issues that were her own prominent concerns.
5 Laurence Sterne (1713–68), writer and Church of England clergyman, author of *The Life and Opinions of Tristram Shandy, Gentleman* (Dublin, 1759–67); Charles Lamb (1775–1834), essayist; John Betjeman (1906–84) né Betjemann, Kt 1969, poet, writer and broadcaster, Poet Laureate 1972–84.
6 During his 'Grand Embassy' 1697–8 Peter the Great visited European capitals, and on his return introduced some of the cultural practices he encountered, determined to make Russia a major European power.

self-consciousness and uneasiness even below that, in these 'county' circles. Rakitin[1] is aware of the anomalous condition of the Russians, and their inferiority to the West: the student Belyaev is subject to radical influences at his university, which blow in from the West, not from any Russian roots. Belinsky is a purveyor of these, and they were more earnestly and deeply believed in than they were in the West, and were transformed by the passionate and religious conviction that this was where salvation must come from – but still, not native. It is a mixture of naivety and a thin layer of sophistication from the West, which makes all Russians (perhaps not all, but most of the famous ones) concerned with 'Who are we Russians, where are we going, what is our fate, why were we created?' The 'top' nations, the French and the English, don't ask that sort of thing; they take themselves for granted quite complacently and justifiably (perhaps); but 'developing' nations, like Africans now, are worried about what is thought of them, whether they are doing well, whether it is all right or not all right to try and imitate more developed nations, etc. That makes people introspective, self-critical etc., often in a very charming, fresh way. That is the best I can do, and I am sorry not to have said that at the time. Perhaps I couldn't have got it all out: I should have talked too fast and nobody would have understood a word.

Yours sincerely,

[Isaiah Berlin]

TO MORTON WHITE

11 February 1981

Headington House

Dear Morton,

Let me begin by saying that we still feel awful about not coming to Princeton. If my pulse had not played up I should have come, flu or no flu, but once that happens I can never know when or whether it will subside, when it may start up again or what to do about it. My cardiologist took the same line, so this relieved me of some degree of guilt. [...]

I did participate in the fellowship election at All Souls, but refrained from making my usual vehement speech, which probably did the winning candidate – a Miss Hurley,[2] an American disciple of Charles Taylor, Ronnie Dworkin, the later Wittgenstein – a good deal of good. The first woman, and I think the first American citizen, to be elected to a proper fellowship.

1 Rakitin and Belyaev are characters from Turgenev's play, centred on events at the Islaev family estate: Mikhail Aleksandrovich Rakitin is a family friend, devoted to Arkady Islaev's wife, Natal'ya; she in turn is taken with Aleksey Nikolaevich Belyaev, the young tutor to her son Kolya.

2 Susan Lynn Hurley (1954–2007), US philosopher, was attending Harvard Law School when she became the 1st woman to be elected to a fellowship at All Souls, 1981–5; DPhil 1983; fellow, St Edmund Hall, 1985–94; prof., dept of politics and international studies, Warwick, 1994–2006; later (2006–7) prof. of philosophy, Bristol; her life was cut short by breast cancer.

Some of my more conservative colleagues could hardly speak for – not exactly indignation, but mortification, inability to absorb into their conscious mind that such a thing had finally happened. Something of the sort happened when we took our first and only black man[1] [...], but this went even deeper. I literally cannot understand such feelings, and am the only member of my age-group who has spoken and voted for this revolutionary step. I am consequently regarded with considerable disfavour by some very old friends, who suspect me, I think, of trying to keep in with the young. Not that all the young were in favour – we have some splendid young fogies. The speeches, the behaviour, the storms in this body of sixty to seventy fellows were extraordinary, impossible to describe in neutral language. But I still feel acute guilt about not being at Princeton, quite apart from regret and a sense of bereftness – not to be described in neutral language either, which brings me to my next point.

Neutral and loaded language: no, I do not believe that historians are obliged to moralise; there is no need for them to say 'Stalin (a scoundrel) viciously massacred an unheard-of number of utterly innocent and honourable people to satisfy his blood-lust', etc. This is rather what E. H. Carr thinks I am advocating, but that is a mere travesty. I do not mind historians moralising if they choose to – it is their right as human beings, although they will, of course, create in the reader's mind some suspicion of their bias [...].

My position is somewhat different: in cases of human activities, especially in dealings of human beings among themselves, some of the central terms inevitably used seem to me, whether one consciously intends them to do so or not, to convey an evaluative attitude. 'Murder', as Russell rightly says,[2] must now carry the implication of culpable homicide; but so in my view do all the other terms. There are various ways of saying that someone deprived someone else of his life, and each of these ways seems to me to have some evaluative force. Thus, although the descriptive element is identical in them all, 'X murdered Y', 'X killed Y', 'X executed Y', 'X inadvertently' – a descriptive word – 'caused Y's demise', 'X poisoned Y', 'X's operation ended in Y's death', etc. etc. all record the same descriptive kernel, yet each conveys a different impression of the writer's attitude. To say, as you suggest, 'Stalin committed adultery', and then add a footnote to the effect that this is not meant as a moral judgement, will surely not make much difference to those who think that adultery is a mortal sin; if you wish to avoid evaluation and convey neutrality of judgement you must say something like 'Stalin lived in an intimate

1 Hugh Worrell Springer (1913–94), barrister; visiting fellow, All Souls, 1962–3; hon. fellow 1988–94; governor general, Barbados, 1984–90.
2 William Oldnall Russell (c.1784–1833), legal writer and judge (in India); author of the influential *A Treatise on Crimes and Misdemeanours* (London, 1819), in which he writes: 'such killing as is accompanied with circumstances that shew the heart to be perversely wicked, is adjudged to be of *malice prepense*, and consequently murder' (3. 1, 'Of Murder', 614).

relationship with X, who had a husband'; but this, in my view, conveys what zealots would condemn as obvious condonation on the part of the writer.

In other words, what I am arguing is that the statement 'I am avoiding moral judgements' is itself a moral judgement about the obligations of historians. And, let us say, a Marxist or a liberal or whoever who recommends looking at the facts in a certain fashion – say in a temperate, cool, detached manner, or alternatively from the point of view of the class alignment in a given situation – is likely to be charged with (and certainly perceived as) emphasising some aspects of the situation much more than others because of presuppositions about values, e.g. the ends of man, or correct or incorrect views of these ends. It does not seem to me to matter much whether you encourage readers to moralise or not. As I say, I am more interested in the force of the words themselves, and do not believe in the possibility of complete neutrality where human relationships are concerned. A chemist or physicist really does get neutrality, or something very, very near it; in human affairs, the mere selection of the facts, the emphasis on this rather than that, indicates one's conception of what matters and what doesn't – that is certainly evaluation (where 'moral' ends and something else, 'political' or 'aesthetic', begins is another question, not easily answered, I think). All such things imply, or even presuppose, scales of value. [...] In short, I do not believe that the effort to avoid giving the impression of bias – if by bias is meant any evaluation at all – can be achieved, because emphasis, the order of events, the omission of this, a detail about that, reference to goals, motives, outlooks (in descriptions which are more than protocol sentences)[1] cannot but involve points of view, a sense of values which, where they are accepted without question, are simply not noticed until viewed from the standpoint of some other moral position.

Do you disagree with all this? When I read E. H. Carr I know perfectly well what his values are: so I do when I read Halévy[2] or Sam Morison[3] or Namier. If I am not sympathetic to them, I notice this; otherwise I probably remain unconscious. None of these people go about saying 'What a splendid achievement!' or 'How disgusting!' or 'steeped in crime', as the well-known neutral Machiavelli did about people he held up for admiration. [...]

Love to Lucia,

Yours,

Isaiah   [...]

---

1 Name given by logical positivism to allegedly uninterpreted descriptions of immediate sense-perception (e.g. 'A red patch appears in the upper right visual field'), claimed to be the foundations of all knowledge.

2 Élie Halévy (1870–1937), French historian and philosopher known for his *A History of the English People in the Nineteenth Century* (Paris, 1912–46; trans. E. I. Watkin, London, 1924–47), incomplete at his death.

3 Samuel Eliot Morison (1887–1976), American historian and Pulitzer-Prize-winning biographer; professor of history, Harvard, 1925–41, Jonathan Trumbull Professor of American History 1941–55.

TO NORA BELOFF[1]
27 March 1981

Headington House

Dear Nora,

[...] First of all, let me go back to the topic we talked about in Fortnum's.[2] Is the Soviet Union inspired by a Marxist ideal of world Communist revolution, or by traditional Russian imperialism plus the government's aim of self-perpetuation? I believe that the answer is somewhat analogous to what could have been said about Islam during the first thousand years of its existence. On the one hand, there is the Muslim doctrine of the need to propagate the faith, if need be by the sword: this inspired early Muslim conquests. But once Islam was 'contained' by Charles Martel or by the re-conquest in Spain or, finally, at the gates of Vienna,[3] the vast Turkish Empire, although officially inspired by the official ideal of the Caliphate and Islam as a fighting religion, in fact settled down to a pattern of hostilities followed by long *de facto* truces. There was a curtain then, just as effective as the iron curtain; not much truck between the two worlds. The Turks conquered whatever they could, and held on to their conquests, until decay set in.

So, too, the Soviet Union, except the difference is that the Turks didn't have ideological allies in the West. All empires bent on [...] acquisition, retention and extension must be animated by some kind of ideology which justifies their conduct to themselves – this is true of Rome, France, Britain, everybody. So, too, the Russians. But it does not dictate the tactics or even the strategy, the purpose of which is the extension of power without consideration of ultimate ends, whatever such extensions may be. Rich men seldom ask themselves what exactly the advantages of being richer and richer may be; nor do states; though usually ideologues try to justify it, and other ideologues criticise it.

So much for my cynicism on this subject. I think the question Pipes v. Solzhenitsyn – imperialism v. ideology – is not a real contrast. The main thing is to eliminate danger by defeating enemies and extending power as far as practical. Who they are enemies to – to the ideology or to the Soviet state – is irrelevant: enemies to the one are enemies to the other. The point is that historically it is clear that ideological objections to power moves are rejected

1 (Leah) Nora Beloff (1919–97), journalist; on staff, *Observer*, for almost 30 years, from 1948, becoming political correspondent 1964, the 1st woman to hold such a post on a British newspaper.
2 The tea salon in Fortnum & Mason's Piccadilly premises, close to the Berlins' London base (a set in Albany), was one of IB's favourite venues for social encounters. After their meeting there Beloff sent IB a draft of an essay on the USSR.
3 The victory of the Frankish leader Charles Martel (c.688–741) at the Battle of Tours in 732 stopped Muslim expansion into Western Europe; Granada, the last Muslim stronghold there, fell to Spain's Christian rulers Isabella I and Ferdinand V 1492; the 2nd and final Ottoman siege of Vienna was lifted 1683, and the Turks forced to retreat, after which their power began to recede in their Balkan stronghold.

in the Soviet Union: anyone who says that one should support Mao against Chiang Kai Shek,[1] not deal with Mussolini,[2] and not support Hitler in 1939, not support de Gaulle[3] against the socialists in France, or Giscard[4] against Mitterrand,[5] etc. – for ideological reasons, loyalty to Marxist ideals, etc. – is told he just doesn't understand the national needs of the Soviet Union or its ideological war against capitalism, which are one and the same thing, whatever means are adopted, at the cost if need be of the destruction of Communists and other allies. [...]

I do not think that 'socialism in one country'[6] means 'socialism in *only* one country' – the idea of encouraging Communist revolutions in other countries, or steps towards them via nationalist anti-imperialism, was surely never abandoned, even officially. I have a feeling that the thing to say is that the Soviet Union *can* be stopped by concerted action, and without atom bombs. They were going to take over Persia in 1945, and certainly stirred up a great Communist Tudeh[7] movement there, but *were* in fact stopped by Byrnes[8] and Bevin. Cuba was, after all, an unprovoked threat, but it *was* coped with; they *were* stopped in Egypt, they *were* stopped in Korea.[9] If foreign rule is regarded as undesirable, and rule by Moscow particularly hideous, and if Western Europe really does not propose to subjugate anyone – nor America after the lesson of Vietnam unless the Soviet Union *conspicuously* makes

1 Chiang Kai-shek (Jiang Jie Shi) (1887–1975), President, Republic of China, 1928–49, Taiwan 1950–75, led the nationalist Kuomintang in the civil war against Communist forces under Mao Zedong; fled to the island of Taiwan after the fall of Peking 1949.

2 Benito Amilcare Andrea Mussolini (1883–1945), founder and leader of Italian Fascism, dictator of Italy ('il Duce', 'the Leader') 1922–43; deposed 25 July 1943, captured and executed by Italian partisans 28 April 1945.

3 Charles André Joseph Marie de Gaulle (1890–1970), French general and statesman; leader, Free French government in exile, 1940–4; head of French provisional government 1944–6; prime minister 1958–9; President, France, 1959–69; his Gaullist movement was broadly anti-socialist, but transcended party politics in the national interest, including some left-wingers.

4 Valéry Marie René Georges Giscard d'Estaing (b. 1926), French statesman, leader, centrist Independent Republicans; minister of finance in the Gaullist administrations 1962–6, 1969–74; President 1974–81; lost to François Mitterrand 1981.

5 François Maurice Marie Mitterrand (1916–96), French socialist statesman; President 1981–95, the 1st socialist President for 3 decades.

6 A principle endorsed by Stalin in December 1924 in the preface to his *On the Road to October* (Moscow, 1925), and turned into a slogan by his 18 December 1925 speech at the 14th Party Congress: industry and military power were to be built up in the USSR before the attempt was made to spread Communism elsewhere.

7 Iranian Communist party founded in September 1941 after the deposition by the Allies of Reza Pahlavi, Shah of Iran; initially liberal, it became overtly pro-Soviet, enjoying its greatest influence in the immediate post-war period.

8 James Francis ('Jimmy') Byrnes (1882–1972), US lawyer, judge and Democrat politician; senator, South Carolina, 1931–41; secretary of state 1945–7; spurred on by Truman, and in tandem with Bevin, he took an increasingly tough line on Soviet influence in Iran 1946.

9 In October 1962 the Soviet attempt to site nuclear missiles in Cuba was thwarted by the Kennedy administration; between 1972 and 1976 Anwar Sadat severed Egypt's close ties with the USSR; and in the Korean War 1950–3 a US-led international coalition prevented a Communist takeover of the whole Korean peninsula by containing the Soviet- and Chinese-backed forces to the north of a demilitarised zone along the 38th parallel.

trouble in Latin America (I think this, but it may be disputed) – if this is so, the idea that force is always answered by force and that Western strength is bound to provoke war seems to me untrue. What reason is there for supposing that if the West were to abandon this or that weapon the Russians would do likewise? After the Second War, the Americans in effect did demobilise, the armament industry did run down – but the Russians showed no sign of following suit, and the Cold War was caused (whatever the revisionists said) by the flexing of Soviet muscles, not American. The crucial moment was when Mrs Roosevelt[1] and her fellow liberals, and large sections of the British Labour Party (not just Bevin, but people like Healey, Aneurin Bevan),[2] understood that the Soviet Union penetrates wherever defences are weak or there is a vacuum of any kind; even Cripps came to believe this. What reason is there to think that the Soviet Union has changed its spots just because Stalin is dead? Stalin was notoriously cautious: his heirs, at best, plan the careful expansion of power and deliberate debilitation of the West, rather than precipitate adventures, which might, as in Cuba, prove counterproductive. [...]

Cultural exchanges, etc. [...] There are very few cases where Soviet visitors to the West have been convinced that the West is worse than, or at least as bad as, they supposed – they may say this to keep their party ticket, but in fact they do learn. Conversely, there are very few cases of Western visitors [to] the Soviet Union who think that things are nothing like as bad as they had supposed: a good example of this is the reaction of most Western correspondents who went to the Olympics. The Muggeridge[3] experience is not only not unique, but there are very few known exceptions. Nobody now comes back from the Soviet Union to point the contrast between reasonable peace-supporting policies of the Soviet leaders versus the sabre-rattling Western imperialists and warmongers – as they used to come back even from Hitler's Germany. It is a comfort that evidently one cannot fool even all the leftists all the time. [...]

Finally: the last three years of campaigning for human rights has not made [the] USSR respect the rights of other societies, or individuals – only their power. [...] Threatening war is always stupid and dangerous; all we can be expected to do (even if we are the most ardent socialists) is to support morally decent forms of government wherever they are, and keep our own powder

1 (Anna) Eleanor Roosevelt (1884–1962) née Roosevelt, niece of the former President Theodore Roosevelt; m. 1905 her distant cousin FDR; diplomat and humanitarian, delegate, 1st UN assembly, 1946, chair, UN Commission on Human Rights, 1946–51.
2 Aneurin ('Nye') Bevan (1897–1960), South Wales miners' leader, socialist and Labour politician; as minister of health in Attlee's government 1945–51 he was responsible for the creation of the National Health Service.
3 (Thomas) Malcolm Muggeridge (1903–90), journalist and broadcaster; editor, Punch, 1953–7; disappointed by the advent of the National Government in Britain, he and his wife Kitty emigrated September 1932 to the USSR, 'which they regarded, like many young nonconformists of the time, as the new Jerusalem. Muggeridge, however, was quickly disillusioned' (Richard Ingrams, ODNB); they left for Switzerland.

dry. With a monstrous regime like the Soviet Union,* one can only achieve
– not a *modus vivendi* but a *modus non vivendi*, which is not at all the same
thing as [a] *modus moriendi*[1] – and this applies to our new Chinese friends too
– however desirable it is to keep on good terms with everybody [...].

Yours ever,

Isaiah

⟨*Radek[2] once said to Charles Bohlen,[3] so B told me, 'Communism is not like
a bath: one cannot make it now colder now hotter'. Read 'Soviet conduct'.
Our effect on its domestic policies is zero: they do relent only if they think
that their allies abroad are likely to be too deeply shocked: & not always then:
& never more than temporarily; there is no evidence that Western rearma-
ment has ever made them more aggressive: nobody thinks Afghanistan or
Cambodia or Korea were provoked by Western acts or threats, or do they?⟩

TO MORTON WHITE

7 April 1981

Headington House

Dear Morton,

[...] You say you are uninterested in the writer's evaluative attitude towards
events and persons. In fact, what you are saying is 'Facts are sacred, comment
is free'[4] – the noble but unrealisable ideal of the old *Manchester Guardian*.
I think that for once Carr, quoting Goethe,[5] is right:[6] there are no 'facts' in
that sense, all facts embody theories, and all theories – if I am right – embody
evaluations. Of course I don't want the reporter evaluating the facts for me,
I only want him to tell me what happened; I don't want him declaring his full
political and religious position, *à la* Eliot; I don't think I want to know whether
the historian is a royalist or not – I think that I can discover that pretty well

---

1 'Way of living [alongside one another]' adopted by parties that disagree; 'way of not living'; 'way
   of dying'. IB means that in the 2nd Latin expression 'not living' should not be taken to mean
   'dying'.
2 Karl Berngardovich Radek (1885–1939) né Sobelsohn, Polish Jewish revolutionary, imprisoned for
   treason 1937 during Stalin's Great Purge.
3 Charles Eustis ('Chip') *Bohlen (1904–74), US diplomat and Soviet specialist; US ambassador to
   the USSR 1953–7, to France 1962–8; IB first encountered Chip and Avis Bohlen in Washington
   during the war, and they belonged to the extended family of his closest friends there.
4 'Comment is free, but facts are sacred': C. P. Scott, 'A Hundred Years', *Manchester Guardian*, 5 May
   1921, 35.
5 Johann Wolfgang von Goethe (1749–1832), German poet, dramatist, novelist and scientist; most
   famous for his 2-part verse tragedy *Faust* (1808, 1832); a writer of enormous range, achievement
   and influence.
6 Goethe wrote that 'Everything in the realm of fact is already theory': *Wilhelm Meisters
   Wanderjahre*, 2nd. ed. (Stuttgart and Tübingen, 1829), book 2, [appendix,] 'Betrachtungen im
   Sinne der Wanderer: Kunst, Ethisches, Natur'. We have not found this view quoted as Goethe's
   by Carr, though he certainly shares it.

from the language he uses about a king and his family; and if he were writing about revolutions, I think I could equally deduce from his language whether he was royalist, anti-royalist, neutral etc. You really do believe, I think, that the historian can furnish you with the 'bare facts' and let you react to them in ways in which you might not be able to help reacting: I do not believe this. In other words, I believe that it is possible to write about geological formations in that way, but not about the motives, goals, outlooks, fears and hopes, loves and hates, 'what Alcibiades did and suffered',[1] his relationships to the society in which he lived and other societies, and the rest of it.

How, you ask, shall we resolve our differences? Only by talking, I expect. I am certainly not saying that historians *must* express attitudes *and* ought to do so – only that they must; and ought not to behave as if they didn't; and thereby mis-express them if they feel them. Is that nonsense?

Yours ever,
Isaiah

TO ARIEH HARELL[2]

16 April 1981 [*carbon*]

Headington House

Dear Professor Harell,

[…] I think you are perfectly right. What is wrong with Generals Pfuel, Bennigsen and Paulucci[3] is that they do not understand what men live by, and try to apply abstract schemata to men and their behaviour, beliefs, lives, which, in Tolstoy's view, breed illusions, sometimes of megalomania. I do not know that he actually concedes that many of these men are 'honest, struggling against hollowness, self-delusion and fraudulence';[4] certainly the Germans, Tsar Alexander,[5] Napoleon do not do that; for Tolstoy, unlike, say, Turgenev, characters in the novels are on either the right or the wrong side; they are good, with an insight into spiritual reality, or blind inflicters of damage on themselves and others. I think the paeans to 'the people'[6] are not

---

1 Aristotle's illustration of the subject matter of history ('suffered' in the sense of 'had done to him'): *Poetics* 1451b11. Alcibiades (*c.*450–414 BCE), Athenian statesman, soldier and orator.

2 Arieh Harell (1911–98) né Steinberg, Kiev-born doctor and diplomat, Israeli ambassador to the USSR 1958–62; head of Ichilov Hospital, Municipal Government Medical Center, Tel Aviv, 1962–80. AH had written to IB about HF.

3 All 3 are military commanders of the Napoleonic era, and also appear in Tolstoy's novel *War and Peace* (1869): Ernst Heinrich Adolf von Pfuel (1779–1866), Prussian general, then minister of war and prime minister; Count Levin August Gottlieb Theophil von Bennigsen (1745–1826), German general in the service of the Russian Empire, and a veteran of the Napoleonic Wars; Philip/Filippo Osipovich Paulucci (1779–1849), an Italian marquis who fought with the Russian army during the Russo–Turkish War of 1806–12.

4 AH to IB, 1 March 1981.

5 Alexander I (1777–1825), Tsar of Russia 1801–25; repulsed Napoleon's invasion of Russia 1812, and participated in the decisive defeat of the retreating French army at Leipzig 1813.

6 A term much invoked in AH's letter to IB, e.g. 'The real hero in Tolstoy's *War and* Peace is […]

principally because they are the people (as against self-intoxicated individuals or individualists) [but] because he thinks simple men have an instinctive
understanding of reality, both material and moral, of what makes life worth
living, of what are the true ends of man, or the relations of man and God,
and all the things that to Tolstoy appeared to matter more than the kind of
knowledge science or history or economics or worldly wisdom of any kind
can bring – for he came to denounce them all.

Kutuzov (who, as you know, is not in the least like the real Kutuzov of
history, who was a cunning courtier and a first-rate intriguer)[1] is a hero because
he feels what the people feel, understands life as they do, they feel he is in communion with them and he feels this about them. It is not, I think, the mere fact
that 'the people', whatever that might mean – and for Tolstoy and the Russian
radicals in general it meant the poor, the ignorant, the exploited, the simple,
not the comfortably-off, the officials, the professors, the bankers etc. – not
because 'the people' feel or know this, but because what they feel and know is
closer to the truth than the civilised world which Tolstoy denounced as corrupt
and involved in false values. In short, he was not, in my view, a populist in
the sense that he believed that one must do what the people wants because it
wants it, so much as a believer that to the simple and [uncorrupted?] truths are
revealed that are no longer acceptable to the corrupt middle and upper classes,
their lackeys and providers of their pleasures.

I think that towards the end of his life Tolstoy came to believe that men
who took the Christian Gospels seriously could know the truth, and that
anyone who departed from these truths was simply wrong and dangerous.
[…] As you know, he disapproved of the revolutionaries, even if he also hated
their government, and the fact that the mass of the people (even if it had
been so) placed their faith in revolutionaries would not have caused him to
think that the revolutionaries and their followers had got it right, so to speak.

One might say, I suppose, that the mass of the German people, particularly peasants, simple folk, etc., were in strong sympathy with Hitler, that
the mass of Huns or Tartars were in sympathy with Attila or Genghis Khan[2]
– but that would not have made Tolstoy suppose that this was sufficient to
guarantee the validity of their beliefs or actions, surely? Nor do I believe
that democracy consists in the instinctive faiths and natural beliefs of what

the Russian People with capital R and P – as a collective existence which emerges out of the
multitude of personalities appearing in the book.'
1 Mikhail Illarionovich Golenishchev-Kutuzov (1745–1813), also portrayed in *War and Peace*, was
commander-in-chief, Russian armies, 1812; he adopted a 'scorched earth' policy in response to
the Napoleonic invasion, and is regarded as an early exponent of total war.
2 Attila (406–53), king of the Huns c.434–453, inflicted devastation on a vast expanse of the Eastern
Roman Empire 445–50 from his base in Hungary; defeated by a Roman–Visigoth alliance at
Châlons in 451. Temujin (1162–1227) united Mongolia and was proclaimed Genghis Khan ('ruler
of all'); captured Beijing 1215, and created an empire that stretched from the Pacific to the northern shores of the Black Sea; the Tartars (including the Mongols) were nomadic central Asian
peoples who threatened settled civilisations in Asia and Europe.

Communists used to call 'the masses'. When these masses killed Jews, or witches – there is, after all, no doubt that it was spontaneous, not enforced – this did not constitute democracy in any modern sense. I do not know what I mean by democracy – I think simply any form of government (not widespread popular desires or activities) which depends on the favour of the electors. Such a government may seek to bribe or flatter or otherwise gain this favour, in which case it can be described as a corrupt or dishonest democracy, but still a democracy. Whereas forms of government can be conceived where the despot is genuinely enlightened, the laws are just, individual liberty quite wide, but this is despotism all the same, and, if one believes in the proposition that the people should participate in the government of their societies, to be rejected.

I do not think that Tolstoy cared for any of these political forms, only for spiritual salvation. He thought that the peasants were spiritually less corrupt, purer, than his own class (although the only people he describes with any degree of veracity, and indeed genius, are the aristocracy – his peasants are wooden and the middle classes absent). He deified the people only because he thought they were the carriers of God's truth, and not because they were the people, so it seems to me; and the Germans, theorisers, manipulators, were to be condemned not because they were not members of the masses, but because they had lost sight of true values, which only a different kind of life, closer to that which was lived by the ordinary peasant, would secure. All this comes from Rousseau[1] as much as from the New Testament – mystical faith in the pure souls of the peasant is not democracy, in my sense at least.

You wonder whether my views do not emerge in the course of that essay. I expect they do: one never knows how much of oneself one reveals in writing about others – I, perhaps, more than most. I certainly do not much believe in the application of the methods of the natural sciences to the explanation of human behaviour, at least, nor of the relationships of individual men and women to each other – although it may do better in areas like geography, food supply, natural factors, the actions of large masses of men over huge periods of time (as in the kind of books that Braudel[2] and his school write).

1 Jean Jacques Rousseau (1712–78), Swiss-born French philosopher, whose *Du contrat social, ou, Principes du droit politique* [*On the Social Contract, or, Principles of Political Right*] ('Amsterdam' [sc. France], 1762) encouraged ideals that inspired the French Revolution, for whose excesses he is sometimes blamed by his critics, among them IB: 'Thank you for "Rousseau's Two Concepts of Liberty". You will not be surprised to be told that I am not convinced by it: it is a rich and deeply sympathetic account of Rousseau's various uses of liberty, autonomy, independence etc. etc., but I do not think the Jacobins misinterpreted his doctrines more than Plekhanov or Lenin those of Marx' (to Robert Wokler [plate 11], 12 March 1985). One of the 6 main subjects of FIB.

2 Fernand Paul Braudel (1902–85), French historian and author of the 2-vol. *La Méditerranée et le monde méditerranéen à l'époque de Philippe II* (Paris, 1949), trans. Siân Reynolds as *The Mediterranean and the Mediterranean World in the Age of Philip II* (London / NY, 1972–3). Braudel's work, combining insights from a number of disciplines, and emphasising long-term social history, exemplifies the approach of the Annales school of French historiography, named after its flagship journal.

Tolstoy thought all history was bunk, to use Henry Ford's phrase,[1] and his attack on sociologists, liberals, intellectuals etc. derives not from a different view of history (of which in the end he confessed despair and ignorance), but because their eyes were directed at the external instead of the inner world. The fact that he wrote the best historical novel ever produced by a human being is a marvellous paradox. [...]

Yours sincerely,

[Isaiah Berlin]

TO NORMAN STONE[2]

30 April 1981

Headington House

Dear Mr Stone,

Thank you for the review.[3] It is very brilliant, and as readable and enjoyable as the works of the master himself. I share your admiration for him, as you know, and am fond of him, and do not mind his quirks; but I am not convinced – as I suspect you are – that Mein Kampf[4] was irrelevant to Hitler's actions. After all, most of the things he wished to happen, he did his best to bring about. Nobody is less disposed to believe in determinism and predictability than I am, but Alan's addiction to the idea that everything, virtually, is contingent, that the faintest suspicion of a theory or a hypothesis indicates a foolish academic preoccupation with ideas, lack of a tough sense of the kaleidoscope of reality, is too much even for me. Only those historians seem to me to survive who provide a genuine vision of a society or a period, like Gibbon, Macaulay,[5] Fustel de

1 'History is more or less bunk': US industrialist and car manufacturer Henry Ford (1863–1947) in the 3rd part of an interview with Charles N. Wheeler, 'Fight To Disarm His Life's Work, Henry Ford Vows', *Chicago Daily Tribune*, 25 May 1916, 10a–e at 10a. Tolstoy's extremely jaundiced view of the possibility of objective historical writing is a main theme of IB's *The Hedgehog and the Fox: An Essay on Tolstoy's View of History* (London/NY, 1953), originally published in shorter form as 'Lev Tolstoy's Historical Scepticism', *Oxford Slavonic Papers* 2 (1951), 17–54.

2 Norman Stone (b. 1941), lecturer in Russian history, Cambridge, 1967–84, fellow and director of studies in history, Jesus, 1971–9, fellow, Trinity, 1979–84; prof. of modern history, Oxford, and fellow, Worcester, 1984–97.

3 'Taylorism', LRB, 22 January 1981, 12–15, in which Stone found much to praise in A. J. P. Taylor's works, notably his controversial and revisionist *The Origins of the Second World War* (London, 1961).

4 Adolf Hitler, *Mein Kampf: Die nationalsozialistische Bewegung* [*My Struggle: The National Socialist Movement*], Hitler's autobiography and political manifesto, first published in Munich in 2 vols 1925 and 1926 (the latter vol. dated 1927). Of Taylor's view, radical at the time, that *Mein Kampf* was not Hitler's blueprint, but rather 'the kind of bad-tempered vapouring you could hear in any Munich beerhouse or Viennese café' (12) Stone argued: 'It is almost certainly right not to bother too much with *Mein Kampf* in a direct sense: but it said a great deal about the moral framework in which its author operated (and for that matter its readers)' (14).

5 Thomas Babington Macaulay (1800–59), 1st Baron Macaulay 1857, historian, essayist and poet; Whig politician and supporter of the 1832 Reform Act; his *History of England* (London, 1849–55) brought him wealth, fame and a peerage.

Coulanges,[1] even Acton,[2] Halévy, Trevelyan[3] – not necessarily working from primary sources. But do you think that Alan does present a picture of a society or an age? His *Bismarck* does, and so do bits of the Oxford History;[4] but *The Origins of the Second World War*? What he mostly loves doing is giving a series of short, sharp jabs to, and placing a series of delicious banana-skins under, the pompous and magniloquent and moralistic. Nevertheless, he is a marvellous writer, and wasn't well treated, though Oxford never did what he says it did – it really did not, for all his fury. You are right that the passion for Beaverbrook derives from the fact that he made a fuss of him, as you say, when he had been let down – as he thought – by others: Namier, Oxford, the establishment, everyone, even old pupils. The mere sight of him scudding along in the street with his head down gives me pleasure and a sense of life – and I cross over if only to get an unappreciative growl. [...]

Yours,

Isaiah Berlin

PS Why do you say that Carr has touched on a large variety of subjects, or something of the sort? Besides Russia, there is only the appeasement book[5] and *Karl Marx*[6] – all that fits into a single pattern: even Dostoevsky and Bakunin are all part of that single pattern.[7] Deutscher,[8] I remember,

---

1 Numa Denis Fustel de Coulanges (1830–89), prof. of history, Strasbourg, 1860–70; lecturer, École Normale Supérieure, Paris, 1870–5; prof. of ancient history, Sorbonne, 1875–8, of early medieval history 1878–89; his greatest work, *La Cité antique: étude sur le culte, le droit, les institutions de la Grèce et de Rome* (Paris, 1864), emphasised the fundamental importance of religious belief in society, in direct opposition to Marx's emphasis on economic relations, and he had considerable influence, not least upon his most remarkable student, Émile Durkheim (1858–1917).

2 John Emerich Edward Dalberg-Acton (1834–1902), 1st Baron Acton 1869, historian and moralist; Regius Prof. of Modern History, Cambridge, 1895–1902; planned and co-edited, but did not contribute to, the 14-vol. Cambridge Modern History [of the World] (Cambridge/NY, 1902–12); his concern as a liberal Catholic was with the capacity of the individual, properly informed, to promote progress and freedom.

3 George Macaulay Trevelyan (1976–1962), historian, educator and conservationist; Regius Prof. of Modern History, Cambridge, 1927–40; Master, Trinity, 1940–51; a prolific historian, with a liberal-Whig bias, he was widely read and admired; his most popular works were *History of England* (London, 1926) and *English Social History: A Survey of Six Centuries, Chaucer to Queen Victoria* (London etc., 1942).

4 *Bismarck: The Man and the Statesman* (London/NY, 1955); *The Struggle for Mastery in Europe, 1848–1918* (Oxford, 1954), the 1st vol. of the Oxford History of Modern Europe to appear.

5 Carr's classic monograph *The Twenty Years' Crisis, 1919–1939: An Introduction to the Study of International Relations* (London, 1939) advocated appeasement.

6 E. H. Carr, *Karl Marx: A Study in Fanaticism* (London, [1934]).

7 2 studies published by Carr early in his career: *Dostoevsky (1821–1881): A New Biography* (London, 1931) and *Michael Bakunin* (London, 1937). Mikhail Aleksandrovich Bakunin (1814–76), Russian anarchist, ideological rival of Karl Marx, believed that 'putting the power of the state in the hands of the workers was as bad as putting it anywhere else' (Simon Blackburn, *Oxford Dictionary of Philosophy*).

8 Isaac Deutscher (1906–67), Polish-born Jewish historian and left-wing commentator, author of *Stalin: A Political Biography* (Oxford, 1949) and a 3-vol. biography of Trotsky (Oxford, 1954–63); regarded by his critics, including IB, as an (albeit not unreserved) apologist for Stalinism; for IB's role in his failure to secure a chair in Soviet Studies at Sussex in 1963 see L3 377–81, 384–7.

reproached his friend Carr for lack of respect for ideas, e.g. Trotsky's,[1] etc.;[2] but what one does not feel at home with, one does not like, and Carr's relation to ideas is all too like that of the Foreign Office, which seems to me a kind of mirror image. Or is that unfair?

TO JOHN GRIGG[3]

26 May 1981

Headington House

Dear John,

Thank you very much for your extremely nice, and, if I may say so, characteristically generous and honourable letter. My sources about Einstein's views are the same as yours;[4] it was on them that I based an address on him,[5] the main purpose of which was to show his courage and independence – whatever may be thought of the wisdom (which, as you may imagine, I do not question) of his Zionist views (as opposed to other views), which so shocked his assimilated Jewish friends and colleagues in the 1920s and later. [...]

I am glad that you now think that Einstein was, even if [not] *tout court*, a Zionist. Of course, if one is writing at length (as I did in that lecture), one has to qualify, as you suggest. Einstein was a pacifist, but when the

---

1 Leon Trotsky (1879–1940) né Lev Davidovich Bronshtein, Ukraine-born Bolshevik revolutionary and theorist; lost the power struggle to succeed Lenin and was expelled from the USSR 1929; assassinated in Mexico by a Stalinist agent.

2 IB may have in mind Deutscher's 'Mr E. H. Carr as a Historian of the Bolshevik Regime' in *Heretics and Renegades and Other Essays* (London, 1955): 'Mr Carr approaches the revolutionary upheaval with the mind of the academic scholar interested above all in constitutional precepts, political formulae and machinery of government, and less in mass movements and revolutionary upheavals. His passion is for statecraft, not for "subversive" ideas' (95–6).

3 John Edward Poynder Grigg (1924–2001), 2nd Baron Altrincham 1955–63 (title disclaimed), author, journalist, broadcaster; owner and editor, *National and English Review*, 1954–60; columnist, *Guardian*, 1960–70; at *The Times* 1986–93.

4 Principally Albert Einstein, *Ideas and Opinions* (based on *Mein Weltbild*, ed. Carl Seeling [Amsterdam, 1934], and other sources), new translations and revisions by Sonja Bargmann (London/NY, 1954). JG had quoted as from 1950 a 1938 remark from this source in 'Chapel-Born Zionist', a review of Harold Wilson, *The Chariot of Israel: Britain, America and the State of Israel* (London, 1981), *Observer*, 10 May 1981, 32: 'Apart from practical considerations, my awareness of the essential nature of Judaism resists the idea of a Jewish state with borders, an army, and a measure of temporal power [...]. I am afraid of the inner damage Judaism will sustain' (190: from 'Our Debt to Zionism', extracted from an address given at the celebration of the 'Third Seder' by the National Labor Committee for Palestine, NY, 17 April 1938, in *New Palestine*, 28 April 1983). From this JG draws the conclusion that Einstein was not a Zionist, a finding challenged by S. I. Levenberg, 'Einstein the Zionist – What He Thought', letter, *Observer*, 17 May 1981, 16. The next day IB wrote to the *Observer*, and to JG privately, supporting Levenberg; a misleadingly cut version of his letter appeared the next Sunday ('In Einstein's Opinion', 24 May 1981, 16), and IB wrote a private letter of complaint to the editor, Donald Trelford, 25 May 1981.

5 IB gave an address 14 March 1979 at the opening of a symposium held in Jerusalem to mark the centenary of Einstein's birth: this appeared with cuts as 'Einstein and Israel', NYRB, 8 November 1979, 13–18, and in full in Gerald Holton and Yehuda Elkana (eds), *Albert Einstein: Historical and Cultural Perspectives*, the Centennial Symposium in Jerusalem (Princeton, 1982), and PI.

hour struck he supported war against Hitler. He was an internationalist, with socialist sympathies; nevertheless, in the case of Jews, he obviously wanted them to have a national existence, with a specific territory, and he said so unequivocally. I think you are right in thinking, if only on the basis of the passage you quoted, that he hated all coercion – all armies, frontiers, state authority, etc. – and probably believed in some kind of vague, egalitarian world state of a peaceful semi-anarchist kind, whatever that might be (perhaps 'state' is the wrong word, but except for his Zionist beliefs, his political opinions were never exactly concrete). Like Weizmann (though he never said so in public), he would have preferred a Jewish Palestine with a friendly Arab minority, having something like dominion status within the British Empire, with its foreign and perhaps its financial policy controlled by London. He may himself have thought this was utopian, and it did make him refrain from all criticism of the state of Israel, some of the policies of which he would surely have disapproved of. [...] A Jewish state was not the ideal solution, but better than the alternative – the continuation of a Diaspora without hope of reconstruction as a nation. That, I am sure, is what he not only said but believed. He thought that all criticism of Israeli policies would play into the hands of its opponents, especially the Arabs, whom he never again mentioned, presumably because he thought that reconciliation in the immediate future was a hopeless goal. He was convinced, too, as he says somewhere in the book we both used as our evidence, that Arab gangs were financed from abroad.[1] I don't know whom he was thinking of: Germans and Italians, I should think, at that date. I only refer to this to show the general direction of his ideas at that time.

Consequently I really do think that you diverge sharply from his entire attitude to the problem. As for my belief in 'the necessity for territorial statehood',[2] I do indeed believe in it. You think that a scattered Diaspora can 'continue to have a most potent and fruitful existence':[3] history seems to me to show that this is not so, that when Weizmann spoke of the Jews as being ground into the dust between the upper and the nether millstone of other powers, he was saying no more than what is true. I am no friend to Begin, as you may imagine, but I do not for a moment believe that the Holocaust would have killed anti-Semitism for ever if there had been no Israel. Do you really think that all those anti-Semitic articles about the Jews

---

1 'Fields cultivated by day must have armed protection at night against fanatical Arab outlaws. [...] Everyone knows that the riots are artificially fomented by those directly interested in embarrassing not only ourselves but especially England. Everyone knows that banditry would cease if foreign subsidies were withdrawn.' 'Our Debt to Zionism' (excerpt from an address in NY, 17 April 1938), in *Ideas and Opinions* (162/4), 188–90 at 189–90.

2 In his letter of 21 May 1981 JG had written: 'When you refer (in your letter to me [18 May 1981]) to "the need to re-establish Jewish national existence", you show a belief in the *necessity* of territorial statehood which – as it seems to me – the history of the Jewish nation supremely disproves.'

3 ibid.

in the Soviet Union, during and after the Holocaust, would have ceased, or not continued to be symptoms of an apparently undying hostility? Or that anti-Semitism in, say, South Africa or Argentina has anything to do with Israel's existence? Or that charges apparently being made in Germany now that Einstein went to America out of greed for money, and that his theory is anyway unproven (unlike Max Planck,[1] who stayed and is a hero) – some newspaper in Germany quotes pamphlets and letters to this effect – would not be being made if Israel did not exist?

You may say that all this is lunatic fringe stuff, and so it is – but Hitler in his day was so thought of. Can you expect his victims to take these things lightly? Anti-Israelism, and at times anti-Semitism, are certainly connected with Israel, the PLO etc.: but there is still plenty of it without that. As for 'fruitful existence', it has been very fitful in the long span of Western history. Such talent and genius as the Jews have generated seem to me to have been the result of pressures sometimes amounting to suffering. The price of being a Diaspora has simply been too high, even before the Holocaust, in terms of what Dostoevsky called 'the insulted and the oppressed'[2] and the wounded and the dead. At least the Jews in Israel, whatever their shortcomings, or their future, are saved from the moral insecurity and uneasiness, and the twisting and the turning, which Einstein bravely denounced in the case of his German Jewish fellow citizens. You may say that this was bought at too high a cost to the Arabs. Of course injustice to the Arabs has been done. It is only a question of whether Weizmann was not right when he said that when there are two valid claims, all one can do is obtain the least degree of injustice, and he believed (and I agree with him) that the injustice to the Arabs (which a different British policy could have avoided, but I won't go into that here) is less than leaving the Jews in a condition in too many countries in which they feel alien and insecure, with all the distortions of personality which this entails.

But I really must not go on, for I shall not convert you, nor you me. I only want to add that I always thought that to ask the Jews to go on as they were because of their contribution to general culture was like telling oysters that they must go on contracting diseases so that one in a million might generate a pearl. Supposing an oyster says that it is not interested in pearls, doesn't want to enrich culture, just wants to live an ordinary, normal oyster's life in the kind of conditions in which other creatures live theirs – if need be, remain ungifted, ordinary and obscure – is that to be forbidden? Is martyrdom, or the risk of it, a duty? You speak of the brute force with which the Jewish nation

1 Max Karl Ernst Ludwig Planck (1858–1947), German theoretical physicist; Nobel Prize in Physics 1918 for his revolutionary quantum theory; opposed Nazism, but remained in Germany after the accession of Hitler; his younger son, Erwin, was executed 1945 after the 20 July 1944 bomb plot against Hitler.
2 Dostoevsky's 1861 novel Unizhennye i oskorblennye, whose title is variously translated into English.

was created in Palestine, and of its fanaticism, and the danger and dishonour this creates. I disagree. It was created not by brute force but by legal decision: this decision was defied, naturally enough, by the Arabs, and after that the long war began in which neither side could possibly escape unscathed.[1] As for fanaticism, the vast majority of the Jews of Israel are anything but fanatical, and detest terrorism as much as anyone – as much as I do, who hate it in all its forms, Begin, the Stern Gang,[2] the IRA, PLO, everyone who is ready to massacre in the name of whatever ideal. Begin, whom I dislike as much as anyone, would not be in power today if it were not for the votes of the oriental Jews, who remember nothing but their treatment – for centuries, not just after Zionism – by the Arabs in the countries from which they immigrated. This is in no sense a justification of Begin or his policies, but it is at least a part-explanation of what makes extremism arise. Where hatred and prejudice have been too strong, insulation seems to me the only solution: for the Jews to govern two million Arabs, or the Arabs to govern three million Jews, in any shape or form, would obviously be disastrous. [...]

Yours,

Isaiah   [...]

TO ANDRZEJ WALICKI

27 May 1981

Headington House

Carissimo amico,

[...] Of course we shall be here in November. If you can pass through England, this would make me happy; if you go to Australia for any length of time, you will get leave and resources to come to Europe – Australia is aware of its somewhat isolated geographical situation, and travel of this kind is part of the system. Leszek Kołakowski is just off to Chicago, where he will spend 1981–2: he seems to be neither happy nor unhappy here, but lonely. He will obviously never be contented outside Poland. He says, convincingly, that England is an island in Europe, that Oxford is an island in England, that All Souls is an island in Oxford, and that he is an island in All Souls. It is a great relief to be able to talk to him. All Souls has grown much more philistine than in your day, perhaps as part of the general decline of intellectual standards in England. When Mitterand had his inauguration, he invited 'humanist' intelligentsia from America, Arthur Miller,[3]

1 Resolution 181 (part II), UN General Assembly, 29 November 1947, proposed the partition of Palestine into a Jewish state and an Arab state: it was accepted by the Jewish side, but not by the Arab; violence broke out almost at once, followed by the Arab–Israeli war of 1948–9 after the British Mandate came to an end 14 May 1948.

2 3/2.

3 Arthur Miller (1915–2005), US dramatist; author of *Death of a Salesman: Certain Private Conversations in Two Acts and a Requiem* (NY/London, 1949), for which he won the Pulitzer Prize, and of the

James Baldwin,[1] Saul Bellow[2] (who would not [come], the company was
too left-wing for him), Elie Wiesel[3] (Holocaust Jews, etc.); some intellectuals from Italy; I do not know whom besides Schmidt from Germany; but in
England, they could think of no one – only Noel Baker,[4] who must be in his
middle nineties. Indeed, who is there? Who are our leading 'humanists' of
whom the French would have heard? Gombrich? Karl Popper? Englishmen?
Henry Moore?[5] There is something wrong about this. The political situation
may have been darker, but the intellectual situation was far better in the
1930s. On this sombre note I close, and wait for November, or at any rate
news of you [...].

Yours,
    Isaiah B

TO GEORGE WATSON[6]

24 September 1981

Headington House

Dear George,

    [...] I wish I could recommend someone to you – someone, I mean, whom
I know about – about NKVD–Gestapo collaboration in 1939–41,[7] but I know
nothing about these things: I am not a Sovietologist, although sometimes
described as one in pejorative language in Soviet publications. I think the
man to turn to is Leo Labedz,[8] of *Survey*, who, even if he did not know

parable of the McCarthyite era *The Crucible: A Play in Four Acts* (NY, 1953), based on the Salem
witch trials.

1 James Arthur Baldwin (1924–87), US novelist, dramatist and social critic, prominent in the civil
   rights movement, whose work confronted the prejudice experienced by the US gay and African
   American communities.
2 Saul Bellow (1915–2005) né Solomon Bellows, Canadian-born US playwright and novelist of
   Russian Jewish descent; Nobel Prize for Literature 1976.
3 Eliezer ('Elie') Wiesel (b. 1928), later (2006) hon. KBE, Romanian-born US writer, academic and
   human rights campaigner who survived Auschwitz and Buchenwald; Nobel Peace Prize 1986 for
   humanitarian activism.
4 Philip John Noel-Baker (1889–1982), life peer 1977, Labour politician; Nobel Peace Prize 1959 for
   contribution to international disarmament; aged 91 at the time of this letter.
5 Henry Spencer Moore (1898–1986), CH 1955, OM 1963, sculptor and artist whose monumental
   bronze sculptures are immediately recognisable; member, Royal Fine Art Commission, 1947–71.
6 George Grimes Watson (1927–2013), Australian scholar of literature and political thought, fellow,
   St John's, Cambridge, 1961–2011.
7 Some 60% of German Communists who fled Nazi Germany to the USSR met their deaths in
   the Soviet terror. During the period of Soviet–Nazi rapprochement 'hundreds of them were
   even handed over to the Gestapo by the Soviet secret police': Archie Brown, *The Rise and Fall of
   Communism* (London, 2009), 88; see also Eric D. Weitz, *Creating German Communism, 1890–1990*
   (Princeton, 1997), 280.
8 Leopold Labedz (1920–93), Russian-born Polish Jew; fought with General Anders's Polish army
   during WW2, settling in London afterwards; having lost family members to both the Nazis
   and the Soviets he devoted his life to fighting totalitarianism, and was fiercely anti-Communist;
   founded the journal *Survey* 1961 to report on the Communist world; championed Solzhenitsyn,
   and later campaigned for *Solidarność* (175/2).

anything himself, would know precisely to whom to turn (always assuming that there exists someone to turn to). The article you sent me seems to me horribly convincing. Not so much the Katyn massacre:[1] killings of that order had, after all, happened before in recent history, if not in Europe then by the Turks, and in the seventeenth century the Ukrainians (Poles and Jews); the slaughter by Bohdan Chmielnicki's[2] bands in the 1660s was probably one of the most extensive since Genghis Khan. But I still think you are absolutely right: it is really the deportation and destruction of the kulaks during the first Five-Year Plan that probably impressed Hitler and his henchmen. On the other hand, it is commonly supposed that it was the Nazi purges of 1934[3] that inspired Stalin to his own Great Purge of the later 1930s.[4] Still, the Russians have primacy in this matter, and you are perfectly right to discount the legend that it was Stalin, and not Lenin, who began the terror and systematic liquidation of whole classes of persons. Do Marx and Engels actually advocate racial extermination? Are you thinking of passages in which the liquidation of Czech institutions by German ones is advocated by Engels?[5] Or the anti-Semitic remarks in '[On] The Jewish Question'?[6] Racism in Marx and Engels is there, of course, but it is not something which any socialist, let alone Communist, has ever conceded. But what passages in particular are you thinking of? [...] When I wrote my little book on Marx, I did remark on his awkward attitude to his Jewish origins[7] – on which I dwelt again in an

1 The massacre of some 15,000 Poles, systematically shot by their NKVD captors during the early days of the Nazi–Soviet Pact of 1939; evidence of the killings, ordered by Stalin, was uncovered by the German army in Katyn forest in the Western USSR 1943, but responsibility for the crime was denied by the USSR until April 1990.

2 Bogdan Zinovy Mikhailovich Khmel'nits'ky (in Polish Bohdan Chmielnicki) (c.1595–1657), Ukrainian Cossack leader who led the 1648–54 uprising against Polish rule, in the course of which his rebels scapegoated the Jews, who were massacred in tens of thousands.

3 The 'Night of the Long Knives', 29–30 June 1934, when Hitler used his personal bodyguard, the SS, to eliminate Ernst Röhm's more radical SA (Sturmabteilung: 'storm troops') or Brownshirts, began a wider purge in Germany designed to eliminate any threat to Hitler's rule.

4 'Stalin relished the news of the Night of the Long Knives: "What a great fellow! How well he pulled this off!" [...] What was characteristic about Stalin is that he meant every word he said about Hitler with passionate intensity, and was willing to act in the same fashion when the opportunity arose.' Robert Service, *Stalin: A Biography* (London, 2004), 340; for Stalin's observation see Anastas Mikoyan, *Tak bylo: razmyshleniya o minuvshem* (Moscow, 1999), 534.

5 Presumably a reference to 'Der magyarische Kampf' ('The Magyar Struggle'), *Neue Rheinische Zeitung*, 13 January 1849, where Engels wrote of the Czechs and Serbs as 'fragments of peoples, the remnant of a former population that was suppressed and held in bondage by the nation which later became the main vehicle of historical development. These relics of a nation, mercilessly trampled under foot in the course of history, as Hegel says, [...] always become fanatical standard-bearers of counter-revolution and remain so until their complete extirpation or loss of their national character.' CW viii 234.

6 'In a celebrated passage in his essay *On the Jewish Question* of 1844, he says that the secular morality of the Jews is egoism, their secular religion is huckstering, their secular god is money. The real God of the Jews is the bill of exchange. "Money is the zealous God of Israel, before whom no other god may be."' IB, 'Benjamin Disraeli, Karl Marx and the Search for Identity' (1970; repr. in AC), citing CW iii 172.

7 KM5 91–2.

essay on Marx and Disraeli[1] – but public advocacy of racial extermination, texts Lenin might have read? If this is indeed so you should write about it, it is a very timely topic.

Yours ever,
Isaiah

TO MICHAEL MORAN[2]

29 September 1981

Headington House

Dear Moran,

Thank you ever so much for sending me your review of *Against the Current*.[3] What can I say? It is at once the most generous, penetrating, interesting and to me – as you might well imagine – unbelievably welcome review of anything I have ever written (my memory is not very good, but I believe this to be absolutely true). It shows more *Einfühlung*[4] into the character and purpose of what I think and believe than anyone has ever shown. Consequently, what can I do but express the most unlimited gratitude to you?

You wonder whether you are perhaps 'wrong' about me? Not at all – at least, so far as I can tell. I think the quotation from Mill about the possibility of revealing to writers that about themselves which can only be perceived by another observer – which no introspection discloses – is absolutely true in this case.[5] And the critical remarks, expressed with the greatest courtesy and concern for my feelings as a human being, seem to me to have much justice in them.

Firstly, you wonder whether my dogmatic summaries of the doctrines of the Enlightenment are valid. I am sure you are right: so far as they are valid, they apply to some (at most), not all, of the eighteenth-century French thinkers among the *philosophes* – it does not allow for the pessimism of many of them, or the scepticism of even so committed a thinker as Voltaire – and certainly

---

1 Benjamin Disraeli (1804–81), 1st Earl of Beaconsfield 1876, Conservative statesman, prime minister 1868, 1874–80; of Jewish ancestry, he was christened an Anglican.

2 (John) Michael Patrick Moran (b. 1935), assistant lecturer in philosophy, Keele, 1960–2; lecturer in philosophy and intellectual history, Sussex (where IB attended some of his lectures), 1962–88, professorial fellow, Eastern Mediterranean, Cyprus, 1989–93; academic adviser to Rauf Denktaş, President, Turkish Republic of Northern Cyprus, 1991–2000.

3 *History of European Ideas* 1 no. 2 (January 1981), 185–90. The review is every bit as positive and perceptive as IB indicates.

4 'Empathetic insight'.

5 'The first question in regard to any man of speculation is, what is his theory of human life? In the minds of many philosophers, whatever theory they have of this sort is latent, and it would be a revelation to themselves to have it pointed out to them in their writings as others can see it, unconsciously moulding everything to its own likeness.' J. S. Mill, 'Bentham' (1838), op. cit. (88/1) x 94. Moran suggests that 'we can gather something of what is doubtless Berlin's *own* theory of life from a description he gives ostensibly – and I do not question plausibly enough – about the leading ideas of Alexander Herzen', and then quotes the description (AC2 165) at length.

not to e.g. Diderot, who cannot possibly be excluded from the Enlightenment.
And in the nineteenth century it perhaps applies only to Comte and his immediate allies and followers. But there is more to the Enlightenment than
that, especially on its negative side: the war against irrationalism, prejudice,
oppression, cruelty, intolerance and stupidity, in both theory and practice,
[and] its often frightful consequences. I tried to say some of this in the brief
and not particularly illuminating introduction to the little anthology called
The Age of Enlightenment[1] – I do not recommend you or anyone else to look
at it now: it is harmless, but rather flat. The positive element, and the rich
variety and undogmatic humanism, of much of the Enlightenment is, for
obviously polemical reasons, not allowed enough by me; and perhaps the
picture of the Enlightenment is too much of an Aunt Sally, and I do not deny
that it is the rectilinear, emotionally blind, unimaginative, rationalist dog-
matism – what Hayek called 'scientism'[2] (my views are sometimes described
as analogous to Hayek's, to my extreme dissatisfaction) – that I think has
caused havoc. This is the dominant theology of the West during the last
two hundred years, despite all the attacks upon it, clerical or Romantic or
populist or sceptical; it is still what you and I and people we respect and
admire rightly believe ourselves to be on the side of; yet the protest against it
of my irrationalist 'clients' seems to me – even though it does, of course, go
too far and produce nonsense and ghastly obscurantism and awful practice
of its own – to bring out weaknesses much more sharply than 'constructive' criticism by allies. But you are perfectly right: I am obviously concerned
with present discontents. The fact that there is a line between the denial of
human rights in totalitarian Communist countries and the noble defence of
reason in the eighteenth century is not accidental. It is, of course, terribly
wrong and unhistorical and altogether disreputable to blame Bentham[3] or
Helvétius[4] for Stalin, or Hegel and Nietzsche for Nazism, etc. Nevertheless,
the tracing of roots does fascinate me, as I am sure it engages your interest.

1 *The Age of Enlightenment: The Eighteenth-Century Philosophers* (Boston/NY, 1956), whose introduction appears as 'The Philosophers of the Enlightenment' in POI.
2 Friedrich August von Hayek (1899–1992), Austrian-born British economist; Tooke Prof. of
Economic Science and Statistics, LSE, 1931–50; prof. of social and moral science, Chicago,
1950–62; prof. of economics, Freiburg, 1962–69; Sveriges Riksbank Prize in Economic Sciences in
Memory of Alfred Nobel 1974 with Gunnar Myrdal; his *The Road to Serfdom* (Chicago, 1944) had
a profound influence on Margaret Thatcher, and his ideas on the free market were precursors
of Thatcherism. In his *The Counter-Revolution of Science: Studies on the Abuse of Reason* (Glencoe,
1952) he defines 'scientism' as 'slavish imitation of the method and language of Science' (15) – 'an
attitude which is decidedly unscientific in the true sense of the word, since it involves a mechanical and uncritical application of habits of thought to fields different from those in which they
have been formed' (15–16).
3 Jeremy Bentham (1748–1832), British philosopher, jurist and social reformer who argued that
social policy should adhere to the theory of Utilitarianism by promoting '*the greatest happiness
of the greatest number*'. [Jeremy Bentham], *A Fragment on Government* (London, 1776), preface, ii;
A Comment on the Commentaries and A Fragment on Government, ed. J. H. Burns and H. L. A. Hart
(London, 1977), 393.
4 Claude Adrien Helvétius (1715–71), French philosopher, one of the principal figures behind

My basic objection is, I suppose, the Dickens–Tolstoyan one:[1] the *lumières* did not, and do not, for the most part, know what it is that men live by. [...]

Again, you are quite right to wonder whether my 'empathy' does not go too far. When I write about someone to whom it seems to me historical justice has not been done, whose ideas are more original, have more in them, are more important and sometimes even valid, than is allowed for by conventional accounts, I do probably get carried away and begin to speak with their voices, or at least their voices as I hear them; this must make it seem to some people that I am too empathetic, for Hamann or de Maistre[2] and their progeny *are* real and dangerous enemies of the Enlightenment and against what I myself believe in; and since I write with equal enthusiasm about unquestionable 'progressives' like J. S. Mill or Herzen or Belinsky, or a sceptical but sufficiently anti-reactionary liberal like Turgenev, the reader doesn't know what to think; I seem to be 'representing' all these opposed clients. I think the charge, mild and generous as it is, that you basically make, and that perhaps should be made against my method, is rather like that which some of the radical *philosophes* made against Montesquieu,[3] when he was accused of being more interested in describing the customs of men than in pointing out their defects and seeking to suggest improvements. At least, the tone is too ambiguous, so that nobody is quite clear where I stand, and this must irritate all the committed. But I cannot help it. My favourite quotation is one I've got into the *Oxford Book of Quotations* (I think) – Kant's (in Collingwood's[4] version) 'Out of the crooked timber of humanity no straight thing was ever made.'[5] Some histories of ideas pay no heed to that.

You are quite right, also, in supposing that most historians of thought must regard my methods as insufficiently academic and detached, too descriptive,

---

the *Encyclopédie*; his *De l'esprit* (1758) influenced Jeremy Bentham and the development of Utilitarianism. The 1st of the 6 main subjects of FIB.

1 Charles John Huffam Dickens (1812–1870), novelist; a favourite author of Tolstoy's. Both Dickens and Tolstoy might be seen as aligned with the 'Counter-Enlightenment' figures who so fascinated IB because they stressed the crucial aspects of life that the tidy scientistic systems of the *philosophes* neglected.

2 'The sympathy for de Maistre's views, which you rightly detect, is due to my general inclination to deal with the enemy, and not with allies in thought; it is they who see the shortcomings and insert blades between the ribs, who teach one something. Hence my interest in Machiavelli, Hamann, Sorel, as well as de Maistre, all of whom I dislike a good deal but from whom I derive genuine intellectual profit' (to Morton White, 24 December 1990).

3 Charles Louis de Secondat (1689–1755), baron de La Brède et de Montesquieu, French political philosopher, historian and novelist; one of the most influential French Enlightenment writers.

4 Robin George Collingwood (1889–1943), lecturer in philosophy and Roman history, Oxford, and fellow, Pembroke, 1912–35; Waynflete Prof. of Metaphysical Philosophy, Oxford, and fellow, Magdalen, 1935–41. For his version (not what IB gives) see CTH2 xxiii.

5 Immanuel Kant, 'Idee zu einer allgemeinen Geschichte in weltbürgerlicher Absicht' ('Idea for a Universal History with a Cosmopolitan Purpose', 1784), *Kant's gesammelte Schriften* (Berlin, 1900–) viii 23.22. The quotation was added to *The Oxford Dictionary of Quotations* (*sic*) in its 3rd edition (1979) as 'Out of the crooked timber of humanity no straight thing can ever be made' (the unnecessary, pedantic, alteration being HH's), and of course provided HH with the title for CTH.

insufficiently accurate, analytic, cautious, detailed. That, too, I cannot help. You very sweetly condone this and let me get away with it; I can imagine that you know of people who do not. I remember a review of *Vico and Herder* by Mary Warnock, in which she made it plain that my exposition might at times be beguiling, but it was not critical in the proper sense, and simply wouldn't do: it was really just rhetoric.[1] [...]

Yours very sincerely,
    Isaiah Berlin

TO JOSEPH ALSOP

30 September 1981

Headington House

Dearest Joe,

[...] Did you really start writing your big book[2] eighteen years ago? 1963? Inconceivable! Time goes rather too fast at my age, and even at yours. Do you think about death much? I occasionally wonder how many years I have to live, will I be able to write a big book in the years left to me, and does it matter whether I can or not? When I see in All Souls College statistics that some given professor will retire in 2003 a very slight cold shiver passes very quickly through me. Very unlike John Sparrow, I am not either depressed or indignant at the thought of the termination of my life; I have a feeling that our political, and I dare say social, system will alter radically in Europe before the end of the century. I cannot see how it cannot – all European countries are declining. America is all right because neither the Republicans nor the Democrats are slaves of ideology; but Conservatives, Liberals, Social Democrats, Socialists, Communists cannot possibly survive in their present form. In that sense, Marx was quite right: whatever the material patterns of life – relations of production, etc. – if the ideologies don't fit, 'the integument bursts'.[3] So I shall really be quite glad to disappear before it all: I feel firmly tied to the values of the nineteenth century – as you are, on the whole, I think, to the values of the inter-war years – or I am mistaken?

I have no doubt about the success of your big book. And certainly your memoir of Roosevelt[4] will go like hot cakes.[5] You know it well. [...] Mere immersion in all those years must, alone, have exhilarated you; and you

1 In her review ('History of Ideas', *New Society*, 26 February 1976, 446) Warnock writes: 'one can hear the voice of the brilliant lecturer, who totally convinces, persuades and excites his audience at the time, but leaves them afterwards wondering whether the brilliance of the lecture was not rather greater than the interest of the text'.
2 op. cit. (29/4).
3 '[Die] Hülle [...] wird gesprengt.' Karl Marx, *Capital*, vol. 1 (1867), chapter 24, part 7: part 7, chapter 32 in CW (xxxv 750).
4 Franklin Delano Roosevelt ('FDR') (1882–1945), Democrat US President 1933–45, the only President to be re-elected 3 times.
5 *FDR, 1882–1945: A Centenary Remembrance* (NY/London, 1982). 'One of the most enduring – and

are in an absolutely unique position to do it – all the other writers about Roosevelt are inevitably a little too class-conscious when writing about this left-wing prince. Which reminds me of Mr Ziegler,[1] who is writing the life of Mountbatten[2] – a left-wing prince, infallibly successful in all democratic societies – Ziegler the biographer of Diana. The extracts in the *Sunday Telegraph* seem a trifle cheap to me: all this dwelling on Duff's[3] amours, drunkenness, idleness etc., and the impression that Diana actually looked for possible mistresses for him – that is certainly untrue – conjures up a 'Let them eat cake'[4] picture which is utterly untrue to our old friend. Why couldn't Susan Mary[5] have written this book? What is Diana's attitude to it? There are many versions: (*a*) that she insisted on it appearing in her lifetime, and is simply delighted with it; (*b*) she insisted on it appearing in her lifetime, and thinks it too awful; (*c*) she did not want it to appear at all, and refuses to read it; (*d*) she doesn't care; and so on.[6]

John Julius[7] rang me up in a state of great agitation the other day – someone, Nigel Nicolson[8] in the *Financial Times*, reviewing the book, said that Duff, although a tremendous pro-Zionist etc., was somewhat anti-

endearing – of his books is his perceptive and affectionate *Centenary Remembrance* of FDR' (Arthur Schlesinger, Jr, 'Joseph Alsop', obituary, *Independent*, 31 August 1989, 29).

1 Philip Sandeman Ziegler (b. 1929), historian and biographer, entered Foreign Service 1952, resigned 1967, joining publishers Collins the same year: editorial director 1972–9, editor in chief 1979–80; author of *Diana Cooper* (London, 1981) and *Mountbatten: The Official Biography* (London, 1985).

2 Louis Francis Albert Victor Nicholas Mountbatten (1900–79), 1st Earl Mountbatten of Burma 1947, OM 1965, naval officer closely connected to the Royal Family; the last Viceroy of India, March–August 1947, when he oversaw the process by which India and Pakistan gained their independence from Britain; governor general, India, August 1947–June 1948; personal ADC to Elizabeth II 1953–79; murdered by the IRA when his boat was blown up off Mullaghmoor harbour 27 August 1979 on a family fishing expedition.

3 (Alfred) Duff Cooper (1890–1954), 1st Viscount Norwich 1952, politician, diplomat and writer, resigned as first lord of the admiralty 1938 in protest against the Munich agreement, but was recalled to Churchill's wartime coalition; UK ambassador to France 1944–7; Ziegler regetted that, because Duff came under his scrutiny largely in the guise of a less than faithful husband, his finer qualities were obscured; elsewhere he was able to record some of these, noting that during his short time on the Western Front 1918 Duff proved himself 'exceptionally courageous, resourceful, and a natural leader of men' (Ziegler, ODNB).

4 Said, according to Rousseau (*Confessions*, book 6, 1736), by a 'great princess' on hearing that the poor had no bread; often misattributed to Marie Antoinette.

5 Alsop's former wife (618).

6 Diana Cooper wrote to Ziegler: 'On reading your book for the second time (the first time I was generally staggered and embarassed [*sic*] and funnily enough unprepared!) I find it a long *love letter*, and as you make quite plain in the story there is nothing which gives me so much joy' (undated). He had been commissioned to write the book by Hamish Hamilton and her son, John Julius (next note), and she had wanted to see it published in her lifetime, not least because of the fun it would give her to see her friends' reactions.

7 John Julius Cooper (b. 1929), 2nd Viscount Norwich 1954, the only child of Duff and Diana Cooper; writer and broadcaster.

8 Nigel Nicolson (1917–2004), son of Harold and younger brother of Ben(edict), director, Weidenfeld and Nicolson, 1948–92; Conservative MP 1952–9; columnist, *Spectator* 1992–5, *Sunday Telegraph* 1995–2002.

Semitic too.[1] John Julius told me this with indignation, and asked me to write and refute it: I referred him to Victor Rothschild,[2] who was a really intimate friend of Duff's, who is ready to write the letter and would rather I did not co-sign it with him – just as well. John Julius told me that when he came back from school at the age of nine, and said that he had met a boy called Davis, whom he liked very much, 'he is a Jew, though'; Diana gave him a tremendous slap and told him that he was never to say such a thing again. He said that his cheek still burns from this. It is a matter of small importance: of course, in a sense Ziegler must be right – Duff, however pro-Jewish, pro-Zionist etc., had the ordinary prejudices of the world in which he was brought up, both the fashionable VD doctor his father, and the duchess his mother;[3] while he strongly disapproved of anti-Semitism, as you or I disapprove of, let us say, anti-Papism, nevertheless we do in fact suspect priests, Jesuits etc. of conducting some underground activity against liberal civilisation. I shall be glad to see Victor Rothschild's letter, and John Julius's indignant rebuttal – I do not entirely believe in them, but think it a very good thing to say this.

So you feel sad about finishing your big book, like Gibbon; only you mustn't turn into what J. S. Mill called 'a pig contented' v. 'Socrates discontented'[4] – I am very nearly the former, but your temperament is different: you must, like Gibbon, continue to scribble, scribble, scribble.[5]

Ah, but you should have seen the Annenbergs with Mrs Reagan here, in Covent Garden, with Princess Margaret at their side.[6] Goodness, if I could

1 Nigel Nicolson, 'Diana and Duff', *Financial Times*, 19 September 1981, 10: 'An unapologetic snob, an anti-Semite [there is no mention of Zionism], a drinker, a gambler, he was capable of losing in one night the money which she earned for both of them, by the *Miracle*, in a week.' Diana Cooper played the Madonna on alternate nights in a 1924 Broadway revival of Karl Vollmöller's play *The Miracle* (1911).

2 (Nathaniel Mayer) Victor Rothschild (1910–90), 3rd Baron Rothschild 1937, GBE 1975; zoologist, government adviser and public servant.

3 Alfred Cooper (1838–1908), Kt 1902, surgeon to kings and princes, with a fashionable private practice, but also a committed surgeon to voluntary hospitals; author of *Syphilis and Pseudo-syphilis* (London, 1884); m. 1882, as her 3rd husband, (Lady) Agnes Cecil Emmeline Flower (1852–1925), daughter of 5th Earl Fife, but not a duchess.

4 'It is better to be a human being dissatisfied than a pig satisfied; better to be Socrates dissatisfied than a fool satisfied.' J. S. Mill, *Utilitarianism* (1861), chapter 2, op. cit. (88/1) x 212. Socrates (c.470–399 BCE), Greek philosopher recognised as one of the fathers of Western philosophy; he left no written work, but his thoughts have lived on in the writings of his disciples, notably the dialogues of Plato and Xenophon's *Memorabilia*.

5 'Another d—mn'd thick, square book! Always scribble, scribble, scribble! Eh! Mr Gibbon?' A reaction to the publication of (probably) vol. 2 (1781) of Gibbon's *The History of the Decline and Fall of the Roman Empire* (London 1776–89) attributed to William Henry, Duke of Gloucester, by Henry Digby Best(e) in his *Personal and Literary Memorials* (London, 1829), 68.

6 Walter Hubert Annenberg (1908–2002), US businessman, diplomat and philanthropist, US ambassador to UK 1969–74; his 2nd wife Leonore ('Lee') (1918–2009) née Cohn, businesswoman and philanthropist, was President Reagan's chief of protocol 1981–2; Nancy Davis Reagan (b. 1921) née Anne Frances Robbins, former Hollywood actress (as Nancy Davis), 2nd wife 1952 of Ronald Reagan, First Lady, US, 1981–9; HRH Princess Margaret, Countess of Snowdon (1930–2002; plate 28), younger daughter of George VI and Queen Elizabeth, younger sister of Elizabeth II: all were

see you, I really could tell you some stories that would delight your heart –
which noses were put out of joint, and how much, over invitations to the
evening party at Buckingham Palace, the actual wedding, *placement* at the
wedding (why was Mrs Reagan so far behind Lady Avon, why was Lady
Spencer[1] further back?), why was the accountant sacked by Lady Spencer
but retained by the Princess of Wales[2] invited to all the ceremonies, why,
why, why; why did Professor Plumb[3] have a heart attack from dancing too
much as Lady Spencer's guest at Buckingham Palace, why was he only
given a green, or yellow, or blue ticket, or whatever it is, to a Buckingham
Palace garden party, and declared, to someone else with the same ticket, 'No!
A green ticket you have? I cannot understand it – nothing for the Enclosure?
You must never come again'? All this delights me – I am still far too frivolous
for what I am supposed to be – a retired old person, asleep in the corner of
a common room, glad to be spoken to by the younger set.

Talking of academics, John Sparrow now is distinctly on the bottle, and
cannot remember in the morning who put him to bed the night before –
and rather truculent. I propose not to go to the dining club we are both
members of because he becomes too uncontrolled too early in the evening:
still, he may recover. He is one of my oldest friends – he used to be the best
company in the world, extremely intelligent, able, amusing, independent,
fearless, comically reactionary but delightful – and now, especially since the
death of Mrs Fleming, is in pieces.[4] [...]

Much love, as always,

Yours ever,

Isaiah

PS My relations with the late Burdon-Muller were not very good towards
the end, after his accusation that my views on Vietnam were influenced by
a desire to please Bundy[5] on account of the grant to Wolfson. But he left me
$2,000 in his will, as well as a pair of cufflinks. More guilt.

in London for the wedding of Diana Spencer and Charles, Prince of Wales, 29 July. The Dance
Theater of Harlem opened their 1st season at Covent Garden 27 July.

1 Raine Spencer (b. 1929) née McCorquodale, Countess Spencer; m. 1976 2ndly Edward John
Spencer, 8th Earl Spencer, the father of Diana, Princess of Wales; she had strained relations with
all of her stepchildren, not least Diana.

2 Diana Frances Mountbatten-Windsor (1961–97), Princess of Wales, née (Lady) Diana Frances
Spencer, 3rd daughter of 8th Earl Spencer; m. 1981 Charles, Prince of Wales, separated 1992,
divorced 1996; died 31 August 1997 of injuries sustained in a car crash in Paris.

3 John Harold Plumb (1911–2001), Kt 1982; fellow, Christ's, Cambridge, 1946–2001, reader in modern
English history 1962–5, prof. 1966–74; Master, Christ's, 1978–82.

4 Ann Geraldine Mary Fleming (1913–81) née Charteris, society hostess, m. 1952 3rdly Ian Fleming
(1908–64), creator of James Bond; d. 12 July 1981.

5 McGeorge ('Mac') Bundy (1919–96), Harvard academic and administrator, and special assistant
for national security affairs 1961–5, in which capacity he was one of the principal architects
and defenders of the Vietnam War; president, Ford Foundation, 1966–79, in which capacity he
was one of IB's greatest supporters in the creation of Wolfson, pledging the very substantial

TO ANDRZEJ WALICKI

11 January 1982

Headington House

Милый Друг!¹

I did indeed receive your letter and the article on your personal impres-sions of the situation in Poland. I did not reply to it because things in Poland began to alter, things began to boil, and your analysis of the situation – although I can see that it is still perfectly valid – was overtaken by history to such a degree that I could not produce a coherent response. People here are uncritically enthusiastic about Solidarność² – naturally enough: a spon-taneous rising against despotism, such as they were in 1831 or 1864,³ without perception of or, indeed, interest in the quality of feeling and ideology of the leaders of this movement. The enthusiasm here is both moving and proper, even though you are obviously perfectly right about the populism and anti-intellectualism and remoteness from what you and I would regard as essen-tial conditions of human liberty on the part of this passionate, indignant, justified, confused, collectivist reaction.

All this I understand – not many other people, I suspect, do, now, at least here; if one tried to explain it, it would be regarded as improper, indecent, almost blasphemous. So I shall keep my peace. The position is all too clear to me – of course you could not do anything to add grist to the mill of your enemies against your friends. You are right to be pleased to be in Australia: you are in no moral dilemma, and moral agony seems to be worse than any other (Marx said that the only antidote to moral pain was physical pain, or something of the sort. I wonder).⁴

Are you surprised that among the arrested there are non-political persons, Jews etc.? Once oppression begins, it nearly always extends to persons who are unpopular for one reason or another. This happens even in the case of the kind of upheavals that you and I would broadly sympathise with; but once there is an upheaval, it acquires its own momentum, and the just suffer with the unjust. Those who realise this are a minority of sceptical intellectuals, out of whom no society can be built, and who are always caught between cross-fires. That is the price we pay. You ask whether there are protests by Western intellectuals, as in the case of Vietnam or El Salvador, South Africa. Yes. The

endowment funds that made the project possible. IB made public his opposition to the Vietnam War 1967, the year after Wolfson was founded: see L3 247–8, 278/5, 601–2.

1 'Dear friend!'

2 'Solidarity', the trade union movement founded in Poland in September 1980 after widespread strikes triggered by increases in food prices; though proscribed by the government, it emerged as a focal point in the resistance to Communist rule.

3 The November Uprising of 1830–1 and the January Uprising of 1863–5 began as spontaneous protests against Russian imperial rule in Poland.

4 'There is only one effective antidote to mental suffering, and that is physical pain.' Letter to Jenny Longuet, 7 December 1881. CW xlvi 156.

British Academy, a pretty immobile body in general, under the impulsion of Seton-Watson,[1] will send a protest to the Polish Academy, whose President I think was arrested and then let out.[2] The greatest shock here among my colleagues is the death of Lipiṅsky, at the age of, I believe, ninety-three, in prison: I do not know if this is right, but some of the economists here seem to believe it – I can well believe it myself.[3]

I went to a meeting of the PEN Club.[4] The evening was not terribly exhilarating in itself (although I am a Vice President of the British Section, I have never been to a single 'function' of it in my life), and there a halting speech was made by the son of the head of the Polish PEN. That assembly, too, not exactly made up of leading intellectuals, but still, decent, high-minded persons, novelists, poets etc., has also sent some kind of indignant message. So there is no lack of that. The English can certainly be trusted to do that; even the one card-holding member of the Communist Party known to me here, Eric Hobsbawm (I believe him to be a card-holding Communist, but I have no concrete evidence; I have not seen his party card, and one never knows),[5] seemed to me unusually distressed about what is happening. Czechoslovakia did not mean so much to him, because that was merely reaction against intellectuals and the like: but here unions are being suppressed, and that is very terrible from the point of view of a Communist of the least degree of sincerity. The British Party, of course, condemned the events – the French Party I do not think did. The French government did, which contains Communist members, but the Party as such has not spoken, so far as I know. The Italians were delighted to thunder against it. Will this make a difference to the Soviet leaders? Or have they discounted this in advance? The latter, I fear. Meanwhile various persons have asked me in a very concerned way about your safety – Leonard Schapiro, Hugh Seton-Watson, people at St

1 (George) Hugh Nicholas Seton-Watson (1916–1984), FBA 1969, historian and political scientist; prof. of Russian history, School of Slavonic and East European Studies, UCL, 1951–83.
2 The BA and Royal Society cabled the Polish Academy of Sciences 15 January 1982 with a joint message of sympathy and support, reported in the press as 'an unprecedented intervention in political affairs' by those bodies 'in support of the many scientists, engineers and scholars locked up or muzzled by the Polish generals' ('A Far Cry from the Ivory Tower', Times, 20 January 1982, 15a). The BA subsequently learned of the severity of the Polish regime's actions towards its country's academicians, all of whom were probably detained in the first days of the martial law that was imposed, including their president, the historian Aleksander Gieysztor (1916–99; later released, as IB reports), and the 94-year-old economist and leading dissident Edward Lipiński (1888–1986), corresponding fellow, BA.
3 The BA subsequently protested to the Polish government over its treatment of Lipiński, reports of whose demise proved premature: a few months later Roger Boyes, the Times correspondent, interviewed him in his Warsaw flat and found him 'buzzing around problems like a summer wasp' ('Polish Elder Dissident Thrives amid Chaos and Cognac', 5 June 1982, 6e–g at 6e).
4 PEN [Poets, Playwrights, Editors, Essayists and Novelists] International, the worldwide association of writers, founded in London 1921.
5 'I became a communist in 1932, though I did not actually join the Party until I went up to Cambridge in the autumn of 1936': Hobsbawm, An Interesting Life (London, 2002), 127. He remained a member even after the Soviet invasion of Hungary (1956).

Antony's, and the like – and when I said that you were in Australia there was great relief and satisfaction. I hope you are being treated well by Kamenka and the others. He is a local liberal apparatchik, if such a thing can be conceived, but a benevolent one, provided that his little kingdom is not adversely affected. And he has done much good: his own works are mediocre in quality, as you know, but he does a great deal of good by simply detecting excellence in others, and on the whole supporting intellectually worthy causes with energy and success. So do not let us look too deeply in the mouths of gift horses. I beg you not to leave this letter on your desk in the History of Ideas Unit. Let me say once again how happy I am that you are not in that terrible cauldron.

I have just received a little book – a collection of Leont'ev's letters to Rozanov, printed by some unknown firm in England,[1] sent by some, to me, totally unknown lady, who is probably some kind of recent émigré. Quite interesting: neither is a figure exactly sympathetic to me; nevertheless their gifts were of a certain quality, a relief from Philistine liberalism and routine, mechanical socialism. I am occasionally accused of too much interest in *mrakobesy*[2] – it is true that I prefer even the malicious detection of shortcomings in liberal and humanitarian doctrines to rose water and high-minded repetitions of familiar platitudes. I cannot help that. A taste for irony is an inescapable attribute of civilised observers, from Petronius[3] to Montaigne, Diderot, Herzen, you, me.

Yours ever,
Isaiah Berlin

---

1 Konstantin Nikolaevich Leont'ev (1831–91), East-oriented Russian writer and essayist who warned against the influence of European economic, social and political transformation; Vasily Vasil'evich Rozanov (1856–1919), controversial Russian writer, religious thinker and journalist. Leont'ev's *Pis'ma k Vasiliyu Rozanovu*, ed. V. V. Rozanov (London, 1982), was published by Nina Karsov (b. 1940), Polish writer and publisher who emigrated to the UK 1968.
2 'Obscurantists'.
3 Petronius Arbiter (*c.*27 BCE–66 CE), Roman politician and courtier in the reign of Nero, generally thought to have written the satirical Latin prose work *Satyricon*.

Mary Fisher, Maire Lynd, Christopher Cox, Ruth Metaxa, Ireland 1934

The main shack on the island in 2011; (*inset left*) the shacks in the 1930s; (*inset right*) Christopher Cox, Mary Fisher, Maire Lynd, 1934

TO MAIRE GASTER[1]

January 1982

Headington House

Dearest BJ,

[...] Do you remember the beginning of our first visit to Ireland? Where did we land? In Rosslare? Or in or near Waterford? What was the name of the lough near Oughterard where Countess Metaxa's island was?[2] (As you see, my memory is gone: an agreeable haze surrounds my recollection of how it all was, then and later – but details ...?) We had decided to go by way of Elizabeth Bowen's House, Bowen's Court, in County Cork near Kildorrery, to which we had been invited for a night by my friend Humphry House,[3] who was staying with her. None of us knew her personally. We knew that she was a famous writer, that she was married to a man called Alan Cameron,[4] that they lived in Headington; she was, I knew, a great friend of Maurice Bowra and John Maud;[5] and Humphry, who had become devoted to her, had said that she would give us a night's lodging.

We approached the grey, somewhat severe stone mansion, I remember (or think I remember), with slight nervousness. Two ladies were seated on the terrace. As we approached them we saw that they were topping and tailing gooseberries. One of them was Elizabeth Bowen; the other was a friend and neighbour. They had evidently not been warned of our coming by Humphry. We introduced ourselves. Although clearly surprised by our arrival, they

1 Maire Gaster (1912–90) née Lynd; m. 1938 Jacob ('Jack') Gaster (1907–2007); nicknamed 'BJ' ('Baby Junior': she had an older sister, Sigle); read classics as a home student 1930–4 and became a close friend and holiday companion of IB, who tutored her in greats, the 2nd part of the classics course; for some 50 years a reader for the publishers William Heinemann. This letter was written for inclusion in a birthday book for her seventieth birthday.

2 With his friends Mary Fisher, Christopher Cox and Maire Lynd (as she then was: previous note), IB visited Ireland from late June to early July 1933 (and again in 1934, 1935 and 1938); the name of the lough is Lough an Illaun ('Lake of the Islands'), near Maam Cross, Co. Galway; the island was owned by a woman who lived in nearby Oughterard, Ruth née Anketell-Jones, Countess Metaxa (1877–1960), widow of an Irishman of Greek descent with an inherited Venetian title, and mother-in-law of James Harford, an Oxford friend of Christopher Cox; the shacks on the island still stand, and the boat in which they rowed across to it survives in its (more recent) boathouse.

3 (Arthur) Humphry House (1908–55), literary scholar; senior lecturer in English literature, Oxford, 1948–55; senior research fellow, Wadham, 1950–5. Elizabeth Dorothea Cole Bowen (1899–1973), novelist, chatelaine of her ancestral home, Bowen's Court. Bowen, married to Alan Cameron (next note), had fallen in love with House, whom she met in early 1933, and they began an affair that carried on after his marriage to Madeline Church in December of that year. The much younger House's attraction to Bowen was not in doubt, but he was also on the lookout for experience.

4 Alan Charles Cameron (1893–1952), educationalist; author, 1932 report of the Commission on Cultural and Educational Films, *The Film in National Life* (officially credited to Benjamin Gott as chair: Cameron was joint honorary secretary), which led to the founding of the British Film Institute; m. 1923 Elizabeth Bowen; their principal home at the time, Waldencote, was in Old Headington, in NE Oxford.

5 John Primatt Redcliffe Redcliffe-Maud (1906–82), life peer 1967, public servant; UK ambassador to South Africa 1961–3; Master, Univ., 1963–76.

On the island in Lough an Illaun: the jetty and boat in 2011 and (*inset*) 1938: IB, Maire
Lynd, Mary Fisher, Lackavrea mountain

behaved with exquisite politeness; I explained, with some embarrassment, that Humphry had encouraged us to come. Elizabeth went into the house to fetch Humphry. The friend, who, I continued to believe for many weeks, was called Miss Prong (in fact her name was Brown), chatted amiably about this and that until the return of Elizabeth, accompanied by Humphry, who was apologetic, but not very. We sat in wicker chairs (not hip-baths filled with cushions, in which, we were told, the Irish gentry used to sit on sunlit afternoons and drink white wine), and after some initial stiffness we all talked easily.

Humphry, dark, heavy, with a lowering brow, formidable, talked slowly and deliberately, principally to you; he was by nature highly susceptible, and plainly found you irresistibly attractive. Elizabeth spoke with immense charm, stammering slightly, about everything in the world. So did Miss Prong, in a slightly lower key. We were given tea indoors; were told about, and taken to see, the wishing well, where you certainly, and Christopher,[1] Mary[2] and I perhaps also, expressed silent wishes; we climbed to the upper landing of the house – a large central room from which our bedrooms opened; it was virtually empty, with huge, craniological heads made of plaster (I think) on the floor, and portraits propped against the walls: it was not exactly crumbling, but dank and abandoned and, as I later learned on a fateful occasion (when neither you nor Mary nor Christopher were present, only Goronwy – but that, of course, is another story), used to play deck quoits in.

Humphry followed you like a huge, lovelorn dog – his feelings were unmistakable. This worried me. In those days I was prudish to a degree: at parties, I am told, I used to look round sharply, like a governess, to see whether anyone was holding hands. Humphry was a friend to whom I was devoted: but he was a man of passionate nature, which he had little wish to control. At this time he was unhappy, jobless, a prey to religious doubts, and only too ready for emotional involvement.[3]

We dined happily and well. But I felt responsible for the visit, a self-appointed duenna, set over Mary and yourself. I was unwilling to confess my worry to Christopher for fear of being accused (justly) of being an absurd fusspot. After dinner, after you had all gone to bed, Humphry duly informed me that he was in love: deeply, irrevocably. I cannot remember what I said: but I was told by him that nothing I had said 'hung on at all', and was totally unreal. We went to bed at 2 or 3 a.m.

1 Christopher William Machell Cox (1899–1982), KCMG 1950, ancient historian and educationalist; fellow, New College, 1926–70; advised successive governments on overseas education and development 1940–70; longstanding friend of IB.
2 Mary Letitia Somerville Bennett (1913–2005) née Fisher, daughter of H. A. L. and Lettice Fisher; civil servant; m. 1955 John Bennett; Principal, St Hilda's, 1965–80.
3 House had been ordained a deacon in the Church of England 1931, and was elected chaplain fellow and lecturer in English at Wadham the same year, but resigned 1932 after experiencing a crisis of faith that caused him to leave the ministry.

I did not report any of this to anyone. I cannot pretend that I passed a sleepless night. In the morning we continued on our journey. Humphry insisted on coming with us to some neighbouring town. I was in a troubled state, like a distracted chaperone, and, out of pure nervousness, sang, clutched at the steering wheel, was accused of jeering at the villagers and peasants we passed in our car, and was reproved by both Christopher and Humphry. You looked disapproving, too: Mary alone remained calm.

We stopped for a meal somewhere. 'You are a prig and spoilsport,' said Humphry as he took his leave of us, 'and you do talk the most terrible nonsense about people and books and everything. It just won't do. Goodbye.' And marched off. 'Please don't answer him,' you murmured, putting your hand on my sleeve. 'I thought Elizabeth Cameron very nice indeed.' 'Yes,' I said, 'I thought she was wonderful, very much my cup of tea.' 'She is all our cups of tea,' said Christopher. 'Oh dear, put down again,' I said. After which we drove off in the best of spirits to the west, bought soda bread and an enormous ham and some butter to sustain us on Countess Metaxa's island.

Humphry and I remained close friends, for all his occasional truculence, until his untimely death.

With lifelong love from an older septuagenarian to a far, far younger one.
Isaiah

TO OLIVIA EMMET[1]

11 March 1982 [carbon]

Headington House

Dear Miss Emmet,

Thank you for your letter, which very properly takes up remarks I made the other night.[2] It has made me realise that I am not at all clear about the issue myself, although I am prepared to defend my original thesis.

I did indeed mean that the alternatives were extinction (however arrived at) on the one hand, and on the other, in your own words, 'centuries of gulags, and the sufferings inflicted on the victims of repressive regimes', to which I would add all the other forms of misery and squalor and degradation and dehumanisation, such as the victims undoubtedly suffered – we, after all, only hear from those who preserved their human semblance and a measure of dignity and freedom. You rightly point out that human history

---

1 Olivia Emmet (b. 1933), pen name of Lily Emmet West née Lily Dulany Emmet, translator of Russian and French texts; sister of Alexandra Schlesinger (629); m. 1952 Anthony West, son of Rebecca West and H. G. Wells.

2 At a dinner at Emmet's sister's IB had remarked, in response to the observation that human life might end in a thermonuclear explosion: 'Some things are worse than extinction.' Emmet understood him to mean hopeless existence under repressive regimes, but this troubled her, and she wrote reaffirming her belief in the value of life, even in conditions of extreme adversity (letter of 22 February).

and prehistory are full of appalling sufferings and horrors perpetrated by human beings on each other, but that nevertheless wonderful things have been created, and that moments of joy and noble achievement, above all unextinguished hope, nevertheless occurred – and does all this not outweigh the darkness and hopelessness of the millions, soon billions? Sums like this are difficult to make, and I do not urge a purely utilitarian scale, whereby the probability of the total sum of suffering could be shown by some rational method to be greater than that of – to call it so for short – happiness. Then there would be no point in going on. There was a philosopher in ancient Greece, a Stoic, I think, who used to persuade people to commit suicide if the prospect of happiness was too poor.[1] I do not mean that. I think in the end that, just as we ask ourselves whether something is worth doing, or life is worth living, just as situations arise in which it seems perfectly reasonable to terminate one's life if the alternative is too awful – where one has no worthwhile motive for going on – so this could arise for whole groups or societies, and, in theory, for the whole of mankind.

I think you are perfectly right. That is, I think that it is difficult to imagine a situation in which there was literally no hope left, no hope of that minimum degree of human relationships, of the capacity for any use of thought, imagination, emotional response to anything. It is difficult to imagine this, but not impossible. I simply cast my mind back to my short term of duty in the Soviet Union in 1945, when I asked myself what I would do if I suddenly found myself with a Soviet passport instead of a British one. I was quite clear then that I would wish to blow my brains out rather than try to adjust myself to the system in the hope of better things, or of being able to help others, or the like. And if I felt this, if I felt that life for me in the Soviet Union was intolerable (though I knew it was not so for everybody), then why not for X and Y and Z, who theoretically might include all mankind? But you are perfectly right: it is an absurd proposition to advance as baldly as I did. The only point I wished to make was that the by now ridiculous formula of 'a fate worse than death'[2] had some genuine content, and that mere clinging to life, mere tenacity, was not enough. That, and something more: that the price for the 'marvels: of beauty and knowledge and joy' (and the 'health and well-being' of animals and plants) might be too high, that not to save mankind

1 This was the general view of ancient Stoicism. Diogenes Laertius writes: 'They tell us that the wise man will for reasonable cause make his own exit from life [...] if he suffer intolerable pain, mutilation, or incurable disease.' *Lives of Eminent Philosophers* 7. 130, trans. Robert Drew Hicks (London, 1925). The doctrine is associated with Chrysippus in particular, though he allegedly also said the opposite (Plutarch, *On Stoic Self-Contradictions* 18).

2 The earliest use of this exact phrase we have found occurs in [George Sale and others], *The Modern Part of an Universal History, from the Earliest Account of Time* (London, 1759–66) xxi (1960) 181 (book 19, 'The History of Spain', chapter 1, section 13), where the Muslim inhabitants of Granada, resigned to the success of the siege laid against them by the Catholic Monarchs Isabella and Ferdinand, are portrayed as 'regretting that a fate worse than death was appointed for themselves'. But the idea behind it – that rape or prostitution is such a fate – is older.

from some appalling fate short of actual extinction might be a disservice to it. And to this appalling proposition, I think I still cling.

I do hope I have made myself clearer. I think we do disagree. I do not think that the marvels necessarily weigh more than the horrors. It may be that they do, but it may also be that they do not, and will not; and unless one believes that life was given one by God and [one] has no right to deprive oneself or others of it because it is not something we are entitled to withhold or extinguish (if one believes that, then of course you are right), the question remains open. You are simply more optimistic than I am: you believe that there is always a possibility of so much light at the end of each tunnel as to make it all worthwhile; I wish I believed that. The only thing that comforts me is that even such reflections make no difference to practice, even in so unsatisfactory a world as we live in at present. But the blessings, I fully admit, still enormously outweigh the horrors, and there is rational ground for hope.

Yours sincerely,
    [Isaiah Berlin]

TO ISAAC STERN

15 March 1982 [*carbon*]

Headington House

Dear Isaac,

I am back from Jerusalem – exhausted, exhilarated (by the vitality of all our friends) and, of course, depressed. If the present policies are followed, they will endure for longer than people think or hope, but in the end they cannot but lead to a huge debacle. When I arrived, Teddy earnestly begged me to put in one of those little prayers into a crevice in the Wall, imploring the Deity for Begin's recovery; his disappearance would, in everyone's view, let in Sharon[1] and Shamir,[2] who are more violent and touched with a certain insanity. Or so people say. The fact that Sharon goes to see my cousin the Lubavitcher[3] in New York whenever he is there does not exactly delight me. Politically we can only shut our eyes and pray for the best, or the 'least worst' – there is certainly nothing that people like us can do. I no longer think that it is wicked to thunder against that government in London or New York, even

1 Ariel ('Arik') Sharon (1928–2014) né Scheinermann, Israeli general and politician; MK 1973–4, 1977–2006, later (1999–2005) Likud leader; minister of defence 1981–3, later (2001–6) prime minister; spent his last 8 years in a coma after a stroke; a brilliant though controversial military commander who fought with distinction in the Six Day and Yom Kippur wars, but also headed the elite anti-terror unit blamed for the deaths of villagers at Kibbiya, Jordan, October 1953; for his resignation as minister of defence after the Sabra and Shatila massacres of Palestinian refugees see 194.

2 Yitzhak Shamir (1915–2012) né Ezernitsky, Polish-born Israeli politician; Likud MK 1974–96, foreign minister 1980–6, prime minister 1983–4, 1986–92.

3 Menachem Mendel Schneerson (1902–94), distant cousin of IB's; leader of the Lubavitcher Jews in NY, one of the most devout sects of Hasidic Judaism.

though I am not disposed to do any thundering myself, partly because I do not know what alternative I could responsibly and conscientiously offer. But enough of that – it is too gloomy. [...]

Teddy, Ruthi [Cheshin] etc. of course send you warmest greetings, although I said I would not see you for some time – they will probably turn up in New York before long, as always. What Teddy has done to the Damascus Gate is marvellous – the diversion of the late Sir Charles Clore's funds from Hurva to David's Tower does nothing but good. The idea of restoring the Hurva as it was in the seventeenth century (which seems obviously right), according to Teddy, is likely to be condemned by the Israel Architects Association: foolish fellows – to wish to be modern at all costs and in all environments is also a kind of vulgarity, don't you think? Now that we have got into abstract issues, better stop. We must be concrete, Comrade, as Koestler's[1] old Communist cronies used to say.

Love to Vera,[2]

Yours ever,

[Isaiah]

TO OLIVIA EMMET

30 March 1982 [*carbon*]

Headington House

Dear Miss Emmet,

[...] I am afraid that what I said to you in my last letter was founded on a mechanical extrapolation of that which applies to one individual, as applying to more than one and in the end to all – that is, mankind at large. I see on reflection that this is patently absurd. I may have a right to put an end to my own life; not only a right, but it is something that can be rationally defended, perhaps even emotionally defended, too; I may even have a right to kill others in some circumstances. But you are perfectly right – indeed, self-evidently so – that neither an individual nor a group nor a nation has a right to decree this for mankind, i.e. [...] put an end to human life (and perhaps all life), for all one can tell, for ever. It is difficult to know when, if ever, I have the right to urge, even compel, others to do things which expose them to mortal danger, e.g. conscript people in wartime. But to condemn the whole of humanity to perish, no matter what the probable horrors of its continued existence, is plainly unthinkable and mad. The question is, whether one is so much as permitted to contemplate the possibilities of universal extinction as

---

1 Arthur Koestler (1905–83), Hungarian-born British author; joined CPGB 1931 and travelled in USSR; appalled by the Moscow show trials, left the party 1938, and his novel *Darkness at Noon* (London, 1940) did much to publicise the horrors of the Stalinist regime; later wrote extensively on science and parapsychology.

2 Vera Stern (b. 1927) née Lindenblit, m. Isaac Stern 1951 (his 2nd wife); they divorced 1994.

a less awful alternative than continued existence, provided, of course, one does nothing towards the former. Since the consequences are not remotely calculable, it is absurd to weigh these alternatives. Consequently, I capitulate. I think I spoke rashly. My arguments and my position are refuted by your simple and unanswerable last letter. My mind is cleared, and I am most grateful to you.

    Yours sincerely,

      [Isaiah Berlin]

TO GALEN STRAWSON[1]

9 April 1982

Headington House

Dear Galen,

I have read your article in *Quarto*[2] with, one might say, excessively total agreement, and great pleasure. 'Excessively' because I *cannot* read the authors of whom you speak: I have done my best with Derrida,[3] and such American offshoots as Paul de Man,[4] and a man whose name I have forgotten who used to be Cultural Attaché in the French Embassy here,[5] and Barthes[6] also [...], and decided that it was not for me. I feel some guilt about not embarking on reading Heidegger, whom I suspect to be a major thinker of some kind, however repellent (at least to me); but none about ignoring the objects of your 'mildly polemical' treatment. I am sure you are perfectly right: there is something to be said about the ambiguity, levels of understanding, differences of meaning to different groups, cultures, times, places; conflicts of meaning, etc. But it has been badly overdriven, and your robust insistence on the fact that we can describe the real world in adequately clear and precise

---

1 Galen John Strawson (b. 1952), philosopher and literary critic; assistant editor, TLS, 1978–87, consultant editor 1987–2012; philosophy lecturer at a series of Oxford colleges 1979–87, fellow and philosophy tutor, Jesus, 1987–2000; son of the Oxford philosopher Peter Strawson (34/2).

2 GS's review of Vincent Descombes, *Modern French Philosophy* (Cambridge, 1980), *Quarto*, March 1982, 16–18.

3 Jacques (né Jackie Élie) Derrida (1930–2004), Algiers-born French philosopher; taught at Sorbonne 1960–4, at École normale supérieure 1965–84; leading representative of the philosophical/literary movement known as deconstruction; hon. DLitt Cambridge 1992. 'My principal emotion at the moment is indignation about the Cambridge degree for Derrida. If you think that "Philosophy in Britain" is likely [...] to make it even slightly less probable that a charlatan of that kind can get an hon. degree at a reputable university, then I am prepared to be the hon. Vice President of this organisation.' To Peter Strawson, 15 May 1992.

4 Pseudonym of Paul Adolph Michel Deman (1919–83), Belgian-born literary critic and theorist, friend and close associate of Derrida; emigrated to US 1948; Sterling Prof. of French and Comparative Literature, Yale, 1970–83. The 1987 revelation that during the war he had written for 2 Nazi-controlled Belgian newspapers damaged his posthumous reputation, and was especially difficult for the Jewish-born Derrida.

5 Claude Lévi-Strauss (192/3), cultural attaché at the French Embassy in Washington 1946–7.

6 Roland Barthes (1915–80), semiologist and literary theorist, regarded as the key figure in structuralism.

language, and reasonably hope to be understood across large stretches of time and space, that the language both of the sciences and common sense can be made sufficiently clear and unambiguous, and is not susceptible to being dissolved or undermined (note the metaphors!) in this way, needs very badly to be expressed. It seems to me to lead to a fantastic kind of linguistic Idealism – a world constituted by languages – to which, in a mild form, the new objectivism of values is addicted. Of course there *is* a genetic fallacy – even if Vico was right in supposing that the history of linguistic usages, and even of individual terms, throws light on cultural history and leads to a valuable kind of self-knowledge, it does not follow that what is being said, or those who say it, can be resolved into, or wholly (or even very largely) accounted for, by reference to impersonal social forces or psychological, physiological, genetic factors (e.g. the social growth of linguistic forms, or anthropology), the very identification of which presupposes a pretty fixed, clear, intelligible kind of use of prose. One must allow, I suppose, the fact that all new ideas usually make an impact by being greatly exaggerated. Plato[1] exaggerated, so did the Stoics, Descartes, Leibniz,[2] Berkeley,[3] Hume, Kant, Hegel, Marx, Nietzsche, Freud etc. etc. Aristotle and Locke[4] perhaps did not, but I can think of few other first-rate philosophers who didn't overstate their cases – it needs something to crack 'the cake of custom',[5] the obstruction of received ideas. But the converse does not follow. Exaggeration is not enough.

The trouble about sending this article to me is that you are adding the most welcome support to my already existing biases. I now feel less inclined than ever to plunge into those murky seas – I feel convinced that most of the stuff you write about is in fact rot, of a very pretentious, boring kind. Sartre[6]

---

1 Plato (*c.*429–347 BCE), disciple of Socrates and teacher of Aristotle; most widely studied of all of the ancient Greek philosophers, effectively the inventor of the modern discipline: 'The safest general characterisation of the philosophical tradition is that it consists of a series of footnotes to Plato.' Alfred North Whitehead, *Process and Reality: An Essay in Cosmology* (Cambridge, 1929), 2. 1. 1 (63).

2 Gottfried Wilhelm Leibniz (1646–1716), FRS 1673, German philosopher, mathematician and logician, trained in law but influential in a wide range of subjects.

3 George Berkeley (1685–1753), philosopher, Bishop of Cloyne 1734–53; advanced the doctrine of immaterialism, which denies the reality of any external world beyond the mind (an approach often called subjective Idealism) in *A Treatise Concerning the Principles of Human Knowledge*, part 1 (Dublin, 1710; no part 2 was published).

4 John Locke (1632–1704), philosopher; founding father of political liberalism, and a central figure in the British empirical tradition, whose influence can be seen in both the European Enlightenment and the drafting of the American Constititution.

5 Walter Bagehot, in 'Physics and Politics: No. I, The Pre-Economic Age', *Fortnightly Review* 8 (NS 2, July–December 1867), 518–38, coins the phrase 'cake of custom' at 531; in 'Physics and Politics: No. II, The Age of Conflict', ibid. 9 (NS 3, January–June 1868), 452–71 at 458, he speaks of 'breaking the cake of custom'; see *Physics and Politics, or Thoughts on the Application of the Principles of 'Natural Selection' and 'Inheritance' to Political Society* (London, 1872), 27, 53.

6 Jean-Paul Charles Aymard Sartre (1905–80), French philosopher, writer, activist and leading exponent of existentialism; became a Marxist, though not a Communist, after WW2.

was, of course, an interesting figure before Marxism overcame him; so was Kojève, who is almost single-handedly responsible for the Hegelianised Marxism of everybody from Sartre and his immediate disciples to Charles Taylor, Alasdair MacIntyre,[1] the old New Left (is there a new New Left? if so, I know nothing of them).

So let me tell you again how much pleasure your piece has given me; the book you are reviewing was described to me as not too good by my friend Jerry Cohen,[2] whose views on the French *fumistes*[3] coincide with yours, but that is merely a peg on which to hang your very timely reflections. No philosophical movement has ever been killed by criticism, I believe; only changes of outlook, new problems, due to who knows what, do that (to that extent, the sociologists of knowledge, from Mannheim[4] to Kuhn,[5] are right, though they, too, wildly exaggerate). But Julien Benda's little book *Sur le succès du bergsonisme*,[6] Russell's strictures,[7] Leonard Woolf's little book *Quack, Quack!*,[8] have done something to keep Bergson from these shores – something Freddie Ayer did not succeed in doing against Sartre (who did have important things to say).[9]

1 Alasdair Chalmers MacIntyre (b. 1929), University Prof. in Philosophy and Political Science, Boston, 1972–80; Luce Prof., Wellesley College, 1980–2; W. Alton Jones Prof. of Philosophy, Vanderbilt, 1982–8; McMahon/Hank Prof. of Philosophy, Notre Dame, 1988–94; Arts and Sciences Prof. of Philosophy, Duke, 1995–2000; author of foreword to CC2.

2 Gerald Allan ('Jerry') Cohen (1941–2009; plate 11), Canadian-born Marxist political philosopher; reader in philosophy, UCL, 1978–84; Chichele Prof. of Social and Political Theory, Oxford, and fellow, All Souls, 1985–2008; he had studied at Oxford (BPhil 1963) under IB and Gilbert Ryle.

3 'Practical jokers'; 'clever men who produce mumbo-jumbo' (to Peter Strawson, 15 May 1992).

4 Karl (né Károly) Mannheim (1893–1947), Hungarian-born sociologist; emigrated to England from Germany 1933; lecturer in sociology, LSE, 1933–45; prof. of education, Institute of Education, London, 1945–7; regarded as the founding father of the sociology of knowledge.

5 The US philosopher of science Thomas Samuel Kuhn (1922–96), in his influential book *The Structure of Scientific Revolutions* (Chicago and London, 1962), posited that scientific understanding of the world is not fully objective, but conditioned by a changing series of 'paradigms' – spectacles or frameworks through which the world is viewed at any given time. For Kuhn there can be no such thing as a paradigm-neutral account of reality.

6 IB identifies 3 writers critical of French philosopher Henri Louis Bergson (1859–1941) for championing intuition against reason. Bergson was a bête noire of Julien Benda (1867–1956), French novelist and philosopher, whose *Sur le succès du bergsonisme: précédé d'une réponse aux défenseurs de la doctrine* (Paris, 1914) was the last of 3 books by him devoted to attacking Bergson's ideas.

7 Bertrand Russell's highly critical article, 'The Philosophy of Bergson', *Monist* 22 no. 3 (July 1912), 321–47, ends: 'those to whom action, if it is to be of any value, must be inspired by some vision, by some imaginative foreshadowing of a world less painful, less unjust, less full of strife than the world of our everyday life, those, in a word, whose action is built on contemplation, will find in this philosophy nothing of what they seek, and will not regret that there is no reason to think it true' (347).

8 Leonard Sidney Woolf (1880–1969), author, publisher and political theorist; founder of the Hogarth Press with his wife Virginia (m. 1912); joint editor, *Political Quarterly*, 1931–59; dedicatee of VH. *Quack, Quack!* (London, 1935), an attack on irrationality in which Woolf writes: 'Bergson must be counted among the intellectual quacks, a teacher of […] metaphysical magic' (178).

9 A. J. Ayer attacked Sartre in 'Novelist-Philosophers: V – Jean-Paul Sartre', *Horizon* 12 no. 67 (July 1945), 12–26, no. 68 (August 1945), 101–10, of which IB wrote to Aline, 3 January 1955, 'What a fool I was to be deceived by Freddie's articles in *Horizon* at the end of the war which concentrated on Sartre's obscure logic & his attitudes to sex & "proved" it all bogus. It is not. It is most imaginative & bold & important' (L2 467).

Who will strike a blow, a really hefty blow, for reason? against froth? Won't you?

Yours ever,

Isaiah

TO OM BAKSHI[1]

22 September 1982 [*carbon*]

Headington House

Dear Professor Bakshi,

I have now read your monograph on the decline of political theory.[2] I read it with much interest, and have learned a good deal from it – it is one of the fullest surveys of recent thought on the subject that I have come across, and I congratulate you on it. At the same time, I have some thoughts about it, which I shall try and formulate [...].

I must confess that I don't distinguish political theory from political phil-osophy – they seem to me so overlapping as to be virtually identical. Perhaps the former is a little more concrete, examining the role and interplay of insti-tutions; but both seem to apply what you call axiological principles to social, political and generally public life. Some have thought political theory to be simply ethics applied not to individuals but to groups, and I have a certain amount of sympathy with this point of view. As for political science, that can no doubt to some degree be defined as who, whom, when, where, how? Politics, said somebody, is about power. I disagree. Political philosophy is about ends, not facts save as illustrations for contributions to the meanings of past users of political terminology. Political philosophy surely asks 'Why should I obey?' not 'Why do I obey?'; 'What is a right?' – which is another way of asking 'What grounds have I for claiming to be able to vote?' and 'Who conferred this liberty?' and 'In what way were they entitled to do so?' and 'What is entitlement? Does it rest on a contract, or the word of God, and if so, why should the contract be carried out, God be obeyed?' and so on and so on. I am sure you do not disagree.

The importance of contexts. Yes, of course, to understand the terms in which philosophers, political or otherwise, in order to understand the thrust, the point, of their statements and arguments, I do require to know what ques-tions they were asking themselves (that much, Collingwood said already); and that, no doubt, has direct relevance to the circumstances in which they lived and their general outlook, cast of thought, method of communicating, search for understanding of themselves, of others, and of the world around them. But then, to seek to reduce their ideas to their temporal or spatial

---

1 Sometime prof. of political theory, School of International Studies, Jawaharlal Nehru.
2 *The Crisis of Political Theory: An Inquiry into Contemporary Thought* (Delhi, 1987). IB had read a draft typescript.

context, to say that we really do not know much about what Athens was like in the days of Plato or Aristotle, we cannot be sure of the meanings of Greek words, is surely not right, for it does not seem absurd to say that Plato was one of the supreme thinkers, about politics as well as almost everything else. When Aristotle accuses him of wanting an over-unified society, he said that this cannot be done, that men are more various and that the rules by which they can seek either life or the good life must be more flexible than Plato demands, we seem to understand what is being said – not merely in relation to Athens and Greece, but to other demands for uniformity, say Spinoza's[1] or those of the Communist Party. So, too, Rousseau may in fact, when talking about the General Will, have had in mind the privileges of the various estates – nobility, the Church, the court etc. – but his plea for independence of the wills of others has wider implications than protest against the particular inequalities of his own time. The doctrine of natural rights, whether stated by Locke or Jefferson,[2] or of human rights today, which is pretty nearly the same thing, may well be enriched and elucidated by explaining precisely what was meant by Grotius[3] or Burlamaqui[4] or the Hebrew prophets, but the general implications are such as interest us today.

There are, it seems to me, issues that transcend their time because men, however various and changeable their natures, have certain qualities, face certain problems, from generation to generation, which do not differ sufficiently to make central issues either obsolete or unintelligible at later dates. The great thinkers are surely those who enunciated these ideas most starkly, at a sufficiently profound and general level; to attempt to dilute them into their times seems to go against all that we think and know. Shakespeare gets through even the worst translators, so does the Bible [...].

This, of course, is not an argument against trying to establish as precisely as possible, in the light of evidence, what these terms mean – that Machiavelli meant by *stato* not what we call 'states', but rather as we use the word in 'He came in great state', is important; but still, we understand the main thrust of his argument and what he was trying to refute in the way of Christian humility, feeble government, even if we do not know about *stato*. This is not a plea for the unhistorical way in which I was taught Plato and

1 Benedict de/Baruch Spinoza (1632–77) né Benedito de Espinosa, Dutch Jewish rationalist philosopher whose naturalistic views (often regarded in his time as atheistic, for all that he spoke of 'God or nature') on a wide variety of topics were an important part of the C17th background that ushered in the Enlightenment.

2 Thomas Jefferson (1743–1826), US President 1801–9; a key member, Continental Congress (first met 1774), he was also the principal author of the Declaration of Independence (1776); his ideas on government were profoundly influenced by the 2nd of John Locke's *Two Treatises of Government* (London, 1690 [sc. 1689]).

3 Hugo Grotius (also Huig/Hugeianus/Hugh de Groot) (1583–1645), Dutch jurist and theologian.

4 Jean Jacques Burlamaqui (1694–1748), Genevan patrician, and legal and political theorist; his principal publications, *Principes du droit naturel* (Geneva, 1747) and *Principes du droit politique* (Amsterdam, 1751), were influential in the American Revolution.

Aristotle when I was young – as if they were Englishmen, giving papers in a philosophical society – but it is a protest against the exaggeration of treating the history of ideas as a history of things that pass and die with their age. It is my experience that those who write the history of, say, political philosophy, do it very mechanically and understand very, very little unless they have themselves struggled with problems of this type, and understand – or want to understand – where the shoe pinched in the sixteenth as opposed to the eighteenth century; and unless it pinches still, these ideas really have died away (as some certainly have: who now cares about the doctrine of Two Swords, Pope and Emperor?).[1] We read Hobbes[2] and Locke, and not Filmer[3] or the pre-Adamitic theorists[4] at whom he is alleged to be tilting, because their words speak to us. Hobbes is marvellously relevant to the discontents of the twentieth century, as Filmer or Althusius[5] are not, at least to the same degree. These may be truisms, but I think that they need stating in view of the powerful influence which, I am sure rightly, you say that the historicists have had or are having.

You say [...] that political theories arise out of upheavals in society. I am sure this is by and large the case. But even if it is true of Hobbes, Rousseau, Hegel, Mill, what about Hume, who lived in a very stable and relatively untroubled society, or at least what seemed to him such? Or, indeed, Kant, who has had a powerful influence on political thought, but before the French Revolution lived in a very stable East Prussian society? What, indeed, about Aquinas?[6] It seems to me that certain central questions can arise at almost any time, and that it is these questions that moral, political, aesthetic, social thought – whether called philosophy or theory – is about, i.e. the ultimate ends of men, based on a certain conception of human nature, which differs from thinker to thinker quite often: Machiavelli's man is very different from Locke's, so is Kant's timeless eternal moral being, or Spinoza's unchanging human nature [...].

You speak of the decline of political theory in English-speaking countries,

---

1 Pope Boniface VIII issued a papal bull 1302 stating: 'We are informed by the texts of the gospels that in this Church and in its power are two swords: namely, the spiritual and the temporal.' Cf. Luke 22:38: 'And they said, Lord, behold, here are two swords. And he said unto them, It is enough.'

2 Thomas Hobbes (1588–1679), philosopher; generally considered the founder of moral and political philosophy in England, and of the social contract tradition in political theory; author of *Leviathan* (1651).

3 Robert Filmer (c.1588–1653), English political theorist, held that 'God had himself ordained the great pyramid of the world' (FIB2 7), and defended the divine right of kings, who inherited from Adam the authority bestowed on him by God at the creation.

4 Who believed that humans existed before Adam.

5 Johannes Althusius/Althaus (c.1557–1638), German jurist and political theorist; developed a theory of federalism and popular sovereignty.

6 Thomas Aquinas (1225–74), Italian scholastic philosopher, theologian and monk of huge influence whose monarchist political views, IB implies, did not stem from exposure to notable social upheavals.

at any rate since, say, the death of T.H. Green; and it is true that until the Second World War this was a very justified complaint. One of the reasons for this, I think – I do not know if you will agree – is the emergence of new disciplines. Parricide is common among theories: it is not only in Freud that the children kill the father. These new disciplines have made the whole thing much more complicated. With the rise of economics, sociology, social psychology, Freudian psychology, when men spoke about freedom people asked: 'Which kind do you mean? Freedom from anxiety? Economic freedom? Freedom of societies, or of the individuals in them?', just as Sismondi[1] asked: 'What is meant by a rich state? That the treasury is full, or that the citizens are prosperous?'[2] The complications which these new disciplines have introduced destroyed the pristine simplicity that made it possible for Locke, Rousseau, even Mill, to talk as they did.

Sociology has on the whole not been a success story; at least, political sociology has no doubt generated much useful and surprising knowledge, but the effort to discover powerful general propositions about the laws, or even tendencies, that govern human history has – at least in our century – not been crowned with much success. That is no doubt why sociology, which, under Comte, started so ambitiously, is at present in a somewhat frustrated condition. And this leads me to the view than Comte's effort to create a natural science of politics founded upon the discovery of irrefutable laws of history, on the analogy of the triumph of the natural sciences, was in principle misconceived. The analogy is not valid: men are not merely objects in nature, governed by discoverable causal laws. To understand human behaviour, one needs to understand how men interpret themselves and their relations to others, how they see themselves in the world, what they think their relationship is to past and future, to nature, and above all to one another. Thinkers like Vico and Herder and Hegel, and the social anthropologists of our day (say Evans-Pritchard, or Geertz, or Levi-Strauss)[3] see this, and are

1 (Jean Charles) Léonard Simonde de Sismondi (1773–1842), Swiss historian and political economist; initially influenced by Adam Smith, he later came to question laissez-faire.

2 Apparently a paraphrase rather than a quotation, though it is hard to prove a negative. Cf. a passage in IB's essay on Machiavelli: 'like Sismondi and the theorists of the welfare state, one may prefer a state in which citizens are prosperous even though the public treasury is poor, in which government is neither centralised nor omnipotent, nor, perhaps, sovereign at all, but the citizens enjoy a wide degree of individual freedom'. AC2 75.

3 Edward Evan Evans-Pritchard (1902–73), Kt 1971, prof. of social anthropology, Oxford, and fellow, All Souls, 1946–70; in his writings 'sociological analysis never deprives the reader of a living and sympathetic impression of the people themselves' (R.G.Lienhardt, ODNB). Clifford James Geertz (1926–2006), US anthropologist; prof., School of Social Science, IAS, Princeton, 1970–2000; Geertz propounded a humanistic anthropology in which 'man is an animal suspended in webs of significance he himself has spun'. He continues: 'I take culture to be those webs, and the analysis of it not to be an experimental science in search of law but an interpretive one in search of meaning.' 'Thick Description: Toward an Interpetive Theory of Culture', chapter 1 in *The Interpretation of Cultures* (NY, 1973), 5. Claude Lévi-Strauss (1908–2009), Brussels-born French anthropologist; of Jewish descent, he was exiled in the US during WW2, and taught at the New School for Social Research, NY, 1941–5; prof. of social anthropology, Collège de France, 1959–82;

not betrayed into pseudo-scientific pursuits. In this sense, logical positivism[1] rendered a disservice, and it and a great deal of modern behaviourism[2] simply don't answer the questions which men want to ask. 'Why should I be treated as a commodity? Why should I not rebel against authority? Is it right for judges, policemen, prime ministers to order me about? Are all values compatible? Why cannot we, even in principle, be both perfectly just and perfectly merciful? I must choose: what must I choose, and why? Why cannot I do what I like, rather than behave decently? What is a minimally decent society?' To all this, behaviouralism (which seems to me on the wane) gives no answers, only examines conduct and tell us what happens, how, when and under what pressures. [...]

    Yours sincerely,
      Isaiah Berlin

In June 1982 the Israeli defense minister Ariel Sharon initiated Operation Peace of the Galilee (the [First] Lebanon War), intended to eliminate Palestinian terrorist groups operating from southern Lebanon. The operation at first had broad support in Israel, but public controversy dogged its course, and dissent intensified after the massacre of Palestinian refugees in the camps of Sabra and Shatila near Beirut, 16–18 September 1982. Calls for a commission of enquiry into the massacre were initially resisted by the government, and on 20 September the President, Yitzhak Navon,[3] met with Prime Minister Menachem Begin to demand action. Navon's office subsequently issued a statement:

We do not have the right to, and should not, ignore the issue: not towards ourselves, not towards our image in our own eyes, nor towards that part of the world which we perceive ourselves as being part of. Our duty is to investigate, as quickly as possible and in an accurate manner, by credible and independent people, everything that occurred in this unfortunate affair, and, if it is warranted, to draw the full conclusions of this investigation.[4]

On 25 September the opposition Alignment Party organised one of the largest demonstrations in Israeli history, in Tel Aviv, and on 28 September the government acceded to the demands for a commission of enquiry; it was headed by

---

a leading proponent of structuralism, he positioned himself closer to the sciences on an arts–science continuum than either Evans-Pritchard or Geertz, but did not posit biological differences as underlying cultural variation, as some earlier generations of anthropologists had done.

1 The theory espoused by the 'Vienna Circle' of philosophers in the early 1930s, who wished to assimilate all enquiry to the natural sciences. It thus ruled out as misconceived attempts to understand human beings interpretatively, 'from the inside' (as claimed by the thinkers IB lists), rather than by appealing to universal scientifically discoverable laws.

2 Behaviourism analyses human mental activity exclusively in terms of outwardly visible behaviour, leaving no role for (and sometimes denying the existence of) inner states.

3 Yitzhak Navon (b. 1921; plate 19), Israeli politician, diplomat and author, fluent in Arabic; member of the centre-left Alignment Party; President, Israel, 1978–83.

4 Tova Tzimuki, 'President Navon Calls to Investigate the Massacre Affair', *Davar*, 21 September 1982, 1.

Justice Yitzhak Kahan.[1] *His report on the Sabra and Shatila massacre was published on 7 February 1983: it found the state of Israel indirectly responsible for the massacre, as the camps were under IDF control when they were attacked by Christian Phalangist militias. Kahan recommended that Sharon should be removed from the post of minister of defence, and not reappointed to that office, which eventually led to Sharon's resignation.*

The massacre caused outrage in the Diaspora as well as in Israel, and IB was one of those deeply affected. At a time when it still seemed uncertain whether the government would set up a commission of enquiy, IB played a central role in drafting, and dispatching, a letter to Ha'aretz in protest. As he explained to Ursula Niebuhr,[2] *29 October 1982:*

I feel deeply distressed [by] that horrible government, as you may imagine, and did indeed draft a letter to *Ha'aretz*, which I got some tycoons to sign as well as worthy academics – worthy tycoons, I must admit, because I thought that would get through, whereas the fact that a lot of academics don't like massacres or violence or coercion is not news. In effect, the letter said 'We have never signed a letter critical of the Israel government before; we have not done so (*a*) because we are told we don't know the pressures and dangers of life in Israel and (*b*) because we didn't want to give aid and comfort to her enemies; but [...] we could keep silence no longer about the reluctance of Mr Begin's government to have an enquiry, which makes us doubt its bona fides' – and more in the same sense. [...] The letter duly appeared: at first they thought it was a bit too late, and so it was; collecting signatures is not easy; I have never done it before and hope never to have to do it again. But in the end it appeared, plus an article[3] saying that Stalin's question 'How many divisions has the Pope?' cannot be answered in terms of military divisions alone, and that the letter was signed by quite a division, etc. (of which I have now been promoted to being the commander).

TO ROBERT MABRO[4]

23 September 1982 [*carbon*]

Headington House

Dear Dr Mabro,

    [...] I entirely agree with you that aggression fosters hatred, but this

---

1 Yitzhak Kahan (1913–85), Galician-born Israeli jurist; justice of Israel's supreme court 1970–83, president 1982–3.

2 Ursula Mary Niebuhr (1907–97) née Keppel-Compton, English-born NY theologian, m. 1931 the American theologian Karl Paul Reinhold Niebuhr (1892–1971); prof. and founder of the dept of religion, Barnard College, 1946–65.

3 Yossi Melman, 'The Divisions of Isaiah Berlin', *Ha'aretz*, 5 October 1982, 11.

4 Robert Emile Mabro (b. 1934), Egyptian-born economist; senior research officer in the economics of the Middle East, Oxford, from 1969; fellow, St Antony's, 1971–2002; founder and director, Oxford Institute for Energy Studies, 1982–2003, later (2003–6) president. Mabro had written (20 September) urging IB to make a public statement against 'Mr Begin and his associates', who were 'turning a deaf ear to world protests', but might be moved 'if prominent Jews voiced publicly

statement, as you well know, cuts both ways. I am indeed horrified by the fact that these Christian militias are permitted to enter the two camps by Israeli authorities – so, as you must know, are many people in Israel. Speaking as a Jew to an Arab (to invert your expression), I should be glad to protest together with you, if you in your turn are prepared to protest against the outrages committed by Arab terrorists, both of the PLO and associated organisations and allies, against innocent Israelis, especially women and children. Massacres are always odious, whoever commits them, whoever the victims are. At least indignation has been expressed in wide sections of the Israeli population – you and I have yet to hear similar indignation against terrorism by Arab parties or public opinion in the Arab states. If that were so, we could sign a joint letter, denouncing both sides for their excesses and brutality. I feel strongly that what is sauce for the Israeli goose must be sauce also for the Arab gander.

Yours sincerely,
[Isaiah Berlin]

TO THE EDITOR OF *HA'ARETZ*

[*Editorial translation of a letter published in Hebrew in* Ha'aretz, *1 October 1982, 22, headed 'Let Israel Regain Its Honour'*][1]

[We have for a long time been among the active supporters of Zionism and the state of Israel, and our support continues. In the past we have hesitated to criticise the government of Israel publicly – not only because we respected the point made by many Israelis that those who live outside Israel's borders cannot really comprehend the severity of the dangers and pressures which are the lot of Jews living in Israel. Moreover, we did not – and still do not – want to join those of Israel's critics who kept their silence when Jews in Israel – men, women and children – had been massacred by Arab terrorists and their allies.

But faced with the massacre perpetrated last week in the refugee camps Shatila and Sabra in Beirut, and the ensuing situation, we feel that he who remains silent in such times is mistaken. We wholeheartedly support the demand of President Yitzhak Navon[2] to set up an independent commission of enquiry to investigate the chain of events leading to this shocking event.

---

their dissent': 'You may find it difficult to criticise the Israeli government in public, in front of the world. But silence also has a price.'

1 We have not found the original English text. An editorial footnote to the published letter says: 'This letter was written and sent before the government decided to set up a commission of enquiry.'

2 In the weeks after the massacre at Sabra and Shatila he 'emerged as the conscience of the nation' (Christopher Walker, 'Begin Rides the Storm, But for How Long?', *Times*, 5 October 1982, 10b–e at 10d).

He who refuses to investigate will cause doubts in the hearts of civilised and honest people in Israel and abroad about the integrity of the government of Israel. We have been and still are devoted friends of the state of Israel and its people, and we hope that everything will be done to clear their conscience and to bring back their honour, which has been a source of pride for Jews all over the world.

Lord (Sidney) Bernstein, Chairman, Granada TV
Lord (Marcus) Sieff, Chairman, Marks and Spencer
Lord (Samuel) Segal
Lord (Arnold) Goodman
Lord (Victor) Rothschild, banker
Baroness (Dora) Gaitskell, House of Lords
Baroness (Alma) Birk, House of Lords
Sir Isaiah Berlin, All Souls College, Oxford
Steven Roth, Director, Institute of Jewish Affairs, London
T. R. Fyvel, writer
Professor Chimen Abramsky, University College, London
Jacob Rothschild, banker
William Frankel, writer
Professor Alfred Neuberger, Director, Institute for Preventive Medicine, London

Ellis Birk
Professor Julius Gould, Nottingham University
John Gross, writer (former editor, TLS)
Professor D. D. Raphael, Imperial College, London
N. M. Dunietz, Oxford
Rabbi Hugo Gryn
Professor David Daiches, Edinburgh University
Professor John Friend, Hull University
Professor Leonard Schapiro, London School of Economics
S. Zipperstein
Peter Oppenheimer, Oxford
Michael Freeden, Oxford
Peter Pulzer, Oxford]

TO SHIRLEY ANGLESEY[1]

15 November 1982

Headington House

Dearest Shirley,

What a wonderful letter! I am so glad you loved Leningrad. It is indeed a beautiful city, very neoclassical and un-Russian, despite everything, not built for the kind of inhabitants that hurry along the streets now – or did, at least, in 1956, when I last saw it, and I cannot believe that much has changed. I ought to have asked you to pay a special visit to the Fontanka canal and look at the exquisite iron railings of the 'Fountain House' of the Sheremetevs,[2]

1 (Elizabeth) Shirley Vaughan Paget (b. 1924), Marchioness of *Anglesey, writer.
2 One of tsarist Russia's wealthiest noble families. Their palace on the Fontanka canal (whence its name) was first built 1712, but replaced in the 1740s by a grander building, donated to the Soviet

1 During his (Peter) Jay Interview, 'In Quest of Our Civilisation, no. 2: Politics',
London Weekend TV, 31 August 1975

2 Members of 'The Club' dining society, *c.*1975: (*back*) E. T. ('Bill') Williams, Kenneth Wheare, Hugh Trevor-Roper, William Hayter; (*middle*) IB, John Sparrow, Peter Strawson, John Masterman; (*front*) Robert Blake, Raymond Carr; 'it was originally meant for conservative, snobbish, well-born fellows of colleges – that's how it was in the nineteenth century, and roughly until I was elected' (to HH, 28 September 1992, 8/3)

3 Tahiti, *c.*10 September 1975: 'it is all too beautiful, sun drenched, remote – very agreeable and not to be seriously tolerated for more than a week' (to Patricia and Bernard Williams, 10 September 1975, 7)

4 Making friends with the locals, Australia, September 1975: 'the kangaroos, emus, koala bears, parrots *are* worth inspecting' (to Jean Floud, 6 October 1975, 9)

5 With Bryan Magee for his *Men of Ideas* interview, 23 May 1976: '"Every time Magee spoke, it all burst into flames", said Professor Laithwaite, until I plunged the whole thing again into ghastly unintelligible patter. Very good for me (presumably)' (to Bernard Williams, 10 February 1978, 65)

6 Montepulciano, summer 1976, with Bob Silvers: 'a very devoted friend – particularly if one is in trouble – he acts as a kind of lifeboatman' (to Massimo Bacigalupo, 10 April 1979)

7 With the violinist Isaac Stern, his accompanist Alexander Zakin, the musical philanthropist Robert Mayer and Aline, Headington House, 8 May 1977, for a concert by Stern in support of the Musicians Benefit Fund and the Wolfson College Music Society in the Sheldonian Theatre, Oxford

8 With Max Mallowan and Aline at the foot of the east stairs, Palace of Xerxes, Persepolis, Iran, late October 1977: 'Max Mallowan, not in the best of health, recognised that this would be his last visit to Iran and wanted to bid farewell to places he knew and loved most. Thus we came to visit Isfahan and Shiraz and Bishapur and Persepolis and Bam, all intensely memorable' (Peter Brown to the editors, 17 November 2013)

9 Anna Kallin (L3 638) and Nicolas Nabokov, November 1977: IB felt specially close to these two Russian-born friends, partly because of their shared cutural hinterland, describing Nabokov as 'an aristocrat in exile with bags permanently packed to return to his native land, which he knew he would never reach, and therefore clinging to every genuine fragment of it' (to Arthur Schlesinger, 2 May 1978, 74)

10 With Jacob Rothschild, Corfu, early September 1978

11 At the lunch for his first Festschrift, Wolfson College, Oxford, 2 June 1979:
(*left to right*) Pat Utechin, Herbert Hart, Robert Wokler, Jerry Cohen, Alan Ryan, HH,
IB, Chuck Taylor, Bernard Williams, Robin Milner-Gulland, Richard Wollheim,
Patrick Gardiner, Stuart Hampshire, Larry Siedentop

12 With Harry Levin, Harvard, for IB's hon. LLD, 7 June 1979: 'I was genuinely flattered by being offered this degree, for I have warm feelings towards Harvard' (to Irving Singer, 19 July 1979, 110)

13 With Sidney Morgenbesser, chez Grace Dudley, New York, c.1980–1: IB greatly enjoyed Morgenbesser's friendship, and wit: 'Pragmatism is as a theory entirely valid, true and accurate and original in every detail. Only one thing is wrong with it – it doesn't work' (quoted by IB to Victor Weisskopf, 20 February 1990)

14 Pat Utechin, the redoubtable secretary and friend who kept IB's life in order, at her son Nick's wedding, 18 July 1981: 'Pat, Why am I lunching in Balliol to-day? am I?' (31 May 1979, 633)

15, 16 At Ugo's Bar, Portofino, December 1980: 'I go to Italy (today), where everything is delightful' (to Yehudi Menuhin, 18 July 1977)

17 With John Tooley, Aline and Liliane de Rothschild, 29 July 1981, for the wedding of Charles, Prince of Wales, and Diana Spencer: 'marriage – I speak from twenty-five years (only) of experience – is a marvellous institution' (to the Prince of Wales, 24 February 1981)

18 With Arthur Schlesinger and Bob Silvers, chez Marietta Tree, New York, 1982

19 With Alfred Brendel (hon. DMus) and Yitzhak Navon in Magdalen College, Oxford, on the New Building lawns, with the Cloister behind, Encaenia garden party, 22 June 1983

where I visited the poet Anna Akhmatova in 1945 – it is, or was, a most exqui-site palazzo.[1] You were quite right to wonder at the fact that Peter the Great could have driven all those miserable slaves to perish in the marshes of that most unhealthy climate in order to build this proud, handsome, aloof monu-ment[2] – 'a window into Europe',[3] as it was called, a challenge to traditional Russia of the most emphatic kind [...].

I was absolutely fascinated by your accounts of those stray characters who attached themselves to you, who hoped against hope to get out, or to get some sort of benefits from the foreigners, or to penetrate in some way the walls that surround them, whether physically or culturally. I wonder how many of them got into actual trouble for attaching themselves to you – not that you could help it. When they did that in the old days, of course, they got picked up at once and sent to fearful camps. Now I dare say it isn't quite so severe, but nevertheless one of my great reasons for not going to the Soviet Union is my feeling that if I talk to anyone, as I am liable to do, and get into a real conversation – which delights me, because there is nothing more agreeable than talking to simple, spontaneous people who have been bottled up for years, and then they realise there is someone from the Western world speaking their language with whom they can actually chat in some very spontaneous free fashion, not just ask questions but enter into a kind of personal relationship – I feel that they will have to pay dearly for this; and therefore although one may enjoy oneself a great deal it is at a cost for them which they themselves sometimes do not realise, since some of them live in a kind of fool's paradise. That happened certainly in 1945, and also in 1956, and I daren't risk it again. To me, the pleasure would be very great – but to them the cost.

I have a feeling that George Galitzine[4] would not be my cup of tea – I may

state 1918. Akhmatova lived (1926–41, 1944–52) in an apartment (now a museum devoted to her life and work) in the south rear wing, as common-law wife (since c.1924), then from 1938 ex-wife, of the art historian and critic Nikolay Punin (1888–1953, her 3rd and last husband), who lived there.

1 It still is.
2 St Petersburg was founded 1703 by Peter the Great on land won from Sweden during the Great Northern War (1700–21); sited in the marshy delta where the Neva river meets the Baltic, it was built largely by conscripted peasants and Swedish prisoners of war; tens of thousands perished in its construction.
3 Petersburg was called a 'gran finestrone, dirò così, novellamente aperto nel Norte, per cui la Russia guarda in Europa' ('a large window, so to speak, newly opened in the north, through which Russia looks at Europe') by Francesco Algarotti 30 June 1739: see *Saggio di lettere sopra la Russia* (Paris, 1760), letter 4, 55. The phrase 'a window into Europe' ('V Evropu [...] okno') was used by Pushkin, citing (inaccurately, evidently without the text before him) a French translation of Algarotti's work, *Lettres du comte Algarotti sur la Russie* (London [i.e. Paris?], 1769), 64, in the prologue to his poem *A Bronze Horseman: A Petersburg Tale* (1833), published posthumously in *Sovremennik* 5 (1837) no. 1, 1–21.
4 The anglicised version of the Russian name Golitsyn. (Prince) George (Georgy Vladimirovich) Galitzine (1916–92), businessman and Russian historian; of aristocratic lineage, his family left Russia 1919, settling in the UK; George Galitzine (Brasenose history 1935–8) served in the Welsh Guards during WW2, attaining the rank of major.

be wrong [...]. I have a slight phobia about White Russians – their charm doesn't work for me; there is always an undercurrent of anti-Semitism, and a desire to defend the indefensible in the old regime, and sometimes even a certain instinctive pride in the splendour of that regime, which did, after all, expand the frontiers of Russia and put an end to all those knock-kneed liberals, socialistic Jews and other subversive elements who did not understand the glories and agonies of the real Russia. All this may to some degree be justified, but Turgenev and I don't like it, whereas Dostoevsky obviously did. Tolstoy detested such people – in some sense, of course, he felt by origin and habits one of them, and that all the miseries and injustices of his country were brought about by his own class. All these complex emotions, which are not too far below the surface, embarrass me, and so I have kept away from White Russians all my life – except the very gentle, tame ones like my friend Dimitri Obolensky,[1] who is a professor here; and dear Nicolas Nabokov, a rotten liberal through and through, had exactly the same feelings about these people as I do.

I have a feeling that the physical appearance of Russians has changed as a result of the Revolution. All those beautiful, tall ladies with aristocratic features, who probably had Swedish and Finnish blood in them, have disappeared to make room for those fat laundresses, doubtless partly the product of the bread and potatoes on which many of them have had to live for too long. The type has actually changed – so has the outlook. Dear me, now I am talking like a White Russian [...].

I loved the anecdotes, I loved your letter.

Yours,

Isaiah

TO NORMAN STONE

15 December 1982

Headington House

Dear Mr Stone (with your permission I shall call you Norman, but not without),

I have read your splendid piece on EHC:[2] I may not be the most unbiased judge, but I can find nothing unjust in it – such minor points as I have, I shall now list.

[...] I am not sure how much insight he had into the Russian past. I think what fascinated him was individuals: Dostoevsky (quite genuinely), but Bakunin and Herzen in a rather curious way. No doubt remoteness from

---

1 (Prince) Dimitri Dimitrievich Obolensky (1918–2001), Kt 1984, Russian-born Oxford historian, student (i.e. fellow), Christ Church, 1950–85, prof. of Russian and Balkan history 1961–85.
2 'Grim Eminence', review of E. H. Carr, *The Twilight of the Comintern 1930–1935* (London/NY, 1982), LRB, 10 January 1983, 3–8. NS had sent IB an advance text.

his own world was a factor, but the thing I felt (particularly with regard to Bakunin, but also to a great extent with Herzen) is that he writes like a detached, ironical observer, a British official, as it were, in a foreign land, amused, even fascinated, by the goings-on of these eccentric, uncontrolled, slightly absurd creatures – their enthusiasms, their love affairs, their over-tense, over-excited relationships with each other, and indeed, with ideas too; with which, however, he feels no personal sympathy. Their agonies are not conveyed in the language of understanding, they are always being looked at through a telescope, and the habits of these odd foreigners are described much in the way that Norman Douglas writes about the 'Little White Cows' on Capri (Nepenthe) in *South Wind*[1] – a mixture, I suppose, of Gorky's Bolshevik summer-school attenders and dotty religious sectarians.[2] And all this for the entertainment of sane, sensible Englishmen who live in the real world (very different from, say, Maurice Baring's[3] genuine insight into at any rate his aristocratic–peasant Russia).

You have called that 'insight'. He reports accurately the movements, letters, political acts, domestic arrangements of these strange characters, but they remain marionettes, much as Roman emperors do to Gibbon. No life is infused into them, they remain on the stage. I think this is part of his entire treatment of people who do not seem to him serious. It extends to the silly liberal professors of the 1930s, Toynbee and Zimmern,[4] ranting away about collective security, liberal values or whatever, when they do not see the telegrams and dispatches and therefore cannot know what is really going on; and to the idiotic Russian émigrés of the 1920s and 1930s and later dates. But the Bolsheviks are serious because, as you of course say, they are in his view successful. They can only be taken really seriously if their success lasts for, I suppose, at least over half a century – that is why Bismarck, in his view,

1 (George) Norman Douglas (1868–1952), Austrian-born British writer. The novel *South Wind* (London, 1917) his best-known work, is set in Nepenthe, a fictional island based on Capri, where he then lived, and portrays philosophical hedonism. The phrase IB quotes is introduced in chapter 2: 'The Russian sect [...] were religious enthusiasts, [...] led by their Master, the divinely inspired Bazhakuloff [...]. They called themselves the "Little White Cows", to mark their innocence of worldly affairs' (16). In chapter 11 Bazhakuloff says he gave them this name because 'cows were pure and useful animals without which humanity could not live' (146). Douglas portrays them as naive devotees.
2 The Russian writer and political activist Aleksey Maksimovich Peshkov (1868–1936), known as Maxim Gorky ('Bitter'), lived 1906–13 on Capri, where he and his acolytes ran a school to teach Bolsheviks revolutionary socialism in terms of a Marxist (and so atheist) religious creed that he had adopted, and which, in his novel *Ispoved'* [*A Confession*] (Moscow, 1908), he dubbed *bogostroitel'stvo*, 'god-building'.
3 Maurice Baring (1875–1945), British diplomat, journalist, playwright, poet, travel writer, essayist, translator, war correspondent, brilliant linguist, and devoted Russophile before the Revolution; travelled extensively in Russia, about which he wrote a number of books, which IB adored.
4 Alfred Eckhard Zimmern (1879–1957), Kt 1936, classicist and internationalist; deputy director, League of Nations Institute of Intellectual Co-operation, Paris, 1926–30; 1st Montague Burton Prof. of International Relations, Oxford, and fellow, Balliol, 1930–44; secretary general to the Constituent Conference of UNESCO 1945.

was not a success, even though some people might think that [in] his own lifetime, at any rate, he had achieved all he had set out to do. You rightly say that Abramsky is obviously wrong in saying that he had interviewed everybody that he could on the Russian Revolution. Not only did he not do so, but he made it a principle not to – failures are only likely to try to exonerate themselves, and what is the use of listening to that? We don't want to hear why some batsmen score ducks, still less why they think they did, etc.

The question is: Why did he hate the Americans? Was that just general leftism? Maybe. But also, I think, because it is connected with the kind of class and type of person from whom he had suffered some humiliation – the British ruling class, the Victorian-Edwardian establishment, a world he wanted overthrown and which was being propped up by the USA. However, that is mere speculation.

You say that he was the most eminent left-wing British historian during his lifetime. I would tend to agree, but will AJPT concede that? Perhaps he would. He would certainly say so now, but not twenty years ago, I'll bet. Certainly he is more readable and, I should say, despite everything, a better historian. [...]

John Gross[1] once told me that an interesting BLitt could be written on the reviews of Russian books in the TLS during the Carr–Deutscher period (Deutscher's review of *Doctor Zhivago* was a famous monstrosity).[2] One of the differences between them was that Deutscher could not quite accept Carr's extreme contempt for ideas as factors in history: Carr had no fault to find with Deutscher. Yet what you say about Deutscher's book on Stalin[3] is absolutely right. The apparently dispassionate tone in which it is written conceals the most violent bias and distortions and suppressions: his treatment of Kronstadt[4] is no better than Carr's. I am glad you refer to the attempted suppression of Leonard Schapiro's first book – he would have had no career as a historian of Communism if this had succeeded.[5] [...]

Your last pages on him [Carr] are very devastating, but I cannot deny that they give me a certain amount of natural satisfaction.[6] I did find it difficult to swallow his genuine lack of interest in the complex nature of the facts – he did not bend the pattern he sought to impose. I feel that the early volumes

1 John Jacob Gross (1935–2011), writer and editor; editor, TLS, 1974–81; book reviewer, *New York Times*, 1983–8; theatre critic, *Sunday Telegraph*, 1989–2005.
2 'Pasternak and the Calendar of the Revolution', *Partisan Review* (1959), 248–65.
3 *Stalin: A Political Biography* (Oxford, 1949), Deutscher's 1st major work.
4 St Petersburg's main seaport, where in March 1921 there occurred the unsuccessful uprising against the Bolsheviks that IB refers to here, played down by Carr and Deutscher for what IB saw as partisan reasons.
5 41.
6 In his last paragraph Stone writes: 'I am nearly tempted to exclaim that no more useless set of volumes has ever masqueraded as a classic. Carr's real talent lay in mathematics. [...] from the mathematical spirit he took a quality not so much of abstraction as of autism, which was carried over into historical work. The result is a trail of devastation' (8).

of the History, which is all that I have ever read (and not much of that, save vol. 1, which I reviewed somewhere – I simply cannot remember where, perhaps in the *Sunday Times*)[1] were rather like reading a highly competent and clearly written official history of the activities of, say, the Foreign Office, based on its documents, without the aid of a single unofficial piece of information, written by a well-trained, highly competent bureaucrat with a gift for exposition, unswerving loyalty to his superiors and colleagues, not much regard for the far from simple, unsymmetrical nature of reality – that, quite apart from a peculiarly powerful contempt for the martyrs and the minorities, and a total disregard of the alternative solutions there were to given problems, even for Soviet rulers: the reasons for which they chose to do what they did, and rejected other alternatives, or ignored them, were sufficient and justifiable.

I must not go on. I think it is a fine piece, and serves much better now that he is dead. Despite his crude Marxist attacks on me personally, we got on, as I told you, quite well. He had not had an entirely happy life, and to add to his cup of misery, although it was not that full, would, perhaps, have been unkind. But now the truth can be told. It really is an object lesson of how not to write history, not to ignore ideas; and how personal resentment and coldness of nature are not the best qualities for those who attempt what men have done and suffered.[2] [...]

Yours ever,

Isaiah Berlin   [...]

TO EDWARD MORTIMER[3]

15 April 1983

Headington House

Dear Edward (I beg you not to stand on ceremony),

[...] What Reni Brendel[4] said to you is quite true. I did tell her, when she mentioned you in conversation, that your articles on Arab–Israeli conflict distressed me, and sometimes caused me bitter feeling: it is not so much their content as their tone that has this effect on me, and I daresay on other friends of Israel. What you say about my friendly feelings towards yourself and your family is entirely true. I felt this years ago, and do so still. [...] It is because

1 'Soviet Beginnings', review of E. H. Carr, *A History of Soviet Russia*, vol. 1: *The Bolshevik Revolution 1917–1923*, *Sunday Times*, 10 December 1950, 3.
2 Cf. 'what Alcibiades did and suffered' (157/1).
3 Edward Mortimer (b. 1943), author and journalist; fellow, All Souls, 1965–72, 1984–6 (and 2006–8; Distinguished Fellow from 2013); foreign specialist and leader writer, *Times*, 1973–85; Foreign Affairs Editor, *Financial Times*, 1987–98.
4 Irene Brendel (b. 1945) née Semler, German-born wife of 1st (m. 1975, later divorced) Alfred Brendel, 2nd (m. 2012) her partner since 2001, Ronald Dworkin; studied music and organ with Karl Richter in Munich, and became a cultural correspondent for German TV in London; sometime trustee, Opera Factory, and director, ROH, the Almeida Theatre and Aldeburgh Music.

of these feelings on my part, and because I know that you are completely honest in your beliefs and speak them without fear or favour, that I like and respect you personally; but I should have found it embarrassing to meet you socially without saying something about our differences. Had I not, I should have felt craven; and then we might have had a sharp argument, and that, I thought, would have been unfair to our hostess, to the Brendels, to all the others. There is nothing I dread so much as public altercation, but to have said nothing or to have said something mild would have made me feel ashamed.

When you say that you are not anti-Semitic, I find it astonishing that you should bother to say this. I find it almost offensive that you should suppose that I could think you anti-Semitic in any degree. I know that the line between anti-Zionism and anti-Semitism can be very thin at times, and that the partisan feelings which Israel engenders sometimes spill over, at times half consciously, into irritation with the Jews as such, and even dislike of them. But never conceivably could I have thought this about you.

Let me go back to the issue between us, and first of all, very briefly, state my own position. I am a Zionist, if only because I believe that neither the Jews nor anyone else should be condemned to be a minority everywhere, for that distorts human development, both of individuals and of peoples. Perhaps it would have been better for the Jews if they had been assimilated – disappeared, as the Assyrians and Carthaginians have.[1] But they have not, and their efforts to do so – at least on the part of some of them – have ended in ghastly and humiliating failure, particularly in countries where it appeared that they had been progressing most rapidly and effectively, e.g. Germany at the end of the last and beginning of this century, and Russia in the early years of the Revolution, before Stalin's real anti-Semitism became permanently respectabilised, *de facto*, as a widespread attitude in the Soviet Union. Also, I think that Palestine was the only country in which the Jews could have set up a genuine establishment of their own, for reasons which of course I could expound to you, and which you probably know very well, but for which there is obviously no space here.

Moreover, it is clear to me that the Arabs of Palestine have suffered an injustice, for reasons which again are self-evident. The question therefore is whether the misery of the Jews, and the danger to them in Muslim as well as Christian countries, did not outweigh the wound inflicted upon the Arabs. When conflicts of this kind arise, the least degree of misery (and injustice) is the only right goal to aim at, though what this is cannot be demonstrated conclusively by any methods that I recognise as valid (least of all historic rights, national self-determination, God's covenant with Abraham,

---

1 The extensive Assyrian civilisation, originating *c.*1300 BCE in northern Mesopotamia, succumbed to the Medes *c.*614–12 BCE. The utter destruction of the Phoenician city of Carthage (on the NE coast of modern Tunisia) by the Roman Empire 146 BCE was the climactic end to the 3rd and final Punic War of 149–146 BCE.

or any other a priori approach). It is a question of a painful empirical adjustment, and partition schemes seem to me to have been the least unjust in
the circumstances: i.e. a Jewish and an Arab state – what the very moderate
Arabs demand now, both Palestinian and others. The Zionists, *à contre-coeur*,[1]
did accept this: e.g. the recommendations in 1937 of the Peel Report;[2] of
the British cabinet plan in 1944[3] or whenever that was (at least Weizmann
regarded this as an acceptable minimum); of the United Nations; etc.

All these were rejected by the Arabs, who, of course, hated the whole
thing. Wars were fought, Jews won them, they held on to their gains to minimise as far as they could the dangers of being attacked again. The Arabs,
quite understandably, did not and do not want the Jews there at all [...]. The
view – which your articles offer to your readers – that the Arabs have been
maltreated, that the Israelis are wicked and often hypocritical aggressors,
and should at the very least be squeezed back into the pre-Six-Day-War, or
-1947, frontiers – with the implication that they should not have been there
at all – is a view held widely. Of course I know that one can be a decent,
fair-minded and honourable person and hold it – after all, the entire British
Foreign Office, with very few exceptions, have held it since virtually Curzon's
day; the entire State Department has held it, and holds it still; there is not
a Foreign Office in the world that, in my view, would not heave a sigh of
relief if Israel went out of existence – its continuance is of value to the Jews
alone. I don't think this is an exaggeration; and your expression of such sentiments is only a particularly sharp and uncompromising form of it.

As a result of the Arab–Jewish wars, and Arab feeling that at any rate
official British opinion was very much on their side, Arab bitterness and hostility to Israel have increased sharply; it is not unnatural that Israeli fears have
increased correspondingly. Most pro-Arabs would, I think, wish the Jews to
return to pre-1947 conditions, even though Hitler and the Russian pogroms
make it understandable that most Jews cannot want this to be the case. Of
course I realise that to be strongly pro-Arab is not to be a villain. What has
wounded me deeply and continuously in your articles is their tone more than
their content.

I say again that you have made yourself in effect the voice of the PLO,
which, as I am sure you will not deny, fundamentally seeks to regain the

1 'Reluctantly'.
2 The Royal Commission of Inquiry to Palestine (the 'Peel Commission') recommended, July 1937,
   the partition of Palestine between Jews and Arabs, the smaller Jewish state extending from the
   midwest to the north, and the Arab state from the mideast to the south; Arabs mostly rejected
   the plan, which they saw as a betrayal; Jewish opinion was divided, but Ben-Gurion favoured
   acceptance, without renouncing the principle that 'the Land of Israel' meant the whole of
   Palestine.
3 In January 1944 the British cabinet approved a proposal for the partition of Palestine after the war,
   based loosely on the recommendations of the Peel Commission (previous note); after the assassination of Lord Moyne (3) the plan, which anyway had determined opponents in the government, was effectively abandoned.

whole of Palestine – *reconquista*[1] – and out with the Jews if necessary; it will only swallow them if it absolutely must (and most of them don't think that even now), because of their inability to drive them out; all of which they blame – naturally enough – on America. So far as I know, you have not at any point conceded anything to the point of view of, or a case for, the immigrants into Palestine – for them and their Israeli children – whose last best hope of a normal life Israel in fact constitutes, and who view a PLO state as dedicated to the destruction of the Jewish state, if not immediately, then by stages, as the Carthaginians were slowly eliminated: or Outremer.[2]

You may think the Jewish case is weaker than that of the Arabs, as I think it stronger; but if one is to be minimally fair, one must balance one's passionate and understandable pro-Palestine indignation with some degree of understanding of, even if one cannot generate any sympathy for, the population which came initially only to live a normal life – the number of aggressive Jewish nationalists in 1918 was minute and uninfluential – and found itself caught in a trap, and like other trapped animals sometimes strikes out blindly and self-destructively

[…] if the Jews are to give up the West Bank, cannot the PLO yield something concrete? Before 1972 a large majority of Israelis were, in my view, ready to give up most of the West Bank for peace. Now they don't think that the PLO means peace. And Arafat's inability to say the word 'Israel', save in execration, reinforces this. […]

I won't argue with you about whether an Israel side by side with a West Bank PLO-dominated state is feasible – I don't think so; but that is an empirical point which does not, at least for me, involve any issue of principle. What I want to stress is that anyone reading your articles cannot help feeling that the Israelis are pretty black, with very few exceptions indeed, and that none of the Arabs are so – at most they are light grey. Is this unfair? […]

We ought to talk this out. I am glad Mrs B[rendel] spoke to you: she simply assumed, from my complaints about your tone, that our meeting might have embarrassed me; I do find my feelings about your pieces difficult to bear or swallow, but a conversation will do much, I hope, to make things easier. You are quite right: angry silence is worst of all […]. Private life and personal relations are not everything, but they are a very great deal; I cannot believe that you believe the opposite.

Yours sincerely,
    Isaiah Berlin

PS It is a historical irony that the PLO is a mirror image of the Zionist

---

1 'Reconquest', 'recapture'.
2 'Beyond the sea', the Frankish name given to the Latin (i.e. Western European) kingdom of Jerusalem established after the First Crusade (1096–9).

Revisionists,[1] created by the Jews: the same passion, slogans, actions. Partition is, I am sure, in principle, the only way out. If only Begin, Sharon, Abu Nidal,[2] Arafat would go.

I have remembered a curious image produced by Isaac Deutscher, for whose doctrines in general I have little sympathy, and who was, of course, wholly anti-Zionist: it was of a man in a burning house jumping out of the window on to the back of another man standing casually in the street, who was knocked out by this.[3] I infer, even if Deutscher did not mean, that room in the street had to be found for both, in 1918, not just 1945. I think there is a good deal in that analogy. Do you disagree?

TO HENDRIK HOETINK[4]

15 June 1983

Headington House

Dear Dr Hoetink,

Thank you for your letter of 11 May: it put very searching and central questions to me, which go to the heart of my entire position. I wish I were one of those people who know the true answers and are not assailed by doubts either about the solutions themselves or their own capacity to reach them. Auguste Comte, the logical positivists of the 1920s and 1930s, my colleagues in Oxford Professors Hare and Dummett, are not, so far as I know, assailed by doubts about their positions. I am. Still, I should like to tell you what I believe at present.

I wish I thought that Goethe was right: that all men in their *dunkelen Streben*[5] nevertheless knew the right path, however different in different times

---

1 Revisionist Zionism emerged in the 1920s under the leadership of Ze'ev Jabotinsky (238/2); it had right-wing overtones, and rejected gradualism, demanding the immediate establishment of a Jewish state in all of Palestine and Transjordan, a project in which the British Mandatory authority was expected to co-operate.

2 Sabri Khalil al-Banna (1937–2002), known as Abu Nidal ('Father of the Struggle'), founder and leader, Fatah (a backwards acronym from the Arabic for 'Conquest by Jihad') Revolutionary Council, also known as the Abu Nidal Organization, ruthless Palestinian splinter group responsible for numerous acts of terror in the 1970s and 1980s.

3 'A man once jumped from the top floor of a burning house in which many members of his family had already perished. He managed to save his life; but as he was falling he hit a person standing down below and broke that person's legs and arms. The jumping man had no choice; yet to the man with the broken limbs he was the cause of his misfortune. If both behaved rationally, they would not become enemies. [...] But look what happens when these people behave irrationally. The injured man blames the other for his misery and swears to make him pay for it.' Isaac Deutscher (in a 1967 interview), *The Non-Jewish Jew and Other Essays* (London, 1968), 136. In 'Israel's Spiritual Climate' (1954) Deutscher had written: 'I have, of course, long since abandoned my anti-Zionism' (ibid. 111).

4 Hendrik Richard Hoetink (b. 1929), Dutch curator; director 1975–99 Praemium Erasmianum Foundation, Amsterdam, which awarded IB an Erasmus Prize 1983; director, Mauritshuis, The Hague, 1972–91.

5 sc. 'dunklen Streben' ('dark urge'). In the 'Prologue in Heaven' in Goethe's *Faust* God says: 'Ein

and places. I don't think this. Men have been responsible for what almost everyone would now regard as frightful acts – massacres of the innocent, destruction of entire societies and cultures (against which God warns Jonah in the last verses of that remarkable book of the Old Testament)[1] – in the full conviction that what they have done is wholly and eternally right; not just because of errors of fact, e.g. that there are *Untermenschen*[2] and that Jews and Gypsies are such, but because of dedication to purposes and values which we may find detestable or barbarous. If I deny, as I do, the absolute authority of universal laws and truths – which hold for everyone everywhere – arrived at by some species of infallible intuition, or metaphysical reasoning, or faith, or revelation, or theological reasoning, am I then committed to some species of relativism or subjectivism, as so many have supposed, and still suppose? I think not. These are my reasons.

I accept the obvious validity of the views of those who believe in an empirical version of 'natural law'[3] (e.g. my colleague Herbert Hart), namely, that minimum of moral values accepted by all men without which human societies would disintegrate, and from which, for quasi-biological causes, men cannot depart without perishing. Such are the perception of the difference of good and bad,[4] of true and false, perhaps of just and unjust. Without this minimum no life can be lived long: nothing is predictable; communication between men (and I daresay animals) cannot occur; no society can begin to exist if there are no hopes or fears; or if there is universal lying (i.e. no predictable behaviour of things or persons), universal murder and so on. So *some* common values are indispensable for the most primitive associations. This does form a kind of universally accepted 'natural law'; but it is not nearly *sufficient* to give us what we need – constellations, systems, of values to govern life.

Next, there is the need for communication between human beings. If I cannot communicate with you, if your behaviour follows no rules that I can understand or grasp (whether I approve or not), you are not a human being for me: we don't live in the same world. If, to use Hume's example, I meet

guter Mensch, in seinem dunklen Drange, / Ist sich des rechten Weges wohl bewußt' ('A good man, in his dark urge, is well aware of the right path').

1 In the last verse of Jonah (4:11) God says: 'And should not I spare Nineveh, that great city, wherein are more than sixscore thousand persons that cannot discern between their right hand and their left hand; and also much cattle?'

2 'Subhumans'; a term infamously employed by the Nazis to identify those, such as Jews and Gypsies, whom they considered racially inferior.

3 See 276.

4 It is unclear here whether IB means simply people's ability to separate (whatever they regard as) good and bad, or whether specific judgements as to what is good and bad are also implied. (The latter interpretation is perhaps suggested by what IB writes elsewhere, e.g. 'there is a great deal of broad agreement among people in different societies over long stretches of time about what is right and wrong, good and evil': CTH2 19.) This apparent ambiguity afflicts many of his statements on this point. Truth and justice are perhaps different, since they can to some extent be established by less controversial criteria.

a man who simply *cannot see* why he should not destroy the world to relieve a soreness on his little finger,[1] I have no means of conducting a wholly meaningful dialogue with him. The minimum values needed for intercommunication are in this sense an objective, not a subjective, need: part of the objective world which we inhabit together, which we literally cannot do without. This will not exclude relativity in a wide sphere. The ends of life – values – can differ widely. So I continue.

If the number of possible human ends is literally infinite, a kind of relativistic 'ideal utilitarianism'[2] would follow: I live for collecting green objects because they are green; you destroy all blue objects because they are blue. These are our ultimate ends: there is no overarching criterion or scale of values to determine whether either of us is right or wrong. We just do have the ends we have: ends cannot be criticised. The only thing we can do is to judge, on the basis of experience, experiment etc. which are the best means to those ends. Such utilitarianism is called 'ideal' because not only happiness or pleasure, but literally *anything* – worship of the one God, destruction of certain types of beetle, creation of works of art, torture of small children – anything – can be an ultimate end which governs someone's life. If I cannot understand why you think about nothing but how to accumulate matchboxes, not because this gives you pleasure (I could understand that – just), but because they are matchboxes, I call you irrational; but nothing follows; it is an end of life, as good as any other, uncriticisable; there is no criterion of criticism. That would lead to pure subjectivism or relativism.

I don't believe that human beings *are* like that. I believe (on the basis of the collective, recorded experience of mankind and the data of observation) that the number of pursuable human ends is not unlimited. You asked me whether I thought that there was a 'core' human nature; not, as you rightly surmised, *quod semper, quod ubique, quod ab omnibus*;[3] but in the sense that only some values, some ends, can be ultimate goals for human beings. Yes. Some of them are indeed incompatible with one another, and this entails the incoherence of the idea of perfection – of the possibility of a harmony of all human values. But there are only 17 or 83 or 117 such, not an infinity.

By value[s] and ends I do not mean isolated values: peace or liberty or happiness or justice or love or artistic activity – too general in any case; capable of much specification and interpretation. I mean reasonably coherent visions

---

1 'It is not contrary to reason to prefer the destruction of the whole world to the scratching of my finger.' David Hume, *A Treatise of Human Nature* 2. 3. 3. 6.

2 According to which the goodness or badness of actions depends on how far they contribute to the achievement of whatever ideals are taken to be intrinsically good. The term was coined by Hastings Rashdall in chapter 7, 'Ideal Utilitarianism', of *The Theory of Good and Evil: A Treatise on Moral Philosophy* (Oxford, 1907) at 184, but the doctrine was previously espoused by G. E. Moore in *Principia Ethica* (Cambridge, 1903).

3 'Quod ubique, quod semper, quod ab omnibus creditum est' ('what is believed everywhere, always, by everyone'): Vincent of Lérins, *Commonitorium* 2. 3.

of life; patterns of behaviour and beliefs and feeling and disposition and ideals grandly called *Weltanschauungen*;[1] entire structures, entire ways of life, in which the values or ends or motives are interconnected in particular ways, so that one cannot simply remove 'a value' or 'a purpose' from one pattern – that of an industrial organiser or a religious army general, a socialist doctor or a sceptical liberal intellectual – and transplant it from one of these patterns into another. They form wholes: 'organic', some call them, though I do not find that this biological metaphor adds all that much.

I believe that the network of values realised in these ways of life – limited by being ends of more or less sane human beings and not angels or lunatics – are objective in the sense that they embrace goals which human beings *can* pursue as human beings, as they can contract pneumonia, but not grow a thousand feet tall. They are such that, even if I myself don't hold them, or reject or even detest them, nevertheless I can understand how, in a given situation, with a given (intelligible to me) character, a man or woman could coherently pursue them.

That is what Vichian or Herderian empathy is for (*Einfühlen*).[2] I can imaginatively enter – have an insight – into what it must have been like to be a Greek slave, or a Roman soldier, or a martyr, a Jacobin, a royalist, a Communist, an ayatollah, a Chinese anti-imperialist, an American hippy. With enough knowledge of the relevant historical facts and enough imaginative insight, I ought to be able to grasp why the Christian 'deadly sins' did not include, say, cruelty or treachery, which I consider far worse than gluttony or accidie, which are included in the list. The spiritual pattern, relation to God, is conceived in a way I may not share or sympathise with, but am able to comprehend. This comprehensibility gives the medieval Christian outlook an objective status as one of 17 or 181 ways of living open to men; pure relativism or subjectivism does *not* require the possibility of understanding of other outlooks or customs or ways of life, public or private.

All these 'varieties of experience' – William James's pluralism is the doctrine I feel closest to[3] – are authentic and capable of being lived through by X and understood by Y, across centuries and vast spaces. It is the inability to allow for this that makes much of the otherwise marvellously liberating French Enlightenment so unhistorical and dogmatically self-centred and blind to what human beings and lives can be – the whole rich tapestry of the

---

1 'Conceptions of life'.
2 Literally 'feeling into'.
3 William James (1842–1910), US psychologist and philosopher, brother of the novelist Henry James. IB alludes to his 1901–2 Gifford Lectures, *The Varieties of Religious Experience: A Study in Human Nature* (London and NY, 1902). James did indeed espouse what he called pluralism – see in particular his Hibbert Lectures, *A Pluralistic Universe* (NY etc., 1909) – but it cannot be said that he fully anticipated IB's value pluralism, for all that there are passages in his work that strongly call IB's view to mind: see ⟨http://berlin.wolf.ox.ac.uk/lists/pluralism/index.html⟩ s.v. 'James, William'.

human past, with its repeated and unrepeated patterns – and gives it a thin lucidity at the cost of variety, and above all depth.

Much of the difference of outlooks is, of course, due to sheer empirical illusions: that there is a Moloch which clamours for human sacrifice; or that burning people at the stake improves their chances of avoiding hell; or that there are subhuman creatures, biologically identifiable – Blacks, Jews etc.; or that self-flagellation opens the gate to spiritual illumination. If these remediable errors and illusions are discounted, the values of different sects and ideologies may turn out to be much more similar than is commonly thought. Basic differences of human outlook have been much exaggerated. But they exist. The world of the rich *is* different from that of the poor; of tycoons from that of artists; of a Jewish atonal composer from that of an Arab peasant; Khomeini's from Voltaire's. But provided they are intelligible, form choosable lives – ones I can conceive of, or imagine, myself as capable of entertaining in a particular place and time and context – then, however remote or odious it may be to me as I am, they are, in my sense, objective: human nature is definable in terms of this diapason.

So Vico tells us that only men who are mean, cruel, oppressive, intensely ambitious, could have generated the *Iliad* and *Odyssey*.[1] In so far as we claim to understand these masterpieces, and recognise them as works of genius, we can enter into the Homeric world as a possible life for us, had we been there then. I reject Homeric life; I am repelled by the world of Wagner's tetralogy; but I can enter into them imaginatively. If there is no 'common ground', there is no understanding or communication. The common ground does not entail a common 'core': Wittgenstein's 'family resemblance' is sufficient.[2] If A has something in common with B, B with C, C with D, etc., I can move along this line and finally arrive at Z; there need be no centre, no 'basic' human nature, no 'natural man' stripped of all his acquired characteristics. This is not like relativism, which says 'I like my coffee black' v. 'I want it white' – two 'brute facts' with no bridge between them; no common ground; where anyone might be of any sort, pursue any end – everyone to his taste.

The real (objective) human values are, as it were, given. They cannot be invented. They are developments of a finite set of humanly leadable lives. Anyone who is identifiable in terms of at any rate some constituents of one of these leadable lives – possible outlooks and dispositions – is for me

1 e.g. 'Nor could the truculent and savage style in which [Homer] describes so many, such varied and such bloody battles, so many and such extravagantly cruel kinds of butchery as make up all the sublimity of the *Iliad* in particular, have originated in a mind humanised and softened by any philosophy.' *The New Science of Giambattista Vico*, trans. Thomas Goddard Bergin and Max Harold Fisch (Ithaca, NY, 1948), para. 785; cf. para. 338.
2 See e.g. Ludwig Wittgenstein, *Philosophical Investigations*, trans. G. E. M. Anscombe (Oxford, 1953), §§66–7. Whether this notion applies to IB's idea of a common human nature may be doubted: in many places, including this letter, he espouses the view that there are some basic universal principles common to all human beings, for all that they may be variously expressed in different cultures. This view seems both true and not captured by Wittgenstein's concept.

a human being. How many constituents it is impossible to specify – a suf-
ficiency. This is what I should like to call objective pluralism: choosable, intelligible lives and outlooks. [...]
        Yours sincerely,
        Isaiah Berlin   [...]

TO PHILIP MOORE[1]

        27 June 1983 [carbon]

                                                          Headington House
Dear Philip,
        I have made a very private enquiry, via a common friend, of Francis Bacon[2]
(he was told that I, who knew him, would like to send an unsolicited letter
to someone at the Palace recommending an OM). He said that he would
not accept it, that he wished 'to remain as he was at birth, with no added
attributes'. Of course, once approached, he *might* take it. But I think, on the
whole, better not.
        I am quite sure there is no other British painter or sculptor of OM quality.
Lucian Freud[3] is nearest, but he has just got a CH, and Moynihan[4] and
Gowing[5] and Spear[6] and Carel Weight[7] and so on are talented but not of
the first class. I wonder if John Betjeman is right for this? He is far from well,
and he *has* created a world of his own, and his verse has made an impact on
writers, as well as gained a popularity with the public unparalleled by any
other poet. He *is* a kind of (minor) genius, in my view. Is he too old? An OM
would be well received, I believe. I wish we had a marvellous architect or film
producer; and one actor is enough.[8]
        The only other person who seems suitable to me is the art historian Sir

1 Philip Brian Cecil Moore (1921–2009), KCVO 1976, life peer 1986; PS to the Queen and Keeper,
  Queen's Archives, 1977–86; director, General Accident, Fire and Life Assurance Corporation,
  1986–91; Permanent Lord-in-Waiting to the Queen 1990–2009; in his capacity as a senior courtier
  he had in the past encouraged IB to suggest names of possible candidates for the OM.
2 Francis Bacon (1909–92), the most acclaimed British painter of the C20th, known for his disturbing exploration of the human condition. It has been supposed that his homosexuality and
  bohemian lifestyle precluded his consideration for any official honour, but IB's letter suggests
  otherwise.
3 Lucian Michael Freud (1922–2011), CH 1983, OM 1993; German-born British painter, draughtsman
  and etcher, grandson of Sigmund Freud; both Aline and IB (plate 38) were later his subjects.
4 (Herbert George) Rodrigo Moynihan (1910–90), Tenerife-born British artist whose work fluctu-
  ated beween the figurative and the abstract; prof. of painting, Royal College of Art, 1948–57.
5 Lawrence Burnett Gowing (1918–1991), Kt 1982, painter and writer on painting; prof. of fine art,
  Leeds, 1967–75; Slade Prof. of Fine Art, UCL, 1975–85; painted 2 portraits of IB, one of which is in
  the National Portrait Gallery, the other at CCC.
6 (Augustus John) Ruskin Spear (1911–90), artist, noted for his portraits and landscapes; visiting
  teacher, Royal College of Art, 1952–77.
7 Carel Victor Morlais Weight (1908–97), British painter and art teacher; prof. of painting, Royal
  College of Art, 1957–73.
8 Laurence Olivier (264/2).

Ernst Gombrich. He *has* made a vital difference to his subject (which is my criterion for scholars in the humanities) – nobody in art history can ignore him. In that respect he stands alone, like Syme, and much more than Kenneth Clark. I think all art historians would acknowledge this, whether they like his views or not.

Yours ever,

Isaiah Berlin

TO CLAUS MOSER[1]

[July 1983, *carbon*]

Headington House

[...] One of the most startling things is that there is no effort in this report[2] to compare British operatic with European experience. Even the most passionate regionalist cannot but profit from knowing how opera is supported in the provincial capitals of e.g. Germany, Italy, and even Switzerland and France; about the dominant part that municipal aid plays there; and how well they do without an Arts Council (but never mind about that). There really are some lessons to be learnt about what to do and to avoid, which it is typical British parochialism to ignore – that does seem to me worth saying, however irritating.

Broadcasts [...]: if Carl Rosa[3] and visits by the troops to the Naples opera at the end of the war have had this splendid effect on hoi polloi, then why are there not more broadcasts, why only on the Third Programme or BBC2? Why not on BBC and TV1[4] as well? This really would be a very good thing. The chief obstacle is surely the unions, I imagine. Isn't that right? We are told that the costs of the big five companies are likely to increase because of 'international producers, designers, conductors, artists'. And what about the unions? NATKE, MU, Equity?[5] It is not the foreign canaries and maestri who cost that much more, as we know, but chorus, orchestra, stage-hands etc.

---

1 There is no salutation in the carbon, and the sign-off is 'Dictated but not read by Sir Isaiah Berlin, before going abroad'. The hypothesis we have adopted is that this is a memorandum sent to CM for distribution to the ROH board, though CM himself is uncertain about this.

2 IB had seen an advance text of the 'Priestley Report': Clive Priestley of the government's Efficiency Unit submitted *The Financial Affairs and Financial Prospects of the Royal Opera House, Covent Garden Ltd and the Royal Shakespeare Company: Report to the Earl of Gowrie, Minister for the Arts* in September 1983.

3 The Royal Carl Rosa Opera Company, founded 1875 by the German violinist and impresario Karl August Nikolaus Rose ('Carl Rosa') (1842–89), who settled in England 1866, and his wife the soprano Euphrosyne Parepa-Rosa (1836–74); it became a touring company, accorded the title 'Royal' by Queen Victoria 1893.

4 Presumably BBC1 and ITV.

5 The National Association of Theatrical and Kine Employees (NATKE), founded 1890, subsumed within the Broadcasting and Entertainment Trades Alliance 1984; the Musicians' Union, founded 1893 as the Amalgamated Musicians' Union; Equity, founded 1930, the UK trade union for professional performers and those in the creative arts.

Tremendously well worth emphasising this point – the talk of snobbish use of foreigners needs refuting.

This comes up again [...]: we are pandering to international stars in the choice of operas, and this is positively bad for opera. Here we must say what John Tooley has repeated so often, that one of the central purposes of any great opera house – one of the big five [sc. four], Scala, Vienna, the Met, us, and, well below that, Paris, West Berlin, East Berlin, Hamburg, Rome, Naples etc. – is to give the public an opportunity of hearing the greatest (or, indeed, the most famous) singers of our times. The history of opera is largely the history of singers, for whom Rossini,[1] Verdi, Donizetti,[2] and indeed Mozart and Wagner, composed parts in their operas. The degree to which we yield to the wishes of these world-famous singers is not great, and if we did not the public would rightly feel cheated and be displeased. And this would be bad, not good, for opera. The objection is a typically priggish-populist-academic resentment of glamour in any form – and yet vocal splendour is the heart of opera in its great period. This can be said with some emphasis: it is part of being first-rate. And [it is] no good saying that Welsh, Scottish, Kent have come on tremendously and are practically the equal of ROH and even ENO: they are not, and this [is] regionalist fanaticism and anti the alleged wealth and fashion supposedly found at Covent Garden.

[...] We are accused of 'an unimpressive record' in respect of 'new works'. Something was said about this at the Board, but we really ought to list the entire *oeuvre* of Britten[3] and Tippett,[4] and the works of Henze,[5] Tavener,[6] Searle,[7] Maxwell Davies,[8] and indeed Schoenberg[9] (we started off *Moses and Aaron* on its world career) and his *Erwartung*, Shostakovich, Janáček,[10]

---

1 Gioachino Antonio Rossini (1792–1868), Italian composer noted for his choral and chamber music, but especially his comic operas, above all *The Barber of Seville* (1816).

2 Domenico Gaetano Maria Donizetti (1797–1848), Italian composer, principally of operas, notably *Lucia di Lammermoor* (1835).

3 (Edward) Benjamin Britten (1913–76), OM 1965, life peer 1976, regarded as the pre-eminent British composer of the mid C20th, famous in particular for his operas, notably *Peter Grimes* (1945); IB was not an unqualified admirer (L3 102).

4 Michael Kemp Tippett (1905–98), Kt 1966, OM 1983, English composer, known especially for his oratorio *A Child of Our Time* (1944).

5 Hans Werner Henze (1926–2012), German conductor and versatile and prolific composer, with wide literary interests.

6 John Kenneth Tavener (1944–2013), later (2000) Kt, English composer and organist; prof. of composition, Trinity College of Music, London, 1968–2013.

7 Humphrey Searle (1915–82), English composer and writer on music, expert on Liszt; prof. of composition, Royal College of Music, 1965–82.

8 Peter Maxwell Davies (b. 1934), Kt 1987, composer and conductor; artistic director, Dartington Hall Summer School of Music, 1979–84; associate composer/conductor, Scottish Chamber Orchestra 1985–94, Royal Philharmonic Orchestra 1992–2000; conductor/composer, BBC Philharmonic Orchestra, 1992–2001.

9 Arnold Franz Walter Schoenberg (1874–51), Austrian-born composer, conductor and teacher; US citizen 1941; a revolutionary figure in C20th music; IB championed the British premiere of his unfinished opera *Moses and Aaron* at the ROH 1964: L3 181–2.

10 Leoš Eugen Janáček (1854–1928), Czech composer, conductor and organist famed for his operas.

whom I think we produced before ENO; and indeed *Lulu*, which counts as modern because hitherto not done in full. It is a monstrous charge. We have, of course, lost a lot of money over this, but still regard it as our sacred duty. This charge should be hit quite hard.

In connection with this [...], we are urged to increase the public's taste for new works by 'education' etc., which the regional companies are said to be doing. In fact, we know perfectly well that nobody has succeeded in doing this: all new works are resisted by the public everywhere, for obvious reasons. *Grimes*, after 40 years (?) and *Wozzeck* after 50, are still money-losers, at any rate in England. Schoolmasters all over England promote school performances of British composers, etc., but this has done little good from the box office point of view. This is a pious wish on the part of the committee, and should be described as such. One of the true reasons for this situation is, of course, that there is very little good modern opera, and people prefer to listen to nineteenth-century works not simply because they are more familiar, but because they are much better. Everyone secretly knows this. If the perfectly worthy champions of new music (even our own Alexander Goehr,[1] naturally) desire this, they must demand a huge subsidy for it, otherwise no good, except flops *d'estime*[2] at best.

[...] What is meant by saying that ROH audiences (apart from ticket prices 'separately mentioned') are 'weighted in favour of the economically and socially privileged'? Does it mean that people in jeans feel ill at ease? This seems to me Hoggartian[3] claptrap all the same. This is bound to be true of all the great opera houses, but it is equally true of the Bolshoi, Zagreb, and I dare say in Siberian towns as well. Perhaps there is nothing to be said about that, although it would be as well to say something in order to make them spell out just what they do mean: would it be a concession to them if we served beer in the crush bar, as I suspect we do not? Does ENO? Anyway, the difference between a great opera house and a Volksoper[4] is bound to exist, and there is plainly a need for both. When the televised Bayreuth *Ring* was looked at by one million persons, it shows that when things are first-rate the public does respond. [...]

It is not true that commercial sponsors only support what is 'known and fashionable'. If composers of the order of Stravinsky or Britten were still writing, business would support that too. The idea of not giving business sponsors too much credit is an old Arts Council demand – it is ridiculous. It is the function and duty of the Arts Council to provide funds, but not that

1 Alexander Goehr (b. 1932), composer; prof. of music, Cambridge, and fellow, 1976–99; director, ROH, 1982–4.
2 'Critical flops'.
3 (Herbert) Richard Hoggart (1918–2014), Warden, Goldsmiths, London, 1976–84, was an enthusiast for popular culture, and for bringing art to the working class.
4 'People's opera house' putting on popular classical operas, operettas and classic musicals.

of commercial enterprises, so why should we be asked to give exaggerated thanks to Roy Shaw[1] (from whom it comes), and not to Commercial Union? This point, in a mild way, should be made. [...]

[IB pp PU]

In 1983 BBC2 TV's Timewatch[2] *interviewed Jenifer Hart[3] for a programme about British Intelligence in the 1930s. Hart had joined the Communist Party in the summer of 1933 at Oxford, and had been told to keep her membership a secret on joining the Home Office in 1935, so that she could act as a 'mole' or sleeper. In her 1998 autobiography* Ask Me No More[4] *Hart claimed to have left the CPGB in 1939, and denied ever passing on any secrets, but during the 1960s she was twice interviewed by MI5, and by 1983 it was public knowledge that she was suspected of having been a Soviet agent. She saw the interview with* Timewatch *as an opportunity to address these suspicions, and spoke candidly of the appeal of Communism for her generation. Soon afterwards she was contacted by an ex-lodger, now a journalist, who alluded ominously to the BBC press releases for the programme, and invited her to set the record straight. This she ill-advisedly attempted to do, describing once again the importance of Communist ideals in the 1930s, and remarking: 'I mean one felt one wasn't a narrow patriot: I never felt much loyalty to my country, but don't say that.'[5]*

The telephone conversation was secretly recorded, and formed the basis of an article in the Sunday Times, *17 July 1983, 'I Was Russian Spy, Says MI5 Man's Wife'. The article not only stated that she had admitted to being a Soviet agent, but implied that her husband was complicit, having known of her involvement while he was at MI5. The Harts subsequently sued the* Sunday Times *for defamation, and won costs, but the paper issued only a 'very brief and wholly inadequate' apology,[6] and in October of that year Herbert Hart suffered a nervous breakdown. While IB had great sympathy for Jenifer, he regarded her husband, also a close friend, as the real victim of the whole affair. 'It is worse for him – all this – than for her,' he wrote to Pat Utechin: 'he is so impeccable & upright – [...] She doesn't care much, I suspect.'[7] Much later he wrote to Diana Hopkinson,[8] a near contemporary of Jenifer Hart at Oxford: 'What a tangled story it is. Nobody seems to have emerged well out of it, except for Herbert, who was so falsely accused. It really was a monstrous attack, disgusting in every detail.'[9]*

---

1 Roy Shaw (1918–2012), Kt 1979; secretary general, Arts Council of Great Britain, 1975–83.
2 Broadcast 27 July 1983.
3 Jenifer Margaret *Hart (1914–2005), civil servant and historian.
4 London, 1998.
5 Nicola Lacey, *A Life of H. L. A. Hart: The Nightmare and the Noble Dream* (Oxford 2004), 338–40 at 340; JH's specific comment about loyalty was reported by her husband in a letter to IB postmarked 28 August 1983.
6 *Ask Me No More* (215/4), 78.
7 To Pat Utechin, n.d. [July 1983].
8 Diana Mary *Hopkinson (1912–2007), writer.
9 To Diana Hopkinson, 21 March 1986; see also 492–3.

TO JENIFER HART

10 August 1983 [*manuscript*]

Paraggi

Dearest Jenifer,

Your letter really did upset us: the lies, bad faith, malice, desire to throw intellectuals to the lions of the political pornography hungry (as Herbert rightly calls it) public is very disgusting. After Stuart's horrible experience at the hands of a similar scoundrel from the *Observer* (did you not see his letter on this in the *Times*?[1] he was helped to draft it, on my pressing advice, by Arnold G[oodman][2] – his pride rebelled against this, but sense prevailed)[3] you shd have known better: & your sharp treatment of whoever it was from MI5 who reasonably called on you, in the 1960ies was it? After Blunt was blown? did not help:[4] & I do see that Herbert must be even more upset: at least you did dabble in Communism – I had *no* idea of it at the time! – whereas he is super-honourable (oh dear does that mean to imply that I think you are *not*? I do *not*, I *cannot*, mean to imply this: you are *far* too wedded to principles, odd ones at times, but lack of integrity is *not* an attribute of yours) and patriotic and Caesar's wife: of course he knew all about your wanderings – but by 1939 you had been converted to reason,[5] & it had no relevance to his war work. Still all that is in the past. My view is (a) that Goodman is a tremendous authority on relations to the Press: he usually advises against proceedings both because the press is very heavily defended by legal experts, but even more because even if you win, you are liable to endless persecution

---

1 In a letter to *The Times* 2 years before, Hampshire had recounted the 'disagreeable experience' of being shown the draft of an article, to be published the next day in a national newspaper 'not ordinarily associated with sensationalism', insinuating that he 'was plausibly suspected of having been a Soviet agent'. After 'a persuasive friend remonstrated with the acting editor', he was told that the article would not appear, but he appealed for an end to 'this selling of newspapers with the aid of speculative spy stories': 'Danger of Taste for Spy Stories', *Times*, 1 December 1981, 11g.

2 Arnold Abraham Goodman (1913–95), life peer 1965, founder and consultant, Goodman Derrick and Co., solicitors; Master of Univ. 1976–86. Among his many roles he had been chair, Observer Editorial Trust 1967–76, Newspaper Publishers Association 1970–6: 'The darker side of this remarkable life was that he used his influence to protect powerful people from the press, and sometimes the quick fixes he put in place caused more long-term harm than good' (Brian Brivati, ODNB).

3 'I thought it right & quite brave, given his sensitivity & natural reticence, to have struck back: it all seems to me a kind of political pornography & quite disgusting. I am sure you agree: am I being priggish? I think not.' To A. J. P. Taylor, 6 December 1981.

4 In her memoirs *Ask Me No More* (London, 1998), Hart recounts being contacted by MI5 1962, and again 1966. Peter Wright, author of *Spycatcher: The Candid Autobiography of a Senior Intelligence Officer* (NY and Toronto, 1987), was present on both occasions, the 2nd of which Hart remembered as 'a long and rather nasty affair'; she afterwards wrote to Wright in connection with this interview, and that may be the 'sharp treatment' that IB refers to here, though in her memoirs (75–6) Hart gives no indication of being severe with Wright.

5 This is generally given as the date when Hart left the CPGB, but IB wrote to Pat Utechin July 1983: 'Poor old Jenifer: I am fond of her & sorry: I had no idea she only lapsed after the war – she told *me* she had been converted by Herbert by 1938 or 1939' (cf. 492).

by journalists (goodness how far less honourable & civilized & decent a profession in England than in America or France or Germany! I wonder why) for the rest of your life. So do listen to me, & consult Goodman privately, no matter what your solicitor says; his advice on writing a letter to a journal wd have saved you much trouble.

b) If you need "conservative" character witnesses or Herbert does (what an irony! Aristides[1] in search of testimony to uprightness!) – [...] Richard Wilberforce is *excellent*; also Beloff[2] who is often silly and strident, but perfectly decent & brave, & has known you as a real friend for years. *Not* Quinton, who looks on Herbert as a detractor (Politics Chair etc.).[3] What about Lord Dacre? Whatever he is thought to be, not a pillar of the Left; & he deeply respects Herbert (pity he left "The Club!").[4] Is Dick White[5] out of [the] question? John Maud wd have done very well: so wd H. W. B. Joseph.[6] Sparrow too far gone. Finnis?[7] Blake (is he a friend or ex-friend of Herbert? I imagine not.) Warnock?[8] Very conservative look: & relevant as Vice-Chancellor; Bullock?[9] *all* possible. End of my imaginative capacity. I'll [be] back in Oxford about 17th or 18th Sept: I imagine all is quiet at the moment: Jean who is coming here on Sept 6 or 7 will tell us more I expect: the Donaldsons[10] who love you & will be here will listen with all their ears – *they* may have some useful ideas. Dear Jenifer I *am* distressed: you do make precipitate moves – *I* find that wonderful – but occasionally it must get you into hot water. Remind Wilberforce about his ancestor – the Bishop's answer about why he was called 'Soapy Sam' "Because I am always in hot water & my hands are always clean'[11]

Love from us both
Isaiah

1 Aristides ('the Just') (530–468 BCE), Athenian statesman and general renowned for his honour. Herodotus dubbed him 'the best and most just man in Athens' (*Histories* 8. 79).
2 Max Beloff (1913–99), life peer 1981, historian; Gladstone Prof. of Government and Public Administration, Oxford, and fellow, All Souls, 1957–74; Principal, University College at Buckingham, 1974–9.
3 Herbert Hart was an elector 1953–73 to the Chichele Chair of Social and Political Theory, which Quinton had hoped to occupy after IB, but John Plamenatz was elected.
4 For 'the Club' see 8/3.
5 Dick Goldsmith White (1906–93), KBE 1955, director general, MI5 1953–6, MI6 1956–72.
6 Horace William Brindley Joseph (1867–1943), philosopher; fellow, New College, 1891–1932.
7 John Mitchell Finnis (b. 1940), fellow and jurisprudence praelector (i.e. tutor), Univ., 1966–2010; called to the Bar, Gray's Inn, 1970; Rhodes Reader in the Laws of the British Commonwealth and the US, Oxford, 1972–89, prof. of law and legal philosophy, 1989–2010.
8 Geoffrey Warnock was vice chancellor, Oxford, 1981–5.
9 Alan Louis Charles Bullock (1914–2004), Kt 1972, life peer 1976, historian; founding Master, St Catherine's, 1960–80; at IB's request he had served on the trust that managed the early affairs of Wolfson.
10 John George Stuart ('Jack') Donaldson (1907–98), life peer 1967, farmer; director, ROH 1958–74, Sadler's Wells 1963–74; minister for the arts 1976–9; m. 1935 Frances Annesley (1907–94) née Lonsdale, farmer and writer, biographer of Evelyn Waugh and P. G. Wodehouse.
11 Samuel Wilberforce (1805–73), bishop of Oxford and of Winchester; for the origin of this story see L3 514/4.

TO ALISTAIR COOKE[1]

19 September 1983

Headington House

Dear Alistair,

I don't see the *New Yorker* at all regularly, and was therefore delighted to receive your excellent piece on my hero[2] – hero, yes, because I think he saved our lives, and I expect that under my old chief Lord Halifax[3] we should have made peace in 1940, and been successfully invaded after (or before) the defeat of Russia, etc. But on the only occasion when I met him to talk to, I was, despite all my passionate admiration, put off by his brutality, his contempt for the lesser breeds without the law, his lust for war, his odious doctrine about the need – eternal need – for a permanent reserve of unemployed as a source of efficiency, and so on. And I had to remind myself that he was a genius, a saviour – and, of course, I did fall under the spell of his very funny and fascinating conversation. [...]

As for our ages, I have (don't laugh, please don't – shed a tear) lost the use of one of my two vocal cords, and only produce a hideous guttural sound, a kind of croak, which distresses and disgusts me; but otherwise I am not too bad for my years – and, my God, nor are you. If we drank like Denis Brogan[4] we should be long since under the cold earth – but we don't. You are wonderfully productive; I moderately. But I wish we could meet: it would make me very happy. Let me say once again, your piece on WSC really *is* a masterpiece.

Yours ever,

Isaiah

1 (Alfred) Alistair Cooke (1908–2004), hon. KBE 1973, journalist and broadcaster; commentator on US affairs for the BBC 1938–2004; broadcast 'American Letter' 1946–50, 'Letter from America' 1950–2004, BBC radio; chief US correspondent, *Guardian*, 1948–72.

2 'The Last Victorian', AC's review of William Manchester, *The Last Lion: Winston Spencer Churchill*, vol. 1, *Visions of Glory, 1874–1932* (Boston/London, [1983]), *New Yorker*, 22 August 1983, 86, 89–93, ends with the closing words of IB's 1949 essay on Churchill (448/5): 'the largest human being of our time' (93; PI 22).

3 Edward Frederick Lindley Wood (1881–1959), 1st Earl of Halifax 1944, statesman; secretary of state for foreign affairs 1938–40, UK ambassador, Washington, 1941–6; elected chancellor, Oxford, 1933, and hon. fellow, All Souls, 1934.

4 Denis William Brogan (1900–74), Kt 1963, historian; professor of political science, Cambridge, and fellow, Peterhouse, 1939–68. 'As a person, despite his shyness, he was an easy and much-liked colleague, a witty companion, who unashamedly enjoyed good food and drink, and a teacher who was generous of his time with undergraduates': 'Sir Denis Brogan: Authority on American Life and Modern French History', obituary, *Times*, 7 January 1974, 12 g–h at 12h.

TO GEORGE KATKOV[1]

21 October 1983 [carbon]

Headington House

Dear G[eorgy] M[ikhailovich],

I hope you are as well as our years permit, and that our many years of friendship will bear the burden of the somewhat disagreeable fact which I wish to bring to your attention. I was horrified to see in Patricia Blake's[2] introduction to *Writers in Russia: 1917–1978*, by Max Hayward,[3] pp. l–li, the following sentence: 'He [i.e. GM] went to Isaiah Berlin and told him that Pasternak wanted the book [i.e. *Doctor Zhivago*] translated and published quickly. "That's all nonsense," Berlin said. "It's an interesting novel, but whether it's published now, or fifteen years from now, doesn't matter." GM says "I decided to give the manuscript to Max"', etc.

I am quite clear that I never uttered, nor could have uttered, the sentence attributed to me, nor anything remotely like it. As you know, Pasternak gave me a copy of *Doctor Zhivago* in Moscow[4] in 1956: I read it at once, and thought it, as I still do, a work of genius. The poet's wife Zinaida[5] begged me to persuade him not to publish it, out of fear of consequences to him, herself and her children. But when I put this to him, he almost lost his temper, and shamed me into silence. All this I have described in my memoir of my visit to him in my *Personal Impressions*;[6] and I recollect repeating it to you on my return. You did not, I am sure, consult me about the English translation at any stage. Pasternak did ask me to translate it: after reading it, I did not think I could do it adequately. It is inconceivable that I could have used such dismissive, almost contemptuous, words as 'interesting novel', or that it did not matter when it was published in English, since I look upon the novel as a masterpiece by a man of genius, one of the most moving writings of our century; and am known to think this by anyone who has ever spoken to me, or read what I have written, e.g. about my visit, and more briefly in the *Sunday Times* or the *Observer* (I cannot remember which).[7]

1 George (né Georgy Mikhailovich) Katkov (1903–85), Russian-born historian and philosopher; archivist, Franz Brentano Gesellschaft, Prague, 1931–9; BBC monitoring service 1939–47; studied and taught philosophy, Oxford, 1947–50; BBC Russian service 1950–9; senior lecturer in Russian studies, St Antony's, 1953–9, fellow 1956–71; lecturer in Soviet economics and institutions, Oxford, 1959–71.

2 Patricia Page Blake (1925–2010), journalist with a special interest in Russian literature of the Soviet period; correspondent, *Life* magazine, NY, 1954–62 (Moscow 1955, 1959, 1962); associate editor, *Time* magazine, 1968–87; 3rd wife of Nicolas Nabokov 1948–52.

3 London, 1983. (Harry) Maxwell ('Max') Hayward (1924–79), Russian scholar and translator; fellow, St Antony's, 1956–79.

4 In fact in the writers' village of Peredelkino.

5 Zinaida Nikolaevna Pasternak (1897–1966) née Eremeeva, previously married to Genrikh Gustavovich Neigauz: Boris Pasternak was her 2nd husband from 1934.

6 PI3 394–5.

7 IB's contribution to 'Books of the Year: I', *Sunday Times*, 21 December 1958, 6, is mainly on *Doctor*

I did question the wisdom of broadcasting the original over the Russian Service of the BBC (though he may well have wished this), since I thought that the harm this would do Pasternak would outweigh anything it could do for the cause of freedom or truth or literature. What followed his Nobel Prize you know. But whether I was right or wrong about this, I look on the attribution to me of these words as not only grotesque but defamatory. I cannot and will not believe that you are responsible for this invention.

My veneration for Pasternak is such that I propose to publish this letter, certainly in the TLS and the NYRB,[1] since I regard the words ascribed to me as a piece of singularly revolting philistinism and vulgarity – something that, in the words of the law, is calculated to bring me into 'ridicule and contempt'. I intend to put the record straight. My love and regard for you are known to you and to everyone who knows us both. I cannot believe that you have libelled me in this way, even in a moment of irritation; I prefer to believe that words have been put been put in your mouth. An assurance from you that this is indeed the case would, as you well imagine, be a source of relief to me. I only hope that this will not upset you as greatly as it has upset me.[2]

Yours,

[Isaiah]

Among the most interesting episodes in IB's life was the time that he spent in New York and Washington during the Second World War in the service of the British government. This brought him into contact with a broad cross-section of American society, and with members of the US administration, so that he was well placed both to gather information, and to share it. He used this vantage-point to strengthen, wherever he could, the position of the Anglophile Zionist leader Chaim Weizmann. He made no secret of his Zionism, but claimed to have had no doubts as to where his ultimate allegiance lay: 'I took the supremacy of total loyalty to England for granted.'[3]

The reality was more complicated, and in July 1943 he intervened secretly to undermine a joint declaration by the British and American governments that would have imposed an effective moratorium on decisions relating to Palestine until the war was over.[4] Both London and Washington feared alienating the Arab states, whose support was seen as vital to the war effort, by appearing to favour the Zionist cause, and the joint declaration would have represented a considerable setback to Jewish interests. Convinced of this, IB leaked news of it to the Zionist newspaper publisher George Backer, who contacted the treasury

---

Zhivago. His remarks there about the novel are reprinted at SM xxiv–xxv.
1 He didn't.
2 In his reply (28 October 1983) Katkov did question Blake's account but insisted that IB (like Katkov himself) had not fully appreciated the novel's genius at the time.
3 97.
4 MI 117–18.

secretary Henry Morgenthau,[1] who in turn made strong representations to FDR.
In consequence Washington abandoned its support for the declaration, to the
consternation of the British government.

   IB was subsequently asked by the Foreign Office to account for the failure of
the plan, and this he did in the form of a personal letter[2] to Angus Malcolm,[3]
a former colleague at the Washington Embassy, in which he painted a detailed
picture of the intricate politics of Washington, and the activities of the Jewish
lobbies there. The letter, dated 9 August 1943, expressed his regret that the
declaration had been aborted; he presumably meant to cover his tracks, but the
letter seemed incomprehensible to the Israeli journalist Louis Rapoport,[4] who in
1983 discovered it at the PRO in London and wrote to IB. IB did not divulge his
role in what Rapoport called 'the Hoskins affair' (after the American diplomat[5]
who initiated the joint declaration) until the end of his life, when he confessed it
to his biographer. In 1983 he still kept cover, as he had done forty years earlier. He
answered Rapoport's queries about his apparently anti-Zionist tone by claiming that his letter to Malcolm was in effect an official dispatch, which had been
amended by an unidentified anti-Zionist at the Embassy. This seems impossible:
the letter shows no signs of tampering, and is signed by IB. That Rapoport came
to accept IB's explanation of its provenance stemmed surely from deference to his
standing as a prominent liberal Jewish intellectual, and not from a dispassionate
assessment of the facts.

TO LOUIS RAPOPORT

2 November 1983

                                                        Headington House

Dear Mr Rapoport,

   [...] you have put several questions to me which I shall attempt to answer;
but you will, I am sure, realise that events of forty years ago are not easy to

1 Henry Morgenthau, Jr (1891–1967), US secretary of the treasury 1934–45; loyal to FDR and the
   New Deal, though opposed to Keynesian economics; forced to resign over a policy difference
   with Truman, July 1945, he then worked for Jewish causes, strongly supporting Israel; from 1943
   urged a more active US policy towards Jews in Nazi-occupied Europe, and was behind the creation of the US War Refugee Board in January 1944.
2 Letter of 9 August 1943, L1 443–51.
3 Angus Christian Edward Malcolm (1908–71), diplomat; UK Embassy, Washington, 1938–42, North
   American dept, FO, 1942–4; UK ambassador and Consul General, Tunis, 1956–61.
4 Louis Harvey Rapoport (1942–91), Los-Angeles-born Israeli journalist; reporter and senior editor,
   JP; 'The Hoskins Affair', chapter 5 of his posthumously published Shake Heaven and Earth: Peter
   Bergson and the Struggle to Rescue the Jews of Europe (Jerusalem, 1999), addresses the topic of this
   letter, and includes none of the remarks to which IB objects.
5 Harold Boies Hoskins (1885–1977), Beirut-born businessman, diplomat and educator working in
   Middle Eastern affairs; appointed US diplomatic emissary in Palestine by FDR 1942; thereafter
   served as a counsellor on economic affairs at US diplomatic missions throughout the Middle
   East; director, Foreign Service Institute, 1955–61; considered anti-Zionist, he advocated a Greater
   Syria.

remember with any precision. I have never kept any record of anything in my life, so I can only try to jog my unreliable memory: I cannot possibly guarantee the accuracy of the result.

You ask about the 'Joint Declaration', as I think it was called, of 1943. It was, I believe, to be issued under the names of Roosevelt and Churchill, and to say that Zionist pressure, propaganda etc. was upsetting the Arabs, and therefore constituted an obstacle to the Allied war effort; and urged either the modification or total cessation (I cannot remember which) of such pressure. I have no doubt, any more than you have, that, if this had been published, it would have inflicted great damage to Zionist activity; not, perhaps, as great as that of the 1938–9 White Paper[1] (in the spirit of which it was clearly conceived by its authors in the State Department and the Foreign Office – I fancy it was initiated by the latter, but I don't know), but still very considerable and lasting.

Churchill's name would certainly have shaken the American Jewish community (not to speak of Jews in the British Commonwealth), but Roosevelt's much more violently. F. D. Roosevelt was at the time a great Jewish hero in America and the entire free world. A statement made on his authority that Zionism was doing harm to the war effort would have produced a deep trauma. Jewish loyalties would have come into conflict with those to America, the Allied cause, the war against Hitler. The great majority of American Jews would surely have been severely shaken, and Zionist activity would have suffered a terrible blow. The fact that Jews were singled out for such a reproof (after all, there was plenty of pro-Indian, anti-colonialist, anti-imperialist agitation going on in the US at the time, supported by liberals, Irish organisations, anti-British – ex-isolationist – etc. groups all over the country) would itself have been an open affront.

I thought the idea – I cannot now remember how or when I came to know of it – I think only after it was dead – as iniquitous as I am sure you think it. In the event, the plan became known (as my letter to Angus Malcolm which you mention probably reports) to important Jews in the administration, such as Henry Morgenthau and the President's speech-writer Samuel Rosenman,[2] as well as influential persons such as Frankfurter[3] and Baruch[4] – I don't really

---

1 The May 1939 White Paper reversed the partition plan outlined by the 1937 Peel Commission, proposing instead a unitary state and restrictions on both future Jewish immigration and the right of Jews to buy land from Arabs; it was regarded by Jews as a betrayal, but was also viewed with suspicion by Arabs. In response to the White Paper the militant Zionist group Irgun began to make plans for armed resistance against the Mandate, and for the establishment of a Jewish state.

2 Samuel Irving Rosenman (1896–73), lawyer and Democrat political activist; justice, NY supreme court, 1932–43; confidential adviser and speechwriter to Presidents Roosevelt and Truman 1943–6.

3 Felix Frankfurter (1882–1965), Vienna-born US lawyer and judge; Byrne Prof. of Administrative Law, Harvard, 1914–39; George Eastman Visiting Prof., Oxford, 1933–4 (when his close friendship with IB began); associate justice, US supreme court, 1939–62; subject of a memoir in PI.

4 Bernard Mannes Baruch (1870–1965), financier made wealthy by stock market speculation;

know who else – and was cancelled. After it was abandoned, news of it was leaked to and published by the columnist Drew Pearson;[1] then there was naturally a storm of protest by Zionist bodies and their well-wishers. Since I was known to be in touch with Zionists, I was asked by the Foreign Office (i.e. Angus Malcolm) to find out what had happened. I told Malcolm what I have told you, in greater detail. [...]

You ask me if the words expressing regret that the statement was aborted were 'camouflage' on my part. No: I was not responsible for them; my job was to write the first draft of what was in fact a despatch, even if it was couched in the form of a letter. This was sent to e.g. the Head of the Chancery (Michael Wright,[2] a passionate anti-Zionist and pro-Arab), or it may have been some other equally anti-Zionist official, naturally displeased by the fate of the statement. I did not see the final text until years later, in the PRO, while looking for something else; the tone of the 'letter' did not, I admit, surprise me. I was personally immensely relieved by the failure of this bitterly anti-Zionist effort. So were some Jews highly placed in the administration to whom I spoke of it after Drew Pearson had given it wide and hostile publicity: they all agreed that it would have appalled the Jewish community and might have led to deep divisions within it. I do *not* think that it would have had as disastrous an effect as the White Paper of 1938/9. [...]

Nevertheless, damage would have been done. The anti-Zionism of the Middle Eastern section of the State Department at that time cannot be exaggerated. So the 'gzerah'[3] passed. This is all I know. But I can quite see that you might be surprised by the tone of the letter to Malcolm, given my known and unchanging pro-Zionist opinions. Such changes were made in other drafts of despatches composed by me – as, indeed, was the right of my superior officers and Lord Halifax himself. I reported the facts faithfully in the line of my duty: how they were ultimately presented was not under my control. [...]

As for Stephen Wise,[4] I simply do not know the truth about all this: at what dates the news of extermination camps reached him; to whom he

adviser on wartime economic mobilisation to Woodrow Wilson's government 1916–18, to FDR's 1941–5.
1 Andrew Russell ('Drew') Pearson (1897–1969), US journalist; with Robert S. Allen (till 1942), the creator and author from 1932 of the 'Washington Merry-Go-Round' syndicated newspaper column, which combined investigative journalism with sensationalist reporting; at the time of his death Pearson was America's best-known newspaper columnist.
2 Michael Robert Wright (1901–76), KCMG 1951, diplomat; British Embassy, Paris 1936–40, Cairo 1940–3, Washington 1943–6; assistant undersecretary of state, FO, 1947–50; UK ambassador to Norway 1951–4, to Iraq 1954–8.
3 'Decree' – often, as in this metaphor for the threat hanging over the Jews, an anti-Jewish one. The word appears in a celebrated prayer, used in the Rosh Hashanah and Yom Kippur services, that recounts God's decision as to who shall live and who shall die (and how), but promises that 'repentance, prayer and charity cancel the harsh decree'.
4 Stephen Samuel Wise (1874–1949), Hungarian-born Reform rabbi, social reformer and Zionist leader; president, American Jewish Congress, 1925–49.

spoke and what he did, or failed to do; what could have been done. I was outside all that, in my embassy enclosure. When I ask myself when I came to realise the full horror of the Holocaust, I do not know the answer: probably not before 1944, or even later.[1] The American newspapers paid little publicity to such horrors.[2] No Zionist leader told me about systematic extermination until 1945. We knew about the Warsaw ghetto, and assumed that all Jews behind German lines were probably doomed in one way or another – prison, or torture, or death – but not the full horror: that, nobody in my world, Jewish or gentile, imagined.

I think it was probably impossible to stop the actual mass killings of Jews by Germans. What could have been done, and was not, was [...] rescue of some Jews from SE Europe – Hungary, Romania, Yugoslavia etc. – by dire threats to Balkan and SE European states of the punishment likely to be visited upon them by the Allies if they harmed Jews, surrendered them to Eichmann,[3] etc. By the time the Allies looked like winning – from the end of 1943 onwards – this *might* have frightened some countries into refraining from killing or surrendering Jews to the Nazis. And this was not attempted, so far as I know, save in very general terms, which did not penetrate. That is my personal view. I cannot tell if I am right. Jewish pressure in the US – especially by eminent Jews (not the population in general – which I still think was not effective till the end of the war, when the camps were entered by US troops and a general sense of horror spread everywhere) – might have worked. Such pressure did not occur on a sufficient scale, for fear, I suppose, of rocking the military boat; such attitudes have occurred before and after, as you know – humanity, courage and persistence are always in short supply.

I hope this is of some help.

Yours sincerely,

Isaiah Berlin

---

1 IB is noticeably unsure and defensive on this point: see L3 503–5, 506–11, 513–19, 520–2.

2 In both the US and Britain, reporting of the systematic extermination of Jews and others in Nazi-occupied Europe was surprisingly scant before 1945, although the essential facts were known and reported as early as December 1942, when both the *Washington Post* and *The Times* covered (on 18 December) the Allies' joint statement of 17 December, which put on record that the extermination was taking place, and that the Allies' intended in due course to bring the perpetrators to justice: L3 507/2, 510/1; see also 451 below. In the US there was also Varian Fry's detailed report, 'The Massacre of the Jews', *New Republic*, 22 December 1942, 816–19. IB surely saw (or was told of) these reports.

3 Karl Adolf Eichmann (1906–62) joined the SS 1932, Lieutenant Colonel 1941; became the Gestapo's expert on Jewish affairs, and directed the assembly, transport and mass murder of c.6 million Jews in Nazi-controlled Europe; lived in hiding in Argentina after the war and was abducted from there by Mossad 1960; tried in Israel for war crimes 1961, hanged 31 May 1962.

TO ROMA SCHAPIRO[1]

3 November 1983 [*manuscript*]

Headington House

Dear Mrs Schapiro,

It was with deep grief that I learnt that Leonard had had a stroke: when the nurse I spoke to said that he had not regained consciousness, I realized that the situation was very grave. I find it hard to accustom myself to the thought that Leonard is no more. He was, as you know, my oldest friend. We were first brought together by our parents in Petrograd in late 1916 when I was seven, and Leonard eight: he was superior to me in every respect. In 1917 & 1918 he educated me in artistic matters: we were both moderately precocious, but he much more so: he told me all about Alexandre Benois, Bakst, Dobujinsky, Kustodiev, other Russian painters;[2] he gave me postcards – coloured illustrations – of their work: he was a sculptor & produced a marvellous head of the dying Marat;[3] he told me about a composer called César Franck[4] & opened all kinds of new horizons; we spent two summers together in Pavlovsk & he was the leader of our little group of boys and girls: I looked up to him in every way. Then in Riga his Latin teacher held him up as a model to me: in England, I chose St. Paul's School, & persuaded my parents to send me there, solely because he was there already & I knew I wd have a friend; & so it went, happily, for years. After I went to Oxford I saw him far less, & our paths diverged: he became a barrister, I a don; still, I went to stay with him in the Black Forest with his charming (paternal) grandmother, widow of Philip[p] Schapiro;[5] I saw him from time to time in the thirties; he was politically well to the right of me – & inclined towards religion & infected me with a desire to visit synagogues (which we did, though not often, together) in the poorer

---

1 (Dorothy) Roma Thewes Schapiro (1917–98) née Sherris, journalist, m. 2ndly 1976 Leonard Schapiro.

2 Alexandre Nikolaevich Benois (1870–1960), Léon Bakst (1866–1924), Mstislav Valerianovich Dobuzhinsky (1875–1957), Boris Mikhailovich Kustodiev (1878–1927), members of the movement *Mir iskusstva* ('World of Art') whose development of Russian culture fed off Western European influences without slavishly aping them.

3 Jean Paul Marat (1743–93), physician and French revolutionary journalist; a supporter of the Jacobins, he conspired with Danton and Robespierre 1793 to overthrow the moderate Girondins, an act avenged that July when he was stabbed to death in his bath by the Girondist Charlotte Corday d'Armont, a scene famously depicted in David's *Death of Marat* (1793; Musées royaux, Brussels).

4 César Auguste Jean Guillaume Hubert Franck (1822–90), Belgian-born French composer and organist; appointed organist, church of Sainte Clotilde, Paris, 1858, where his admirers included Liszt, who compared his virtuosity to that of Bach; from 1872 prof. of organ at the Conservatoire de Paris.

5 Philipp Schapiro was a wealthy owner of a sawmill (like IB's adoptive great-grandfather, Isaiah Berlin, after whom IB was named) at Bolderāja (then a village north of Riga, at the mouth of the Daugava river; now a district of Riga), Latvia, and of forests in the hinterland: one of many parallels between the lives of IB and Leonard Schapiro. Max (1878/9–1953), son of Philipp and his wife Doris, took over the family business 1912.

part of London, where the services were more sincere & devout, it seemed to us. But I must not go on so: it is only that his loss leaves a terrible gap in my life, even though we did not see each other all that often in the last ten – twenty – years. You do not need me to tell you how greatly his learning, capacity for writing, courage, but above all unswerving integrity, total honesty and devotion to truth as he saw it, gained the admiration of almost everyone who came into any kind of relationship with him: the denunciation of him from the Left, did him nothing but honour: his enemies were not honourable people.[1] I admired him & loved him & mourn his passing and offer you my warmest feeling: after my parents' death – & but for an aunt aged 96[2] – he is the oldest root of my life. [...]

Yours very sincerely
Isaiah Berlin.

TO HUGH TREVOR-ROPER

3 January 1984

Headington House

Dear Hugh,

I was delighted by your letter. In your beautiful, clear hand you paint the inferno in which you are forced to live in almost Dantean colours.[3] They sound a dreadful crew, and I only hope that you will be able to go on to the end, unflinching, if only to show them the stuff the elect of Oxford are made of. I am thinking of the statistics of Oxford immigrants to Cambridge, and what became of them. Roger Mynors,[4] as you know, loathed it from start to finish; A. H. M. Jones[5] did not like it; Bernard Williams likes it less than he did to begin with; C. S. Lewis detested it, or so he told me; my friend Wynne Godley,[6] the economist at King's, cannot bear it; on the other hand,

---

1 Possibly an allusion to the controversy over the publication of Schapiro's *The Origin of the Communist Autocracy* (41, 200).

2 Ida Samunov (1887–1985) née Volshonok, IB's aunt (younger sister of Marie Berlin), widowed after the death of her husband Yitzhak Samunov (1886–1950).

3 'Cambridge is dreadfully dull and Peterhouse just dreadful. I have been a fellow of three Oxford colleges but have never known anything like this [...]. The worst of the Fellows here are barbarians – and incredibly malevolent: *childishly* malevolent' (HTR to IB, 10 December 1983). IB wrote to Ron Kitaj, 21 April 1986, of 'the rather terrible fellows of Peterhouse (the head of that College, Lord Dacre, [...] spends his entire time in denouncing them as a bunch of corrupt reactionaries).'

4 Roger Aubrey Baskerville Mynors (1903–89), Kt 1963; fellow and classics tutor, Balliol, 1926–44; Kennedy Prof. of Latin and fellow, Pembroke, Cambridge, 1944–53; Corpus Christi Prof. of Latin Language and Literature, Oxford, and fellow, CCC, 1953–70.

5 Arnold Hugh Martin Jones (1904–70), fellow, All Souls, 1926–46; lecturer in ancient history, Wadham, 1939–46; prof. of ancient history, UCL, 1946–51; prof. of ancient history, Cambridge, and fellow, Jesus, 1951–70.

6 Wynne Alexander Hugh Godley (1926–2010), New College PPE (philosophy pupil of IB) 1943–7; professional oboist 1950; joined economic section, treasury, 1956, deputy director 1967–70; fellow, King's, Cambridge, 1970–98, prof. of applied economics 1980–93; director, ROH, 1976–87.

Denys Page[1] took to it like a duck to water, Jean Floud could not but enjoy
it because she was made so much more of there than at Nuffield, but is
relieved to come back. So will you be when your thorny path leads back to
our happier world.

That reminds me of the Club. I fully intend to go to its next dinner, despite
the occasional sense of unease that I have before and during our feasts, caused
by the nervous anticipations of the behaviour of our secretary[2] – I think that
all the Brethren feel this in some degree, save for Charles Stuart,[3] who seems
wholly unperturbed by the permanent possibility of embarrassment which
prevails throughout the evening.

Back to academic affairs. All Souls, as you know, is offering two research
fellowships – one for the over-forties, one to those below that age. About
two hundred entries. The short list, which is quite long, contains the names
of Conrad Russell,[4] whom you must know; Pagden,[5] whom I rescued from
being eliminated; Norman Stone, whom I think a clever man, but who will
not be able to clear the hurdle of his 'bad taste' in his piece on E. H. Carr in
the London Review of Books,[6] about which there was a good deal of priggish
comment ('Is he some kind of scoundrel?', the Warden[7] asked me, on the
basis of a letter from an old friend of mine and an acquaintance of yours) –
Cobb[8] had written a wonderfully characteristic testimonial for him, saying
how marvellous it was that he should have done in that old wretch Carr,
partly on information derived from him, Cobb, what a splendid historian he
is, how glad he is that the 'old monster' got what he so richly deserved, etc.
I am afraid that won't do him much good with the great philistine block,
with its pronounced anti-intellectual and anti-academic bias (led by e.g.
Quintin H[ogg] and various other contemporaries of mine in various stages
of decomposition), which has led to some unworthy elections.

You speak of your colleague Norman.[9] Let me tell you that one of
the junior fellows of my College earnestly enquired of one of his seniors

1 Denys Lionel Page (1908–78), Kt 1971; student (i.e. fellow) and classics tutor, Christ Church, 1932–
50; Regius Prof. of Greek, Cambridge, 1950–73; Master, Jesus, Cambridge, 1959–73; President, BA,
1971–4.
2 John Sparrow.
3 Charles Harborne Stuart (1920–91), C18th British historian, student (i.e. fellow) in modern
history, Christ Church, 1948–87; in his prime in the 1950s he was a stalwart figure in the running
of the college.
4 Conrad Sebastian Robert Russell (1937–2004), 5th Earl Russell 1987; lecturer in history, Bedford,
London, 1960–74, reader 1974–9; prof. of history, Yale, 1979–84; Astor Prof. of British History,
UCL, 1984–90; prof. of British history, King's London, 1990–2002.
5 Anthony Robin Dermer Pagden (b. 1945), political theorist and author; lecturer in history,
Cambridge, 1980–93, reader in intellectual history 1993–7; fellow, Girton, Cambridge, 1980–3,
King's 1985–97; Harry C. Black Prof. in History, Johns Hopkins, 1997–2002.
6 198/2.
7 Patrick Neill.
8 Richard Charles Cobb (1917–96), FBA 1967, historian of France and the French Revolution specialising in popular history; prof. of modern history, Oxford, and fellow, Worcester, 1973–84.
9 Edward Robert Norman (b. 1938), lecturer in history, Cambridge, 1965–88; Dean and fellow,

whether Cowling[1] could be induced to apply for the chair of political theory, or even invited to do so! To do him justice, Patrick Neill is aware of a kind of militant middle- or even low-brow front at work. Exactly the same is going on in Section 15 of the British Academy,[2] where Lord Beloff is trying to reproduce his kind. I long for all academic institutions – colleges, academies, universities – to put up a large notice upon which might be inscribed in bold letters Hinshelwood's[3] words 'There is no quicker way of making a first-class institution third-class than by appointing second-class men.' [...]

Yours,

Isaiah

TO LANA PETERS

6 January 1984 [*carbon*]

Headington House

Dear Svetlana,

I have received your bitter, violent and very wounding letter of 3 January, in which you tell me that you think me a vile hypocrite, a promise-breaker, and call down the justice of God upon me. I realise that your circumstances are difficult, that you are very unhappy, and that this may account for your wild statements, which amount to a kind of curse upon me and all my works. I do not suppose that anything I can say could make much impression upon you in your present state of mind; nevertheless, I do not think that such statements, no matter how baseless, can be left without an answer. I should therefore like to repeat what I have said to you before, both in speech and in writing: that, contrary to your allegation, I never tried to persuade you to come to England. You told me that you found your life in America intolerable and wondered whether England or Switzerland could be more congenial. I thought that they might, but that Switzerland might be more expensive than England. I can quote in evidence of this your own letter to me of 18 October 1983, in which you say:

> I DO NOT 'ACCUSE' you of tempting me to move to GB, or to have some persuasion on my own opinions in this respect: *to bring Olga to England* for her

Peterhouse, 1971–88; dean of chapel, Christ Church College, Canterbury, 1988–95; canon residentiary, York Minster, 1995–2004.

1 Maurice John Cowling (1926–2005), lecturer in history, Cambridge, 1961–75, reader in modern English history 1975–88; fellow, Peterhouse, a college 'widely regarded as a conservative seminary, partly because several of Cowling's pupils went to work for the Conservative research dept or Conservative newspapers' (Jonathan Parry, ODNB), 1963–93.

2 *Political Studies*.

3 Cyril Norman Hinshelwood (1897–1967), Kt 1948, OM 1960; lecturer in chemistry, Trinity, 1921–36; Dr Lee's Prof. of Chemistry, Oxford, 1937–64; senior research fellow, Imperial College, London, 1964–7; Nobel Prize in Chemistry 1956 with Nikolay Nikolaevich Semenov for their researches into the mechanism of chemical reactions.

education had been MY IDEA *since many years ago*; it was only now that I finally came to grips with all practicalities to fulfil this in action. [...][1]

Two months later, you have said the opposite to all this. I can only repeat once again that I have done all that you had requested me to do: recommended you to my publisher, who to my knowledge has treated you courteously throughout; written a letter which I think has had some effect in causing the Home Office to give you temporary residence; when you asked advice about a school for your daughter, Aline and I did our best to provide it.

You say in the letter which I have already quoted, 'So, by now, I can say that there is *hardly anything* that I could ASK you to do to help me.' Only to read the book you are writing and to help you to place it with a publisher in England. I have not offered to do this because I know that I have little influence with publishers, and that Hugo Brunner[2] or an agent recommended by him could do this far better than I. I am quite certain that my reading of your manuscript would be of no use to you.

I have written all this because I believe it to be wrong to leave false charges unanswered. I do not suppose that any of this is likely to make any impression upon you, given your opinion of the kind of person I am.

Your last letter makes it purposeless to continue this correspondence, or, indeed, any further communication between us. You call down divine justice upon me: so far as my behaviour towards yourself is concerned, I have no fear of it.

Yours sincerely,
[Isaiah Berlin]

TO ROBERT ARMSTRONG[3]

30 January 1984 [*carbon*]

Headington House

Dear Robert,

[...] I am so sorry not to be able to come to the next meeting of you-know-what.[4] I am a little shocked about the substitution of Sir S. Sitwell[5] (the

1 IB's quotations from this letter are given in the idiosyncratic form in which they appear in LPs letter.
2 Hugo Laurence Joseph Brunner (b. 1935), later (2008) KCVO, publisher; sales director, Chatto and Windus, 1966–76; Deputy General Publisher, OUP, 1977–9; managing director, Chatto and Windus, 1979–83, chair 1983–5; Lord Lieutenant of Oxfordshire 1996–2008.
3 Robert Temple Armstrong (b. 1927), KCB 1978, life peer 1988, civil servant; PPS to the prime minister 1970–5; deputy undersecretary of state, Home Office, 1975–7, permanent undersecretary 1977–9; cabinet secretary and *ex officio* chair, honours committee, 1979–87; joint head, Home Civil Service, 1981–3, head 1983–7.
4 The Maecenas Committee, which made recommendations for honours to the government of the day. Both its membership and its proceedings were confidential.
5 Sacheverell Reresby Sitwell (1897–1988), 6th Baronet, writer.

credit for this is claimed by Lords Donaldson and Hutchinson[1] – I have told them that there is nothing to claim), whose works no one has read for years, in place of the Librarian of the University of Hull,[2] who by general (and I think just) acclaim is our best living poet, bar only Robert Graves,[3] but he is now too old for anything. I think, therefore, that we should put up Larkin again. I should myself be inclined to add Brendel[4] for an hon. knighthood (he is an Austrian citizen, but lives here, is extremely Anglophile, and seems to me of the right calibre) – but that could wait, I think. I should like to repeat my support for a knighthood for Geoffrey Warnock, now upstaged by the damehood of his wife Mary: he has been an excellent vice chancellor during a very difficult period, and is in my view a good philosopher. His name is before the British Academy, though it is never certain who will be elected; and there was (sent to 10 Downing Street, I think) that long round robin of his academic admirers, instigated by Rex Richards[5] – merited, in my opinion.

I am quite sure that no painter or writer deserves either a CH or a knighthood, but I think a CBE could properly be offered to Bridget Riley.[6] Sooner or later I expect we shall have to do something for Keith Thomas,[7] who was, after all, recommended by the History Faculty for the Regius Chair – but the P[rime] M[inister] thought differently.[8] And there is Professor Richard Cobb, FBA – eccentric, unsober, but brilliant, a unique specialist on France. Lord

1 Jeremy Nicolas St John Hutchinson (b. 1915), life peer 1978, barrister; Magdalen PPE 1933–6, when he shared lodgings in Beaumont Street with Stuart Hampshire and Ben Nicolson; Recorder of Bath 1962–72, of the Crown Court 1972–6.
2 Philip Arthur Larkin (1922–1985), poet and novelist; librarian, Hull, 1955–85; declined offer of UK Poet Laureateship 1984; CH June 1985, died in December.
3 Robert von Ranke Graves (1895–1985), poet and novelist; prof. of poetry, Oxford, 1961–6; his best-selling historical novel *I, Claudius: From the Autobiography of Tiberius Claudius, Emperor of the Romans, Born BC 10, Murdered and Deified AD 54* (London, 1934), and its sequel *Claudius the God and His Wife Messalina: The Troublesome Reign of Tiberius Claudius Caesar, Emperor of the Romans (Born BC 10, Died AD 54)* (London, 1934) had been made into a successful BBC TV series 1976.
4 Alfred Brendel (b. 1931; plate 19), hon. KBE 1989; Austrian-born concert pianist (1948–2008), writer and poet; a noted interpreter of the works of Haydn, Mozart, Beethoven, Schubert, Brahms and Liszt; a close friend of IB's later years (from 1975), he played Schubert at IB's 1998 memorial events at the Hampstead Synagogue (14 January: the Andante sostenuto from the B flat major sonata, D960, also chosen by IB in a Brendel version on *Desert Island Discs* 1992) and the Sheldonian Theatre, Oxford (21 March: the G major sonata, D894); 'The wonderful pianist Alfred Brendel, who is a friend of mine, made me understand what Schubert conveys: particularly the tragic in his works' (CIB 118); awarded hon. DMus at Oxford 22 June 1983.
5 Rex Edward Richards (b. 1922), Kt 1977; Dr Lee's Prof. of Chemistry, Oxford, 1964–70; fellow, Exeter, 1964–9; Warden, Merton, 1969–84; chancellor, Exeter University, 1982–98.
6 She already had one: Bridget Louise Riley (b. 1931), CBE 1972, later (1998) CH, painter, writer and curator; a pioneer of the optical art (op art) movement.
7 Keith Vivian Thomas (b. 1933), Kt 1988, early modern historian; fellow, All Souls, 1955–7 (and 2000–15), St John's 1957–86 (history tutor 1957–85, reader in modern history 1978–85, prof. of modern history January–September 1986); President, CCC, 1986–2000, BA 1993–7.
8 Though officially crown appointments, Regius Professors are effectively appointed by the prime minister. Margaret Thatcher installed the military historian Michael Howard in the Oxford Regius history chair 1980, 'causing an outcry among those Oxonians who thought that left-leaning Keith Thomas should have been appointed' (Simon Targett, 'A Regius Rumble', THES, 1 March 1996, 19).

Dacre would certainly support, so would others in the British Academy. It would show real imagination to make him a knight. [...]

Yours ever,

[Isaiah]

TO ALISTAIR COOKE

31 January 1984

Headington House

Dear Alistair,

[...] Your enclosure is absolutely delightful. How could I possibly have read *The Journals of Lady Monkswell, 1873–1895*?[1] The silliness, naivety and unself-conscious, disarming snobbery seem to me to show that she had no eye to publication, unlike e.g. Harold Nicolson or my ex-colleague A. L. Rowse – he is certain that his diaries will form a great twenty-first century industry, like Pepys[2] or Horace Walpole;[3] since he considers that he is an insufficiently recognised man of genius, towering far above the envious pygmies who seek perpetually to drag him down to their miserable level, he is preparing bomb-shell after bombshell. Last time I met him at the Athenaeum he said to me 'My God, the College [i.e. All Souls] is in for it – they'll catch it!'[4] I expect they will, too: all kinds of reputations will be founded on these paranoiac out-pourings. Do you know Rowse at all? The temperament of a genius, without the genius – and that is quite a serious condition to be in.

But I must curb my malice, and thank you again for those wonder-ful extracts. I should have liked to meet the agreeable, curly-haired Oliver Holmes, and dear young Mrs Holmes, and the little dried-up old Dr Holmes who loved Longfellow 'but not intensely';[5] and somebody – I cannot remem-

1 *A Victorian Diarist: Extracts from the Journals of Mary, Lady Monkswell, 1873–1895*, ed. E. C. F. Collier, 2 vols (London, [1944, 1946]).

2 Samuel Pepys (1633–1703), diarist and outstanding naval administrator; President, Royal Society, 1684; best known for the journal that he secretly kept, in cipher, in the 1660s, published unbowd-lerised in 11 vols as *The Diary of Samuel Pepys: A New and Complete Transcription*, ed. Robert Latham and William Matthews (London, 1970–83).

3 Horace Walpole (1717–97), 4th Earl of Orford, author, politician and patron of the arts known for his letters and memoirs; he left the latter in a sealed chest ready for posthumous publication, and among the numerous editions in IB's lifetime was John Brooke's *Memoirs of King George II* (New Haven and London, 1985).

4 'Rowse insisted that his many publications represented only "the tip of the iceberg" of his writing. He was alluding primarily to the diary that he kept for most of his adult life. At breakfast in All Souls he would often tell colleagues, especially any who had displeased him, that they had been included in the entry written the night before: "You're in it and you're in it". [...] The diaries remained unpublished at his death, and those colleagues who read them agreed that full publica-tion would require both courage and good legal advice.' John Clarke, ODNB, citing personal knowledge. A selection was published as *The Diaries of A. L. Rowse*, ed. Richard Ollard (London, 2003).

5 The US jurist Oliver Wendell Holmes, Jr (1841–1935), associate justice, US supreme court, 1902–32; his wife, the reclusive Fanny Bowditch Holmes (1840–1929) née Dixwell; and his father Dr Oliver

ber who – who has 'a beautiful nose'.[1] I wonder, however, whether they would have liked me much. Still, I would have taken the risk of being snubbed. Have you ever thought about people who are snubbable as against those who are not? The late Lord Halifax, for example, was absolutely unsnubbable, whereas the late Lord Simon[2] was very snubbable indeed. Lord Curzon, I think, thought he was unsnubbable but in fact was[n't]. Those are only the famous men, but in one's own private acquaintance it's quite an interesting classification: unsnubbability is a very enviable quality. I see that I am writing in the style of Lady Monkswell,[3] and must therefore stop. [...]

Yours ever,

Isaiah

TO KARL MILLER[4]

[c.22 February 1984, carbon]

Headington House

Dear Karl,

I *have* had a bad time with the *London Review*: first Aarsleff[5] (I did not much like Nigel Hamilton's wholly contemptuous review of 'my' Washington dispatches,[6] but I thought that what he said was quite just); then a nasty piece about the domination of America by the 'Elders of Zion', with their mysterious, unlimited power, by the fanatical Ian Gilmour,[7] who obviously really

Wendell Holmes, Sr (1809–94), physician and poet, who is quoted as saying of the US poet Henry Wadsworth Longfellow (1807–82): 'We love him but not intensely.' ibid. i 92.

1 'Kindly young Mrs. Winthrop came in the afternoon: her forehead & eyes & nose are beautiful.' ibid. i 88. Elizabeth Mason Winthrop (1844–1924) née Mason was the wife of Robert Charles Winthrop, Jr (1834–1905), son of Robert Charles Winthrop, Sr (1809–94), speaker, US house of representatives, 1947–9. The family were typical Boston Brahmins.

2 John Allsebrook Simon (1873–1954), Kt 1910, 1st Viscount Simon 1940; barrister and Liberal/Liberal National politician; fellow, All Souls, 1897–1954; attorney general 1913–15, chancellor of the exchequer 1937–40, lord chancellor 1940–5.

3 Mary Josephine Collier (1849–1930) née Hardcastle, Lady Monkswell 1886, diarist; m. 1873 Robert Collier, 2nd Baron Monkswell.

4 Karl Fergus Connor Miller (1931–2014), British literary editor, critic and writer; Lord Northcliffe Prof. of Modern English Literature, UCL, 1974–92; founding editor, *London Review of Books*, 1979–89, co-editor 1989–92.

5 Hans Christian Aarsleff (b. 1925), Danish-born US scholar of linguistics; prof. of linguistics, dept of English, Princeton; author of 'Vico and Berlin', LRB, 5–18 November 1981, 6–7; IB responded in the same issue, 7–8, and in a subsequent letter, 3–16 June 1982, 5.

6 (Charles) Nigel Hamilton (b. 1944), British-born US biographer; in 'In the Field', LRB, 5 November 1981, 16–17, a review of H. G. Nicholas (ed.), *Washington Despatches 1941–45: Weekly Political Reports from the British Embassy* (London/Chicago, 1981) and 5 other books, he asks: 'Why should this gifted man have failed to deliver something more rewarding? The answer is, of course, censorship. Not imposed – though that, too, possibly – so much as self-imposed' (16).

7 Ian Hedworth John Little Gilmour (1926–2007), 2nd Bt 1977, life peer 1992; Conservative MP 1962–92; secretary of state for defence 1974, lord privy seal 1979–81. Gilmour was disturbed by Eden's Suez venture 1956 and later 'was to be accused of over-zealousness in his Arab sympathies'; he had been deeply affected by a visit to the defeated Arab side after the Six Day War, and 'having seen at first hand the treatment of the Palestinians, [...] made theirs a lifelong cause' ('Lord

does think there is a conspiracy and that American senators are manipulated
– even in States like Idaho, where there are virtually no Jews – by horrid
methods that he only mysteriously hints at, but I know what he means, and
it won't do. […] The present government of Israel is, in my view, wicked and
odious, but that is not the point. Your Middle Eastern experts seem to me
possessed – and have been for some time – by a hatred beyond reason of the
entire horrid enterprise of Zionism, of the springs and nature of which they
show not the slightest knowledge, as if it was something frightful, exploding
out of nothing.

Stuart telephoned me the other day and asked me if I had seen the latest
copy of the LRB. I said I had not. He begged me not to look at it, since the
article by Edward Said[1] would surely cause me to cancel my subscription,
and would send me into a sharp decline. I did, of course, read it at once.
Stuart's disapproval was concerned not too much with the first part of the
article, which, we agreed, was routine PLO stuff, only more repetitive, pretentious and confused than the shorter and clearer statements by Arafat, but
with the encomium to Chomsky.[2] I know Chomsky quite well, and like him
– he is a man of brilliant gifts and great personal charm; but his polemical
writings are not exactly notable for scruple or unswerving adherence to the
truth. This is true about all his writings, including linguistics,[3] but he lost all
political credibility after he maintained that the reports of massacres by the
Khmer Rouge were largely inventions of the American media,[4] and after

  Gilmour of Craigmillar', obituary, *Times*, 24 September 2007, 60a–e at 60a, 60b). The 'nasty piece'
  is 'America and Israel', LRB, 18 February to 3 March, 7–9.
1 'Permission to Narrate' (LRB, 16 February 1984, 13–17), a review of 8 books on the Palestinians,
  including Noam Chomsky, *The Fateful Triangle: Israel, the United States and the Palestinians*
  (Boston/London, 1983). Edward Wadie Said (1935–2003), Jerusalem-born Palestinian American
  literary critic and political activist, internationally known for his advocacy of the rights of the
  Palestinian people; joined faculty, Columbia, 1963, full prof. 1970, University Prof. 1992–2003.
2 After expressing some reservations about Chomsky's approach – 'his work is not only deeply
  and unacceptably pessimistic: it is also a work not critical and reflective enough about its own
  premisses' – Said writes: 'These criticisms cannot be made at all lightly, or without acknowledging the unparalleled energy and honesty of his achievement. There is something deeply moving
  about a mind of such noble ideals repeatedly stirred on behalf of human suffering and injustice.
  One thinks here of Voltaire, of Benda, or Russell, although more than any of them, Chomsky
  commands what he calls "reality" – facts – over a breathtaking range' (16).
3 An unfair comment: Chomsky's achievement in linguistics is widely recognised. In 2014 he was
  the first recipient of the British Academy's Neil and Saras Medal for lifetime achievement in the
  scholarly study of linguistics.
4 In his writings on Cambodia during and directly after the period of Khmer Rouge rule Chomsky
  kept an open mind on the total number of Cambodians murdered by the Pol Pot regime, but
  viewed with extreme scepticism Western media reports depicting state-sponsored genocide,
  later proved to have occurred. Steven Lukes's highly critical commentary on this position –
  'Chomsky's Betrayal of the Truths', THES, 7 November 1980, 31 – met with several emphatic
  rebuttals (e.g. Laura J. Summers, letter to the editor, 19 December 1980, 22), and there was
  later a direct exchange between Chomsky and Lukes (Chomsky, 'The Truth about Indochina',
  6 March 1981, 13; Lukes, 'Suspending Chomsky's Disbeliefs', 27 March 1981, 31; Chomsky, 'The
  Dispute about Atrocities in Kampuchea', letter, 12 June 1981, 35).

a piece by him[1] was published, with his permission, as an introduction to a book by a man called Faurisson,[2] who said that the Holocaust had never occurred, but was a Zionist invention. The tribute to Chomsky's integrity irritated Stuart because of its patent falsity. (He said that this was intended to support the right to free speech, but it went too far even for his followers.) One cannot, of course, blame any Palestinian Arab for hating Israel, whatever he writes; but so far as serious students of the subject are concerned, Said was laid out once and for all by the formidable Bernard Lewis,[3] in an article in the NYRB:[4] his Harold-Bloom-hypnotised[5] critical essays seem to me, in their own silly way, no better, though I expect Frank K.[6] might defend them on principle.

What I really want to ask you is: Must you use only zealots in writing about the Middle East? If you employ members of the Council of the PLO or CAABU, should not this be balanced with pieces by some ghastly ex-member of the Irgun[7] or the Stern Gang? It is clear that nobody can be neutral about either the Soviet Union or Israel. Nevertheless, there are degrees of rabidity – there must be more temperate people who can write. In Israel itself there exists a movement called 'Peace Now', which is entirely decent and very moderate – prepared to talk to the PLO, give up the West Bank, etc. They organised huge meetings to protest about the invasion of Lebanon, the treatment of Arabs, and everything that goes with it (one of its members, the novelist Amos Oz,[8] who is a genuinely brave protester, is one of the people whom Chomsky – approved by Said – regards as a greater menace than the nationalist fanatics).[9] These people are not favoured by the government, nor even by sections of the Israel Labour Party, for whom they go too far, but

1 'Some Elementary Comments on the Rights of Freedom of Expression', published in French translation as a preface to Robert Faurisson, *Mémoire en défense, contre ceux qui m'accusent de falsifier l'histoire: la question des chambres à gaz* (Paris, [1980]), and in English in Noam Chomsky, *Chomsky on Democracy and Education*, ed. C. P. Otero (NY and London, 2003).
2 Robert Faurisson (b. 1929), British-born French academic and Holocaust denier; taught French literature, Lyon II, 1973–91; deprived of his professorship in 1991 after conviction under the 1990 Gayssot Act, which makes it an offence to deny officially recognised crimes against humanity.
3 Bernard Lewis (b. 1916), Cleveland E. Dodge Prof. of Near Eastern Studies, Princeton, 1974–86; director, Annenberg Research Institute, Philadelphia, 1986–90.
4 'The Question of Orientalism', NYRB, 24 June 1982, 49–56.
5 Harold Bloom (b. 1930), US literary critic; Yale faculty 1955, Sterling Prof. of Humanities 1983; Berg Visiting Prof. of English, NYU, 1988–2004. Cf. 434/1.
6 (John) Frank Kermode (1919–2010) Kt 1991; Lord Northcliffe Prof. of Modern English Literature, UCL, 1967–74; King Edward VII Prof. of English Literature, Cambridge, 1974–82, and fellow, King's, 1974–87.
7 Irgun Ts'vai L'umi, or Etsel (National Military Organization), right-wing Zionist paramilitary group founded 1931.
8 Amos Oz (b. 1939) né Klausner, Israeli writer, novelist, journalist and intellectual; prof. of Hebrew literature, Ben-Gurion University of the Negev, 1987–2005; since 1967 a prominent advocate of a 2-state solution to the Israel–Palestine conflict, and one of the founders of the Peace Now movement 1978.
9 'The truth of the matter is that Amos Oz is no more an advocate for peace than the mainstream of the PLO, maybe less so': Chomsky interviewed in May 1988 by Burton Levine, *Shmate:*

I admire them greatly. Can't there be something by, or at least about, them? There are no other moderates in the Middle East. They write calmly and well.

But why am I going on like this? What right have I to write a letter simply to say that I keep having an awful time with your otherwise excellent periodical? My unfortunate experience is probably unique. It is only that I wanted to get all this stuff off my chest, but there is no reason why you should be subjected to a tirade. Please forgive me. I should have preferred to *say* this to you, but we see each other, sadly, so seldom, that the only way of dealing with this is in writing. No doubt the Edwards – Said, Mortimer etc. – would say that my letter is precisely the kind of attempt at censorship that the wicked Zionists are so good at. They are impervious to argument. Anyway, Stuart encouraged me to write to you, else I don't think I should have. [...]

Yours, in unbroken friendship,

[Isaiah]

TO HENRY ROSOVSKY[1]

24 February 1984

Headington House

Dear Henry,

After reading the letter addressed by Abba Eban[2] to the Nobel Peace Prize Committee in Oslo, I think that the award of the Nobel Peace Prize to 'Peace Now' would be justified, both politically and morally, and would have a good effect. Would you consider writing to the Peace Prize Committee a letter, however brief, indicating your support for Eban's initiative (they will presumably have received his letter and thought about it by now)? I should like to add that in my view 'Peace Now' is made up of entirely decent persons. Their number is not large, but their influence has turned out to be considerable, and their activity as a kind of conscience of Israel – especially as many of them are soldiers who have fought in Israeli wars – is doing nothing but good. Of course, if for some reason you do not wish to write to Oslo, I would entirely understand, and apologise for intruding upon you in this way.

Yours sincerely,

IB

A Journal of Progressive Jewish Thought, 20 (Summer 1988), 24–32: see ⟨http://www.chomsky.info/ interviews/198805--.htm⟩.

1 Henry Rosovsky (b. 1927), Russian-born US economic historian specialising in East Asia; prof. of economics, Harvard, 1965–96, acting president 1984, 1987.

2 Abba Eban (1915–2002) né Aubrey Solomon, South-African-born Israeli diplomat and politician; Israeli representative to UN 1948–59, Israeli ambassador to the US 1950–9; held numerous ministerial posts 1959–74 (foreign minister 1966–74); advocated a withdrawal from the occupied territories.

TO WILLIAM PHILLIPS[1]

9 April 1984 [*carbon*]

Headington House

Dear William,

Ex nihilo nihil fit.[2] My mind is empty and if you would like to impersonate me I shall raise no objection. I am too old to mind about anything much now, even Reagan and Mrs Thatcher, Shamir and even the Ayatollah,[3] and that is going very far – but you will see the helpless and hopeless condition I am in.

Yours,

[Isaiah]

TO ARTHUR SCHLESINGER

II April 1984

Headington House

Dear Arthur

Your letter to the Peace Prize people is absolutely marvellous[4] – its superiority to that of e.g. David Astor[5] cannot be overstated. I cannot remember if I sent them my own letter or not, but I do not think it could have any weight – for ethnic reasons. But I shall fire one off anyway, stirred by your encouragement.

So Joe is still lecturing? He was in far better form here than I have seen him for a long, long time – didn't drink, no enormous 'Ah's, no tirades against 'liber*als*',[6] altogether a return to the best years. Extraordinary. It must all be the work of doctors, for I know of no political or personal events that could have caused such splendid return to form. My feeling is that we are in for Mrs Thatcher and Reagan for a good long time – that all the old hacks should look for other professions. There is a faint ray of hope in Israel, but that

---

1 William Phillips (1907–2002), US editor, co-founded the revolutionary socialist, but anti-Stalinist, *Partisan Review* 1934 and edited it until shortly before his death.

2 'Nothing comes from nothing', a principle common to all the ancient Greek physicists, and canonically expressed by Lucretius, *De rerum natura* 1. 150, though not in this exact form, whose origin is unknown.

3 Khomeini.

4 Schlesinger had written to the Nobel Peace Prize Committee, 21 March 1984, in support of the candidacy of Peace Now: 'It is hard to imagine a more effective and dramatic demonstration of dedication to peaceful solutions in difficult and dangerous circumstances than Peace Now. In a time and region swept by bitter emotions, Peace Now has been the unwavering voice of conciliation and rationality.'

5 (Francis) David Langhorne Astor (1912–2001), editor, *Observer*, 1948–75. IB knew Astor from Oxford in the early 1930s; their mutual friends included Adam von Trott, whom Astor revered more than IB did.

6 'Although foreign policy monopolised his last years, and although he liked to tease friends as "liber-*als*" to the accompaniment of his booming laugh, he was [at] least something of a liberal himself.' AS, op. cit. (171/5).

might mean the return of the old hacks too. The sight of the Walt Rostows[1] here, together with that of the man who used to write Johnson's[2] speeches (what is his name?[3] he is an academic, Jewish, dark hair, dark face, rode very high at the end of Kennedy and beginning of Johnson), reminded me of old hacks – and the state I was in when I told Henry Luce[4] that it was faith that did all the harm and spilt all the blood. You can imagine how ill received that was. Still, I would not like to go with 'pas trop de zèle'[5] inscribed on my tomb.

Yours ever, ⟨Much love from us both⟩

Isaiah   [...]

TO LOUIS RAPOPORT

7 May 1984

Headington House

Dear Mr Rapoport,

[...] So far as the issue of Wise, Goldmann[6] and the official Zionist leadership in America during the war versus Bergson[7] are concerned, I have told you all I know in the letter of 2 November: the Zionist leaders thought that Bergson's activities were likely to irritate, and possibly alienate, important American individuals and groups, whose support they regarded as crucial to the fulfilment of Zionist aims. [...] I am not clear even now how much difference Bergson's agitation actually made – whether e.g. the petitions signed by senators, congressmen and influential persons in fact made a significant

1 Walt Whitman Rostow (1916–2003), US economist and political theorist; as a special adviser to JFK he was a passionate defender, and an architect, of the Vietnam War; special assistant for national security affairs to President Johnson 1966–9; m. 1947 Elspeth Vaughan Davies (1917–2007), political scientist, educationalist and academic administrator.

2 Lyndon Baines Johnson (1908–73), Democrat US President 1963–9; senator, Texas, 1949–61, John F. Kennedy's running mate 1960, Vice President 1961–3.

3 Richard Naradof Goodwin (b. 1931), US lawyer, academic and writer; speechwriter and adviser to Presidents Kennedy and Johnson and to Senator Robert F. Kennedy.

4 Henry Robinson Luce (1898–1967), Republican editor and publisher; founder of *Time* magazine 1923 (with Briton Hadden) and *Life* 1936, and editor in chief of all his publications until 1964.

5 This maxim is attributed to Talleyrand in various forms. The earliest published citation of this version we have found is 'Surtout pas trop de zèle' ('Above all, not too much zeal') in 'Bien mal acquis ne profite jamais' (by 'Marcant'), *Revue de Marseille et de Provence* 5 no. 7 (July 1859), 335. An earlier version is 'N'ayez pas de zèle' ('Don't be zealous'), in C.-A. Sainte-Beuve, 'Madame de Staël' (1835): Sainte-Beuve, *Oeuvres*, ed. Maxime Leroy ([Paris], 1949–51), ii 1104; 'point de zèle' ('no zeal at all') is also found.

6 Based in NY during WW2.

7 Peter Bergson, pseudonym of Hillel Kook (1915–2001), Lithuanian-born Revisionist Zionist; as a founding member and representative of the Irgun, he accompanied Ze'ev Jabotinsky to the US 1940, remaining there after Jabotinsky's death; as Peter Bergson he became a spokesman for Revisionist Zionism, agitating for a Jewish army, and from 1942 publicising the extreme plight of Jews in Nazi-controlled Europe; Bergson bypassed conventional diplomatic channels, and instead made direct appeals to the US public and to Congress, and this directness, accompanied by a sometimes bombastic tone, alienated established Zionist and Jewish groups in the US.

difference to the policies of the Roosevelt administration. What did make an enormous difference, of course, were the first reports and photographs from the death camps. This turned the tide throughout America in a pro- Zionist direction. But even if agitation, shouting, did not work – at any rate after the war had started – it certainly could have made a difference in the 1930s; and even if it might not have done so, given the rigid opposition to immigration by Congress, government departments, etc. [...] I agree with you that Jews should have shouted, even if this frightened some of the timorous rich among them; that it was shameful not to have done so; that there are circumstances in which decent people can only do one thing. At least the British Home Office let in a much larger proportion of Jewish refugees than did the Americans.

Now, let me turn to your observations about myself. Of course I cannot ask you not to be critical of what I did or said or was – if I really said or did or was what you take me to have done or been. But I do, naturally enough, take exception to being seriously misrepresented – I suspect this to be due to my failure to make myself sufficiently clear in my replies to your questions. [...]

You say that 'both the ostensibly pro-Zionist Berlin and his colleague William Hayter ... thought that the Anti-Zionist Declaration should be issued immediately', etc.[1] I simply cannot understand this. Issues of policy were not referred to me on this, or anything else. I knew nothing of the Joint Declaration until the whole thing was over and the Declaration dead.[2] My job was to report general political opinion in the US and the views of influential individuals and groups – I was a kind of foreign correspondent, save that some of my reports went in a code and to a limited official readership. The Joint Declaration had been killed before it was leaked to Drew Pearson, I don't know by whom; and when the storm of Jewish protest naturally occurred I was asked by the Foreign Office (in the person of Angus Malcolm) to tell them what I could discover about what had happened. [...] I drafted an official letter to Malcolm and told him what was being said, but the sentence you quote [...] about how melancholy it was that the State Department should have failed to implement the Declaration was certainly not written by me. I did tell you, in my letter of 2 November, that this sentence was not mine – and I stand by that. I cannot understand why you should fail to believe me [...]. Since my pro-Zionist sentiments were no secret from my colleagues, such a sentence by me would have caused astonishment and comment, I am sure, at the time. I must therefore ask you to withdraw this

---

1 In the long letter of 9 August 1943 (220/2) IB writes: 'Both William Hayter and I thought that it was now or never, and that delay would automatically invite intrigue. We were, therefore, somewhat dismayed to learn that the statement had been postponed in order to get the War Department to vet it and if necessary strengthen it' (L1 445).

2 But cf. 'Goldman came rushing to see me to ask if anything could be done to stop the declaration' (ibid.).

wholly unjust charge against me: I do not want to have to deny the truth of
what you have said, and feel sure that you do not wish to put me under this,
to me disagreeable, necessity. The sentence in question was not one which
I was capable of uttering. I have never indulged in any kind of camouflage in
my life, and hope I never shall.

[...] The impression you give of some kind of double-dealing on my part
is, I assure you, false – and indeed gravely defamatory. Again (on the same
page) you speak of my 'delicate game'. I played no game. I gave no confidential information to Dr Weizmann and his colleagues, and it should be said
for them that, close as my relations were to Dr Weizmann, then and later,
he never asked me for 'classified' information – if only out of a desire not to
embarrass me, I imagine – and this held for other Zionists also. [...]

I am perfectly ready to accept responsibility, and if need be criticism, for
what I truly did or said, e.g. my underestimate of Jewish influence in 1945, or
my acceptance of the official Zionists' view of Bergson's activities, but not
for what I did not believe or say or do. Memory may be a fallible guide, but
not as fallible as that in matters which mean a great deal to one. And this
applies no less to your words in the Epilogue on my being 'on the wrong side
of the Hoskins affair'. I was not.

Let me add two relevant footnotes. First, about Hoskins. I did not know
him at the time of the Joint Declaration. I met him only once, a month or
two later, at the home of a colleague of mine who had served in Baghdad,
and was a mild anti-Zionist. Hoskins launched a diatribe against the Zionist
intrigues which had scotched his excellent plan, which he described to
me – Joint Declaration and all. I told him what I thought of his plan and
his motives, and the likely consequences. We began to argue; it ended in
a violent row, I think the worst row I have ever had with anyone, and finally
he left in a state of great anger. He told one of my friends, a British official,
still alive and still a friend,[1] that I was a Zionist agent and that he would try to
convey to the British Embassy that they should get rid of me. For all I know
he may have tried to do this, but I heard nothing of it, although our common
friend could never understand why Hoskins conceived such hatred for me. It
was, in fact, reciprocated.

Secondly, about the Jewish Army. While I was an official of the British
Information Services in New York in 1941 I was called on by Peter Bergson,
and later by one of Jabotinsky's[2] people (I cannot remember the name), both
of whom asked me about why I thought the British government objected to

1 Presumably William Hayter.
2 Ze'ev Jabotinsky (1880–1940) né Vol'f Evnovich Zhabotinsky, Odessa-born Revisionist Zionist
leader; orator, editor, writer – using the pseudonym Altalena ('swing': cf. 362/2) – and soldier;
MBE 1919 for his service in the British army during WWI, but subsequently played a major role in
challenging the British Mandate in Palestine, becoming identified with a nationalist, right-wing
Zionism, though in fact a democrat who loathed totalitarianism.

the idea of a Jewish Army. I cannot remember what I said to Bergson, but
I do remember that, when the other man asked me whether I thought that
the proposal was blocked for political reasons, I said that this might well be
the case, that Lord Lloyd,[1] whom I had met at a dinner in London in 1940,
had talked about the proposal for a Jewish Army made to him by Weizmann
(he was at that time Secretary for War), and then muttered something about
the fact that the price paid for Weizmann's services as a chemist in the First
World War had been too high – or some such remark. Jabotinsky's man
reported my response in a letter sent to someone in London. The letter was
duly intercepted by the British censors, and I received a stern reprimand from
the Ministry of Information for having committed a monstrous blunder.
Later, in the Foreign Office papers in the PRO, I discovered that a suggestion had been made that I should be sacked for taking an anti-government
line (the official reason for refusing the Army was lack of equipment). I was
defended by a friendly official, who said that no great harm, in his opinion,
had been done, and that a severe warning might be enough. So much for my
'ostensible pro-Zionism'.

[…] I cannot persuade myself that you could allow the offending passages
about me to stand in view of what I have said. I am sure that your purpose,
like mine, is to establish the truth, or get as near to it as one can. I hope that
you agree with me – I shall be glad to hear that you do.

Yours sincerely,
Isaiah Berlin

TO PATRICIA GORE-BOOTH[2]

5 July 1984 [*manuscript*]

Headington House

Dear Pat,

I was very distressed to see the obituary of Paul[3] in the *Times* – I liked
and respected and admired him very much: & he was wonderfully nice to
me in Washington & forever after – I remember him as a contemporary
at Oxford – at lectures – at classes – in the streets – we did meet then, but
only really came to know each other in Lord Halifax's embassy: what first
astonished and delighted me about him was that he preserved his humanity

1 George Ambrose Lloyd (1879–1941), GCIE 1918, 1st Baron Lloyd 1925, Conservative politician and
   diplomat; secretary of state for the colonies (not for war, *pace* IB) 1940–1.
2 Patricia Mary Gore-Booth (1921–2012) née Ellerton, daughter of Montague Ellerton, company
   secretary, of Adelaide, Australia, and latterly Kobe, Japan; it was in Japan that she met Paul Gore-
   Booth (next note), then at the British Embassy in Tokyo; m. 1940 in Tokyo.
3 Paul Henry Gore-Booth (1909–84), KCMG 1957, life peer 1969; Balliol 1928–32 (greats [classics]
   1931, PPE 1932); entered diplomatic service 1933; 2nd secretary, Tokyo, 1938–42; 1st secretary,
   Washington, 1942–5; UK high commissioner, India, 1960–5; permanent undersecretary of state,
   FO, 1965–9; head, diplomatic service, 1968–9.

intact – mysteriously, given the smoothing out, & (I can't help noticing) somewhat dehumanizing effect of the diplomatic service. I don't mean the naturally smooth or unreal: but the need to suppress one's natural moral reactions and feelings to fit in with policy decided above one: to find bad reasons to justify the wicked or stupid behaviour of other governments (and one's own) with the perfectly good purpose of preventing conflict – the pot from boiling over – & defending the national interest – that is bound (as with lawyers) to atrophy human responses – spontaneity – to petrify feeling. We've all known diplomats who were totally honest, brave, decent, charming, upright, able, excellent, devoted servants of the state: but after, say, 35, a mask, a carapace, develops: & feelings turned in on themselves sometimes rot inwardly[1] & lead to terrible bitterness as in Cadogan's memoirs.[2] Well: what I want to say – I do apologise for all [th]is maundering [–] is that Paul miraculously (or not [–] perhaps it was marriage to you, which is evidence in itself) escaped this: remained open, human, warmhearted, in touch with the human feelings of others – in the world outside the office – with a great variety of social, religious, personal kinds of experience which made him about the most understanding servant of the Crown I have ever known: and all this with immense expert skill at the business of the Foreign Office, scrupulous observance of the rules, justice, kindness, and fearless integrity. There: I must not go on: I am not composing a memorial oration: but it *was* unusually intelligent of the office – or of someone – to make him its head. Wherever I saw him in some public assembly, my spirits rose: & his love for you and what you were to him & for his life & happiness in all the tribulations of health and thorns of life, everyone who knows you, knows. Words are not much good at saying what one feels when really fateful things happen: & mine are pretty illegible into the bargain. God bless you for many years – & *don't* acknowledge this in any way, please. Aline feels as I do, we send you our warmest wishes –

    Isaiah.

---

1 'The hungry sheep look up, and are not fed, / But swoln with wind, and the rank mist they draw, / Rot inwardly, and foul contagion spread.' St Peter in John Milton, 'Lycidas' (1637; a poem of which IB had parts, at any rate, by heart), lines 125–7.

2 Alexander George Montagu Cadogan (1884–1968), KCMG 1934, OM 1951, diplomat; permanent representative to the UN, NY, 1946–50. 'In his official life he was reserved, impeccably correct, and buttoned up. But when he went home to the privacy of his Diary he let fly with all the vituperation and abuse at a gentleman's command at the politicians and officials with whom he had to deal during his overworked day.' Thomas Barman, review of *The Diaries of Sir Alexander Cadogan, OM, 1938–1945*, ed. David Dilks (London, 1971), *International Affairs* 48 no. 2 (April 1972), 272–4 at 272.

TO BRYAN MAGEE

13 July 1984

Headington House

Dear Bryan,

I have read Kundera's second article:[1] I do not find it disturbing, because I believe in the truth of his general thesis – indeed, that is in part why I ceased to be a philosopher in 1950 and applied myself to reading nineteenth-century Russians, who are morally and psychologically more sympathetic to me than the great rationalist and empirical thinkers of the West. In fact, I find his thesis something that many of us 'have thought but ne'er so well expressed'.[2] Is it news to you? Only out of your excessive devotion to Popper – after all, after the scientists and the disciples in LSE (only one now, so far as I know, namely Watkins),[3] I am the greatest admirer of Popper after you, but even I think that your faith in his immortality is, perhaps, not wholly well founded. On this, Kundera is right. He is right to quote Broch,[4] who thinks that what the novel can do, only the novel can do – that Freud is wrong, who said science cannot answer all our questions, but what it cannot do, nothing else can. I don't share Kundera's enthusiasm for Thomas Mann;[5] Broch I haven't read – Heidegger, no matter how splendid, cannot reveal what artists, novelists and poets can about the contradictory and many-faceted moral and religious visions. He is wrong to say that Tolstoy wrote about the power of the irrational: he tried to expose rational planning of the German kind, to

1 Milan Kundera (b. 1929), Czech academic and novelist, whose 1st novel, The Joke (1967), explored, with ironic intent, the lives of Czechs under Stalinist repression; officially proscribed after the Soviet-led invasion of 1968, and allowed to emigrate, he has lived since 1975 in Paris, becoming a French citizen 1981. The 'second article' is 'The Novel and Europe', NYRB, 19 July 1984, 15–19, in which Kundera asserts the overriding importance of the novel, especially the European novel, as a means of approaching the complex and unfathomable nature of being – a function not performed by the rationalism of the sciences, technology, politics and history, indeed one ignored by them. 'The novel's essence is complexity. Every novel says to the reader: "Things are not as simple as you think." That is the novel's eternal truth, but its voice grows ever fainter in a world based on easy, quick answers […]. In this world, it's either Anna or Karenin who is right, and the ancient wisdom of Cervantes, which speaks of the difficulty of knowing and of a truth that eludes the grasp, seems cumbersome and useless' (18).
2 'True Wit is Nature to Advantage drest, / What oft was Thought, but ne'er so well Exprest': Alexander Pope, An Essay on Criticism, 2nd ed. (London, 1713), 15 (lines 297–8). In the 1st edition (London, 1711), 19, Pope writes 'ne'er before Exprest'.
3 John William Nevill Watkins (1924–99), philosopher; studied politics at the LSE 1945–9, where he came under the conflicting influences of Karl Popper and Harold Laski; lecturer, dept of government, LSE, 1950; transferred to Popper's dept of philosophy, logic and scientific method 1958 as reader in the history of philosophy; prof. of philosophy 1966–89.
4 Hermann Broch (1886–1951), Austrian writer of Jewish descent, emigrated to US 1938 after a brief imprisonment in the wake of the Anschluss (459/9); he was deeply concerned with human rights and mass pyschology, and his works exemplified his belief that art should be of service to its age.
5 Thomas Mann (1875–1955), German novelist and essayist; Nobel Prize in Literature 1929; emigrated from Germany soon after Hitler came to power; domiciled, 1938, in US, whence he wrote and broadcast against the Nazi regime; US citizen 1940; returned to Europe 1952.

him a hollow fraud, because of our ignorance, because of the greater grasp
of truth in the intuitive sense of reality (peasants, Kutuzov etc.). But he was
himself rational through and through – that, indeed, was part of the trouble
he had with religion. He simply believed that too many causes – 'small
causes'[1] – governed the world, causes which we cannot know or integrate;
but that in principle, if we could, rational behaviour would be possible. He
denounced the arrogance of science and system-building, but did not celebrate dark, irrational forces as Hamann or Nietzsche or D. H. Lawrence[2] did.
But that is enough – I must go to Italy. I shall see you, I hope, on return – I am
sorry you won't be in Salzburg. Up Kundera! I must sit down and read his
novels.

Yours,
    Isaiah

PS I cannot value *Jacques le fataliste* or *Tristram Shandy* as Kundera does[3] – the
first is brilliant and interesting but not a masterpiece (it is scarcely a novel
in our sense); the second is, of course, an enormously admired classic, with
a huge following, particularly among German Romantics – did Schopenhauer
like it?[4] For me it is the beginning of a kind of wistful, self-deprecating
fantasy, which generated Lamb and Betjeman, full of charm, and deliberate
inconsequentiality – but too deliberate, too contrived, too fey. [...]

*In his views on architecture IB was no reactionary, and greatly admired the
Japanese architect Kenzō Tange,[5] designer of the modernist Hiroshima Peace
Memorial Museum (1949–56). But he also prized neoclassical harmony and*

1 'Only by taking infinitesimally small units for observation (the differential of history, that is, the
   individual tendencies of men) and attaining to the art of integrating them (that is, finding the
   sum of these infinitesimals) can we hope to arrive at the laws of history.' *War and Peace*, vol. 3,
   part 3, chapter 1: L. N. Tolstoy, *Polnoe sobranie sochinenii* (Moscow/Leningrad, 1928–64) xi 265–6.
   In a letter of 5 January 1954 to Meyer Schapiro IB writes of Tolstoy's attraction to 'the hypothesis
   that an omniscient rational being could integrate all the infinity of small causes' (L2 420).
2 David Herbert Lawrence (1885–1930), novelist and poet who stressed the central role in life of
   (especially) sexual feelings.
3 Kundera wrote that Denis Diderot's *Jacques le fataliste et son maître* (Paris, [1796]) and Sterne's
   Tristram Shandy (149/5) 'are for me the two greatest novelistic works of the eighteenth century.
   These two novels are playful on a grandiose scale and reach pinnacles of unseriousness never
   scaled before, or since. After Sterne and Diderot, the novel tied itself down to obligations of
   verisimilitude, realistic setting, and chronological order, and abandoned the seam opened up by
   these two masterpieces, which could have led to a different development of the novel (yes, an
   alternative history of the European novel can be imagined ...).' op. cit. (241/1), 18.
4 Arthur Schopenhauer (1788–1860), German post-Kantian philosopher famous for extreme
   pessimism. In 'On the Metaphysics of the Beautiful and Aesthetics' (1851) Schopenhauer
   described *Tristram Shandy* (149/5) as one of 'four novels [...] at the top of their class': *Parerga and
   Paralipomena: Short Philosophical Essays*, trans. E. F. J. Payne (Oxford, 1974), ii 440. The other 3 top
   novels were Goethe's *Wilhelm Meister['s Apprenticeship]* (1795–6), Rousseau's *Nouvelle Héloïse* (1761)
   and Cervantes' *Don Quixote* (1605, 1615).
5 Kenzō Tange (1913–2005): his approach balanced Western and Japanese aesthetics, and the traditional with the modern.

proportions, and was one of the National Gallery trustees strongly opposed to the Hampton extension proposed by the Ahrends, Burton and Koralek (ABK) partnership in 1983. In order to pay for itself the extension was to combine gallery space with a prestige office development, and at the trustees' behest ABK were obliged to modify their original design. Their revised plan included a 120-foot-high glass-faced tower topped by aluminium masts, and this proved the most controversial part of a vision that elicited strong opposition, to which the Prince of Wales gave voice in a famous image. On 30 May 1984 he addressed the guests at the 150th anniversary gala evening of the Royal Institute of British Architects at Hampton Court, making a much quoted speech in which he appealed for greater harmony between the aspirations of architects and the feelings of 'the mass of ordinary people'. He took the Hampton extension as a case in point:

Instead of designing an extension to the elegant facade of the National Gallery which complements it, [...] it looks as if we may be presented with a kind of vast municipal fire station, complete with the sort of tower that contains a siren.

I would understand better this type of high-tech approach if you demolished the whole of Trafalgar Square and started again with a single architect responsible for the entire layout, but what is proposed is like a monstrous carbuncle on the face of a much loved and elegant friend. Apart from anything else, it defeats me why anyone wishing to display the early Renaissance pictures belonging to the gallery should do so in a new gallery so manifestly at odds with the whole spirit of that age of astonishing proportion.[1]

The Prince's intervention was welcomed by IB and came at a crucial time. Shortly afterwards IB wrote to Noel Annan, then chairman of the board of trustees of the National Gallery, seeking to galvanise resistance to the ABK design, and the government subsequently announced that it had been rejected, the tower being singled out for particular criticism. Meanwhile the trustees sought private funding to enable the extension to be devoted exclusively to gallery space, and on 2 April 1985 it was announced that John Sainsbury[2] and his brothers[3] would donate some £50 million. This gift transformed the situation, and the Sainsbury Wing, designed by the postmodernist partnership of Robert Venturi and Denise Scott Brown,[4] opened to general acclaim on 9 July 1991.

1 The Prince of Wales, 'Give us Design with Feeling', *Times*, 31 May 1984, 16b–e at 16d–e.
2 John Davan Sainsbury (b. 1927), Kt 1980, life peer 1989; director, Sainsbury's (J. Sainsbury plc), 1958–92, vice chair 1967–9, chair 1969–92, president since 1992; director, ROH, 1969–85, chair 1987–91; trustee, National Gallery, 1976–83.
3 Simon David Davan Sainsbury (1930–2006), businessman and philanthropist; director, J. Sainsbury, from 1959, deputy chair 1969–79; trustee, National Gallery, 1991–8; chair, Wallace Gallery, 1992–7. Timothy Alan Davan Sainsbury (b. 1932), Kt 1995, businessman and politician; director, J. Sainsbury, 1962–83; Conservative MP 1973–97; minister of state for trade 1990–2, for industry 1992–4.
4 Robert Charles Venturi (b. 1925) and Denise Scott Brown (b. 1931) née Lakofski, American architects; partners in the firm Venturi, Scott Brown and Associates.

TO NOEL ANNAN

14 July 1984 [*carbon*]

Headington House

Dear Noel,

[...] I believe we ought to tell the Minister[1] that the majority of the Board are now against this building altogether [...], that we have a duty to the public not to outrage it with a building in which we never ourselves believed much – it is not as if we were defending a bold scheme against the philistines – and that our 'change of heart' was a gradual process, as the design progressed and became less and less tolerable. [...]

I do believe in immediate action. Michael Levey[2] may well explode, but never mind – I do not need to tell you that I realise that you will stand up to him on this issue, whether he goes to the Tuesday meeting (which I, alas, cannot attend) or not. You behaved admirably at the last meeting, with splendid courage and firmness (that we shall be accused of infirmity of will does not matter – better candour and truth than mere obstinacy, and it is marvellous that you do not mind our making ourselves ridiculous). Of course John Baring,[3] Michael Sacher[4] and, no doubt, Stuart Young[5] may wish to dissociate themselves from the majority, and this, no doubt, will have to be made clear – i.e. that the entire Board is against the scheme as it stands, that a minority think that with a modified tower it might do, but the majority are dead against what has emerged from the drawing board, and believe (I think this quite important) than no architect can be trusted to produce a satisfactory revamped scheme if the heart of the old one (and the architect insisted that it was that) has been torn from it. To force a man to produce something he does not believe in cannot turn out well.

We may well be threatened with the need to wait for the report, which I am sure would be unwise, with the collapsing morale of the staff (moral blackmail, to be ignored); and the possibility should not be suppressed that someone may resign. If you and I do, the plan really would be dead, I think – you and I and Bridget[6] and Caryl[7] could mount the pyre with some dignity,

---

1 Charles Patrick Fleeming Jenkin (b. 1926), life peer 1987; Conservative MP 1964–87; (inter alia) secretary of state for the environment 1983–5.

2 Michael (Vincent) Levey (1927–2008), Kt 1981; assistant keeper, National Gallery, 1951–66, deputy keeper 1966–8, keeper 1968–73, deputy director 1970–3, director 1973–86.

3 John Francis Harcourt Baring (b. 1928), Kt 1983, 7th Baron Ashburton 1991; managing director, Barings Bank, 1955–74, chair 1974–89; chair, Barings plc, 1985–9; director, BP, 1982–92, chair 1992–5; trustee, National Gallery, 1981–7.

4 Michael Moses Sacher (1917–86), vice chair, Marks and Spencer, 1972–82, joint vice chair 1982–4; trustee, National Gallery, 1982–6.

5 Stuart Young (1934–86), senior partner, Hacker Young (chartered accountants), 1960–86; chair, BBC, 1983–6; trustee, National Gallery, 1980–6.

6 Bridget Riley was a trustee, National Gallery, 1981–8.

7 Caryl Hubbard (b. 1933) née Whineray, director of Pallent House Gallery; trustee, National Gallery, 1983–92.

I believe, lamented by Howard[1] and viewed nervously but with crocodile tears by the minority. What a marvellous letter we could send, roughly following *Country Life*, which apparently urges the Board to come to its senses.[2] We fly the colours of the Prince of Wales, *In hoc vinces*.[3]

[...] If Michael blows up, so be it. The faithful will march to the edge and over into the abyss. I believe that we can win, and have a perfectly good building; that we should let things sleep for a year or two and recommence. Even Broackes[4] might come round to this – but even if not, others could be found after the dust has settled. I apologise for all this; I am sure it is otiose and that you have it all and more in mind. *Avanti!*[5] I had a talk with Jacob[6] and John Sainsbury – very sound. [...]

Yours,

Isaiah

TO IRVING SINGER

20 November 1984

Headington House

Dear Irving,

The Nature of Love[7] has not arrived yet, but your letter has, and that, I feel, is almost as good – in fact, rather better – shorter and more personal. My health is only moderate, my spirits fairly low but not very. The loss of voice does not get me down, because it liberates me from lectures, classes, after-dinner speeches and other horrors. Otherwise, given my enormous age, I really am quite mobile and active. I sit in the British Museum, day by day, reading about German Romantics, on whom in principle I wish to write a huge book – but whether I have enough years to do this in is the question. Did Freud read Proust? Did Proust read Freud?[8] If they'd met they certainly would not have got on, that is clear. Nor would either have got on with Joyce,[9] that is equally clear. Certainly Freud would have denied that you, or anyone else, is ever too old for love – but for purely physiological

1 (Gordon) Howard Eliot Hodgkin (b. 1932), Kt 1992, painter and print-maker; trustee, National Gallery, 1974–85.
2 Article/letter untraced.
3 In full 'In hoc signo vinces', 'In this sign thou shalt conquer', motto used first by Constantine the Great, subsequently by others, but not by the Prince of Wales, whose motto is 'Ich dien[e]', 'I serve'.
4 Nigel Broackes (1934–99), Kt 1984; chair, 1969–92, Trafalgar House, the property developers employed by the government to build the extension to the National Gallery.
5 'Forward!'
6 Lord Rothschild was chair, board of trustees, National Gallery, 1985–91.
7 The 2nd vol. (1984) of IS's 3-vol. work on *The Nature of Love* (Chicago, 1966–87) was subtitled *Courtly and Romantic*. IB viewed IS's philosophical treatment of love with a measure of scepticism.
8 It is unclear how much of each other's work, if any, these contemporaries read.
9 James Augustine Aloysius Joyce (1882–1941), Dublin-born writer, author of (inter alia) *Dubliners* (London, 1914), *A Portrait of the Artist as a Young Man* (NY, 1916) and *Ulysses* (London, 1922).

reasons it does not happen all that frequently. As for the meaning of life, I do not believe that it has any: I do not at all ask what it is, for I suspect it has none, and this is a source of great comfort to me – we make of it what we can, and that is all there is about it. Those who seek for some deep, cosmic, all-embracing, teleologically arguable libretto or god are, believe me, pathetically mistaken. [...]

Yours ever,
  Isaiah

TO MARTIN GILBERT

8 January 1985 [*carbon*]

Headington House

Dear Martin,

[...] Now you ask me about WSC. I met him in all on four occasions, only once properly to speak to. The three earlier occasions were (*a*) in the White House on one of his visits to Washington, when I was handed some kind of message to him from the embassy, which I delivered, and received a few kindly words of general encouragement: he asked me what I did and did not listen, and said 'Carry on, carry on, do your best, my boy', or something of the kind; (*b*) at Hatfield,[1] where he devoted his entire attention to the American ambassador – Douglas[2] – and paid no attention to anyone else, including his host. I remember David Cecil was there, determined to secure his attention, and finally got through with 'Isaiah and I were arguing about the meaning of the word "pettifogging" – what do you think it means, exactly?' ' "Pettifogging" means deliberately obfuscating the issue in a pedantic manner', Winston replied, and then turned his back on him and back to Douglas and Anglo-American relations. (*c*) at Oliver Lyttelton's,[3] discussing the possibility of the Third World War: he wondered which of the great centres of culture we would be forced to bomb first – Paris? Rome? Someone said 'I am told that Crossman says that armies and navies will be quite useless in the next war', to which Winston replied 'Crossman – double-Crossman – behind the bars with him, he is no true friend of liberty or of England.' I may

---

1 Hatfield House, a Jacobean country house in Hertfordshire, seat of the Cecils. Churchill's host would have been Robert Arthur James ('Bobbety') Gascoyne-Cecil (1893–1972), Viscount Cranborne 1903, 5th Marquess of Salisbury 1947; a Unionist MP 1929–41, he had resigned with Eden in February 1938 in protest at the government's foreign policy, but returned to office under Churchill as paymaster general 1940, and was leader, Lords, 1942–5, 1951–7; secretary of state for commonwealth relations 1952; lord president of the council 1952–7.

2 Lewis Williams Douglas (1894–1974), Democrat US politician, businessman, diplomat and academic; representative, Arizona, 1927–33; US ambassador to UK 1947–51.

3 Oliver Lyttelton (1893–1972), 1st Viscount Chandos 1954, KG 1970; Conservative MP 1940–54, cabinet minister in Churchill's wartime government, secretary of state for the colonies 1951–4; turned thereafter to business, and sat on the board of a number of high-profile companies.

have got this wrong but that is what I remembered – or rather, remember having remembered at the time.

The only real meeting I had with WSC was when Bill Deakin[1] took me to lunch at Chartwell[2] during the first post-war Labour government, probably in 1947 or so. He conceived the idea that I knew something about Russia, and wished me to vet his account, in the first volume of his memoirs, about the Moscow trials. I knew no more than anyone else who read the newspapers, although I knew Russian (which did not particularly help with this). He propped up the page proofs against some object on the luncheon table, as if wishing me to read it there and then; then felt that this was not exactly courteous, withdrew the proofs and chatted. He seemed convinced that Stalin was right to execute Marshal Tukhachevsky[3] and the others, because he had been told by Beneš that these men were traitors. I said that no evidence had been discovered for this, so far as I knew, in the German papers captured by the allies; but he was very insistent. I imagine that what probably happened was that the NKVD – or whatever it was called then – fed information through Prague so that it appeared to come from a reliable friendly source. Anyway, Winston seemed to believe it and could not be shaken […].[4]

He then proceeded to denounce the Astor family,[5] saying that none of its members had done England any good, that they were really a pretty dismal and disastrous lot: he sang a song to the effect that 'We will hang the Astors from a mulberry tree.' He asked me who my ambassador was during the war. When I said 'Lord Halifax', he said, so far as I can remember, something that went as follows: 'Edward is a man compounded of charm. In his presence I invariably melt. He is no coward. No gentleman is. But there is something which goes through him like a yellow streak: grovel, grovel, grovel. Grovel to the Germans, grovel to the Indians, grovel to the Americans' – or

1 (Frederick) William Dampier ('Bill') Deakin (1913–2005), Kt 1975, historian, research assistant to, and literary collaborator with, Winston Churchill; seconded to SOE (Special Operations Executive) during WW2; founding Warden, St Antony's, 1950–68; close friend of Aline Berlin.

2 Churchill's home near Westerham, Kent, which he had bought 1922.

3 Mikhail Nikolaevich Tukhachevsky (1893–1937), Soviet military commander; a veteran of WW1, he is credited with reorganising the Red Army in the interwar years; appointed a Marshal of the USSR 1935; arrested 2 years later and found guilty, with 7 other senior army commanders, of conspiring with Nazi Germany; the execution of all 8 presaged Stalin's purge of the officer corps.

4 Robert Conquest in The Great Terror: Stalin's Purge of the Thirties (London, 1968), 219, relates that Tukhachevsky was framed by German intelligence, which, in order to destabilise the Soviet military, fed incriminating information to Stalin through the Czech leader Beneš. More recent accounts suggest that the forged German case merely gave Stalin and his henchmen in the NKVD (as it was indeed then called) the pretext that they needed to eliminate the only force in Soviet society capable of challenging Stalin's absolute rule.

5 Waldorf Astor (1879–1952), 2nd Viscount Astor 1919, politician and newspaper proprietor, and his wife, Nancy Witcher Astor (1879–1964) née Langhorne; Nancy succeeded her husband as Unionist MP for Plymouth 1919, the 1st woman elected as an MP to take her seat in the Commons; they both supported appeasement in the 1930s, their grand Buckinghamshire home, Cliveden, hosting the 'Cliveden set', which became synomyous with that policy – a strong reason for Churchill taking against them.

'to everybody'. When I said something feeble like 'I imagine that he had really had little experience of foreign affairs or foreigners before being put in charge of the Foreign Office', he said 'If you believe that, you would believe anything', à la the Duke of Wellington.[1]

Then he drew me into a corner and asked me what honorarium I would accept for reading his first volume and commenting on it. I said that it was a great honour and that I should not dream of expecting payment or agreeing to be paid: he said 'That is very monkish of you, much too unworldly. Anyone who does a job must be paid for it. You must not behave in this absurd way.' Bill Deakin, who was there, may or may not corroborate all this; the conversation, or fragments of it, is as I remember his words. I remember little else. Except, of course, that he did then tell me the story about the confusion between Irving Berlin and myself,[2] in detail – you know the story, so I need not tell it to you in his or anybody else's words. When I asked him 'Mr Churchill, when you asked him those questions, what did he reply?', he said 'Oh, he said "It'll be all right" and that kind of thing.' And said goodbye. Mrs Churchill[3] said goodbye too, and said, 'Winston is rather sad today. His little dog has been killed' – or had died – 'He doesn't really like dogs at all, but he feels that he should.'

I then read the volume and produced my comments. I received a letter which said, I think, 'Thank you for your observations. I will send you my rejoinders presently.' But no rejoinders ever came. The thing I noticed about the first volume – I do not know if it is in the final version – is his account of the visit to Munich, when he said to Hanfstaengl[4] something to the effect that he admired men who raised their countries from a low condition, the patriots who stood up and lifted people when they needed it, etc. This Hitler appeared to him to have done, but what had he against the Jews?[5] Of course,

1 The story goes that Arthur Wellesley (1769–1852), 1st Duke of Wellington, who looked very like the painter George Jones (1786–1869), was once accosted in the street by a man who said, 'Mr Jones, I believe?' Wellington is said to have replied, 'If you believe that, you'll believe anything.'
2 L1 478–80. Irving Berlin (1888–1989) né Israel Isidore Baline, Russian-born Jewish American composer who helped define American popular song: his many hits included *White Christmas*.
3 Clementine Ogilvy ('Clemmie/Clemmy') Spencer-Churchill (1885–1977) née Hozier, life peer 1965; m. 1908 Winston Churchill.
4 Ernst Franz Sedgwick Hanfstaengl (1887–1975), Munich-born German American Harvard-educated businessman; supporter and confidant of Hitler, and from 1931 a Nazi Party member; he defected 1937, and was interned in England at the outbreak of war; subsequently assisted the US government by supplying detailed information on the Nazi leadership, particularly Hitler.
5 In a proof of *The Gathering Storm* [*The Second World War* i] (London, 1948) which IB saw, Churchill reports himself as saying: 'Why is your chief so violent against the Jews? I can quite understand being angry with Jews who have done wrong or are against the country, and I understand resisting them if they try to gain too much power in any walk of life; but what is the sense of being against a man simply because of his birth? How can any man help how he is born?' IB underlines 'power in any walk of life' and comments in the margin: 'the view that Jews ought to be kept in their place might attract some criticism: it is a very live issue in the U.S.A. at the moment'. Churchill changes 'gain too much' to 'monopolise', which is the reading of the published book (65). But the addition in the proof of 'as a community' after 'power' is not made in the book.

if the Jews were against the country, they had to be put down, but surely the German Jews were among the most patriotic of German citizens, and perfectly loyal: why, then, all this? Hanfstaengl must have realised that if he brought this up during his interview in Munich with the leader of the National Socialist Party, it might lead to an altercation or a scene, the Führer might lose his temper, and the interview be off. You will find all that in vol. 1 of the war memoirs. I pointed out that requiring no opposition from Jews put them, as it were, on probation, and might not be well received by some of his readers – but I received no 'rejoinder' about this or any other point. [...]

Yours ever,

[Isaiah]

TO CHARLES, PRINCE OF WALES

2 April 1985 [*manuscript*]

Headington House

Sir,

I cannot resist – I hope Your Royal Highness will forgive me – saying how grateful London, the nation, and above all the National Gallery should be to Y.R.H for the part which the carbuncle has played in paving the way to the magnificent act of generosity on the part of John Sainsbury and his brothers, which has saved the situation. The Trustees seemed to me to have shown weakness (I include myself among them, of course) in letting themselves be rolled along as far as they were by our friend Hugh Casson[1] and the Royal Fine Arts Commission (which acclaimed the carbuncle) towards the abyss. A minority of us did try to arrest this fatal course, but not very effectively; in the end the entire Board of Trustees did recoil: but it would have been too late if it weren't for your remarks to the R.I.B.A which radically changed the entire atmosphere. Until you spoke, the opposition was none too effective: vocal, but the voices were too few; then the tide turned. If it weren't for that, God knows what the ministry's inspector – who was much too favourable to the scheme as it was – might not have said: and posterity would have denounced all those responsible, bitterly and with justice. May I warmly congratulate Your Royal Highness in saving us all from this hideous fate; I do apologise for this uncontrollable personal outburst.

I have the honour to remain Your Royal Highness's humble and obedient servant.

Isaiah Berlin

1 Hugh Maxwell Casson (1910–99), Kt 1952, architect, interior designer, artist, writer and broadcaster; prof. of environmental design, Royal College of Art, 1953–75, Provost 1980–6; President, Royal Academy, 1976–84. Casson was a member of the Royal Fine Art Commission 1960–83 'and was thus able to influence the choice of architects for major commissions during a period when the commission was eager to promote modern architecture in place of traditional survival' (Alan Powers, ODNB).

TO GEORGES NIVAT[1]

4 April 1985

Headington House

My dear Nivat,

Thank you for sending me your review of my collection of articles on Russian topics.[2] I do not, of course, begin to question your right to make whatever criticisms you think just (although I shall come to these in a moment). But I do not think that your opening remarks about Oxford high tables or my discreet and frequently rewarded diplomatic activities (I did serve in embassies, but had no executive duties of any kind and engaged in no diplomacy, discreet or otherwise) are worthy of a serious review in a serious periodical.[3] These sentences seem to me to trivialise the opening of your piece, unexpectedly – at least to me – from the man and scholar whom I have admired for all these years. You will think this too sharp, but believe me, any reader of your article cannot but be affected by the ironical tone of your little vignette, which sounds more like George Steiner than yourself. [...]

Yours ever,

Isaiah Berlin

PS I have just read your most interesting and rightly harrowing article on literature as witness to inhumanity.[4] I am glad that I can this time, without serious reservations, tell you how much I like it and respect it, particularly your reflections on Solzhenitsyn and Shalamov. (Did you ever see the film based on the Czech Communist London's book[5] about his experiences during

1 Georges Nivat (b. 1935), Russianist, one of the translators of Solzhenitsyn; prof., Geneva, 1974–2000.

2 Nivat wrote to IB, 20 March 1985, enclosing his review of RT, 'Les Penseurs russes', Le Monde, 8 March 1985, 24–5.

3 'Diplomate et professeur, Sir Isaiah Berlin est un maître typiquement oxonien, en litote et en nuance, plus authentiquement lui-même dans la dispute intellectuelle à la "haute table" d'un collège que dans le déballage publié auquel on le sent vaguement rétif' (ibid. 24) ['Sir Isaiah Berlin, diplomat and teacher, is a typical Oxford tutor, understated and sophisticated, more authentically himself in intellectual argument at a college high table than on public display, when he seems vaguely awkward'].

4 Nivat was then engaged in writing about Russian nationalism 'mainly through the arts' (letter to IB of 20 March), and enclosed an article on 'some extreme forms of literature such as Shalamov and Grossman' (ibid.), 'La littérature témoin de l'inhumain', in Symposium: les enjeux (Paris, 1985), 64–72. Varlam (né Varlaam) Tikhonovich Shalamov (1907–82), Russian journalist, writer and poet who survived the Gulag and wrote Kolyma Tales (written 1954–73), a collection of short stories drawn from that experience. Vasily Semenovich (né Iosif Solomonovich) Grossman (1905–64), prominent Soviet war correspondent who became disillusioned with Stalin's anti-Semitism: his major works Everything Flows and Life and Fate (English editions London, 2010 and 1985) were censored in the USSR and first published in the West; Sakharov was among those involved in smuggling them out.

5 Artur London (1915–86), a co-defendant in the Slánský trial (251/1): sentenced to life imprisonment but released 1955 and later rehabilitated; subsequently lived in France. L'Aveu, dans l'engrenage du procès de Prague, trans. Artur and Lise London (Paris, 1968); trans. Alastair Hamilton as The Confession (NY, 1970).

and after the Slánský Trial?[1] It bears out painfully Bettelheim's[2] account of the pathetic dependence of the victims on their torturers.)

The phenomenon of Faurisson is truly frightening[3] – I cannot understand even now how Chomsky, with all his bouts of fanaticism, came to allow his writing to be used as an introduction to Faurisson's book. And all your admirable lines on prison literature, from Dostoevsky[4] onwards [...]. But the Russian memoirs, as well as Margaret Buber-Neumann,[5] haunt one and always will. I wonder how soon they will be forgotten, except by specialists.

I do not believe that Kafka,[6] as usually thought, is in some way a prophet of this. His combination of minute realism with the sinister and irrational trap in which his heroes find themselves seems to me really different from the frightening but alas not unintelligible monstrosities of Hitler and Stalin – their purposes are not obscure. The extermination of the Jews and the reasons for it were set out clearly enough; Stalin's desire to beat his subjects into a kind of pulp out of which he could fashion whatever he liked is brutally clear. So long as there were laws men could obey, they could escape (e.g. non-Jews under Hitler) – but *arbitrary* rule leads to helplessness and therefore to malleability. The late Professor A. Kojève once said this to me and I think

1 A show trial staged in Czechoslovakia in November 1952, directed against CP members suspected of siding with the Yugoslav leader Tito in his break with Stalin; the leading figure of the 14 arrested was the Party general secretary Rudolf Slánský (1901–52), one of the 11 who were subsequently hanged.
2 Bruno Bettelheim (1903–90), Vienna-born US psychologist; assistant prof. of psychology, Chicago, 1944–7, associate prof. 1947–52, prof. 1952–73, head, Sonia Shankman Orthogenic School, a residential school for emotionally disturbed children, 1944–73; interned in Dachau and Buchenwald 1938–9, in October 1943 he wrote an article based on his experiences there, 'Individual and Mass Behaviour in Extreme Situations', *Journal of Abnormal and Social Psychology* 38 no. 4 (October 1943), 417–52: 'The main goal [of Gestapo methods] seems to be to produce in the subjects childlike attitudes and childlike dependency on the will of the leaders' (452).
3 Faurisson was judged by Christopher Hitchens to be 'an insanitary figure who maintains contact with neo-Nazi circles and whose "project" is the rehabilitation, in pseudo-scholarly form, of the Third Reich': 'The Chorus and Cassandra: What Everyone Knows about Noam Chomsky' (a spirited defence of Chomsky), *Grand Street* 5 no. 1 (Autumn 1985), 106–131 at 120. Hitchens averred that among Chomsky's very few mistakes was to have once 'unguardedly' described Faurisson as ' "a sort of relatively apolitical liberal" ' (ibid. 124): the 'unguarded' comment came in Chomsky's article 'Some Elementary Comments on The Rights of Freedom of Expression' (233/1): 'As far as I can determine, he is a relatively apolitical liberal of some sort' (xiv–xv; quoted from the English original, 123).
4 Dostoevsky's novel *The House of the Dead* (1862) depicts the life of prisoners in a Siberian camp like the one that he himself survived 1850–4 after his conviction for association with the progressive discussion group known as the Petrashevsky Circle.
5 Margarete Buber-Neumann (1901–89) née Thüring, German Communist and concentration camp survivor; m. 1922 Rafael Buber, divorced 1929; afterwards lived with Heinz Neumann, a leading German Communist, and went into exile in the USSR with him 1933; imprisoned in a Soviet labour camp 1938–40; handed over to Nazis after the Nazi–Soviet Pact, and imprisoned in Ravensbrück 1940–5; wrote of these experiences in Margarete Buber, *Fånge hos Hitler och Stalin* (Stockholm, 1948), trans. Edward Fitzgerald as *Under Two Dictators* (London, 1949); strongly anti-Communist, she returned to Germany in the 1950s.
6 Franz Kafka (1883–1924), Prague-born German-speaking Jewish novelist whose works have given rise to the epithet 'Kafkaesque', describing the surreal, nightmarish world of his characters.

he is right – he saw himself as Hegel, and Stalin as Napoleon, and wrote him letters, strangely enough unanswered; but he was a very perceptive man. This is not so in Kafka. It may be that the fate of the Jews is what inspired his concept of the victims, or it may be that God appeared to him in the guise of the source of total authority, if guided by his own rules, not those of our human morality, unintelligible to us, too absolute, à la Kierkegaard;[1] something terrifying enough, but profounder than the workaday horrors of deliberate human invention. There is something numinous in the terrors of Kafka's nightmares – the prison from which the helpless victims seek to escape is somehow of supernatural origin: not so in earthly cells.

I see no merit, I admit, in Steiner's view that the corruption of language, if it is that, is a harbinger of the inhumanity to come[2] – that, I think, is wholly implausible; and Hitler's appeal to the Jewish 'chosen race' concept is a very typical piece of Jewish self-laceration, of which Steiner is an obvious example,[3] as the somewhat greater figure of Heine was before him.[4] Steiner seems to me to have too professional an interest in the Holocaust, and [to] glory in being obsessed by it. Or is this unjust?

I must admit that Miss Arendt is a *bête noire* of mine – I see nothing in her writings of the slightest value or interest, and never have. The pages you admire in the book on totalitarianism seem to me either truisms (about the Nazis: 'everything is possible'[5] was not true of them – Aryans had to be preserved, while Celts and Latins were neutral; I believe in interpreting words literally) or inaccurate (about Russia – her attitude to Russian totalitarianism seems to me mechanical and [to] show no insight at all) – it is all a kind of metaphysical free association: no bones, no argument, a kind of patter. [...]

IB

1 Søren Aabye Kierkegaard (1813–55), Danish philosopher and theologian, founder of modern existentialism.

2 Steiner holds that language is corrupted by mass communication. In *After Babel: Aspects of Language and Translation* (London, 1975) he argues that the multiplicity of languages, blurred by globalisation and the mass media, is a blessing, not a curse, since each language contains a world-view that is worth preserving; in *Language and Silence: Essays 1958–1966* (London, 1967), later sub-titled *Essays on Language, Literature, and the Inhuman* (NY, 1976), he addresses the vulgarisation of language by the media. 'The inhumanity to come' is the Holocaust.

3 In Steiner's controversial novella *The Portage to San Cristobal of AH* (London and Boston, 1981), adapted for the stage by Christopher Hampton (1982), Hitler has survived the war, and is caught in the Amazon jungle by a team of Nazi hunters, led by an Israeli Holocaust survivor, Emmanuel Lieber, who bases himself in the Ecuadorian Galapagos island of San Cristóbal. Under pressure of circumstance they decide to put Hitler on trial immediately, against Lieber's wishes: he fears Hitler's persuasiveness, and Steiner has the Nazi leader defend himself partly on the ground that his notion of the 'master race' is copied from the Jewish concept of the 'chosen people'.

4 (Christian Johann) Heinrich Heine (1797–1856), German-born Jewish poet and influential radical thinker; converted from Judaism to Christianity 1825; mocked medieval Jews in his unfinished historical novel *The Rabbi of Bacharach* (1840).

5 Arendt had argued that totalitarian regimes believed in, and applied, the principle that 'everything is possible' – *The Origins of Totalitarianism* (NY, 1958), 441 – as an expression of their absolute power; and, moreover, that the concentration camps were places where 'the fundamental belief of totalitarianism that everything is possible is [...] verified' – *The Burden of Our Time* (London, 1951), 414.

TO SIDNEY BRICHTO[1]

29 April 1985 [*carbon*]

Headington House

Dear Rabbi Brichto,

[…] I was interested to see that at the last meeting[2] the BBC World Service, particularly programmes to the Third World, was discussed. I have no doubt myself that it is heavily biased against Israel – the constant repetition, both on the external service and the domestic services, of the hatred shown by Israeli troops among the Shias,[3] the brutality of Israel against unarmed Arab boys of fifteen, whom they are described as murdering in a mindless way (without remarking that boys of fifteen in that part of the world perpetrate brutalities of their own), and so on, is no accident. I shall never forget the pride with which the present director of the BBC, Alasdair Milne,[4] told my wife […] that his son was the Oxford representative of the Friends of the PLO.[5] I abhor the Likud more than most, and believe the Lebanese war to be both a blunder and a crime, but I do hope that someone will tell people like Ian Gilmour and his son,[6] and Mr Fisk,[7] that Jews have the longest memory of any known human community, and that when their names have been totally forgotten elsewhere, they will linger on on an unforgotten list of ill-wishers of the Jewish people. […]

Yours sincerely,
[Isaiah Berlin]

TO SHIELA SOKOLOV GRANT

12 July 1985 [*manuscript*]

All Souls

Dearest Shiela

I am just off to Italy for the summer – but cannot part without saying how sad it is that there you sit in Ireland – isolated, insulated; what drove

---

1 Sidney Brichto (1936–2009), US-born British rabbi and author; executive vice president and 1st director, Union of Liberal and Progressive Synagogues, 1964–89; governor, Oxford Centre for Hebrew and Jewish Studies, 1994–2003.
2 Presumably of the Israel–Diaspora Trust, a forum of influential Jews in British public life established by Brichto 1982 in an attempt to counter the ebbing support for Israel after the Lebanon War; it operated under Chatham House rules.
3 The Shia Muslims were Israel's opponents in the Lebanese War.
4 Alasdair David Gordon Milne (1930–2013), director of programmes, BBC TV, 1973–7, managing director 1977–82; deputy director general, BBC, 1980–2, director general 1982–7.
5 Seumas Patrick Charles Milne (b. 1958), younger son of Alasdair Milne; Balliol PPE 1976–9; left-wing journalist; comment editor, *Guardian*, 2001–7; secretary of the undergraduate Oxford Palestine Campaign 1977–9.
6 David Robert Gilmour (b. 1952), 4th Bt (succeeded 2007), writer; deputy and contributing editor, *Middle East International*, 1979–85; research fellow, St Antony's, 1996–7; elder son of Ian Gilmour.
7 Robert Fisk (b. 1946), Middle East correspondent, *Times* 1976–88, *Independent* since 1989. IB was strongly critical of Fisk's coverage of Israel, which he found lacking in balance.

you there? desire for rural life: some ancestral pull, some British longing
– nostalgia for an idyllic past, away from the racket? You always did prefer
fields covered with flowers to the beau monde of Oxford: a mixture of social
idealism with romantic idealization of men of action – heroes – martyrs,
and a desire for self realization. Goronwy does not fit into all this: but your
view of him was coloured with love and the exhilaration which he brought
to everything when he was young (he did rather lose his way in later years:
but still wrote very well & vividly – & had a genuine gaiety not entirely
ruined by drink and resentments) but – there: I did not want to write about
our innocent & reputable pasts: only to wish you well. 'Have a nice life' say
American graduates occasionally, after, at even rarer moments 'wonderful to
know you'. It is too. Do let us meet at least *a little* more often – in the South:
I have begun to hate travel: but you are younger not only literally but in
many other ways: still hopeful, not, like me, comfortably resigned –

   yours with all my love (as we used to say)
   Isaiah

*Shiela Sokolov Grant's lifelong friendship with IB was forged in the early 1930s
when, as Shiela Grant Duff (SGD), she read PPE at LMH. Passionately moral
in her approach both to personal relations and to international politics, she
became a close friend of the charismatic German Rhodes Scholar Adam von
Trott,[1] then reading PPE at Balliol, who was also a friend of IB. Trott viewed
with alarm Hitler's accession to power in 1933, and, unable to condone emigration, returned to Germany that year to continue his legal studies, keeping in
close contact with his English friends while he sought to build connections
with the German resistance to Hitler. SGD meanwhile became a foreign correspondent, a prominent anti-appeaser, and a defender of what she believed
was a strategically vital Czechoslovakia.[2] She and Trott were both idealists,
she from a Liberal background, more than decimated by the First World War,
he from a family steeped in Prussian civil service ideals; both in their own way
failed in their efforts to avoid a second world war. Trott, the most studied of the
Kreisau Circle/Stauffenberg[3] plot martyrs, could not understand the depth of*

1 (Friedrich) Adam von Trott zu Solz (1909–44) studied law at Munich and Göttingen before spending a term at Mansfield Hilary 1929; returned to Oxford 1931 (Balliol PPE) as one of the first
   German Rhodes Scholars since WW1; went back to Germany 1933, and actively opposed Nazism;
   entered information service of German FO 1 June 1940; arrested 25 July 1944, and executed 26
   August on Hitler's orders by hanging from a beam with piano wire; commemorated on the
   WW2 memorial plaque outside Balliol chapel.
2 Shiela Grant Duff, *The Parting of Ways: A Personal Account of the Thirties* (London, 1982), 162–88.
3 Claus Philipp Maria Schenk, Graf von Stauffenberg (1907–44), German army officer, central
   figure in the final resistance to Hitler; planted the briefcase bomb that very nearly killed Hitler
   in his headquarters at Rastenberg, East Prussia, 20 July 1944; with several co-conspirators he was
   captured and executed the same day; of Swabian aristocratic descent, and a practicising Catholic,
   he was never a Nazi Party member. The 'Kreisau Circle' was the Christian-oriented German
   resistance movement against Nazism centred on the estate at Kreisau, Silesia, of Helmuth von
   Moltke (257/2), one of its founders and leading members, which met from 1941.

*SGD's anguish after Munich, and failed to take her into his confidence when,
in 1939, he sought, through the Astor family and their circle, to persuade Britain
to make concessions to Nazi Germany, at the expense of the Poles and the
Czechs, as part of building an anti-Hitler coup.*[1] *Until late August of that year
they conducted an intense correspondence, at the heart of which was their joint
desire to unite Europe on the foundations of Anglo-German understanding, but
Trott's bid for further appeasement undermined SGD's faith in him, and their
last letters 'were not without bitterness'.*[2]

The disintegration of their friendship was a personal tragedy that mirrored
events on a wider stage. IB's own respect for Trott survived the breach caused
by Trott's controversial 1934 letter to the Manchester Guardian *denying
anti-Semitism in the German courts.*[3] *He accepted Trott's explanation of his
conduct, and his 'friendly feelings towards Adam' continued 'until the summer
of 1939', the last time he saw him, when, 'although his anti-Nazi views were not
in doubt, his talk was too ambiguous. This shook me, but did not lead to real
doubts until the reports of what he said in England in 1939 [...] reached me.'*[4]

IB's conflicting feelings were not simplified by Trott's martyrdom in the cause
of German resistance to Nazism. After the 20 July 1944 bomb plot to kill Hitler
Trott was arrested and executed, which endowed his memory with a special
status, not least for most of his Oxford friends. When, almost forty years later,
Shiela Sokolov Grant asked IB to review Klemens von Klemperer's forthcoming
edition of her correspondence with Trott, the aptly named A Noble Combat,[5]
IB declined, having no wish to enter public controversy over Trott's character
and motives. As he had written to her on a previous occasion: 'Peace be to his
ashes: he died a heroic death and perhaps that is all that matters now.'[6]

TO SHIELA SOKOLOV GRANT

27 August 1985

As from Headington House

Dearest Shiela,

[...] As for letters – Adam's to you and yours to him, mine to you, etc.

---

1 Giles MacDonogh, *A Good German: Adam von Trott zu Solz* (London, 1989), 120–32; Christopher
Sykes, *Troubled Loyalty: A Biography of Adam von Trott zu Solz* (London, 1968), 221–55.
2 Tim Mason, review of *A Noble Combat: The Letters of Shiela Grant Duff and Adam von Trott zu Solz
1932–1939*, ed. Klemens von Klemperer (Oxford, 1988), *History Workshop Journal* 27 no. 1 (Spring
1989), 212–16 at 214.
3 L1 83–5, 89–91, 718–19; L3 345.
4 L3 349.
5 Note 2 above. Klemens Wilhelm von Klemperer (1916–2012), historian of modern Europe, and of
the German resistance to Nazism; born in Berlin of Jewish descent, he studied in Vienna, leaving
Austria for the US after the *Anschluss*; L. Clark Seelye Prof. of History, Smith College, Mass.,
1979–87.
6 Letter of 2 July 1962.

– this is most unjust. I have certainly sent you spontaneous letters, particularly when we were very young, and on other occasions too, though I cannot remember which – your oblivion in this matter I forgive. But the notion that I only write to you in response to demands of one kind or another from you is most baseless. However, in this case, there is something, after all, in what you say, for the next topic on which I am bound to address you is von Klemperer's book, of course. You ask me to review it. I cannot. Not only because I don't write reviews – as you know – but also because I cannot bear to go back to Adam and all that. Even so, it was with blood that I wrote those few pages that were read aloud before David Astor's lecture on Adam at Balliol.[1] I have said my say, my views on him are known to the few people who take an interest in them, and, after all, I only saw Adam literally twice after he left Oxford for Germany – once when he came back en route from America, and we had to have our 'explanation' about his letter to the *Manchester Guardian*, and once in 1938, when he said that Germany must be surrounded, otherwise it was all up with all of us. I have no idea what he did in China; I have no idea what he did in America before the war, nor what he did when he went there after our war had begun. All that, so far as I am concerned, is hearsay. Therefore his views, his attitudes, at times when I didn't see him are something I cannot possibly pronounce about; and the whole thing is half a century away. No, no, I don't want to think about him any more, least of all to say anything in public about which I can never feel at all sure. I have no doubt the book of letters ought to be reviewed by serious people – one or two, no doubt, will be stimulated by David Astor and the German friends, so you must expect something not entirely just or pleasing in one or two English periodicals (but I hope I am wrong); but otherwise it will enter into the corpus of what went on ideologically in Germany in the 1930s.

I am very glad that Tim Mason[2] has been a help to you. He is an exceedingly nice man. When he came to Oxford he looked to me rather ill and distraught, and I was told that he had had some kind of mild breakdown: but I expect all that is over. Is it a case of left versus right? That all those more or less right-wing friends of Adam's in Germany want to believe one thing, partly out of conservatism, partly out of German patriotism, and that Tim and his friends want to believe that Communists and socialists and other politically sympathetic (at any rate to them) individuals did more resisting than they are commonly credited with having done? I wonder. At any rate, controversy about this (though not, I suspect, very prominently) will,

1 'A Personal Tribute to Adam von Trott (Balliol 1931)', *Balliol College Annual Record* 1986, 61–2; repr. in L1, 718–19, and as 'Adam von Trott' in PI3. Astor's lecture was one in a series held in honour of von Trott in Balliol Hall during Hilary Term 1983, marking the 50th anniversary of the advent of Nazi rule in Germany.

2 Timothy Wright ('Tim') Mason (1940–90), social historian and expert on labour relations in the Third Reich; research fellow, St Antony's, 1963–71; fellow and history tutor, St Peter's, 1971–84.

I suppose, go on for years, until we are all dead and it all dies down and enters into some corners and footnotes – which is all that I have ever had anything to do with either deserves or anyway will get. [...]

Anyway, it was delightful to hear from you; I look forward to seeing you; don't, I beg you, press me about von Klemperer's book – of course I shall read it, of course I shall talk to you about it, but wild horses wouldn't make me say a word in public about Adam, the Germans, except before 1850, when I find them dangerous and fascinating and am reading about them all the time – and propose, perhaps, even to say something in print, perhaps post-humously. One cannot possibly pronounce about one's attitudes and beliefs of half a century ago without feeling that it may be quite, quite wrong. Still, I shall read the book with absolute fascination, as I do everything you write, as well you know. Your last book,[1] after all, got some perfectly favourable and deserved reviews, and this one even more so, of that I am convinced. The view of Adam as a saint and martyr is inevitable – he was more interest-ing, knew many more people, was much more widely liked and taken an interest in, than the other anti-Nazis; certainly than Stauffenberg, who had been a straight pro-Nazi before, or Moltke,[2] who was honourable, pious, utterly decent and brave, but personally much less interesting. So that was inevitable, given that [that] particular group of persons had to have a hero who somehow cast a better light on them too. But this attitude will not go on for long. Christopher Sykes's book,[3] and your book, are likely in the long run to have much, much more influence, supported as they are by much solider data and a wider context. So rest in peace!

Now, as for Goronwy – a much more delightful subject to me, in spite of everything, rogue and scamp as I am afraid he most definitely was. God knows what Goronwy was vis-à-vis Communism. Rosamond Lehmann,[4] as you know, says that he told her, when he was living with her, that he was not only a Communist but an agent; and it seems generally agreed that if he was, he ceased to be at the time of the Russo-German pact. The only thing I found odd was that in his account of his past, when he says that Guy Burgess asked him to be an agent and he took no notice of it and simply

1 *The Parting of Ways* (254/2).
2 Helmuth James (Graf) von Moltke (1907–45), great-nephew of the Prussian general Helmuth von Moltke; jurist, conscripted into German intelligence 1939; becoming convinced of the need for active resistance to Nazism, co-founded the Kreisau Circle (254/3); arrested by the Gestapo January 1944, tried for treason, and executed 23 January 1945.
3 Christopher Hugh Sykes (1907–86), writer and traveller; deputy controller, Third Programme, BBC, 1948, features dept 1949–68; author of *Troubled Loyalty* (255/1), commissioned by von Trott's friend and staunch defender David Astor; Sykes felt pressurised to produce a favourable account, writing to SSG 22 May 1968: 'This Trott Committee is out for praise, and nothing but praise, and any criticism is held to be treacherous betrayal of the most horrible kind. They ought to have got a nice tame hack.'
4 Rosamond Nina Lehmann (1901–90), novelist; married Wogan Philipps 1928 (divorced 1944); began an affair with Goronwy Rees in September 1936, and they then lived together until Rees married in 1940.

regarded it as a joke, he never says then, or anywhere else, whether in fact he was a Communist at any stage; and I now, retrospectively, believe that he may well have been, like everybody else. But that is a matter of very small importance.

You speak of him as an artist 'with all the wild creativity of his Celtic blood'. 'Wild creativity'? I really do not see that. I don't think he was wild at all: he had great charm, a beautiful voice, he was a good writer, he was very bright, he was all the things that we know him to have been. I don't think Celts are particularly wild, though they are usually held to be – perhaps some Irish have been, but very few Welsh. And I don't believe that he was tremendously creative. You think he was not a very reassuring character, but what do you mean? Highly intelligent, very fetching, delightful to be with, gay, set one up a great deal. I remember how wonderful it was when I met him in Salzburg in 1933, and he immediately said in German 'Wie ist die Lage?',[1] and giggled excitedly, and wrote to me to say that he had taken part in a German, rather pro-Nazi, film, if you remember, by saying 'I move in film circles, I am very much their cup of tea and a fresh one at that.' All that was simply splendid, but I don't believe in the wild creativity; and I admit I know nothing about Communist friends [...].

　　Yours, ⟨with fondest love⟩
　　　Isaiah

TO MIRIAM BERLIN[2]

28 August 1985

Headington House

Dear Mimi,

You ask, about Leonid Pasternak,[3] why nothing about Jews? Because, descended from rabbis in Odessa as he undoubtedly was, he and his family were, so to speak, on the way out: he got himself to Moscow, where Jews by and large were not permitted to live, met Tolstoy, various Russian painters, and, with relief, plunged into an entirely Slav scene. He did not have any particular phobia about the Jews: when he went to Berlin after the Revolution, he painted some prominent Jews [...], and painted the opening of the Hebrew University in Jerusalem. I don't think he minded whether he knew Jews or not, he was quite relaxed on the subject; but didn't care for his origins or for anything to do with Judaism – not uncommon with assimilated Russian Jews. His son Boris was a very different matter; and suffered from acute phobia;

---

1 'What is the situation?'
2 Miriam H. ('Mimi') Berlin (1926–2015) née Haskell, assistant prof., Russian, European and Middle Eastern History, Wellesley College, 1958–75; no relation.
3 Leonid Osipovich Pasternak (1862–1945), Odessa-born Russian Impressionist and portraitist, father of Boris Pasternak; moved to Berlin 1921, England 1938; among his sitters were his friend Tolstoy, and Einstein and Lenin.

and ran away from anything remotely Jewish as energetically as possible, and ladled off everything he had to say about them [...] into the figure of Gordon in *Zhivago*, which liberated him to be a blue-eyed, fair-haired Slav hero. Having discharged all this justifiable (but nevertheless perhaps superfluous) malice, I rest my case. [...]

Yours ever, ⟨with much love from⟩
Isaiah

TO CAROL FELSENTHAL[1]

16 September 1985 [*carbon*]

Headington House

Dear Miss Felsenthal,

[...] I met Alice Longworth at dinner with Mr and Mrs Eugene Meyer[2] in Washington in 1941, when I was a British official (serving first in New York and later at the British Embassy in Washington). I sat next to her at dinner, and she was very friendly and infinitely exhilarating and amusing, and I thought that she was one of the most brilliant and remarkable persons I had ever met. When I lived in Washington, 1942–6, I got to know her well. She was very hospitable to me, and I greatly enjoyed seeing her, both in her own house and at dinner with common friends [...], because of the brilliance, verve and charm of her conversation, and her general style, her tenue. She was a grande dame of the first order, and would have been so in any society at any time. Above all, I think, she wanted to be amused, and therefore liked clever, interesting people of intellectual vitality, or those who had achieved something strange and interesting, or those who fed her acute sense of the ridiculous in life, for which she had an undying appetite. She was always described as being extremely right-wing, and this, of course, in a sense is perfectly true. It sprang, it seemed to me, from several sources: partly because she genuinely liked to shock, *épater*,[3] the solemn and the earnest – she genuinely disliked the [...] liberal, high-minded, idealistic do-gooders of every kind, and delighted in mocking, and holding them up to ridicule and laughter. But if these liberals turned out to be intelligent, amusing, full of vitality, original, fascinating in any way, their politics or their idealism did not stand in the way of friendship. Thus she was a friend of Justice Felix Frankfurter, who was nothing if not an idealistic liberal; but that was because of his love of life and of amusement, and his ebullient and delightful temperament. Another source was, I think, the fact that she felt that Franklin Roosevelt had outshone her father, to whom

1 Carol Felsenthal (b. 1949), US journalist, blogger and biographer; she had written to IB in connection with her research for her biography *Princess Alice: The Life and Times of Alice Roosevelt Longworth* (NY, 1988).
2 The parents of IB's close friends Philip and Katherine ('Kay') Graham (623). Eugene Meyer was the owner/publisher of the *Washington Post*.
3 French for 'shock'.

she was totally devoted and whom she regarded as a far greater man than the second Roosevelt. She particularly disliked Eleanor for her high-mindedness, her earnestness, her humanitarianism – qualities which she held in genuine contempt. What she liked was heroism, boldness, power, pride, unashamed ambition, grandeur of character: she disliked dimness, servility, convention. She liked Renaissance virtues, pagan qualities, and therefore took pleasure, in a defiant, perverse sort of way, in denouncing liberals, do-gooders etc., which is what gave her the reputation (not undeserved, of course) of being an acute reactionary. She believed in elites, and felt herself to be part of one, and disliked democracy and general American ideals, save in the form in which her father accepted them.

She had great wit, and considerable malice, though I never found it to be cruel.[1] She certainly never in my presence referred to Senator Borah,[2] and I never heard that she had any relationship with Senator Joseph McCarthy.[3] But she was quite capable of saying something complimentary about him in order to shock, excite, annoy, hold up to ridicule. She was perfectly irresponsible, but it was a mistake to take her political pronouncements seriously – she certainly never did herself. She was a very clever, indeed very brilliant, talker – deliberately unfair, but loyal and affectionate towards those she liked, and open about her likes and dislikes. There was no touch of hypocrisy or desire to appease those for whom she did not care, in any degree.

[...] Kind she was not, and did not wish to be, save to those she liked or loved – towards mankind in general, not at all. She was, I think, intensely jealous of Eleanor Roosevelt, whose column outshone her own brief one, and was wonderfully disparaging about Franklin Roosevelt, whom I vastly admired. She said 'My poor cousin, he suffered from polio, so he was put in a frame; and now he wants to put the entire United States into a frame, as if it was a crippled country – that is all the New Deal is about, you know.' That kind of analogy, with all its injustice but brightness, was typical of her. She did make some marvellous jokes: epigrams, perhaps, would better describe them. Someone said to her that he could not understand how it was that Philip Lothian, the British ambassador, who, after all, was born a Catholic, could have been converted to Christian Science. Whatever one might say against the Catholic Church, it was a great, historically rich, profound and

1 Visitors to Longworth's Washington home were invited to sit near a pillow with the needlepoint motif 'If you can't say something good about someone, sit right here by me' (Thomas Mallon, 'Washingtonienne', NYT, 18 November 2007, G14).

2 William Edgar Borah (1865–1940), US lawyer and politician of independent and outspoken views; Republican senator, Idaho, 1907–40; for his affair with Longworth see 100/2.

3 Joseph Raymond McCarthy (1908–57), Republican senator, Wisconsin, 1947–57, progenitor of 'McCarthyism', the 1950s anti-Communist witch-hunt of those suspected of 'un-American activities'. Longworth had little time for him, on personal rather than political grounds: 'She cut short his attempt to first-name her by saying: "No, Senator McCarthy, you are not going to call me Alice. The truckman, the trash man and the policemen on the block may call me Alice, but you may not."' loc. cit. (note 1 above).

magnificent affair. How could a man brought up in it, even if he was in love with Lady Astor (who was, of course, a Christian Scientist), change from that to something so thin, artificial, to some people's minds almost vulgar, as Christian Science? How could he? She said 'All poor Philip did was to swap virgins in midstream.' That seems to me an epigram worthy of Voltaire. [...]

   Yours sincerely,

   Isaiah Berlin   [...]

TO LEON EDEL

17 September 1985 [*carbon*]

                                           Headington House

Dear Professor Edel,

   [...] As you know, I loved and admired Edmund [...], and still do. His friendship meant a very, very great deal to me, since his late forties when we met and until his death. The pages of his diary which you have kindly sent me[1] contain a fairly continuous disparagement of me, which naturally enough I find profoundly wounding[2] – together with a great deal of straight invention of facts. I do not suppose any of the latter was ever deliberate. When he missed his target, he missed it by many miles, as I am sure you know, and uttered some absurdities in his life (cf. the egregious review of *Doctor Zhivago* in the *New Yorker*, filled with really grotesque fantasies).[3] Whether these pages were meant to be published, whether he was entirely sober when he wrote some of them, seems to me dubious. [...]

   All this about Maurice Bowra and David Cecil (who were not friends at all) blackballing people, etc. is pure nonsense, whatever Connolly[4] may have said: nor do I believe that Connolly said it. But as for Roth,[5] it is true that I held against him the fact that after the war he tried to keep out all the bourgeoisie, the shopkeepers and merchants who came to live in Oxford, from the Synagogue, which he regarded as sacred to the University alone; and I was appealed to, and did think that any Jew who wished to worship in the Synagogue should have a right to enter it under ordinary circumstances. My

1 From a draft of the 4th vol. of Wilson's diaries, edited by Edel, *The Fifties: From Notebooks and Diaries of the Period* (London/NY, 1986). Of the passages that IB discusses a number survived: on blackballing and Roth (ibid. 136), on the stammering don etc. (137–8), and on IB and Tolstoy (139).

2 For instance, Wilson sometimes sensed IB 'scraping bottom when he has sailed into the shallows of his mind' (ibid. 139).

3 'Doctor Life and His Guardian Angel', *New Yorker*, 15 November 1958, 201–26. IB praised this review to the skies in 1958 (L2 667–8), and said he agreed 'with every line' in 1959 (L2 677), but wrote to Rory Childers on 12 June 1980 of Wilson's 'absurd attempts to "decipher" things in *Doctor Zhivago* – Vetchinkin as Hamlet, and the like. I loved and respected Edmund Wilson, but this was one of his most absurd ventures.'

4 Cyril Vernon Connolly (1903–74), critic, author and journalist; founder co-editor, *Horizon*, 1939–50; joint chief literary critic (with Raymond Mortimer), *Sunday Times*, 1950–74.

5 Cecil Roth (1899–1970), reader in post-biblical Jewish studies, Oxford, 1939–64, president, Jewish Historical Society of England, 1936–45, 1955–6.

relations with Roth somewhat deteriorated after that. However, all that is Edmund's typical perversity, which you must know as well as I do. [...] I don't go about saying 'The Jew is a kind of hunchback', though I did once write a long piece for the Hebrew University in which I compare the attitude of assimilated Jews who pretended that there was no difference between them and non-Jews to hunchbacks who had certificates showing that they had no humps.[1] But I don't think that Edmund ever read that – still, someone may have said something to him about it, and that is what this may have come from. Harry Levin's[2] gloss is one of typical malice.[3]

[...] The young Don with an impediment in his speech was John Bayley:[4] the 'young woman who had written a book on Sartre' was Iris Murdoch, Bayley's wife.[5] Edmund simply hated them all, including the philosopher (that was Stuart Hampshire, whom he came round to later). It is true that Edmund was grumpy, bored and rather disagreeable to Iris, and the evening had plainly not been a success. I had only asked them because Edmund had asked to meet such intelligentsia as might be found in Oxford; they were distinguished representatives of it at the time. I did not invite Maurice Bowra, because I thought he would take against him – as, indeed, he did, if you look at *Europe without Baedeker*, where there is a violent onslaught on my poor old friend.[6]

[...] the idea that the last bit of my essay on Tolstoy is really autobiographical and that, 'like all serious Jews', I long to be a hedgehog is simply not true: one may not know oneself at all well, but one knows oneself well enough to know that that is not one's ideal, secret or overt. This judgement

1 'Jewish Slavery and Emancipation', first published in the *Jewish Chronicle* 1951, then in Norman Bentwich (ed.), *Hebrew University Garland* (London, 1952); repr. in POI. Jews 'acted like a species of deformed human beings, let us say hunchbacks, and could be distinguished into three types according to the attitudes they adopted towards their humps. The first class consisted of those who maintained they had no hump. If challenged, they were prepared to produce a document signed and countersigned by all the nations, in particular by their most enlightened leaders, solemnly declaring that the bearers were normal, full-grown persons, with no marks to distinguish them from other healthy human beings, and that to think otherwise was an offence against international morality.' POI 174–5. Cf. 285/2.

2 Harry Tuchman Levin (1912–94; plate 12), literary critic and author; Irving Babbitt Prof. of Comparative Literature, Harvard, 1960–83; cordially disliked by IB.

3 EW had written: 'It may be, as Harry Levin suggests, that they take this line ['The Jew is a kind of hunchback'] as a way of apologising, vis-à-vis the other Jews, for their own popularity.'

4 John Oliver Bayley (1925–2015), literary critic and writer; fellow and English tutor, New College, 1955–74; Thomas Warton Prof. of English Literature, Oxford, and fellow, St Catherine's, 1974–92; m. 1956 the philosopher and novelist Iris Murdoch, whose affliction by Alzheimer's he charted in 3 vols, the 1st, *Iris: A Memoir of Iris Murdoch* (London, 1998), appearing shortly before her death in 1999.

5 Murdoch's study of Sartre, *Romantic Rationalist* (Cambridge, 1953), was her 1st book; she had briefly met Sartre while working in Brussels with UNRRA 1945.

6 In *Europe without Baedeker: Sketches among the Ruins of Italy, Greece, and England* (NY, 1947), 21, Wilson wrote of meeting 'an Oxford don [...], a scholar of enormous reading' who 'remarked that he had never read Walt Whitman, who was considered, he understood, a great writer in South America': hardly a violent onslaught.

is not offensive, but merely a total misconception – a typical piece of wild lunging by Edmund, which we all know.

Edmund, as you know, was a genuine, old-fashioned Anglophobe – all this must have begun before the First World War, when he came to England and evidently had a not very good time, and this rubs off on to the pages that you have sent me. I really feel upset about these pages – I mean, about the references to myself. Of course we were friends and of course he stayed with me and of course he probably said worse things about other people to whom he was equally, or more, attached. But I know that Mary McCarthy,[1] for example, did manage to arrange for the omission of particularly embarrassing or offensive remarks about herself, and I, too, must admit that I crave for some degree of protection. I would, of course, rather not be mentioned at all than mentioned in this fashion in Edmund's diaries. I remember that when Nigel Nicolson edited Virginia Woolf's letters,[2] he wrote to people mentioned in them in some disagreeable way, asking them if they minded these passages being included. Some, so Nigel told me, like Peter Quennell,[3] asked for them to be expunged; others, like Raymond Mortimer,[4] who thought himself a very intimate friend of Virginia's, and about whom she was quite singularly nasty, had the courage to say 'Let them be printed' – and shortly afterwards died (not necessarily cause and effect!). I do not aspire to that degree of courage, and would much rather that passages were left out that would cause too much malicious pleasure, too much relish, among people whom I regard as friends and who probably will remain friends – let alone those who are not. After my death, I do not care.

[...] You must obviously do what you think right, but I do think that human beings have some right to a degree of protection against wild statements and sheer spleen. I had a curious impression, quite apart from my personal feelings, as I read these pages, of a certain odd unworldliness on the part of Edmund. What he writes about people has a certain unrealism about it – it is as if he moved rather sightless through the human world as opposed to that of books. He writes like a man who has led his life in a library, and not really moved among people with a sense of what was what and who was who in human relationships. Do you think I am mistaken? You may think that I am being altogether oversensitive. But the degree of pain is not diminished by one's knowledge of the thinness of one's skin.

Oh dear. As someone once said to me, 'It is only one's friends who can

1 Mary Therese McCarthy (1912–89) novelist, critic and social commentator; m. 1938 (divorced 1946) the writer and literary critic Edmund Wilson (his 3rd wife).
2 *The Letters of Virginia Woolf*, ed. Nigel Nicolson, assistant ed. Joanne Trautmann (London/NY, 1975–80).
3 Peter Courtney Quennell (1905–93), Kt 1992, writer and editor; editor, *Cornhill Magazine*, 1944–51, *History Today* 1951–79.
4 (Charles) Raymond Bell Mortimer (1895–1980), critic; literary editor, *New Statesman*, 1935–47; book reviewer, *Sunday Times*, 1948–52; joint chief literary critic (with Cyril Connolly) from 1952.

betray one, one's enemies cannot.' Believe me, I am not over-reacting, and I beg you to be not just but merciful.

Yours sincerely,

Isaiah Berlin

TO LEON EDEL

5 November 1985 [*carbon*]

Headington House

Dear Leon Edel,

Thank you ever so much for your letter of 30 October. The introductory piece seems to me quite admirable. There are one or two things I should like to comment on, but as a general account of EW's attitude to England it is, I am sure, just and needed. [...].

I should like to tell you a story, told me from both ends, about his wartime visit to London. The man attached to him and instructed to look after him and give him a good time was Hamish Hamilton,[1] the well-known publisher (still alive at an advanced age, living in Florence), who is half American, was attached to the Ministry of Information, and I suppose a regular liaison with writers, top-class journalists and the like. I do not know if you have ever met him: he is an amiable, slightly nervous club man, married to an Italian, madly upper-class wife, and they used to have a salon in London for literary persons – literary and artistic figures. Their intimate friends were Laurence Olivier,[2] Iris Origo,[3] the Kenneth Clarks[4] and the like; he was a popular member of the Garrick Club, where those kinds of people congregated, not unlike American publishers of the same kind – say, his great, great friend Cass Canfield.[5] He was told to look after EW, who took an instant hatred to him (as he told me himself); he was given a party, at which he met the Sitwells,[6] and T. S. Eliot, to neither of whom he wished to speak. I rather

1 Hamish (né James; 'Jamie') Hamilton (1900–88), US-born British publisher; founder, Hamish Hamilton publishers, 1931, managing director 1931–72, chair 1931–81, president 1981–8; m. 1940, 2ndly, Yvonne Vicino Pallavicino (1907–93), an Italian countess from Rome and a highly successful literary hostess.

2 Laurence Kerr Olivier (1907–89), Kt 1947, life peer 1970, OM 1981, actor, one of the foremost Shakespearians of his generation, equally famous for his performances on stage and screen; director, National Theatre, 1962–73, associate director 1973–4.

3 Iris Margaret Origo (1902–88) née Cutting, Anglo-American writer and biographer; m. 1924 Antonio Origo (1892–1976), living for much of her life in Tuscany; became a close friend of Bernard Berenson, once the lover of her mother, Sybil.

4 Kenneth Clark m. 1927 Elizabeth Winifred ('Jane') Martin (1902–76), a leading hostess, innovatory in style, wearing dresses by Elsa Schiaparelli and jewellery by Alexander Calder; before WW2 the Clarks entertained London high society in their house in Portland Place

5 (Augustus) Cass Canfield (1897–1986), US publishing executive and author; president, Harper & Brothers (later Harper & Row), 1931–45, chair of board 1945–55, of executive committee 1955–67, senior editor 1967–86.

6 The literary siblings Edith Louisa Sitwell (1887–1964), DBE 1954, poet and biographer; (Francis)

doubt if Angus Wilson[1] would at that date have been invited. The only person he spoke to was Compton Mackenzie.[2] He liked him because he was an old, bearded rogue, a man of letters of the old-fashioned kind, whom he rather favoured.

David Cecil told me afterwards, after meeting him, that he thought that Edmund was rather like writers and critics before 1914: when people like Kipling, Wells, Shaw, Chesterton, Henry James[3] met at dinner in some club – as they certainly did – they did not talk about literature or art, they talked about publishers, royalties, personal affairs; a certain amount of scabrous talk about their amorous lives; it was all very jolly and masculine and hearty, with gusts of laughter, not at all like the dinners given by Elizabeth Bowen at which I used to meet, say, T. S. Eliot or Mrs Woolf, and their friends. There may be something in that. Anyway, he told me the party was ghastly, that the only man he could talk to was Compton Mackenzie, and that he wished this hadn't been done: his particular dislike, of course, was concentrated on T. S. Eliot, whom he described as 'somewhere deep inside himself a scoundrel' – whatever he may have meant by that.

The one man he wanted to see was his old Princeton professor of philosophy, the eminent Kantian scholar, Kemp Smith,[4] who went back from Princeton to Edinburgh, where by that time, I think, he was living in retirement. He said that Hamilton made difficulties about the journey to Edinburgh, but he managed to give him the slip, and went. When he came back he apparently went to another party, reluctantly, and wished to walk home from it to the hotel at which he was staying – which apparently involved going via Piccadilly and Park Lane. Hamilton, according to him, did his best to persuade him to get a taxi, as it was raining etc., and anyway for the sake of general comfort. But he, Edmund, knew that Hamilton's real motive was to keep him from seeing the prostitutes who were walking the streets, which the Ministry of Information wished to keep secret, but which he, Edmund, was determined to see. So he did get into the taxi, and got out of it five minutes later, and, by God, he did walk the streets and he did see the prostitutes – so he had succeeded in cheating poor old Hamilton. All this

Osbert Sacheverell Sitwell (1892–1969), 5th baronet, writer; and Sacheverell Sitwell: the children of George Reresby Sitwell (1860–1943), 4th baronet, antiquary and original.

1 Angus Frank Johnstone Wilson (1913–91), KBE 1980, novelist and biographer, prof. of English literature, East Anglia, 1966–78; President, Royal Society of Literature, 1983–8.

2 (Edward Montague Anthony) Compton Mackenzie (1883–1972), Kt 1952, novelist, came to prominence with *Carnival* (London, 1912) and *Sinister Street* (2 vols, London, 1913–14).

3 (Joseph) Rudyard Kipling (1865–1936), Bombay-born English poet, novelist and short-story writer, Nobel Prize in Literature 1907; H(erbert) G(eorge) Wells (1866–1946), novelist and social commentator; G(ilbert) K(eith) Chesterton (1874–1936), journalist, novelist, critic, poet; Henry James (1843–1916), OM 1916, NY-born US novelist, British citizen 1915.

4 Norman Kemp Smith (1872–1958), prof. of psychology, Princeton, 1906–14, McCosh Prof. of Philosophy 1914–19; prof. of logic and metaphysics, Edinburgh, 1919–45; translator of, and authority on, Kant.

is a very typical piece of paranoiac imagination, to which he was certainly given, particularly in England. I am telling you this story to indicate his mood when he came here as war correspondent, which of course got into *Europe without Baedeker*.

It was then that he met Maurice Bowra, at dinner with Sylvester Gates[1] (I was not in London at that time), and there they had a row, which he reports in *Europe without Baedeker*.[2] Something like this happened: EW said, according to himself, that he thought that perhaps Walt Whitman[3] was the greatest of all American writers; MB, contemptuously, 'Even better than Whyte-Melville?'; by which Wilson correctly took him to mean Herman Melville,[4] which he had casually got wrong, out of general contempt for America. After which they had a proper row, according to Sylvester Gates, to which EW would go back in conversations with me [...]. About Bowra he said 'There is no doubt that he absolutely loves literature. Pity that he has nothing of the slightest interest to say about any of it, isn't it?' When he was told by someone, I think Gates, that Maurice Bowra, on being given some French decoration, had said that the French ambassador had formally kissed him on both cheeks (normally done in such situations) – 'Il m'a baisé deux fois'[5] (as you know, 'baiser' has an obscene sense, and the correct word should have been 'embrassé') – he, EW, was delighted, and used to repeat it with loud guffaws every time he remembered Maurice Bowra in England: particularly when talking to me. He would never tire of this particular quotation. [...]

England to Edmund was the home of class distinctions, privilege, snootiness, everything that was thought in America by a large number of average Americans during the war. Big Bill Thompson[6] of Chicago was not far away. [...]

1 Sylvester Govett Gates (1901–72), barrister and banker, pupil of Felix Frankfurter as a Commonwealth Fund Fellow, Harvard, 1925–7. His lifelong friendship with IB began in the 1930s.

2 The quotation at 262/6 continues: 'When I said that *Leaves of Grass* was probably the greatest American book, he asked me whether I thought it even more important than the writings of Whyte-Melville.' That Bowra, 'a scholar of enormous reading', could confuse the author of *Moby-Dick* with the Victorian novelist and poet George John Whyte-Melville (1821–78), an authority on hunting and field sports, seemed deliberate disparagement to Wilson, and another instance of the anti-American sentiments, often expressed by 'the old offhand methods' (ibid.), that he had experienced since arriving in London.

3 Walter ('Walt') Whitman (1819–92), US poet; Ralph Waldo Emerson, on receiving from Whitman a copy of the 1st edition of his self-published collection *Leaves of Grass* (Brooklyn, 1855) famously hailed 'the most extraordinary piece of wit and wisdom that America has yet contributed. [...] I greet you at the beginning of a great career.' Emerson to Whitman, 21 July 1855: ' "Leaves of Grass" ', *New-York Daily Tribune*, 10 October 1855, 7.

4 Herman Melville (1819–91), US novelist, poet and (briefly) sailor; author of *Moby-Dick, or, The Whale* (NY, 1851; as *The Whale*, London, 1851).

5 'He fucked me twice.'

6 William Hale ('Big Bill') Thompson (1869–1944), Republican mayor of Chicago 1915–23, 1927–31; notoriously corrupt, he sought re-election 1927 on a demagogic, anglophobe platform: 'I wanta make the King of England keep his snoot out of America!' Lloyd Wendt and Herman Kogan, *Big Bill of Chicago* (Evanston, 2005), 248.

The last occasion, I think, on which I saw Edmund was when I stayed with him at Wellfleet and was made to cut out my name with a diamond on his window. I refused to offer an aphorism of my own, and was made by him to inscribe a verse from the Prophet Isaiah. I realise from the letters that he regarded me as in some way inspired by, almost identifying myself with, the Hebrew prophets of old, let alone the Hasidic sect[1] in which he mistakenly thought me to have been brought up. I really do not think he knew much about people – mis-shots are too frequent, the absurdities too many. There is no doubt that I did rather hero-worship him, and to an extent do still, in spite of those remarks. [...]

Yours very sincerely,
Isaiah Berlin

TO MICHAEL WALZER

12 November 1985

Headington House

Dear Michael,

[...] You say, quite justly, that I 'run (mostly) with the foxes'.[2] I think this undeniable, but I found it entertaining, and mildly intriguing, that François Bondy,[3] reviewing the book in some German newspaper, I think the *Frankfurter Allgemeine Zeitung*,[4] said (with some irony) that the same ideas ran through all my writings that he was acquainted with – pluralism, incompatibility of ultimate values, negative liberty, incoherence of the concept of a final solution to all our ills, a kind of anti-positivist empiricism, etc. – and that this recurrent pattern, from which I seem unable to detach myself, makes me a kind of hedgehog. I do not know if you would agree. Perhaps it is true – it is certainly not a conscious or deliberate perception of single, overarching principles. [...]

It never struck me that there were no hedgehogs who wanted to be foxes: it is an original idea on your part, as so many are, and I agree. Are there people brought up in some rigid, all-embracing religious discipline who long to escape it and enjoy life in all its variety for its own sake, but cannot abandon their overwhelming sense of the claims of the faith in which they were brought up or to which they were converted? But of course you are

---

1 Lubavich Hasidism, a mystical Jewish revivalist movement which reacted against the rigidity of traditional Judaism; founded in C18th Poland by IB's direct ancestor Shneur Zalman of Liady (1745–1812), it had a strong popular following, but declined in the C19th and early C20th, subsequently reviving and engaging in vigorous outreach throughout the Jewish world.
2 MW had sent IB an advance text of his introduction to a new edition (NY, 1986) of HF, in which this quotation appears at [xi].
3 François Bondy (1915–2003), German-born Swiss novelist and journalist.
4 Review untraced.

right, such cases do not easily come to mind, though I suppose they are not entirely impossible. [...]

Yours ever,

Isaiah   [...]

TO DAVID COOPERMAN[1]

15 November 1985 [carbon]

Headington House

Dear Mr Cooperman,

[...] Let me answer your questions, so far as I am able. What Weizmann feared was that the Jews were fundamentally an unpolitical society, and that their long existence as a scattered community, not used to collective decisions and national life, would [lead them to] quarrel bitterly among themselves and, as they say, 'tear themselves apart'. I think that at one time he hoped that Israel might remain part of some wider and more experienced political entity – say the British Empire, which, of course, he admired, and for the admiration of which he is now so sternly criticised by Israelis. He would not, I think, have minded if a very wide measure of home rule had been granted to the Yishuv,[2] whereby foreign policy and perhaps financial policy would be governed by agencies of the British Empire, everything else being left to the Jewish inhabitants of Palestine. Bevin and the Foreign Office made that quite impossible, and Weizmann, of course, in the end was passionately in favour of an independent state, but only because all other expedients proved unavailing and the alternative was intolerable. Do I think the same? I wish not to. Under Ben-Gurion and Eshkol[3] and even Golda [Meir] it looked as if a liberal republican tradition, with a slant towards a good deal of a social role – in fact, a welfare state – might be coming to maturity. Now the eruption of religious and political fanaticism frightens me. If ever Israel declines – I do not believe even now that it will be extinguished in any foreseeable future – the fault will lie in internal, not external, danger.

Did Weizmann fear secularism as a danger to the preservation of Jewish tradition? It is difficult to answer for the dead, but I should say no. He was himself steeped, as I said in that lecture,[4] in traditional religious Jewish education; his Yiddish was interspersed with Biblical and Talmudical phrases; he looked on the influence of the Orthodox rabbinate with suspicion; he believed that the Jews would remain Jews wherever they were – that, indeed,

1 David ('Dan') Cooperman (1927–98), US sociologist, studied and (from 1948) taught at Minnesota for his entire career; assistant prof. 1956, associate prof. 1958, prof. 1964–98; among his special interests was the Danish reaction to the Holocaust.
2 'Settlement', the pre-1948 Jewish community in Palestine.
3 Levi Eshkol (1895–1969) né Levi Shkolnik, Mapai MK from 1951, leader of Mapai 1963–5, of Alignment 1965–9; prime minister 1963–9 in succession to Ben-Gurion.
4 Chaim Weizmann, 2nd Herbert Samuel Lecture (London, 1958), repr. in PI.

was the basis and reason for Zionism, in the end – but he wanted a secular, democratic republic, and thoroughly approved of the fact that there was no state religion in Israel (nowadays more of a formal than a real state of affairs). He was a democrat, a liberal and a man of wide European outlook. The outlook of Mr Begin horrified him; he did not imagine that a phenomenon like Kahane[1] could occur. He did not think about the Arabs much – that was a genuine weakness. In that sense, he was somewhat narrowly nationalistic. Consciously or not, he wanted something like the British welfare state, which was created in his lifetime but came to fruition after his death.

What are my views on the subject? I agree with him – or with what I take to be his opinions. I think that the development of acute nationalism and religious intolerance, the control of social and personal life by ultra-Orthodox, or even just Orthodox, rabbis constitutes an enormous step backwards in the history of the Jews, and if pursued spells disaster, both morally and materially, both spiritually and politically. I am sorry to finish this letter on so sombre a note. [...]

Yours sincerely,
Isaiah Berlin

TO ALISTAIR COOKE
5 December 1985

Headington House

Dear Alistair,

Thank you for your most fascinating letter. Anti-Semitism: goodness me, Mr Poliakov's fourth (I think) volume on the subject has just appeared, and no doubt there will be seventeen more.[2] It is a subject which is, of course, endlessly referred to and written about, and nobody has got it quite right, and I daresay nobody will. What you say about Balfour[3] is no doubt true:[4] I know perfectly well that one of his motives for Zionism, perhaps the strongest, was his belief that unless you give the Jews a safety-valve – some way of 'normalising' themselves – they will breed revolutionaries, subverters of the order which he believed in and which he wished to preserve at all costs.

1 Meir David Kahane (1932–90), Brooklyn-born US Orthodox rabbi and ultra-nationalist; MK for the extreme right-wing Kach party, which he founded and led 1984–8, and which advocated the transfer of Arabs from Israel, and was banned 1988 under the law excluding parties that incited racism; assassinated by an Arab gunman in Manhattan 5 November 1990.

2 Léon Poliakov (1910–97) wrote many books on anti-Semitism; the 4th and last vol. of his *Histoire de l'antisémitisme* (Paris, 1955–77), *L'Europe suicidaire*, was trans. George Klin as *The History of Anti-Semitism: Suicidal Europe, 1870–1933* (Oxford, 1985).

3 Arthur James Balfour ('AJB') (1848–1930), OM 1916, KG 1922, 1st Earl of Balfour 1922, Conservative and Unionist statesman; prime minister 1902–5, first lord of the admiralty 1915–16, foreign secretary 1916–19.

4 Cooke had quoted Piers Brendon: 'The truth was that Balfour was a Zionist because of his anti-Semitism, not despite it.' *Eminent Edwardians* (London, 1979), 121. Letter of 25 November 1985.

Moreover, he was certainly a somewhat cynical man, and was not moved by the condition of the poor or the horrors of the Ireland of his day[1] or by the abandonment of the Georgian republic in the Caucasus by British troops when things got too hot.[2] Curzon, then Secretary for India,[3] demanded that the social democratic Georgian republic be supported against the Bolsheviks, otherwise there might be a massacre. 'An extraordinary massacre, or an ordinary one?', asked Balfour, according to the account in the Milner papers.[4] All this I know. Nevertheless, he was spurred by some kind of romantic vision of the restoration of the Jews in their ancient homeland, as Disraeli was, as Lloyd George[5] undoubtedly was, as many of the supporters of the Zionists among the British [...] were. [...]

Of course you are right. The upper classes of England, and indeed, in all countries, have a large dose of anti-Semitism circulating in their veins (sometimes it becomes acute) – the Belloc-influenced[6] Catholics among them, or those who look on Jews as a mixture of Fagin[7] and cigar-chomping bankers (Bevin had a bit of that in him, undoubtedly – the Jews to him in his Foreign Office days were a mixture of Laski,[8] who had humiliated him, I suspect, and horrible New York Jewish millionaires who were sending poor Jewish scum in leaky ships to Palestine to madden the innocent Arabs, primitive fellows but ordinary human beings like himself, victims to the clever-clever machinations of cunning Jewish businessmen and intellectuals).

But where is the root of all this? Of club anti-Semitism (the normal kind), or acute anti-Semitism – Wagner, Hitler, Henry Ford,[9] Houston Stewart

1 As Chief Secretary for Ireland 1887–91, a difficult portfolio, Balfour revealed 'the steel underlying his languid demeanour', and was dubbed 'Bloody Balfour' by Irish nationalists in consequence (Ruddock Mackay and H. C. G. Matthew, ODNB).
2 A British military force attempted to galvanise anti-Bolshevik forces in the Caucasus 1918; in June 1920 it withdrew in the face of an inevitable Bolshevik victory; the Democratic Republic of Georgia gave way February 1921 to the Socialist Soviet Republic of Georgia.
3 Curzon was foreign secretary 1919–24, never secretary of state for India.
4 Alfred Milner (1854–1925), KCB 1895, 1st (and last) Viscount Milner 1902; German-born British Unionist politician and imperialist; high commissioner, South Africa, 1897–1905; a member of Lloyd George's war cabinet 1916–18. We have not been able to trace the quotation.
5 David Lloyd George (1863–1945), OM 1919, 1st Earl Lloyd George 1945, Liberal statesman; MP 1890–1945, Prime Minister 1916–22.
6 (Joseph) Hilaire Pierre Belloc (1870–1953), French-born British poet and author; a polemical apologist for Roman Catholicism, and an anti-Semite despite his avowals to the contrary; he had the prejudices of the French right, believing throughout his life in the guilt of Dreyfus (271/2).
7 In 'Boz' [Charles Dickens], Oliver Twist, or, The Parish Boy's Progress (London, 1838), the master of the pickpocket gang led by the Artful Dodger; the portrayal drew on Jewish stereotypes, Bill Sikes denouncing him as 'an infernal, rich, plundering, thundering old Jew' (chapter 13, i 198).
8 Harold Laski, son of a prominent figure in Manchester's Jewish community, had at an early age married a gentile, in defiance of his parents' wishes. The experience of the Holocaust made him a passionate Zionist, and a strong opponent of Bevin's policy in Palestine.
9 In the early 1920s Henry Ford's weekly newspaper The Dearborn Independent published a series of articles claiming to expose a Jewish conspiracy to subvert US society; the articles appeared against the background of the publication of the The Protocols of the Learned Elders of Zion (London, 1920), which Ford republished in his paper.

Chamberlain,[1] the anti-Dreyfusards[2] and the rest? Everyone has their own pet explanation of this. I feel convinced (how can one have concrete evidence for this?) that it really does have its roots in Christianity. The Gospels refer to 'the Jews' as the people who killed God:[3] little children, who are taught about this, have no idea who the Jews are in concrete terms, but there is an obviously sinister connotation which attaches to the word 'Jew' as a result of this; so that when actual Jews are referred to there is a sense of their being connected in some way with an alien, sinister, vaguely dangerous and certainly not at all nice sect.

I do not say that this is conscious in, say, British breasts, but it is that ember of a flame lit by those early Christians who wished to detach themselves from, and therefore libelled, their enemies, the orthodox Jews in Rome. This ember glows throughout history. When it merely glows it is, perhaps, not very dangerous or harmful, but any wind can blow it into a flame. The winds do differ: that is why there are all those theories of anti-Semitism – the search for a scapegoat, the economic tensions, xenophobia, fear of clever crooks and intriguers who mislead not very bright but honest men, of whom the bulk of the nation is composed, etc. etc. etc. There is, for example, an essay by Sartre which is well-meaning in the sense of being anti-anti-Semitic, but which does not begin to penetrate to the heart of the problem.[4]

Since these winds, as I call them, will probably never cease to blow, there will be anti-Semitism so long as groups of Jews live in the midst of other peoples. The ultimate cause of it is that they have not assimilated. A minority have, and have melted away. Namier once had a brilliant image about the Jews of Eastern Europe:[5] they begin as a frozen mass, devout, self-insulated, plunged into their religious habits, a survival from the Middle Ages, squeezed by the Russians into adjacent territories, and thus rendered into a kind of artificial national minority. Then the sun of the Enlightenment starts melting this frozen mass. Some of it evaporates (conversion, intermarriage, assimilation into the surrounding peoples), some of them remain stiff and frozen (the Orthodox religious un-surrendering ones), and some are turned into rushing streams – socialist and Zionist. The socialists wish to destroy the

1 Houston Stewart Chamberlain (1855–1927), British-born Germanophile racialist writer whose works prefigured Nazi Aryan ideology; m. 2ndly 1908 Wagner's only daughter, Eva, and died at Bayreuth, which he regarded as his spiritual resting-place.

2 Those convinced of the guilt of Alfred Dreyfus (1859–1935), a Jewish Captain in the French Army falsely convicted of treason in December 1894, defended by Émile Zola in his famous open letter *J'Accuse: lettre à M. Félix Faure, Président de la République* (*L'Aurore*, 13 January 1898, 1–2), and exonerated 1906. The Dreyfus affair became a touchstone for attitudes towards Jews in French society.

3 Not in those exact terms: 'When Pilate saw that he could prevail nothing, but that rather a tumult was made, he took water, and washed his hands before the multitude, saying, I am innocent of the blood of this just person: see ye to it. Then answered all the people, and said, His blood be on us, and on our children.' Matthew 27:24–5.

4 *Réflexions sur la question juive* (Paris, 1946), trans. George J. Becker as *Anti-Semite and Jew* (NY, 1948).

5 In 'Zionism', *New Statesman*, 5 November 1927, 103–4, reprinted in his *Skyscrapers and Other Essays* (London, 1931). Cf. POI 162.

regime which has oppressed them, and make common cause with its other victims; the Zionists believe that the only solution is to get out and live a free life somewhere else.

Weizmann had no illusions about this: he was not, as you charitably say, saintly, far from it; he liked civilised values and was an absolutely fanatical moderate: he believed that all extremism leads to ruin, however noble the ideals that inspire it. He liked Balfour not only for what Balfour did for his cause, but also because Balfour was genuinely charmed by him, and being a famous charmer himself, charmed him in turn. Weizmann liked refinement, subtlety and aristocratic qualities, which Balfour, despite his anti-Semitism and heartlessness, certainly possessed. Balfour saw in him some ancient Jewish prophet carrying great historical charisma, speaking out of the depths of the biblical tradition, etc., and this obviously fascinated him in a historic-aesthetic sort of way. Neither Weizmann nor anyone else would pretend that Balfour was a warm-hearted idealist/altruist and friend of the oppressed.

The Weizmann I knew was not a Hebrew prophet, but a very strong-willed, highly rational, exceedingly wise old gentleman (by the time I knew him), who had come to the conclusion that assimilation had been a failure (and who would deny it today?); that the Jews had not only not assimilated but were not assimilable, whatever the circumstances; that to be a minority everywhere was an intolerable moral condition; that in every country, to have to look over one's shoulder to see how others were regarding one, how one 'fitted in', with indelible historical memories of what happened when one didn't, and the unforgettable stations of martyrdom, particularly in Christian countries (not that the Muslims treated Jews much better: there were sufficient pogroms in, say, Morocco, or even Muslim Spain, throughout the later Middle Ages and the eighteenth and nineteenth centuries; otherwise the famous loi Crémieux[1] establishing Jewish rights in North Africa would [not] have been needed), was intolerable; or, if the desire to fit in and get by, or, better still, do well, become prosperous, get titles, influence affairs in one's adopted country – if that didn't work, then the opposite: out of frustration, resentment and defiance came radicalism, revolution, Karl Marx, Lassalle[2] (it is said that he once said that had he been born a Prussian, he would have liked to have been a Guards officer, but as it was he had to make do with creating the German Labour Party, as a great model of all labour parties elsewhere), Jewish Bolsheviks (Lenin of course was not a Jew, but who his mother was remains uncertain to this day: her name was 'Blank',[3] and none

---

1 This 1870 law, named after the French Jewish minister of justice Adolphe Crémieux (1796–1880), gave French citizenship to Jews in Algeria.

2 Ferdinand Johann Gottlieb Lassalle (1825–64) né Lassal, German Jewish lawyer and socialist; founder, 1863, Allgemeiner Deutscher Arbeiterverein, an antecedent of the Weimar SPD.

3 Lenin's mother Maria Aleksandrova Ulyanova (1835–1916) née Blank was the granddaughter of Moshe Itskovich ('Moshko') Blank (c.1758–1846), a trader in wine and spirits in the province of Volyn' who, although born into a Jewish family, did not observe the faith; he was baptised an

of his ten million biographies say one word about her origins – German? Jewish? the NKVD won't tell us).

Zionism was an alternative to this. If the Jews could be found a corner in which to create their own establishment, then all the Jewish attributes which result from persecution – survival of the fittest, the cleverest, the scepticism, the artistic talent born of traumata, the violinists, chess-players, tailors, comedians, bankers, fixers, agents, and agents of agents (seldom the owners of real basic materials – oil or steel or iron or coal) – all this would disappear, and the Jews would be made ordinary men and women: farmers, artisans, shopkeepers, soldiers, with a mere sprinkling of intellectuals, artists etc.

And this, of course, is how it was realised in Israel. No great chess-players, no splendid novelists – fiddlers, yes – no great conductors, no tortured writers, no Kafkas, no Heines, no Harold Laskis, no Einsteins, no Freuds, no Marxes. Mediocrity, perhaps not an altogether unhealthy development from an earlier situation in which endless, at best discomfort, at worst persecution and extermination, bred the flowers of art and literature.

To return to anti-Semitism: I cannot see how it could possibly disappear. It might greatly diminish if Israel were ever allowed to cease to be a source of friction and anxiety (the problem of the Arabs and Palestine has no clean solution; it's a matter of time, patience and some kind of trade-offs, it seems to me). The Jews of the rest of the world would breathe more easily, and perhaps assimilate more successfully, as they are more or less doing in parts of America, perhaps. But even the most friendly, unbiased, unprejudiced Englishman today certainly does not think of Jews as English. They may be all right, he has nothing against them, but they are Jews first and foremost. They are Jews not in the sense in which Presbyterians or Methodists, or even Catholics, are what they are – English Catholics, Scottish Presbyterians, Presbyterian Scotsmen, Catholic Englishmen. Jewish Englishmen? Perhaps a few are – perhaps Keith Joseph is so conceived. But neither Lord Rothschild nor Mr Leon Brittan[1] is so thought of, and not just in Conservative purlieus alone. [...]

Oh dear, I didn't mean to write you a sermon on anti-Semitism, and I think the definition of 'intellectual' is very funny and does touch a nerve.[2]

Orthodox Christian (as Dmitry) after the death of his wife, and his 2 sons converted to Christianity, Aleksandr Dmitrievich (1804–70) né Srul (Yiddish for Hebrew 'Israel') Moshevich, Maria's father, marrying a Lutheran, Anna Ivanovna Großschopf (c.1799–1838); the Soviet authorities attempted to suppress the fact that Maria's ancestry was partly Jewish.

1 Leon Brittan (1939–2015), Kt 1989, later (2000) life peer, Conservative politician and European minister; minister of state, Home Office, 1979–81; chief secretary to treasury 1981–3; secretary of state, Home Office, 1983–5, for trade and industry 1985–6; European commissioner 1989–99.

2 Cooke had written: 'The Chronicle (of San Francisco, where I was last week) interviewed people on the street and [in] offices for a definition of "an intellectual". This is my favorite – from a 24-year old real estate man: "An intellectual is somebody that everything they do they give it a lot of thought. They analyze everything to the point they don't enjoy themselves." I think the second sentence touches a nerve.'

But where Winston said 'He never stooped but he never conquered', I do not know – but it is very good.[1] I do not share your contempt for Balfour. He was no better and no worse than the class and time into which he was born: more imaginative, more interesting than most of them; more so than Curzon or any of the Dukes; a Zionist not just because he wanted to get the Jews to leave Europe for fear of what they might do, rather more because he thought it interesting, perhaps amusing, to see whether a new nation could be created with a fascinating history. And Winston too, who was a stout Zionist, certainly did not particularly like Jews. He may have liked Baruch, as Balfour may have liked Natty Rothschild[2] (the father of the man to whom his Declaration was addressed), but they quite definitely thought of them as for-eigners of some kind, *métèques*,[3] resident foreigners; some of them perfectly nice, but still not Englishmen, not Scotsmen, not Welshmen, not Irishmen – Jews. Like the rich Greeks who live in London: Stavrides, Calvocoressis.

There is an old joke about the fact that if you ask a native of Czechoslovakia what he is, some will say 'I am a Czech', some will say 'I am a Slovak', some will say 'I am a Ruthenian'; but Jews will say 'I am a Czechoslovak.' Therein lies the perfectly real tragedy to which Israel is the greatest step towards a solution [...], despite the injustice to the Arabs, despite the appalling behav-iour of the fanatics and the zealots and the fools and the knaves, who are there as frequent as they are today almost everywhere else – despite all this, nevertheless, an achievement.

Weizmann is largely forgotten by the Israelis now, regarded as an old-fashioned, anglophile, gentlemanly snob (or almost). But if Israel survives at all, his outlook will be resuscitated. So I believe. [...] (I do not think that some of my Jewish friends – Keith Joseph, the late Justice Lionel Cohen[4] and his surviving family, Edward Warburg[5] in New York – would find my thesis at all attractive, or even valid, though in their heart of hearts – such of them as still possess hearts – they would know it to be largely true.)

Forgive me for this unconscionably long outpouring. Next time we meet I shall be quite willing to carry on in this strain for hours and hours, so do be warned – this is a threat – I promise you I won't if I see the least sign of resistance, which would be only too natural, on your part.

1 'He would not stoop; he did not conquer', said of the 5th Earl of Rosebery (prime minister 1894–5): 'The Earl of Rosebery', *Great Contemporaries* (London, 1937), 13–30 at 19.
2 Nathan Mayer Rothschild (1840–1915), 1st Baron Rothschild 1885, GCVO 1902, father of Lionel Walter Rothschild (1868–1937), 2nd Baron Rothschild, to whom the Balfour Declaration of 2 November 1917 (479/3) was addressed.
3 Metics: aliens with citizenship rights.
4 Lionel Leonard Cohen (1888–1973), Kt 1943, life peer 1951; judge, chancery division, high court of justice, 1943–6, lord justice of appeal 1946–51, lord of appeal in ordinary 1951–60.
5 Edward Mortimer Morris ('Eddie') Warburg (1908–92), US philanthropist, art collector and patron of the arts; founding father of the American Ballet, precursor of the NY City Ballet.

Warmest regards,
Yours ever,
    Isaiah   [...]

TO PETER GAY[1]

[1985?, *manuscript draft*]

                                                               Headington House
Dear Peter,
    [...] The man who arranged my visit to Siegmund Freud was a pious Jewish
metal merchant, Oscar Philipp,[2] now dead, who was a cousin of Freud's
wife. I called some time – I cannot recollect when – Netherhall Gardens[3] – in
I think the late summer of 1938 – but it may have been later, on a Friday afternoon at about 5 pm. While we were talking about various things – his arrest
in Vienna[4] & psychoanalysis in Britain, Frau Freud came in & said (I quote
from memory) 'Since you know my cousin Oscar Philipp, you must know
that on Friday evenings good Jewish women light candles for the approach of
the Sabbath. But this *Unmensch*[5] (I *think* we talked in German) will not allow
this, because he says that religion is a superstition.' It was said with feigned
indignation – humorously with affection – to which Freud nodded gravely &
said 'Yes, indeed, religion *is* a superstition (ein Überglauben)'[6] & Frau Freud
said 'you see?' It was all very charming – obviously this was a regular inter-
change for more than half a century – & a standing joke for the benefit of
relevant & sympathetic visitors. I cannot, of course, vouch for the details of
this – but that is what I now remember, after more than forty years. [...]
    Yours ever,
        Isaiah

TO MICHAEL WALZER

14 January 1986

                                                               Headington House
Dear Michael,
    [...] As for relativism, I understand your problem very well, since this is

1 Peter Gay (b. 1923) né Peter Joachim Fröhlich, Berlin-born US historian; prof. of history,
   Columbia, 1962–9; prof. of comparative and intellectual European history, Yale, 1969–84, Sterling
   Prof. of History 1984–93.
2 Oscar Isaac Philipp (1887–1965), metal-broker, lived until the beginning of WW2 at 33 Ferncroft
   Avenue, London NW3; Ferncroft Avenue adjoins Hollycroft Avenue, where IB and his parents
   lived (at no. 49, visible from Philipp's house) from 1928. Cf. L1 316/6.
3 In fact 20 Maresfield Gardens, London NW3, now the site of the Freud Museum.
4 It was Freud's daughter Anna, not Freud himself, who was (briefly) arrested in Vienna 1938,
   leading to Freud's emigration to London later the same year.
5 'Brute'.
6 sc. 'Aberglaube'.

also mine.[1] 'Common ground' is, I suppose, what Herbert Hart tried to formulate as a kind of empirical version of natural law,[2] i.e. those laws without which no society could survive – if everybody lied, killed (or even, I suppose, if the majority did), no society could survive and this is therefore almost a kind of biological necessity, however the word 'necessity' is interpreted. But clearly this is not enough as a minimal code – even if sufficiently universal. So what does one say? If I am right, and ultimate values can be incompatible, how does one in fact decide between love and honour? How does one decide whether Antigone was right or wrong in what she did?[3] There has been disagreement about this for some time: Hegel sat on the fence (I think rightly);[4] Sartre thought Creon was right. And what about Dido and Aeneas? When he found that she was madly in love with him, and he was not at all with her – although he lost his head (one might say) in that cave into which the storm had driven them – what was he to do? Marry her and condemn them both to conflict and misery? Or abandon her as he did? Of course Virgil tells you that Mercury came and told him that his duty was to create Rome, etc., but that is what Kant used to call a miserable subterfuge.[5] The nineteenth-century editors all thought that Aeneas was a howling cad, and poor Dido a victim,

1 While agreeing with IB that a 'minimum of common moral ground' precludes relativism, Walzer nevertheless struggled to define this: 'I still have trouble, inclined to say too much or too little (too much when I find myself in one sort of argument, too little when in another)' (to IB, 11 December 1985). In his letter Walzer alludes to IB's 'Note on Alleged Relativism in Eighteenth Century European Thought', *British Journal for Eighteenth-Century Studies* 3 (1980), 89–106; repr. in CTH.

2 In *The Concept of Law* (Oxford, 1961) Hart argued that there was an empirical foundation to natural law, arising from the need of the individual, and group, to survive: 'our concern is with social arrangements for continued existence' (188); 'there are certain rules of conduct which any social organisation must contain if it is to be viable' (ibid.); 'Such universally recognised principles of conduct which have a basis in elementary truths concerning human beings, their natural environment, and aims, may be considered the *minimum content* of Natural Law' (189).

3 Antigone is a figure in Greek myth who defies an order by Creon, king of Thebes, that her brother Polynices not be buried after his death in an attack on the city. Her predicament exemplifies the irresolvable clash between two rival moral systems, in this case 'the unwritten laws, the eternal code which Antigone obeys, and Creon's belief that the state is the ultimate source of authority' (UD 102); 'whether Creon or Antigone wins, there is tragedy because something has been lost: if Creon prevails, then the principles in which Antigone [...] believes are violated; if she wins, then the state's authority is undermined' (UD 101).

4 In his *Lectures on Aesthetics* of 1835 Hegel gave weight to both countervailing principles, referring to 'the collision of equally justified powers and individuals [...]. The chief conflict [...] is that between the state [...] and the family [...]. These are the clearest powers that are presented in tragedy, because the full reality of ethical existence consists in harmony between these two spheres [...]. Antigone honours the bond of kinship, the gods of the underworld, while Creon honours Zeus alone, the dominating power over public life and social welfare.' G. W. F. Hegel, *Aesthetics: Lectures on Fine Art*, trans. T. M. Knox (Oxford, 1975), ii 1213.

5 Mercury's speech to Aeneas is at Virgil, *Aeneid* 4. 265–75. 'Miserable subterfuge' ('elender Behelf') was the term applied by Kant in the *Critique of Practical Reason* to the theory of self-determinism, which attempts to reconcile free will and determinism by saying that the proximate cause of human action is a decision, albeit itself caused, made by the individual. *Kant's gesammelte Schriften* (170/5) v 96.15, cf. L 7, where IB describes the theory as holding that 'I am free if I can do what I wish [...]. But my choice is itself causally determined.'

and her self-immolation[1] rather wonderful; and the fact that Hannibal[2] had to avenge himself on Rome, as her descendant, a pleasing aetiological myth.

But what do you and I think? Should the Jewish leaders under Nazi rule have agreed to save a certain number of Jews at the cost of giving the names and addresses of others and condemning them to immediate slaughter, or should they, when they were asked to do this, have done nothing, or committed suicide? Surely, *pace* Miss Arendt, who I think is terrible on this (as on many things),[3] we are in no position to moralise about this: in painful and agonising situations of this order, surely any criterion that one would regard as in any sense objective (though I shall never quite know what that means) must be condemned.

In cases of such conflict, even if it is not agonising, but simply a conflict between ends of life which we hope can be harmonised, if only by a trade-off, but sometimes cannot, we are, I think, forced to plump and defend our choice in terms of the values that we regard as ultimate for ourselves and, let us add, assume to be such for a good many members of the society in the times in which we live.[4] Since we can, if I am right, in principle not seek for an overarching objective order, true for all times, in all places, and for all men, then disagreements between cultures are in the same box as all other conflicts of values. We follow our own; but we cannot be converted to a religion, to a code of ethics, almost to another culture, perhaps. If we say 'This is it at last, now I really do see what is right and good', as people certainly have done, and do, and will do, we ought to be able to explain why this is so to others. We can only do so if we have enough common ground with others, i.e. enough to make it possible to be able to carry conviction by, e.g., pointing out similarities of the values they are now preaching to some which the interlocutor already holds too. Surely that is about as near to objectivity as we can get? If people object to saying 'How can we know how to live?', a combination of Hart-like arguments about the minimum requirements of a functioning society (even if immoral) plus examples of lives, outlooks, characters, the anti-Kantian morality which Bergson, in *Two Sources of Morality and Religion*,[5] talks about, seems to me about all that we can do. And that is surely how we actually act in practice. Ayatollahs, Leo Strauss,[6] Kant, the council of sages in Jerusalem who dictate the policy of the

---

1 According to Virgil Dido committed suicide when Aeneas left her to found Rome.

2 Hannibal Barca (247–c.182 BCE), descendant of a brother of Dido; Carthaginian military leader, enemy of Rome.

3 Cf. 463–4.

4 'That is, I can give reasons: it is not irrational plumping.' To MW, 17 October 1995. This of course only kicks the question of relativism upstairs, since the background constellation of values appealed to here itself needs justification as against alternative constellations.

5 *Les deux sources de la morale et de la religion* (Paris, 1932); *The Two Sources of Morality and Religion*, trans. R. Ashley Audra and Cloudesley Brereton, with the assistance of W. Horsfall Carter (London, 1935).

6 Leo Strauss (1899–1973), German-born political philosopher and interpreter of classical political

religious parties in the Knesset, G. D. H. Cole, others who derive light from revelation, or a priori knowledge of moral values and rules, might disagree, and ask what, if this is not so, does 'moral blindness' mean?[1] But I think that anyone who does not understand the conflict of Antigone, or the Jewish leaders under the Nazis, or anyone subjected to moral blackmail, whether in his own mind or by others, is morally blind. Beyond this, I cannot go, but I do not claim this to be entirely satisfactory.

Do let us discuss it when next we meet – it is an issue which nobody yet has written about in a magisterial[2] fashion which one can accept and say 'At last the problem has been, if not solved, enormously clarified.'

Yours ever, ⟨most gratefully⟩

Isaiah

TO BEATA POLANOWSKA-SYGULSKA[3]

24 February 1986

Headington House

Dear Mrs Polanowska-Sygulska,

Thank you very much for your most interesting letter, which I read with great pleasure and attention [...]. First [...] let me talk about the difficult question of 'human nature'. Do I believe in a fixed and unalterable human nature? You rightly quote me as saying that I do not, and then again rightly quote me as referring to it as the basis of human communication. What, then, do I believe? I wish I could answer this question with extreme precision, but it does not seem to me to lend itself to that. What, I think, I believe is that there are thinkers, principally believers in natural law, who propose that all men are created, whether by God or nature, endowed with innate know-ledge of certain truths – some 'factual', some normative. The lists differ, from Aristotle, the Stoics, Isidore of Seville, Gratian, Grotius[4] etc., but for the most

theory; emigrated to US 1938 (naturalised 1944); prof. of political science, New School for Social Research, NY, 1938–49, Chicago 1949–68, Claremont (California) Men's College 1968–9, St John's College, Annapolis, 1969–73; alleges that IB is a relativist in ' "Relativism" ', in Helmut Schoeck and James W. Wiggins (eds), *Relativism and the Study of Man* (Princeton, 1961), 135–57.

1 If the morally right decision when values clash is revealed to us as part of objective reality, one can be metaphorically blind to it just as one can be literally blind to the physical world: this is the view IB attributes to the persons he lists, who might argue that if there is no incontrovertible criterion enabling us to decide in difficult cases, 'moral blindness' would have no clear meaning. IB rejects this argument, and holds that the lack of a definitive way of choosing between the plural, conflicting values in which he believes is itself part of objective moral reality, so that failure to recognise the true nature of clashes between these values is in turn a form of moral blindness.

2 Word deleted, but without a substitution.

3 Beata Maria *Polanowska-Sygulska (b. 1954), philosophically inclined lawyer.

4 Isidore (*c.*560–636), Archbishop of Seville, author of the *Etymologiae*, an etymological encyclopedia drawn from classical sources; Gratian (b. C11th, d. not later than 1159), author of the *Decretum Gratiani*, the major source of Roman Catholic canon law; Hugo Grotius (also Huig/ Hugeianus/ Hugh de Groot) (1583–1645), Dutch jurist and theologian.

part they include the existence of God, the knowledge of good and evil, right and wrong, the obligation to tell the truth, return debts, keep promises (*pacta sunt servanda*),[1] some or all of the Biblical ten commandments, and so on. I do not know who first questioned this – I dare say Epicurus or Lucretius.[2] But in modern times the main attack upon this was delivered by thinkers like Vico and Herder and Marx (and, indeed, Hegel and his followers), and, of course, the empiricists – not Locke, but Hume and his followers – according to whom, whatever the status of these natural laws, primitive men did not possess knowledge or even awareness of them, and they came into consciousness, or, indeed, formed objects of belief or certainty, in the course of evolution, or under the influence of changes in material circumstances and the growth of culture (whatever factors enter into that). For this entails that human beings go through a process of moral or metaphysical growth and development; and this is as valid as that empirical knowledge is an onward-going process, whether one believes that it tends to progressive development towards some kind of perfection (which it may never reach) or not – that it is cumulative but possesses no identifiable structure or teleological tendency.

This is certainly what Vico and Marx believed. That is, they believed that what is called human nature varies and differs from culture to culture, or even within cultures – that various factors play a part in the modification of human responses to nature and each other; and that therefore the idea that all men, at all times, in all places, are endowed with actual or potential knowledge of universal, timeless, unalterable truths (whether such truths exist or not, though for the most part such people did not believe them to exist) is simply false. The belief in such a priori knowledge and such unalterable truths does form the heart of the central European tradition, from Plato and the Stoics, through the Middle Ages, and perhaps in the Enlightenment as well, to our own day, indeed.

But if Vico and Marx etc. are right, and I think they are, this is not a valid conception. Human beings differ, their values differ, their understanding of the world differs; and some kind of historical or anthropological explanation of why such differences arise is in principle possible, though that explanation itself may to some degree reflect the particular concepts and categories of the particular culture to which these students of this subject belong. I do not think this leads to relativism of any kind; indeed, I have an essay on the alleged relativism of the eighteenth century, of which I enclose an offprint.[3]

But even though there is no basic human nature in this sense[4] – in the sense in which, for example, Rousseau believed that if you strip off all the increments,

1 'Agreements must be kept', a principle deriving from Roman civil law.
2 (Titus) Lucretius (Carus) (*c*.95–55 BCE), Latin poet whose long poem *De rerum natura* (*On the Nature of Things*) presents and defends the philosophy of Epicurus.
3 276/1.
4 The completion of (the sense of) this sentence is lost sight of until the next paragraph.

all the modifications, corruption, distortion etc. (as he thought of it) brought about by society and civilisation, there will be discovered a basic natural man, sometimes identified with, say, Red Indians, who have not had the unfortunate experience of having their natures distorted by European culture – this is the position attacked, for example, by Edmund Burke, who says that the idea that there is a natural man (about whom he thinks the French revolutionaries speak, and whose rights they wish to restore) is false, that there is no such creature; that the arts, which according to Rousseau are a later and perhaps disastrous development, are, as he says, parts of man's nature;[1] that there is no central, pure, natural being who emerges after you have scraped off all the artificial beliefs, habits, values, forms of life and behaviour which have been, as it were, superimposed on this pure, natural being – that is what I mean by denying a fixed human nature: I do not believe that all men are in the relevant respects the same 'beneath the skin', i.e. I believe that variety is part of human existence and in fact (though this is quite irrelevant) that this is a valuable attribute, though that is a very late idea, probably not to be met much before the eighteenth century.

What, then, do I mean by saying that men do have a common nature? Well, I think that common ground between human beings must exist if there is to be any meaning in the concept of 'human being' at all. I think that it is true to say that there are certain basic needs – for example, for food, shelter, security and, if we accept Herder, for belonging to a group of one's own – which anyone qualifying for the description of 'human being' must be held to possess. These are only the most basic properties. One might be able to add the need for a certain minimum of liberty, for the opportunity to pursue happiness or the realisation of one's potentialities for self-expression, for creation (however elementary), for love, for worship (as religious thinkers have maintained), for communication, and for some means of conceiving and describing themselves, perhaps in highly symbolic and mythological forms, [and] their own relationship to the environment, natural and human, in which they live. Unless there is that, communication between human beings, even within a society, let alone understanding of what others have wished to communicate in other ages and cultures, would become impossible.

I believe in the permanent possibility of change, modification, variety, without being able to state that there is some central kernel which is what is being modified or changed. But there must be enough in common between all the various individuals and groups who are going through various

1 'The state of civil society [...] is a state of nature; and much more truly so than a savage and incoherent mode of life; for man is by nature reasonable, and he is never perfectly in his natural state, but when he is placed where reason may be best cultivated, and most predominates. Art is man's nature. We are as much, at least, in a state of nature in formed manhood, as in immature and helpless infancy.' Edmund Burke, *An Appeal from the New to the Old Whigs, in Consequence of Some Late Discussions in Parliament, Relative to the Reflections on the French Revolution* (London, 1791), 130–1.

modifications for communication to be possible; and this can be expressed by listing, almost mechanically, various basic needs – 'basic' for that reason – the various forms and varieties of which belong to different persons, cultures, societies etc. The need for food is universal, but the way I satisfy it, the particular foods I crave, the steps I take to obtain them, will vary. So with all the other basic needs: my mythology, metaphysics, religion, language, gestures will widely vary, but not the fact that these are attempted ways of trying to explain to myself, to find myself at home in, a puzzling and possibly unfriendly environment or, indeed, world.

Wittgenstein once explained the concept of 'family face':[1] that is, among the portraits of ancestors, face A resembles face B, face B resembles face C, face C resembles face D, etc., but there is not a central face, the 'family face', of which these are identifiable modifications. Nevertheless, when I say 'family face' I do not mean nothing, I mean precisely that A resembles B, B resembles C and so on, in various respects, and that they form a continuum, a series, which can be attributed to family X, not to family Y. So with the various natures of various cultures, societies, groups etc. This is what I mean: that there is not a fixed, and yet there is a common, human nature. Without the latter there would be no possibility of talking about human beings, or, indeed, of intercommunication, on which all thought depends; and not only thought, but feeling, imagination, action. I do not know if I make myself clear, but that, I think, is what I believe. [...]

Yours sincerely,
    Isaiah Berlin

                                                           [...]

TO IMOGEN COOPER[2]

21 March 1986

Headington House

Dearest Imogen,

I was terribly distressed to read in *The Times*, in Jerusalem, about Martin's death.[3] I was ill all last week, and this somehow seemed to close the heavens utterly and for ever. I absolutely adored him. I telephoned your mother and spoke to your brother, who told me that Martin had died in his sleep – so

1 Usually translated as 'family resemblance': cf. 209/2.
2 Imogen Cooper (b. 1949; plate 32), daughter of Martin Du Pré Cooper and his wife Mary (next note), concert pianist, studied at the Paris Conservatoire 1961–7 (Premier Prix 1967), and at Vienna with Alfred Brendel 1970; her many international performances have included regular appearances at the Proms since her 1975 debut.
3 Martin Du Pré Cooper (1910–86), music critic and musician, St Edmund Hall modern languages 1928–31; his friendship with IB began with a chance meeting at the Holywell Music Room in Oxford; m. 1940 Mary Stewart, and had 4 children (a son and 3 daughters); joined music staff, *Daily Telegraph*, 1950, music editor 1954–76; he died on 15 March, and his *Times* obituary described him as 'one of the most gifted, stylish and intelligent music critics of his time' ('Martin Cooper: Music Critic and Author', 17 March, 14g); subject of a memoir in PI3.

may we all. I have written a long letter to your mother in longhand, from Jerusalem – it is torture to read my handwriting, hence this impersonal typewriter. I won't repeat what I said to Mary about my first meeting with Martin in the anteroom of the Holywell Music Room, and all our subsequent meetings when I went to stay with your grandparents in York. Did you ever know your grandfather? He was a sweet, gentle, charming old man when I was an undergraduate; and as I used to sit in front of the fire in the Canon's house, trying to read Kant, he would come towards me, offer me some comfort – a chocolate or a glass of wine (not that I could drink it) – and say 'Stiff? Very stiff?', and I would say 'Yes, yes, very stiff, awful'; 'Well, then, why don't you stop and listen to Martin play a little.' It was absolutely idyllic. Nor will I forget Martin in Salzburg: sheaves of music paper on which he inscribed various songs in the style, he said, of Schumann, for the approval of Professor Egon Wellesz.[1] Or the spoof piece we wrote together about a composer called Fillink, whose principal work was *One Step Forwards, Two Steps Backwards*,[2] and a translation of whose Slav romance in English went 'Dabchick, dabchick, dabchick hey'.

But I must not go on in this flippant and sentimental vein of reminiscence – although, deeply painful as I find the thought that I shall never see Martin again, something of the sense of fun with which our entire relationship was bound up, and which we expected and I think obtained from each other, keeps breaking through.

That he felt intensely proud of you, you must know: I think you realised all his unfulfilled ambitions as a pianist. This really did fill him with joy. [...]

I must not go on, all I really want to say is that I am upset, that nothing will make up for the place that he held in my life, and that Aline and I send you our warmest love.

Yours ever, ⟨with much love⟩

    Isaiah

TO WOO-YEUNG SHIN[3]

14 May 1986 [*carbon, heavily corrected in manuscript*]

                        Headington House

Dear Mr Shin,

[...] Historicism and value judgement: this, of course, is a famous crux, made, e.g., by Momigliano in his (in my opinion somewhat wrong-headed) review of my book in the *New York Review of Books* some years ago, attributing

---

1 Egon Joseph Wellesz (1885–1974), prof. of the history of music, Vienna, 1929–38; fellow and music tutor, Lincoln, 1939–74; reader in Byzantine music, Oxford, 1948–56.

2 *One Step Forwards, Two Steps Backwards: The Crisis in Our Party* (Geneva, 1904) is a pamphlet by Lenin.

3 Unidentified.

relativism to Vico, with which, he says, I did not adequately cope.[1] But, as you know, my view is that Vico is not a relativist, but a pluralist. Let me try and answer your question.

How can we judge other cultures in terms of our own values? And if not, if Montesquieu and Vico are right, must we try to probe into their value systems and only judge them in terms of theirs, and not our own? There was a famous controversy between Lord Acton and Bishop Stubbs[2] about the crimes of the Borgias in the Renaissance: Acton simply condemned them as wickedness; Stubbs tried to defend them on the ground that the morality of the Renaissance was very different from ours, so that, in terms of people's thoughts and behaviour of that time, their deeds must appear in a different light, be differently judged, etc.[3]

Let me explain: I do believe that Vico and Herder were both right in saying that cultures can only be understood in terms of the values they, and not we, pursue; and that this is a very difficult thing to do – it means a great deal of sympathy, research, knowledge, insight, imagination, every faculty and every effort we can bring into play: that is why the history of culture is such an absorbing and *appallingly* difficult subject. The point is that, to understand men in the past, one must be able to understand how it must have been to have felt and thought as they did, how values alien to us, or repellent to us, can have been valid, or valid-seeming, ends that were authoritative to men in remote times and places. As may be the case, and as your letter implies, we may find it too difficult to understand how it is possible that these savages, or barbarians, or medieval Franks, or fourteenth-century Japanese, can have thought what they thought, wanted what they wanted, judged men or institutions or themselves as they did.

If we really cannot understand this, if it seems to us totally unintelligible, or even totally disgusting, something we cannot conceive of human beings as pursuing, as it were, then it seems that we don't understand them at all, and they are not, in some sense, wholly human beings at all. Communication has broken down. Our language is not their language. We cut reality too differently to be able to understand each other. What, however, must be possible, is for us to be able to enter into a foreign scheme of values, to think of what it could

1 Arnaldo Momigliano, 'On the Pioneer Trail', NYRB, 11 November 1976, 33–8, to which IB replied in 'Note on Alleged Relativism in Eighteenth Century European Thought' (276/1).

2 sc. Creighton. William Stubbs (1825–1901), historian, Bishop of Oxford from 1889; Regius Prof. of Modern History, Oxford, and fellow, Oriel, 1866–84. Mandell Creighton (1843–1901), historian, Bishop of London from 1897; Dixie Prof. of Ecclesiastical History, Cambridge, 1884–91; author of *A History of the Papacy during the Reformation* (London, 1882–94): 'His great Catholic contemporary, Lord Acton, attributed Creighton's detachment as a commentator to his "serene curiosity" [...]. He looked for much more explicit censure on the Renaissance popes' (C. M. D. Crowder, ODNB).

3 'I am with Acton against Creighton: understand whatever you can, but this is no reason for not condemning, even if you can imagine yourself as perpetrating these evils if you were a different person in a different place under different influences, etc.' To HH, 5 July 1993.

have been like for us to have lived then and thought like this; and then, if we want to, simply condemn it, say 'These are not our own values.' They *are* possible human values, one could live like that, there could have been a perfectly genuine culture of that kind, but we reject it in terms of what are ultimate values for us, or our civilisation, or *Kulturkreis*.[1] We are perfectly entitled to explain religions and the Borgias, or other persons we might regard as wicked or strange, in the light of their values, and yet be able to condemn them – either because they failed to pursue what they thought good and right, or, even if they did think it good and right, because these things are not considered in terms of our values to be good and right. Their values simply clash with ours, but they must be the kind of values which we can imagine ourselves as capable of pursuing without ceasing to be human or decent or intelligible.

That is my answer to the relativism of which Montesquieu or Vico or Herder stand accused. Herder, like Mao, said that there are many flowers, cultures each quite different from the others.[2] Optimistically, he believed that they would all form a beautiful cosmic harmony. About that, no doubt he was mistaken: they can collide, they can be incompatible, within cultures, between cultures, even within human beings, and then we have to do what we can and live in terms of imperfect compromises. But, because we belong to one kind of flowerbed, not to understand that the other flowers have their own beds and are equally flower-like flowers – that, I think, is Herder's great contribution, of which Vico in some sense was an anticipator, Vico in terms of historical periods, Herder in terms of different nationalities, past and contemporary cultures, etc. That is what historicism means to me, and I think did to Vico. [...]

Yours sincerely
Isaiah Berlin

TO DANIEL BELL[3]

3 June 1986

Headington House

Dear Professor Bell,

[...] I am not so sure that assimilation has as little meaning as you give

1 'Culture' (literally 'cultural circle').
2 'Letting a hundred flowers blossom and a hundred schools of thought contend is the policy for promoting progress in the arts and the sciences and a flourishing socialist culture in our land.' Mao Zedong, 'On the Correct Handling of Contradictions among the People', speech to the 11th Session, Supreme State Conference, Beijing, 27 February 1957: *Selected Works of Mao Tse-Tung* (Peking, 1961–77) v 408. If Herder did not use the same image, he subscribed to the same idea, e.g. in *Yet Another Philosophy of History* (1774): 'Every nation has its own inner centre of happiness, as every sphere its own centre of gravity.' *Herder's sämmtliche Werke*, ed. Bernhard Suphan and others (Berlin, 1877–1913), v 509.
3 Daniel Bell (1919–2011) né Bolotsky, NY-born US journalist and sociologist, son of immigrant Jewish garment-workers from Eastern Europe; spent his early career in journalism, specialising

it. A great deal of melting is undoubtedly going on through intermarriage and general evaporation, so much so that the Jewish Board of Deputies in England has set up some kind of statistical unit to discover why the community is losing so many members. I am not at all against that: people must do as they wish. But as a doctrine, a 'solution', it is no longer advocated. I do come across ambivalent figures who are uneasy about their status, certainly in England; less so, I admit, in America. Oddly enough, I think the 1967 war – the Six Days War – did have a powerful emancipating effect on Jews everywhere. It almost went beyond Hitler in causing Jews not only to feel as Jews but to accept that they were what in fact they were. I did write, years ago, an essay on 'Jewish Slavery and Emancipation',[1] in which I spoke about hunchbacks (it caused a good deal of offence in the Anglo-Jewish community at the time), and indicated three phoney ways of meeting this condition, and one difficult but genuine one.[2] I never let this essay be reprinted in English (for some odd reason it appeared in French), because I didn't want to stir too great a controversy in a community with which I should have to live for too many years.

But although the situation of the 1950s, when this was written, has undoubtedly altered as a result of what happened in Israel, I think I disagree with you in maintaining [...] that all Jews outside Israel to some degree or other feel a certain social unease. In America particularly, they may feel fully realised inside their own marvellously successful and powerful Jewish community; still, at any rate some of the ones I know, either apologetically or defiantly, feel that the eyes of others (not just Wasps, but gentiles in general) are upon them, and that they are in some sense watched.

The situation is different from what Weizmann once described it as being when some Irish lunatic – in 1938, I think – threw a pistol at the feet of the horse which King Edward VII[3] was riding, and was duly arrested. Jews said 'Thank God it was not a Jew.' If it had been a Jew, all Jews would have felt

---

in social subjects; prof. of sociology, Columbia, 1959–69; prof. of social science, Harvard, 1969–80, Henry Ford II Prof. of Social Science 1980–90.

1 262/1.

2 The 'phoney ways' were to maintain that (1) there was no hump; (2) a hump was a source of pride; (3) the hump would in time disappear. The 'difficult but genuine way' was to remove the hump. POI 174–6.

3 sc. Edward VIII: Edward Albert Christian George Andrew Patrick David Windsor (1894–1972), King Edward VIII January–December 1936. A loaded revolver was thrown at the King 16 July 1936 by George Andrew McMahon (né Jerome Bannigan) as the King rode back to Buckingham Palace after presenting new colours to the Brigade of Guards in Hyde Park. McMahon was found guilty of producing a firearm 'with intent to alarm' the King, and sentenced to 12 months' hard labour. The popular press reported that he was an Irishman of unstable temperament, prone to drink. His claim to be the unwilling agent of an international conspiracy to assassinate the King was rejected in court; more probably he sought redress for what he regarded as his continuing persecution by the Home Office, and in particular the Home Secretary (from 1935) Sir John Simon, having been sentenced to 12 months' imprisonment for criminal libel 1933 and then released after 3½ months, without compensation, when his conviction was quashed on appeal.

nervous, fingers would have been pointed at them as a community. That may no longer be so. But still, outside Israel, even in Yale, Harvard, Princeton, there is a certain social uneasiness which I detect quite easily, not only on the part of old men like Harry Levin, let us say, or John Clive, but younger ones as well. They no longer conceal their origins as, let us say, Bobby Wolff,[1] the Russian historian, more or less did; but they haven't quite come to terms with it, so long as they live in a non-Jewish environment.

Am I totally mistaken? You say that, by a paradox, normalisation, which was the purpose of Zionism, has led to an exceedingly abnormal society in Israel – besieged, distorted by the need to defend itself [in]to an exaggerated and dangerous nationalism, as in the case of Gush.[2] But my point is that the Israeli sabras are the only people who do not feel in an ambivalent situation [...] – they simply don't feel the Jewish problem as a personal problem. The problem of the security of their state is, of course, another matter: they think about which states are friendly, which movements are against them, etc., but when one goes to Israel I, at any rate, have a feeling that in Tel Aviv there are fewer people noticeably Jewish, as it were, than there are in Miami or Brighton – they are simply a somewhat brown-skinned population, most of them, like Cypriots or Maltese. Of course their problems are appalling, but the purpose of Zionism ('normalisation' in the sense they meant it) has been realised: not to the satisfaction of those who wanted some morally superior, intellectually lofty community to arise, the dream of Zion as a great spiritual centre, but 'normalisation' – yes, I think so. [...]

Yours very sincerely,
Isaiah Berlin

PS [...] Of course Jews in the West do not feel themselves to be pariahs, but given e.g. Gore Vidal's[3] intemperate attack on Podhoretz[4] as an Israeli fifth-columnist, etc.,[5] no matter how much part of the American scene *Commentary* and its influence has become, do you think that a similar attack could have been delivered against some IRA-supporting prominent public figure, or some philhellene or Turcophile supported by their side in Cyprus?[6]

1 Robert Lee Wolff (1915–80), Coolidge Prof. of History, Harvard, 1965–80; expert on Balkan and Byzantine history.
2 Gush Emunim ('Bloc of the Faithful'), Israeli extra-parliamentary national religious movement founded February 1974, advocating the *de facto* extension of Israeli sovereignty to the Golan Heights, the Gaza Strip, Judaea and Samaria by means of massive civilian settlement, established if needs be in defiance of the government and the IDF.
3 (Eugene Luther) Gore Vidal (1925–2012), US novelist, playwright, essayist and commentator.
4 Norman Podhoretz (b. 1930), US neoconservative, editor 1960–95 of *Commentary*, monthly US public affairs magazine with an emphasis on Jewish issues. Author of the hostile 'A Dissent on Isaiah Berlin', *Commentary* 107 no. 2 (February 1999), 25–37; letters and response by Podhoretz, ibid. 107 no. 5 (May 1999), 20–3.
5 Stigmatising Podhoretz, whose 'first loyalty would always be to Israel', as a right-wing Israeli fifth columnist: 'The Empire Lovers Strike Back', *Nation*, 22 March 1986, 350.
6 After gaining independence from the UK 1960 Cyprus was riven by communal strife;

When Lindbergh,[1] all those years ago (is he still alive?), made that famous attack on British propagandists, Jews etc. as driving America into war in 1941 – by which I remember he managed to discredit himself (I was a British propagandist myself in New York at the time) – the British did not mind a bit, but the Jews did, violently. Do you think that is all past? Do you think the Jews no longer fidget, however much at ease they feel in New York or Chicago or California? Do you think the proportion of Jewish members of the faculty in, say, Harvard, is not a subject for the kind of jokes other minorities are not exposed to (like references to Mrs T's kosher cabinet?).[2] Or am I exaggerating or living in the past? Both are perfectly possible, and if you tell me so, I shall believe it. [...]

One of the most distinctive qualities of IB's personal correspondence is the lack of self-editing. After writing critically to his friend Jack Donaldson about mutual acquaintances in the opera world, in December 1966, he added: 'P.S. I haven't reread this, but perhaps there is too much salt, pepper etc: if so, discount it, be charitable, you are.'[3] He seems to have hoped that his correspondents would make allowance for his tendency to exaggerate, whose consequences he was well aware of: 'I am an intemperate writer and probably made a number of unjustifiable remarks about all kinds of good people.'[4] By contrast, he studiously avoided public controversy, and on public issues could be circumspect to the point of silence. He fully understood what this might imply: 'I am attacked in periodicals and have to answer; I am told I am a charlatan and ignoramus, I make feeble replies to that; I am accused of hollow conformism or cowardly evasiveness, and do not reply'; 'it may be natural cowardice on my part, but I get a sense of nightmare a little too quickly, and hate fights perhaps too much'; 'I wish I had not inherited my father's timorous, rabbity nature! I can be brave, but oh after what appalling superhuman struggles with cowardice!'[5]

The point can be overstated: IB was more active in support of public causes, and in taking stands on political issues, than many allow. But he gave voice to strong opinions more in private than in public. In 1986 these traits embroiled him in a public controversy that ended his friendship with Noam Chomsky. The controversy arose because IB objected to a journal of the civil liberties movement,

a Greek-backed coup in July 1974 was swiftly followed by a Turkish invasion, and the island was (and remains) divided along ethnic lines.

1 Charles Augustus Lindbergh (1902–74), US aviator, was widely cricitised for his activities on behalf of the America First Committee, and in particular for the anti-Semitic content of a speech in Des Moines, Iowa, 11 September 1941 (L3 590/5).

2 Margaret Thatcher's cabinet included several ministers of Jewish descent, including Michael Howard, Keith Joseph, Nigel Lawson, David Young, and Malcolm Rifkind and Leon Brittan (who were cousins); among the comments this elicited was one attributed to Harold Macmillan, to the effect that the cabinet was more Old Estonian than Old Etonian.

3 To Jack Donaldson, 28 December 1966.

4 To Kyril FitzLyon, 11 December 1990.

5 To Irving Singer, 15 June 1982; to Morton White, 22 March 1973; to Jean Floud, 27 August 1969.

Index on Censorship, *publishing an article by Chomsky about* de facto *censorship in US media reporting on Israel.*[1] *This was special pleading, even though he had long been convinced of an anti-Israeli bias in the British media. Instead of writing a public letter to* Index, *he wrote privately to the chair of* Index, *Mark Bonham Carter, and talked to the journalist Nora Beloff. 'The last thing I want', he later wrote to William Frankel,*[2] *'is a public row with Chomsky, which never ends – hence my cowardly act of keeping my head down in public and making a fuss privately.'*[3] *The unfortunate irony of this approach was that it created the circumstances for a lasting breach with Chomsky. In objecting to Chomsky's article IB had made some sharply derogatory comments on its author, and through a mole at* Index *this fact reached the radical New York journalist Alexander Cockburn,*[4] *who gave it publicity, so that IB found himself in the invidious position of having his privately expressed feelings made public.*

TO MARK BONHAM CARTER[5]

18 July 1986 [*carbon*]

Headington House

Dear Mark,

   Index: Israel again. As you may imagine, I dislike raising the subject actually more than you will mind my writing to you about it. Some time ago an Arab poet in Israel wrote a pretty violent article complaining of being suppressed, arrested, harassed etc., with some obvious exaggeration but nevertheless clearly some basis for what he said.[6] Dear Lois[7] rang me up saying she was being pressed to resign from *Index* because of gross unfairness to Israel, and would I do the same? I said that neither she nor I must do it, because there was no reason why censorship in Israel should be exempt from criticism any more than [in] any other country. But I did talk to somebody

---

1 'Thought Control in the USA: The Case of the Middle East', *Index on Censorship* 15 no. 7 (July 1986), 2, 11, 23.
2 William Frankel (1917–2008), barrister and influential editor, JC, the world's oldest Jewish weekly newspaper, 1958–77.
3 To William Frankel, 9 October 1986.
4 Alexander Cockburn (1941–2012), Scottish-born, US-based radical left-wing journalist and author.
5 Mark Raymond Bonham Carter (1922–94), life peer 1986; publisher, public servant and Liberal politician; 1st chair, Race Relations Board, 1966–70; director, ROH, 1958–82; governor, Royal Ballet, 1960, chair 1985–94; chair, *Index on Censorship*, 1978–89, editorial board 1980–9, advisory board 1978–88 (chair 1979–88).
6 IB probably refers to the translator's interview with the poet that introduces Samih al-Qasim, 'Slit Lips and Other Poems', trans. Abdullah al-Udhari, *Index on Censorship*, December 1983, 30–2; see also Samih al-Qasim and Emile Habibi, 'Palestinian Writers in Israel: Two Views on the Forms of Censorship and the Limits of Freedom', interviews with Roger Hardy, ibid., August 1982, 19–20.
7 Lois Mae Sieff (b. 1923) née Ross, m. 1952 2ndly Joseph Edward ('Teddy') Sieff (1905–82), president, Marks & Spencer, 1979–82; she had personally helped, 1982, to raise funds for *Index on Censorship* in addition to the financial support provided by the Edward & Lois Sieff Charitable Trust.

– I think Spender,[1] and possibly Theiner[2] – and told them that whereas in totalitarian countries checking information is difficult or impossible, in Israel everyone looks, and there are totally honest liberals, and above all extreme civil libertarians, who know all about these cases and tell the truth. Certainly the ferocious but entirely dependable Miss Ruth Gavison,[3] Herbert Hart's devoted pupil, knows most of the facts, and *Index* certainly does not check up with her or anyone like her, but only with the pro-Arab lawyer[4] who, I am told, is a straight Communist and takes the party line (I, in my turn, have no way of checking this last, but I believe it, from reading her statements to the press). Evelyn Rothschild[5] took the same line, and so we lowered the temperature over this.

But this time the situation is somewhat different. There is an article in the July–August issue by Noam Chomsky, called 'The United States and the Middle East'.[6] I know Chomsky well and I like him; he has considerable charm and remarkable gifts as a highly original writer on linguistics. However, [...] his polemics are very violent, and he is liable, in my view, to distort (don't circulate this letter, as I don't want to choose my words cautiously) pretty unscrupulously. I cannot help liking him when we meet, but that is neither here nor there. His only real disciple in England, as you may imagine, is Richard Wollheim.

His article, which contains howling inaccuracies, e.g. that Arafat is perfectly prepared to recognise Israel on reasonable conditions[7] – it is only Israel and America who brutally repel his advances (now my language is becoming intemperate) – is designed to show that, while there is technically no censorship in America, the press and the media are so violently pro-Israel and so violently anti-Arab that they play up every atrocity against the Jews and hush up every atrocity committed by Israel against the Arabs; that American opinion is in effect brainwashed, and that this *de facto* acts as a kind of psychological censorship, worse than in totalitarian countries, which only control

---

1 Stephen Spender was then a director, and on the editorial board, of *Index on Censorship*.

2 George Theiner (1928–88), Czech-born translator; interned in a Czech labour camp 1948–51 for refusing to join the CP or its youth wing; left for UK after Soviet invasion of 1968, repeating the journey he had made with his parents after Munich 30 years before; editor, *Index on Censorship*, 1982–8.

3 Ruth Gavison (b. 1945), St Anne's 1971–5 under H. L. A. Hart's supervision (DPhil 1975); taught in faculty of law, HUJ, 1969–71, 1975–2010, Haim H. Cohn Prof. of Human Rights since 1984.

4 Presumably Felicia Langer (b. 1930) née Felicia-Amalia Weit, Polish-born German Israeli lawyer and human rights activist known for her work in defence of Palestinian political detainees in Israeli-occupied Gaza and the West Bank.

5 Evelyn Robert Adrian de Rothschild (b. 1931), Kt 1989; chair, *Economist* 1972–89, N. M. Rothschild 1976–2003, later (since 2003) E. L. Rothschild; at this time on advisory board, *Index on Censorship*.

6 288/1.

7 '[I]n April–May 1984, Yasser Arafat issued a series of statements calling for negotiations leading to mutual recognition. The national press refused to publish the facts; *The Times* even banned letters referring to them' (23).

what people [do] but not what they think (*sic*)[1] – you can see that it is not a credible thesis.

Chomsky went too far for liberals in two cases: (*a*) when he tried to deny that there had been a huge massacre in Cambodia – all American propaganda;[2] and (*b*) when he wrote an introduction to a book by a Frenchman called Faurisson which (the book) denied the fact of the Holocaust, called it Zionist propaganda, etc.[3] There was difficulty about publishing the book, and Chomsky defended his writing of the introduction on the grounds of supporting freedom of speech, not the author's thesis.

But that is not my point. A piece denouncing the American media for distortion, suppression etc. is not an exposure of censorship, which is *Index*'s business. If I were to write a passionate piece saying that the Gilmours, *père et fils*, Grey Gowrie's[4] brother 'Skimper',[5] Mr Fisk, Karl Miller, Edward Mortimer, David Hirst[6] *et hoc genus omne*[7] are distorting British perception of what goes on in Israel (which, despite the horrors of the Likud and the West Bank, I more or less believe they do), I would expect *Index* to reject it, on the ground that it had nothing to do with revealing political censorship. Do look at the article – it does contain a mass of falsehood, and is governed mainly by Chomsky's implacable hatred of American politics everywhere, and New York Zionists who are happy about this: a perfectly tenable position with which I have little sympathy. Hatred of all American establishments governs him, I think, much more than thoughts about Israel as such, or fear of a world war triggered off by Israel.

But be that as it may, *Index* in my view had no business to publish this or any other piece merely directed against the media in a free country, however irritating the BBC, the *Guardian* etc. may be to friends of Israel. I do not see how I can go on receiving *Index* – as you know, I did once perform a service to it,[8] but I think this has gone too far. I wonder, therefore, if you would be kind enough to see that my name is removed from the list of recipients. Please do not show my letter to Mr Theiner or anyone else, because my impression of Chomsky is founded on general acquaintance with his political writings (he occasionally sends me his books and articles), and if pressed for precise evidence for some of my statements I should find it very annoying

1 IB's '*sic*'.
2 Chomsky never attempted to deny that mass murder had taken place, but see 232/4.
3 More accurately, Chomsky was asked to write an article on the civil libertarian aspects of the Faurisson affair. This was then used as a preface to Faurisson's book (233/1).
4 Alexander Patrick Greysteil ('Grey') Hore-Ruthven (b. 1939), 2nd Earl of Gowrie 1955, Conservative politician: minister for the arts 1983–5; chancellor, duchy of Lancaster, 1984–5; director, Sotheby's Holdings, 1985–98; chair, Sotheby's Europe, 1987–94.
5 Malise Walter Maitland Knox ('Skimper') Hore-Ruthven (b. 1942), writer and editor, BBC External Services, 1966–70, 1976–86; lecturer, dept of divinity with religious studies, Aberdeen, 1994–9.
6 David Hirst (b. 1936), journalist; Middle East correspondent, *Guardian*, 1963–97.
7 'And all his kind'.
8 Possibly IB's efforts to raise funds for *Index* in 1974.

to have to fish it out. The issue is one of principle, of the categories of what *Index* exists to publish, and not whether what Chomsky said is true or false. Besides, despite his often shocking actions, I wish to preserve my remote friendship with him.

I do apologise for inflicting all this upon your innocent head. We go to Italy on Sunday, and obviously there is no urgency. I shall be back in the second week of September. The Italian postal system is appalling, but we could talk about this when I get back if you are here.

Yours,

[Isaiah]

TO LOUIS RAPOPORT

12 August 1986

Headington House

Dear Mr Rapoport,

I have just read your article 'Refuseniks' in the international edition of the *Jerusalem Post*, week ending 5 July.[1] I can only tell you that I was profoundly moved by it. Of course I have read the stories about refuseniks, both in Martin Gilbert's books and articles[2] and in the regular bulletins about them which are sent to me; but I have never read anything which has touched me so deeply and directly as the quotations you give from the actual people, from Ida Nudel[3] onwards. It is clear that by writing as you have, you do nothing but good. The one thing one gathers from all they say is that they are terrified of being forgotten – that one must talk about them and talk about them and go on talking, however boring this may be for the rest of the world, and, indeed, for some Jews also – in spite of the complaints of foreign offices and state departments that this endless harping on their misfortunes on the part of the Jews is really irritating, goes too far, complicates diplomatic relationships beyond the actual good that it can do, etc. etc. (that, after all, in a much more hideous form, was the resistance shown to 'harping on' what

---

1 'Refuseniks: The Captive Israelis', a special 12-page supplement (including an interview with Ida Nudel) to the weekly *Jerusalem Post International Edition*, week ending 5 July. The interview with Nudel, 'Ida Nudel's Long White Night' (x–xii), also appeared in the weekend *Jerusalem Post Magazine*, part of the daily JP, 27 June 1986, 4–6. It concludes with a quotation from Nudel: 'If you forget us, all this suffering is in vain.' The main text of the supplement (ii–viii) was reprinted as 'The Refuseniks after Shcharansky' in a JP book, *Anatoly and Avital Shcharansky: The Journey Home* (San Diego etc., 1986), 282–317. A later article on this topic by Rapoport, 'The Refuseniks', appears in the *Encyclopaedia Judaica Year Book: 1988–89: Events of 1987–1988* (Jerusalem, [1989]), 76–83.

2 See for example Gilbert's *The Jews of Hope* (Basingstoke, 1984), in which he tells 'the story of some of those Soviet Jews whose hopes have been roused and whose Jewishness has been reborn, but who are now faced by the bleak prospect that they may never be allowed to leave' (ix).

3 Ida Nudel (b. 1931), Russian Jewish activist; refused permission to leave USSR 1971; campaigned on behalf of the 'Prisoners of Zion' (Jews imprisoned for Zionist activities); sentenced to internal exile in Siberia 1978–82; granted an exit visa 2 October 1987, after an international campaign, and arrived in Israel 15 October.

was happening to the Jews in Germany, as one can read in the minutes of British Foreign Office officials before and during the war, and I daresay those of other countries as well). Despite all that, one must go on 'harping on', which obviously does good, and keeps the problem burning, or at least festering. The danger is that these uncomfortable Jewish customers could one day be treated as Caucasians and Balts, and, indeed, as the Volga Germans were – packed away, and no more was heard of them, simply because of absence of interest in them abroad.

I used not always to think that: I remember when Iliav[1] – the one who died, who originally came from my home town of Riga – asked me, I suppose thirty or so years ago, whether one should scream about these people or whether, on the contrary, it did harm in the sense that they might be treated worse as a result of fuss being made in Israel, I thought at one time that perhaps it did endanger, or at any rate worsen, their condition. But, as so often, I was wrong. Since so far as anything was done for them, it was done directly in response to agitation, if not directly by Jews, at least by public opinion in countries with which the Soviet Union at that time wished to be in more favourable relations, principally, of course, the United States, but also in countries likely to have influence with the United States – Britain, France and whoever they thought might help the Soviet Union to extract concessions from the West.

Consequently I think that the more widely your article can go – in the original, in translation, by whatever means – the better for Jews and mankind. [...]

Yours,

IB pp PU

TO KYRIL FITZLYON

19 August 1986

Headington House

Dear Kyril,

I have just finished your excellent translation of 'Winter Notes'.[2] As you said at Martin's memorial meeting,[3] it is all there. The entire world is horrible: the Russians are either barbarous (but that is better than being hypocritical: better to whip people – at least that is spontaneous and natural – than hypocrisy and artificial existence, self-deception) – either Russians are barbarian peasants and peasant-whippers, or they imitate the ghastly West and

---

1 Untraced.
2 Dostoevsky's essay 'Winter Notes on Summer Impressions' was published in *Vremya* 1863. FitzLyon's translation, with his introduction, was published in London 1985.
3 A memorial concert had been held for Martin Cooper at St John's, Smith Square, London SW1, 29 June.

think that all blessings come from there. Germany is comical, grotesque, all small-minded, neat and horrible (memories of your excellent translation of Saltykov).[1] England is a great [den?] of the most horrible iniquity – Haymarket,[2] women for sale (interesting that he thought English women so beautiful); everything is venal, the hypocrisy of writing about the pretty Vicarage gardens and the blue-eyed daughters of the idyllic vicar and his wife side by side with the brutality of the prostitution, loathsome, in that frightful hell, London, like an inferno and the negative of all that is good and sacred. Then Paris, vanity, hollow eloquence, bourgeois pettiness, falsity, graceless, and again, profound hypocrisy, total destruction of true values, Voltaire and the awful Rousseau, Napoleon III, Jules Favre.[3]

What, then, is to be done? Only sacrifice, attempts by town-dwellers to achieve communion with the peasants – 'going into the people'[4] – false Herzenism, convincing immersion into some idyllic rural state; still worse, imitation of the odious and worthless West. The only solution – Christian sacrifice of all I am to mankind; only by losing my soul can I save it, by total reciprocal sacrifice of all to all. Did he really believe in the remotest possibility of this on earth? I suppose that in his deepest feeling he did. But it is almost unbearable to read. The loathing of ordinary life, such contempt, such corrosive destructiveness – that was certainly the foundation of his genius. Surprisingly unhostile about Turgenev, and even Belinsky, in this, yet at other times they are, of course, the principal enemy.

I cannot help feeling that as a man it is actually darkness he liked best – in the underground is where he felt in some sense real. None of this is exactly original on my part. Critical as I have always been of the smoothness and shallowness of the great French enemies of superstition, ignorance, oppression etc. in the eighteenth and indeed nineteenth century too – for a profound lack of understanding of what it is that man lives by – nevertheless if I have to vote … […]

Yours ever,
    IB pp PU

PS There is, of course, an element of all this in Solzhenitsyn, but the misanthropy and pessimism and suffocation do not seem to me to be quite so great, don't you think? […]

1 i.e. Saltykov-Shchedrin (17/6). Translation untraced.
2 In Dostoevsky's time London's Haymarket Street was a notorious centre of prostitution.
3 Charles Louis Napoléon Bonaparte (1808–73), Napoleon III, Emperor of France 1852–70; nephew of Napoleon I; became President, Second Republic, after the February Revolution 1848; seized power in a coup December 1851, becoming ruler of the Second Empire; defeated in the Franco-Prussian War, 1870–1, and went into exile in Britain. (Claude Gabriel) Jules Favre (1809–80), French politician; led the republican opposition to Napoleon III's Second Empire, and negotiated the end of the Franco-Prussian War.
4 A slogan used by the Russian Narodniks ('populists') 1874 when they attempted to foment revolution among the peasantry.

TO ARCHIE BROWN[1]

22 September 1986

Headington House

Dear Archie (if I may call you that),

I am invited [...] to suggest names of possible candidates for the Wardenship of St Antony's. Since you are the only member of the committee whom I know, may I address myself to you? [...]

It seems to me that the most needed qualities in a head of house are justice, kindness, imagination and intellectual power. [...] I do not believe that outsiders, no matter how eminent, who have been made heads of houses, have proved an unqualified success either at Oxford or at Cambridge. This is not really due to personal qualities: it is that academic communities are really rather special, and such people cannot get used to what seems to them to be the parochialism of university life. I think one has to have tasted life in the Cathedral Close to be able to return to it happily and successfully: e.g. Rab Butler[2] *had* been a don for some years; he knew what Cambridge life was like. With the exception of Lord Goodman, who is an exception to all rules, and who anyway only came to his College for a few days each week but has benefited it in many ways, I cannot think of any outsider – no ambassador, politician, of whatever kind, no matter how brilliant and successful in public life – who has proved successful as head of college in our community. I base this on sixty years experience of Oxford (I really am very old).

This seems a very sweeping statement, and I daresay there are probably exceptions to it and qualifications that should be made – but I feel convinced that unless one has had academic experience for a reasonable period of time, as a teacher or researcher, unless one can function easily and freely as a natural member of the academic world, and in particular as someone involved in college life, then the cost of [being] the head of a college is bound to prove, after a short while, tedious, and what seem to be the trivial issues which occupy governing bodies, irritating, to inhabitants of wider worlds. I could produce a list of persons to whom this applies, but that would be invidious and I must not do so, at any rate in this letter; but it is a truth of which I am deeply, I do not think too deeply, convinced. [...]

Yours ever,

Isaiah Berlin

---

1 Archibald Haworth Brown (b. 1938), lecturer in Soviet institutions, Oxford, 1971–89, fellow, St Antony's, 1971–2005; director, Russian and East European Centre, St Antony's, 1991–4 (and 1999–2001); prof. of politics, Oxford, 1989–2005.

2 Richard Austen ('Rab') Butler (1902–82), KG 1971, life peer 1965, Conservative politician; Home Secretary 1957–62, deputy prime minister 1962–3, foreign secretary 1963–4; fellow, Corpus Christi, Cambridge, 1925–9, Master, Trinity, 1965–78.

TO MARK BONHAM CARTER
23 September 1986 [*carbon*]

Headington House

Dear Mark,

I have just received a copy of a letter which Nora Beloff has sent to *Index*, and wishes to be published there.[1]

In the last sentence she plainly refers to me as having withdrawn my subscription. She came to see me about 'reds under the bed' in general, which is, indeed, her central preoccupation, and, among other things, I told her that I thought that Chomsky, whom she referred to as a wicked man, had had an article published in *Index* to which I had taken some exception. The last thing I wanted was to provoke her into writing a fulmination of the kind she has perpetrated (can one perpetrate fulminations? perhaps not).

My only objection, as you know, is not at all hers – namely, the character of Chomsky, the contents of the article, etc. as such – but merely the fact that charges of heavy bias in the public media in a free country, where in this case the author could get his piece published anywhere, is not suitable for a magazine dedicated to uncovering censorship. The last thing that I wanted to do was to enter into the rights and wrongs of the case, whatever I might feel – as you said in your letter, every time Israel is mentioned Jews blow up. This is inevitable, and perhaps quite natural, but I don't wish to be reckoned among them. At any rate, I don't wish to be accused of steaming up Nora, who needs no steaming up.

I don't wish to be associated with any of her campaigns, and wish I had not mentioned the matter to her. Oh dear. I don't want to start a conflagration. My letter to you was simply written on an issue of principle; I gather from both you and Stephen that the general issue of what constitutes censorship is to be discussed by the *Index* committee. I do beg you not to mention my name in this connection, for the reasons I have given.

Yours ever,

[Isaiah]

---

1 Beloff's letter protesting against Chomsky's article, as published in *Index on Censorship* 15 no. 10 (November/December 1986), 2, does not refer to IB. It concludes: 'Many of us will cancel our subscriptions unless, in future, *Index* shows greater discrimination.'

In August 1986 IB learned that a letter he had written to Clarissa Avon at the
beginning of the Suez crisis, expressing support for the conduct of her husband,
Anthony Eden,[1] *had been used by the historian Robert Rhodes James*[2] *in his*
biography of Eden, due to be published in London later that year. IB had
written: 'I should like to offer the Prime Minister all my admiration and sym-
pathy. His action seems to me very brave very patriotic and – I shd have thought
– absolutely just' (1 November 1956, L2 547), and it was on the strength of this
that Rhodes James mistakenly identified IB as being 'among those who publicly
supported the government' (552). A group of senior dons at Oxford did indeed
publicly back the Anglo-French military operation, including John Sparrow and
Gilbert Murray,[3] *but IB was not among them. He was characteristically torn,*
able to see all of the elements in a complex situation, but unable to offer a simple
solution. Soon after writing to Lady Avon he changed his mind. In public,
though, he remained non-committal, writing to his stepson Michel Strauss:[4]
'I have kept very silent and signed no letters or counter-letters, appeared on no
platforms or counter-platforms' (8 November 1956, L2 551). That his conduct
should later be misrepresented upset him, and he wrote to Pat Utechin: 'I am not
pleased that Clarissa shd have sent my letter to her to Rh. James without at least
telling me – not friendly like – so I'll quarrel with her sometime. Meanwhile
I expect (deserved evidently) snide references in reviews: tho' I may not be
noticed much – as I deserve' (24 August 1986).

TO CLARISSA AVON

26 September 1986 [*manuscript*]

Headington House

Dear Clarissa,

Thank you for your letter about my grievance. Although you advise me
not to answer, I cannot do that, for you have misinterpreted my feelings,
and I must clarify the issue. It is true that I had absolutely no recollection
of writing you, or anyone else, a letter about Suez [...]. What I felt, I felt:
what I have written, I have written: I have no intention of withdrawing or
retracting anything. It is true that I had changed my mind after two days and
for that reason refused to sign the pro-government letter signed by Gilbert
Murray, John Sparrow and others. But that is not relevant. I cannot possibly

1 (Robert) Anthony Eden (1897–1977), 1st Earl of Avon 1961; Conservative MP 1923–57; secretary of
   state for foreign affairs 1935–8, 1940–5, 1951–5; deputy prime minister 1951–5; prime minister 1955–7.
2 Robert Vidal Rhodes James (1933–99), Kt 1991, historian and Conservative politician; fellow, All
   Souls, 1965–8, 1979–81; Conservative MP 1976–92.
3 (George) Gilbert Aimé Murray (1866–1957), OM 1941, Australian-born classical scholar and internationalist; Regius Prof. of Greek, Oxford, 1908–36; his prominent support of the League of
   Nations carried great moral authority.
4 Michel Jules *Strauss (b. 1936; plate 35), son of Aline Berlin and André Strauss, art expert and
   connoisseur.

object to my letter being referred to or used by the biographer. What does offend me is that you shd have passed on, however inadvertently, a private letter for public use without so much as telling me that you intended to do so.[1] This is, in my view, a breach of the rules governing personal relations, privacy, especially where it affects a friend. However the letter reached Robert Rhodes James, once you knew he had it and wd use it, it was surely your duty if only out of friendship, to have told me. It is not the content of the letter that is relevant, nor its use by Rhodes James of which I cannot complain, but the fact that a private letter was supplied for a publication, without so much as consulting the writer: that seems to me highly improper, quite apart from our old friendship: though the latter seems to me to make it worse. Still, what has occurred has occurred, & there is nothing to be done. I thought it right to explain to you what I found painful. There is, I agree, no need to mention the matter again. [...]

Yours ever,
Isaiah

TO DERWENT MAY[2]

1 October 1986

Headington House

Dear Derwent May,

First let me thank you for sending me your little book on Hannah Arendt. I lost, alas, your copy with its nice inscription, but procured another immediately – the lost copy is (or was) somewhere in the Sheldonian Theatre, where I began reading it during an interval of a singularly boring concert, which only loyalty to the organisers had made me go to. Nobody has returned it to me; it may generate another reader or two for her works – I am not so ill-disposed to her as to begrudge her that additional fragment of posthumous reputation. Nevertheless, I think that it will not last very long – that, unlike Heidegger, who will be remembered for all kinds of reasons, intellectual as well as political, as in some sense a major figure, she will be swallowed into a large philosophical limbo in which most of the French, German and Italian thinkers after Hegel and before Husserl[3] and Bergson will lead their forgotten existences, mentioned only by the most fanatical taxonomists of the history of thought. And that not so much because of any particular views that she held, but because of insufficiently strong and individuated philosophical personality, which is what keeps Schopenhauer, Nietzsche, Russell,

---

1 Clarissa Avon had in fact handed over her late husband's files rather than individual letters, and IB's charge seems harsh.
2 Derwent James May (b. 1930), journalist, critic, author; literary editor, *Listener*, 1965–86; literary and arts editor, *Sunday Telegraph*, 1986–90; author of *Hannah Arendt* (Harmondsworth, 1986).
3 Edmund Gustav Albrecht Husserl (1859–1957), German philosopher and logician, founder of modern phenomenology.

Wittgenstein, William James, even Bergson, probably Sartre, alive. However, I may be wrong. I very often am.

You will not be altogether astonished to learn that, in spite of my assiduous attention to your every word, my opinion of the good lady remains unaltered. My trouble is not, as I think I have told you, that her historical facts are jumbled and wrong, nor that there is an arrogantly dogmatic tone not justified by sufficient intellectual power in her pronouncements, or a total incapacity for continuous argument – too few 'becauses' and 'therefores' – but principally because I simply cannot fish out any doctrine, attitude, let alone proposition, which seems to me worth defending or attacking. You will accuse me of blind prejudice; and it may be that the fact that I found her so personally deeply unattractive on the four occasions on which I met her to talk to has something to do with this – I wish I could deny it with conviction.

But believe me, be that as it may, I have done my very best to find something in her writings which is neither commonplace – sometimes dramatised commonplace (like the participatory democracy, derived from a totally imaginary vision of the Greek *polis*; or the 'banality of evil', the second- and third-rate executors of policy arrived at by more powerful figures: who did not know about the thousands of Soviet commissars, similar to Eichmann, [or] Inquisitors in sixteenth-century Spain, who, Herzen says, probably went to bed with quiet consciences and the smell of roasted human flesh still in their nostrils?)[1] – [nor] shallow interpretations of historical phenomena like anti-Semitism: nationalism pitching on scapegoats, aliens as victims. True enough, but what about the huge massacres along the Rhine of Jews by Crusaders,[2] pogroms of various sizes right through the Middle Ages and well after the Renaissance? It is absurd to ignore the continuity of anti-Semitism and simply talk about the rich Jews of Germany as stimulating it. This is the illusion which German Jews (and Jewesses) right through the nineteenth century lived under: that if only they could get rid of the unattractive face of plutocracy (the Rothschilds, the Warburgs, the post-1918 crooks and operators, who probably did make widows and orphans bankrupt), they would remain good Germans and be loved by their fellow citizens, or at any rate regarded as normal members of German society.

The illusion went on particularly strongly after 1918, when most German Jews of Miss A's type said that they would be all right, as far as their good German neighbours were concerned, if it wasn't for all those horrible East European Jews pouring in from Poland and the Baltic and God knows where,

---

1 'Doktor Krupov' (1847), op. cit. (22/1), iv 264.

2 In the winter of 1095–6 Jews in cities along the Rhine, and further afield in Germany and France, were massacred by popular armed bands formed in response to the appeal by Pope Urban II for the liberation of Jerusalem; the attackers were not officially part of the First Crusade (1096–9), which left Europe in August 1096, and the violence fitted into a pattern of religious hostility towards Jews in Europe during the Middle Ages.

with their awful manners and their side-curls, their Asian habits – bigots, bar-barians, who naturally create anti-Semitism wherever they go. That is exactly what American Jews felt about the unfortunate Jewish refugees when they poured into New York in the 1930s and early 1940s; and [they] thought that Congress could never stand them, and the [loss of the] jobs they were alleged to take away from good solid Wasps. Alas, every group of Jews at a certain stage blamed anyone but themselves for what happened.

The classical exposition of this position was made by Moses Hess, himself a German Jew of solid origins, who wrote a book called *Rome and Jerusalem*,[1] which I recommend to you, about the illusions under which what Namier called his 'co-racials' (since he had no religion) lived. It was a wonderful exposure, and duly denounced or ignored at the time.

Poor Miss A. Her book about Rachel von Varnhagen[2] is a real piece of nostalgic self-romanticisation – of course, she is Rachel. And let me tell you, you take from her book the proposition that her poor husband was really rather a feeble character, well known only for being married to his brilliant wife; when he was in fact a brilliant diplomat and a friend of Goethe and very much a man in his own right – unlike Miss A's somewhat trivial, though I dare say perfectly decent and harmless, first and second husbands.[3]

I mustn't go on like this. I see that I am provoking myself into paeans of indignation. I must find something favourable to say about your protégé. I will say this: Kurt Blumenfeld,[4] with whom I met her in New York in 1941, and with whom she was then having an affair, told me afterwards, in Jerusalem, that there was a time when she was a touching, though never very intelligent, seeker after truth; but that after the war he found it impossible to talk to her. It wasn't just the book on Eichmann; she had become conceited, fanatical, and talked terrible nonsense both about Jews and about history in general; and what a strange thing it was that all those intellectuals in New York should be taken in by all this cultural rhetoric. The same was said to me by our friend Scholem[5] – genuinely a man of genius, or very near

1 Hess's 'best and most famous book', whose subject is 'the Jews, what they are, and what they should be' (AC2 291, 292): *Rom und Jerusalem, die letzte Nationalitätsfrage: Briefe und Noten [Rome and Jerusalem, The Last Problem of Nationality: Letters and Notes]* (Leipzig, 1862), discussed by IB in 'The Life and Opinions of Moses Hess' (1959), repr. in AC.

2 *Rahel Varnhagen: The Life of a Jewess* (London, [1957]). Rahel Antonie Friederike Varnhagen (1771–1833) née Levin, German writer, salonnière and correspondent; converted from Judaism to Christianity 1814; m. the same year Karl August Varnhagen von Ense (1785–1858); they were prominent figures in a leading Berlin salon; she was an important influence on his work, and after her death he published two collections of her writings.

3 Arendt m. (i) 1929 the German journalist and philosopher Günther Anders (1902–92) né Günther Siegmund Stern; they divorced 1937; (ii) 1940 the German poet and Marxist philosopher Heinrich Blücher (1899–1970).

4 Kurt Yehudah Blumenfeld (1884–1963), German-born Zionist; director, dept of information, Zionist Organization, Berlin, 1910–14; president, German Zionist Federation, 1923–33; emigrated to Jerusalem 1933.

5 Gershom Gerhard Scholem (1897–1982), German-born Israeli philosopher and historian;

it – with whom, you remember, she had that correspondence in *Encounter* about Eichmann.[1] He said that she had no capacity for thinking whatever, that only men of letters were taken in by her, not a single genuine philosopher – like me, he thought Jaspers[2] a nice, decent, upright but very undistinguished thinker, and Heidegger a nasty, able, remarkable villain, but not in any degree interested in or influenced by her, save in a purely sexual sense.

I can go on like this: Marcuse, who had known her very well in Berlin, said, when I mentioned her name – and he was a clever, amusing, cynical but very perceptive old rogue – 'Hannah? Typical conceited Berlin blue-stocking': *Berliner blauer Strumpf.* But I admit that Auden could not understand why I didn't care for her – as 'she was so nice', and her book on the human condition,[3] of which I have spoken to you, seemed to him a wonderful book, as it did to Robert Lowell. Not quite such praise came from Chiaromonte,[4] whom I met with Mary McCarthy, and to whom I complained about the nonsense in that book. He said, 'Yes, she does talk nonsense, historically all she says doesn't hold up, but she is nice, her views are nice, her attitude is nice, and that's enough for me.' Mary was rather angry with him, and more or less stormed out of the room. Mary was certainly her greatest conquest – to this day I cannot understand why.[5]

No matter, I won't go on. All I can say is that you have done her proud, far more than she deserves, and your motives are still to me totally unclear. Next time we meet, I may ask you again, and if you complain about being bullied about this, as you may well do, I promise you not to mention the matter again, and talk about gayer (not in the modern sense) and jollier and more interesting things.

Yours ever,

Isaiah   [...]

professor of Jewish mysticism and Kabbalah, HUJ.

1 '"Eichmann in Jerusalem": An Exchange of Letters between Gershom Scholem and Hannah Arendt', *Encounter* 22 no. 1 (January 1964), 51–6.

2 Karl Theodor Jaspers (1883–1969), German psychiatrist and philosopher, one of the founders of German existentialism, alongside Martin Heidegger; prof., Heidelberg, 1920–48 (dismissed by Nazis 1937, reinstated 1945); prof. of philosophy, Basel, 1948–61.

3 *The Human Condition* (Chicago, 1958): cf. L2 676/4.

4 Nicola Chiaromonte (1905–72), Italian writer and left-wing political activist; fled Italy for France 1934, moving to NY 1941; drawn to the leftist anti-Stalinist movement there, contributing to *Partisan Review, New Republic* etc.; with Ignazio Silone, founded and edited the liberal cultural-political journal *Tempo presente* 1956–68; close friend of Mary McCarthy.

5 For McCarthy's defence of Hannah Arendt, and IB's incomprehension, see L3 192/2.

TO SHIRLEY ANGLESEY

27 October 1986

Headington House

Dearest Shirley,

Thank you ever so much for your fascinating travelogue. I can see the combination of the CND missionaries and the two American fairies (what are we to call them? I hate 'gays', I hate 'queers', I hate all the other American equivalents – and they object to 'homosexual' as being a pompous medical term: so what are we to say? Betjeman used to call them 'homos': perhaps that's best, even though we don't talk about 'heteros'); your motley company came very clearly before my eyes.

You ask me about some conference in Cambridge, with Russian studies. The general level of contemporary (and, indeed, uncontemporary) Russian studies in this country is exceedingly low. I do not say that it is any higher in Europe, but it is a good deal better (I feel convinced, without too much evidence, but some) in the United States. The only conferences I have ever been to, usually small, special ones, were very depressing in the quality of the questions asked, answers given. It does not consist of people mainly interested in a genuine way in Russian literature, but in half-hearted, semi-ex-fellow-travellers, if you know what I mean, not endowed with too much intelligence, critical sense or knowledge. This may be too harsh, but I wonder. Far worse is the fact that I have never heard of the modern Russian writers whom your students read with avidity – Bulgakov,[1] yes, but the others, who are they? Unless they are crypto-dissident, I suspect that they are on a level with our own not terribly good novelists – the good Miss Drabble,[2] the Booker Prize winners,[3] the wicked A. N. Wilson[4] and the rest, nothing really to write home about. But it may just be my old age and remoteness from contemporary life.

Talking of which, I have to confess that the general papers and essays done by the candidates at All Souls this year do not seem to me to offer one whit of the kind of papers written in the 1930s. What is this a symptom of? Are we frozen? I suspect perhaps yes, with all that that entails, like Spain in the late seventeenth century, let us say, or, worse still, the eighteenth

1 Mikhail Afanas'evich Bulgakov (1891–1940), Kiev-born Russian satirical writer and playwright favoured by Stalin; his Faustian masterpiece *The Master and Margarita* was written 1928–40, but published only posthumously 1966–7.

2 Margaret Drabble (b. 1939), later (2008) DBE, m. 1982 Michael Holroyd; novelist, biographer and critic.

3 The Booker–McConnell Prize (1968–2002; from 2002 the Man Booker Prize), awarded annually to an original work in English, and sometimes considered to reward commercial sucess as much as literary merit; the winners 1984–6 were Anita Brookner, *Hotel du Lac* (London, 1984); Keri Hulme, *The Bone People* (London, 1985); Kingsley Amis, *The Old Devils* (London, 1986).

4 Andrew Norman Wilson (b. 1950), acerbic writer, editor and broadcaster; lecturer, St Hugh's and New College, 1976–81; literary editor, *Spectator*, 1981–3, *Evening Standard* 1990–7.

and nineteenth. Ex-empires are curious places in which to live, or, indeed, flourish. I don't wonder that Golitsyn (spelt with pedantic accuracy,[1] as in Mussorgsky's[2] *Khovanshchina*) talked about the Jews thrusting themselves forward in the way of emigration. I think there is some truth in that – they wish to get out more acutely than anyone else simply because, unlike any other ethnic group in the Soviet Union, they have no country, no territorial base: unlike Bashkirs, or Chukchas[3] (a Siberian tribe who have become the chosen carriers of various Soviet jokes: for example, a Chukcha tries to park his car somewhere near Red Square in Moscow; he is told by a policeman that he cannot do this, for it is rather near the government and the Party; the Chukcha says 'Yes, I realise that, it's quite all right, I've locked the car' – this is highly typical).

But you speak of latent anti-Semitism in Russia – latent? Patent, I should say: there's no concealing it, and no effort to do so. There was a brief period in the early 1930s when anti-Semitism was regarded as a property of Whites, Guards officers, wicked pogrom-makers and the like, and socialists of all hues were, I think genuinely, free from it, and horrified by the thought that any of them might be tainted by it [...]. But now it is very open, and much used by the government and the Party as a weapon against imperialism, American–Zionist plots (rather like the President of Syria[4] at the moment), etc. etc. Russia, by and large, was and is an anti-Semitic country, and that in itself stimulates the desire to leave it on the part of Jews – the resentment is genuine enough, but not justified. [...]

Much love to Henry and, indeed, to you.

Yours,

Isaiah

TO NOAM CHOMSKY

1 December 1986

Headington House

Dear Noam,

I was much irritated by the piece by the, in my opinion, not very respect-worthy Cockburn, and propose to send the enclosed letter[5] to the *Nation*. My

---

1 The name is sometimes transliterated as 'Golitsin' (or anglicised as 'Galitzine'). The aristocratic Russian statesman Vasily Vasil'evich Golitsyn (1643–1714) is a character in Mussorgsky's opera *Khovanshchina* (319/3). Presumably IB refers to Anatoly Mikhailovich Golitsyn (b. 1926), defector from the Soviet KGB, author of *New Lies for Old: The Communist Strategy of Deception and Disinformation* (NY, [1984]).

2 Modest Petrovich Mussorgsky (1839–81), Russian composer.

3 The Bashkirs are a Turkic people from the Urals, while the indigenous Chukcha people inhabit lands around the Bering Sea and Okhotsk Sea, at the eastern extremities of Siberia.

4 Hafez al-Assad (56/2).

5 The next letter.

point, as you will see, is that I did not in my private letter discuss the contents of your article, only its relevance to *Index*.

I have no reason for thinking that what you said is incorrect. But, given my views, I suspect I may not think the rejoinder as mistaken as I imagine you will.

I wish we could occasionally meet and talk about these things, which worry me too, in my own way.

Yours,

Isaiah

TO THE EDITOR OF THE *NATION*

2 December 1986 [*carbon; revised 8 December; not sent*]

Headington House

Sir,

A friend has sent me a cutting of an item by your contributor Mr Alexander Cockburn (22 November, p. 541),[1] in which a largely false account is given of my comments in a private letter on the article by Professor Noam Chomsky. I have not followed Mr Cockburn's writings, if only because I have never been able to take Mr Cockburn seriously, nor have I ever heard of anyone who has: discovery of the truth, if the item in question is any evidence, does not seem to me to be his main objective, as it used to be of earlier muck-rakers. Nevertheless, your readers, who may be insufficiently aware of this, deserve to have the record set straight.

According to your contributor, I wrote 'anonymously' that Professor Chomsky's thesis about the bias of the American press in favour of Israel was not valid. Whatever my opinion about this, I said nothing of the kind. My present knowledge of the American media is too small to enable me to assess the justice of Professor Chomsky's accusation. Be that as it may, the point I made in a private letter to a friend,[2] which I did not fail to sign, was that the censorship with which *Index* has been dealing, and for the most part dealing very well indeed, is censorship in the proper sense of the word, that is, suppression of writings or other forms of expression by institutions or their representatives – Churches, political parties, courts of law, juntas of various kinds, and, of course, government departments empowered to do

---

1 'Index Fingered' appeared in Cockburn's fortnightly column, 'Beat the Devil', in the weekly *Nation*, 22 November 1986, 540–1 at 541. Referring to an unpublished draft of Beloff's letter to *Index on Censorship* Cockburn identified IB, 'supposed by many to be a glorious emblem of high-minded liberal tolerance', as the author of an 'anonymous denunciation of Chomsky': 'the sagacious Berlin asserted flatly that it is inaccurate to say, as Chomsky had, that while there is technically no censorship in the United States, the press is so pro-Israel and anti-Arab that it exaggerates atrocities committed against Israel and suppresses atrocities committed by Israel. Berlin also maintained, rather comically, that a piece denouncing the US media for distortion and suppression is not an exposure of censorship and hence is beyond the purview of *Index*.'
2 18 July 1986 to Mark Bonham Carter, 288–91.

this by kings, popes, dictators or parliaments: whoever may be sovereign in a given state or community.

Other forms of interference with freedom of speech – by pressure groups, blackmail, threats, corruption, arm-twisting – are evils but not forms of censorship; activities which legislation is largely incapable of checking; and so are partiality or bias or whims on the part of editors or journalists or broadcasters or those who influence them, whom Professor Chomsky condemns. People sometimes speak of 'self-censorship' – that seems to me a metaphor, like promises made to oneself. The 'useful little periodical', as Mr Cockburn so patronisingly calls *Index*, has done the excellent job it has because it has confined itself to cases of censorship proper, which can be accurately pinned down and described (since they are official). It has its hands full enough with these cases, as it is. If it tried to go into a wider field, and deal with general cases of interference and obstruction, it would necessarily take on too much – and dilute its strength in the vast grey territory which this would open up. Professor Chomsky's article could very well have been published in your pages – and more than one British publication which I could mention would, I think, have been glad to have it. Its publication in *Index* seems to me to have opened the door to a new policy, which in my opinion would damage its effectiveness. This is an issue on which rational persons can disagree; at any rate, that is my view.

Mr Cockburn refers to my cancellation of my subscription to *Index*. I should find that difficult to do, since I had rendered some service to the periodical and it kindly placed my name on its free list.[1] So much for Mr Cockburn and his revelations: perhaps not too high a price to pay for an uncensored press.

Yours faithfully,
    Isaiah Berlin

TO NOAM CHOMSKY
8 December 1986

                                                    Headington House

Dear Noam,

I have decided, after all, not to send my letter to the *Nation*, of which I sent you a copy a few days ago.[2] I have met Alex Cockburn and did not take to him, and his methods seem to me so unattractive that to roll about in the mud with him, however just my cause, seems a somewhat horrible prospect. At the same time I wish you to know the truth of the matter. While I thought

1 Though IB had no subscription to cancel, he had asked Mark Bonham Carter (letter of 18 July 1986) to remove his name from the free list (290).
2 The possibility that a mole at *Index* might divulge the contents of IB's letter to Mark Bonham Carter (288–91) may have influenced IB's decision not to send his letter to the *Nation*, since on key points it could be refuted.

that your piece was one which, even in my ignorance, I should instinctively somewhat disagree with, that was not my private and not at all anonymous point which I made to someone on *Index* – which was that I thought that your piece did not really deal with censorship as I understand it, but with bias, violent partiality, etc., and that *Index* would do a better job if it confined itself to what, perhaps somewhat pedantically, I call censorship than if it spread its tentacles to embrace all forms of obstruction, selectivity, decisions by editors, publishers (some, sometimes, after all, virtuous and useful ones) etc. etc., to which there is no end. I said nothing about the contents of your piece and stressed the fact that it was not what I was talking about. I just wanted you to know that, in case you were taken in by Cockburn's highly misleading and hostile account.

We have had friendly relations for so long now, and I believe enjoy a mutual liking and respect for each other, despite profound disagreements, that I did not want you to think that I had done what Cockburn charged me with doing.

I wish we could meet occasionally, but I scarcely ever come to America now. I did come to Cambridge for a few hours more than a year ago, but have no plans to come again in the near future; and you, I imagine, are not planning to come to England: if you do, please let me know.

Yours ever,

Isaiah   [...]

The above letter to Chomsky tested the water after the embarrassing revelations in Cockburn's Nation *article. How would Chomsky react? Chomsky's reply (18 December) left IB in no doubt as to where he stood. 'I do not want to conceal from you', Chomsky wrote, 'that a certain amount of material has been leaking about the sordid affair at Index on Censorship, and some of it has reached me indirectly.' This included an unsigned memorandum about a letter to the chairman of Index (Mark Bonham Carter) from 'a long-term supporter of Index who wishes to remain anonymous'. IB must have known that Chomsky guessed this was him; and he suffered the humiliation of having his sharply critical but privately expressed opinion on Chomsky quoted back to him by Chomsky himself. Of this underhand mode of expressing criticism Chomsky remarked:*

This, I should say, is quite typical of many examples I have seen over the years of the behaviour of elite British intellectuals, spewing forth their malice in secret, knowing that the arrangements of power will enable them to vilify those whom they regard as having breached the limits of decorous conformity. The reactions you mention to Alexander Cockburn's honest and forthright work are simply another example. I saw enough of the infantile senior common room antics while I was there [in Britain] so that I am not very much surprised.[1]

There was no further contact between them.

1 Chomsky to IB, 18 December 1986.

TO ARTHUR SCHLESINGER

8 December 1986

Headington House

Dear Arthur

I enclose a letter which I was going to send to the *Nation*, but have decided
not to. [...] It worries me a bit that there should be a mole at *Index* who
supplies Miss Nora Beloff's drafts to Cockburn or his friends, but that's their
lookout. In a periodical such as theirs it is particularly undesirable to have
moles, but that is none of my business. I am merely sending you a copy of
my unsent letter in order to tell you what exactly occurred. I did not blow
up at the content of Chomsky's article – though it was clearly a characteristic outburst of violent feeling, occasioned, in my view, not by hostility to
Zionism or the state of Israel as such (he certainly does not wish to obliterate
the state, as the PLO would like, and does not think it a wicked nationalist
experiment – he holds the views of the Zionists of twenty or thirty years ago,
which are not in themselves disreputable), but by his deep hatred certainly of
the American Jewish establishment in New York – Podhoretz and his friends
– and of the whole what he conceives of as the American imperialist structure. A kind of anti-Americanism seems to me to be the underlying motive,
but one can never tell what goes on inside people's souls.

Podhoretz's nephew[1] is the kind of target that I think that Chomsky wants
to shoot at. I am sure [...] it is undesirable to engage with Cockburn – with
a genuinely (I believe, from what I have heard) somewhat disreputable figure;
quite apart from his views. No doubt some of them are due to his loyalty to
the memory of his father,[2] whom some people admired but I never did – the
Week[3] did nothing but harm in its day, and as you know, was the basis of
Senator Borah's isolationist speeches in the Senate.

I see no good in Communism of whatever kind, and never have. In view
of all the recent revelations I seem to be almost alone in my generation to

1 Joshua Moravchik (b. 1947), neoconservative foreign policy commentator; resident scholar,
  American Enterprise Institute for Public Policy Research, 1987–2008.
2 Claud Cockburn (1904–81), journalist; joined the CPGB *c.*1932 and soon afterwards founded the
  Week, which he edited 1933–46; diplomatic and foreign correspondent, *Daily Worker*, 1935–46;
  Alexander Cockburn's fortnightly column in the *Nation*, 'Beat the Devil', took its title from his
  father's 1952 novel of the same name, made into a film by John Huston (1953).
3 The *Week* was a shoestring, subscription-only, radical news-sheet, claiming an influence far
  beyond its circulation: 'Cockburn was not an orthodox journalist. He pooh-poohed the notion
  of facts as if they were nuggets of gold waiting to be unearthed. It was, he believed, the inspiration of the journalist which supplied the story' (Richard Ingrams, ODNB). Both of the journals
  that Cockburn was associated with during WW2, the *Week* and the *Daily Worker* (the organ of
  the CPGB), were suppressed by the Home Secretary, 21 January 1941, on the grounds that they
  systematically published material 'calculated to foment opposition to the prosecution of the war
  to a successful issue' ('The "Daily Worker": Mr Morrison on Its Suppression', *Times*, 23 January
  1941, 2a): at this time the USSR was in alliance with Nazi Germany. Senator Borah, 'the lion of
  Idaho', opposed US involvement in both World Wars.

have these feelings. No doubt inoculation by the 1917 Revolution was in my case a dominant fact. [...]

Yours ever,

[Isaiah]

TO SHIELA SOKOLOV GRANT

28 January 1987

Headington House

Dearest Shiela,

[...] You ask me about Mr Gorbachev.[1] I am totally pessimistic. I know that isn't fashionable, but my pessimism in the past about all his predecessors and their alleged breakthroughs have been fully justified. The only man who made any difference at all was Khrushchev,[2] who really did break the Stalin terror to a high degree: since then, nothing. Clearly Gorbachev is an intelligent man, who knows the Soviet economy is in a bad state, or needs resources, who doesn't want to spend too much on armaments, who wants to be modern, to talk the kind of language that is fresher, more attractive than that of his dreary predecessors, etc. etc. But what I believe is this: so long as the system in Russia does not radically alter, all the rest is necessarily cosmetic. It is intended to improve the atmosphere, intended to lower the temperature somewhat, that kind of thing (not that war between the United States and Russia is in any degree probable in our lifetime, or, I should have thought, for longer after); but unless the system, which is rigid, can be altered – and I don't believe that any Russian leader can do that without risking too great an upheaval, too violent a collapse in unexpected quarters – nothing will basically alter. People in the West will go on hoping and underlining Gorbachev's modernity, Madame Gorbachev's alleged (not in my eyes) good looks[3] – I have seen her close to, and I can assure you that this is a total myth; she doesn't look like a battleaxe, but that's about all, nor like one of those enormous laundresses to whom Soviet commissars used to be married. I am complacently pessimistic, I am afraid; I don't fear war; the only thing that

---

1 Mikhail Sergeevich Gorbachev (b. 1931), elected general secretary, CPSU, 1985, embarked on a policy of glasnost (openness) and perestroika (restructuring), liberalising society and beginning a détente with the United States aimed at reducing defence spending in favour of civil society; resigned 25 December 1992 as the USSR disintegrated after the fall of the Berlin Wall (November 1989); Nobel Peace Prize 1990; honorary citizen of Berlin 1992.

2 Khrushchev launched an unbridled personal attack on Stalin and the 'cult of personality' at the Twentieth Party Congress, 25 February 1956, accusing him, inter alia, of mass murder, cowardice, bullying and anti-Semitism: 'Mr Khrushchev is said to have painted a vivid picture of a regime of "suspicion, fear, and terror".' 'Terror during Last Years of Stalin', Times, 17 March 1956, 6g.

3 Raisa Maksimovna Gorbacheva (1932–99) née Titarenko; m. 1953 Mikhail Gorbachev, whom she met while studying philosophy in Moscow. Her glamour and looks helped project a new image of the USSR, but it was not one that was admired there at the time: 'Diehard Comrades Regret that the Lady is not a Frump' (Sunday Times, 29 November 1987, 16).

saddens me is the rapid, uncontrolled decline of England in almost every sphere – perhaps not in that of armaments, but apart from that, intellectually, academically, artistically. All the symptoms of a genuine culture are very clear signs of hyper-decline. I shall be dead before it gets too bad, but that is cold comfort, I fear. Compared to the United States, we are inexorably going downhill – even compared to Germany, I fear. Who would have thought [it] when we were young? [...]

You ask about our friendship – that is, fortunately, unalterable, much more certain than the existence of God or a future life. So be comforted, and come and see us.

Yours ever, ⟨with much love⟩
    Isaiah   [...]

TO OSCAR WOOD[1]
    2 February 1987

                               Headington House

Dear Oscar,
    [...] I am perfectly willing to see Mr Ray Monk[2] about that evening[3] – and indeed, to tell him, if he wants to know, about my own encounter with Wittgenstein in Cambridge in 1940, when, in fear and trembling, I read a paper about solipsism to the Moral Sciences Club. If and when we meet – and I do not know why we meet so seldom – I can tell you about that, to me, unforgettable episode.[4]

My memories largely tally with yours about the Magdalen evening. The only point on which I think I differ is this: I remember that after your paper he began talking about psychological verbs, and said something like 'I can say when the bell rang, but if I say "At that time Mr Wood began to dress very well", I cannot, in answer to the question "Precisely when did this happen?", give the hour.' Then Prichard[5] did indeed get up and said, 'I thought we were discussing Deṣcartes' *cogito ergo sum* – does Professor Wittgenstein' – both the 'W' and the 'st' were pronounced in an English and not a German fashion

1 Oscar Patrick Wood (1924–94), philosopher; lecturer in philosophy, Christ Church, 1955–6, student (i.e. fellow) 1956–87.
2 Raymond ('Ray') Monk (b. 1957), prof. of philosophy, Southampton, since 1992; author of the biography *Ludwig Wittgenstein: The Duty of Genius* (London, 1991).
3 On 14 May 1947. OW, as undergraduate secretary, Jowett philosophical society, 1946–7, had invited Wittgenstein (LW) to give a paper. LW had instead agreed to reply to a paper by an undergraduate, which OW had to deliver himself, as preparation time was short. He spoke on Descartes' famous principle 'cogito ergo sum' ('I think, therefore I exist'), to a large audience at Magdalen, including most of the philosophy subfaculty. LW took little notice of the paper or its subject. At his suggestion the meeting was adjourned to the next day in All Souls, where he stayed the night as the guest of John Holloway (309/2).
4 See MI 94–5.
5 Harold Arthur Prichard (1871–1947), White's Prof. of Moral Philosophy, Oxford, and fellow, CCC, 1928–37.

– 'believe that this is a valid inference?' To which Wittgenstein replied, 'I did not come here to discuss Descartes: honest, I didn't', and then began talking about psychological verbs again, and said, 'I can say "I have started believing, doubting, wondering" but I cannot say "I started knowing"; this does not *demonstrate* anything, but it is an important pointer.' At which Prichard rose again and said, 'Would Professor Wittgenstein mind saying whether *cogito ergo sum*, in his opinion, is true or false: yes or no?' It was at this point that I think Weldon[1] looked very cross, indeed angry, and said, 'We really must ask Professor Wittgenstein to continue, and not interrupt in this fashion.' At which point Prichard got up, looking furious, and stumped out of the room – and I think he died a few weeks later. Otherwise it was precisely as you say, according to my recollection. Do you remember none of this? I also remember Wittgenstein saying, 'I am on an ascending curve and I should like to go on talking'; and Holloway[2] said, 'My name is Mr Holloway and I have a room in All Souls', and offered it for the next day. I did not go to All Souls – or perhaps I did – but I think you did.

I only saw Wittgenstein once again, in the street, when he was walking with, I think, Smythies;[3] he stopped and said, 'We have met before', and then marched on.

Yours ever,
Isaiah

TO MORTON WHITE
4 February 1987

Headington House

Dear Morton,

Thank you very much for your marvellous piece on William James.[4] I have read it twice, with increasing enjoyment. [...]

Naturally you send it to me in particular because of the issue of freedom of the will. On introspection I find that this is deeply true of myself. I do not think temperamentally I want the universe to be spick and span, tidy, follow rigorous rules and be reducible to as few (if possible one) presuppositions [as possible] from which all other rules and laws would flow – the unified field theory is not to me in the least an attractive prospect. Of course I realise its

---

1 Thomas Dewar ('Harry') Weldon (1896–1958), MC and Bar 1918; fellow and philosophy tutor, Magdalen, 1923–58.
2 John Holloway (1920–99), temporary lecturer in philosophy at New College 1946–7; fellow, All Souls, 1946–60, Queens', Cambridge, 1955–82, reader in Modern English 1966–72, prof. 1972–82.
3 Yorick Smythies (1917–80), philosopher and librarian; read moral sciences 1935–9 at King's, Cambridge, where he was a pupil of Wittgenstein (the two subsequently corresponded); some of his notes on Wittgenstein's lectures have been published.
4 'Good in the Way of Belief', review of Gerald E. Myers, *William James: His Life and Thought* (New Haven, [1986]), *New Republic*, 29 December 1986, 25–8, 30.

rationality, and even desirability, and the noble aim of Einstein etc. in trying to develop a system in which everything would follow from everything else – not like that wonderful thing you said to me about William James on Hegel, about the small boarding-house in which all lodgers touch each other all the time.[1] No, I do not want the universe to be tidy in that sense, and would like breaks in the continuity, unexpected events, surges, swerves, what the Epicureans called – I have forgotten the Greek name[2] but the Latin is *clinamina* – which was their way of protecting free will against the determinism of the Stoics.

You are quite right that for more than two thousand years thinkers have argued about determinism with no very concrete result – perhaps precisely because this is not an intellectual problem that is in principle soluble, but simply shows the way people want the world to be. It isn't simply that I want to blame someone for the Holocaust or the poison gas the Iraqis are using at present[3] – though I do, of course – and think it unnatural not to do so (at least for me); but I wish to go further, as you know, and to say that if you tell me that everything is caused and that cause is caused etc., then blame in that sense, or responsibility, or all the cluster of concepts which accumulate round it, are literally inapplicable[4] [...].

I have been trying to think of determinism as an empirical hypothesis. [...] But I don't think that is right, I think it is a matter of wanting the world to be X or not-X, rigorously determined or capable of being modified by uncaused human wishes, acts, decisions. And then on the other side, the estimable scientific desire to account for everything in what is ultimately a somewhat mechanistic model. All the stuff about indeterminism, undecidability, rival hypotheses which account equally well for what occurs, which may or may not be saying the same thing in different symbolisms, Feyerabend[5] etc.

1 'The "through-and-through" universe seems to suffocate me with its infallible impeccable all-pervasiveness. Its necessity, with no possibilities; its relations, with no subjects, make me feel as if I had entered into a contract with no reserved rights, or rather as if I had to live in a large seaside boarding-house with no private bedroom in which I might take refuge from the society of the place.' William James, 'Absolutism and Empiricism', *Mind* 9 no. 34 (April 1884), 281–6 at 285.

2 *Paregklisis – clinamen* (plural *clinamina*) was coined by Lucretius.

3 The UN Security Council, in a presidential statement, 21 March 1986, had condemned Iraq's use of chemical weapons in its war against Iran; in the New Year of 1987 Tehran alleged that mustard gas was being used against its front-line troops.

4 One might extend this point to cover rational activity as a whole, as normally understood, since this characteristically involves free choice between alternatives, weighing evidence and arguments, etc. If this is right, the consequences of the truth of determinism for our conceptual resources are even more devastating than IB says. Indeed, the very statement of determinism as a rational conclusion seems ruled out, which would make the doctrine self-refuting.

5 Paul Karl Feyerabend (1924–94), Vienna-born philosopher of science; associate prof. of the philosophy of science, Berkeley, 1958–62, prof. of philosophy 1962–90; prof. of philosophy of science, Federal Institute of Technology, Zurich, 1970–90; famous for his scepticism about the possibility of universal scientific method or scientific objectivity, he drew on the work of Thomas Kuhn (188/5): for both thinkers scientific progress was at crucial moments revolutionary in ways that would not be possible if the classical view of scientific progress as cumulative were correct.

etc. seems to me a mere irrelevance to all this – as I am sure it does to you (I remember Stuart Hughes[1] made a lot of that in explaining why historians in the past were slaves of a nineteenth-century causal model, and how different it was now that Heisenberg[2] had discovered mere probabilities, and cited E. H. Carr to the purpose).[3] Everything that can be causally explained, predicted, arranged, connected, should be. But freedom of the will, or consciousness of choice, is a basic datum, and in perfect rivalry to the observation of the external world. The two things glare at each other and you pays your money and you takes your choice, as your old friend C. I. Lewis[4] would have said.

So it is a matter of temperament. Do you differ from me? I think you do. I think the Quine in you resists my old libertarian tutor Frank Hardie[5] (of whom you never will have heard) in me. I am all for Leibniz's 'causes that incline but do not necessitate'[6] – I think I know what that means, but am not prepared to explain, if you see what I mean. So I think 'Dad', as both Billy James and his brother Harry[7] referred to him when talking to me, was quite right, as about so many things. As for God, this may be a matter of temperament too, don't you think? A form of making the universe cosier for oneself, however angry the followers of Kierkegaard would have been with this vulgar phrase on my part.[8] [...]

    Yours ever,
      Isaiah

1 (Henry) Stuart Hughes (1916–99), cultural and intellectual historian; prof. of history, Harvard, 1957–69, Gurney Prof. of History and Political Science from 1969.

2 Werner Karl Heisenberg (1901–76), German theoretical physicist; prof. and director, Max Planck Institute for Physics, Göttingen, 1946–58; 1932 Nobel Prize in Physics for his contribution to quantum mechanics. The implications for philosophy of his uncertainty principle (1927) have been much discussed.

3 Stuart Hughes, *History as Art and as Science: Twin Vistas on the Past* (NY, [1964]), 2, cites both Carr and Heisenberg, though not quite as IB here remembers; probabilities are mentioned at 21.

4 Clarence Irving Lewis (1883–1964), US philosopher; taught at Harvard 1920–53, Edgar Pierce Prof. of Philosophy from 1946.

5 William Francis Ross ('Frank') Hardie (1902–90), fellow and philosophy tutor, CCC, 1926–50, President 1950–69; for Hardie's profound intellectual influence on IB, and IB's enormous admiration for him, see L1 709–10.

6 Leibniz discusses this idea at many points in his *Theodicy*, writing, for example, 'la predetermination que j'admets est tousjours inclinante, et jamais necessitante' ('the predestination I allow is always one that predisposes, never one that necessitates'). *Essais de théodicée sur la bonté de Dieu, la liberté de l'homme et l'origine du mal* (1710), preface: *Die philosophischen Schriften von Gottfried Wilhelm Leibniz*, ed. C. I. Gerhardt (Berlin, 1875–90), vi/2 47.

7 William ('Billy') James (1882–1961), painter, and Henry ('Harry') James (1879–1947), lawyer, sons of the psychologist William James, who set out his belief in free will in an address on 'The Dilemma of Determinism', *Unitarian Review and Religious Magazine* 22 no. 3 (September 1884), 193–224, repr. in his *The Will to Believe: And Other Essays in Popular Philosophy* (NY, 1897).

8 Presumably because for Kierkegaard religious belief was too serious a matter to be treated so flippantly.

On 12 and 14 March 1987 Oxford MAs turned out in unprecedented numbers to
elect the University's next chancellor, in succession to Harold Macmillan, who
had died the previous December. The front runners were the former Labour
cabinet minister and founder member of the SDP, Roy Jenkins; his erstwhile
parliamentary opponent, the former Conservative prime minister Edward
Heath; and the Provost of Queen's, Robert Blake. On the eve of the poll the
bookies made Jenkins the favourite, followed by Blake, and then Heath, and this
proved to be the finishing order, much to the delight of IB, whose candidate had
won. He had not given very serious consideration to a proposal that he should
himself stand, and once Roy Jenkins had declared his interest such a candidacy
could only have divided the liberal vote, just as Ted Heath and Robert Blake had
divided the conservative one.

TO SHIELA SOKOLOV GRANT

21 April 1987

Headington House

Dearest Shiela,

[...] Why would you have wished to vote against Roy? I was one of his
ardent supporters – what have you against the poor man? You cannot think
him a traitor to socialism (are you one? were you ever exactly that?), nor can
you be anti-European, nor can you prefer Lord Blake or Heath, who is by
now a mass of resentments, wounds, anger and total inability to connect
with human beings, though he is, for a politician, honest and, I suppose, in
view of the Brandt Commission, decently progressive.[1] He was dreadfully
upset to come third and I doubt if he will ever come to Oxford again – rather
like the other wounded victim, Mrs T.[2] I think that Roy Jenkins is superior
to the other candidates – or, as an Italian professor once said about some
paper of mine he heard at a society, 'the least worst' – but in fact much
better than that. He resigned on an issue of principle, he has never cheated
or lied, his views seem to me entirely reputable – and his taste for gracious
living is slightly absurd and has done him much political damage, but is not
a mortal sin.

1 In his later years Heath gained a reputation for discourteousness, and at the dinner table was 'apt
   to relapse into morose silence or completely ignore the woman next to him and talk across her
   to the nearest man': Philip Ziegler, *Edward Heath: The Authorized Biography* (London, 2010), 142.
   He was invited to join the Brandt Commission 1977 as its UK representative: the Commission,
   chaired by Willy Brandt (1913–92) né Herbert Ernst Karl Frahm, chancellor of West Germany
   1969–74, was charged with investigating international development issues, and specifically the
   gap between the wealth of the nations in the northern and southern hemispheres.
2 Mrs Thatcher, a graduate of Somerville, had been denied an hon. DCL 29 January 1985 by Oxford
   after dons voted by 738 votes to 319 against at a specially convened meeting. She became the 1st
   Oxford-educated prime minister not to be accorded this honour, and the vote, which was highly
   controversial, revealed the extent of concern in academic circles about the effects of her government's policies on higher education.

You ask about Provence, or Digne[1] – Aline may, I certainly don't, know. My passion for France is limited – I dare not confess this fully to my wife, who takes it slightly amiss, but I find the French not at all sympathetic, intellectually, morally or personally. There are obviously some exceptions, but I prefer the corrupt and easygoing Italians, and even the awful but at least intellectually interesting Germans, who have some kind of inner lives, awful as these may often be. Have you seen *Shoah*?[2] It really is unforgettably horrifying, worse in a way than the extermination camps and corpses and skeletons and shoes and teeth. There is an excellent series on Channel 4 on *Europe at War*, which contains something about the concentration camps etc., which we recorded yesterday but which I haven't yet had the courage to look at – but I shall. I feel one must. And yet all those young Germans seem charming. [...]

What will you do after the Grant Duff memoirs?[3] Have you a book in mind? Or would you be content, say, to live somewhere near, or in, Oxford, travel to London occasionally to see plays, concerts, operas, and call on us and the Jays[4] and make new friends? Ann Fleming, now dead, believed strongly that in order to have a happy old age one must make friends much younger than oneself, for obvious reasons (most of ours really are dead or dying). So will you set yourself to do that? I can't, but why shouldn't you? Enough appetite for life, enough interest, and they will flock. [...]

What are you to read? Buckle's list is wonderful.[5] You would certainly go mad if you began reading that particular list, even Brown on cause and effect,[6] a somewhat forgotten work, I fear. Anyway, reading masterpiece after masterpiece would be extremely unsettling. [...] I find pleasure in looking at

1 SSG and her husband Micheal contemplated a visit that June to Digne-les-Bains, capital of the French *département* of Alpes-de-Haute-Provence, to meet a sculptor friend attending 'some sort of Art conference' there (SSG to IB, n.d. [1987]).
2 *Shoah* (1985; the title is Hebrew for 'catastrophe'), a 9-hour long documentary by the French film-maker Claude Lanzmann, who eschewed archival footage, instead using interviews with survivors, perpetrators (often filmed surreptitiously) and witnesses to create a highly detailed picture of the Holocaust.
3 IB's reference to 'memoirs' is misleading. SSG had been working for many years, with more than one book in view, on the papers of her grandfather, the author, colonial administrator and Liberal MP Mountstuart Elphinstone Grant Duff (1929–1906), who published 14 vols (in 2-vol. instalments) of *Notes from a Diary* (London, 1897–1905), edited extracts from his diaries covering 1851–1901. She applied (unsuccessfully) for an All Souls fellowship 1985 to work on this project, but this did not prevent her from completing much of a biography of Grant Duff, and a book about the friendship between his wife Anna Julia and the lawyer and author James Fitzjames Stephen, neither of which has been published.
4 Douglas Jay and his 2nd wife Mary Lavinia Thomas (b. 1942, m. 1972), lived near Oxford.
5 Henry Thomas Buckle (1821–62), historian, author of *History of Civilization in England* (London, 1857–61), was asked to recommend a course of reading 1861, and SSG asked IB the same question (n.d., [1987]), sending him a summary of Buckle's list, which comprised Aristotle, Bacon, Berkeley, Thomas Brown, Bunyan, Cervantes, Comte, Dante, Descartes, Goethe, Grotius, Hegel, Hobbes, Homer, Kant, Locke, Malthus, Mill, Plato, Ricardo, Shakespeare and Adam Smith: Alfred Henry Huth, *The Life and Writings of Henry Thomas Buckle* (London, 1880) ii 63–4.
6 Thomas Brown (1778–1820), Scottish philosopher and poet, author of *Observations on the Nature*

the second- or third-rate novels of my youth, like Maurice Baring or *A Room With a View*[1] or Aldous Huxley, who say far more to me than the writers of the present. But I daresay that is the condition of all old persons, though I say, self-consciously, that I do see the new ones to be quite talented, only acutely uninteresting to me; the worst is Rebecca West,[2] who is dreadful and not gifted at all;[3] and dear Elizabeth Bowen, whom I loved but whose works I simply cannot read (do you remember what she said about Mary Fisher? 'I don't like girls who say "Alas" ').

You ask about the Hopkinsons: no, we don't see them. Diana must be against you entirely because of inadequate appreciation of Adam, who is her past and her present in her life – the same as David Astor's disapproving view of me.[4] I used to hate people, but don't any more – I think they are all dead. It is rather like the brigand whom the priest was trying to persuade on his deathbed to say that he forgave his enemies: 'I have none, Father, for I have killed them all.'[5] I have killed nobody – but dreadful people like Lord Cherwell or Hannah Arendt or that woman (what is her name?) who wrote *The Little Foxes*,[6] ⟨Lillian Hellman – old Stalinist & hideously ugly – not just in face, but expression.⟩ are really dead. If you read Mary McCarthy's *Groves of Academe*,[7] I think you would enjoy it – but literature it is not.

So tell me when you are coming.

Yours ever,

Isaiah

TO ANDRZEJ WALICKI

21 April 1987

Headington House

Dear Andrzej,

Your *Legal Philosophies*[8] has arrived, but when I shall look at it God only knows. I cannot tell you how overwhelmed I am by theses, British Academy documents, Royal Opera House committees and other things which old men have to do – but I shall push all that aside as soon as I can, and sit down

and *Tendency of the Doctrine of Mr Hume, concerning the Relation of Cause and Effect* (Edinburgh, 1806).

1 E. M. Forster's novel was published in London 1908.
2 Pseudonym (borrowed from an Ibsen heroine) of Cicily Isabel Andrews (1892–1983) née Fairfield, DBE 1959, writer, critic and journalist.
3 When West reviewed RT – 'Sir Isaiah's Brand of History', *Sunday Telegraph*, 15 January 1978, 14 – IB wrote to HH (n.d.): 'her views are worthless & don't annoy me – it is like being kicked by a superannuated old cow'.
4 Because of IB's lack of enthusiasm for Astor's and other friends' efforts to canonise Adam von Trott, about whom he had deeply ambivalent feelings.
5 Variously attributed.
6 Lillian Hellman, *The Little Foxes: A Play in Three Acts* (NY, 1939).
7 Mary McCarthy, *The Groves of Academe* (London, [1953]).
8 Andrzej Walicki, *Legal Philosophies of Russian Liberalism* (Oxford, 1987).

and read it, for, as you may imagine, the subject is near my heart. [...] As for democracy – participatory democracy, particularly in the form of the demands for it of the rebellious students of the late 1960s, or Sheldon Wolin,[1] who wrote a good book once, and then turned into a kind of left-wing mystical Arendt-loving semi-anarchist guru (his magazine duly collapsed): I had quite a lot of respect for him twenty years ago; now, although he is personally a clever, subtle and rather nice man, my respect has totally evaporated; liking, some, is left; admiration, respect, attention to his theses, none – Miss Arendt's dream about ancient Athens mixed with Tocqueville, New England town meetings, Quaker gatherings, mystical interpretations of Rousseau, General Will[2] – all that is not for me, and I am sure not for you. As a reaction against corruption, plutocracy, oppression of various thoughts it is intelligible, but that does not make it intrinsically more attractive.

As for Gorbachev, we shall see: so far, he has played his cards extremely well. It is obvious that he is in some danger, but I think that people who have gone through his hard school and walked over a sufficient number of corpses will know what to do. Perhaps matters will be somewhat improved, but I fully sympathise with my fellow Europeans, who do not wish to be exposed to the 'Russian conventional force steamroller'.

As you see, I am going through your letter point by point with great pleasure. What you say about American students is perfectly true:[3] in my day at Harvard and elsewhere they believed that objective truth was discoverable; that the professor may well have possessed it; that with enough pressure he might reveal it; not much was understood of selective and critical reading. But I used to recommend bibliographies, and students used to ask which chapters, or even sections, of these books they were to read, as they read every word, without skipping, without the slightest sense of what was important and what was not. Their search for the truth, their belief that anything new, or even true, was worth earnest endeavours to extract from the professor, was touching; and for the professor often rather moving and flattering, after the *blasés*[4] of English students. But in the end it turned out to

---

1 Sheldon Sanford Wolin (b. 1922), US political theorist; prof. of politics, Berkeley 1954–71, Princeton 1973–87; founding editor 1981 of the short-lived *Democracy: A Journal of Political Renewal and Radical Change*; the 'good book' is *Politics and Vision: Continuity and Innovation in Western Political Thought* (Princeton, 1960).

2 Arendt's ideal of direct democracy, drawing on the political traditions of ancient Athens and the New England settlers, figures in her comparative study of France and America, *On Revolution* (NY, 1963). IB rejected both the utility and legitimacy of Arendt's analysis, but her interpretation of Rousseau as a precursor to C20th totalitarian terror is closer to his own position than he cared to acknowledge.

3 Walicki, who had joined Notre Dame, in Indiana, the previous year, had written: 'Unfortunately, graduate students here have difficulties even with summarising texts read by them, completely unable to make their own comments or to reconstruct what is not explicitly said in the text' (10 April 1987).

4 If this apparent use of *blasé* to mean '*blasé* attitude' is intentional, it is very unusual, though not completely unattested. But there may be an error of transcription.

be a little too naive – the graduates were sometimes very good at Harvard, the undergraduates seldom.[1] [...]

As for Oxford, goodness me, nothing is happening here of the slightest interest, except that money is being withdrawn, the brain-drain of the best philosophers, for example, is continuing. Did you ever know Alan Ryan at New College, or Lukes,[2] or a philosopher called McDowell[3] (you wouldn't have known him), or Bernard Williams, the Provost of King's College at Cambridge, where Aileen Kelly is still writing, and writing well? They are all going to America (not Aileen), and they are only the beginning. Hence the refusal of an honorary degree to Mrs Thatcher, described by her champions as a mixture of greed and spite (the motives for the refusal, I mean).

I have been to Israel since I last saw you, and there too the situation seems to me highly unsatisfactory. Why is everyone rushing towards religious obscurantism, *mrakobesie*[4] of the most awful kind? Colonels, terrorists, tyrants, ayatollahs, moral majorities, the Reverend Moon;[5] Sakharov and Alfonsín[6] the only persons one can look up to at all? I think that is what Herzen & Co. felt in the 1850s. Why must the end of my life be covered in this growing darkness? [...]

Yours ever,
Isaiah

TO BEATA POLANOWSKA-SYGULSKA

22 April 1987

Headington House

Dear Mrs Polanowska-Sygulska,

[...] You write about Popper. It is true that I never mentioned him much, but I don't mention anyone much unless I am specifically writing about them. I think he regards me as some kind of disciple of his, which I am not exactly; nevertheless he thinks that we have some kind of common liberal individualist standpoint – which to a certain degree is true, though he has

1 Cf. IB's 'The Intellectual Life of American Universities', L2 749–60.
2 Steven Michael Lukes (b. 1941), political and social theorist; fellow and sociology and politics tutor, Balliol, and lecturer in politics, Oxford, 1966–88; prof. of political and social theory, European University Institute, Florence, 1987–95; prof. of moral philosophy, Siena, 1996–2000.
3 John Henry McDowell (b. 1942), fellow and philosophy praelector (i.e. tutor), Univ., 1966–8; lecturer, Oxford, 1967–86; prof. of philosophy, Pittsburgh, 1986–8, University Prof. of Philosophy 1988–2009.
4 The Russian word for obscurantism.
5 Sun Myung Moon (1920–2012) né Young Myung Mun, Korean religious cult leader, industrialist and self-proclaimed Messiah; advocated Christian unity against atheistical Communism, founding the Unification Church, with headquarters in NY; his followers were dubbed 'Moonies'.
6 Raúl Ricardo Alfonsín (1927–2009), Argentinian lawyer and Radical Civic Union politician; came to prominence during the military dictatorship 1976–83 as a defender of human rights; as President 1983–9 he failed to control the economy, but brought the military under democratic civilian countrol.

gone far further in the direction of a kind of conservative laissez-faire liberalism than I should be disposed to or have ever embraced. [...]

You tell me that my doctrine seems to be essentialist, in Popper's terms. That I should deny flatly. Popper's essentialism, in particular as part of his attacks on Plato, Aristotle, Hegel, Marx etc., takes the form, so far as I remember it (and goodness knows how many years ago I read *The Open Society* or *The Poverty of Historicism*),[1] of saying that these thinkers take it that there is a kind of inner structure to human beings, to their associations – tribes, societies, states – which makes it inevitable that certain courses should be pursued. In other words, that there is a kind of set libretto which people cannot help following, whether they want to or mean to or not – in other words, a form of historical inevitability, which, as you know, I am wholly opposed to. That is what I take Popper's essentialism to be mainly about. The proposition that history has no libretto – which, as you know, Herzen makes so much of – is precisely what I do believe, particularly with my unpopular opinion that individuals make more difference [to] the twists and turns of human history than is commonly supposed by the system-builders – the exact opposite of what Engels said, when he said that if Napoleon had not existed a number of persons would collectively have produced the self-same result.[2]

I am prepared to believe that men are to a large degree conditioned by the society into which they are born – see Herder – by the habits, outlook, way of life, language, beliefs, from which they can of course rebel, but which nevertheless form and condition the means by which they do so, and the set of their minds and emotions and hearts. Nevertheless, this is not totally determined: at crucial moments, when conflicts arise within a society – particularly then – the impulse given freely by an individual acting through his own free will and not in some predictable fashion (which some psychologist or sociologist armed with sufficient data could have foretold) can send things spinning in some unforeseen and unforeseeable direction. If Alexander[3] or Caesar[4] had not lived, history would certainly have taken a different turn. This is true of a good many individuals, or perhaps groups of individuals,

---

1 *The Open Society and Its Enemies* (London, 1945); 'The Poverty of Historicism', *Economica* 11 (1944) no. 42, 86–103, no. 43, 119–137, 12 (1945) no. 46, 68–89 – revised as *The Poverty of Historicism* (London, 1957). Both works were written during WW2, when Popper was in New Zealand. 'The *Poverty* and *The Open Society* were my war effort': 'Autobiography of Karl Popper', in Paul Arthur Schilpp (ed.), *The Philosophy of Karl Popper* (La Salle, Ill., 1974), i 91.

2 In a letter to Walther Borgius of 25 January 1894: 'in the absence of a Napoleon, someone else would have taken his place'. CW l [i.e. vol. 50] 266. Not quite what IB says.

3 Alexander the Great (356–323 BCE), king of Macedonia 336–323 BCE; tutored by Aristotle, and considered the greatest general of classical times; his conquests spread Greek culture throughout the Eastern Mediterranean and into Asia.

4 Gaius Julius Caesar (100–44 BCE), Roman general and statesman, conquered Gaul (58–49 BCE), invaded Britain (54 BCE), crossed the Rubicon (49 BCE), and became dictator of Rome 49–44 BCE; assassinated in the senate on the Ides of March (15 March).

certainly of Napoleon, of Hitler; even Churchill by behaving as he did in 1939–45 prevented a situation in Europe – when Hitler's victory seemed highly probable to most rational political calculators – and things would have been exceedingly different; and the same is certainly true of 1917 in Russia – if a brick had fallen on the head of Lenin, goodness me, there might have been an upheaval, a revolution, civil war between the peasants, proletarians, landowners, officers, liberals, heaven knows what, I don't deny that; but the particular outcome could very well have been wholly different from what in fact took place.

So I am a believer, more than most people, in the influence, both conscious and sometimes unintended, of men of unusual power – certainly not virtuous or humane, quite often – who give an impulsion which produces results quite different from those which Tolstoy, for example, insisted on in his highly determinist, though in some ways ambivalent and self-contradictory, theory of historical determination. That is what I take to be the heart of essentialism.

What essentialism, then, is it that you take me to hold? [...] I am far from saying that human nature 'is always the same': or that there is a kernel inside every human being, his 'essential' nature, which does not alter however much other attributes do, so that by looking into this basic nature it is possible to discover 'natural laws', true of all men everywhere at all times – *quod semper, quod ubique, quod ab omnibus*[1] – as held, I suppose, by Aristotle, the Christian Fathers, Isidore of Seville, Gratian, Grotius (I suppose Spinoza), Rousseau, Jefferson etc., and denied only by people like Vico or Hegel, who thought it was a matter of growth and development, though even they were teleological and thought that nature, God, built us to pursue certain goals which we cannot avoid or deviate from too far. None of this do I believe; only that *de facto* there is sufficient common ground between men at most times in most places – not, perhaps, always and everywhere – to make understanding and communication and explanation possible. [...]

With my best wishes and gratitude,

Yours,

Isaiah Berlin

TO JOHN GRIGG

1 May 1987

Headington House

Dear John,

[...] I am naturally deeply flattered by the idea, and by the fact that *The*

Times should wish to entrust me with this remarkable task.[1] But I am afraid I shall be of no use for this purpose. I do not find it entirely easy to explain why, but I shall try.

I did meet Solzhenitsyn once, at lunch with Professor Prince Sir Dimitri Obolensky, and realised then, as has become clear since, that S. is not interested in Russian literature, history, politics as such, but only in the Revolution and its aftermath. He is sometimes described as a Slavophil – that is quite wrong; he does not take the faintest interest, so far as I can tell, in any Slavs except Great Russians. What he most resembles is the Old Believers: when (but I expect you know all this) the Patriarch Nikon[2] tried to reform the Russian Church in the seventeenth century, there were those who rejected the reforms; their leader, the Archpriest Avvakum (Slavonic for Habbakuk), whose spiritual biography is a great masterpiece, was duly burnt at the stake by his friend the Emperor Alexis, his followers, when Peter's soldiers tried to arrest them for non-payment of tax and refusal to serve the state in any way, burnt themselves in groups, singing and holding crucifixes (Mussorgsky's *Khovanshchina*,[3] which you could have seen at Covent Garden, is all about that). The Old Believers regarded Peter's modernisation as a horrible evil and the state itself as a satanic power to be resisted to the point of death, in order to restore the original purity of the Church. These people persist to this day in an underground sort of way.

Solzhenitsyn's attitude to the Soviet Union seems to me very similar – his life is devoted to the destruction of the spiritual evil of Communism. Western Europe is feeble and useless, Latin America worse; only the US seems to have some power of resistance to the evil empires (China etc.). I really do not think he is interested in anything else. He is not primarily a man of letters at all – his books, in my view, are not novels of genius, as sometimes described, but the most powerful and devastating documents of our time. So far as I know, his time is entirely spent in collecting material for another instalment

---

1 Grigg, who had 'a loose advisory role on *The Times*' (letter to IB, 29 April 1987), had written to ask if IB would be interested, in principle, in participating in a dialogue with Solzhenitsyn about 'Russian literature, history and politics, including of course the most recent developments'; an edited version of their talk would then be published in *The Times*, and doubtless reproduced worldwide: 'Without labouring the point, it seems to me that such a conversation between you and him would be of unique interest and value. Wary, difficult and defensive though he is, I feel confident that he would respond to the idea of talking to you.'

2 Nikon (or Nikita Minin) (1605–81), patriarch of Moscow 1652–8, fundamentally reformed the Russian Orthodox Church's liturgy, meeting persistent opposition from the schismatic 'Old Believers'; his reforms were rigorously enforced by the civil authorities, and the Old Believers faced continuing persecution and penal sanctions until the early C20th.

3 Mussorgsky's opera *Khovanshchina*, unfinished at the time of his death, was completed and orchestrated by Rimsky-Korsakov (St Petersburg, 1886), and deals with the 1682 uprising against Peter the Great led by Prince Ivan Andreevich Khovansky, a supporter of the Old Believers. It was performed at the ROH 1963, 1972 and 1982; IB's 'Historical Note', a programme note written for the opera's ROH premiere 1963, was reprinted in the 1972 and 1982 programmes.

of *1914*,[1] plus materials for a history of Russia which will make the scales fall
from the eyes of both Russians and foreigners. His entire attitude to literature, the arts etc. is governed by their relationship to his crusade. He would
not find it in the least interesting to talk to me, or anyone like me, about
Pushkin, Turgenev, Pasternak etc.; he only wanted to meet me because he
had heard that I was a friend of Akhmatova, whose independence had made
her into a kind of icon for every dissident, in and out of Russia. Every effort,
during the lunch in question, to get him talking about anything other than
the fight against Communism was contemptuously waved aside.

The Soviet Union is basically outside my range. He would be far more
likely to talk freely to some sovietologist – I do not know who they are nowadays – [...] than to me.

Believe me, I am not simply dodging a conversation with a daunting
prophet – certainly he sees himself in that role – but I know for certain that
it would not work. I am so sorry that this should be so. The opportunity in
principle is marvellous, and somebody could do it – but do not expect S. to
talk like a man of letters: he has only one purpose and will not deviate from
that in talk or any other respect.

    Yours ever,
      Isaiah

TO GODFREY LIENHARDT[2]

5 May 1987

                                   Headington House

Dear Godfrey,
    [...] Thank you [...] for that wonderful review from the *L[iterary] R[eview]*[3]
[...]. By the time Auden came back to Oxford[4] he heartily disliked Rowse,
and told me so. They did, just, speak to each other, at least Rowse spoke,
but Auden studiously and successfully avoided him, even while he lived for
a short while in All Souls (where he was robbed by some falsely religious

1 *Avgust chetyrnadtsatogo* (Paris, 1971), trans. Michael Glenny as *August 1914* (London, 1972), dealing
   with the Russian defeat at the Battle of Tannenberg, 23–31 August 1914, was the 1st in a series of
   what turned out to be 4 novels, *Krasnoe koleso* [*The Red Wheel*], in which Solzhenitsyn offers an
   alternative account of Russian/Soviet history. At the time of IB's letter 2 further instalments,
   Oktyabr' shestnadtsatogo [*October 1916*], later trans. H. T. Willetts as *November 1916* [the date according to the Western calendar] (London, 1999), and *Mart semnadtsatogo* [*March 1917*], had appeared
   in Russian (Paris, 1984, 1986–8); the latter instalment and its successor *Aprel' semnadtsatogo* [*April
   1917*] (Paris, 1991) have not (yet) been translated into English.
2 Godfrey Lienhardt (1921–93), anthropologist, expert on Southern Sudan; reader in social anthropology, Oxford, 1972–88; fellow, Wolfson, 1967–72, professorial fellow 1972–88.
3 Edmund White, 'The Swabbling of Auden', review of A. L. Rowse, *The Poet Auden: A Personal
   Memoir* (London, 1987), *Literary Review* (May 1987), 38–9.
4 Auden returned to Oxford (where he had been an undergraduate) as prof. of poetry 1956–61, and
   at the very end of his life he returned again, taking up residence at his old college, Christ Church,
   in the autumn of 1972.

ne'er-do-well who came to him for help). I don't think there had ever been any homosexual bond between them. T. S. Eliot, I think, did take Rowse seriously, and wrote him letters, of which Rowse was intensely proud – more fool TSE, who in some ways was extremely naive, save that one ought to add that in the 1920s Rowse's left-wing boutades were more readable than during his later nationalist, Union-Jack-waving phase. He is not exactly a stupid man, but the megalomania and the vanity are (as everyone points out) of a loony variety. The thing about Rowse which is not so often noticed is that, underneath the nonsense, the vanity, the ludicrous and dotty and boring and egotistical layers, he is quite a nasty man – very cruel to those who do not recognise his genius if they are weak and defenceless, and filled with hatred if they are in any degree formidable: a man who I think perhaps has some of the temperament of genius without a spark of genius, which is quite difficult to live with. He has written a gigantic diary, to be published only after his death, on which I expect much [of] the impression of us all in this century will ultimately be based – people won't realise how mad he is. He once told me 'In the twenty-first century there'll be a Rowse industry, as there is a Pepys industry now' – and maybe there will be.[1] The people he will have written about will, I think, be dead by then – still … on the provision of facts, one cannot say he has any conscience at all. […]

   Yours gratefully,
   Isaiah

TO TEDDY KOLLEK

II May 1987

                                                    Headington House

Dear Teddy,
   […] Whoever told you about the Chancellorship? I never thought it was very serious, although virtually everybody has conspired to tell me that, if I had stood, there would have been no question that I should have been elected. I am sceptical. But even Aline is not. Anyway, how would it have been if I had had to welcome people 'In nomine Patris, Christi [sc. et Filii] et Spiritus Sancti'?[2] What would Rabbi Schach[3] have said? Fried[4] is very proud

---

1 There was not (230/4).
2 'In the name of the Father, of Christ [sc. and of the Son] and of the Holy Spirit', the standard Christian ritual formula originating in Matthew 28:19, traditionally intoned by OU chancellors on public occasions. As a Jew IB could hardly have used these words.
3 Eliezer Menachem Man S[c]hach (1899–2001), Lithuanian-born rabbi and Talmudic scholar, leader of the strictly Orthodox Haredi Jews in Israel; regarded as an ideologue who exercised considerable political influence in Israeli politics.
4 Arthur William Fried (b. 1941), Brooklyn-born managing director and chief financial officer, Lehman Bros, before becoming CEO, Rothschild Foundation, Jerusalem/Geneva, 1981–99.

of the fact that his rabbinical college has been condemned by that worthy –
he telephoned at once, thinking that it would give me pleasure. It did [...].

You must certainly stand for the mayoralty again. Eighty-two is no age
for that particular purpose (the Oxford Chancellorship is for life – a very different matter). I have said to you times without number that your position
is unique, that your mere occupancy of that post does more to create good
will for Israel, not just among Jews (though that, too, is after all of some
importance) but in much wider, Christian, atheist, I daresay Moslem, not
to speak of Buddhist, circles – but I mean that seriously. It would be a grave
dereliction of direct obligation to the Jewish people if you withdrew simply
in order to live a more comfortable life (which is what you, with some justice,
accuse me of having chosen).

I have just seen Rosa Goldberg.[1] She would talk of nothing but her
projected museum of Biblical musical instruments (I don't quite see Mrs
de Rothschild[2] being wildly enthusiastic about that) and your merits – ten
minutes of the museum, one hour and a half on your merits. As she belongs
to my Riga pre-1914 generation, I listen to her and to Yeshayahu Leibowitz[3]
with particular trust and attention – we pre-1914 Rigenser are always right, so
don't think of not standing. [...]

Yours, ⟨with much love⟩
    Isaiah

TO ARCHIE BROWN

12 May 1987

Headington House

Dear Archie,

I ought to have written to you long ago to thank you for your letter of 23
March about *Requiem*.[4] If indeed it was released for general circulation, I am
to some degree shaken, as I promised you I would be; evidently something
is happening. And yet, in my horribly suspicious way, I feel convinced that
this is all done in order to win favour among the Russian writers, painters
etc. – I hesitate to call them intelligentsia – and consequently, in the West,

1 Unidentified.
2 Dorothy Mathilde ('Dollie') de Rothschild (1895–1988) née Pinto, wife of James de Rothschild;
   like him a Jewish (and Zionist) activist and philanthropist; IB corresponded with her often, and at
   length, about her charitable causes.
3 Yeshayahu Leibowitz (1903–94), outspoken polymathic Riga-born scientist, philosopher, Zionist
   and devout Orthodox Jew; prof. of biochemistry (1941–52), organic chemistry and neurology
   (from 1952), HUJ; subject of a tribute by IB (published in Hebrew translation as 'The Conscience
   of Israel', *Ha'aretz*, 4 March 1983, 8).
4 In conversation with AB, IB had expressed scepticism about perestroika, saying that he would
   believe things were really changing only when the Soviet authorities allowed publication of
   Akhmatova's *Requiem*. The poem had just appeared in the literary journal *Oktyabr'* (1987 no. 3,
   130–5).

which is extremely responsive to what happens to the cultural section of the Soviet population. My feeling is that of course Gorbachev wants to get the country going, greatly improve the economic structure and economic performance; that for this he needs to reduce military expenditure, which he can only do by bold offers to the United States; so far, so good; but that the political set-up will not necessarily alter much as a result. Soviet visitors to the West seem to me to have been positively instructed to speak critically about the government and about Soviet arrangements in general, to display unwonted freedom of view, and otherwise to impress the West in the way that Gorbachev realises it needs to be impressed if good will is to be obtained; but [...] these things are done to order – just as I think that secret ballots will doubtless occur, but people will know for whom to vote.

I don't doubt that he is taking a risk, that large sections of the bureaucracy, perhaps even the army, will be discontented with the upheaval he is creating, and that what he is doing is, of course, better than to preserve the frozenness of his predecessors. What I am not convinced of is that one can talk about genuine liberalisation so long as the Iron Curtain persists, [...] free communication of persons is obstructed, [... and] people live in accordance with an imposed discipline without any real possibility of open opposition. The optimum result from Gorbachev's point of view is a great strengthening of the Soviet Union and a consequent danger to the West. At present I feel convinced that all this playing up to European public opinion is really intended to divide it from the wicked regime of the United States. I am sure that if one goes to the Soviet Union today one would notice a great many changes for the better; but I still remain obstinately sceptical about fundamental change or the real belief in peaceful coexistence on the part of the Soviet authorities.

Still, I may be wrong, this may just be insensitiveness on my part to genuinely radical changes that are going on – not just in the economy, which I am prepared to believe, but in the rigorous militarised set-up of the whole thing. I suspect that you are more optimistic and you may be right. I shall need more evidence, rather a lot more.

Yours ever,
Isaiah

TO KAY GRAHAM

20 May 1987 [*manuscript*]

As from Headington House

Dearest Kay,

I have just spoken to Lally,[1] but I have a feeling that I did not, perhaps

---

1 Elizabeth Morris ('Lally') Graham Weymouth (b. 1943), eldest of the 4 children, and only daughter, of Kay and Phil Graham; US journalist; contributing editor to publications such as *Esquire*, the *New York Times Magazine*, the *Atlantic Monthly* and the *Los Angeles Times*.

could not, convey to her the full extent of my distress at not coming to your birthday party in June:[1] I have a feeling that Joe & I are about the only people, apart from your family, who have been close friends of yours since 1940? Joe longer than I, obviously. It was in 1940 that I pronounced you to be the "perfect American couple" – a solid public man – and wealthy father's – idealistic leftish daughter married to a brilliant, ardent, irresistibly charming, upward moving, wildly witty young lawyer, burning with New Deal flame, put through College by a radical senator – a wonderful couple, very different & to me unbelievably more attractive than any family in England – (I'll never forget that Phil said to me practically at our first meeting, that he had thought of volunteering for the Soviet Union against the Finns – it was not meant too seriously, but it was unlike what anyone in the whole wide world could have said) – since then much has changed, but not my love for you and my happiness when we meet. But besides a natural wish to be an active celebrant of your birthday – gesture, acts, being present on occasions of joy or sorrow, are, I think, important – ritual does matter – symbolic acts express one's character and feeling – besides that, the event will be *stupendous* – unlike anything in either hemisphere, & I am a connoisseur of such occasions – I love them – I observe them with infinite pleasure and often amusement – all those speakers each with a typical rhetorical style – who is present, who is absent – why – how have relationships changed over the years – all that fascinates me almost too much: & I love formulating hypotheses & explanations of what goes on. So it is terribly disappointing to stay at home, eaten with frustration and acute moral discomfort (I no longer mind about not having gone to Joe's party[2] – you were right about that – he can take it, & so can I). But then why can't I come? Because of a fatal conjunction of circumstances: On the very day there is a meeting of the Board of the Royal Opera – my last – I've been on it longer than anyone has ever been – quite illegally – & some kind of "presentation" is to be made – & the date is fixed – & they are "all" coming – if I were ill, I suppose it wd not happen – but as it is – I cannot well stay away: then on the very next day, at 11 a.m. or so there is a meeting of a Rothschild Charity, on the tiny committee of which I sit, which dispenses large sums of money: there are two applications which, I feel pretty sure, if I am not there fervently to plead for them, will be turned down: & two persons' careers & prospects are literally dependent on this particular – quite large – help [...]. As if this is not enough there is an event on the night of July 1[3] at the British Academy of which I used to be the head – which again morally involves me – if it were only *that*, I wd come most eagerly. But I fear guilt – I am liable to it – it preys on me – so hence the awful

1 For KG's seventieth birthday, 16 June 1987.
2 In a letter of 16 April 1987 to KG, IB had confessed to feelings of guilt at not having taken the trouble to attend a party to celebrate Joe Alsop's birthday – presumably his 75th, 1985.
3 In 1987 the annual general meeting and dinner, BA, were held 2 July.

voice of duty – all v. Hebraic I suppose – oh if I had Alan Pryce Jones's or Mrs Longworth's character! – I just had to go on pouring this out to you – tedious for you it must be – if only to alleviate my own mortification (it doesn't alleviate it much) – if I cd have come without horrible gnawing conscience, I wd fly to your side (& that of the five hundred others) with passionate eagerness & certainty of a marvellous evening. [...]

    All my love –

    darling Kay –

      Isaiah

You won't be able to read this without torture: but I *could not* dictate it. [...]

TO SHIRLEY ANGLESEY

    22 June 1987

                                   Headington House

Dearest Shirley,

    [...] I have never seen *Storm* by Ostrovsky;[1] I know *Katya Kabanova* uses it as a libretto – but I like almost all Ostrovsky that I have ever seen. I saw it only in Moscow during my 'years of government service', i.e. my four months in 1945, and would love to see it again, even in English. Meanwhile, we are about to do *Onegin* in Russian at Covent Garden, with surtitles, which I passionately believe in – they make a huge difference to me, even in 'easy' operas like *The Magic Flute* or *The Barber of Seville*, or, indeed, English operas, when not a word can ever be understood as sung nowadays, at ENO or anywhere else. Anyway, Covent Garden is gradually moving towards doing all its operas with surtitles, not every night but, say, on two or three nights out of six, which I welcome.

    I leave the board of that great institution in July. There are tremendous changes about to occur. The opera committee, over which I have presided with indifferent success for two stretches, is being abolished by John Sainsbury; so is the ballet committee. Instead of that, two boards with their own budgets are being introduced – I think rather a good idea. And all the 'oldies', as Colette Clark[2] unkindly calls us, are being swept out in one fell swoop, I dare say rightly [...]; and a body, I should guess, of young, vigorous City tycoons, who may or may not distinguish one note from another, are being imported to give Covent Garden a totally new facelift – face, because

1 *Groza* [*The Storm*], an 1859 social realist play by Aleksandr Nikolaevich Ostrovsky (1823–86) about the unhappily married Katerina Kabanova, her domineering mother-in-law Marfa Ignat'evna Kabanova and her weak husband Tikhon Ivanovich Kabanov, is the basis for the libretto by Vincenc Červinka (1877–1942) for Janáček's 1921 opera *Katya Kabanova*.

2 Colette Elizabeth Dickson Clark (b. 1932), daughter of the art historian Kenneth Clark; friend and assistant of Margot Fonteyn; director, ROH.

the real work will be done by Jeremy Isaacs,[1] who is very energetic and im-aginative and tough, above all tough. How he will live with the equally tough John (Sainsbury), whose last remark at the board which I attended was, in answer to some underling's complaint that unless certain facts were in by a certain date the printers couldn't print the tickets, 'I am not used to taking no for an answer' – 'That is quite true,' I said, thus producing a slight relaxa-tion of tension during the giggles that followed – well, how they will live together, we shall see. [...]

Now, to more important matters. *Lady Macbeth of the District of Mtsensk*:[2] I haven't been to see it. I am inhibited from doing so, perhaps unreason-ably: the critics went overboard and said how marvellous the production, as well as the orchestral playing, was, and how wonderful Barstow[3] was; it may all well be true. I am very put off by Pountney[4] – his *Queen of Spades*[5] was a nightmare (actually, he produced it as one, a nightmare in the anti-hero's head); so was *Mazeppa*,[6] though I don't think that was him, only some disciple. He twists things, adds, takes away, distorts – in this case, all those butchers' corpses, in other cases all kinds of other additions of a, to me, highly distracting kind. The characters who are supposed to be off the stage cover themselves with blankets and sit on it, dark figures not in the libretti appear and disappear.

Perhaps there is something to be said for all this, I think a second or third look at masterpieces is permitted; but in the case of classical masterpieces these effects are totally, to me, vulgar and destructive – and indeed this is the view of one or two critics, who keep begging him to keep his hands off the classics. It may be said that *Lady Macbeth* is not among them – that is perfectly true. My hesitation about going to the Coliseum is somewhat different: I knew Shostakovich, he stayed with us when he got his degree at Oxford;[7] I then went with him to the rehearsals of the amended, or weak-

1 Jeremy Israel Isaacs (b. 1932), Kt 1996; television producer and executive; chief executive, Channel Four TV Co., 1981–7; director, ROH, 1985–97, general director 1988–97.

2 *Lady Macbeth of the Mtsensk District*, opera by Dmitry Shostakovich, premiered in Leningrad 1934; though a success with audiences, and apparently with the authorities, it was anonymously con-demned in *Pravda* 1936, and henceforth effectively banned. Shostakovich subsequently reworked the piece, which was reborn as *Katerina Izmailova* (327/1). Its British stage premiere was David Pountney's production at the London Coliseum, home of the ENO, 22 May 1987: a staging 'not easily [...] forgotten for its sardonic brilliance' (*Opera*, September 2001, 110).

3 Josephine Clare Barstow (b. 1940), DBE 1995, opera singer; debut 1964 with Opera for All; studied at London Opera Centre 1965–6; Katerina in the ENO production of *Lady Macbeth*.

4 David Willoughby Pountney (b. 1947), freelance director; director of productions, Scottish Opera 1976–80, ENO 1982–93; has undertaken guest productions for all the major Britsh opera companies.

5 First presented at the ENO 20 January 1983, and described as an 'unnerving success' by Paul Griffiths: 'Through a Madman's Eyes', *Times*, 21 January 1983, 9a.

6 Tchaikovsky's 1884 opera, produced by David Alden at ENO 1984 in a low-budget staging, 'complete with bloody chainsaw massacre', hailed by Andrew Clements as one of the 'Ten Productions That Changed British Opera': *Guardian*, 20 August 2011, supplement, 11.

7 Shostakovich was made an hon. DMus at the Encaenia ceremony of 26 June 1958: L2 637–41.

ened, *Lady Macbeth* (called then *Katerina Izmailova*) at Covent Garden,[1] and translated for him, for his English was non-existent. In the course of this he more or less made plain to me what he intended this piece to be, how he intended it to be performed; although, being a man of appallingly timorous disposition, he was still shivering and trembling at the thought of too much sex, too much violence, all the things which Stalin had condemned, and every time the heroine approached the bed on which the lover, after his beating, is nursing his wounds, he would rush forward to the stage with me, and say to me (which I would then have to yell at the producer), 'Further away, further away, don't let her approach the bed, at least three yards to the side', and so on. However this may be, I think I do know the piece quite well, having seen it at Covent Garden three times, as I say, once with commentary and explanations by the composer. The earlier version, I am sure, is more gifted, 'stronger', more surrealistic, more obviously influenced by Berg[2] and Mahler,[3] and therefore more worth hearing, and I should be glad to hear it on the radio; but I think I should be too upset at seeing the mauling which Pountney cannot not have given it, for he plays nothing straight, there always has to be some kind of ferocious distortion – he imposes a personality on these works ruthlessly, and to me destructively. Hence my reluctance. [...]

Much love from Aline, and to Henry, [...]

Isaiah

TO ARYE CARMON[4]

1 July 1987 [*carbon*]

Headington House

Dear Professor Carmon,

Thank you very much for your letter of 15 June. I realise, of course, that the antidotes to the false and damaging charges, and disgusting inventions, about Nazi–Zionist collaboration[5] etc., cannot be successfully rebutted by

---

1 *Katerina Izmailova* was first staged at Covent Garden 2 December 1963: Shostakovich spent the last 2 months of that year travelling between London and Riga to work on productions of the opera.

2 Alban Maria Johannes Berg (1885–1935), Austrian composer of modest output but wide influence; his opera *Lulu* (1935) was contemporaneous with Shostakovich's *Lady Macbeth* (1932), and his other works include *Wozzeck* (1922).

3 Gustav Mahler (1860–1911), Austrian composer, conductor and pianist; conducted the Vienna State Opera 1897–1907, the Met 1908–10.

4 Arye Zvi Carmon (b. 1943), expert on political reform (and photographer); founding president (1991) and senior fellow, Israel Democracy Institute, Jerusalem; has published extensively on the Holocaust and on Israel–Diaspora relations.

5 *Perdition*, a play by Jim Allen, had been due to open at the Royal Court 22 January 1987. Its 'central thesis is that Zionists collaborated with Adolf Eichmann, the SS chief, in Hungary in 1944 in an operation which led to the death of hundreds of thousands of people at Auschwitz' ('Play Attacked for "Slur" on Zionists', *Times*, 15 January 1987, 6b–c at 6b). The cancellation of the play after protests from the British Jewish community led to letters in *The Times* from, among others, Allen, Martin Gilbert and Bernard Levin. The *Times* columnist Barbara Amiel wrote that the play

the mere publication of a kind of solid, possibly dull, authoritative work, such as I spoke of to Mr Barclay. [...]

But I must repeat that I still think that the book I am contemplating is indispensable. *The Protocols of the Elders of Zion*[1] would never have been nailed as a forgery if a series of articles in *The Times*, written by their correspondent Philip Graves,[2] had not, point by point, refuted the entire thing and told the true story of the original in the 1860s, the transference of the charges from the Jesuits to the Jews by Nilus in Russia, etc; and whenever the thing crops up again, as of course it has done since, one can refer to that notorious exposure as compelling evidence of the falsification. Exactly this has to be done with regard to Nazis and Zionists. I do not think that schoolchildren or ordinary readers or the left-wing extremists in Britain, Europe or America – Trotskyites and the like – would read this book, but that is not the point. Provided that there is a single, solid, dependable exposé of the facts, even if some of them are delicate and uncomfortable, this can be used as a crushing weapon from time to time. Of course this will not work in the Middle East, where the *Protocols* are also busily circulating, or among lunatic-fringe groups – White Russians, the new Soviet nationalists, certain somewhat degraded Catholic circles, etc. [...].

I do not think that it will be 'thin'. When someone at the Institute of Jewish Affairs suggested that such a work ought to be published under their auspices, I explained that in my view this would have no effect whatever on the people at whom it is aimed – gentiles, quite decent uninformed people who are today taken in to a large degree by propaganda, both from the right and the left. No doubt Jewish anti-defamation activities are of value, but the books which really put across the notion of the neglect, indifference to the fate, of the murdered Jews in the Holocaust are not Martin Gilbert's, who could be accused of bias, not Wasserstein,[3] but the man whose name I cannot

'argues that Hungarian Zionists collaborated with the Nazis on the grounds that the more awful the massacre of the Jews, the better the chances of establishment of the state of Israel. The play's author, Trotskyist Jim Allen, went even further in interviews, saying that all over Europe "Jews were massacred because their leaders covered up for the Nazis"' ('Perdition: Killed by its Blatant Lie', 24 January 1987, 16b–e at 16b).

1 This forgery by the Russian religious writer Sergey Aleksandrovich Nilus (1862–1929), supposedly the manifesto of a Jewish conspiracy aiming at worldwide domination, first appeared in the Russian newspaper *Znamya* 1903, and was widely circulated after the Russian Revolution. It was published in London 1920 in Nilus' *The Jewish Peril*, but a series of articles by Philip Graves (next note) in *The Times* 1921 revealed that it consisted largely of 'clumsy plagiarisms' from Maurice Joly's satire against Napoleon III, *Dialogue aux enfers entre Machiavel et Montesquieu* (Geneva, 1864) ('The End of the "Protocols"', *Times* leader, 18 August 1921, 9c–d at 9d), which made only passing reference to Jews, and itself drew on the works of the French novelist (Joseph Marie) Eugène Sue, where the conspirators were Jesuits. Despite these and other exposures, the *Protocols* were used for anti-Semitic purposes by the Nazis, and resurfaced as anti-Jewish propaganda during the conflict between Israel and Palestine.

2 Philip Perceval Graves (1876–1953), journalist, *Times* correspondent in Constantinople/Istanbul 1908–14, 1919–46; served in Near East while in the army 1915–19.

3 Bernard Wasserstein (b. 1948), British historian of Israel and of modern Jewish history; associate

remember who wrote *While Millions Died*.[1] The man who is believed when he writes letters denouncing Irving[2] for falsification of the facts about Hitler and the Holocaust is not a Jew but an Englishman of impeccable Church of England loyalties.

That is my case.

Yours sincerely,

Isaiah Berlin

TO DANIEL BELL

7 November 1987

Headington House

Dear Dan (surely after all these years we could be permitted to symbolise the friendship that we feel – I don't know whether it is you or I who has been responsible for this formal style, but I am perfectly willing to take the blame),

I greatly enjoyed your lecture, and shall be glad to read it if you have a text. About your reference to my view: I was not troubled but was indeed somewhat puzzled about the need to 'bend' principles, which you attributed to me.[3] I don't think I talk about principles much (or do I?), so much as values or ends, and I do believe, as you know, that ultimate values can clash, and that in such situations one has to choose, and that to sacrifice one value in favour of another can be exceedingly painful, and not, as some utilitarians seem to think, leaving one with a perfectly quiet and contented conscience, and no regret, since one has obeyed the rules (whatever they may be). Sometimes, of course, one has to perform a trade-off – so much for value *a*, so much for value *b* – if that can be done, and how much, for how long, and where and when, are matters for individual judgment, which can often be defended on consequentialist grounds.

So all I niggle at is your use of the words 'bending principles', while

---

prof. of history, Brandeis, 1980–2, prof. 1982–96; president, Oxford Centre for Hebrew and Jewish Studies, and fellow, St Cross, 1996–2000.

1 Arthur D. Morse (1920–71), US WW2 historian, best known for his *While Six Million Died: A Chronicle of American Apathy* (NY, 1968).

2 David John Cawdell Irving (b. 1938), British historian of WW2 and Holocaust denier (409/1).

3 Bell had given the Leonard Schapiro Lecture at the LSE, 'The End of Ideology Revisited', 29 October, and, as he wrote in a letter to IB of 1 November, he had been asked afterwards for his views on 'the principle[s] of merit and affirmative action in the US as contrary objectives'. He replied that he 'upheld the merit principle in selection' but that in specific situations 'would "bend" the principle, knowing full well that I had done so, for sometimes such compromises are necessary to redress specific injustices, but I did so as a compromise but not the surrender of the principle'. He continued: 'I remarked, as I recall, that this was the position you had taken when there were often contrary objectives that seemed incompatible, that while you held to the primary belief in one principle you would be ashamed if this stood in the way of remedying specific instances of injustice, but that such a compromise was not the surrender of a principle.' And he quoted from *Four Essays on Liberty* (423/5): 'To avoid glaring inequality or widespread misery, I am ready to sacrifice some, or all, of my freedom: I may do so willingly and freely' (125; L 172). Values generate principles, and IB's point here seems pedantic. Cf. 361, 435, 474.

retaining them. Principles for me imply rules, and while of course there can be a clash between rules, what I am mainly concerned with is values embodied in policies or decisions or ways of life – e.g. how much freedom for how much equality, how much justice for how much compassion, and the like, rather than the general prevalence of Kantian rules.[1] [...]

Yours,
Isaiah

TO ALISTAIR COOKE
17 November 1987
                                                                    Headington House

Dear Alistair,

How delightful to hear from you – it has cast a great shaft of light upon these dark days. I may be one full year younger than you, but you live in the world and I vegetate in Oxford with bewildered visits to the great metropolis, where I am too old for the gentlest pontifications – quite apart from the fact that the gods have rightly punished me by removing the use of one of my vocal cords, as a lesson that other people should occasionally be allowed to get a word in edgeways. Still, not to be able to speak in public – strictly forbidden by the doctors – is a source of enormous relief, and a great blessing, if they but knew it, to potential audiences of all kinds.

[...] You live in a much more turbulent milieu[2] – out with Bork,[3] out with Ginsburg,[4] the best of the White House, Camarilla, wobbling tight-ropes, no predictable successor to the Presidency, and, upon it all, crooks, chaos, voices of doom. Have I any money left? I have no idea. So long as I have meals, if reduced, each day, and shelter, I do not ask: I have a feeling that whether one is rich or poor or in the middle, as in 1931, provided one did not need to sell everything in order not to starve, literally, but held on to what one had, then eventually it was a gain. At least I hope so.

We live under a matriarchal dictatorship – there is not a cabinet minister who can act without permission or develop views of his own. All chance of that is gone [...]. It is a more than Periclean dictatorship;[5] not exactly

---

1 i.e. universal, exceptionless rules.
2 The Reagan presidency had run into difficulties over the Iran–Contra Affair, in which National Security Council staff had secretly sold arms to Iran and, in defiance of Congress, used the proceeds to fund the Contra rebels in their fight against the left-wing Sandinista government of Nicaragua.
3 Robert Heron Bork (1927–2012), US federal appellate judge; solicitor general 1973–7; nominated to supreme court by President Reagan 1 July 1987, but rejected by the Democrat-controlled senate, after intense interest-group lobbying, on the basis of his conservatism 23 October 1987.
4 Douglas Howard Ginsburg (b. 1946), US federal appellate judge; nominated to supreme court after Bork's rejection, but withdrew 7 November 1987, before his nomination was formalised, when it emerged that he had smoked marijuana while on the Harvard law faculty.
5 Pericles (c.495–429 BCE), Greek statesman, leader of Athens from 461; according to the Greek

malevolent, but anti-intellectual, philistine, suspicious of ideas, hearts, the least expensive embellishments of life, to a degree unequalled in this country in my time. I remember that when Montague James[1] was the Provost of King's, an aged fellow – perhaps Nathaniel Wedd[2] or some such name – said 'So this is the end of thinking at King's.' *Mutatis mutandis* I feel the same. You and I, Cassandra to Cassandra, perhaps it all cancels out in the end.

Yours ever,

Isaiah

TO THE EDITOR OF THE *FINANCIAL TIMES*

[19? December 1987][3]

Garrick Club

Sir, – Critics are entitled to some degree of aberration, but Dominic Gill,[4] in his now notorious notice of one of Alfred Brendel's Schubert recitals, seems to me to abuse the privilege. Mr Brendel does not need defence from anyone – it is rather Mr Gill who stands in need of it. I have no doubt that his piece will do far more damage to his reputation than it could conceivably do to that of Mr Brendel.

I remember that similar charges – an intellectual approach, didacticism and so on – were made in London before the Second World War against Artur Schnabel;[5] in effect, that he thought when he played. These are now, at best, historical curiosities.

Isaiah Berlin

historian Thucydides, under Pericles 'What was democracy in name became in practice rule by its first citizen': *History of the Peloponnesian War* 2. 65. 9.

1 Montague Rhodes James (1862–1936), OM 1930; Provost of King's, Cambridge, 1905–18, of Eton 1918–36.

2 Nathaniel Wedd (1864–1940), fellow, King's, Cambridge, and for many years classical lecturer and assistant tutor there; lecturer in classics, Newnham, and lecturer in ancient history, Cambridge.

3 'He Thinks When He Plays', *Financial Times*, 22 December 1987, 19; see also the reply by Robert Snaith, 'The Honest Music Critic and a Question of Technique', 31 December 1987, 11: 'Sir Isaiah […] invokes the comparison with the late Artur Schnabel, and it is apt: both artists in their different ways are notable for a profusion of interesting insights and ideas coupled with technical limitations which tend to obstruct their projection.'

4 Dominic Gill, music critic of the *Financial Times*. 'Brendel/Festival Hall', Gill's excoriating review of Brendel's Schubert recital at the Royal Festival Hall, London, on 8 December appeared in the *Financial Times*, 10 December 1987, 25: 'What sort of great Schubert playing was this of the famous E flat and A flat Impromptus, flat and didactic, as technically undistinguished as it was expressively unsurprising?'

5 Artur Schnabel (1882–1951), Polish-born pianist and composer. Of his playing before the war *The Times* remarked: 'That it is the result of an exceptionally long and deep study of every detail of the music will not be questioned. But that the listener cannot fail to be aware of this suggests, perhaps, a criticism of its manner as a whole.' 'The Musician's Gramophone', 10 August 1938, 10d.

TO JOSEPH BRODKSY

21 December 1987

Headington House

Mileishii drug,[1]

I wish I could write Russian, in Russian, but I cannot – I can read, I can speak (up to a point), but if I try to write it, Latin letters come creeping in and the whole thing is a kind of Nabokovian kaleidoscope.

I think about you continually (like Stephen Spender, in his poem 'I think continually of those who were truly great'),[2] and wish you were here. One often says that out of politeness, but you will realise how genuine these words are – I suspect that you, too, would not strongly object to my intermittent presence in your neighbourhood. But although I was coming to New York this *sochel'nik*[3] (I am becoming more and more like Nicolas Nabokov, this must stop), we have decided not to – too far, too old, too exhausting. We go to our house in Italy, then *Don Giovanni* in Milan, then home again, and the ghastly prospect of having to write a piece to celebrate a prize[4] (not quite Nobel, far from it; but not totally, in the literal sense, valueless, but entailing television, a lecture etc.; goodness, why do I accept? – vanity, weakness, anxiety to please, to show that there is somewhere where I too am appreciated?). All this is a burden – I have no fresh ideas. Simply to dip into the old pot and extract spoonfuls of the old familiar broth, slightly warmed up, is too depressing. But it is all I am capable of doing.

But what I really want to say, apart from all this, is thank you, thank you, for Shestov[5] (how much do I owe you? – it would genuinely distress me not to pay). Your respect for him moves me deeply – who else besides you and me even think about him now? (It is a great nuisance that John Bayley has praised him somewhere – how dare he? They say that a cat may dare to look at a king, but I am not sure.)

I have suddenly received a postcard, asking me whether I know whether Akhmatova had an affair before the Revolution with some Grand Duke, or, my correspondent suggested, with Nicholas II[6] – that was the most likely

---

1 'Dearest friend'.
2 The 1st line of Spender's 'The Truly Great' (1931?), no. 33 in *Poems* (London, 1933), 37–8.
3 'Christmas Eve'.
4 The inaugural Senator Giovanni Agnelli International Prize for the Ethical Dimension in Advanced Societies, 1988 (334–5).
5 Lev Isaakovich Shestov (1866–1938) né Yehuda Leyb Schwarzmann, Russian existentialist philosopher; unable to accommodate himself to the Soviet regime, he left Moscow 1918, and Russia 1920, settling in Paris 1921: IB owned several books by Shestov, and perhaps one or more of them had been sent to him by Brodsky.
6 Nicholas II (1868–1918), last tsar of Russia 1895–1917; discontent with his autocratic rule contributed to the revolution of 1905; he abdicated March 1917, and was imprisoned with his family after the October 1917 Bolshevik Revolution; they were executed by the Bolsheviks at Ekaterinburg 11 July 1918.

indication. How do you think Anna Andreevna would have received this suggestion? With how much annoyance, how much amusement? The thought of secret meetings in Tsarskoe Selo;[1] the suspicious Gumilev,[2] Aleksandra Fedorovna,[3] both in heavy disguise, creeping along the neoclassical wall in an attempt to surprise them, like the last act of *Nozze di Figaro*[4] – an absurd yet deeply unworthy thought, like a surrealist scene by a totally giftless, deservedly unsuccessful hack writer.

But I must not go on.[5] Do let me know when you are back in Europe. I shall not come to the United States for at least a year, but I hope to see Bob in Leningrad. I expect he will have told you: I want to go when Brendel is playing.[6] He has just received very hostile notices in two or three London papers:[7] it really upsets one, me much more than him ⟨(but it *did* upset him: encomium by Bern[ard] Levin[8] in the Times[9] does *not* compensate.⟩. I have written a ferocious letter to one of the papers, the *Financial Times* – I think too tough for them to print, but we shall see. As I never read this paper, I may never know, unless my victim answers, and even then I doubt if I shall learn of it.

But I am beginning to talk nonsense again: I must stop, I must stop.

Yours,

Исайя[10]   [...]

---

1 'Tsar's Village' (because the tsars had a palace there), south of St Petersburg/Petrograd, where Akhmatova lived as a child, and again when she married Gumilev (next note); now part of the town of Pushkin.

2 The poet Nikolay Stepanovich Gumilev (1886–1921), Akhmatova's 1st husband 1910–18.

3 Alexandra Feodorovna Romanova (1872–1918) née Victoria Alix Helena Louise Beatrice von Hessen und bei Rhein, from 1894 (last) Empress consort of Russia, wife of Tsar Nicholas II.

4 In the last act of Mozart's opera *The Marriage of Figaro* the Countess Rosina Almaviva is disguised as her maid Susanna, and vice versa, and there is an assignation in a garden.

5 Pat Utechin interpolates: '(I agree! P.U. secretary)'.

6 See 336.

7 For example, Nicholas Kenyon, 'Prophet of Doom', *Observer*, 13 December 1987, 19: 'I don't know why Brendel [...] should feel the need to pound the second group of themes so awkwardly.' And Meirion Bowen, in 'The True Challenge of Schubert', *Guardian*, 17 December 1987, 10, calls Brendel's performances 'characteristically intense, though sometimes wayward'.

8 (Henry) Bernard Levin (1928–2004), writer and broadcaster, studied at LSE under Karl Popper and Harold Laski; became a television star through his 1963 appearances on the satirical show *That Was The Week That Was*; enjoyed a wide readership as a political columnist for *The Times* 1970–97; interviewed IB for BBC2 TV 1981.

9 'Music's Sublime Summit', 21 December 1987, 10b ff.: 'we, under the benign presidency of Sir Isaiah, constitute the Brendel Groupies, mutually pledged not to miss any of his concerts or recitals unless we are abroad, jailed, in hiding from our creditors, undergoing open-heart surgery or fighting drunk. [...] To explore [the greatness of Schubert] in the company of Alfred Brendel's playing is to reach as far into the mystery as mortals can hope to get.'

10 'Isaiah'.

*In November IB had learned that he was to be the first recipient of the bien-
nial Senator Giovanni Agnelli International Prize for the Ethical Dimension
in Advanced Societies, endowed by the Fiat company in honour of its founder,
Giovanni Agnelli.*[1] *The prize was intended*

to draw attention to the need for reflection on the role of ethical principles
in modern society. Economic, scientific and technological progress has been
accompanied by a growing uncertainty about the moral and cultural values
that are fundamental to modern society. The prize, by recognising outstanding
contributions to our understanding of the ethical dimension in modern society,
seeks to strengthen public thought and action concerning the ethical problems
that confront us.[2]

*IB replied to numerous letters of congratulation by confessing that he was sur-
prised at the award, since he had neither written on ethics as it was understood
in academic circles, nor taken the slightest interest in advanced industrial societies. This typical self-deprecation is not to be taken at face value: IB spent much
of his life, and his last years in particular, grappling with ethical issues, and
the need to deliver a lecture at the prize-giving ceremony in Turin in February
inspired him to compose a succinct statement of his 'general credo', 'On the
Pursuit of the Ideal', published in the NYRB the next month.*[3]

*The Agnelli Prize came with a substantial sum of money, half of which
(some £70,000) IB used to create an Oxford fund to facilitate exchanges between
British and Italian scholars in the fields of modern history, art and literature.*

TO KEITH THOMAS

22 December 1987 [*manuscript*]

[Headington House]

Dear Keith,

[…] Thank you ever so much for your congratulations. The whole thing
was a total surprise to me, as you may imagine. I had never heard of the
foundation; I didn't know that anyone had thought of me in connection with
any prize, anywhere; and when the two Italians who represented it came to
see me in London, they beat about the bush for about half an hour before
half rising from their chairs and announcing that I was the first recipient
of this great (in financial terms, certainly) prize, and that I was to deliver
some kind of address indicating my ethical views, as it was for ethics that
I had been chosen. I did my best to convey to them that I had never written
an essay on moral philosophy, as such, in my life, and that I was not really

---

1 Giovanni Agnelli (1866–1945), Italian industrialist; co-founder of the Fiat car company 1899; managing director 1900, chairman 1920, in control until his death; senator for life 1923.
2 'The Senator Giovanni Agnelli International Prize', NYRB, 17 March 1988, 15.
3 *On the Pursuit of the Ideal* (Turin, 1988); NYRB, 17 March 1988, 11–18; repr. as 'The Pursuit of the
   Ideal' in CTH and PSM; for 'general credo' see 466.

suitable for their purposes, and that Rawls,[1] e.g., or even Hare, Hampshire, Williams etc. etc. would meet the case more obviously. But it was no use. I am to go to Turin.

In the meanwhile, the *Daily Telegraph* has announced that I come from Lettonia[2] (wherever that may be) and that I occasionally lecture at Oxford – and that is roughly all, but for a few journeys to America and the like. The *Corriere della Sierra* is more precise in describing me as a Latvian philosopher – there are not many of that breed, and I can without excessive vanity claim to be a leading Latvian philosopher (so far as I know, there are literally none, and never have been any – it is the only Baltic state of which I believe this to be true). Some strange things were apparently said about me in the *Guardian*, which I haven't seen, such as that I was Warden of All Souls?[3] I gather this from the fact that Neill has offered to resign in my favour instantly, if I so want it. I relieved his feelings.

I thought from the words of my Italian ambassadors that I was getting one-tenth part of the sum which has in fact been awarded, and thought even that rather a lot: as it is, I shall be expected to disburse quite a lot of it to a good cause, and have thought of at least one in Oxford which might not take it amiss. I mustn't go on babbling. Thank you ever so much for your very nice and very welcome letter, especially as it is virtually the only one on the subject that I have received from any academic – hence the rapidity of my reply.

Yours ever,

Isaiah

The First Intifada ('uprising') against the Israeli occupation of Palestinian territories began in December 1987, and throughout that month The Times *carried reports of violent confrontations between Palestinian youths and the IDF, principally in Gaza. The Israeli government's response to the crisis attracted international condemnation,[4] and gravely concerned IB, whose thoughts turned to his friends in Jerusalem.*

---

1 John Bordley Rawls (1921–2002), John Cowles Prof. of Philosophy, Harvard, 1975–9, James Bryant Conant University Prof. 1979–91; Rawls emphasised the rights of the individual over utilitarian notions of the common good, and his *A Theory of Justice* (Harvard, 1972) is credited with rejuvenating the study of political philosophy, though IB's work also played its part in this, especially *Two Concepts of Liberty* (Oxford, 1958). IB later wrote to Rawls acknowledging *A Theory of Justice* as a 'masterpiece – for such I, too, truly think it to be' (9 May 1978).

2 Italian for Latvia. Announcement untraced.

3 Untraced.

4 See e.g. Mohsin Ali, 'US Castigates Israel over Crackdown in Occupied Areas', *Times*, 16 December 1987, 6c–d, a report that ran directly beneath Ian Murray, 'Stones against Guns as Gaza Toll Grows', ibid. 6c–g.

TO TEDDY KOLLEK

19 January 1988

Headington House

Dear Teddy,

You must be having a terrible time. Aline and I tried to telephone you last night, because of the situation described in a famous line from a poem by Lermontov:[1] 'Tedium, sadness, and no one to shake by the hand'.[2] As usual, you are the only light in all this rapidly gathering darkness. We shall try to telephone all the same, just to hear your voice. We didn't realise until the radio this morning that last night (or yesterday sometime) you were talking to some Mufti or other. Thank God you are still there to do even as much as that. It looks dreadful from here and only dear Mrs de R[othschild] remains desperately uncritical, although uncharitably I propose to shake her a little. Jacob is thinking of other things. I must not go on in this unkind fashion. Let me shake you by the hand. [...]

Much love to both,

Isaiah

IB's prediction to Dita Shklar in December 1980 that he would never again visit the Soviet Union proved mistaken: in March 1988 he overcame his inhibitions, and, rather than 'watch from outside', went to see 'that terrible world' again at first hand.[3]

TO SHIRLEY ANGLESEY

5 April 1988

Headington House

Dearest Shirley,

We are indeed back from Moscow and Leningrad, and my only impressions are those of private visits: all the public things you know as well as I do – there is nothing new in my observations or, I dare say, Aline's. Once more, I had the acute and lasting impression (the same as in 1945 and 1956) that when one meets people they are either in some official position – guides or officials or heads of galleries or theatres – in which case what they say is guarded and designed to forward whatever they regard as their professional interest within the framework of Soviet orthodoxy, old or new; these people are not really worth talking to as individuals, even though they may have

1 Mikhail Iur'evich Lermontov (1814–41), Russian Romantic poet, novelist and dramatist; an army officer, he was exiled to a regiment in the Caucasus for his elegy to Alexander Pushkin, *Death of the Poet* (1837), which was highly critical of the Russian court; like Pushkin he died in a duel.
2 The 1st line of an 1840 poem known by its opening words as 'I skuchno i grustno' (literally 'Bored and sad').
3 147.

quite interesting things to say about what goes on within their realms. And, on the other hand, people not so connected – private individuals whom one can meet in buses, trains, wherever, plus the disapproved-of figures who live on the edges of official society, who are full of imagination, life, humour, and touching and delightful in the most enormous – to me, at least – degree. I did meet several such, and from them I carried away extremely vivid impressions: including, of course, the noble Sakharov, than whom there is no more morally wonderful person in the world – unless it be Mother Teresa,[1] but she is somehow professionally so, as well as genuinely – he, on the other hand, doesn't need to be and is. All that I can tell you about when we meet. [...]

Yours ever,

Isaiah

TO BERNARD LEVIN

5 April 1988

Headington House

Dear Bernard,

I did as you instructed me to do. I talked about the Uspenskys[2] to various people in the Soviet Onion (as Foreign Office officials used to refer to it during the war – on a par with 'Uncle Joe', etc.). The British ambassador said that the Embassy was in touch with refuseniks in general, they certainly knew Alex Ioffe[3] and they knew the case of the Uspenskys, and brought it up to whomever might be thought to be influential. I had a similar request from Abe Harman,[4] of the Hebrew University, and Martin Gilbert, about a refusenik called Kosharovsky;[5] I managed to telephone him and get him

1 Ajezë Gonxhe Bojaxhiu (1910–97), Macedonian-born ethnic Albanian, known by her religious name, Teresa, after joining the Loreto Convent, Darjeeling, 1931; Roman Catholic nun and missionary who founded the Missionaries of Charity, 1950, to bring relief to the poor of Calcutta; Nobel Peace Prize 1979; later (2003) beatified.

2 Igor Uspensky (b. 1939) and his wife Inna (b. 1932) née Ioffe were both research entomologists at the Moscow Institute of Physics and Technology; their requests for exit visas were refused between 1979 and 1989 on the spurious grounds that Igor's mother, the retired biologist Irina Voronkevich, had had access during her career to state secrets, as had Inna's brother, Alexander Ioffe (next note). Their son Vyacheslav ('Slava') (b. 1969) was also refused permission to leave. Their case was taken up by the American and British governments, and in July 1989 all three received their visas; Igor and Inna subsequently continued their scientific research at the HUJ.

3 Alexander Davidovich Ioffe (b. 1938), mathematician; research engineer (military) 1961–72; associate prof. of applied mathematics, Moscow Institute for Automobile and Road Construction, 1972–6, dismissed when he applied for an exit visa, granted January 1988, when he took up a professorship of mathematics at Technion (Israel Institute of Technology), where he had been given a post in 1979.

4 Avraham ('Abe') Harman (1914–92), British-born Israeli diplomat and administrator; Israeli ambassador to the US 1959–68; president, HUJ, 1968–83.

5 Yuli Kosharovsky (1941–2014), Russian radio electronics engineer; one of the early refuseniks, and subsequently a refusenik leader, among the last to be granted an exit visa; emigrated to Israel January 1989, where he became a leading spokesman for Soviet Jews; one of the dedicatees of

invited to a party the ambassador was giving for the Brendels, etc. He was on
a hunger strike and said he would come but might faint – he came, did not
eat or drink, did not faint; he seemed a very nice man and I had a talk with
him, although all I could do for him was to promise to mention his name,
together with the Uspenskys', to Soviet notables. I did not in fact meet any
Soviet officials or important academics (the head of the Hermitage[1] or of the
Moscow Conservatoire[2] are hardly relevant); so I mentioned these names to
people I did meet, although most of them were like Sakharov, on the wrong,
or decent, side of the line. I am sorry that I could not do more, but I am not
a *persona grata* in influential Soviet circles. Do you know the Soviet ambassador in London?[3] He is among the worst.

> Yours ever,
> Isaiah

TO ED CONE[4]

5 April 1988

Headington House

Dear Ed,

[...] Now, about the Jews. It is awful. You are quite right about giving
money not to the U[nited] J[ewish] A[ppeal], but to specific organisations.
I do the same – not necessarily to those interested in peace (though in effect
I belong to the Peace Now group), but also to universities and the like, all
of whose members – no, not all, but say seventy to eighty per cent – are
perfectly right-minded, and half certainly belong to Peace Now. I think the
Jewish leaders in America ought not to be shy of speaking out. It seems to
me, as it does to the Peace Now people, that the chief obstacle to anything
being achieved on Shultz-like[5] lines is the solid and unwavering support for
the Israel government's policies, no matter how obstinate and fatal, on the

---

Finest Hour, 1939–1941, the 6th vol., by Martin Gilbert, of Randolph Churchill and Martin Gilbert,
Winston. S. Churchill (London, 1966–88).

1 Boris Borisovich Piotrovsky (1908–90), Soviet archaeologist, director, State Hermitage Museum,
St Petersburg, 1964–90.

2 Boris Ivanovich Kulikov (b. 1932), teacher of choral conducting, Moscow Conservatoire, from
1958, prof. from 1977, rector 1975–90; has visited the West on numerous occasions to conduct.

3 Leonid Mitrofanovich Zamyatin (b. 1922), diplomat; USSR ambassador to UK 1986–91; forced
to resign after refusing to condemn the attempted coup by Communist hardliners against
Gorbachev August 1991.

4 Edward Toner Cone (1917–2004), US music scholar, pianist and composer; instructor, dept of
music, Princeton, 1946–7, assistant prof. 1947–60, prof. 1960–85.

5 George Pratt Shultz (b. 1920), US economist, academic, statesman and businessman; President
Reagan's secretary of state 1982–9; in response to the violence of the First Intifada Shultz
embarked on intense shuttle diplomacy, aiming to bring the interested parties into negotiations
according to an agreed timetable; fundamental stumbling blocks were the Shamir government's
extreme reluctance to deal with the PLO, its resistance to any internationalisation of the talks,
and its rejection of the principle, central to Shultz's thinking, of land for peace, adopted in UN
Security Council Resolution 242, passed in the aftermath of the Six Day War.

part of the American Jewish establishment; and anything which can make these people doubt, seriously, the utility from Israel's point of view of their blind support would be a good thing. All I have done so far is to sign a letter[1] with four academic colleagues (Herbert Hart, Ronnie Dworkin, Freddie Ayer and someone else I can't remember – Freddie insisted on signing although only fifty per cent Jewish)[2] supporting the excellent letter in the *New York Times* signed by Henry Rosovsky, Irving Howe,[3] Michael Walzer etc.[4] – you must have seen it. All that was duly reported in the Israeli press, though probably not anywhere else. And another letter, which I think is going the rounds in America or somewhere, again with Rosovsky, and Lord Rothschild, the British Chief Rabbi (Lord Jakobovitz!), Isaac Stern and Saul Bellow, saying more or less the same thing.[5]

I fully understand why Jews don't like doing that sort of thing. The amount of not only anti-Israeli-ism but somewhat cognate and overlapping anti-Semitism has risen so high in the word today (and indeed, in the Soviet Union, where I have just been, where the younger students appeared to be filled with it) that one does not like putting weapons in the hands of the enemies either of Israel or of the Jews. Nevertheless, unless they do give up the West Bank, or large parts of it, they will be overwhelmed by the sheer tide of the Arab birth rate. Quite apart from moral considerations such as the corrupting influence of imposing foreign rule over the Arabs, etc. We have not been deceived by a biased press: no doubt they exaggerate, and like exaggerating – the media have never been particularly in favour of Israel since the Six Day War, when from being underdog they turned into a kind of top dog. Nevertheless, I regret to say that much of what they say is only too true. It really is very depressing, particularly to a lifelong and unrepentant Zionist like me, who continues to believe that the Jews are entitled not to be a minority everywhere, and that the foundation of the Israeli state was entirely justified, even at the expense of Arab rights. [...]

Yours ever,
Isaiah

---

1 Untraced, if indeed it was published.
2 Ayer's mother, Reine Citroën, came from the same Dutch Jewish family as the founder of the car manufacturer of that name.
3 Irving Howe (1920–93) né Horenstein, Bronx-born Jewish American literary and social critic, educator and democratic socialist.
4 'American Jews Must Let Israel Know', NYT, 26 January 1988, A24.
5 This letter was sent to 100 Jewish intellectuals attending a conference on 'The Future of Democracy in Israel' at the Israel Democracy Institute in Jerusalem in March 1988; it urged compromise, and the abandonment of measures that 'are likely sooner or later to lead to moral and political disaster': 'We are committed supporters of Israel. We have its welfare at heart. Consequently we consider it our right and our duty to urge all concerned Jews, both in Israel and outside its borders, to advocate a compromise compatible with the security of the state, without necessarily expecting favourable Arab reactions, before it is too late' (undated letter faxed to Teddy Kollek 10 March 1988). The 7 signatories were the 5 listed by IB, IB himself and Arnold Goodman.

TO SHIRLEY ANGLESEY
    8 April 1988

Headington House

Dearest Shirley,

[...] I did call on Chukovskaya, and a very good two hours it was too. I was sorry to leave when I did, and shouldn't have done – I should have stayed, as she begged me to do, until midnight; but what with the embassy car and ambassadorial arrangements, I couldn't. She was in good health, not blind, not deaf, and absolutely fascinating – a very tough old lady and sharp, stern and extremely nice. The whole Akhmatova circle seem to be marvellous people, and they all know each other, and I was very gratified that I did not need to explain to them who I was – I was just passed from hand to hand. Apart from them and the people who came to the ambassador's[1] party, I really met nobody else of note – or of no note.

    Yours, ⟨with much love⟩
    Isaiah

TO JOSEPH ALSOP
    18 April 1988

Headington House

Dear Joe,

Thank you ever so much for your sweet card about my Agnelli lecture.[2] You would, I think, have enjoyed the occasion – not the lecture or the concert so much as the attendant circumstances. First of all, a tremendous fuss beforehand about what was to be done about the lecture – it was clear to me that it could not be read in English to an audience whose English was imperfect, and particularly if rendered at my pace, in my voice, in the Turin opera house, seating about 1,700. So with difficulty I persuaded the Agnelli Foundation to invite my publisher to get it translated into Italian to read it himself. But it was clear from the beginning that it might actually last (you will not be surprised) more than an hour. That was clearly out of the question, even for more patient persons than the Avvocato;[3] so, after much painful discussion (not at all painful to me, but to the officials of the foundation), the

1 Bryan George Cartledge (b. 1931), KCMG 1985; entered Diplomatic Service 1960; UK ambassador to the USSR 1985–8; Principal, Linacre, 1988–96.
2 334/3.
3 Giovanni ('Gianni') Agnelli (1921–2003), Italian industrialist; grandson of (Senator) Giovanni Agnelli, founder in 1899 of the Turin car manufacturers Fiat (Fabbrica Italiana Automobili Torino); took control of Fiat 1966 and attempted to diversify its operations during a challenging era for European car manufacture; one of the wealthiest men in Italy, Agnelli was known for his playboy lifestyle and dress sense; nicknamed 'L'Avvocato' ('The Lawyer') because he held a law degree, though he did not practise.

thing was cut to about a third or less of its size, and read at breakneck pace by my very nice Italian publisher.[1] I rose, and uttered a few broken words in Italian to thank both Agnelli and the reader, but totally forgot the latter's name. Covered with confusion, I came and sat next to the great Avvocato himself, between him and Helmut Schmidt, Mr Rohatyn,[2] the President of the Italian Senate,[3] [the] seven times prime minister[4] and that sort of thing, and the Avvocato nervously asked me how long Tchaikovsky's Fifth Symphony, which was the next item on the agenda, was likely to last – would it last for longer than a quarter of an hour? (He fidgeted very violently during the Beethoven 'Emperor' Concerto with which we led off.) I said I feared it would last as long as three-quarters of an hour. He looked displeased at that. I told him that Dr Johnson, in such circumstances, recommended people to avert their thoughts and think upon Tom Thumb[5] – I didn't actually say Tom Thumb, which I thought was beyond my benefactor's horizon, but told him to think about something else, as agreeable as he could. He said 'Yes, I will take your advice, I will now think of all the most beautiful women I have ever met; I think this could easily fill up three-quarters, or even an entire hour' – and fell into a delicious reverie.[6]

Lord Weidenfeld[7] was a member of the audience of 1,500. My last glimpse of him was standing at the supper on the upper floor, by himself, with a huge dish piled high with the richest Italian food that could be found, gobbling away, oblivious of all the distinguished friends of Agnelli whom he would by that time already have spoken to and suggested books, conferences, parties and other lollipops to. You would have enjoyed it had you been there, not so much the official part of the proceedings as the social aspects of this enjoyable but, in an Edwardian way, slightly ludicrous event.

Yours ever,

Isaiah

1 Roberto Calasso (b. 1941), writer and publisher; editor, Adelphi, 1962, editoral director 1971, CEO 1990, later (since 1999) president.

2 Felix George Rohatyn (b. 1928), Austrian-born US investment banker, diplomat and adviser to the Democratic Party; US ambassador to France 1997–2000 during the 2nd Clinton administration.

3 Giovanni Spadolini (1925–94), Italian Republican Party politician; prime minister 1981–2; President, Italian senate, 1987–94.

4 Amintore Fanfani (1908–99), Italian Christian Democrat politician, one of the best-known political figures in Italy in the post-war period; prime minister on 6 occasions between 1954 and 1987.

5 Hester Thrale once asked Dr Johnson about the conversational powers of an acquaintance of his: ' "He talked to me at club one day (replies our Doctor) concerning Catiline's conspiracy – so I withdrew my attention, and thought about Tom Thumb" ': Hester Lynch Piozzi, *Anecdotes of the Late Samuel Johnson, LL.D. during the Last Twenty Years of His Life* (London, 1786), 81. Tom Thumb was the eponymous minuscule hero of a C17th English folk tale, and of the celebrated theatrical farce by 'Scriblerus Secundus' (Henry Fielding), *Tom Thumb: A Tragedy* (London, 1730).

6 L'Avvocato (340/3) was linked with the actresses Rita Hayworth and Anita Ekberg, and the socialite Pamela Harriman, among others.

7 (Arthur) George Weidenfeld (b. 1919), Kt 1969, life peer 1976, Vienna-born British publisher; emigrated to UK 1938; co-founder 1948, with Nigel Nicolson, and chair, Weidenfeld & Nicolson; the original publisher in book form of IB's *The Hedgehog and the Fox*.

TO MORTON WHITE
 18 April 1988

Headington House

Dear Morton,

[…] I adored our evening – it is a terrible thing, when one knows people so well and likes them so much, to be divided by enormous spaces, so that one can only see them at huge, irregular intervals. […]

We shall probably be in the USA towards the end of October/beginning of November – possibly Washington rather than New York. But in any case, ask me about Russia then – no matter what might have happened in between, my impressions will still be exceedingly fresh. I did not meet a single person there who did not in fact wish to be somewhere else; and that, in spite of the genuine hope among the artists and intellectuals that their greater freedom will last. But it is all rather like the old story about the rabbi to whom a very poor Jew went saying that his life was intolerable – poverty, squalor, and apart from his wife and many children, a goat tethered in his room, so that he could hardly breathe. What was he to do? The rabbi said 'Bring in another goat.' After some months the man came back and said things were suffocatingly awful. 'Bring in another goat,' said the rabbi sternly. At the end of the year the man came back and said he could not go back, he had decided to commit suicide, life under these conditions was literally unliveable. The rabbi said 'Remove one goat.' The man reported immense relief; the second goat was removed and he became totally content with his life. So, too, in the Soviet Union. Some goats have been removed, but that is about all.

You ask me about my recollections of Washington. My visits to London I remember vividly, and what I was doing in England or Russia during my periods of absence from Washington. The rest is surely somewhat general. The atmosphere I remember very well, better than more recent events – that often happens to old men, doesn't it? When I go to Washington now, and sometimes visit the house where we lived, it is all extremely vivid. It may, of course, be imaginary – I cannot judge – but I do relive it all. I was happy and interested, not quite continuously, but still, for long enough at a time, during my life in Washington. Guilt about horrors which were going on to other people, both in the war and behind German lines, while we, the 3,000 officials, lived in comfort and relative bliss, away from everything – still, it seems to me to have been idyllic, now. Harvard, fairly soon afterwards, and indeed Oxford immediately afterwards, were not at all the same. The work was so infinitely less demanding – five hours' teaching a week. It was all so routine, so mechanical; one could get through the files so easily and simply mark them 'The proof of the pudding is in the eating' or 'Time will show', and that counted for a unit of work done!

Love to Lucia.
Yours ever,
Isaiah

TO HENRY S. RICHARDSON[1]
20 April 1988

Headington House

Dear Richardson,

Thank you very much for your letter of 4 March. I read your paper[2] with the greatest interest and profit, and think that some of your criticisms and strictures have a great deal in them. I naturally tend to think that any criticisms made of me are always just and deserved, but in this case I really do think some of this is true. Nevertheless, I shall attempt to answer your points as best I can. If what I say is not entirely satisfactory, do write back to me and I shall try again. I think correspondences of this kind can do nothing but good, they really do clear one's mind – at least mine – and I am grateful for such exchanges. I tend to be suspicious of my own responsiveness and sense of self-criticism because, in spite of all the attacks, both offensive and based on, it seemed to me, true misunderstanding, that have been made upon me – or sometimes perfectly intelligible criticisms from determinist or Catholic or Marxist positions – I have never really changed my mind about the basic issues about which you have written to me. There must be something wrong with that: I, who have received so many more kicks than ha'pence, should surely consider whether, in view of this, I can be as certain of what I believe as I seem to myself to be. But let that be, and let me begin.

[...] The passage which you quote about Acton:[3] there are two things I'd like to say about that. (a) There are, as I should have made clear and haven't in my writings, two considerations about choice and freedom. There is a basic sense of freedom, in which it is presupposed by the possibility of choice, i.e. either the illusion or the reality of being free to choose between the minimum of two alternatives, to do or be X or not to be or do it. If that minimal degree of choice is removed or aborted in some way, then I don't

1 Henry Shattuck Richardson (b. 1955), assistant prof. of philosophy, Georgetown, 1986–94, associate prof. 1994–2002, later (from 2002) prof.
2 A draft of HSR's 'Constructive Liberalism and Conflicts of Values' (never published), enclosed with a letter dated 4 March which made clear that he had been inspired by several meetings with IB a decade or so earlier, and explained that his paper focused on IB's 'treatment of the themes of plurality and incommensurability among competing ideals and the necessity of living with less than final solutions to this conflict'.
3 From 'Two Concepts of Liberty' (335/1), where IB argues that, because of the essential incompatibility of the ends that men seek, the possibility of conflict 'can never be wholly eliminated from human life [...]. This gives its value to freedom as Acton conceived of it – as an end in itself, and not as a temporary need, arising out of our confused notions and irrational and disordered lives, a predicament which a panacea could one day put right' (L 214)

think anyone in that position could be regarded as capable of human activity in the full sense – it reduces the agent to some sort of animal or robot-like condition. Choice seems to me to be one of the *sine quibus non*[1] ingredients of what it is to be a human being – if one cannot choose at all, I think it is difficult to say that one is, in the ordinary sense of the word, human. It is not just a basic right, it is a basic characteristic – people who are asleep or hypnotised or anaesthetised in some way are not human beings for the purposes of moral philosophy of any kind. That is the basic sense of choice, which underlies everything.

(*b*) Then, of course, there is negative versus positive liberty, etc., and I do not ever say, or hope I do not, that positive liberty is in some sense less of a liberty, or less important than negative liberty. There are two questions we can ask: (1) How many doors are open before me? – how many are open, how many are blocked? – and of course, as I think I say in my piece,[2] the degree of openness or the quality of the doors, etc.; that cannot be defined – but degree of negative liberty simply means the kind and number of doors that are open versus those that are blocked, by human action, direct or indirect (I am only speaking of political liberty, of course). (2) Who is in charge? The state, the Church, the party, the class, the family, the factory manager, my 'real' self or 'true' self, embodied in whom or in what, or how identified?

These are not the same questions; the answers to them are different, though of course they overlap. Benjamin Constant[3] and others are, of course, right in supposing that unless I can determine, to some degree, what it is that I do – i.e. that I am in charge – the number of doors open and closed will be directly affected. So the two questions are not unconnected, nor the two answers, nor the two senses of liberty. The main point, as I am sure you know, is to say that the notion of positive liberty has been far more abused, and led to far more despotism, than that of negative liberty – though that has of course been badly abused too, in the form of untrammelled laissez-faire, child labour, the mockery of the poor if they are told that they are free, at liberty, to live in the Ritz Hotel; or if we tell the weak that there is no law against their subduing the strong, or the carp that it is legally entitled not to be eaten by the pike, etc. Of course I do not deny any of that, although I have been, in my opinion unjustly, accused of it.

[...] you talk of my sense of tragedy in the case of choices. I do not, of

---

1 'Indispensable' (literally 'without which not'; the plural form of *sine qua non*).

2 L 177/1, without the metaphor of the doors, introduced at L 32: 'Such freedom ultimately depends [...] on how many doors are open, how open they are, upon their relative importance in my life.'

3 In 'De la liberté des anciens comparée à celle des modernes' (1819), in Benjamin Constant, *Collection complète des ouvrages publiés sur le gouvernement représentatif et la constitution actuelle, ou Cours de politique constitutionnelle* (Paris and Rouen, 1818–20) iv, part 7, 238–74; trans. as 'The Liberty of the Ancients compared with that of the Moderns', in id., *Political Writings*, ed. Biancamaria Fontana (Cambridge, 1988), 309–28.

course, mean that every choice entails tragic consequences – that would be absurd – only that every choice entails the loss of the unchosen alternative – one of which may be unimportant, or anyhow not to be dignified by the name of 'tragic' in any sense. My point was that in the case of the incompatibility of ultimate ends – of ultimate values such as honour, freedom, love, life – the sacrifice of one of these to the other, which is inevitable, entails the equal inevitability of a tragic loss to the agent, or even community. [...]

Let me make it clear that I do not derive evaluation of freedom from the fact of the conflict of values. These two ideas are different ones – they may affect one another but they are not directly connected; there is no logical relation that I can see. Pluralism is one variety of freedom from oppression or imposed uniformity, but liberty is something different – whether it is negative or positive. It involves, as I said above, a possibility of choice – and even those who believe that all values are in the end compatible, or even entail each other, do not deny the reality of choice, even though it may be, for the rational man or Kantian, always something which does not entail any kind of loss, being what any rational man will be fully satisfied with if he has thought the situation through: the perfect answer, at any rate in principle, entailing no possible regret, remorse or tragic loss. Let me reiterate: liberty in one sense is basic, the one value which is presupposed by all others in human life – without that no choice, no action, subject or object of moral thought; in my sense, no humanity.

Then, of course, there is a question of liberty as one value among many, and that I try to make plain in the text of 'Two Concepts ...'.[1] Certainly, freedom of action – after the basic freedom of choice has been guaranteed – must compete with security, justice, social welfare and all kinds of other things. About that, there need be no neutralism. I put liberty above equality or peace; you put peace or equality above liberty. The social contract requires trade-offs, compromises. Why am I not neutral about which value to choose? I do say there is no overarching criterion of an objective kind which tells us what to do – that is true enough. But in choosing which value to realise, how far to compromise, what is to be done if too many goods – happiness, justice, whatever – are not to be altogether extinguished by some arbitrary choice, what I have to keep in mind is not a non-existent single criterion, in which, as you know, I do not believe, but a pattern of living, a form of life. I do not just choose arbitrarily, I do not say 'I opt for peace', 'I opt for war', 'I opt for mercy', or justice, or whatever, when these conflicts arise, or competition occurs in which something can be given to each of these values without totally crushing any of them. What I have to think about is what fits best into the general form of life which I (and, inevitably, that portion of society with

1 'The extent of a man's, or a people's, liberty to choose to live as he or they desire must be weighed against the claims of many other values, of which equality, or justice, or happiness, or security, or public order are perhaps the most obvious examples.' L 215.

which I am, as a self, bound up, since even I don't think that man is an island) am living, what kind of general pattern a particular solution or intended action fits into.

Let me put it this way. Supposing you are in a moral dilemma – sometimes you decide to go and speak to someone you morally respect in order to discuss what to do. You don't think that the person whose advice you value highly knows more about the facts – the facts are probably much better known to you and perhaps not at all to him – nor that he is in possession of some powerful criterion which is better than yours, more objective, based upon a deeper understanding of some teleological process of life: you may not believe in that in any case. You go to him, I think, because you believe that he understands what goes with what: that if you say to him 'Should I do X or Y?', he has enough insight to point out that if you do X it will conflict with A and B and C and D and E, all of which are part of the pattern of the life which you lead, in which you believe, which you wish to realise, and which the culture of which you are a part – or perhaps even nation, tribe, whatever society you know yourself to be deeply associated with – pursues. Whereas Y will not conflict with these other values, ways of behaviour, purposes. In which case, you should prefer Y to X. All that he can do is parade before you a number of goals which you think you are in pursuit of already, and then try and work out what goes with what, what cancels or irretrievably conflicts with what, etc. That, of course, entails harmonisation, competition, compromise, fitting in, etc. – which, indeed, is what our lives are like, I think.

So in that sense I do not – and I am sorry if my text gave the impression that I did – believe in liberty above everything: of course some liberties have to be pushed aside, to feed people, or save their lives, or increase their welfare, or whatever. In this sense, I think that people who accuse me of atomism (like Taylor), or inclination towards liberal laissez-faire, rugged individualism, obedience to market forces which produce the best solutions, etc. are wrong. Of course men are what they are largely because of the impalpable links, as Burke calls them,[1] which connect them to each other and to generations past and perhaps future, etc. But to deduce from this that the unit of

---

1 Probably a typically Berlinian creative 'quotation' deriving from a passage in *Reflections on the Revolution in France* about 'the great primeval contract of eternal society, *linking* the lower with the higher natures, connecting the visible and invisible world, according to a fixed compact sanctioned by the inviolable oath which holds all physical and all moral natures, each in their appointed place. [...] The municipal corporations of that universal kingdom are not morally at liberty [...] to separate and tear asunder the *bands* of their subordinate community, and to dissolve it into an unsocial, uncivil, unconnected chaos of elementary principles' (our italics). *The Writings and Speeches of Edmund Burke*, ed. Paul Langford (Oxford, 1981–), viii, *The French Revolution*, ed. L. G. Mitchell (1989), 147. The 'bands' become 'links' under the influence of 'linking' – elsewhere 'strands' by assonance and relatedness of meaning – and are then dubbed 'impalpable' or 'unanalysable' by IB. There may also be an elision with what Taine calls the 'myriad threads' connecting C18th French society: *Discours de M. Taine prononcé à l'Académie française* (Paris, 1880), 24–5; cf. CC2 160–1.

action – the agent – is not the individual but a group, a class, an army, seems to me a *non sequitur* of a dangerous kind.

Charles Taylor used to say to me that of course every soldier doesn't know what the general goals of the army are, he doesn't particularly say to himself 'I must attack this, I must win that' etc. – perhaps not. But in the end the army is its components. As sociologists we cannot enumerate them – Collingwood was right, we don't want to know the names and addresses of every member of Wellington's army.[1] But unless the individuals are each drawn by some kind of purpose, if only out of fear, the army cannot march; if enough individuals conceive of ends not compatible with whatever it is the commanders want, there will be a mutiny, and the mutiny will be the action of A and B and C and D – not of groups acting as a unit. I think that the idea of groups not as legal fictions, but as genuine subjects capable of activity, of which individuals in some sense only form component parts – which philosophers have thought (nobody will persuade me that Hegel or Marx did not think in these terms) – is a distortion of the truth. Moral philosophy is about the relations of individuals to each other, not collections of them; and political philosophy is the application of moral philosophy to social groups on the assumption that they are composed of individuals each with not only the capacity for choice but the right to prefer one thing to another, which may lead to a particular consequence in terms of the operations of the market, financial or otherwise, which in turn individuals can reject as socially undesirable, thereby curtailing the freedoms of choice of A and B and C and D. I don't know whether I am making myself clear, I only hope so. [...]

Yes, I do not deny it, I do prefer variety (simply as one value among others)! I fear monistic bullying. I understand the bullies, and they understand me. They understood perfectly well what Turgenev lived by; they lived in the same moral world; he just pursued different goals; but there was a constellation of common values. With people like [this] it is simply a conflict, not tragic. [...]

'Civil conversations'[2] of course take place – there is common ground. But in the end, when there is a real collision between patriotism and personal relations – do I hand over my greatest friend to the police because I discover that he is a traitor to my country? – civil conversations are no good. No doubt I do decide in the end, unless I shoot myself first. Let us say that I do tell the

---

1 Not found in his published writings. Perhaps from the lectures on the philosophy of history that IB attended 1929 (CTH xi).

2 HR had written 'The absoluteness with which the conflicting ideologies are held squashes any chance for a "civil conversation" that could rebuild a common ground', attributing the phrase 'civil conversation', 'with its nice dual overtones of civics and civility', to John Courtney Murray: see Murray's *We Hold These Truths: Catholic Reflections on the American Proposition* (London, 1960), 14, where his introduction of the idea begins: 'Barbarism [...] threatens when men cease to talk together according to reasonable laws. There are laws of argument, the observance of which is imperative if discourse is to be civilised. Argument ceases to be civil when it is dominated by passion and prejudice.'

police: the loss, the sacrifice, of the value of friendship is clearly something that I cannot ignore on the grounds that [a] utilitarian calculus, or something of the sort, gives a clear answer to such a conflict of values. I do not know if you read that Agnelli lecture which the *New York Review of Books* has printed,[1] but there I do give instances of this kind of thing. If I am a member of a resistance movement, and the alternatives are to see my parents tortured to death before my eyes or to betray my comrades, nothing that I can do can avert a tragic result.

It is all very well to discuss these matters in the relatively peaceful Anglo-Saxon context – particularly the American context, which I think is all that Rawls is really thinking about, perhaps quite rightly. But what is the good of that to the Romantic politics which seem to dominate various countries at present? The heroic values of Nietzsche, the absolutes of Dostoevsky – in *The Possessed* is it clear that the revolutionary conspiracies are wholly evil and satanic?[2] What about those who believe in reason of state, of Church, or revolution? When the Russian socialist Plekhanov,[3] at the Congress of 1903, which split the Bolsheviks from the Mensheviks, said 'Everything must be sacrificed to the success of the revolution – *salus revolutiae*' – if he had known more Latin, he'd have said *revolutionis* – '*suprema lex esto*',[4] do you think that it is possible to have a civil conversation between the absolute demands of a revolution and the absolute demands of not torturing children, or mass slaughter of innocents? You may say that these things do not happen all that often – but with the ayatollahs, and swords of every kind, religious, political, personal, roaming the earth, this cannot be said so easily. Of course I agree with you: in practice we must do everything possible to adjust, to steer between the extremes of which you speak – fanatical monism and unprincipled pragmatism. But tell that to people in Beirut, or to Mishima – they, too, must be brought into considerations of what morality (above

1   He had (he refers to it in his letter of 4 March); for the lecture see 334/3.
2   Dostoevsky's novel *Besy* (St Petersburg, 1813), variously translated as *The Possessed*, *The Devils* and *Demons*, depicts as a demonic force the radicalism of a small cell of revolutionaries whose plans ultimately unravel in murder and suicide.
3   Georgy Valentinovich Plekhanov (1856–1918), Russian revolutionary and Marxist theorist; exiled 1880, he collaborated with Lenin, but sided with the Mensheviks in the 1903 split; returned to Russia 1917, but died shortly after the Revolution; his works were an important source for KM, and indeed for IB's later work.
4   'Let the safety of the revolution be the highest law.' IB first paraphrases Plekhanov, who said that 'the success of the revolution is the highest law', and then quotes what Plekhanov says a little later in Latin, importing 'esto' from the ancient principle that inspired Plekhanov's, 'salus populi suprema lex esto' ('let the safety of the people be the highest law': Cicero, *On the Laws* 3. 3. 8). *Protokoly s"ezdov i konferentsii Vsesoyuznoi Kommunisticheskoi Partii (B): vtoroi s"ezd RSDRP, iyul'–avgust 1903 g.*, ed. S. I. Gusev and P. N. Lepeshinsky (Moscow, 1932), and *Vtoroi s"ezd RSDRP, iyul'–avgust 1903 goda: protokoly* (Moscow, 1959), 182 in both editions. The erroneous 'revolutiae', which appears in Plekhanov's notes and in the 1932 edition, has been replaced by the correct 'revolutionis' in the 1959 edition: see 1932 ed., 182/**, and cf. L 69–70.

all, political morality) must embrace. These are the things which I think are strictly tragical.

One more word and I stop. Back to the concept of liberty. Let me once again say that for me the basic sense of liberty is, as you may well suspect, the notion of freedom from chains. I am told by MacCallum[1] and others that freedom is a triadic relation – the liberty of X, from Y, to do Z or to be Z. This is plausible, but I think false. If I am in chains, what I want is for the chains to be struck off – never mind what I want to do next. What I want is to get rid of the chains. If I am tied to a tree I wish to be untied, and at that moment I don't wish to be asked 'And if I untie you, what will you do with your freedom, what do you want to be untied for the sake of, for what purpose?' Freedom can be freedom from being ordered by somebody [who], or something which, I do not identify with what I know to be myself at this moment. This freedom may not be realistic or even morally desirable – of course I have to be ordered at times, of course I can say, 'At my best I wouldn't have done this, therefore if you stop me from doing it you are acting in my "true" interest', but nothing follows about a 'true self'. Of course I must obey – in democracies, at least I invent my own straitjacket, which prevents me from acting freely when it may be improper to try to do so. But the basic sense of freedom is still freedom from obstacles, freedom to act. Equally important, I don't deny for a moment, equally valuable, equally an ultimate end, is self-realisation, the development of my potentialities and powers; or of the potentialities and powers of the group or class or nation to which I am indissolubly connected by Burke's impalpable, unanalysable strands. If in some more primitive sense I am not free from what prevents me from getting going at all, then this noble sense of positive freedom can't be realised. That is really what that lecture was about, though perhaps I didn't make it clear. Perhaps I make it slightly clearer in the Agnelli lecture, which I hope you have [read] or will read.

There now, I don't think I can say much more. I only hope that this is of the slightest use to you – do tell me if it is not.

Yours sincerely,
Isaiah Berlin

1 Gerald Cushing MacCallum, Jr (1925–87), assistant prof., Wisconsin, 1961–6, associate prof. 1966–9, prof. 1969–77; his critique of IB's conception of liberty appeared as 'Negative and Positive Freedom', *Philosophical Review* 76 (1967), 312–34.

TO AHMAD KHALIDI[1]

11 May 1988 [*carbon*]

Headington House

Dear Mr Khalidi,

[...] Of course the subject is as near my heart as it is yours, and you are right to suppose that I have reflected about it as painfully and long as I have, and as you doubtless have also. I have read your letter most carefully, and have this to say.

In the first place, it expresses a perfectly just condemnation of the mal-treatment of the Arab inhabitants of the West Bank; in the second place, it pleads for an international conference, which in your view will – or at least may – succeed in solving this agonising problem. Of course, if one feels morally outraged by a situation, one is perfectly justified in expressing one's feelings – with that I naturally sympathise. My feelings may not be as acute as yours, because I can also see the problems of Israel, and its reaction to being surrounded by enemies who, whatever may be done to redress injustice, will, I am sure (as Conor Cruise O'Brien,[2] in my opinion rightly, maintains), go on hating it. I think that is probably natural and unavoidable, however unfortu-nate it may be in the circumstances. But during my long life I could not help observing that expressions of purely moral condemnation have seldom if ever had much effect on the political behaviour of nations or parties. If one really wants to change things, it is more effective, in my view, to appeal to self-interest, moral, political and social, than simply to denounce, even if this is justified.

In this case, I believe that the preservation of the state of Israel prob-ably entails the evacuation of at least part of the West Bank, or at any rate measures which result in the abandonment of Israeli rule over one million and a half Arabs – which might not have occurred but for the Six Day War, which could not but increase the siege mentality of the Israelis, to which I think much of the present trouble is inevitably due. I do not believe that an international conference, for which Jordan and the PLO are calling – of the kind you, too, advocate – would help much. There is no common ground between the parties at present which would make negotiations feasible. I think Mr Shultz's plan is much more promising, but that has been rejected by the PLO, Jordan and, more or less, the Israeli government. Unilateral

---

1 Ahmad Samih Khalidi (b. 1948), Palestinian academic and writer; adviser to the PLO delegations at the Israel–PLO peace talks 1991–3; senior adviser to Presidents Arafat and Abbas; associate fellow, Royal Institute of International Affairs (Chatham House), 1994–5; senior associate member, St Antony's, since 1997.

2 (Donal) Conor David Dermot Donat Cruise O'Brien (1917–2008), Irish diplomat, politician and author. In a long and varied career he was, inter alia, on the staff of Ireland's Dept of External Affairs 1944–61; vice chancellor, Ghana, 1962–5; Labour Teachta Dála (Irish MP) 1969–77, minister for posts and telegraphs 1973–7; fellow, St Catherine's, 1978–81; editor in chief, *Observer*, 1979–81.

abandonment of at any rate part of the West Bank by Israel is probably the only way to alleviate the situation.[1]

However that may be, my principal reason for declining to sign your letter – to much of the substance of which I am naturally sympathetic – is that I have already signed three letters,[2] two of which I drafted myself, together with other people (Profs Hart and Ayer signed one), which were highly critical of the present policy of the Israel government, urged negotiation on Shultz-like lines, and appealed to Israeli self-interest, at once moral and political. There are a good many people in Israel who share my view. Would that any articulated voices of a similar kind were heard in Arab countries – you know yourself the reason why, even if there are such people, they are unlikely to give voice to their feelings. And, having signed these three letters, I simply cannot bring myself to sign any more. The value of one's name, even if it is not great, declines even further the more letters one signs – it is no use becoming a professional letter-signer on the same topic within a relatively short period of time. That in itself is to me a conclusive reason for reluctantly declining to sign your letter. But the considerations I tried to outline above also weigh with me: to utter a moral protest, however justified, with the proposal of a conference which seems likely to be doomed from the outset, will not in my view help matters, as both you and I desire. I do not expect you to agree with me about this: I only beg you to believe me when I say that I feel just as strongly, friend of Israel and Zionist though I am, as you do against the present policies of the government of Israel. I hope you will forgive me, both for these sentiments, and for not feeling able to support your proposal.

With great respect,

Yours sincerely,

Isaiah Berlin

TO LOUIS RAPOPORT

30 August 1988

Headington House

Dear Mr Rapoport,

[...] I agree with you, of course, that the comments of the British press, and more particularly the BBC, on the Israel–Arab situation are heavily biased. I have always thought that. There are exceptions. There was a very good TV

1 In late February Henry Kissinger had publicly called for Israel to make a unilateral declaration of its readiness to put Gaza and parts of the West Bank under Palestinian control, as an 'interim solution' to the violence. Israel must 'face the fact that it cannot permanently occupy territory inhabited by a reluctant population': Michael Binyon, 'Kissinger Call for an Israeli Withdrawal', *Times*, 22 February 1988, 8d–h at 8g.

2 The letter signed by Hart and Ayer has already been mentioned (339/1); a second must be that identified at 339/5; the third is untraced.

series of three dialogues, arranged by a man called Michael Ignatieff (BBC),[1] first four Jews quarrelling among themselves – very fruitfully, I thought – then four Arabs, all of whom sang the same song, then two Jews and two Arabs – quite good; very fair-minded and decent. [...]

I feel about your article that while you are critical of what is going on on the West Bank – as what decent man could fail to be? – you nevertheless think that although the accounts of the oppression are much exaggerated, nevertheless there is a case for what is going on. I won't argue with you about that on moral or even political grounds – in the sense of whether it is right, just, politically wise, etc. – but there is a case (most forcefully produced by General Harkabi)[2] about the Arab birth rate. Do you not think that if the West Bank and its inhabitants are kept in some form by the state of Israel, whether as occupied territories, or annexed, or even with some form of home rule, then quite soon, by, say, the year 2000 or shortly thereafter, there will be parity of populations and then a rapid increase?[3] And that, quite apart from moral considerations, about which there can be disagreement (though I sympathise with Peace Now, and always have), the danger to the sheer survival of Israel as a Jewish state is such that, unless Israelis cease to govern, even in the most enlightened fashion (which is, alas, not the case), two million or more Arabs, the thing will blow up inevitably? No doubt people other than Rabbi Kahane, in their hearts, hope that somehow the inhabitants of the West Bank can be made to leave it, whether by persuasion or other means; but you and I know perfectly well that this cannot be, that expulsion, in whatever form, even if it is called exchange of populations, will not be allowed by the UN, and least of all by the USA; and that therefore it simply isn't on, quite apart from the injustice; and that the elimination of the Arabs by any other means had better not be thought about by sane men. Consequently, is it not better to have a demilitarised little Arab state, even under [the] control of the PLO, uncomfortable and in some ways dangerous as this might be – but [a] lesser evil than a process which must end in the overwhelming of the state of Israel, no matter how great an immigration of Jews from other countries (very unlikely at present) can be in the future?

Those are my feelings, and I know they are shared by a great many quite sensible people. So while I welcome your reaction to unjust reports and remarks, what about the substance? I am sure Peres would like to give up

1 Michael *Ignatieff (b. 1947), writer and broadcaster; authorised biographer of IB; author of foreword to HF2; his BBC2 TV series *State of Conflict* comprised 3 programmes: 'Through Israeli Eyes' (28 May), 'Palestinian Perspectives' (29 May), and 'This Land is Our Land' (30 May). It was in 1988 that Ignatieff began the conversations with IB that continued until IB's death.

2 Yehoshafat Harkabi (1921–94), Israeli soldier, defence strategist and academic; prof. of international relations and Middle Eastern studies, HUJ, 1978–89; a hawk turned 'Machiavellian dove' – his phrase: 'Dissent on the West Bank from Israeli Insider', NYT, 25 May 1980, E5 – he advocated negotiations with the PLO over the establishment of a Palestinian state; author of *Israel's Fateful Decisions* (London, 1988).

3 Not true in 2015, but the movement is in this direction.

the West Bank if he can, but Likud will never let him do it. There are those who think that a real adventurer like Sharon, just because he is an adventurer, and has no principles, might come to an agreement with Arafat or whoever about the West Bank, and urge that only a right-wing government can make a peace that sticks, because a left-wing government will be stabbed by the right wing. There is, I fear, something in that. What do you think? I feel deep discouragement.

Yours ever,

IB pp PU

PS I ought to add that of course I realise that what you say is entirely true about the Israeli army – that they hate having to do what they are doing, they don't indulge in sadism or violent hatreds and unprovoked assaults, and that to that degree reports which circulate in England and other countries, which do damage to Israel's reputation, are rather wicked. I am also impressed by the fact that – is it forty? – Israeli generals have signed a document urging the yielding of land for peace,[1] whether the whole of the West Bank or large portions of it I am not sure. The army commanders are among the most decent Israelis there are, and in general I have that opinion about army officers – I think they are a much maligned body, and are usually morally and personally much more decent than either journalists or politicians (do not take this to heart!).

TO ED CONE

31 August 1988

[Headington House]

Dear Ed,

Thank you very much indeed for the piece on Eliot. I don't propose to take any notice of this idiotic controversy.[2] [...] Let me tell you that when

1 This was widely reported in the press, e.g. in Milan J. Kubic, 'A Generals' Revolt', *Newsweek* ('Atlantic' edition), 6 June 1988, 24: ' "We want to tell our people that peace is a major security asset, that peace is worth territory and more peace is worth more territory," said retired Maj. Gen. Yosef Geva, one of the leaders of the Council for Peace and Security, a two-month-old group that includes 32 reserve major generals and more than 100 reserve brigadier generals – almost half of Israel's retired top brass.'

2 On 23 August EC had sent IB part (269–71) of John Malcolm Brinnin's essay 'Mr Eliot, I Presume', in his *Sextet: T. S. Eliot and Truman Capote and Others* (London, 1982), 249–75. Brinnin gave his personal view on Eliot's alleged anti-Semitism – 'that Eliot was perhaps not so much anti-Semitic as he was the unwitting victim of the myths of his class and kind' (269) – and quoted a letter (355/3) from Eliot rejecting anti-Semitism. The topic threatened to cloud the centenary of the poet's birth, and caused at least one prominent member of Britain's Jewish community, the MP Greville Janner, to decline to support a £100,000 appeal launched by the London Library to commemorate Eliot, its president when he died. IB was one of the patrons of the appeal, alongside (among others) Lord Goodman, and Cone hoped that the excerpts from Brinnin's book might help IB to justify his involvement, should he think it necessary.

I was at Bryn Mawr in 1952, in the spring, I received a letter from Eliot on this topic also.[1] I had written a rather provocative piece[2] for a kind of Festschrift for the Hebrew University, which appeared in instalments in the *Jewish Chronicle* in London – not widely read outside the Jewish community – in the course of which I made various observations (which I have never had republished because I think they would cause a row, in which I should not wish to be involved, even though there is nothing I would wish to withdraw, I say truculently) about the fact that Jews can often be uncomfortable members of gentile society, but that any society that calls itself liberal in any degree had no right to wish them out on those grounds (except secretly, perhaps); and that the only three thinkers who wanted a totally homogeneous society, and no disturbing foreigners, were Plato, T. S. Eliot and Arthur Koestler. The latter had written a very amusing article, saying what was all this about Jews praying three times a day to be returned unto Zion when for $312 a TWA plane would take them there at any time?[3] Why should they pray for rain in October because some forgotten pastoral people three thousand years ago may have needed it in their parched country, when outside the synagogues in which they pray it was raining cats and dogs? And still worse, they pray for dew – and so on. They really must stop this rot, intermarry or go to Israel, and stop driving other people mad. That's why I included him – and oh, H. G. Wells said something very similar,[4] and I daresay lots of people think it.

I don't think Eliot minded being compared with Plato, but I am sure he didn't want to be compared with Koestler. Some kind friend must have sent this very obscurely published piece to him, and I then received a very long letter from him – very friendly, telling me all about his visit to Bryn Mawr, the bronze bed which Miss Thomas,[5] the founder, had presented, how uncomfortable he was in it, how very badly the heating system worked in winter, how he hoped I was not too much disturbed by that, and other

---

1 Letter of 28 November 1951: L2 277–8.
2 262/1.
3 'Since the burning down of the Temple [orthodox Jews] have never ceased to pray for the restor-ation of the Jewish state, for "next year in Jerusalem". On 14 May 1948, their prayer was suddenly fulfilled. [...] No obstacle prevents any longer any orthodox Jew from obtaining a visa at the Israeli Consulate, and booking a passage on the Israeli Line': 'Judah at the Crossroads' (1954) in his *The Trail of the Dinosaur and Other Essays* (London, 1955). In *Promise and Fulfilment: Palestine 1917–1949* (London, 1949) Koestler writes that the Diaspora Jews 'kept praying at the proper season for rain to fall in a country on which they have never set eyes'. Are the other examples invented by IB? (For dew see 47.)
4 In *The Shape of Things to Come* (London, 1933) Wells anticipated a future in which the 'antiquated obdurate culture' of the Jews would disappear, and be 'completely merged in the human com-munity'; meanwhile the Jews were 'preoccupied with a dream called Zionism, the dream of a fantastic independent state all of their own in Palestine [...]. Only a psychoanalyst could begin to tell for what they wanted this Zionist state. It emphasised their traditional wilful separation from the main body of mankind. It irritated the world against them, subtly and incurably' (387).
5 M(artha) Carey Thomas (1857–1935), US educator, suffragist and linguist; appointed dean-elect and prof. of English, Bryn Mawr College for women, Pennsylvania, 1884 (it opened 1885); dean 1885–1908, (2nd) president 1894–1922.

amiable small talk. Then he came to the point, and said that Jewishness was purely a religion, and he certainly didn't think of them as a people, had no views on that subject, felt perfectly friendly, and so on and so on. I did reply to say that that couldn't be quite right because 'freethinking Baptists' didn't make sense, whereas 'freethinking negroes' did – or something like that, I cannot just remember.[1] Anyway, I got a very long answer saying he was not an anthropologist and anyway he didn't mind the Jews going to Israel but he didn't think they could all be fitted in because there were too many, and uttering generally friendly sentiments. He then said in a grand way 'One day, when we both have more time at our disposal, we must continue this correspondence', rather like Voltaire writing to Rousseau or vice versa, or Mill to Tocqueville. I think that Mrs Eliot intends to reprint the whole thing in her edition of Eliot's letters[2] – I made no objection.

All this fits in beautifully with what he wrote to you;[3] he obviously didn't like being called anti-Semitic; he was obviously, in fact, an anti-Semite though it was not in the forefront of his consciousness or his image or what he cared about. I think his views are not at all dissimilar to those of his friend Ezra Pound,[4] but at a much lower temperature, much more cautiously expressed – he was not the bravest of men. At the same time, I didn't go along with my friend Edmund Wilson's view that inside Eliot 'there was a kind of scug',[5] which his verse and prose cannot wholly conceal. In fact I think Eliot hated the modern world, industrialism, liberalism, science, the kind of world which the Jews who had emerged from the ghetto, some of them at least, prospered in – and like Toynbee wanted to go back to some kind of imaginary Middle Ages. It is an irony that he should be regarded as a modernist, quite rightly, when he loathed everything about the Western world since roughly the seventeenth century – Lancelot Andrewes[6] was about the last man he could reasonably bear.

Thank you ever so much for writing. If I needed ammunition[7] I would use

1 See L2 278–9.
2 Valerie Eliot died before reaching this point in her edition of Eliot's letters, but encouraged the inclusion of both sides of the exchange in the present edition of IB's. See L2 277–83.
3 Eliot wrote to William Kolodney, one of the signatories of an enquiry sent 12 February 1953, that 'any country which denies the rights of its own citizens or makes pariahs of any body of its own nationals – and most especially the Jews – will sooner or later have to pay the full price for so doing.' Letter of 17 February 1953, quoted in op. cit. (353/2), 271.
4 Ezra Weston Loomis Pound (1885–1972), US modernist poet and critic, friend and artistic collaborator of T.S. Eliot; settled in Rapallo 1925, and studied economics and international capitalism, becoming anti-Semitic and supportive of Mussolini.
5 Public-school slang for an undistinguished, ill-mannered boy.
6 Lancelot Andrewes (1555–1626), bishop of Winchester and dean, Chapel Royal, 1618–29; the prose style of his sermons was much appreciated by C20th literary critics, among them T.S. Eliot, whose unsigned essay 'Lancelot Andrewes' appeared in the TLS 23 September 1926, 621–2: 'His sermons are too well built to be readily quotable; they stick too closely to the point to be entertaining. Yet they rank with the finest English prose of their time, of any time' (621).
7 To justify his support for the London Library appeal.

it. It was very good of you to suggest it, but I don't propose to go to war, not unless something much worse blows up – I think it will blow over.

Yours ever,

IB pp PU   [...]

TO DIANA HOPKINSON

14 September 1988

Headington House

Dearest Diana

[...] Thank you for congratulating me on my old age. How well I remember the vanishing silver matchbox when you were twenty-one. You described it in one of your books very accurately.[1] I am shocked and appalled by the fact that you should have kept anything I ever wrote to you, but since you quote something from a letter which I must have written in 1933, I do not think that there is anything false in it – my universe began contracting then, expanded, contracted, expanded again mainly through war and travel abroad – then contracted, and is now rapidly reaching vanishing point. I have not the faintest desire to celebrate my eightieth birthday – the older I am the more displeased I am at having to die so soon. I have no wish to die. I am not afraid of death, only of the process of dying; I am still curious about life, I still feel moderately well, and therefore the approaching prospect I regard as a grave nuisance.

Aline still arranges roses. And BJ has written a most moving letter to me about our common past. She did say that Tommy,[2] by not marrying her, broke her heart. That I never knew – I thought that she had jilted him.[3] Of course they came together towards the end, but of course it isn't the same thing – I know all about what happens in old age and it is by no means what happens at the height of one's sensibilities and openness to life. [...]

Isaiah

1 In a November 1933 letter to DH (L1 74) IB confesses to the recent inadvertent removal and subsequent loss of a silver-framed matchbox. The quotation from this letter in DH's autobiography, *The Incense-Tree* (London, 1968), 121, was slightly falsified at the request of IB (L3 346).
2 Thomas Lionel Hodgkin (1910–82), Balliol classics 1928–32; his engagement to BJ was broken off before he went to Palestine on archaeological research in December 1932; m. 1937 the chemist and crystallographer Dorothy Crowfoot; Hodgkin did much to establish African studies in Britain, and was lecturer in the government of new states, and fellow, Balliol, 1965–70.
3 As is strongly implied in IB's letter to Diana Hopkinson of 28 September 1990 (392).

TO ELIZABETH MCKANE[1]

14 September 1988

Headington House

Dear Mrs McKane,

[...] I have no idea whether the significance or circumstances or essence of the work of a poet can possibly be conveyed in the kind of films that you project. However, on that my opinion is quite worthless and I do not wish to discourage you unnecessarily – perhaps something very creative and worthwhile can be achieved in this way. What I am clear about is that I cannot possibly participate in any way in this enterprise. I do not know, no one knows, and no one has ever written or speculated on, what the relationship of my meeting with Akhmatova had with the various poems – the cycles which you speak of.[2] I should consider it both useless and vulgarly presumptuous to try to seek to enter the creative process which led to the writing of this poetry. Of course external circumstances have some influence, and plenty has been written about the personal relations of poets and the connection of these with the poetry they wrote – never very convincingly. Least of all do I think this can be reproduced in the form of a play or a film or a representation of that type. In any case, my visit, memories of it (which I have described in print), my experience and feeling, are both private and impalpable – not analysable, not describable; and in any case private to a degree that I should regard any comment upon them as pure invasion of my deserved privacy.

For that reason you must count me out of anything you may wish to do. [...]

Yours sincerely,

Isaiah Berlin

TO WALTER LIPPINCOTT[3]

20 December 1988 [*carbon*]

Headington House

Dear Mr Lippincott,

Thank you for your letter of 6 December, which touches on a very sensitive nerve. I delivered my Mellon lectures twenty-three years ago, and was rightly not paid the full emolument because I failed to deliver the manuscript, then or subsequently.

---

1 Presumably Elizabeth McKane – who, with her husband, Richard, translated Osip Mandel'shtam's *The Moscow Notebooks* (Newcastle upon Tyne, 1991) and *The Voronezh Notebooks* (Newcastle upon Tyne, 1996).

2 But see 114/2.

3 Walter Heulings Lippincott (b. 1939), American publisher; editorial director, Cambridge University Press (America), 1974–81; executive editor, Cornell Univerity Press, 1981–3; director 1983–6; director, Princeton Uiniverity Press, 1986–2005.

Morally tormented by guilt from time to time during the intervening years, I have in a confused way begun thinking again about doing something with the transcripts of the broadcasts that the BBC made of these lectures. To look through twenty-four thick files of notes – a task on which I am soon to embark – and to turn these into a book will probably occupy the rest of my already overlong life. If, however, this comes to fruition, either before I die or posthumously, you will, I hope, be duly informed. I am so sorry to return so unsatisfactory a reply, but as you can yourself judge there is nothing much else that I can do.

Yours sincerely,

[Isaiah Berlin]

TO JOHN LOWE[1]

27 February 1989

Headington House

Dear Mr Lowe,

[...] I do indeed know that you have agreed to write John Sparrow's biography for Collins. I think it is a very interesting but, I cannot conceal from you, a very difficult task to write the real life of our friend. There is almost nothing I wouldn't do to avoid having to do this myself. The reason is not simply that I am not good at biography or the like – it is honourable, successful and conventional – but that his public life is of little outstanding interest. What is really remarkable and worth going into is, of course, his private life, which offers terrible obstacles to the writer. As you yourself remark, the delicate (or 'indelicate') aspects of it are exceedingly difficult to investigate, assess, discuss, describe: yet they are his real life.

It is all very well for John to say 'publish and be damned', but it affects too many others, and too much is half-unknown, and would have to be delved into, if anything like even semi-completeness is to be achieved.

At any rate, if you are set on this task, which I truly do not envy you, fascinating as it undoubtedly could be, I should be very glad to talk to you whenever you wish. [...]

In my view, John's interests in order of priority could be described as follows:

1. Himself.
2. Sex.
3. At a great remove from these, old books.
4. English literature in the seventeenth and nineteenth centuries.

1 John Evelyn Lowe (1928–2010), writer, expert on Japanese culture; visiting prof. in British cultural studies, Doshisha, Japan, 1979–81; author of *The Warden: A Portrait of John Sparrow* (London, 1998).

5. The classics, the visual arts, friendships with colleagues and school friends etc., and the edges of political life.

The College comes low in the list, even though he felt it to be his home for all those years. He was the best company in the world, so far as I am concerned. His wit, his irony, his charm, his sheer intelligence, indeed his brilliance, and his total lack of fear, moral and physical, and his independence, were unique in my experience. I have known him, I suppose, since 1931, and he did not change very much during my lifetime. There were certain qualities which, given his ostensible respect for public values and 'the establishment', as it is now called, were unusual. He totally lacked public spirit, and it was that, I think, that prevented his being given an honour by the state, in spite of efforts on the part both of Kenneth Clark and of Harold Macmillan to get him one. When Macmillan was prime minister he did nothing, but he did suggest it once or twice after he had ceased to be a minister, as Chancellor of the University. I do not know who was consulted, but if any academics or persons in public life were among them, they would be bound to say that he was totally devoid of any altruistic interest in the lives or activities of his fellow citizens, individual or collective. This is perhaps too harsh, indeed I am sure it is, but that is the impression he both conveyed and wished to convey. He was, of course, as you must know, something of an actor – one of his motives for wishing to go for the Bar, and not, for example, staying in the Bodleian, which he could so easily have done.

In College, to which he was in a sense devoted, his principal achievement was blocking – with the greatest ingenuity, style and brilliance – the slightest change in its arrangements. He did not always succeed, of course, but his efforts in that direction were wonderful to behold. I was, as you must know, devoted to him personally, and, of course, still am, and that is why I never took part in any opposition – except once or twice on very outrageous methods of preventing desperately needed changes, or recognising human needs, on his part. I cannot deny that I watched his manoeuvres to outwit and stymie his colleagues with the most fascinated, if somewhat disapproving, admiration. His virtuosity in that respect was, in my experience, unparalleled. He saw it as saving the College. Few of his colleagues saw it in that light.

It must be admitted that when he declined to take on the Vice Chancellorship – when it fell to him in the rota – there was a great deal of relief among the senior members of the University. I think they feared, not without reason, that he would be liable to make some sudden intemperate attack on hippy beards [...] (he had an *idée fixe* about that, and kept inviting any rough and unkempt youths he met in the High Street to his study to argue with them: that added to his reputation for oddity), or the admission of women to academic life, or the raising of salaries (to any degree) of academics and, still more, of college servants. This would be very difficult for the University to shake off, and would give an unfortunate impression to the world.

Towards the end of his life, as you must also know, he was represented as a kind of almost comical diehard, brilliant resister of all change, symbol of reaction among portions of the public, especially in the progressive press. He was perfectly aware of this and gloried in it. His jokes are marvellously good: e.g. when elected Warden he told me: 'In ten years time the Warden will, under the rubric "Warden's Business" in the agenda of College meetings, write: "The Warden will mind his business, if the fellows mind theirs." After twenty years, "They say he has grown a beard and only sees the Manciple[1] now." In thirty years, "The Warden passed away this morning angrily in his sleep."'

His personal charm, which was usually irresistible, overcame some of the disapproval that he excited, and his essays, being beautifully written – he had a wonderful prose style – were in general well received. He had deep friendships – not many, but very genuine – throughout his life, and some acute hatreds, particularly among his colleagues in All Souls, which the latter naturally returned in kind. All this can be discussed and reported without necessarily hurting the feelings of living persons, or even the relatives of the dead. But it was, of course, his sexual life which dominated him to a profound degree and affected his attitudes to life and people and literature and politics […]. I remember the particular passion with which he attacked any attempt to relax the anti-homosexual laws on the grounds that this went against received opinion, which he venerated. He wished his own behaviour in that respect to remain dangerous and illegal, which added something to its attraction for him. His respect for genuine learning, particularly in the classics, was great – for academic excellence as such, much weaker. He preferred the idiosyncratic, the odd, even among classical scholars, and saw the academic community in terms of its more unusual, picturesque inhabitants rather than solid or distinguished learning, for which fundamentally he did not care that much. Certainly, the two ablest of the prize fellows elected in his day at All Souls – two persons who earned world reputations[2] – bored him, and jokes were made about them (of which he was a great master) simply because they were serious, and that he found inexpressibly tedious. He was, as you know, easily bored, and responded to vitality, wit, charm and, above all, youth, and was profoundly bored by worth, virtue, serious dedication to academic life. His values were worldly – he respected statesmen,

---

1 A member of the All Souls College staff, more akin to a major domo than a steward (the sense in which the term is generally used).
2 Possibly Michael Dummett, elected 1950, not long before Sparrow became Warden (1952), and the philosopher Derek Parfit (b. 1942), elected 1967; 'prize fellows' are officially known as fellows by examination.

politicians, judges, bankers much more than dons. He wanted to be admired and amused. Personal relations meant far more to him than academic ones. [...]

I ought to add that the College in the last ten or fifteen years was his life; he saw himself as its protector against all kinds of, from his point of view, undesirable reforms. [...] I think that probably his collapse was due to the fact that he had to leave the College – he was deeply hurt by the fact that he was not to be prolonged, which may have been legally possible, although no one, so far as I know, so much as suggested this – and, having no other hobbies or purpose in life, he began, I fear, to decay. Maurice Bowra once said about him that when he, Sparrow, was a boy at Winchester [...], he found the world to be somewhat chaotic, something he did not want to entertain, and so he imposed upon it his own schema, a kind of fantasy which he lived for the rest of his life – and which caused him not to wish to be taken seriously, at any rate in academic circles, although he did wish to be taken seriously in London among lawyers and politicians, for example. That is why he turned almost everything into some kind of ironical comedy, and that it was that made him such marvellous company, since what might be called an 'earnest' conversation was impossible with him on any topic, and that surprised and sometimes distressed some of his more serious-minded colleagues, and was a source of infinite delight to others, like me, who were, perhaps, less solemn in these matters.

Well now, I have been as indiscreet as I think he might have preferred me to be. But perhaps not? At any rate, let us meet.

Yours sincerely,
    Isaiah Berlin

TO ARTHUR SCHLESINGER

28 February 1989

Headington House

Dear Arthur,

I read your two pieces – 'War and the Constitution'[1] and 'New Viewpoints Revisited'[2] – with the greatest possible pleasure. Your exposition of the degree of authority and decision without careful authorisation by Congress on the part of Abraham Lincoln[3] seemed to me very fascinating. It supports my *idée fixe* about the incompatibility of values, principles etc. – in this case, the need to seek proper constitutional authority, to abide by the rules, not to

1 Presumably part of *War and the Constitution: Abraham Lincoln and Franklin D. Roosevelt* ([Gettysburg], 1988).
2 'New Viewpoints in American History Revisited', *New England Quarterly* 61 no. 4 (December 1988), 483–501.
3 Abraham Lincoln (1809–65), Republican US President 1861–5, 'the Great Emancipator': 543/1.

bend them, because this was not a policy that appeals to persons in authority; and, on the other hand, the opposite – that in a critical situation, not even a very desperate one but simply a critical one, action has to be taken for the purpose of defending the morally desirable establishment to which one is dedicated even if this involves precisely such bending or ignoring: the whole problem of *raison d'état* is a very tormenting one.

Sometimes turning a blind eye must surely be right. The Nuremberg trials[1] were clearly not justified by any legal rules, yet does one condemn them for that reason? When Ben-Gurion sank a ship called the *Altalena*, in which the Irgun were bringing weapons to Israel to arm their movement in 1948, and were forbidden to do so by the prime minister, and defied his ban, and were then shot down and sunk (which probably averted a civil war)[2] – whatever the condition of the law might have been, one could defend it, and I do. I don't know much about events in the [American] Civil War [...] – but when you get to Roosevelt and the last war, then I am much more at home, and your account is fascinating beyond words. I was in Washington during part of the arguments about sending the destroyers to England,[3] and I remember the people you speak of – Ben Cohen[4] etc. Byrds [sc. Byrnes][5] also played a decisive role in the Senate – of course it was strictly illegal, and even if the law is supposed to be the nearest approximation to civil or political justice that we have (not that it is, but let us suppose that), unjust as well: but I have never accepted the late, sainted Hannah Arendt's somewhat frenzied defence at a seminar which we both attended of *ruat coelum, fiat justitia*[6] – another nail in her coffin so far as I am concerned, I say with ill-concealed satisfaction. [...]

1 The 1945–6 trials, by an Allied military tribunal, of 23 Nazi leaders accused of war crimes; the first such trials in history, they resulted in the execution of 10 of the accused; the proceedings were held in the Bavarian city of Nuremberg, previously the site of the Nazi Party's annual congress.
2 In June 1948 the *Altalena* (named after Jabotinsky: 238/2) sailed from France for Israel with a substantial cargo of arms and men intended to augment the ranks of the Irgun. Though it was being absorbed into the IDF after the proclamation of the state of Israel, the Irgun remained an independent force, and its leader, Begin, refused Ben-Gurion's demand that the *Altalena*'s cargo be handed over to the government. After a tense stand-off, interspersed with fighting (with fatalities on both sides), Ben-Gurion ordered the destruction of the *Altalena*, which was shelled from the shore near Tel Aviv. This action, though deeply controversial, established the authority of the government, which Begin was forced to recognise, and a civil war may have been averted.
3 FDR's administration agreed 2 September 1940 to transfer to the Royal Navy 50 mothballed destroyers, in return for leases on land in British overseas possessions, to be used for US military bases; this anticipated the lend-lease programme of March 1941. Both measures were designed to circumvent the neutrality acts of 1935–9, allowing the US to give military aid to the Allies in their war against Nazi Germany, which the President now deemed essential, though sections of Congress did not.
4 Benjamin Victor Cohen (1894–1983), graduate of Harvard Law School who became a key adviser in the Roosevelt and Truman administrations; in 1941 he helped to draft the lend-lease plan (previous note).
5 Byrnes (154/8) was much relied upon by FDR in the senate, especially during the progress 1941 of the lend-lease scheme (previous note but one).
6 'Let the sky fall so long as justice is done.'

Yours
   Isaiah   [...]

The publication in September 1988 of the novel The Satanic Verses *by the British writer Salman Rushdie[1] was greeted with anger by many Muslims, who regarded it as blasphemous; and on 14 February 1989 the Iranian supreme leader Ayatollah Khomeini issued a fatwa, or Islamic legal judgement, condemning Rushdie to death. Rushdie was given protection by the British government, and lived in hiding for many years, but elsewhere some of those associated with foreign editions of the novel were killed by Islamic fundamentalists. Shortly after the fatwa was issued Mark Le Fanu,[2] the general secretary of the British Society of Authors, attempted to organise a 'world statement' expressing solidarity with Rushdie. Karl Popper was among those who declined Le Fanu's request to sign this statement, and he wrote to IB explaining why. At the heart of Popper's case was the belief that Rushdie's offending material should not have been published: 'I do believe that every freedom involves duties: to use your freedom responsibly. Those who don't may kill the freedom. Every freedom can be misused. And our ancestors in this struggle – so Voltaire, Kant, Mill – believed that we will be civilised enough to live up to this almost obvious demand.'[3]*

TO KARL POPPER

2 March 1989

                                      Headington House

Dear Karl,

Thank you very much for your letter of 25 [sc. 24] February and the enclosure of your letter to Mark Le Fanu. I entirely agree with your first point, namely that 'the undersigned' are [not] 'involved in the publication' of Rushdie's book. I do not in the least feel involved in this, nor would I wish to be, any more than yourself. That point is unanswerable.

On the other hand, when you say that every freedom involves a duty (e.g. the duty not to hurt people), I am not sure that I agree. Telling the truth is certainly not always compatible with not hurting feelings, and yet there are obviously circumstances in which there is a duty to do so – nor would it have been right to suppress Voltaire ('whether we agree with him or not' – I know what you and I would say) from publishing his attacks on the Bible

---

1 *The Satanic Verses* (London/NY, 1988). (Ahmed) Salman Rushdie (b. 1947), later (2007) Kt; Indian-born British writer of Kashmiri descent; his second novel, *Midnight's Children* (London/NY, 1980), won the 1981 Booker Prize. In his letter Popper says: 'the W[orld] S[tatement] contains an untruth [...], both in fact and in intention. "We, the undersigned ... declare that we also are involved in the publication."' Letter of 5 March: *After the Open Society: Selected Social and Political Writings*, ed. Jeremy Shearmur and Piers Norris Turner (London, [2008]), 203.
2 Mark Le Fanu (b. 1946), solicitor; general secretary, Society of Authors, 1982–2011.
3 op. cit. (note 1 above), 204.

and Christianity on the ground that these must obviously be received with violent indignation by believers. At the same time, I do not deny that there are plenty of occasions when hurting feelings is worse than telling the truth – and so on. True values, as we both know, can be incompatible.

What I should have said, in place of their letter, is simply that whatever one may feel about causing such pain to believers in Islam, instructions to kill the author of the offending document are an outrageous offence against the morality we hope to live by (who is 'we'? 'we' is we – we all know what that means). If, as a result of this, hostages are killed in Lebanon, should we feel collective guilt about protesting in any terms, however carefully chosen, against the Ayatollah's monstrous act and the incitements to murder in this country? I wish I knew.

Yours ever,
    Isaiah

TO SHIRLEY ANGLESEY
    13 March 1989

                                       Headington House

Dearest Shirley,
You know very well that the pleasure you speak of is always reciprocal – it was pure good luck that I was put to sit next to you, and all Gladwyn's[1] incoherent cross-talk did not spoil things in the least. It was, I think, the most geriatric party that even I have ever been to, comparable only to the quinquennial lunches for the OMs which the Queen gives, where virtually everybody walks on two sticks and seldom lasts until the next one – I cannot think how I have.

As for the Soviet general,[2] I wish I could have gone to him – a very intelligent, very tough man, whose official life of Stalin is alleged to be very revealing indeed (so at least Lord Thomas[3] has informed me – he has been allowed to see all the papers), and is full of damaging stories about the late JVS: not nearly as damaging as they should be, I am sure. The question is, at what stage will the put-down of V. I. Lenin be permitted? Even now one is allowed to say things against him, but certainly not publish them, perhaps not even write them privately. But I think the day will come. I cannot get it out of my head that Stalin was merely a violently brutal and totally horrible

---

1 (Hubert Miles) Gladwyn Jebb (1900–96), 1st Baron Gladwyn 1960, diplomat; UK permanent representative to UN (which he had helped to create) 1950–4; UK ambassador to France 1954–60; deputy Liberal leader, Lords, 1965–88.

2 Dmitry Antonovich Volkogonov (1928–95), historian, head of Soviet psychological warfare 1979–84, author of *Triumf i tragediya: politicheskii portret I. V. Stalina* (Moscow, 1989), ed. and trans. Harold Shukman as *Stalin: Triumph and Tragedy* (NY, 1991).

3 Hugh Swynnerton Thomas (b. 1931), life peer 1981, historian and writer; professor of history, Reading, 1966–76.

continuation of Lenin, but not a distortion or 'betrayal' of him, as the late Trotsky maintained.[1] Indeed, I heard one of the leaders of the New York Trotskyites, a revered figure among them, say at the centenary of the Second International in Stanford that Trotsky found great difficulties in manufacturing disagreements of an ideological kind with Stalin – hatred, yes, corruption, barbarism etc., but profound differences of ideas? Such as Trotskyites are supposed to be divided from Stalinists by? About this he had great difficulty. The Trotskyites who were in his audience were totally stupefied by such remarks from one of the great leaders of the American Trotskyite movement. I giggled quietly. [...]

When shall we meet? We won't be off to Italy till mid July, so do proposition us, or we shall think of something to do with you – perhaps we could go to *Rigoletto* together? My faith in Covent Garden is wavering. There is, I think, a very regrettable famous German film producer called Schaff[2] who has done *Figaro*, and now *Così* – the critics, I am sure rightly, are against it:[3] we have to go with Jeremy Isaacs to the box, so doubtless I shall not be able to say what I think, although my pursed lips may say more than anything. He is supposed to do all the Mozart operas. Nightmare. I am glad for this reason, if for no other – there are plenty of others – that I am no longer on the board. What heaven it is to be able to talk loudly, freely and if necessary trenchantly.

Yours ever, ⟨with much love⟩

Isaiah

TO ARTHUR SCHLESINGER

17 April 1989

Headington House

Dear Arthur

It's always delightful to hear from you, and this time I propose to reward you with an anecdote. [...]

We went to Paris the other day for the weekend to hear my friend Alfred Brendel play in two Beethoven concerti. After the second a party was given

---

1 In *The Revolution Betrayed* (London, 1937) Trotsky wrote that the Stalin-led Soviet bureaucracy 'conquered more than the Left Opposition. It conquered the Bolshevik Party. It defeated the programme of Lenin, who had been the chief danger in the conversion of the organs of the state "from servants of society to lords over society". It defeated all these enemies, the Opposition, the party, and Lenin, not with ideas and arguments, but with its own social weight. The leaden rump of the bureaucracy outweighed the head of the revolution' (93–4).

2 Johannes Schaaf (b. 1933), Stuttgart-born film, theatre and opera director, and actor; produced *Le nozze di Figaro* (1987), *Così fan tutte* and *Idomeneo* (1989), and *Don Giovanni* (1992) at Covent Garden.

3 'Only 18 months have passed since Johannes Schaaf staged a *Figaro* for the Royal Opera which probed well beneath the skin of all those on stage. But he has found *Così fan tutte* [...] a far more slippery proposition.' John Higgins, 'German rather than Germane', *Times*, 8 March 1989, 21a–d at 21a.

by Baroness Élie de Rothschild,[1] for them, for their various friends, for us, for various eminent musicians in Paris, etc., etc. On my right at dinner was a charming woman,[2] the new Russian wife of Daniel Barenboim[3] – pretty, gifted, cosy, charming, and I could talk Russian to her, which is always a great pleasure to me and in which all kinds of pleasing interchanges can occur which cannot happen in any other language. I was absorbed in talking to her, and also to Daniel B., who was sitting on her other side; and then after a bit I felt I really must address myself to the neighbour on my left, a middle-aged-looking, quite handsome lady with fairish hair, whom I took to be some distinguished Frenchwoman, an acquaintance of our hosts. So very politely I turned to her, and in my not very good French said to her 'Habitez-vous Paris?' She said 'Non, je n'habite pas Paris. Et vous, vous habitez Paris? Vous êtes français?' I said 'Non, j'habite Oxford.' 'Est-ce que vous connaissez, par hasard, Isaiah Berlin?' 'C'est moi.' Astonishment, a brief stunned silence. I then said 'Qui vous parlait de moi?'[4] 'Oh, hell, we've surely met – my name is Lauren Bacall.'[5] This time *I* collapsed. At once she said 'Arthur Schlesinger – I love him, don't you? I do love Arthur.' I said 'Ditto.' Then we tried to remember where we'd met – certainly at dinner with you in Cambridge, somewhere in the early 1950s; and again, I thought, after that in a hotel in London, whether with or without you I can't remember. Anyway, neither of us obviously had the faintest recollection of face, voice or any characteristics of each other. Too awful. After that we chatted amiably but did not agree to meet again. Perhaps you will bring us together again one day and we could laugh about it: at the time it was distinctly embarrassing for us both – except that at least the offence was equal on both sides, and she is obviously great fun. [...]

Yours ever,

Isaiah

---

1 Liliane Elisabeth Victoire de Rothschild (1916–2003; plate 17) née Fould-Springer, youngest of the 4 children of Eugène Fould-Springer, and a lifelong friend of Aline Berlin, who as a child had lived in the same apartment building in Paris on the avenue d'Iéna, near the Arc de Triomphe; m. 1942 Élie de Rothschild (1917–2007; plate 25), then a prisoner of war in Colditz Castle, head, Château Lafite Rothschild, Médoc, 1946–74: the marriage took place by proxy, Élie having proposed by letter 7 October 1941.

2 Elena Dmitrievna Bashkirova (b. 1958), Moscow-born pianist and musical director; later founder (1998) and artistic director, International Jerusalem Chamber Music Festival; m. 1988 2ndly Daniel Barenboim (next note).

3 Daniel Barenboim (b. 1942), later (2011) hon. KBE, Argentinian-born pianist and conductor; m. 1967 British cellist Jacqueline du Pré (1945–87); 1988 Elena Bashkirova (previous note); debut as a pianist with the Israel Philharmonic Orchestra 1953; music director, Orchestre de Paris, 1975–88, Chicago Symphony Orchestra 1991–2006, Berlin State Opera from 1992; later (1998) co-founder with Edward Said, West–Eastern Divan Orchestra.

4 'Do you live in Paris?' 'No, I don't live in Paris. And what about you: do you live in Paris? Are you French?' 'No, I live in Oxford.' 'Do you by any chance know Isaiah Berlin?' 'I am he. [...] Who told you about me?'

5 Lauren Bacall (1924–2014) née Betty Joan Perske, US actress famous for her seductive appeal, m. 1945 Humphrey Bogart, with whom she starred in 4 films.

'I have avoided birthday celebrations all my life, since the age of about seven, and if I am expected to say even a very few words the prospect is a genuine nightmare to me'.[1] So it was with special misgivings that IB wrote to Arthur Schlesinger, after the non-celebration of his seventy-ninth birthday in June 1988: 'it may be difficult to avoid something when I am eighty – but I shall try very, very hard'.[2] Inevitably he failed. Radio 3 broadcast a tribute on 6 June – 'An Evening With Isaiah Berlin', a four-hour programme of music and talk[3]– and while this was on air IB was feted at a dinner at his old undergraduate college, Corpus Christi, given by the Chancellor of the University, Roy Jenkins. As IB later wrote to Joe Alsop: 'thank God it is over. I had to speak (ordeal 1); as Maurice used to say "they laughed at my jokes" thank God. Next, Wolfson College – more civilized, no speech. (3) Concert on 17th July. Will I have to speak to them all? a worse nightmare, climb on to the stage? I think I can evade the latter & minimize the former. My God, I shall be glad to be 81!'[4] In fact the last event, a concert given in his honour at the Royal Festival Hall, proved the most enjoyable of all. Neville Marriner[5] conducted the Academy of St Martin-in-the-Fields in an all-Mozart programme: Júlia Várady[6] and Dietrich Fischer-Dieskau[7] sang concert arias; the oboist Heinz Holliger[8] played the flute concerto K313, and Alfred Brendel the piano concerto K459. 'The musicians really were marvellous – all four of them seemed to me, as I sincerely described them, to be artists of genius; and the fact that they offered me this without a fee is, I cannot deny, the greatest compliment ever paid to me in my life. Now I can face my Maker peacefully, there is no more to do.'[9]

1 To Shirley Anglesey, 4 May 1989.
2 To Arthur Schlesinger, 13 June 1988.
3 The broadcast began at 7.05 p.m. and consisted of: a conversation between IB and John Drummond, controller, Radio 3; Alfred Brendel playing Schubert; a recording of the 1st of IB's 1965 Mellon Lectures on Romanticism; IB's reminiscences of Stravinsky, with excerpts from the latter's works; a dramatic reading of Turgenev's short story 'A Fire at Sea' in IB's 1957 translation; and Mozart's clarinet quintet in A, K581.
4 Letter of 20 June 1989.
5 Neville Marriner (b. 1924), Kt 1985, conductor and violinist; founder, Academy of St Martin-in-the-Fields, 1958, director 1958–78, chair 1978–92; conductor, Los Angeles Chamber Orchestra, 1969–79; principal conductor, Minnesota Orchestra, 1979–86; conductor, Stuttgart Radio Symphony Orchestra, 1983–9.
6 Júlia Várady (b. 1941) née Tözsér, Hungarian soprano; debut 1962; Cluj State Opera 1960–70, Frankfurt 1970–2, Munich 1972–98, when she retired from opera; m. 1977 Dietrich Fischer-Dieskau (next note).
7 Dietrich Fischer-Dieskau (1925–2012), German baritone, one of the greatest singers of his generation, noted for his rendering of German lieder, particularly Schubert's song cycles.
8 Heinz Holliger (b. 1939), Swiss oboist, composer and conductor; principal oboist, Basle Orchestra, 1959–64; solo debut at the Salzburg Festival 1961.
9 To Teddy Kollek, 12 September 1989.

    14 June 1989

Headington House

Dearest Shiela,

I am terribly sorry that you are laid up in hospital, and I should have been much upset if, even if you were in Oxford, you had come hobbling in on crutches, just to sit next to Douglas or Herbert, not far away from Thingmajig,[1] who were there, of course. It all went off quite peacefully. It is agony to me to make speeches of any kind, least of all on this kind of occasion. I have lectured for, I suppose, more than forty years and I have never enjoyed a single lecture I have ever delivered – always agony, always a sense of shame afterwards at not having said what I wanted to say or making mistakes or whatever. Hence my nervousness about looking at the audience. I never do, my eyes securely fixed on the top right-hand corner; and a certain low-church unction enters my voice, simply because of the angle of my head, which I cannot prevent. Anyway, it's all over. Before and after my speech I enjoyed myself; so did they all, on the whole, and I am very, very sorry that you weren't there. You might have thought it rather nice: friendly old familiar faces, memories – rather a sentimental occasion in many ways. [...]

[...] All after-dinner speeches are shaped in a fixed art form – sonata form, in fact. First, light matter, allegro; then grave things which you really wish to impart, if any; then allegro again, jokes, light matter, desire to please the audience; and in some awful cases a rondo, i.e. you go back to the beginning and start again. After-dinner speeches only occur where the British flag has waved: not only in the UK, but North America, anglophone Africa, India, Burma, Israel, Malta, Cyprus, even Corfu, I think – nowhere else. In France, Germany, Italy there are formal orations read from paper, containing elaborately constructed sentiments which could go into handsome print at any moment, but none of the at any rate intendedly charming, audience-pleasing bricks without straw. So if you ask what I said, fortunately it has gone from my mind, and I shall never think about it again, although it seemed on the whole not too bad at the time.

[...] When you were twenty, had you ever met anyone of eighty? I never did. I did at All Souls at the beginning of 1933: there was Cholmondeley,[2] Rector of Adlestrop, whose booming voice made it impossible to communicate with him because one never understood anything he said (the same could be said of me from time to time); the other one, of course, was

---

1 Nickname for Jenifer Hart that arose when SGD forgot her real name (L2 59/1).
2 Francis Grenville Cholmondeley (1850–1937), rector of Broadwell-cum-Adlestrop in Gloucestershire, and fellow, All Souls, 1874–1937. He followed in his father's footsteps in both his clerical and academic appointments: 'Hardly known to the University at large, he was ever a welcome sojourner in the College' ('Mr Cholmondeley', obituary, *Times*, 28 July 1937, 16c).

Spenser Wilkinson,[1] a retired military historian who knew Bismarck. He was a tremendous bore and people ran from him in all directions, but sometimes, with a bony hand, he gestured one to stay and it was cruel to abandon him – no story ever lasted less than one hour and a half. Neither of these persons were strictly similar to human beings – scarcely human by the time I saw them. Do you think that the grandchildren look on me like that? I hope not, but I cannot be altogether sure. Douglas seems all right, Herbert seems human, even Franks,[2] who is older, is hale and hearty – but is that only to my eye and not to those of the young? However, I do not worry about that.

[...] You ask about the future. No, no, I know nothing about that, the past and present are enough for me; but if you want to ask me questions and put propositions to me – verbally, I mean – I promise to bend all the feeble energies I have, such ideas as weakly straggle across my failing consciousness, to try and satisfy you. So do come here soon, let me know, and we will have a talk. It is ridiculous that you go on living in Ireland, however good the reasons. Sell everything and come and live here, whatever this may entail, and we will spend – at least, I will – my last years in your neighbourhood, which would be a great comfort to me.

All my love (as Goronwy used to say), and as I fully mean,
Isaiah

TO BAILLIE KNAPHEIS[3]
16 June 1989

Headington House

Dear Baillie,

[...] Don't talk to me about Israel. I think it is frightful. I was rung up the other day by the *Jewish Chronicle*, which had discovered that I was not prepared to go to a meeting to proclaim my solidarity with the government of Israel, to which I was invited.[4] I was asked why not; I said it was because

---

1 (Henry) Spenser Wilkinson (1853–1937), military historian; the 1st Chichele Prof. of Military History (now the History of War), Oxford, 1909–23, fellow, All Souls, 1909–37; he continued to write in his retirement.

2 Oliver Shewell Franks (1905–92), KCB 1946, life peer 1962, OM 1977, philosopher, college head, diplomat, banker, public servant, played an important role in initiating both the Marshall Plan and NATO, and was UK ambassador to the US 1948–52; as head, Commission of Inquiry into Oxford University, 1964–6, he gave steadfast support to IB's plans for Wolfson, and was made an hon. fellow there 1967.

3 Baillie Jean Knapheis (b. 1941) née Klass, born in Winnipeg, IB's personal secretary 1965–7; m. 1963–4 Brian Knapheis, 1967 Christopher Tolkien; editor of J. R. R. Tolkien's *The Father Christmas Letters* (London, 1976).

4 Shamir wrote to many leading Jewish figures: 'In view of recent developments in the Middle East, there is an urgent need to strengthen the relationship of solidarity between Israel and all Jews around the world. The Government of Israel expects the entire Jewish people to stand at Israel's side in its quest for peace, security and prosperity.' David Goldberg, 'Israel Rallies the Troops in the Diaspora', *Independent*, 20 March 1989, 19.

I felt no solidarity with it. They then said, what is your view of Mr Shamir? I could only say that I thought that although stone walls had many excellent uses […], talking to them is wholly counterproductive, and that is what conversation with Mr Shamir is bound to be. This was then reproduced in the JC, the *Sunday Telegraph* and everywhere else,[1] and has become a kind of stock phrase to be applied to that terrible man. I could have said something much ruder, but I thought that in public utterance one ought to try and be moderate, even when unfriendly. […]

Yours ever,

Isaiah

TO KYRIL FITZLYON

19 June 1989

Headington House

Dear Kyril,

[…] It is no joke being eighty, as you will discover in due course. I do indeed remember Meyendorff[2] – what a charming, distinguished old gentlemen he was. I liked him very much – and his absurd letter to me about peace between Jews and Arabs. He wished me to go and see Ben-Gurion, Nasser, whoever was in Jordan, I can't remember if the Emir Abdullah was still there or his feeble-witted son or the present King[3] – to bring all these people together and create a harmonious solution to the troubles of that appallingly troubled region. I replied to him and said that I was quite incapable of such a thing, and that these persons would not listen to me for a second (which is obviously true). He was rather displeased, and thought that a golden opportunity had been missed. He was a sweetly idealistic person, but this particular proposal was, I fear, ridiculous.

As for the horrors that are going on at present, the shooting, the intifada,[4] the killing of children, etc., you can very well imagine what I feel. I should say that the majority of British Jews feel as I do – at the very minimum, troubled; at the maximum, indignant. In Israel my very strong views about

---

1 Untraced in the newspapers IB names; but Barbara Amiel reported in *The Times* that IB, 'when invited by Shamir last March to come to Israel and support the government, remarked that "stone walls have many uses, but talking to them isn't very fruitful"'. 'Guardian of the Third Temple', 19 May 1989, 15a–g at 15f.

2 Aleksandr Feliksovich von Meyendorff (1869–1964), Octobrist, member, imperial Duma for Livonia, 1907–17; domiciled in England from 1919; reader in Russian institutions and economics, LSE, 1922–34.

3 Members of the Hashemite dynasty ruling Jordan: Abdullah bin al-Hussein (1882–1951), emir of Transjordan 1921–46; 1st king of independent Jordan 1946; assassinated in Jerusalem 1951; succeeded by his son Talal bin Abdullah (1909–72), king of Jordan 1951–2, who abdicated on health grounds (reportedly schizophrenia); succeeded by his son Hussein bin Talal (137/2), the 2nd Arab head of state to recognise Israel (1994, after Anwar Sadat 1978–9).

4 335.

this are widely disseminated – I do not need to proclaim them in public to get them to the attention of the only people who will listen. Even if you are right about any possible effect which people like me might have on English Jews, let me make it plain to you that, alas, what English Jews do or do not feel does not have the faintest effect on the present administration of Israel. It is like water off a duck's back. They could not care less. They are fanatical, true believers. Most of them are prepared (or think they are) to die, after selling their lives dearly to the horrible PLO, etc. There is no point whatever in making appeals in the English or any other non-Israeli press. [...]

The only thing which would shake these people is a split among the American Jewish supporters of Israel, which is certainly beginning – vast cracks have appeared. If they went to town I think there might be some effect – but they are very resentful of advice from British Jews, as I found to my cost. I must have signed at least half-a-dozen violently protesting letters about the present policies of the Israeli government, particularly of its Likud section – both in Israel and here, and joined in American documents of that kind as well. It does no good whatever, so far as I can tell. I do not believe in signing these things – except to relieve one's conscience, which is what I have done – unless one thinks that it can be even minimally effective. In this case it will not be. The Jews in Israel are convinced that the murder of their children by the PLO – which of course has occurred on a pretty wide scale – justifies them in a tit-for-tat form of violence; and if one says anything against it they complain that they live a dangerous life, surrounded by a vast number of bitter enemies, they are trying to save their lives and traditions and honour, and it is very well for those who sit comfortably in New York or Oxford to tell them what to do. In fact it is counterproductive, even in the case of mildly liberal persons, hence no good.

I am very distressed that this should be so, but it is the case.

Yours ever,

Isaiah

TO JOHN HILTON[1]

28 June 1989 [*manuscript*]

Headington House

Dear John,

Thank you for your jolly and to me enchanting letter. It is hell being 80 – wasn't for [...] you, I daresay; but I have attracted an unwelcome degree of attention, and feel like an aged performer in the worst sense of that word. I *long* to be 81. I truly tried to circulate the fact that by some oversight I had

---

1 John Robert Hilton (1908–94), Corpus contemporary of IB (classics 1926–9), archaeologist and architect turned intelligence officer; officially with the diplomatic service, he served with the Secret Intelligence Service (MI6) 1943–69.

misread my birth certificate, & that I was in fact 81 – but didn't do it. I wish
I had. There *was* a nice programme on the 3d Channel on June 6, I daresay:
I didn't hear it, for I was otherwise engaged[1] – but did you *really* enjoy
Stravinsky's Abraham & Isaac?[2]

Why am I so meaninglessly busy all the time? I have retired from everything God knows how long ago – yet I feel totally spent every evening &
morning – old & grey & full of sleep is entirely true about me: are we the
only great survivors from the great age of Corpus? Not quite. Frank Hardie
is 87: there may [be] a few other ancient persons with one foot in the grave
knocking about somewhere; when I received your most welcome letter
I remembered a story about a man who received a letter from an octogen-
arian contemporary & wrote back to thank him – & added – how nice to
hear from you. I rather thought that we were both dead! I am quite clear
that such career as I have had was securely founded on being systematically
overestimated. Not that I mind: I hope this will continue – it buoys me up.
But eighty is enough – now the decline – the order is one forgets names, then
nouns, then everything: gagahood – the end. On this cheerful note let me
thank you very very much.

    Love,
      Isaiah

TO KYRIL FITZLYON
30 June 1989

                                            Headington House

Dear Kyril,

I understand the purpose of your letter only too well.[3] There is no doubt
that the majority of the Jewish establishment in England are horrified at what
is going on in Israel. But there is not the slightest hope of their producing
a manifesto on the lines you indicate, because they don't want to be called
traitors, even by the present wicked government – and its supporters in
England (who are more numerous than they ought to be). They will say they
don't wish to add to the difficulties of a beleaguered state and be accused of
playing into the hands of its enemies, that anti-Semitism is anyhow here to

---

1 367/3.
2 Stravinsky's sacred cantata for baritone and chamber orchestra, to a Hebrew text, 1962–3, dedicated to the people of Israel. This and Stravinsky's *Les Noces* were introduced by IB as part of *An
   Evening with Isaiah Berlin* (367/3). For IB's role in the genesis of *Abraham and Isaac* see L3 72–3.
3 KF had written to IB, 26 June, to explain that in his letter of 14 June, to which IB replied 19 June
   (370–1), his aim had been 'to ward off or at least weaken any feeling of anti-Semitism fostered
   or provoked by such actions of Shamir's government as child murder by suggesting to distinguished members of the Jewish community (such as you) that they should publicly disassociate
   themselves and the Jewish community here from these atrocities and thus help to clear the Jewish
   name and reputation. Too many people are only too eager to impute to all Jews the crimes committed by very few (relatively fewer, perhaps, than is the case within most other communities).'

stay and its increase or decrease cannot be compassed by public disassociation. All this I think is mere nervousness, not to say cowardice, but I am sure there is nothing to be done about it. A counter-manifesto would duly appear, signed by Lord Weidenfeld, Captain Maxwell,[1] Mr Ronson,[2] Lionel Bloch,[3] rich and influential persons – most of the backbone of the Conservative Party, solid British citizens (I don't include Captain M) who have in the past regarded similar pronouncements by me and others as mere feeble liberalism, virtually left-wing propaganda, pandering to the murderous Arabs, etc. etc. I am very sorry that this should be so, but alas, it is.

Yours ever,

Isaiah

TO SAM GUTTENPLAN[4]

14 July 1989

Headington House

Dear Sam,

[...] You are perfectly right: my interest in people is perhaps almost obsessive. It is so great that I am happy to sit in a café in Paris or stand in a queue in London, absorbed in the looks, shape, gait of passers-by – and if their head or face has a particular structure, or bears a particular expression, which in some way interests me, I stare unashamedly until they look embarrassed and I lower my eyes in shame. I watch them almost as a birdwatcher watches birds. This extends right through everything I do – my interest in the history of ideas extends principally, as you know, to the possessors or expounders of these ideas, their characters, their personal circumstances, the ways of life to which they belong and therefore to their times and places and circumstances, etc. Some people must find this too personal and too frivolous for serious

---

1 (Ian) Robert Maxwell (1923–91) né Abraham Lajbi/Leiby (later Jan Ludvik) Hoch, Czech-born British publisher and newspaper proprietor; fought in British army during WW2, promoted captain, MC 1945; died at sea in mysterious circumstances November 1991, as his business empire, which he had run fraudulently, stood on the brink of collapse.

2 Gerald Maurice Ronson (b. 1939), business tycoon and philanthropist; chief executive of Heron Corporation from 1976, of Heron International from 1983.

3 Lionel Herbert Bloch (1928–98), Romanian-born multilingual British solicitor, Zionist and anti-Communist, sometime London correspondent, JP, and hon. legal adviser to the Israeli Embassy; 'never happier than when puncturing the modish delusions of Arabists and fellow travellers, whether on the BBC World Service or in the letters columns of newspapers': 'Lionel Bloch', obituary, *Daily Telegraph*, 7 November 1998, 27.

4 Samuel David Guttenplan (b. 1944), graduate student and lecturer, CUNY, 1965–71, research assistant to IB 1966–7; philosophy graduate student, Wolfson, 1971–6 (DPhil 1976), supernumerary fellow 1975–6; lecturer, Open University, 1975–6; lecturer, Birkbeck, London, 1976, reader 1992, later (2004–10) prof. of philosophy. In the opening of this letter (omitted above), IB writes, 'we have always possessed a certain moral affinity – what else can I call it? – which has made it easy for us to talk to each other without explaining things in detail, because of a certain instinctive understanding of our respective and very similar points of view'.

scholarship: certainly Habermas,[1] for example, was shocked when I tried to say to him that part of the anti-French reaction on the part of the German thinkers in the eighteenth century was due to the fact that the Germans were all of humble origin, whereas the French were by and large aristocratic – and that there was a certain tension on the part of the Germans and a certain condescension and lack of interest on the part of the French. He said 'Oh, of course, if you reduce all this to personal factors ...' etc. He wanted, naturally enough, a more structural Marxist analysis.

Well, that is how I am made, it is true. And I am grateful to you, and touched, indeed moved, that you know this about me, that you sympathise with it, and even by the fact that you claim – I don't know with what validity – to have been influenced by it in some way. I have always been afraid of responsibility, especially of influencing people – who can tell to what that might lead them? And I have always been terrified of being blameworthy for the things they became or did. Hence no disciples, as you know, in any real sense, which is a great relief to me. Still, I cannot deny that, quite apart from the fact that I am not indifferent to praise, as you so rightly remark, I am genuinely honoured and delighted by the fact that you should maintain that I have had this effect. [...]

Yours ever, ⟨with much love⟩
    Isaiah

TO DAVID VITAL

27 September 1989

Headington House

Dear David,

[...] Of course I have never thought Jabotinsky was an evil man in any way, and of course he was brilliant, remarkably gifted, unique in his generation and altogether someone who deserves to be remembered in all kinds of ways; occasionally a little too sentimental for my taste (e.g. *Pyatero*).[2] No, what I meant by saying he was unscrupulous was founded on an incident in Oxford in the 1930s. He came to address the Zionist Society, about 1934. Walter Eytan, in those days Ettinghausen, asked him: 'Mr Jabotinsky, why do your young men fight the Histadrut[3] young men in the streets of Tel-

---

1 Jürgen Habermas (b. 1929), prof. of philosophy and sociology, Goethe, Frankfurt am Main, 1964–71, 1983–93; director, Max Planck Institute for the Study of the Scientific–Technical World, Starnberg (near Munich), 1971–83; recipient of Germany's highest award for research, the Leibniz Prize, 1986; best known for his magnum opus *The Theory of Communicative Action* (Boston, 1981).

2 *Pyatero* (Paris, 1936, in Russian), trans. Michael R. Katz as *The Five: A Novel of Jewish Life in Turn-of-the-Century Odessa* (Ithaca, NY, 2005), Jabotinsky's paean to the experiences of his youth.

3 'General Organisation of Workers in the Land of Israel'; founded 1920, it could claim to represent the vast majority of the Jewish workforce in Mandatory Palestine by the end of the decade, and is today a powerful economic and social force in Israel.

Aviv, and wear brown jackets?' It was a time when there were street fights between the two youth organisations, some of them, as you know, quite savage. Jabotinsky said, speaking slowly, 'Professor Ettinghausen, the next time you hear that Jews use Christian blood for the baking of *matza*[1] for the Passover, do not believe them at once.' That is what I call unscrupulous. But nothing worse than that.

Goodness, what a mess now. How and when will it end, and in what way? The late George Lichtheim[2] used to say that in the end Dayan would make a deal with Arafat and there would be peace. Not so.

Yours ever,
Isaiah

TO ROBERT KAISER[3]

17 October 1989

Headington House

Dear Bob,

[...] All that you say about Joe Alsop rings entirely true. It is related to the substance of that play written about him by Art Buchwald,[4] which was put on in Washington and which it was thought improper of his friends to see. However, like most of his other friends we went to it and rather enjoyed it; but it was a caricature (a visit to Vietnam by a paranoiac war correspondent throwing his weight around).

I have known Joe Alsop since 1940 and we were warm friends. Let me tell you what I think, as briefly as I can and as my secretary, who is typing this letter, will tolerate. When I first met him in 1940 and got to know him in 1941, he was a stout New Dealer, devoted to FDR, a friend of Felix Frankfurter, Philip Graham (a left New Dealer at that time) and his wife Kay, an admirer of Ben Cohen, a passionate interventionist (*The American White Paper*[5] was a pamphlet in that direction); and these loyalties remained solid to the end of his life. He was totally fearless, independent, patriotic and a super Wasp – that he could not help being. His father,[6] whom I knew, was exactly the same;

---

1 'Unleavened bread'.

2 George Lichtheim (1912–73), German-born socialist intellectual and authority on Marxism; sometimes used the pseudonym G. L. Arnold; emigrated from Nazi Germany to England and settled there, but held no tenured university post, though his works were greatly admired.

3 Robert Greeley Kaiser (b. 1943), US journalist, joined *Washington Post* 1964 and had assignments in London, Saigon and Moscow before joining its national staff 1974–82; managing editor 1991–8; came to know Alsop, a diehard supporter of the war in Vietnam, during Alsop's visits there 1969–70.

4 *Sheep on the Runway: A Comedy in Two Acts* (NY, [1970]), which premiered in NY 1970, features a character described by its publisher as 'an antidisestablishment columnist who smells red subversion round every corner': ⟨http://www.samuelfrench.com/p/1024/sheep-on-the-runway⟩.

5 Joseph Alsop and Robert Kintner, *American White Paper: The Story of American Diplomacy and the Second World War* (NY and London, 1940).

6 Joseph Wright Alsop IV (1876–1953), gentleman (tobacco) farmer, sometime president, New

so was his mother,[1] Theodore Roosevelt's niece, a very nice and amusing woman. He was a warm-hearted and loyal friend, totally truthful, highly intelligent and very civilised – his knowledge of French literature, particularly Saint-Simon,[2] of Chinese political writings, of art, furniture, Greek history and God knows what else was pretty exceptional for an ordinary American political correspondent or columnist.

He was not at that period conspicuously right-wing, though of course he became it later. He did have an obsessive and somewhat apocalyptic vision of the conquest of the civilisation he believed in by barbarians from the East, i.e. the Russians. The Chinese he admired so much that, even though they might conquer the world, he thought that that would be to America's disadvantage but not to that of the world. Russian Communism would mean total extinction of all values which he believed in (and in which I think I believe too).

With all this, he was bad-tempered, bibulous (as you say),[3] could be a bully – but only towards people whom he suspected of opportunism, running with the tide, above all of holding views, whether in a weak and flexible way or in an obstinate and unyielding way, which he regarded as against the interests of the United States. Hence his dislike for Walter Lippmann[4] (whom I knew well and who was indeed a twig that bent in the wind, honest, intelligent but of no character really, undone by his appalling embarrassment about his Jewish origins, which rattled like a skeleton in a half-opened cupboard); ditto my hero Stevenson, whom he regarded as a weakling, over-high-minded; Scotty Reston,[5] for whom he had no moral or intellectual respect; but equally right-wingers like Arthur Krock,[6] whom he despised as one of the vicious defenders of the extreme, slightly Fascist right. He was a deeply neurotic character, lonely, liable to periods of gloom and depression – hence, for the most part, the drink – and certainly to some extent undone by his crypto-homosexuality, which he sought to conceal all his life, but which became

England Tobacco Growers' Association, and insurance executive from Avon, Connecticut; active in Republican politics, he served in his state legislature (house of representatives 1907–9, senate 1909–13), leading the Connecticut effort to elect Teddy Roosevelt 1912; described by Arthur Schlesinger, Jr, as 'a Bull Moose Republican' in *A Life in the Twentieth Century: Innocent Beginnings, 1917–1950* (Boston, 2000), 379.

1 Corinne Douglas Alsop (1886–1971) née Robinson, later (1956) Cole, cousin of both Eleanor Roosevelt and Alice Longworth; a leading Connecticut Republican, she served in the state legislature's house of representatives 1925–9, 1931–3; 'a frank and flavoursome lady' (ibid.).

2 (Claude) Henri de Rouvroy, comte de Saint-Simon (1760–1825), French social theorist who sought, in response to industrialisation, a more equitable reorganisation of society, and profoundly influenced thinkers such as Comte and Marx. One of the 6 main subjects of FIB.

3 RK to IB, 6 October 1989: 'One of my most vivid memories is of him getting drunk twice a day. Too much before and at lunch, then a nap, then too much before, at and after dinner.'

4 Walter Lippmann (1889–1974), US journalist and essayist; author of the widely syndicated and influential 'Today and Tomorrow' column in the *New York Herald Tribune* 1931–67.

5 James Barrett ('Scotty') Reston (1909–95), Scottish-born newspaperman and author; chief Washington correspondent, NYT, 1953–64, associate editor 1964–8, executive editor 1968–87.

6 Arthur Bernard Krock (1886–1974), newspaper manager and Pulitzer-Prize-winning columnist; Washington correspondent, NYT, 1932–53.

more and more widely known, although he never knew the extent to which it was known. [...]

His domestic habits and temperament were those of a rather headstrong eccentric British aristocrat. When he arrived to stay, he wanted the servants to run around, and brought baskets of dirty laundry which had to be washed immediately, and longed to dress every night. If you had seen his room at Avon in Connecticut, and his father, the tobacco-growing squire, and his mother, and the ancestral portraits, you'd have seen where he came from. It certainly involved a high degree of straight social snobbery, but at least you could say it was absorbed at birth – the entire world in which he grew up was affected by it. Nevertheless, in spite of his fanatical anti-Communism, and the fact that he was virtually the first Cold Warrior, there were certain countervailing tendencies – to begin with, what you know already, his passionate concern with civil liberties, his resistance to McCarthyism, the fact that various persons accused by McCarthy, people whom he disliked for their fellow-travelling views and suspected of dishonesty (sometimes legitimately), were nevertheless asked by him to stay with him in order that he might defend them. His most glorious hour was when he defended Henry Wallace, whom he politically detested, from the charge of being a Communist agent.[1] He appeared before the committee, I think the McCarran,[2] and testified – naturally the committee could do nothing with so rock-ribbed an anti-Communist as Joe Alsop, and at the end they said 'Thank you, Mr Alsop, that will be quite sufficient', to which he replied 'No, senator, it will not be sufficient ...', and carried on for another half-hour, bawling at them.[3] So the bawling was not reserved for social inferiors, fellow-travellers, feeble liberals, etc., but was sometimes directed against the grand and powerful.

He could not resist charm and intelligence. Naturally, he began by violently denouncing Bob Silvers. When they met, they became fast friends. He was a great friend of my friend Stuart Hampshire, who is a lifelong socialist and whose views coincided with Joe Alsop's at very few points. He became a friend of a man called Burdon-Muller, of whom I do not expect you to have heard (he was a rich, eccentric pro-Soviet who lived in Cambridge and Boston) as well as Franklin Roosevelt; and Ben Cohen, whom one cannot accuse of illiberal views – Joe thought him a saint and almost invariably right,

---

1 Henry Wallace was called before the McCarran Committee (next note) in autumn 1951. The conservative Alsop did not share Wallace's liberal political views, but believed that he was entitled to a proper defence, and persuaded the diplomat George Ball (1909–94) to act as his counsel, which he did when Wallace appeared before the committee 17 October 1951.

2 Patrick Anthony ('Pat') McCarran (1876–1954), strongly anti-Communist Democrat senator, Nevada, 1933–54; chair, 1950–3, Senate Internal Security Subcommittee (SISS; 'the McCarran Committee'), which had extensive powers to investigate alleged subversive activities in the US; Alsop appeared before the committee 18 October 1951 in Wallace's defence.

3 There is no record of such an exchange in the official transcript of the proceedings; an anecdote of this kind is told of various persons, including the inevitable Oscar Wilde, and seems to be a story that does the rounds without being properly sourced.

though politically, of course, there were disagreements. He was friends, to my great indignation, with the horrible Lillian Hellman, who had praised his stance on civil liberties. But of course, as time went on he became more and more reactionary, even though one could tease him about that and to some degree he laughed at himself for his lonely, rock-like attempt to stem the irresistible tide of vulgarity, decline in intellectual rigour, betrayal of the old civilisation, etc. which he perceived at Harvard, Washington and wherever.

[...] He was hideously unpopular among his fellow journalists always, partly because of the upper-class manner, grandeur, snobbery, ordering waiters about, demanding special treatment, etc. He was not one of the boys, ever, but a somewhat eccentric and often appallingly aggressive, bad-tempered shouter. I have been present at dinner parties in his house, attended, as always, by whoever was important in the administration of the day, plus personal friends, which ended in some kind of row – violent altercations between him and the equally conservative Charles Bohlen, frightful scenes with Dean Acheson,[1] whom he rightly suspected of a certain lack of stoutness of character, despite his looking like the Laughing Cavalier, but who, of course, as against Joe, was almost invariably right. All this was very disagreeable, and his violent pro-Vietnam war line was a trifle mad. His attitude later was friendship and approval for those who had supported the war, even if they changed their mind afterwards, e.g. Robert McNamara,[2] but who did not try to work his passage back by what he regarded as the methods used by e.g. Mac Bundy, whom he regarded as a miserable traitor. All this is true. His political attitudes were often dotty, unacceptable and even odious.

Now if you ask me why I remained such friends with him, let me say again: he was a man of incorruptible integrity; affectionate, loyal, civilised, a devoted friend – nothing said of someone, if he really was a friend, would shake his devotion. You could argue with him quite openly, denounce his views, and he remained courteous, inflexible. If ever there was a middle-of-the-road liberal, extreme left of the right, extreme right of the left, it is myself – yet our friendship never wavered. He knew perfectly well that I didn't like Eisenhower,[3] that I was not all that pro-Kennedy (with whom he was virtually in love), that I thought Nixon and Reagan too awful – it made no difference to our relationship. He disliked Nixon, he was not a buddy of Reagan's, but voted for them, no doubt, and supported their policies, but was

1 Dean Gooderham Acheson (1893–1971), US lawyer and public servant; secretary of state 1949–53; one of the founders of NATO and the Marshall Aid programme, subsequently a foreign policy adviser to Presidents Kennedy and Johnson.
2 Robert Strange McNamara (1916–2009), US defense secretary in the Kennedy and Johnson administrations 1961–8; president, World Bank, 1968–81; came publicly to regret his early advocacy of the Vietnam War, and published a memoir of the conflict with Brian VanDeMark, *In Retrospect: The Tragedy and Lessons of Vietnam* (NY, 1995).
3 Dwight David Eisenhower (1890–1969), US soldier and Republican statesman; supreme commander of Allied expeditionary forces in Western Europe 1943–5; of NATO 1950–2; US President 1953–61.

repelled by them, socially and personally; he was not comfortable during the reign of Truman,[1] whom I greatly admired.

He was a total original: the cruel bullying of which you speak did no doubt occur, and so did the drunkenness – if I had been there, even shivering in a corner, and said 'Now, Joe, stop this, don't go on like this', I think he would have stopped. He prized friendship above almost everything – not above his patriotism, perhaps, but certainly everything else. Arthur Schlesinger's obituary of him was fundamentally just and generous:[2] he basically did not care for Arthur, unlike everyone else – he seemed too far to the left (!) – but adored his second wife, who is the daughter of a lady[3] he once paid court to. So they remained on terms. Given this, Arthur's piece about him is very creditable indeed. But they were not friends personally in the way that Chip Bohlen, Philip Graham [...], Fritchey,[4] Evangeline Bruce[5] or Aline and I were friends. In the end, it was his private person, his warm heart, his honesty, courage and integrity, which no political combination or personal advantage, of whatever kind, ever affected in the smallest degree, that drew one to him. In the end, one simply likes people for what they are, not for this or that reason – I think Montaigne said that.[6] The way people look, speak, the expressions on their faces, what one experiences when they enter a room – this is what determines one's fundamental feelings. He was a man on his own: his marriage was a disaster. He remained incurably solitary; his politics were more often than not deplorable – in personal conversation it became a joke – but you are right, in the kind of situations you describe he must have been often unspeakable.

I have done my best. I don't know if that explains anything,[7] I only hope it does. Please give my love to both your parents.

Yours ever,
　　Isaiah

1　Harry S. Truman (1884–1972), Democrat US statesman; senator, Missouri, 1935–45; FDR's Vice President 1945, assuming office on the death of FDR that April; US President 1945–53.

2　The article (171/5) ended: 'My wife and Aline Berlin called him two weeks ago from the Berlin eyrie in Paraggi. His voice sounded infinitely weak, but his spirit was, as always, indomitable. He embraced life, rejoiced in friends, laughed and raged at human folly, cherished human courage, was a civilised man, a gentleman and a patriot.'

3　Lily Dulany Cushing (1909–69) of NY, artist whose works have been displayed in the Museum of Modern Art, NY, and are also held in private collections.

4　Clayton Fritchey (1904–2001), US journalist and public servant; a syndicated columnist, he was press secretary to Adlai Stevenson in his 1952 and 1956 presidential campaigns, and subsequently Stevenson's director of public affairs, US mission, UN, 1961–5.

5　Evangeline Bruce (1914–95) née Bell, m. 1945 David Kirkpatrick Este Bruce (1898–1977), US diplomat, ambassador to UK 1961–9; one of IB's oldest friends from his wartime years in Washington.

6　'If you press me to say why I loved him, I feel that the only explanation is to reply: "Because it was he; because it was me." ' Michel de Montaigne, Essays 1. 28.

7　RK and IB had both attended Alsop's memorial service the previous month, and RK wrote 6 October (cf. 376/3) expressing bafflement at their mutual friend's contradictory character.

TO HERBERT NICHOLAS[1]

20 October 1989 [carbon]

[Headington House]

Dear Herbert,

Your letter, naturally enough in the circumstances, caused me probably as much pain as my original letter inflicted on you. Perhaps I exaggerated my negative feelings about New College – I was perfectly happy there immediately after the war, with David Cecil, Joll,[2] Bullock, and I thought I loved the Warden,[3] whose election was not communicated to me in 1944 or whenever it was. My less affectionate feelings only began towards the end of the 1940s, and I think I exaggerated them even in my letter to you – in fact, I feel guilt about my outburst. I think it all comes from the imperfectly healed scar of my dismissal – not, of course, from my fellowship, which I resigned while I was Sub-Warden, but as a lecturer, kept on as I was when I was back in All Souls – as K. G. Davies[4] kindly informed me, for incompetence, apparently agreed to by the Warden and tutors.[5] It is not for me to say that this was not justified, but I had been lecturer of the College continuously for twenty years, so I cannot deny that it came as a shock.

However, my guilt about my letter to you is so acute that to purge it, despite your last paragraph,[6] I cannot help but send you £100 (which will arrive shortly from a charitable trust).

I shall miss the St Thomas's Dinner[7] this year out of tact towards myself, but no doubt come next year.

When you were my pupil (you cannot possibly remember that time) I was totally happy in my relationship with New College, even with Crossman [...].

Yours ever,

[Isaiah]

1 Herbert George Nicholas (1911–98), fellow, New College, 1951–78; Rhodes Professor of American History and Institutions, Oxford, 1969–78. As director, New College development fund, HGN had asked IB for a contribution, which IB had declined to make, pleading dissatisfaction with the College. In his reply (18 October) HGN had written: 'Your letter administered the severest jolt I've sustained in a long time. To find that the tutor/colleague who influenced me most & the institution which has shaped & sheltered me the most are so wildly discordant comes as a very painful shock.'

2 James Bysse Joll (1918–94), fellow and politics tutor, New College, 1946–50; fellow, St Antony's, 1951–67; Stevenson Prof. of International History, LSE, 1967–81.

3 Alic Halford Smith (1883–1958), fellow and philosophy tutor, New College, 1914–44, Warden 1944–58.

4 Kenneth Gordon Davies (1923–94), historian of the British Empire; fellow, New College, 1952–63; prof. of history, Bristol, 1963–9; Erasmus Smith's Prof. of Modern History, Trinity, Dublin, 1977–86.

5 IB had failed to fulfil all his teaching obligations at New College, and his contract was terminated 1955 not for incompetence but for lack of commitment: he was travelling too much, and/or was too absorbed with his fellowship at All Souls.

6 'In the circumstances I think it would be quite wrong of you to pay any attention to my letter. Don't give any thought to a contribution. It would make me even more unhappy.'

7 The St Thomas's Day (21 December) dinner was the annual College feast, for reasons that are somewhat obscure: it is unclear even which St Thomas was originally celebrated.

PS My God! Coals of fire! A letter from Harvey![1] Election to hon. fellowship! The Soviet Press normally says 'It is no accident that ...'. But I firmly intend to regard this as pure serendipity, miraculous coincidence. After this, nothing less than £250 will do. And I will come to the St Thomas's Dinner (can I bring my wife as my guest? I shall assume it unless you tell me not to).

Worth waiting eighty years for. If I see you at the dinner, I may repeat to you all the horrid things I said about the New College common room, which I fear obtained enthusiastic agreement from the former Warden. As Sir Zelman Cowen[2] said at a public dinner where some honour was given to him, 'I am choking, I cannot go on ...', and then went on for an unconscionable time.

TO SHIRLEY ANGLESEY

13 November 1989

Headington House

Dearest Shirley,

[...] The Mariinsky Theatre has genuinely moving memories for me. It was there that I heard my first opera, namely *Bohème* – totally forgotten – and then *Boris Godunov* with Shalyapin (better in English than Chaliapine),[3] which I still remember, particularly the moment when Boris sees the ghost and Shalyapin climbs under the table and pulled the tablecloth over his head and sang in a hollow sepulchral voice from underneath the table: that gave me (I was then seven), as you may imagine, acute pleasure and has never been forgotten.

But what is this about Pushkin lying in state?[4] He was buried secretly at night, because the Emperor feared that there might be riots about the death of a worshipped national poet killed by a White Frenchman[5] who was connected with the court. I don't believe in the lying in state, I think that is an invention, like the attack on the Winter Palace by the sailors of the cruiser

---

1 Harvey McGregor (b. 1926), barrister; fellow, New College, 1972–85, Warden 1985–96; his letter of 18 October 1989 told IB that he had been elected to an hon. fellowship (1990–7), and extended an invitation to the St Thomas's Day dinner (380/6).

2 Zelman Cowen (1919–2011), Kt 1976, Australian-born barrister, legal scholar, public servant and college head; governor general, Australia, 1977–82; Provost, Oriel, 1982–90; director, John Fairfax Holdings, 1992–6.

3 Fedor Ivanovich Shalyapin (conventionally 'Chaliapin') (1873–1938), Russian bass; IB recalled hearing him sing the title role of Mussorgsky's *Boris Godunov* at the Mariinsky Theatre, Petrograd, 1916.

4 Pushkin died 10 February 1837, 2 days after being wounded in a duel fought in St Petersburg with baron Georges D'Anthès, a French royalist in the service of the Tsar's army who had paid court to Pushkin's wife, Natalya. As he lay dying a large crowd gathered outside his house, alarming the authorities, who, fearing that the poet's funeral would become a focus for political protest, ignored calls for a state event, and changed both the venue and the time of the service at the last moment, deploying troops to watch over the reduced number of mourners.

5 i.e. d'Anthès (previous note): IB uses 'White' to mean 'tsarist'.

Aurora, which occurs in Eisenstein's film but not reality.[1] Stroganov[2] I do not know, but as I'm never likely to go back there perhaps it doesn't matter. I am sorry about the loo,[3] very funny. The Yusupov Palace – that I know because that is where Brendel refused to play a concert specially arranged for him because the piano, which no doubt dated back to 1910, was no good. They made a tremendous fuss, practically broke open doors, produced another piano – still no good.[4] So no concert in the Yusupov Palace. But I adored the concert hall, so vulgar, so luxurious, so typical of the last days of the imperial regime.

Thank you for the photograph of Akhmatova's window – but believe me, that is pure fantasy. It was quite different, it was nothing like your photograph, it was a grey little window much higher up than the one they showed you, in a much more squalid part of that not wholly restored Fountain House. I know about the museum: it's rather more than the students;[5] there is an organisation in Moscow subsidised by the government which really is making a museum for her. Emissaries have arrived in London to collect stuff for it, including my few unimportant fragments – and a real fuss is to be made of her. It is extraordinary, the dates follow continuously: 1889 Akhmatova, 1890 Pasternak, 1891 Mandelstam, 1892 Tsvetaeva[6] [...] – the centenaries follow each other in a row, but I think they may get a little bored and I doubt if poor Marina will get as much homage as the first two, or, indeed, as much as she deserves – for did not Akhmatova say to me 'Marina is a better poet than I am'? You never saw the rooms in which I had my unforgettable and unforgotten evening, or rather night; I dare not say that to the people who come and take tapes of it back to the Soviet Union – my fragmentary memoirs, I mean, for reproduction for God knows who – because to say that I spent

---

1 Eisenstein's film *October 1917 (Ten Days that Shook the World)* (1928) depicts a piece of Soviet mythology: 'Technically there was a group of sailors who went to the Winter Palace, which had no real defence. The sailors went straight into the Winter Palace and found that there was a provisional government there, which they tried to arrest. Some escaped, some did not. There wasn't a great assault, a magnificent battle with machine guns' (UD 167).

2 The Stroganov Palace, on Nevsky Prospekt and the Moika canal, was being restored.

3 When SA asked for a toilet at the Stroganov Palace she 'was shown very reluctantly all that was available – very crummy stalls' that provided their users with 'sheets of Pravda (what will they do if its circulation drops further?!)'. SA to IB, 3 November 1989.

4 The problem was that the layout of the palace did not allow a proper concert grand to be brought in. The recital was, at short notice, transferred to the Old Stock Exchange as an afternoon event, and was sold out within a day. This was Alfred Brendel's 1st visit to Russia, where he was joined by IB, Aline and a few other friends.

5 SA had visited Fountain House (196/2), where IB and Akhmatova had met in 1945–6, and wrote that 'students – I believe – have opened a small Akhmatova museum in the building'. IB is right that it was not just students who were involved: the fully professional museum resulted from a decision of the Leningrad City Council taken in 1988.

6 Marina Ivanovna Tsvetaeva (1892–1941), Moscow-born poet and prose writer whose works have been much translated into English; she rejected the October 1917 Revolution and went into exile, but returned to the USSR to be with her husband, June 1939; later that year he was arrested and shot; she committed suicide 1941.

'a night' carries the wrong implications; there is a widespread belief that
I had an affair with Akhmatova, which I cannot wholly scotch, but nothing is
further from the truth. [...]

Yours ever, with much love
Isaiah

TO DIANA HOPKINSON
27 November 1989

Headington House

Dearest Diana,

Thank you for your letter, particularly about BJ (Maire to you). I am in
sporadic – is that the word? – correspondence with her; our letters to each
other are fairly long but not very frequent. However, each letter refers to its
predecessor, so in some sense it is a continuous-discontinuous correspondence. I realise that she is not well; she does indeed invite me to go and see
her [...]. I think she really is a wonderful human being – her views were and
are absurd,[1] but there must have been plenty of people in the eighteenth and
nineteenth centuries who were equally eccentric in their views, although this
took nothing away from the beauty of their characters or the touching nature
of all they thought and felt and did. It is a pity that BJ's views connect with
some of the most horrible crimes in the entire span of human history, but
somehow these have made no impression on her whatever. I dare not bring
them up with her: the distress would be too great and she obviously has not
much longer to live (I hope I am wrong, but it seems so to me). What can
such people have been thinking during these years? That it is all bourgeois
propaganda, all lies, even after Khrushchev's speech? And as you say, what
about now? What can they think? I think people like her, and there aren't
perhaps many, somehow manage to block out whole ranges of experience,
views, human qualities, etc., and live in a very imaginary world. Otherwise
I cannot explain the views of a good many of our friends of those days. What
about Goronwy? He only ceased to be a Communist in 1939, very late – what
about the horrors before that which were well documented? Guy Burgess
had no moral basis to his life; but Philip Toynbee,[2] who also lapsed in 1939 –
what could he have thought? How could Christopher Hill[3] have gone on like
this? Goodness, I'll never understand. It broke my friendship with several of

1 Maire Lynd followed her sister, Sigle, into the CP while at Oxford; after Hungary 1956 she
  remained in the Party only for the sake of her marriage (179/1).
2 (Theodore) Philip Toynbee (1916–81), son of the historian Arnold Toynbee; writer and critic;
  foreign correspondent, *Observer*, and a member of its editorial staff 1950–81; an undergraduate at
  Christ Church (history, 1936–8), he was the first Communist president of the Oxford Union, but
  left the party 1940 over the Soviet invasion of Finland.
3 (John Edward) Christopher Hill (1912–2003), Marxist historian of the C17th; CPGB member until
  1957; fellow and history tutor, Balliol, 1938–65, Master 1965–78.

these people, but I cannot regret that, it was inevitable; and if I lived my life over again it would still happen. [...]

Do telephone, and we shall meet.

Yours ever,

Isaiah

TO JACK DONALDSON

10 May 1990

Headington House

Dear Jack,

I feel tremendously flattered that you should seek my opinion on the war crimes issue. My mind is not very clear about that, but I will do my best to tell you what I think – not to change anything you believe: I think your case is excellently summarised.[1]

1. '45 years is too long'.[2] I don't think I believe that we change much through time – the people I have known for forty-five years seem to me not radically changed. I may have changed, they may have changed, but identity is not quite so unstable or variable as your argument seems to imply. We've known each other for over thirty years: what radical changes do we observe in each other? Any? Have e.g. Quintin Hailsham or Frank Longford[3] changed one relevant iota since you knew them at school? I don't believe it. However, this point is not very amenable to conclusive argument. But if you believe that, it does weaken the argument for ever punishing or rewarding anyone for acts committed forty-five years ago. [...]

2. Now about punishment. Here I hold somewhat heterodox views, which may shock you. You think that the deliberate infliction of pain can be justified only if it improves the world in some way, e.g. by reformation, deterrence, compensation for injury, protection of the public, expression of society's condemnation. All this I accept. These are all utilitarian arguments, none the worse for that. But I have always believed, on the whole against all my decent, enlightened, humane and rational friends (what others could I possibly have?), that the concept of punishment is based on something else, namely – here is the shock – the idea of retribution. That is what Kant

1 JD had written to IB, 8 May 1990, enclosing a draft speech he proposed making in the Lords on the 2nd reading of the War Crimes Bill, 4 June, and asking for feedback. The Bill allowed UK courts to try those accused of war crimes in Nazi Germany or its occupied territories 1939–45 who subsequently became British citizens or residents; it was rejected by the Lords 4 June by a large majority, but became law in May 1991 under the provisions of the (rarely used) Parliament Acts of 1911 and 1949.

2 This phrase appears early in JD's draft as an argument against prosecution.

3 Francis Aungier ('Frank') Pakenham (1905–2001), 7th Earl of Longford 1961; Labour politician, writer, social reformer and philanthropist; a cabinet minister under Clement Attlee and Harold Wilson, he was leader, Lords, 1964–8. He, Hailsham and Donaldson were all near contemporaries at Eton: the former 2 went on to Oxford, the latter to Cambridge.

believed.[1] You and most of the people you and I respect may think that this is a relic of our primitive and barbarous past – of something like lust for revenge – and that it is right to be ashamed of it. Yet I do not agree: when we say 'Serve him right' or 'Poetic justice' – as indeed most of us do – this does mean retribution. If someone falls into a pit which he has dug, for the worst of motives, for an innocent person, we experience satisfaction. Why, if not because we believe something like that the punishment should fit the crime (to quote the Mikado)?[2] I think this is of the essence of punishment proper. Perhaps, for enlightened reasons, punishment in that sense should be abolished. What would be left would be done for your reasons, i.e. utilitarian ones, and very good ones. But the rescue of, creation of better conditions for, individuals or society is not what I think punishment means. This may seem a question of definition: but I cannot help stating what I think is a common motive for punishment. I do not, of course, hope to convince you for one single moment. Still, surely there is something in what I say? But if you condemn retribution, why don't you attack it firmly? I am sure that some of the supporters of the Bill do believe in it.

There is one point where I do genuinely disagree with you and do hope to convince you. I agree with all you say [to the effect] that punishing old men won't deter them from repeating their crimes, or reform them, or stop people in the middle of a war from doing awful things – and perhaps there ought to be a statute of limitations on society's expressions of horror also (presumably the only justification for Nuremberg on your premisses – but not on mine). But I believe that punishing old men can act as a deterrent to others from repeating crimes. Let me tell you what I mean. It seems clear to me that during the war nothing could have stopped the Nazis from exterminating Jews. All this talk about bombing the camps, the trains etc. would have done little good; they would have rebuilt them immediately. In the last months, and indeed weeks, before the end of the war, when the Germans were obviously losing, they went on killing the Jews till the last moment. I believe that they wanted to exterminate the Jews more than they wanted to win the war – that is what undeterrable fanaticism is. But if the Allies had uttered blood-curdling threats, in about 1943, to the Hungarians, Romanians, Slovaks, Croats etc., that if they did anything to the Jews terrible things would be done to them (for by that time it did not look at all certain that Germany was bound to win), then I think such threats might have had an effect, and so do some American historians of the period I have talked to. My only point is that this kind of deterrence *can* work (though it wasn't done in this case),

---

1 In *The Metaphysics of Morals*. See *Kant's gesammelte Schriften* (170/5), vi 332.19–21: 'Only the law of retaliation (*ius talionis*) [...] can determine the quality and quantity of punishment.'
2 From the Mikado's song in Act 2 of Gilbert and Sullivan's comic opera *The Mikado, or, The Town of Titipu* (London, 1885): 'My object all sublime / I shall achieve in time – / To let the punishment fit the crime.'

that you can frighten other people into not committing crimes by conspicuously punishing people who have, at whatever date. That is the only point on
which I really disagree with you. Again, there is no way of proving it.

My principal reason for myself being against the Bill (apart from the
immorality of retrospective legislation, which I do feel – as for the fact
that the crimes were not committed by British subjects on British soil, that
touches me less, because that would make Nuremberg totally wrong) is
a much less reputable one. I think that such trials would strengthen the view
– more or less expressed by one of the bishops in the original debate – that
this might be thought to originate in ferocious Jewish agitation, and would
increase anti-Semitism (presumably, as I should put it, by being thought to be
typical of the horrid Jewish eye-for-an-eye mentality, unacceptable in decent
society).[1] If I am right, as I believe I am, the harm done to the Jews in this
country might outweigh any deterrence or expression of horror that could
be achieved by the trials.

I think if you made the speech on the lines you indicate, and not on [those
of] Quintin's silly speech,[2] it would be a very noble utterance, and I wish to
encourage you to do so. So there. Let me add that my secretary, Pat Utechin,
to whom I am dictating this, wishes me to know that she wholly agrees with
all you say, and not at all with me; I think most of the Lords will echo her
views and I shall not regret this.

Yours ever,
Isaiah

TO BEATA POLANOWSKA-SYGULSKA
29 May 1990

Headington House

Dear Beata (if I may?),

[...] First, let me tell you that I never predicted the recent events any more
than anyone else succeeded in doing. Whatever may happen to Gorbachev

1 In the debate on the War Crimes Inquiry Report the previous December John Taylor, Bishop
of St Albans, had stated: 'I am becoming conscious of a revival of anti-Semitism in this country.
I have seen it in my diocese. A school chaplain spoke of it to me a few days ago. It makes me
fearful, and I pledge myself to do all that I can to stamp it out. However, I fear lest the proposal
to pursue the last remaining war criminals may be turned by the enemies of Judaism into yet
more hostility, not against the criminals but against the victims and those who seek justice on
their behalf. They may be seen to be the driving force behind this legislation. I believe that they
are not.' *Parliamentary Debates* (Lords) 513, 4 December 1989, cols. 604–79 at col. 624.
2 Lord Hailsham (Quintin Hogg) opposed retrospective war crimes legislation on the grounds of
legal practicality, but also, by implication, of its unfairness: 'Nobody suggests that the murderers of the Katyn massacres – which were every bit as bad in their own way because they were
intended to destroy the Polish middle class – should be brought to justice. It is only those who
happen to be on the losing side.' Unable to recommend a change in the law he took comfort in
a final court of judgement: ' "it is written, Vengeance is mine; I will repay, saith the Lord". And
you may bet your life that he will.' ibid. cols 629–32 at col. 632; Romans 12:19.

in the Soviet Union, there is no doubt that statues should be put up to him in Poland, Czechoslovakia, even Romania. Without him, the collapse of the old system could, in my opinion, not have occurred so soon. I realise only too well what you mean by saying that you and others are 'too tired' to glory in the fruits of this situation, welcome as it must be, with all its dangers and deficiencies. I have just read an interesting article by Michnik[1] (a German translation of something he had written for some organisation in Vienna) in which he says, I think with great understanding, that the alternatives before the liberated central European countries are the path of Sakharov versus the path of Solzhenitsyn – democracy, individual liberty, modernisation, use of scientific methods, the kind of liberal regimes that the Russian intelligentsia of the nineteenth century believed in, versus nationalism, anti-modernism, return to ancient values, chauvinism, authoritarianism, anti-Semitism etc., not perhaps quite so violent an overturn as recommended by really disreputable bodies like Pamyat[2] or their allies, but nevertheless the kind of thing that the right wing of both the Russian emigration in the West and, evidently, many people in the Soviet Union still hanker after. I do not suppose either will come to pass, but some unsatisfactory compromise between the two, as usually happens in human affairs. [...]

Your daughter[3] seems to me to be gifted with an exceptional sensibility and imagination, and I do not wonder that this is so – genes are important, we are told, and she has obviously inherited excellent ones. I am glad you gave her that washing powder – once one's imagination fixes on something it is right to increase people's happiness as you have done. About advertising: of course I would not deny that advertisements create desires which were not there previously for things which in fact may not be good for one. What I disagree with Charles Taylor about is that these artificially awakened desires are not real desires. All desires are stimulated by something, whether the depths of one's own character or one's experience – some unexpected physical, moral, emotional or intellectual event in one's mind, heart, soul. Of course the causes are many and obscure, and difficult to trace, and the psychoanalysts may be right at any rate about some of them. What I do not

1 'Zwei Gesichter Polens, zwei Gesichter Europas' (presumably translated from Polish), written for *Osteuropa: Übergänge zur Demokratie?*, the 1st issue of the journal of the Vienna Institute of Human Sciences, *Transit* (autumn 1990), 185–9; trans. Mariusz Matusiak and Christian Caryl as 'The Two Faces of Europe', NYRB, 19 July 1990, 7. Adam Michnik (b. 1946), Warsaw-born author, dissident and political activist, co-founder 1976 of the Polish Workers' Defence Committee (KOR), precursor to Solidarity; Michnik was an adviser to Solidarity and became editor in chief of its journal *Gazeta Wyborcza* (*Electoral Gazette*), which became Poland's largest daily newspaper.

2 'Memory', extreme nationalist, anti-Semitic Russian political movement which evolved from the late 1970s, gaining strength after the breakup of the USSR: in essence, Slavic neo-Fascism.

3 Paulina Julia Sygulska (b. 1984), BP-S's first child, had seen a TV advertisement for washing powder and conceived an irrepressible desire to acquire it. Advertising was virtually unknown under Communism and this was one of Paulina's first exposures to it. BP-S called this an 'artificial desire'. UD 29, 67–8 (letter of 18 May 1990).

think is that [...] what man desires 'truly' is something different from what
he thinks he desires under the influence of these commercial or political
stimuli. I take a crudely empiricist position: what one desires, one desires;
it may not be a good thing to satisfy certain desires, it may do one (or other
people) harm, but I do not think that a rigid distinction [should be drawn]
between 'real' desires – which flow from one's 'true' nature and are part of
the purpose (at least for Taylor) towards which one's being is directed by
God or nature or whatever directs one's life to certain individual goals – as
against these other desires which are not part of this teleological process.
[...] all that is wrong with advertising is that it directs or conditions one's
yearnings towards something which turns out not to be as described, which
is a 'false prospectus', a false description, and that is something which can
justly be objected to – as [one can make objections] against every kind of
deception or manipulation – but should not be taken as leading to a distinction between 'true' and 'false' desires. If one does that, one goes back again
to the two selves, one of which is entitled to dominate the other, and that, as
you know, leads to my horror of the perversion of that into arguments used
by every despotic regime in history. [...]

    Yours affectionately,
        Isaiah Berlin

*'I have yielded to the temptation to appoint an "official" biographer,' IB wrote
to Morton White in December 1990, 'provided that I am in no condition to read
what he has to say.'[1] The biographer in question was Michael Ignatieff, who
had been interviewing IB since 1988, capturing on tape the memories that IB
had made clear he would never commit to paper. Ignatieff's conversations with
IB were conducted over the course of a decade, and were a principal source for
the biography, with IB's letters and the testimony of his friends (and enemies).
Ignatieff drafted the biography while IB was still alive, but on the condition,
imposed by IB, that it would be published posthumously.*

TO STEPHEN SPENDER
29 May 1990

                                            Headington House

Dear Stephen,
    [...] You suspect me of acquiring or developing an archive. Believe me,
this is not so. If it is true that I don't destroy letters, I throw them into heaps,
bags, boxes, and anyone who wants to write about me will, I suppose, have
to go through them in some fashion – I have no idea what it all contains. [...]
You ask what happened to your letters to me: I cannot tell, for I dare not look

1 To Morton White, 24 December 1990.

at letters written to me in the past. I only once put my hand in a drawer full of letters, and pulled out two or three, and was horrified – one's relationships became so changed after the years. There are letters which are obviously warm and intimate from people from whom one has become totally distant – and again, angry letters from people with whom one is now on the best of terms and one has forgotten what the friction can have been about. The whole thing reminds one of a world which has gone – my memory is not good, despite all that is thought of it by others (mistakenly) – and suddenly to plunge into the past and be faced with one's own past life and past experience terrified me. So I never did it again.

There are two ladies from the Bodleian who are supposed to sort out my letters, such as survive – no doubt yours are among them; at least, I hope so. But I don't think that Michael Ignatieff will look at them while I am still alive, or if he does I shall not allow him to tell me anything about them unless he simply wants to ask factual questions – to have something written about me in my lifetime horrifies me beyond words. Nor have I ever written an autobiography or a journal, as you know (though, as you may imagine, publishers have occasionally suggested it), because I am so deeply uninterested in myself [...]. If one is like that one cannot possibly try to reconstruct, to resuscitate, one's life, one's feelings, one's opinions. I really live from hour to hour, from moment to moment, in the most superficial way. I do not exactly despise myself, for such as I am, I am, and I have led a, to me, happy life, largely through lack of depth of character, which probably has saved me a great deal of agony, which deeper natures, such as yours or Edmund Wilson's or T. S. Eliot's, or Auden's, must have gone through. Indeed, I believe that in my own way I am as superficial as the contemptible Hannah Arendt – I cannot insult myself more than that. But I have never laid claim to any kind of depth of insight or wisdom. I am so surprised to be alive at my age that every time (or almost) that I wake in the morning, I congratulate myself on having yet another day, in the course of which anything may happen. My life is really – though it seems so regular and in a way conventional – a kind of hopping from island to island in some enormous ocean, some thorny, some with soft and velvet grass, some large and comfortable to be on, some jagged and frightening, but all passing soon, none lingering too long. How could someone like me write a journal or an autobiography, I ask you? I have never consciously thought about what material I am likely to leave when I am dead, nor have I the faintest interest in what will be written about me. Stuart never believed [me] when I said I didn't really mind what happened if I was dead, but in the end even he came to recognise that what I was saying was true, that life is life and once it's over it's over. I have no wish to be remembered or forgotten or written about or praised or insulted – I could not care less about what happens once I am dead. It is a horrifying confession, but I make it to you: to whom else could I say all this?

You say that you suspect that I have a low opinion of Curtius.[1] Surely this is not so. I have not read much of him, but my impression is that he is a truly great scholar about the Latin Middle Ages and classical literature in France as well. I should have read him, and your quotations are wonderful: they make one think, and that is the best that one can expect from any writing. Of course it's true that Shakespeare is the greatest arouser of Romantic literature there has ever been. I do not think one could describe him as a Romantic himself, if by romanticism one means what I mean by it – a denial of fixed points, absolute values, classical patterns, a kind of perpetual movement, in which both oneself and the universe are involved, which creates its own purposes, ideals, as it moves forward in an unpredictable but constantly creative fashion. That, I think, is what the German Romantics thought. And Goethe didn't. Shakespeare for them was the great destroyer of what seemed to them dead French classicism, the prison house of Boileau;[2] 'wood-notes wild',[3] which liberated one from what Blake,[4] who was a true Romantic, hated most – the cage (as he thought it) created by Newton, Locke and other rational thinkers [for] 'Robin Red breast',[5] that is himself and people like him, who were caught. I do not know whether Curtius thought of romanticism in these terms. It is a German invention, it is the product of Francophobia, humiliation at the hands of the grand, proud, soulless, materialistic (as they thought of them) and world-loving French, who humiliated them so deeply in the seventeenth and eighteenth centuries.

But I mustn't go on. When you come back, will you tell me what to read by Curtius, and what he says about romanticism? I shall pounce upon it eagerly. So few people have written sense about romanticism, and so many have attacked it without understanding what it was, that anything illuminating is to me tremendously valuable. [...]

Love to Natasha.

Yours ever,

[Isaiah]

---

1 Ernst Robert Curtius (1886–1956), German humanist, scholar of European (particularly medieval) literature, taught at Bonn from 1929.

2 Nicholas Boileau-Despréaux ('Boileau') (1636–1711), French satirist, poet and critic, self-appointed legislator of French classicism, revered in England by the likes of Dryden, Pope and Addison.

3 'Or sweetest *Shakespear*, fancies child, / Warble his native Wood-notes wilde': John Milton, 'L'Allegro', in *Poems* (London, 1645), 36, lines 133–4. The phrase became something of a literary trope, signifying untutored poetic genius as against regimented classicism: in his *The Enthusiast: Or, The Lover of Nature, A Poem* (London, 1744), 12, lines 130–1, Joseph Warton asked: 'What are the Lays of artful *Addison*, / Coldly correct, to *Shakespear*'s Warblings wild?'

4 William Blake (1757–1827), engraver, artist, poet and visionary; his C20th reputation was enhanced by Northrop Frye's *Fearful Symmetry: A Study of William Blake* (Princeton, 1947), which 'established Blake as a defining presence in the pantheon of English Romantic poetry, the equal of Wordsworth and Coleridge' (Robert N. Essick, ODNB).

5 'A Robin Red breast in a Cage / Puts all Heaven in a Rage.' William Blake, 'Auguries of Innocence' (1803), lines 5–6.

TO SHIRLEY ANGLESEY

25 June 1990

Headington House

Dearest Shirley,

[...] How wonderful all those photographs are of the Upper Volga regions. I cannot quite understand who the lady is who is researching into the 'blue clapboard house'.[1] There is no doubt that in 1915 my family inhabited precisely such a house in Andreapol' – a tiny company union townlet plus railway station – not far from the city of Toropetz, where my grandparents and uncles established themselves during the same period, and a little further from Ostashkov. All this I remember, or think I remember, vividly; particularly, of course, Andreapol', which was an establishment backed by a village called Velikoe Selo,[2] where the peasants lived who cut the trees and bound them into rafts and floated down on them – like Canadian lumber – down the Dvina river to Riga, where my father's firm was. I remember the soldiers who drove me about in lorries – the smell of slightly burning tyres is still in my nostrils, rather like corresponding memories in Proust (that famous macaroon).[3] I remember soldiers playing balalaikas in wooden huts, officers waiting to be sent to the front, reading to my mother in the evenings and mildly flirting with her; an old, sick landowner called Kushelov, descendant of a long line of Andrey Kushelovs, after whom Andreapol' is of course called, dying slowly in his dilapidated manor house, allowing himself occasionally to be called on by parties of children and slightly older boys and girls, relations of the various clerks, timber controllers, Russian officials and tutti-frutti who were allowed to go picking mushrooms and berries in his tangled woods and gardens – all that straight out of the nineteenth century, Turgenev and Chekhov all mixed up.

So if anything is known about the blue clapboard house, with its barefoot peasant girls who looked after us – an idyllic form of life for nine months – I should be deeply moved, I know it. Ostashkov I only remember has a railway station; Toropetz I remember well, with a river, high reeds growing along it; my uncles,[4] who told me all about Garibaldi[5] and La [Spedizione dei] Mille and the redshirts on the one hand, and the Niebelung songs on

1 In her letter of 17 June SA mentioned an unidentified 'Leningrad correspondent' whom she appears to have charged with taking (untraced) photographs of the house in Andreapol' where IB and his parents lived from June 1915 to early 1916, before moving to Petrograd.

2 'Big Village'.

3 An eccentric translation of 'madeleine' in Proust's À la recherche du temps perdu, the small cake whose taste has become the paradigm of a sense-impression that recalls the past.

4 Presumably the youngest of Mendel Berlin's brothers, the twins Leo and Samuel Berlin, born 1897, and so 17–18 in 1915–16, when the family was in Andreapol'.

5 Giuseppe Garibaldi (1807–82), Italian patriot active during a crucial phase of the movement for the unification of Italy, the Risorgimento; in the 1860 Expedition of the Thousand (Spedizione dei Mille), he led his legion of 'Redshirts' to victory over the Kingdom of the Two Sicilies.

the other, all of which they appeared to be learning in the upper forms of a school at the same time; I knew all about Hagen, Gunther, Siegfried etc., all mixed up with Garibaldi, the conquest of Sicily and long poems by Pushkin which I was made to read, plus a book on Egypt which gave all the original Egyptian spellings of the names (Izi for Isis, Osire for Osiris), and Persian names (Kambudjia for Cambyses, Ksharsha for Xerxes, and so on) – all this mixed up in my mind as a kind of panorama of my childhood. So you see how sentimental one can get as a result of the references in your letter. [...]

Much love,

Isaiah

TO DIANA HOPKINSON

28 September 1990

Headington House

Dearest Diana,

The news about BJ, as I have always called her, even though I knew that she had been ill for a long time, was a shock, and a cause of deep distress. Have you ever known anyone of purer, sweeter character, with infinite moral charm and, incidentally, beauty, physical as well as spiritual? Oh dear. I never answered her last letter, which of course causes great guilt. But she remained a friend for over sixty years, and H. A. L. Fisher, the Warden of New College, once wrote a poem about her and me which began 'Her raven locks he seeks to bleach', then I can't remember, then 'Higher still and ever higher / To Isaiah, to Isaiah': this would be about 1933.

You are right, Tommy's death was very painful to her; she idolised and idealised him, and bitterly regretted not having accepted him when he proposed in the very early 1930s – all because her head was turned by that awful Howard.[1]

Thank you very much for giving me this sad news, which I might not otherwise have known for months. I must write to Jack.

⟨yrs with much love –⟩

Isaiah

11 October 1990: publication of IB's The Crooked Timber of Humanity: Chapters in the History of Ideas, *edited by HH.*

---

1 Peter Dunsmore Howard (1908–65), Wadham 1928–31, but left without taking a degree; represented Oxford (1929, 1930) and England (8 caps 1930–1) at Rugby football; political columnist, Express Newspapers, 1933–41; farmer from 1937; underwent religious conversion *c.*1940, and from 1941 campaigned for the Christian renewal movement Moral Re-Armament, which he led 1961–6.

TO KYRIL FITZLYON

11 December 1990

Headington House

Dear Kyril,

[...] Russia: oh dear, oh dear, I fear you are right. No goods, friction everywhere, and dislike and distrust of Gorbachev. Nevertheless, I regard him as a natural survivor. If there is a coup of some sort, and there is a new dictatorship, I have a feeling that Gorbachev would somehow be at the new dictator's side rather than buried by him.[1] But I may, as so often, be wrong. The thing which cheered me, when I was there two or three years ago, and now when they come to see me, is the survival of the Russian intelligentsia. I thought it had been killed stone dead by Communism, but not so. There are young men, educated, sensitive, morally sympathetic, with interest [in] and understanding of the arts, literature etc. – I cannot understand how this could have, not exactly survived, but been reborn. There is something marvellous about Russia after all; as Tyutchev said, 'Russia is not to be understood by the brain',[2] etc.

The theories about why this terrible regime came to pass are bound to be many and various. The only ones which threaten any danger to human lives are the anti-Semitic ones, e.g. that the Tsar and his family were murdered by Jews, that the Politburo was entirely Jewish (certainly at least half was), that Lenin was a Jew (his mother's name was Blank, clearly the name of a baptised Jew from Odessa), as against the official version that his mother was half German, half Swedish, and his father a straight Kalmyk[3] – so much for his pure Russian origin as hitherto believed, in comparison with the rootless cosmopolitan[4] Trotsky. Like you, I hate them all and I always have; and I don't exclude Bukharin[5] either, who was weaker and more amiable than the others, but did not do a single good thing, did not help a single persecuted writer or artist, when appealed to; his 'rehabilitation' as the more acceptable side of Bolshevism I reject with both hands.

I am glad you like Maistre; some people who adore him have written to

---

1 In August 1991 Gorbachev survived a coup staged by hardliners, but was then politically sidelined as Communist rule in the USSR effectively ended and power swung to Boris Yeltsin (484/2), recently elected President, Russian Federation.

2 Fedor Ivanovich Tyutchev (1803–1873), Russian Romantic poet, wrote an untitled quatrain 1866 whose 1st line is 'Russia cannot be understood with the mind alone.'

3 Ilya Ulyanov, Lenin's father, was born in Astrakhan to a Chuvash (an ethnically Turkic group) family; but on his mother's side there was Western Mongolian Oirat (Russian Kalmyk) blood.

4 A phrase coined 1948 by the editor of the Russian journal *Ogonek*, Anatoly Vladimirovich Sofronov, to refer to Soviet Jews. It appeared in his article 'For the Further Development of Soviet Dramaturgy', *Pravda*, 23 December 1948, 3.

5 Nikolay Ivanovich Bukharin (1888–1938), Russian revolutionary, close associate of Lenin; editor, *Pravda*, 1918–29; expelled from the Politburo by Stalin 1929, but politically rehabilitiated 1934, becoming editor of *Izvestia*; denounced as a Trotskyite 1937; executed for treason.

protest against his being put in the same company as Hitler and Mussolini. I don't quite do that; nevertheless I think he would have preferred them, *malgré tout*,[1] to feeble liberals – Kerensky,[2] as it were – whom he disliked and despised beyond everything. [...]

Yours ever,
Isaiah

TO LOUIS RAPOPORT

13 December 1990 [*carbon*]

Headington House

Dear Mr Rapoport,

[...] You rightly suppose that my anti-inevitability views are powerfully reinforced by what has happened in Eastern Europe. So far as I know, only Mrs Thatcher and the British ambassador[3] in Moscow of seven years ago predicted this – and now hooray! it has happened. But the Jews, of course, are in a panic. Any radical change exposes them to ghastly destinies – this is not the first time, nor, I fear, the last.

But when will your government change? I hope its fall is close, if unpredictable. The mere sight of Shamir's face in the newspapers disgusts me. I dare say he is a better man than I think him, for he could scarcely be worse.

You ask me about my views in the 1930s and 1940s about the Marxist dream. I never had the faintest sympathy for Marxism at any time in my life, and earned a good deal of disapproval from dear friends, particularly in the later 1930s. Except for the Leonards Schapiro and Woolf, I know of no contemporary of mine who was proof against it. But I am beginning to boast, so it is time to wish you well during the troublesome period through which we, and particularly you, are going.

Yours sincerely,
Isaiah Berlin

TO KYRIL FITZLYON

27 December 1990

Headington House

Dear Kyril,

[...] I do not deny that the original Politburo did contain a hefty proportion of Jews, and that they did fill all kinds of jobs in the most odious parts of

1 'In spite of everything'.
2 Aleksandr Fedorovich Kerensky (1881–1970), moderate socialist, one of the leaders of the February 1917 Revolution in Russia (March in the Western calendar); prime minister, provisional government, from July onwards, he was ousted after the Bolshevik October Revolution.
3 Iain Johnstone Macbeth Sutherland (1925–86), KCMG 1982; joined diplomatic service 1950; UK ambassador to Greece 1978–82, to USSR 1982–5.

the bureaucracy, at least until the big purges of 1936–7. But I don't think that is the only cause of Soviet Russian anti-Semitism. Anti-Semitism is an ancient, endemic thing in Russia, as you know – indeed, you say that yourself. Funny about the praise given to Nicholas I,[1] who I suppose tried to russify Russian Jews, and was to that extent not too badly disposed towards them. I can't refrain from telling you the story of a Jewish village which Nicholas visited. As you know, there is a passage somewhere in the Bible which says 'Blessed be He in his coming and blessed be He in his going.'[2] They wrote this down in Hebrew. Naturally, the Russian officials demanded a translation, in case there was something improper. The Jews supplied the best translation they could: 'Thank God that he came, thank God that he left.'

Interesting that you should mention the Russian Jews and the Zionist anti-Arab feelings. I have a theory about that. As you know, the Pale of Settlement[3] squeezed the Jews into living in adjacent towns, townlets, *mestechki*[4] etc., and by the sheer process of compressing them into comparatively narrow territory created an artificial national minority, which they did not constitute in other countries, where they tended to scatter to some degree. They were surrounded by peasants, with whom they had no real contact. The peasants were pious Christians, largely illiterate, and had a culture wildly different from that of the Jews, who could read, at least Hebrew letters, and had a long scholastic tradition, and were totally dedicated to a different religion, not compatible with that of Russia. And so there was virtually no contact – there was at most a kind of exchange of goods with the natives. They didn't hate the peasants, but they feared them, no doubt much as the British colonists feared the Red Indians: pogroms were always possible, and whenever there was a *krestnyi khod*[5] the Jews trembled lest this turn into some kind of attack. Then a great many of them went to Palestine. They carried their portable culture with them. Their attitude towards the Arabs was a direct copy, as it were, so it seems to me, of their feelings about the Russian peasants – the Arabs were illiterate, spoke Arabic, were barbarous, etc. etc. Of course, some cultured Jews from Germany tried to get into contact with the Arabs and formed organisations for friendship with them. But you must imagine what it must have been like for some civilised musical critic from Mannheim trying to talk to an Arab landowner, or Jerusalem merchant. They met once, at most twice; after that the Arabs didn't come back. So it all failed miserably.

1 Nicholas I (1796–1855), Tsar of Russia 1825–55; authoritarian ruler who confronted, and crushed, the Decembrist revolt of 1825, and the Polish uprising of 1830–1.
2 A misquotation of Deuteronomy 28: 6: 'Blessed shalt thou be when thou comest in, and blessed shalt thou be when thou goest out.' But the anecdote still works if we substitute 'Thank God that you came, thank God that you left.'
3 The area in the Russian empire between the Baltic and the Black Sea, where Jews had been confined by statute since the end of the C18th.
4 'Shtetls'.
5 '(Religious) procession'.

Now, of course, they have an appalling government of religious bigots and nationalist fanatics and God knows what will happen. Nevertheless, there is a large number of liberal-minded Jews still there, with whom I can comfortably associate, who deplore the present situation and want to give up the West Bank. Unless this happens the Arabs will overrun the Jews by sheer numbers. Of course the behaviour of the Jews on the West Bank and [in] Gaza must have increased hostile feelings, especially on the part of the left, who strenuously deny that it became anti-Semitic, only anti-Israeli, they maintain. However, the dividing line can be extremely thin, and anti-Zionism, anti-Israelism, easily spill over into anti-Semitism.

I do not think that Zionism is racist in any degree. That proposition I am prepared to defend to the death. The worst among them don't want the Arabs there – bad enough, but there is no question of hatred of them because of their origins, their blood, etc. Whatever the laws about 'Who is a Jew?'[1] – and conversion is an open door to it as well as being born of a Jewish mother – there is no racist propaganda, the Arabs are not denounced as biologically inferior, intermarriage is not condemned more than with rich American Wasp ladies. There is a great deal of *Erde*, but not *Blut*.[2] Hatred of the Arabs is both inevitable and abominable, but it has nothing to do with the Nazis, much more with the Spaniards versus Indians. Herzl was right: once Jews say they are a nation in some sense, that they are not Russians as the Russians are Russians, or English as the English are English,[3] that to some degree coincides with what anti-Semites say, and that is why the entire liberal Jewish establishment of the late nineteenth and twentieth centuries denounced Zionism as a form of Jewish anti-Semitism. One knows what they meant. Myself, I have nothing against complete assimilation of the Jews: but it isn't on; it hasn't worked; the survival of the Jews is a mystery, but it is a fact. So one might as well make the best of it. So long as every Jew in the world, including baptised Jews, feels some minimal degree of social unease – it need be no more than that – there has to be a country in which they don't feel that, however deplorable the behaviour of some of them may be in other respects. The original Zionists always talked about having 'our own thieves, our own murderers, our own forgers'.[4] To belong completely to a nation,

1 For IB's views on this recurrent question see L2 671–3, 763–7.
2 'Earth'; 'blood'.
3 In his address to the 1st Zionist Congress in Basel 1897 Herzl says that the Jews are a nation, not a religious community, and hence deserve a polity of their own. ⟨http://zionism-israel.com/ hdoc/Theodor_Herzl_Zionist_Congress_Speech_1897.htm⟩.
4 This well-known Zionist witticism, which often continues 'and then having our own policemen to put them in our own jails', is sometimes attributed to the poet Chaim Nachman Bialik (1873–1934) in the form 'We shall be a normal state only when we have the first Hebrew prostitute, the first Hebrew thief, and the first Hebrew policeman' ('Hebrew' here being used to refer to the *Ivrim* or 'new Jews' of the Zionist state), but we have found no documentary evidence for this. Cf. 'a Jewish state will not be a success when the Jews in it are successful, or even when the Jews in it are statesmen. It will be a success when the Jews in it are scavengers, when the Jews in

a community, a group, is a basic human desire, and that the Jews have had, in a very twisted kind of way – hence my Zionism. You are wrong about Zionism, you really are – your position is intelligible but founded on very light support, misunderstandings.[1] Still, I do not hope to convert you, either at your or my time of life.

The root of anti-Semitism is in the Gospels. [...] The Muslims are not in that sense anti-Semitic: they look down on the Jews as they did on Christians, as second-class people because not Muslims. However they may have pretended otherwise here and there, they do all believe this if they are true Muslims. But their dislike of the Jews is due to political circumstances of this century, and is not a rooted, indelible sort of anti-Semitism, the kind which fed the Christian Middle Ages and does still, and will so long as (a) people read the Gospels, (b) there are Jews. To that I am – all Jews should be – resigned. Hence the need of a country of their own – at a high price, but not as high as would be paid if they didn't. [...]

Yours ever,

Isaiah Berlin

TO KARL POPPER

27 December 1990

Headington House

Dear [Karl,]

[...] I was delighted to receive your letter, and feel greatly honoured by the thought of being associated with you in remaining unbowed by the enormous waves of ideological folly, conformism, the onslaughts of all the enemies of truth and reason through which we have lived.[2] Events in Eastern Europe really are a kind of miracle; whatever may happen, even if things go wrong here and there, even if they go wrong badly, it cannot go back to the

---

it are sweeps, when they are dockers and ditchers and porters and hodmen. When the Zionist can point proudly to a Jewish navvy who has *not* risen in the world, an under-gardener who is not now taking his ease as an upper-gardener, a yokel who is still a yokel, or even a village idiot at least sufficiently idiotic to remain in his village, then indeed the world will come to blow the trumpets and lift up the heads of the everlasting gates; for God will have turned the captivity of Zion.' G. K. Chesterton, *The New Jerusalem* (London, 1920), 293–4.

1 KF had written: 'Any defence of anti-Semitism or an attempt to excuse it – for whatever reason or against whomsoever directed – is, of course, utterly abhorrent to me and is, indeed, one of the reasons why Zionism – at least as practised and even verbally articulated by Israelis – with its numerous other Nazi overtones – racism, Blut-und-Erde, violence and much else – is to me quite unacceptable' (19 December 1990).

2 KP had written: 'We have both lived through an amazing end of a most dangerous age – dangerous for the survival of mankind; and although it is not quite over, it looks very hopeful now, in spite of this appalling story of Iraq. I think that our views of all that must be similar, and nothing need be said. [...] But the intellectual situation is, I think, awful. [...] Everywhere [...] there seem to be only silly fashions: people are too cowardly to go their own way or to swim against the current. I greet you as one of the few who did' (4 December 1990).

awful past. I had a long talk about that with Sakharov – he was pessimistic, he said that Gorbachev was a tyrant, didn't understand democracy, etc. etc. I tried to persuade him that things never return to the full horror of their beginnings. He said 'Yes, I understand; as a worker in the laboratory I know that there are always residues in the pipes and the retorts with which chemists work, so the good is never emptied entirely. I cling to that.' [...]

I wish you a very, very Happy New Year, and, as Jews sometimes say at services, a long life.

Yours ever,

Isaiah Berlin

TO KYRIL FITZLYON

16 January 1991

Headington House

Dear Kyril,

Thank you for your letter of 30 December, which I think is a masterpiece of indictment – at times just, at times unjust. My God, you have managed to dredge up some pretty frightful examples of odious remarks by Zionists, for which I cannot take responsibility – nor do I seek to condone [them]. [...]

Firstly you speak of the 'desire of the Jews' to have a country of their own. Not desire, but desperate need, which is somewhat different, even in previous centuries – hence this unceasing nostalgia for Zion, which animates the whole of the Jewish religion and, by the usual stages, enters into their secular consciousness as well. But then, after pogroms, massacres and the Holocaust, it reaches a maximum point. But I don't think you want to deny that.

Now, Verwoerd.[1] Certainly that monster approved of Israel precisely for the reason he gave.[2] But my case is that the apartheid, which is perfectly genuine, is not based on racial grounds but on something else, which can then be well treated. Given the situation, this was not a morally defensible position, and most Zionists, certainly the dominant Labour Party of the whole pre-Begin period, accepted this. The desire not to have strangers, above all strangers who had virtually nothing in common with them, is natural, but has to be overcome – about that I would agree. I still do not believe that it has

1 Hendrik Frensch Verwoerd (1901–66), Dutch-born South African National Party politician; as minister for Bantu affairs 1950–8 he established apartheid; prime minister 1958–66; banned the African National Congress after the Sharpeville Massacre (21 March 1960), and withdrew South Africa from the British Commonwealth 1961; assassinated by a white extremist in parliament 1966.

2 KF: 'Zionism, whatever we think of its ideals and asipirations, manifests itself, & can for the time being manifest itself, only on racist terms, with all that this entails. This is the main reason why the former South African prime minister Verwoerd, a great friend of Israel, said in praise of it that "Israel, like South Africa, is an *apartheid* state."'

anything to do with race, as it did in South Africa, or in America with regard to the blacks, or in Russia with regard to the Jews, or Poland or Rumania, both of which I was taught to regard as totally anti-Semitic countries. And there is a case for that, save that lately, for whatever reason, I have lost my dislike of these countries, let alone their individual citizens, of which I can be quite fond, and have begun to understand what historically must be the cause of this – social, economic but above all religious and Christian. I can see that those who kill God must always have a shadow over them. There has been the ember of this for two thousand years, and the winds can and do blow it into a flame. [...]

Now, the anti-Semitism of the 'pillars of Zionism' – and indeed Herzl too. That is easily explained: the anti-Semitic belief that Jews are not Englishmen as Englishmen are Englishmen, for Weizmann and his friends, was valid, and in that sense they believed that they were on the side of the anti-Semites as against the assimilationist Jews. The vast majority of Jews in Herzl's and Weizmann's early days were violently opposed to Zionism, as you must know, because they believed that, if not now, then tomorrow, or the day after tomorrow, they would become Englishmen, Germans etc., and were indeed already that to a large degree, and that to regard them as somehow different was itself a form of irrational prejudice. Weizmann did not think it irrational; but it was not a racial difference that he was concerned with (even if the anti-Semites did look on the Jews as a race), but the Jews as a nation – coinciding with race, perhaps, [...] but not at all identical. There was never any proclamation of racial superiority by any of these people. As for 'Arab trash', that is terrible and inexcusable, of course;[1] it derives, as a phrase, from 'poor white trash', the despised white poor in the southern American States. It is a terrible phrase, but it isn't racist; a horrible expression of hostility or contempt, but there is no reason for thinking it was said on a racial basis.

Then you speak of the equally disgusting statement by the Sephardic Chief Rabbi on blood transfusions.[2] Of course there are religious bigots everywhere, and the notion of racial purity, or the purity of blood, is not something which is intrinsic to the Jews, whatever this horrible man may have said. You can become a Jew by conversion – this would not be the case if blood is what mattered. As for the attitude itself, my goodness me, rabbis in Israel have [made], and will doubtless continue to make, a frightful fuss about non-Orthodox Jews – for example, those who are married by Reform rabbis,[3]

---

1 KF had condemned as racist Weizmann's 'reference [...] to Palestinians as "Arab trash" ruled by the Turks, rightly, he thought, "with sword and fire" & his consequent *complaint* that the British, instead of using whips on the Arabs, "mete out the same justice to Jews and Arabs"'.

2 Mordechai Tzemach Eliyahu (1929–2010), Sephardic Chief Rabbi of Israel 1983–93, held that Jews should if possible not accept blood transfusions from non-Jews. KF quotes him as saying that 'it takes Jewish blood to cure Jews'.

3 Adherents to the progressive, liberal, non-orthodox Judaism that has its roots in the Reform movement in C19th Germany.

who are regarded as not rabbis at all, so the marriages are not marriages and the children are bastards; and conversions are not conversions, so that their children are not Jews at all.

At the present moment, with the inpouring of Russians, all this is going to become much more acute so far as the religious fundamentalists are concerned. Plenty of Russian Jews are only half Jews, or even a quarter: some have brought with them Russian wives, some [are] Jewish wives who have brought Russian husbands. All this will be thunderously denounced by the rabbis. But I can assure you that the great majority of the Jews of the world do not hold with this. And if it goes too far there will be a serious *Kulturkampf*.[1] I hope this doesn't happen, but one of the most powerful rabbis in Jerusalem, aged, I think, ninety-six, says that insufficiently pious Jews may not be admitted to communal prayer and the like, and, indeed, denounces the Hasidim (from whom I admit I am descended)[2] as not Jews at all, because of differences of ritual and the like. That is a case of real religious fanaticism of the most odious kind, to which Jews are of course liable; and, of course, to talk of blood is racist – but this cannot apply to the vast majority of either Jews or Zionists, I do maintain, whatever the extremists may scream.

There was Rabbi Kahane, assassinated in New York a few weeks ago – he certainly believed this kind of thing; but at least he did go to jail in Israel three times for his views.

The whole problem of racial purity is a sinister and interesting topic, about which I do not know much. It begins, so far as I can discover, in Spain, in the sixteenth century, where there is a doctrine of *limpieza de sangre*;[3] those who did not have Jewish or Moorish blood in their veins were regarded as less suspect of the secret practice of Jewish or Muslim rites, though officially Christian, than those who did have such blood. Hence, paradoxically, bishops and archbishops were very suspect to the Inquisition, because a good many of them apparently did have Jewish blood in their veins, whereas the peasants were OK because few Jews seemed to have intermarried with them, or bred children with them. So on that point I can only say that racism is odious wherever it is, and the Jews no doubt have their share in it; but the Europeans, who invented it, I think, have a far larger proportion of persons affected by it. Are you really prepared to deny that? I can assure you that what the Chief Rabbi said is in no sense an official state doctrine or ideology, even on the part of the present awful government. Racism is on the whole confined to the right wing of the Jews. Israel grew under a Labour government, which was free of racism in any conscious sense [until] the sudden injection

1 'Culture struggle', a term originally applied to the policies adopted by the Prussian chancellor, Otto von Bismarck, in the 1870s to reduce the power of the Roman Catholic Church and promote secularisation.
2 267/1.
3 'Purity of blood'.

of, above all, religious racism by rabbis who for a very long time, until almost the present, were bitterly anti-Zionist – because human beings have no right to usurp the role of the Messiah, who alone can bring the truth back to their ancient kingdom. Anyway, that is my impression, against which I do not see sufficient evidence.

As for the way the Arabs are depicted in Israeli films, etc., there is some correspondence here to the *Der-Stürmer*-like[1] cartoons and statements about Jews in every Arab country. Both are loathsome, but that there should be a Jewish response to all this is, perhaps, not altogether surprising, however regrettable. Of course this kind of thing would be banned in this country, because at present, let us say, the Asians and Africans here are not regarded by most people as a sufficient danger to English culture (in the sense in which Powell spoke of it);[2] whereas in Israel it obviously does constitute such a danger. [...]

You speak of anti-Arab land and employment legislation. Of course that is unjust. A great many people I know in Israel would condemn it as such, and there is a journal which exists solely for the purpose of exposing and condemning this.[3] Indeed, you would not have heard of it if it weren't that Israeli publications are relatively uncensored, and these things are written about, cause indignation in government circles, etc., whereas similar treatment of Jews, say, in Syria, Iraq, even Egypt, is not widely known because nothing about it is permitted to be published. I don't think two blacks make a white, but if racism is to be condemned, the number of countries in which it is rife is not inconsiderable. Still, in so far as there are Jewish racists, they should of course be restrained.

Again, you speak of punishments meted out to Arabs but not to Jews. No doubt there is much injustice done, but the reason for it is precisely that

1 *Der Stürmer* (*The Stormer*) was a virulently anti-Semitic Nazi tabloid weekly founded 1923 by Julius Streicher, the propagandist and party leader, and published (with some brief gaps) until the end of the war 1945.
2 (John) Enoch Powell (1912–98), English politician and classical scholar; MP 1950–87 (Conservative 1950–74, Ulster Unionist 1974–87); minister of health 1960–3; sacked from the Shadow Cabinet 21 April 1968 for making what many considered an incendiary speech the day before against immigration in Birmingham, describing the concept of integration as a 'dangerous delusion': 'Now we are seeing the growth of positive forces acting against integration, of vested interests in the preservation and sharpening of racial and religious differences, with a view to the exercise of actual domination, first over fellow immigrants and then over the rest of the population.' 'To the Annual General Meeting of the West Midlands Area Conservative Political Centre', in *Reflections of a Statesman: The Writings and Speeches of Enoch Powell*, ed. Rex Collings (London, 1991), 373–9 at 378, 379.
3 If IB means the short-lived daily newspaper *Hadashot* (1984–93), whose weekend edition might be thought of as a journal, what he says is an exaggeration, but he may have in mind the closure of the paper by the military censor for 4 days in April 1984 when, in the wake of the hijacking of a bus by 4 Arab terrorists, it defied the authorities by printing a photograph of the 2 terrorists who survived the rescue operation being led away to their deaths, when the official story was that they had died of their wounds.

which caused the British to bomb villages in Iraq[1] as a form of collective punishment; which caused them to act as they did towards mutineers after the Indian Mutiny;[2] which caused the French to act as they did in Algeria,[3] and other horrid colonialist activities. Colonialism may be condemned as such, but so long as a country regards the behaviour of some of its inhabitants as an open mutiny, by violence, against its government, this is surely bound to happen to some degree? The only way to stop it is by partition, by exchange of populations, or other drastic measures; so long as there are minorities there will always be a danger of injustice, discrimination, sometimes violence, sometimes by more peaceful if sometimes no less invidious means. I still see no racism. And even 'qualitative and quantitative difference between Jews and non-Jews' – why is 'qualitative' racial? People denounce lower cultures, but that is not racism; it may be unjust and wrong, but there are few people who do not think of some culture as inferior to their own – 'lower' – but I do not think this entails racism.

Consequently, I still hold to the view that, deplorable as some of Israel's policies are, and unrealistic and self-defeating as the blind loyalty of a good many Jews to the policies of its present government may be (which is founded largely on their sense of the precariousness of Israel's military and political position, their fear – not ungrounded – for its future), racism does not greatly enter into it. It may, as I said above, in some marginal groups, but not among either the majority of the Jews or the majority of the Israelis, at any rate that is my impression.

So, finally, the answers to your two questions. (1) Is Zionism racist? I say firmly no, even if it has racists amongst its adherents, as there are racists in most parties in most countries. (2) Could Zionism have been promoted, and Israel established, without racism? I would answer in equally firm terms, it could have been and was. But of course there are always fanatical rabbis who believe that eating non-ritually-slaughtered food would make the composition of human bodies physically and biologically different, and 'de-Judaised' – and similar nonsense.

I do not suppose for one moment that I shall have convinced you. I can only reiterate your friendly last paragraph, and say that in my, in its turn overlong, letter I have said not only what I believe to be true, but have produced some arguments to justify it. Still, I think we shall continue to differ.

---

1 In the early 1920s: see L3 404/1.
2 The Indian Mutiny, which began at Meerut 10 May 1857, and petered out after the recapture by British forces of Delhi 14 September, saw numerous massacres of Europeans; the British 'Army of Retribution' exacted a terrible revenge, including a systematic wholesale execution of prisoners; the Mughal punishment of tying victims to the mouth of a cannon and blowing them apart was also revived.
3 During the Algerian War of Independence, 1954–62, the French routinely used torture against prisoners from the Algerian Front de libération nationale (FLN); the war saw extreme brutality on both sides.

I only hope that history does not justify your pessimistic interpretation of what Zionism is, and that after the present awful government goes – all governments go in the end – and not necessarily by the destruction of Israel (which has never been impossible), a decent society will emerge, and your analysis will be refuted by the facts.[1] Inshallah.[2]

Yours ever,

IB pp PU

On 2 August 1990 Saddam Hussein,[3] dictator of Iraq, ordered the invasion of neighbouring Kuwait, which he accused of stealing Iraqi oil resources. In defiance of UN resolutions Kuwait was annexed as the nineteenth province of Iraq. The UN Security Council imposed economic sanctions on Iraq and authorised (29 November) an international military coalition, led by the US and based in Saudi Arabia, to reverse its gains. Diplomatic efforts failed, and an air and ground offensive, Operation Desert Storm (17 January–28 February 1991), successfully evicted the Iraqi forces from Kuwait: they were routed and largely destroyed in the deserts of southern Iraq. But Saddam Hussein remained in power, and soon violated the terms of the UN ceasefire that had brought the Gulf War to an end.

TO ARTHUR SCHLESINGER

5 March 1991 [carbon]

Headington House

Dear Arthur,

Thank you for that odious review of Noel's book.[4] [...] I entirely agree with you about Podhoretz [...]. I remember that he and Diana Trilling[5] set upon Stephen Spender and myself with great ferocity for contributing to a pro-Communist and pro-PLO periodical called the New York Review of Books: Pod said, 'How can you, a Zionist, betray the cause so openly?' We

1 KF had signed off: 'I can only hope that my total frankness has not in any way whatsoever either hurt you or offended you. I hope too, in view of the emotional feelings raised by Zionism and its achievements in many fields, that I can be proved wrong (by you perhaps?) in my estimation of it.'

2 Arabic: 'If Allah wills it', 'God willing'.

3 Saddam Hussein Abd al-Majid al-Tikriti (1937–2006), Iraqi dictator 1979–2003; a Sunni Muslim from a peasant family in Tikrit, he joined the radical Ba'ath Party 1957; played a leading role in the coup that brought the party to power 1968; led Iraq in the Iran–Iraq War 1980–8, Gulf War 1990–1, and later (2003) Iraq War (captured by US forces near Tikrit 2003; found guilty of crimes against humanity by the Iraqi Special Tribunal and hanged 2006).

4 Norman Podhoretz, 'Portrait of a Generation', review of Noel Annan, Our Age: Portrait of a Generation (London, 1990), New Criterion 9 no. 5 (January 1991), 70–2.

5 'She is obsessed by anti-Communism. I remain on good terms with her, because she is so eccentric, and peculiar, and articulate about her past (her autobiography was not very kind to Lionel), and in the end, though I fear to say it, she continues to be entertaining to me. But she is possessed.' To Morton White, 27 December 1994.

defended ourselves without difficulty, and enjoyed the evening in an awful sort of way. I have sent the review to Noel on the assumption that he may not have seen it. I don't think that he will mind it much; but he has received, if not a beating, a very mixed bunch of reviews in England. I cannot remember who is doing it for Bob, but he will not be too badly treated there, I expect, and in general I expect he will get a better reception in the US than in England, where personal factors play a considerable part. I think one of the nastiest reviews I have ever seen in my life was perpetrated by a New College don called Christiansen, in the *Independent*.[1] Every sentence was both malignant and funny, so one read it with a certain degree of guilty amusement – but it was a dreadful piece, and could have been written, by an enemy, about you or me, on roughly the same sort of grounds. But I enjoyed Pod without qualification – it is precisely what one would expect [...].[2]

As for the dumb war,[3] I must put my cards on the table – I am a hawk. There has in fact been no enthusiasm for the war in England, though much approval – no machismo, no sabre-rattling (when I say 'no', I exclude the worst example of our yellow press, which in my view has never had any effect on anybody, since the days of Beaverbrook onwards). Why am I a hawk? You may suspect pro-Israeli feelings. No doubt these may play a part, but I am prepared to defend myself on higher ground. I believe that every aggressive dictator who shows savagery and is therefore an obvious menace to decent people can, if he begins to be a threat beyond his frontiers, be stopped, if need be by force. There was not quite enough force to stop Alexander, Caesar, Genghis Khan; but we are supposed to be pleased about the defeat of Xerxes[4] (by force). Mussolini could have been stopped if we had imposed oil sanctions at the time of the Abyssinian war.[5] He apparently

1 Eric Christiansen (b. 1937), historian; lecturer in history, Oxford, and fellow, New College, 1965–2002. 'Me and My Chums Aboard a Sinking Ship' (also a review of *Our Age*: 403/4), *Independent*, 6 October 1990, 32: 'the earliest memories of their juniors are fouled with the relentless emissions of autobiographical verbiage, and our last moments will be disturbed by the sprightly or solemn voices of their many disciples blathering on about Me and Virginia Woolf, Me and Pacifism, Me and Oxford, Me and Munich, Me and Wittgenstein, Me and the whole worm-eaten toy-cupboard of Twentieth-Century Reminiscence'.

2 Podhoretz attacked Annan's 'rapturous canonisation of Isaiah Berlin. [...] the fact remains that Berlin has neither an original mind nor even a particularly unconventional one; and if the English philosopher Roger Scruton goes too far in characterising him as shallow, Scruton is entirely justified in attacking this famous defender of liberty for maintaining a discreet silence since liberty came under assault in the universities from the left and for failing to take on such "polluters" of scholarship as the Marxist historians E. J. Hobsbawm, Christopher Hill and E. H. Carr' (72). IB had a greater capacity than most for maintaining friendly relations with those with whom he disagreed politically, notably Hobsbawm and Carr; but see L2 58/2.

3 Schlesinger had asked (19 February 1991): 'Why are the British so much more in favor of this dumb war than the Americans? I asked Michael Howard this question the other day. Memories of Suez? of Munich? of T. E. Lawrence? of Chinese Gordon? He replied, "You must remember that the British have not lost a war since 1783." '

4 Xerxes I (c.519–465 BCE), king of Persia 486–65 BCE; forced to withdraw from his invasion of Greece after defeats at Salamis in 480 BCE, and Plataea in 479 BCE.

5 When Italy invaded Abyssinia, 3 October 1935, the League of Nations declared Italy the aggressor,

told Hitler that he would have had to stop if this had been done; and the late Lord Simon once said in my hearing in the common room at All Souls (from which nothing ever leaked, surprisingly), 'You young men want me to impose oil sanctions on Italy. Supposing I do, and Mussolini falls. What then, Communism?' Hitler could have been stopped in 1936. The French wanted to, came to London, we said no go: 'He is only recovering his back garden', in the words of Archbishop Lang.[1] I suspect, though that shocks everybody, that continued intervention in 1918 could have stopped Lenin, who certainly thought so himself. Then we might have had a civil war between the left and the right, which, whatever the result, might have been better than what happened. [...] the action against Galtieri,[2] even Noriega,[3] seemed to me perfectly OK. Cuba was the only failure.[4]

I genuinely believe that if one does not stop those who swallow neighbouring states, far worse must always follow – hence my hawkhood. Suez does not count, because he[5] did not seize foreign soil. I cannot deny that the prospect of the effect on Western industrial life, let alone Third World life, of Saddam lording it over the Middle East does enter into the picture. So, in short, perhaps for the first time in my life, I think you are mistaken, and suspect that your worthy anti-Republican feelings are not entirely irrelevant to your stance. The thought of a handsome press prize to Pilger,[6] which is anticipated, is in my view scandalous. [...] Now you and Teddy Kennedy[7]

and imposed economic sanctions; but neither Britain nor France were fully committed to punitive action, fearing it would drive Mussolini into alliance with Hitler, and the omission of oil from the list of embargoed goods was an obvious, fatal, weakness in the League's response.

1 Cosmo Gordon Lang (1864–1945), 1st Baron Lang 1942; fellow, All Souls, 1889–93, 1897–1928; Archbishop of Canterbury 1928–42. At the time of Hitler's military reoccupation of the Rhineland, March 1936, Philip Henry Kerr, Lord Lothian, was widely reported as saying that the Germans were only occupying 'their own back garden': J. R. M. Butler, *Lord Lothian* (1960), 213. Multiple signs were given to the French in February and early March 1936 that Britain did not regard the Rhineland as its frontline, and France, isolated, could not act alone.

2 Leopold Fortunato Galtieri (1926–2003), Argentinian general, dictator 1980–2, President 1982; led Argentina to defeat in the Falklands War against Britain, April–June 1982, and subsequently resigned; democratic elections for a new President followed.

3 Manuel Antonio Noriega Morena (b. 1934), dictator of Panama 1983–9; though an ally of the CIA from the 1960s, his involvement in drug trafficking eventually led the US government to disown him; after he voided the result of democratic elections 1989 US President Bush ordered US troops into Panama City; Noriega was captured in January 1990 and subsequently sentenced to 40 years' imprisonment by a US court.

4 JFK's support for the Bay of Pigs invasion of Cuba by anti-Communist exiles, 17–19 April 1961, was disastrous: their defeat consolidated the power of Fidel Castro.

5 Gamal Abdel Nasser (1918–70), Egyptian army officer, a key figure in the group that deposed King Farouk 1952; prime minister of Egypt 1954–6, President 1956–70; his nationalisation of the Suez Canal Company in July 1956 precipitated the Suez Crisis.

6 John Pilger (b. 1939), Australian-British journalist and documentary film-maker; an outspoken critic of US and UK foreign policy, and of the mainstream Western media; controversially awarded the Richard Dimbleby Award for factual television reporting at the Baftas 17 March 1991; news of the award was leaked a fortnight before the ceremony.

7 Edward Moore ('Ted') Kennedy (1932–2009), later (2009) hon. KBE; US Democrat politician, younger brother of President John F. Kennedy and Senator Robert F. Kennedy; US senator,

can throw pillows at me. Schwarzkopf[1] has become my pin-up boy – after his reference to Hannibal at Cannae[2] I cannot think too highly of him. I fear you may disagree.

We could discuss this matter in detail in the summer if only you would come and see us again. But I admit that to find myself on the same side as Pod and Luttwak[3] is rather lowering.

Much love,
[Isaiah]

TO HENRY HARDY
2 April 1991

Headington House

Dear Henry,

[...] You ask, as is your wont, important – central and difficult – questions, to which I do not know of any firm answer. I'll do my best to reply to you, but it is all, as you will see, painfully tentative.

First, about anxiety to please (a relatively easy question). I still think that my own comes from the need, no doubt hereditary, and I daresay by now genetic, of outsiders exposed to peril – the Jews, for two thousand years – to accommodate themselves in a hostile environment, which can be done either by aggressive self-defence (which usually ends badly) or attempts to appease, which may well be undignified and pathetic but do, I suppose, lead to self-preservation of a minimum degree, social acceptance. It was so in the ancient world and the middle ages, and in the modern world something of that lingers. You are quite right to suppose that I am perfectly comfortable in my present existence. I am not conscious of having to make compromises or of having to appease, suck up to potentially dangerous or powerful people or institutions; nothing of that, I admit, do I feel or practise; but my natural tendency towards trade-offs, compromise, peaceful settlement – whatever

Mass., 1962–2009; he voted against the resolution to authorise US military action against Iraq in the key senate vote of 12 January 1991 (carried 52–47).

1 (Herbert) Norman Schwarzkopf (1934–2012), hon. KCB 1991; US General, commander of all Allied forces in the Gulf War, January–February 1991; a larger-than-life figure, 6′ 3″ tall and weighing 240 pounds, 'Stormin' Norman' proved adept at handling news briefings, and became a celebrity in the West after orchestrating the liberation of Kuwait; but he had had at his disposal in Operation Desert Storm massively superior forces, ranged against an enemy 'with a gross national product equivalent to North Dakota's'. Robert D. McFadden, 'Lionized for Lightning Victory in '91 Gulf War, Gen. H. Norman Schwarzkopf Dies at 78', NYT, 28 December 2012, A1.

2 At Cannae in Southern Italy (now on the SP3, 10 km WSW of modern Barletta) in 216 BCE the Carthaginian general Hannibal executed a now fabled battle plan to inflict one of the worst defeats ever suffered by imperial Rome; it was a victory much admired by General Schwarzkopf, who subsequently claimed that it inspired his strategy in the Gulf War.

3 Edward Nicolae Luttwak (b. 1942), neoconservative US historian, military strategist and consultant, political theorist and combative contributor to *Commentary*, a journal which was in some ways anathema to IB.

their objective justification and validity – probably does spring from unconscious efforts to fit myself into a totally new environment in 1919.[1] As it is successful, the need for it evaporates, I suppose, but its traces cannot but remain in all kinds of subconscious, unexpected and perhaps rather central ways. That's the best I can do. But I admit with some pleasure that whatever the roots of my temperament and habits, I am not conscious of them, and perhaps never was – my theory is a mere hypothesis, though I still think not implausible.

Now, your more serious question. My God, what do I answer about 'the common human moral core'?[2] All general propositions of the kind I utter about that kind of thing are in a sense amateur observations, general reflections not founded on accurate knowledge of history, sociology, psychology etc., which in theory would be needed to give them any kind of objective or scientific respectability. One just says 'Most human beings, at most times, in most places, surely ...' etc. What is this founded on? A general sense of what human beings are like – which may well have not merely gaps but be seriously mistaken in places – but that cannot be helped: all vast generalisations of this kind are neither avoidable nor demonstrable.

You ask if they apply to the non-Western world[3] – in my opinion, they do. Japanese culture, for example, which seems to me remoter than any other I have ever encountered, and its values, which differ sharply from our own, nevertheless is a culture of human beings – that is, *nos semblables*.[4] I mean something very simple: that unless there are common values, however different in detail, twisted this way or that by circumstances, genes or whatever – unless there are these, communication becomes impossible; but it is not impossible. Missionaries correctly assumed that they could try to convert

---

1 sc. 1921, when the family emigrated to England.
2 HH had asked (25 March 1991) about 'the scope of your view of the common human moral core (if I may so describe it) – the bulwark against relativism'. This exact phrase is not used by IB in his writings, but he does speak in the relevant sense of 'common values' – L 21 ('the common values of men'), 24; RR2 167–8; CTH2 317; POI 12 – as he does in the next paragraph and in letters to Hendrik Hoetink, 15 June 1983 (206 above), and Beata Polanowska-Sygulska, 28 June 1987 (UD 100).
3 HH's letter (previous note) continues: 'I have always assumed that, though your examples have naturally most often been Western ones, your canvas is (at least potentially) the whole of humanity.' The stimulus for seeking clarification on this point was a request to HH from Michael Ignatieff to comment on a draft of his review of CTH, 'The Ends of Empathy' (*New Republic*, 29 April 1991, 31–7), in which he reported IB as holding that the common moral framework he identifies applies only to the West – 'When Berlin speaks of universal values, he means European ones' etc. (34) – which would render it useless as a bulwark against those who flout it, especially in other parts of the world. This interpretation stems from unclarity on IB's part: he does sometimes say things like 'at any rate in the West' (e.g. L2 757; cf. 413), but this is merely a disclaimer recognising that his knowledge of the East is restricted. As this letter shows, he believes that the framework is humanity-wide, as indeed it has to be to have any teeth. HH passed on IB's clarification to Ignatieff, but the information appears to have reached him too late to influence the text of the article.
4 'People like us'.

Trobriand Islanders or, for all I know, African pygmies, in spite of the vast chasm which lay between the forms of life. They could only do this by appealing to something which in the end the others understood – in some cases allowed themselves to be persuaded by, in other cases not, but in both cases in some degree intelligible.

The question is, how widely does this go? Herbert Hart, as you probably know, once tried to work out an empirical theory of natural law,[1] by saying that there were certain principles which all men accepted because otherwise society would collapse, and there was an almost biological need to continue living together: e.g. no murder, otherwise society couldn't go on; no lying, otherwise nobody could believe anyone else (again, no communication); presumably food, drink, shelter etc. etc., without which men would perish. But in the end, although these things are true, they form too thin a basis for what we like to think of as human rights, which are presumably founded on some kind of general moral acceptance.

So what can I say? Only that in my opinion – but only in my opinion – differences between nations, cultures, different ages of human life, have been exaggerated. We do not, surely, entirely misunderstand Plato, though we don't know what Athens looked like (was it like Beirut, or like an African kraal?), even though Skinner would have us believe that, unless we do know such things, we don't really understand what thinkers mean.[2] If this is so then there is a pretty wide common ground between human beings as such, upon which one can build. It must be possible to preach to Muslim bigots, or Communist fanatics, in terms of values which they have in common with the preacher – they may reject, they may argue, they may murder and torture, but they have to construct special hypotheses in order to account for the fact that the preacher is mistaken, and explain the cause or root of the mistake, which entails some degree of common understanding. At some times, of course, the preacher is successful, at least in weakening, if not refuting, violently held views. This I firmly believe, and this applies to the whole of mankind. If Michael Ignatieff thinks differently, do correct him.

Now, about pluralism and toleration. My God, another terrible question. Your formula is the well-known – and in my opinion correct – one, that democracies should tolerate all doctrines save those which threaten to subvert democracy; liberalism should tolerate everything except what will put an end to liberal thought and action; etc. All that is true, and I do accept that. But it does not go far enough. I do not wish to say that I tolerate, and

1 206, 276.
2 Quentin Skinner's 'historical contextualism' holds that ideas have to be understood in their historical setting, not anachronistically: we cannot have a conversation with Plato as if he were in the same room, sharing our cultural and intellectual baggage. Works of political theory written in the past cannot be treated as straightforward contributions to perennial debates. This view IB substantially rejects.

do not wish to suppress, the opinions of those who think it all right to torture children to amuse themselves, or preach or practise other enormities – even racial or national hatreds – even if my presumably tolerant society is not actually endangered by it in a serious degree. You ask me, do I want to imprison David Irving[1] or the National Front?[2] Not imprison, perhaps, because that is not needed: I would not in the least mind a degree of censorship which would not permit certain things to be published, much as the race relations legislation does.[3] And yet society is not in serious danger: it is not the kind of intolerance which might subvert the foundations of our liberal society.

On the other hand, I can't say that I wish to suppress all intolerance, as such. All believers in universal values are presumably at some point intolerant of what they regard as falsehood or perversion – but far be it from me to say that a check ought to be put on the preaching or practice of Islam, Christianity, Buddhism or whatever. I believe Judaism also believes in universal truths, which those who depart from them do at their own peril and should if possible be stopped from doing. But some Jews maintain that Judaism is only for the Jews, and they take no interest in anybody else – about that there is some controversy. I cannot say that I wish to tolerate everything except intolerance: only either (a) your case – intolerance which endangers pluralism, tolerance etc. – or (b) what I regard as evil (which others may not so regard) because I do have the sort of beliefs that I have, I do believe that there is a certain interwoven set of values – a horizon of them which underlies a form of life – without which, in my opinion, my life (and that of people who think like me, i.e. the society communication and life in which is part of my own life and thought and feeling) would be impossible.

You will ask, but what about pluralism, what about life in societies which hack off limbs for theft or send people to torture and death? I maintain the somewhat uncomfortable, but to me nevertheless fairly clear, notion that, while pluralism entails that I can understand other cultures (because they are human and because with a sufficient degree of imaginative empathy I can enter into them at times – at least, I think I can, though this may be an illusion), I remain wedded to my own, and am prepared to fight, or exterminate if extreme cases arise, forms of life which I understand but abhor. Pluralism

1 Irving, author of 'revisionist' works on WW2 Germany, was denounced as a Holocaust denier and serial falsifier by the US historian Deborah Lipstadt in her *Denying the Holocaust: The Growing Assault on Truth and Memory* (NY, 1993); Irving subsequently lost his widely publicised libel action against Lipstadt and her publishers. Richard Rampton, Lipstadt's QC, concluded that Irving was 'a right-wing extremist, a racist and, in particular, a rabid anti-Semite' who had 'prostituted his reputation for the sake of a bogus rehabilitation of Hitler': Michael Horsnell, 'Holocaust Trial about Freedom, Says Irving', *Times*, 16 March 2000 5a–c at 5c, 5a.

2 British far-right political party founded 1967; fielded 573 candidates in general elections 1970–2010, never securing sufficient votes to retain a single deposit.

3 The Race Relations Acts of 1965, 1968 and 1976, designed to make discrimination on the grounds of race illegal in British society; the 1976 Act established a Commission for Racial Equality to oversee the implementation of the legislation.

is the remedy against relativism, not against intolerance of what I regard as evil.

In other words, I do not believe, as, for example, Hampshire does, in the existence of 'absolute evil', in an objective way. I don't know what this would mean: objectivity of values is an old conundrum, and I don't quite understand what people believe who believe that; I only know that they believe it – perhaps my empathy doesn't go far enough for this. But I claim (*a*) that I understand why the Nazis believed what they believed (at least, the genuine ones among them) – namely that Jews, or gypsies, were subhuman, and termites, who undermined the only societies worth preserving – their own – and therefore had to be exterminated. This in the end is an empirical error (though it sounds tame to call it that): there are no subhumans; there are no gammas; Jews etc. don't undermine, nor does anyone else, etc. But if you really believe that they do, then of course you do what the Nazis did, and it is not insane (people too easily said they were mad, i.e. unintelligible): it is sane but founded on a colossal delusion, which had to be exterminated, very likely by force – as, indeed, it more or less was. 'Understanding', however, does not preclude a violent 'battle against'. I defend my – our – form of life against the enemy. The fact that I understand the enemy does not make me more tolerant towards him – but the fact that I do understand him precludes relativism.

You ask about universalist doctrines, e.g. Christianity. Of course I am not prepared to exterminate it, or even argue against it, particularly vehemently. Pluralism does not entail intolerance of non-pluralism, only, as you yourself say, the kind which does too much harm – harm towards what I regard as the minimum set of values which makes life worth living for me and mine – i.e. the culture in which I live, the nation, society etc. of which I see myself as a member.

Does this answer your question? I am not sure. [...]

Yours ever

Isaiah

TO CHIARA MERLO[1]

9 April 1991 [*carbon*]

Headington House

Dear Signora Merlo,

[...] Oxford and Cambridge philosophy. I was brought up in that movement, empirical-analytic-rational – and remain to a high degree part of it. But what I have in common [with it] is the belief that philosophical thought and language ought to be as clear as one can make them and refer to [...] empirical reality, both external and internal – introspective, capable of some

1 Then studying philosophy at Padua, and writing a thesis on IB.

degree of self-knowledge, self-understanding, consciousness of hopes and fears and emotions as something in time and not transcendent. In short, I do belong to this school of thought, even though in a moment I shall tell you about some of my differences with it. That is, I neither sympathise with nor really understand the metaphysical tradition that seems to me to prevail in the greater part of the European continent. My ideas are shaped by the English-speaking and Scandinavian worlds, in which, interestingly enough, may be included Finns, Poles and Israelis – I have no real grasp of what Heidegger, or Jaspers, or most Italian philosophers under their influence, are really about. Nor have I any sympathy for the Idealistic tradition, Hegel and his disciples, Croce[1] and all – that is different from Heidegger, who seems to me to be some kind of gifted charlatan, as do Derrida and most post-structuralists, deconstructionists and most of the French philosophers of the 1940–80 variety. I may be mistaken, but they seem to me exactly what the French call *fumiste*.[2] [...]

From that tradition I am totally alien; so is most of the English-speaking and Scandinavian world. The chasm between the two traditions must have been created around 1900, I think, and a great pity, for until then they more or less understood each other. I daresay the great Kant, certainly the greatest modern philosopher, was in some way responsible for this. He was certainly a dominant genius, but, in order to express himself, he invented a complicated philosophical vocabulary which could be abused only too easily by some of his disciples. Fichte, Schelling[3] and Hegel, of course, had a great deal to say; sometimes it is sheer night and darkness, but when you emerge out of the wood into a comparatively clear space there is a great deal that is original, important and influential. I am very far from condemning these people as idle [*flâneurs?*],[4] in the way in which English philosophers of the early part of the century, Russell and his friends and disciples, were apt to do. But there is no need to talk like that. What can be said, can be said more clearly – and if it is not, it leads to confusion in theory and sometimes dreadful consequences in practice.

Now about my differences with the empiricist tradition. I believe that, in the case of social and political thought, the most important thing is to understand what the vision of a given thinker – or indeed, society or tradition – is; for unless one grasps what that is, one cannot know what it is that is really being thought and said. Of all people, the positivist Bertrand Russell once said that the most important thing about understanding a philosopher

---

1 Benedetto Croce (1866–1952), Idealist Italian philosopher and politician concerned mainly with the philosophy of history and of aesthetics. IB reviewed his *My Philosophy* in *Mind* 61 (1952), 574–8, in somewhat hostile terms.
2 'Practical joker'.
3 Friedrich Wilhelm Joseph von Schelling (1775–1854), German philosopher, one of the principal German Romantics; a Tübingen contemporary of Hegel and a collaborator with Fichte.
4 'Loafers'.

is to understand his basic outlook, which is relatively simple. The ingenuity, the complicated and important arguments which are produced, are mainly instruments of attack or defence used upon real or imaginary opponents – very important in themselves, to be taken wholly seriously, but one cannot understand what Kant, Descartes, Spinoza, Einstein, Russell himself, I daresay even Croce (who is a half-closed book to me, I admit) thought unless you can understand the vision which they had, of which the arguments are props, instruments, weapons, but are not intrinsic.[1]

In other words, I don't think that by following the rational arguments produced by philosophers for the positions which they hold, these positions will become adequately clarified. I think my colleagues do not think this, but I do. I am sure it is true of social and political thought. So did Vico, so did Herder – hence my admiration for them. So, to do him justice, did Hegel, who approached Aristotle (who had a huge influence on him) in exactly that way.

Moreover, in ethics some of this also holds. Sheer analysis is not enough. One wants to know what is the constellation of values, the – as it were – moral horizon of a given thinker, or a given group of thinkers, or indeed of a culture, or a society, if one is to understand or evaluate what they believe, in the light of which they lead their lives. Some writers on ethics in the empirical tradition (what you call Oxford–Cambridge) have not exerted themselves in this direction. Certainly a considerable philosopher like G. E. Moore, who had a huge influence [on] literary and artistic as well as philosophical thought, did not approach the matter in this way; nor did Russell; nor do most other writers on morals in Oxford and Cambridge now; nor do my friends Rawls or Bernard Williams, whom I greatly admire, usually do this, though there are times when they do exactly this and then I feel in kinship with them.[2] I can talk to them about ethics, which I cannot do with the philosophers of Paris or, I suspect, of Milan or Turin (though I may be wrong about this – there are some clear and valuable thinkers in Italy, but few). [...]

Yours sincerely,
Isaiah Berlin

---

1 'Every philosopher, in addition to the formal system which he offers to the world, has another, much simpler, of which he may be quite unaware. If he is aware of it, he probably realises that it won't quite do; he therefore conceals it, and sets forth something more sophisticated, which he believes because it is like his crude system, but which he asks others to accept because he thinks he has made it such as cannot be disproved. The sophistication comes in by way of refutation of refutations, but this alone will never give a positive result: it shows, at best, that a theory *may* be true, not that it *must* be. The positive result, however little the philosopher may realise it, is due to his imaginative preconceptions, or what Santayana calls "animal faith".' Bertrand Russell, *History of Western Philosophy* (NY, 1945; London, 1946) 1. 2. 23 ('Aristotle's Physics'), 2nd paragraph. One of IB's favourite observations.

2 IB wrote to Rawls on 31 August 1988: 'your defence of pluralism speaks to both my heart and my mind – it is to me, as it is to you, "a permanent feature of [the] public culture of modern democracies"'.

TO CLAUDE GALIPEAU[1]

15 April 1991

Headington House

Dear Galipeau,

[...] You ask me questions which I find exceedingly difficult to answer, not so much because of confusion on my own part, or uncertainty about what I think, but because the questions are intrinsically difficult to answer. What you ask brings up the very topic which I keep trying to deal with: namely, the conflict of ultimate values, the impossibility of reconciling them, and the need, if the worst is to be avoided, to invent trade-offs, compromises etc. which keep things going, never very neatly but better than if either value was fulfilled at the total cost of the other, or others.

[...] I still believe that 'believers' have a right to cause their children to be educated in the schools of their faith, but that these schools need not be supported by the state. Whether they ought to get tax rebates I do not know – I do not mind about that. You are perhaps more generous in this respect than I should be. But at this point I have to say this: although individuals and groups have the right, in a liberal society of a pluralist kind, to pursue their ends and support the beliefs, religious faith, moral outlooks and so on which they hold, this right has its limits. Let me explain what I mean.

There are certain values which one can assume – rightly, and if you like dogmatically – to be sufficiently universal to put reins on freedom of action. This is what, broadly speaking, makes men able to intercommunicate, and forms the moral and political basis – perhaps not very wide, but real – for human beings, certainly for societies in the Western world (outside that, I don't feel too sure).[2] That is what justifies one in keeping people from committing obvious crimes, oppression, injustice, all that is opposed to life, liberty and the pursuit of happiness, etc. You can extend the list very easily yourself. Hence the British were perfectly justified in stopping the suttee in India, no matter what Hindu custom might dictate. I daresay other forms of physical improprieties – perhaps the circumcision of women, marrying out of one's caste in India. Somebody the other day was forced to be killed, together with her wrong-caste husband, for daring to get married. And so on.

You see what I wish to say? These things do put a limit on tolerance, and rightly so. In addition to the right to arrest intolerance, or bans and laws which endanger a minimum degree of tolerance and civil liberty in a liberal society, measures can be taken against extremists, right-wing and left-wing, if their activities begin seriously to endanger the very bases of the liberal

---

1 Claude Jean Henry Joseph Galipeau (b. 1959; plate 34), Canadian political scientist and digital media executive; his Toronto PhD thesis (1990) was published as *Isaiah Berlin's Liberalism* (Oxford, 1994); policy adviser to the Ontario government 1990–6; thereafter in digital media.

2 Cf. 407/3.

pluralist society. In other words, the choice of education for one's family must stop at the frontier of what might be regarded as either criminal or excessively repressive or impossibly anti-social. There is a universal code – I do not say absolute, but one which a great many people in a great many countries over very long periods of time have observed; and that creates a solid basis for legislation.

In the second place, so far as education is concerned, there is such a thing as a general standard of education, and indeed of culture, which prevails in a given society – which is the expression, if you like, of the traditions of the majority of its members. Very few societies are so cut up into minorities as not to have what might be called a solid majority culture and a solid majority standard of education. Private schools, religious schools etc. are entitled to exist, but they must be compelled (I say harshly, but firmly) to teach a syllabus of subjects which we all, or almost all, regard as indispensable. A religious school cannot be permitted to exist which refuses to teach the current alphabet of the majority culture, which confines its pupils to Hebrew or Arabic or Armenian alphabets or vocabularies; nor one which does not teach what might be called general history, not affected by any strong bias in any direction – that is, so strong as to be ruled out by what we should regard as normal, impartial, decent, reasonably objective standards, taken from the majority of the community in question. This applies to other subjects as well. No school should be allowed to practice which has not, in other words, a strong overlap with the curriculum of the schools of the majority culture. [...] In other words, too much deviance cannot be allowed: it undermines the minimum of social solidarity. [...]

Thus, I would certainly not allow religious Muslim or Jewish schools in England not to teach any English literature at all, no matter how penetrated by Christian values. The obligation of the majority of schools to teach Pakistani, Hebrew literature in order to create a wider horizon for its pupils I regard as much less compelling – indeed, not compelling at all. Children cannot be burdened with too much, and I repeat that I think that the central culture, as one might call it, of a given community is rightly given primacy of place, provided that other forms of knowledge, culture, tradition etc. (provided that the conditions I outlined above are preserved) can be imparted privately, or in all schools marginally – rabbis, imams should be allowed to come once a week and [be] paid for.

Let me continue. My subjective view is against segregation. I do not like Jewish schools, which I am constantly invited to support by the Chief Rabbi, as you may imagine; nor do I approve of Catholic schools, to which a great many important and distinguished British citizens have gone and go. I think it creates a sense of – not of segregation, but of cultural difference, which in my view is not good for human beings. I think there is a great deal to be said for an integrated society in which everyone – or, at least, as many people as possible – understand each other half instinctively, without the need for mental translation of what the others mean, making allowances, etc., for differences of outlook bred by schools or teachers. For this reason, the law in England, which is that all children must be sent to school, does preclude private tuition at home as the exclusive form of education, save for parents who can make a strong case for doing this, for whatever reason. Such may be exempted by the schools inspectorate – I regard that as about right. In other words, I do not consider 'communal and familial autarky'[1] as essential in order to preserve cultural pluralism within a society. On the contrary, what you call a universal and public school system, free of religion and unilingual, is not a threat to cultural pluralism and the rich fabric of our societies. It must be promoted quite strongly, provided that opportunities are given for the existence of schools which are founded on religions or traditions different from those of the general community. [...]

Yours sincerely,
Isaiah Berlin

TO NORMAN BROWN[2]

6 May 1991

Headington House

Dear NOB,

Your letters always give me the greatest pleasure. I am sorry that they come so seldom. I am glad that my latest 'collection' stirred you to express yourself in your usual inimitable and to me always most attractive fashion. [...]

You are [...] right that I am drawn to the extremes – to the irrationalists, to those who upset, and not to those who smoothly assert. I explain this to myself by saying that I don't want to read allies – those who simply confirm what I know and believe already, and in any case am sceptical about by temperament. I'd rather read the critics, the sceptics, the enemies, however extravagant, because they uncover the cracks, the flaws, the places between the ribs where the dagger can successfully be inserted – and that teaches one something and makes one revise one's earlier view. Hence my fascination with Vico, Hamann, and indeed Nietzsche. Not that I have read the last – and Schopenhauer even less. That is due to idleness; to addiction to easy reading, to newspapers; to irresponsibility, to a desire to have a peaceful old age, I think, free from duty, given over to inclination, to obedience to sudden desires and urges – desire to read now this book, now that article, in no order,

1 CG to IB, 2 April 1991.
2 Norman Oliver ('NOB', 'Nobby') Brown (1913–2002), left-wing US philosopher and historian; Balliol classics 1932–6, taught by IB; prof. of classics, Wesleyan, 1946–56, Jane A. Seney Prof. of Greek 1956–62; Wilson Prof. of Classics and Comparative Literature, Rochester, 1962–8; prof. of humanities, Santa Cruz, 1968–81.

in a kind of self-indulgent irregularity. I have always been like that, and it is in curious conflict with my respectable, conformist, on the whole well-ordered and pedestrian sort of life. But I am strongly drawn to the wild riders beyond the frontier of received good sense – and this is what I think irritates Stuart, who is an addict, a genuine addict, to rationality, and wants a world capable of being regulated by reason, science, order, all that Spinoza, Aristotle and perhaps even Freud believed in. [...]

How can I stimulate you to write to me again? What would you like me to do, to say, to tell you? I must admit that the latest turn of the wheel in Eastern Europe does leave too many ideologists high and dry – it could easily lead to some hideous contradictory propositions, some opposite extreme. Never mind, we are both quite old, we shan't live to see the worst, let us cultivate our gardens as best we can – tell me what plants you want from mine, and which you would like to offer me from yours, and we shall remain contented and affectionate.

Yours ever,
Isaiah

⟨P. S. You are quite right: I always tend to make my "subjects' – resemble myself – others have remarked this – and it is sadly true. The only method of empathy – like an actor playing a part – that I turn out to have –⟩

TO LEON WIESELTIER[1]

21 May 1991

Headington House

Dear Leon,

I began reading your answer to Todorov[2] (whom I have met, and did not really make much of – some years ago) before I read him. And I still haven't read him. But it is clear to me from your piece that I agree totally (as so often) with you: about the justifiability of hatred; about the specious attempts to make analogies between the torturer and the tortured; that to say that to return hate for hate, whereby the victim cannot avoid, does not wish to avoid, hate for his torturer, comes gradually to create an equation between

---

1 Leon Sol Wieseltier (b. 1952), Jewish-American author, critic and public intellectual; literary editor, New Republic, 1983–2014; author of Kaddish (NY, 1998); later (since 2015) Isaiah Berlin Senior Fellow, Brookings Institution, Washington. A close bond with IB began when LW was a BLitt student at Balliol, 1974–6.

2 Tzvetan Todorov (b. 1939), Franco-Bulgarian cultural critic and philosopher, spoke on 'Facing Evil: Shoah and Primo Levi' 8 April 1991 at Columbia, as part of the Lionel Trilling Seminar series; LW was one of 2 'discussants'. Todorov's lecture arose from his book Face à l'extrême (Paris, [1991]), trans. Arthur Denner and Abigail Pollack as Facing the Extreme: Moral Life in the Concentration Camps (London, 1999). A good part of LW's reply appeared in 'After Memory', New Republic, 3 May 1993, 16–26.

the hate that fills the torturer and the counter-hate which fills the tortured – that all this is, to me, wicked nonsense.

When I am told by the late Professor Butterfield, quoting a famous Christian source, that one must hate the sin and not the sinner,[1] I flatly disagree and don't quite know what it means. This may be true of saints, but I have never experienced this condition. Sins don't exist by themselves – acts are acts of actors, and sins are the acts of sinners; and if you hate the sin what you hate is the perpetrator's act, and that is not divorceable from the perpetrator himself. You can forgive, and you can forget, and you can ignore, and you can be indifferent to, but the sin and the sinner, the act and the actor, are one and indissoluble; and the Todorov thesis,[2] which, as you say, smacked too much of the late Mademoiselle Weil,[3] is to me a kind of sentimental, spiritually bogus, phoney attempt at charity towards what – if the concept of desert means anything – deserved the opposite.

You are perfectly right: if there are such things as radical evils, and there surely are, within a moral horizon of an individual group or culture, then to say that to detest them may make one similar to their perpetrators seems to me nauseating nonsense. I know nothing about the causes of Levi's[4] suicide – no one does: nothing that has been said is convincing – but I simply do not believe that it is 'guilt' at having been in a concentration camp. At most, in order to meet the Todorov theory, one could say that some of those who survived felt shame at having survived when all the others around them died so hideously. That is felt even by soldiers in a war when their comrades are slaughtered. But that that can lead to suicide seems to me exceedingly improbable, whatever psychobabblers may say. He was, of course, highly neurotic, fell into gloomy states from time to time, may have thought that he suffered mentally or physically; but the idea that the victims gradually begin to resemble the 'victimisers' seems to me totally implausible. You and I will be told that we do not know enough modern psychopathology, etc. Ordinary

1 A recommendation originated by Augustine, who writes of 'love for the person and hatred for the sin' in a letter to a convent of consecrated virgins, Letters 5, trans. Sister Wilfrid Parsons (NY, 1956), 46 (letter 211, written c.423).

2 Todorov argued that hatred of the Nazis is an obstacle to understanding and a perverse replication of their own reprehensible attitude.

3 Simone Weil (1909–43), French philosopher, Christian mystic and social activist whose reputation rests on her posthumously published works, notably Cahiers (Paris, 1951–6), trans. Arthur Wills as The Notebooks of Simone Weil (London, 1956). 'According to Simone Weil, who displays an unpleasant silence on the Nazi persecution of the Jews, Hitler is no worse than Napoleon, than Richelieu, than Caesar.' Susan Sontag, 'Simone Weil', NYRB, 1 February 1963, 22.

4 Primo Michele Levi (1919–87), Italian Jewish chemist, writer and Holocaust survivor; captured when fighting with partisans 1943 and sent to Auschwitz; his subsequent works dealt with his experiences there, notably his memoir Se questo è un uomo ([Turin, 1947]), trans. Stuart Woolf as Survival in Auschwitz: The Nazi Assault on Humanity (NY and London, 1958) and as If This is a Man (London, 1959); his Il sistema periodico (Turin, 1975), trans. Raymond Rosenthal as The Periodic Table (NY, 1984; London, 1985), a collection of autobiographical short stories, consolidated his international reputation; died in a fall in his Turin apartment building 11 April 1987; the verdict of suicide has not been universally accepted.

perception of what human beings are like is, perhaps, enough to resist all the theoretical fantasies. Anyway, as usual I line up with you. [...]

I talked to old Natalie Sarraute[1] the other night – she is ninety-two and a Russian Jewess by origin. She has just been to Russia after God knows how many years, and she says that anti-Semitism is bubbling everywhere, which I do not doubt. Russia, Germany, Poland, France, the United States are basically anti-Semitic countries; Britain, Italy, Scandinavia, Bulgaria and Georgia are not. About Latin America I know nothing – Argentina clearly is: people were slaughtered there under the military dictatorship simply for being Jews.[2] About Chile I simply don't know.[3] On this very gloomy note, I end, with much love to you both,

Yours,

Isaiah

As part of the celebration of IB's eightieth birthday a symposium was held in his honour at the Israel Academy of Sciences and Humanities in Jerusalem, and its proceedings published in Israel.[4] The organiser of this conference and his wife, Avishai and Edna Margalit,[5] also edited a Festschrift, Isaiah Berlin: A Celebration *(London/Chicago 1991), originally intended to appear for the same birthday, but in the event published only in time for his eighty-second. It was the second Festschrift of IB's career. In 1979, in conditions of great secrecy, HH had organised* The Idea of Freedom: Essays in Honour of Isaiah Berlin *(Oxford, 1979), edited by Alan Ryan. 'I am opposed to Festschrifts,' IB wrote, soon after being presented with this text: 'they seem to me coffins of the works of the unfortunate authors, who often write under considerable moral pressure; but I cannot deny that I was deeply moved by the fact that so many friends were better men than I – I had refused to contribute to their Festschrifts and they*

1 Nathalie Sarraute (1900–99) née Natal'ya Il'inichna Chernyak, French writer born into an assimilated Jewish family in Russia, emerged in the 1950s as a leading proponent of the *nouveau roman* ('new novel').

2 According to one investigator, Juan Pablo Jaroslavsky, 'Jews represented more than 12 per cent of the victims of the military regime while constituting under 1 per cent of Argentina's population': Uki Goñi, 'Jews Targeted by Argentina's Dicatorship', *Guardian*, 17 March 1999, 18.

3 'Unlike its Argentinean counterpart, the Chilean authoritarian regime had repudiated anti-Semitism from the outset. Pinochet himself flirted with the Jewish community. [...] Pinochet, of course, maintained excellent relations with the state of Israel, where Chile acquired weapons. This relationship made Israel vulnerable to criticism from both inside and outside the country.' Luis Fleischman, 'Pinochet – Good for Jews, Tragedy for Human Rights', *Jewish World Review*, 4 November 1998, ⟨http://www.jewishworldreview.com/0798/pinochet1.asp⟩.

4 Avishai Margalit and others, *On the Thought of Isaiah Berlin: Papers Presented in Honour of Professor Sir Isaiah Berlin on the Occasion of his Eightieth Birthday*, in the case of some papers trans. Gabriel Piterberg (Jerusalem, 1990); also published in Hebrew.

5 Avishai Margalit (b. 1939), Israeli philosopher; taught at HUJ, where he undertook his doctoral studies, from 1970; later Shulman Prof. of Philosophy (1998–2006) and George F. Kennan Prof. (2006–11), Princeton, and trustee, IBLT (from 2014); author of foreword to POI2. His wife (m. 1968) was Edna Ullmann-Margalit (1946–2010), Israeli philosopher; doctoral student, Somerville (DPhil 1973); taught at HUJ from 1976, associate prof. 1994.

contributed to mine, and my debt is unrepayable.'[1] *The same sentiment guided his response to* A Celebration, *and he took the trouble to write full letters to some of those 'better men'.*

TO MICHAEL IGNATIEFF

7 June 1991

Headington House

Dear Michael,

[...] I must talk to you about your views about my views. I read your piece[2] with great admiration, and was much moved by it – it is beautifully written, and gets me nearly right. Nearly, because I do not regard the Nazis as, in my and your sense, outside the pale; some of them, perhaps, but not Nazis as such, not moral idiots, not simply pathological murderers, pathological torturers as some of Stalin's and Hitler's people certainly either were or became. But (as you yourself say) I regard them as people trapped by emotions which are universal – namely, nationalism – driven to the point of pathological extreme; but still not inhuman; and fed by empirical nonsense, but intelligible nonsense, just false, and false in a way that indicates a profound misunderstanding of life in general – but still not inhuman. I think they would go to hell rather less if they were in the literal sense outside the pale, if they were just unintelligible maniacs. We must talk about this. In the meanwhile, thank you, thank you – you have acted with great nobility and I shall be eternally grateful.

Yours ever,

Isaiah

PS One more thing. The idea of the subhumans is a piece of odious nonsense; but it cannot be said to be beyond the pale, unintelligible. That is roughly what I think the Dominicans thought about the South American Indians in the sixteenth century when Jesuits opposed them, and said that they were human beings.[3] Some Catholic orders thought that these were not creatures for whom Christ died – that is certainly an allegation of subhumanity. But that is not unintelligible, merely appalling, from the point of view of semi-universally accepted human values. From that there is no very great distance to the racialism of Gobineau[4] and the Nazi horrors.

IB

1 To Brian Knei-Paz, 20 June 1979.
2 'Understanding Fascism?', in IBAC.
3 When the Jesuit order arrived in South America in the mid C16th the Franciscans and Dominicans were already established there; inspired by Thomas More's *Utopia* (Leuven, 1516), the Jesuits adopted a protective and paternalistic attitude towards native peoples, organising them in self-sustaining communities or 'reductions'.
4 Joseph Arthur, comte de Gobineau (1816–82), French diplomat, writer and ethnologist, whose *Essay on the Inequality of Human Races* (Paris, 1853–5) argued that the white Aryan race was

TO RICHARD WOLLHEIM

14 June 1991

Headington House

Dear Richard,

I am immensely grateful to you for your wonderful piece[1] in my *Celebration*. I did my best to prevent the book, but I think my editors took my extreme reluctance for granted. I know what a bore it is to have to contribute to Festschrifts (I have been very bad about that myself – I have done it twice)[2] – people have gone to heaven for less.

There is only one point I'd like to make, and it is looking a splendid gift horse not too deeply in the mouth, so forgive me. You praise me for responding to personal characteristics of the people who views I write about. So I do. Consciously or unconsciously I usually tend somewhat to introduce my own autobiographical elements into them – even de Maistre, I fear. But the thing I wanted to say is that I am no good at knowing what people's moods are. I am totally insensitive to whether they are sad or gay, embarrassed, secretly distressed, or whatever, unless this is made very obvious by tears or laughter. In a room, I have no antennae for emotional conditions. What I do think I may know something about is basic characters of people, the skeleton more than the flesh or skin. But, as you may imagine, your attribution to me of virtues I only, at most, half possess has given me only undeserved but nevertheless warm pleasure. [...]

Yours ever,
    Isaiah

TO BERNARD WILLIAMS

17 June 1991

Headington House

Dear Bernard,

I read your essay on opera[3] in the Festschrift with the greatest pleasure and enjoyment and admiration – and, oddly enough, agreement. To have been forced to write about me to the extent which you have is really too much – heroic martyrdom on your part, to which I can only bow the head

---

superior to all others, but would maintain this status only so long as it remained racially pure. Gobineau's crude determinism had a profound influence on, among others, Houston Stewart Chamberlain and Adolf Hitler.

1 'The Idea of a Common Human Nature', in IBAC.
2 In fact thrice: 'L. B. Namier: A Personal Impression', in Martin Gilbert (ed.), *A Century of Conflict, 1850–1950: Essays for A. J. P. Taylor* (London, 1966); 'Georges Sorel', in Chimen Abramsky (ed.), *Essays in Honour of E. H. Carr* (London, 1974); 'Decline of Utopian Ideas in the West', in J. M. Porter and Richard Vernon (eds), *Unity, Plurality and Politics: Essays in Honour of F. M. Barnard* (London and Sydney, 1986).
3 'Naive and Sentimental Opera Lovers', in IBAC.

in gratitude – thank you very, very, very much. It really is an act of sublime friendship.

I think perhaps that on Puccini[1] and Wagner I have something to add. In the case of Puccini what I object to is not so much the cynicism and the contrivance and the manipulation, which of course are all there, but the mixture, not merely of cruelty, but of cruelty with sex, in every one of his famous operas other than *Bohème* – and I like *Bohème* well enough: I mean, I listen to it with some degree of pleasure and no twinges of discomfort or disgust, as happens in the case of *Butterfly* or the great masterpiece, for it is one, *Tosca*, which on the whole I hate. No, my trouble is not only the combination of sex and cruelty (the only comparable work in which this occurs is Evelyn Waugh's *Helena*),[2] but the cheapness, the vulgarity, of much of the music; combined with a no doubt perfectly genuine sincerity. Not to put too fine a class point on it, it is sentimentality of an Italian hairdresser, if you know what I mean – it's proof that sincerity and vulgarity can go together, that commonness and genius can combine, for there is no doubt that he is a genius. I have always thought that about poor Bernard Levin: he is utterly sincere, I think, despite all the grimaces and gestures, and yet totally vulgar – even when, as occasionally he does, he hits the nail on the head. The same is true of Leonard Bernstein, whom I find intolerable for that reason – his writings, his music, everything – and yet he was a very nice, generous, wonderfully gifted, perfectly sincere sort of man; but the kitsch is there. As it is in Weill.[3] It is only when these people let themselves go that something superficial, frivolous and charming like Bernstein's *On the Town*, an early work which is perfectly agreeable and unpretentious – that this particular element of vulgarity is not present.

Now for Wagner. I am sure that I do not suffer from fear of dark vistas within oneself, which one cannot face, evoked by his works; and there are huge portions of *The Ring* – not huge, but large – which I greatly admire and listen to with actual delight; perhaps 'fascination' is the word. What I don't like is, I think, the atmosphere, the quality, of his world – of *Tristan*, of *The Ring*, even of *Tannhäuser*. The teutonic medievalism, the brutal relationships of the protagonists, the deeply neurotic relations of the men and women – that entire world is repellent to me. And I have to admit that stretches of him just do bore me – my thoughts wander. Curiously enough, the neurotic

1 Giacomo Antonio Domenico Michele Secondo Maria Puccini (1858–1924), Italian composer; considered the heir to Verdi, and known especially for his operas *La bohème* (1896), *Tosca* (1900) and *Madama Butterfly* (1904).
2 Evelyn Arthur St John Waugh (1903–66), novelist, considered *Helena* (London, 1950) his best novel, but it met with an indifferent reception: 'the greatest disappointment of his whole literary life'. Christopher Sykes, *Evelyn Waugh: A Biography* (London/Boston, 1975), 337.
3 Kurt Julian Weill (1900–50), German-born composer; developed a new school of satirical popular opera with Bertolt Brecht as his librettist; they had a notable success with *Die Dreigroschenoper* (*The Threepenny Opera*; Berlin, 1928); of Jewish descent, Weill left Germany for Paris 1933, settling in NY 1935 (US citizen 1943), and there wrote a series of successful Broadway musicals.

elements in Berg do not bother me in that way. I admire, like and am upset by his work in a way which one cannot mind being upset – which in fact can have a transforming effect, not only in *Wozzeck* but by the chamber music too, and by *Lulu*. To return to Wagner for a second: he is *sentimentalisch*,[1] as you rightly say, in every possible way – that is what Schiller's word means. But I think all forms of self-consciousness, of awareness of your own relationship, both to other musical styles, from which you derive or which you oppose, and to other forms of art in your own day, and a certain attitude to your entire *Weltanschauung* – that is *sentimentalisch* too, and it is true of Debussy and Berg. I think perhaps the only naive composer after Verdi whom I could have mentioned is Bruckner,[2] who in his own way is as naive as Bach. Mahler is wonderfully the opposite of all this, the absolute apotheosis of *Sentimentalismus* as opposed to *Sentimentalität*.[3] But enough – I can go on like this, no doubt, at great length; it will bore you a great deal and if I go on too long it'll end by boring me too. [...]

    Yours ever,
    Isaiah

TO STUART HAMPSHIRE

17 June 1991

Headington House

Dear Stuart,

I read your piece[4] in my *Celebration* [...]. I think you have got me to a T; I think all you say about the effect upon me of Hume is probably right.[5] I know you think – and Chuck thinks it even more – that it is an unfortunate empirical wodge inside me which prevents me from seeing greater truths, above all of his views, but also of your own. Your antipathy to Hume I know well. Nevertheless, I think there is something that I can comment on. While

1 'In [...] *Über Naive und Sentimentalische Dichtung* [*On Naive and Sentimental Poetry* (1795–6), *Schillers Werke: Nationalausgabe* (Weimar, 1943–2012), xx 413–503], Schiller distinguished 2 types of poets: those who are not conscious of any rift between themselves and their milieu, or within themselves; and those who are so conscious.' IB, 'The "Naivety" of Verdi', AC2 361. Cf. IB's frequent reference, when praising a critic, to there being 'nothing between him and the object': e.g. PI2 277 (David Cecil); PI2 352 and L1 717 (Stephen Spender); POI2 102 and RT 162 (Belinsky); interview with Allegra Mostyn-Owen and Hugo Dixon (97/2), 8 (Wittgenstein).
2 (Josef) Anton Bruckner (1824–96), Austrian composer, organist and teacher, wrote 9 symphonies and many sacred and secular choral works.
3 The former term means sentimentality in a pejorative sense, the latter in a descriptive sense.
4 'Nationalism', in IBAC.
5 'I *love* Hume. He got some things wrong – sense data, causality, justice – but not only was he one of the nicest men who ever lived, but his ideas, when one is agonized, always return one to sanity: he did not allow for heroic martyrdom: but [...] his moral & political ideas are a marvellous antidote to Ayatollas, G. E. Moore, J. S. Mill (I mean Bentham), Ludwig W., Hegel, Marx, the Roman Church, et al. Hurray for Montaigne, Erasmus (antisemitic like T.S.E), Diderot, Hume & the welfare state.' To Noel Annan, 12 September 1988.

it is true that I do attach great importance to Herderian 'belonging', which I regard as a basic human need, and think of the need to appraise things empirically and not in terms of schemas or blueprints, however enlightened – while all this is true, yet I do believe in ultimate human values, mediated by local circumstances but nevertheless as universal as empirical things can be: namely equality, justice, the pursuit of knowledge, truth etc. However the prisms of local circumstances may refract these values, they are objective, i.e. accepted by a very great many people at a very great many times in a very great many places – universal in the same sense – and while they may collide with each other, they do not have to be justified by tradition or national, still less local or other particular, frameworks. They are valid in their own right, if anything is. In other words, I think you make me out too localised, too like Oakeshott (*horribile dictu*),[1] too like the trendy right-wingers of our day, both in England and America. There is enough of Millian belief in central human values in me to modify strongly the claims of communities, traditions, ways of life. Apart from that, I think your piece really does make the best analysis of what I have thought over the years – so far as I think at all – that anyone has ever tried to give. Not that I deserve it, I say with genuine, not assumed, humility. […]

Yours ever,

Isaiah

TO FREDERICK ROSEN[2]

17 July 1991

Headington House

Dear Professor Rosen,

Thank you for your very courteous letter and for sending me your lecture *Thinking about Liberty*,[3] which I have read with great attention and interest. It was very good of you to send it to me, and I feel an obligation to reply to the points you raise.

You will not be astonished to hear that nothing that I have ever published brought so much criticism, sometimes highly personal, as this lecture of mine.[4] I tried to answer the first objections in my introduction to *Four Essays on Liberty*,[5] but this did not placate some of my opponents, among whom I must now reckon yourself. I had better come clean without further ado,

1 'Ghastly to relate'.
2 Frederick Rosen (b. 1938), US-born academic, expert on Jeremy Bentham; lecturer, dept of government, LSE, 1970–83, senior lecturer 1983–6; general editor, Bentham Project, UCL, 1983–2003, director 1983–2002; reader in the history of political thought, UCL, 1986–90, prof. 1990–2003.
3 *Thinking about Liberty*, an inaugural lecture delivered at UCL 29 November 1990 (London, [1990]) (hereafter TAL).
4 *Two Concepts of Liberty* (335/1).
5 London, 1969.

and say that I think that you have largely misunderstood what I was trying to say, and in consequence misrepresented me to a degree. [...]

I am not at any stage an advocate of what you call 'maximum non-interference';[1] I am as aware as anyone else that any kind of community requires restraints upon negative liberty. Of course civil and political liberties cannot obtain without the guarantee of law or custom or authority of some kind, and perhaps sanctions too; of course I am as well aware as anyone that the complete liberty of the carp is not compatible with the complete liberty of the pike; indeed, I say that in my lecture – the liberty of sheep is not possible if complete negative liberty is accorded to the wolf. And that, I take it, is what you wish to say when you speak of civil and political liberties. That I fully recognise, and it is for that reason that I do not offer the absurd proposition that a society could subsist if maximum negative liberty were granted to all, or even some, members of such a body.

But I go further than that: I consider that, given other human values – ends of life, as it were – and the sheer needs of social life as such, some of which can, in some degree, be incompatible with each other – given this, liberty of whatever kind must make room for these other values if a decent society is to be established. Values sometimes conflict, compromises have to be made, trade-offs are needed, and in my lecture I say, again quite specifically, that liberty is not the only end of a man, and therefore it must on occasion yield, at any rate in some degree (and in some cases of acute crisis perhaps almost completely) to other needs. If that is to be the case, of course machinery for this is indispensable: law, authority, traditional values, the state etc. etc. – all the Burkean framework in which even the freest and most liberal society must live.

Of course basic human rights cannot be exercised in a society which imposes no constraints on potential infringements of them – only a totally anarchist society, I suppose, the possibility of which rests on assumptions which few of us are ready to accept, for reasons of the most minimal realism. I think that you mistakenly look upon my lecture as a defence of Hayekian or Thatcherite unbridled laissez-faire and a minimal state. That is not so. I am prepared to go further and say that civil liberties and rights, e.g. the freedom to live in the Ritz Hotel, which someone cannot exercise because he is penniless, can be hollow in a Benthamite[2] as well as the real world. Nevertheless, they are freedoms, and negative liberty embraces them. Given that I allow, as I do, the necessity of restraining not only the liberty of wolves (to protect

1 TAL 8.

2 i.e. according to Bentham's Utilitarianism. In a Benthamite calculation of the best course of action – the one that achieves *the greatest happiness of the greatest number* (169/3) of people – the (theoretical) freedom to live at the Ritz should not be accorded a high value for those who cannot afford its rates, precisely because its value is merely theoretical if the means to enjoy it are not to hand. IB is saying, then, that, whether or not you are a Benthamite, you can recognise that negative freedom isn't everything.

the sheep), but the demands of other values – rivals to liberty – as well, I do not think that [...] you are correct in accusing me of 'oversimplifying the ideas of civil and political liberty'.[1] Of course all liberties that belong to men in society require restraint. My only point was that law is not liberty, but a diminution of it, however necessary. What I obtain from Constant, whom I greatly admire, and in particular the essay you refer to,[2] by which I was deeply influenced, is that in any decent society (at any rate of a modern kind) a minimum – not the maximum – of negative liberty is needed for individuals; an area in which laws, institutions, individuals and other agencies do not normally operate to restrain. That is all that Constant is asking for, and all that I do too.

[...] you speak of the 'cold-war rhetoric' which portrayed the 'totalitarian democracies (so-called)'[3] in a manner that you think was false. Indeed. I do not think that what you call 'cold-war rhetoric', much of which, as you yourself recognise, turned out to be valid, referred to them as 'democracies' at all, for they were not. The question of an oppressive democracy is another problem to which I shall come a little further on. Nor is it true that it is the Communist states in Eastern Europe and elsewhere that 'haunted'[4] me when writing my lecture. Certainly I accepted the Orwellian view of them, as anyone who has ever lived under one could not, if he was sane and honest, fail to do. But I was thinking just as much of right-wing despotisms. Let me make it plain that I was thinking, to begin with, of Europe in, let us say, 1938–9, the Europe of Stalin, Hitler, Mussolini, Franco, Salazar,[5] dictators in the Balkans and the Baltics and some parts of Asia. That is where civil rights were trampled upon, both negative and positive liberties, in the name of making it possible for the citizens to realise themselves in a manner in which their 'real self' demanded – in the name of the liberty of this 'real self' to dominate over the unfortunate empirical selves of the oppressed individuals and peoples.

At the time when I drafted my lecture, all that remained of this was the Soviet Union and its East European satellites, China, Spain, Portugal and various African states. But that was enough. I do not think I was 'haunted' at all, I merely wished to stress the perversion of the concept of liberty in an Orwellian manner, as a synonym for total control, indeed, oppression. The 'higher destiny'[6] which you mention here has often been represented as

1 'Berlin simplifies almost to caricature the crucial point regarding civil and political liberty' (TAL 8).
2 344/3.
3 TAL 9.
4 ibid.
5 António de Oliveira Salazar (1889–1970), Portuguese dictator 1932–68; personally austere, he introduced a modified Fascism to Portugal, but maintained the country's neutrality during WW2, while upholding its ancient alliance with Britain; awarded an hon. DCL by Oxford 1941.
6 TAL 9.

a form of liberation of men from liberal or democratic or atheistical or other heretical fallacies, which the 'real self' was there to see through and reject. To that extent we agree. But my lecture was not an exercise in cold-war rhetoric – it replied to despotisms in the remoter past and in our present just as much.

[...] you say that you do not understand how my account of the relationship of negative liberty and democracy can stand.[1] Quite apart from your expression 'the cold-war rhetoric', which is both a slur and completely unjust, let me point out that democracies can be exceedingly oppressive, and diminish civil and political liberties very greatly indeed. Do you really think that the Athenian democracy, in its actual functioning (and as very brilliantly described by Constant),[2] was compatible with the basic liberties, whether negative or positive, of Socrates, Anaxagoras, Diagoras and other thinkers punished by exile or death (Aristotle only just escaped such a fate)?[3] Do you think that American democracy, which is real, in spite of the flaws in practice which we all recognise, was not oppressive vis-à-vis all kinds of minorities, not merely in McCarthy's day but in New England in the seventeenth century – the witches of Salem?[4] Would you say that the New England communities were not democratic, ruled by majorities? Would you say that the majority of Iranians under the Ayatollah Khomeini would not have voted to repress those who disagreed with them, or, as some did, looked forward to the rule by a majoritarian populist Islam over the world, and the elimination of the basic rights of, say, 'the great Satan' (the USA)? Would you describe this as cold-war (or some other version of mere) rhetoric on my part?

[...] you ask why men and women are willing to fight and die for liberty, and you say it is not negative liberty they are fighting for, not the liberty to starve, be homeless, to lie in a coma, etc.[5] Indeed not. But what kind of liberty do you suppose Sakharov was fighting for? A utilitarian society? He fought for basic human rights, and he knew, as you and I know, that laws, constitutions, the source of authority of whatever kind, are needed to protect these. The liberties he enunciated were in my sense largely negative

---

1 TAL 12.

2 op. cit. (344/3).

3 Socrates drank the fatally poisonous hemlock given him after he was charged with corrupting the young and impiety, and sentenced to death, in 399 BCE. Anaxagoras (500–428 BCE), a Presocratic philosopher born in Asia Minor, lived most of his life in Athens under the patronage of Pericles, whom he tutored; obliged to leave Athens for the safety of Lampsacus around 450 BCE, despite Pericles speaking in his defence at his trial, again for impiety; buried with high honours on his death. Diagoras, Greek poet and Sophist active in the last decades of the C5th BCE; also charged with impiety, and condemned to death c.415 BCE, he fled Athens for Corinth, where he died.

4 Seaport in Mass. gripped 1692 by a frenzy of suspicion, after an epidemic swept through the community, convincing many that evil spirits were at work: hundreds of innocents were accused of witchcraft, and 19 hanged – one, Giles Corey, being crushed to death. When suspicions fell even on the family of the governor, William Phips, the hysteria began to subside, and many recanted their accusations.

5 TAL 12–13.

liberties – freedom from hideous interference of the kind to which he was subjected, both politically and physically, by the Soviet authorities. Do you really wish to maintain that democracy is a sufficient guarantee of these? Or a utilitarian system? Do you think that the oakum-picking prisoners who were to increase Bentham's private fortune[1] were an example of a minimum degree of freedom which even prisoners might be thought to be entitled to in their lonely cells?

It seems to me that the only guarantee of civil liberties, or indeed any kind of freedom, negative or positive, is, in the end, their establishment by laws beyond the interference of majorities, laws that guarantee Constant's minimum private space, and therefore [by] constitutions, whether written or as good as written, accepted without much question; bills of rights; basic principles and laws, perhaps of such a kind (if much more egalitarian, applying to all the inhabitants of a country) as a group of slave-owning American landowners (not keen supporters of total popular liberty) drew up for their country. That constitution has plenty of flaws, but it has preserved liberties more successfully than utilitarian denials of natural or any other liberties save those which laws – the only purpose of which is to maximise happiness – allow. Clearly the happiness of the many can be purchased by injustice to the few, or by arresting scientific progress and the search for the truth for fear of dangerous social consequences. I do not believe that either utilitarianism or representative democracy as such are obvious guarantors of individual, or indeed communal or sectional, liberties. No doubt Constant was right, and [...] the best way of obtaining such liberties is in a democracy [...], just because other forms of government are likely to jeopardise it more. It is a necessary but not a sufficient condition – accountability is not enough: governments can be accountable to majorities which can be turned this way or that way by unscrupulous demagogues or charismatic leaders. No doubt democracy does presuppose the existence of more than one party – to that extent it does allow some degree of competition between them which can be helpful for securing liberties. But it still seems to me that unless there is some firmer basis to protect individuals or groups – what liberals but not necessarily democrats seek to obtain – the dangers of liberty, whether under an over-strenuous, over-interfering yet perhaps entirely honest democracy, let alone a corrupt or stupid one, can be considerable.

Let me repeat: my defence of negative liberty is not a Hayekian–Thatcherite doctrine (far from it), which I think you are liable to reduce it

---

1 Oakum ('off-combings') is tarred fibre used for caulking ships' timber joints; oakum used to be recycled by unravelling ('picking') old tarred ropes into their constituent fibres, a task often assigned to prisoners, though Bentham did not see it as a source of profit in the kind of prison he envisaged. He also advocated the management of the poor in profitable 'industry houses', where the work done by inmates would generate income for the proposed National Charity Company that would run the proposed institutions; but again he did not see oakum-picking as a potentially significant contributor to any profits, though he did intend to profit from their work.

to. I merely wish to insist at this point that guarantees against invasion of a minimum degree of privacy and negative liberty that human beings need are more important than simply accountability. [...]

    With best wishes,

    Yours sincerely,

      Isaiah Berlin

Shirley Morgan and IB in a punt, Oxford, 1946

TO SHIRLEY ANGLESEY

  24 September 1991

                           Headington House

Dearest Shirley,

    Thank you for your, as always, splendid letter. The photographs are remarkable – I long to see a vivider version of it. Where could we have been? A punt?[1] Surely not. Somebody's sofa? And as you say, who took it? Marcus[2] is a good idea, who else did we ever know in common who could have done it?

---

1 SA must have sent him a very poor copy of the photo, since in the original, reproduced here, the punt and river are clearly visible.

2 Marcus William Dick (1920–71), fellow and philosophy and politics tutor, Balliol, 1947–63; prof. of philosophy, East Anglia, 1963–71; an old friend of IB's.

Not the Harts, where you used to stay when helping me; not some common friend in London, for who could that be? [...]

As for what Jock Balfour,[1] who was Minister in Moscow, used to call the Soviet Onion, I cannot help feeling that horrors may accumulate, massacres may occur, minorities will be oppressed and seek to manufacture nuclear devices to save themselves – all that may happen, and yet, and yet, it is much the best thing that has happened in our lifetime; the lifting of a gigantic burden, an act of liberation not just for Russia but for a great many other people as well. Well may you ask about G. A. Cohen. Both he and Hobsbawm are in a state of some depression, but Cohen has not been a Marxist for some years; and Hobsbawm gets out of it by smooth talk, I fear, about how nationalism, kept under by Stalin, will now be rampant. So it will – a terrible thing – but nothing can be as awful as what occupied seventy years of our lives. So I feel cock-a-hoop.

Pipes doesn't know much about Marxism or ideas in general, but he is a good historian, and his account of the Revolution is bound to be reliable – he is so right-wing that Aline doesn't really want him in the house, but he is an old student of mine and I like him despite certain defects – and think him a learned and useful man, to be respected. [...]

Yours, ⟨with much love – & to Henry⟩

Isaiah

TO HENRY HARDY

7 October 1991

Headington House

Dear Henry,

No good. I realise that all you say is perfectly sensible, but this is the wrong time, even if these things are to be published.[2]

I am quite prepared to help you with editorial notes, arcane allusions, etc., but I think at the moment, when the Soviet Union has gone under, to add to works which dance upon its grave would be inopportune. There is far too much of this going on already – the various ways of showing the inadequacies of Marxism, Communism, Soviet organisation, the causes of the latest putsch, revolution, etc. And I think these essays, if they are of any worth,

---

1 John ('Jock') Balfour (1894–1983), KCMG 1947; Russian-speaking UK minister, Moscow 1943–5, Washington 1945–8; UK ambassador to Argentine Republic 1948–51, to Spain 1951–4.

2 HH had proposed publishing a collection of essays that eventually appeared posthumously under his editorship thirteen years later (Washington, 2004) as *The Soviet Mind: Russian Culture under Communism*, with a foreword by Strobe Talbott. Reviewing the book for the *Moscow Times* (26 March 2004), Walter Laqueur wrote: 'While Berlin was alive, he was somewhat of a supreme authority in the West as far as Russian culture was concerned. At present, there are many excellent specialists to be found in the Western world, but it is difficult to think of a figure of similar intellectual curiosity, wide knowledge and sure judgement who is equally at home in the cultural traditions of several major countries.'

which, as you know, I permanently doubt, had much better be published in ten or fifteen years time, perhaps after my death – as interesting reflections, at best, of what things looked like to observers like myself in the 1950s, '60s, '70s etc. Believe me, I am right.

Yours ever,
    Isaiah

TO ROBERT SILVERS

18 November 1991 [*carbon*]

Headington House

Dear Bob,

[...] Marietta's[1] memorial service: it was perfectly nice. [...] A lot of people came who did not know Marietta particularly well, largely because of what Cyril Connolly once said about memorial services – 'Cocktail parties of the old.' I quite liked to mingle among the interesting and possibly well-born persons whom I had assumed, rightly, might be present. Roy Jenkins placed himself firmly in the front row [...]. Behind me, Lords Zuckerman[2] and Sherfield – perfectly right to be there – but I won't go on: there is really nothing to report except that it was dignified, the church was full and all went very well. [...]

Now let me turn to a very different subject. I am visited occasionally by a young man of about twenty-eight, from Alma-Ata in Kazakhstan. The astonishing thing about him is that he speaks English perfectly, studies political theory, is very civilised, very Western in the way he thinks, delightful to be with, confident, intelligent, Westernised – all in Alma-Ata. He spent some time in Moscow but not long, and then came to Oxford for three weeks and longs to come back. I was deeply impressed. He said to me that Kazakhstan was divided into three sections: the Muslims of his sort, who were gentle and decent; the Russians, who are perfectly reasonable; and the Muslim bigots, who are unspeakable but have great influence and could easily ruin the country. He also says that corruption is everywhere, and that the oil companies from Europe and America, which have now pounced on his country, which is the second largest oil repository after Saudi Arabia, have created a world of bribes and pressures such as that peaceful country had never

1 Mary Endicott ('Marietta') Tree (1917–91) née Peabody, US socialite and Democrat political activist; m. as his 2nd wife (Arthur) Ronald Lambert Field ('Ronnie') Tree (1897–1976), English gentleman of American descent and independent means; they were good friends of the Berlins; Marietta died 15 August in NY; a memorial service was held in the Grosvenor Chapel, South Audley Street, London W1, on 12 November.
2 Solly Zuckerman (1904–93), Kt 1956, life peer 1971, scientist and public servant; Sands Cox Professor of Anatomy, Birmingham, 1943–68; professor at large, East Anglia, 1969–74; trustee, Wolfson Foundation, 1965–87, strongly opposed to IB's application for funding for Wolfson College.

known. All this makes him lament. I asked him if there were many people like him in the country: he said, 'Yes, we form quite a decent intelligentsia but there are not many of us. We hope to have some influence, but goodness me, we have a lot of opponents. Still, we struggle, we try, and we are not persecuted.'

Anyway I am telling you about him partly because he is what is called a phenomenon, and Amartya Sen[1] says he might get him to come to Harvard for a term or so. If you are in touch with Amartya, do remind him and tell him that I think it a very good idea. Meanwhile I shall try and get him back to Oxford for a month or so – it may not be impossible, as he has friends in St Antony's. His difficulty is that he can't get any books in Alma-Ata, so I wonder if you could do me a favour. Could you (only at my expense, if you will send me a proper bill, otherwise it won't work), send him some books? [*A list follows.*]

The rest I think I can provide from England; but if you could get some bookshop to send these to him it would be a great service.

[Isaiah]

TO THE EDITOR OF THE *OXFORD MAGAZINE*

14 December 1991[2]

Headington House

Sir,

In your last issue (Eighth Week, Michaelmas Term), in the course of his review of *Oxford 1919–1939* (Éditions Autrement, Paris, 1991),[3] Emeritus Professor A. F. L. Beeston[4] says that my account of the attacks at the end of the 1920s by 'athletes' upon 'aesthetes' 'is at the very least a gross exaggeration', and goes on to add that 'drunken sprees' of destruction took no account of persons, but were 'ragging of which the victim would be a member of their own group'; and continues, 'The only instance of room-wrecking ... in which the boat club made havoc of a room was of a man who was himself a member of the club.'[5]

---

1 Amartya Kumar Sen (b. 1933), Indian economist; Drummond Professor of Political Economy, Oxford, and fellow, All Souls, 1980–88; professor of economics and philosophy and Lamont University Professor, Harvard, 1988–98; Master, Trinity, Cambridge, 1998–2004; Sveriges Riksbank Prize in Economic Sciences in Memory of Alfred Nobel 1998.

2 Published as 'Mixing It', *Oxford Magazine*, Noughth Week, Hilary Term 1992, 8; Beeston's article had appeared in the issue for Eighth Week, Michaelmas Term 1991, 17–18.

3 Françoise du Sorbier, *Oxford 1919–1939: un creuset intellectuel ou les métamorphoses d'une génération* (Paris, [1991]), contained an interview with IB, 'Sir Isaiah Berlin, esprit hardi', 57–71.

4 Alfred Felix Landon ('Freddie') Beeston (1911–95), orientalist; Laudian Prof. of Arabic, Oxford, and fellow, St John's, 1955–78.

5 op. cit. (note 2 above), 18. The wording of the last quotation is garbled. Beeston wrote: 'The only instance of room-wrecking [...] was one in which the boat club made havoc of the room of a man who was himself a member of the club.'

Mr Beeston's generalisation can easily be shown to be false. My reminiscences of what occurred are based on personal knowledge. I begin with Mr Beeston's 'room-wrecking'. I do not know what he is describing, but I suspect that it refers to an episode which occurred in Balliol in my first year (1928–9), where I knew the victim[1] personally. He was anything but a member of the wreckers' own group: he was an 'aesthete' of French extraction, possibly of Near Eastern origin, whose extreme exhibitionism made him very notorious in various ways. There was a rumour that the boat club, after an anticipated bump supper,[2] was going to attack him. His friends locked him in a cupboard outside his rooms, with vents for air and a bottle of brandy to keep him going. He spent the night there. The boat club, finding him absent, destroyed a large part of the walls, floor and ceiling of his room, as well as furniture, books etc. The College authorities exacted a huge fine. Conducted tours of the wrecked rooms took place, in which I took part. The victim was sent down. Years later, when I asked the Master why the College had punished the victim, the late Lord Lindsay said that a man who had made himself so hated could not be kept.

The next example is of an undergraduate at New College, suspected of homosexual inclinations; he later became a well-known Roman historian in a northern university. Again rumours of an impending attack began to circulate. The gang of 'hearties', armed with various weapons, reached the first floor of the staircase, but the metal part[s] of the banisters had had electric current put through them and the invaders received violent shocks and fell over each other. The raid had failed. I happened to be passing through the front quad of New College at the time and saw the melee with my own eyes. It was much talked about afterwards. The Roman historian was not exactly a member of the gang who tried to beat him up.

My next case is that of a Peruvian who lived in a flat in King Edward Street. Aesthetes gathered there on certain nights and one day were attacked by a mob of 'hearties'. The room was duly wrecked and one or two guests were physically damaged. The Proctors did deal with the case, and Bulldogs were stationed for some weeks to protect the flat. The Peruvian left Oxford very soon after this.

My last example occurred in my own college, Corpus Christi. Corpus was, and probably still is, a gentle and highly civilised society and what occurred was exceptional, but it did occur. One of my neighbours was the

1 Unidentified, as are the victims in the next two paragraphs.
2 A celebration of the achievement by a college eight of a 'bump' (i.e. contact with the boat in front) on each of the 4 days of one of the biennial 'bumps races' at Oxford and Cambridge (styled Torpids and [Summer] Eights in Oxford, Lent and May races in Cambridge). Bump suppers are high-spirited occasions at which drink is liberally consumed, and an old boat sometimes ceremonially burned in a college quadrangle.

late Bernard Spencer,[1] a gifted poet whose verse can still be found in more than one anthology. He was certainly an uncompromising aesthete, a friend and disciple of Louis MacNeice.[2] One morning a neighbour woke me in my bedroom in the Corpus Annexe in Magpie Lane and said something unusual was happening which might be worth seeing. I saw about a dozen Corpus undergraduates burst into Spencer's bedroom – he was asleep – and fall upon him and cut off one of his long whiskers (a typical mark of an aesthete in those days), beat him up and throw his books out of the window. It was a horrible sight, like a lynching bee. Spencer uttered not a sound, and bravely did not cut off his other whisker, but let the original one grow again. No disciplinary steps were taken.

Perhaps this is enough. I do not think that the ritual cutting to pieces of Stephen Spender's red tie by the hearties at Univ. can quite qualify.

These were by no means isolated incidents at the time. I cite only those of which I have direct personal knowledge. I think this is sufficient to dispose of Mr Beeston's ill-considered effort to convict me of 'gross exaggeration'. His world is not the one I was acquainted with.

Yours sincerely,
Isaiah Berlin

TO ERIC MACK[3]

3 February 1992

Headington House

Dear Professor Mack,

[...] I could not be more deeply in agreement with you about the effect on universities – very strong in the USA but no doubt coming here soon: the beginnings are noticeable – of the absurd claims of differences in ethnic, gender and, for all I know, all kinds of other needs (or alleged needs), which are directed against, and no doubt are doing much to destroy, the pursuit of knowledge and its dissemination, which is the principal object of institutions of learning. Equally, I abhor the absurdities of people like Derrida, de Man

---

1 (Charles) Bernard Spencer (1909–63), CCC classics 1928–32, poet, broadcaster and teacher; IB had shared lodgings with him in St John Street during his PPE year.

2 (Frederick) Louis MacNeice (1907–63), poet and dramatist; Merton classics 1926–30; lecturer in classics, Birmingham, 1930–6; lecturer in Greek, Bedford, London, 1936–40; feature writer and producer, BBC, 1940–9.

3 Eric Mitchell Mack (b. 1946), assistant prof. of philosophy, Tulane, 1975–8, associate prof. 1978–91, prof. since 1991. EM had sent IB the typescript of 'The Limits of Diversity: The New Counter-Enlightenment and Isaiah Berlin's Liberal Pluralism', which had been accepted for publication in Howard Dickman (ed.), *The Imperiled Academy* (New Brunswick, NJ, and London, 1993), where it appears at 97–126. Some time after Berlin responded, EM sent him the typescript of 'Isaiah Berlin and the Quest for Liberal Pluralism', which had been accepted for publication in *Public Affairs Quarterly* 7 no. 3 (July 1993), where it appears at 215–30. He remembers enclosing a note saying that this article took a more critical view of IB than the other essay. IB did not reply.

and the sages of Yale,[1] which seem to me to be a kind of game – a form of perhaps not wholly unconscious, clever, amusing, frivolous quackery, which its more gifted exponents enjoy putting across, without, I think, actually believing all that they are saying, but delighted to find such a market for them. The same was certainly in part true of the Marxism of people like Marcuse, who confessed to me to being astonished by the degree of support he suddenly obtained when he used the same charges against the United States which he had formulated against the Weimar Republic in the late 1920s and early 1930s. He enjoyed being followed by the students, but thought most of them had no brains – but cynically did not mind that, and adored his fame and influence. No doubt he did believe in part of what he said, but not the full-blooded doctrine. I suspect the same, to an even greater extent, is true of the deconstructionists, post-deconstructionists, etc. etc. I cannot believe that this bogus activity will not evaporate. However, that may be baseless optimism on my part.

Now let us come to more serious issues, where I feel that you have made some important criticisms which I recognise as valid and which I wish to answer.

You have made it clear to me that I should have laid greater emphasis on the limits both of negative and of positive liberty. The absurdities of women's studies, black studies, Puerto-Rican studies, Lesbian studies etc., and the rejection of the alleged despotism of the views of Dead White European Males, are of course a form of blowing up of positive liberty – self-promotion, the imposing of one's free personality against all kinds of enemies who are trying to control, shape and perhaps ignore all these 'rights' for the benefit of some establishment over which they preside and which they wish to impose on universities and other institutions.

But the same considerations apply to negative liberty. Let me explain: it was perhaps not enough for me simply to say that the ultimate values sometimes collide and cultures are incommensurable, etc., and that, for that reason, single ideals – say, even of liberty in certain respects, or of justice or of happiness, etc. – must on occasion be made to yield to some degree to each other. I should have made it far clearer that what I believe is not merely that where there is a clash of values, each individual or group or for that matter nation must choose one of the ultimate values, for the sake of which one exists – or make an attempt at a compromise between several of these; but something further. [...] Obviously if the framework of society is to be

---

1 In addition to Derrida (186/3) and Paul de Man (186/4), these were Geoffrey Heumann Hartman (b. 1929) né Gert Heumann, Joseph Hillis Miller (b. 1928) and Harold Bloom (233/5). Styled by Miller 'the Yale school of criticism', they published *Deconstruction and Criticism* (London/NY, 1979). 'It may not have been intended as a manifesto, but it was received as one': Louis Menand, 'The De Man Case', *New Yorker*, 24 March 2014, 87–93 at 92. De Man and Miller were strong adherents and proponents of Derrida's 'deconstruction'; Hartman and Bloom were fellow-travellers who drifted away from the 'school's' agenda.

preserved, which I take for granted, then excess of self-determination must be restrained. You speak of a universally valid norm to preserve society or university.[1] The reason for it is, of course, that unless there is peace, order, a degree of toleration, understanding etc., societies can scarcely be preserved. All that I accept, and should have made it clear that constraints of this kind are indispensable, and that negative liberty – and positive liberty too, which is involved in self-assertion of ethnic, gender etc. claims – must be confined within a certain radius. But I do not believe in universally valid norms – I am content, as an empiricist, to confine myself to principles which a great many people, in a great many places, for a very long time, have accepted: principles, values, rules. That is what creates the possibility of coexistence, of social life, of communication. [...]

Yours sincerely,
    Isaiah Berlin

TO HENRY HARDY
10 February 1992

Headington House
Dear Henry,

Thank you for saying that you liked the Ignatieff show. God knows what'll happen with Magee[2] – anyway, I am past minding. Now to your queries.

[...] The privacy of religious views. My inspirer is John Stuart Mill, who, when he stood for Parliament, said he was ready to answer all questions except those about his religious views, which he said were no business of the public.[3] Rightly or wrongly, I admire that very much. There are certain things which people are not prepared to talk about, and why on earth should people who may be thinkers confess these things, even if they have had an influence on their views? After all, one may have all kinds of complicated views about one's parents – hatreds, resentments, sexual complications, God knows what, according to modern psychopathology. Yet even now I think probing enquiries about whether Major[4] could be said to have an Oedipus

1 EM had written: 'I provide a sketch of the sort of common norms without which the liberal society and the liberal university cannot survive.' 'The Limits of Diversity' (433/3), 99.
2 IB was interviewed by Michael Ignatieff for an episode of BBC2 TV's *The Late Show* broadcast 5 February; Bryan Magee interviewed him for 'Nationalism: The Melting-Pot Myth', broadcast 19 February as the last in the series *What's the Big Idea?*
3 'I should positively and deliberately refuse to allow myself to be interrogated on any subject whatever of purely religious opinion. I do this on principle. I conceive that no one has any right to question another on his religious opinions.' Letter of 21 June 1865 to Charles Westerton, published in Charles Westerton, 'Mr John Stuart Mill and Westminster', letter of 23 June 1865, *Times*, 24 June 1865, 5e.
4 John Major (b. 1943), later (2005) KG, Conservative MP 1979–2001; foreign secretary 1989, chancellor of the exchequer 1989–90, prime minister 1990–7, coming to power by winning the Conservative leadership election that ended the career of Margaret Thatcher, whose nomination as leader he had himself proposed.

complex would not be regarded as altogether proper, at least by me and people who think like me.

However, I am perfectly prepared to tell you about myself and my religion. It is really quite simple. I was brought up in a Jewish family which was not strictly Orthodox – rather relaxed, like the kind of Church of England families who go to church once in a while but certainly not every Sunday, and have a vague belief about what Anglican Christianity teaches but don't allow it to disturb their daily thoughts. I remember that Lord Melbourne[1] once said something like 'What are things coming to if religion is allowed to interfere with one's private life? That will never do.'[2] Anyway, I used to be taken to synagogue in Russia and in London, found it frightfully boring but not disagreeable, and rather enjoyed the hymns.

My difficulty was that when I began thinking about these things I could attach no meaning to the concept of 'God'. To me, he is either an old man with a beard, as Michelangelo[3] paints him, and in that I cannot believe any more than a very, very great many other people of even a mildly sophisticated kind; or I don't know what is meant. The idea of a transcendent spiritual person, or a divine force which rules the world, or someone who created all things and directs the course of them, etc., means absolutely nothing to me. With my rigid, I fear, empiricism, I can attach no meaning to it.

So it's no good saying I'm an atheist – they know what the word 'God' means and just deny His existence. Nor an agnostic, who is not sure whether He exists or not. I am well beyond these things: I simply don't know what is meant. I am like a tone-deaf person who realises that other people listen to music with pleasure or even total absorption – I have no idea what the experience is.

On the other hand, I understand what are called religious feelings, up to a point, as expressed, let us say, in the cantatas or oratorios of Bach, or the masses of Mozart or Beethoven or Bruckner, and I have a certain empathy with that – the feelings, but not their object. Moreover, I go to synagogue, say four times a year at most, partly for sentimental reasons, to say a prayer for my parents when their anniversary falls, as they would have liked me to; partly because I like the hymns; also I like to identify myself with the Jewish community – I like to feel a member of a community which has existed

1 William Lamb (1779–1848), 2nd Viscount Melbourne 1805, Whig statesman; prime minister 1834, 1835–41; political mentor to the young Queen Victoria.
2 'When Lord Melbourne had accidentally found himself the unwilling hearer of a rousing Evangelical sermon about sin and its consequences, he exclaimed in much disgust as he left the church: "Things have come to a pretty pass when religion is allowed to invade the sphere of private life!"' One Who Has Kept a Diary [George W(illiam) E(rskine) Russell], Collections and Recollections (London, 1898), 79.
3 Michelangelo (di Lodovico) Buonarroti (Simoni) (1475–1564), Florentine sculptor, painter, architect, draughtsman and poet; among his masterpieces is the fresco cycle in the Sistine Chapel of the Vatican (1508–12, 1533–41), which depicts (inter alia) God creating Adam.

continuously for three thousand years. But I perfectly understand the feelings of those of my Jewish friends who don't want to feel any of this, and never go.

How am I to explain all this, particularly in relation to my social, political, philosophical views? I don't see that it has much relevance.

The only occasions, I think, on which I am filled with religious feelings are not at church or mosque or synagogue services (all of which I enjoy up to a point), but when listening to certain types of music – say the Beethoven posthumous quartets.

On the other hand, I find that those who, like Freddie Ayer or Trevor-Roper, are bone-dry atheists and simply deny and denounce the whole thing (as Freddie used to, and Trevor-Roper, more cautiously, still does) – they do not begin to understand what men live by, which I claim to be able to do, because of this understanding, which I believe I possess, of religious emotion and the effect and influence which it has upon people's characters and lives. What more can I say to you?

You speak of great philosophers. Some would have agreed with me – Spinoza certainly, though God knows what he meant by 'God'. I don't know what *deus sive natura*[1] meant to him or to anyone. Matthew Arnold's description of him as a God-intoxicated man[2] seems to me absurd. I doubt whether Kant, who theoretically believed in God, or Hegel, who claimed to be Lutheran, could have made plain what they actually believed in. My master in this, as always, is David Hume, who would have agreed with me. I ought to add that religious poetry, say parts of the Bible, or the poetry of people like Herbert and Crashaw and Vaughan,[3] certainly moves me; but what this has to do with my philosophical or political views, only God (if he exists – whatever that may mean) knows. [...]

Do democrats have a right to elect an anti-democratic government? In a democracy, where people have a right to vote for anyone they please, they certainly do. They'd be bloody fools if they did, and every legal step should be taken to dissuade them from doing so; but if they want to commit suicide I cannot see how this can be prevented, except by depriving democratic voters of the right to vote for anti-democratic governments – and that seems to me to go too far. This is hard on the democratic minority which is overcome by

---

1 'God or nature', Spinoza's equivocal characterisation of the universe, sometimes thought atheistic or pantheistic.

2 It was Novalis, not Arnold, who first so described Spinoza, 11 February 1800: 'Spinoza ist ein Gott-trunkener Mensch.' Novalis, *Schriften*, ed. Ludwig Tieck and Fr[iedrich] Schlegel, 5th ed. (Berlin, 1837), [ii, comprising] part 2 [Zweiter Theil], Fragmente vermischten Inhalts, III. Moralische Ansichten, 261.

3 George Herbert (1593–1633), metaphysical poet and cleric, best known for his sacred poetry (*The Temple* appeared posthumously, 1633); influenced Richard Crashaw (c.1612/13–1648), English poet, who converted from high Anglicanism to Catholicism in Paris after fleeing puritans at Cambridge, and Henry Vaughan (1622–95), religious poet and mystic.

a huge, let us say pro-Fascist, majority – quite apart from Algeria[1] – which is nearly what happened in Germany. But nobody can deny that the appointment of Hitler as Chancellor was legitimate in terms of the democratic laws of the Weimar Republic. It's rather like the question of censorship: should there be censorship of anti-social films, writings etc.? Why should pornography be censored, or racist attacks? I have to modify the above statement. If there is a party, say the National Front, which begins to threaten to take over British institutions, then I think there is a case for trying to prevent it from doing so, by legislation of a non-democratic kind. But when this point is reached it is very difficult to say, and democrats might well disagree with me about this. Let me cite an old story to you. German conservatives in the Weimar Republic with authoritarian inclinations said to liberals, 'Under the liberal system, we are allowed to say whatever we like and vote whichever way we want to vote; that is your principle. Under us, you will be forbidden to express your views or vote in the wrong direction, because that's our principle. Anything wrong with that?' So we go back to the old business of having to ban, in free countries, any forces which seriously threaten freedom. Make of that what you will.

Yours ever,

[Isaiah]

TO HENRY HARDY

18 February 1992

Headington House

Dear Henry,

I am the last person to deny that fearful crimes have been committed by religious intolerance. Everyone knows that: Jews, the Inquisition, Muslims, Catholics in seventeenth-century Paris, etc. etc. I think only Buddhists are comparatively innocent. But I don't think it is religion that is at fault, but clericalism – religion in authority, institutional religion. I am not engaged in writing the history of political doctrines, or giving marks to political thinkers, or analysing their views altogether. My writings, I should have thought, if anyone was interested in them, are enough to convey that I take an interest in the perversion of words such as 'liberty', that I am opposed to despotism, particularly of those who believe in the perfect solution (e.g. theologians), and therefore need not be explicit about all this. [...]

Of course philosophers' views of God make a difference to their views; but I don't see why I need go into that; I am not writing biographies of philosophers, and I don't attack Fascism as such, except indirectly; Communism,

---

1 Where the issue was whether a Muslim majority might properly vote for an undemocratic Islamic government: see 446/2.

yes, because that depends on misuse of certain liberal concepts. In general my position with regard to persecution is clear enough, I think. What is not so clear is what room should be made by people like me for religious sects: is it all right for Muslims to insulate themselves and take very little part in general English culture? What do I feel about Sikhs and their battles against (Muslim) Pakistan and (Hindu) India? or about the union of a certain section of the Russian Church with nationalism and neo-Fascism, as well as the Communist *nomenklatura*?[1] I don't think I need go into that: it is quite clear [...], if one is a liberal, what one's views must be about all that, and there I rest it. The part played by religion in the thought of political philosophers is a subject for philosophical biography or motivation of their political views, not of great interest to me. [...]

Yours ever,

I.B

TO HANNAH ROTHSCHILD[2]

6 March 1992

Headington House

Dear Hannah,

[...] Aline and I met Picasso in the house of Douglas Cooper[3] in France. He and Cocteau[4] had just been to a bullfight, and he and Cocteau and the man who made his pots in Vallauris were present; maybe also one or two other people. Anyway, I found myself standing next to Picasso. He was silent. So was I. Out of pure nervousness, in order to break the silence, I thought I would tell him a story, since it was fresh in my mind, having been told it about a fortnight before. It is this. The famous Spanish dramatist, Lope de Vega,[5] when he was dying, asked his doctor whether he would die soon (the story is best in French): 'Est-ce que je meurs aujourd'hui, Monsieur?' 'Oui, Monsieur.' 'Vous en êtes sûr?' 'Oui, Monsieur.' 'Vous êtes absolument sûr?' 'Oui, Monsieur.' 'Est-ce que je meurs dans une heure ou moins?' 'Oui, Monsieur.' 'Vous en êtes sûr?' 'Oui, Monsieur, absolument sûr.' 'Alors, Dante m'emmerde.'[6]

1 Holders of posts filled by Communist Party appointees.
2 Hannah Mary Rothschild (b. 1962), writer and film-maker, daughter of Jacob Rothschild; co-founder, 1997, Artists on Film Trust.
3 (Arthur William) Douglas Cooper (1911–84), art historian, collector, critic; Slade Prof. of Fine Art, Oxford, 1957–8; Picasso was a neighbour and frequent visitor to his house in the south of France.
4 Jean Maurice Eugène Clément Cocteau (1889–1963), avant-garde French poet, playwright, designer and film-maker; he associated with many of the leading artistic figures of the day, including Picasso, Diaghilev and Stravinsky.
5 Félix Lope de Vega y Carpio (1562–1635), prolific Spanish Baroque playwright.
6 'Will I die today, sir?' 'Yes, sir.' 'Are you certain?' 'Yes, sir.' 'Are you absolutely certain?' 'Yes, sir.' 'Will I die in a hour or less?' 'Yes, sir.' 'You are sure?' 'Yes, sir, absolutely sure.' 'Well then, Dante bores me.'

I told this story to Picasso, hoping it would amuse him, but it didn't: he said not a word and crossed the room to the other end, and then, about a quarter of an hour later, apparently, said to someone there, it may have been Douglas Cooper, 'Who is this man who talks about death?' So it was not a successful meeting, I fear. Meanwhile Cocteau behaved like a trained monkey, leaping about, taking books out, looking at them, putting them back, chatting, trying to draw every kind of attention to himself; while Picasso was quiet, dignified, extremely impressive, like a man who knew he was a man of genius and did not need to try to make himself amusing or interesting. [...]

Yours ever,
Isaiah

IB was the castaway on BBC Radio 4's *Desert Island Discs* on 19 April 1992; drawing by Hugh Casson

TO SHIELA SOKOLOV GRANT
  20 April 1992

Headington House

Dearest Shiela,

Thank you ever so much for your letter of 10 April. No, I cannot begin to write letters to you – or anybody else – on serious subjects. But I do wish hastily to inform you that the fifth[1] Tory government is not the worst thing that could happen to England or Europe or anywhere else. Your dismay at it I understand fully, and it is shared by practically everybody I know; I am

1 sc. fourth (counting from and including Margaret Thatcher's victory 1979).

ashamed to say that I don't mind it as much as most, because somehow I could get up no enthusiasm for any of the three parties, and virtuously voted for the Lib. Dems, knowing that it would have no effect: we duly elected a Labour man for our constituency.

No, all I wanted to say to you was that the events of, let us say, 1935–45, particularly the age of Hitler, Mussolini, Franco, Stalin, was much, much, much worse than anything that happens now, however we may regret this or that – there is no comparison with those black days. That is how I console myself every time some public disaster happens: at any rate, it is not worse than what happened then. I don't believe that could quite happen again. [...]

Yours ever, ⟨with much love as always⟩

Isaiah

TO RICHARD WILBERFORCE

15 May 1992 [*carbon*]

Headington House

Dear Richard,

[...] You have brought everything back to me about the 1930s. You are perfectly right – I am a man of the '30s. I think I remain one. I am not so sure that you do – do you? My musical taste is fixated in that period – that's when Schnabel[1] transformed me, so did Busch and his quartet,[2] so did Toscanini,[3] so did the whole experience of Salzburg,[4] much more than Glyndebourne, excellent as that was. I am like those very old men; indeed, I am one – we both are – who thinks that things can never be as good as they were fifty years ago. But I am convinced that artistically that is so, in spite of my idol Alfred

---

1 'It is by now a well-established fact that Artur Schnabel is much the most original figure among the pianists of our day. The records made of his performances of Beethoven's sonatas and concerti are probably the greatest single contribution which the gramophone companies have made to the musical culture of our times.' [IB], 'Gramophone Notes', *Oxford Magazine* 54 (1935–6), 370.

2 Adolf Georg Wilhelm Busch (1891–1952), German-born violinist and composer, founded the Busch Chamber Players in England in the late 1930s; the quartet made many famous recordings. '[A]ll the frightful patter about self-realizing individuals & freedom in obedience to law appears unsullied & true in the playing of the Busch family.' IB to Cressida Bonham Carter, n.d. [1938?], L1 273.

3 Arturo Toscanini (1867–1957), Italian conductor, passionately admired by IB because of his musical genius and his refusal to conduct under Fascist regimes. Reviewing a 1937 concert conducted by Toscanini, IB wrote: 'It was a personal experience of the first magnitude for everyone present: those who had never heard him before may well have found that for them it shifted the boundaries of artistic possibility, and in this respect fundamentally altered the nature of their musical experience.' [IB], 'Toscanini', *Oxford Magazine* 55 (1936–7), 719–20 at 719; cf. L1 236.

4 '[W]e all find Salzburg the fulfilment of all our dreams (I have for the past 4 years)' (to Christopher Cox, 25 August 1933, L1 58); 'it is the only town in which I know that I shall be entirely happy all the time' (to Lettice Fisher, 27 August 1935, L1 131).

Brendel and the wonderful Perahia[1] and the wonderful Bach player Andras Schiff[2] – have you heard him? If not you must, you must, you must.

I remember you had a to me somewhat unaccountable taste for Miss Tureck,[3] remarkable as she was and is; but I never quite took to her playing of Bach. Perhaps it is my fault.

I remember there were two quartets playing in the 1930s – indeed, at the end of the 1920s. One was the Busch, noble, austere, north German (as I thought of them, I don't know if they were), pure; the other, Léner,[4] Hungarian, delicious tone. Everything covered with the most exquisite butter, beautifully played but only delicious, not admirable enough, not serious enough, in fact. I remember they were frightfully ugly, all four of them. I couldn't conceive how they could go on travelling together, day in, day out, and look at each other without a certain degree of disgust. But perhaps that isn't fair.

Toscanini's performance of the *Eroica* at the Queen's Hall[5] was something the like of which I never heard before – until I heard him do *Falstaff* and *Fidelio* in Salzburg in 1936 and 1937.

But I mustn't go on – my point being, however much it may be delusion, that the 1930s was the serious time for music. There are occasionally returns to it, like Brendel, like Schiff, like the late Klemperer,[6] but this somehow all dates back to the golden age – it was golden for me at least.

I am glad you remember *Traviata*: it always moves me. So does the last Schubert sonata.[7] Why didn't you like Schnabel in Schubert? This reminds me of something odd. I remember going to a concert by him in the Albert Hall, towards the end of his not very long life.[8] All the British pianists were there, lined up in the front rows – Solomon, Clifford Curzon, Myra Hess, for all I know Lady Maud, the then Mrs Spender, Lady Drogheda, old Aunt Harriet Cohen and all.[9] He played [the] op. 111 sonata. The first movement

1 Murray Perahia (b. 1947), US pianist and conductor; debut in NY 1968; played Scarlatti, Handel, Bach and Beethoven in IB's honour in the Sheldonian Theatre, Oxford, 30 September 1994; later (2009) appointed president, Jerusalem Music Centre, in whose creation IB had been closely involved (139/2).

2 András Schiff (b. 1953), later (2014) Kt, Hungarian-born British pianist and conductor celebrated especially for his interpretations of Bach; artistic director, September Chamber Music Festival, Mondsee, Austria, 1989–98; he had given a concert of Bach concertos 10 August with the Camerata Academica Salzburg at the Salzburg Festival.

3 Rosalyn Tureck (1914–2003), US keyboard player, conductor and music teacher; toured Europe from 1947, specialising in Bach; formed the Tureck Bach Players in London 1959.

4 Hungarian string quartet formed 1918 by four members of the Budapest Opera Orchestra: Jenö Léner, Josef Smilovits, Sándor Roth and Irme Hartman; after their debut in Budapest, 1919, they became one of the leading quartets of the inter-war period.

5 4 June 1930.

6 Otto Klemperer (1885–1973), German-born conductor, noted interpreter of Beethoven.

7 Piano sonata in B flat major, D960: see also 229/4.

8 Schnabel played a special Beethoven programme 29 May 1946, including the piano sonata no. 32, op. 111; he last appeared at the Royal Albert Hall June 1947.

9 Solomon Cutner ('Solomon') (1902–88); Clifford Michael Curzon (1907–82), Kt 1977; Myra Hess (1890–1965), DBE 1941, founder and director of the famous WW2 lunchtime recitals at the

was flawless. He began the second movement. He played the theme, then the first variation, the second, the third, then a slight pause, then the third again – then again the third, then the third for the fourth time. Agony. He had obviously forgotten. It was not clear what was going to happen; people began shifting uneasily and then, thank God, he remembered and went on triumphantly to the end. An inferior pianist might have apologised, but this heroic man did not.[1] I also remember him in the Town Hall, when Tom began to peal at 9.05 or whatever it was,[2] in the middle of the Diabelli Variations.[3] He played a bit, for a minute or two, then a tiny bit more, then stopped dead, got up, and said in a very county-like voice 'I can't go on in this infernal row ...'. He never came back to Oxford at all after that. [...]

Now, although Mozart is divine, as who can doubt, I feel totally dedicated to Bach. As you say, the cantatas are beyond everything; not so much for me, I hate to admit, the B Minor Mass – the beginning, sublime, and portions of it, like everything else he wrote. I like to think that in the eighteenth century there was Rameau[4] sitting in Paris, sure that he was the greatest composer in the world, that his music would be played every day by someone somewhere so long as music was played at all, and correspondingly so treated by his French contemporaries, and perhaps Italians and Germans too; and there was Bach, a good organist in Leipzig – he knew he was pretty good – he knew he was a good composer, better than some, better than Telemann,[5] perhaps as good as Vivaldi;[6] but the thought that he would become a model, a kind of Zeus, could never have occurred to him. I am sure he was too busy to think about anything except begetting children and writing music. His excitement

National Gallery, London; (Margaret) Jean Redcliffe-Maud (1904–93) née Hamilton, Baroness Redcliffe-Maud (m. 1932 John Redcliffe-Maud); Natasha Gordon Spender (1919–2010) née Litvin (m. 1941 Stephen Spender as his second wife); Joan Eleanor Moore (1903–89) née Carr, Countess of Drogheda (m. 1935 Garrett Drogheda); Harriet Cohen (1895–1967).

1 'Asked once what he felt at those supreme moments when, as in the last movement of Beethoven's sonata, op. 111, he seemed to pierce through the veil of matter into a realm of pure spirit, he replied, "I move in time and space." It was this transcendental quality which gave his playing its unique value.' D. and R. M., 'Mr Artur Schnabel', supplementary obituary, *Times*, 29 August 1951, 6f.

2 Great Tom, the bell of Tom Tower in Christ Church (Oxford's largest college, near the Town Hall), sounded 101 times every evening at 9:05 p.m. (once the equivalent in 'Oxford time' of 9:00 p.m. GMT) as a curfew for undergraduates: Christ Church originally had 100 original scholars, plus 1 added 1663. At Tom's peal all the colleges used to lock their gates; no longer, though the bell rings still.

3 Beethoven's *33 Variations on a Waltz by Anton Diabelli*, op. 120.

4 Jean Philippe Rameau (1683–1764), Dijon-born French composer, harpsichordist and organist; settled in Paris 1722.

5 Georg Philipp Telemann (1681–1767), German composer and organist; appointed Kantor of the Johanneum and music director of the 5 main churches in Hamburg 1721; appointed Kantor at the Thomaskirche, Leipzig, 1722, in preference to J. S. Bach, but chose to remain at Hamburg after his salary was increased and he was given the additional post of music director of the opera.

6 Antonio Lucio Vivaldi (1678–1741), Italian composer and virtuoso violinist; a master of the concerto, and a prolific writer of operas; much of his sacred music was written for performance at the Ospedale della Pietà in Venice, where he held dicontinuous posts 1703–40.

at being summoned by Frederick the Great[1] to Berlin is typical – Rameau
wouldn't think it at all surprising if Louis XV[2] had invited him, as he probably did, to play at Versailles. [...]

Yours,

[Isaiah]

TO JOHN BAYLEY
10 June 1992

Headington House

Dear John,

[...] I get on quite well with A. N. Wilson – to the horror of my progressive friends – if only because he is extremely polite to me, which I can never
resist. For some reason I get upset every time I see my name in a newspaper,
whether for good or ill. It is a kind of neurosis, insecurity – whatever it is,
very unlike my great friend Stephen Spender, who once said in an interview
that he was disappointed whenever he opened a newspaper and did not see
his name in it.

Suez has always slightly haunted me, because I took one step forwards,
two steps backwards (the title of one of Lenin's pamphlets),[3] which showed
deplorable infirmity of will and opinion. Still, perhaps it was a little pompous
of me to ask Wilson to produce a *démenti*.[4]

I do not believe that cookery, clothes and women's magazines are your
principal interest – nor, perhaps, do you. But whenever one is accused of
anything one immediately feels a sense of guilt and wonders whether it may
be so. I think if I were accused of murder I should still feel a twinge of guilt –
because one believes that all bad things said about one, however disagreeable
and uncalled for, may well be true.

About Graham Greene, I agree – but we are the only people in the English-
speaking world who do not boil with indignation because they do not get
the Nobel Prize. About 'all right to like ...', I cannot forbear telling a story.
I had been given a lift by K[enneth] and Jane Clark from Glyndebourne to
Brighton, where we were all staying (not together!). After the talk about the
music had died down, I said during a silence that I had been looking with
pleasure at paintings by Hubert Robert.[5] Jane said 'He's not a very good

---

1 Frederick II (1712–86), king of Prussia 1740–8 (cf. 478/2), was a composer, flautist and patron of
   music; he established a court orchestra at Berlin 1740, and an opera house there 1742.
2 Louis XV (1710–74), king of France 1715–74; great-grandson of Louis XIV.
3 282/2.
4 In an article on JB, 'Mad Don and English Man', dealing with (inter alia) JB's domestic habits and
   alleged fondness for *Woman's Own* magazine, Candida Crewe quoted A. N. Wilson as saying that
   JB and IB had signed a petition in support of Suez 1956: *Times*, 23 May 1992, *Saturday Review*, 4–6
   at 6c; Wilson's démenti was a letter to the editor, 'Sir Isaiah and Suez', 29 May, 15c. Cf. L2 547–8.
5 Hubert Robert (1733–1808), French landscape painter, draughtsman and garden designer.

painter, but it is quite all right to like him.' Bad painters whom it is all right to like, good painters whom it is not all right to like – the vista spreads before one. [...]

Yours ever,

Isaiah

PS Russian authors: I think they will actually do better without protest and tyranny, but that may be mere misplaced patriotism on my part.

TO MORRIS ABRAM[1]

12 June 1992 [*carbon*]

Headington House

Dear Ambassador Abram,

[...] You ask me three questions, which I shall do my best to answer – perhaps not as briefly as I should like.

Negative and positive liberty. I do not know whether this has a direct relation to human rights as conceived by the United Nations. I do not think that by positive liberty I do refer to economic and social rights. I wasn't writing about rights. If I were to use the language of rights, I should maintain that human beings have some degree of right (never absolute, as I am sure you will agree) both to negative and to positive liberty, i.e. both to the liberty of choice uninterfered with by other human beings, and to liberty as determination by oneself rather than being directed or coerced by other agents. However, that is not, I think, what you really want me to answer you about.

My initial difficulty is that the whole language of rights has always been somewhat puzzling to me. You may be astonished to hear this, as, after all, we all talk about rights and we all think we know what we mean. I have no difficulty about legal rights. They are entailed by rules which are enacted by the sovereign body in question, whatever it may be – God, the King, Parliament, the popular assembly, whatever the ultimate legislative body may be in a given society. So far so good. But about human rights I am not so clear. Who enacts them? How do we know what they are? Can one, as in the case of legal rights, lose them, waive them, transfer them, acquire them? From whom can one claim them? Who decides? I have never known any of that, although of course there is a vast literature about it. I have tried to interpret these natural, or human, rights to myself as being simply this: there are certain forms of conduct which we regard as right or wrong (whatever our criteria may be, but all human beings have notions of these, even if they disagree). If something is right and to my interest, then I claim it so as a right; if something is right and against my interest, I am not likely so to claim it; if

---

1 Morris Berthold Abram (1918–2000), US lawyer and public servant; a prosecutor at Nuremberg; subsequently active in the US civil rights movement and in US Jewish associations; US representative to the UN in Geneva 1989–93; co-founder of UN Watch 1993, chair 1993–2000.

something is wrong, then neither I nor anyone can justifiably claim it. I don't know if that analyses rights properly, but I have always gone on some such notion as this. What makes these right or wrong are no doubt moral rules or political rules: whatever I regard as that which is accepted in the society in which I live, and perhaps in every human society, at all times, at any rate by a great many men at a great many times in a great many places. In other words, my right simply consists in something which, if right, it is in my interest in being done – or, if wrong, avoided. People have to specify rules – lists of natural rights, lists of natural laws, as it were – but that is a large subject and goes back to ancient times. There is much disagreement about this.

[...] You say: 'while freedom alone may not guarantee economic success, repression almost certainly guarantees economic failure'.[1] What about Japan? The big step forward in economic life, and indeed political organisation, which Japan made in the late nineteenth century was done under conditions of pretty rigid repression, from which Japan has hardly recovered, in some ways, even now. I wish I thought that liberty was a prerequisite of, for example, culture. But a great many wonderful works of art were created under tyranny. So I think your view of that is somewhat optimistic. I should like to believe it to be true, but I do not think that history entirely bears you out.

But there is a greater difficulty, and that is this. It has often been pointed out, particularly to me by my critics, that the right of a man to live in the Waldorf Astoria Hotel may be absolute, but if he has no money it is a mere mockery to tell him this. This applies to civil liberties as well, and political rights too. I have a political right to vote in a democracy, but if I am too illiterate, and can get no help, and have no idea what goes on, my right is not worth much, and the use of it is not going to be very profitable, either to myself or to society. Consequently I do see that there is a clash of values in society, as there always is, say between liberty and equality: complete liberty means that the wolves are free to eat the sheep, the strong destroy the weak; equality means curtailment of liberty, sometimes quite severe, in order to create the absolute equality of which you speak as being enjoyed in prison. So, too, a minimum of security may be incompatible with a maximum of liberty. In the case of civil or political rights I cannot with my hand on my heart say that the ban in Algiers on free elections[2] in order to prevent a takeover by Muslim fanatics was to be utterly condemned as curtailment of basic liberties, which in some sense it could be thought to be. It is a curtailment, but are there not

---

1 MA to IB, 18 May 1992.

2 On 12 January 1992 Algeria cancelled the 2nd round of its parliamentary elections, the first free elections that the country had seen, to prevent the fundamentalist Islamic Salvation Front (FIS) party, the clear victor in the 1st round of voting, from coming to power, and the FIS was officially dissolved 4 March by the military government that had assumed power as Algeria descended into civil war.

circumstances that justify it? So, too, it might be thought that any decent society must accept [that it ought] to provide a certain degree of freedom from hunger, from insecurity, from ignorance, even [...] free exchange of goods between persons, and so on – some of which could be regarded as 'economic rights'. In other words, the primacy of the civil and political rights of which you speak is an idea deeply sympathetic to me, but I can conceive of situations in which some of these do have to be curtailed in order to make a situation tolerable for at any rate the great majority of a society. Do you disagree? Perhaps you do.

As to *Language, Truth and Logic*: I shall certainly try and find a copy for you, although I ought to warn you that the author, in a broadcast not long before his lamented death, said that most of the things in it, in his opinion, were wrong or false, although the general approach was correct.[1] Very little of that book has been left standing in contemporary English-speaking philosophy. But, of course, in its day it was a marvellous manifesto which liberated a great many people (though not in a civil or political sense!), and it is beautifully written. Anyway, I'll try and find it for you.

Yours sincerely,

Isaiah Berlin

[...]

TO ALAN MONTEFIORE[2]

6 July 1992

Headington House

Dear Alan,

[...] As for Mr Helfgott,[3] I cannot sign the letter. (*a*) I think that the Holocaust has become a commercialised affair, particularly in the USA but also here, even at the Oxford Centre,[4] and this is having a counterproductive effect on otherwise sympathetic and humane people; (*b*) I do not believe that refuting people who deny the Holocaust, or try to minimise it (as some German historians are of course trying to do), is likely to impress those who can be taken in by pro-Fascist propaganda. The House of Lords debate on war criminals has certainly had a mild but noticeable counter-effect. In short, I do not believe in the value of continuing to reveal the horrors of what happened, except from time to time with particular connections, e.g.

---

1 See 619. We have been unable to trace the broadcast that IB refers to here.
2 Alan Claude Robin Goldsmid Montefiore (b. 1929), philosopher; fellow and philosophy tutor, Balliol, 1961–94; member of a prominent British Jewish family.
3 Ben Helfgott (b. 1929), Polish-born British Holocaust survivor, businessman and Olympian; captain of the British weightlifting teams, Melbourne 1956, Rome 1960; lost his parents and sister, and 27 other members of his family, in the Holocaust, and devoted his life to ensuring the proper commemoration of its victims.
4 IB regarded Yarnton as 'not only the best Centre of Hebrew, Yiddish and general Jewish research in England [...], but one of the very best, if not the best, in the world'. To David Patterson, 19 March 1990.

in answering the enemy or commemorating the Kristallnacht, and that sort of thing. I may be wrong but I have felt this now for a good long time, and have for that reason not associated myself with 'Holocaust' activities, e.g. Mrs Maxwell[1] etc.

If you think I am mistaken I can only ask you to forgive my invincible error. I cannot bring myself to say all this to the obviously worthy Mr Helfgott, partly because it might, given his past, hurt his feelings, partly because he might wish to reply, and I do not wish to enter into correspondence on the subject if I can help it. So could you be so angelic as to reply to him for me, in whatever way you think best? I am perfectly willing to send £50 for his in my view superfluous periodical, to salve my conscience.

Yours ever,

Isaiah

TO MICHAEL O'REGAN[2]

28 October 1992 [*carbon*]

Headington House

Dear Mr O'Regan,

[…] The story about Churchill[3] is wonderful – it is exactly what would have happened at that date. He was literally a prophet without honour in his country at that time. I fully understand why you and other people felt that he was just an absolute bully, a relic of a discredited imperialism calling for war. Nevertheless, as you rightly say, he saved not only civilisation (your word) but, literally, our lives. That is why I wrote an encomium to him in about 1949 or 1950, in an American journal, which was afterwards reprinted in one of my books of essays.[4]

I did not terribly like him when I met him: he was aggressive and coarse. But he was a marvellous man, certainly the largest human being I have ever met, composed of fewer pieces, as it were, than most of us; and I felt that all the criticism of him in the late 1940s and early 1950s – there are always revisionists trying to modify earlier opinions – was unjust and ungrateful, and so I wrote a review of the first volume[5] of his memoirs in the form of

---

1 Elisabeth Jenny Jeanne ('Betty') Maxwell (1921–2013) née Meynard, French-born wife of the newspaper proprietor and publisher Robert Maxwell (m. 1945, separated 1990). Of an aristocratic French Protestant lineage, she developed an interest in genealogy, and, through researching her husband's family, the Holocaust, becoming a recognised scholar in that field.

2 Michael Lionel Victor Rowan Hamilton O'Regan (1916–95), St John's PPE 1936–9, from 1948 a schoolmaster at Marlborough Grammar School (known as St John's School from 1975), 'an inspirational teacher to generations of schoolchildren' (Personal Column, *Times*, 4 March 1995, 18c).

3 Untraced (MO'R had sent IB some of his pieces, but these have not survived among IB's papers).

4 'Winston Churchill in 1940', in PI and PSM; 1st published 1949 as a book review (next note).

5 In fact the 2nd vol. of Churchill's war memoirs, *Their Finest Hour*; the review, 'Mr Churchill', was published in *Atlantic Monthly* 184 no. 3 (September 1949), 35–44, and as 'Mr Churchill and FDR',

a tribute. He apparently read it, but reacted not at all.[1] Never mind. I do not at all repent of having done it. I would have done the same today.

Your stories about life in Austria [...] correspond to a good many experiences of others. The Austrians are people full of charm, gifts, and some of them are exceedingly handsome, but I have a feeling that inside there is not very much; that they have little conscience – enthusiasm, passion, yes, but anybody can lead them in any direction, above all right-wing directions, as now, of a rather sinister kind.[2] There is no doubt that they are more agreeable to meet than the Germans, but the Germans do have souls, they do suffer tortures after painful experiences; they are not exactly attractive, but they are much more genuine and three-dimensional than the charming but feckless Austrians. That has been my experience.

The scene in Nuremberg has been described by many, and a lot of people – including one of my gifted pupils in New College, later a prominent Conservative politician[3] – felt exactly what you felt, and it took him time to disabuse himself of the fascination of Hitler. I listened to Hitler on the wireless in 1939 and 1940, and those frenzied shrieks never made any impression on me. I could not really understand how decent or civilised people could be so deeply influenced by that screaming and hysteria. Still, there is no doubt that it happened, and it could happen again. I find all your reactions natural, perfectly intelligible, and I sympathise with every word you say.

As for your Pole who could not understand why Communists were allowed to preach in Hyde Park,[4] that is an ancient problem: how far a liberal society which believes in freedom of speech should go in allowing sentiments directed against its own existence, the very bases on which it is founded, to be expressed. I don't know the answer: I am not in favour of total toleration, nor, of course, of rigid censorship. I can only say rather feebly that a society which feels genuinely menaced has a right to suppress those who desire its destruction, however sincerely, and who[ever] they may be; but that liberal societies can wear a certain amount of criticism, however irrational and even evil, provided they do not feel menaced. That is our policy about the National Front, which few people think could ever come into power, even

Cornhill Magazine 981 (Winter 1949/1950), 219–40. It also appeared as a separate slim volume, *Mr Churchill in 1940* (London, [1964]; Boston/Cambridge, n.d. [1964/5?]).

1 IB has apparently forgotten that Churchill sent him a telegram, 4 December 1949, which reads: 'I HAVE READ WITH SO MUCH PLEASURE WHAT YOU WROTE IN YOUR AMERICAN ARTICLE BEST WISHES FOR CHRISTMAS AND NEW YEAR WINSTON CHURCHILL'.

2 The far-right Austrian Freedom Party, led by Jörg Haider (1950–2008), performed surprisingly well in the 1991 local elections in Vienna, where Haider's campaign slogan had been 'Vienna for the Viennese': 'Austria Shifts Right', leader, *Times*, 12 November 1991, 15a–b at 15b.

3 Not securely identified.

4 i.e. Speaker's Corner, at the NE corner of Hyde Park, near Marble Arch, Westminster; from 1872 the park authorities were granted the right to permit public meetings, which gave *de jure* recognition to its long-established *de facto* status as a venue for political protests (Marx and Lenin spoke there).

in a coalition. I don't feel quite so certain about the Germans or the French today, but I think probably they are right not to take steps against these people. So long as there is a high probability of their merely talking and not doing serious harm to the liberal society in which they live, there is no case for applying sanctions. But at a certain point I should certainly be prepared to arrest, suppress etc.

But thank God we are very far from it in the West as yet: long may this last. With all the disasters looming before us, I don't think Fascism is a real possibility; nor, after what has happened, Communism either. When I was young, perhaps because I was born in Russia, I disliked Communism and Fascism equally. But there weren't many like me, and I got into grave trouble with some of my friends for my anti-Stalinism, much as you will have done for similar crimes. [...]

Yours sincerely,
    Isaiah Berlin

In conversation with the Iranian philosopher and academic Ramin Jahanbegloo[1] in December 1988, IB was asked about his experience, as a Jew, of the Second World War. He answered that he did not think his experience different from the vast majority of Jews outside Nazi-occupied Europe, adding:

There is something in this connection which I must confess with a degree of shame. I assumed from the very beginning that Hitler meant to inflict terrible sufferings on the Jews – he was a fiend and implacable, that was obvious. We all knew that Jews had been imprisoned, and some were killed, in concentration camps, from 1933 onwards. And this was not publicised sufficiently in the West. [...] After the invasion of Poland, I assumed that terrible things were happening to Jews, that they would be arrested, persecuted, tortured, perhaps killed, but none of us knew what was going on. Before the events of the Warsaw ghetto, no news came. We just assumed appalling horrors. Before 1944 I knew nothing about systematic extermination – the gas chambers. Nobody told me, in England or America; there was nothing about it in anything I read – perhaps that was my own fault. That makes me feel ashamed.[2]

On 20 November 1992, two members of Britain's Jewish community, Lea and Ansel Harris,[3] having read Jahanbegloo's interviews with IB, wrote to IB about

1 Ramin Jahanbegloo (b. 1956), Iranian philosopher; lecturer in political philosophy, Academy of Philosophy, Tehran, 1993–4; senior researcher, French Institute for Iranian Studies, Tehran, 1994–5; adjunct prof. of political science, Toronto, 1997–2001; completed his first book, *Conversations with Isaiah Berlin* (London/NY, 1992; first published in French 1991) (CIB), while a doctoral student at the Sorbonne.
2 ibid. 19–22; cf. L3 507–10.
3 Ansel Zev Harris (1925–2001), retail executive and charity worker, born in London to an Orthodox Jewish Lithuanian family; emigrated to Israel 1950 after serving with the RAF 1944–7, but returned to the UK 1954, joining Marks and Spencer, for whom he worked as a senior executive till 1981; honorary treasurer, Oxfam, 1981–7; chair, UK Jewish Aid and International Development, 1990–2001; described by Rabbi Jonathan Sacks as 'one of Anglo-Jewry's unforgettable characters.

his 'honest confession', to ask how he could not have known. They cited two
clear examples of news reports that suggested that he must have done. One was
Anthony Eden's statement in the House of Commons on 17 December 1942 on the
extermination of European Jews by the Nazis; the other the BBC broadcast, in
June 1942, of the testimony of the Polish-Jewish historian Emanuel Ringelblum, [1]
who documented everyday life in the Warsaw ghetto, and who estimated that
700,000 Polish Jews had been killed. 'Allow us to ask,' they wrote, 'without, we
hope, creating offence, how was it at all possible that a sensitive Jew like yourself
and in such a privileged position could not have not known?'

TO LEA AND ANSEL HARRIS

27 November 1992

Headington House

Dear Mr and Mrs Harris,

[...] First, my confession in the *Conversations* [...]. I think you partly misunderstand what I said, but only partly. Of course I knew, as who did not, that
Germans were maltreating, indeed, killing Jews. I knew, of course, about the
uprising in the ghetto in Warsaw. I assumed that frightful things were being
done – murder, slaughter of every kind. Of that there is no doubt. I did not
know that Eden had got up and made that statement; I knew only well after
the war that Members of Parliament rose as an act of homage to the victims
– I think something of the sort happened when James de Rothschild made
a similar speech at some stage. [2] That was not reported in any American
newspaper that I read – or, if it was, I missed it. [3] Similarly, I knew that an
eminent Polish Jew, member of the Polish government committee in London
– I think Siegelboim [4] – publicly committed suicide as a protest against the
failure of the Allies to do anything about what was happening to the Jews in
Poland [...].

Obstinate, single-minded, impossible to argue with and equally impossible not to admire' ('Tears
Are the Universal Language, Help the Universal Command', *Times*, 8 December 2001, 26c–h
at 26c); m. 1986 2ndly Lea Harris (b. 1934), formerly Josse, née Ber, Kraków-born solicitor and
mediator who escaped from Antwerp with her parents 1940, arriving at Liverpool that July on
a Dutch cargo boat from Bordeaux.

1 Emanuel Ringelblum (1900–44), Polish historian and social activist; the leading figure in the creation of the Warsaw ghetto archive by the group calling itself Oneg Shabbat ('Sabbath Delight').
The archive survived by being buried just before the ghetto was liquidated.

2 Eden read a prepared statement in the Commons 17 December 1942 on the 'cold-blooded extermination' by the Nazis of European Jews: *Parliamentary Debates* (Commons) 385, 17 December
1942, col. 2083 (cf. L3 507/2). At the end of Eden's speech the House rose in silence, in a gesture
of respect for the victims. For IB's confusion about the circumstances of this, and de Rothschild's
role: L3 516/1 and 2. James Armand Edmond de Rothschild (1878–1957), French-born British politician and philanthropist; Liberal MP 1929–45.

3 It was reported as 'Nazi Retribution Widened by Eden', NYT, 18 December 1942, 10; cf. L3 507/2.

4 For the circumstances in which Szmul Zygielbojm (1895–1943), Polish trade unionist, Bund party
politician and witness to the Holocaust, committed suicide in London 12 May 1943 see L3 516/5.

I knew, therefore, that unspeakable things were happening. What I did not know – and what makes me feel ashamed, and is responsible for my confession – was the existence of the gas chambers and the extermination of millions. That, of course, was reported by a member of the World Jewish Congress in Geneva in a message to Rabbi Stephen Wise, and reported to Roosevelt, but of all this we knew nothing, since Roosevelt had advocated silence – shamefully, I think. But there were people, like my future wife's relations and other refugees, who knew a good deal more than I did. Neither Chaim Weizmann nor Felix Frankfurter, whose Zionism cannot be doubted, ever said one word about it to me – I saw both of them at frequent intervals. I only learnt of it, as I said in my confession, towards the end of 1944, beginning of 1945 – and that is a cause of great distress to me. But the news of that only became worldwide when American troops liberated the camps, and the terrible photographs appeared.[1] That is the truth. I think my life in the British milieu in Washington may have been somewhat circumscribed; nevertheless I did meet Jews and Zionists, and none of them spoke of gas chambers. Why not, I cannot conceive. [...]

Yours sincerely,
Isaiah Berlin

TO FUMIKO SASAKI[2]

30 November 1992

Headington House

Dear Miss Sasaki,

[...] George Orwell:[3] I admire his views because, although he was in favour of the oppressed, the victims, the losers – which is surely one of the essences of a liberal attitude – he saw through the false claims of e.g. Soviet Communists to provide the liberties which the poor and the oppressed craved for; and was the first writer, virtually, to speak openly about the fact that the word 'freedom' was used by them to mean slavery; that 'truth' was used to mean what the governing group imposes upon the population, in disregard of its normal meaning; that 'representatives of the people' turned out to be gangs of mass murderers; and the like. It was the first real blow struck against left-wing totalitarianism, addressed to those who were anti-Fascist and anti-Conservative but liable to illusions about the Soviet Union. And at

---

1 *The Times* of 19 April 1945 displayed photographs of the shocking scenes at Buchenwald and Nord-hausen, both recently liberated by US troops: 'German Concentration and Labour Camps', 6b–f.
2 Fumiko Sasaki (b. 1964), student of international relations; assistant prof., Ogaki Women's College, 1991–9; later (2005) PhD in international relations / Asian studies, School of Advanced International Studies, Johns Hopkins.
3 Eric Arthur Blair (1903–50), political writer and essayist, wrote under the pseudonym George Orwell; a socialist and anti-Communist, he attacked totalitarianism and social injustice; author of *Animal Farm* (London, 1945) and *Nineteen Eighty-Four* (London, 1949).

20 In Paraggi, September 1983

21 On 1 January 1985

22 At a press conference after his Agnelli Prize address, Turin, 15 February 1988:
'The press conference which I was compelled to hold resulted in *Il Messaggero* saying
that I had never heard in my life of Signor Agnelli, […] and declared that I had said that my
opinion of Mrs Thatcher was not worth hearing. So you see, much fun was had by all'
(to Arthur Schlesinger, 7 March 1988)

23 With Noel Annan, c.1987: 'I love Noel truly:
the causes he defends are often just and unpopular,
& he is a good, decent, sensible, administrator,
pro-highbrow' (to Claus Moser, c.1987)

24 Joseph Alsop at Headington House, 20 October
1987, for IB's and Arthur Schlesinger's hon.
Oxford DLitts: 'In the end, it was his private person,
his warm heart, his honesty, courage and integrity,
which no political combination or personal
advantage, of whatever kind, ever affected in the
smallest degree, that drew one to him'
(to Robert Kaiser, 17 October 1989, 379)

25 With Aline and Élie de Rothschild, Headington House, 1987

26 At the launch of the Bodleian Library campaign, Oxford, 5 July 1988

27 Stephen Spender and Kay Graham chez Drue Heinz for an eightieth birthday lunch in IB's honour, summer 1989

28 With Tony Quinton and Princess Margaret on the same occasion: 'As for Mrs Heinz, the food was indeed delicious, and the Yquem – I never drink, but I drank a glass of it, was transported by it, not literally but in some spiritual sense – I am prepared to drink a glass a year if it is as good as that' (to Anthony Quinton, 14 September 1989)

29, 30 With Andrey Sakharov (hon. DSc) at Headington House, 21 June 1989:
'Sakharov is my man, as he is, I am sure, yours: that is the authentic noble liberal voice,
very like Herzen's – everything he says seems to me true, unanswerable and more simply
and better put, braver and more moving, than any other voice in the world today'
(to Arthur Schlesinger, 12 July 1978, 82)

31 With Graeme Standen, Cecilia Dick and Aline, Wolfson College, 10 July 1989,
with eightieth birthday gifts: in his right hand a pomander (made by CD), and in his
left framed photographs of the College's opening in 1974 (presented by GS)

32 With Imogen Cooper at the Barbican, 11 July 1992, after her performance of Mozart's piano concerto no. 25 in C major, K503, with Colin Davis and the LSO

33 With David Campbell (publisher), Charles, Prince of Wales (President, Royal Shakespeare Co.; guest of honour), Trevor Nunn and Tom Stoppard at the Savoy Hotel, London, for the Everyman's Library Shakespeare Luncheon, 26 October 1992, held to launch the Everyman edition of Shakespeare's sonnets and narrative poems

34 Hon. Doctor of Laws, Toronto, 24 November 1994, with (*left to right*) Jon Cohen, John Gardner, Rose Wolfe, Barry Brown, Michael Marrus, Robert Prichard, Bob Rae, Claude Galipeau (*behind*), Paul Gooch: 'I regret that I shall not see this brighter future, which I am convinced is coming. With all the gloom that I have been spreading, I am glad to end on an optimistic note. There really are good reasons to think that it is justified' (from his acceptance address, 581)

35 Aline Berlin and members of her family, gathered for her eightieth birthday, January 1995: (*back*) Andrew Strauss, Peter Halban, Patrick Mahony; (*middle*) Aline, Rosane Halban, Julia Strauss, Martine Halban, Michel Strauss, Margery Strauss; (*front*) Emily Halban, Tania Halban, Alexander Halban, Claudia Strauss, Victoria Strauss, Amanda Mahony, Philippe Halban

36 With Michael Ignatieff, mid-May 1995, during filming of the interviews broadcast posthumously on BBC2 TV, 14 and 15 November 1997

37 HH and Peter Halban at the launch of Michael Ignatieff's biography of IB, British Academy, 26 October 1998

38 Unfinished portrait by Lucian Freud, 1997

the same time he preached a political life which was in a sense influenced by socialist ideals, equality, non-exploitation, democracy; but found a kind of mean between the need for collective self-rule, which sometimes diminished the liberties of individuals, on the one hand, and the moral rights of individuals to certain values, no matter what the government said – truth, a degree of liberty (not infinite), the American ideals of life and the pursuit of happiness, and the like: in short, what makes life tolerable for normal individuals. It is a difficult compromise and a difficult line to draw, but he drew it – although he did not formulate it – as well as anybody in our day.

[...] Yes, I supported the Spanish republican government.[1] When I did my reporting from Washington, that government had collapsed and the policy of the British government by that time was, of course, anti-Fascist, and therefore to that degree against the allies of Hitler anywhere – Italy, Spain, as well as others. I have to admit that, in the days of the Spanish Civil War, like many others I was somewhat taken in by the simple pattern which, as it were, repeated the revolutions of 1848. On one side, the bad men – generals, the rich, the Roman Church, unbridled capitalism. On the other workers, students, intellectuals, artists – good men. The situation turned out to be much more complicated. The destruction of the Anarchists by the Communists, the internecine feuds among the various republican factions, the murderousness of both sides, which sometimes threw liberal persons into the arms of Franco, and Franco's followers into the arms of the Republicans – all this produced a pattern so complex that the simple dichotomy [in] which people like myself, in England particularly, believed proved in some ways illusory. But that didn't prevent me from preferring the republicans, with all their faults, even though they were supported by the odious Stalinist regime, to the oppression of army, Church and the rich, who seemed to me to make for a greater degree of misery and injustice. And so I think it proved, even though Franco was comparatively mild, certainly more so than Hitler or Stalin, or indeed Mussolini.

[...] I had no views as to whether the USA and the USSR could co-exist peacefully [after 1945]. Remarks to that effect were made by Stalin, but of course I knew that could not be taken at face value, like everything else that he said. No, I was not happy about the possibility of peace. I thought that on the whole the Soviet Union was expansionist and would take over as much territory as it could, provided there was no strong resistance – as, indeed, it did in Eastern Europe. At one time it looked as if France and Italy were liable to have Communist regimes, and I feared that. I believed, with the then doctrines of George Kennan, that the proper policy was 'containment', i.e. resistance to Soviet ambition wherever necessary. How long a tension of

---

1 The Second Spanish Republic, 1931–9, dissolved after the victory of General Franco's Nationalist forces in the Spanish Civil War, 1936–9, with military support from both Hitler and Mussolini.

that kind could last I could not tell. No, I was not too optimistic; I thought that Stalin's intentions were too ambitious, as well as evil. Still, of course I hoped that some kind of equilibrium could be found, like that between Islam and Christianity between, say, the sixteenth and seventeenth centuries, and thereafter. [...]

Yours sincerely,
    Isaiah Berlin

TO EDWARD ADEANE[1]

4 May 1993 [*carbon*]

Headington House

Dear Edward,

I feel like Goethe, in *Faust*, when he said 'Ihr naht euch wieder ...' – 'You are approaching again, flickering images.'[2] Well, let us begin.

[...] It is a sad condition for our country to be in, that there should be no novelist, poet, even painter (even Freud), historian, classical scholar, of such shining quality as to even begin to seem obvious. However, I agree with you, one must not be too defeatist, so let me continue and go over all your suggested names – you really have gone over the ground with a toothbrush, it seems to me. Forward!

I agree about S. Runciman,[3] H. Casson and John Gielgud.[4] (With regard to the last, I don't know whether the blot on his reputation – the skeleton – is quite enough to disqualify him. I regard him as possible – in the absence of all others, I would rather have him than most of the others in your letter: but, once again, let us go forward.)

Lucian Freud: he is indeed the best contemporary painter; I don't think he would decline; his private life is exactly as you describe it. He is very polite to me – on the very few occasions when we meet he is always extremely courteous, and quite interesting. He is not a good character, far from it. He is a gifted painter, but in my view not quite up to the Bacon standard. [...]

---

1 (George) Edward Adeane (b. 1939), called to Bar, Middle Temple, 1962; PS and treasurer to the Prince of Wales 1979–85, treasurer to the Prince and Princess of Wales 1981–5, PS to the Princess of Wales, 1984–5, extra equerry to the Prince of Wales from 1985.

2 'Ihr naht euch wieder, schwankende Gestalten', the opening line of the dedication in Goethe's play. EA had sought IB's advice on candidates for admission to the OM.

3 James Cochran Stevenson ('Steven') Runciman (1903–2000), Kt 1958, the pre-eminent historian of the Byzantine empire and the crusades; of independent means, he held no tenured academic post after 1945, but lectured widely and published regularly.

4 (Arthur) John Gielgud (1904–2000), Kt 1953, OM 1996, actor; first appeared on stage at the Old Vic 1921, and enjoyed a brilliant career on stage and screen. Gielgud was homosexual, and in an era when such relations were criminalised was cautious about his liaisons; he was nevertheless arrested in London on the evening of 20 October 1953, charged with soliciting, and fined the next day; the case became public, but his intense anxiety about the public's response was allayed by a standing ovation he received when opening at Liverpool the next week; a few months later he suffered a nervous breakdown.

There would be some shock if this was done for him, because his private life is regarded as too disreputable by most of those who know – even like – him. If you want to consult a real expert in that group, it might be worth asking David Sylvester,[1] who is quite discriminating – I think you would get a just verdict. Sylvester told me that the person who deserved it most was Brendel, whom he puts above everyone; but he can't get it because he is an Austrian citizen. So I am not that keen.

I am much keener, curiously enough, on Sir N. Foster:[2] he is much the best architect we have, far better than the other famous ones. The buildings he has so far built really are excellent by international standards – I have never seen the enormous one in Hong Kong, but it is much admired. [...] You can think for yourself who I think he is better than – one died recently,[3] the other[4] built the Pompidou Centre. Foster is better than these, and the fact that he has gone off with the wife of the supremo of the Murdoch papers[5] is neither here nor there in these days.

We then speak of scientists. I think that Sir R. Doll[6] is a good name, not so much because he is an eminent doctor as because he created the great anti-smoking campaign, which must have saved a great many lives, and I think it would be a wonderful thing to reward somebody for benefits conferred upon society, not just by discoveries or curative methods or inventions but by sheer moral and public pressure – which he did superbly. He is pretty old but perhaps that doesn't matter so much – so, after all, are you and I, and who are we to scorn our juniors? Katz[7] is a pretty good example, but since being Foreign Secretary of the Royal Society I think he has receded into some kind of background. I don't think he has been heard of lately: I think it would be some surprise to scientists if he were suddenly lifted out of the mist – but

1 (Anthony) David Bernard Sylvester (1924–2001), writer, broadcaster, critic and art curator.

2 Norman Robert Foster (b. 1935), Kt 1990, OM 1997, later (1999) life peer, British architect of world renown; his works include the Hong Kong and Shanghai Bank, Hong Kong, 1979–86, and the remodelling of the Reichstag in Berlin, 1992–9.

3 James Frazer Stirling (1926–92), Kt 1992; highly individual, eclectic and non-conformist architect appreciated posthumously more than in his lifetime; among his earlier works are the controversial history faculty wing at Cambridge, 1964–8, and the Florey Building for Queen's, Oxford, 1966–71.

4 The Centre Georges Pompidou in Paris, an example of high-tech, postmodern architectural style, was designed by a team that included the distinguished British architect Richard George Rogers (b. 1933), Kt 1991, life peer 1996.

5 Sabiha Rumani Malik (b. 1948), Foster's wife 1991–5, wife 1975–91 of Andrew Stephen Bower Knight (b. 1939), who was chair 1990–4 of News International, the newspaper empire of the Australian media mogul (Keith) Rupert Murdoch (b. 1931), director, News International, 1969–2012.

6 (William) Richard Shaboe Doll (1912–2005), Kt 1971, British physiologist and epidemiologist; Regius Prof. of Medicine and student (i.e. fellow), Christ Church, 1969–79; 1st Warden, Green, 1979–83; honorary consultant, Cancer Research UK, Radcliffe Infirmary, 1983–2005; with Austin Bradford Hill (1897–1991) he was among the first to demonstrate a statistical link between lung cancer and smoking (Richard Doll and A. Bradford Hill, 'Smoking and Carcinoma of the Lung: Preliminary Report', *British Medical Journal*, 30 September 1950, 739–48).

7 Bernard Katz (1911–2003), Kt 1969, German-born British experimental physiologist; prof. and head of biophysics dept, UCL, 1952–78; Nobel Prize in Physiology or Medicine 1970; FRS 1952.

I may be wrong. If you consulted someone like Atiyah (who has it already, I imagine?),[1] he would know; so would the existing members of the Order: Todd,[2] Hodgkin, Huxley[3] could tell you very firmly whether he is of the right standard, and if what they said was favourable I should be in favour too.

No, there is no classicist of the order of Murray or Syme or Jebb[4] (Mackail[5] did not deserve it). K. Dover is probably the best classicist we have, and was President of the British Academy. He would be very astonished to get it, as he is a man of extreme modesty, and a very nice one, too – rather destroyed by the awful time he had over the Anthony Blunt non-expulsion from the Academy. But I don't think he is either well-known enough or, indeed, quite grand enough; quite apart from being attacked by Lord Beloff in the House of Lords, very disgracefully, for taking an interest in Greek homosexuality.[6]

We come to Roy Jenkins: […] he is not quite of the stature, in my view, friend of mine though he is, but it would be perfectly well received – the combination of having been a very good Minister, both at the Home Office and the Treasury, and a highly competent biographer, and Chancellor here (I don't think the Royal Society of Literature counts for much). He is now regarded as vaguely above the parties, and I think he does fit the slot of which you speak. He is not a Franks, but he is not far below, indeed level with, Waverley,[7] in spite of not having the commanding Roman stature of that formidable man. […]

Pinter[8] I do think possible. He is the most distinguished living British dramatist, without a doubt, and of very, very considerable gifts. It might be thought that someone of his passionate left-wing views – not that he is anywhere near Communism or anything politically disreputable – might refuse, but I don't think he would: I think he would accept, provided there

1 Michael Francis Atiyah (b. 1929), Kt 1983, OM 1992; mathematician and geometrician; Royal Society Research Prof., Oxford, and professorial fellow, St Catherine's, 1973–90; director, Isaac Newton Institute for Mathematical Sciences, Cambridge, 1990–6, and Master, Trinity, 1990–7.

2 Alexander Robertus Todd (1907–97), Kt 1954, life peer 1962, OM 1977, organic chemist; Nobel Prize in Chemistry 1957; prof. of organic chemistry, Cambridge, 1944–71, and Master, Christ's, 1963–78.

3 Andrew Fielding Huxley (1917–2012), Kt 1974, OM 1983, physiologist and biophysicist; Royal Society Research Prof., UCL, 1969–83; Master, Trinity, Cambridge, 1984–90; Nobel Prize in Physiology or Medicine 1963 (with Alan Hodgkin and John Eccles); half-brother of the writer Aldous Huxley, and grandson of the biologist Thomas Henry Huxley.

4 Richard Claverhouse Jebb (1841–1905), Kt 1900, OM 1905; prof. of Greek, Glasgow, 1875–89; Regius Prof. of Greek, Cambridge, and hon. fellow, Trinity, 1889–1905.

5 John William Mackail (1859–1945), OM 1935; classical scholar, literary critic and poet; examiner and assistant secretary, Board of Education, 1885–1919; prof. of poetry, Oxford, 1906–11.

6 We have not been able to trace Beloff's Lords attack on Dover's pioneering *Greek Homosexuality* (London/Cambridge, Mass., 1977), but cf. Richard Davenport-Hines, 'The Throne Trembles', TLS, 5 January 2007, 11. Dover was not appointed OM.

7 John Anderson (1882–1958), 1st Viscount Waverley 1952, KCB 1919, OM 1957, civil servant and politician; chair, ROH board, 1946–57.

8 Harold Pinter (1930–2008), playwright, actor, theatre director, one of the most influential modern British dramatists; later (2005) Nobel Prize in Literature.

was no handle to the name; people like him regard it as perfectly proper to be honoured in this way, as you know. Graham Greene,[1] for example, would never have accepted a knighthood.

Of the two musicians, there is no doubt that Birtwistle[2] is better than Maxwell Davies: he really is now a composer of world renown, a kind of leader of modernism, and a very considerable musical figure. It would not be wrong to think of him – he is less famous than, but in my opinion fully as good as, anyone we have had in that category. Rattle:[3] I really don't see why not. It would be a very bold move – he was not even given a knighthood because he was thought to be too young, which was absurd. He certainly deserves a CH – perhaps that would be right at the moment; after all, one can have both. I think that would be absolutely appropriate, and better than a knighthood, with a view to supreme honour ultimately, which I am sure in principle he does and will deserve – he is much the best British conductor of our time, by miles.

The last man on your list (S. Hawking)[4] has somehow missed it. I don't know why I feel that – I used to urge him on you, you remember, year by year [...]. But as a result of his book,[5] which serious scientists do not in fact think much of, and all the publicity and hoo-ha, perhaps he has rather forfeited it. His serious work was done in the past, and he probably does deserve it on that. Again, I would consult the people already in that class in the Royal Society – at any rate, the physicists among them. There is a kind of consensus in that world which is pretty universally accepted internationally, unlike in the humanities and the rest. [...]

I hope this is of some use. I suspect it isn't. I wish I could think of new names not on your list. Peter Brook[6] I think a man of genius – but no, doesn't live in England, and in general not quite right. An hon. degree, yes, but not this. There is our old friend Trevor-Roper: he is the best British historian now writing, and writes like an angel; but he hasn't produced a major work, and I fear that when he is dead his reputation will somewhat, though not steeply, decline. One other name I would urge you to investigate, or get the Queen's

1 OM 1986.
2 Harrison Paul Birtwistle (b. 1934), Kt 1988; associate director (of music), National Theatre, 1975–81; Henry Purcell Prof. of Composition, King's College London, 1994–2001.
3 Simon Rattle (b. 1955), Kt 1994, later (2014) OM; principal conductor, City of Birmingham Symphony Orchestra, 1980–98; later (since 2002) chief conductor and artistic director, Berlin Philharmonic Orchestra.
4 Stephen William Hawking (b. 1942), CH 1989, theoretical physicist; afflicted since 1963 with motor neurone disease, which has left him almost completely paralysed; fellow, Gonville and Caius, Cambridge, since 1969; Lucasian Prof. of Mathematics 1979–2009.
5 The international bestseller (allegedly more bought than read) *A Brief History of Time: From the Big Bang to Black Holes* (London/NY, 1988); 20 years after its publication there were an estimated 9 million copies in circulation.
6 Peter Stephen Paul Brook (b. 1925), French-domiciled British theatre and film director; director of productions, ROH, 1947–50; founder and artistic director, International Centre for Theatre Research (CIRT), Paris, 1970–2008; later (1998) CH.

Secretary to do so, and that is Penrose:[1] he is a very, very gifted man, not even a knight, I think, who got some kind of world prize together with Hawking. He is certainly of the calibre, but of course one would have to consult; if he hasn't a Nobel Prize it is mainly because he is a mathematician, for which there are no Nobel awards – he must have got other things. Anyway, do get someone to look into him. Oh dear, I wish I could think of somebody in the humanities, the so-called social sciences, in addition to those already mentioned.

Yours ever
Isaiah   [...]

TO SHIRLEY ANGLESEY
11 May 1993

Headington House

Dearest Shirley,

[...] It is terrible [...], I agree, not to have seen you for so long. I keep mistaking other people for you (this doesn't sound entirely polite, but it only is evidence of my profound feeling). At a reception at the National Gallery to which I thought you might have been invited – but I suppose there was no particular reason for it except I saw what seemed to me a double of you mounting the steps – I began to move forward ardently, but checked myself just in time to see a total stranger, who gazed at me curiously, intelligibly so.

No, I shall not go to *Elektra* at the Proms.[2] It is unquestionably a masterpiece, though I doubt if it will be conducted as it deserves; but I don't really like it. There is such a thing as greatly respecting a work without positively enjoying listening to it – I feel that about much Wagner, unlike Henry. Still, I have now gone through four *Rings*, and still it hasn't taken – like an inoculation which fails. Never mind: I am quite content with Monteverdi,[3] Verdi, Haydn, Mozart, Beethoven and lots of Russian and Spanish music – and Berlioz. Later French composers the same as in the case of Strauss[4] and Wagner: admiration, respect, prepared to listen if it is more or less on the doorstep, e.g. in Oxford, or London, but to make an effort, no. I am at last old enough to treat myself in this connection. When I was younger, I felt a certain kind of duty – however that is to be analysed – to listen to

1 Roger Penrose (b. 1931), Kt 1994, later (2000) OM; Rouse Ball Prof. of Mathematics, Oxford, and fellow, Wadham, 1973–98.
2 *Elektra* opened the 1993 Proms 16 July and was well received: Richard Morrison, 'Strauss's Bloodstained Elektra Thunders Forth', *Times*, 17 July 1993, 3a–c.
3 Claudio Giovanni Antonio Monteverdi (1567–1643), Italian composer and musician famous for his contributions to the development of opera and to church music.
4 Richard Georg Strauss (1864–1949), German-born composer, conductor and pianist; Austrian citizen 1947; best known for his symphonic poems and operas.

unsympathetic, 'important' music. Strauss for me is simply Wagner turned to sugar. Is this wrong?

Now we go on to our common topic, Russia and the Russians. So you are going to Kazan – remember that it is the capital of the Tatar Republic. I am on friendly terms with an eminent Tatar poet[1] who comes from there, and his quite pretty wife[2] writes poems in my honour in Moscow – that is my only connection with the university to which both Lenin and Tolstoy went.[3] You mention Gorbachev. Poor Gorbachev! No man, we are told, is more hated by every man, woman and child in Russia, Ukraine etc., and I can see in a way why they feel this. But in Poland, Romania, Bulgaria statues ought to be put up to him – it was after he told his East German colleague Honecker[4] 'Erik, it's no good, I can't come to your help' that the crumbling began. To have liberated Eastern Europe is an achievement, whatever else may be said about him. But at the moment all he can look forward to is well-rewarded lecture tours in the USA, just like all the other ex-Prime-Ministers – Kerensky, Schuschnigg,[5] Beneš, Brüning,[6] Thatcher etc. etc. Still, I am sorry for him.

The two men who really caused the Soviet downfall (though some would certainly disagree) are (1) Reagan, because of the Star Wars:[7] that caused the Russians to compete in a somewhat irrational way, and ultimately it

1 Ravil Raisovich Bukharaev (1951–2012), poet, novelist, playwright, historian and publicist based in London from 1992.

2 Lidiya Nikolaevna Grigor'eva (b. 1945), prolific Ukrainian poet living in London; has worked with the BBC World Service, Russian radio and TV, and the British Library; in an interview with the cultural journalist Ivan Tolstoy broadcast 24 October 2001 in a Radio Svoboda [Radio Liberty] programme, *Poverkh bar'erov* [*Over the Barriers*], she said, 'I only got to London in the early 1990s. I still managed to meet, thank God, Sir Isaiah Berlin, and we were in touch a lot, and there is even a video recording of a conversation between the two of us.' ⟨http://www.svoboda.org/content/transcript/24200444.html⟩.

3 Both left without taking their degree: Lenin was expelled shortly after enrolling in the law faculty, autumn 1887, for participating in anti-tsarist demonstrations; Tolstoy, who enrolled 1844, abandoned his studies in law and oriental languages in mid course.

4 Erich Honecker (1912–94), East German Communist; head, GDR, 1971–89; Gorbachev's visit to the GDR, 7 October 1989, as guest of honour at its 40th anniversary celebrations, intensified popular opposition to the Honecker regime, which had stubbornly resisted glasnost and perestroika; unable to count on Soviet military backing, Honecker was obliged to resign 18 October in the face of a rising tide of protest.

5 Kurt Alois Josef Johann Schuschnigg (1897–1977), Austrian politician; chancellor 1934–8, forced to resign 11 March 1938 by Hitler, who then effected the *Anschluss* (union) with Austria; subsequently imprisoned in Dachau and Sachsenhausen; released to US troops in May 1945, he became prof. of politics, Saint Louis, 1948–67.

6 Heinrich Aloysius Maria Elisabeth Brüning (1885–1970), German statesman; leader, Weimar Catholic Centre Party; chancellor and foreign minister 1930–2; escaped the Nazis' 1934 purge and emigrated to the US 1935; Lucius N. Littauer Prof. of Government, Graduate School of Public Administration, Harvard, 1939–52; prof. of political science, Cologne, 1951–6.

7 Popular name (deriving from the *Star Wars* film franchise) for the Strategic Defense Initiative (SDI) first proposed by President Reagan March 1983, and intended to harness cutting-edge science in a comprehensive ground, air and space missile detection and interception system; despite political controversy and technological difficulties SDI has been credited with hastening the end of the Cold War.

ruined them financially; and (2) the Pope,[1] who channelled a lot of money, in devious ways, to the Church in Poland, which supported Solidarnost',[2] which I think might not have survived otherwise – and then visited Poland, which created an enormous anti-Communist upheaval. It was there that the rot began, and spread to the other parts of the empire.

I have a friend called Hobsbawm, who is the last card-carrying member of the Communist Party known to me. He is a clever, amusing and interesting man, very gifted, very agreeable, and a great friend of all kinds of very non-Communist characters – a kind of favourite Communist of the anti-Communists. When I tell you that Hugh Seton-Watson proposed him for the Athenaeum Club, you will know what I mean. Well, I occasionally needle him about what has happened. He, not very plausibly, told me that all that had been wrong was that it was the wrong time, the wrong place and the wrong people who made the Revolution – otherwise, perfectly OK. Not a position he took in the last, let us say, sixty years, as I don't fail to point out to him. The other left-wing view is of course that, terrible as Stalin may have been, he did hold nationalism down. Now it is rampant everywhere and, my goodness, its victims may in the end exceed even those slaughtered by the Stalin regime.

I am not terribly impressed by either of these arguments, but the poor left, what can it say? Still, funny to think that the Khmer Rouge are still slaughtering people in the name of Stalin, let alone Marx;[3] that China is still in effect Stalinist; that North Korea is preparing large nuclear weapons; that Yemen, Libya, Syria, Iraq are not exactly parts of the civilised and more or less humane world in which we still live. Never mind, I am quite selfish about this, I am too old to see the direst consequences. You, I fear, are not. Still, it may well happen after we are all dead and buried – I think better so. But in the long run I am not optimistic, though I think in the end that humanity, culture, liberalism, decency, the kind of moral values we almost instinctively live by, will not perish from the earth. But I mustn't go on with this sermon.

Yes, I saw *Wittgenstein*: it amused me more than shocked me. The director[4] is of course a rather dotty homosexual: hence all those pictures of Ludwig in bed with a boy, originally Keynes's boy, which is total rubbish. Keynes did not pursue boys, only grown men; Wittgenstein certainly was accused of

1 Karol Józef Wojtyła (1920–2005), later (2014) Saint John Paul II, born in Wadowice, Poland; bishop of Rome and head of the Catholic Church 1978–2005; his visit to his homeland as pope June 1979 galvanised popular resistance to the Communist government there, and encouraged the foundation of Solidarność. His advocacy of non-violent political activism is credited with helping to end Communist rule in Eastern Europe.

2 The Russian form of 'Solidarność'.

3 Though overthrown as the government of Cambodia in January 1979, the Khmer Rouge continued to wage a guerrilla war from bases near the border with Thailand, rejecting the UN-backed peace settlement of 1991, and the multi-party elections of 1993; it continued its war against the elected government of Cambodia until 1999.

4 (Michael) Derek Elworthy Jarman (1942–94), film-maker, painter and passionate campaigner for gay rights; his *Wittgenstein* premiered at the Cambridge Arts Cinema 31 January 1993.

having a taste for rough trade, but it was never established. The only lover he might have had was somebody at school with me,[1] a very modest, grave, pale mathematician, who was totally dominated by him, and it may be that they had some kind of physical intercourse – but that is the maximum that is known. Keynes as a multi-coloured queer, smiling roguishly, could not be further from the man I knew. Russell in cap and gown (which he never wore – certainly not a doctor's gown, and certainly not after he went to jail in 1917 or whenever it was)[2] was badly treated just because he was so rigidly heterosexual. As for Lady Ottoline,[3] I did meet her. She was totally caricatured: she wasn't this grand, snobbish, ironical lady – she was well born, certainly, but eccentric, a sort of odd lady with a whining voice, who didn't make jokes, but was a hostess to Bloomsbury etc., all of whom mocked her and treated her badly. They wouldn't have done if she'd been as grand as that, for they were, one and all, with the possible exception of Leonard Woolf, very definite snobs.

I didn't hate the film, but it was ludicrous; the relation to reality very, very remote; except, I admit, that the man who acted Wittgenstein did look in a way rather like him – save, of course, he represented him as being continuously hysterical, which was anything but true. I must tell you one day about the only time [I met him,] when I read a paper, which he in effect replied to – but that's another story. [...] All the well-known quotations from Wittgenstein, which everyone knows, were built into the film, but the real substance of what he was and believed was certainly not there – nobody who read him or knew him or has any regard for him at all could have associated the film with the truth. I wonder why they need produce such appalling caricatures – amusing as parts of it undoubtedly were. Don't believe a word of it, it really is remote from the truth. [...]

Much love, and from Aline,
    Isaiah

1 David Hume Pinsent (1891–1918), Trinity, Cambridge, mathematics 1910–13; reputedly a brilliant student, Pinsent met Wittgenstein, two years his senior, 1912; a test pilot during WW1, he was killed in a flying accident in May 1918; Wittgenstein was deeply affected by the loss, which he learned of while on leave from the Austrian army in summer 1918, and dedicated his *Tractatus Logico-Philosophicus* (London, 1922) to Pinsent's memory.

2 Russell served a 6-month prison sentence 1918 for prejudicing Britain's relations with its ally, the US: he had written an article for *Tribune* alleging that US troops would be used to break up strikes in Britain.

3 Ottoline Violet Anne Morrell (1873–1938) née Cavendish-Bentinck, literary hostess, entertained Bloomsbury and assisted the careers of Mark Gertler, Stanley Spencer, Henry Lamb and others; she inherited a title, but not a fortune, and even after her 1902 marriage to Philip Edward Morrell of the brewing family she struggled financially; but that did nothing to cramp her inimitable style, complete with huge velvet hats 'the size of a small cartwheel. This was the arresting and easily mocked figure who, in 1907, began holding weekly parties at Bedford Square for the artists and writers she met and whom she hoped to help by offering introductions to rich patrons. Henry James was among those who feared that her generosity would be abused. He was right.' Miranda Seymour, ODNB.

TO LEON WIESELTER

11 May 1993

Headington House

Dear Leon,

Thank you for the Holocaust Museum.[1] Of course I agree with you, I think there is something terribly unattractive about the entire commercialisation and publicity for the Holocaust – and talk about its theological, moral significance, etc. etc. We all know what happened; we all regard it with an equal measure of horror. I cannot help agreeing with Yeshayahu Leibowitz, who, on an occasion in Paris to which I went God knows why, presided over by Nahum Goldmann, about how to spend restitution money, when someone began to ask for money for 'Holocaust Studies' etc., said in his usual exaggerated and somewhat violent way, 'The Holocaust is the worst disaster which has ever happened to the Jewish people, including the destruction of both Temples.[2] Nevertheless, the spiritual and moral significance of this event, which is like an earthquake or the eruption of a volcano – a hideous disaster unexplained and virtually inexplicable – is zero!' Of course everyone there was very shocked, and I dare say even I think that its philosophical significance does exist in that the historical patterns of Hegel and Marx are gravely disturbed by it, don't you think? Nevertheless, fundamentally what he said was to me sympathetic – and so was your article. [...]

Yours ever,
    Isaiah

TO HENNING RITTER[3]

24 May 1993

Headington House

Dear Herr Ritter,

[...] Miss Arendt: quite apart from the fact that I found her dreadfully unsympathetic personally, which probably colours my view of her writings (you may be right, she may have said interesting things) what I really held against her most of all was not so much her, to me, disconnected, ignorant metaphysical association of ideas – no rational structure at all, and an awful lot of inflated platitudes, repetitions of always the same texts from Aristotle

1 LW's article 'After Memory' (416/2).
2 The Temple on Mount Moriah in Jerusalem, where the people of Israel offered sacrifices to God, was built in the reign of Solomon (c.970–930 BCE), and destroyed by the Babylonians c.586 BCE. The building of the 'Second Temple' began c.520 BCE, and was reconstructed by Herod from 20 BCE; it was destroyed when the Romans sacked the city in 70 CE.
3 Henning Ritter (1943–2013), German journalist, author and translator; son of the philosopher Joachim Ritter; humanities editor, Frankfurter Allgemeine Zeitung, 1985–2008.

– but what really provoked me to some indignation was her lecture to the Jews about what they should have done when threatened with deportation, death etc. She says very firmly that they should have fought and not gone like sheep to the slaughter, should have resisted, should have displayed heroism, pride etc. This is the most terrible arrogance, especially from someone who was sitting safely in New York.[1]

Supposing I were a Jew in Hungary, and the Gestapo came to me and said, 'You know most of the Jews here. Can we have their names and addresses? We can, of course, discover them ourselves, but it would be a convenience if you co-operated with us; and, if you do, you will be allowed to go, and take sixty-five people with you.' I don't know how a man should behave in these circumstances.[2] You have four choices: to refuse to collaborate, in which case you are deported and that is the end of that; to commit suicide, an obvious way out; or to agree, and then warn the Jews what is in store for them – almost none can escape, and when it is discovered what you have done you are destroyed as well as they; or you can accept their offer, and take out sixty-five people from among your friends and relations, which of course has the awful implication that you are condemning the rest to perdition.

It seems to me that anything that a person does in that situation is in order. Ordinary moral and political principles don't apply to appalling extremes of this kind. For Hannah Arendt to lecture people in that situation about what they should or shouldn't have done seems to me the most monstrous [arrogance].

After that, I saw no reason for meeting her again. No matter what my great friends Mary McCarthy, Robert Silvers, Elizabeth Hardwick,[3] Auden, Lowell, to all of whom I feel devoted, saw in her, I did not care: there is something radically wrong with someone like that. [...] You may well think that I am being tediously moralistic: plenty of morally dubious people have possessed noble gifts – Wagner was not exactly a nice man. But Hannah

---

1 In *Eichmann in Jerusalem* (41/7) Arendt explored Jewish complicity in Nazi war crimes in occupied Europe: 'To a Jew this role of the Jewish leaders in the destruction of their own people is undoubtedly the darkest chapter of the whole dark story. [...] In Amsterdam as in Warsaw, in Berlin as in Budapest, Jewish officials could be trusted to compile the lists of persons and of their property, to secure money from the deportees [...], to supply police forces to help seize Jews and get them on trains' (104).

2 IB's refusal to pronounce judgement on the Judenräte – the Jewish councils established by the Nazis in the ghettos of occupied Europe from September 1939 – was central not only to his critique of Arendt, but also to his loathing for her. The Judenräte took on the role of municipal authorities, and its members were in the invidious position of having to co-operate with the Nazis in order to secure concessions for the communities that they represented; for some members of the Judenräte, but by no means all, this co-operation ceased, often at the cost of their own lives, once they were faced with the cruel dilemma of compiling lists of those to be deported to the concentration camps, and thus to certain death.

3 Elizabeth Hardwick (1916–2007), US literary critic, novelist and short-story writer; co-founder and advisory editor, NYRB; m. 1949 the poet Robert Lowell, divorced 1972.

Arendt set herself up as a moralist – that is what Mary McCarthy so admired in her – so I think my disgust is not entirely unfounded. [...]

Yours very sincerely,

Isaiah Berlin

TO CARL ROLLYSON[1]

31 May 1993

Headington House

Dear Mr Rollyson,

[...] I ought to explain that I was not a friend of Rebecca West's. I met her, I think, not more than twice or thrice: I think the first occasion was lunch with the Warden of New College, H. A. L. Fisher, when I heard her talk but did not speak to her myself – she was lively, made jokes and interrupted her host continually with various anecdotes and reminiscences. I doubt if he greatly enjoyed this – he was old, dignified and distinguished, and probably preferred more conventional manners. All this was before the war, in the middle 1930s, I should say. After that I did not see her until about the late 1950s or early 1960s, when I was a guest at lunch with my colleague Geoffrey Hudson,[2] a fellow of All Souls. Miss West and her husband Henry Andrews[3] were also there, and, as before, she told anecdotes, overheard and interrupted conversations, and in general behaved in the kind of lively manner which I think was, on the whole, expected of her – and probably did give pleasure to that company. Her host, Hudson, made some mildly friendly comment on Yugoslavia, which led to a short explosion on Miss West's part.

At the end of lunch she asked me if she might pay me a private visit, to discuss the matter on her mind. I think it must have been a few days later that I asked her and Mr Andrews to lunch. Nothing happened at lunch, but at the end of it she asked her husband to leave the room; then, leaning towards me confidentially, she said, 'Mr Berlin, I have a question to ask which of course you do not need to answer if you would rather not, but I feel I must know the truth about this matter. When did Mr Charles Bohlen, in your opinion, leave the Communist Party?'

I was completely taken aback. Bohlen was a great friend of mine, and a more consistent anti-Communist I have never known in my life. The idea of his ever having anything to do with the Party, let alone been a member

1 Carl Edmund Rollyson (b. 1948), US biographer and critic; assistant prof. of humanities, Wayne State, Michigan, 1976–82, associate prof. 1982–7, prof. 1987; prof. of journalism, Baruch College, CUNY, from 1987; his *Rebecca West: A Saga of the Century* (London, 1995) appeared in the US as *Rebecca West: A Life* (NY, 1996).

2 Geoffrey Francis Hudson (1903–74), historian of the Far East; fellow, All Souls, 1926–54; director of Far Eastern studies, St Antony's, 1954–74.

3 Henry Andrews (1894–1968), merchant banker with extensive business links to Germany, where he was interned during WW1; m. Rebecca West 1930.

of it, was absolutely grotesque. He was a considerable expert on the Soviet Union, before and after he had been American ambassador to Moscow. I knew him intimately, and did not know what to answer. I think I must have said that I did not believe for a moment that Bohlen had had anything to do with the Party, or indeed any left-wing movement. I received a withering look, rather as if I was attempting to protect him, or was myself somehow involved with the Party, and she said, so far as I recollect, 'There's no more to be said, I must go', opened the door, called for her husband, and marched off.

I realised then that she was obsessed with Communism, and, in spite of the fact that I shared her views, I thought that on that subject she had gone somewhat round the bend. I remember thinking the same when I read an article by her on the trial of John Amery,[1] who had been a pro-Nazi broadcaster from Berlin during the war (and who I think was subsequently executed). In the course of reporting this trial she spoke about my friend John Foster,[2] a barrister, later a Member of Parliament, also a fellow of All Souls, who had volunteered to defend Amery, as a typical Renaissance bravo – who enjoyed that kind of occasion and simply showed off – or something to that effect. The truth was that Leo Amery,[3] John's father, was a fellow of All Souls and a friend of John Foster. Nobody was prepared to defend him. He was very sorry for the appalling condition of both Leo and his wife,[4] the staunchest Conservatives and defenders of the Empire in the world, whose lives had been virtually destroyed by their son's treason – and out of pure friendship offered to defend him, when nobody else wanted to do so. In the end I don't think he had much to do, since Amery's guilt was clear, and he had not denied it. [...]

Yours sincerely,

Isaiah Berlin

1 John Amery (1912–45), elder of the 2 sons of Leopold and Florence Amery (notes 3 and 4 below); lived on the Continent after being declared bankrupt 1936, and ran guns across the Pyrenees for Francoist forces during the Spanish Civil War; agitated for an Anglo-German anti-Bolshevik alliance during WW2, and tried unsuccessfully to raise a pro-Nazi legion from British prisoners of war 1942–4; broadcast messages to UK urging his countrymen to change sides; captured in Italy April 1945, arraigned 28 November on 8 counts of treason at the Old Bailey; pleaded guilty, and was hanged 19 December.

2 John Galway Foster (1904–82), KBE 1964, lawyer; fellow, All Souls, 1924–82; Conservative MP 1945–74; Foster defended Amery with Gerald Slade KC, who had defended William Joyce, 'Lord Haw-Haw'.

3 Leopold Charles Maurice Stennett ('Leo') Amery (1873–1955), Conservative politician, journalist and historian; fellow, All Souls, 1897–1912, 1939–55.

4 Florence Louise Adeliza ('Bryddie') Amery (1885–1975) née Greenwood, sister of Hamar Greenwood, 1st Viscount Greenwood, barrister and Liberal MP.

TO ANDRZEJ WALICKI

19 August 1993

Headington House

Dear Andrzej,

[...] I am glad that you are having a good time in Warsaw, and that you find a response there which, I am not surprised to learn, you miss at Notre Dame. There is a ferment going on in Eastern Europe, despite and amid all the horrors, and something will come of it in the end – a new intelligentsia will surely be born. The young men I met in Moscow three years ago,[1] and some of those I occasionally see here, fill me with confidence that the old intelligentsia – pure-hearted, infinitely curious, totally honest, with a rich and real inner life, morally deeply sympathetic – is far from dead.

I realise that our nineteenth-century friends – Herzen, Belinsky & Co. – are nauseous to the present generation of the ex-Soviet young. They were rammed down their throats in a distorted form for so long that nausea was bound to set in. [...] One day our heroes will return. Herzen is not dead yet in the East; he is gaining adherents in the West and is much more widely read [...] than ever before. There is hope. Your duty is plain: to bring up successors imbued with the true values, with intellectual sensitiveness to the moral, political and social issues with which these people struggled. This cannot succeed while people are looking for bread, water, candles, bits of paper to write on, but the line ought not to be severed. I am sure you will find in Warsaw successors, disciples, whom you can look to as continuers of what we have thought about for so long and with such personal profit. [...]

Yours ever,

Isaiah B

TO MIRKO WISCHKE[2]

30 August 1993 [carbon]

Headington House

Dear Dr Wischke,

[...] My general credo you will find in the Agnelli Lecture published [in] the latest volume of my essays, *The Crooked Timber of Humanity*.[3] Those are my fundamental beliefs, and in the light of them one can probably read and criticise other things that I have written. You are quite right to say that the horrors of our time have somewhat compromised the idea of progress, not only continuous, but even discontinuous, in dialectical leaps, quantum

---

1 sc. five (March 1988).
2 Mirko Wischke (b. 1961), German academic; research assistant to Manfred Riedel, Institute of Philosophy, Martin Luther University, Halle-Wittenberg, 1993–2000.
3 392.

jumps, as some people try to interpret the history of the modern world. But there is something else, more radical, that I believe and ought to explain.

My criticism of the idea of ideal solutions to human problems, particularly political and social ones, is based not only on the view that they are utopian and impracticable (that, I am sure, is what makes us call them utopian). Ordinary commonsense opinion formulates it as 'One cannot change human nature', which I do not regard as valid: one can, and sometimes radically for the worse, perhaps for the better – but human nature is not static, it can be altered; about that Vico, Saint-Simon and Marx are right. No, my criticism is more fundamental than that. I believe that some ultimate human values are incompatible with each other – conceptually incompatible, not just in practice. It does not make sense, in any intellectual framework that shapes our thought, to suppose that perfect liberty is compatible with perfect equality, or perfect justice with mercy; nor is a capacity for planning compatible with complete spontaneity. These are all human values which men pursue, quite apart from destructive ones (which I do not mention). So also one could say that knowledge is not always compatible with happiness: if I know that I have cancer, my knowledge does not increase my happiness, as many rationalists since Plato have maintained.

Thinkers from Plato to our day, through the Stoics, the Christian Middle Ages, the Renaissance, eighteenth-century materialism, Hegel, Marx, modern empiricism, analytic philosophy, have tended to believe that a perfect state of affairs, a rational harmony, is in principle possible, or thinkable, even if it will never be reached, given the obstacles. But I do not believe that even this can be maintained. If ultimate values are (a) sometimes incompatible, and (b) incommensurable, by which I mean that unless one is a metaphysical or theological dogmatist, and knows for certain what the ultimate criterion for the hierarchy of human values is (God's word, or perfect rational insight) – unless one believes that, there is no single, overarching criterion in terms of which ultimate values can be measured against each other on a single hierarchical pillar. Those who believe that there is a perfect solution to human problems, and are completely convinced of it (like Marx and his followers), believe that, no matter what the sacrifices en route, they are worth bearing for the sake of ultimate happiness, the eternal happiness of all mankind. So any number of eggs can be broken, provided one is sure that there will be an omelette. But we know from our own experience, if nothing else, that the eggs can be broken and the omelette is not in sight.

But – apart from the empirical fact that the actions of those who believe in these ultimate solutions almost invariably, if in power, lead to cruelty, the shedding of blood as the means to paradise – if I am right, then it is even conceptually incoherent to suppose that such a solution is thinkable. This is a more radical attack on final solutions than that made by most anti-utopian political thinkers. That is the point I should like to emphasise. If you are writing about my views, I should value it if you bring in this notion, which, without trying to be too vain or boastful, I do not think is to be found in most of the political philosophers of whatever age. [...]

Yours sincerely,
Isaiah Berlin

On 13 September 1993 Yitzhak Rabin and Yasser Arafat shook hands in a public ceremony at the White House in the presence of President Clinton,[1] thereby affirming their commitment to the so-called Oslo I Accord, intended as the first step towards a permanent settlement between Israel and the Palestinians. The agreement was the outcome of secret talks at the Fafo Foundation in Norway which provided for mutual recognition as a basis for negotiation. The PLO recognised the state of Israel and renounced violence, while Israel recognised the PLO as the representative of the Palestinian people. Oslo I dealt with Palestinian self-rule, Israeli withdrawal from the occupied territories, economic co-operation and regional development, creating a framework for future progress, and on 28 September 1995 an interim agreement on the West Bank and the Gaza Strip, known as Oslo II, was signed by Rabin and Arafat in Washington. The Oslo Accords represented genuine progress, but their implementation was made increasingly difficult by political events in the region, notably the assassination of Yitzhak Rabin on 5 November 1995, the Hamas-inspired terrorist attacks in Israel in February and March 1996, and the election of the conservative hardliner Binyamin Netanyahu[2] as prime minister of Israel on 29 May 1996. An attempt was made to revive negotitations with the Wye River Memorandum of October 1998, but within a few years all forward momentum had effectively ceased.

TO LESLIE LIPSON[3]

30 September 1993 [*carbon*]

Headington House

Dear Leslie,

It was very nice to hear from you – there has indeed been what you call a hiatus, and it ought to be bridged. I am waiting for your book.[4] I must have

---

1 William Jefferson ('Bill') Clinton (b. 1946), Democrat governor, Arkansas, 1979–81, 1983–92; US President 1993–2001.

2 Binyamin Netanyahu (b. 1949), Israeli diplomat and politician; prime minister 1996–9 (and since 2009); succeeded Yitzhak Shamir as leader of Likud 1993; outspoken critic of the peace negotiations that led to the Oslo Accords; narrowly defeated Shimon Peres in the May 1996 direct elections for prime minister, and headed a coalition government, his electoral success influenced by the resurgence of Islamist terrorism; a supporter of West Bank Israeli settlements.

3 Leslie Michael Lipson (1913–2000), London-born US political scientist and writer; prof. of political science, Berkeley, 1950–84.

4 *The Ethical Crises of Civilization: Moral Meltdown or Advance?* (Newbury Park, CA, and London, [1993]).

mislaid the typescript that you sent me: I have looked for it everywhere, but if you saw the chaotic mountains of documents, books, periodicals, letters, theses that still clutter my desk despite my enormous age, you would not be surprised, even though you might be slightly narked. Anyway, do send me your book: I read about three pages a day now, on account of old age and general hebetude – but I read. And your book I certainly shall read, slowly, with great profit, respect, agreement, admiration and every other positive quality that it demands.

You are right about the contemporary world. I must say, it is a breakthrough, no question of that. I, who have seen everything – the First World War, the Russian Revolution, Hitler, the creation of Israel, the collapse of the USSR (enough for one lifetime) – in about the worst century that mankind has had since I don't know when, even I must say that I was moved by the TV spectacle of Rabin and Arafat. Peres is really the hero of this, and I daresay some of the Arabs from Jerusalem. No doubt horrors will accumulate: Syria will not behave well, the fundamentalists from Lebanon will go on killing, so will Hamas[1] (yet Syria could stop it tomorrow if it wanted to, by blocking the Persian money and the Lebanese groups), other things will blow up, Likud will sabotage, the awful rabbis will say and do unspeakable things. And yet and yet, there is no complete going back. Once such a thing has happened, it may to some extent recede, but never go back to the horrible earlier phase. So, old as I am, I am glad to have something still to live for. As for the Arab–Israeli 'peace', I can only repeat what Napoleon's mother said to someone who said 'Madame, your position in history is unique, you are the mother of an Emperor, three kings and a queen, this has never happened in history before' – to which, as I am sure you know, she replied 'Pourvu que ça dure',[2] with a strong Corsican accent.

Pourvu, pourvu,

Yours ever,

[Isaiah]

TO ARTHUR SCHLESINGER

4 October 1993

Headington House

Dear Arthur,

[...] The situation in Israel, and Arafat, really is extraordinary. Of course

---

1 Arabic acronym meaning 'zeal' and designating the 'Movement of Islamic Resistance'; established in the Gaza Strip December 1987, and largely funded by Iran, it took a leading role in the Intifada, as well as making provision for schools, hospitals and other social services, challenging the PLO's claim to be the representative of the Palestinian people; inflexibly opposed, on religious grounds, to the existence of, and peace with, the Jewish state.

2 'Provided it lasts', said to be the motto of Napoleon Bonaparte's mother (Maria) Laetitia (1750–1836); the story, often told of Napoleon's coronation as Emperor 1804, may be apochryphal.

it must give delight to all decent human beings, whether Jews or not. [...] Did you read Edward Said's attack on it, on the ground that the Palestinian diaspora has not been taken care of?[1] Ridiculous, like most of what he says and writes. It proves that sincerity and weak-mindedness and vanity can all go together. I always knew that sincerity and vulgarity can be combined, because of the writings of Bernard Levin, some of which I like and some of which give me gooseflesh, particularly when it's about art, music etc. [...]

I am glad Clinton is on the up and up. I wish him very well, and in particular wish ill to all his enemies and critics. At our end, John Smith[2] has done very well, and poor John Major is under fearful attack from all quarters. Have you read the memoirs of Alan Clark?[3] Nicko Henderson[4] told me that it was unputdownable, and so have others: so, slightly ashamed, I bought it and read it. It is not at all that, for me, unputdownable; occasionally I got fearfully bored; but it is an extraordinary performance – a cad, bounder and worse (I do not put the other word for fear of shocking my prudish secretary), and doesn't mind appearing such, indeed insists upon it. He has one of the most brutal faces I have ever encountered, and I do encounter it in Albany from time to time, where he occupies his father's rooms. And yet, on nature, on buildings, on animals he is quite good; but the passion for Mrs Thatcher, and the wild hatred for everything even faintly liberal or decent, in the end got me down. Still, I think you would enjoy it. [...]

Yours as ever ⟨with much love⟩,
    Isaiah

14 October 1993: publication of IB's The Magus of the North: J. G. Hamann and the Origins of Modern Irrationalism, *edited by HH.*

TO LEON WIESELTIER

29 October 1993

Headington House

Dear Leon,
    Thank you ever so much for all the things that you sent me – I read them

1 Edward Said, 'The Morning After', LRB, 21 October 1993, 3, 5: 'So first of all let us call the agreement by its real name: an instrument of Palestinian surrender, a Palestinian Versailles' (3).

2 John Smith (1938–94), lawyer (Scottish QC 1983), Labour MP 1970–94; leader, Labour Party and opposition, 1992–4; his untimely death cut short a promising career; he was succeeded by Tony Blair.

3 Alan Kenneth Clark (1928–99), elder son of Kenneth Clark; Conservative politician, author and diarist; his *Diaries* (London, 1993), covering 1983–92, when he had been a minister in Mrs Thatcher's government, were a publishing sensation, earning its author wealth, fame and notoriety.

4 (John) Nicholas Henderson (1919–2009), KCMG 1972, diplomat and author; PS to foreign secretary 1963–5; minister in Madrid 1965–9; UK ambassador to Poland 1969–72, to FRG 1972–5.

avidly and with great interest and pleasure. The review of Diana Trilling's
book[1] by that excellent man[2] seems to me very good indeed – better, I am
sure, than what anyone else will write about it. I don't know if it will be
published in England, or make the faintest impact here – if not, it'll be
another grievance to the angry old lady, to whom I remain devoted. I had
no idea before that Lionel was liable to rages and depressions, and violently
blamed Diana for things which happened to him. She seems to me to skate
rather lightly over his Jewish difficulties: she does talk about them, and
her own, but not altogether fully. For example, the story of how Lionel
managed to obtain tenure at Columbia is told by her as if it was Nicholas
Murray Butler[3] (Miraculous) whose love of Matthew Arnold determined
this, because Lionel had written a book about him.[4] I don't believe this.
I believe the account by the wicked Sidney Hook, in, I think, *Midstream*,[5]
who tells a marvellous story about Lionel coming to him in gloom and
despair about not being kept on, how he told him how to be tough with the
Dean, and how it was obvious to him that Lionel didn't have the character
to do that: he couldn't possibly bang the table and say, 'I know why you are
doing this to me, it is because I am a Jew. There are three million of us in
New York, and by God they will all hear about it', etc. etc. Then the Dean,
again according to Hook, would say 'Sit down, Lionel, don't shout. We all
love you, you know that. Nothing has been decided. Keep your shirt on, do
sit down, don't stand there glowering at me. We must talk this through', etc.
etc. And how then Lionel in fact did exactly what Sidney told him to do,
and the Dean behaved exactly as Sidney said he would. It is a very well told
story, and I recommend it. [...]

Farewell, do come here again, all my love, and Aline's,

Yours ever,

Isaiah

1 A review by Robert Alter of Diana Trilling's *The Beginning of the Journey: The Marriage of Diana
  and Lionel Trilling* (NY and London, 1993) appeared under the title 'In Responsibilities Begin
  Dreams', *New Republic*, 1 November 1993, 30–6. 'During his depressions, which Mrs Trilling says
  occurred five or six times a year, he would subject her to vehement verbal abuse, blaming all his
  unhappiness on her' (31).
2 Robert Bernard Alter (b. 1935), Hebrew scholar and literary critic; prof. of Hebrew and comparative literature, Berkeley, 1969–89, Class of 1937 Prof. of Comparative Literature since 1989.
3 Nicholas Murray Butler (1862–1947), educator; President, Columbia, 1902–45; dubbed 'Nicholas
  Miraculous' by his friend Theodore Roosevelt, Butler was an adviser to 7 US Presidents, held 37
  honorary degrees, received decorations from 15 foreign governments, and was awarded the 1931
  Nobel Peace Prize.
4 Diana Trilling had a premonition that Butler would give Lionel tenure after reading his *Matthew
  Arnold* (London, 1939), which Lionel had given Butler; and she was convinced that this happened
  when Butler personally appointed Lionel assistant prof. of English, the 1st Jew to be admitted to
  that dept: *The Beginning of the Journey* (note 1 above), 318–21.
5 Sidney Hook, 'Anti-Semitism in the Academy: Some Pages of the Past', *Midstream* 25 no. 1
  (January 1979), 49–54.

8 November 1993

Headington House

Dear Mr Garfinkle,

Thank you for sending me the essay by Voll[2] and Esposito.[3] I read it with some interest but total disagreement. I do not believe that democracy, as the West understands it, whether one is in favour of it or not, has much in common with the kind of fraternity, ‹populism (v. different from democracy)› unity and theoretical equality which, according to the essay, is preached by Islam. There is nothing in this essay to indicate that in any Muslim state individuals are protected by law in their freedom to speak, vote for anyone they wish to elect to a democratically organised institution, or indeed enjoy most of the civil liberties, as we call them, which exist in various measures in the West, and are the centre of the ideologies of liberalism. Nothing in this essay indicates that such institutions exist or are permitted in Islam. So whatever the merits of these societies (and I do not, of course, deny the right to coexist of societies with very different beliefs and modes of behaviour, provided they do not coerce others into accepting their ways of life), I see nothing in this essay that begins to establish the point that the authors wish to defend. The general view that one ought to try and understand societies different from our own, and tolerate them so far as they do not endanger our own forms of life, is of course perfectly valid ‹tolerant pluralism is the heart of liberal democracies›; but from that there does not seem to me to follow their very heterodox interpretation of Islam, despite all the quotations brought up to support their view.

I am not, I am afraid, disposed to discuss these issues in public, since I know too little about Islam and take too little interest in it. My feeling is that at present militant Islam is the greatest danger to free, democratic societies to be found anywhere; consequently this attempt to throw bridges, while no

1 Adam Morris Garfinkle (b. 1951), US editor, speechwriter and foreign policy analyst; visiting prof. of political science, Pennsylvania, 1989–91; from 1993 editor, *National Interest*, principal speechwriter to Colin Powell and founding editor, *American Interest*; professorial lecturer in US foreign policy, School of Advanced International Studies, Johns Hopkins, 1995–8. As temporary joint editor with Daniel Pipes of the newly established *Middle East Quarterly* he had invited IB's comments on an article by John Obert Voll and John L. Esposito, 'Islam's Democratic Essence', which appeared in the September 1994 issue (1 no. 3), 3–11; not wishing to become involved in a public controversy, IB refused, in a letter of 26 November, AG's request to publish an edited version of the letter published here.
2 John O. Voll (b. 1936), prof. of history, New Hampshire, 1965–95; prof. of Islamic history, Georgetown, 1995–2014.
3 John Louis Esposito (b. 1940) taught religious studies at Holy Cross, Mass. 1972–93, then at Georgetown (prof. of religion and international affairs from 1993).

doubt commendable in itself, seems to me to bear no relation to the existing situation in Islamic countries. [...]

Yours sincerely,

Isaiah Berlin

TO FRANCISCO VERGARA[1]

8 November 1993 [carbon]

Headington House

Dear Mr Vergara,

Thank you for your interesting essay on Mill and the ends of life.[2] For me, ultimate ends and the ends of life are identical; I mean exactly the same by both, namely ends not means, the ultimate values in the light of which men, groups, societies, religious organisations lead or try to lead their lives. Some of these conflict, but they remain ultimate all the same, and choices between them are often very hard to make; and since I do not believe in a single ultimate end (unlike Mill), I know of no criterion in terms of which these conflicts can be settled.

You distinguish feelings from beliefs.[3] But I must explain to you that in my view (and those of many other thinkers) morality, religion and other forms of what may loosely be called experience of, belief in or pursuit of, values, of whatever kind, are ultimately founded on what Adam Smith called sentiment. Hume, Kant, Adam Smith,[4] and indeed Mill, for all that he discovered that happiness is the only true ultimate value, in the end found their beliefs on what you call feeling. Other thinkers have supposed that there is a faculty called reason, which identifies the right ends of life: I do not know what is meant by this. By 'reason' I mean the capacity for reasoning, capacity for giving reasons for one's beliefs (whatever such reasons are, whether founded on feeling or otherwise), capacity for generalisation, capacity for understanding coherence, consistency and the like, empirically obtained knowledge of what means lead to what ends, and so on. But as a faculty that uncovers ends, ultimate values, indeed values of any kind – I do not recognise such a capacity. Nor did most of the thinkers who have written about this subject,

1 Francisco Vergara (b. 1945), Chilean-born economist and journalist, living in Paris since 1970; author of *Introduction aux fondements philosophiques du libéralisme* (Paris, 1992).

2 'Utilitarianism and the "Ends of Life"' (typescript), inspired by IB's 'John Stuart Mill and the Ends of Life' (in L): 'According to Professor Berlin, Mill strays away from utilitarianism, since for a utilitarian *the only* "ultimate end" (end pursued for its own sake) should be "the happiness of the community". It seems that Professor Berlin is confusing two different concepts: the first concept is what in Ethics is called "the ultimate end", the second concept is what a biographer would call "the end in life".'

3 'I think that Professor Berlin has also confused a person's *feelings* with a person's *beliefs*. [...] If one distinguishes between the two basic psychological categories of *feeling* and *thinking*, then Mill's position becomes very clear.'

4 Adam Smith (1723–90), moral philosopher and political economist.

for all their talk about rational ends, a rational life, etc. Values, ideals, principles are either accepted as issuing from some final authority (God, sacred writings, prophets, dictators, sovereigns etc.), in which case there is nothing particularly rational about it; or they are our own, or those of our group, culture, nation, period etc., which enables us to communicate with others who may differ from us in their values but not so much that there is no common ground, therefore no argument or communication possible. These values are ultimately founded on what we believe life is for; and that, in turn, is ultimately a matter of what we believe in. 'Believe in' and 'believe that' are different: the first is founded on sentiment, the second on empirical observation of facts, or scientific findings, or other forms of knowledge or belief, or what there is in the world. Consequently I cannot accept the distinctions which you ask me to face, or your proposition that I have made a cardinal error in my interpretation of Mill or anyone else.

Yours sincerely,

Isaiah Berlin

TO MARK LILLA[1]

13 December 1993

Headington House

Dear Professor Lilla,

[...] You say that my case for Hamann is not original. Far be it from me to boast of originality in this or any other context, but I would claim, though not too strongly, that the representation of Hamann as the first and most passionate and uncompromising assailant on the Enlightenment – more so than the people who followed, and with few if any predecessors – is something that so far as I know nobody else has expressed. When my hero Alexander Herzen says about the Jacobins, with admiration, that they rejected the entire *ancien régime*, its virtues as well as its vices, it seems to me that Hamann had the same uncompromising and excessive attitude towards the Enlightenment, of which you rightly believe me to be a genuine disciple. Certainly I would vote with even Helvétius[2] and Holbach[3] against Hamann if it came to that – these

---

1 Mark T. Lilla (b. 1956), US political theorist and historian of ideas; assitant/associate prof., dept of politics, NYU, 1990–9; later prof. of social thought, Chicago (1999–2007), of the humanities, Columbia (since 2007); co-editor, *The Legacy of Isaiah Berlin* (NY, 2001); author of foreword to AC2. In this letter IB comments on a typescript of 'The Trouble with the Enlightenment', Lilla's review of IB's *The Magus of the North* (London, 1993; 470), which appeared in the LRB, 6 January 1994, 12–13.

2 Claude Adrien Helvétius (1715–71), French Enlightenment philosopher who attempted to treat human society, morals and politics by the methods of natural science; he was a utilitarian *avant la parole*, and his *De l'esprit* (1758) was an important influence on the thought of Jeremy Bentham and his successors; 1st of the 6 main subjects of FIB.

3 Paul Henri Thiry, baron d'Holbach (1723–89), German-born French philosopher and leading Encyclopedist, proponent of an atheistic natural philosophy: 'Morality', he wrote, 'is the science

thinkers did a great deal of good; they effectively attacked superstition and ignorance, cruelty, darkness, dogma, tradition, despotism of all kinds, and for that I truly honour them. But by temperament I am liable not to write about thinkers I approve of – I take those for granted. I find it not very interesting to praise thinkers for what I agree with, but prefer the enemies, who, however vicious and destructive at times, as they certainly were, discovered chinks in the armour of the Enlightened, important chinks, which do make valid points against them; and which cause one at any rate to think, to realise that one can't swallow them whole, that some of the results of their teachings did lead to deplorable results.

Of course I agreè that Diderot, Lessing,[1] two of my favourite thinkers in the eighteenth century, did not in any way lead to the horrors of uniformity, and in the end the Gulag. Nor can I accuse any of the Enlightened thinkers, however fanatical their devotion to monism, rationalism, true answers to all questions, etc., of directly leading to authoritarianism, bullying and in the end totalitarianism itself, at least in the Soviet Union (Hitler is another story). But I do think that their interpreters in later times, in particular, of course, Marxists, but also Comte (as you rightly remark), did lead to something of the sort, in its exaggerated, sometimes distorted but nevertheless traceable form. Thinkers who know the answer and maintain that if others fail to be persuaded, then force, law, in the end coercion, may have to be used to improve the world, have much to answer for. I did deliver a course of lectures on the Enlightenment, or parts of it, for the BBC, years and years ago, which was never published because I thought, as you do, that my charges against them were somewhat extreme.[2] All this sprang, I think, from my interest in Marxism and my reading of Plekhanov, that brilliant and mordant writer, certainly the most brilliant of the Russian Marxists, who wrote an entire book (called, because of the censor, something like *On the Monistic Conception of History*)[3] where he does write about the French Enlightenment extremely

---

of the relations which exist between the minds, wills and actions of men, in the same manner as geometry is the science of the relations that are found between bodies.' *Esquisse d'un tableau historique des progrès de l'esprit humain* (Paris, 1795), 365; *Outlines of an Historical View of the Progress of the Human Mind* (London, 1795), 353; cf. FIB2 12–13. Wealthy and generous, he was the host of a major, influential, Paris salon.

1 Gotthold Ephram Lessing (1729–81), German dramatist and critic; remembered less for his philosophical writings than for the influence he had on the German thinkers of his day.

2 *Freedom and Its Betrayal*, 6 lectures given on the BBC Third Programme October–November 1952; published 50 years later as FIB.

3 *On the Question of the Development of the Monist View of History: A Response to Messrs Mikhailovsky, Kareev and Co.* (St Petersburg, 1895); trans. Andrew Rothstein as *In Defence of Materialism: The Development of the Monist View of History* (London, 1947), reviewed by IB in *Slavonic Review* 28 (1949–50), 257–62 (letter, 607–10): 'The clumsy title under which the treatise translated by Mr Rothstein was published was given it deliberately in order to avoid the attentions of the Russian censorship; as the translator relates in his preface, this ruse succeeded, and it duly became one of the basic texts of revolutionary Marxism in Russia' (260).

clearly and persuasively, readably, but obviously with a view to making them prop up his own, pretty intolerant, Marxism.

You rightly say that I do not advocate the doctrines of Hamann – far from it. But you do imply that I think better of them than in fact I do: perhaps I have not expressed myself clearly enough. My only wish in investigating these thinkers was to identify the interesting and worth-thinking-about objections which they had to the over-dogmatic, naive, opportunistic and on occasions shallow doctrines and prophecies of the Enlightenment. In my view, if one is to understand the world, one must take both sides into account, and not hasten to clear conclusions, given the 'crooked timber'[1] of mankind. You speak of the scepticism of the men of the Enlightenment. Certainly Voltaire was not optimistic about the future of what he believed in; but he did believe in it, and wanted it to happen, and influenced others directly. Not much scepticism in Helvétius, Holbach, La Mettrie,[2] or indeed the admirable Condorcet,[3] one of the best men who ever lived; in Diderot, yes, in Lessing too – and that leads to the ambivalences of Tocqueville, Humboldt,[4] J. S. Mill, and my adored Herzen, not to the rigid authoritarianism of Comte or scientism, as Hayek called it, or in the end to Marx, Lenin, Stalin, Mensheviks and Bolsheviks, H. G. Wells, Shaw etc. – all of whom did want to smooth out the world, make it spick and span, trample on inconvenient human variety – fatal reductionism, if you know what I mean (and of course you do).

[...] I think you really do exaggerate my criticism of the Enlightenment. I don't discuss them in detail, because the people Hamann attacked, including Rousseau of the *Social Contract*,[5] and the philosophical rather than emotional writings, were pretty uniform in their views. But to say that my characterisation of the Enlightenment is 'almost black' really is an exaggeration. I think that monism does lead to the trouble I describe; but I don't think my view of the monists, i.e. the whole central current of European philosophy, is of something 'black': Plato, Aristotle, Hegel, Marx are not 'black' for me as they are for, say, Popper – my book on Marx shows that sufficiently, I think. I just think that from small acorns great oaks do grow,[6] and that monism in the end led to consequences for which the early monists cannot strictly be

1 170/5.
2 Julien Offray de La Mettrie (1709–51), French physician and philosopher; developed his materialist and atheistical ideas with great originality, though the results were profoundly shocking to contemporaries.
3 Marie Jean Antoine Nicolas Caritat, marquis de Condorcet (1743–94), French humanist philosopher; wrote on educational reform, women's rights and the abolition of the slave trade.
4 (Friedrich) Wilhelm Christian Karl Ferdinand, baron von Humboldt (1767–1835), German humanist philosopher, diplomat and linguist.
5 J[ean] J[acques] Rousseau, *Du contrat social, ou Principes du droit politique* ('Amsterdam' [sc. Paris?], 1762), his principal political work, 'seeks to derive the right of some men to authority over others from a theory of the transference of power in accordance with the social contract' (RT 53, hf2 48, PSM 469).
6 C14th English proverb often worded 'Great oaks from little acorns grow.'

blamed. I hate people who say that Hegel is responsible for the Nazis – but of course they used him, as they used Fichte, as they used everybody, for their terrible ends.

[…] My view of the Enlightenment is not 'cloudy'. I do believe that some of the doctrines, particularly as interpreted in the nineteenth and in our own century, did much to undermine individual liberty, civil rights, liberalism, tolerance – and that, I would not retreat from. But in a little collection of texts called *The Age of Enlightenment*,[1] in the introduction, I do pay genuine homage to the eighteenth-century champions of these very values,[2] even if their views did by various means lead to the opposite of what, perhaps, some of them believed. I do not deny […] that the *lumières* very usefully and effectively attacked medieval scholasticism, as well as modern rationalism; but not, I think, by means of what you call 'sceptical empiricism', but by appeals to reason, science, experience etc. They were in their own way just as dogmatic as their opponents, except that by and large they were right and the opponents wrong. Again, I have to except Diderot and Lessing. Of course they were not unfeeling, of course they were tolerant, of course it was Saint-Simon who began the true process of imposing the rules and leading to the oppression – which you and I recognise. But Saint-Simon was a true disciple of the Enlightenment, and, while he did not acknowledge it, Marx was a true disciple of Saint-Simon […].

Forgive me for all these comments, but I thought that I would just let you know that I admired your review, and shall read it again when it appears in the next issue of the *London Review of Books*. I think it is by and large generous, and for the most part just. But when you say that I am not sure that I know where I myself stand – that I oscillate, as it were, between the Enlightenment and the Counter-Enlightenment – I know what you mean. What I truly believe is that we are children of two traditions, which we have not reconciled in our own breasts – not merely my own breast, but most people's. Let me give you an example. Sincerity is a virtue not found before the eighteenth century: if people are wrong – Muslims, Protestants – then true Christians give them no marks for being sincere in the wicked doctrines they hold; they don't say 'This Protestant is driving souls to perdition, but he doesn't do it for personal glory, but because he truly believes what he says, and one ought to admit that as something in his favour.' That was never said: on the contrary, the more sincerely held a false belief was, the more dangerous, wicked and deserving of elimination the holder. But in the nineteenth century, and today, we do give marks for sincerity, for approval of variety (for Spinoza, a sure sign of error); if things go too far, then sincerity – on the

1 169/1.
2 The introduction concludes: 'The intellectual power, honesty, lucidity, courage and disinterested love of the truth of the most gifted thinkers of the eighteenth century remain to this day without parallel. Their age is one of the best and most hopeful episodes in the life of mankind.' POI 52.

part of Lenin or Hitler – is not often pleaded; but in other cases, quite often. Supposing one asks oneself, 'Do you value Torquemada[1] above or below Frederick the Great?'[2] The first tortured innocent men to save their souls (as he sincerely believed), to make their passage to heaven easier, so in this respect he was an honest man who did what he truly believed was right and good; whereas Frederick the Great was in many ways a villain, a cynic etc., but the standard of living in Prussia under him rose, as people were made happier, their chances greater than ever before. Do you give more marks to Torquemada's sincerity or to Frederick for utilitarian reasons? I don't think we know: people oscillate between the two, and no doubt I oscillate with them. To that extent you are right. In the end I come down on the side of the Enlightenment, but the other side should be listened to: they have identified grave flaws, they have a vision too.

With this I close, and thank you again.

Yours sincerely,

Isaiah Berlin

TO MORRIS ABRAM

14 December 1993

Headington House

Dear Mr Abram,

Thank you very much for sending me your lecture.[3] I thought it was a powerful and persuasive indictment of UN attitudes to Israel; but I think that in putting the case you perhaps may, occasionally, somewhat overstate it.

For example, [...] you say that human rights and fundamental freedoms have been observed by the Jewish state in its treatment of its Arab citizens, even while defending its life in four Arab wars. I doubt if this is strictly true. I think that if you consulted the Israeli monitoring organisation, B'tselem[4] (a reliable body), they could supply you with details of a good many failures to observe the human rights of the Arabs, of which there are a number of reports. Even if not all of them are totally reliable, a good many of them certainly are. I would therefore qualify this passage, or perhaps omit it altogether and simply confine yourself to saying that Israel is the only democracy

---

1 Tomás de Torquemada (1420–98), Spanish Dominican descended from a line of converts from Judaism (*conversos*); supported the Alhambra edict of 1492 banishing Jews from Spain; the 1st Grand Inquisitor, 1483–98, of the revived Spanish Inquisition; his tribunals burnt an estimated 10,000 or more victims.

2 Frederick II was regarded as both a brutal militarist and the most progressive ruler of his age, a practitioner of 'enlightened absolutism', a term coined by Wilhelm Roscher in the 3rd part of 'Umrissen zur Naturlehre der drei Staatsformen', published in 5 parts in *Allgemeine Zeitschrift für Geschichte* 7 and 9 (1847, 1848), at 7, 451; established Prussia as a major European power.

3 MA had sent a 14-page typescript entitled 'United Nations, Israel and the Peace Process: Help Mate or Check Mate'.

4 'Israeli Information Center for Human Rights in the Occupied Territories'.

operating by the rule of law in the entire Middle East. Indeed, you could refer to B'tselem as an example of Israel's own internal vigilance in trying to act up to the highest possible standards – something totally absent in other Middle Eastern countries, as I need hardly say. I think that might be more impressive. [...]

Israel's title deeds: three thousand years[1] is surely not right, even if you begin with Joshua[2] (when was he? 1500 BC?) and continue to the Second Temple and after. The Balfour Declaration and the Palestine mandate do not give the Jews the right of occupation of the whole of Palestine.[3] 'National home' was a deliberately ambiguous formula, and interpreted, both by the British Foreign Office and by the League, as not permitting any kind of total occupation, let alone a sovereign state. So one has to be careful about that too, if your excellent document is not to be open to objections. The same applies to the UN partition of 1947.

[...] you say that 'No act of the infant state of Israel was the cause of that war':[4] would you not think that Deir Yassin or Kibbiya[5] could be regarded as provocations? Not sufficient to unleash a war, nevertheless acts which even during a troubled period are difficult to defend (at any rate in my view). No doubt the leaders of the Irgun and Stern Group thought differently, but the memory of these massacres – for that is what they were – has done a lot of harm to the Israeli cause in the eyes of quite friendly observers.

The rest is, as they say, 'just fine'. I think it is a powerful and eloquently stated case. And there is a true need for it: it does all need to be said.

Yours sincerely,
    Isaiah Berlin

---

1 MA had written: 'Israel's title rest[s] on continuous occupation for 3,000 years.'

2 Successor to Moses; according to biblical chronology he lived 1355–1245 BCE; led the Israelites into Canaan after the exodus from Egypt; his story is told in the biblical book of Joshua.

3 The Declaration, conveyed in the form of a letter from Arthur James Balfour, then foreign secretary, to Lord (Walter) Rothschild, 2 November 1917, states in full: 'His Majesty's Government view with favour the establishment in Palestine of a national home for the Jewish people, and will use their best endeavours to facilitate the achievement of this object, it being clearly understood that nothing shall be done which may prejudice the civil and religious rights of existing non-Jewish communities in Palestine, or the rights and political status enjoyed by Jews in any other country.' *Zionist Review* 1 no. 7 (November 1917), 102; *Times*, 9 November 1917, 7e.

4 The sentence that IB quotes here reads in full: 'No act of the infant state of Israel was the cause of that war [the 1948–9 Arab–Israeli war], but all subsequent history in the area is a consequence of this failure of will by the UN and its member powers' (i.e. to uphold General Assembly Resolution 181, 29 November 1947, partitioning Palestine).

5 Deir Yassin was the site of the massacre, 9 April 1948, of up to 254 Arab civilians by Irgun and Stern Gang terrorists. The Jordanian village of Kibbiya was targeted in a revenge attack by an elite unit of the IDF, October 1953: many homes were destroyed, and nearly 70 villagers killed. IB either forgets the later date of Kibbiya, or interprets 'that war' to mean the ongoing Arab–Israeli conflict, not solely the 1948–9 outbreak.

TO LEON WIESELTIER

14 December 1993

Headington House

Dear Leon,

[...] Your piece on Sarajevo[1] is splendid; a collection of maxims or epigrams sometimes merely shine by their own brilliance, and do not hit the
target – yours do. And you are absolutely right about Milošević[2] – he could
have been stopped, in your view and in my view, and one knows how; and
it was simply not done, out of a kind of collective nervousness and lack of
confidence in each other of the Western states. Invasion, even when it is not
ethnic cleansing, is invasion: I was in favour of the Falklands War and of the
Gulf War. That divides me from some of my friends and allies, nevertheless
I am quite clear about that, and so I think are you. Perhaps one has to belong
to a minority to have these feelings, but if so it merely opens one's eyes; it
is not to be attributed to particular kinds of partiality, or historically conditioned sensitivity. You really do speak for men as men (I mean, of course,
persons as persons).

    Yours, with much love
        Isaiah

TO RICHARD ROBBINS[3]

19 January 1994 [carbon]

Headington House

Dear Mr Robbins,

[...] You ask why no women occur in my sketches and essays. I can assure
you that it does not come from the slightest form of misogyny on my part.
But if you could think of some female political thinker, not necessarily even
of importance but of originality and interest, I would try to do justice to such
a one. There were all kinds of revolutionary ladies in Russia, of course, and
they did write – but not significantly enough. It was their character, courage
and sometimes fanaticism which made them famous, not their contribution
to thought. I could not bear to write about Mrs Webb.[4] George Eliot is not
systematic enough to be treated in this way. So what am I to do?

1 'Curses' ('Washington Diarist' column), New Republic, 25 October 1993, 46.
2 Slobodan Milošević (1941–2006), Serbian nationalist politician, widely regarded as having instigated regional war 1991 to secure a 'greater Serbia' after the break-up of the former Yugoslavia;
   President, Serbia, 1989–97, Federal Republic of Yugoslavia 1997–2000; later (2001) arrested, and
   tried at the International Criminal Tribunal for the former Yugoslavia in the Hague on charges of
   genocide, crimes against humanity and war crimes; died in prison while on trial.
3 Richard Robbins (1927–2009), painter, sculptor and art teacher, only son of the economist Lionel
   Robbins; taught at Camberwell School of Art 1958–60, Hornsey School of Art (Middlesex
   University 1973) 1960–93 (head of painting 1984–90, of the school of fine art 1990–3).
4 (Martha) Beatrice Webb (1858–1943), social reformer and diarist; with her husband Sidney James

God! Nature! Humanism! Bosnia, indeed. The number of periods during which human beings could justly be called enlightened, tolerant, even decent, is so much smaller than the enormous areas of darkness [...]. I remember the late Warden of All Souls, Hubert Henderson, saying something of this kind at dinner: he was pounced on by Rowse, at that time a Marxist, and Christopher Hill, who thought it absolute rubbish, and gave him a disagreeable time. I came to his defence, but not very effectively, perhaps, in those days. [...]

Yours gratefully,
[Isaiah Berlin]

TO BERTELL OLLMAN
22 February 1994 [*carbon*]

Headington House

Dear Burt,[1]

I was profoundly moved by your last letter, as surely you would have wished me to be. Our entire relationship has been a source of very great pleasure to me – particularly our disagreements. We took to each other quite early in your life, and reasonably early in mine – and have shared a mutual devotion ever since, which will certainly last until the end of my life, you may be sure of that.

So you are still a revolutionary. I do not think that you will see the desired revolution, whatever may happen after you are gone. Nor do I wish you to, for reasons that I need not reiterate. Nevertheless, if you succeed in promoting your revolution, please remember me and save me from the dire fate which would otherwise await me. You once saved me from having tear gas, or some other substance, sprayed over me – you and Marshall Berman,[2] do you remember? In the basement of CUNY, at a political meeting, at which Charles Taylor used politically proper words but I displayed non-politically-sound sentiments, and was warned that I might be assailed physically, and given instructions as to what to do – including pressing a specially prepared

Webb (1859–1947), Baron Passfield 1929, she was half of a dynamic partnership pioneering social science in Britain, which may help to explain why IB was not an unqualified admirer, and declined 1972 to write an introduction to one of their works: 'I am somewhat allergic to Beatrice's work, although I have much respect for the quiet, dull but very respectworthy Sydney [...]. He was comical, but very decent and learned, and intellectually honourable. She was – or seemed to me to be – profoundly unsympathetic both morally and intellectually' (to Maurice Cranston, 25 January 1972).

1 IB sometimes spelt BO's name 'Burtol' or 'Burt'. BO himself did not use a nickname, but the nickname he didn't use would have been spelt 'Bert'. BO sometimes spelt IB's name 'Isiah', and wonders whether IB's mauling of 'Bertell' might have been his revenge (BO to HH, 22 August 2014).

2 Marshall Howard Berman (1940–2013), US Marxist philosopher and Upper West Side NY radical intellectual; student of IB's at Oxford (BLitt 1963); assistant prof. of political science, City College, CUNY, 1967–71, prof. from 1972.

handkerchief to my face – and the means of a rapid escape.[1] As you saved me then, so may you save me in the event of the inevitable revolution.

In the meanwhile, I wish you well in your subversive activities, especially as I do not believe that they will be crowned by the intended result. I send you my and Aline's warmest love, and hope to see you soon in Headington House, with Paule if possible.

Yours ever

[Isaiah]

PS I'll send you my latest shocking work, on the monstrous reactionary J. G. Hamann, who certainly shares none of your opinions and very few of mine, but nevertheless was a remarkable man. As you know, I take more interest in the enemies of the views that we do share than in their friends [...].

TO LEON WIESELTIER

23 February 1994

Headington House

Dear Leon,

Thank you for the editorial essay on Bosnia.[2] I think I agree with you that the whole ghastly slaughter could have been stopped, particularly by Clinton if he had accumulated ships and aircraft in Italy and threatened to bomb Belgrade. I don't think he would have had to do that; in any case, in the end he might have decided not to. But I think that Milošević would have yielded if these forces looked threatening enough, and enough great powers had supported Clinton, which I think they might have done. I am very depressed by our statesmen and your statesmen, by the right and the left who say that giving arms to the Bosnians would merely increase the number of deaths, etc. Even if they did, it is better to die with arms in one's hand, and taking some of the enemy with you, than being slaughtered like sheep. Wars are dreadful, but they are less dreadful than massacres. I believed that about Vietnam too – and that is the trouble with the right and the left, as usual. For once, the government lag behind public opinion. I am sure that most people in Britain and the USA passionately want something done – by 'something', I mean an attack against the Serbs and the Croats, and it is Parliament, Congress and the governments which hang back, mainly out

1 Christopher Hitchens, in 'Moderation or Death', LRB, 26 November 1998, 3–11, disbelieves this story: 'Well, I know Bertell Ollmann [sic] and Marshall Berman [...]. They both love "Isaiah", and they would both gladly have done that for him, and more. But they say they can't recall the event [...]. One begins to see how myths are made.' Asked about this in 2014 Ollman wrote: 'my best guess is that the incident at CUNY either happened or, for some reason I don't know, Berlin believed it happened. Berlin was simply not one to make things up' (BO to Nicholas Hall, 30 June 2014).

2 IB here returns to the article he commented on earlier (480/1).

of fear of losing votes, which no doubt they would risk. Anyway I won't go on; you recognise my sentiments. Nevertheless, I think your piece is slightly overdone, rather like your piece on the Holocaust Museum. Our prime minister and your President are in a difficult position – they do not have enough political support for anything they might want to do. You cannot altogether blame them for not wanting to lose their heads and still do no good. [...]

Yours ever, ⟨with much love⟩

Isaiah

TO ANDRZEJ WALICKI

14 March 1994

Headington House

Mileishii[1] Andrzej,

I beat my breast in repentance at not having replied to your letter sent so long ago. What explanation, let alone excuse, can I give you for such behaviour? Old age, indolence, mental decay, preoccupation with trivia (newspapers, radio, anything to take one away from the hard labour of genuine thought). I cannot think why, in my nonage, I get so many documents – theses, essays, reports, books, even portions of encyclopedias – which demand more or less immediate comment. Naturally I ignore most of them: but not all, and this, too, is a good enough reason for not doing serious work. Indeed, I look for every possible excuse for avoiding intellectual labour. Still, this does not excuse the fact that I have not replied to someone I love and admire as much as I do yourself.

I am glad that you are to retire. You will have more time to do all the things that I no longer do: to think, to research, to write, about topics of genuine importance which are at present widely ignored. I am melancholy about the world in general, in this sense: twenty or thirty years ago there were still writers, artists, thinkers whom one could call great, or at any rate to whom one could attribute some measure of genius. Today I can think of only two provinces for which this is true: no great writers, historians, poets, novelists, sculptors, painters, philosophers, critics – I could go on. The two provinces where this can still be found are the cinema – there are still some great directors, especially in China and Japan, but some perhaps in France and even Hollywood – and architecture: there are great architects alive, as I am sure you will agree. But the decline in what I can only call culture is quite steep, and unless the new ex-Communist countries suddenly burst forth in a creative stream – and I fear they will take some time to do that, even if in the end they do – I shall end my life in a comfortable intellectual desert.

You speak of Russia: and what you say is sadly true. My heroes, and to

1 'Dearest'.

some degree yours – Belinsky, Herzen, Turgenev – are now regarded as the forerunners of all that is hated: Soviet Communism, horrible radicalism, odious populism, etc. etc.; and the reaction against it takes them to theologians of the second and third order. Even completely inferior journalists, of whom you will never have heard, e.g. Douglas Reed,[1] are now apparently widely read – because he was wildly anti-Semitic, semi-Fascist, anti-Soviet etc. I am only quoting this to show that something like a real reactionary wave has begun, quite apart from Yeltsin[2] and his policies. Are you sure that Zhirinovsky[3] will never come to power? – if things go on as they do in Russia now for, say, two years, that he will not rise to the top of the wave of indignation? The fact that he is a mountebank and a clown may not prevent it – Hitler could have been regarded as that in the 1920s, and the rise of neo-Nazism in Europe now cannot be wholly ignored.

You speak of liberals like us. Who are the first-class liberals among the Russians, or the Poles? Whom would a book called *Russian Liberalism* contain? Leonard Schapiro's favourite Chicherin, Granovsky, Kavelin, Stasyulevich, Milyukov?[4] First-rate thinkers? Men of original ideas or moving eloquence? Petrunkevitch, Koni?[5] It is all very well to say, quite correctly, that the Russians did have a liberal society, that a great many professionals – doctors, engineers, *agronoms*,[6] professors, journalists – were, in fact, liberals in the European sense; but there was a singular lack of leaders. Unlike the West, where there

---

1 Douglas Launcelot Reed (1895–1976), journalist and author; assistant Berlin correspondent, *Times*, 1929–35, Central Europe correspondent 1935–8 (resigned after Munich); his *Insanity Fair* (London, 1938) warned of the dangers posed by Nazism, but he elsewhere displayed 'virulent anti-Semitism'. 'Mr Douglas Reed', obituary, *Times*, 23 September 1976, 16g–h at 16h.

2 Boris Nikolaevich Yeltsin (1931–2007), reformist Russian politician; elected president, Russian Soviet Federative Socialist Republic, 1990; rallied support for Gorbachev during attempted coup of 1991, and on breakup of USSR became President, Russian Federation, 1991–9; survived attempted coup 1993, ill health and impeachment proceedings, but resigned unexpectedly 1999, designating Vladimir Putin acting president.

3 Vladimir Vol'fovich Zhirinovsky (b. 1946) né Eidelstein, controversial, outspoken Russian politician, a former colonel in the Russian Army; founder 1991 and leader from 1992 of the far-right ultra-nationalist Liberal Democratic Party of Russia, which scored a notable success in the 1993 Duma elections, winning 23% of the vote: 'An Estonian deputy said prophetically two years ago [i.e. 1991]: "When Zhirinovsky first appeared, we thought he was a good joke. Then we thought that he was a bad joke and now we don't think that he is a joke at all."' Anatol Lieven, 'He Was a Good Joke, Then a Bad Joke – Now He's No Joke at All', *Times*, 14 December 1993, 12a–f at 12b.

4 Boris Nikolaevich Chicherin (1828–1904), liberal Russian historian and philosopher, and social and political reformer. Timofey Nikolaevich Granovsky (1813–55), Russian historian influenced by Hegel and Ranke, and admired by Herzen. Konstantin Dmitrievich Kavelin (1818–85), Russian historian, jurist, sociologist, and architect of early Russian liberalism; with Granovsky and Herzen, a leading Westerniser. Mikhail Matveevich Stasyulevich (1826–1911), Russian writer, scholar, historian, journalist, editor and publisher. Pavel Nikolaevich Milyukov (1859–1943), Russian liberal politician and historian, a founder of the Constitutional Democratic ('Kadet') party.

5 Alexander Ivanovitch Petrunkevitch (1875–1964), Russian-born arachnologist, naturalist, poet and political activist; left Russia for political reasons, settling in US; professor of zoology, Yale, 1917–64. Anatoly Fedorovich Koni (1844–1927), St-Petersburg-born liberal jurist, public figure and writer.

6 The Russian for 'agronomist' is 'agronom'.

were a few: Constant, J. S. Mill, Mazzini,[1] Michelet,[2] Renan had something to say, surely a head above their Russian equivalents? Or do you disagree? Am I wrong to think that all America provides is McDonald's, Coca-Cola and scandals in the White House? Even the dissident Jewish intelligentsia in New York seems finished.

And yet I have a blind hope, founded on very little empirical evidence, that out of America and Russia something big and valuable will come.[3] [...]

Yours ever

Isaiah

TO PETER HAMM[4]

31 March 1994 [carbon]

Headington House

Lieber[5] Peter Hamm,

[...] The spontaneity of which you speak is genuinely natural to me. I love talking; I do not think of what I am saying when I am talking; I do not think beforehand of what I shall say, nor after of what I have said, and once it is over I would rather not see the result. I live from moment to moment, in a sense, and that could be held against me. So you are right – chatting, Plauderei,[6] is my natural medium, and whatever I know or think certainly enters it quite naturally, for better or for worse. You say that one feels leicht[7] because my words are light – I think that is true, and I am glad you like that. I believe in personal relations and communication even more than Habermas. With him, it is a kind of official doctrine, with me it comes naturally – he is very un-leicht, I am perhaps too leicht.

I am glad you are not devoted to Wagner. There is something about

1 Giuseppe Mazzini (1805–72), Italian nationalist leader, republican and democrat, who spent most of his life in exile; one of the leading figures in the Risorgimento (391/5).

2 Jules Michelet (1798–1874), French historian, keeper, national historical archives, 1831–52; author of the 17-vol. Histoire de France (Paris, 1833–67).

3 Cf. 'Why am I pessimistic about Russia's future? Because the Russians are not a political people: that is to say, the basic institutions which guarantee co-operation, mutual respect, freedom of individuals, security, justice, human rights, accepted machinery for settling differences – all that was largely missing in previous Russian history. There is not enough of, as it were, "civil rights" development – the natural behaviour of human beings in liberal and civilised countries, which does not need coercion – not enough settled acceptance of common norms of behaviour. That is why I think there will be a great deal of disorder, injustice and suffering, as there is today in the Balkans or the Middle East, until some progress towards peace, security, justice and decent government develops.' To Fumiko Sasaki, 6 April 1994. See also 488.

4 Peter Hamm (b. 1937), German poet, essayist, music and literary critic, film producer and director, directed the video Alfred Brendel Plays and Introduces Schubert Piano Works (Berlin, 2007; recorded at Radio Bremen 1976–7). Hamm had written to IB (13 March 1994, in German) about the German edition of CIB.

5 'Dear'.

6 'Gossip'.

7 'Weightless'.

Wagnerians, whatever their other merits, which in my case creates a certain distance between us. It is not so much the quality of the music itself – I realise his genius and importance even if I cannot respond to it – but because of the whole content and atmosphere of the libretti, the quality of his imagination, the dark, sinister atmosphere of *The Ring*, the combination of eroticism, rhetoric, the chauvinism of his evocation of myths, legends, the real absence of humanity, even in *Die Meistersinger*: all those inhuman giants, dwarves, gods, the sense of sin, doom, the general inhumanity, remoteness from everything I like and believe in. All this came between me and Wystan Auden, who was a dedicated Wagnerian; he has an excellent short essay on him, in which he says, about his anti-Semitism (that does not disturb me particularly: almost everybody in the nineteenth century was anti-Semitic in some degree, unless they clearly were not – a tiny minority), that most writers and composers in the Victorian age disliked the Jews but did not speak about exterminating them; with Wagner, he says, one cannot be so sure.[1] And that, I think, is true – there is a kind of murderous hatred there, which emerges in the music, as it does not, for example, in Chopin, who was virulently anti-Semitic in a Polish sort of way.[2] Dostoevsky has something of it, I fear, and when I read him I feel that I am in a kind of nightmare: the whole of reality is somehow transformed by him, and changed into his own world. It is with relief that I stop reading him, and return to ordinary life.

I fear that what you say must be true – I like things as they are, perhaps too much. Tolstoy is sunlit even in his most severe and tragic passages – Dostoevsky is always night. I think it is the night of which Novalis[3] speaks, that kind of Romantic vision that I cannot enter properly, much as I admire the genius which often goes into it. Nietzsche is not night, and his love of *Carmen* is very sympathetic. [...] I feel no *doch ... und doch*,[4] although I understand very, very well what it is that you mean.

What you say about *kindlich*[5] is absolutely true. I realise that poetry, if it is gifted at all, is about the childhood of the poet in some way. Pasternak says that,[6] and he is right; it is memories of the child's world that shape the words and the vision of the artist, at whatever age; if that does not occur, as for

1 'Most nineteenth-century anti-Semites would have been genuinely horrified by Auschwitz, but one has the uncomfortable suspicion that Wagner would have wholeheartedly approved.' 'The Greatest of the Monsters', *New Yorker*, 4 January 1969, 72–82 at 75.

2 Frédéric François Chopin (1810–49) né Fryderyk Franciszek Szopen, Polish French pianist and composer. 'Chopin's attitude toward Jews was in tune with the Polish-language culture of the nineteenth century [...], which allowed mocking and patronising – but seldom vicious – remarks about Jews.' Tad Szulc, *Chopin in Paris: The Life and Times of the Romantic Composer* (NY, 1998), 60.

3 Pseudonym of Friedrich Leopold von Hardenberg (1772–1801), German Romantic author.

4 'And yet ... and yet'.

5 'Childlike'. IB had observed that 'Pierre [in *War and Peace*] is not childlike' (CIB 191). Hamm commented: 'But I think childlikeness – intentional childlikeness – is the most important requirement for being any kind of artist.'

6 In various ways and places: see for example his 1922 poem 'Tak nachinayut. Goda v dva ...' ('That's how they start. At about two ...').

instance, in my view, in Balzac,[1] then there is no poetry. Tolstoy was full of his childhood – even if Pierre[2] is not either childish or childlike, and Myshkin[3] fully is so, Tolstoy's genius is deeply bound up with his early experience, and remained so even during the most solemn, pompous preaching of his later years.

I am glad, too, that you approve of my sympathy for, and I believe understanding of, religious feeling, quite apart from my total inability to understand what is meant by God [...]. I do not know that Goethe was right in saying that it is mankind's best part that lies in the kind of holy awe – almost terror – of which he speaks;[4] but that it is essential to aesthetic sensibility, I fully recognise. Alfred certainly won't agree – I have had sharp arguments with him about that – and although he is undeniably affected by religious feeling in music, and probably in literature also, he stoutly denies it. There is much in him that he himself, I believe, does not fully understand. Perhaps that is true of all artists – total self-understanding must surely kill a good deal of spontaneous expression. Alfred's *Tiefe*[5] is unintelligible without religious feeling – but I shall never say this to him again, otherwise I shall be denounced. Reni, I think, understands this all too well. That is why I came to his children's confirmation, when it happened in a church, and Alfred refused sternly to come.[6]

To receive letters such as yours, so much rather than 'stealing' valuable time, adds something irreplaceable to one's pride and happiness. I am very grateful to Marianne[7] for telling you to do this. I do hope to meet you both again soon. Our conversations are always a source of deep pleasure to me, and illumination too, even on political issues, on which you must surely have changed your mind somewhat since your admiration for the culture of East Germany as opposed to the corruption of the capitalist West. Why do you not come to Feldkirch, at least when Alfred is playing? Then we could meet again. I cannot tell you how delighted I should be. Thank you, thank you, thank you for your wonderful letter.

Yours ever,

Isaiah

---

1 Honoré de Balzac (1799–1850), French novelist and playwright.
2 Petr Kirillovich ('Pierre') Bezukhov, the favourite of the several illegitimate sons of Kirill Vladimirovich Bezukhov in *War and Peace*.
3 Lev Nikolaevich Myshkin, the central protagonist of Dostoevsky's *The Idiot* (1868–9).
4 'Das Schaudern ist der Menschheit bestes Teil' ('The shudder of awe is the best part of mankind'). Faust to Mephistopheles, *Faust* 2. 6,272.
5 'Profundity'.
6 IB refers to the confirmation of the Brendels' son Adrian Johannas Brendel (b. 1976), the cellist, in Sherborne Abbey.
7 Marianne Koch (b. 1931), German actress, medical practitioner and television presenter; partner of Peter Hamm from the mid 1980s.

TO SHIRLEY ANGLESEY

5 April 1994 [*carbon*]

Headington House

Dearest Shirley,

[…] I am fascinated by your continuing connection with Russia – it obviously gives you pleasure, and stirs your interest, and there is no subject I like thinking about or talking about more, even now. But I am very depressed, as you may imagine, about what is going on. It is in a far, far worse condition than the other trouble spots – the Balkans will be settled one of these, if not days, then months; the Jews and Arabs will come to some understanding, however uncomfortable, although it may take some years; but Russia? (Ireland I really don't know about. I am getting a degree in Dublin,[1] and may stay with the American ambassador,[2] if she invites us. She is a Kennedy sister or daughter. I propose to tell her that I think the IRA is a murder outfit. I am not sure that that will be entirely well, or indeed other than very badly, received, but I shall be brave, and say it. I follow the line of my new friend Conor Cruise O'Brien,[3] who is quite clear on this issue, and ought to know, as all his life he has been a semi-Marxist of some kind,[4] and quite late in life discovered that the Marxism of the IRA is entirely counterfeit.)

About Russia: the trouble is that there is no tradition of civil life – the normal network of human relationship through associations, professions, clubs, groups etc. such as other countries have – no pattern of ordinary peaceful living together, apart from whatever the political structure may be. It did not exist under the tsars, nor under the Communists. There was a faint effort at it between February and October 1917, but it was too clumsy, too short, too feeble. So that is what has gone wrong. Now that the iron discipline has gone, everything falls to pieces. There is no natural cement to hold it, as there is in Western countries, whatever their regimes – not much of it in the Balkans either, nothing developed under the Turks, but still more than is to be found in Russia.

---

1 An hon. LittD from Trinity College Dublin, bestowed 8 July 1994.
2 Jean Ann Kennedy Smith (b. 1928), US diplomat, younger sister of JFK; US ambassador to Ireland 1993–8.
3 O'Brien entered Irish politics just as 'the Troubles' began in Northern Ireland, and controversially 'preached unremitting hostility to the IRA, as its terrorist atrocities became bloodier'. As minister for posts and telegraphs he banned Sinn Féin from appearing on the public service network RTE: 'This was censorship by any name, and O'Brien did not deny it, though even some of those who disagreed with him conceded that he had not followed the ignoble tradition of some Irishmen of hypocritical condemnation of terrorists whose aims they shared' (Geoffrey Wheatcroft, ODNB).
4 'I was never a Marxist, and the more I studied Marx, the less of a Marxist I became. The nearest I ever was to being a Marxist was as a very young undergraduate when I had read absolutely no Marx at all.' 'In Search of Morality: Conor Cruise O'Brien Talks to Brian Inglis', *Listener*, 23 August 1973, 235.

I went to lunch with Roy, and sat next to his daughter-in-law,[1] a Croat, and she told me that she goes to Moscow from time to time, and in Moscow does not feel safe but thinks she can walk the streets comparatively confidently – in St Petersburg, not: the mugging, the gangsterism, the insecurity of life and limb are beyond words, so she says. I don't wonder that people wistfully look back on to the terrible Soviet regime, in which people were perfectly safe in the streets. The Communist police were effective; the present police are evidently both inefficient and corrupt. Oh dear.

The Russians are a great people, as I need not tell you, and full of gifts, and will rise; but whether they will rise in some horrible imperialist Zhirinovsky manner, and try and reconquer the Caucasus, the Baltics etc., I don't know. This could happen, but I somehow think that will be cut short; it is too much to swallow; it is too pessimistic to think that the Zhirinovsky programme – the great world power again, stretching over a fifth of the world's surface, as used to be said – will come into being. But still, the future is very murky, and I feel gloomy. Yet people write poetry, paint pictures (not much, and not good); the intelligentsia in some sense survives; people I met there, and meet here occasionally, are wonderfully like the noble old nineteenth-century liberal intelligentsia, which puts me in good heart; and yet, and yet, the gangsterism is terrific, and all these Russians who are buying huge, rich houses in London, as the Arabs used to – where do they come from? I feel, uneasily, that there must be Jews among them – I wish I didn't think there were – but my natural anti-Semitism tells me that there must be a proportion.

Let me stop talking about this gloomy subject. Gorbachev has no future, I am sure – the question is, does Yeltsin? It's all very strange – Zhirinovsky is half a Jew, but denies it;[2] Rutskoy[3] is half a Jew, and doesn't look it and doesn't behave like that. Are the old gang, the old Soviet bureaucrats, plus the nationalists, plus the Church (which is not behaving well) – are they gathering force? Do they want a tsar? But I mustn't go on in this depressing fashion. [...]

[Isaiah]

1 Ivana Alexandra Jenkins (b. 1948) née Sertic, daughter of Ivo Vladimir Sertic; m. 1971 Charles Arthur Simon Jenkins (b. 1949), son of Roy and Jennifer Jenkins.
2 Until 2001 Zhirinovsky denied his father's Jewishness; thereafter he attempted to come to terms with it. His father, Vol'f Andreevich Zhirinovsky né Eidelshtein, was a Polish Jew who left Zhirinovsky's mother when his son was still a child, and emigrated to Israel with a new family 1949.
3 Aleksandr Vladimirovich Rutskoy (b. 1947), Russian politician and former Soviet military officer; Vice President, Russia, 1991–3; governor, Kursk Oblast, 1996–2000; his mother was Jewish.

TO ANAND CHANDAVARKAR[1]

18 April 1994

Headington House

Dear Mr Chandavarkar,.

Thank you for your clear and admirable piece about Keynes and anti-Semitism. I read it with great interest, and indeed instruction [...].[2]

I did not know Keynes at all well, but I met him two or three times, and I know something about his milieu and outlook. I think that Skidelsky is probably right to attribute his anti-Semitic remarks to his class and time and milieu.[3] I do not think one can call him an anti-Semite as one can, let us say, Evelyn Waugh, T. S. Eliot, Harold Nicolson, Vita Sackville-West,[4] and even, I think, Virginia Woolf (despite the fact that she was married to a perfectly self-identified Jew). In the case of Keynes, as [in] that of several members of Bloomsbury, it seems to me that they simply did not care for Jews socially, did not like their company; they sometimes rationalised this by picking on certain real or alleged characteristics of Jews as a reason for this, even a justification; but I think in fact that it was not that most of them disliked this or that attribute of the Jews they knew or heard of, so much as simply not liking them. Some people in England couldn't, and can't, bear Germans, or Frenchmen – as many Americans don't like, say 'Hispanics', and indeed Jews too. I mean that if Jews were persecuted anywhere, or an act of grave injustice was done to a Jew (as in the case of Dreyfus), people like Keynes would certainly have signed a note of protest, and feel genuine indignation – quite independently of the fact that they could avoid meeting them, or at any rate feel uncomfortable in their presence, feel them to be unsympathetic or alien or ungentlemanly in some way.

This was true of Bertrand Russell, probably true of E. M. Forster (though I am sure he would have denied it – but there is a piece by him on an exhibition in, I think, the Royal Academy, where there was a portrait of the late Sir Philip Sassoon,[5] and he expostulates that this oriental should have any-

1 Anand G. Chandavarkar (1925–2011), Indian economist; director, Reserve Bank of India; assistant director, IMF; author of *Keynes and India: A Study in Economics and Biography* (London, 1989).

2 The piece in question was a draft of AC's article 'Was Keynes Anti-Semitic?', *Economic and Political Weekly*, 6 May 2000 (35 no. 19), 1619–24, where IB's letter appears at 1623. AC concluded: 'In retrospect, Keynes's anti-Semitism will be seen more as a peripheral fringe of an inherently compassionate personality, an unamiable foible rather than a fatal flaw of character, a blind spot which never blurred the totality of his social and political vision' (1623).

3 Skidelsky observed, for example, that Louis-Lucien Klotz, the French finance minister before and after WWI, 'represented, to Keynes, the other face of France's grasping sterility; a view not uninfluenced by the anti-Semitism which was normal to his class and generation'. *John Maynard Keynes: A Biography* i, *Hopes Betrayed 1883–1920* (London, 1983), 360.

4 Victoria Mary ('Vita') Sackville-West (1892–1962), daughter of Lionel Sackville-West, 3rd Baron Sackville; wife of Harold Nicolson; mother of IB's friend Ben Nicolson; poet, novelist, short-story writer and biographer.

5 Philip Albert Gustave David Sassoon (1888–1939), 3rd Bt 1912, GBE 1922, Unionist politician,

thing to do with the way England was governed).[1] In short, it is a kind of club anti-Semitism, but it is not a deep, acute hostility to Jews, as in the case of, say, Hilaire Belloc or Chesterton or, some would say, though I have no evidence of it myself, Kipling or Henry James, which went beyond social disdain or looking down on Jews as somewhat inferior people, vulgar, obsequious, aggressive etc. etc., which has been said against them, quite apart from greed, dishonesty and so on. No doubt all forms of anti-Jewish feeling derive from common roots, but in the case of Keynes it was at once genuine and superficial.

You mention Richard Kahn,[2] who worked with Keynes and was a devoted follower and much admired by Keynes. Kahn was a true friend to him, and promoted his interests in every way; nevertheless, I remember being told at King's College, of which both were fellows, that he sometimes said (of Kahn) 'my little Jew' – half affectionately but half contemptuously, I fear. You must remember that unfriendly feeling for the Jews is centuries old, whatever the cause (which I suspect to be ultimately the Christian Gospels); that if you ask who, even in the nineteenth century in civilised society, showed a positive attitude towards the Jews they met or wrote or spoke about, very few names come to mind. George Eliot was notorious for liking them; Dickens has a famous Jew villain, and then to make up for it creates a kind of half-hero in another novel;[3] Trollope has at least one noble Jew and several Jewish villains;[4] and so on and so forth. They are felt to be in some sense outsiders, not quite acceptable – with exceptions. Leonard Woolf and Arthur Waley[5] (the Chinese and Japanese expert) were fully received in Bloomsbury, as real members of the group and personal friends. One or two Jewish judges who

government minister and art collector; trustee, National Gallery 1921–8, Wallace Collection, Tate Gallery and British School at Rome 1929–39.

1 'Here my attention was drawn by a young Oriental, subtle and charming and not quite sure of his ground. I complimented him in flowery words. He winced, he disclaimed all knowledge of the East. [...] I ought to have looked first at the clothes. They were slightly horsey and wholly English, and they put mine to shame. Why had he come from Tabriz, or wherever it was, and put them on? Why take the long journey from Samarcand for the purpose of directing our aeroplanes and denouncing our Socialists?' E. M. Forster, 'Me, Them, and You: Sargent at the Royal Academy', New Leader, 22 January 1926, 3.

2 Richard Ferdinand Kahn (1905–89), life peer 1965; fellow, King's, Cambridge, 1930–89, First (i.e. principal) Bursar 1946–51; prof. of economics, Cambridge, 1951–72.

3 Fagin in Oliver Twist (London, 1838) and Riah in Our Mutual Friend (London, 1865).

4 Anthony Trollope (1815–82), novelist, famous for his 'Barsetshire' and 'Palliser' novels; drew on Victorian stereotypes of Jews for some of his characters, for example the rapacious moneylender Jabesh M'Ruen in his comic novel The Three Clerks (London, 1858); but he also satirised anti-Semitism, and in Ezekiel Brehgert, the Jewish banker in The Way We Live Now (London, 1875), evoked a man more noble than the upper-class Longestaffes who presumed to look down upon him.

5 Arthur David Waley (1889–1966) né Schloss, sinologist and translator of Chinese and Japanese literature; his father, the economist and civil servant David Frederick Schloss, was one of the first Jews to be elected to a college scholarship at Oxford (CCC classics 1869–73).

went to Eton or some other grand pubic school were similarly accepted; but these were to some degree exceptions.

So you are basically right. Keynes did suffer from the prejudices and tastes of his milieu. He greatly admired e.g. Lord Samuel,[1] who served in various Liberal administrations, but nevertheless could certainly bring himself to crack some joke about him in what might be thought doubtful taste – but it was no more than that.

Thank you ever so much again for your very interesting piece.

Yours sincerely,

Isaiah Berlin

TO MORTON WHITE

4 July 1994

Headington House

Dear Morton,

[…] Herbert Hart – I really was devoted to him, as you can see. The story about his going off his head is quite simple. His wife Jenifer was a Communist in the 1930s, indeed became a Soviet agent at some point, although she swears – and I have no reason to doubt her – that she never did anything of a concrete nature, e.g. never reported the secrets in the Civil Service, where she worked. However that may be, an agent she was, and ceased to be some time before the beginning of the war, largely as a result of association with Herbert, who regarded this aspect of her as ridiculous, and must have talked her out of it quite quickly – in those days he was not even a Labour Party supporter, as he became, but a Liberal.

Years later various articles and books began to appear about 'the spies', stimulated mainly by the escape of Burgess and Maclean to the Soviet Union in 1951, the exposure of Philby,[2] later Anthony Blunt, etc. etc. Indirect references, without names, began to be made to Jenifer. MI5 agents must have called on her to ask her for confessions of various kinds, which, I daresay from instincts of loyalty, even though by then she was strongly anti-Communist (and had been since the beginning of the war),[3] she declined to supply. Then, finally, an ex-paying-guest of the Harts who had become a *Sunday Times* journalist telephoned her to say that the BBC was about to produce a programme on the spies, in which she was mentioned, and if she talked to

1 Herbert Louis Samuel (1870–1963), GCB 1926, 1st Viscount Samuel 1937, OM 1958, Liberal states-man; high commissioner, Palestine, 1920–5, Liberal leader, Lords, 1944–55; his ancestors, of German Jewish origin, settled in England in the C18th.

2 In November 1955 Harold Macmillan, then foreign secretary, cleared Philby's name in the Commons, even though MI5 were by then persuaded of his treachery; confronted with evidence of his guilt by British intelligence services January 1963, Philby fled to the USSR at the end of the month.

3 Cf. 215/5.

him and told him the facts, he might be able to avert the worst.[1] What she did not know was that he had a recording instrument, so that everything she said to him on the telephone was recorded, and was used by the journalist in a piece in the *Sunday Times* which said more or less 'nest of spies in Oxford uncovered' – and these were Herbert and Jenifer.

Herbert, as you may imagine, was totally innocent. His loyalty to England, the government, MI5 (where he worked) was total. He was a rigid anti-Communist, anti the spies, from the beginning of the war (when he was first employed by the government). It upset him frightfully. He was already in a rather shaky state, because there was going to be a conference on his work in Jerusalem,[2] he had decided that much of what he had written was obscure, confused, false etc. etc.: how would he defend himself? – all the things which you and I might feel about our past work if it was to be scrutinised by non-friends, or even by fair-minded friends. Anyhow, the Jenifer/ *Sunday Times* business upset him terribly, and he literally went off his head, had to be sent to a psychiatric hospital, was actually given electric shocks – he babbled nonsense during this period, and really was mad. But he recovered.

Poor Jenifer was invited to appear on a TV programme to tell her story.[3] She thought she would stop the rumpus by doing so, but did herself no good by typically candid words ('But when you were a Communist, were you not affected by patriotic feelings?' 'Oh no, patriotism, no, nothing like that, no, I never felt that much ...', etc.). Herbert recovered, was made an Honorary Queen's Counsel (a high legal honour), just to show that he was trusted and admired by the authorities, and towards the end was, as you might say, OK. The fact that he and Jenifer had a motor accident when she was driving did not do him much good. He died in much pain and agony. I have never known a better, more upright, man. [...]

Yours ever, ⟨with much love to Lucia from Aline & me⟩
    Isaiah

TO JOHN GOODWIN[4]
22 July 1994

Headington House

Dear Mr Goodwin,
    Thank you very much for your letter of 20 July. I may have gone a little

---

1 214.
2 A conference on 'The Legal Philosophy of H. L. A. Hart' was held in Jerusalem, on the initiative of the Van Leer Jerusalem Foundation, 13–15 March 1984, and resulted in a book: Ruth Gavison (ed.), *Issues in Contemporary Legal Philosophy: The Influence of H. L. A. Hart* (Oxford, 1987).
3 The *Timewatch* episode mentioned earlier in the letter.
4 John Digby Goodwin (b. 1944), merchant banker, S. G. Warburg, from 1965: executive director 1977–93, vice chair, S. G. Warburg International 1993–95, its successor companies 1995–2000.

too far in describing Geoffrey Dawson[1] as being like a White Russian officer.[2] What I meant to convey is that he seemed to me to be a representative of the most reactionary, uncompromising element in the Conservative
Party – those who wanted to have nothing to do with liberal social policies
of any kind, wanted to defend the Empire at all costs, and were principally
influenced by fear and hatred of the Soviet Union, which was then regarded
as a genuine menace to Britain, the Empire and the West: I think that was
probably the principal motive for appeasement, and not just fear or hatred of
war. I remember that when Salter[3] (by no means a man of the left, although
elected to Parliament by a kind of popular front against the Conservative
candidate for the University, in the middle 1930s – a supporter and ex-official
of the League of Nations) took up an anti-Franco position in Spain, Geoffrey
Dawson, talking to me, pointed a finger at him and said, 'Look at Salter: he
is the man who wants to put weapons in the hands of the rabble in Madrid'
– gentlemen versus rabble was the image, I think. Salter ended up as a brief
minister in Churchill's caretaker government in 1945, so he can hardly be
accused of leftism. But what I said implied a certain brutality on Dawson's
part, and I don't think that was there. All I remember is that in 1938, when
people were digging trenches and getting fitted for gas masks in town halls,
Dawson declined to have anything to do with it, as being politically provocative – presumably to Hitler and Mussolini.

You ask me, what about the opera?[4] I thought that musically it was rather
good; the two ladies seemed to me excellent, though Roocroft[5] seemed
mis-cast as Elvira; but the production seemed to me both ugly and vulgar
– there is no reason why Don Giovanni should be a low-class, or déclassé,

1 (George) Geoffrey Dawson (1874–1944) né Robinson, historian and newspaper editor; fellow, All
  Souls, 1898–1906, 1911–44; editor, Times, 1912–19, 1923–41; for IB, a main architect of appeasement.
2 JG had met IB during the interval of Don Giovanni at Glyndebourne a few days earlier and
  their conversation had turned to Geoffrey Dawson, maternal grandfather to Goodwin's wife.
  Goodwin: 'How well did you know him? Was he a good man or a bad man?' IB: 'I knew him very
  well. Oh, he was a bad man, a bad man. I'm sure he was a good husband and father but definitely
  a bad man. No doubt at all. He reminded me of a White Russian officer – he was that kind of
  reactionary. Mind you, he was always kind to me: he thought I had the same views as him. I've
  always felt rather ashamed of that.' JG to Mark Pottle, 27 November 2014.
3 (James) Arthur Salter (1881–1975), KCB 1922, 1st Baron Salter 1953, civil servant, politician, political theorist; Gladstone Prof. of Political Theory and Institutions, Oxford, and fellow, All Souls,
  1934–44; Independent MP for Oxford University 1937–50; Conservative MP and government minister 1951–3.
4 Deborah Warner's production of Don Giovanni, then in rep at Glyndebourne, proved controversial with the critics, but so too did the loud boos that greeted her curtain call on the opening
  night; these were identified in some reports as coming from the most expensive seats: 'They
  hadn't got dressed up in black tie to see Mozart massacred by some young woman director on
  only her second opera, who thought it clever to put the singers in modern dress on a brutalist
  grey set, then have them jive and fondle a plaster Madonna' (Geraldine Bedell, 'Disturbing the
  Picnic', Independent, 17 July 1994, 17). Don Giovanni's spooning of a statuette of the Virgin Mary
  was perhaps the most provocative element of the staging.
5 Amanda Jane Roocroft (b. 1966), English soprano; professional debut, Cardiff and WNO 1990,
  ROH and Glyndebourne 1991.

cad and bounder. Although he was of course wicked, immoral, cynical etc., he is nevertheless an aristocrat – elegant, grand, impresses everyone by his dash and style, even when he is discovered to be supremely wicked. Nor should Donna Anna and Donna Elvira be dressed like prostitutes, or at any rate rather louche young women. In short, I am on the side of the squares against the 'progressives'. But still, just to show that I am not as square as all that, I once saw a TV *Don Giovanni* where both he and Leporello were drug-pushers:[1] it seemed horrifying at first, but in the end it worked, and I enjoyed it – so there. I am not quite to be lined up with the extreme party of respectability and reaction.

Yours sincerely,

Isaiah Berlin

TO FRED WORMS[2]

10 January 1995

Headington House

Dear Mr Worms,

[…] You ask me about Nahum Goldmann and Mr Hayter. I think I can throw light on all this. Nahum Goldmann was the principal representative of World Zionism in America. From time to time he used to come and see me in the British Embassy, and chatted about the latest policies of the American Zionists, and similar topics. On this occasion, he came in order to say that the official Zionist organisation disapproved of the demonstrations organised by Bergson (the son, or grandson, of the rabbi Kook).[3] Bergson organised something which was known as 'The March of the Rabbis'[4] – marches to

1 The 1990 TV production of Peter Sellars's startlingly modern adaptation of *Don Giovanni*, staged in NY in summer 1989. 'Sellars has become so identified in the United States as the Newest Thing in opera that to protest at his stressed and skewed updatings is to identify oneself as resisting the very century we live in. […] In this particular nightmare world Donna Anna is a heroin addict, Elvira a hysterical punk, and Ottavio a local cop. Occasionally, the Sellars twisting and turnings yield moving results.' David Littlejohn, 'Kitchen Sink Mozart', *Times*, 5 August 1989, 36e–g at 36e.

2 Fred Simon Worms (1920–2012), Frankfurt-born businessman, entrepreneur and philanthropist, emigrated to England 1937; supported many cultural and charitable enterprises in Jerusalem, and was active in the B'nai B'rith Housing Association of Great Britain.

3 Bergson's father was Dov Kook, the 1st chief rabbi of Afula, and his uncle Dov Kook's older brother Abraham Isaac Kook (1865–1935), the 1st Ashkenazi chief rabbi of Mandatory Palestine, and one of the most influential rabbis of the era, a prolific author on the Halakha (560/1) and Jewish thought.

4 Some 500 mostly Orthodox rabbis marched 6 October 1943 from Union Station in Washington to the senate steps of the capitol, where a petition was read aloud to the Vice President, Henry Wallace, calling for 'immediate and practical measures of rescue and [the] use of all possible means to end the murders committed by Nazi criminals'. FDR's absence on this occasion was criticised by the marchers, whose protest was held under the auspices of the 'Emergency Committee to Save the Jewish People of Europe'; Peter Bergson, who was present at the march, was identified in the press as co-chair of this body. Kurt Kelman, 'Wallace Addresses 500 Presenting Petition for Help', *Washington Post*, 7 October 1943, 1; cf. 'Rabbis Present Plea To Wallace', ibid. 14.

Washington to demand the opening of the gates of Palestine, steps towards the rescue of the Jews in the Nazi-occupied territories. He explained that the reason for disapproval was that the Zionist organisation believed in cultivating good relations with important persons in the US government, Congress and other influential bodies. They had had considerable success in this regard by the time he came to see me. He knew that Roosevelt was infuriated by these marches, which denounced the American government, the British government, etc. for their failure to do anything about European Jews. He and the other Zionist leaders took the line that there was nothing which either America or Britain could do to alleviate the state of the Jews – it was clear that the Nazis intended to destroy them in one way or another (I cannot remember whether the crematoria were already known about at this time; I think probably they were),[1] and demonstrations of this kind, while quite natural expressions of indignation and despair, antagonised a good many influential persons whom it was in the interests of Zionism to make allies, in order to secure their help in creating what at this time was known as the 'Jewish Commonwealth' – the word 'state' was never used.

This, in a sense, was reasonable. Of course there was something absolutely awful about the fact that the Jews in America didn't cry out as they could have done about the horrors in Europe. It is true that Roosevelt persuaded Stephen Wise not to spread information about the terrible events, which had been reported by the World Jewish Congress representative in Geneva by the end of 1942 (I think). What arguments the President used I do not know, but Wise was convinced that Jews, and in particular Zionists, had nothing to gain by demonstrations against American authorities, and had something to lose. (The British, of course, talked about the likelihood of this, to excite the Arabs, whose acquiescence the Anglo-Americans needed.) In a sense this was an intelligible policy. What could the British or Americans in fact have done? It was quite clear that the Nazis were determined to exterminate the Jews – they wanted this more than any other single thing. If you remember, in even 1945, by January, February, March, when Soviet troops first entered Auschwitz, and British troops liberated Belsen,[2] such Nazis as were still in charge of camps went on killing Jews. It is clear to me that they

---

1 The existence of gas chambers, though not specifically crematoria, was certainly known. Gas chambers were reported to have been used to kill 30% of the surviving inmates of a small sub-camp of Auschwitz at Mysłowice (a town c.20 km to the north) after an outbreak of typhoid there: 'Poles' Martyrdom: Horrors of Prison in Upper Silesia', Times, 6 March 1943, 3d. A 27 July 1943 report referred to the Majdanek death camp: 'On July 2 and 5 two trains of 30 trucks each, 100 persons to a truck, arrived there. Within a few hours, on each of those days, more than 3,000 people were murdered in the gas chambers. Such executions [...] are taking place every day': 'Massacre in Poland', 3d. The Times reported 1 September 1943 that 6,000 had been murdered in gas chambers at Oświęcim (Auschwitz) in SW Poland,: 'Poland's Martyrdom: Four Years of Nazi Occupation and Terror: A Policy of Extermination', 5f–g.

2 Soviet troops liberated Auschwitz on 27 January 1945; British troops liberated Bergen-Belsen, near Hanover, on 15 April (Anne Frank had died there the previous month).

wanted to kill Jews more than they wanted to win the war – it was the centre of the entire Nazi enterprise, more than any other single objective. Given this, what could the Allied governments have done? Protests were obviously useless; the two minutes' silence which Eden, as Foreign Secretary, asked the House of Commons to observe as an expression of grief and indignation at the persecution of the Jews was no doubt a dignified act, but had no practical significance.[1]

There was a great deal of talk about the need to bomb the trains which carried Jewish victims to the gas ovens.[2] I never myself believed in the utility of this (I think I was in a minority in this view), because if a train was bombed no doubt three hundred Jews and thirty Nazi guards might be killed; but the trains would be rebuilt immediately; the entire policy of bombing traffic in Germany didn't work too well, and in this case the passion to keep the traffic to the camps was for the Nazis overwhelmingly strong, so that I do not see that this could have done much good – as a demonstration, as a piece of symbolic action, perhaps, but whom was it intended to impress? There is no doubt that the state Department was one hundred per cent anti-Zionist – anti-Semitism played its part, of course. The same is true about the Foreign Office. There were, however, three members of the FO known to me who were not anti-Zionist (I knew of no others). They were my friend the late Sir Anthony Rumbold[3] (son of one of the British ambassadors in Berlin at the beginning of the Nazi period);[4] William Hayter (then a First Secretary in the British Embassy in Washington; later, as Sir William Hayter, British ambassador in Moscow, then Warden of New College – and still, like me, alive); and – I cannot remember his name, the Principal Private Secretary to Eden, who later became ambassador in Paris and a peer, and was by way of being a friend of Dr Weizmann.[5] Goldmann wanted me to convey to the relevant officials of the British Embassy that they, the Zionists, were not in favour of the violent demonstrations against the British Embassy, the White House, Congress etc. which were then going on in Washington under the leadership of Bergson (who I think became a member of the Irgun). I duly reported this, and it no doubt gave some satisfaction to the British Embassy (and later the Foreign Office).

You speak as if these demonstrations did something which the silence of Stephen Wise & Co. failed to do. But what was that? I repeat again that it

1 IB variously attributes this gesture to the initiative of Eden or James de Rothschild, but it was William Cluse who suggested it: L3 507/2, 516/2; cf. 451.
2 IB elides the gas chambers used to kill concentration camp victims with the ovens that were used to dispose of their bodies. Cf. 504.
3 (Horace) Anthony Claude ('Tony') Rumbold (1911–83), KCMG 1962, diplomat, Washington, 1937–42.
4 Horace George Montagu Rumbold (1869–1941), 9th Bt 1913, KCMG 1917, diplomat; UK ambassador to Germany 1928–33; Anthony Rumbold was his nephew, not his son.
5 Pierson John ('Bob') Dixon (1904–65), KCMG 1950; PPS to foreign secretary 1943–8; permanent UK representative, UN, 1954–60; UK ambassador to France 1960–4; not a peer.

was shameful that there was no great cry of horror by the Jews. It might have done no good, but at least it would have been testimony to what was felt – but the practical consequences, I do believe, would have been zero. Hayter told me that he fully understood what the feelings of Jews must be about the horrors then going on in the Germany-occupied lands, and that he deeply sympathised; but that he did not know what either the British officials in America, or indeed Congress or the government, could in practice do. Roosevelt, I think, was rather hard-hearted about the whole thing, and not the warm ally of Jews and Zionism which the American Jews fondly believed him to be. His last policies before he died were not favourable to the Zionist cause – as those of Truman were.[1] The most interesting thing that Goldmann ever told me was that there was a secret cabinet committee which by 1944 had decided on the partition of Palestine between Jews and Arabs, and that this was to be kept secret until the end of the war. But that is another story, which I will be glad to tell you if and when we meet.

With my best wishes,
Yours ever,
Isaiah B.

TO ANDRZEJ WALICKI

13 February 1995

Headington House

Dear Andrzej,

[...] I fully understand why you do not wish to return to Poland. I have no doubt that you would be enormously admired and flattered there, and regarded as an object of great national pride; but the pressures upon you would be considerable. Every time you spoke it would either be too much or not enough for some people; everything you said would be followed with too much concentrated attention, both by allies and by opponents – and in those conditions it is very difficult to write. [...] I remember once when I was offered a job in the Israeli Foreign Ministry (in about 1948, to be head of some department, with all kinds of prospects of advancement), and I knew then that, Zionist as I have always been, and happy as I was at the emergence of the state of Israel (even in the very different conditions in which it was born, both morally and materially) – I knew it was no good my going there, that

---

1 FDR paid increasing attention to Arab opinion in the latter stages of WW2, as exemplified by his meeting with Ibn Saud, king of Saudi Arabia, on board the USS Quincy, 14 February 1945. The assurances that FDR there gave on Palestine were reiterated in a letter 5 April 1945, in which FDR renewed his promise to 'take no action [...] which might prove hostile to the Arab people': 'Attitude of American Government toward Palestine', Department of State Bulletin 13 no. 330 (21 October 1945), 623. Truman, by contrast, backed substantial and immediate Jewish immigration into Palestine from Europe after the war, and was prepared to put pressure on the British government to achieve this end.

I would sooner or later, and probably sooner, be torn to pieces by contending parties, and would be completely frustrated and made totally impotent. I am not by nature ambitious, and do not think well of my own powers, but such as they are I thought that if something was to be made of myself it could not be done in that cauldron, which was inevitably destined to be such. And there is something cauldronish in Poland too, and likely to continue, and in a way for much the same reasons – the lack of political balance in the character of the nation. Dr Weizmann once said to me, 'The Jews are not a political nation: sooner or later they will tear each other to pieces.' I hope this is not so, but the possibility – both in Poland and in Israel, and a number of other ex-colonial countries, so to speak – exists. [...]

You and Kołakowski between you have performed a work of analysis, dissection, judgement on Marxism and its predecessors – and in your case liberalism and [...] legalism as well – which is second to none. If I were a young Russian, or even a young Frenchman, only recently in the clutches of French existentialist or 'scientific' Marxism, I would spend my time in reading nobody but him and you. You could add pinches from my scattered essays, and between us we really could account for a good deal. I do not think this is exaggerated; I think it really about right. But I do not know that the intellectual world realises it, or ever will; still, we have done our work and have nothing to be ashamed of. Far less, for example, than my poor friend Nathan Rotenstreich[1] in Israel, who has written no fewer than forty-five books, none of any value whatever; or, as Roman Jakobson once said to me about the Czechs, 'There are at least two hundred Czech novels in the nineteenth and early twentieth century, none of any value at all.' Hegel once said that quantity changes into quality[2] – it is one of the least true things which even that not very dependable thinker ever said. I genuinely feel sorry (though not very much so) for those energetic and eloquent Marxists who dominated the scene for so long – outside France, I mean – like Hobsbawm, Perry Anderson,[3] Christopher Hill, Deutscher. Deutscher died before the final disillusionment, but the others continue writing out of vanity, respect for their own, sometimes considerable, abilities, the need to function – but

1 Nathan Rotenstreich (1914–93), Galician-born Israeli philosopher; senior lecturer in philosophy, HUJ, 1950–5, prof. 1955–82; dean, faculty of humanities, 1958–62, rector, HUJ, 1965–9; published prolifically.

2 In the section on 'measure' in the *Encyclopedia of the Philosophical Sciences* (1817 etc.), §111, Hegel writes: '[Quality and quantity] have passed over, quality into quantity, and quantity into quality.' In the editorial additions to §108 taken from his lectures he gives the examples of water turning into ice or steam as a result of quantitative changes of temperature, and of the political constitution of a state changing if its population and/or size grows sufficiently. *The Logic of Hegel: Translated from the Encyclopaedia of the Philosophical Sciences*, ed. and trans. William Wallace (Oxford, 1874), 176, 173–4.

3 Francis Rory Peregrine ('Perry') Anderson (b. 1938), British Trotskyite and public intellectual; editor, *New Left Review*, 1962–82 (and 2000–3); taught at Cornell, and at the New School for Social Research, NY; latterly prof. of sociology and history (now Distinguished Prof.), UCLA.

the spirit is not the same. As a Russian diplomat whom I met in Washington in 1940 said to me, when I asked what he was doing, 'Il faut circuler, Monsieur, il faut circuler.'[1] You and I are not circulators, and so much the better.

With all my affection and respect,

Yours,

Isaiah

TO KYRIL TIDMARSH[2]

20 February 1995

Headington House

Dear Kyril,

Thank you both for your letter and for your pamphlet.[3] I am sure you are absolutely right. The Russian peasants never were particularly enterprising, and they were, no doubt, a cowed collection of serfs who took some time to recover after emancipation. But there is no doubt that by the time of the great economic surge forward of the Russian economy – in the 1890s and the beginning of our century – something had happened; and you remember that Lenin said 'If Stolypin[4] goes on like this, our cause is lost'[5] – because Stolypin was creating, as you know, these independent farmers, and gradually dissolving the *mir*.[6] Then came the Russo-Japanese war, when things went down again – and then the Soviet regime.

Your article about that seems admirable to me – it is clear why these people became flattened out, dispirited, discouraged, dishonest, malingering. And no possible economy can be built on that base. So what is to happen now? At the top a lot of powerful crooks and adventurers and self-made millionaires (self-made by criminal activity); at the bottom, peasants poorer than they were during the worst parts of previous centuries. The gap is bigger than even in Italy or Latin America. Obviously nobody knows what to do. You do have a few optimistic remarks, about the fact that, if the West helps as it is doing, this can be overcome. I wonder. If not, I have an awful feeling, which I hope is mistaken, that some kind of hierarchical command economy will be established again – not Marxist, Communist, but simply a lot of authoritarian persons reorganising the mob below – rather like south-east Asians

---

1 'One must circulate, Sir, one must circulate.'
2 Kyril Ralph Tidmarsh (b. 1931), Russianist and administrator; Nuffield politics DPhil 1956, supervised by IB and E. H. Carr; Moscow correspondent, *Times*, 1965–9; International Labour Organization 1969–93.
3 Presumably his 'Russia's Work Ethic', *Foreign Affairs* 72 no. 2 (Spring 1993), 67–77.
4 Petr Arkad'evich Stolypin (1862–1911), prime minister, Russia, 1906–11; ruthlessly punished the 1905 Revolutionaries but introduced agrarian reforms that improved the legal status and living conditions of the peasantry; remembered as the last effective tsarist statesman, he was assassinated in a Kiev theatre.
5 Usually cited as 'If Stolypin continues ruling, there's no point in a revolution.'
6 A peasant commune in imperial Russia.

and indeed the Chinese, a kind of centralised, authoritarian, capitalist dictatorship. Or is that impossible?

Anyway, thank you ever so much for sending me this deeply depressing piece. I was delighted to see you, I do hope we shall meet again before I am completely gone. It must be twenty years since we have seen each other. Don't let that happen again – come and see me, do, if you feel inclined; I should be delighted to see you and have a long talk about everything in the world.

Yours ever,
Isaiah

TO TEDDY KOLLEK

22 February 1995 [carbon]

Headington House

Dear Teddy,

Here are some notes on Jerusalem.[1]

1. City holy to three faiths.

2. Nevertheless, unique to the Jews – Christians have Rome. All three faiths call it 'the Holy Land', but to the Jews it was the centre of their lives for three thousand years, and every prayer and every secular movement towards the restoration of the destroyed Jewish state speaks of Jerusalem as the heart and centre of what their religion means to them.

3. Of course the Crusades occurred, but they were duly defeated, and after that I do not know of any Christian pilgrims who went to the Holy Land in order to settle there as their natural, historic home, whereas Jews did, e.g. Yehuda Halevi,[2] Rabbi Isaac Luria[3] etc. in the late Middle Ages and the Renaissance – which shows a bond which I do not think, emotionally or politically, existed for either the Christians or the Muslims. Mecca and Medina are the great Muslim sites. Of course Jerusalem is a holy place to them, but one of three, not unique.

4. The idea of internationalisation, put forward both by the Vatican and by UN Commissions, was natural enough, in order not to reward one religious community at the expense of the others. The motive is clear, the idea might

---

1 Kollek had asked IB (5 February 1995) for 'a few sentences' on the unique status of Jerusalem for Jews, in advance of the city's trimillennium 1996. He understood IB's 'uneasiness about marking the anniversary', but observed: 'As the peace process progresses, we come closer to the day that Jerusalem will become part of the negotiations. I am very concerned that world opinion may not be in our favour.'

2 Yehuda Halevi (c.1075–1141), Spanish Jewish poet and religious philosopher; in his later years he resolved to settle in the land of Israel, his yearning for which was a poignant feature of his verse; he duly left Spain, but died en route to Egypt.

3 Isaac Luria Ashkenazi (1534–72), Jewish mystic and founder of the Lurianic Kabbalah; probably born in Jerusalem, he was raised in Egypt, but settled in Safed, Galilee, c.1570.

have something in it, but it is clear that every city governed in this way in the end collapses. Free cities can flourish in countries where the citizens are of the same culture and nationality as the rest of the country in which they are situated, e.g. in Germany, Russia etc., but these are not internationally controlled – I am thinking of the fate of Danzig and Memel, which flourished when they were German and to some degree when they became Polish and Lithuanian, but never under international rule. Occupied Berlin, occupied Vienna, the Saar, the Ruhr could not have gone on indefinitely being un-self-governing. Unless Jerusalem becomes directly occupied and governed by, say, the Vatican – which nobody has suggested (I hope) – the idea of international control cannot possibly succeed.

5. After all, when the Byzantine Empire fell and the Turks occupied Palestine and governed Jerusalem, nobody seemed to display indignation or desire to oust them – the Crusades were regarded as an episode of the medieval past. Why should Israeli rule be regarded as more offensive by – I do not say the Arabs, who of course mind – but by the rest of the world, than Turkish rule (which was for half a millennium)? The Turks did not interfere in any way with the holy sites, Catholic or those of the Orthodox Church, or, indeed, Jewish. Of course Israel will have to behave similarly, and fanatics will have to be restrained (it doesn't look like this at present, does it?). But provided guarantees backed by police powers were given, and effective resistance to rabbinical ambitions were established, this would be the least contentious solution.

I can't think of anything else to say, but I could expand all these points. Is there anything else? It doesn't seem a very convincing document to me: if I was a Monsignor in Rome, or an Imam in Pakistan, or a Bishop in England or Germany, I would feel uncomfortable about this. Is it necessary to produce this argument at all, given that it is bound to be criticised, and indeed attacked? The alternative is simply a noble piece about the part Jerusalem has played in Jewish life from the beginning – and that could be produced much better by some head of Hebrew studies at Harvard or Columbia (above all, not liberal rabbis or Zionist officials) than it would be by me. It has to be produced with deep historical and religious feeling, of a kind likely to touch non-Jewish hearts; and I am not really capable of dignified emotionalism of this kind. Indeed, I know of nobody in England who could do it well – for this purpose we need a Buber[1] or a Namier. I feel too self-conscious about the whole thing to be able to do it well. It needs someone with a gift for political eloquence, and deep spiritual feeling – which I don't think I possess. I am by nature

---

1 Martin Buber (1878–1965), Vienna-born Jewish theologian, philosopher and acclaimed translator of the Bible into German; embraced Hasidism; wrote on the relationship between man and God, influencing modern Christian as well as Jewish theology; emigrated to Palestine 1938, where he advocated a bi-national Arab–Jewish state, and taught anthropology and sociology at HUJ.

too sceptical, too secular, too unpolitical, even, to do this job. Do you not agree?

Yours ever,

[Isaiah]

[...]

The impossible dilemmas and awful responsibilities faced by members of the Judenräte in Nazi-occupied Europe were epitomised in the life and death of the Hungarian Jew Rudolf Kastner.[1] *Kastner assisted in the escape of Jewish refugees to Hungary from other parts of occupied Europe, and after the Nazi occupation of Hungary in March 1944 he enabled refugees to escape from Hungary itself, negotiating with Adolf Eichmann the safe passage to Switzerland of more than 1,600 Jews (the so-called Kastner train), including members of his own family, in return for cash, gold and diamonds. Although by then aware of the Nazis' extermination policy, he is alleged not to have shared that information, and later stood accused of abandoning the many to save the few.*

Kastner emigrated to Israel in 1947, becoming a government civil servant and Mapai activist, but in 1953 a radical pamphleteer accused him of being a Nazi collaborator. The government sued for libel on Kastner's behalf, but on 22 June 1955 the district court of Jerusalem found him guilty on several counts. That verdict was mostly overturned by a majority in the Supreme Court in January 1958, but by then Kastner was dead, fatally wounded on 4 March 1957 in a gun attack in Tel Aviv by nationalist extremists.

IB was deeply interested in the unusual ethical implications, as well as the human dimension, of Kastner's sad plight, and in March 1995 he used it in an epistolary exchange with the philosopher Jonathan Dancy to illustrate his belief, pace Hannah Arendt, that posterity does not always have the right to judge. The agonising moral quandaries in which the Judenräte found themselves were, for him, not amenable to clear-cut solutions, let alone ones theoretically derived, but could be addressed only by profoundly unsatisfactory compromises, always entailing terrible wrongs, and arrived at in extreme circumstances with which later commentators could scarely begin to empathise.

TO JONATHAN DANCY[2]

28 March 1995 [*carbon*]

[Headington House]

Dear Dancy,

Thank you for your letter about the conflict of values. I am afraid that

1 (Israel) Rudolf Kastner (1906–57), also known as Rezső Kasztner, journalist and lawyer; from 1952 a spokesman in Israel's ministry of trade and industry.

2 Jonathan Peter Dancy (b. 1946), philosopher; lecturer, Keele, 1971–87, senior lecturer 1987–9, reader 1989–91, prof. 1991–6; prof. of philosophy, Reading, 1996–2004.

your account of my views is somewhat at variance with what I believe myself to hold. Let me begin.

You speak of an 'anecdote' as being a 'refreshing change'. The story I tell is so horrible that there is something totally inappropriate in calling it an 'anecdote'. You say that I tell it as a true story, which implies that though I tell it so it may not be – but I can assure you that the trials in Tel Aviv have revealed the full horrible story in all its gruesome details. So the story is true and not merely, as you take it to be, an example of an extreme case of the conflict of what you call disvalues.[1] Before we get on to the substance of this letter, let me continue a little with the 'anecdote'. You say that the Gestapo chief tells the Jewish leader that the Jews are to be transported 'somewhere where their chances of survival are not good'. By this time the Jews of Hungary, where this episode occurred (as well as many similar ones in other countries), knew perfectly well where people were being transported to: the news about the gas ovens[2] was by this time widely known even in the West. So it is very likely that this phrase describes what was known. [...]

I ought to add that this story is not, for me, a case of a conflict of 'disvalues', but [of] quite a different paradigm. My point when telling this story is that there are situations so extreme, and indeed appalling, that ordinary moral categories are not fitted to cope with such cases; and that therefore the attempt to judge the conduct of the Hungarian Jewish leader as being right or wrong does not arise. We are in no position to pass judgement on behaviour in a situation so unspeakable; ordinary moral criteria do not apply to situations so far outside the range of normal experience. I said all this because I was against Hannah Arendt, and others like her, who criticised German, Hungarian etc. Jews for not standing up more to the Nazis, and letting themselves be taken like sheep to the slaughter. This seemed to me not only wildly unrealistic, but a piece of inexcusable arrogance on the part of people living in safety, daring to dictate what people in that situation should or should not have done. No doubt there are religious doctrines or ideologies which do dictate a clear answer to this kind of dilemma: but if they exist, I do not share them. I am concerned [with] the normal ethical views of the great majority of mankind, in many times and places.

[...] You speak of adopting certain values or disvalues. But this is not a realistic piece of moral psychology. We simply find that these values are such that we can, being what we are and [believing] what we believe, live our lives by them. I do not believe that we 'adopt' values, as if a variety of them were offered to us in some ethical shop window, and we decide on reflection that we propose to try and realise no. 3 or no. 7. We are born with certain values as a result of all the forces that create us – tradition, education, the

1 The opposite of values, i.e. outcomes to avoid.
2 See 497/2.

views of the people we live among, the books we read, our own thoughts, etc. etc. Of course we can reject any of them, and of course we can imagine different ones – the latter must be true of the first people to conceive Jewish, Christian or Muslim, or Communist or Fascist, values, or the first aesthetes, or pacifists or internationalists or whatever. Novelty occurs. 'Adoption' is too weak a word for what I mean; where people are converted to a set of values, they do not simply 'adopt' – nor yet when they pursue conventional or traditional values at the cost of their lives.

It would be idle to ask a normal person 'When exactly did you adopt your outlook?' We begin with some kind of constellation of values and disvalues, some kind of outlook, and can alter it as a result of thought or imagination, or some shock of recognition or crisis in our or other people's lives. This is not selection or adoption: we live our lives in the light of a constellation of values, perhaps uncritically accepted (but not 'adopted'), or perhaps critically – emerging as a result of reflection or self-criticism or the like. You speak as if we simply decide to choose this or that value out of those available to us, and this is surely psychologically not true. If you go to a wise friend for advice on which of two conflicting values to realise, in what does his wisdom consist? Not in knowing more facts than you do (which may or may not be so), nor because he is a specialist in values (whatever that may mean – not much to me), but because he is capable of showing you [that] value X is much more like the horizon of your existing values, of life as you wish to live it, than is value Y. He points out that following value X is likely to lead to consequences which [do] not collide with something you seek – or collide less than if you realise value Y. [...]

Yours,

[Isaiah Berlin]

TO JONATHAN DANCY

25 April 1995 [carbon]

[Headington House]

Dear Dancy,

[...] You ask me whether it makes any philosophical difference if the story I told is truth or fiction. I do tell it as truth, but I do not think that is essential. I do not think philosophy need concern itself with empirical facts: examples is all it needs, and therefore fiction is quite sufficient. As you rightly say, all that the actual truth can do is to throw light on how human beings can behave, and in fact did behave – and that, no doubt, is relevant to such moral psychology as we inevitably bring into moral discussion. The fact that what happened was so horrible I do not think is relevant, at any rate to the topic we are discussing.

[...] You ask the very interesting question (particularly interesting to me) about what is the difference between recognising values and committing oneself to them. I certainly think there is a vast difference. Anyone who reads biographies or histories must know that other persons in other situations at other times and places pursue certain values – avoid certain courses of action – which one can understand, that is, recognise as genuine human values, the kind of values the pursuit of which does not dehumanise people. Of course, I can take the position that I commit myself to none of these, although I can intuitively enter into what it is like to pursue them – and to that extent I can display a certain sympathy for values which may be repellent to me personally. That is my case for what I call moral pluralism – where one recognises values (to which one does not commit oneself) as true values, but not values for me [...]. Indeed, I can go so far as to admire a culture which pursues values which I recognise as values though they are emphatically not mine – the values of the Homeric world, of the Italian Renaissance, etc. You see what I mean? [...]

Now let me offer you a *bonne bouche* of a case where whatever you do may be to some extent morally wrong (again, this is a true story, though it doesn't need to be). I was told by a British Intelligence officer that towards the end of the war he went to see a French Resistance unit which had captured a French traitor who had worked for the Gestapo. He wished to interrogate him, and the Resistance people said, 'Certainly you can interrogate him as much as you wish, but whatever happens he dies tomorrow morning. That is a decision which, no matter what the result of your conversation may be, we shall not change.' The British officer goes to interrogate the young traitor, probably eighteen or nineteen years old, in order to find out facts which may enable him to save victims of the Gestapo. The young man says, 'Why should I talk to you? If you can guarantee that I shall not be executed, then I will talk; but if you cannot, why should I?' What should the British officer have done? He did not tell me what he had done. But it was clear to me that he was troubled by the thought that if he had obeyed his duty as an intelligence officer, and indeed perhaps his duty as a human being, he would perhaps have promised the young man that he would be spared (in order to get the information which might save lives). But if he did that – and perhaps he did – then he would realise that the last thought on the part of the young traitor was that he had been lied to. I don't know what he did – I had the impression that he did lie, telling the young man that he would be spared, and for the rest of his life was troubled by the thought of the young man's last minutes. If he had chosen otherwise he might have been more troubled by the thought of having failed to obtain life-saving information. It may be clear what one should do, but if he was a sensitive human being he would never say to himself afterwards, 'I did what was right. I have no remorse. I would do it again if I had to.' That is just to indicate tragic possibilities of a rather different kind. [...]

Yours sincerely,
    [Isaiah Berlin]

TO MICHAEL IGNATIEFF

22 May 1995

Headington House

Dear Michael,

[...] I enjoyed the inquisition and am glad that everyone was happy.[1]

I have decided to relent. Do you think if I said at the age of ninety or death, whichever is the earlier?[2] I cannot believe that I shall mind anything being done about me if I am ninety, so I think I shall write in those terms. But I may regret it.

One more thing. If, in the course of all this, not a word is said about my marriage to Aline, she will take that very hard, I know. I don't think I need go over the story of my courtship and the agonies of the divorce (preceding it, I mean), the early years with stepchildren, etc. etc. Presumably the TV cannot be altered – no postscripts possible, for the whole *équipe*[3] would have to come back here: obviously out of the question. Could you, if you make an introduction to the programme, say something about falling in love (1941), courtship (begins in 1952), difficulties and obstacles made by her then husband, Professor Hans Halban,[4] the happy solution (1956), and happiness for ever after – Darby and Joan?[5] Some liability to *amitiés amoureuses*,[6] only mildly resented, no effect upon continuously happy family life – and my surprise and gratification at such wonderful good fortune, encountered not so very often, perhaps due to my late marriage, or just to luck. [...]

Yours ever,

Isaiah

TO TATIANA MATSKOVSKY[7]

2 June 1995 [*carbon*]

Headington House

Dear [Tatiana],

[...] This is only to ask you how you and your family are. I am always delighted to receive your letters, and the last one seemed to me to show that

1 MI interviewed IB on camera 15–17 May 1995, and their discussion formed the basis of *Isaiah Berlin*, 2 programmes first broadcast on BBC2 TV 14 and 15 November 1997, subtitled *The Making of a Hedgehog* and *Freedom and Its Enemies*. See plate 36.
2 IB had originally agreed to these interviews only on condition that the result would not be screened in his lifetime.
3 'Crew'.
4 Hans Heinrich *Halban (1908–64) né von Halban, nuclear physicist, Aline Berlin's 2nd husband.
5 A devoted old married couple who first appeared ('Old DARBY with JOAN by his side') in Henry Woodfall's poem *The Joys of Love Never Forgot: A Song* in the *Gentleman's Magazine* 5 (1735), 153.
6 'Romantic friendships'.
7 IB's 1st cousin: daughter of his youngest paternal uncle Samuel Berlin (1897–1988); wife of Alexander Matskovsky.

things were getting on not too badly. I am sure you are careful not to ask for anything, complain about anything, criticise anyone or anything – but perhaps you go too far in that direction. If you do need something, it would be a pleasure to me to do it for you if I possibly can – after all, I am very old, I have very few relations left, and you are among the closest. So don't hesitate to let me know.

What can I tell you? I have just received a book called something like *The Slaves of the Red Pharaoh: The Last Ten Years of Stalin's Life*,[1] in which there is a fantastic account from the KGB papers (which the author collected from all over the place), reporting that I was at the centre of a spy ring in Moscow in 1945 (when I served in the British Embassy), and that the other members of the ring were my uncle Lev Berlin[2] – the professor – who was one of the nicest men in the world; also my father in London; and a mysterious figure called Pevsner.[3] I think the secrets came from Lev Borisovich; they were passed on, presumably, to me, from me to my father, from my father to Pevsner. It is not specified what this secret information was or what Mr Pevsner was supposed to do with [it]. Naturally the whole thing is a fantastic web of lies. Nobody more unpolitical or innocent than my father ever lived; as for me, being at the embassy I was of course automatically regarded as a secret agent, as all foreigners were, particularly in Stalin's last terrible years. No doubt that is what poor Leva was made to confess when he was arrested. According to this book he was tortured three times but did not break. Then they applied some new, unheard-of torture, which nobody could bear: that did break him, and he talked (I can imagine that all he did was to sign some fantastic collection of false and ridiculous statements). I did not realise that he had actually been tortured in the camp; but now I realise how he came to die – this, I think, is your story – when he saw his 'examiner', or maybe torturer too, walking on the opposite pavement of the street. I think you

1 G[ennady Vasil'evich] Kostyrchenko, *V plenu u krasnogo faraona: politicheskie presledovaniya evreev v SSSR v poslednee stalinskoe desyatiletie – dokumental'noe issledovanie* [*Imprisoned by the Red Pharaoh: The Political Persecution of Jews in the USSR in Stalin's Last Decade – A Documentary Study*] (Moscow, 1994); translated as Gennadi Kostyrchenko, *Out of the Red Shadows: Anti-Semitism in Stalin's Russia* (Amherst, NY, 1995). The section on IB is at 331–2 in the original, 282–3 in the translation.
2 Lev/Leo Borisovich Berlin (1897–1955), IB's uncle, a younger brother of his father Mendel; prof. of dietetics, Moscow. The 3 February 1954 resolution of the ministry of internal affairs releasing Lev has him confessing 7 March 1952 that IB, 'when he met with me and my brothers […] and other relatives, expressed hostile fabrications about the USSR, strongly criticised Soviet reality, and slandered the policy of the CPSU and the Soviet government': 'Postanovlenie MVD SSSR ob osvobozhdenii L. B. Berlina, byvshego zaveduyushchego otdeleniem kliniki lechebnogo pitaniya', in G. V. Kostyrchenko, *Gosudarstvennyi antisemitizm v SSSR ot nachala do kulminatsii: 1938–1953* (Moscow, 2005), 442–8 at 444.
3 Manuil Isaakovich Pevsner (1872–1952), gasteroenterologist; director, dept of digestive diseases and clinical nutrition, USSR Academy of Medical Sciences, 1930–52; head, dept of clinical nutrition, 1932–52; board member, *Terapevticheskii arkhiv* [*Therapeutic Archive*] (journal).

told me that he saw him, had a heart attack, and subsequently died not long after.[1]

I wonder if this would have happened if I had not so unwisely called on him and his family in 1945. I think this was an act of great folly on my part – I did not realise how dangerous it was. It took some years to produce its terrible result. Maybe he would have been arrested anyway, with the other Jewish doctors – who can tell? But it is an awful story.

I am so glad that you are in Israel. Anything might have happened to you in the ex-Soviet-Union. I remember thinking when I was at the embassy: Supposing one day somebody came to see me and said 'You were born a subject of his late Imperial Majesty Nicholas II, therefore you became a Soviet citizen automatically at the end of 1917; you only left Petrograd in 1920. You are therefore our subject, our citizen, so you are to stay here and do what we tell you.' I was a naturalised British subject, and I think there is a paragraph which says that the country which adopts you can defend you everywhere except in the country of your origin; so legally they would have been able to arrest me. I daresay that because I was at the embassy, efforts would have been made to liberate me, so my danger was not really very great; but it came to me as a kind of nightmare. I asked myself: Supposing this happened, what would I do? And I said to myself, 'I am not very brave; still, rather than work with them, I would shoot myself.' My hatred of the regime in 1945 – if one knows the language, one sees what goes on – was so deep that the very idea of serving such people would have been more than even I, weak as I am in some ways, could have borne.

On this absurdly melodramatic note I end my letter. Do write again.

Yours ever,

Isaiah

TO NATASHA SPENDER

1 August 1995 [*carbon*]

Headington House

Dearest Natasha;

When we met after Stephen's funeral, I apologised for not having written to you.[2] There seemed to me too much to say and I can only try to make up for not writing to you immediately by this probably quite long letter about Stephen, in particular the part he played in my life, and the part that, I think, I played in his. In the course of our long lives (both born in the same year) we each had many friends and acquaintances, but our deep friendship was,

1 Cf. L3 341/1.
2 Stephen Spender died of heart failure 16 July 1995; he was cremated, and his ashes buried 21 July at St Mary's, Paddington Green.

I believe, a unique ingredient of both our lives, and never faltered, whether we saw each other or not.

We were divided by the war – he was in London, I in Washington – but when I came back it was exactly as it had been before, and so remained to the end. I think I first met him in Oxford late in 1929, or very early in 1930. I think the man who introduced me to him was my friend Bernard Spencer, a very nice, gentle, charming man, a good minor poet, who knew Stephen before I did. By that time the golden period of Oxford aestheticism was over: Harold Acton,[3] Brian Howard,[4] Cyril Connolly, Auden, Betjeman, Evelyn Waugh had all gone down. The dominant figure was Louis MacNeice, whom I did not know, and never – after I met him – entirely liked. Stephen knew him and tried to persuade us to feel sympathetic to each other, but it never worked, either way. Be that as it may, my first impression of Stephen was, as it remained, of a wonderfully handsome, friendly, open, gifted, disarmingly innocent, generous man, irresistibly attractive to meet and to know – indeed I remember vividly the sheer pride with which I could claim his acquaintance at that early period. I saw him in Oxford from time to time. He read his poetry to me: I think his early verse, of those days, is among the best he wrote. We used occasionally to go for walks in Christ Church Meadow or the University Parks. I was, as during the rest of our lives, uniquely exhilarated by contact with him, and became devoted to him very soon indeed – and he, on his side, seemed to like me well enough to invite me to go and see him in London after he went down.

I remember well his comical accounts of his academic life – the boring tutorials with his philosophy tutor E. F. Carritt[5] – according to him, after Stephen read his essay he would take out some notes, look through them, quote one or two things based on them, then say 'That pretty well covers the field', at which Stephen bowed, and left. What happened to the politics and economics tutorials I have no idea: he never mentioned them.

He was extremely popular as an undergraduate. That is to say, he was equally happy in the company of aesthetes, contributors to the *Oxford Outlook* (of which I became editor), and rowing men, footballers and the like: they all fell under the spell of his great charm. In that respect, if in no other, he was unique – the gap between the 'aesthetes' and the 'hearties' was pretty wide at that time, and he alone, so far as I could tell, bridged it easily,

---

3 Harold Mario Mitchell Acton (1904–94), Kt 1974, art historian, aesthete, poet and novelist; Christ Church 1922–6, graduating with a fourth in modern languages; inherited the villa La Pietra, Florence (where he was born and died), from his mother 1962.

4 Brian Christian de Claiborne Howard (1905–58), aesthete, hedonist, poet and occasional contributor to the *New Statesman*; of American Jewish descent, he was one of the leading figures of his generation at Eton and Oxford: 'Exotically handsome, after the manner of a Disraeli hero, rich, brilliant in conversation, and endowed with great physical courage': 'Mr Brian Howard', obituary, *Times*, 24 January 1958, 11f.

5 Edgar Frederick Carritt (1876–1964), lecturer in philosophy, Oxford, and fellow, Univ., 1900–45.

unselfconsciously (and very happily – he liked liking even more than being liked).

Then I remember, before he went down (I don't think he knew that he had not done well in his final examination), he asked his friends to come and see him in his rooms in St John Street – no. 53,[1] I seem to remember. He told them that they could take with them anything that they found there – desks, chairs, tables, clothes, books, manuscripts, whatever there was: it was a general distribution of all his worldly goods. I remember Richard Crossman walking off with a book of manuscripts of Stephen's poems. As for me, I think he gave me a book: I cannot remember what it was, I think a book of his early poems, inscribed 'To Isaiah, this book made valuable by the author', i.e. by bearing his signature. This sounds vain, but he was not given to any kind of vanity: he was neither modest nor vain, he was perfectly natural in all situations – he knew his own value, he did not exaggerate it, but neither did he underestimate it. And his comments on other writers – both senior to him, and influential, like T. S. Eliot, or his great friend and mentor Wystan, as well as later contemporaries, writers and artists of various kinds – were remarkably penetrating and sometimes devastating. Writers he reviewed and people he met sometimes took offence; yet in a sense he was more vulnerable than the people he saw through.

In spite of wearing an air of a certain solemnity – in later life people thought of him, very falsely, as solemn, humourless, earnest, dreary – he was in fact sharply observant. His books of criticism, for example *The Destructive Element*,[2] and his later ones too, are remarkably original and striking, and above all penetrating; just as his comments about people were often very funny, almost always entirely valid, and liable to hit the nail on the head, sometimes with almost too much force – that's what made conversation with him not merely fascinating in general but extremely entertaining and delightful, in the way in which conversation with the very intelligent and observant Auden, or T. S. Eliot (whom I did not know well, but did know), was not. I remember meeting Auden at Stephen's house in Frognal, it must have been about 1934; Auden took violently against me: I was everything that at that time he was against – middle-class, fat, conventional (he felt sure), bourgeois, obviously not homosexual, over-talkative; I met him again only in 1941, in New York, when we made friends and so remained for the rest of our lives.

But to go back to Stephen. Our love of music was an additional bond, particularly the chamber music of Beethoven. As you know, the late 'posthumous' quartets meant a great deal to him (too much, T. S. Eliot said to me,

---

1 In fact no. 63.
2 *The Destructive Element: A Study of Modern Writers and Beliefs* (London, 1935): 'it is good in parts, but sticky, very moralistic & extremely depressing & guilt inducing' (IB to Elizabeth Bowen, 13 March 1935, L1 116).

about Stephen), and that mask of Beethoven to which he wrote a poem[1] came from a book I gave him, I think after he had gone down from Oxford. We both were transported by the performance of Beethoven's sonatas by Artur Schnabel – word from a new world to both of us: we went to every single performance, I think, he ever gave in London. We went to every performance of the Busch Quartet, who were a kind of moral equivalent of Schnabel – they inhabited the same world. We were both great admirers of the conductor Toscanini. Music meant a very, very great deal to us both; we used to talk about it incessantly, and I think neither of us talked about it so often, and with such feeling, with anybody else [...].

Our moderate political views to a large degree coincided. We were both what might be called left of centre – Lib–Lab – typical readers of the *New Statesman*. Stephen was taken up by Bloomsbury, and Harold and Vita Nicolson – I remained remote from them. We were both deeply affected by the hunger marchers,[2] by the Spanish Civil War, as so many of our friends and contemporaries were, by Fascism in Germany, Austria, Spain (for some reason Italy, although of course its regime was disapproved of, was somewhat regarded as more comical than tragic, perhaps wrongly). Stephen was deeply affected by his journey to Spain during the Civil War, to bring back one of his friends who went to fight for Franco, but I rather think deserted and had to be rescued from danger from each side. I remember begging him most earnestly not to join the Communist Party, which I thought was not at all the kind of thing he believed in or would find himself comfortable in. But he insisted – his reason, I remember, was that everything else around us was decayed, soft, too flexible; that Communism was the only firm structure against which one could measure oneself (that was his phrase), and so find oneself, identify one's personality and task in life. As you know, it lasted a very short time, and he rightly removed himself from the Party. I rather think that the head of the British Communist Party in effect told him that he was not one of them – rightly. His book *Forward from Liberalism*[3] is perhaps the weakest of all his works, but it breathes the same air of sincerity, humanity, passion for the truth, decency, liberty and equality, not to speak of fraternity (which meant a great deal to him), as all his writings, at every period of his life.

I remember introducing Stuart Hampshire to him, I think in 1935, when Stuart was an undergraduate. I remember Stuart saying about him, as we

---

1 'Beethoven's Death Mask', in *Poems* (332/2).

2 During the 1930s Great Depression a series of 'hunger marches' took place in Britain against the shortage of jobs, and of social welfare for the unemployed; the largest, the National Hunger March of September–October 1932, met with heavy, some said excessive, police resistance on arrival in Hyde Park.

3 In which he argued that the show trials of Zinov'ev and other Trotskyites exposed the need for internal reform of the Soviet state, and for greater liberalism there: see L1 229/1. The book was published by Victor Gollancz's Left Book Club (London, 1937).

walked away from the Spaniards Inn on Hampstead Heath, where we had met, 'There is nothing between him and the object' – i.e. his vision is direct, not mediated by anything, not framed by categories, preconceptions, a desire to fit things into some framework: direct vision, that was one of his outstanding and most wonderful characteristics, both as a man and as a writer. He was, I suppose, the most genuine, the most authentic, least arranged human being I have ever known, and that had an attractiveness beyond almost every other source of one's sympathy, love and respect. Whatever situation he found himself in, his natural dignity and instinctive human feeling never deserted him. He was never a detached observer, never, I am happy to think, someone who looked upon men or situations with a cold, objective eye; he took sides; he identified himself with the victims, not the victors, without sentimentality, without tears, without feeling that he was behaving generously or kindly or nobly or importantly, without a dry sense of obligation, but with a kind of total commitment which moved me, I think, more than the character of anyone I ever met. [...]

I have said nothing about his experiences in Germany. As you know, he and his friends Auden, Isherwood, John Lehmann[1] went to Germany and sometimes Austria, because the Weimar Republic and its cultural colonies seemed to them an ideal form of free existence and the satisfaction of all their spiritual and physical needs.[2] Nevertheless, even there his acute sense of the ridiculous – which was always present in him, and which was one of his most delightful attributes – did not desert him. His experiences in Hamburg, on which his only novel,[3] issued much later, was based – the embarrassing behaviour of his hosts, in particular of a man called Eric Alport[4] (I rather think that he threatened to sue for libel if the novel was published, soon after it was written, in the early 1930s) – I myself read it at the time, with the greatest pleasure and amusement.

He was terribly bullied at that period by his great friends Auden and Isherwood. They were at that time totally opposed to what might be called

---

1 (Rudolph) John Frederick Lehmann (1907–87), publisher, poet and author peripherally associated with the 'Auden group' at Oxford; younger brother of Rosamond Lehmann; partner and general manager, Hogarth Press, 1938–46; managing director, John Lehmann (publishers), 1946–54; he lived as a poet in 1930s Vienna, 'a city he monitored as Christopher Isherwood did Berlin. The 1st of his 3 vols of autobiography, *The Whispering Gallery* (London, 1955), reflects the hardening of his anti-Fascist view of that "pink" decade' (David Hughes, ODNB).

2 In Weimar Berlin the persons IB mentions could practise their homosexuality with a freedom impossible in Britain.

3 *The Temple* (London, 1988), which Spender began writing in 1929.

4 Eric Adolf Alport (1903–72) né Erich Adolph Alport, born in Posen, grew up in Hamburg; undertook research at Univ. for 2 terms in 1926, successively in politics and English; emigrated to Britain 1937; a lover of the arts, and a friend of Auden and his circle, he bequeathed his library to his old college; Alport did indeed believe that the novel, which is scarcely disguised autobiography, libelled him (in the guise of Dr Ernst Stockmann, a homosexual Jew given a sex scene), and said that he 'would be prepared to take any steps in [his] power to prevent publication' (Geoffrey Faber to Alport, 31 July 1933), whereupon Faber declined the book.

middle-class culture – one was not allowed to like Beethoven, or Dickens, or Thomas Mann, certainly nothing by any French writer. Only homosexual experiences counted, that alone was where salvation lay. Stephen was unsatisfactory in that respect: he did not accept or practice this particular doctrine, and so, on the island of Rögen, in the North Sea, where they took their holidays, he was mercilessly persecuted about some of his bourgeois tastes. But he did not surrender – and his love of England, his natural patriotism, was in sharp contrast with the escape from the decaying Old World, from which his friends duly fled. Nevertheless they remained friends through it all. They lived in a world to which war, destruction, was inevitably coming, and everything that they wrote was conscious of that mounting cloud. I felt that myself, quite acutely, but as I was not an artist or a writer it did not affect my life or work as it did theirs; but I remained in sympathy with them, then and retrospectively.

After the war, when I came back from Washington and Moscow, where I had been as a servant of the government, Stephen had married you. His first marriage was a disaster: I have always blamed myself for having been party to it. I think that he met Inez[1] at lunch with me, though I hardly knew her. It was over almost from the beginning, though when Inez left him he was very unhappy – humiliated, lonely and miserable, and his poetry of that date reflects all that very directly. But his marriage to you filled him with happiness [...].

And our lives, as earlier, became interlaced: we saw each other frequently, as you know; and you were both part of Aline's and my life, and we were, I sincerely believe, part of yours. I cannot even now bring myself to realise that I shall not see him again. His face, his figure, his voice, haunt me, and will I expect haunt me till my dying day. I have never loved any friend more – nor respected, nor been happier to be his friend.

That is all I have to say. I expect I have left a great deal out, both of what I felt and of what he did and of what we did together and what we talked about; but at the moment nothing more comes to mind. Forgive me – this is all I can say at the moment. My memory in deep old age is none too good – forgive me for that too. I really have tried to do my best to convey what he meant to me. I wish I could do it more adequately. Stephen deserves better, but I am not gifted enough to do it.

Yours, with much love, ⟨from us both⟩

Isaiah

---

1 Stephen Spender's first wife, Marie Agnes ('Inez') Pearn (1913–76), Somerville modern languages 1933–6; m. Stephen Spender 1936, divorced 1941, m. Charles Madge 1942; novelist as 'Elizabeth Lake'; cf. 631.

TO JONATHAN HASLAM[1]

27 September 1995

Headington House

Dear Dr Haslam,

Thank you for sending me the relevant part of your chapter about Ted Carr and me.[2] Let me begin by telling you that I think that your account of our duel is reasonably 'objective',[3] and I have no real complaint on that score, although I have some queries to put, some modifications to suggest. [...]

In my review,[4] from which you very rightly quote, I do say that if Carr's methods continue, there will be a challenge to the ideal of impartiality, objectivity etc. [...] which historians have so far – at any rate most of them – tried to practise. Curiously, he did not mind this review; when the *New York Times* asked him to nominate a reviewer (very improperly) of his volume, he nominated me as far the best. It shows a curious generosity, and imperviousness to criticism, which I think you underestimate – I think he minded attacks upon him less (certainly he believed he minded them less) than you maintain. [...]

My general objection to his history of the Soviet Union is a very plain one, which I don't think I ever explicitly expressed: it is that it is based entirely on official documents. It is as if the Soviet Foreign Office asked for an official history, and opened its official archives to him (not the secret ones, of course); and that he then wrote an excellent account of what the government wanted people to believe, to think true. Trotsky comes in so long as he is in power (that may have irritated Soviet historians a little), but he drops out as he falls from power. I did ask Ted why he totally ignored the critical books about the Soviet Union, by émigrés and others [...]. He replied exactly as you cite him later – that one didn't want to know what failures said, whether what they said was true or false: one only had to know about the actions, and therefore the views, of those who scored centuries, not ducks. He truly believed in ignoring the martyrs and the minorities (unless they turned out to be influential or 'successful' in the end – like, say, the earlier Christians). He paid

1 Jonathan George Haslam (b. 1951), historian of international relations; lecturer, Birmingham, 1975–84; associate prof., Johns Hopkins, 1984–6; visiting associate prof., Stanford, 1986–7, Berkeley 1987–8; senior research fellow, King's, Cambridge, 1988–92, fellow, CCC, since 1993; assistant director of studies (i.e. lecturer), Cambridge, 1991–2000.

2 Haslam sent IB a draft of chapter 8 of *The Vices of Integrity: E. H. Carr, 1892–1982* (London, 1999); the published chapter (192–204) is substantially the same as the draft.

3 The scare quotes presumably reflect Carr's insistence that 'Objective history does not exist': 'Truth in History', editorial, TLS, 1 September 1950, 549.

4 'Soviet Beginnings', IB's review of the 1st vol. of E. H. Carr, *A History of Soviet Russia* (London, 1950–78), *The Bolshevik Revolution 1917–1923*, vol. 1 (London, 1950), *Sunday Times*, 10 December 1950, 3, ends: 'If Mr Carr's remaining volumes equal this impressive opening they will constitute the most monumental challenge of our time to that ideal of impartiality and objective truth and even-handed justice in the writing of history which is most deeply embedded in the European liberal tradition.'

no attention to the alternatives which existed before someone embarked on a policy. There was no discussion of what made the accepted alternative more or less realistic than the ones rejected; still less, of course, any speculation on what might have happened if a particular course of action had not been taken but some alternative embraced.

I know of no other historian, of any nation (except, of course, official Soviet historians, and Nazi ones), who ever practised this principle. Surely you ought to bring this out? It really is so unlike anything that other historians, even biased ones – even as heavily biased as Ted – did and do. His method was unique in that respect for someone not employed by a government. I always felt that there was some unconscious continuity with his work at the Foreign Office, where one worked on official documents. But whether or not I am right about this, it is a very great deviation from the norm, and I think you would be wrong not to remark it. [...]

It is true that I mentioned Carr, in my Auguste Comte Lecture,[1] as judging from a morally relativist point of view. But I was wrong: I don't think there was any morality at all in Carr's approach, except unconsciously. His History is written without any apparent moral awareness of anything. Quite apart from uttering moral judgements in history, which I do not particularly wish to defend, the very language a historian uses gives away what his moral attitude is – and this is certainly true of Ted. [...]

History for me is not the history simply of what happened, the occurrence of human acts, the time and place, the character of the actors, but what people hesitated between, wanted to do but did not, might have done, might not have done, what other people were doing which clashed with the main decisions, the ambience and human texture within which acts and decisions took place – and all that seems to me entirely missing in Ted's work; it is missing from Hegel, too, by and large. [...]

Finally, about my remark in the *Listener* about the Trevelyan Lectures, that Carr was not too confident in the regions of the philosophy of history – that was not his metier.[2] This is confirmed by two separate conversations which I had with Deutscher and Marcuse, who admired Carr, but who both complained that he paid no attention to ideas, in Marx, Bakunin or anyone else. For 'no attention', I am willing to substitute 'far too little attention', but on that I stand.

To end on a lighter note: the Trevelyan Lectures were originally offered to me; I wrote and declined them; Dom Knowles[3] (the organiser) begged

---

1 9/9.

2 In 'What is History?', an exchange of letters with E. H. Carr in the pages of the *Listener*, IB wrote that Carr's intervention in the field served as a 'warning' to others tempted to 'venture into regions too distant from their own'. *Listener*, 18 May 1961, 877; L3 42.

3 Michael Clive Knowles (1896–1974), known by his religious name, David, joined the Benedictines in 1914 (priest 1922, hence 'Dom[inus]', 'master'); fellow, Peterhouse, Cambridge, 1944–63, Regius Prof. of History 1954–63.

me to reconsider – I said I couldn't do it, and when he asked me if I wished to nominate anyone, I said 'E. H. Carr.' He never knew that he owed this to me, for – rightly, I am sure – I never told him this: it would have irritated him somewhat.

I think you could sum up our relationship by saying that Carr thought that what I was saying was arrant, obvious nonsense. He really meant this. I thought that his advocacy of appeasement, first of Germany, then of Russia, must have fatal consequences, and that his dedication to Stalin's Soviet Union led to a considerable perversion of history. Given this, it is extraordinary that during our very long acquaintance we continued to like and respect each other to the end. [...]

Yours sincerely,
    Isaiah Berlin

TO MICHAEL WALZER

17 October 1995

Headington House

Dear Michael,

I am writing to you, somewhat belatedly (because I have had a not very important operation,[1] and am recovering rather too slowly from it), to say how deeply grateful I am for what you say about me in the review of Gray's book in the NYRB[2] – that you have probably come nearer to understanding (and sympathising with) what I believe than anyone else has done [...].

At this point I have to make an admission. There is something that I now believe, and I think believed then, which I did not make clear in my essay on positive and negative liberty. It is this: there are two kinds of liberty (apart from positive and negative). One is [...] liberty as one value among others, which certainly may have to be curtailed or modified in some way if other values in a concrete situation seem more urgent or important (security, justice etc.) – that is the kind of liberty I mostly talk about. But there is another more basic sense of liberty, which is ability to choose *telle quelle* – as such. Unless a human being is in a position either to do or to be X, or not to do/be it (that is the minimum); either to act in this or that way, or to commit suicide, or be hypnotised for the rest of one's life and become a kind of zombie – unless this capacity for choosing, i.e. freedom, is present, then I hold that human beings cannot remain human at all, and to the degree to

1 To insert a pacemaker.
2 John Nicholas Gray (b. 1948), prolific and controversial author; fellow and politics tutor, Jesus, 1976–98, professor of politics, Oxford, 1996–8; professor of European thought, LSE, 1998–2007; author of foreword to RR2; MW, 'Are There Limits to Liberalism?', review of Gray's *Isaiah Berlin* (530/1), NYRB, 19 October 1995, 28–31.

which it is diminished, to that degree there is dehumanisation. In this sense, being human entails this basic freedom, entails it conceptually, as it were, metaphysically as others would put it, but I do not. This is a more fundamental sense of freedom than the political liberty about which in general I speak. If I did not say it in that essay it is, I suppose, because I was talking about political liberty and nothing else – not moral or spiritual or economic liberty or whatever. But when I speak as I do of inalienable ingredients, then I mean this basic, non-political, personal liberty – which is, of course, connected with the others in all kinds of ways, but nevertheless can be differentiated from them. [...]

[Y]ou speak of my view that love of liberty, or the need for it, has some basis in human nature – hence liberalism is the best politics for beings like us. At this point I really do have to uncover my views. I do not think that liberty has a unique status, in some sense the master idea; it does so for *me* as an individual, but it needn't for either liberals or pluralists as such. In the sense of liberty as a basic capacity to choose, yes – in that sense it is intrinsic to human nature. But political liberty, a value among other values: I wish I could maintain that, as some liberals I am sure would wish to do (Mazzini and the like), 'Give me liberty or give me death'; that represents this position. But I was terribly impressed by a passage in my hero Herzen's book *My Past and Thoughts*, in which he says that men do not really all seek liberty – security, yes, but liberty?[1] He says it is as if one said about flying fish that that is the natural way for fish to be, and that fish in water all long, whether they know it or not, to fly.[2] But most are quite comfortable living in water. They may not dislike or fear the idea of flying (the, for me, mistaken view of that psychoanalyst – what is his name?[3] – who wrote a book called *Fear of Freedom*); they might be pleased if they could fly; but if faced with a choice between their life in water and the perils of flying they would unhesitatingly choose the former; i.e. all men seek security, only some seek liberty. And even if Rousseau denounces the former as a disgraceful choice of slavery, they still are as they are. I cannot pretend that human beings as such (even if I do) put liberty as a primary value, with a special status. I think that simply as a fact that is not the case. Hence my distinction between the basic liberty which men cannot be without and remain men, and some degree, or at least the minimum, of the more familiar kind which I personally regard as having

---

1 IB must be thinking of a passage in *From the Other Shore* (1850): 'The masses [...] are indifferent to individual freedom, to freedom of speech; the masses love authority. [...] The masses want a social government that would govern *for* them, and not, like this existing one, *against* them. To govern themselves doesn't enter their heads.' Chapter 6, 'Omnia mea mecum porto', op. cit. (22/1) vi 124; Alexander Herzen, *From the Other Shore* and *The Russian People and Socialism* (115/2), 133–4. Cf. RT2 100, 226.

2 ibid. 94–5; 108–9. Cf. RT2 107, AC 207, L 51/3, PSM 519.

3 Erich Seligmann Fromm (1900–80), German-born US psychoanalyst and writer; author of *The Fear of Freedom* (London, 1942).

superior status but do not attribute to men as such as a conceptual or even empirical notion. [...]

Yours ever,

Isaiah   [...]

TO JOSHUA CHERNISS[1]

18 October 1995

Headington House

Dear Mr Cherniss,

What can I say in answer to your wonderful letter of 10 October but that you are quite right: I, too, am a sceptical, 'humanistic' Jew, an Anglophile and a Zionist. So our kinship is genuine.

I am always astonished to hear that my works should have any influence, but there is no doubt that your appreciation of the transforming effect they have had on you moves me deeply. [...]

Thank you ever so much for writing to me as you have – and I predict an intellectually honourable and successful career for you.

Yours sincerely

Isaiah Berlin   [...]

TO ANDREW STOKES[2]

11 December 1995 [*draft*]

Headington House

[Dear Mr Stokes,]

You ask me what Verdi's operas mean to me. My love for his music has virtually no limits. The unquenchable vitality, the use of primary colours which express the full depth of basic human passions – love, hatred, jealousy, envy, faith, trust, despair, suspicion, triumphant joy, devotion to freedom (personal and political), above all the love of men and women, parents and children, friends, country – all these are conveyed with a directness and depth of understanding within the framework of the conventional rules of Italian opera, without need for aesthetic extravagance, iconoclasm for its own sake. His operas do not embody some megalomaniac world-transforming vision,

---

1 Joshua Laurence Cherniss (b. 27 September 1979) had written to IB that his work 'has had a great impact on me. Like you, I am a Jew (albeit a somewhat sceptical, "humanistic" one), an Anglophile and a Zionist.' IB's reply exemplifies IB's encouragement of young enthusiasts (and strangers). This young man was barely sixteen, and his early interest in IB grew into a dominant intellectual preoccupation, leading to many essays on IB's work, and also *A Mind and Its Time: The Development of Isaiah Berlin's Political Thought* (Oxford, 2013).

2 Andrew John Stokes (b. 1962), director, sales and marketing, ROH, 1994–8, had asked for 'a couple of sentences [...] saying what Verdi means to you personally' for their 1996 Verdi Festival brochure (letter of 5 December).

nor a search for salvation, nor personal problems or neuroses. Nothing is contrived, sentimental, nor is it even addressed to the head or heart – but to the nerves. Everything is on a human scale, sane, natural; it has a noble simplicity in conveying the deepest human feelings.

Verdi's genius is capable of a deep moral and political grasp of reality, a degree of universal understanding which for me, at least, is without parallel. What more can I say?

[Isaiah Berlin]

TO ADELHEID GOWRIE[1]

1 January 1996

Headington House

Dearest Neiti,

The three (according to me) indispensable attributes for a marriage that will not end in tears are: (*a*) that the intended consort should be a nice person – we all know what that means – 'nice' and 'nasty' are intelligible to everybody since the first moment of creation; (*b*) one must feel completely at ease with him/her – this is not quite Hegel's formula, but similar;[2] (*c*) one must know oneself to love the other person – not necessarily be in love with – simple love alone guarantees a very great deal.

Yours ever,

Isaistotle ⟨(you remember Aquinas calls him "the Master of all who know"[3] […])⟩

TO JEAN FLOUD

25 January 1996 [*manuscript*]

Headington House

Dear Jean,

Thank you for sending me Arnaldo's piece.[4] As always, it was brilliant and

1 Adelheid ('Neiti') Hore-Ruthven (b. 1943) née von der Schulenburg, Countess of Gowrie; m. 1974 Grey Gowrie, and met IB soon afterwards. IB's letter probably follows one from AG accepting an invitation to the Berlins' forthcoming 40th wedding anniversary party, held at Brooks's club 7 February 1996, or a Christmas card referring to marriage in the context of this event.

2 In §163 of *Elements of the Philosophy of Right* Hegel writes: 'The ethical aspect of marriage consists in […] love, trust, and the sharing of the whole of individual existence.' He believes, indeed, that man and wife 'constitute a single person' (§162). Quoted from the edition by Allen G. Wood, trans. H. B. Nisbet (Cambridge, 1991), 202, 201.

3 Aristotle is described as '[i]l maestro di color che sanno' ('the master of those who know') by Dante, *Inferno* 4. 131. Aquinas doubtless thought the same, but doesn't say so in these words in his published works.

4 Arnaldo Dante Momigliano (1908–87), hon. KBE 1974, Italian Jewish ancient historian; Professore Incaricato di Storia Greca, Rome, 1932–6, Professore Titolare di Storia Romana 1936–8; emigrated to Britain as an academic refugee March 1939; prof. of ancient history, UCL, 1951–75. IB was shocked to learn in the pages of the TLS in early 1996 (W. V. Harris, 'The Silences of Momigliano',

fascinating, and I read it at once and with exhilaration. Nevertheless, I have to tell you that I think he does not make out his case.

His thesis is that the English, contrary to what was said (e.g. by me), were interested in the history of ideas. There is a sense in which they weren't and aren't. He does not mention Buckle (*History of Civilisation in England*), who doesn't talk much about ideas. Bury,[1] whom he does mention, talks much more about institutions, and it is a poor book anyway.[2] Collingwood was not strictly interested in the history of ideas, except about history – he lectured on this but did not write what might have been a good book.

The only real case for Arnaldo is Leslie Stephen,[3] whose books on Utilitarianism and English political ideas in the eighteenth century are genuine histories of ideas – somewhat narrow and dry and dullish, but authentic – and convey information on the history of this particular topic better than anyone else does.

The strange thing, which I repetitively emphasise (of course), is that in the nineteenth century any educated or would-be educated Peruvian or Bengali had to have heard of Bentham, Mill, Carlyle,[4] above all Spencer[5] – and some, like, say, Tolstoy, would have read Ruskin[6] and Matthew Arnold. Apart from one or two Frenchmen and, say, one American, they were the dominant idea-mongers in Europe and the Western world. There are monographs on them, of course, but no continuous history of the development or spread or conflicts of their ideas – as there are in most countries. In France you have de Bodin[7] à Montesquieu, de Montesquieu à Rousseau, de Rousseau

12 April 1996, 6–7) that his great friend had a hidden Fascist past, having joined the Party in Italy in the 1930s; but university teachers were then obliged to conform to the regime, and only 11 academics among thousands had refused to take an oath of loyalty 1931; as the TLS reviewer observed, 'This is not another Paul De Man case (186/4), for Momigliano wrote nothing criminal on behalf of the regime, and would have been incapable of doing so' (7). The piece JF had sent IB is 'National Versions of an International Phenomenon', TLS, 24 November 1972, 1417–18.

1 John Bagnell Bury (1861–1927), Irish-born classical scholar and historian; Regius Prof. of Modern History, Cambridge, 1902–27; his inaugural lecture on 'The Science of History' (the title printed on the 1st page of the text) was published as *An Inaugural Lecture, Delivered in the Divinity School, Cambridge, on January 26, 1903* (Cambridge, 1903).

2 IB probably means *The Idea of Progress: An Inquiry into Its Origin and Growth* (London, 1920), though Momigliano also mentions *A History of Freedom of Thought* (London, 1913).

3 Leslie Stephen (1832–1904), KCB 1902, author, literary critic, mountaineer; 1st editor, *Dictionary of National Biography*, 1882–91; father of Virginia Woolf; author of *History of English Thought in the Eighteenth Century* (London, 1876) and *The English Utilitarians* (London, 1900).

4 Thomas Carlyle (1795–1881), historian, essayist and political thinker, won enormous prestige in his lifetime as a social commentator and critic of industrialisation; established his reputation as a historian with his *The French Revolution: A History* (London, 1837).

5 Herbert Spencer (1820–1903), philosopher and social theorist; an advocate of social and economic laissez-faire, and an early and lifelong exponent of Darwin's ideas on evolution (coined the phrase 'the survival of the fittest' 1864).

6 John Ruskin (1819–1900), author, artist, critic, 1st Slade Prof. of Fine Art, Oxford, 1870–8, 1883–4; Tolstoy was an admirer, in particular of *Unto This Last: Four Essays on the First Principles of Political Economy* (London, 1862).

7 Jean Bodin (c.1529–1596), French lawyer and political philosopher, author of *Six livres de la*

à Comte, de Comte à Leon Bourgeois[1] etc. In Germany there are chairs in *Geistesgeschichte, Ideengeschichte*[2] etc. In Italy also, in America too. In England – two minor posts, occupied by pretty inferior people. That is my case. [...]

Yours with love

Isaiah

TO MARIA BRODSKY[3]

30 January 1996 [*carbon*]

Headington House

Dear Maria,

The shock to me of the death of Joseph was very great, but naturally cannot begin to be as great as it is to you.[4] What can I say? When really fateful things happen, words are like sticks, and convey too little or nothing. Given his heart condition, you must have imagined at times what his passing would be like, but when it happens it is always much, much worse. So what can I say but that for me, as for many, many others, this is an enormous misfortune which cannot help changing our lives. What comfort is there in telling you that? I send you my fondest love, and beg you not to give up your future or your child's for too long.

My relations with Joseph were, as you know, very close. Stephen Spender arranged for me to see him on the second or third day after his arrival in London: and at any rate on my part it was love at first sight. I felt, unlike some people, totally easy in his presence. Quite apart from my admiration for his genius – that one would take for granted – I found that, to my relief (I did not know what to expect), we had a very great deal to talk about, that all he said was new, fascinating and indeed totally absorbing. I did not wish him to leave. I wanted him to go on and on. I felt both warmed and excited by his presence, his tone of voice, the words he used – and I have felt that ever since, with all our meetings and conversations as well as his published works. Of course Akhmatova had something to do with all that, but I think it would have happened anyway. His path in life, as everyone knows, was heroic at all stages. Usually one feels daunted in the presence of heroes so superior to

république (1576–7); regarded undivided monarchical authority, tempered by constitutionalism, as the best safeguard of order and defence against anarchy.

1 Léon Victor Auguste Bourgeois (1851–1925), French politician and statesman; president, French senate, 1920–3; worked tirelessly to promote international co-operation in the cause of world peace; 1st president, Council of the League of Nations; Nobel Peace Prize 1920.

2 'Intellectual history', 'history of ideas'.

3 Maria Sozzani, a translator and scholar of Russian literature, met Joseph Brodsky when, as a docotoral student, she attended a series of lectures he gave at the Collège international de philosophie in Paris, where he was teaching literature; they married 1990 and their daughter Anna was born 1993; after her husband's death she became president, Joseph Brodsky Memorial Fellowship Fund, of which IB was a founding member.

4 Joseph Brodsky, who had a history of heart trouble, died of a heart attack in NY City 2 days earlier, 28 January, at the age of 55.

oneself in every way; but in his case an intimate relationship sprang up and developed. His passing cuts off a slice of my own life. It would be banal to say that this is irreplaceable, but in fact I know it to be so. I know of no other way of conveying this.

I have never met anyone in my life – none of the English poets whom I knew and whom he admired – who was as obviously inspired as he was; nor anyone who understood so much, who instinctively rejected anything that was even faintly false or artificially constructed, both in human beings and [in] their attitudes and works; nor anyone whose search for what he valued was so unswerving, so uncompromisingly dedicated. And this involved him in seeing through and rejecting a lot of what more ordinary people uncritically accept and regard as normal. That made his life a continual sacrifice on his self-constructed altar, and the degree to which your love for him and his life with you lighted his difficult path was unbelievably great and wonderful. I am sure you saved him from all kinds of risks that might have destroyed him, every day and in every way.

Of course you are in a state of inconsolable grief, as in some degree we, his friends, all are. But your achievement has been very great: do not doubt it, it is so.

Every contact with him – meetings, letters, books he sent me – changed the quality of my life. I have never had such a relationship with anyone, at any time, at any rate since my first meeting with Stephen Spender and my long visit to Akhmatova. A great deal will be written about him, and ought to be written about you too – for your union was indissoluble. I always wondered whether he could achieve it with anyone, until you opened that door and it was done. Dear Maria, I must not go on with these platitudes; I am not worthy of this event.

I cannot help comparing his loss with the deaths of Pushkin, Lermontov, victims of duels; it is quite different from the despair and suicide of Esenin,[1] Mayakovsky, who spiritually seem to me altogether inferior to Joseph. He is the last great modern poet, not only in Russia but, it seems to me, in the entire world, for the time being – there may be others, but he will remain a unique, agonised, burning genius for ever.

With much love, and I hope somewhere, sometime, we can meet again. I am too old and frail to come to the funeral or the memorial service – I would if I could – but he was surrounded by the devotion of those who will come, and mine, believe me, was as deep as anyone's, and will always remain so.

Yours,

[Isaiah] [...]

---

1 Sergey Aleksandrovich Esenin (1895–1925), Russian poet of peasant life noted for his lyrical gifts; greeted the October 1917 Revolution with optimism, but became alienated by Bolshevism; drunk and dissolute in his last years, he hanged himself in a hotel room in Leningrad after a brief hospitalisation for a nervous breakdown.

TO CHIMEN ABRAMSKY

26 February 1996

Headington House

Dear Chimen,

I have read Diana Trilling's article on Goronwy Rees,[1] because she sent me an early version of it. I know her, and I knew Goronwy extremely well. The trouble with her piece, which I do not recollect in detail, is that her love and loyalty blinds her to certain facts to do with Rees. His daughter's book is the best thing written about him,[2] and I strongly recommend it to you – it is very just and very good, written with love and fairness. As for Diana, she says things which seem to me plainly inaccurate (I do beg you not to let her know this, or repeat it to others who might repeat it to her – she can be very ferocious if one contradicts her, though she is a great friend of mine and I love her). For example: the notion that the hostility to Rees, because of the four notorious articles,[3] was due to the fact that he attacked his friend Burgess is absurd. Nobody except Communists and fellow-travellers could have objected to that. None of us who were shocked by the articles had the faintest objection to an attack on Burgess, who deserved it – and we all knew it. Again, the idea that homosexuals were unfair to him because Burgess was one is again an absurdity. She means Maurice Bowra, who did indeed write a letter to Rees saying 'What will you do with the thirty pieces of silver? Grow a row of Judas trees, I suppose':[4] unkind, but not due to the anti-homosexual tone of the piece, but to the fact that it had a kind of McCarthyite quality, it said that the Foreign Office was full of homosexual Communists, and that kind of thing – it had a real tone of hysterical McCarthyism about it.

Again, she omits the fact that one of the bad things my friend did – and remember, I was very fond of him, and he of me, and despite our coolness as a result of the article (which I don't think he actually noticed), we became

1 Diana Trilling, 'Goronwy Rees – and Others: A Remembrance of England', *Partisan Review* 63 no. 1 (Winter 1996), 11–47.

2 *Looking for Mr Nobody: The Secret Life of Goronwy Rees* (London, 1994), by Margaret Jane ('Jenny') Rees (b. 1942), eldest of the five children of Goronwy and Margaret Rees; journalist and author. 'Mr Nobody' was the self-deprecating name that Rees gave to himself, and according to *The Times* his daughter's biography was 'An excellent investigation of this brilliant but flawed man of letters and his tortured relationship with the Cambridge spy ring': Daniel Johnson, 'The Traitor's Conscience', 24 December 1994, *Weekend*, 12a–f at 12b–c.

3 Five, in fact: 122/6.

4 Rees subsequently wrote: 'My sense that I had committed a double offence, against good taste and decent feeling, was confirmed by letters and protests which I began to receive soon after the first of the articles was published. The Warden of an Oxford college, for whom I felt an affection which dated from my undergraduate days, wrote to suggest that I should plant a screen of Judas trees around the college athletic fields': Goronwy Rees, *A Chapter of Accidents* (London 1972), 267. Contrariwise, Mary Bennett and George Huxley told Bowra's biographer that Bowra *said* to Rees 'Go hang yourself from a Judas tree': Leslie Mitchell, *Maurice Bowra: A Life* (Oxford, 2009), 173. In any event, it is a phrase that Bowra regretted: 'I wrote him a very nasty letter' (Bowra to Cecil Day Lewis, 13 March 1970).

friends again, and I went to his deathbed, and was terribly moved by what he said to me then – to begin again, one of the bad things he did was to attack perfectly innocent people as Soviet agents, among them a man who stood by him through thick and thin during his period of unpopularity, namely Professor R. C. Zaehner,[1] whose loyalty to him was beyond words, when other people were scornful of what he had done. The idea of Zaehner as a Soviet agent was grotesque. He attacked similarly Stuart Hampshire, who was perfectly innocent and a perfect patriot, whatever his political views; and a number of others.

The people who remained loyal to him were not just Diana and me, but Zaehner, John Sparrow, and above all Freddie Ayer, who wrote a very nice piece about him in the *Dictionary of National Biography*. At the end of his life Goronwy was seldom sober, very unhappy, and his only friends really were the *Encounter* group, on the grounds of anti-Communism (which I shared).[2] When the famous *Encounter* scandal occurred,[3] Goronwy telephoned me to say that it was ridiculous to object to the fact that the CIA supported this journal. When I said I had no objection to support from anti-Soviet sources, but thought it a little much if a periodical which prided itself on its independence was in fact subsidised from secret funds – when I said that, he became somewhat hysterical. Yet we did not quarrel, we remained friends to the end. But he did behave badly, of that there is no doubt, and Diana was too fond of him ever to notice that – the very notion that the four articles were due to patriotism is patently untrue.

Still, it is a very interesting piece, you are quite right to praise it, and I am moved that she should have offered this posthumous tribute to a man who in general has been partly forgotten, partly unjustly disliked.

Yours ever,
Isaiah   [...]

TO LILIAN SCHAPIRO[4]
7 March 1996 [*carbon*]

Headington House

Dearest Lilian,
You can imagine my grief at the news that Meyer was no more. You know

---

1 Robert Charles Zaehner (1913–74), orientalist and intelligence officer; acting counsellor, British Embassy, Tehran, 1943–7, 1951–2; Spalding Prof. of Eastern Religions and Ethics, Oxford, and fellow, All Souls, 1952–74.
2 After his resignation as Principal, University College of Wales, Aberystwyth, 1957, Rees contributed a strongly anti-Communist monthly column to *Encounter* under the *nom de plume* 'R'. Not long before he died he reviewed AC here (122/4).
3 See L3 432/1.
4 Lillian Milgram Schapiro (1902–2006) née Milgram, paediatrician, specialist in childhood tuberculosis; lecturer, NYU medical school, 1933–77; m. 1928 the art historian Meyer Schapiro (136/2), who had died 3 March; they had a daughter and a son.

that we were very old friends – we used to say that when Meyer made time for me in New York when he was busy or unwell. Old friendship removed barriers, you thought, and rightly so.

I first met him, as you must also know, before the war, as a result of a meeting arranged by Freddie Ayer. From that moment onwards we became friends – as time went on, closer and closer friends. There is nobody in the world I admired so much, and this is literally true not only of me but of a great many other people as well. I have just read a worthy obituary of him in the *Guardian*, with a little friendly postscript by Ernst Gombrich, which does not begin to do him justice.[1] Why did we all admire him so much? Because he was the most universal spirit of his time: his knowledge was vast, accurate and deep; the relationships he traced between thought in general, philosophy in particular, social conditions, individual character and works of art have not been paralleled by any other writer on the subject, so far as I know [...].

I was frightfully pleased that he was all the things that he was – that he was a Jew, that he came from Eastern Europe, that like my grandparents he was brought up in Yiddish, that he understood my origins and his own so clearly, that we could talk so directly, without any intervening medium, let alone obstacles, that I understood every word he said about life and people almost before he had finished the sentence – and he paid me in the same coin. I shall always cherish the little drawings he made for me when he illustrated some point he wanted to make [...].

I have never been prouder of not merely knowing but being treated with warm friendship by anyone else in my life. Of course I could go on and on amplifying his wonderful qualities; and other people will no doubt offer, I hope, discerning and eloquent meeds of praise to him, all over the world.

I remember his Marxism, in *Partisan Review* days, in 1941, bothered me a little, for I was born anti-Marxist. But his Marxism was so humane, so profoundly civilised and illuminating, that this evaporated extremely early. Unlike some, too, I admired his stern attitude towards the student unrest in Columbia[2] – no man ever stood more four-square for civilisation, for light and order. He threw light on everything he touched (there I go again – I must not go on so), at once a unique scholar and a saint in character, and indeed appearance. His mere head and face were part and parcel of what was most sacred in the Hasidic tradition in which we were both brought up – and that too, as you may imagine, never failed to move me, and moves me still, even as I grieve and lament the passing of my great, great friend.

1 John Russell's obituary, 'Peeping into Glory' (*Guardian*, 5 March 1996, 16). In his note on the same page Gombrich wrote that 'there will never be another Meyer Schapiro'.
2 Violent confrontation between police and students at Columbia April 1968 was the climax of a long-running protest there, organised by activists from the radical Students for a Democratic Society movement.

The famous story of the monastery in Spain, which he visited on a mule sixty years ago, when there were no motor roads, and the account, much later on, by one of the monks to an American art scholar, saying, 'An American art scholar visited us sixty years ago to see one or two of the paintings in our monastery, and some of us thought that Abraham looked like that; some of us thought that Moses may have looked like that; and some thought' – at this point his finger pointed to heaven – 'that *He* looked like that.' I have never forgotten it, and somehow it was one of the most moving tributes to his personality ever made.

I'll stop now, and beg you not to acknowledge this is any way. You will have too much to do replying to all the true admirers – true and false, all will write to you, but that is the penalty of being a wonderful person oneself, as you are, a wonderful wife, a wonderful mother, and a wonderful companion to a great, great man. [...]

Yours, with infinite love,
    Isaiah

In March 1996 Robert Silvers, editor of the NYRB, asked IB whether he might publish his 1952 exchange of letters with T. S. Eliot on anti-Semitism,[1] mentioned by Anthony Julius in T. S. Eliot, Anti-Semitism, and Literary Form *(Cambridge, 1995). Julius's book had forced a reappraisal of Eliot's attitude to Jews, and IB asked HH to look out his correspondence with Eliot. There Eliot had insisted that he was not anti-Semitic, as IB had seemed to imply in his 1951 article 'Jewish Slavery and Emancipation';[2] and when the article was republished in 1952,[3] Eliot's name was excised. IB's response to revisiting this controversy led to the reinstatement of Eliot's name when the essay was republished in POI in 2000.*

TO HENRY HARDY

n.d. [before 18 March 1996; *manuscript Post-it note*][4]

[Headington House]

Henry:
    I had forgotten the texts. I feel embarrassed at having been so excessively polite – almost obsequious – to Eliot: at that time I had not read his

---

1 IB decided that the exchange should await posthumous publication.
2 262/1, L2 278/3.
3 In *Hebrew University Garland* (262/1), the 'Jerusalem volume' that IB refers to (528).
4 Attached to the 1952 correspondence, later published at L2 277–83.

antisemitic lines of poetry: much worse than the text I refer to.[1] Did I really leave out his name in the Jerusalem volume? I should not have done

has Michael [Ignatieff] seen this – he should?

TO RUTH CHANG[2]

15 April 1996

Headington House

Dear Ruth,

[...] You ask me various questions. At the age of eighty-six and three-quarters as you so precisely put it, there is not much to do except go on as long as one can. Herzen once said that the purpose of life is life[3] – if the purpose of life were some goal towards which it tended, that goal would be death; and I am not yet ready for that. You ask me what I have learnt by my enormous age. I cannot tell you that offhand, or probably at all, but off the cuff – love, liberty, love of life are worth all the other great virtues, justice, security, truth etc. put together. Still, they are all of an ultimate status. Do I feel that I know what love and happiness are? Yes. How would I like to be remembered? I could not care less: I do not mind in the least if I am completely forgotten – I really mean that. What do I think about most these days? One thing and another – I cannot tell you that there is something I think about more than about anything else. You see how basically frivolous I really am. [...]

Yours ever, ⟨with much love⟩

Isaiah

TO GEERT VAN CLEEMPUT[4]

22 April 1996 [carbon]

[Headington House]

Dear Dr Van Cleemput,

I have read your piece and reviews on nationalism[5] with great interest. In

---

1 In *After Strange Gods: A Primer of Modern Heresy* (NY/London, 1934), 20, Eliot had written: 'reasons of race and religion combine to make any large number of freethinking Jews undesirable'.

2 Ruth Elizabeth Chang (b. 1963), US philosopher; junior research fellow, Balliol, 1991–6; later taught at Rutgers – assistant prof. 1998–2004, associate prof. 2004–13, prof. since 2013.

3 Not in so many words. Herzen wrote, 'a goal must be closer – at the very least the labourer's wage, or pleasure in work performed. Each epoch, each generation, each life has had, has, its own fullness; and en route new demands grow, new experiences, new methods [...]. The end of each generation is itself. Not only does nature never make one generation the means for the attainment of some future goal, but she doesn't concern herself with the future at all; like Cleopatra, she is ready to dissolve the pearl in wine for a moment's pleasure' etc.: op. cit. (22/1) vi 34–5; op. cit. (115/2), 36–7. Cf. RT2 105, 222.

4 Geert Van Cleemput (b. 1965), Belgian classicist and nationalist politician; taught ancient Greek language and history and classical humanities, Chicago, 1989–98; later (1999–2003) parliamentary aide to Flemish Independence Party (Vlaams Blok).

5 Van Cleemput had sent IB 2 book reviews and an article on nationalism. The reviews were of

the course of the following remarks you will see in what respect I think you have not put my position precisely enough, at any rate for my taste. [...]

Let me start by saying that I am in considerable sympathy with your general position. Alien rule is a terrible thing, and you are perfectly right to say that the emphasis on citizenship and the unity of the political state can lead to the oppression of communities other than the leading community in the state, and to tyranny of a very painful and repellent kind. About this, let me make the following observations.

It is not entirely correct to say that imperialism, or alien rule unwelcome to the ruled, has necessarily inflicted damage on these subjects. What I am thinking of is Karl Marx's very shrewd remark that the British in India have driven the Indians, by their rule, into three or four centuries of normal development from a totally agrarian society to a comparatively modern one.[1] He adds, of course, that the British did not do this for the benefit of the Indians, but for their own benefit; nevertheless, he says that the idea that once upon a time there was a peaceful, rural society of contented peasants, free from the horrors of industrialism and modernisation, is a myth – that the brutality of the pre-British rulers of India was very great, and that the lot of the average Indian was in a sense greatly improved by British rule, whatever the motives of the British may have been. This is, of course, in harmony with Marx's general view that there is an objective succession of phases from the most primitive to the most industrially developed, ending in classless communism. Nevertheless, even if this particular ladder is faulty, and it certainly is; even if history is not a play with acts which follow each other in some inevitable sequence, which is what Hegel and Marx believed: even if this is so (as I believe), it remains true that foreign rulers have often, whatever their motive, benefited the ruled, of different classes and societies.[2] This is true even of Central Asia under Soviet rule.

Misha Glenny, *The Fall of Yugoslavia: The Third Balkan War* (London, 1992), in *International Journal on World Peace* 11 no. 1 (March 1994), 81–8, and Roger Michener (ed.), *Nationality, Patriotism, and Nationalism in Liberal Democratic Societies* (St Paul, MN, 1993), in Jan Knappert and Geert van Cleemput, 'Nationality, Patriotism and Nationalism in Liberal Democratic Societies: A Review Symposium', ibid. no. 3 (September 1994), 72–88 at 81–8; the article was probably 'Clarifying Nationalism, Chauvinism, and Ethnic Imperialism', ibid. 12 no. 1 (March 1995), 59–77 (cf. 'Rejoinder', ibid. 88–97).
1 'England, it is true, in causing a social revolution in Hindustan, was actuated only by the vilest interests, and was stupid in her manner of enforcing them. But that is not the question. The question is, can mankind fulfil its destiny without a fundamental revolution in the social state of Asia? If not, whatever may have been the crimes of England, she was the unconscious tool of history in bringing about that revolution.' 'The British Rule in India' (1853), CW xii 125–33 at 132; cf. KM5 187–8.
2 'I never said that India should not be allowed independence until the Indians had the knowledge or skill to establish proper democracy. I am sure I could not have said that, for I never believed it. Government by an alien people, however benevolent, is always to some degree oppressive and humiliating. It is true that Karl Marx says somewhere that the English pushed India through various stages of social development quite rapidly – not, of course, in India's interests, but in their own. But nevertheless they did achieve it, and therefore did Indians good by doing so,

Let me now go on to the central subject – nationalism, chauvinism etc. My view is somewhat similar to that of Herder. If you read my essay on him in *Vico and Herder* I think you will get a juster perception of what I mean by national consciousness than you would derive even from John Gray's interesting and on the whole perfectly just book.[1] My position is comparatively simple. I think that the desire to belong to a community is as natural for human beings as a desire to eat or sleep or drink or move, or any other basic human need. I do not think, in spite of Hobbes, that human beings are ever solitary, brutish etc., but they have always lived in communities of some kind because the desire to live among people who understand one's language, among whom one feels at home (whatever feelings may be between individuals), who form a natural unit, so to speak, is permanent. In the case of nations – however they may have arisen – national consciousness I regard as a normal human feeling which is not at all to be condemned, which creates solidarity, loyalty, patriotism and other feelings which unite human beings to one another and make co-operation possible and valuable. I do not call that nationalism.

My view is that when national consciousness develops a pathological condition – becomes inflamed – then that is, properly speaking, nationalism, and in its extreme case chauvinism; that is the condition where members of the nation regard themselves as superior to others, and entitled to dominate them as being selected by God or by Providence to play a special role in the development of mankind, inasmuch as they possess certain properties not possessed by others – political wisdom, a correct interpretation of history, racial purity (which alone generates true creativeness), etc. – all of which entitles those who are so fortunate to dominate, and if need be attack and conquer, inferior societies. All this goes with a great deal of hypocrisy about the fact that this domination does the dominated nothing but good, etc.

So I draw a sharp line between national consciousness, which is so to speak OK, and nationalism, which is not. This, I think, you do not bring out when you talk about my conception of nationalism. I admit that this is only my usage – nationalism in general may not mean the kind of pathological condition which I condemn. But the difference between patriotism and nationalism consists precisely in this overweening pride, xenophobia, sense of mission, being chosen to transform the world – which is the source of the evils which you and I condemn.

In principle I agree with you. The best situation would be where

which primitive, patriarchal India could never have done for itself. However that may be, I do not believe in the coercion of one nation by another, even for its own good. I disagree with Marx, although what he says has some truth in it.' To Fumiko Sasaki, 6 April 1994.

1 *Isaiah Berlin* (London, 1995; Princeton, 1996); retitled *Berlin* for the paperback edition in the Modern Masters series (London, 1995); reissued with a substantive new introduction by the author as *Isaiah Berlin: An Interpretation of His Thought* (Princeton, 2013).

communities – defined quite properly in terms of language, custom, common memories (whether genuine or mythological), and perhaps a long life on a limited part of the globe, but especially language and common memories – [I agree] that these communities would be best off if they could be entirely self-governing, not governed by others; and that all efforts to combine such communities into states or empires – as the Russians, Austrians, French, British, Chinese and lots of others have done – lead to oppression and are fundamentally destructive in character. Above all, they are an enemy to individual freedom, which in the end is what every good society rests on. I have to admit that even pure democracies of an ethnically uniform kind can be oppressive to various groups of individuals among them – oppressive democracies are not uncommon in history.

But I have to plead Churchill's formula: democracy is not a particularly good form of government, but every other is much, much worse.[1] Any government where the individual can to some degree control the way in which he and his fellows live (by voting, or influence, or persuasion, or a free press, or whatever) is better than any other. A true democracy, according to me, is one where the government does not feel too safe: they feel they must please the people if they are not to be turned out; unless the government feels that at any moment it might be got rid of, it is liable to become a tyranny. It may be a benevolent and wise tyranny, as Plato warned, but a tyranny nevertheless.[2] And however enlightened to begin with, a tyranny almost invariably degenerates into something much less satisfactory.

I think of the Balkans. I am sure the squeezing together of Serbs, Croats, Slovenes, Bosnians led to a great deal of oppression and misgovernment. If each of these little communities could be self-governing, it would be better – in so far as Wilson's self-determination[3] (or your own use of the term) is valid, it leads one to suppose that the splitting up of the world into a great many small, uniform or reasonably uniform, communities would do more for human

---

1 'No one pretends that democracy is perfect or all-wise. Indeed, it has been said that democracy is the worst form of government except all those other forms that have been tried from time to time; but there is the broad feeling in our country that the people should rule, continuously rule, and that public opinion, expressed by all constitutional means, should shape, guide and control the actions of ministers, who are their servants and not their masters.' Churchill speaking in the Commons on the 2nd reading of the Parliament Bill, *Parliamentary Debates* (Commons) 444, 11 November 1947, cols. 203–321 at 206–7.

2 It is not clear what IB has in mind here. For Plato, tyrants are anything but benevolent and wise: see the long discussion in books 8–9 of the *Republic*.

3 (Thomas) Woodrow Wilson (1856–1924), Democrat US President 1913–21; sought a peace settlement 1918 based on his 'Fourteen Points', which he outlined to Congress 8 January. Point 5 called for 'A free, open-minded, and absolutely impartial adjustment of all colonial claims, based upon a strict observance of the principle that in determining all such questions of sovereignty the interests of the populations concerned must have equal weight with the equitable claims of the government whose title is to be determined.' *Congressional Record* 56, *Proceedings and Debates of the Second Session of the Sixty-Fifth Congress of the United States of America*, part 1 (3 December 1917–19 January 1918), 690–1 at 691.

liberty and happiness than the great combined states and empires. Herder believed that, and that is why he was a cultural nationalist but not a political one, and hated the Austro-Hungarian Empire, and hated all conquerors, for instance Alexander the Great, for stamping out all kinds of native cultures in Asia Minor – and Julius Caesar for the same kinds of reasons.

So far so good. At this point I have to make a qualification. If you allow the possibility of minorities at all – and it is difficult (indeed perhaps wrong) to demand that states should be entirely uniform, as, for example, Plato and T. S. Eliot wanted them to be – room must be made for minorities, whether ethnic, religious or of whatever kind. The first attribute of a liberal democracy is toleration of a certain degree of multiplicity of cultures. In spite of that, I have to say that I think that, given the need for states at all (and the abolition of the state is not a very practical proposition, whatever anarchists may say), there has to be a central culture and a central language, to which the minorities must adjust and adapt themselves, and not cut themselves off from – otherwise things disintegrate and hatreds are bred.

I am thinking of America, which after all started as the purest democracy of all: the fact that Spanish-speaking parts of that country sometimes declare that they don't wish to learn English, that they have their own culture, that they wish to remain Iberian, etc. – if pushed too far that does lead to the splitting of such a state into mutually hostile groups, which is bad for everybody. I therefore do not believe in total self-determination of minorities in a state which consists of more than a totally uniform ethnic or religious or cultural group. I think that the Pakistanis in England – who for the most part of course speak English and for the most part do try and assimilate with the rest of the population – are right, and that the intolerant Muslim minority, which denounces education in English schools because they do not teach Islam, are in the end troublemakers to be condemned. I expect you will not agree with this – at least, I think not, if your thesis is to be fully implemented.

The Jews in England are a fairly good example of a minority which has integrated itself quite successfully with the country at large. They teach the Jewish religion: they do have the Hebrew language, in which they read the Bible and say their prayers; nevertheless, they do go to English schools – they do not attend Christian prayers, but they do not demand services of their own. They behave as a minority which wishes to live at peace must behave, with due respect to the central culture which every political state must basically possess.

There are other minorities which have behaved in this way – say, the Germans and Scandinavians and for the most part the Italians, Jews, Greeks in the United States. A Greek Vice President was elected (he turned out to be a crook) in Nixon's time;[1] he did not feel it an obligation to encourage Greek

---

1 Spiro Theodore Agnew (1918–96), US lawyer (till disbarred) and Republican politician; governor,

separatism of any kind. When President Johnson, whatever his faults, did so much for the Mexican and Puerto Rican immigrants, he did not take steps – nor was he expected to take them – to create independent communities of these people, insulated to some degree from the majority, merely obeying the laws of the state but otherwise not connected with the majority population. This I do feel rather strongly. Like you, I believe that where there is intolerable friction there ought to be partition; as between Norway and Sweden,[1] in Cyprus (whatever either side may say), certainly in Palestine – the Arabs who choose to live among Israelis do tend to learn Hebrew, and do not harry the Jews. Those who do, and who find it intolerable to be dominated by these foreign invaders, must certainly be separated from them – hence the justice of cutting off the West Bank.

I do not know if I have made myself clear, but I think my general position must by now be fairly easy to understand. [...]

Yours sincerely,
Isaiah Berlin   [...]

TO SHIRLEY ANGLESEY
2 May 1996 [*carbon*]

                                                            Headington House
Dearest Shirley,

[...] I don't envy you your visit to Chernobyl.[2] The mere thought that there must be farmers in Scotland still affected by what happened then, and their children too, and that this pollution is in a thin but persistent way going on and on, is something that maddens me. The mixture of restlessness and economy, which operated in Soviet nuclear defences, reminds me only of France. I remember I used to think that their pilots were very brave but the planes were made too economically, with the result that if we duly crashed in Paris,[3] which we nearly did thirty years ago – I thought my last moment had come, but we came down to earth very quickly about ten miles outside Paris; both wings had fallen off; I saw one of them fall off but attached no importance to it – all I wanted was to save my new little American radio set,

Maryland, 1967–9, Nixon's running mate 1968, Vice President 1969–73; resigned in the face of corruption charges; his father, a Greek immigrant, shortened the family name from Anagnostopoulos to Agnew.

1 After a brief war between Sweden and Norway 1814 the 2 countries formed a union under the king of Sweden, becoming the United Kingdoms of Sweden and Norway; in June 1905, after a period of tension, the Norwegian parliament unilaterally declared the country's independence, an act approved that October by Sweden.

2 Ukrainian town near Kiev, scene of probably the world's worst nuclear power generation disaster (cf. the accident at Fukushima Daiichi, Japan, 2011): workers at the Chernobyl plant lost control of a reactor core 26 April 1986, resulting in a fire and explosion that sent radioactive material far across Europe, with severe implications for the health of humans and livestock.

3 No apodosis follows.

to which I was much attached.[1] So once we were on the ground, I felt we were quite safe, and didn't move unduly. Everyone else rushed for the exit, since it was clear that the plane might well be on fire – first the crew, no question of women and children, then the rest of us. By the time I got out the rest were specks in the distance. I realised the danger, and myself began to race towards the airfield sheds; there we were given cups of coffee or glasses of brandy; we were packed into another plane, though some people were too shattered to go into it. All I remember is sitting next to a very drunken black man, who tapped me on the knee and said, 'C'est le bon Dieu qui nous a sauvé. Rappelez-vous, Monsieur, c'est lui-meme qui a participé en cette affaire.'[2] Another black man sitting next to him said, 'My mummy always told me not to fly, she always said, "Don't fly, Jimmy, don't. They're terrible, they're devils, those machines."' In the end we got to London. I was slightly shaken, but not so much as I should have been. After that I felt nervous about flying, but got used to it in the end, and now feel perfectly safe, however irrationally.

Goodness, how you dash about – Chernobyl, Lvov (Lemberg: to me, the centre of Auberon Herbert's[3] Uniates[4] – very tiresome people they are, too, neither one thing nor another).

Ivinskaya: the Pasternak relations loathed her, thought she was a prostitute who ruined their brother/cousin; others said she had great charm, was very nice, a sweet, simple woman. So you can take your choice. As for Lydia Chukovskaya, she certainly was a saint and very, very incorruptible, inflexible, fearless – without her I don't think Akhmatova would have had half the reputation she has now. I know her daughter,[5] [...] who went to pieces when her mother died and is taking some time to recover. She may be coming to England soon, in which case I will try and look after her – Lyusha is her name, and she is extremely nice too. The fact that families like that survived the Soviet regime is a compliment to the human race. I don't know

1 A dramatically exaggerated account of a 1952 episode, recounted at the time to Vera Weizmann and Alice James: L2 299, 307–8. There *was* a fire, but the contemporary account makes no mention of wings, though a blazing propeller does fall off; a clear instance of IB embellishing to entertain.
2 'It is the good Lord who has saved us. Remember, Sir, it is he himself who was involved in this episode.'
3 Auberon Mark Henry Yvo Molyneux Herbert (1922–74), Liberal politician, patron of the arts, writer for the *Daily Telegraph* and supporter of refugees, notably from Eastern Europe; co-founder and vice chair 1954 (later chair), Anglo-Belarusian Society; accepted late in life by Bishop Ceslaus Sipovich into the Belarusian Greek Catholic Church; subject of a memoir in PI.
4 The Eastern Catholic Churches (including the Church that Herbert joined) which remained in communion with Rome, while observing the liturgical practices of the East; a derogatory term when used by members of the Eastern Orthodox Church.
5 Elena Tsezarevna ('Lyusha') Chukovskaya (1931–2015), Lidiya's only child. She did come to England 1996, after her mother's death, and met IB in Oxford and London, as she had done on an earlier visit in April 1989, when she organised an interview of IB (in Russian) by Vsevolod Shishkovsky, London correspondent of Russian state TV and Radio.

of any similar cases in Germany – one or two in Poland, perhaps, none in the Ukraine.

Since I dictated this, you have met Aline at lunch in Sotheby's. She says you looked very well; you probably thought that she did too; we all suffer from various ailments, Aline more than I, which is unfair considering our difference of age. [...]

Yours ever,

Isaiah

On 9 May IB attended the lecture 'Eliot v. Julius' given at Oxford by the profes-
sor of poetry, James Fenton.[1] The lecture was stimulated by the publication
of Anthony Julius's book on Eliot and anti-Semitism,[2] which, Fenton argued,
would have to be taken into consideration in any future assessment of Eliot's life
and work: 'Julius says an anti-Semite is a scoundrel. What is it that holds us
back from saying that Eliot was a scoundrel?'[3] On leaving the lecture theatre IB
apparently spoke to a journalist, and an account of their conversation appeared
in 'The Talk of the Town' column in the New Yorker *of 20 May: 'Very good*
indeed! Excellent! Every word he [Fenton] said seems to me to be true. [...] Eliot
tried to get out of it. He said "I'm not an anti-Semite." But Eliot's beliefs were
the same as Ezra Pound's. Only more cautious.'[4] Soon afterwards IB was obliged
to defend his words to Eliot's widow.

TO VALERIE ELIOT[5]

19 June 1996

Headington House

Dear Mrs Eliot,

Henry Hardy has shown me your letter to him of 11 June.

Let me assure you that I never supposed that Mr Eliot was ever unfriendly to any particular Jew or group of Jews on the ground that they were Jews; or had ever done anything against them. This was made plain in our correspondence, which you hold, and I never thought otherwise.

But I have to admit that the notorious sentence in *After Strange Gods*[6] is critical of the position of the Jews in gentile society. My feeling was that he was close politically to Charles Maurras[7] and other members of the Action

---

1 James Martin Fenton (b. 1949), poet, journalist and literary critic; professor of poetry, Oxford, 1994–9.

2 527.

3 Ian Parker, 'Eliot v. Julius' (opening 'The Talk of the Town'), *New Yorker* 20 May 1996, 29–30 at 29.

4 ibid. 30.

5 (Esme) Valerie Eliot (1926–2012) née Fletcher, 2nd wife and literary executor of T. S. Eliot (m. 1957); a watchful guardian of his works and reputation, she edited *The Letters of T. S. Eliot* i, *1898–1922* (London, 1988) and co-edited four further vols (1922–31) (London, 2009–14).

6 528/1.

7 Charles Marie Photius Maurras (1868–1952), ultra right-wing French political theorist and author;

française, whose contributions he occasionally published in the *Criterion*, and there is no doubt of their political hostility to the Jews, particularly in France, of course.

I repeat that of course I did not suspect Mr Eliot of any personal anti-Semitism,[1] and his relations to me, as you know, were always very friendly. Political anti-Semitism was a major phenomenon since the end of the nineteenth century, and Mr Eliot's alliance with the French extreme right is evidence of his political views in this respect.

I am terribly sorry if your feelings were hurt by what I casually said to some unknown journalist. I cannot deny that I was impressed by the weight of the evidence which the Professor of Poetry adduced from the sentence in the essay and the famous anti-Semitic lines in the poems.[2] But that was all. My personal respect and liking for Mr Eliot remain unimpaired. Do not, I beg of you, think of me as one of his detractors; when some people tried to enlist me in opposing the renaming of the Carlyle Trust as the Eliot Trust in the London Library, I declined to have anything to do with this, and supported the change. So do not think ill of me, I do beg you. ⟨But Mr Eliot, I ought to remind you, did speak of race as well as religion among his objections to too many 'unbelieving[3] Jews' –⟩

Yours sincerely,

Isaiah Berlin

TO MICHAEL IGNATIEFF

25 July 1996

Headington House

Dear Michael,

Gratified as I deeply am by your failure to discover totally black attributes or actions on my part, I had better send you a list of my surviving enemies,[4] to whom you could address yourself (one of them I have just forgiven, so he is no good).

Yours ever,

Isaiah

prominent in the Action française political movement founded 1899, and a contributor of anti-Semitic writings to its daily, *L'Action française*; collaborationist supporter of the Vichy regime.

1 Cf. 355: 'he was obviously, in fact, an anti-Semite'.
2 IB must have in mind lines from some or all of the 5 poems identified by Anthony Julius as being anti-Semitic: 'Burbank', 'Gerontion', 'Sweeney Among the Nightingales', 'A Cooking Egg', and the posthumously published (in 1971) 'Dirge'. op. cit. (527), 5.
3 sc. 'free-thinking'.
4 MI remembers no such list arriving.

TO IMMANUEL JAKOBOVITS[1]

27 July 1996

Headington House

Dear Lord Jakobovits,

I was shocked to see my piece on death etc. in *The Times*.[2] A year or so ago a perfectly nice woman came to see me and asked me my views on the subject. I had not thought about it, and simply improvised as best I could; she included my views in a collection of such pieces which she wished to edit and publish. I forgot all about it – she must have sent me the book, but I have no recollection of seeing it. Imagine my surprise, and indeed horror, at seeing that large extract in *The Times*, plus a photograph; I never intended these reflections to speak to hundreds of thousands of readers, and I am not at all sure that I would have formulated my views as I did.[3]

Your sermon is wonderful – and by wonderful I mean wonderful.[4] Your analogy of the children in the womb, and the prediction by one of them that beyond the womb is nothing, not a wider, richer life, is brilliant.[5]

For myself, I should be very happy if I thought that there was the other world, the *ha-olam ha-ba*;[6] in spite of fears for my own fate in it, I should like to believe that there is this world after death. I even want to hope that it exists. But I cannot persuade myself that it does. I realise that the teaching of our sages demands some kind of leap of faith, not rational argument; and if I suddenly found that I had made this leap and began to believe that there is a life after death, I should be happy to be in that state – but at present I am not. When I told my father that I believed in it, I did it not to distress him, but it was not a true account of my state of mind.

The sages seem to me to preach a wonderful truth in emphasising that the rewards and punishments of 'the other world' are not held out in order to influence human beings in this life – it is not a utilitarian, sticks and carrots, argument, but goals to be sought after for their own sakes. Marxism held out the rewards in this world, but our religion does not in that sense hold

---

1 Immanuel Jakobovits (1921–99), Kt 1981, life peer 1988; chief rabbi, Jewish Communities in Ireland, 1949–58; rabbi, Fifth Avenue Synagogue, NY, 1958–67; chief rabbi, United Hebrew Congregations of the British Commonwealth, 1967–91.

2 'Why I Do Not Regret Lying to My Father about Death', *Times*, 19 July 1996, 16e–h, an extract from *Death: Breaking the Taboo*, interviews by Anna Howard (Evesham, 1996), 30–7. IB reported falsely telling his father Mendel, who was dying (probably unawares) of leukaemia, that he believed in an afterlife.

3 Not for the first time IB displays a perhaps surprising unawareness of the extent and implications of his celebrity.

4 Having been 'extraordinarily intrigued – challenged – even bemused' by IB's article, IJ sent IB his thoughts on the subject: 'If they can serve as the slightest source of hope and comfort I shall be happy indeed. Wishing you a robust postponement of the encounter for many good years to come.' IJ to IB, 19 July 1996.

5 Apparently a version of Plato's allegory of the cave.

6 'The world to come', i.e. the afterlife.

out rewards in the next one. The heaven and hell which orthodox Judaism believes in are what they are in themselves, and not simply means of attracting people in one direction or another. That, I think, is noble and right.

And of course I could not agree with you more strongly about the mortality of those whose example we follow – our parents, or other heroes, about whom we can say that they would have approved of what we are doing, or before whom we would feel ashamed that we had fallen below their standards for some unworthy motive.

My position is somewhat like that of that Christian Father who said 'Lord, help thou mine unbelief.'[1] If one morning I awoke believing in what our sages taught about the world hereafter, I should be perfectly happy, and report it to you immediately if I could. I wish I could believe this. This is a genuine wish, but does not go very far. [...]

Yours very sincerely,
    Isaiah Berlin

TO ANDRÁS SCHIFF

28 August 1996 [*manuscript*]

Albany

Dear Andras,

This is only to tell you that your Bach concertos in Salzburg[2] (which I rightly preferred to attend to going to Sir G. Solti's[3] conducting of Fidelio on the same night – though I falsely promised him to do so) was one of the most moving experiences of my life: it was a totally unforgettable event – I have never heard Bach played like this – I was too deeply moved to visit you after the performance – because I thought you might take my enormous degree of congratulation to be a mere courtesy. I don't know where you are – I am just off to Italy – & back at the end of September – so I send this to your excellent agent. I'll never forget the concertos.

    Isaiah

---

1 'Lord, I believe; help thou mine unbelief': the words of the father whose epileptic son is cured by Jesus (Mark 9:24).
2 Under the auspices of the Salzburg Festival, Schiff performed 6 piano concertos by Bach at the Mozarteum Foundation 10 August 1996.
3 Georg Solti (1912–97) né György Stern, KBE 1971, Hungarian conductor; principal conductor and artistic director, LPO, 1979–83; music director, Chicago Symphony Orchestra, 1969–91; conducted the Vienna State Opera chorus, and the Vienna Philharmonic, in 7 performances of Beethoven's *Fidelio* 10–29 August 1996.

TO DENIS NOËL[1]

14 October 1996

Headington House

Dear Mr Noel,

Thank you for your very interesting letter – I am fascinated by the vagaries of your life. I wish I could answer your question. I simply don't know what first stimulated me to write the various things which I have done. I think I have always written to order, in answer to commissions; like a taxi, unless summoned I stay still. *Karl Marx* was written because it was commissioned by a firm which could find nobody else to write it – and I thought that, though I knew nothing about Marx, unless I wrote about him I should never bring myself to read him. As for other things, I think the strongest influence on me was probably the Russian revolutionary Alexander Herzen, whose views I find deeply sympathetic. I strongly recommend you to read his autobiography *My Past and Thoughts* – it is a wonderful work – and, perhaps, a work called {*Letters*} *From the Other Shore*, also by Herzen.

As for what you should be doing, I have no specific advice to give – only this: do not do anything that bores you. If you go to a lecture or read a book and find it boring, no matter how important the lecture or famous the book, stop at once; only do things which grip you, truly interest you – not out of duty but out of a wish to do them.

I wish you very well.

Yours sincerely,

Isaiah Berlin

TO PAOLO GALLI[2]

22 October 1996 [*carbon*]

Headington House

Dear Mr Ambassador,

[...] I do not know what I can possibly say to add to the minutes of the Herzen Conference,[3] but shall do my best to justify my appointment as president of this conference (I have no idea who attended the conference):

[...] What can I possibly say about Herzen, having written so much about him over the years, which could be regarded as even a minor contribution?

1 Then a graduate student in computer science at Laval, Quebec; he had also written to other prominent persons making similar enquiries.
2 Paolo Galli (b. 1934), Italian diplomat and author; served in the ministry of foreign affairs from 1958; minister to the EEC, Brussels, 1980–5; Italian ambassador to Poland 1986–8, to Japan 1992–5, to UK 1995–9.
3 IB had accepted the presidency of this conference, held in Naples 11 November 1995, but his operation to insert a pacemaker had prevented him from attending.

All I can say is that I still regard him as a man of genius, both as a writer and as a thinker, who has not received his full due even now. I do not think he is much read in Russia now, because his name is associated with Lenin's praise of him, which wrongly associates him with the rise of the Communist movement. There is nothing he detested so much as Communism, not merely Marxian Communism, but the earlier communism of thinkers like Étienne Cabet.[1] There is, therefore, a certain irony in the fact that during the Soviet period so many streets and institutions were called after him – he would have been the first to enjoy an irony of that kind. His essay of the greatest relevance to the world today is perhaps *From the Other Shore*; I do not know if this has been translated into Italian[2] – if not it certainly should be. In the course of this brilliant piece of writing about the revolution of 1848–9, he speaks of idealists who go through terrible torments in order to reach some kind of perfect society, for which no sacrifices can be too great. When it is pointed out that various crimes and enormities are committed in search for this ideal world, people of this kind say that one cannot make an omelette without breaking eggs. Herzen says that the eggs are broken easily enough, the trouble is that the omelette never materialises. They are like worshippers of Moloch, trying to move towards him through seas of mud and blood, but, as they approach, the Moloch is constantly receding, and therefore they never reach him, nor will they ever reach him.[3]

That is the fate, in Herzen's opinion, of those who believe that there is some perfect political society, which with enough knowledge and enough effort can be created by human beings. His view (and I share it deeply) is that the belief that a perfect society can be created, or is even clearly conceivable, either in detail or on general lines, invariably leads people to commit crimes which they normally would not dream of committing; that political fanaticism of this type, no matter how pure the motive, how noble the goal, invariably leads to blood. There is no century in which this has not been illustrated in a more dreadful fashion than ours. It is probably the most terrible century of any in the history of the Western world: the amount of deliberate cruelty, destruction, extermination of millions of innocent victims, has, I think, never been paralleled.

And yet, if one asks oneself how this came about, one cannot, in my

1 Étienne Cabet (1788–1856), French teacher, lawyer and utopian thinker, whose romance *Voyage et Aventures de Lord William Carisdall en Icarie* (Paris, 1840) imagines a Communist society based upon the principle expressed by others in variants of the formula 'From each according to his abilities, to each according to his needs.'

2 It had been translated twice, both times as *Dall'altra sponda*, by Bruno Maffi (Milan, 1945) and by Pia Pera (Milan, 1993) – in the latter case from the edition introduced by IB (115/2).

3 'Who is this Moloch who, as the toilers approach him, instead of rewarding them, draws back; and as a consolation to the exhausted and doomed multitudes, [...] can only give the [...] mocking answer that after their death all will be beautiful on earth?' op. cit. (22/1) vi 34; op. cit. (115/2), 36. Cf. RT2 104–5, 193.

opinion, deny that it is ideas which have done it all[1] – not, as some historians would like to believe, social conditions, the factors involved in social or political change or development, the relationship of economic classes, the effect of technology on culture. In my view it is ideas – Marxism, Fascism, National Socialism – ideas born in the heads of individuals who bound their spell upon a mass of credulous followers: it is these ideas in the end, and these individuals, who are responsible; without them it is not credible that anything of this kind could have happened.

Herzen is the most eloquent and convincing preacher of this particular truth. I can only say that the sooner people learn the lessons of history, and especially this particular lesson, and the more people who read Herzen's wonderful pages, the better for us all. [...]

Yours sincerely,
[Isaiah Berlin]   [...]

24 October 1996: publication of IB's The Sense of Reality: Studies in Ideas and their History, *edited by HH, with an introduction by Patrick Gardiner.*[2]

TO FRED WORMS
29 October 1996 [*carbon*]

                                                                    Headington House
Dear Fred,
[...] As you may imagine, I share your sentiments entirely. I think the present government is terrible, and is likely to make mistakes and commit crimes of a very peace-endangering sort.

I wish I could believe in your theory (in which you do not believe too much yourself) of Netanyahu's cunning plan to take a step, under the pressure of the post-election American President, to get rid of the extremist right-wing fanatics and then extend a hand to Peres, and form a national government. That would be a very good thing – at least, the best that could happen in these confused circumstances. But I wonder if so obstinate, vain and foolish a man would ever follow so rational a course. [...]
    Yours ever,
    Isaiah

---

1 An allusion to Voltaire's 'Les livres ont tout fait' ('Books did it all'). 'Epître au roi de Danemark, Christian VII, sur la liberté de la presse accordée dans tous ses états' (1771): *Oeuvres complètes de Voltaire* [ed. Louis Moland] (Paris, 1877–85), x 427.
2 Patrick Lancaster Gardiner (1922–97; plate 11), lecturer, Wadham, 1949–52; fellow, St Antony's, 1952–8; fellow and philosophy tutor, Magdalen, 1958–89; best known for his work on Schopenhauer and Kierkegaard, and for encouraging a renewed interest in German idealism among British philosophers in the 1960s. IB admired his fastidious taste.

TO PETER SMITHERS[1]

11 November 1996 [*carbon*]

Headington House

Dear Peter,

I read your letter with great pleasure and interest.[2] Basically our views don't disagree. My fundamental thesis is that the qualities which go towards making a competent scientist, e.g. the capacity for formulating general propositions, deducing various particular results from them, interrelating these general propositions into higher hierarchies so that perhaps a great many of them follow from each other and form a deductive system – all this is not what constitutes the qualities needed by a successful statesman. The assumption of a scientist is endless rotatability of the phenomena: you formulate a hypothesis on the basis of 1, 2, 3 observations in the laboratory, but you know from the general scientific rules which guide you that no matter where, when or how, given the ingredients of these particular experiments, the results are bound to be the same wherever, whenever they occur.

History is not like that, nor is human nature: each situation is in some way uniquely different. To understand what was common to the British revolution of the seventeenth century, the French Revolution in the eighteenth, the Russian in the nineteenth [*sic*] will not help you to promote a successful revolution in Ecuador. An attempt to generalise, to deduce conclusions, to apply scientific method to human materials – if I may so speak – is doomed to failure. Quite different attributes are needed for success. What you say in your letter is correct: to be a successful statesman you certainly need ambition, but even more you need this capacity for integrating a great many relevant facts (and a sense of what is relevant and what is not), which Kissinger's sixty-odd researchers could not possibly do, nor could a machine. It is the kind of understanding of the material which an artist has – to know what can be done with stone, wood, clay without being able to formulate precise rules about what you are doing.

Statesmanship, like art, is a way of manipulating human beings, based on an understanding of what effect this or that political move is likely to have on this or that group of people – which can only be learnt through some kind of experience of public life, for which there is no theoretical substitute. That is

---

1 Peter Henry Berry Otway Smithers (1913–2006), Kt 1970, politician, diplomat and amateur botanist; Conservative MP 1950–64; secretary general, Council of Europe, 1964–9; senior research fellow, UN Instititue for Training and Research, 1969–72; general rapporteur, European Conference of Parliamentarians and Scientists, 1970–7.
2 Inspired by IB's essay 'On Political Judgement', NYRB, 3 October 1996, 26–30 (repr. in SR), Smithers hazarded his own foray 'into the question what constitutes statesmanship. [...] In the following note you will see that I arrive at most of your conclusions though by a different process' (letter of 26 October).

why I think that the successful politicians – Julius Caesar, Abraham Lincoln,[1] Tito, Mao – were successful not only because they had the willpower, the ambition, the driving force, but because they understood the nature of the 'material' with which they were dealing, in these cases elements of human societies, groups, classes, Churches, traditions: the ability to predict what kind of effect this or that move was likely to have on some given plurality of people. Nothing can teach you this except native intelligence (not intellect, I agree with you: politicians do not need to be intellectuals, and when they are it probably works against them: see Balfour, the French prime minister Painlevé[2] – an excellent mathematician, who got things into a condition where Clemenceau[3] was needed to put them right). Even Mitterrand managed very skilfully to manoeuvre into all kinds of positions which less intelligent, less adroit, less cunning people could not have done. He actually managed to conceal, and then cause to be ignored, his Vichy past, his associations with various scoundrels – he had the particular kind of qualities which make a man successful in political life. I think you feel that quite clearly, and so do I; you think you come to it by a different route from me, but I don't think that is so, I think our routes are very similar.

Yes, Henry Kissinger can be regarded as a successful statesman, until the end, when he made a blunder. His great achievements were the breakthrough with Nixon in China (Nixon could never have done that for himself) and his build-up of Nelson Rockefeller[4] until he became a presidential candidate, which he could never, never have done for himself, with his relative lack of intellect, intelligence etc. His blunder was ambition. You quite rightly say that if an ambition comes into conflict with other factors it may ruin the whole thing: you give an example of Iain McLeod,[5] who upset the situation in Africa by putting too much money on the blacks, and ignoring the whites and Indians. Kissinger did the same when he wanted to govern

---

1 Lincoln's 1861 election on an anti-slavery platform helped precipitate the US Civil War 1861–5, which he pursued to a successful, though costly, conclusion; with the Emancipation Proclamation, 1 January 1863, he laid the foundations of the end of slavery; assassinated shortly after the Confederate surrender in April 1865.

2 Paul Painlevé (1863–1933), French politician and mathematician; prime minister, France, September–November 1917, April–November 1925; Painlevé's 1st premiership coincided with the disastrous Nivelle offensive on the Western Front, April–May 1917, and it is unrealistic to blame the difficult condition of France in November 1917 on his brief spell in office.

3 Georges Benjamin Clemenceau (1841–1929), prime minister, France, 1906–9, 1917–20; a strident critic of the French government and military from the outbreak of war, he assumed office at a perilous time for his country, but successfully instilled a sense of unity and inspired a belief in ultimate victory; led the French delegation at the Paris Peace Conference 1919.

4 Nelson Aldrich Rockefeller (1908–79), grandson of John D. Rockefeller, Sr, who founded Standard Oil; a liberal Republican, he unsuccessfully sought his party's nomination as its presidential candidate 1960, 1964, 1968; Gerald Ford's Vice President 1974–7.

5 Iain Norman Macleod (1913–70), Conservative politician; secretary of state for the colonies 1959–61; chancellor, duchy of Lancaster, and leader, Commons, 1961–3; editor, Spectator, 1963–5; chancellor of the exchequer 1970 (died shortly after taking office); as Colonial Secretary he hastened Britain's withdrawal from Africa, prioritising majority rule.

the country. He couldn't become President, because he wasn't born in the USA, but he persuaded Ford, when he was a candidate, to promise him that if he was elected President he, Kissinger, would be wholly responsible for foreign policy – one of the factors which lost Ford the Presidency (I don't say he wouldn't have failed for other reasons). The mere fact that Kissinger thought that a known promise to lift him to a height where he could ignore the President, almost ignore Congress, shows something overweening; the ambition, and the imagination which goes with it, distorted his view of what was and was not feasible. About all this I think we agree. [...]

You speak of the avalanche of papers and problems and situations which rain in upon modern prime ministers – the only time when they can think calmly is in their bath. That need not be so. In the end, the capacity for integrating all these bits of information is a unique gift, and it does occur. Kohl[1] in Germany – he is not a genius and he must have had absolute avalanches of stuff pouring in on him; nevertheless, he has so far done much better than anyone could have anticipated, on account of some native capacity for knowing how to act, when to act, how strongly to act, against whom, with whom, for whom, etc., for which there is no substitute. It is a native gift which can take the forms of artistic creation or public activity, but is most unique, indescribable and indispensable.

I do not believe, as you do, that social scientists can be useful in practical matters, but about that I may be old-fashioned and wrong. Political philosophy, yes, because it at least helps one to identify the ends for which one is working, the distinction of ends and means, the collision of possible ends between [which] one has to choose what to try and implement, what to ignore or drop. But I agree, none of it is reducible to a system. For all this I think one needs some other term than intelligence: political talent, political genius.

I have said enough. Yes, indeed, I remember my comparison [between] the Soviet Union and a public school, and the startled reaction of your political school.[2] A very nasty school, governed by very unscrupulous, Jesuitical figures – but all that is over, and the result is chaos. I am glad to be as old as I am, and I am glad that you are. Long may we live. Thank you again for your letter.

Yours ever,
Isaiah

---

1 Helmut Josef Michael Kohl (b. 1930), German statesman who oversaw the reunification of his country; chair, Christian Democratic Union, 1973–98; chancellor, FRG, 1982–90, Germany 1990–8.

2 'Let me recall a delightful moment, as you opened your address to the retired colonels and their ladies at the Conservative Party Political School which I had arranged at Bournemouth in, perhaps, 1948. Your subject: "The Soviet Union". "Ladies and Gentlemen, the Soviet Union – is rather like a Public School" (shocked gasp from the audience). "Yes, you see – there are the masters – and the prefects – and then there are the boys." It was a great triumph on what might have been a somnolent occasion.' PS to IB, 26 October 1996. By 'very nasty school' in the next sentence IB of course means the USSR.

TO MICHAEL IGNATIEFF

30 December 1996

Headington House

Dear Michael,

Aline has read your biography,[1] and I swear by all the gods that I have not read a single word of it, nor had it read to me. She agrees with and admires the greater part of it very much, but finds certain things puzzling. Consequently I have decided to send you an account of some of the things she has raised. I am sending it as a tape because I imagine you would not wish any other ear but yours to hear what I say.

Yours ever,

IB

A transcript of the cassette tape follows.

Let me begin with the most central point, which Aline, more or less, told me about: my alleged feelings as an outsider in a world to which I came as a stranger, etc., and its relevance to my view of the Jews as hunchbacks, etc.[2] This really is not the case. The thing about me, the thought of which occasionally embarrasses me, is that I adjust myself too rapidly and easily to almost any group of persons I am thrown together with. I have no recollection what happened when I was in Russia, of course, but, let me tell you, thrown into a group of English schoolboys in Surbiton, who were as remote from me as anyone could be, I felt no sense of alienness – I fitted in very quickly, became quite popular and felt totally at home among them all. I played cricket and football quite easily and naturally, and accepted all their values – followed them whole, uncritically. So too later.

The only moment at which something unlike this happened was when (as I think I told you), having been accepted by Westminster, my Latin coach told me that the name 'Isaiah' might cause boys to tease me and mock me, and would it not be better if I changed it to something ordinary, English, like 'John' or 'Robert' or 'Henry'? I then thought: No, I don't wish to go to a school where this is liable to happen. That was the only moment of, as it were, a foreigner's self-conscious resistance that ever occurred in my life, I think. And so, boldly, I chose St Paul's, where there were plenty of Jews, some whose parents came from abroad.

I was totally happy in St Paul's and fitted in from the beginning. I had only two Jewish friends:[3] all the others were English Gentiles. The English

---

1 She read a draft typescript at MI's request. IB had consistently said that he would not read the book.

2 262, 285, 550–1, 554.

3 Excluding his childhood friend (since 1916) and St Paul's contemporary Leonard Schapiro.

Gentiles were a great deal closer to me than the two Jews – one of them was only half Jewish and was killed as a pilot in the Battle of Britain;[1] the other, called Ettinghausen, then became a Zionist, became called Eytan, and became a high Israeli official, ambassador in Paris, etc. I still know him of course, he's my age, but our relationship has become very, very remote. My friends in St Paul's were naturally English. I never felt alien – so far as I can recollect, of course – for one second.

After that, Oxford. Corpus Christi College had scarcely any Jews, and no foreigners, mainly boys from the middle public schools from Winchester downwards, no Eton or Harrow. From the first week, after some feeling of strangeness, but immense relief at being free at last and not at my parents' home, I made almost too many friends almost too easily, and there is no doubt that during my entire period there I felt totally at ease, completely natural, and nobody ever tried to embarrass me or talked to me about my strange origins or non-Christian religion, ever. Odd but true. There *were* Jews in Oxford then, to the number of I think seventy or eighty, and I was of course always a Zionist from the beginning, but my Zionism entirely consisted in the general idea of getting a Jewish state going, and had no relation to any particular Jews or my relation with them. Again, this may sound odd but it is true. There was a Zionist Society in Oxford to which I regularly once a year addressed myself with Zionist propaganda. I met these people and was perfectly amiable to them, and they to me, but we did not belong to the same society, I did not make real friends with them.

There was indeed a Jew called Beddington at Corpus, of a fairly old British Jewish family, originally called Moses. He did come and see me very late at night and told me how awkward he felt about being a Jew, how he hated it, and how he hoped that nobody was taking him for one. In fact nobody did. Incidentally, there's a funny story. There was a perhaps not very nice schoolmaster at Rugby where Roy Beddington (still alive, a painter) was, who used to say to the boys, 'And the Lord said unto Moses, good morning, Mr Beddington.'

I was very sorry for Roy Beddington, but felt that this could never happen to me. Anyway, I made friends in other colleges, none from my old school except the two I mentioned. I presumed that everybody knew I was a Jew – I have been so one hundred per cent from the very beginning, as indeed any child of my parents couldn't help but be. I didn't go to chapel; still, nobody ever brought it up in any connection, however polite and friendly, and yet I had very good and genuinely intimate friends at Corpus at this time. When I moved into digs it was with three Marlburians,[2] one from Corpus,

---

1 Wolf Abiram ('Abe') Halpern (1909–43), German-born, IB's contemporary at St Paul's and Oxford, naturalised 1932, worked for Derby & Co., London metal-brokers; killed in action 1943 (i.e. not in the Battle of Britain, July–October 1940); cf. L1 18.
2 Old boys of Marlborough College (a public – i.e. private – school founded 1843) in Wiltshire.

two from elsewhere, with one of whom, Bernard Spencer – quite a good poet – I remained on intimate terms for the rest of his life (he fell out of a train from Vienna while working for the British Council, nobody knows how, whether voluntarily or by accident). The only Jew in Oxford I really knew was Herbert Hart, who was a very marginal one, and although we talked about how boring he found his minister's sermons in Bradford, we never talked about Judaism much, and a great many people, including the last Warden of New College[1] and the last Master of Univ.,[2] of both of which he'd been a fellow, had no idea he was a Jew: I discovered that when I went to his funeral. He did not hide it, but he was super-English.

After that, two months at New College, and then All Souls. Again you might think that, since I was the first Jew ever to be made a fellow, this would somehow come up. It didn't. Again I felt all too much at home, particularly among my contemporaries, and made lifelong friends of John Sparrow, Douglas Jay, Goronwy Rees, Ian Bowen,[3] John Austin, and to a certain extent, before our breach about Communism, with Christopher Hill (who was violently anti-Zionist), in whose room I argued about this occasionally.

I have to report that the important persons among the senior fellows who governed England, Halifax, Geoffrey Dawson (editor of *The Times*), Simon (then not yet a Lord), Lionel Curtis the fanatical imperialist, Dougal Malcolm[4] (who succeeded Cecil Rhodes[5] as head of the South Africa Company and was a civilised and amiable old rogue) – all these people loved being at All Souls, loved coming back as to the old school, talked to the junior fellows easily and sometimes quite interestingly and tried to behave as if they were still at school, still junior jellows: relations between the old and young were very good. Wilfrid Greene,[6] later Master of the Rolls, who had made more money at the English bar than anyone before him – even Simon – I think was probably a Roman Catholic anti-Semite at heart, but none of this ever emerged. I only learnt of it in connection with the blackballing of Hart from a club in London as a Jew, in which apparently he had played some part. I think you will not find it easy to credit all this, but it is the absolute truth.

Then the war, New York and Washington, my friend Guy Burgess, and

---

1 Harvey McGregor had recently retired as Warden.

2 Kingman Brewster, Jr (1919–1988), diplomat and educator, Master, Univ., 1986–8; but IB may mean Arnold Goodman, Master 1976–86.

3 (Ivor) Ian Bowen (1908–84), economist; fellow, All Souls 1930–7; prof. of economics, Western Australia, 1958–73; editor, *Finance and Development*, 1974–7.

4 Dougal Orme Malcolm (1877–1955), KCMG 1938, historian, fellow, All Souls, 1899–1915, 1924–47, director, British South Africa Company, 1913–37 (not Rhodes's immediate successor), president 1937–55.

5 Cecil John Rhodes (1853–1902), imperialist, colonial politician, mining entrepreneur; prime minister, Cape Colony 1890–6; founder, British South Africa Company, director 1889–96, 1898–1902; a graduate of Oriel, he made provision in his will for the Rhodes Scholarships to Oxford.

6 Wilfrid Arthur Greene (1883–1952), Kt 1935, Baron Greene 1941, lawyer and judge; Master of the Rolls 1937–49. Greene took silk 1922 and built one of the largest Chancery practices of the day; though made wealthy by this work, he also did a great deal pro bono.

all that. When I arrived in New York as an official I discovered that my post had been created for me by John Wheeler-Bennett,[1] who is extremely affectionate about me in his autobiography,[2] and Aubrey Morgan,[3] a Welsh patriot, brother-in-law of Lindbergh. They had decided that I was suitable for the non-U[4] clients of the United Kingdom: other people would deal with the Wasps, but I might be suitable for Catholics, Jews, Negroes, Mormons and other minor tribes without the law. In this connection they consulted Weizmann and Frankfurter. I had known Frankfurter from his Oxford visits in the 1930s, and of course I became a friend, an admirer, of Weizmann, in about 1938. They both testified that I could make it, so I was told later that I would be suitable. But they certainly had nothing to do with the initiation of the appointment, nothing whatever, whatever you may have been told or read.

Anyway, to go back. My friends in New York in 1941, such as they were, and there were not many, were my colleagues in the office, all English of course, no Jews, no foreigners except me; and one or two American friends I had somehow made. Then the embassy and Washington, 1942. You might easily assume that the Foreign Office, which was violently anti-Zionist, with few exceptions, might form a group into which I didn't naturally fit as a Jew – they're always accused of anti-Semitism – and, as a Zionist, not altogether without reason. Again I felt totally at ease: not only John Foster and Tony Rumbold, my friends from earlier days who were in post there, but the other members of the diplomatic corps, and of course of the information service in which I worked,[5] behaved to me as if I was one of them, and I behaved to them in similar fashion. My immediate assistant, Archie Mackenzie,[6] a Buchmanite[7] (the Oxford Group), later a British diplomat, was as close to

1 John Wheeler Wheeler-Bennett (1902–75), KCVO 1959, historian; lecturer in international politics, New College, 1946–50; fellow, St Antony's, 1950–7; historical adviser, Royal Archives, 1959–75; a wartime colleague of IB's in the US, where he was, inter alia, personal assistant to the UK ambassador.

2 Wheeler-Bennett wrote that on meeting Berlin in Washington 1940 he 'fell under the spell of his brilliant intellect': 'one of Isaiah's most priceless attributes is that he evokes genius in others with whom he talks'. *Special Relationships: America in Peace and War* (London, 1975), 87, 88.

3 Aubrey Niel Morgan (1904–85), born in Wales; deputy director general, BIS, 1942–5, personal assistant to UK ambassador to the US (Oliver Franks) 1948–52; m. 1st 1932 Elisabeth Reeve Morrow (1904–34), eldest daughter of Dwight Morrow, former US ambassador to Mexico, 2nd 1937 her youngest sister Constance Cutter Morrow (1913–95); they were the sisters of the aviator and author Anne Spencer Morrow (1906–2001), m. 1929 her fellow aviator Charles Lindbergh.

4 Non-upper-class, as opposed to 'U', a social distinction drawn by Nancy Mitford in *Noblesse Oblige: An Enquiry into the Identifiable Characteristics of the English Aristocracy* (London/NY, 1956).

5 In NY 1940–2 IB had worked for BIS, but he seems to be referring here to his information-gathering activities in Washington 1942–6.

6 Archibald Robert Kerr Mackenzie (1915–2012), diplomat; based at Washington 1943–5; UK ambassador to Tunisia 1970–3; minister for economic and social affairs, UK mission, UN, 1973–5.

7 Member of the Christian Oxford Group (subsequently known as Moral Re-Armament) that emerged c.1931 from the First Century Christian Fellowship founded in England 1921 by the US Lutheran and missionary Frank Buchman (1878–1961).

me as anybody; somehow the fact that I was a Jew and a Russian, which he and I daresay everybody knew perfectly well, never came up, or, if it did, in a quite casual and natural fashion. You know me well enough to know that I'd be unlikely to conceal anything about either my origins or my opinions: e.g. my Zionist views were known to some of the diplomatic corps, but they did not seem to mind. Now and then they would ask me to find out from 'your Zionist friends' what agitation was going on among them, but nothing beyond that.

The Americans: I made the best friends I ever had very quickly indeed. First the New Dealers: Benjamin V. Cohen, a prominent New Deal lawyer who held high office under Roosevelt, a wonderful noble figure whom I met quite early on in Washington as a friend of John Foster; Philip Graham and his wife Kay (now the famous Mrs Kay Graham), then a left-wing couple who were very, very New Deal types, he very left-wing, charming, brilliant and interesting, with whom I immediately made friends; Donnie – Donald – Hiss, brother of Alger;[1] Edward Prichard, who worked in the White House, again a lifelong friend; Rauh,[2] a really noble Jewish lawyer, a friend in turn of all the principal New Dealers (he was never thought of as a Jew either, oddly enough). And then the other end, the wicked Mrs Longworth, daughter of Theodore Roosevelt, a right-wing hostess but a grande dame of the first order, brilliantly amusing and witty and charming and distinguished, politically extremely right-wing; and then Joe Alsop the columnist, who became a really intimate friend till his dying day. I think I was probably the best friend, the most intimate, he ever had, with all his quirks. I was very close to him at all times. Then Charles Bohlen, the diplomat, with whom, and with whose wife, Aline and I became very great friends – they remained lifelong friends also – and Johnny Walker,[3] the director of the Mellon Gallery, married to a Scottish noblewoman,[4] daughter of Lord Perth,[5] a Scottish Catholic peer who had been Secretary to the League of Nations, an ambassador in Rome.

1 Donald Hiss (1906–89), US lawyer employed by the state dept during WW2, younger brother of US public servant Alger Hiss (1904–96), who was one of FDR's advisers at the Yalta Conference in February 1945. Both were denounced as Communist agents in testimony given before the House of Representatives Committee on Un-American Activities 1948: Alger was imprisoned 1950–4, but there were significant doubts about his guilt, and he always maintained his innocence; the release of Soviet files after the end of the Cold War convinced many historians that he had in fact been a spy.

2 Joseph Louis Rauh, Jr (1911–92), labour attorney and Democrat political activist of German Jewish descent; one of the foremost US civil rights lawyers of the post-war era, he was closely associated with the National Association for the Advancement of Colored People; posthumously awarded the Presidential Medal of Freedom by President Clinton 30 November 1993.

3 John Walker (1906–95), chief curator, National Gallery of Art, Washington, 1939–56, director 1956–69.

4 Lady Margaret Gwendolen Mary Walker (1905–87) née Drummond, eldest of the four children of Eric Drummond, 16th Earl of Perth; m. John Walker 1937.

5 (James) Eric Drummond (1876–1951), KCMG 1916, 16th Earl of Perth 1937; diplomat and Liberal peer, deputy leader, Lords, 1946–51; secretary general, League of Nations, 1919–33; UK ambassador to Italy 1933–9.

When Johnny, who was sickly, at one time thought he really was dying of some disease, he told Margaret, his wife, that if he died she was to be sure to marry me, for we would be very happy together. All this boasting is in order to tell you how surprising it is that I was so cosy and utterly unselfconscious in these societies. The idea of being odd, different, watching them as it were from outside, as Proust watched the French aristocracy, was totally not the case.

Then back to England. New College, All Souls. I used to be thought of before the war as a very donnish don, more don than anything else. I remember being accused by Lord Hailsham, my colleague at All Souls in the 1930s, of being 'such a don, such a terrifically typical don – I have never met a don as donnish as you; still, we all love you', etc. After the war I was not so donnish. There were of course a few fellows of All Souls who didn't like me, possibly because I *was* a foreigner and a Jew, though they never, never let on – E. L. Woodward;[1] Humphrey Sumner,[2] the historian, later Warden; J. L. Brierly,[3] professor of international law. But they thought of me as a talkative flibbertigibbet who would never do any serious work in his life, and disapproved of me, I think, for that reason, but maybe as a Jew as well, for all I know. All I can tell you is that, after I was a success in Washington, that attitude totally altered: they all became extremely friendly, very polite. So much for worldly values in academia. It has been so for the rest of my Oxford life. The curious thing about me is that I knew very few Jews, then or now: acquaintances, yes, but friends, no. With all my Zionist passion I have friends among Israelis, but English Jews, American Jews? Only Frankfurter, Ben Cohen; up to a very limited point, Keith Joseph at All Souls. I was the only Jew elected to All Souls; I was the only one who was a tutor and fellow of a College since the days of the late Professor Alexander[4] in the 1890s, and yet it somehow wasn't commented on. No, the idea that I somehow felt an outsider ever in my life is simply not so.

Now about the hunchbacks. The idea came, as you know, from that funny joke about Otto Kahn,[5] which I heard from one of the very pro-British

1 Ernest Llewellyn Woodward (1890–1971), historian; fellow, All Souls, 1919–44, lecturer, New College, 1922–39; Montague Burton Prof. of International Relations, Oxford, and fellow, Balliol, 1944–7; prof. of modern history, Oxford, and fellow, Worcester, 1947–51; prof., IAS, Princeton, 1951–62.
2 (Benedict) Humphrey Sumner (1893–1951), fellow and history tutor, Balliol, 1925–44; prof. of history, Edinburgh, 1944–5; Warden, All Souls, 1945–51.
3 James Leslie Brierly (1881–1955), fellow, All Souls, 1906–13, 1922–47, of Trinity 1913–20; Chichele Prof. of International Law, Oxford, 1922–47.
4 Samuel Alexander (1859–1938), philosopher; fellow, Lincoln, 1882–93 – 'According to the *Jewish Chronicle* this was the first election of a professing Jew to a fellowship in either of the ancient English universities' (John Laird rev. Michael A. Weinstein, ODNB) – prof. of philosophy, Manchester, 1893–1924.
5 Otto Hermann Kahn (1867–1934), banker and philanthropist, was walking past Temple Emanu-El Synagogue on East 65th Street in Manhattan with Charles Proteus Steinmetz (1865–1923), a US

Ministers in the American Embassy in London, who realised it was a bit anti-Semitic as a story but safe to tell me – as indeed it was; that and Moses Hess, who was the first to preach to the American Jews about the pathetic, useless efforts to become assimilated Germans. He didn't have much effect on them, as you know: some German Jews, to the end, felt one hundred and fifty per cent German; but Hess told them that it was their long noses, their curly hair which would make the Germans never accept them, and so it has proved. These stories together produced the image of the hump, which perhaps was an over-violent metaphor, but I liked these metaphors, like the hedgehog and the fox: it concentrated things. And myself, I never felt in the least bit hump-ridden, not even the tiniest hump. I felt it about certain American Jews, the owners of the *New York Times* – Walter Lippmann – who terribly didn't want to be Jews, but knew they couldn't avoid it; and others like them in England; but not many prominent people. Hunchbacks are entirely confined to Jews who have what Diana Cooper once succinctly called to me 'Jewish trouble' – her very clear formula – not those who did not suffer from it: the pious fundamentalists, the Zionists, Herbert Samuel, Hore-Belisha,[1] politicians of that kind not at all. But the judge Lord Cohen, my friend Victor Rothschild, [...] those to some degree, yes. When one is so complete a Jew as I am in my own consciousness, one is free from this, and that is true of several Russian Jews I knew. It is not a universal Jewish characteristic, far from it, but a very widespread one all the same. Again, the hump has nothing to do with being an outsider, which according to Aline you somehow connect.

Now about my snobbery and clubs. I expect I *am* something of a snob. Most people are, and I am perfectly aware that I am pleased to be friends with people of distinguished lineage – not very pleased, but pleased. You say David Cecil: nobody who was at New College with him could have failed to know him quite well; as for me, we became intimate friends. I was his best friend and he mine, at any rate in Oxford, and lifelong it was, and his being a Lord may have had something to do with what attracted me in his character, but it was not a consciousness of his title, if you see what I mean. So too Lord Oxford,[2] a gentle, grey, Catholic scholar of Balliol, brought up by priests and women, a friend of various friends of mine in Oxford at that time among the undergraduates. I was quite a popular don among the 'smart set', I'm

electrical engineer with a hump. Kahn: 'I used to attend services there'; Steinmetz: 'And I used to be a hunchback.'
1 (Isaac) Leslie Hore-Belisha (1893–1957), 1st Baron Hore-Belisha 1954; National Liberal politician and government minister; from a family of Sephardic Jews who settled in Britain in the C18th.
2 Julian Edward George Asquith (1916–2011), 2nd Earl of Oxford and Asquith 1928, KCMG 1964; grandson of H. H. Asquith, and son of Raymond, both of whom he followed to Balliol 1934–8 (greats); colonial governor; governor and commander in chief, Seychelles, 1962–7; commissioner, British Indian Ocean Territory, 1965–7.

afraid; that is, I used to be asked to lunch by Father D'Arcy[1] or Ronnie Knox[2] or Maurice Bowra or Roy Harrod or Freddie Ayer. Lord Oxford was a minor figure in that world, but he took to me very warmly, and told me about Archilochus, hence the hedgehog and the fox[3] – his being a Lord really was irrelevant. Not but what the smart set was of course partly sons of peers, and I graduated from them to London hostesses during my smart social period, which undoubtedly occurred. But let me go back to clubs for a moment.

I never tried to become a member of any club in my life. Before the war I lived with my parents when in London, and if I wanted to meet people, met them in little Soho restaurants. After the war, and with some degree of public position, there were people who wanted to see me who I didn't particularly want to give lunch to or spend more than an hour with; so I needed somewhere. I didn't look round for anything, but suddenly my friend Sylvester Gates, a famous lawyer and banker, asked if I'd like to become a member of the Reform Club. So I said yes, and was elected, and there, I add, it was a perfectly nice club, except that whenever I went there I was invariably, or almost invariably, surrounded by terrible bores who fixed on me, and I found it difficult to get time to write a letter. Some were indeed Jews, some were not. It was there I had a series of political rows with Anthony Blunt and Guy Burgess after the war, but never mind that.

Then I was asked by my friend Raimund von Hofmannsthal[4] if I would like to become a member of his club at St James's. I said I'd like to become a member of any club where I didn't know people, could go in, have lunch, read a newspaper, write two letters and go. I was then asked by my friend John Wheeler-Bennett, would I like to become a member of his club? – Brooks's – so I said the same.

Then the episode occurred which you know, in which I received an ambiguous letter from Oliver Lyttelton in which he said how wonderful it would be if I became a member of the St James's, of which he was chairman, but that he'd heard a rumour from the secretary that there was 'a prejudice against

1 Martin Cyril D'Arcy (1888–1976), Jesuit theologian and philosopher; taught philosophy, Oxford, 1927–45, Master, Campion Hall, 1932–45; provincial, English province, Society of Jesus, 1945–50; one of the most widely known and respected Roman Catholic priests in England.

2 Ronald Arbuthnott Knox (1888–1957), Roman Catholic priest and writer; Anglican ordination 1912, Catholic conversion 1917, ordination 1919; Catholic chaplain, Oxford, 1926–39; lived from 1947 at Mells, Somerset, also the home of Katharine Asquith, widow of Raymond and mother of Julian (next note).

3 In 1939 Julian Oxford told IB of a line by the Greek lyric poet Archilochus (*c.*680–*c.*645 BCE), 'The fox knows many things, but the hedgehog knows one big thing', fragment 201 in M. L. West (ed.), *Iambi et elegi graeci ante Alexandrum cantati*, 2nd ed., vol. 1 (Oxford, 1989). This provided the starting-point for IB's celebrated essay on Tolstoy and history, *The Hedgehog and the Fox* (London, 1953); cf. HF2 1/2, 114–15.

4 Raimund von Hofmannsthal (1906–74), US Anglophile and sometime London correspondent of *Time*, son of the Austrian poet Hugo Laurenz August Hofmann von Hofmannsthal (1874–1929; the librettist of *Der Rosenkavalier*).

members of your race'.[1] I won't bore you, because I've told you already what I replied, and what then happened, but I withdrew my name immediately. So I was never formally blackballed, because I never came up for election, but apparently things were written on the page on which my name originally appeared which caused two members of the club to resign in indignation. Ten years later, as you know, I was offered honorary membership of the club, and accepted, but made it plain that I would never go there in my life. Then they went bankrupt, joined Brooks's, and all the Jews in St James's now crowd the corridors of Brooks's – that is just a funny outcome.

But I never tried to become a member of a club. I said yes if anyone suggested it, or no as the case might be. I have refused at least four smart clubs, dining clubs in particular, just because I thought I'd be terribly bored and would have to go to London too much. The Garrick is another story. The second wife[2] of Lord Rothschild said to my wife what a pity it was that one could never bring wives to any club but the Garrick, and she said wouldn't it be nice if I joined it. Then she put up two of her friends to do it, I was rung up and asked if I was serious. I said 'Oh yes, Aline would love it', became a member by some fast-rate machinery – other people had to wait years, I was told – and did use it for the purpose of inviting ladies and wives and so on. I am very happy in all of them. As for the Athenaeum, when I complained to Lord Robbins about my having no time to myself in the Reform Club, he rapidly made me a member of the Athenaeum, and I was duly grateful. But I never, never asked for it, so the idea that I aimed to become a member of clubs is not the case, believe me.

Incidentally, among the list of your peers comes Lord Halifax, who was never a friend, but because we used to chat at All Souls, as all junior fellows did, and then, when he was ambassador, he quite enjoyed having me to meals, we did develop quite a friendly relation, terrible man though in some ways he was, but a friend, no.

The femme fatale who I loved, Lady Patricia,[3] was a peer's daughter. You think I might not have fallen in love if she had been a commoner? A very unlikely hypothesis, besides which she was enormously déclassé and worked as a religious missionary in squalor and poverty.

I am something of a snob, to some degree, but not in the way I think you think, that is my point. Jewishness did not have that dominant an influence

1 IB misremembers the wording used by Lyttelton, chairman of the club, who reported that 'there may be one or two who are determined to have no one of Jewish extraction in the Club'; Lyttelton was prepared to resign his membership if IB's canditature were rejected, and urged IB: 'My strong advice to you is to allow your candidature to go forward.' Lyttelton to IB, 4 July 1950.

2 Teresa Georgina ('Tess') Rothschild (1915–96) née Mayor; Cambridge graduate who worked at MI5 during WW2, where she became a close friend of Stuart Hampshire, and also met Victor Rothschild (m. 1946).

3 Patricia Sybil de Bendern (1918–91) née Douglas, later Hornak, daughter of Francis Douglas, 11th Marquess of Queensbury; IB's (unrequited) first love; they met in Washington 1942, when her 1st husband, John de Bendern, was a prisoner of war in North Africa (see MI 111–12).

on all I was and did and thought and felt, as, according to Aline, you say. It was not a burden I ever carried, and not an attribute I ever felt made a difference to my philosophical opinions, to my friendships, to any form of life that I lived. I felt a Jew exactly as I felt I had two legs, two arms, two eyes – nothing to be proud or ashamed of, just an attribute, something one was, something one couldn't help be. Some people didn't like it, but I was perfectly comfortable with it, always. Consciously, it didn't make a difference to anything I was or did. To me it's odd that it should be so – a Jew born in Latvia, St Petersburg, then England, then Washington, etc. etc. – and yet, believe me, I naturally fitted in to every society I was ever a member of, almost too comfortably, too frictionlessly. You could say that it indicated a certain failure of personality, of strength of personality or the like. But it is so.

I forgot to add that among the factors which entered the notion of the hunchback was Namier's wonderful phrase used to me about English Jews as the 'Order of Trembling Israelites', OTI, which Chip Bohlen and I in Washington changed into OTAG, 'Order of Trembling Amateur Gentiles' – Walter Lippmann and Co. He knew perfectly well what I meant, and I was delighted to enjoy myself in talking about him and other 'gentiles' in those terms. They may have regarded it as a mild form of anti-Semitism, and I daresay it was and is.

These I think are the only points Aline made. There may be others that may come up when she finishes the book, which she is reading with evident enjoyment. By the way, do you feel outsiderdom as half Canadian, half Russian? I don't believe it. The same is true for me. The case of Jews is often worse. No need to reply to this letter, whose purpose is really only to convince you of the truth of what I say for the benefit of your estimate of me. I honestly don't think that I have exaggerated this or invented it to protect myself against some fearful dark inner complex which in fact threatens me day and night. I don't believe that anyone who's ever known me ever doubted that I was a Jew, but oddly enough I think half the embassy in Washington and half All Souls did not think it always.

Now three postscripts:

1. Aline thinks that I ought not to have written to you at all about all this, that subjects of biographies have no right to tell their biographers how to interpret their lives. But I must say that I do not agree, and I hope that you agree with me. If not, what can I do but apologise for inflicting this upon you and ask you to ignore it, or at worst ask me a few new questions which might perhaps induce you to modify some of your ideas about me? Anyway I apologise for sending it to you: I do hope it doesn't irritate you; of course I don't mean it to do, but one never knows the effect of one's words. Forgive me, forgive me, forgive me.

Postscript 2. There is one thing about my life which perhaps you haven't stressed sufficiently, if Aline is right, and that is the enormous part that music has played in it since, say, the age of fourteen or fifteen. My life has been lived against the background, or indeed as part of a tissue, of musical listening. I play no instrument, but since my schooldays I have loved music to a very, very high degree. Listening to Schnabel playing Beethoven,[1] or the Busch Quartet, transformed the limits of my experience, widened them, gave me a new sense of what art is: above all, of course, what music can be. They are not the only influences. I have listened to more soloists, chamber music, opera, symphonies, choral works than almost, I think, anyone living. This may sound an extravagant claim. My only point is that it is an intrinsic part of my life, not just one of its great pleasures. If you want to know more about that, do talk to me about this, because it wouldn't impinge on the general picture, but might add to it. So next time we meet, bring it up if you want to, or not, as you please.

Postscript 3. I suddenly thought in this connection that while the BBC keep plying me for various interviews on TV and radio, which I systematically refuse, a programme on the part that music has played in my life might perhaps be something I could just do – but without illustrations, of course. I think I could talk about a succession of musical experiences, and in this connection I should like to add, if I haven't already, that while snobbery may indeed be an element in me, hero-worship is much more such: I've had such heroes as Stravinsky, Toscanini, Edmund Wilson, Weizmann, Pasternak, Akhmatova, not quite but nearly Brodsky, people in whose presence I felt humble and whose every move I followed with dedicated admiration and fascination. I really am a hero-worshipper, more than I suspect anyone else you've ever known. But Lord Halifax, Lord David Cecil and Lord Oxford, and sundry other Lords, particularly Labour Lords, have not been objects of worship. Whatever made me like some of them was due to quite different motives. There now, I must stop. Once again, forgive me. This really is the end.

TO TEDDY KOLLEK

17 January 1997

Headington House

Dear Teddy,

Thank you for inviting me to become Chairman of the international editorial board for the *Jerusalem Review*.[2] Since I imagine this entails no duties or responsibilities, and since I have no idea who the other members of the board

---

1 'Schnabel of course was my God in those years in England. The performances of the Beethoven sonatas made a permanent impression upon me. [...] These two men, Toscanini and Schnabel, altered my notion of how music could be done, while my contemporaries preferred Backhaus and Furtwängler.' MI Tape 11, 18 June 1989.

2 The *Jerusalem Review of Near Eastern Affairs*, whose editor in chief was (and is) Gabriel Moked.

are – and do not even ask – and since I am far too old to contribute anything to anyone ever again, if you want to make use of my name – if you think it will do the periodical the slightest good – then in view of my friendship for you and the very eccentric but to me dear Moked[1] – then I formally accept.

Yours ever, ⟨with much love⟩,

Isaiah

TO DAVID LANDAU[2]

28 January 1997

Headington House

Dear David,

Thank you ever so much for your piece in the *Wall Street Journal*.[3] I think all that you say is perfectly true, but it is said to some degree from the Likud standpoint, as if what mattered was the degree to which Arafat is able to extract from Israel more and more concessions, which, under the Oslo Agreement, were not promised. But I do not think that is quite right. Quite apart from what Oslo did or did not propose, and what the various leaders of Israel and the Palestinians do or fail to do, I have always held the view (which I am sure you reject) that the danger to Israel is mainly that of the enormous growth of the Arab population in the West Bank, as contrasted with the low birth rate of the Israelis. My view was that unless Israel cut off the West Bank, and all those Arabs, it would never become what it was – and rightly – intended to be, a Jewish state. The Arabs in Galilee and the Bedouin etc. do not constitute a real danger. But a rapidly growing population in the West Bank could in time outnumber the Israelis – and then, goodbye the state of Israel. Consequently my view was that they should have cut off the West Bank pretty early, established a strongly fortified frontier against it, and then let the Arabs do what they wished with it – create a state, attach to Jordan, govern it in some other way – of no immediate concern to Israel. Otherwise I think the future of Israel is unnecessarily uncertain.

But I am sure you won't agree. You feel that you want to protect Israel against intolerable steps taken against it by the Arabs, whether Palestinians or not. And it is true that in our time, and I daresay for a good many years to come, the two sides will continue to hate each other: that was not inevitable, but has become so as a result of a failure of any positive Arab policy on the part of the Zionists, and vice versa. You and I will continue to hope for the best for Israel, but I do not believe that the present Likud policy would lead

1 Gabriel Moked (b. 1933) né Munvez, Polish-born Israeli literary critic; prof. of philosophy, Ben-Gurion, since 1971; co-founded the literary journal *Ah'shav* in Tel Aviv 1949.

2 (Maurice) David Landau (1947–2015), British–Israeli journalist and newspaper editor; diplomatic correspondent, JP, 1985–97; founder and editor in chief, English edition of *Ha'aretz*, 1997–2004.

3 Unidentified; possibly attributed to the wrong organ by IB.

to anything but increased friction, bloodshed, explosions – it does not augur well either for the Palestinians or the Israelis. When you speak of Zionism, I think you think of it as a demand for the whole of Palestine. Originally, no doubt, they wanted Transjordan as well, but when this was cut off by Winston Churchill only Jabotinsky resigned from the Zionist organisation.[1] Weizmann accepted it; and if he were alive, I am sure that he would accept an Israeli state minus the West Bank – just as Ben-Gurion wanted. In those respects I am a Weizmannite.

So we agree and disagree. Why not? I was delighted to see you the other day, and always am.

Yours ever,

Isaiah

TO MIRIAM GROSS

30 January 1997 [*by fax*]

Headington House

Dear Miriam,

The torment was inconceivable. However, I have generated the following:

1. Marcel Proust, *In Search of Lost Time* (is that the latest title?).[2]
2. James Joyce, *Ulysses*.
3. Primo Levi, *If This Is a Man* (please check title).[3]
4. T. S. Eliot, collected poems.
5. W. B. Yeats,[4] collected poems.
6. W. H. Auden, collected poems.
7. Max Weber, *The Rise of Capitalism and the Protestant Ethic* (please check).[5]
8. Virginia Woolf, *To the Lighthouse*.

---

1 As secretary of state for the colonies 1921–2, Churchill grappled with the implications for British policy of the collapse of Ottoman power in the Middle East. After complex negotiations with the regional powers, the British Mandate for Palestine was divided into two administrative areas. West of the Jordan was Palestine, administered by the British until 1948. East of the Jordan was Transjordan, treated as an autonomous British protectorate under the rule of the Hashemite family; it gained its independence 1946, becoming the Hashemite Kingdom of Jordan 1948. For Jabotinsky and Zionists of his temper Transjordan was an integral part of the land of Israel, not to be bartered away by the British. Pragmatists such as Weizmann, however, were more flexible, and this difference in outlook was among the reasons that Jabotinsky withdrew 1923 from the Zionist Organization, founding his Revisionist Zionist Alliance 1925.
2 It was the overall title given to the revision by Terence Kilmartin and D. J. Enright (London, 1992) of *Remembrance of Things Past* (London, 1922–31), C. K. Scott Moncrieff's translation of Proust's *À la recherche du temps perdu* (Paris, 1913–27).
3 Correct (NY, 1959).
4 William Butler Yeats (1865–1939), Irish poet, dramatist and prose writer; Nobel Prize for Literature 1923.
5 Max(imilian) Carl Emil Weber (1864–1920), German philosopher and economist, one of the founders of modern sociology; *The Protestant Ethic and the Spirit of Capitalism* (1904–5), trans. Talcott Parsons (London, 1930).

9. Evelyn Waugh, *A Handful of Dust*.
10. Ludwig Wittgenstein, *Philosophical Investigations*.

Could you please say that my assumptions are: (1) that the twentieth century begins in 1914 (otherwise Tolstoy,[1] Chekhov, Ibsen, Kipling, Henry and William James, Mark Twain, Thomas Hardy[2] etc. would have to be considered – according to me they are all nineteenth-century authors – if not, I cannot cope). (2) I only choose works translated into English. (3) This list leaves out Orwell, *Animal Farm*; D. H. Lawrence, *Sons and Lovers*; Joseph Conrad,[3] *The Heart of Darkness*; Boris Pasternak, *Doctor Zhivago*; J. M. Keynes, *The General Theory of Money and Investment* (please check title);[4] William Faulkner,[5] *The Sound and the Fury*; Paul Valery,[6] translations of *Poems*; Luigi Pirandello,[7] *Henry IV* or *Short Stories*.

If two more could be included, I would choose Lawrence and Conrad. I have also left out Thomas Mann (whom many will choose), Fèvre, Pirenne, Gide, Sartre and Camus.[8]

Yours in torment,
   Isaiah Berlin

Shortly afterwards a second fax replaced Primo Levi and Weber with Henry James's The Golden Bowl *(1904) and William James's* The Varieties of Religious Experience *(1902), in first and second positions. The other entries remained in the same order. A third fax added the observation that 'Henry [sic] James (1902) begins the twentieth century.' An explanatory letter followed on 4 February. IB's selection was published in 'Books of the Century', Sunday Telegraph, 9 February 1997, Sunday Review, 12.*

---

1 '*War and Peace* is certainly the greatest work of fiction ever composed.' To Louis Rapoport, 4 February 1991.
2 Henrik Johan Ibsen (1828–1906), Norwegian playwright and poet; Mark Twain, pseudonym of Samuel Langhorne Clemens (1835–1910), American writer, journalist and lecturer; Thomas Hardy (1840–1928), OM 1909, novelist and poet.
3 Joseph Conrad (1857–1924) né Józef Teodor Konrad Korzeniowski, Ukraine-born British novelist, short-story writer and master mariner of Polish descent.
4 *The General Theory of Employment, Interest and Money* (London, 1936).
5 William Cuthbert Faulkner (1897–1962) né Falkner, American novelist and short-story writer; Nobel Prize for Literature 1949.
6 (Ambroise) Paul Toussaint Jules Valéry (1871–1945), French poet, essayist and critic.
7 Luigi Pirandello (1867–1936), Italian playwright, novelist and short-story writer; Nobel Prize for Literature 1934.
8 Henry Fèvre (1864–1937), French writer; Henri Pirenne (1862–1935), Belgian medieval historian; André Paul Guillaume Gide (1869–1951), French writer, humanist, and moralist, Nobel Prize for Literature 1947; Albert Camus (1913–60), French novelist, essayist and playwright, Nobel Prize for Literature 1957.

TO EMMANUEL KAYE[1]

4 February 1997

Headington House

Dear Emmanuel,

I wish I could answer the questions in your very nice letter of 29 January. I contracted two kinds of flu, which kept me in London for a week, so we never went to Israel. So I cannot say whether a visit to Israel would have changed my views.

I cannot get out of my head the idea that while nothing can stop Hezbollah[2] – except peace with Syria – or Hamas from terrorist murders in Israel, if the full Rabin/Peres programme had been fulfilled the Palestinians would have had to take more gradual steps against individual terrorism if they were to keep in with world opinion, and particularly America, which they need. It is perfectly true that Arafat did not fulfil his promises, but neither did the other side if you assume that the Oslo programme was that of Rabin.

But never mind, we can talk about that after I've been to Israel; we intend to go there for the Passover, so after that, if alive, I'll tell you about my opinions, such as they are – not that they are really worth much.

Yours, with much love
    Isaiah

20 February 1997: publication of The Proper Study of Mankind: An Anthology of Essays, *co-edited by HH and Roger Hausheer, with a foreword by Noel Annan and an introduction by Roger Hausheer.*

TO AVRUM EHRLICH[3]

10 March 1997 [*carbon*]

[Headington House]

Dear Rabbi Ehrlich,

    [...] I wish I could agree with your ideas, but I don't.[4] The kind of life you

1 Emmanuel Kaye (1914–99), Kt 1974, Russian-born industrialist and philanthropist, founded Lansing Bagnall 1943, which became the largest manufacturer of electric forklift trucks in Europe; founder, Kaye Organisation, 1966, chair 1966–89 (of Kaye Enterprises from 1989); supported many charities in Britain and Israel.

2 'Party of Allah', radical Islamist organisation devoted to ending the Israeli occupation of Lebanon 1982–4, and to the destruction of Israel and the establishment of an Islamic Palestinian theocracy; its attacks on northern Israel in 1996 were also *de facto* attacks on the peace policy promoted in Israel by Yitzhak Rabin and Shimon Peres.

3 (Mark) Avrum Ehrlich (b. 1968), rabbi and academic, doctoral student, dept of Semitic studies, Sydney, 1994–7; director and administrator, L'Chaim Society, Oxford, 1997; later (since 2009) director, Israel–China Institute for Co-operation and Research.

4 AE had sent IB a copy of his article 'The Judean Alternative' (AE has forgotten its publication details), which advanced, as an alternative to the secularism of the state of Israel, a religiously inspired utopia based exclusively upon the laws and traditions comprising the Jewish heritage.

describe, totally obedient to the rules of Halakha[1] (or, if you prefer it, to the 613 positive and negative enactments of the Well-Laid Table),[2] would be ruled theocratically. There have been people who lived, and live, in this way: Christian monks in monasteries; Jewish students in *yeshivot*;[3] the priesthood of the Vatican; and no doubt in other societies covered by rigidly religious rules, e.g. in modern Iran and Sudan.

But that is not my view of a (to me) tolerable society. I have always been a liberal, and therefore believed in individual and social liberty, which precludes total obedience to a rigid set of rules. Without the degree of liberty and variety of views and conduct, within the framework of, say, the rule of law of a liberal democracy, which the Halakha opposes, no society which I would regard as honourable, decent and free can exist. Even the application of the commandment which forbids the making of graven images (woven images?), let alone the harmless statues with which the world is filled (not that it was always applied in ancient Palestine, e.g. the paintings in the synagogue of Dura-Europos),[4] strikes me as irrational.

So, you see, our views differ; and I have a feeling they always will. But I greatly enjoyed meeting you and all those nice, pious scholars, all the same.

Yours sincerely,
Isaiah Berlin

TO ALFRED BRENDEL

7 June 1997 [*manuscript card*]

Albany

Dear Alfred,

I cannot – and in fact do not wish to – refrain from telling you that your playing at Plush on June 6[5] was truly divine: no other word will do: Far, far more than any of us who listened deserved: I don't know how many of those present felt this: but if they did not, they should not have been invited. There was an old German pianist – I can't remember his name – who said about Bach: "it is too good for wretched creatures that we are". I felt somewhat the same –

It really was a most sublime experience – this has happened on other occasions too, of course; but it is always different, always comes from regions

---

1 Jewish religious laws.
2 Shulhan Arukh, a Jewish legal code.
3 A *yeshiva* (plural *yeshivot*) is an institue for Jewish religious training.
4 When a synagogue was discovered 1932 at the ruined ancient city of Dura-Europos in Syria, it was thought to be a Greek temple because of its extensive figurative wall paintings; further research dated it to c.245 BCE, making it one of the oldest synagogues in the world.
5 IB's 88th (and last) birthday, in celebration of which AB played Schubert's last 3 piano sonatas, D958–60. Plush is the Dorset village in whose church summer concerts have been given since the 'Music at Plush' series was founded 1995.

far above ordinary human life. No one's birthday has ever been so marvellously celebrated. What more can I, should I, I am permitted, to say? *Nunc dimittis* ....

Yrs

Isaiah

TO BEATA POLANOWSKA-SYGULSKA

28 June 1997

Headington House

Dear Beata,

[...] Why political democracy? Why not, for example, theocracy, or, for that matter, traditional life with blind obedience to traditional rules? Let me begin by saying that there are certain foundations on which all ethical and political beliefs rest [...]. Men cannot do without – call it psychological, physiological, biological, etc. – food, sleep, breathing, sex, security, the possibility of communication, the life of the senses. This presupposes a basic liberty of choice: Do I choose to get up or lie in bed? Do I rest or work? – etc. Without this, we are reduced to mere material objects, or at best animals who do everything by instinct. Hence you can say that without such conditions we are dehumanised – these are liberties that men require basically, all human beings require them; this is not an a priori statement (because I do not believe that there are a priori truths about life), but based on observation. In addition to this, men, as men, i.e. pretty universally, need society – Hobbes's solitary savages never existed (this is true even of animals in some unselfconscious way). And the need for society and communication, which all men require, presupposes certain values to be followed. For example: truth – if everyone lies, nobody can rely on anybody [...].

But this does not entail political liberty. Men can live under tyranny, theocracy, obedience to traditional authority. This does not dehumanise – so why liberal democracy? It is a fact, discoverable by anthropological observation, that men seek different values – negative liberty, positive liberty, equality, justice, mercy, rational organisation, family life. Some of these clash, as we know, but the question is, why seek them at all, what makes them values? The answer to this is that everything is ultimately psychological – that that is how men are made, some differing from others, and so people choose values as they do because they are so made; and if they clash, then they can compromise between them, as, for example, between traditional authority and liberty from it by means of rebellion, resistance to tyranny by – usually – minorities, etc. The chief compromise, of course, is between institutions and individual liberty. Without institutions society cannot persist; if it is totally institutionalised, political liberty is extinguished. So we choose democracy: that means that governments cannot rule unless they obtain enough support from the members of society, unless the government knows that it can be turned out (by whatever the machinery may be – usually votes in elections). The government may even be despotic if enough people like that – that is still democracy, even if libertarians don't like it – but that must depend on the fact that the government is not totally safe, that there are rules under which it can be overturned, rules which they accept – that makes it democratic, that is what gives individuals so-called political rights etc. Then there is individual liberty – that is what makes the democracy liberal, the possibility of individual choice – that there are doors open. I repeat that this can clash. So we compromise to survive, and get what we can. Democracy means that the government can be turned out, liberty means that there are enough roads open for me to take, whatever the government may decide. If the government stops me from taking these roads, then I ask myself whether I want to turn out the government and start agitating under the rules – that is how societies proceed. [...]

Then again, why particularly liberal democracy? Not for the reason Gray gives,[1] i.e. that all value systems are what they are and it is a non-rational toss-up between them – because we can give reasons for our choice, give reasons why we prefer this to that; whether because we cling to tradition or defy it, whether we want to live under a republic or a monarchy. We could not argue about that, and give our reasons for it, we could not try to convince slaves to rise, we could not reasonably adhere to certain general rules which may not be universally, but which are widely, accepted – none of this would be possible unless our reasons were intelligible to those who reject them. So liberal democracy is a cross between having institutions and having a degree of liberty, which we prefer – not just because we prefer it, but for reasons which we can give, although these reasons may not be convincing to others.

I don't know if I have made this clear, as against Gray. If argument between followers of different constellations of values is to be possible at all, then it is not a matter of a toss-up between them, each system being what it is, unable to condemn any of the others. Of course I can condemn systems which I hate, what I cannot do is pretend not to understand them (pluralism). I can see how one might prefer to live under some, to me odious, system, but it is odious because my life, and that of a great many other people with whom my life is bound up – my entire society in fact – chooses to live under another system. Why did they so choose? You may say it is psychological – but in that sense everything is: nothing is logical in this region. [...]

Your query about 'the truth': I am a pluralist in the realm of values, but not in epistemology.[2] Truth does not vary with cultures or societies: if true, it

---

1 op. cit. (530/1), *passim*, esp. chapter 2, 'Pluralism'.
2 BP-S writes: 'Berlin ascribes to me here an erroneous interpretation of his views which I actually did not make. This is a result of a piled-up misunderstanding for which I was originally responsible, having asked a misconceived question' (UD 102/1).

remains so 'for ever'. While I cannot be sure that my beliefs are true – infallibility, absolute knowledge, are not, according to me, within our grasp – yet I can regard some judgements as incorrigible, and such judgements do not depend on milieu. If someone says to me that $2 + 2 = 193$, I do not say that the rules of arithmetic [that are] 'universally accepted' make this nonsense, but that in some cultures it seems acceptable: I say that it is untrue and does not make sense, and given what arithmetic is, it is nonsense – and remains nonsense whoever says it, wherever and whenever. I do not add that on the planet Venus another arithmetic may operate, unknown to us. No pluralism here.

Yours,

Isaiah

TO MATTHEW ALTHAM[1]

3 July 1997

Headington House

Dear Mr Altham,

Thank you very much indeed for sending the issue of *Zvezda* with the article by Anatoly Zykov in it.[2] I was much touched by the dedication, and should be very grateful if you could forward a copy of this letter to Mr Zykov and the other signatories. Now to the substance of the article itself.

Let me begin by saying that I did not know, after I left Moscow in 1946, that Anna Akhmatova had written or dedicated any of her poetry to me,[3]

1 Matthew John Arnold Altham (b. 1975), management consultant and conductor; reading modern languages, New College, when this letter was written.

2 Leonid [*sic*] Zykov, 'Nikolay Punin – adresat i geroi liriki Anny Akhmatovoi' ['Nikolay Punin: The Addressee and Hero of Anna Akhmatova's Poems'], *Zvezda* 1995 no. 1, 77–103 (followed by 'Iz perepiski A. A. Akhmatovoi i N. N. Punina' ['From the correspondence of A. A. Akhmatova and N. N. Punin'], ed. Leonid Zykov, 104–14). On 1 July 1997, shortly before his final illness began, IB dictated a note to HH about this article: 'This article is by a man called Zykov, the husband of the granddaughter of Punin, AA's 3rd husband. The article, as you see, was written some years ago, and now Zykov, his wife Anya Kaminskaya and someone else have sent me this old article, with affectionate greetings, via one Matthew Altham, of New College (I do not know him). The article maintains that the references to me in AA's poem, and especially in *Poem Without a Hero* ("the Guest from the Future") are, for the most part – they do not quite say entirely – in fact references to Punin, who died in a Siberian camp (I think in the 1970s) – with whom a very intimate, loving correspondence with AA is printed in the same issue. The thesis is that it was the critics, led by the great Zhirmunsky and supported by virtually everyone else, who invented me as the addressee of the relevant poems. Zhirmunsky came to see me in Oxford some years ago (he was getting an honorary degree) and gave me the full list of poems relevant to me – on, he said, the direct request of AA. The apparatus is enormous, and I think the intentions are sincere. No clear reason is given about why the true addressee is Punin, for whom I act as a "mask". They do not think this is my fault, but that the critics, for no known reason, invented me as the addressee.' A reply to the article was published by Anatoly Naiman: 'Vot s kakoi tochki nuzhno smotret' na predmet!' ['What a way to look at it!'], *Segodnya*, 10 March 1995, 10. Leonid Aleksandrovich Zykov (1940–2001), artist, husband of Anna Kaminskaya (564/1); researcher and publisher of the Punin family archives.

3 Not strictly true: on 5 January 1946 'I repeated the performance with the poetess in Leningrad, who finally inscribed a brand new poem about midnight conversations for my benefit, which is

or that I was relevant to anything she wrote after my visit. I was first told about the details of this by Zhirmunsky, who was of course an old friend of Akhmatova, and who came to see me in Oxford when he received an Honorary Degree here – I cannot remember exactly when, probably in the late 1950s or early 1960s. He told me that he was visiting me at the express wish of Akhmatova, who wished him to convey to me which of her poems related to me; he did this not hesitantly, as the article says, but with great clarity and firmness, having been – he said – commissioned to do so by Akhmatova herself. So I had no hesitation in believing his every word on the subject. He was, as you know, a deeply respected and honourable man, and would not have done this had he not believed what he told me. All this was confirmed to me later by Amanda Haight, who of course accompanied Akhmatova on her visit to England, together with Anna Kaminskaya,[1] and who asked me to see her in connection with her biography – which in my view is still the most dependable, and deeply sincere, work on Akhmatova's life that has yet been written. Gleb Struve, for some reason, harshly condemned it – I never understood why. Perhaps he thought that she was treading on his territory. At any rate, she spoke to me in detail about the relevance of the poems; and so later did one other person in a position to know, namely the late Joseph Brodsky, who became a very great friend of mine and who said that Akhmatova often told him about who the unmentioned, 'secret' subjects of various poems were. He, too, told me that she said to him that she was Dido, and that I was Aeneas, who had abandoned her – I did not realise until then how deeply she felt about the act in my life which had evidently wounded her so much.

You must realise that I spent not two or three hours, as the article says, but fourteen hours with Akhmatova: I came to see her, after the episode with Randolph Churchill,[2] at 9 p.m., and left her at 11 a.m. the next morning. It was perhaps the most transforming episode in my entire life, and I think she, too, responded to our talk, and the readings of her poems to me (including large sections of *Poem without a Hero*), during that magical night. I won't go on about our relationship, save to say that, although there were rumours in Russia that we had something approaching 'an affair', this is wildly untrue. I did not touch her physically, even to kiss her hand in the usual fashion, during those wonderful fourteen hours; nor when I last called on her in January 1946 to say goodbye. [...]

Now back to the contents of the article. One of the most vivid reasons

the most thrilling thing that has ever, I think, happened to me' (IB to Frank Roberts, 20 February 1946, L1 619). The poem, written by Akhmatova in a presentation copy of her volume of poems *From Six Books* (Leningrad, 1940), is the 2nd in the cycle *Cinque*: see PI3 429.

1 Anna Genrikhovna ('Anya') Kaminskaya (b. 1939), art historian; granddaughter of Nikolay Punin, step-granddaughter, companion and friend to Anna Akhmatova.

2 Randolph Frederick Edward Spencer Churchill (1911–68), journalist and Conservative politician, only son of Winston Churchill; for his unexpected call on IB when the latter was visiting Akhmatova in Leningrad see PI 190–1, MI 155, 161.

for knowing that *Cinque* was written about my visit in 1945 is that the first poem is a precise description of the ice breaking in the Neva that night; and the second line, which directly refers to me and cannot refer to anyone else, in my view, is the one about the thin smoke of the cigar.[1] I did indeed smoke a thin Swiss cigar – one after the other – during the evening. I know precisely what the cigar of which she spoke looked like, and why the smoke was thin – that again is a very direct and irrefutable evidence, at any rate of something denied in the article.

The article itself is a wonderfully researched, fascinating, deeply informative and altogether interesting piece, written obviously with the deepest sincerity and belief in its validity. But the proposition that I am a mask for Punin cannot be true. I spoke of being deeply moved, and more, by the visit; and of her feelings, as I recognised them. But I did not know of the image I acquired in her mind, until Brodsky told me about Dido and Aeneas. Then I realised that she regarded herself as the abandoned Dido, because she believed that we had established an immortal relationship, transcending all earthly and mundane facts, and that although we were probably destined never to see each other again, this was a mystical bond which would never be broken. I say this because, when I was in Moscow in 1956, and, as the article correctly says, I did not see her (because Pasternak told me that while she was in Moscow she was nervous of seeing foreigners, because her son had just been released from his third internment, and she had to display extreme caution, because she believed that my earlier visit had been responsible for, at least in part, her and her son's fate after 1946), nevertheless she had told Pasternak that she wished me to telephone her – that 'they' listened to telephone conversations with foreigners, and therefore would know what we might say to each other, and therefore it was in a sense perfectly 'safe'. I did telephone her. The first thing she said was 'Pasternak told me that you married'; I said 'That is true'; she asked exactly when, I said 'Six months ago, this year.' There was then a long silence, at the end of which she said, 'What can I say? Congratulations'; then again a long silence; then we talked about ordinary things – the coming publication of Korean translations of her poems, and the circumstances of her life in general.

I realised then that in her eyes I had committed an unforgivable crime – the unbelievable vulgarity of marrying someone – and indeed this was borne out when I saw her in England in 1964. She did not speak of my marriage; we talked about many other things; she said she would have stayed with us had it not been forbidden by the Soviet Embassy; and when she came to dinner

---

1 There seems to be no relevant mention of ice in any of Akmatova's poems. As for the cigar, IB is presumably thinking of 'the cigar's blue smoke', which appears not in *Cinque* but in the 2nd poem of *A Sweetbriar in Blossom*, and in *Poem without a Hero* 1. 1, 'The White Hall'. For IB's belief that this image was a reference to him see e.g. Anatoly Naiman, 'Sir', BI 76, and L3 460.

with us, at this address – I think she refers to it (the Obolenskys[1] were there; I am not sure whether Anya Kaminskaya was present or not)[2] she treated my wife with the most unbelievable coldness; she was chilly whenever she turned to her, to speak a little in French, which my wife never forgot and did not understand until I explained the nature of the sacred relationship in which Akhmatova had evidently believed.

Let me make it clear that this is the full and sufficient reason for Akhmatova crossing out my name in the text of 1956;[3] it was a sign of real anger or indignation, which I only came to understand after our telephone conversation; it took me a little time to realise the pain I had caused. When I saw Lydia Chukovskaya, she confirmed this; and indeed, in her account of Akhmatova's reference to our telephone conversation in Moscow the evidence for this is clear. She, too, confirmed the identity of the addressee of the poems which related to me.

For these reasons I cannot accept the interpretation given by the author of the article: the evidence is too directly incompatible with it. Of course, in interpreting literature and its relationship to real persons and real life, if I may call it that (Akhmatova would never have permitted the word 'real' to be used in this connection), endless hypotheses are possible, and have indeed been used in trying to explain the lives of Wordsworth, Shelley,[4] Dostoevsky, to name but a few. Consequently it is impossible to refute hypotheses of this kind; and I have no doubt that the author believes every word of his article to be valid. But the idea that critics, the great majority of them, as he admits, including Zhirmunsky and Chukovskaya and all others, including, I believe, Naiman,[5] invented the idea that I was the subject of various lines of Akhmatova's poetry, that I was simply 'inserted' for reasons which Zykov does not give – for they surely could not wish to put a mask on Punin – this idea cannot be right. [...]

1 Dimitri Obolensky m. 1947 (divorced 1989) Elisabeth Nikolaevna Lopukhina (b. c.1915), a fellow Russian exile.
2 According to her diary she was: Anna Kaminskaya, 'Angliiskskaya "akhmatovka": iz dnevnika' ['English "Akhmatoviana": From a Diary'], *Zvezda* 2014 no. 6, 111–20 at 115.
3 It is unclear what IB means here, since AA never mentioned him by name in anything she wrote; nor had Akhmatova seen Lidiya Chukovskaya's diaries. Perhaps he is simply mistaken. It is true that in *A Sweetbriar in Blossom*, poem 7 (written 20–3 August 1956), AA changed lines that originally read 'and I was ready to meet / the Messenger of snow-white cliffs' to the less personal 'and I was ready to meet / the ninth wave of my destiny', but IB may not have known of this change, even if the original lines referred to him as a messenger from a country known for the white cliffs of Dover; and we cannot know whether the change was made because of IB's marriage, for creative reasons, or in response to censorship.
4 William Wordsworth (1770–1850), poet, and one of the progenitors of the English Romantic movement, which included the peerless poet Percy Bysshe Shelley (1792–1822).
5 Anatoly Genrikhovich Naiman (b. 1936), Leningrad-born Russian poet, writer and translator; friend and literary collaborator with Anna Akhmatova in the 1960s; author of the memoir *Remembering Anna Akhmatova* (Moscow, 1989; trans. Wendy Rosslyn, London, 1991), and the novelistic *Ser* [*Sir*] (Moscow, 2001), about Akhmatova and IB, part of which is translated by Josephine von Zitzewitz in BI.

I won't go on, save to say that I do not intend to publish anything about Akhmatova and myself, privately or otherwise, and that the book written by a Hungarian (whose name I can't remember) called *Anna Akhmatova and Isaiah Berlin*[1] is an inflated and totally superfluous piece of writing – with various groundless hypotheses which add nothing to the sum of known facts. He makes much of the Dido and Aeneas idea. It is true that when I realised that she saw me as a kind of Aeneas – my marriage constituted the great betrayal – it filled me with grief and guilt; not because of what I had done (marry), but because I had not understood until then what her image of our relationship was; certainly nothing of this was conveyed during my night in November 1945.

Do please thank the author and the others on my behalf, and convey to them, if you will, the contents of this letter. I shall do nothing to assert [my disagreement with] what I believe to be a largely (if not entirely) mistaken interpretation of events. I should, of course, be wounded if I thought that what the article said was true, but I do not, and for that reason only feel sorrow and guilt, as well as unforgettable exaltation when I think of Anna Andreevna, as I cannot help doing, from the first moment until now.

Yours sincerely,
Isaiah Berlin

TO ARTHUR SCHLESINGER
16 October 1997

Headington House

Dearest Arthur,

We are both terribly sorry not to be able to come to your eightieth birthday party – I have known you longer and loved you more warmly than anybody living. Aline has known you for fewer years, but her feelings are equally warm for both of you, like my own.

I shall say nothing about your public life – others will do this better – save that no more warm-hearted, honest, brave, dedicated devotion to public causes has ever existed.

So, warmest congratulations to you and warmest good wishes to you both. How much more can we say? Make that up out of your own infinitely fertile imagination.

Love, love, love,
Isaiah and Aline   [...]

---

1 György Dalos, *Der Gast der Zukunft: Anna Achmatowa und Sir Isaiah Berlin: Eine Liebesgeschichte*, trans. (from the original Hungarian) Elsbeth Zylla (Hamburg, 1996); subsequently published in an English translation by Antony Wood, *The Guest from the Future: Anna Akhmatova and Isaiah Berlin* (London, 1998; NY, 2000).

TO AVISHAI MARGALIT

16 October 1997

Headington House

Dear Avishai,

This is my formula: of any use to anyone? If not – waste-paper basket.

Yours ever, the still far from well, ⟨– hence this superfluous 'advice'⟩

Isaiah

ISRAEL AND THE PALESTINIANS

Since both sides begin with a claim of total possession of Palestine as their historical right; and since neither claim can be accepted within the realms of realism or without grave injustice: it is plain that compromise, i.e. partition, is the only correct solution, along Oslo lines – for supporting which Rabin was assassinated by a Jewish bigot.

Ideally, what we are calling for is a relationship of good neighbours, but given the number of bigoted, terrorist chauvinists on both sides, this is impracticable.

The solution must lie somewhat along the lines of reluctant toleration, for fear of far worse – i.e. a savage war which could inflict irreparable damage on both sides.

As for Jerusalem, it must remain the capital of Israel, with the Muslim holy places being extra-territorial to a Muslim authority, ⟨+ a smallish Arab quarter⟩ with a guarantee from the United Nations of preserving that position, by force if necessary.

16 October 1997

Isaiah Berlin

TO EMMANUEL KAYE

31 October 1997

Headington House

Dear Emmanuel,

You had no idea that I was ill, and I had no idea that you were the generous benefactor of the Isaiah Berlin Visiting Lectures,[1] which are said to be in full flood.

As for myself, I have had a bad time, with two periods in hospital – said

1 The six lectures in that year's series, entitled 'The Politics of History and the English Enlightenment', were given in the Examination Schools, Oxford, by the Isaiah Berlin Visiting Prof. in the History of Ideas 1997–8, J. G. A. Pocock. After the 1st lecture, which began with an encomium to IB, HH acquired a text from the lecturer and read IB the encomium on a visit to Headington House during IB's final illness. IB's verdict during this reading was 'Complete rot so far.'

to be splendid, but I did not enjoy it for a moment. I am about to embark on two operations,[1] neither of them agreeable but both said to be indispensable. After the first I shall be fed by a machine, which, considering my extreme reluctance to eat naturally, will actually be a relief. So next time you go to your synagogue, pray for me. [...]

What more can I say, but once again, thank you, thank you, thank you.
Yours ever,
    Isaiah

IB's letter of 16 October to Avishai Margalit was sent by normal airmail. Margalit was struck by the fact that IB had never before been so explicit about his position in public, and he showed the statement to the Israeli daily newspaper Ha'aretz, asking whether they would publish it and, if so, in which section. After some delay he was told that they did not find it that significant, but were willing to print it in a somewhat obscure part of the paper. Margalit, aware of IB's extreme sensitivity to publicity, wanted his explicit confirmation of what the letter already implied, that the statement was for publication. His wife Edna called Headington House in his presence, but IB could not take the call. The confirmation was sent by fax on what was to be the last day of IB's life. Ha'aretz published both the statement and the news of IB's death on their front page on 7 November.

TO EDNA ULLMANN-MARGALIT[2]
    5 November 1997 *(fax)*

The answer is 'Yes.' [...]
    IB pp PU

On 5 November, after authorising publication of the statement, IB was taken to the Acland Hospital in Oxford to have a feeding tube inserted, because of a persistent difficulty in swallowing. He had previously resisted this step, but his wife had finally prevailed on him – too late, she subsequently felt.[3] As he left Headington House, Pat Utechin said to him, 'Grin and bear it, Isaiah!' 'I'm bearing it,' he replied, 'but I'm not grinning.'

Shortly before midnight on the same day he died of heart failure. His last recorded words, addressed to the nurse attending him at the time of his death, were entirely characteristic of him: 'And where do you come from?', he asked her.

---

1 The 1st operation, to insert a feeding tube, occurred on 5 November (see editorial commentary at foot of this page); IB died later the same day, and no 2nd operation was performed.
2 Edna Ullmann-Margalit (1946–2010), Israeli philosopher; doctoral student, Somerville (DPhil 1973); taught at HUJ from 1976, associate prof. 1994; m. 1968 Avishai Margalit.
3 However, a post-mortem revealed that he was also suffering from cancer; so earlier intervention, even if successful, may have been a mixed blessing.

The need for an answer to this question, asked in a deeper sense, was for IB, as we have seen, among those that are of primary importance for human beings: 'people should know where they come from'.[1] *This was especially true for the Jews of the Diaspora; and it was the justification of Berlin's Zionism that the only acceptable answer for many of them, after 1948, was 'Israel'.*

The next day a Telemessage arrived for Aline from Buckingham Palace. The Queen recalled her happy memories of many meetings with IB, describing him as 'a man of the utmost distinction who was held in respect and affection by all who knew him'.

---

1 To Felix Posen, 14 September 1989.

APPENDICES

ANSWERS TO QUESTIONS FROM
LARS ROAR LANGSLET

Lars Roar Langslet had first been in touch with IB in 1961 to request permission to publish his work in Norwegian translation. He met IB later that year and asked his advice on a thesis he was planning. Thirty years later, working as a commentator for the Norwegian daily newspaper Aftenposten, *he approached IB for an interview, sending his questions in advance, and following these up with a long conversation in IB's London home. His account of the interview was published soon afterwards.*[1]

1. I think many would join me in seeing your defence of 'negative liberty' (absence of coercion) as the nucleus of your political thought. Would you agree?

2. It would seem that the 'negative' definition of liberty provides a much more stable and well-defined safeguard of human freedom than the various interpretations of 'positive' liberty, which are 'sliding' towards absolutist forms, undermining or eliminating individual freedom of choice. How would you comment on that?

[...] No view I have ever expressed created so much controversy or has been so often attacked. I can't think why. All I tried to do is to clarify two senses of the notion of political liberty, to distinguish them from identifying it with other values – inner liberty, say (as conceived by Spinoza or Kant), power, security, happiness, human rights, freedom from poverty, creation of beauty. My point was that the basic sense of political liberty is what a prisoner seeks – the open door, the breaking of his chains. That is what I called *negative liberty* – its degree consists in how many doors are open for one to enter by. Positive liberty is an answer to a different question: 'Who determines what I am and do? Do I? Or someone else?' Of course men are shaped by physical, biological, psychological, social etc. factors. But that is nothing to do with *political* liberty. Here the question is: 'Who controls me? Whom do I obey? The nation? Society? The Church, the party? Or is it myself, within certain limits?' Both senses of liberty can, of course, be abused: 'negative' by demanding a maximum of social or economic laissez-faire – the liberty of the strong has led to injustice, cruelty, poverty, oppression of the weak; the liberty of the wolf is death to the sheep. (Perhaps Friedman and Hayek haven't thought about that quite enough.) Positive liberty can be interpreted

---

1   See Lars Roar Langslet, 'Mennesket lever i kraft av ideologiene' ['Man lives by the power of ideologies'], *Aftenposten*, 18 January 1991, 40; repr. in *Minerva* 2008 no. 3, 68–73. The advance questions, IB's written responses to which are excerpted here, are dated 2 January 1991.

in even more sinister ways: if there are infallibly true answers to how life should be lived, which say that it must be guided by reason, or tradition, or the Church or the party or the leader, then ordinary men either understand these truths or they do not. If they do, there can be no disagreement between them and the supreme authority – state, party, leader, whoever it may be. They know that this authority cannot be wrong – *Il Duce ha sempre ragione*.[1] If they don't know this, then they live by false values; yet they are capable of rising above this and knowing the truth if they are properly guided. Some teach this by distinguishing two selves: the ordinary, empirical, common self, which makes mistakes and requires guidance, and the 'true', 'real', self, which sees the light of truth. Coercion by superior authority is only applied to those who do not themselves spontaneously do what the right authority – or real self – knows to be right, since they only fail to do it if their 'real' or 'true' self is not in command. Therefore, since the true authority and the 'real' self coincide in their purposes, true freedom – the freedom of the 'true' self – is at one with the party, the state, the leader etc. This doctrine rests on the fallacy of the two selves – one's self as one is ordinarily aware of it, and the 'true' or 'real' self, which should be in charge. This doctrine – identification of [the] supreme authority's orders, my true interests, my 'real' wishes as opposed to what I think them to be – can lead to the most monstrous oppression. That is what I mean by saying that positive liberty, interpreted in this way (as it often has been throughout history), is probably responsible for more injustice and suffering than the perversions of negative liberty, undesirable as these have often been, particularly in the last two centuries.

3. Your defence of 'negative liberty' is closely associated with a pluralist universe where ultimate values are always in principle colliding, and where no universally agreed hierarchy of values can be established. Is this a fair summary?

Some commentators have remarked that your scepticism about the ultimate truth of moral principles leaves you powerless to adjudicate between rival values (Barry).[2] How would you answer that argument?

4. Would you reserve a privileged position for 'liberty' as compared with other human values, such as happiness, equality etc.?

---

1 'The Leader is always right', Italian Fascist slogan.
2 It is not entirely clear what LRL is referring to here (and he doesn't remember): probably Brian Barry, *Political Argument* (London, 1965), chapter 3, 'Political Principles', section 4B, 'Interpersonal Comparisons', though this Barry does not discuss Berlin. There is also Norman Barry, *An Introduction to Modern Political Theory*, 3rd. ed. (Basingstoke, 1995), 123: 'liberalism, in all its versions, has been proposed as a value system that has compelling hold on our reason. Yet from Berlin's perspective it is simply one doctrine amongst a plurality of competing ones. From within the doctrine itself no decisive reason can be produced to show why its emphasis on liberty and equality should theoretically rule as inadmissible those orders that might value traditional hierarchy.'

[...] Since I do not believe that all values are compatible with each other, and hold that therefore there can be no objectively, universally agreed, hierarchy for values; since values can be incompatible not merely between cultures or between different communities or individuals within a culture, but also within one individual self – 'Socrates discontented or the pig contented' (J. S. Mill):[1] do I choose troubled freedom or contented subjection, even slavery? – if this is so, what reason is there for allowing those who pursue one set of values, one constellation of values which determines an entire way of life, to dominate those who pursue other such constellations, ways of life? Freedom of choice between different ideologies must, of course, be restrained (a) because otherwise there is war of all against all (Hobbes),[2] and a minimum of order and common laws, customs, values is clearly indispensable to any decent society, and (b) because the claims of other ultimate values should also be considered – of justice, security, peace, truth, loyalty, happiness, honour and so on. [...]

Of course liberty is a central, ultimate value; without a modicum of it no human being can live a fully human life. But arrangements must be made whereby these other ends of life also have their claims satisfied to some degree, and that demands skill, sympathy, wisdom and everything that is needed for producing a minimally decent society. Liberty is not the paramount virtue – it is only one among other ultimate ends of man, ends in themselves, not all of which can be fully, and sometimes even partially, satisfied. Choices are made, and you ask me: [...] How do we 'adjudicate between rival values (Barry)'? How indeed? To begin with, different value systems between different groups, or even cultures, can be exaggerated. There is a good deal of common ground between them, otherwise there would be no understanding across time or space – we would be totally puzzled by Greek ideals, or those of the Jews, or the Chinese, if we did not have a good deal of imaginative understanding of what they were at. But in the end, you may well say, like Barry, if there is no overarching criterion, no ultimate principle to appeal to when values clash, how should we decide? We decide as we decide, as meetings, parties, parliaments decide, governments decide, men and women, with very different interests, decide whatever seems to be most likely to preserve their forms of life, of the minimum they have in common, of what constitutes their vision of their communal life. Of course there must be exceptions: when fanatics clash there is no solution either in principle or in practice; then there are those who pursue their own path, and must only be restrained if they obstruct too many others from pursuing the ways of life to which they are equally entitled – that is what J. S. Mill preached, and I think basically that he is right. That is what 'Live and let live' in the end

1 173/4.
2 'Bellum omnium contra omnes': De cive, preface.

means – that as well as 'It takes all sorts to make a world.' This is the inescapable framework within which choices are made, and, if I am right, always will be. [...]

5. You have constantly attacked monism as a prevailing feature of European thought, because of its authoritarian tendencies, denying man the opportunity of choosing between values and purposes. Generally speaking, why is it that the inclination to monism has been so dominant, even in recent history, and why is it that the liberal pluralism you advocate so brilliantly has been a rather rare phenomenon?

[...] Monism in general is a doctrine according to which the structure and behaviour of everything in the world is governed by some central principle, summarised in some central concept, which, at any rate in principle, makes it possible to describe, account for and, I suppose, predict everything that has been, is or will be. Monism in ethics rests on the proposition that there is a central dominant objective value or combination of values in terms of which everything that human beings crave can be graded, accepted and rejected. The monism that I oppose is that according to which, guided by this dominant universal goal, one can establish some ideal situation in which all humanity lacks will be made good – where justice, happiness, knowledge, truth, liberty will reign, and perhaps entail each other in a perfect harmony. According to some doctrines, e.g. those of Hegel and Marx, history is a drama with many acts, some happy, some tragic, which end in an ultimate culmination that will be the solution of all problems in a seamless web of total human fulfilment. The Judaeo-Christian tradition teaches that human history is moving inexorably towards this culmination, if not in this world, then in the next. Others think it depends on concerted human effort. It is usual to suppose that this goal is utopian because human beings are too imperfect, bearers of original sin, or too ignorant or weak or stupid or incompetent, or in other ways incapable of reaching this conclusion, at any rate in this life.

But my objection goes deeper than that: it is not merely that human *inability* cannot generate this happy state of affairs, but that the very notion of a perfect society is *incoherent*. If, as I believe, some ultimate values are incompatible – if it is conceptually impossible for perfect liberty and perfect equality to coexist, or for perfect justice and unlimited mercy, or for spontaneity and rational calculation, or for a sense of duty and infinite generosity, or the like (there are many other possible examples of incompatible final ends), then the very conception of a perfect society, that is one in which all aspirations are realised, the ultimate harmony, is itself internally contradictory, that is, incoherent. And my concern is that because people have, intelligibly enough, wanted to believe in such an earthly paradise, and since they quite logically drew the consequence that no price could be too high to pay for reaching this perfect state, it followed that all kinds of brutal acts, coercion, slaughter and the like, painful as these might be, may have to be perpetrated in order to realise this supreme goal. Hence the famous doctrine of the need to break eggs to make omelettes. My hero Alexander Herzen denied this. He said – in different words – that the eggs have been broken but there has been no sign of the omelette. Because the omelette is unmakeable in principle, the breaking of the eggs turns out to be sheer crime and vice and folly – and a great deal of human misery is caused by this terrible and continuing fallacy. Whenever men have believed that there was one ultimate solution to all human ills, and have tried to work towards it against all odds, all moral considerations, the result has too often been only the suffering and torture and blood of innocent victims. That is my case against ethical, but above all political, monism and the dream of the perfect life on earth. [...]

A MESSAGE TO THE TWENTY-FIRST
CENTURY

On 24 November 1994 IB accepted the honorary degree of Doctor of Laws at the University of Toronto. He prepared this 'short credo' (as he called it in a letter to a Canadian friend)[1] for the ceremony, at which it was read on his behalf.

'It was the best of times, it was the worst of times.' With these words Dickens began his famous novel *A Tale of Two Cities*. But this cannot, alas, be said about our own terrible century. Men have for millennia destroyed each other, but the deeds of Attila the Hun, Genghis Khan, Napoleon (who introduced mass killings in war), even the Armenian massacres, pale into insignificance before the Russian Revolution and its aftermath: the oppression, torture, murder which can be laid at the doors of Lenin, Stalin, Hitler, Mao, Pol Pot, and the systematic falsification of information which prevented knowledge of these horrors for years – these are unparalleled. They were not natural disasters, but preventable human crimes, and whatever those who believe in historical determinism may think, they could have been averted.

I speak with particular feeling, for I am a very old man, and I have lived through almost the entire century. My life has been peaceful and secure, and I feel almost ashamed of this in view of what has happened to so many other human beings. I am not a historian, and so I cannot speak with authority on the causes of these horrors. Yet perhaps I can try.

They were, in my view, not caused by the ordinary negative human sentiments, as Spinoza called them – fear, greed, tribal hatreds, jealousy, love of power – though of course these have played their wicked part. They have been caused, in our time, by ideas; or rather by one particular idea. It is paradoxical that Karl Marx, who played down the importance of ideas in comparison with impersonal social and economic forces, should, by his writings, have caused the transformation of the twentieth century, both in the direction of what he wanted and, by reaction, against it. The German poet Heine, in one of his famous writings,[2] told us not to underestimate the

---

1 To John Roberts, 5 December 1994.
2 *On the History of Religion and Philosophy in Germany*. 'Note this, you proud men of action, you are nothing but the unconscious tools of the men of thought, who in humble stillness have often drawn up your most definite plans of action. Maximilian Robespierre was merely the hand of Jean Jacques Rousseau, the bloody hand that drew from the womb of time the body whose soul Rousseau had created. [...] Hence, spectres! I am about to speak of a man whose mere name has the might of an exorcism; I speak of Immanuel Kant. It is said that night-wandering spirits are filled with terror at the sight of the headsman's axe. With what mighty fear, then, must they be stricken when there is held up to them Kant's *Critique of Pure Reason*! This is the sword that slew deism in Germany. [...] Implacable Kantians [...] with sword and axe will dig up the soil of our

quiet philosopher sitting in his study; if Kant had not undone theology, he declared, Robespierre might not have cut off the head of the King of France.

He predicted that the armed disciples of the German philosophers – Fichte, Schelling and the other fathers of German nationalism – would one day destroy the great monuments of Western Europe in a wave of fanatical destruction before which the French Revolution would seem child's play. This may have been unfair to the German metaphysicians, yet Heine's central idea seems to me valid: in a debased form, the Nazi ideology did have roots in German anti-Enlightenment thought. There are men who will kill and maim with a tranquil conscience under the influence of the words and writings of some of those who are certain that they know perfection can be reached.

Let me explain. If you are truly convinced that there is some solution to all human problems, that one can conceive an ideal society which men can reach if only they do what is necessary to attain it, then you and your followers must believe that no price can be too high to pay in order to open the gates of such a paradise. Only the stupid and malevolent will resist once certain simple truths are put to them. Those who resist must be persuaded; if they cannot be persuaded, laws must be passed to restrain them; if that does not work, then coercion, if need be violence, will inevitably have to be used – if necessary, terror, slaughter. Lenin believed this after reading *Das Kapital*, and consistently taught that if a just, peaceful, happy, free, virtuous society could be created by the means he advocated, then the end justified any methods that needed to be used, literally *any*.

The root conviction which underlies this is that the central questions of human life, individual or social, have one true answer, which can be discovered. It can and must be implemented, and those who have found it are the leaders whose word is law. The idea that to all genuine questions there can be only one true answer is a very old philosophical notion. The great Athenian philosophers, Jews and Christians, the thinkers of the Renaissance and the Paris of Louis XIV, the French radical reformers of the eighteenth century, the revolutionaries of the nineteenth – however much they differed about what the answer was or how to discover it (and bloody wars were fought over this) – were all convinced that they knew the answer, and that only human vice and stupidity could obstruct its realisation.

This is the idea of which I spoke, and what I wish to tell you is that it is false. Not only because the solutions given by different schools of social

European life in order to tear out the last roots of the past. Armed Fichteans will enter the arena, [...] restrained neither by fear nor by self-interest [...], like the first Christians, whom neither physical pleasure nor physical torture could break. [...] A drama will be performed in Germany in contrast with which the French Revolution will seem a mere peaceful idyll.' Heinrich Heine, *Zur Geschichte der Religion und Philosophie in Deutschland* (1835), book 3: *Heines Werke*, Säkularausgabe. ed. Renate Francke (Berlin, 1970–), viii, ed. Fritz Mende, 193. 5–9, 35–9; 194. 1–2; 228. 20–4; 229. 24–6.

thought differ, and none can be demonstrated by rational methods – but for an even deeper reason. The central values by which most men have lived, in a great many lands at a great many times – these values, almost if not entirely universal, are not always harmonious with each other. Some are, some are not. Men have always craved for liberty, security, equality, happiness, justice, knowledge and so on. But complete liberty is not compatible with complete equality – if men were wholly free, the wolves would be free to eat the sheep. Perfect equality means that human liberties must be restrained so that the ablest and the most gifted are not permitted to advance beyond those who would inevitably lose if there were competition. Security, and indeed freedoms, cannot be preserved if freedom to subvert them is permitted. Indeed, not everyone seeks security or peace, otherwise some would not have sought glory in battle or in dangerous sports.

Justice has always been a human ideal, but it is not fully compatible with mercy. Creative imagination and spontaneity, splendid in themselves, cannot be fully reconciled with the need for planning, organisation, careful and responsible calculation. Knowledge, the pursuit of truth – the noblest of aims – cannot be fully reconciled with the happiness or the freedom that men desire, for even if I know that I have some incurable disease this will not make me happier or freer. I must always choose: between peace and excitement, or knowledge and blissful ignorance. And so on.

So what is to be done to restrain the champions, sometimes very fanatical, of one or other of these values, each of whom tends to trample upon the rest, as the great tyrants of the twentieth century have trampled on the life, liberty and human rights of millions because their eyes were fixed upon some ultimate golden future?

I am afraid I have no dramatic answer to offer: only that if these ultimate human values by which we live are to be pursued, then compromises, trade-offs, arrangements have to be made if the worst is not to happen. So much liberty for so much equality, so much individual self-expression for so much security, so much justice for so much compassion. My point is that some values clash: the ends pursued by human beings are all generated by our common nature, but their pursuit has to be to some degree controlled – liberty and the pursuit of happiness, I repeat, may not be fully compatible with each other, nor are liberty, equality and fraternity.

So we must weigh and measure, bargain, compromise and prevent the crushing of one form of life by its rivals. I know only too well that this is not a flag under which idealistic and enthusiastic young men and women may wish to march – it seems too tame, too reasonable, too bourgeois, it does not engage the generous emotions. But you must believe me, one cannot have everything one wants – not only in practice, but even in theory. The denial of this, the search for a single, overarching ideal, because it is the one and only true one for humanity, invariably leads to coercion. And then to destruction, blood – eggs are broken, but the omelette is not in sight, there is only an infinite number of eggs, human lives, ready for the breaking. And in the end the passionate idealists forget the omelette, and just go on breaking eggs.

I am glad to note that towards the end of my long life some realisation of this is beginning to dawn. Rationality, tolerance, rare enough in human history, are not despised. Liberal democracy, despite everything, despite the greatest modern scourge of fanatical, fundamentalist nationalism, is spreading. Great tyrannies are in ruins, or will be – even in China the day is not too distant. I am glad that you to whom I speak will see the twenty-first century, which I feel sure can be only a better time for mankind than my terrible century has been. I congratulate you on your good fortune; I regret that I shall not see this brighter future, which I am convinced is coming. With all the gloom that I have been spreading, I am glad to end on an optimistic note. There really are good reasons to think that it is justified.

REMARKS FOR ATHENS

In October 1996 IB received a letter from Dimitris Dimitrakos, professor of political philosophy in the University of Athens, offering him an honorary doctorate in philosophy.

TO DIMITRIS DIMITRAKOS
30 October 1996 [*carbon*]

Headington House

Dear Professor Dimitrakos,

I am naturally deeply honoured by your proposal to confer an Honorary Degree upon me at the University of Athens. As you may imagine, the name of that city has meant more and more to me since my early schooldays (my ancient Greek was never up to much). I shall look forward to hearing from the Rector in due course.

There is only one thing I should like to add. I am totally incapable of speaking in public – this may seem somewhat ungracious on the part of the recipient of an honour, but one of my vocal cords is paralysed, and although my ordinary speech is not too much impaired, I have had to decline to speak in public for many years now. Other universities who have been kind enough to offer me similar honours have always agreed to arrange for one of the other Honorands to offer thanks on behalf of them all. I do hope this will not create a problem.

With renewed expressions of gratitude to you personally – I am glad of the closeness of our subjects – and with best wishes,

Yours sincerely,
[Isaiah Berlin]

Given what he said in the second paragraph of his letter, IB drafted the remarks below for delivery at the degree ceremony, which took place on 17 April 1997 in the Grand Hall of Ceremonies, the central building of the University. Professor Dimitrakos gave the official speech as IB's proposer, and IB's remarks were translated into Greek by George Christodoulou, professor of comparative literature in the University of Athens, who also delivered his translation. IB stayed with Aline at the Hotel Grande Bretagne. On the evening of the ceremony, he returned to the hotel to change for a reception and dinner in his honour. When he made his appearance, he said that he had lost his wallet. After some discussion Professor Dimitrakos's wife suggested it might be in the back pocket of the trousers he had changed. It was. IB was delighted with Mrs Dimitrakos and

together, after dinner, they sang some operatic arias. IB amazed everyone with
his vitality and panache in spite of his eighty-seven years.

Rector of the University of Athens, Ladies and Gentlemen:

To receive this honour from the University of Athens means a great deal
to me. Before I thank you for it, let me make an apology. I am sorry not to
be able to able to speak this directly to you, but that is due to the fact that
one of my vocal cords has been paralysed for a good many years, and this
prevents my voice from being audible to more than a few people in a room.
I am very sorry about this but I am afraid it cannot be helped – there is no
known remedy for this defect.

Let me now once again say how deeply honoured I feel by this great gift on
your part, in particular because of the way in which I was brought up at my
school in England. I studied on what was called the classical side. This meant
that for six or seven years I was expected to read only classical literature – the
Greek and Latin classics. I was never a good scholar; nevertheless this kind of
education shapes one's entire existence, and it has shaped mine. The names
and works of Aeschylus, Sophocles, Euripides, Aristophanes, Herodotus,
Thucydides, Xenophon, Plato, Aristotle, Demosthenes – these names were
as familiar to us as those of Shakespeare, Milton, Dickens, Gibbon, Darwin;
or, since I was born in Russia, Pushkin, Tolstoy, Turgenev, Dostoevsky. And
indeed, even the names of lesser-known figures, like Isocrates, Aeschines,
Zeno, Epicurus, come into this list. That was the world I was brought up
in, and it still remains with me, even though I have forgotten much of what
I knew then.

Of course I had to read Latin authors too, and wonderful as Virgil,
Catullus, Lucretius, Livy, Tacitus are, in my view they are not fit to tie the
shoelaces of the great Greek writers. The Greeks shaped my life for ever, and
they entered the texture of my thought and feeling, and that of many other
British schoolboys of my time.

Jerusalem and Athens are the twin roots of European civilisation; they
are the greatest trees, the most powerful pillars on which it rests. To receive
degrees from the universities of both – what greater privilege can anyone
ask for? Of course I do not begin to deserve it; but, as someone once said, it
is more delightful to receive more than one deserves than exactly what one
deserves. That is why this is one of the proudest moments of my very long
life.

A question I have asked myself – and perhaps others have too – is: How
did Athens come to be the home of all art, all philosophy, mathematics, the
sciences, of the Western world? Why not Argos, Corinth, Thebes? Nobody
has ever explained this. Nor can it be explained. The great explosions of
human genius cannot be explained, whatever historians may say. Why did so
much art emerge from Florence, and to some degree Venice, and not from

the equally prosperous and powerful Genoa or Rome or Naples? Why was there a sudden rise of literary genius in Germany towards the end of the eighteenth century, and of poetry in England and Russia at the beginning of the nineteenth – and not in France or Italy? These sudden upward curves are genuinely inexplicable – no one has given a credible explanation for them: this may be true everywhere, but certainly in the West. The history of genius has no libretto – one creative period is not a stepping stone into the next.

And so with human history as a whole. The natural sciences may develop in a progressive line, but the history of mankind does not. Hegel and Marx and their disciples were mistaken. Nobody did and nobody could predict when and how the French and Russian Revolutions would break out, nor the rise of nationalism, racism, religious fanaticism in our time. As the British Bishop Butler said many years ago, 'Things are as they are, and their consequences will be what they will be: why then should we seek to be deceived?'[1]

It is time I stopped, but I cannot do so without once again expressing my profound feeling of gratitude for this to me entirely unique honour.

---

[1] 'Things and Actions are what they are, and the Consequences of them will be what they will be: Why then should we desire to be deceived?' Joseph Butler, *Fifteen Sermons Preached at the Rolls Chapel* (London, 1726), sermon 7, 136 (§16). One of IB's favourite (mis)quotations.

A Month in the Country

by Ivan Turgenev   translated by Isaiah Berlin

The National Theatre receives financial assistance from the Arts Council of Great Britain and the Greater London Council and stands on a site provided by the GLC.

				Director	Lighting
Francesca Annis	Betty Hardy	Susan Porrett	Ewan Stewart	Peter Gill	Rory Dempster
Paul Bentall	Holly De Jong	Jake Rea	Robert Swann		
Paul Bradley	Caroline Langrishe	John Rees	Nigel Terry	Designer	Music
Clare Byam Shaw	Mary Macleod	David Ryall	Di Trevis	Alison Chitty	George Fenton
Leonard Fenton	Alex Paterson	Kate Saunders	David Troughton		
Michael Gough	Ron Pember	Peter Sproule			

Poster for Turgenev's *A Month in the Country*, directed by Peter Gill in IB's specially commissioned translation, National Theatre, London, opening 19 February 1981

CHRONOLOGY

The second column of this concise chronology records events of biographical significance, the third, world events, focusing on those mentioned in the letters. At the end of each year IB's publications are listed in concise form: full references are at ⟨http://berlin.wolf.ox.ac.uk/lists/bibliography/index.html⟩. We have given as continuous and accurate a record of IB's movements as the sources, primarily his letters and appointments diaries, allow, but there are naturally gaps in our understanding, and the chronology should not be considered either exhaustive or infallible.

Aline generally, but not always, accompanied IB on his travels. When IB was in Oxford his home address was Headington House, Old High Street, Headington, and he also had a room in All Souls; in London (where they were to be found most weekends) the Berlins lived in their set in Albany, Piccadilly; in Italy (in the late summer) at their house in Paraggi; in New York they often stayed at the Ritz Towers Hotel on 57th Street and Park Avenue, in Jerusalem generally at the King David Hotel.

1975

1 January–mid July **(IB 66 on 6 June)**	Oxford/London	
11 February		Margaret Thatcher elected leader of Conservative Party
15 March (the Ides)	Retires as President of Wolfson	
April	Elected Distinguished Fellow, All Souls	
17 April		Khmer Rouge capture Phnom Penh, inaugurating a genocidal regime that claims $c.1.7$ million lives
30 April		Saigon government surrenders to North Vietnam, ending Vietnam War
5 June		British referendum on membership of European Community: 67% vote in favour on a turnout of 64%
12 June	Appointed Trustee of National Gallery	
10 July	BA AGM	
Mid July– late August	Paraggi	

Early September	Oxford/London	
3–16 September	Flies to Canberra via Tahiti and Fiji	
16 September–mid November	Visiting lecturer, History of Ideas Unit, ANU; visits to Sydney, Melbourne, New Zealand, Tasmania, Adelaide	
29 October		Franco's dictatorship ends with announcement that Prince Juan Carlos will become provisional head of Spanish state
10 November		UN resolution 'that Zionism is a form of racism and racial discrimination'; revoked 16 December 1991
Mid November–8 December	Return journey via Bali, Jakarta, Singapore, Hong Kong, Bangkok, Jerusalem	
8–31 December	Oxford/London	

1975 publications

John Petrov Plamenatz, 1912–1975

Foreword (on Avraham Harman) to Dov Noy and Issachar Ben-Ami (eds), *Studies in the Cultural Life of the Jews in England*

'L'apoteosi della volontà romantica: la rivolta contro il tipo di un mondo ideale' ['The Apotheosis of the Romantic Will: The Revolt against the Myth of an Ideal World'] (*Lettere italiane*)

'Performances memorable and not so memorable' (*Opera*)

Presidential Address (*Proceedings of the British Academy*)

Speech at the Official Opening of Wolfson College, Oxford, 12 November 1974 (*Lycidas*)

(unattributed) 'Sir John Wheeler-Bennett' (obituary, *Times*)

'Sir John Wheeler-Bennett' (supplementary obituary, *Times*)

(with others) 'Writers and the Closed Shop' (letter, TLS)

1976

1–26 January	Oxford/London	
21 January		Supersonic airliner *Concorde* enters service with British Airways and Air France
26 January–c. 17 February	NY: keynote speaker at conference on 'Vico and Contemporary Thought'	
5 February	Lectures at MIT on romanticism	

8–14 February	Lectures at Yeshiva University, NY, on romanticism	
17/18 February–15 April	Oxford/London; IB 'now installed in a large panelled room [5.2] in All Souls' (letter to Burdon-Muller, 17 March)	
16 March		Harold Wilson resigns as prime minister
5 April		James Callaghan elected Labour leader and becomes prime minister
15–25 April	Paraggi	
25 April–18 July **(IB 67)**	Oxford/London	
16–17 May	Zurich	
16 June		Soweto protest turns violent, leaving many dead; beginning of popular uprising against South African apartheid state
1 July	Presidential address at annual dinner marking 75th BA anniversary	
18 July–mid September	Paraggi	
9 September		Mao Zedong dies
Early September–31 December	Oxford/London	
3 November		Democrat Jimmy Carter wins US presidential election, defeating the incumbent, Gerald Ford
Early December	Hernia operation in Oxford	

1976 publications

Vico and Herder: Two Studies in the History of Ideas
Contribution to John Jolliffe (ed.), *Auberon Herbert: A Composite Portrait*
'Comment on Professor Verene's Paper' (*Social Research*)
'Go There to Find Your Identity' (JC)
Presidential Address (*Proceedings of the British Academy*)
'Vico and the Ideal of the Enlightenment' (*Social Research*)
Letter to Douglas Villiers, in id. (ed.), *Next Year in Jerusalem: Jews in the Twentieth Century*
'Vico's Doctrines' (letter, *History Today*)

1977

1 January–3 April	Oxford/London	
3–10 April	NY: speaks on nationalism in Trilling Seminar series 7 April	
10 April–1 May	Japan: visits Tokyo and Kyoto at invitation of Japan Foundation	
1 May–mid July (**IB 68**)	Oxford/London	
17 May		Likud under Menachem Begin win historic landslide in Knesset election, the first victory by a party other than Alignment/ Mapai; popularly known as the Mahapakh ('upheaval')
20 June		Begin prime minister of Israel
30 June	Presidential address at BA annual dinner	
18 July– 15 September	Paraggi	
14–19 August	Salzburg for festival: at Hotel Goldener Hirsch and with Hofmannsthals in Schloss Prielau, Zell am See	
12 September		South African anti-apartheid activist Steve Biko dies in custody
15–17 September	Basle and Geneva	
17 September– 17 October	Oxford/London	
17–26 October	Tehran, for BA, to open new British Institute of Persian Studies; stays at British Embassy	
26 October– 4 November	Jerusalem	
4 November– 31 December	Oxford/London	
19 November		Egyptian President Muhammad Anwar al-Sadat becomes first Arab leader to visit Israel; addresses Knesset 20 November
17–22 December	Paraggi	

1977 publications

Sir Harry d'Avigdor Goldsmid, 1906–1976

Contribution to the programme *Mstislav Rostropovich: 50th Birthday Gala Concert*

'Hume and the Sources of German Anti-Rationalism', in G. P. Morice (ed.), *David Hume: Bicentennial Papers*

'Old Russia', review of Marvin Lyons, *Russia in Original Photographs 1860–1920*, ed. Andrew Wheatcroft, and Kyril FitzLyon and Tatiana Browning, *Before the Revolution: A View of Russia under the Last Tsar* (*Guardian*)

Presidential Address (*Proceedings of the British Academy*)

Contribution to 'Reputations Revisited' (TLS)

1978

1 January–7 April	Oxford/London	
c. 12 January	Hospitalised for more than a week (after diagnosis of atrial fibrillations) with high fever and hepatitis-like symptoms; cancels lectures	
16 March		Former Italian prime minister Aldo Moro kidnapped in Rome, and later murdered, by Red Brigade terrorists
7–c. 15 April	Paraggi	
c. 15 April–14 July (**IB 69**)	Oxford/London	
29 June	Retires as President of BA	
14 July–1 September	Paraggi	
20 August		2 killed, 9 injured in attack on London El Al staff by Popular Front for the Liberation of Palestine
1 September–17 September	48 hours in UK, then Corfu for a week, then Jerusalem for Isaac Stern's Music Foundation	
17 September		President Carter brokers talks between Begin and Sadat at Camp David that lead to a framework for peace ('the Camp David Accords')
17 September–5 November	Oxford/London	
16 October		Polish cardinal Karol Józef Wójtyła elected Pope John Paul II

27 October		Sadat and Begin joint winners of 1978 Nobel Peace Prize
5–19 November	Ritz Towers Hotel, NY	
8 November	Lecture at Yale	
11–12 November	Weekend in Washington	
19 November– 31 December	Oxford/London; awarded 1979 Jerusalem Book Prize	
6 December		Spanish voters endorse a new, democratic, constitution

1978 publications

Russian Thinkers
Concepts and Categories: Philosophical Essays
Decline of Utopian Ideas in the West
Introduction to *Derek Hill: Portraits*
'Comments' (on Abraham Kaplan, 'Historical Interpretation', in the same volume) and (with
    others) 'Is a Philosophy of History Possible?', in Yirmiahu Yovel (ed.), *Philosophy of
    History and Action*
'Marx's *Kapital* and Darwin' (*Journal of the History of Ideas*)
'El nacionalismo: descuido del pasado y poder actual' ['Nationalism: Past Neglect and Present
    Power'] (*Diálogos*)
Presidential Address (*Proceedings of the British Academy*)
'Corsi e Ricorsi', review of Giorgio Tagliacozzo and Donald Phillip Verene (eds), *Giambattista
    Vico's Science of Humanity* (*Journal of Modern History*)
'Tolstoy Remembered', review of Tatyana Tolstoy, *Tolstoy Remembered* (*New Review*)
'Mr Nicholas [sc. Nicolas] Nabokov' (obituary, *Times*)

1979

1 January–8 March	Oxford/London	
3 January		Lorry drivers' strike begins, intensifying the labour unrest of Britain's 'Winter of Discontent'
8 January		Victory of Vietnamese-led rebels over Khmer Rouge in Cambodia
16 January		Shah of Iran flees country after months of violent protests against his regime
1 February		Ayatollah Khomeini returns to Iran from 14 years' exile and takes over the revolution
8–*c.*17 March	Jerusalem: meetings about Stern's Music Centre; Rothschild Fellowship interviews; speaks on Einstein at centenary celebrations 14 March	

c.17 March–17 April	Oxford/London	
26 March		Egypt–Israel peace treaty signed in Washington by Sadat and Begin, in presence of President Carter
30 March		Shadow Northern Ireland Secretary Airey Neave killed by car bomb as he leaves Parliament; Republican terror group Irish National Liberation Army claims responsibility
17–c.25 April	Israel; presented with Jerusalem Book Prize 19 April	
c.25 April–6 June	Oxford/London	
3 May		Conservative General Election victory with 43-seat majority; Margaret Thatcher becomes Britain's first female prime minister
c.6–10 June	NY, Ritz Towers Hotel	
7 June (IB 70)	Receives hon. LLD, Harvard	
10–25 June	Oxford/London	
18 June		President Carter and Soviet leader Leonid Brezhnev sign Strategic Arms Limitation Treaty (Salt II) in Vienna
25 June–11 September	Paraggi	
11–20 July	Oxford/London	
17 July	Receives hon. LLD, Sussex	
27 August		IRA murders Earl Mountbatten, the dowager Baroness Brabourne and 2 teenage boys at Mullaghmoor, Co. Sligo, and 18 British soldiers at Warrenpoint, Co. Down
30 August–1 September	Pisa for conference lecture on relativism on 1 September	
11 September–31 December	Oxford/London	
3 October	Aborts planned trip to China as head of BA delegation to Chinese Academy of Social Sciences after contracting high fever	

4 November		Islamist students storm US Embassy in Tehran, taking many hostages: 52 are held until January 1981
15 November		Mrs Thatcher identifies Anthony Blunt as 4th man in Cambridge spy ring
10 December	Declines Mrs Thatcher's offer of peerage	
c.27 December		Soviet invasion of Afghanistan begins, in support of a coup against government of Hafizallah Amin

1979 publications

Against the Current: Essays in the History of Ideas
'Einstein and Israel' (NYRB)
'Professor Scouten on Herder and Vico' (*Comparative Literature Studies*)
Note on Lydia Chukovsky, *Notes about Anna Akhmatova*, in 'In absentia: Some Books of the Year' (TLS)
Letter to Adam Podgorecki (on the intelligentsia), in Adam Podgorecki and Maria Los, *Multi-Dimensional Sociology*

1980

1–13 January	Oxford/London	
13 January–14 February	NY and Princeton	
20 January		President Carter announces US boycott of Moscow Olympics unless Soviet troops withdraw from Afghanistan
22 January		Andrey Sakharov sent into internal exile in USSR after calling for withdrawal of Soviet troops from Afghanistan
14–27 February	Oxford/London	
27 February–5 March	Jerusalem, with Herbert Hart, for Rothschild Fellowship interviews	
5 March–14 July (**IB 71**)	Oxford/London	
13 May	Bowra Lecture, 'Conversations with Russian Poets'	
14 July–16 September	Paraggi, via Aix in France	

20 August	Via Genoa to Salzburg	
20–8 August	Salzburg	
28 August–1 September	Vienna	
31 August		Polish trade union federation Solidarność (Solidarity) emerges under leadership of Gdańsk shipyard-worker Lech Wałęsa
16 September–9/10 November	Oxford/London	
22 September		Beginning of 8-year Iran–Iraq war
10 October		Mrs Thatcher tells Conservative Party Conference 'The lady's not for turning'
4 November		Republican Ronald Reagan elected US President by a landslide, defeating the incumbent Democrat Jimmy Carter
9/10–16 November	Jerusalem, for Stern's Music Centre	
10 November		Michael Foot elected Labour leader
16 November–31 December	Oxford/London	
31 December–3 January 1981	Paraggi	

1980 publications

Personal Impressions
Story in *Pass the Port Again: The Best After-Dinner Stories of the Famous*
'The Incompatibility of Values' and 'Virtue and Practicality', in Melvin Kranzberg (ed.), *Ethics in an Age of Pervasive Technology*
'Meetings with Russian Writers in 1945 and 1956', in PI
'Conversations with Russian Poets' (Bowra Lecture, TLS and – with additions – NYRB)
'Note on Alleged Relativism in Eighteenth Century European Thought' (*British Journal for Eighteenth-Century Studies*)
'On Philosophy' (*Good Book Guide*)
'A Tribute to my Friend' (Jacob Talmon, *Forum*)
'Upon Receiving the Jerusalem Prize' (*Conservative Judaism*)
Contribution to 'Books of the Year' (*Sunday Times*)
'The Hedgehog and the Fox Continued' (letter, NYRB)

1981

31 December 1980– 3 January	Paraggi	
3 January– 26 March	Oxford/London	
21 January		US hostages freed in Tehran
February	Viral infection and arrhythmia force cancellation of planned trip to Princeton	
19 February	Turgenev's *A Month in the Country* opens at the National Theatre in IB's translation	
26 March		Formation of Social Democratic Party (SDP) by Roy Jenkins, David Owen, Bill Rodgers and Shirley Williams
26 March–1 April	Jerusalem: Rothschild Fellowship interviews	
1 April–28 May	Oxford/London	
11 April		Riots in Brixton, south London
5 May		Bobby Sands first IRA prisoner to die on hunger strike, in Northern Ireland prison protest
28 May–3 June	Baltimore, Washington, NY	
3 June–14 July (**IB 72**)	Oxford/London	
16 June		Formation of SDP–Liberal Alliance
July		First cases of HIV/Aids in US
14 July– *c.*20 September	Paraggi (returning 25 July for royal wedding)	
29 July		Wedding of Prince Charles and Diana Spencer, St Paul's
5–7 August	Venice	
7–*c.*21 August	Salzburg	
*c.*20 September– 31 December	Oxford/London	
6 October		President Sadat assassinated by members of Egyptian Islamic

6 October (*cont.*)	Jihad opposed to peace with Israel

1981 publications

For Teddy Kollek

Introduction and unattributed contributions to H. G. Nicholas (ed.), *Washington Despatches 1941–45: Weekly Political Reports from the British Embassy*

Translation, with Introduction, of Ivan Turgenev, *A Month in the Country*

Reply to Hans Aarsleff, 'Vico and Berlin' (LRB)

'Russian Thought and the Slavophile Controversy', review of Andrzej Walicki, *A History of Russian Thought (From the Enlightenment to Marxism)* and *The Slavophile Controversy (Slavonic and East European Review)*

Contribution to 'Books of the Year: A Personal Choice' (*Observer*)

'Plea for a Library' (letter, JC)

Contributions to Sandra Martin and Donald Hall (eds), *Where Were You? Memorable Events of the Twentieth Century*

'How Russian and English Lines Can Get Crossed' (letter, *Guardian*)

1982

1 January–6 February	Oxford/London; IB ill with mumps, subsequently contracted by Aline	
6–20/21 February	NY	
20/21 February–6 June	Oxford/London	
2 April		Argentina invades Falkland Islands, precipitating the Falklands War
3 June		Shlomo Argov, Israeli ambassador in London, shot and severely wounded by Arab assailants
6–11 June	NY, staying in an apartment at 110 East 57th Street	
6 June (**IB 73**)		Begin uses Argov shooting as pretext for invading Southern Lebanon to drive out PLO
11 June–*c.*21 July	Oxford/London	
14 June		Argentine surrender ends Falklands War
17–23 June	Jerusalem	
18 June	Notification of award of Erasmus Prize	

20 July		IRA bombings in central London parks: 11 dead, nearly 50 injured; 7 horses killed/destroyed
21 July– 20 September	Paraggi	
18–26 August	Salzburg	
16–18 September		Massacre of Palestinians and Lebanese Shiites in Sabra and Shatila refugee camps (in an area under IDF control) by a Christian Phalangist force
20 September– 17 December	Oxford/London	
12 November		Poland: Lech Wałęsa released from 11 months' internment
17–31 December	Princeton, as member of committee of visitors at school of historical studies, IAS; then joins Aline at 110 East 57th Street, NY	

1982 publications

'A Letter from Sir Isaiah Berlin' (*Intellectual History*)
'Mrs Salome Halpern' (obituary, *Times*)
'Prof. Roman Jakobson' (supplementary obituary, *Times*)

1983

1 January–*c.*2 March	Oxford/London	
10 January	Writes to Shiela Sokolov Grant: 'I have lost my voice – that is, one of my vocal cords is paralysed (don't laugh)'; forbidden by his doctors to speak in public	
8 February		Israeli government's Kahan Commission finds Israel indirectly, Defence Minister Ariel Sharon personally, responsible for Sabra–Shatila massacre
14 February		Sharon resigns
*c.*2 March–8 April	Jerusalem, later joined by Herbert Hart, for Rothschild Fellowship interviews; remains abroad with Aline for health reasons	

23 March		President Reagan announces 'Star Wars' strategic defence initiative (SDI)
31 March–8 April	Italy	
8 April–mid July **(IB 74)**	Oxford/London	
4–17 May	NY	
9 June		Landslide Conservative General Election victory
Mid July–29 September	Paraggi	
23 June		Pope John Paul II meets Lech Wałęsa in Poland
22 July		Polish government ends martial law and takes steps to create civil society
1 September		Korean Airlines Flight KAL 007 shot down by Soviet jet after straying off course; all 269 on board are killed
29 September– 5 October	Jerusalem	
5 October– 31 December	Oxford/London	
23 October		Over 300 servicemen, principally US Marines, killed by truck bombs in Beirut planted by Islamist terror group
25 October		US invasion of Grenada
10–15 November	NY to receive an hon. Doctorate of Humane Letters (DHL) from CUNY 14 November	

1983 publications

'Giambattista Vico and Cultural History', in Leigh S. Cauman and others (eds), *How Many Questions? Essays in Honor of Sidney Morgenbesser*

'The Conscience of Israel' (tribute to Yishayahu Leibowitz, *Ha'aretz*)

'Maynard and Lydia Keynes', in Milo Keynes (ed.), *Lydia Lopokova*

'The Gentle Genius', review of *Turgenev's Letters*, trans. and ed. A. V. Knowles (NYRB)

'Isaiah Berlin et le progrès' (letter, *Monde Dimanche*)

'Reply to Robert Kocis' (*Political Studies*)

Contribution to 'Books of the Year' (*Sunday Times*)

(with others) 'Charges against KOR Repudiated' (letter, *Times*)

Contribution to Linda Sternberg Katz and Bill Katz, *Writer's Choice: A Library of Rediscoveries*

Contribution to Morris Halle and Paul E. Gray (eds), *A Tribute to Roman Jakobson 1896–1982*

1984

1 January–10 March	Oxford/London	
10–15 March	Jerusalem	
12 March		National Union of Mineworkers begins 51-week strike over threatened pit closures
15 March–15 July	Oxford/London, with an early visit to Paraggi	
8 May		Moscow, followed by almost the entire Eastern bloc, announces boycott of Los Angeles Olympics
30 May		Prince Charles denounces design for an extension of the National Gallery in London as a 'monstrous carbuncle on the face of a much-loved and elegant friend' (243)
6 June (**IB 75**)		Indian troops opposed to Sikh militants storm Amritsar's Golden Temple; many hundreds killed
15 July–9 September	Paraggi	
31 July–6 August	Salzburg	
9 September–31 December	Oxford/London	
26 September		Britain and China finalise agreement to hand Hong Kong to China in 1997
12 October		IRA bombs Grand Hotel, Brighton, during Conservative Party conference: 5 killed; Mrs Thatcher narrowly escapes injury
31 October		Indira Gandhi, Indian prime minister, assassinated in New Delhi by Sikh bodyguards
6 November		Ronald Reagan re-elected US President, defeating Democrat Walter Mondale
16 December		Future Soviet leader Mikhail Gorbachev and his wife Raisa entertained by Mrs Thatcher at Chequers
29 December		Indira Gandhi's son Rajiv wins landslide election victory

1984 publications

'A New Woman in Russia', review of John Carswell, *The Exile: A Life of Ivy Litvinov* (*Sunday Times*)

'Mozart at Glyndebourne Half a Century Ago', in John Higgins (ed.), *Glyndebourne: A Celebration*

Foreword to Sir Immanuel Jakobovits, *'If Only My People ...': Zionism in My Life*

Tribute to Sir Hugh Casson (*RA*, the magazine for the Friends of the Royal Academy)

1985

1 January–15 July **(IB 76)**	Oxford/London	
29 January		Oxford votes against awarding Mrs Thatcher hon. DCL
3 March		National Union of Mineworkers votes to end coal strike without winning any concessions over pit closures
11 March		Mikhail Gorbachev becomes Soviet leader and adopts 'glasnost' ('openness') in politics and society and 'perestroika' ('restructuring') in the Soviet economy
15 July–9 September	Paraggi	
26 July–3 August	Salzburg	
9 September–31 December	Oxford/London	
28 September and 1 October		Hostility to the police triggers riots first in Brixton, then in Peckham and Toxteth
6 October		Police officer Keith Blakelock murdered in riot at Broadwater Farm estate, Tottenham
15 November		Mrs Thatcher and Eire Taoiseach Garret FitzGerald sign Anglo-Irish Agreement at Hillsborough, Co. Down, giving Dublin a role in Northern Ireland government
19–21 November		Geneva summit between President Reagan and Mikhail Gorbachev
27 December–4 January	Planned trip to NY: called off because of Aline's ill health	
27 December		18 killed and over 100 injured in gun attacks at Rome and Vienna airports:

27 December (*cont.*)   Palestinian terror group Abu Nidal
                                                held responsible

1985 publications

'Nahum Goldmann (1895–1982): A Personal Impression', in William Frankel (ed.), *Survey of
    Jewish Affairs 1983*
'On Vico' (reply to Zagorin) (*Philosophical Quarterly*)
Contribution to 'Terence Cornelius Farmer Prittie, 15 December 1913 – 28 May 1985, In Me-
    moriam' (*Britain & Israel*)

1986

c. 1 January	IB in Jerusalem for funeral of his aunt Ida Samunov	
2 January–31 May	Oxford/London	
28 January		US space shuttle *Challenger* explodes after lift-off, killing all 7 astronauts on board
15 April		US air raids, mostly from British bases, target Libya's President Mu'ammer Gaddafi
28 April		Soviet authorities admit to accident at Chernobyl reactor, Ukraine, as probably the worst civil nuclear disaster in history unfolds
31 May–5 June **(IB 77)**	Jerusalem, on panel overseeing design of new Supreme Court building	
5 June–20 July	Oxford/London	
19–22 June	Hohenems, Austria, for Schubert festival	
27 June		International Court of Justice finds US guilty of backing the armed insurgency of Contra rebels in Nicaragua
20 July– *c.* 11 September	Paraggi	
22–28/9 August	Salzburg	
c. 11 September– 18 December	Oxford/London	
12 October		Soviet–US disarmament summit at Reykjavik ends in failure, with President Reagan's refusal to abandon SDI

27 October

UK government introduces
deregulation of financial markets,
notably the stock exchange, in City of
London (the 'big bang')

Late–31 December   Oxford/London

23 December

Andrey Sakharov vows to continue
public advocacy of human rights after
returning to Moscow from 7 years'
internal exile

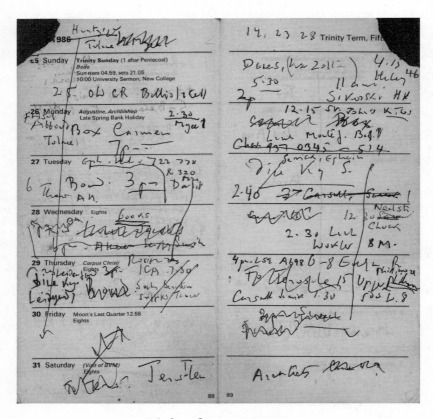

IB's diary for 25–31 May 1986

1986 publications

'The Cost of Curing an Oyster' (*Jerusalem Post*)

'Martin Cooper: In Memoriam', in programme for memorial concert by Lindsay String
     Quartet, 29 June 1986

'Memories of Brief Meetings with Ben-Gurion' (*Jewish Quarterly*)

'A Personal Tribute to Adam von Trott (Balliol 1931)' (*Balliol College Annual Record*)

'A Personal View of Super-Titles', in *Glyndebourne Touring Opera 1986* programme

'On Yitzhak Sadeh' (*Davar*)

'Spender's "Journals" ' (letter, TLS)

Entry on J. P. Plamenatz in Lord Blake and C. S. Nicholls (eds), *The Dictionary of National Biography 1971–1980*

(with others) 'Polish-Jewish Studies' (letter, NYRB)

Contribution to 'Greetings' (*Secular Humanistic Judaism*)

Foreword to Neil Cornwell, *The Life, Times and Milieu of V. F. Odoyevsky 1804–1869*

1987

1 January–15 July	Oxford/London	
8–13 March	Jerusalem	
21–30 March	Germany	
May	Hon. DHL (Doctor of Humane Letters) from New School of Social Research, NY	
11 June (**IB 78**)		Conservatives win General Election with 102-seat majority; Mrs Thatcher first prime minister since Lord Liverpool (1812, 1818, 1820) to win third successive term
12 June		President Reagan, at the Brandenburg Gate in Berlin, urges Mikhail Gorbachev to 'Tear down this wall!'
24 June		Roy Jenkins installed as Oxford Chancellor
3 July		Klaus Barbie, former head of the Gestapo in Lyon, sentenced to life imprisonment for his role in the Holocaust
14 July	Leaves ROH board	
15 July–mid September	Paraggi	
30 July	Flying visit to London for performance of *The Queen of Spades* during historic visit of Kirov Opera to Covent Garden	
31 July–10 August	Salzburg for 10 days	
22–3 August	Pesaro for Rossini operas	
Mid September–31 December	Oxford/London	

20 October	Hon. DLitt, Oxford
22 October	Joseph Brodsky wins Nobel Prize in Literature
8 November	IRA bomb kills 11 at Remembrance Day service in Enniskillen, Co. Fermanagh
8 December	President Reagan and Mikhail Gorbachev sign Intermediate-range Nuclear Forces (INF) treaty
9 December	First intifada ('uprising') against Israeli occupation of Palestinian territories of Gaza and West Bank begins

1987 publications

'David Cecil (1902–1986)', in *Reports for 1985–86 and 1986–87* (Royal Society of Literature)
'Edmund Wilson at Oxford' (*Yale Review*)
Contribution to 'Books of the Year: Who Read What in 1987?' (*Sunday Times*)

1988

1 January–14 February	Oxford/London
14–16 February	Turin, to receive inaugural Agnelli Prize 'for the Ethical Dimension in Advanced Societies' on 15 February
16–28 February	Oxford/London
28 February–3 March	Jerusalem: Rothschild Fellowship interviews
First half of March	Oxford/London
3 March	Liberal Democrat party created by SDP–Liberal merger
16 March	Iraqi dictator Saddam Hussein launches chemical weapons attack on Kurdish city of Halabja, northern Iraq, killing thousands
18–29 March	Moscow and Leningrad
29 March–28 April	Oxford/London
14 April	USSR commits to withdrawal from Afghanistan (begins in May, completed February 1989)

28 April–4 May	Israel: hon. DPhil from Ben-Gurion University of the Negev 2 May	
4 May–17 July (**IB 79**)	Oxford and London	
3 July		USS *Vincennes* shoots down Iranian passenger airliner over Persian Gulf, mistaking it for a hostile fighter
17 July–12 September	Paraggi	
28 July–9 August	Salzburg	
31 July		King Hussein announces the severance of Jordan's legal and administrative ties with the West Bank, effectively recognising PLO sovereignty there
12 September–1 November	Oxford/London	
9 October		Mass movement launched in Riga, seeking greater independence for Latvia from USSR
1–30 November	Washington and NY	
1 November	HH begins full-time work on IB's papers at Wolfson	
8 November		Republican George H. W. Bush wins landslide victory in US presidential election, defeating Democrat Michael Dukakis
30 November–31 December	Oxford/London	
21 December		Libyan terror plot causes Pan Am Flight 103 from London to NY to blow up over Lockerbie, Scotland, killing all 259 on board and 11 on ground

1988 publications

Foreword to Ada Rapoport-Albert and Steven J. Zipperstein (eds), *Jewish History: Essays in Honour of Chimen Abramsky*

On the Pursuit of the Ideal

'Dorothy de Rothschild' (obituary, *Independent*)

'Israeli Solution' (letter, *Independent*)

'Wybór listów od Isaiaha Berlina' (letters to Beata Polanowska-Sygulska), in Beata Polanowska-Sygulska, *Filozofia wolności Isaiaha Berlina*

1989

1 January–5 March	Oxford/London
14 February	Ayatollah Khomeini issues fatwa condemning British author Salman Rushdie to death for publication of his novel *Satanic Verses*
5–9 March	Jerusalem
9 March–26 May	Oxford/London
27 March	Many Communist Party candidates defeated in unprecedentedly open Soviet parliamentary elections; Boris Yeltsin wins landslide in Moscow constituency
26–31 May	NY
31 May–22 July **(IB 80)**	Oxford/London: celebration of IB's 80th birthday includes a dinner at Corpus (6 June) and a concert in London (17 July)
3 June	Tiananmen Square massacre, Beijing: unknown number of civilian protestors killed by Chinese military in bloody suppression of political protest centred there
26–9 June	Hohenems
22 July–21 September	Paraggi
18–19 August and 6–7 September	Pesaro
21 September– 31 December	Oxford/London
18 October	Erich Honecker, leader of GDR, forced to step down by widespread public discontent
9 November	GDR opens its border with West, allowing protestors access to West Berlin: effective demise of Berlin Wall
10 November	Demolition of Berlin Wall begins, prefiguring the end of the Eastern Bloc and the reunification of Germany

| 25 December | Nicolae Ceauşescu, deposed Communist President of Romania, and his wife Elena shot by firing squad |

1989 publications

'Writers Remembered: Virginia Woolf' (*Author*)
Foreword to Anatoly Nayman, *Remembering Anna Akhmatova*
Contribution to *Academy of St Martin in the Fields 1959–1989*

1990

1 January–27 June	Oxford/London	
11 February		Nelson Mandela freed from prison in South Africa as President F. W. de Klerk takes steps towards ending apartheid
31 March		Violent anti-Poll-Tax riot in London's West End, centred on Trafalgar Square
24 April		US Hubble space telescope launched from Cape Canaveral, Florida
4 May		Latvia declares independence
27 June–1 July (**IB 81**)	Hohenems	
1–mid July	Oxford/London	
Mid July–*c.*15 September	Paraggi	
2 August		Iraqi invasion of Kuwait starts train of events leading to Gulf War; Saddam Hussein annexes Kuwait as 19th Iraqi province
4–6 August	Pesaro	
22–9 August	Salzburg	
29 August–3 September	Mondsee	
*c.*15 September–31 December	Oxford/London	
3 October		East and West Germany reunited
14 November		Michael Heseltine stands as Conservative leader, forcing an election
22 November		Mrs Thatcher resigns as Conservative leader and prime minister after failing

22 November (*cont.*)		to win outright in first ballot of leadership contest
27 November		John Major wins second ballot, becoming Conservative leader and prime minister

1990 publications

The Crooked Timber of Humanity: Chapters in the History of Ideas
'Joseph de Maistre and the Origins of Fascism', in CTH
Contribution to *The Evolution of the Symphony Orchestra: History, Problems and Agenda*
Contribution to *Robert B. Silvers*
Contribution to 'The State of Europe: Christmas Eve 1989' (*Granta*)
Contribution on Mozart (*Vita*)
Contribution to ROH programme insert on Garrett Drogheda
(with others) 'An Open Letter on Anti-Armenian Pogroms in the Soviet Union' (letter, NYRB)
Contribution to 'Boris Pasternak' (letters, TLS)
'No Conservative' (on Herder; letter, NYRB)

1991

1 January–mid July	Oxford/London	
17 January–28 February		US-led coalition (Operation Desert Storm) drives Iraq from Kuwait
7 February		IRA attempts to assassinate British cabinet in mortar attack on 10 Downing Street
21 May		Former Indian prime minister Rajiv Gandhi assassinated while campaigning in Tamil Nadu
13 June (**IB 82**)		Boris Yeltsin elected President of Russian Federation
25 June		Slovenia and Croatia declare independence from Serb-dominated Yugoslav Federation, beginning years of ethnic conflict in Bosnia and Herzegovina
Mid July–20 September	Paraggi	
20–5 July	Hohenems	
27–8 July	Verona	
10–18 August	Salzburg	
13–21 August		Hard-line Communists try to depose Mikhail Gorbachev: the coup fails, signalling the end of the Communist Party in Russia

Early September	Brief visit to London	
20 September–mid/ late December	Oxford/London	
Mid/late December	Israel (Dead Sea and Jerusalem), where IB contracts 'a mysterious illness': admitted to Hadassah Hospital	
25 December		Mikhail Gorbachev formally resigns as President of USSR; Boris Yeltsin effectively succeeds him as President of Russian Federation
26 December		USSR formally ceases to exist, replaced by Commonwealth of Independent States
31 December	Oxford/London	

1991 publications

'Der Vetter aus Oxford' (Yehudi Menuhin), in Jutta Schall-Emden (ed.), *Weder Pauken noch Trompeten: Für Yehudi Menuhin*
Letter to Antonio Verri, in id. (ed.), *Vico e il pensiero contemporaneo*
(with others) 'The Detention of Sari Nusseibeh' (letter, *Independent* and NYRB, in slightly different forms, and with more signatories in the NYRB)
'Position on the Chair' (letter, *Observer*)

1992

1 January–23 June	Oxford/London	
9 April		Conservatives win General Election with reduced majority of 21
19 April	Castaway on *Desert Island Discs*, BBC Radio 4	
23–9 June (**IB 83**)	Hohenems	
29 June–7 August	Oxford/London	
18 July		John Smith elected Labour leader, succeeding Neil Kinnock
7–c.11 August	Salzburg	
c.11–25 August	Baden-Baden	
25–31 August	Salzburg	
31 August– 1 September	Mondsee	

1–25 September	Paraggi

16 September	'Black Wednesday': John Major suspends British membership of European Exchange Rate Mechanism as pound plummets

25 September–31 December	Oxford/London

4 November	Democrat Bill Clinton defeats incumbent Republican George H. W. Bush for US presidency

1992 publications

'Alexander and Salome Halpern' (in Russian translation), in Mikhail Parkhomovsky (ed.), *Jews in the Culture of Russia Abroad: Collected Articles, Publications, Memoirs and Essays*

'The Early Years', in Freda Silver Jackson (ed.), *Then and Now: A Collection of Recollections*

'Reply to Ronald H. McKinney, "Towards a Postmodern Ethics: Sir Isaiah Berlin and John Caputo"' (*Journal of Value Inquiry*)

Introduction to *Founders and Followers: Literary Lectures Given on the Occasion of the 150th Anniversary of the Founding of the London Library*

Introduction to inaugural concert programme for Israel's new Supreme Court Building, November 1992

Letters to Conor Cruise O'Brien in his *The Great Melody: A Thematic Biography and Commented Anthology of Edmund Burke*

'Mixing It' (letter, *Oxford Magazine*)

'No Trace of Roguery' (letter, *Spectator*)

(unattributed) 'Professor H. L. A. Hart' (obituary, *Times*)

Contribution to feature on the literary canon (*Times Higher Education Supplement*)

Appreciation of David Patterson (*Centre Piece*, newsletter of the Oxford Centre for Postgraduate Hebrew Studies)

Comment in Charles C. Brown, *Niebuhr and His Age: Reinhold Niebuhr's Prophetic Role and Legacy*

1993

1 January–16 June	Oxford/London

26 February	Islamist terrorists detonate car bomb in World Trade Center, NY, killing 5 and injuring scores more

20 March	IRA bombs Warrington, killing 2 boys and injuring over 50 people

16–20 June (**IB 84**)	Feldkirch (formerly Hohenems) music festival, Austria

20 June–late July	Oxford/London

Late July–26 September	Paraggi

1 August	Munich
2–11 August	Salzburg
11–29/30 August	London

13 September	Israeli prime minister Yitzhak Rabin and PLO leader Yasser Arafat shake hands at White House, affirming the Oslo I Accord, aimed at ending the Israel–Palestine conflict
26 September–31 December	Oxford/London
4 October	US forces in Mogadishu, Somalia, in fierce battle after failed attempt to capture local warlord
15 December	British and Irish premiers sign Joint Declaration of Peace in effort to end Northern Ireland 'Troubles'

1993 publications

The Magus of the North: J. G. Hamann and the Origins of Modern Irrationalism
'England's Mistaken Moralist' (G. E. Moore in *Principia Ethica*), contribution to 'Speaking Volumes' (*The Times Higher Education Supplement*)
'A Reply to David West' (*Political Studies*)
'Yitzhak Sadeh' (*Midstream*)
Contribution to Sir Isaiah Berlin and others, *Herbert Lionel Adolphus Hart 1907–1992: Speeches Delivered at Memorial Ceremony on 6 February 1993*
Contribution on books read during 1992 (*Misuzu*)
Contribution to tenth anniversary CD booklet for Music at Oxford

1994

1 January–31 August	Oxford/London
5 February	Mortar bomb in Sarajevo marketplace kills 68, wounds 200; Serb artillery then withdraws from Sarajevo after threat of NATO airstrikes
6 April	Death of Rwandan President Juvenal Habyarimana triggers ethnic violence: at least 800,000 Tutsis and moderate Hutus killed by Hutu militants in *c.*100 days
10 May	African National Congress wins South Africa's first democratic elections; its leader, Nelson Mandela, becomes the country's first black President

27 May		Alexander Solzhenitsyn returns to Russia from 20 years' exile in US and is highly critical of new leadership
19–25 June	Feldkirch	
1 July (**IB 85**)		Yasser Arafat returns to Gaza after 27 years' exile
8 July	Dublin to receive hon. LittD from Trinity College	
21 July		Tony Blair elected Labour leader after untimely death of John Smith in May
14–23 August	Salzburg	
31 August		IRA announces complete ceasefire; Russian troops withdraw from Estonia, Latvia and other former Eastern Bloc states
31 August–26 September	Paraggi	
26 September–mid October	Oxford/London	
Mid October	NY	
13 October		Loyalist paramilitaries in Northern Ireland announce ceasefire
14 October		Yasser Arafat, Shimon Peres and Yitzhak Rabin share Nobel Peace Prize for their peacemaking efforts in Middle East
Mid October–31 December	Oxford/London	
26 October		Yitzhak Rabin and King Hussein of Jordan sign treaty ending 46 years of war between Israel and Jordan
24 November	Created hon. Doctor of Laws, Toronto	
9 December		British officials meet representatives of Sinn Fein for talks

1994 publications

'La rivoluzione romantica: una crisi nella storia del pensiero moderno' ('The Romantic Revolution: A Crisis in the History of Modern Thought'), in Isaiah Berlin, *Tra la filosofia e la storia delle idee: intervista autobiografica*, ed. Steven Lukes

(with Bernard Williams) 'Pluralism and Liberalism: A Reply' (to George Crowder, *Political Studies*)

Introduction to Joseph de Maistre, *Considerations on France*, ed. Richard A. Lebrun

Introduction to James Tully (ed.), *Philosophy in an Age of Pluralism: The Philosophy of Charles Taylor in Question*

Contribution to Brian Harrison (ed.), *Corpuscles: A History of Corpus Christi College, Oxford, in the Twentieth Century, Written by Its Members*

Contribution to 'Brushes with Genius' (meetings with Picasso, *Independent on Sunday*)

Contribution to 'Classics of Our Time' (*Sunday Telegraph*)

Contribution to 'Referred Pleasures: Fifteen writers celebrate their favourite reference books' (TLS)

Tribute to Sir Neville Marriner, in souvenir programme for his 70th birthday concert, 5 April 1994, Royal Festival Hall

1995

January–December	Oxford/London	
17 January		Earthquake strikes Japanese city of Kobe, killing more than 6,000
3 May	Hon. DPhil, Bologna	
19 May		Bomb in government building in Oklahoma City kills 168; Gulf War veteran with grievances against Federal government convicted
11–13 June (**IB 86**)		More than 8,000 Bosnian Muslims sheltering in a UN 'safe area' massacred by units of Bosnian Serb army in Srebrenica
29 June		*Mir* Russian space station and US shuttle *Atlantis* dock in orbit, starting new era of space co-operation between former Cold War adversaries
3–*c.*19 September	Paraggi	
28 September		Yitzhak Rabin and Yasser Arafat sign Oslo II Accord in Washington
September/early October	Pacemaker fitted	
4 November		Yitzhak Rabin assassinated by radical Orthodox Jew opposed to Oslo accords; succeeded by Shimon Peres
10 November		Nigeria suspended from Commonwealth after government of General Sani Abacha executes writer and activist Ken Saro-Wiwa and 8 other dissidents

14 December	Presidents of Bosnia, Serbia and Croatia sign Dayton Accord in Paris, aiming to bring an end to ethnic conflict in Bosnia-Herzegovina
20 December	Buckingham Palace announces that the Queen has advised the Prince and Princess of Wales to divorce

1995 publications

'Liberty', in Ted Honderich (ed.), *The Oxford Companion to Philosophy*
Contribution to 'Remembering Stephen' (a tribute to Stephen Spender, *Index on Censorship*)
(with Andrzej Walicki) 'Sir Isaiah Berlin do Andrzeja Walickiego' (letters from IB to AW, *Res Publica*)
(with Robert Grant) 'Tolstoy and Enlightenment: An Exchange' (*Oyster Club*)
'Nin Ryan' (obituary, *Independent*)
Foreword to '*... from the fruits of her labour she planted a vineyard.*', Essays on the Role of Private Philanthropy in Israel to Mark the 100th Anniversary of the Birth of Dorothy de Rothschild, 7 March 1995
Contribution (on Boris Pasternak, *Doctor Zhivago*) to 'On the Shelf' (*Sunday Times*)

1996

1 January–4 August	Oxford/London	
2 January		US troops enter Bosnia as peacekeeping force under Dayton accords
10 January		King Hussein of Jordan visits Tel Aviv in a sign of rapprochement with Israel
31 January		Tamil Tiger rebels kill more than 50 in a suicide bombing in financial district of Colombo during Sri Lanka's long-running civil war
9 February		IRA bomb in London's docklands ends 18-month ceasefire
18 April		17 Greek tourists and an Egyptian tour guide shot dead by Islamist terrorists in Cairo
29 May		Binyamin Netanyahu, having campaigned against Rabin–Peres peace plan, becomes Likud prime minister of Israel, narrowly defeating Labor's Shimon Peres
15 June (**IB 87**)		Massive IRA car bomb devastates busy Manchester shopping centre
4–11 August	Salzburg	

11–16 August	London
16–21 August	Pesaro
21 August–2 September	London
23 August	

23 August	Osama bin Laden, founder of militant Islamist al-Qaeda network, issues a fatwa declaring war on 'the Zionist–Crusader alliance'
28 August	Divorce of Prince and Princess of Wales
2–late September	Paraggi
Late September–31 December	Oxford/London
27 September	Taliban fighters in Afghanistan's civil war take Kabul, declaring an Islamic state and imposing Sharia law
6 November	Bill Clinton first Democratic President since FDR to be re-elected, defeating Republican Bob Dole
13 December	Ghanaian diplomat Kofi Annan elected Secretary-General of UN in succession to the Egyptian, Boutros Boutros-Ghali, a second term for whom was opposed by US

1996 publications

The Sense of Reality: Studies in Ideas and their History
'Berlin', in Thomas Mautner (ed.), *A Dictionary of Philosophy*
Contribution to 'Why be Jewish?', *The UJS Haggadah*
Supplementary obituary note on Lydia Chukovskaya (*Guardian*)
'A Flick Back' (letter, *Guardian*)
'No Smoking in Class' (letter, *Sunday Telegraph*)
(with others) 'Solidarity with Turkish Writers' (letter, *Independent*)

1997

1 January–5 November	Oxford/London
January	Illness leads to cancellation of plan to visit Israel
17 April	Athens for hon. doctorate in philosophy
22 April	Visit to Israel for Passover fails to materialise

1 May		Labour Party wins landslide victory in British General Election; Tony Blair becomes prime minister
1 July **(IB 88)**		Hong Kong transferred from UK to China
8 July		NATO invites Czech Republic, Hungary and Poland to join
19 July		IRA announces new ceasefire from next day
22 July	IB's final illness begins	
31 August		Diana, Princess of Wales, dies of injuries sustained in car crash in Paris
6 September		Funeral of Princess of Wales
11 September		Scottish voters decisively endorse proposals for a Scottish Parliament in Edinburgh, with powers devolved from Westminster
23 October	Tony Blair writes to IB about liberty and the left; IB too ill to reply	
5 November	IB dies in Oxford	

1997 publications

The Proper Study of Mankind: An Anthology of Essays
'Literature and Art in the RSFSR' (1945) (*Kulisa NG*)
'Sir Thomas Armstrong (1898–1994)', in *Christ Church 1996*
Contribution to 'Books of the Century' (*Sunday Telegraph*)
Contribution (on his favourite images) to *RA* (The Royal Academy Magazine)
Letters to Rocco Pezzimenti in his *The Open Society and its Friends, with Letters from Isaiah Berlin and the Late Karl R. Popper*

SELECT BIOGRAPHICAL GLOSSARY

These notes on some important and/or frequently mentioned dramatis personae include rather more information than can be accommodated in a footnote of manageable proportions. The existence of these supplementary notes is flagged by asterisks attached to the relevant surnames on their first occurrence in a footnote, and in the index, thus: Isaiah *Berlin. Like the footnotes, the entries concentrate mainly on the period covered by the present volume; inclusion in the equivalent glossaries in earlier volumes is indicated at the end of the relevant entries.

Akhmatova, Anna Andreevna (1889–1966), pseudonym of the Russian poet Anna Andreevna Gorenko. Akhmatova became famous as a pioneer of the Acmeist group of poets with the publication of her first collection in 1912. After the Bolshevik Revolution, however, she was criticised for failing to conform to Soviet literary orthodoxy, and remained unpublished 1923–40. Choosing not to emigrate, she bore witness to two decades of Stalinist repression. She was briefly rehabilitated during WW2, when the popularity of her verse made her useful to the authorities, but this policy was reversed soon afterwards, partly at least because of suspicions raised by IB's unexpected visit of 15/16 November 1945, and its sequel(s). Late in life Akhmatova was permitted some freedom, and accepted in person the inaugural Etna–Taormina prize in 1964, and an hon. DLitt from Oxford in June 1965. She married: (i) 1910 (divorced 1918) the pre-Revolutionary poet and critic Nikolay Stepanovich Gumilev (1886–1921), who was executed by the Cheka; (ii) 1918 the poet and orientalist Vladimir Kazimirovich Shileiko (divorced 1926); (iii) 1926 the Russian writer and art critic Nikolay Nikolaevich Punin (1888–1953) – a common-law marriage that ended 1938; Punin later died in a Siberian prison camp. Akhmatova's son by Gumilev, her only child, Lev Nikolaevich Gumilev (1912–92), historian, was sentenced in 1938 to ten years in the Gulag, but released to fight with the Soviet Army during the war; his re-arrest and imprisonment 1949–56 were attributed by Akhmatova to IB's visits to her in Leningrad. These visits inspired the love cycle *Cinque*, and IB has also been identified as the 'guest from the future' who appears in her masterpiece, *Poem without a Hero*. IB's hatred of totalitarian systems meant that he would always have admired Akhmatova as an exemplar of the heroic resistance of the individual, and the artist, against state repression, but the fact that he had witnessed her struggle, and become entwined in her narrative, endowed their meeting with a timeless significance: 'My visit was, I think, the central event of my entire life' (to John Russell, 23 January 1995).

Alsop, Joseph Wright ('Joe') (1910–89), newspaper columnist and commentator on foreign affairs. IB first met Alsop in America in 1940, when he had 'the twin attractions of being a relative of the President and a loquacious observer of wartime Washington' (MI 100). 'Joe originally asked me to dinner', IB later recalled, 'I remained silent and inhibited throughout and he did not give me up. For that I shall be eternally grateful to him' (to Susan Mary Alsop, 5 October 1962, L3 115). Alsop wrote the influential 'Matter of Fact' column syndicated by the *New York Herald Tribune* 1945–74 (co-authored by his younger brother Stewart until 1958). He was fiercely anti-Communist, but a strong proponent of civil rights and opponent of McCarthyism; in spite of his Republican roots he was, with the likes of Phil Graham (see Graham, Katharine) and Chip Bohlen (q.v.), one of the 'maréchaux' – 'marshals' – who surrounded the young Napoleon, JFK, in the early 1960s (L3 121). A closet homosexual, he married, 1961, Susan Mary Patten (1918–2004) née Jay, widow of Alsop's close friend the diplomat William Patten, Jr, and a famous Washington political hostess; they divorced in 1973. 'His political attitudes were often dotty, unacceptable and even odious. Now, if you ask me why I remained such friends with him, let me say again: he was a man of incorruptible integrity; affectionate, loyal, civilised, a devoted friend; nothing said of someone, if he really was a friend, would shake his devotion' (to Robert Kaiser, 17 October 1989, 378). Plate 24. L1 703, L2 786, L3 629.

Anglesey, Shirley: (Elizabeth) Shirley Vaughan Paget (b. 1924) née Morgan, DBE 1983, writer, daughter of the novelists Charles and Hilda Vaughan, became the Marchioness of Anglesey after her marriage, 1948, to (George Charles) Henry Victor Paget (1922–2013), 7th Marquess of Anglesey. IB attended their wedding, and often visited the couple at Plas Newydd, their home on Anglesey. Shirley helped him prepare his translation of Turgenev's *First Love* (1950). IB regretted that in his last years they saw one another all too infrequently (458). L2 795.

Annan, Noel Gilroy (1916–2000), life peer 1965, historian and academic administrator; Provost, King's, Cambridge, 1956–66, UCL 1966–78; vice chancellor, London, 1978–81; director, ROH, 1967–78; trustee, National Gallery, 1978–85, chair 1980–5. Annan shared IB's interest in the history of ideas, but IB was unconfident about his friend's judgement, and their relations were tested by IB's repeated requests for the redrafting of Annan's biographical sketch of him in the introduction to *Personal Impressions* (1980). The difference in their outlooks was also evident in their responses to the threatened closure of the historic round reading room in the British Library in the late 1980s, as part of its move to a new site at St Pancras. IB opposed this, but suspected that Annan would not, and wrote to the historian Hugh Thomas, who shared his own views:

> Dear friend though he is, [Noel] is so bent on being 'of our time', and hates anything savouring of antiquity. Do you not remember his constant reproaches to me about not controlling or stopping the election of classical scholars, medieval historians, experts on Renaissance literature, etc. to the British Academy? All unnecessary people: one should reach out to sociologists, educationalists, scholars of modern aesthetics and the like. Hence his passionate advocacy of the Euston Road. (To Hugh Thomas, 8 May 1989)

Plate 23. L3 630.

Ayer, Alfred Jules ('Freddie') (1910–89), philosopher. Grote Prof. of the Philosophy of Mind and Logic, London, 1946–59; Wykeham Prof. of Logic, Oxford, and fellow, New College, 1959–78. Having read classics at Christ Church 1928–32, Ayer was an exact contemporary of IB, and in the later 1930s joined the informal discussion group of young philosophers – including Stuart Hampshire (q.v.) and John Austin – who met in IB's rooms in All Souls. Ayer emerged from this period a strong adherent of logical positivism, the wellspring of his most famous work, *Language, Truth and Logic* (1936): as IB observed, Ayer's treatise had a 'terrific impact' and 'for all that he has no ideas of his own, [...] the manifesto altered a great many people's outlooks' (to Miriam Gross, 26 November 1993). In spite of this achievement, IB believed that Ayer was given less recognition than he hoped for, and certainly than he deserved – the exact opposite of his own case: 'no doubt he deserves an OM, but that is done by the Queen alone, and seems to be done (as I know too well) in accordance with no recognisable criteria' (to Ted Honderich, 11 June 1980). Ayer married: (i) 1932 Renée Orde-Lees (see 624; divorced 1941); (ii) 1960 Alberta Constance ('Dee') Wells (1925–2003) née Chapman, journalist, novelist and broadcaster (divorced 1983; remarried 1989); (iii) 1983 Vanessa Mary Addison Lawson (1936–85) née Salmon. L1 703, L2 786, L3 630.

Ben-Gurion, David (1886–1973) né Gruen, Polish-born Israeli statesman, one of the leaders of Zionist resistance to the British Mandate in Palestine, and one of the principal architects of the emergence of the state of Israel after WW2. With political roots in the Jewish labour movement, he was a central figure in Mapai, the Workers' Party, which he represented in the Knesset 1949–65; he served as prime minister 1948–53 and 1955–63, and came out of retirement to lead the breakaway RAFI (Israel Workers' List) party 1965–7, representing that party in the Knesset 1965–9; in May 1970, after a brief period representing a minority party in the next Knesset, he resigned his seat; he died at Sde Boker, the kibbutz in the northern Negev mountains that he had made his home, in 1973. IB was temperamentally averse to Ben-Gurion, but by no means indifferent to his achievements, and in a lecture delivered in Jerusalem in October 1972 attempted to explain how 'obsessed dervishes like Ben-Gurion sometimes have a deeper insight into events than splendidly gifted but sane and rational men like Weizmann' (q.v.) (to Samuel Sambursky, 13 November 1972, L3 506). L3 630.

Berlin, Aline Elisabeth Yvonne (1915–2014), the youngest of the four children of Baron Pierre de Gunzbourg, Russian-born banker who settled in Paris, and Yvonne Deutsch de la Meurthe, daughter of a prominent French Jewish industrialist. Aline had an English nanny, and grew up speaking both French and English; she was sent to London for safety in 1915, and escaped only with difficulty from Vichy France to the US in early 1941; her older brother, Philippe, fought with the resistance in France for the duration of the war, liaising with the Special Operations Executive in London. It was in New York, in 1942, that Aline first met IB: he soon contemplated proposing to her, but was too timid, and in 1943 she married Hans Halban; their friendship deepened, however, in Oxford after the war. Aline married: (i) 1934 André Strauss (1903–39), son of the art collector Jules Strauss; they had one son, Michel Strauss (q.v.); (ii) 1943 Hans Halban (q.v.); they had two sons, Peter and Philippe Halban (qq.v.), and divorced in 1955; (iii) 1956 Isaiah Berlin (q.v.). 'All my life, it seems to me, I have received more than I deserved. I doubt if I deserved my fellowship at All Souls in 1932. I am quite sure that I did not deserve my chair, my knighthood, my election to the British Academy and, above all, my marriage to Aline' (to John Sparrow, 30 April 1975). Plates 16, 17, 25, 29, 35. L2 792 (s.v. Halban), L3 631.

Berlin, Isaiah (1909–97), born in Riga on 6 June 1909, only surviving child[1] of Mendel and Marie Berlin (qq.v); educated at St Paul's School, London, 1922–8; CCC 1928–32 (firsts in classics – 'greats' – 1931, in PPE 1932); lecturer in philosophy, New College, 1932–8, 1950–5, fellow 1938–50, hon. fellow 1990–7; fellow by examination, All Souls, 1932–8; war service with Ministry of Information in New York 1941–2, at British Embassies in Washington, 1942–6, and Moscow, September 1945 to January 1946; All Souls, 1950–67 (Robertson Research Fellow 1950–7, Chichele Prof. of Social and Political Theory 1957–67), 1978–97 (Distinguished Fellow); founding President, Wolfson, 1966–75; prof. of humanities, CUNY, 1966–71; Vice President, BA, 1959–61, President 1974–8. Died in the Acland Hospital, Oxford, 5 November 1997; buried in Wolvercote Cemetery.

Honorary posts: director, ROH, Covent Garden, 1954–65, 1974–87; Committee of Awards for the Kennedy Scholarships 1967–79; Trustee of the National Gallery 1975–85.

Prizes: Jerusalem Prize for the Freedom of the Individual in Society 1979 (a biennial award for authors given by the organisers of the Jerusalem International Book Fair); Erasmus Prize 1983 (to mark the 25th anniversary of the Praemium Erasmianum Foundation four prizes were awarded that year, the other recipients being Raymond Aron, Leszek Kołakowski and Marguerite Yourcenar); the inaugural Senator Giovanni Agnelli International Prize for the Ethical Dimension in Advanced Societies 1988.

Lectures: Bowra Lecture, Oxford, 1980.

Hon. fellowships: Wolfson 1975, St Antony's 1983, New College 1985.

Honorary doctorates: Harvard 1979; Sussex 1979; Johns Hopkins 1981; Northwestern, Illinois, 1981; NYU 1982; Duke, NC, 1983; City, NY, 1983; New School of Social Research, NY, 1987; Oxford 1987; Ben-Gurion, Israel, 1988; Yale 1989; Trinity College, Dublin, 1994; Toronto 1994; Bologna 1995; Athens 1996.

Publications (edited by HH except those marked †) include: †*Vico and Herder* (1976); *Russian Thinkers* (1978, co-edited by Aileen Kelly); *Concepts and Categories* (1978); *Against the Current* (1979); *Personal Impressions* (1980); †(trans.) Ivan Turgenev, *A Month in the Country* (1981); *The Crooked Timber of Humanity* (1990); *The Magus of the North* (1993); *The Sense of Reality* (1996); *The Proper Study of Mankind* (1997, co-edited by Roger Hausheer); 8 posthumous volumes; and 4 volumes of letters (the second co-edited by Jennifer Holmes, the third and fourth by Mark Pottle).

IB married, 1956, Aline Halban (see Berlin, Aline), was knighted in 1957, appointed OM in 1971, and declined a life peerage in 1979. L1 704, L2 787–8, L3 631.

Berlin, (Mussa) Marie (*c*.1880–1974) née Volshonok ('Wolfson'), IB's mother, married her first cousin Mendel Berlin (q.v.) 1906, and their only surviving child Isaiah (q.v.) was born 6 June 1909. IB's parents spoke Russian and German, but, from 1921, English – always to him, and almost always to others. Marie did more than her husband to shape their son's character, imbuing the young Isaiah with an ineradicable sense of his Russian Jewish identity: 'She had been the real unacknowledged source of his Herderian beliefs – in Jewishness, in belonging, in the very necessity of having roots. She had given him that existential certainty, that confidence in his own judgement, which had allowed him to *live* his life and

---

1 An elder sister was stillborn, and the complications of the birth led IB's mother's doctors to forbid her to have further children.

not merely inhabit it, as his father had done' (MI 272). 'Although it is many years since my mother died, and she was ninety-four even then, the scar remains' (to Brian Knei-Paz, 28 October 1988). L1 704, L2 788, L3 631–2.

Berlin, Mendel (1884–1953), IB's father, a timber and bristle trader by profession, who married his first cousin, Marie Volshonok (see Berlin, Marie), in Riga 1906; Isaiah (q.v.), their only surviving child, was born on 6 June 1909. Mendel is depicted by IB as a timid husband and a somewhat ineffectual though intelligent and thoughtful man, but there can be no denying his resourcefulness, which has perhaps been under-appreciated: he secured the passage of his family first from post-Revolutionary Russia to Riga, in October 1920, and thence to England in February 1921, and provided a comfortable life for them there, putting Isaiah through public school and Oxford, two of the foundation stones of all his later success. After his father's death from leukaemia in December 1953 IB replied to a letter of condolence from his old friend Christopher Cox: 'You know what it is to lose parents in middle age and how it removes a frame one had taken much too much for granted and leaves one suspended and not very well able to find bearings [...]. Excess of personal affection and devotion carries excessive punishments it seems to me; but if one is born soft shelled there is no possible escape' (c.1 January 1954). Mendel wrote an autobiographical memoir to record the family history for IB; it was published as 'For the Benefit of My Son' in BI. L1 704–5, L2 788, L3 632.

Bohlen, Charles Eustis ('Chip') (1904–74), US diplomat, specialised in the USSR, and it was on one of his regular trips to Moscow, in 1934, that he met his future wife, Avis Howard Thayer (1912–81), whose brother was a junior diplomat at the US embassy there; they married in 1935. IB first met them in Washington in 1942, and the three enjoyed a close friendship, in which Aline later fully shared. L2 788, L3 632.

Bowra, (Cecil) Maurice (1898–1971), Kt 1951, classicist, academic administrator and celebrated Oxford personality and wit. Bowra's life centred on Oxford, and on Wadham, of which he was a fellow 1922–38, and Warden 1938–70. He died there on 4 July 1971. IB was taken up by Bowra in the summer of 1931, and was 'acquired for life': 'I really do owe him an unbelievable part of what I am, think, feel' (to Noel Annan, 31 August 1973, L3 547). He returned from Jerusalem specially to deliver the eulogy at Bowra's memorial service, emphasising his friend's 'goodness & life affirming qualities': while his conservative critics were 'Blind & foolish, inhibited & inhibiting', Bowra had 'opened doors & windows' (to Osbert Lancaster, 2 August 1971, L3 461). IB nevertheless found that towards the end of his friend's life he loved him more than he respected him: 'there was *no* peace or quiet underneath his extremely insecure and worried personality; a great personality, certainly – a great man? I think the term ought to be used perhaps more cautiously' (to HH, 17 April 1991). L1 705–6, L2 789, L3 632–3.

Carr, Edward Hallett (1892–1982), historian and diplomat, entered the Foreign Office during WW1, but left for a chair at the University of Wales, Aberystwyth, 1936–47; he was senior research fellow, Trinity, Cambridge, 1955–82. Given the extent of disagreement between IB and Carr – moral, political and philosophical – their relations remained surprisingly friendly, though some of Carr's published criticisms undoubtedly irked IB. After one such unexpected instance in March 1975 he wrote to Chimen Abramsky: 'What an obstinate, resentful, prejudiced, frozen-up old monster he is – if I had known that he was going to do this, would I have contributed to his Festschrift? Someone ought to point out that for this, and this alone, my chances of getting to heaven are marginally better than his. Do stimulate someone to say something irreverent about him – mere age should not be a protection against justice' (25 March 1975). Later he expressed a milder view: 'I feel sure you are right about Carr; I do not know about admiration, but he certainly is quite fond of me in a left-handed sort of way [...]; if you did, somewhere, sometime, refer to his systematic misrepresentation of my views, and his inability to keep off the subject, it would not, I think, do any harm, or indeed hurt his feelings much – he pretends to be so very tough!' (to Chimen Abramsky, [18 June 1975?]). L3 634.

Chukovskaya, Lidiya Korneevna (1907–96), Russian writer and poet, daughter of the prominent children's writer Korney Ivanovich Chukovsky. Lidiya Chukovskaya's husband, the scientist Matvey Petrovich Bronshtein (1906–38), fell victim to Stalin's Great Purge, but this did not deter his widow from her literary activities, and she met the inevitable conflicts with authority 'with a kind of fearless stoicism to which there are few parallels in the Soviet Union as it used to be' (IB, supplementary obituary note on LC, *Guardian*, 9 February 1996, 13). Her defence of the dissident physicist and Nobel laureate Andrey Sakharov led to her expulsion from the Union of Soviet Writers in January 1974. Chukovskaya was a lifelong friend of Anna Akhmatova, and IB considered her memoirs of Akhmatova to be of great importance, because they not only revealed much about that great poet but also bore witness to the times in which author and subject lived. Of the second volume IB wrote:

> Your book, I think, is written without anger, without the wish for revenge, without apologetics or self-accusation (even when you write about the Congress of the Writers' Union at which Pasternak was expelled). This makes it a masterpiece, literary and moral. I don't read many books nowadays, but yours I read day and night, just as I read *Zhivago* in Moscow in 1956. Don't lose heart! It really is a fundamental work. It will be read by people – both Russians and foreigners – and they will be moved by it after you and I are gone, in the twenty-first century. (To Lidiya Chukovskaya, 16–17 June 1981, trans. Katharine Judelson and Sylva Rubashova: see 637/1)

In her reply, dated 27 February 1982, Chukovskaya quoted the last two lines of Mayakovsky's poem *Treating Horses Nicely*: 'Dear sir Isaiah! [*in English*], Today is a very special day for me: I received your letter of 16–17 June 1981. I could hardly believe your appraisal of my book about AA. You are infected by generosity à la Pasternak. For whatever reason, you have grown fond of my book. This means: "Life is worth living / And work worthwhile".' (trans. Katharine Judelson and Sylva Rubashova: see 637/1).

FitzLyon, Kyril (b. 1910) né Kyril L'vovich Zinovieff, diplomat and literary translator born into an aristocratic Russian family from St Petersburg, where his grandfather, Alexander Zinovieff, had been governor, and his mother a lady-in-waiting to two tsarinas. After the Bolshevik Revolution his family emigrated to Britain, and he took British citizenship, assuming the name FitzLyon (a play on his father's name, Leo). He joined the Foreign Office, and was in Prague when the Nazis invaded Czechoslovakia in March 1939. He later worked for the Ministry of Defence, retiring in the early 1970s. FitzLyon married, 1941, April Mead (1920–98), who learned Russian from his mother, and became a translator in her own right; they collaborated on successful translations of lesser-known works by Chekhov and Tolstoy, before completing a new translation of *Anna Karenina*; they also pursued independent careers, April publishing history and biographies, and Kyril concentrating on the Russian translations for which he is best known. The FitzLyons were well known among Russian émigré circles in London, where they lived. IB especially valued Kyril FitzLyon's opinions on Russia, and also on Israel and Zionism, even though they seemed rarely to be in agreement.

Floud, Jean Esther (1915–2013) née McDonald, social scientist and college head. She married, 1938, the civil servant Peter Floud (1911–60), who was alleged to have had connections with the Oxford spy ring to which Jenifer Hart (q.v.) had belonged. Floud taught sociology at the University of London (LSE and Institute of Education) 1947–62, was a fellow, Nuffield, 1963–72, and Principal of Newnham, Cambridge, 1972–83. It was as a member of the Commission of Inquiry into Oxford University (the Franks Commission) 1964–6 that she first came to know IB well, and they became the closest of friends. L3 636.

Graham, Katharine ('Kay') (1917–2001), daughter of Eugene Isaac Meyer (1875–1959), owner and publisher of the *Washington Post* 1933–46) and his wife Agnes Elizabeth (1887–1970) née Ernst, social activist; married, 1940, Philip Leslie ('Phil') Graham (1915–63), lawyer and journalist, who succeeded her father at the *Washington Post* 1946. The manic-depressive Phil Graham took his own life in 1963, whereupon his wife became his *de facto* successor, though she was officially publisher only 1969–79. Kay Graham gave strong leadership at a time when the Nixon administration was using unscrupulous and intimidatory methods in an attempt to block the paper's investigation into the Watergate conspiracy, whose unravelling led to President Nixon's resignation in August 1974. As a result of this cause célèbre her reputation preceded her, and IB wrote to Shirley Anglesey (q.v.) of 'Mrs Graham ("the most powerful woman in the world" – absurd) a *very* old friend (since 1940)' (1 October 1987).

> We go back almost half a century – I am trying to think of who is still alive of that troubled but for us not ungolden time in Washington in the year of Pearl Harbor [...]. And what in fact was a kind of family to me, apart from one or two people at the British Embassy, and, of course, Chip and Avis [see Bohlen, Charles], is no more. So my passion to hold on to what was one of the happiest and gayest times of my life is – quite apart from my deep love for you, of which you are fully aware – very, indeed desperately, strong. (To Kay Graham, 16 April 1987).

Plate 27. L2 791–2, L3 636–7.

Halban, Hans Heinrich (1908–64) né von Halban, nuclear physicist, married (1943–55) to Aline Strauss née de Gunzbourg (see Berlin, Aline); father of IB's stepsons, Peter and Philippe Halban (qq.v.). L2 792, L3 637.

Halban, Peter Francis (b. 1946), publisher; Aline Berlin's second son, stepson to IB; married, 1982, Martine Mizrahi; trustee, IBLT, from 1996. Plates 35, 37. L2 792, L3 637.

Halban, Philippe Alexandre (b. 1950), cell biologist specialising in diabetes; Aline Berlin's third and youngest son, stepson to IB; prof. of genetic medicine and development at the University of Geneva, Switzerland, since 1987; married to Rosane Mahony née de Moerloose. Plate 35. L2 792, L3 637.

Hampshire, Stuart Newton (1914–2004), philosopher. On election to a fellowship at All Souls in autumn 1936 Hampshire joined the discussion group recently established there by John Austin and IB, and became IB's closest male friend (this volume is dedicated to his memory). The paucity of letters from IB to 'Hants' in this volume and its predecessor indicates not a lack of closeness but exactly the reverse: they wrote less because they talked virtually daily. Hampshire was Grote Prof. of Mind and Logic at the University of London 1960–3, then left to take a chair at Princeton 1963–70, a move that IB opposed, and which he ascribed to the malign influence of Hampshire's wife Renée. In 1961 Hampshire had married (Grace Isabel) Renée Ayer (1909–80) née Orde-Lees, with whom he had had a long affair that produced two children, Julian Ayer (died in the 2004 Indonesian tsunami) and Belinda Hampshire, while Renée was still married to Hampshire's friend and colleague A. J. Ayer (q.v.). IB never understood Renée's hold over his friend, but their relations were cordial enough by the time the Hampshires returned to Oxford in 1970, Stuart having been elected Warden of Wadham in succession to Maurice Bowra (q.v.). Hampshire's wardenship lasted until 1984, and he was knighted for his services to philosophy in 1979. On retiring at the mandatory age of seventy he was appointed to a chair at Stanford, where he met his second wife, the philosopher Nancy Lynn Delaney Cartwright (b. 1944); they married in 1985. After Hampshire's retirement from Stanford in 1991, he and Nancy moved to Oxford, and a home close to the Berlins in Headington. Plate 11. L1 709, L2 792–3, L3 637.

Hardy, Henry Robert Dugdale (b. 1949), editor, publisher and occasional author; undergraduate at CCC 1967–71 (classical mods 1969, PPP[1] – psychology and philosophy – 1971); teacher, Shrewsbury School, 1971–2. HH became IB's editor in 1974 while engaged in graduate studies in philosophy at Wolfson 1972–6 (BPhil 1974, DPhil 1976), and continued in that role while working as an editor at Oxford University Press 1977–90. From 1990 to 2015 he worked full-time on IB's papers as a fellow of Wolfson, preparing new works for publication, and revising old ones, with the aim of giving IB's published and previously unpublished ideas their widest possible dissemination in editions that combine clarity with accuracy: 'I really am grateful to you for compelling me to tell the truth, i.e. conform to my claim to remain faithful to the text[s] on which I endeavour to build the thoughts and views of various thinkers. Do continue doing this! Nobody is more inaccurate than I: my quotations are caricatures, sometimes positive improvements (in my view); but never mind, accuracy is all' (to HH,

---

1 Psychology, philosophy and physiology (1947–2010): undergraduates chose two options on which to concentrate.

13 March 1989). Without HH's impetus, and his deep-seated belief in the value of IB's works, which their author did not always share – 'every line I have ever written and every lecture I have ever delivered seems to me of very little or no value' (to Anthony Storr, 29 September 1978, 83); 'I cannot deny that you are treating me rather too well' (to HH, 29 November 1993) – the major part of IB's legacy would have remained hidden: 'Herbert Hart says that you have transformed my reputation for ever, and had a more decisive effect on it, and indirectly me, than anyone has ever had. It may well be so. What a charge to labour under!' (to HH, 2 October 1979). Trustee, IBLT, from 1996; hon. fellow, Wolfson, from 2015. Plates 11, 37.

Hart, Herbert Lionel Adolphus (1907–92), legal philosopher and college head. After reading classics at New College 1926–9 Hart pursued a successful career at the Chancery Bar 1932–40. In May 1940 he began war work with MI5, a role suggested for him by Jenifer Williams (q.v.), then a civil servant in the Home Office, with whom he had fallen in love: they married the next year, and were among IB's oldest and closest Oxford friends. After the war Hart decided not to return to his well-paid legal practice, and instead accepted the post of fellow and philosophy tutor at New College that had been offered to him before the war. He held this post 1945–52; was prof. of jurisprudence, Oxford, and fellow, Univ., 1952–68, research fellow 1969–73; and Principal of Brasenose 1973–8. He declined a knighthood in 1966. Hart's return to Oxford had been influenced by his wife's left-wing views, and her former membership of the Communist Party cast a shadow over his later years, when there was speculation in the media that both husband and wife had betrayed their country. This furore contributed to Hart's nervous breakdown in 1983 (214). Plate 11. L1 710, L2 793, L3 637–8.

Hart, Jenifer Margaret (1914–2005) née Williams, civil servant and historian, read modern history at Somerville 1932–5, and became a close friend of IB from their first meeting in 1934. In 1941 she married the lawyer Herbert Hart (q.v.), with whom she had lived since 1937. To the freethinking Jenifer marriage did not mean monogamy, and among her many affairs there was one with IB, which began in 1950, and was centrally important in both their lives. She took a first in history in 1935, and joined the Civil Service (coming third of 493 candidates in the entrance exam); she worked for the Home Office 1936–47, with special dispensation to remain in her post after 1941 in spite of a ban on marriage for female civil servants. After the war she followed her husband to Oxford, becoming philosophy tutor at New College in 1945, research fellow, Nuffield, 1951–2, and fellow and history tutor, St Anne's, 1952–81. While at Oxford she had joined the CPGB, but agreed to keep this fact secret at the Home Office in order to be of service to the Party. She was interviewed by MI5 in the 1960s about her role as a sleeper, or 'mole', in the civil service, and in 1983 became the subject of scrutiny by the BBC and the *Sunday Times*, which searched for an Oxford equivalent of the Cambridge spy ring. Hart later denied in her 1998 autobiography *Ask Me No More* that she had ever been asked to pass on any secrets (214). L1 722 (s.v. Williams), L2 793, L3 638.

Hopkinson, Diana Mary (1912–2007) née Hubback, of maternal German-Jewish ancestry; childhood and lifelong friend of Shiela Sokolov Grant (q.v.); after St

Paul's Girls School, and LMH 1931–2, trained and worked as a copywriter before refugee work for Basque, German and Czech children 1936–40. She was a great-great-great niece of Jane Austen, and her husband, the author and educator David Hopkinson (married 1939), completed Austen's *The Watsons* as 'Another' (1977). Diana Hubback was one of the 'bevy of bright young undergraduate women' who went to IB for tutorials in the early 1930s; others were Shiela Grant Duff (see Sokolov Grant, Shiela), Maire Lynd and Jenifer Williams (see Hart, Jenifer), who all attended him like 'the beautiful young parishioners of some witty, glamorous, but sexless village priest' (MI 64).[1] Diana became an intimate friend of Adam von Trott, and his lover until 1935, as described in her autobiography *The Incense-Tree* (1968), whis is in part an elegy to him.

Ignatieff, Michael Grant (b. 1947), writer and broadcaster, and IB's chosen biographer as author of *Isaiah Berlin: A Life* (1998); assistant prof. of history, British Columbia, 1976–8, and senior research fellow, King's, Cambridge, 1978–84; thereafter he held numerous visiting fellowships and professorships, later becoming Carr Prof. of Human Rights Policy, Kennedy School of Government, Harvard, 2000–6, Liberal MP, Etobicoke-Lakeshore, Canada, 2006–11, and leader of the Liberal Party of Canada (and of the Opposition) 2009–11, losing the 2011 election to Conservative Stephen Harper; since 2012 he has been professor, Munk School of Global Affairs, Toronto, and prof. of practice, Kennedy School of Government, Harvard. Ignatieff's father had been a St Paul's contemporary of IB, and was later taught by him at Oxford, and the younger Ignatieff's Russian roots were among his attractions for IB, who concluded that he 'would probably be a better biographer, if one is needed, than anyone else I know' (to HH, 10 July 1989). The caveat is significant: IB took some convincing that a biography was worthwhile, and wrote to HH, 'Of course he will try to get you to help him as much as he can, and I hope you will not mind doing this – but that is entirely up to you. I don't really mind what happens after my death – never have – so provided nothing happens in my lifetime I don't terribly mind what is arranged now. I hope this doesn't sound too casual – but you know better than anyone else how I am' (ibid). At the initial urging of their mutual friend Reni Brendel, Ignatieff conducted a series of (mostly recorded) interviews with IB over a decade, 1988–97, at first simply to preserve a record of his conversation, but later as a basis for his biography. Plate 36.

Kollek, Theodor ('Teddy') (1911–2007), mayor of Jerusalem 1965–93, one of IB's closest and most faithful friends in Israel. Born in Hungary, Kollek emigrated to Palestine in 1935, was involved in both Haganah and the Jewish Agency in Europe, and served as director general of the prime minister Ben-Gurion's office 1952–64; he was also chair of the Government Tourist Corporation 1958–65. Kollek was mayor of Jerusalem for 28 years, and was re-elected five times, having first stood, reluctantly, at Ben-Gurion's urging. IB regarded him as

---

1 Cf.the 2nd stanza of Maurice Bowra's satirical poem about IB, 'Major Prophet', which reads in part: 'See the young girls' enraptured faces / To the adagio listening. / Oh, hark, for sex-appeal is calling / And ripples down those bended necks. / The master calls them to attention, / Unveils the mysteries of sex. / What would they give to call him husband, / To pluck the roses from his lips, / With Mrs Halpern, Mary Fisher, / The Granta, both the Lynds and Tips?' *New Bats in Old Belfries, or Some Loose Tiles*, ed. HH and Jennifer Holmes (Oxford, 2005), 32.

a moderating and unifying influence in a city riven by division, and urged him to remain in his post for as long as his health could stand it: 'All my life I have felt for you a mixture of admiration, affection, respect and every other kind of warm feeling – a synthesis I do not think I have ever felt so strongly about anyone – but words couldn't begin to convey adequately this virtually lifelong feeling during my excessively long life' (to Teddy Kollek, 1 June 1987). 'We are going to Israel for two days precisely to celebrate Teddy Kollek's eightieth birthday. I don't feel great enthusiasm for a visit to Israel just now, for reasons you can understand, but this event is unavoidable: he is the last pillar of decency left in that degenerating establishment' (to Leon Wieseltier, 21 May 1991). L2 795, L3 638–9.

Nabokov, Nicolas (1903–78) né Nikolay Dmitrievich, cousin of the novelist and poet Vladimir Nabokov. Composer, teacher, writer and cultural ambassador, Nabokov left Russia for Crimea after the Bolshevik Revolution. He lived in Germany 1919–23, then 1923–33 in Paris, where he associated with Diaghilev and the Ballets Russes, and encountered Igor Stravinsky; he then settled in the US, like Stravinsky, becoming a naturalised citizen in 1939. As the director of cultural relations/secretary general of the Congress for Cultural Freedom 1951–63 Nabokov organised major cultural events, but the exposure of the CIA's covert funding of that body was a personal as well as a professional disaster, and he never found again the standing in society which that role had given him. In IB's eyes he had the air of 'an aristocrat in exile with bags permanently packed to return to his native land, which he knew he would never reach, and therefore clinging to every genuine fragment of it' (to Arthur Schlesinger, 2 May 1978). That IB was a 'genuine fragment' of this lost land helps explain the closeness between them, even though IB readily acknowledged that Nabokov could be 'exhausting company'. He was married five times, on the last occasion, in 1970, to Dominique Cibiel (b. c.1945); all of his five wives attended his funeral. Plate 9. L2 795–6, L3 639.

Pasternak, Boris Leonidovich (1890–1960), Russian poet, novelist and translator; after increasing Soviet state censure in the mid 1930s he ceased publishing his own poetry and turned to translating the works of others, including the plays of Calderón de la Barca, Goethe, Schiller, Shakespeare and Shelley; his editions of several of Shakespeare's plays became classics of Russian literature. He began his only major novel, *Doctor Zhivago*, in 1945, and completed it in 1955; unable to find a Soviet publisher, he managed to deliver the text to the Italian left-wing activist and publisher Giangiacomo Feltrinelli, who issued an Italian translation in 1957; an English version followed in 1958, and in the same year Pasternak was awarded the Nobel Prize in Literature 'for his notable achievement in both contemporary poetry and the field of the great Russian narrative tradition'.[1] The Soviet authorities forced him to decline the prize, and he was expelled from the Union of Soviet Writers. Although Russian editions of *Zhivago* subsequently appeared in the West, the book was banned in the USSR until 1988. IB had met Pasternak several times during his 1945 visit to the Soviet Union (L1 593), and had been given an early draft of part of *Zhivago*; on his next visit in 1956 he was

1 *Les Prix Nobel en 1958* (Stockholm, 1959), 37.

entrusted with a complete text, which he read overnight. His immense appreciation of the literary quality of the work was tempered by his fears for the fate
of its author, should it be published.

Boris was the eldest of the four children of the painter Leonid Pasternak
and his wife Rosa, a concert pianist; Leonid and Rosa, with their two daughters
Josephine and Lydia, left the Soviet Union for Berlin in 1921; IB came to know
Josephine and Lydia after the war in Oxford, where they were then living. Boris
was born in Moscow and lived there and, from 1936, in the writers' village at
Peredelkino; he married (i) 1922 Evgeniya Vladimirovna Lur'e; (ii) 1934 Zinaida
Nikolaevna Neigauz. The companion of his last years was the Russian translator of poetry Olga Vsevolodovna Ivinskaya (1912–95), whom he met in 1946
when she was working as literary editor for the journal *Novyi mir* (*New World*);
she is thought to be the model for Lara in *Zhivago*. Ivinskaya's involvement with
Pasternak was the probable cause of her arrest and imprisonment in the Gulag
1949–53; after Stalin's death she was released and worked as Pasternak's literary
assistant. In December 1960, after his death, she was sentenced to eight years'
imprisonment, and her daughter to three, for smuggling money (i.e. receiving
royalties from the West), convictions seen in the West as acts of political repression and vengeance.

Polanowska-Sygulska, Beata Maria (b. 1954), Kraków-born Polish lawyer of philosophical bent, awarded her doctorate at Warsaw University 1988 for a thesis
on 'Arguments about Liberty in the Context of Isaiah Berlin's Doctrine of
Freedom', has worked at the Jagiellonian University, Kraków, since 1977: teaching assistant, Dept of Humanistic Applications of Computer Science, 1977–90;
lecturer, Faculty of Law and Administration, 1990–8; later senior lecturer in
legal theory, Sub-Faculty of Legal Theory (1998–2013), and university prof.
(from 2013). She made a number of visits to Oxford in the last decade of IB's
life and met him many times to discuss his (and her) work, continuing a correspondence that began in 1983; her publications include *Filozofia wolności Isaiaha
Berlina* [*Isaiah Berlin's Philosophy of Freedom*] (1998), *Unfinished Dialogue* (with IB,
2006) and *Pluralizm wartości i jego implikacje w filozofii prawa* [*Value Pluralism and
Its Implications for Legal Theory*] (2008). She was the recipient of the last serious
intellectual letter that IB wrote (17 July 1997): five days later his final illness
began, and he was unable to deal with corrrespondence of this nature thereafter. That letter, on the possibility of rational resolution of conflict, had ended:
'I am so old, my thoughts are often so confused, that I am not sure that I can be
as clear about my own opinions as perhaps in my printed works I seem to be.
Nevertheless, I think I have a position, and I think you have grasped it perfectly
well. So let me offer you my gratitude and hope that your work will have the
success which it surely most richly deserves.'

Sakharov, Andrey Dmitrievich (1921–89), Moscow-born Russian theoretical physicist
and dissident. A key figure in the Soviet thermonuclear programme, Sakharov
is often described as the father of the Soviet hydrogen bomb, but he later campaigned against nuclear proliferation, and publicly opposed the Soviet atmos-
pheric nuclear tests in 1961, the beginning of a campaign that led to the test-ban
treaty of 1963. From the mid 1950s he began to be increasingly concerned with
the moral implications of his work, and this culminated in the publication in the

West of his June 1968 article *Progress, Coexistence and Intellectual Freedom*, which established his international reputation as a public intellectual, and proved a turning point in his life: henceforth he devoted himself to human rights and the defence of the victims of political trials, and in 1975 this work was recognised by the Nobel Peace Prize. He was prevented from travelling to Oslo to receive the award, which was accepted on his behalf by his wife, the physician Elena Georgievna Bonner (1923–2011), who participated in his dissident activites, and shared the persecution they brought. In 1980 Sakharov was banished to the closed town of Gorky (from 1990 called Nizhny Novgorod), whence he continued to speak out on human rights, staging several hunger strikes; his wife joined him there in 1984. International pressure, and the spirit of glasnost, led to their release in 1986; in 1988 Sakharov was permitted to travel abroad, and he was awarded an hon. DSc at Oxford 21 June 1989: 'Sakharov is the only Russian alive today whom I admire without qualification in everything he does and is' (to James Billington, 20 December 1988); 'Sakharov is my man – he speaks with [an] unaffected, unembarrassed, liberal voice, and enormous courage – not very different from Herzen in the last century: certainly the purest and most civilised voice to come from Russia yet' (to Myron Gilmore, 12 July 1978). Plates 29, 30.

Schlesinger, Arthur Meier, Jr (1917–2007), writer, academic and liberal political commentator, one of IB's oldest US friends, on a par with Joe Alsop (q.v.): indeed this pair, who were political opposites, and eventually became estranged over their differing responses to the escalating Vietnam War, which led Alsop to write a savage review of Schlesinger's *The Bitter Heritage: Vietnam and American Democracy, 1941–1966* (1967; L3 322), were often coupled in IB's correspondence. Schlesinger was associate prof. of history, Harvard, 1946–54, prof. 1954–61; he left to become a special assistant to President Kennedy 1961–3; he was Schweitzer Prof. of the Humanities, CUNY, 1966–95. He married (secondly) 1971 Alexandra Temple Allan (b. 1936) née Emmet. 'We were delighted to see you, and our impression was that you were both very happy. I am sure that we are right – this corresponds to the general impression. The number of happy marriages is not great: yours, ours, David Cecil's, and that's it' (to Arthur Schlesinger, 25 February 1976). Plate 18. L2 797–8, L3 639–40.

Silvers, Robert Benjamin (b. 1929), co-founder in 1963, with Barbara Epstein (1928–2006), of the *New York Review of Books*, which they edited jointly until her death, and which Silvers has since run single-handedly. The fiftieth anniversary of the NYRB in 2013 was marked with a documentary film by Martin Scorsese, *The 50 Year Argument*, directed by Scorsese and David Tedeschi, which includes clips of IB. Silvers began his publishing career as managing editor of the *Paris Review* 1954–8, and on returning to New York became associate editor of *Harper's Magazine* 1958–63. IB first met him in April 1964 in the suitably literary company of the poet Robert Lowell and his wife, the writer Elizabeth Hardwick: 'Silvers I got on with; and he got on with me' (to Noel Annan, 1 May 1964). Their understanding deepened in the years that followed, and IB wrote an encomium to his friend for *Robert B. Silvers* (1990), which concludes:

> Bob combines a warm heart, an all-absorptive and sympathetic intellect and an undeceivable moral insight with a degree (unequalled in my experience) of interest in and understanding of a vast variety of ideas and movements,

social, political, moral, artistic. He responds without fail to every manifestation, small and great, of culture, of original creative power – and, indeed, to an infinity of human issues – and shows an extraordinary understanding of the characters and aims of those involved in them. His contribution to contemporary culture is outstanding.

Plates 6, 18. L3 640.

Sokolov Grant, Shiela (1913–2004) née Grant Duff, author and journalist; LMH PPE 1931–4; trained as a foreign correspondent in Paris 1934, covering the Saarland Plebiscite 1935, then Czechoslovakia, of which she became a strong defender, personally advising Churchill about Czech affairs from 1937; her bestseller *Europe and the Czechs* (1938) contributed to a growing public disillusionment with appeasement; she joined the BBC Czech Service during the war and wrote *A German Protectorate: The Czechs Under Nazi Rule* (London, 1942). At Oxford she was a close but platonic and sceptical friend of Adam von Trott. IB once grouped her with others who fell uncritically under Trott's spell, and who defended Trott over his controversial letter to the *Manchester Guardian* 1934 (see L3 348–9): in fact SSG, then taking her final exams, had taxed Trott on this specific issue, and 'had expressed a hope that [he] had been right about the comparative absence of Jew-baiting in Hessen [Hesse] and had nervously suggested [...] that he was veering in the dangerous direction of aggressive nationalism'.[1] Of her 1982 autobiography *The Parting of Ways* (254/2), the Oxford historian Tim Mason wrote that it 'captures the urgencies and the moral dilemmas of the 1930s liberal politics as no diplomatic history can [...] and it should be on every student's reading list'.[2] Shiela Grant Duff married, 1942, Noel Francis Newsome (1906–76), creator and wartime director of the BBC European Service; they divorced 1952, and the same year she married Micheal (Vikent'evich) Sokolov (1923–98), a White Russian RNVR officer (both changing their surnames to Sokolov Grant). Together they farmed in Cumberland, and later retired to Ireland. L1 709.

Solzhenitsyn, Aleksandr Isaievich (1918–2008), Russian writer and dissident. Joined the Red Army 1941 after the German invasion, and served in the artillery; arrested 1945 and sentenced to eight years in the Gulag on the basis of letters written from the front in which he criticised Stalin and proposed a political alternative to Communist rule. Developed stomach cancer 1952; after the death of Stalin in 1953 he was released into 'administrative exile' and worked as a teacher. In 1962 his autobiographical novel of the Gulag, *One Day in the Life of Ivan Denisovich*, was published, with the personal approval of Khrushchev. His subsequent work treated similar themes, and in 1969 he was expelled from the Union of Soviet Writers after the foreign publication of *Cancer Ward* (1968) and *The First Circle* (1969). In 1970 he was awarded the Nobel Prize in Literature 'for the ethical force with which he has pursued the indispensable traditions of Russian literature'.[3] *The Gulag Archipelago* was published in the West in 1973, and in February 1974

1 Giles MacDonogh *A Good German* (255/1), 64.
2 Tim Mason and David Astor, 'The Terrible Failure of Two Dedicated Loners', *Guardian*, 11 March 1982, 12.
3 Emeka Nwabunnia and Emeka Ebisi, *The Nobel Peace Prize, 1901–2000: Handbook of Landmark Records* (Lanham, MD, 2007), 83.

Solzhenitsyn was arrested, charged with treason, deprived of his citizenship and expelled from the USSR. He lived in Zurich 1974–6 and in Vermont 1976–94. With the dawn of perestroika he was readmitted to the Writers' Union (1989), and his works were published in the Soviet Union; he returned to Russia in May 1994 and died in Moscow. 'For me, he is a Soviet man turned inside out, as it were – a mirror-image of his enemies. Still, I prefer the mirror-image to the original, and if I had to march under either banner I know which it would be, although I should do so with appalling reservations, and am glad I do not have to' (to Myron Gilmore, 12 July 1978); 'Sakharov is patriotic, Solzhenitsyn nationalistic (would you not agree?)' (to Kyril FitzLyon, 22 October 1979). Plates 29, 30.

Sparrow, John Hanbury Angus (1906–92), classicist, barrister and Warden of All Souls 1952–77. If Sparrow's life was dominated 'to a profound degree' by his homosexuality (IB to John Lowe, 27 February 1989, 360), it was also defined by his headship of All Souls, and once this came to an end he began a slow and inglorious decline. When this descent was already well advanced, IB was approached by Sparrow's appointed biographer, John Lowe, who made clear to him what a difficult book it would be to write: 'I am not, as most people presume, referring to "delicate", or rather indelicate, material. "Publish and be damned" says John. Much harder is the central question, "Why did John, given his brains and his opportunities, do so little?"' (Lowe to IB, 16 February 1989). IB recognised this as the central paradox of Sparrow's life. He delighted in his friend's company, and even enjoyed aspects of his reactionary peformance at All Souls, but found it impossible to support a proposal to honour the Warden publicly as he approached his retirement: 'I do not know what to say about John Sparrow. He is one of my oldest and best friends [...]. I should not dream of obstructing a proposal, and if it were put to the vote could not conceivably vote against it: but neither can I make a passionate speech in his favour' (to an unknown correspondent, 10 January 1977). Plate 2. L1 716–17, L2 798, L3 640.

Spender, Stephen Harold (1909–95), poet, critic and playwright. Spender read PPE at Univ. 1927–30, and in his first year came to know W. H. Auden, then in his last year at Oxford, and through him Christopher Isherwood, with whom Spender had a close relationship that was important to both men. Spender's sexuality was not straightforward: he had male lovers but married (i) 1936 (divorced 1941) Marie Agnes ('Inez') Pearn (1913–76), novelist; (ii) 1941 Natasha Gordon Litvin (1919–2010), concert pianist. Spender met IB in his second year at Oxford, after Auden had gone down, and they became lifelong friends. He was coeditor of *Horizon* 1939–41, of *Encounter* 1953–67; held many visiting lectureships and professorships; and was prof. of English, UCL, 1970–7. He was knighted in 1983. On 13 October 1988 Spender's new play *Creon*, a retelling of Sophocles' *Antigone*, opened at the Haymarket Theatre, Leicester, and IB wrote to Shirley Anglesey: 'Thank God that Stephen's play went off well [...]. He needs all the praise he can get. I wish him better almost than anyone living. He is so nice and has had such a rackety life' (17 November 1988). 'I am indeed deeply upset by Stephen Spender's death. I think he had no enemies, only nasty reviewers. He was my oldest friend and perhaps the best – I find it difficult to imagine that he is not alive and will not come into the room in two or three hours' time' (to Morton White, 14 August 1995). Plate 27. L1 717.

Strauss, Michel Jules (b. 1936), Aline Berlin's first son, stepson to IB, and director of the Impressionist and Modern Art Department, Sotheby's, 1961–2000; married (i) 1959 Margery Tongway (divorced 2003); (ii) 2003 Sally Lloyd-Pearson. Author of *Pictures, Passions and Eye: A Life at Sotheby's* (2011). Plate 35. L2 792, L3 640.

Taylor, Alan John Percivale (1906–90), historian, journalist and broadcaster; lecturer, Manchester, 1930–8; modern history tutor, Magdalen, 1938–63, fellow 1938–76. In spite of a prodigious output, command of primary sources in several languages, and widespread acclaim for his authoritative study of international relations, *The Struggle for Mastery in Europe, 1848–1918* (1954), Taylor was passed over for the Regius chair at Oxford in 1957; it went instead to Hugh Trevor-Roper (q.v.). While the details of the case were unclear, particularly the role played by his former mentor at Manchester, L. B. Namier, this did not prevent 'an embittered' Taylor from turning against Oxford, and thereafter 'denigrating the university he loved' (A. F. Thompson, ODNB). IB regarded Taylor's disappointment over the Regius Chair as the reason behind his irresponsible desire always to puncture the certainties of received or established opinion, a trait evident in his revisionist study *The Origins of the Second World War* (1961), of which IB wholly disapproved: 'he seems to me to be activated by a certain, possibly unconscious, wish to oppose all his very great friend Namier believed – all since their famous & unhealed breach towards the end of N's life: a sad business' (to Jacob Talmon, 1 June 1977). Taylor's animus against establishments, though, must also have stemmed from his left-wing political convictions, which made him an early critic of the Cold War, and a long-time supporter of CND. With typical perversity, he wrote a column for Beaverbrook's right-wing *Sunday Express*. IB learnt of Taylor's death only after returning from Paraggi, and wrote to Taylor's widow, Eva: 'I came from abroad yesterday, and learnt to my distress that Alan was no more. I procured the obituaries, *none* of them seemed to me adequate – not Skidelsky, not Trevor Roper, not The Times, none of them brought out the combination of human warmth (however disguised, as it were, for fun) charm and life giving qualities for which I loved him (more than he loved me – but never mind)' (17 September 1990). L3 641.

Trevor-Roper, Hugh Redwald (1914–2003), life peer 1979, historian; Regius Prof. of Modern History, Oxford, and fellow, Oriel, 1957–80; Master of Peterhouse, Cambridge, 1980–7. He married, 1954, Lady Alexandra Howard-Johnston (1907–97), eldest daughter of Field Marshal Earl Haig and former wife of Rear-Admiral Clarence Howard-Johnston (with whom she had three children). IB regarded Trevor-Roper as 'the leading seventeenth-century historian of our time' and 'a superb writer of English prose' (to R. L. Sharp, 25 August 1978). He was somewhat taken aback, however, by Trevor-Roper's comparison, in a 1980 book review,[1] of Zionism with Nazism, a thesis that attracted much criticism, which IB regarded as valid; he was nevertheless prepared to defend his friend against accusations of anti-Semitism, just as he had defended him from a similar charge a few years earlier, over the Bhutto controversy in Oxford (L3 595–7): 'Trevor-Roper is not in fact an anti-Semite, in my view. [... He] likes bold paradoxes, brilliant original hypotheses, something to *épater*[2] the dreary middle-class

1 128/9.
2 'Shock'.

historians, etc. All this, I think, is the ultimate spring of this article. However, it is of course what you say it is, and does great harm' (to Brian Knei-Paz, 29 April 1980). Plate 2. L3 641.

Utechin, Patricia ('Pat') (1927–2008) née Rathbone, IB's devoted, long-serving and long-suffering private secretary 1961–5 and 1972–97: the gap was caused by her move from Oxford to Glasgow with her husband Sergei; after their amicable separation in 1972 she rejoined IB, who relied upon the formidable Pat to keep his life in order, and his time relatively free, and when away from Oxford peppered her with letters, in each of which there might be a score or more of points to deal with, ranging from the domestic to the academic, from the straightforward to the downright difficult: 'The Principal of St. Anne's: *please* tell her that the 3^d & 9th November are *impossible* for me: it is a *nightmare* dinner & I don't want to go: *please* be extra-tactful! If she suggests other dates, say you *cannot* get me to answer (*you* happen to know 3 & 9th no good) as I alone know my diary, & am *inaccessible* etc.' (6 August 1977); 'Pat, Why am I lunching in Balliol to-day? am I? with Montefiore? Is it with Melvin Richter which Montefiore knows about?' (31 May 1979); 'I'll give no *further* trouble, I swear (how much is *that* worth, I wonder?) & cd you post all the enclosed (goes without saying) – & *do* be well! This is a terribly selfish wish on my part, but not entirely! Preserve yourself *whatever* you do – physical health is *everything*' (30 July 1975). Plates 11, 14. L3 641–2.

Walicki, Andrzej (b. 1930), Polish philosopher and historian of ideas, regarded by IB as 'far and away the most distinguished authority on Russian and Polish [...] thought, at any rate in the last two centuries, to be found anywhere' (to Hugh McLean, 30 January 1981). Born in Warsaw, Walicki studied at the universities of Łódź and Warsaw, where he became full professor 1972. IB helped him to visiting fellowships at All Souls 1966–7, 1973; to a senior research fellowship at the History of Ideas Unit, ANU, 1981–6; and later to the founding O'Neill Professorship of the History of Ideas at Notre Dame, Indiana, 1986–99. Their mutually fulfilling intellectual friendship is described in Walicki's *Encounters with Isaiah Berlin: Story of an Intellectual Friendship* (2011). In 1987 IB wrote to HH (then at OUP) about Walicki: 'He does push his own works a bit. I don't blame him entirely: he feels surrounded by strangers who don't appreciate what he writes; he is in a kind of permanent exile from the politics of Poland and the social life of the West. It was very much so when he came to All Souls. My immediate reaction is that his most popular work, most likely to sell, is the *History of Russian Thought*, whatever he may think of that himself, because it is in fact the best book on the subject in print' (5 October 1987). L3 642.

Weizmann, Chaim (1874–1952), chemist and statesman; president, World Zionist Organization and Jewish Agency for Palestine, 1921–31, 1935–46; president, provisional council of the state of Israel, 1948–9; first President of Israel 1949–52. Born near Pinsk, Belorussia, in the Jewish pale of settlement, Weizmann studied chemistry in Berlin, took his doctorate at Fribourg (Switzerland), and then lectured at Geneva, where he met his future wife, the Russian-born paediatrician Vera Chatzman (1881–1966); they married in England in 1906. From 1904 Weizmann held a junior post at Manchester, becoming a reader in 1913. His skilful advocacy of the Zionist cause to Britain's elite was the driving force behind the Balfour Declaration of November 1917, which committed the British government to the principle of a Jewish homeland in Palestine. The Declaration appeared to endorse Weizmann's moderate, pro-British policy, but this eventually cost him the presidency of the World Zionist Organization, and by the time he was appointed first President of Israel he had been politically sidelined. Whatever Weizmann's limitations, IB felt intense pride at his association with him, and was always prepared to defend his gradualist Anglophile approach. L1 721, L2 799, L3 642–3.

White, Morton Gabriel (b. 1917), philosopher and historian of ideas; prof. of philosophy, Harvard, 1953–70, IAS, Princeton, 1970–87. He married Lucia Perry (1909–96) in 1940. Although bound to White 'by ties of ancient friendship' (to Joseph Alsop, 30 September 1981), IB eventually tired of their extended debate over free will and determinism, writing to him that 'the gulf between us is unbridgeable' (9 September 1991). Ten years earlier, in the same letter to Alsop, he had written: 'Meanwhile, I keep thinking how not to offend my friend Morton White, who keeps asking me back to the Princeton Institute to continue conversations with him about the philosophy of history, which I don't want to go on with: the subject is not without interest for me; I should like to give one more swipe at E. H. Carr before we both perish; but the pedantic philosophical way in which Morton does it, although entirely correct and estimable, does bore me terribly – and every time I get a letter from him saying how fascinating our last exchange was, a view I don't share, I am penetrated by guilt, and don't know what to answer. It keeps me away from the United States.' For White's long friendship with IB, which resulted in an extensive correspondence, see his autobiography *A Philosopher's Story* (1999), especially chapter 17, 'Isaiah Berlin: A Bridge between Philosophy and the History of Ideas'. L2 799, L3 643.

Williams, Bernard (Arthur Owen) (1929–2003), later (1999) Kt, philosopher; fellow, All Souls, 1951–4, Distinguished Fellow 1997–2003; New College 1954–9; lecturer in philosophy, UCL, 1959–64; prof. of philosophy, Bedford, London, 1964–7; Knightbridge Prof. of Philosophy, Cambridge, and fellow, King's, 1967–79; Provost, King's, 1979–87; Monroe Deutsch Prof. of Philosophy, California (Berkeley), 1988–2003; White's Prof. of Moral Philosophy, Oxford, and fellow, CCC, 1990–6. He married (i) 1955 Shirley Vivienne Teresa Brittain Catlin (b. 1930), life peer 1993; the marriage was dissolved in 1974; (ii) 1974 Patricia Law Skinner (b. 1942) née Dwyer, formerly senior commissioning editor in history and the social sciences at Cambridge University Press, later European editor for Harvard University Press, publisher for the National Gallery in London, and (from 2010) trustee, IBLT. IB had tremendous admiration, as well as liking, for Bernard Williams, and in addition to their philosophical interests they shared a love of opera: Williams was a director of English National Opera (formerly Sadler's Wells Opera) 1968–86, and IB hankered after recruiting him to Covent Garden. Bernard and Patricia Williams were close friends of Aline Berlin also, and frequent visitors to Headington House and Paraggi: when, in May 1989, IB learned that Bernard would not be able to visit him in Italy that year, he wrote 'I really will miss you very greatly', a sentiment that applied on a larger scale to Williams's emigration to Berkeley in 1988, part of the 'brain drain' across the Atlantic that characterised the Thatcher era. IB unashamedly sought his return: 'I think that one day you will feel a pang of nostalgia for this, whatever you may say, not at all unworthy little island […], and when you do, yield to it!' (letter of 19 May 1989). In fact Williams returned much sooner than IB could have expected, in 1990, to become White's Prof. of Moral Philosophy at Oxford, though he retained his connection with Berkeley for the rest of his life. Plate 11. L3 643–4.

INDEX OF CORRESPONDENTS
AND SOURCES

Nicholas Hall

This index doubles as a reference list for those who wish to consult the copy-texts (which are sometimes carbon copies or photocopies) of any of the letters included in this volume, except that those previously given a reference in another volume, e.g 'to Susan Mary Alsop, 5 October 1962, L3 115', are not included again here. References to plates are in **bold**.

Sources are given in square brackets after the correspondents' names, or, when there is only one letter in question, after its page reference. If there is more than one source for a correspondent's letters, the main source appears after the name of the correspondent, and other sources after the relevant page reference(s). If no source is given, the letter (or copy) was supplied by the relevant correspondent or his or her heir(s). The provenance of one or two letters has become obscured by the passage of time and imperfect record-keeping: in these cases an educated guess has been made.

When both a top copy and a carbon of a letter were available, the source given is that of the top copy. When only a carbon was available, '[*carbon*]' is inserted in the text, after the date of the letter. In some cases, top copies are in the Isaiah Berlin Papers in the Bodleian Library, Oxford, notably when a correspondent's letters were returned to Berlin after the death of the correspondent. Page numbers in italics show letters *to* Berlin.

Where archives have requested specific references, these are provided. Otherwise, except for the Isaiah Berlin Papers in the Bodleian, no specifics are given: these can usually be readily ascertained from the archive in question.

Abbreviations

[123/4]	Oxford, Bodleian Library, MS. Berlin (by shelfmark/folio)
Beinecke	Beinecke Library, Yale University
Chatto	Chatto and Windus Archive, Reading University
CT	connective tissue, i.e. editorial commentary
HUA	Harvard University Archives, Pusey Library, Harvard University
IBLT	Isaiah Berlin Literary Trust archive, Wolfson College, Oxford
ISA	Israel State Archives
JFK	John F. Kennedy Memorial Library
LOC	Library of Congress
Maruyama	Maruyama Library, Tokyo Woman's Christian University
NYPL	New York Public Library
RBML	Rare Book and Manuscript Library, Columbia University
UCLA	Special Collections Library, University of California, Los Angeles
Weizmann	Weizmann Archives, Rehovot, Israel

1 For the entire correspondence between IB and LC see Elena Chukovskaya (ed.), '"… esli by vdrug pozvonil Evgenii Onegin ili Taras Bul'ba": perepiska sera Isaii Berlina s Lidiei Chukovskoi' ['"… if you have suddenly been phoned by Eugene Onegin or Taras Bulba": The Correspondence of Sir Isaiah Berlin and Lydia Chukovskaya'], *Novyi mir* 2009 no. 12 (December), 148–72, and at ⟨http://www.chukfamily.ru/Lidia/Proza/berlin.htm⟩; English version, trans. Katharine Judelson and Sylva Rubashova, at ⟨http://berlin.wolf.ox.ac.uk/lists/bibliography/bib271.pdf⟩.

1   For a fuller selection see UD.

1 For other letters see Walicki's *Encounters with Isaiah Berlin: Story of an Intellectual Friendship* (Frankfurt am Main etc., 2011).
2 For other letters see White's *A Philosopher's Story* (University Park, Pennsylvania, [1999]).

GENERAL INDEX

Christopher Phipps

References in *italics* are to pages where a note provides basic biographical information on a person; references in **bold** are to illustrations. An asterisk preceding a name indicates an entry in the Glossary. Works by IB appear under their titles, works by others under their authors' names. The Chronology is not indexed.

Aarsleff, Hans Christian: 'Vico and Berlin' 13 n1, 231
Abbado, Claudio *30*
Abdullah bin al-Hussein, king of Jordan *370*
Aberbach, David *103*
Abraham, Edward Penley ('Ted') *84*
Abram, Morris Berthold *445*; 'United Nations, Israel and the Peace Process' 478–9
Abramsky, Chimen *97*, 196, 200, 622; (ed.) *Essays in Honour of E. H. Carr* 420 n2
Abu Nidal (Sabri Khalil al-Banna) *205*
Abu Nidal Organization 129 n1, 205 n2
Abyssinia: Italian invasion (1935) 404
Acheson, Dean Gooderham *378*
Acmeist movement 15, 617
Action française 535–6
Acton, Harold Mario Mitchell *510*
Acton, John Emerich Edward Dalberg-Acton, 1st Baron *161*, 283, 343
Addison, Joseph 70 n2, 390 nn2,3
Adeane, (George) Edward *454*
Adelaide 10
Aeneas *see* Dido and Aeneas
Afghanistan: Soviet invasion 124, 131 n3, 156
Aftenposten (newspaper) 573
afterlife 537–8
Against the Current (IB) 49 nn2,5,6, 60 n2, 107, 167 n6, 192 n2, 299 n1, 422 n1; reviews 107–8, 115, 122, 168, 525 n2
Age of Enlightenment, The (IB) 169, 477
Agnelli, Giovanni *334*, 340 n3
Agnelli, Giovanni ('Gianni') *340–1*
Agnelli Prize *see* Senator Giovanni Agnelli International Prize for the Ethical Dimension in Advanced Societies
Agnew, Spiro Theodore, US Vice President 18 n5, *532–3*
Ahrends, Burton and Koralek (ABK; architectural practice) 243
*Akhmatova, Anna Andreevna *4*, 555, 617; biographies and memoirs of 4, 15, 39–40, 51–2, 113, 128, 564, 622; and Chekhov 14; IB's visits to 39–40, 51, 112–14, 197, 357, 382–3, 523, 564–5, 567, 617; arrest of son 51 n4,

565, 617; bugging and harassment of 51, 128, 565; 'started the cold war' with IB 51–2, 113, 147; and Pasternak 112, 128, 146–7, 565; and Joseph Brodsky 127 n4, 522, 523, 564, 565; and Russian Revolution 144; and IB's marriage 147, 565–6, 567; life with Nikolay Punin 196 n2, 563 n2, 617; reputation 320, 534; suggested relationship with tsar 332–3; IB declines taking part in proposed film on 357; centenary 382; museum in Fountain House 382; IB as addressee of poetry 563–5, 566–7, 617; visits England 564, 565–6; *Cinque* 51, 113, 565, 617; 'In Praise of Peace' ('Stalin cycle') 51; *Poem without a Hero* 51 n5, 112–13, 114, 563 n2, 564, 565 n1, 617; *Requiem* 322; *A Sweetbriar in Blossom* 565 n1, 566 n3
Albany (London) 153 n2, 470
Alcibiades *157*, 201 n2
Alden, David 326 n6
Alexander the Great, king of Macedonia 108 n1, *317*, 404, 532
Alexander I, Tsar *157*
Alexander II, Tsar 61 n4; assassination 76 n3
Alexander VI, Pope 116 n1
Alexander, Samuel *550*
Alexis, Tsar *63*, 82 n2, 319
Alfonsín, Raúl Ricardo *316*
Algarotti, Francesco 197 n3
Algeria 272 n1, 402, 438, 446
Ali, Mohsin: on Israeli response to intifada 335 n4
Ali, Tariq 59 n6, 97
All Souls, Oxford: wardenship election (1976) 25–6, 34–5, 50, 335; College meetings 26, 35; admission of women fellows 92–3, 150–1; 'more philistine' 165; candidates for two research fellowships 226; and Rowse's diaries 230; standard of candidates' essays and papers 301–2; Wittgenstein stays at 308 n3, 309; Auden lives at 320–1; Sparrow's wardenship 359–61; IB recalls his experiences at 547, 550, 553
Allen, Carleton Kemp *8*
Allen, James ('Jim'): *Perdition* 327 n5
Allen, Robert Sharon 222 n1

[M]y world dies with me!

IB to Michael Ignatieff, n.d.